3-10
11-46
69-123
125-77
179-205
223-38
241-66
267-346
PP 7 & 8 of <u>Hooters</u>

367-80
381-98
445-538

EMPLOYMENT LAW

**MICHIE CONTEMPORARY
LEGAL EDUCATION SERIES**

EMPLOYMENT LAW

CASES AND MATERIALS

Second Edition

STEVEN L. WILLBORN
Cline Williams-Flavel A. Wright and
 Warren C. (Bud) Johnson Professor of Law
University of Nebraska

STEWART J. SCHWAB
Professor of Law
Cornell University

JOHN F. BURTON, JR.
Dean, School of Management
 and Labor Relations
Rutgers, The State University of New Jersey

LEXIS® LAW PUBLISHING
CHARLOTTESVILLE, VIRGINIA

To Ted St. Antoine and Clyde Summers,
inspirational leaders in the field of
employment law

and

To Mom and Dad,
my first and best teachers
— SLW

To Norma and
Justin, Whitney, Weatherly, Zachary, and Quintin,
and now Soren and Lehman too
— SJS

To Janet
— JFB

Preface to the Second Edition

Our goal in the second edition has been to update and enhance the materials. Much has happened since we wrote the first edition in 1992 and it was time to bring the materials up to date. At the same time, however, we used a general presumption against change. We tried to retain as many of the cases and as much of the structure of the book as possible, both to ease the transition for teachers and for substantive reasons. The cases, for the most part, worked very well as teaching tools and the structure of the book provided flexibility for the many different types of courses professors offer as "employment law."

We offer thanks again to all who have helped us in this project including the many professors who responded to our request for comments on the first edition. In addition to those listed in the Preface to the First Edition, we would like to extend special thanks to Professor Rick Bales at Northern Kentucky; Professor Kathleen Engel at Case Western; Professor Dan Foote at the University of Washington; Professor Alan Hyde at Rutgers; Professor Sam Issacharoff at Texas; Professor Pauline Kim at Washington University; Professor Deborah Malamud at Michigan; Professor Bob Schopp at Nebraska; Elizabeth H. Yates, who provided research and editorial assistance to John Burton; and Rafael Morell, Anne Marie Pisano, Deborah Steiner, and Leo Tsao, for their able research assistance.

Steven L. Willborn
Lincoln, Nebraska

Stewart J. Schwab
Ithaca, New York

John F. Burton, Jr.
New Brunswick, New Jersey

April 1998

Preface to the First Edition

The law that touches the working lives of most Americans today is not the law dealing with collective bargaining and unions that traditionally has dominated the curriculum in law schools. Rather, the workplace law that is important outside of the law schools is what has come to be known as employment law — that unruly matrix of laws that substantively regulates virtually every aspect of the employment relationship.

Employment law, however, poses formidable pedagogical challenges. Unlike the course in collective bargaining, which can be organized around the National Labor Relations Act (NLRA), employment law has no obvious organizing principle. No central, federal source of employment law exists. Instead, employment law is found in hundreds, if not thousands, of separate statutes and cases.

The organizational problem is exacerbated by the broad range of issues subsumed under the category of employment law. Courses in collective bargaining can be limited, somewhat artificially, to the NLRA's procedure for establishing the terms and conditions of employment. The outcomes of that procedure, the substance of the employment relationship, can be considered only very briefly, if at all.

Employment law cannot be limited in that way. Employment law directly affects the substance of the employment relationship. And the substantive areas are many — wages, hours, protection from discharge, employee health and safety, and many more. Understanding employment law requires one to consider the causes of and justifications for governmental regulation in all these areas. It also requires one to analyze not one, all-purpose procedure, but the diverse, overlapping, and often conflicting procedures found in the multitudinous sources of employment law.

The broad range of issues covered in employment law poses the risk that the course will turn into "a grab bag of miscellaneous problems which gain no coherence or illumination from each other." Clyde W. Summers, *What We Should Teach in Labor Law: The Need for a Change and a Suggested Direction,* in THE PARK CITY PAPERS 193, 195 (1985). To avoid this problem, a textbook on employment law must contain strong unifying themes. This book uses four overlapping themes. First, the book regularly examines the proper roles of economic incentives and legal regulations in achieving desirable outcomes in the workplace. By harnessing the economic incentives of workers and employers where appropriate, society can avoid some of the costs of promulgating and enforcing regulations. When economic incentives produce results that society considers unacceptable, however, legal rules to regulate employer or employee behavior may be necessary. One theme, then, will explore the appropriate blend of economic incentives and legal regulation as methods of achieving desirable outcomes. Although economics in this sense is a principal theme, we want to emphasize that this is not a Law-and-Economics text. Rather, it is a law textbook that uses economics to relate seemingly disparate issues and to explore issues in a rigorous way.

Second, the book pursues a theme focusing on the struggle for authority over the workplace. We encourage students to question the common assumption of overwhelming employer authority over the workplace and to begin to think about the different ways in which employers, employees, and the legislature all exert authority over the workplace and are, conversely, limited in their ability to exert authority.

A third theme focuses on the tension between simple rules and effective rules. A goal of much of employment law is to have rules that are easily and broadly understood, applied, and followed. At the same time, however, employers (and often employees) have many strategies to avoid the intended effect of laws. Employment laws have perhaps an inevitable tendency to become complex in order to counter evasive strategies. As we shall see, much of employment law is complex, and this theme explores the need for and costs of this complexity.

A fourth theme focuses on the structure of legal responses to problems in the workplace. One issue is determining the best level of government to regulate a particular problem. A variety of answers to this question are found in current employment law. The states are the primary regulators on a number of issues (such as job security and employee privacy and loyalty), the federal government has taken control in other areas (such as employee benefits), and various mixes of state and federal authority exist in still other areas (such as employment discrimination and employee safety and health). The text will regularly ask students to consider how authority ought to be allocated between governments. Another related issue is identifying the best enforcement mechanism for a particular regulatory scheme. Once again, the mechanisms for enforcing employment laws vary widely. Students will regularly be asked to consider both the ability of various mechanisms to further substantive goals and the cost of the mechanisms relative to others that might be used.

We are convinced that these themes satisfy the need for organizing principles in a course on employment law. First, they are general enough to apply to all of the substantive areas covered. As a result, we use them to tie the materials together, to provide foci that will be present throughout the volume. And second, the themes are sufficiently rigorous to provide an intellectually stimulating framework for the course.

We have attempted to edit the materials unobtrusively. We did not provide any indication when we deleted footnotes and citations to authority, but when we deleted anything other than footnotes or citations, we used ellipses. Citations in cases were often revised without indication (for example, by removing parallel citations), and footnotes that remain have retained their original numbers. For our own citations, except for headings for principal materials, we have followed *The Bluebook: A Uniform System of Citation* (15th ed. 1991).

We owe thanks to many who helped us with this project. We inflicted prior versions of these materials on students at Cornell, Michigan, Nebraska, Rutgers, and Virginia. We appreciated our students' willingness to bear with our typos and downright mistakes (most of which, we hope, have now been excised) and benefited greatly from their willingness to share with us their insights, confusions, comments, and suggestions. Several colleagues also deserve thanks. Professor Rip Verkerke merits special appreciation since he used our materials in manuscript form at Virginia at a time when we were sometimes able to keep only a few days ahead of him. Similar thanks go to Andrew Morriss at Case Western for teaching from the manuscript. Others read various portions of the materials and provided us with helpful comments, including Cynthia Farina, Peter Martin, Russell Osgood, Katherine Stone and Charles Wolfram at Cornell, Charles Craver at George Washington, Kent Syverud at Michigan, William Lyons and Robert Works at Nebraska, Barbara Lee at Rutgers, and Ramona Paetzold at Texas A&M. Rob Denicola also contributed generously by answering many of our questions on copyright issues, or by letting us know authoritatively that there were no answers. Student research assistants, as always, were invaluable. Thanks in this category go to Melissa Barber, Ann Juliano, Andrea Loux, Katherine McMahon, Michael Nolan, Gregory Porter, and J. Michael Roebuck at Cornell and Dan Muffly and Audra Mitchell at Nebraska. Thanks, too, go to the following librarians who performed their usual heroic feats for us: Mitch Fontenot and Anna Kurtz at Nebraska, Beth McWilliams at Michigan, and George Kanlzer, Jeff Katz, and Eugene McElroy at Rutgers. A special thanks to Carolyn Singleton at Cornell for enduring without complaint numerous printings of numerous drafts. And thanks, finally, to Fran Warren, our principal contact at Michie.

Steven L. Willborn
Lincoln, Nebraska

Stewart J. Schwab
Ithaca, New York

John F. Burton, Jr.
New Brunswick, New Jersey

December, 1992

Summary Table of Contents

PART I. INTRODUCTION TO EMPLOYMENT LAW

PART II. THE RISE AND FALL OF EMPLOYMENT AT WILL

PART III. EMPLOYEE PRIVACY

Table of Contents

PART VI. REGULATION OF COMPENSATION

PART VII. EMPLOYEE BENEFITS

Part I
Introduction to Employment Law

THEMES OF EMPLOYMENT LAW Chapter 1

This book considers the role of the law in regulating the complex and crucially important relationship between employer and employee. In modern society, the law plays a role in defining virtually every aspect of that relationship. From the time people are first permitted to enter the workforce under the child labor laws until they leave the workforce under the protection of the age discrimination laws, the law has something to say on nearly every issue arising out of the relationship — wages, hours, fringe benefits, safety, job security, discrimination, employee privacy.

Despite its pervasiveness, however, the law is a secondary force in the relationship. No law requires employers to hire any particular worker or any workers at all, nor are employees required to work. And, on most issues, the law permits a wide range in the terms of employment. On wages, for example, the minimum is currently $5.15 an hour for most employees, but the maximum wage is infinity, which is about what baseball players and CEO's are getting these days. Thus, the law is secondary in structuring the employment relationship: individual employers and employees establish the relationship and most of its terms by agreement.

The law is also secondary to the actions of employers and employees in the aggregate — to the labor market. Relatively few workers, for example, are paid the minimum wage. Ralph E. Smith & Bruce Vavrichek, *The Minimum Wage: Its Relation to Incomes and Poverty,* 110 MONTHLY LAB. REV. 24, 27, 30 (June 1987) (about 3.5% of all workers are paid the minimum wage). The wages of the rest are determined by the labor market, although the precise manner in which that market operates is in many ways still a mystery. Indeed, one way of viewing all of employment law is as a reaction to the outcomes produced by the primary forces of the labor market: employment legislation is enacted when society, or at least some segment of society, is dissatisfied with the level of wages, safety, or job security produced by the labor market. Employment legislation attempts to change those outcomes by influencing the workings of the labor market.

To say, however, that the law is a secondary force is not to say that it is unimportant. Indeed, for the current generation of workers, the law has become an increasingly significant force. In 1960, the only major federal employment law applying to nonunion workers was the Fair Labor Standards Act, which set the minimum wage, required premium pay for overtime work, and restricted child labor. Since then the federal government has enacted several major laws to regulate various aspects of the employment relationship. The Equal Pay Act of 1963 and Title VII of the Civil Rights Act of 1964 were the first of several laws enacted to prohibit discrimination in the workplace. The Occupational Safety and Health Act of 1970 brought the health and safety of workers under the federal aegis. And in 1974, the Employee Retirement Income Security Act was enacted to protect the interests of workers in their pensions and other employee benefits. This federal legislative activity continues. The employment sections of the Americans With Disabilities Act, for example, became effective in July, 1992, and the Family and Medical Leave Act was enacted in 1993.

State government also greatly increased its influence on the employment relationship during this time period. Beginning in the mid-1970s, state courts began to examine more closely the employment decisions — and especially termination decisions — of employers. The employment at will doctrine, which had operated for more than a century to shield termination decisions from judicial oversight, began to erode, and today all but a few states have limited the doctrine to some degree. State and local legislatures also began to enact laws on a variety of employment-related topics so that today hundreds of state statutes exist on a wide variety of issues. On testing alone, there are statutes regulating drug testing, polygraphs, genetic testing, and even "truth" testing.

A major, although undoubtedly partial, explanation for this surge of governmental interest in the employment relationship was the failure of the National Labor Relations Act, which regulates the relationship between unions and employers:

> The basic assumption of the National Labor Relations Act was that the labor market would be regulated by collective bargaining, not by legislation. Workers would be protected by their union, not by government officials. Workers' rights would be guaranteed by the collective agreement, not by law. Those rights would be defined and enforced through grievance procedures and arbitration, not through administrative agencies and courts....
>
> Collective bargaining, where established, served its intended purposes.... Collective agreements not only established wage rates and benefits, but also defined rights of employees in the workplace and provided, through grievance and arbitration, a system for adjudicating and enforcing those rights. Through their union, employees obtained a voice in many decisions affecting their working lives....
>
> [The National Labor Relations Act, however,] failed to achieve its purpose. Collective bargaining never became established except in segments of industry.... Instead of expanding, collective bargaining began shrinking in relation to total employment in the 1950's. It now covers less than [20% of all employees and its coverage] continues to shrink.
>
> Why collective bargaining has not been more widely extended is, for present purposes, unimportant. The significant fact is that collective bargaining does not regulate the labor market.... The consequence is foreseeable, if not inevitable; if collective bargaining does not protect the individual employee, the law will find another way to protect the weaker party. The law, either through the courts or the legislatures, will become the guardian. Labor law is now in the midst of that changing of the guard. There is current

recognition that if the majority of employees are to be protected, it must be by the law prescribing at least certain rights of employees and minimum terms and conditions of employment.

Clyde W. Summers, *Labor Law as the Century Turns: A Changing of the Guard,* 67 NEB. L. REV. 7, 9-10 (1988).[*]

Understanding this newly emerging employment law is no easy task. Employment laws, especially statutes, often pursue broad social goals — to eliminate employment discrimination, reduce the number of workplace injuries, or increase the job security of workers. As a result, an understanding of employment law requires one to analyze what those goals are (or should be) and whether the law is (or can be) effective in pursuing them. But employment law, especially case law, is also interested in the individual interactions between particular employers and employees. When employer and employee enter into a relationship, both parties operate with a considerable degree of uncertainty about such things as the precise work the employer needs done, the ability of the worker to perform it, the employer's long-term need for the worker, and other opportunities which may present themselves to the worker. The agreement between employer and employee, either explicitly or by relying on legal presumptions, must deal with these uncertainties. When should explicit agreements between employer and employee be recognized and enforced by the courts? When should they not? What rules should apply when circumstances arise that the parties have not explicitly considered in their agreement?

In beginning to address these issues, it is useful to distinguish between two types of legal rules: "immutable" rules that the parties cannot change by agreement and "default" rules that state the applicable rules unless the parties agree to alter them. Laws requiring employers to pay a minimum wage are an example of immutable employment laws. An employee cannot legally contract with an employer to work for a wage lower than the minimum wage. Employment at will is a default rule; it determines when an employment contract can be terminated, but applies only when the parties do not agree to another rule.

Some argue that immutable rules are presumptively undesirable. Consider, for example, the issue of workplace safety. A worker who is deciding between two jobs, one very safe and one quite dangerous, will obviously choose the safer one if the wages for the two jobs are the same. As a result, to attract workers, the employer offering the more dangerous job must pay a higher wage. If the wage difference between the two jobs is great enough, the worker may prefer to work at the more dangerous job. The employer offering the dangerous job will pay higher wages, however, only to the extent that the cost of the extra wages is less than the cost of making the job safer. Otherwise, the employer would spend the money to make the job safer and offer lower wages.

---

[*]Copyright © 1988 by Nebraska Law Review. Reprinted with permission.

Good Example

Viewed in this way, an immutable rule that required the employer offering the dangerous job to make the job safer would be undesirable. From the perspective of a worker who would prefer to work at the more dangerous job for a higher wage, the rule would mean that that job (and its higher wage) would no longer exist. The worker would be required to work at a safer but lower-paying job. From the perspective of the employer offering the dangerous job, the rule requires the employer to expend the money required to make the job safer even though it might be cheaper to pay higher wages instead. The immutable rule requiring safer jobs is undesirable, then, because it frustrates the preferences of both workers and employers. Indeed, some argue that it infringes on an important type of individual liberty — in this case, for example, the freedom of workers to decide for themselves the trade-off they want between wages and workplace safety. Richard A. Epstein, *In Defense of the Contract at Will,* 51 U. CHI. L. REV. 947, 953-55 (1984).

The argument that immutable rules are presumptively undesirable, however, depends on a number of assumptions. Even in our simple example, for instance, the worker must have more than one job available to her and she must know about the danger and wages of the two jobs. An immutable rule requiring the dangerous job to be made safer may be justified if one or more of these assumptions are not satisfied:

> Knowing that they must compensate workers to [accept dangerous jobs,] employers would like to keep job hazards secret. Therefore, the market will only work efficiently if potential new employees can observe the riskiness of jobs. One way such information might be provided is through a learning process. The first round of employees are uninformed, but after they are injured, other members of the labor force observe their injuries and illnesses and demand that the company pay a wage premium or reduce workplace hazards.

> There are many reasons why this learning process will work poorly in the real world. First, many hazards take a long time to produce injuries. Second, even if they happen quickly, participants in a large labor market will not observe many of the injured. Third, the level of hazard depends on workers as well as workplaces. Some workers are more susceptible to hazards because of their genetic characteristics or their life style — for example, whether they smoke. Therefore, it may be difficult for job applicants correctly to infer their own risk by observing the harm suffered by others. Fourth, workplace conditions change with technology — so the past may be a poor guide to the future. For all these reasons, regulations that require employers to inform employees of hazards are easy to justify....

> But the mere provision of information may not be sufficient for two different reasons. The first turns on the limited information-processing capacities of people, especially regarding probabilistic information. Rather

than engage in a massive educational campaign, it may be more efficient to regulate workplace health and safety directly ....

A second reason why an information strategy may be inadequate concerns ... "local public goods." If dust collectors are installed, they will benefit all employees on a shop floor; [however, individual workers may understate how much they value the benefit in an attempt to minimize the extent to which their wages are reduced to pay for it.] If employers do not know the value workers place on safety, they may be unwilling to experiment with costly changes that may not pay off in lower wage increases or improved productivity....

There is a final argument for regulating workplace health and safety. Given the widespread existence of health insurance, welfare and publicly subsidized health care for the poor and old, individuals do not bear all of the costs of their illnesses and injuries. Furthermore, individuals may not properly weigh the pain and suffering of their relatives and friends. [Hence,] individuals may fail to take into account all the social costs of their risky employment decisions.

Susan Rose-Ackerman, *Progressive Law and Economics — And the New Administrative Law*, 98 YALE L.J. 341, 355-57 (1988).[*]

Another common justification for immutable employment laws, one that in our experience is intuitively appealing to students, is that individual workers lack the bargaining power necessary to protect their own interests and to obtain socially acceptable terms of employment. Thus, immutable employment laws are required to protect employees, the weaker party to the employment contract. Clyde W. Summers, *Labor Law as the Century Turns: A Changing of the Guard,* 67 NEB. L. REV. 7, 7 (1988). But consider:

[From the law and economics perspective] workers ... are said to be in a position analogous to that of consumers in the product market. We would not ordinarily say that even a lone consumer has no power in dealing with a large supermarket chain, because we realize that this individual relationship is located amidst a host of supermarkets or other grocery stores competing for the patronage of a large number of customers. Thus if a particular shopper does not like the products, services, or prices in one store, he can go elsewhere.... It takes only a limited number of comparison shoppers with the same tastes and resources of this customer to impose the discipline of the marketplace on the decisions made by the store about the mix of product quality and price that will be offered to each and every one of its customers. By the same token, in almost any occupation or locality the individual employee knows that there is and will be a variety of job openings among a

---

[*]Reprinted by permission of The Yale Law Journal Company and Fred B. Rothman & Company from *The Yale Law Journal*, Vol. 1988, pp. 341-68.

number of alternative employers that provide some measure of choice if the employee does not like the specific features of the job he now has.

PAUL C. WEILER, GOVERNING THE WORKPLACE 17 (1990).[*] Thus, in this view, the bargaining power rationale for immutable employment laws is unpersuasive because workers are adequately protected by the existence of other employers offering alternative jobs.

Regardless of one's opinion on these issues, one's understanding of immutable employment laws can be enhanced by considering the extent to which they infringe on the preferences of workers and employers and the justifications offered for the infringements. In this book, we will regularly encourage you to do both.

Default rules raise a set of related, but distinct, issues. Consider, for example, the employment at will rule. One articulation of the rule is that every employment relationship can be terminated by either side, for any reason or no reason at all, unless the parties reach a different agreement. This is a default rather than an immutable rule because the parties can contract around it. The traditional view of default terms is that they should reflect the arrangement that *most* bargainers would prefer. If most workers and employers prefer the employment at will rule, then reading it into employment relationships that are silent on the issue means that most parties will not have to incur the transaction expenses of negotiating and drafting a termination provision at all. Instead they can simply rely on the default term and split the savings on transaction costs between them. Charles J. Goetz & Robert E. Scott, *The Mitigation Principle: Toward a General Theory of Contractual Obligation,* 69 VA. L. REV. 967 (1983).

Accepting that rationale, the employment at will doctrine raises the issue of whether it actually *is* the arrangement that most workers and employers would prefer. In situations where both sides make investments in training (situations that should be increasingly more common as the need for technical skills in the workplace increases), the parties may instead prefer a termination provision that only permits an employer to discharge a worker for good reasons. Consider, for example, the figure on the next page, which illustrates one model of an employee's work life — the implicit life cycle model. The employee enters the workforce by accepting employment with the employer at age *a* and retires at age *f*. The employer pays the employee wage (W). The opportunity wage (OW) curve represents the best wage the employee could earn with another employer and the marginal productivity (MP) curve represents the productivity of the worker in her current job with the employer. At age *a*, both the worker and the employer are investing in job training. The worker would be able to earn higher wages with another employer (OW is more than W), but prefers to work for this employer because she is receiving valuable job training which will permit her to

---

[*] Reprinted by permission of the publishers from *Governing the Workplace: The Future of Labor and Employment Law* by Paul Weiler, Cambridge, Mass.: Harvard University Press, Copyright © 1990 by the President and Fellows of Harvard College.

earn more later in her career (from age *d* to *f*). The employer is paying the worker more than she is producing (W is more than MP) because the employer also anticipates a long-term relationship which will permit it to recoup its investment later (from age *b* to *e*). A rule that limited the ability to terminate the employment relationship might better reflect the intentions of this employer and worker than the employment at will rule. If the increasing need for job training means that the majority of employment relationships fits this implicit life cycle mold, employment at will may not be the appropriate default term.

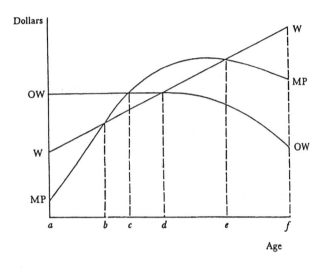

Source: Michael L. Wachter & George M. Cohen, *The Law and Economics of Collective Bargaining: An Introduction and Application to the Problems of Subcontracting, Partial Closure, and Relocation*, 136 U. PA. L. REV. 1349, 1362 (1988). Copyright © 1988 by University of Pennsylvania Law Review. Reprinted with permission.

The employment at will doctrine also raises questions about the traditional view of how to determine default terms. Under the traditional view, one response to the argument based on the implicit life cycle model is that, even if true, it does not matter very much because the parties can contract for the termination provision they prefer. To the extent, however, that the parties do *not* contract around the default term, even though it is in their joint interest to do so, the precise setting of the default term is critical.

Assume, for example, that employers know that employment at will is the default term, but that workers believe incorrectly that the default term provides them with some protections against discharge. It may be that in implicit life cycle situations, the employer would not seek to change the default term even though it would be in the joint interests of the parties to do so. Not changing the default term would permit the employer to discharge the worker at age *e*, and thus avoid the losses it would otherwise incur after that age. The discharge may cause other employees to begin shirking between ages *b* and *e*, which would reduce the employer's gains between those ages (the difference between MP and W), but it may be that the employer's savings from the discharge would exceed those losses. In essence, the default term was not contracted around because that process would have required the employer to disclose its superior knowledge. With that knowledge, the employer was able to get for itself a larger piece of the smaller contractual pie.

Even if a particular worker knows that employment at will is the default term, the parties may not contract around it. A worker who asks for protection against discharge sends a signal to her employer that she might *need* such protection, which may decrease the employer's willingness to hire her. As a result, the worker may decide not to commence negotiations to revise the employment at will default; instead, she may prefer to accept the risk that the employer will breach the implicit lifetime contract at age *e,* rather than the risk that the employer will refuse to hire her if she commences negotiations on the termination clause and sends a signal that she may not be a capable worker. Once again, a strategic consideration results in a contract with the employment at will default, even though other language on termination would better serve the joint interests of the parties.

If these types of problems are common, one response would be to set the default not where most parties would want it to be, but at a point where the parties would *not* want it to be. Instead of using employment at will as the default, for example, the default termination term might be established as "no termination for any reason during the life of the employee." This type of "penalty" default would force the parties to bargain over the term, and in the process reveal valuable information to each other. Ian Ayres & Robert Gertner, *Filling Gaps in Incomplete Contracts: An Economic Theory of Default Rules,* 99 YALE L.J. 87 (1989).

In considering the role of the law in regulating the employment relationship, this book will often consider, as this introduction suggests, the ways in which employment law in its various guises affects the interests and bargaining positions of workers and employers. We will use this type of perspective to explore rationales for regulatory programs and to describe the likely effects of laws on employers, employees, and society. Our hope is that this will consolidate the diverse materials of employment law into an understandable and cohesive package, while simultaneously, and somewhat paradoxically, expanding the horizons of the course beyond the confines of employment law to any area of law (or indeed of discourse) where economics is relevant. At the same time, though, we will also call on a number of other perspectives — for example, comparative law, history, and feminism — which may provide insight into the complex and fascinating field of employment law.

Chapter 2

LEGAL BOUNDARIES OF THE EMPLOYMENT RELATIONSHIP

Employment law regulates the employment relationship. An immediate question is what is employment, and how does it differ from other work relationships? Each particular employment law can and usually does define coverage in its own way. Still, some general principles can be found. In this chapter we ask three basic questions: (1) What factors distinguish employees from other workers, particularly independent contractors? (2) Why does a law cover certain employees and not other employees? (3) Why does a law cover certain employers and not others?

A. EMPLOYEES VERSUS INDEPENDENT CONTRACTORS

SECRETARY OF LABOR v. LAURITZEN

United States Court of Appeals, Seventh Circuit
835 F.2d 1529 (1987), *cert. denied,* 488 U.S. 898 (1988)

HARLINGTON WOOD, JR., CIRCUIT JUDGE.

This, as unlikely as it may at first seem, is a federal pickle case. The issue is whether the migrant workers who harvest the pickle crop of defendant Lauritzen Farms, in effect defendant Michael Lauritzen, are employees for purposes of the Fair Labor Standards Act of 1938 ("FLSA"), or are instead independent contractors not subject to the requirements of the Act.[2] The Secretary, alleging that the migrant harvesters are employees, not independent contractors, brought this action seeking to enjoin the defendants from violating the minimum wage requirements and to enforce the record-keeping and child labor provisions of the Act. [The district court denied the motion of some migrant workers to intervene to protect their claimed independent contractor status; held that the migrant workers were employees; and] entered final judgment on the issues of record-keeping and child labor violations, enjoining the defendants from further violations of the Act. [Lauritzen appeals.]

I. *Factual Background*

We must examine the factual background of the case to determine whether the employment status of the migrant workers could be concluded as a matter of law.

On a yearly basis the defendants plant between 100 to 330 acres of pickles on land they either own or lease. The harvested crop is sold to various processors in

---

[2] All the parties refer to the crop to be harvested as the "pickle crop," and so shall we. Perhaps the defendants have developed a remarkable new "pickle" seed. But whether they grow pickles or only potential pickles in the form of cucumbers, the law is the same.

the area. The pickles are handpicked, usually from July through September, by migrant families from out of state. Sometimes the children, some under twelve years of age, work in some capacity in the fields alongside their parents. Many of the migrant families return each harvest season by arrangement with the defendants, but, each year, other migrant families often come for the first time from Florida, Texas and elsewhere looking for work. The defendants would inform the families, either orally or sometimes in writing, of the amount of compensation they were to receive. Compensation is set by the defendants at one-half of the proceeds the defendants realize on the sale of the pickles that the migrants harvest on a family basis. Toward the end of the harvest season, when the crop is less abundant and, therefore, less profitable, the defendants offer the migrants a bonus to encourage them to stay to complete the harvest, but some leave anyway....

All matters relating to planting, fertilizing, insecticide spraying, and irrigation of the crop are within the defendants' direction, and performed by workers other than the migrant workers here involved. Occasionally a migrant who has worked for the defendant previously and knows the harvesting will suggest the need for irrigation. In order to conduct their pickle-raising business, the defendants have made a considerable investment in land, buildings, equipment, and supplies. The defendants provide the migrants free housing which the defendants assign, but with regard for any preference the migrant families may have. The defendants also supply migrants with the equipment they need for their work. The migrants need supply only work gloves for themselves.

The harvest area is subdivided into migrant family plots. The defendants make the allocation after the migrant families inform them how much acreage the family can harvest. Much depends on which areas are ready to harvest, and when a particular migrant family may arrive ready to work. The family, not the defendants, determines which family members will pick the pickles. If a family arrives before the harvest begins, the defendants may, nevertheless, provide them with housing. A few may be given some interim duties or be permitted to work temporarily for other farmers. When the pickles are ready to pick, however, the migrant family's attention must be devoted only to their particular pickle plot.

The pickles that are ready to harvest must be picked regularly and completely before they grow too large and lose value when classified. The defendants give the workers pails in which to put the picked pickles. When the pails are filled by the pickers the pails are dumped into the defendants' sacks. At the end of the harvest day a family member will use one of defendants' trucks to haul the day's pick to one of defendants' grading stations or sorting sheds. After the pickles are graded the defendants give the migrant family member a receipt showing pickle grade and weight. The income of the individual families is not always equal. That is due, to some extent, to the ability of the migrant family to judge the pickles' size, color, and freshness so as to achieve pickles of better grade and higher value.

The workers describe their work generally as just "pulling the pickles off." It is not always physically easy, however, because the work involves stooping and kneeling and constant use of the hands, often under a hot sun. Picking pickles requires little or no prior training or experience; a short demonstration will suffice. One migrant worker recalled that when he was ten years old it had taken him about five minutes to learn pickle picking. Pickles continue to grow and develop until picked, but not uniformly, so harvesting is a continuing process. The migrant workers' income depends on the results of the particular family's efforts. The defendants explain that the migrants exercise care for both the plants and the pickles, which results in maximum yields, a benefit to the family as well as to the defendants. Machine harvesting, although advantageous for other crops, is not suitable for pickle harvesting. The defendants leave the when and how to pick to the families under this incentive arrangement. The defendants occasionally visit the fields to check on the families, the crop, and to supervise irrigation. The defendant, Michael Lauritzen, who actually operates the business, is sometimes referred to as the "boss." Some workers expressed the belief that he had the right to fire them....

II. *Standards of Review*

....

It is well recognized that under the FLSA the statutory definitions regarding employment[5] are broad and comprehensive in order to accomplish the remedial purposes of the Act. Courts, therefore, have not considered the common law concepts of "employee" and "independent contractor" to define the limits of the Act's coverage. We are seeking, instead, to determine "economic reality." For purposes of social welfare legislation, such as the FLSA, "employees are those who as a matter of economic reality are dependent upon the business to which they render service." *Mednick v. Albert Enterprises, Inc.,* 508 F.2d 297, 299 (5th Cir. 1975) (quoting *Bartels v. Birmingham,* 332 U.S. 126, 130 (1947)).

In seeking to determine the economic reality of the nature of the working relationship, courts do not look to a particular isolated factor but to all the circumstances of the work activity. Certain criteria have been developed to assist in determining the true nature of the relationship, but no criterion is by itself, or by its absence, dispositive or controlling.

Among the criteria courts have considered are the following six:

1) the nature and degree of the alleged employer's control as to the manner in which the work is to be performed;

---

[5] The Act defines an employee simply as "any individual employed by an employer." 29 U.S.C. § 203(e)(1). An "employer" is defined to include "any person acting directly or indirectly in the interest of an employer in relation to an employee." 29 U.S.C. § 203(d). To "[e]mploy includes to suffer or permit to work." 29 U.S.C. § 203(g).

2) the alleged employee's opportunity for profit or loss depending upon his managerial skill;

3) the alleged employee's investment in equipment or materials required for his task, or his employment of workers;

4) whether the service rendered requires a special skill;

5) the degree of permanency and duration of the working relationship;

6) the extent to which the service rendered is an integral part of the alleged employer's business.

This court previously has held that the determination of workers' status is a legal rather than a factual one, and therefore not subject to the clearly erroneous standard of review. The underlying facts, however, are necessarily subject to that standard....

III. *Analysis*

In a number of agricultural cases, albeit nonpickle cases, courts have applied the six criteria to find an employment, rather than a contractual, relationship. In some other cases involving migrant workers in similar circumstances, an employment relationship was either admitted or assumed, and was therefore not an issue.

In one case, however, *Donovan v. Brandel,* the Sixth Circuit affirmed the district court in classifying migrant workers harvesting pickles, under circumstances similar to those here, as independent contractors, not employees. 736 F.2d 1114 (6th Cir. 1984)....

A. *Control*

The *Brandel* court found that the landowner, under a sharecropping arrangement, had effectively relinquished control of harvesting to the migrants. The court considered this to be a factor in its finding that the migrant workers were independent contractors. In view of the pervasive overall control retained by the defendants here, we do not reach the same finding. We view the wage arrangement as no more than a way to effectively motivate employees, and to provide a means of determining their wages.

Brandel, according to the Sixth Circuit, did not retain "the right to dictate the manner in which the details of the harvesting function are executed." *Brandel,* 736 F.2d at 1119. For example, he did not appear in the fields to supervise the workers, or set hours for them to work. In this case, the defendants did occasionally visit the families in the fields. The workers sometimes referred to Michael Lauritzen as the "boss," and some of them expressed a belief that he had the right to fire them. Moreover, unlike the Sixth Circuit, we believe that the defendants' right to control applies to the entire pickle-farming operation, not just the details of harvesting. The defendants exercise pervasive control over the operation as a whole. We therefore agree with the district court that the defendants did not effectively relinquish control of the harvesting to the migrants.

B. *Profit and Loss*

The Sixth Circuit found that the migrant workers had the opportunity to increase their profits through the management of their pickle fields. Although the court found little or no evidence in the record supporting a finding that the workers were exposed to any risk of loss, it found the fact that their remuneration would increase through their management efforts to be dispositive of the profit and loss analysis. We do not agree. Although the profit opportunity may depend in part on how good a pickle picker is, there is no corresponding possibility for migrant worker loss. As the *Gillmor* court held, a reduction in money earned by the migrants is not a loss sufficient to satisfy the criteria for independent contractor status. [*Donovan v. Gillmor*, 535 F. Supp. 154 (N.D. Ohio), *appeal dismissed*, 708 F.2d 723 (6th Cir. 1982)]. The migrants have invested nothing except for the cost of their work gloves, and therefore have no investment to lose. Any reduction in earnings due to a poor pickle crop is a loss of wages, and not of an investment.

C. *Capital Investment*

The capital investment factor is interrelated to the profit and loss consideration. The *Gillmor* court characterized the investment in this context to be "large expenditures, such as risk capital, capital investments, and not negligible items or labor itself." The workers here are responsible only for providing their own gloves. Gloves do not constitute a capital investment. As in *Gillmor*, "[e]verything else, from farm equipment, land, seed, fertilizer, [and] insecticide to the living quarters of the migrants is supplied by the defendants." Although in *Brandel* the migrant furnished the pails, the *Brandel* court minimized this factor by saying that in pickle harvesting by hand there is no need for heavy capital investment by the worker, and the overall size of the investment by the employer relative to that by the worker is irrelevant. To the contrary, we believe that the migrant workers' disproportionately small stake in the pickle-farming operation is an indication that their work is not independent of the defendants.

D. *Degree of Skill Required*

Although a worker must develop some specialized skill in order to recognize which pickles to pick when, this development of occupational skills is no different from what any good employee in any line of work must do. Skills are not the monopoly of independent contractors. The *Brandel* court found that a high degree of skill is involved in caring for the pickle plants and picking the pickles. We agree that some skill is required, but we do not find that this level of skill sets the pickle harvester apart from the harvester of other crops. The migrants' talent and their physical endurance in the hot sun do not change the nature of their employment relationship with the defendants.

E. *Permanency*

Another factor in the employment analysis is permanency and duration of the relationship. The Sixth Circuit in *Brandel* found that the vast majority of harvesters have only a temporary relationship with the employer which suggested to the court an independent contractual arrangement. Many seasonal businesses necessarily hire only seasonal employees, but that fact alone does not convert seasonal employees into seasonal independent contractors. Many migrant families return year after year. In *Brandel* the returning migrant families comprised as high a proportion as forty percent to fifty percent of the work force. In this case the district court found that the migrant workers did not have the sort of permanent relationship associated with employment. Nevertheless, when the district court considered its finding in light of the economic reality of the parties' entire work relationship, the court did not consider this one criterion to be dispositive. Although we have serious doubts about this particular district court determination ... we need not disturb that finding for the purposes of this case. We agree with the *Gillmor* court that however temporary the relationship may be it is permanent and exclusive for the duration of that harvest season. One indication of permanency in this case is the fact that it is not uncommon for the migrant families to return year after year.

F. *Harvesting as an Integral Part of Defendants' Business*

Another factor we consider briefly is the extent to which the service of migrants may be considered an integral part of the pickle-picking business. The district court held that the migrants' work was an integral part of the business, as even the court in *Brandel* conceded. The defendant here takes a contrary view on appeal claiming that the record is insufficient to sustain the district court finding. It does not take much of a record to demonstrate that picking the pickles is a necessary and integral part of the pickle business unless the employer's investment, planting, and cultivating activities are only to serve the purpose of raising ornamental pickle vines. That result would likely disappoint all good pickle lovers.

G. *Dependence of Migrant Workers*

Our final task is to consider the degree to which the migrant families depend on the defendants. Economic dependence is more than just another factor. It is instead the focus of all the other considerations.

> The [other] tests are aids — tools to be used to gauge the degree of dependence of alleged employees on the business with which they are connected. It is *dependence* that indicates employee status. Each test must be applied with that ultimate notion in mind. More importantly, the final and determinative question must be whether the total of the testing establishes the personnel are so dependent upon the business with which they are connected

that they come within the protection of the FLSA or are sufficiently independent to lie outside its ambit.

Usery v. Pilgrim Equipment Co., 527 F.2d 1308, 1311-12 (5th Cir.) (emphasis in
original), *cert. denied,* 429 U.S. 826 (1976). The district court held that the
migrants were economically dependent on the defendants during the harvest
season. If the migrant families are pickle pickers, then they need pickles to pick
in order to survive economically. The migrants clearly are dependent on the
pickle business, and the defendants, for their continued employment and
livelihood. That is why many of them return year after year. The defendants
contend that skilled migrant families are in demand in the area and do not need
the defendants. Were it not for the defendants the migrant families would have to
find some other pickle grower who would hire them. Until they found another
grower, they would be unemployed. It is not necessary to show that workers are
unable to find work with any other employer to find that the workers are
employees rather than contractors.

We cannot say that the migrants are not employees, but, instead, are in
business for themselves and sufficiently independent to lie beyond the broad
reach of the FLSA. They depend on the defendants' land, crops, agricultural
expertise, equipment, and marketing skills. They are the defendants' employees.

IV. *Conclusion*

No trial is needed to sort out the material facts in these circumstances in order
to come to the conclusion of law that these migrant workers are employees,
entitled to the protection of the FLSA. The purpose of the Act is to protect
employees from low wages and long hours, and "to free commerce from the
interferences arising from the production of goods under conditions that were
detrimental to the health and well-being of workers." In this case, for example,
some children under twelve years of age are in the fields. Although there is no
suggestion in the record that the defendants are abusing the children in any way,
the child labor provisions of the Act are intended for their benefit. It may be that
the defendants' pickle operation is exemplary and conducted pursuant to standards even higher than those of the FLSA, but that does not allow the defendants
to circumvent the Act. Neither does the defendants' gloomy prediction that
application of the Act will have a devastating economic impact on the pickle
business relieve them from complying with the Act's provisions. In any event,
that argument is one for the Congress, not the courts. The basic arrangement
between the defendants and the pickle pickers which, according to the defendants, produces the highest economic return for both grower and picker, need not
be altered. All that need change is the label which the defendants apply to the
arrangement. The defendants need only think of the proceeds paid to the pickle

pickers as wages, keep the necessary records, and make sure they abide by the protection that the Act accords to working children.

Affirmed.

EASTERBROOK, CIRCUIT JUDGE, concurring.

Are cucumber pickers "employees" for purposes of the Fair Labor Standards Act? *Donovan v. Brandel,* 736 F.2d 1114 (6th Cir. 1984), says "no" as a matter of law. My colleagues say "yes" as a matter of law. Both opinions march through seven "factors" — each important, none dispositive. As the majority puts it: "Certain criteria have been developed to assist in determining the true nature of the relationship, but no criterion is by itself, or by its absence, dispositive or controlling." Courts must examine "all the circumstances" in search of "economic reality."

It is comforting to know that "economic reality" is the touchstone. One cringes to think that courts might decide these cases on the basis of economic fantasy. But "reality" encompasses millions of facts, and unless we have a legal rule with which to sift the material from the immaterial, we might as well examine the facts through a kaleidoscope. Which facts matter, and why? A legal approach calling on judges to examine all of the facts, and balance them, avoids formulating a rule of decision. The price of avoidance should be committing the decisions to the finders of fact, as our inability to fulfill Justice Holmes's belief that all tort law could be reduced to formulas after some years of experience[1] has meant that juries today decide the most complex products liability cases without substantial guidance from legal principles. Surely Holmes was right in believing that legal propositions ought to be in the form of rules to the extent possible. Why keep cucumber farmers in the dark about the legal consequences of their deeds?

People are entitled to know the legal rules before they act, and only the most compelling reason should lead a court to announce an approach under which no one can know where he stands until litigation has been completed. Litigation is costly and introduces risk into any endeavor; we should struggle to eliminate the risk and help people save the costs. Unless some obstacle such as inexperience with the subject, a dearth of facts, or a vacuum in the statute books intervenes, we should be able to attach legal consequences to recurrent factual patterns. Courts have had plenty of experience with the application of the FLSA to migrant farm workers. Fifty years after the Act's passage is too late to say that we still do not have a legal rule to govern these cases. My colleagues' balancing approach is the prevailing method, which they apply carefully. But it is unsatisfactory both because it offers little guidance for future cases and because any balancing test begs questions about which aspects of "economic reality" matter, and why.

---

[1] OLIVER WENDELL HOLMES, JR., THE COMMON LAW 111-13, 123-26 (1881).

I

Consider the problems with the balancing test. These are not the factors the *Restatement (Second) of Agency* § 2(3) (1958) suggests for identifying "independent contractors." The *Restatement* takes the view that the right to control the physical performance of the job is the central element of status as an independent contractor. My colleagues, joining many other courts, say that this approach is inapplicable because we should "accomplish the remedial purposes of the Act":

> Courts, therefore, have not considered the common law concepts of "employee" and "independent contractor" to define the limits of the Act's coverage. We are seeking, instead, to determine "economic reality."

This implies that the definition of "independent contractor" used in tort cases is inconsistent with "economic reality" but that the seven factors applied in FLSA cases capture that "reality." In which way did "economic reality" elude the American Law Institute and the courts of 50 states? What kind of differences between FLSA and tort cases are justified? A definition under which "in the application of social legislation employees are those who as a matter of economic reality are dependent upon the business to which they render service" does not help to isolate the elements of "reality" that matter.

Consider, too, the seven factors my colleagues distill from the cases. The first is the extent to which the supposed employer possesses a right to control the workers' performance. This is the core of the common law definition. The parties agree that Lauritzen did not prescribe or monitor the migrant workers' methods of work but instead measured output, the weight and kind of cucumbers picked. Lauritzen did not say who could work but instead negotiated only with the head of each migrant family. Lauritzen did not control how long each member of the family worked. This absence of control over who shall work, when, and how, strongly suggests an independent contractor relation at common law.

My colleagues admit that the migrant workers controlled their own working hours and picking methods, but discount these facts on the grounds that what counts is Lauritzen's "right to control ... the entire pickle-farming operation." If this is so, Pittsburgh Plate Glass must be an "employee" of General Motors because GM controls "the entire automobile manufacturing process" in which windshields from PPG are used. This method of analysis makes everyone an employee.

The second factor is whether the worker has an opportunity to profit (or is exposed to a risk of loss) through the application of managerial skills. My colleagues say that this indicates "employment" here because each worker has "invested nothing except for the cost of ... work gloves, and therefore [has] no investment to lose." But the opportunity to obtain profit from efficient management is not the same as exposing a stock of capital to a risk of loss. (*That* subject is the third factor, discussed below.) A consultant analyzing the operation of an assembly line also may furnish few tools except for a stopwatch, pencil, and clipboard, but such a person unquestionably is an independent contractor. The "managerial" skill may lie in deploying a work force efficiently. The head of each migrant family decides which family members work, for how long, on what plot of land. That is the same sort of managerial decision customarily made by supervisors in a hierarchical organization.

Third in my colleagues' list is the worker's investment in equipment or materials, that is, physical capital. The record is clear that the migrant workers possess little or no physical capital.[2] This is true of many workers we would call independent contractors. Think of lawyers, many of whom do not even own books. The bar sells human capital rather than physical capital, but this does not imply that lawyers are "employees" of their clients under the FLSA.[3]

The fourth factor, whether the worker possesses a "special skill," would exclude lawyers and others rich in human capital. The migrant workers, by contrast, are poor in human capital, so this factor augurs for a conclusion of employment.

Fifth in the list is "the degree of permanency and duration of the working relationship." This can be measured, but it is hard to see why it is significant. Lawyers may work for years for a single client but be independent contractors; hamburger-turners at fast-food restaurants may drift from one job to the next yet be employees throughout. The migrant workers who picked Lauritzen's cucumbers labor on many different farms over the course of a year, but work full-time at the pickle operation for more than a month. Surely an engineering consultant who worked full-time on a given job, and frequently worked with a single manufacturer, but did five to ten jobs a year, would be an independent contractor. What matters for the migrant workers: that they have many jobs and float among employers, or that they work full-time for the duration of the harvest? Without a legal theory we cannot tell.

Factor number six, the "extent to which the service rendered is an integral part of the employer's business," is one of those bits of "reality" that has neither significance nor meaning. *Everything* the employer does is "integral" to its business — why else do it? An omission to pick the cucumbers would be fatal to Lauritzen, but then so would an omission to plant the vines or water them. An omission to design a building would be fatal to an effort to build it, but this does

---

[2] Physical capital is not, however, the same thing as a "disproportionately small stake in the pickle-farming operation." The laborers' share of the farm's gross income exceeds 50%, giving the migrant workers a very large stake indeed in the successful harvest and marketing of the crop. (The migrants receive 50% of Lauritzen's gross, plus housing and end-of-season bonuses.)

[3] A story current among electrical engineers has it that after analyzing a destructive harmonic vibration in one of Edison's new generators, Prof. Steinmetz submitted an invoice for $5,000. An irate Edison demanded itemization. Steinmetz's new bill said:

1. Telling you to remove the third coil from the top...$10.00
2. Knowing which coil to remove $4,990.00

Steinmetz, selling only expertise, was the paradigm of an independent contractor.

not imply that architects are the "employees" of firms that want to erect new buildings. Acquiring tires is integral to the business of Chrysler, but the tires come from independent contractors. Perhaps "integral" in this formulation could mean "part of integrated operation," which would distinguish tires but leave unanswered the question why the difference should have a legal consequence.

Seventh and finally we have "dependence." "Economic dependence is more than just another factor. It is instead the focus of all the other considerations." The majority proceeds:

> The district court held that the migrants were economically dependent on the defendants during the harvest season. If the migrant families are pickle pickers, then they need pickles to pick in order to survive economically. The migrants clearly are dependent on the pickle business, and the defendants, for their continued employment and livelihood. That is why many of them return year after year. The defendants contend that skilled migrant families are in demand in the area and do not need the defendants. Were it not for the defendants the migrant families would have to find some other pickle grower who would hire them. Until they found another grower, they would be unemployed. It is not necessary to show that workers are unable to find work with any other employer to find that the workers are employees rather than contractors.

This is the nub of both the district court's opinion and my colleagues' approach. Part of it is factually unsupported. There is no evidence that the migrant families pick only pickles or are "dependent on the pickle business." For all we can tell, these families pick oranges in California, come to Wisconsin to pick cucumbers, and move on to New York to harvest apples. We know they work year-round, and cucumbers are not harvested year-round in the United States. The point of my colleagues' discussion of factors 2-4 is that these migrant workers are not specialized to pickles.

Now the families may be dependent on the pickle business once they arrive at Lauritzen's farm and settle down to work. If a flood carried away the cucumbers, the migrants would be hard pressed to find other work immediately. This, however, is true of anyone, be he employee or independent contractor. A lawyer engaged full-time on a complex case may take a while to find new business if the case unexpectedly settles. Migrant workers are no more dependent on Lauritzen than are sellers of fertilizer, who rely on the trade of the locality and are in the grip of economic forces beyond their control, and the person who fixes Lauritzen's irrigation equipment, a classic independent contractor. The conclusion of dependence in this case is an artifact of looking at the subject *ex post* — that is, after the workers are in the cucumber fields. To determine whether they are dependent on Lauritzen, we have to look at the arrangement *ex ante*.

The usual argument that workers are "dependent" on employers — frequently a euphemism for a concern about monopsony — is that they are immobile. The coal miner in a company town, the weaver who lives next door to one textile mill and 50 miles from the next, may be offered a wage less than the one that would be necessary to induce a new worker to come to town. The employer takes advantage of the family ties and other things that may fracture some labor markets into small regions, each of which may be less than fully competitive. Migrant workers, by definition, have broken the ties that bind them to one locale. They sell their skills in a national market. It is unlikely that they receive less than the competitive wage. That wage may be low — it will be if the skills they possess are common — and the FLSA may have something to say about that wage. It is not possible, however, to get to that conclusion by talking about "dependence." Lauritzen is dependent on migrant labor; he cannot move his farm, or change his crop after planting cucumbers. The workers, by contrast, can and will go elsewhere if Lauritzen offers too little money. The majority's observation when dealing with the fifth "factor" that families come back to Lauritzen year after year, indicates that he offers a satisfactory return on their labor.

So the seven factors are of uncertain import in theory and cut both ways in practice. The list also is curious by its omission. It does not mention the method of compensation. One common feature of an independent contractor relation is compensation by a flat fee (common in the construction business) or a percentage of revenues (the sharecropper and the investment bank). The migrants who picked Lauritzen's crop received more than half of the proceeds of the sales. True, piecework and commission sales are not inconsistent with status as an "employee," but the wrinkle here is that the migrants share the market risk with Lauritzen. Each gets part of the sales price, which may rise or fall with the demand for pickles and the supply of cucumbers each season. If the price collapses, the workers and Lauritzen share the loss; so too they share the gain if the price rises. This is not an ordinary attribute of employment. Employees' "profit sharing" arrangements rarely provide for loss sharing. Why should this be irrelevant to the status of the migrant workers?

If we are to have multiple factors, we also should have a trial. A fact-bound approach calling for the balancing of incommensurables, an approach in which no ascertainable legal rule determines a unique outcome, is one in which the trier of fact plays the principal part....

II

We should abandon these unfocused "factors" and start again. The language of the statute is the place to start. Section 3(g), 29 U.S.C. § 203(g), defines "employ" as including "to suffer or permit to work." This is "the broadest definition '... ever included in any one act.'" *United States v. Rosenwasser,* 323 U.S. 360, 363 n.3 (1945), quoting from Sen. Hugo Black, the Act's sponsor, 81 Cong. Rec. 7657 (1937). No wonder the common law definition of "independent contractor" does not govern. The definition, written in the passive, sweeps in almost any work done on the employer's premises, potentially any work done for the employer's benefit or with the employer's acquiescence.

We have been told to construe this statute broadly. *Rutherford Food Corp.* [*v. McComb,* 331 U.S. 722 (1947)]; *Tony and Susan Alamo Foundation v. Secretary of Labor,* 471 U.S. 290, 296 (1985). Knowing the end in view does not answer hard questions, for it does not tell us *how far* to go in pursuit of that end.... To know how far is far enough, we must examine the history and functions of the statute.

Unfortunately there is no useful discussion in the legislative debates about the application of the FLSA to agricultural workers. This drives us back to more general purposes — those of the FLSA in general, and those of the common law definition of the independent contractor. Section 2 of the FLSA, 29 U.S.C. § 202, supplies part of the need. Courts are "to correct and as rapidly as practical eliminate," § 2(b), the "labor conditions detrimental to the maintenance of the minimum standard of living necessary to health, efficiency, and general well-being of workers," § 2(a). We recently summarized the purposes of the overtime provisions of the FLSA — which turn out to be the important ones here (in conjunction with the child labor provisions) in light of the parties' apparent belief that the migrant workers regularly earn more than the minimum wage. *See Mechmet* [*v. Four Seasons Hotels, Ltd.,* 825 F.2d 1173, 1176 (7th Cir. 1987)]:

> The first purpose was to prevent workers willing (maybe out of desperation ...) to work abnormally long hours from taking jobs away from workers who prefer to work shorter hours. In particular, unions' efforts to negotiate for overtime provisions in collective bargaining agreements would be undermined if competing, non-union firms were free to hire workers willing to work long hours without overtime. The second purpose was to spread work and thereby reduce unemployment, by requiring the employer to pay a penalty for using fewer workers for the same amount of work as would be necessary if each worker worked a shorter week. The third purpose was to protect the overtime workers from themselves: long hours of work might impair their health or lead to more accidents (which might endanger other workers as well). This purpose may seem inconsistent with allowing overtime work if the employer pays time and a half, but maybe the required premium for overtime pay is intended to assure that workers will at least be compensated for the increased danger of working when tired.

[margin note: Purposes of FLSA]

To recite these purposes is not to endorse them; maybe, as Lauritzen says, the FLSA does more harm than good by foreclosing desirable packages of incentives (such as payment by reference to results rather than hours) or by reducing the opportunities for work, and hence the income, of those, such as migrant farm workers, who cannot readily enter white-collar professions and make more money while working fewer hours. The system in place on Lauritzen's farm may be the most efficient yet devised — best for owners, workers, and consumers

[margin note: Potential Problems of FLSA]

alike — but whether it is efficient or not is none of our business. The judicial function is to implement what Congress did, not to ask whether Congress did the right thing.[4]

The purposes Congress identified in § 2 and we amplified in *Mechmet* strongly suggest that the FLSA applies to migrant farm workers. We also observed in *Mechmet* that the statute was designed to protect workers without substantial human capital, who therefore earn the lowest wages. No one doubts that migrant farm workers are short on human capital; an occupation that can be learned quickly does not pay great rewards.

The functions of the FLSA call for coverage. How about the functions of the independent contractor doctrine? This is a branch of tort law, designed to identify who is answerable for a wrong (and therefore, indirectly, to determine who must take care to prevent injuries). To say "X is an independent contractor" is to say that the chain of vicarious liability runs from X's employees to X but stops there. This concentrates on X the full incentive to take care. It is the right allocation when X is in the best position to determine what care is appropriate, to take that care, or to spread the risk of loss. Alan O. Sykes, *The Economics of Vicarious Liability,* 93 Yale L.J. 1231 (1984). This usually follows the right to control the work. Someone who surrenders control of the details of the work — often to take advantage of the expertise (= human capital) of someone else — cannot determine what precautions are appropriate; his ignorance may have been the principal reason for hiring the independent contractor. Such a person or firm specifies the outputs (design the building; paint the fence) rather than the inputs. Imposing liability on the person who does not control the execution of the work might induce pointless monitoring. All the details of the common law independent contractor doctrine having to do with the right to control the work are addressed to identifying the best monitor and precaution-taker.

The reasons for blocking vicarious liability at a particular point have nothing to do with the functions of the FLSA. The independent contractor will have its own employees, who will be covered by the Act. Electricians are "employees" of someone, even though the electrical subcontractor is not the employee of the general contractor. Indeed, the details of independent contractor relations are fundamentally contractual. Firms can structure their dealings as "employment" or "independent contractor" to maximize the efficiency of incentives to work, monitor, and take precautions. Paul H. Rubin, *The Theory of the Firm and the Economics of the Franchise Contract,* 21 J.L. & Econ. 223 (1978). The FLSA is designed to defeat rather than implement contractual arrangements. If employees voluntarily contract to accept $2.00 per hour, the agreement is ineffectual.... In this sense "economic reality" rather than contractual form is indeed dispositive.

---

[4] Or whether, as seems likely, the parties can cope with a change in the legal rule. If the Act applies, Lauritzen can maintain a system of incentives tied to the price the cucumbers will fetch. The farm must keep records and ensure that the total payment exceeds the statutory minimum; if it does this, the FLSA is indifferent to the device by which the excess is determined.

The migrant workers are selling nothing but their labor. They have no physical capital and little human capital to vend. This does not belittle their skills. Willingness to work hard, dedication to a job, honesty, and good health, are valuable traits and all too scarce. Those who possess these traits will find employment; those who do not cannot work (for long) even at the minimum wage in the private sector. But those to whom the FLSA applies must include workers who possess only dedication, honesty, and good health. So the baby-sitter is an "employee" even though working but a few hours a week, and the writer of novels is not an "employee" of the publisher even though renting only human capital. The migrant workers labor on the farmer's premises, doing repetitive tasks. Payment on a piecework rate (e.g., 1 per pound of cucumbers) would not take these workers out of the Act, any more than payment of the sales staff at a department store on commission avoids the statute. The link of the migrants' compensation to the market price of pickles is not fundamentally different from piecework compensation. Just as the piecework rate may be adjusted in response to the market (e.g., to 1 per 1.1 pounds, if the market falls 10%), imposing the market risk on piecework laborers, so the migrants' percentage share may be adjusted in response to the market (e.g., rising to 55% of the gross if the market should fall 10%) in order to relieve them of market risk. Through such adjustments Lauritzen may end up bearing the whole market risk, and in the long run must do so to attract workers.

There are hard cases under the approach I have limned, but this is not one of them. Migrant farm hands are "employees" under the FLSA — without regard to the crop and the contract in each case. We can, and should, do away with ambulatory balancing in cases of this sort. Once they know how the FLSA works, employers, workers, and Congress have their options. The longer we keep these people in the dark, the more chancy both the interpretive and the amending process become.

NOTES

1. *Myriad Definitions of Employee.* The FLSA defines employer and employee curtly but vaguely. Other statutes are more long-winded, in an attempt to be more precise. For an example of a detailed definition, complete with special rules for racing jockeys, see the New York Workers' Compensation Law §§ 2.3-4 (in the Statutory Appendix). In 1994, the U.S. Departments of Labor and Commerce released a report prepared by the Commission on the Future of Worker Management Relations (the "Dunlop Commission"), which recommended that all laws adopt "economic realities" as the definition of employee:

> The definition of employee in labor, employment, and tax law should be modernized, simplified, and standardized. Instead of the control test borrowed from the old common law of master and servant, the definition should

be based on the economic realities underlying the relationship between the worker and the party benefiting from the worker's services.

Is the Dunlop Commission correct in calling for a single definition of "employee" to replace the various common law and statutory tests? Judge Easterbrook concurring in *Lauritzen* suggests otherwise, arguing that whether a worker should be considered an employee depends on the reason for coverage. The policies behind various employment laws differ, suggesting that some workers should be covered employees in one situation but not in another. For example, the FLSA is designed to protect vulnerable workers from employer abuses, such as excessive work hours or low pay. In this case, broad coverage of low-skilled workers would be the desired goal, and the "economic realities" test is appropriate.

Judge Easterbrook, citing Professor Sykes, argues that a different test would be more appropriate when determining whether a general contractor should be liable when a sub-contractor's employee is injured. In that case, liability should be placed on the "cheapest cost avoider" of the accident, the party who is in the best position to determine the costs and benefits of steps that might be taken to reduce the risk of accidents. The "right to control" test works well here because the person who controls the details of work is generally in the best position to make the necessary evaluation. *See generally* Alan O. Sykes, *The Economics of Vicarious Liability*, 93 YALE L.J. 1231 (1984).

2. *The IRS and Independent Contractors*. The largest day-to-day consequence of the employee/independent contractor label is the differing tax obligations. For employees, the employer must withhold federal and state income taxes, pay the FUTA (unemployment) tax, pay the employer's portion and withhold the employee's portion of FICA taxes (social security and Medicare), and pay state unemployment taxes and workers' compensation premiums. In addition, employers must file various tax forms for employees, such as W-2, W-3, 940 and 941 forms.

The tax rules for independent contractors are simpler. A person in a trade or business must file a Form 1099-MISC to report compensation in excess of $600 paid to a nonemployee. I.R.C. § 6041. The business does not have to pay or withhold any taxes, however, because independent contractors are responsible for making their own estimated income tax payments and paying their own federal income taxes.

The Internal Revenue Code relies on the common law to make the employee/independent contractor distinction. I.R.C. § 3121(d) defines "employee" to mean "any individual who, under the usual common law rules applicable in determining the employer-employee relationship, has the status of an employee." Recognizing that this is a bit vague and, as always, trying to be helpful, the IRS has identified the following twenty factors as relevant to the determination:

1. Instructions. Workers required to comply with the instructions of others *This will not be on the exam* about when, where, and how to work are ordinarily employees.
2. Training. Workers provided training tend to be employees.
3. Integration. Employees tend to be more integrated into overall business operations.
4. Services Rendered Personally. Requiring services to be rendered personally indicates employment.
5. Hiring, Supervising, and Paying Assistants. If the worker hires her own assistants, she is more likely to be an independent contractor.
6. Continuing Relationship. A continuing relationship between the worker and the person for whom services are performed indicates employment.
7. Set Hours of Work. Set hours of work indicate employment.
8. Full Time Required. Full-time work indicates employment.
9. Doing Work on Employer's Premises. This factor indicates employment.
10. Order or Sequence Set. If the person for whom services are performed sets the order or sequence in which work must be performed, workers tend to be employees.
11. Oral or Written Reports. Workers who must submit reports tend to be employees.
12. Payment by Hour, Week, or Month. Payment by hour, week, or month indicates employment, while payment by job or commission indicates independent contractor status.
13. Payment of Business and Traveling Expenses. This factor indicates employment.
14. Furnishing of Tools and Materials. If the person for whom services are being performed furnishes tools and materials, workers tend to be employees.
15. Significant Investment. Investment by the worker in facilities used to perform services indicates independent contractor status.
16. Realization of Profit or Loss. A worker subject to a real risk of economic loss due to investments or liability for expenses tends to be an independent contractor.
17. Working for More than One Firm at a Time. Working for more than one firm at a time indicates independent contractor status.
18. Making Service Available to the General Public. Workers making their services available to the general public indicates independent contractor status.
19. Right to Discharge. If the person receiving services can discharge workers, the workers tend to be employees.
20. Right to Terminate. If workers can terminate the relationship at any time without liability, they tend to be employees.

Rev. Rul. 87-41, 1987-1 C.B. 296. *See also* 26 C.F.R. §§ 31.3121(d)-1, 31.3306(i)-1, 31.3401(c)-1 (definitions of "employee" for purposes of FICA, FUTA, and federal tax withholding, respectively).

The IRS is clear, however, that there is no set formula for weighting these questions, or for how many of them need to be satisfied before a worker is classified as an employee. They are "designed only as guides for determining whether an individual is an employee." Rev. Rul. 87-41, 1987-1 C.B. 296, 298. Bills are regularly introduced in Congress to simplify and clarify the IRS definition of employee.

3. *Firm Organization. Lauritzen* indicates that the FLSA creates incentives for employers to structure their relationships with workers as principal-independent contractor, rather than employer-employee, relationships. Other regulatory programs may also influence this decision one way or the other. The desire to limit unionization or to avoid taxes, for example, may push employers towards a principal-independent contractor relationship, while immunity from tort liability under the workers' compensation laws may work the other way.

Independently of incentives created by regulatory programs, however, some parties prefer an employer-employee relationship to a principal-independent contractor relationship, and vice versa. One goal of regulatory law should be to avoid inadvertently distorting these decisions. For example, if employees are more risk averse than employers, an employer-employee relationship may be optimal. In other situations, the decision may depend on the cost of acquiring information:

> [O]pportunities for profitable team production by inputs already within the firm may be ascertained more economically and accurately than for resources outside the firm. Superior combinations of inputs can be more economically identified and formed from resources already used in the organization than by obtaining new resources (and knowledge of them) from the outside. Promotion and revision of employee assignments (contracts) will be preferred by a firm to the hiring of new inputs .... Efficient production with heterogeneous resources is a result not of having *better* resources but in *knowing more accurately* the relative productive performances of those resources.

Armen A. Alchian & Harold Demsetz, *Production, Information Costs, and Economic Organization,* 62 AM. ECON. REV. 777, 793 (1972). How do these reasons for having employees versus hiring independent contractors interrelate with the incentives created by the FLSA and similar laws?

4. *Are Independent Contractors an Exploited Group?* Because the FLSA does not protect independent contractors, the *Lauritzen* court wanted to analyze the economic reality and prevent the migrant workers from being termed independent contractors. But are independent contractors an exploited group? According to recent statistics, 92.3% of all independent contractors are white and two thirds are male. In addition, most independent contractors were found to be well educated; 34% hold a college degree, compared to only 29% of workers in traditional employment settings. Typical occupations for independent contractors are artists, writers, insurance and real estate agents, construction trade employees, and miscellaneous managers and administrators. Sharon R. Cohany, *Workers in Alternative Employment Arrangements*, MONTHLY LAB. REV., Oct. 1996, at 31, 32-33. Indeed, in the *Lauritzen* case, what did the migrant farmers want? Recall that some of them intervened on Lauritzen's side.

B. COVERED EMPLOYEES

Even if a worker is clearly an employee rather than an independent contractor, he or she may not be subject to the protections of a particular employment law. Often an employment statute exempts part-time workers, home workers, leased workers, or other so-called "contingent" workers. The following case, in addition to wrestling with the consequences of the independent contractor label, addresses whether an employer can avoid paying benefits to some employees while offering benefits to its core workforce.

VIZCAINO v. MICROSOFT CORP. *Tough case*

United State Court of Appeals, Ninth Circuit (*en banc*)
120 F.3d 1006 (1997), *cert. denied,* 118 S. Ct. 899 (1998)

FERNANDEZ, Circuit Judge [with whom BROWNING and TASHIMA, Circuit Judges, join]:

Donna Vizcaino [and seven others] brought this action on behalf of themselves and a court-certified class (all are hereafter collectively referred to as "the Workers"). They sued Microsoft Corporation and its various pension and welfare plans, including its Savings Plus Plan (SPP), and sought a determination that they were entitled to participate in the plan benefits because those benefits were available to Microsoft's common law employees. The district court granted summary judgment against the Workers, and they appealed the determinations that they were not entitled to participate in the SPP or in the Employee Stock Purchase Plan (ESPP). We reversed the district court .... *See Vizcaino v. Microsoft Corp.*, 97 F.3d 1187 (9th Cir. 1996) (*Vizcaino I*). However, we then decided to rehear the matter en banc ....

BACKGROUND

At various times before 1990, Microsoft hired the Workers to perform services for it. They did perform those services over a continuous period, often exceeding two years. They were hired to work on specific projects and performed a number of different functions, such as production editing, proofreading, formatting, indexing, and testing. "Microsoft fully integrated [the Workers] into its workforce: they often worked on teams along with regular employees, sharing the same supervisors, performing identical functions, and working the same core hours. Because Microsoft required that they work on site, they received admittance card keys, office equipment and supplies from the company." *Id.* at 1190. However, they were not paid for their services through the payroll department, but rather submitted invoices to and were paid through the accounts payable department.

Microsoft did not withhold income or Federal Insurance Contribution Act taxes from the Workers' wages, and did not pay the employer's share of the FICA taxes. Moreover, Microsoft did not allow the Workers to participate in the SPP or the ESPP. The Workers did not complain about those arrangements at that time.

However, in 1989 and 1990 the Internal Revenue Service examined Microsoft's records and decided that it should have been withholding and paying over taxes because, as a matter of law, the Workers were employees rather than independent contractors. It made that determination by applying common law principles. Microsoft agreed with the IRS and made the necessary corrections for the past by issuing W-2 forms to the Workers and by paying the employer's share of FICA taxes to the government.

Microsoft also realized that, because the Workers were employees, at least for tax purposes, it had to change its system. It made no sense to have employees paid through the accounts payable department, so those who remained in essentially the same relationship as before were tendered offers to become acknowledged employees. Others had to discontinue working for Microsoft, but did have the opportunity to go to work for a temporary employment agency, which could then supply temporary Workers to Microsoft on an as-needed basis. Some took advantage of that opportunity, some — like Vizcaino — did not.

The Workers then asserted that they were employees of Microsoft and should have had the opportunity of participating in the SPP and the ESPP because those plans were available to all employees who met certain other participation qualifications, which are not relevant to the issues before us. Microsoft disagreed, and the Workers asked the SPP plan administrator to exercise his authority to declare that they were eligible for the benefits. A panel was convened; it ruled that the Workers were not entitled to any benefits from ERISA plans — for example, the SPP — or, for that matter, from non-ERISA plans — for example, the ESPP. That, the administrative panel seemed to say, was because the Workers had agreed that they were independent contractors and because they had waived the right to participate in benefit plans. This action followed....

Although the Workers challenge both their exclusion from the SPP and their exclusion from the ESPP, the two plans are subject to rather different legal regimes. The former is a 26 U.S.C. § 401(k) plan, which is governed by ERISA; the latter is a 26 U.S.C. § 423 plan, which is not governed by ERISA. It, instead, is governed, at least in large part, by principles arising out of the law of the State of Washington. Nevertheless, certain issues, perhaps the most critical ones, cut across both regimes, and we will address them first.

I. GENERAL CONSIDERATIONS

A. *The Workers' Status*

It is important to recognize that there is no longer any question that the Workers were employees of Microsoft, and not independent contractors. The IRS clearly determined that they were. In theory one could argue that what the IRS said was fine for withholding and FICA purposes, but that is as far as it goes.

....

That question is obviated here for, perhaps more to the purpose, both Microsoft and the SPP have conceded for purposes of this appeal that the Workers were common law employees. In fact, they have asserted that the Workers' status is a "nonissue" because they concede that the Workers were common law employees. That is to say, they were employees of Microsoft.

B. *The Employment Agreements*

The concession that the Workers were employees would, at first blush, appear to dispose of this case. It means that for legal purposes they, along with the other employees of Microsoft, were subject to Microsoft's control as to both "the manner and means" of accomplishing their job, that they worked for a substantial period, that they were furnished a workplace and equipment, that they were subject to discharge, and the like. If that were all, this would be an exceedingly easy case. Of course, it is not all.

Microsoft also entered into special agreements with the Workers, and it is those which complicate matters to some extent. Each of the Workers and Microsoft signed agreements which stated, among other things not relevant here, that the worker was "an Independent Contractor for [Microsoft]," and nothing in the agreement should be construed as creating an "employer-employee relationship." As a result, the worker agreed "to be responsible for all of [his] federal and state taxes, withholding, social security, insurance, and other benefits." At the same time, Microsoft had the Workers sign an information form, which explained: "As an Independent Contractor to Microsoft, you are self employed and are responsible to pay all your own insurance and benefits.... Microsoft ... will not subject your payments to any withholding.... You are not either an employee of Microsoft, or a temporary employee of Microsoft." We now know beyond peradventure that most of this was not, in fact, true because the Workers actually were employees rather than independent contractors. What are we to make of that?

We now know that as a matter of law Microsoft hired the Workers to perform their services as employees and that the Workers performed those services. Yet we are also obligated to construe the agreements. In doing so, we could take either a negative or a positive view of Microsoft's intent and motives. We could decide that Microsoft knew that the Workers were employees, but chose to paste the independent contractor label upon them after making a rather amazing series of decisions to violate the law. Or we could decide that Microsoft mistakenly thought that the Workers were independent contractors and that all else simply seemed to flow from that status.

....

Absent evidence that the officers of Microsoft used their daedalian talents to follow the first route we have just outlined, we must decide that the second route is a more accurate portrayal of what occurred here. In other words, we should, and we do, consider what the parties did in the best light. In so doing, we do not believe that we are being panglossian; we are merely acting in accordance with the ancient maxim which assumes that "the law has been obeyed."

....

... Viewed in the proper light, it can be seen that the Workers were indeed hired by Microsoft to perform services for it. We know that their services were rendered in their capacities as employees. The contracts indicate, however, that they are independent contractors, which they were not. The other terms of the contracts do not add or subtract from their status or, indeed, impose separate agreements upon them. In effect, the other terms merely warn the Workers about what happens to them if they are independent contractors. Again, those are simply results which hinge on the status determination itself; they are not separate freestanding agreements. Therefore, the Workers were employees, who did not give up or waive their rights to be treated like all other employees under the plans. The Workers performed services for Microsoft under conditions which made them employees. They did sign agreements, which declared that they were independent contractors, but at best that declaration was due to a mutual mistake, and we know that even Microsoft does not now seek to assert that the label made them independent contractors.

....

One additional matter must detain us for a moment. It could, perhaps, be argued that the statements about benefits, unlike statements about withholding, stand on their own footing as a waiver of benefits, regardless of the Workers' true status as employees. As we have said, we think that would be an incorrect interpretation of these agreements, and Microsoft assured us at argument that this is not a waiver case. Were it one, we would have to consider whether the waivers based, as they would have been, on the mistaken premise of independent contractor status were knowing and voluntary under ERISA and Washington law. Moreover, at least as far as the SPP is concerned, we would have to consider whether the mistaken waiver must and would withstand special scrutiny designed to prevent potential employer or fiduciary abuse. *Cf. Holt v. Winpisinger*, 811 F.2d 1532, 1541 (D.C. Cir. 1987) (ERISA vesting provisions cannot be waived); *Amaro v. Continental Can Co.*, 724 F.2d 747, 752 (9th Cir. 1984) (ERISA's minimum standards cannot be waived). However, these issues need not even be mooted once it is recognized that there was no separate waiver at all. Moreover, we need not consider what the result would be if the agreements were of a different form or character.

In short, Microsoft has already recognized that the Workers were employees and that the "no withholding" consequence of the independent contractor label has fallen; we now hold that the "benefit" consequence has fallen also. Having thus burned off the brumes which threatened to obscure our view, we will now turn to the plans themselves.

II. THE PLANS

A. *The SPP*

The SPP is an ERISA plan. The Workers seek enforcement of the terms of that plan. That is, they seek to have us review the determination of the plan administrator and to require that the plan make its benefits available to them. As we have already pointed out, the administrative panel of the SPP determined that the Workers are not entitled to benefits. The reasons appear to have been that the Workers were independent contractors and that they waived the benefits. We must review those determinations to see if they were arbitrary or capricious. Based upon what we have already said, it is pellucid that they were. To the extent that the decision was based upon the supposed independent contractor status of the Workers, the plan conceded that the decision was wrong when it conceded that the Workers were, in fact, employees. To the extent that the decision was based upon a supposed waiver of benefits, the plan administrator purported to construe the agreements rather than the plan itself. But, as we have pointed out, our construction is the opposite. We, therefore, determine that the reasons given for denying benefits were arbitrary and capricious because they were based upon legal errors which "misconstrued the Plan and applied a wrong standard to a benefits determination."

The SPP now concedes as much, but it and the Workers asked the district court, and ask us, to decide a different issue of plan construction, one on which the administrator has not opined. The district court accepted that invitation.... We are tempted to do the same, but upon reflection we have determined that we should not allow ourselves to be seduced into making a decision which belongs to the plan administrator in the first instance.

We are asked to decide what is meant by the SPP's restriction of benefits to common law employees who are "on the United States payroll of the employer." ... No doubt the plan administrator should pay careful attention to what was said there. We have also pointed out that we are dubious about the proposition that Microsoft would manipulate plan coverage by assigning recognized common law employees to its accounts payable department or to its payroll department, as it saw fit. We have our doubts that it could properly do so. But it is the terms of the SPP which control, and the plan is separate from Microsoft itself. Thus, we cannot, and will not, predict how the plan administrator, who has the primary duty of construction, will construe the terms of the SPP.

We do not know whether he will rely upon an "is" construction — you must actually be on the payroll — or upon an "ought" construction — you must be a person who should be on the payroll. Nor do we know if he will accept the domestic versus foreign gloss on the provision in question. What we do know is that the decision is his in the first instance. We would set a poor precedent were we to intrude upon that exercise of discretion before he has even considered and ruled upon the issue. We would encourage the dumping of difficult and discretionary decisions into the laps of the courts, although one of the very purposes of ERISA is to avoid that kind of complication and delay. Of course, should he rule in favor of the Workers' position, he must then go on to determine what benefits they are entitled to and under what conditions, but that, too, is exactly the kind of decision that he should be making for each of the Workers in the first instance....

B. *The ESPP*

The ESPP was a plan adopted for the purpose of taking advantage of the benefits conferred under 26 U.S.C. § 423. It was approved by the board of directors and by the shareholders of Microsoft. Their action was an offer to employees, as that term is defined in § 423. As we have already suggested, we doubt that the corporate officers set out to withdraw the offer from some employees, even if they could have done that. The Workers knew about the fact of that offer, even if they were not aware of its precise terms. Under the law of the State of Washington, which all agree applies here, a contract can be accepted, even when the employee does not know its precise terms. *See Dorward v. ILWU-PMA Pension Plan*, 452 P.2d 258 (Wash. 1969). In *Dorward* the court pointed out that a pension is not a gratuity, but "rather is deferred compensation for services rendered." *Id.* at 261. We think that that same form of reasoning applies to all employee benefits. Few of them are mere gratuities or a result of unadulterated altruism. Most are for services rendered or for the purpose of inducing the further rendering of services. They help to guarantee a competent and happy labor force....

The ESPP was created and offered to all employees, the Workers knew of it, even if they were not aware of its precise terms, and their labor gave them a right to participate in it. Of course, Microsoft's officers would not allow that participation because they were under the misapprehension that the board and the shareholders had not extended the offer to the Workers. That error on the officers' part does not change the fact that there was an offer, which was accepted by the Workers' labor. Of course, the ESPP provides for a somewhat unusual benefit. An employee, who chooses to participate, must pay for any purchase of stock, and the Workers never did that. We, however, leave the determination of an appropriate remedy to the district court.

CONCLUSION

Microsoft, like other advanced employers, makes certain benefits available to all of its employees, who meet minimum conditions of eligibility. For some time, it did not believe that the Workers could partake of certain of those benefits because it thought that they were independent contractors. In that it was mistaken, as it now knows and concedes.

The mistake brought Microsoft difficulties with the IRS, but it has resolved those difficulties by making certain payments and by taking other actions. The mistake has also brought it difficulties with the Workers, and the time has come to resolve those.

Therefore, we now determine that the reasons for rejecting the Workers' participation in the SPP and the ESPP were invalid. Any remaining issues regarding the rights of a particular worker in the ESPP and his available remedies must be decided by the district court upon remand. However, any remaining issues regarding the right of any or all of the Workers to participate in the SPP must be decided by the plan administrator upon remand.

Reversed and Remanded to the district court as to the ESPP. *Reversed and Remanded* to the district court for further remand to the plan administrator as to the SPP.

FLETCHER, Circuit Judge, with whom HUG, Chief Judge, and PREGERSON, HAWKINS, and THOMAS, Circuit Judges, join, concurring in part and dissenting in part:

We concur in the substance of Judge Fernandez' opinion except that we would not remand the issue of eligibility to participate in the SPP to the Plan Administrator and would hold that the Workers are eligible to participate. Remand is inappropriate and further unnecessary in that we conclude that interpretation of the phrase "on the United States payroll of the employer" is not required....

Remand to the Plan Administrator to determine the meaning of the phrase "on the United States payroll of the employer" is improper because a plan should not be permitted to assert on judicial review reasons for denial that were not contained in the plan administrator's decision. Because it was raised for the first time before the district court, the Plan Administrator waived this argument....

O'SCANNLAIN, Circuit Judge, joined by HALL and T.G. NELSON, Circuit Judges, concurring in part and dissenting in part:

I respectfully dissent from all but Part II-A of the court's opinion [dealing with the SPP] because Microsoft and the plaintiffs never formed a valid contract under Washington law for the benefits now claimed. I concur in the result of Part II-A of the court's opinion but not in its analysis.

I

I do not disagree with the court's statement of facts, but it has failed to mention some and may leave a mistaken impression of others. Thus, I suggest that the following additional facts from the record be taken into account.

Freelancers The plaintiffs were temporary "freelancers" for Microsoft. Instead of calling them by this label — which was ubiquitously used within the Microsoft community and by the plaintiffs themselves — the court styles the plaintiffs as "workers." It then engages in a long discussion of why they were in fact "common law employees" of Microsoft. Both labels may be true — the plaintiffs did work, and Microsoft has conceded that the plaintiffs satisfy the definition of common law employees for some purposes. Neither of these labels are relevant to the question before us, however, and both are potentially misleading. Both *Important* labels imply that the plaintiffs were just like any other regular Microsoft employees, and hence should be eligible for the same benefits as regular staff. The evidence in the record, however, points to the contrary. I will refer to the plaintiffs by the same term the plaintiffs themselves use — "freelancers".

Before going further, it is also important that the statement of facts identify precisely what period of activity is at issue in this case. All plaintiffs were hired before 1989. In the fall of that year, the IRS determined, for employment tax purposes, that the freelancers were common law employees. After that, in late 1989 and during 1990, Microsoft directly hired some of the freelancers as "staff"[1] (with Microsoft benefits) and arranged for the remainder to become employees of unrelated employment agencies (without Microsoft benefits) who had contracts with Microsoft. For the sake of clarity, I note that all we decide today is whether the freelancers should have been allowed to participate in the ESPP and the SPP during the period leading up to the 1989-90 conversion. All agree that those freelancers who were converted into employees of outside employment agencies have no valid claim for participation in the ESPP and SPP after the date of their conversion.

When the freelancers were originally retained by contract with Microsoft, they were expressly told that they were not eligible for any Microsoft employee benefits, and that they would have to provide their own benefits. Indeed, the named plaintiffs admit that they did not think they were entitled to benefits, and did not think benefits were a part of their compensation package.

Moreover, the freelancers each signed contractual documents which expressly stated that they would not receive any benefits, and would have to pay their own taxes and benefits. Specifically, Microsoft required that each plaintiff sign an "Independent Contractor Agreement" ("ICA"). I think it is appropriate to set out the complete text of the relevant ICA provision:

> CONTRACTOR is an independent contractor for MS [Microsoft]. Nothing in this Agreement shall be construed as creating an employer-employee relationship, or as a guarantee of a future offer of employment. CONTRACTOR further agrees to be responsible for all federal and state taxes, withholding, social security, insurance and other benefits.

---

[1] "Staff" was the term Microsoft and the plaintiffs use for regular employees.

Attached to the ICA was a one-page document entitled "independent contractor/freelancer information," which the freelancers also signed. It stated:

> [A]s an Independent Contractor to Microsoft, you are self-employed and are responsible to pay all your own insurance and benefits.

In the district court, Microsoft's uncontested extrinsic evidence established that the plaintiffs were told, and knew, that benefits were not a part of their compensation. Instead of providing benefits, Microsoft paid the freelancers at a higher hourly rate than Microsoft's regular employees. The freelancers were also treated differently in a host of other ways. They had different color employee badges, different e-mail addresses, and were not invited to company parties and functions. Instead of receiving a regular paycheck from Microsoft's Payroll department (like Microsoft's regular employees), freelancers submitted invoices for their services to the Accounts Payable department.

With these additional relevant facts in mind, we may consider the merits.

II

As I see it, this is a simple contracts case. The Washington law of contracts governs the freelancers' claim of entitlement to benefits under the Employee Stock Purchase Plan ("ESPP"). No law, state or federal, mandates that Microsoft provide such benefits even to its employees. Plaintiffs are eligible to participate in the ESPP only to the extent that they entered into a valid contract with Microsoft for such participation.

Offer, acceptance, and consideration are requisites to contract formation under Washington law. In order to be entitled to benefits under the ESPP, therefore, Microsoft must have offered the benefits to the freelancers, and the freelancers must have accepted that offer.

The court claims that Microsoft's board of directors offered ESPP benefits to the freelancers when they promulgated the ESPP, reasoning that an offer of benefits in a pension plan extends to and may be accepted by employees who do not know its precise terms, as long as they generally know of its existence .... But in a line of general employment law cases apparently ignored by the court's opinion, Washington courts have held that an employer revokes a generally promulgated offer when it enters into a specific agreement with an employee which is inconsistent with the offer. *Thompson v. St. Regis Paper Co.*, 685 P.2d 1081, 1087 (Wash. 1984); *Hill v. J.C. Penney, Inc.*, 852 P.2d 1111, 1117 (Wash. Ct. App. 1993); *Grimes v. Allied Stores Corp.*, 768 P.2d 528, 529-30 (Wash. Ct. App. 1989); *see also Swanson v. Liquid Air Corp.*, 826 P.2d 664, 672 (Wash. 1992) ("It is generally recognized that an employer can disclaim what might otherwise appear to be enforceable promises in handbooks or manuals or similar documents."). As a matter of standard contract law, that principle is unassailable: an offer can be revoked by giving specific notice to the offeree at any time prior to acceptance or substantial performance.....

Exactly such a revocation occurred here. Microsoft's board offered the ESPP to employees generally, and then Microsoft told the freelancers: "We aren't offering the ESPP to you; ESPP benefits are not included in your contract." Knowing that they wouldn't get ESPP benefits, the freelancers nevertheless agreed to work for Microsoft. Their contract therefore does not include ESPP benefits because the offer of those benefits was revoked.

Likewise, there was no mutual assent (or "meeting of the minds") as is required for the formation of a unilateral contract. Microsoft did not think it was offering ESPP benefits to the freelancers, and the freelancers did not think they were accepting an offer of ESPP benefits. Had the parties known that a court would force them to include ESPP benefits in their contract, the bargain undoubtedly would have been different.

If this is not enough, the court's alleged contract suffers from another defect: a lack of consideration. There was no detrimental reliance on the ESPP by the freelancers — they did not think they would get ESPP benefits, and they still chose to work for Microsoft on Microsoft's terms. Indeed, it is hard to imagine what consideration the freelancers could have given for the ESPP benefits since they chose to work for Microsoft for several years without benefits. If anything, the freelancers received consideration (a higher hourly rate) for their agreement that they would *not* get ESPP benefits.

The court conjures up two reasons to disregard the express and unambiguous revocation of the offer of benefits to the workers, and to find a contract for benefits where none exists. First, the court says, the statements in the employment contracts were the result of a mistake since Microsoft's officers incorrectly thought the freelancers were independent contractors. The statements were not meant to have independent legal significance, but were "simply a helpful disclosure" explaining the meaning of independent contractor status — a status, it later turns out, that the freelancers did not have. I am unpersuaded.

....

The court's second argument, albeit not fully developed, is that under Delaware's corporations law, Microsoft's officers did not have authority to modify or to revoke the offer of the ESPP made by Microsoft's board of directors. There are two problems with this analysis.

First, as an entity without a physical existence, Microsoft can only act through its agents.... The only way to enter into a contract with Microsoft, therefore, was through Microsoft's officers and employees as agents of the corporation....

Second, even if the officers did not have the actual authority under Delaware corporations law to make a "no ESPP benefits" offer to the freelancers, the contract formed by the freelancers' acceptance of the offer exists nonetheless. The "no benefits" provision is an important term of the overall contract and should not be treated apart from the bargain as a whole. The freelancers cannot, with perfect hindsight, pick and choose among the parts of the contract they want to enforce while discarding the provisions they don't like, premised upon the notion that the officers lacked authority to form the contract. Furthermore, a contrary ruling undermines Delaware's carefully crafted rule that only the corporation (or a shareholder suing derivatively) can seek a remedy for unauthorized acts of corporate officers. *See Dieter v. Prime Computer, Inc.*, 681 A.2d 1068, 1072 (Del. Ch. 1996)....

NOTES

1. *Employment Contracts as Simple Contracts.* Judge O'Scannlain, dissenting in *Microsoft*, wanted to treat the case as a regular contracts case. Whether employment relationships should be treated like any other contract, or must be given extra scrutiny for fear of exploitation, is a recurring theme in employment law. But even under the majority's analysis, could not Microsoft have given some employees benefits and denied them to others, if the employment contracts were drafted clearly enough?

2. *When is an Employee an "Employee?"* Microsoft tried by contract to exclude certain employees from company benefits. Often an employment law itself excludes workers who clearly are "employees" from its protection. Many workers' compensation laws, for example, exclude "casual" employees. The Fair Labor Standards Act contains long lists of employees who are not covered by some or all of its provisions, ranging from executive, administrative and professional employees to babysitters and taxicab drivers. 29 U.S.C. § 213. The National Labor Relations Act does not cover agricultural workers or supervisors. 29 U.S.C. § 152(3).

On the other hand, statutes sometimes cover workers who actually are *not* employees. For example, under the Internal Revenue Code, leased workers are considered to be employees of the recipient of their labor if certain criteria are met, even though their employment contracts may be with another party. If the workers perform services for the recipient for a full year on a substantially full-time basis and the services historically have been performed by employees, the worker "shall be treated" as an employee of the recipient for some purposes. I.R.C. § 414(n). Similarly, sometimes protections initially developed to protect employees have been extended to others. *See O'Hare Trucking Serv., Inc. v. City of Northlake*, 116 S. Ct. 2353 (1996) (First Amendment protection generally afforded to public employees also covers independent contractors).

Finally, there are situations where the worker is clearly an employee, but whose employee is unclear. Some courts have declared such workers to be "joint employees" of both the party with whom the workers have employment contracts and the party for whose benefit the workers perform under these contracts. In *Torres-Lopez v. May,* 111 F.3d 633 (9th Cir. 1997), the court held that leased employees who worked for a farm labor contractor picking cucumbers (or should we say pickles?) were protected under the FLSA as employees of the farm on whose land they worked. In reaching its conclusion, the court reasoned that "joint employment should be defined expansively under the FLSA," *id.* at 640, and that "without the land the worker might not have work," *id.* at 639.

3. *Core and Contingent Workers.* Microsoft is typical of modern corporations in employing a permanent core workforce surrounded by contingent workers.

> A company's labor force can be comprised of a mix of two general types of workers — core workers and contingent workers. Core workers have a strong affiliation with an employer and are treated by the employer as having a significant stake in the company. Core workers can be thought of as being part of the so-called corporate family. They show long-term attachment to a company and have a real measure of job stability. In the language of economists, core workers have an implicit contract with their employers: if they follow certain rules and norms and meet certain standards, their employers will provide a long-term home of employment and some measure of advancement. In contrast, contingent workers have a weak affiliation with a specific employer and do not have a significant stake in a company. Contingent workers are not considered part of the corporate family. They do not show long-term attachment to a company, and they often do not have a real measure of job stability. Employers generally do not make implicit contracts with contingent workers.

RICHARD S. BELOUS, THE CONTINGENT ECONOMY: THE GROWTH OF THE TEMPORARY, PART-TIME AND SUBCONTRACTED WORKFORCE 5-6 (1989).

Workers often labeled contingent include casual workers, part-time workers, temporary workers, on-call workers, leased workers, independent contractors, subcontractors, flex-time workers, job-sharing workers, self-employed workers, home workers, and workers employed by temporary staffing agencies.

C. COVERED EMPLOYERS

Some employment laws only make the corporate employer liable; others make managers or supervisors subject to liability as well. Further, employment laws vary dramatically in the scope of covered employers. The following case examines whether supervisors, who are employees themselves, can be sued as employers.

MILLER v. MAXWELL'S INTERNATIONAL, INC.

United States Court of Appeals, Ninth Circuit
991 F.2d 583 (1993), *cert. denied*, 510 U.S. 1109 (1994)

Before FLETCHER, WIGGINS, and KOZINSKI, Circuit Judges.

WIGGINS, Circuit Judge:

....

Phyllis Miller, proceeding pro se, filed sex and age discrimination claims in the district court under Title VII of the Civil Rights Act of 1964, the Age Discrimination in Employment Act of 1967 (ADEA), and the Equal Pay Act of 1963 (EPA), § 206(d) (incorporated into and enforced through the Fair Labor Standards Act of 1938 (FLSA)). She also asserted claims for retaliation and emotional distress. Miller appeals from the district court's dismissal of her claims as untimely (barred by statutes of limitations and laches) or for failure to state a claim.

I. Facts

Miller is pursuing sex and age discrimination claims against six defendants in their individual capacities: Donald Schupak, Dino La Rosa, Carlo Galazzo, Bui Duc Huy, Don Bohn, and Robert Stewart. Donald Schupak was CEO of Maxwell's International, the corporate owner of Maxwell's Plum restaurant, Miller's employer. La Rosa and Galazzo were both general managers of the restaurant; La Rosa was manager from Miller's initial hiring in 1982 until 1985, and Galazzo was manager from 1985 until Miller's third and final termination in 1986. Huy, Bohn, and Stewart were all lower level employees of Maxwell's Plum.

Miller alleges that when she was hired she was told that she would be promoted, but was not because of her sex and age, and that she worked as a manager of the "Terrace Garden" room but was not paid manager's wages. Miller also alleges that La Rosa reduced her hours and subjected her to a hostile work environment because of her sex and age and retaliated against her for complaining of discrimination to La Rosa. Miller further alleges that in retaliation for her having complained to her union about these actions, La Rosa fired her in July, 1984.

After her firing, Miller filed charges with the Equal Employment Opportunity Commission (EEOC) and the National Labor Relations Board (NLRB). NLRB proceedings resulted in Miller's reinstatement as a Maxwell's Plum employee. Thereafter, Miller alleges that Galazzo harassed her and denied her a full time schedule in retaliation for her previous EEOC and NLRB charges. She filed a second NLRB charge on October 30, 1985. Miller alleges that Huy and Bohn gave her notice that she had been fired a second time on November 8, 1985, and that Stewart and Galazzo issued a formal termination notice the next day. Miller also alleges that Galazzo, Bohn, and Stewart refused to write her letters of recommendation in retaliation for her earlier charges and because of sex and age discrimination. These allegations led to a second EEOC charge filed on November 13, 1985.

Sometime in March, 1986, Miller alleges that she was reinstated but then terminated for the third and final time because of retaliatory motives and sex and age discrimination. Miller also alleges that a lawsuit filed by Galazzo against her in March, 1986, constituted malicious prosecution, and she alleges that Galazzo and Schupak denied her unemployment benefits sometime in the Spring of 1986.

After receiving her right-to-sue letter from the EEOC, Miller timely filed an action in the district court on April 24, 1987. Proceeding pro se, Miller was given four opportunities to allege facts that stated a claim against the defendants. After her third amended complaint, the district court finally dismissed Miller's claims on May 18, 1990....

[T]he defendants argue that they have no personal liability under Title VII and the ADEA and that Miller received all of the relief to which she was entitled when she settled her claims with her corporate employer, Maxwell's International. We agree.

In ruling on this issue, the district court noted that "it is unlikely that Congress intended to impose personal liability on employees," but determined that the text of the statute does not necessarily preclude such individual liability and refused to dismiss Miller's claim on this basis without more definite guidance from this court. The liability schemes under Title VII and the ADEA are essentially the same in aspects relevant to this issue; they both limit civil liability to the employer. *See* 42 U.S.C. § 2000e-5(g) (1988) (Title VII); 29 U.S.C. § 626(b) (1988) (ADEA) (allowing actions against an employer by incorporating the procedures under 29 U.S.C. § 216(b)). Because Congress assessed civil liability only against an employer under Title VII, this court has held that "individual defendants cannot be held liable for back pay." *Padway v. Palches*, 665 F.2d 965, 968 (9th Cir.1982).

Nevertheless, the interpretation of the statutes to bar individual liability merits discussion because it conflicts with the reasoning of some courts. The term "employer" under the Title VII and the ADEA liability schemes is defined to include any agent of the employer. 42 U.S.C. § 2000e(b); 29 U.S.C. §§ 630(b), 203(d). Thus, some courts have reasoned that supervisory personnel and other agents of the employer are themselves employers for purposes of liability.

Although this statutory construction argument is not without merit, we are bound by *Padway*, which, in any event, announced the better rule. As the district court below noted, "[t]he obvious purpose of this [agent] provision was to incorporate respondeat superior liability into the statute." This conclusion is buttressed by the fact that many of the courts that purportedly have found individual liability under the statutes actually have held individuals liable only in their *official* capacities and not in their individual capacities. Indeed, these courts have joined this circuit in protecting supervisory employees from liability in their individual capacities.

The statutory scheme itself indicates that Congress did not intend to impose individual liability on employees. Title VII limits liability to employers with fifteen or more employees, 42 U.S.C. § 2000e(b), and the ADEA limits liability to employers with twenty or more employees, 29 U.S.C. § 630(b), in part because Congress did not want to burden small entities with the costs associated with litigating discrimination claims. If Congress decided to protect small entities with limited resources from liability, it is inconceivable that Congress intended to allow civil liability to run against individual employees.

Thus, this court's ruling in *Padway* that individual defendants cannot be held liable for damages under Title VII is good law,[2] and, because of the similarities

---

[2] At the time *Padway* was decided, damages were not available under Title VII. Since that time, Congress enacted the Civil Rights Act of 1991, which permits compensatory and punitive damages

in the Title VII and ADEA statutory schemes, is applicable to suits under the ADEA.[3] Although one court has determined that this holding "would encourage supervisory personnel to believe that they may violate Title VII with impunity," *Hamilton*, 791 F.2d at 443, the court's reasoning is unsound. No employer will allow supervisory or other personnel to violate Title VII when the employer is liable for the Title VII violation. An employer that has incurred civil damages because one of its employees believes he can violate Title VII with impunity will quickly correct that employee's erroneous belief.... There is no reason to stretch the liability of individual employees beyond the respondeat superior principle intended by Congress. Under our interpretation of *Padway* and the Title VII and ADEA statutory schemes, Miller's claims against the defendants in their individual capacities properly were dismissed for failure to state a claim.

....

FLETCHER, Circuit Judge, dissenting:

I respectfully dissent from [the] Part of the majority opinion that individuals (employees of the employer) cannot be individually liable under *either* Title VII or the ADEA.

In respect to Title VII, the majority relies on *Padway v. Palches*, 665 F.2d 965 (9th Cir.1982), which held that an "employer," not an employee, may be liable

---

for intentional discrimination. *See* 42 U.S.C. § 1981a (1992 Supp.). However, in drafting that section, Congress specifically limited the damages available depending upon the size of the respondent *employer*. *See id.* at § 1981a(b)(3)(A)-(D). Because we think that if Congress had envisioned individual liability under Title VII for compensatory or punitive damages, it would have included *individuals* in this litany of limitations and would have discontinued the exemption for small employers, we resist Judge Fletcher's urging specifically to limit *Padway* to back pay.

[3] Judge Fletcher argues that we should refrain from extending the conclusion that individual defendants cannot be held liable for damages under Title VII to suits under the ADEA based on *House v. Cannon Mills Co.*, 713 F. Supp. 159, 160 (M.D. N.C. 1988). *House* distinguished between Title VII and the ADEA for two reasons: one, because of the difference in the scope of relief, i.e., at the time *House* was decided, liquidated damages were available for willful violations of the ADEA, *see* 29 U.S.C. § 626(b), but damages were not available under Title VII; and, two, because "the ADEA incorporates the remedies and procedures of the Fair Labor Standards Act ("FLSA") ..." *House*, 713 F. Supp at 160. We do not find the *House* distinction persuasive. First, we note that Congress has amended Title VII to allow for both compensatory and punitive damages under Title VII. *See* note 2, *supra*. This reinforces our statement that "the liability schemes under Title VII and the ADEA are essentially the same in aspects relevant to this issue; they both limit civil liability to the employer." Second, we note that, although the ADEA incorporates *some* provisions of the FLSA, it does not specifically incorporate the provision that defines "employer." *See* 29 U.S.C. § 630(b). Although the *House* court correctly pointed out that the specific and selective incorporation of FLSA enforcement provisions into the ADEA evidences a Congressional intent to adopt existing interpretations of those provisions, we think logically that adoption must be limited to those provisions that specifically are incorporated. Accordingly, we find *House* unpersuasive for our purposes, and we resist Judge Fletcher's suggestion that we apply it in this case.

for an award of back pay. *Id*. at 968. Part of the rationale in *Padway* was that the employer, not a mere employee (regardless of that employee's supervisory powers), should pay *back wages*. General or punitive damages were not available under Title VII because the statute limited remedies to back pay and injunctive relief. Employees, however, can be sued in their official capacities, allowing a successful plaintiff to obtain injunctive relief.

I am concerned that the majority's overbroad language may unnecessarily cloud decisionmaking under the Civil Rights Act of 1991, which now permits compensatory and punitive damages for intentional discrimination. 42 U.S.C.A. § 1981a (1992 Supp.). This significant revision may permit suits against individuals for compensatory and punitive damages where the discrimination was intentional. *But see id.* at § 1981a(b)(3)(A)-(D) (establishing compensatory damage sum limitations by categories determined by "respondent[s']" number of employees). What can be said, and all that should be said, is that under Title VII prior to its amendment, an employee could not be held individually liable for back pay.

As for individual employee liability under the ADEA, I do not believe Miller's claims can be dismissed on the basis that "[t]he liability schemes under Title VII and the ADEA are essentially the same in aspects relevant to this issue." Notwithstanding the many similarities between the two statutory schemes, at the time of the enactment of the ADEA its "scope of relief [wa]s much broader" than that afforded by Title VII.[1] *See House v. Cannon Mills Co.*, 713 F. Supp. 159, 160 (M.D. N.C.1988). The difference in the scope of relief, in the *House* court's view, foreclosed reliance on *Padway* in determining individual liability under the ADEA. *Id.*

Perhaps a more significant difference between the two statutory regimes is that "the ADEA incorporates the remedies and procedures of the Fair Labor Standards Act, which differ from those under Title VII." There is no question that an individual can be personally liable as an employer under the FLSA; adverse employment actions attributable to individuals as a consequence of their authority over employment decisions can lead to individual liability where those actions violate the FLSA. The same result should apply to actions brought under the ADEA.

In *House*, the key inquiry centered on whether the employer's agents "had authority and discretion over [p]laintiff's discharge for allegedly discriminatory reasons." ... According to the court in *House*, "the clear import of the statutory language [in the ADEA], including the incorporation of the FLSA provisions and their accompanying case law, is imposition of personal liability on all 'employers,'" including supervisors. *House*, 713 F. Supp. at 161-62.

---

[1] 29 U.S.C. § 626(b) provides as a remedy "liquidated damages" "in cases of willful violations." As discussed above, the 1991 amendments to Title VII may or may not have brought Title VII's scope of relief nearer to that available under the ADEA. If they did not, as appears likely given the construction of the limitations categories, ADEA still affords more expansive relief possibilities.

... I conclude Miller should not be precluded from bringing an ADEA claim against those supervisors who took part in the termination decisions; those supervisors can be held liable, in their individual capacities, if their actions violated the ADEA. I would reverse.

NOTES

1. *Counting Employees.* Title VII covers employers with "fifteen or more employees for each working day in each of twenty or more calendar weeks in the current or preceding calendar year." 42 U.S.C. § 2000e(b). Suppose an employer has fourteen full-time employees and one part-time employee who does not work on Fridays. Is this employer subject to Title VII? The issue arose in *Walters v. Metropolitan Educational Enterprises, Inc.*, 117 S. Ct. 660 (1997). The Court of Appeals held that the employer was too small, reasoning that employees should be counted only on days they are actually compensated and determining that the employer did not have fifteen employees "each working day" as required by statute. The Supreme Court reversed, upholding the payroll method of counting employees, which counts all workers as an employee for each working day after they began work until the employment relationship terminates.

2. *Statutory Exemptions for Small Employers.* The coverage of small employers in employment statutes varies greatly. Most statutes define employer coverage by the number of employees, but the number varies statute by statute. The Federal Unemployment Tax Act applies to employers with one or more employees, Title VII and the Americans with Disabilities Act require fifteen employees, the Age Discrimination in Employment Act requires twenty employees, and the Family and Medical Leave Act requires fifty employees. *See* 26 U.S.C. § 3306(a)(UI); 42 U.S.C. § 2000e(b) (Title VII); 42 U.S.C. § 12111(5) (ADA); 29 U.S.C. § 630(b) (ADEA); 29 U.S.C. § 2611(4) (FMLA). Occasionally employer coverage is defined by the dollar volume of the business. Under the Fair Labor Standards Act, for example, "enterprise" coverage generally applies only to employers with $500,000 or more in annual sales. 29 U.S.C. § 203(s). Similarly, the National Labor Relations Board only exerts jurisdiction over employers with a certain amount of sales, for example, $500,000 annually for retail businesses and $250,000 annually for law firms. State employment laws also usually exempt small employers, but typically state laws extend to smaller employers than their federal analogues. For example, most state discrimination statutes extend to employers with fewer than fifteen employees, so they have broader coverage than Title VII, but most also exempt very small employers, for example, employers with less than four or five or ten employees. One of the principal purposes of state equivalents of federal statutes is to extend the reach of the policy.

Should small employers be exempt? On the one hand, the procedural or paperwork requirements that accompany these statutes are often particularly burdensome for small employers. On the other hand, an exemption would seem to let small employers violate the policies underlying the act. Or does it? In *Collins v. Rizkana,* 652 N.E.2d 653 (Ohio 1995), an employee in a three-person veterinarian office quit after accusing her employer of sexual harassment. The substance of the employer's actions clearly violated Title VII and the analogous Ohio Human Rights Law, but just as clearly the small employer did not meet the fifteen-employee threshold of Title VII nor the four-employee threshold of Ohio law. The Ohio Supreme Court allowed the employee to bring a common law wrongful discharge claim in violation of public policy, refusing to find a substantive policy in the four-employee threshold.

> [W]e cannot interpret the [four-employee threshold] as an intent by the General Assembly to grant small businesses in Ohio a license to sexually harass/discriminate against their employees with impunity. Instead, we can only read [the provision] as evidencing an intention to exempt small businesses from [the statute's] burdens, not from its antidiscrimination policy. ... [W]e cannot find it to be Ohio's public policy that an employer with three employees may condition their employment upon the performance of sexual favors while an employer with four employees may not.

Id. at 660-61.

3. *Exemptions for Public Employers*. Many employment laws cover only private employers, exempting government employers. Two conflicting explanations are sometimes given for treating private workplaces differently. On the one hand, government workers have constitutional protections and thus do not need statutory protections. As we shall see in Chapter 9, this reason was given to explain the governmental exemption to the Polygraph Protection Act of 1988. On the other hand, the statutory requirements are sometimes thought to be too burdensome to inflict upon governments.

Title VII, the major federal statute prohibiting sex and race discrimination in employment, illustrates the variation in applying employment laws to government employers. When originally passed as part of the Civil Rights Act of 1964, Title VII applied only to private sector employers. In 1972, however, Congress extended Title VII's coverage to the public sector. Finally, in 1993 Congress imposed the requirements of Title VII and numerous other employment laws on itself. Congressional Accountability Act, 2 U.S.C. §§ 1301-1438.

In some situations, the Constitution may prohibit Congress from extending employment laws to the states. In *National League of Cities v. Usery,* 426 U.S. 833 (1976), the Supreme Court held that Congress violated the Tenth Amendment (powers not delegated to the United States are reserved to the States or to the people) when it extended the minimum-wage and overtime rules of the Fair Labor Standards Act to state and municipal employees. In 1985, however, the case was overruled by *Garcia v. San Antonio Metro. Transit Auth.,* 469 U.S. 528.

Part II

The Rise and Fall of Employment at Will

"Why are you firing me, Mr. Ford?" asked Lee Iacocca, president of Ford Motor Company. Henry, looking at Iacocca, said: "I just don't like you!"
— from David Abodaher, *Iacocca: A Biography* 202 (1982).

"I put thirty-four years into this firm .... You can't eat the orange and throw the peel away — a man is not a piece of fruit."
— Willy Loman, in Arthur Miller's *Death of a Salesman,* Act II.

In this Part, we explore the basic common law principles governing the termination of private-sector employees. Modern contract and tort law have placed considerable limits on the nineteenth century idea that, because the workplace belonged to the employer, employees could be fired for a good reason, a bad reason, or no reason at all. Using similar principles, the law has also begun to protect worker privacy and autonomy from arbitrary action by employers. The following Part will explore these privacy developments.

Chapter 3

HISTORICAL FOUNDATIONS OF EMPLOYMENT AT WILL

STATUTE OF LABOURERS

23 Edw. III (1349)

EDWARD by the grace of God, &c. to the reverend father in Christ, William, by the same grace archbishop of Canterbury, primate of all England, greeting. Because a great part of the people, and especially of workmen and servants, late died of the pestilence, many seeing the necessity of masters, and great scarcity of servants, will not serve unless they may receive excessive wages, (2) and some rather willing to beg in idleness, than by labour to get their living; we, considering the grievous incommodities, which of the lack especially of ploughmen and such labourers may hereafter come, have upon deliberation and treaty with the prelates and the nobles, and learned men assisting us, of their mutual counsel, ordained:

CHAPTER I. Every person able in body under the age of sixty years, not having to live on, being required, shall be bound to serve him that doth require him, or else committed to the gaol, until he find surety to serve.

THAT every man and woman of our realm of *England,* of what condition he be, free or bond, able in body, and within the age of threescore years, not living in merchandize, nor exercising any craft, nor having of his own whereof he may live, nor proper land, about whose tillage he may himself occupy, and not serving any other, if he in convenient service (his Estate considered) be required to serve, he shall be bounden to serve him which so shall him require. And take only the wages, livery, meed, or salary, which were accustomed to be given in the places where he oweth to serve, the xx. year of our reign of *England,* or five or six other common years next before. Provided always, That the lords be preferred before other in their bondmen or their land tenants, so in their service to be retained: so that nevertheless the said lords shall retain no more than be necessary for them. And if any such man or woman, being so required to serve, will not the same do, that proved by two true men before the sheriff or the bailiffs of our sovereign lord the King, or the constables of the town where the same shall happen to be done, he shall anon be taken by them or any of them, and committed to the next gaol, there to remain under strait keeping, till he find surety to serve in the form aforesaid.

CHAPTER II. If a workman or servant depart from service before the time agreed upon, he shall be imprisoned.

ITEM, If any reaper, mower, or other workman or servant, of what estate or condition that he be, retained in any man's service, do depart from the said service without reasonable cause or license, before the term agreed, he shall have pain of imprisonment. And that none under the same pain presume to receive or to retain any such in his service.

    ....

STATUTE OF ARTIFICERS

5 Eliz., c. 4 (1562)

SECTION 1. ALTHOUGH there remain and stand in force presently a great number of acts and statutes concerning the retaining, departing, wages and orders of apprentices, servants and labourers, as well in husbandry as in divers other arts, mysteries and occupations; (2) yet partly for the imperfection and contrariety that is found, and doth appear in sundry of the said laws, and for the variety and number of them, (3) and chiefly for that the wages and allowances limited and rated in many of the said statutes, are in divers places too small and not answerable to this time, respecting the advancement of prices of all things belonging to the said servants and labourers; (4) the said laws cannot conveniently, without the great grief and burden of the poor labourer and hired man, be put in good and due execution: (5) and as the said several acts and statutes were, at the time of the making of them, thought to be very good and beneficial for the commonwealth of this realm (as divers of them are:) so if the substance of as many of the said laws as are meet to be continued, shall be digested and reduced into one sole law and statute, and in the same an uniform order prescribed and limited concerning the wages and other orders for apprentices, servants and labourers, there is good hope that it will come to pass, that the same law (being duly executed) should banish idleness, advance husbandry, and yield unto the hired person, both in the time of scarcity, and in the time of plenty, a convenient proportion of wages....

    ....

SECTION 3. And be it further enacted by the authority aforesaid, That no manner of person or persons, after the aforesaid last day of *September* now next ensuing, shall retain, hire or take into service, or cause to be retained, hired or taken into service, nor any person shall be retained, hired or taken into service, by any means or colour, to work for any less time or term than for one whole year, in any of the sciences, crafts, mysteries or arts of clothiers, woolen cloth weavers, truckers, fullers, clothworkers, sheremen, dyers, hosiers, taylors, shoemakers, tanners, pewterers, bakers, brewers, glovers, cutlers, smiths, farriers, curriers, sadlers, spurriers, turners, cappers, hatmakers or feltmakers, bowyers, fletchers, arrow-head-makers, butchers, cooks or millers.

SECTION 4. [Establishes compulsory service for able-bodied, propertyless adults, along the lines of the Statute of Labourers.]

SECTION 5. And be it further enacted, That no person which shall retain any servant, shall put away his or her said servant, (2) and that no person retained according to this statute, shall depart from his master, mistress or dame, before the end of his or her term; (3) upon the pain hereafter mentioned; (4) unless it be for some reasonable and sufficient cause or matter to be allowed before two justices of peace, or one at the least, within the said county, or before the mayor or other chief officer of the city....

NOTES

1. *The Black Death.* As its preamble suggests, the Statute of Labourers was enacted in response to the labor shortages caused by the "Black Death," a bubonic plague that swept England (and Europe) in 1348, killing perhaps half the population. Historians often point to this Statute as the beginning of Anglo-American labor legislation. The Statute illustrates the feudal conception of individuals as having fixed positions in society with set rights and duties. In particular, the Statute compels workers to accept employment at pre-Black Death wages and forbids them to quit before the end of the employment term. The control of labor was a central feature of England's laws in this period. *See* ROBERT R. PALMER, ENGLISH LAW IN THE AGE OF BLACK DEATH, 1348-1381 (1993).

As with the Statute of Labourers 200 years earlier, the immediate impetus for the Statute of Artificers in 1562 was an epidemic, this one reducing England's population by five percent. The Statute of Artificers remained in practical force for perhaps 200 years and was not formally repealed until 1875.

2. *Symmetry.* The Elizabethan statute, unlike the earlier statute, established employer as well as worker duties, suggesting a desire to treat the parties symmetrically. This symmetry rationale reappears often in contemporary employment law arguments. Nevertheless, the penalties were not symmetrical. A worker who quit before the end of the year or who failed to give proper notice could be imprisoned and might lose the year's wages. A master who dismissed a worker prematurely or without notice was subject to a fine of 40 shillings.

3. *Modern Issues in Elizabethan Language.* Section 1 of the Statute of Artificers complains about the proliferation of laws regulating employment and addresses the problem by enacting another statute. Does not this complaint have a modern ring?

In addition to combating the shortage of labor problem, the Statute of Artificers was designed to shift the burden of caring for the poor from the local parishes to employers. This issue — whether benefits should be provided through the workplace or government programs — remains current nearly half a millennium later.

4. *Yearly Contracts and Just Cause Dismissal.* Section 3 of the Statute of Artificers establishes a minimum duration of one year for employment contracts. Does Section 5 require just cause for terminating employment contracts, and specify a procedure for handling wrongful discharge claims? As we shall see at the end of this Part, the Model Employment Termination Act similarly requires good cause for termination and establishes an arbitration procedure to resolve disputes. Are we returning to the Elizabethan model?

1 WILLIAM BLACKSTONE, COMMENTARIES *413 (1765)

If the hiring be general without any particular time limited, the law construes it to be a hiring for a year; upon a principle of natural equity, that the servant shall serve, and the master maintain him, throughout all the revolutions of the respective seasons, as well when there is work to be done, as when there is not: but the contract may be made for any larger or smaller term.

NOTE

Developments in the English Rule. Consider the explanation of Blackstone's rule from Professor Feinman.

> [Blackstone's] rule thus stated expressed a sound principle: injustice would result if, for example, masters could have the benefit of servants' labor during planting and harvest seasons but discharge them to avoid supporting them during the unproductive winter, or if servants who were supported during the hard season could leave their masters' service when their labor was most needed. But the source of the yearly hiring rule was not solely, as might be supposed from Blackstone's statement, in the judges' concern for fairness between master and servant. The rule was also shaped by the requirements of the Statutes of Labourers, which prescribed a duty to work and prohibited leaving an employment or discharging a servant before the end of a term, and by the Poor Laws, which used a test of residence and employment to determine which community was responsible for the support of a person. Thus, despite a concern with the "revolution of the seasons," the rule articulated by Blackstone was not restricted to agricultural and domestic workers. The presumption that an indefinite hiring was a hiring for a year extended to all classes of servants. Because the rule was designed for domestic servants broadly construed, however, those who were clearly not in that group were sometimes excluded. The types of employment now considered usual — where the hours or days of work were limited, or the employment only for a certain job — would sometimes be held not to import a yearly hiring, indicating some sophistication by the law in not extending a concept designed for one purpose beyond its reasonable reach.
>
> The presumption of a yearly hiring could also be rebutted in specific cases by other means, especially, as the necessity of the rule for settlement cases diminished, when the parties were alleged to have contracted with reference

to a custom of the trade for a shorter period of employment. The frequency of periodic payments was a material factor in determining whether the parties intended the contract to be for a shorter period, but periodic payment of wages alone would not ordinarily rebut the presumption. Because the central question in each case was the factual one of the intention of the parties, the court decisions are sometimes apparently in conflict.

As the law was faced with an increasing variety of employment situations mostly far removed from the domestic relations which had shaped the earlier law, the importance of the duration of the contract in question diminished and the second issue, the notice required to terminate the contract, moved to the fore. Even when they recognized hirings as yearly ones, the courts refused to consider the contracts as entire and instead developed the rule that, unless specified otherwise, service contracts could be terminated on reasonable notice. This principle was recognized as early as the time of Blackstone, who stated that certain yearly hirings could be terminated on a quarter's notice. What constituted reasonable notice was a question of fact to be decided anew in each case, but certain conventions grew up. Domestic servants, who presumably no longer needed the benefit of the seasons, could be given a month's notice. Other types of employees could also be given a month's notice; three months was another common term, although some special cases required six or even twelve month's notice. Although notice was a separate question in each case, the custom of the trade was often determinative. In the twentieth century the required notice decreased considerably and is now regulated for many employees by the Contracts of Employment Act of 1963, which prescribes periods of required notice from one to eight weeks.

English law thus attempted to adapt to changing conditions and new situations, but more was involved than a simple desire to do justice between the parties. The Master and Servant Act of 1824 made breach of a service contract by an employee a criminal offense, while breach by an employer was still only a civil wrong. Thereafter, workers often sought shorter periods of notice. Among miners, for example, a fortnight's notice was common; in Scotland colliers had achieved "minute contracts" terminable on a minute's notice, allowing the workers to avoid criminal liability for sudden strikes. On the employers' side, the opportunity to hire lower-priced workers and fluctuations in the need for laborers made long notice periods somewhat undesirable, except when organized labor activity was great, in which case the employers desired longer periods of notice to protect themselves from damage from sudden strikes. The involved procedure for obtaining damages from an employee who breached without notice made the requirement of notice nugatory as to the employer, frequently resulting in imprisonment of the employee for debt but no payment to the employer. The real beneficiaries of the notice rule in the nineteenth century may have been the newly enlarged "middle class" employees: newspaper editors, commercial and business agents, etc. The cases suggest that their employers would have preferred to discharge them more easily, but the employees were protected by the notice requirement. Later, however, the shortening of the period of notice reduced the benefits to the employees.

Jay M. Feinman, *The Development of the Employment at Will Rule,* 20 AM. J. LEGAL HIST. 118, 120-22 (1976).[*]

HORACE GAY WOOD, MASTER AND SERVANT 272-73 (1877)

With us [in America, unlike in England,] the rule is inflexible, that a general or indefinite hiring is *prima facie* a hiring at will, and if the servant seeks to make it out a yearly hiring, the burden is upon him to establish it by proof. A hiring at so much a day, week, month or year, no time being specified, is an indefinite hiring, and no presumption attaches that it was for a day even, but only at the rate fixed for whatever time the party may serve.[4] It is competent for either party to show what the mutual understanding of the parties was in reference to the matter; but unless their understanding was mutual that the service was to extend for a certain fixed and definite period, it is an indefinite hiring and is determinable at the will of either party, and in this respect there is no distinction between domestic and other servants. But when from the contract itself it is evident that it was the understanding of the parties that the time was to extend for a certain period, their understanding, fairly inferable from the contract, will control. Thus, if A agrees with B to work for him eight months for $104, or $13 a month, this will not only be treated as a contract for eight months' service, but also as an entire contract, performance of which is a condition precedent to a recovery of any portion of the wages, and in *all* cases where a definite term is fixed, the fact that the wages are to be so much a month, and no time is fixed for a payment of the wages, does not make the contract divisible, and full performance is a condition precedent to a recovery of wages. Thus, in one case, the defendant [*sic*] contracted to work for the defendant seven months, at $12 a month, and it was held an entire contract, and that no part of the wages could be recovered until the contract was fully performed, or performance is waived or prevented by the defendant. So where the contract is to work at so much a day for one month or any other period, or at so much a month for six months, no time being fixed for payment, full performance is a condition precedent to a right thereto.

---

[4] *De Briar v. Minturn,* 1 Cal. 450 (1851); *The Franklin Mining Co. v. Harris,* 24 Mich. 115 (1871); *Tatterson v. Suffolk Manuf. Co.,* 106 Mass. 56 (1870); *Wilder v. United States,* 5 Ct. Cl. 462 (1869); [citations of 2 English cases omitted].

NOTES

1. *Rate-of-Pay Rule.* Most employment contracts state the rate of pay in terms of hourly or weekly wages, or monthly or yearly salaries. Does the fact that a contract calls for a salary of $80,000 per year indicate that the parties intended the employment to last for at least that amount of time? If the employee continues working into the second year, would the yearly presumption continue for the second and subsequent years? Or should the period between actual payments be assumed to be the contract period? Although Wood firmly rejected the rate-of-pay rule, one can find many "yes" answers to these questions in the older cases, and the rule refuses to die completely.

Consider S.D. CODIFIED LAWS ANN. § 60-1-3: "The length of time which an employer and employee adopt for the estimation of wages is relevant to a determination of the term of employment."

In *Winograd v. Willis,* 789 S.W.2d 307, 309-10 (Tex. Ct. App. 1990), the letter "outlin[ing] our agreement regarding your employment" called for an annual salary of $52,000. In upholding a jury verdict of wrongful termination, the court said:

> Texas has long adhered to the employment at will doctrine which states that when the term of service is left to the discretion of either employer or employee, either of those parties may terminate the employment relationship at will and without cause. In the absence of special circumstances, however, Texas also follows the general rule practiced in England, which dictates that a hiring at a stated sum per week, month, or year, is a definite employment for the period named and may not be arbitrarily concluded.

The New Jersey Supreme Court rejected the rate-of-pay "feudal custom," allowing summary judgment against an employee fired after eight months who was promised compensation at $80,000 per year. The Court declared that the English view "was appropriate for the agrarian economy of medieval England, where the relationship between masters and servants was governed in part by seasonal and agricultural cycles. With the establishment of a market economy in the United States, there is no longer a need for rules based on feudal custom." *Bernard v. IMI Systems, Inc.,* 618 A.2d 338, 341 (N.J. 1993).

2. *Rejection of Quantum Meruit.* Wood clearly acknowledges that the parties can write a contract of a definite duration. He emphasizes the dangers to employees of such a contract. According to Wood and the cases he cites, an employee who works two months on a yearly contract and then leaves is not entitled to any wages. Wood thus rejects the ability of breaching employees to recover on a quantum meruit theory for the value of services actually performed. Today, state wage laws require frequent payment of wages (monthly, biweekly or weekly) and payment for actual services.

3. *Sloppy Scholarship.* Horace Wood was a lawyer and prolific treatise writer from Albany, New York. A contemporary review of his Master and Servant treatise declared that "Mr. Wood obtained an excellent reputation as a learned, accurate, and original law author.... To bring order, simplicity and symmetry out of [the conflicting common law principles] was the work of a man of genius, and this we have before us." Book Notice, 15 ALBANY L.J. 378-79 (1877).

Later reviewers have not been so kind. Professor St. Antoine has described the employment at will rule as springing "full-blown in 1877 from [Wood's] busy and perhaps careless pen." Theodore J. St. Antoine, *You're Fired!,* 10 HUM. RTS. Q. 32, 33 (1982). *See also* Clyde Summers, *Individual Protection Against Unjust Dismissal: Time for a Statute,* 62 VA. L. REV. 481, 485 (1976) (the rule has "doubtful antecedents").

4. *Wood's Footnote 4.* In particular, scholars and courts often complain that the four American cases Wood cites in footnote 4 do not support the American rule. Professors Freed and Polsby have defended Wood, however, insisting that the four American cases "do indeed support the principle for which Wood cited them." Mayer G. Freed & Daniel D. Polsby, *The Doubtful Provenance of "Wood's Rule" Revisited,* 22 ARIZ. ST. L.J. 551, 554 (1990).

The problem is that the cases are not direct holdings for the employer's right to fire at any time. *Wilder v. United States* is not an employment case at all. A hauler (analogous to an employee?) contracted with the army to transport supplies for a certain rate of compensation, but for no definite duration. When Indian hostilities greatly increased the cost of transportation, the army agreed to the hauler's demand for a higher price. The army later refused to pay the higher price, but the court upheld the hauler's claim for the full price. In what way does this support an employer's right to fire at any time?

In *Franklin Mining Co.* and in *Tatterson,* the appellate courts affirmed jury verdicts for employees with contracts calling for $1,800 per year and $2,000 per year, respectively, finding sufficient evidence for the jury to infer that the employment was for a definite duration. In what way are these cases consistent with Wood's Rule?

In *De Briar,* the case reads in full:

> The defendant was an innkeeper. He employed the plaintiff as a bar-keeper, and was to give him three hundred dollars per month for his services, and allow him the privilege of occupying a room so long as he remained in the defendant's employ. The plaintiff was not hired for any definite period, and he was discharged by the defendant. After such discharge, the defendant notified the plaintiff to leave the room which he occupied, at the end of the month. The plaintiff did not comply with the notice, and the defendant put him out of the house by force; and this action is brought to recover damages for being thus ejected. The jury rendered a verdict in favor of the plaintiff for six hundred dollars.

We do not see how any action can be maintained upon the facts presented. The plaintiff had no right to remain in the defendant's house after being notified to leave, and the defendant had a right to eject him. It does not appear that any more force was used than was necessary, or that the facts would warrant anything more than nominal damages, even if an action could be sustained at all. We think a new trial should be granted.

Is *De Briar* more consistent with Wood's Rule, with the English practice requiring an employer to give reasonable notice, or with a rate-of-pay presumption? The headnote to *De Briar* does state: "Where no definite period of employment is agreed upon between a master and servant, the master has a right to discharge the servant at any time ...." Perhaps this is a good illustration for the common warning that lawyers should not rely on headnotes when reading cases.

5. *An Inflexible Rule.* Horace Wood describes the American at-will rule as "inflexible." In what respect is it inflexible? Consider the following argument:

The Wood formulation has been characterized as unduly rigid, in that it "force[s]" courts to ignore facts and circumstances indicative of the intention of the parties. But there is nothing "rigid" or inflexible about Wood's formulation. Wood does not suggest that it should be impermissible or even difficult for a plaintiff to prove that the parties intended that the employment relationship would last for a certain length of time. All it says is that plaintiff has the burden of proving that a contract of employment with no express duration was nevertheless intended by the parties to continue for a fixed duration. Nothing in the rule forecloses a jury from considering all the facts and circumstances from which inferences might be drawn concerning what the contract had been.

Of course, that is the role of a presumption: to decide issues where facts are skimpy or absent; presumptions are not supposed to keep facts from being introduced into evidence, nor are they supposed to decide what "surrounding circumstances" may count as a fact.

Mayer G. Freed & Daniel D. Polsby, *The Doubtful Provenance of "Wood's Rule" Revisited,* 22 ARIZ. ST. L.J. 551, 553 (1990).*

6. *Profound Influence.* Wood's treatise has been credited with the quick spread of the employment at will rule throughout the United States. As Professor Feinman says:

Whatever its origin and the inadequacies of its explanation, Wood's rule spread across the nation until it was generally adopted.... It is possible, of course, to attribute too much influence to Wood himself. Seldom has one individual been able to shape the law so dramatically through a mere published, ill-supported statement, and this article argues that primary impor-

---

*Reprinted with permission of Arizona State Law Journal and the authors.

tance must be given to factors external to the law itself. But treatises were important to the bar and bench in this period; a modern, comprehensive treatise stating a clear rule of practical application would almost inevitably attract a wide following and be cited as authority. Wood's treatise alone could not have caused the change to employment at will, but without it, the rule would likely not have developed as quickly and as uniformly as it did.

Jay M. Feinman, *The Development of the Employment at Will Rule,* 20 AM. J. LEGAL HIST. 118, 126-27 (1976).

SANFORD M. JACOBY, THE DURATION OF INDEFINITE EMPLOYMENT CONTRACTS IN THE UNITED STATES AND ENGLAND: AN HISTORICAL ANALYSIS, 5 Comparative Labor Law Journal 85, 116-18 (1982)[*]

Perhaps the most common explanation for the courts' embrace of the at-will doctrine was the rise of a formalistic approach to contract interpretation. The law focused narrowly on the contract to determine what the parties had intended. According to this logic, if the parties had intended the employment to last for a definite period they would have made that an express term of the contract. The at-will rule was the apotheosis of the laissez-faire conception of a contractual relation: The parties had a limited commitment to each other; they were free to enter or end a relation and define its terms without judicial interference. The period from 1890 to 1910, when the at-will rule became preeminent, marked the zenith of laissez-faire reasoning by the courts. However, the explanation is not entirely convincing, since the at-will doctrine was at variance with the contrac-tarian principle that the courts were supposed to give effect to the parties' manifest intentions.

The rigid presumption of terminability-at-will forced the courts to ignore evidence of the parties' intentions. In cases where the contract specified a rate of payment, a presumption of at-will terminability contradicted the parties' intentions that the relation should last as long as the period of payment. Strict contractarians like Williston argued that by ignoring the payment period, the

> ... courts had failed to observe that such a construction should, if possible, be put upon the language of the parties who enter into an agreement as will give rise to a legal obligation. [I]t seems a fair presumption that the parties intended the employment to last for at least one such period ... and should the parties continue their relation after the expiration of the first period, another contract by implication of fact would arise for another similar period.[216]

---

[*] Reprinted with permission of Comparative Labor Law.
[216] S. WILLISTON, [1 THE LAW OF CONTRACTS 62 (1920)].

Also, the at-will doctrine flatly contradicted contractarian logic in cases involving permanent employment contracts. The courts in most jurisdictions after 1890 held that contracts for "permanent" or "lifetime" employment were indefinite as to duration and thus terminable at will. Often the plaintiff had been promised permanent employment in return for dropping an injury claim against his employer. The parties clearly had intended that employment should continue as long as the employee remained able to perform his job. Holding such contracts to be indefinite and terminable at will was a negation of these intentions, an outcome that Williston also found unacceptable. English courts in the late nineteenth century considered these contracts to be perpetual in duration and enforceable, as did some American courts. But most American courts refused to enforce these contracts, which weakens the contractarian explanation for the doctrine.

JAY M. FEINMAN, THE DEVELOPMENT OF THE EMPLOYMENT AT WILL RULE, 20 American Journal of Legal History 118, 131-33 (1976)[*]

I suggest an alternative explanation for the rise of the employment at will rule: that the rule was an adjunct to the development of advanced capitalism in America....

The participants in the litigation that resulted in the change to Wood's rule were what could loosely be called middle-level employees and their employers. During a period when annual wages in the United States averaged considerably less than $1,000, many of the discharged employees bringing the duration of contract suits received salaries of several thousand dollars .... Typical positions held by these employees included corporate secretary, sales agent, attorney, plant superintendent, general manager and cashier, and chief building engineer.

Of course, there had always been managers, sales agents, and factory superintendents better paid than average workers. But through the first half of the nineteenth century owners and managers of smaller businesses comprised the bulk of the commercial middle class. Enterprises were not usually impersonal; the managers were frequently the owners of the businesses. The primary identifying feature of the old middle group of workers was that most members had an "independent means of livelihood." As the century progressed and the scale of production increased, however, enterprises became larger and more impersonal and many workers became farther removed from ownership. There were still many independent business people, of course, but salaried employees with little control of their employment situation became a larger proportion of the work force and an important segment of the economy. Engineers, foremen, and the new specialists in the management of larger enterprises were an important component of the new economic system, but for the most part they had less control over their positions than many of their predecessors. Thus the many suits

---

[*]Reprinted with permission of American Journal of Legal History.

brought to establish interests in their jobs were an attempt by a newly-important group in the economy to apply a traditional doctrine to their new situation, but the courts rejected the attempt and instead announced the new principle of employment at will. The reasons for this lie in the class division fundamental to the capitalist system: the distinction between owners and non-owners of capital. The effects of this division are felt in the control of labor and the discharge of employees.

An essential component of a capitalist system is the labor market. The owner of capital — the employer — and the non-owner of capital — the employee — enter into a wage bargain by which the employer becomes entitled to the worker's labor for a certain period and all its fruits in exchange for the payment of wages. The benefit of the bargain to the employer arises essentially because the worker produces more than the wages paid; the benefit to the worker is that wage labor is his sole source of subsistence. A corollary of the wage bargain is that, because the employer has purchased the total effort of the employee for the period, authority over the manner of work and the workplace belongs to the employer, not the employee. In this way the employer can conform the work to the requirements of production, enforcing the most efficient division of labor, for example.

Employment at will is the ultimate guarantor of the capitalist's authority over the worker.[120] The rule transformed long-term and semi-permanent relationships into non-binding agreements terminable at will. If employees could be dismissed on a moment's notice, obviously they could not claim a voice in the determination of the conditions of work or the use of the product of their labor. Indeed, such a fleeting relationship is hardly a contract at all.

The change to Wood's rule takes on added significance when its specific target — middle managers — is considered. This newly-important economic group presented perhaps a greater potential threat to the dominance of the owners of capital than did common laborers. Educated, responsible, and increasingly numerous, the middle level managers and agents of enterprises might have been expected to seek a greater share in the profits and direction of enterprises as the owners had to rely more heavily on them with the increasing size of business organizations. But the employment at will rule assured that as long as the employer desired it (and as long as the employee was not irreplaceable, which was seldom the case) the employee's relation to the enterprise would be precarious. An effective way to assert the owners' control and their right to management and profits and a clear division between owners and non-owners of capital was a legal declaration that the employees had no interest in the firm in the form of employment tenure or a right to a long period of notice. So the legal formula conformed to the economic necessities and to the beliefs of the owners

---

[120] Of course, the worker need not enter the wage bargain, or may do so only on favorable terms, but in practice most of the advantages in this regard belong to the purchasers, not the suppliers, of labor.

in the existence of and the need for an industrial elite of owners of capital with absolute control of their businesses.

NOTE

Spread of the At-Will Rule. In a detailed empirical study of the adoption of the at-will rule by various states in the late nineteenth century, Professor Andrew Morriss attempted to shatter four myths about the rule's creation:

Myth 1: A treatise writer [Horace Wood] made up the employment at-will rule in 1877.

Fact: Employment at-will did not spring from "the busy and perhaps careless pen of an American treatise writer." The at-will rule was adopted by seven states before Horace Wood published his 1877 treatise, was present in the first draft of the proposed New York Civil Code drafted by David Dudley Field in 1862, and was included in the National Currency Act of 1863 for bank officers, as well as in earlier state banking statutes.

Myth 2: The at-will rule was the product of nineteenth century industrialization.

Fact: The pattern of adoption among states strongly suggests, and an empirical analysis confirms, that the at-will rule's spread was not linked to industrialization.

Myth 3: The at-will rule was the result of judicial class prejudice.

Fact: The at-will rule was adopted earlier in states where judicial class prejudice was less (the Midwest) and gained acceptance relatively late in states where judicial class prejudice was greater (New England).

Myth 4: The treatment of employment contracts in the United States was heavily biased against employees by the at-will rule, while European nations provided rules more favorable to employees.

Fact: The European civil law systems did not address the issue of indefinite employment contracts, while the United States' legal system treated employees more favorably than the British legal system in many respects.

Andrew P. Morriss, *Exploding Myths: An Empirical and Economic Reassessment of the Rise of Employment At-Will*, 59 MO. L. REV. 679, 681-82 (1994).

Central to Morriss's argument is a detailed empirical study of the timing of adoption of the at-will rule by various states. Maine (1851) and Mississippi (1858) were the first states to adopt the rule through the common law. In general, adoption of employment at-will rule moved from the west to the south and midwest and only after several decades to the more industrialized northeast states. For example, Pennsylvania adopted the rule in 1891 and New York in 1895; those two states accounted for 1/5 to 1/3 of the entire American economy in 1890, depending on the measure used. One interesting finding of Morriss is that, even after controlling for measures of industrialization and political leanings, states whose supreme court judges were popularly elected were significantly more likely to adopt the at-will rule. Assuming that elected judges are more responsive to middle-class interests than are appointed judges, this finding casts doubt on Feinman's argument that the at-will rule comes from the interests of capitalists in controlling middle managers.

The following run-of-the-mill case shows the severity with which courts applied the employment at will doctrine during its heyday.

SKAGERBERG v. BLANDIN PAPER CO.

Supreme Court of Minnesota

266 N.W. 872 (1936)

JULIUS J. OLSON, JUSTICE.

Defendant's general demurrer to plaintiff's amended complaint was sustained, and he appeals.

....

Plaintiff is a consulting engineer, a specialist in the field of heating, ventilating, and air conditioning. As such he had developed a clientele bringing him a weekly income of approximately $200.

Defendant operates a paper manufacturing plant at Grand Rapids, this state. It had employed plaintiff in his professional capacity in 1926 and again in 1930. He was paid at the rate of $200 per week while so employed. Defendant was planning extensive enlargements of its plant, the estimated expense being about $1,000,000. Ordinarily a consulting engineer's fees for doing the necessary planning and supervision of the contemplated improvements would involve from $35,000 to $50,000. During plaintiff's employment in 1930 there was some discussion between the parties with respect of plaintiff's employment to take this work in hand. At that time, too, he was negotiating with the executive officers of Purdue University relative to taking a position as associate professor in its department of engineering, particularly that branch thereof relating to heating, ventilating, and air conditioning.

The Purdue position carried a salary of $3,300 per year and required only nine months' work in the way of instructions. This would leave plaintiff free to continue his practice as a consulting engineer during a period of three months of each calendar year. He was also privileged, if he entered that position, to continue his practice as a consulting engineer at all times in so far as his professional work at the university permitted him so to do. In addition thereto, he was privileged to contribute to engineering magazines and other publications. All income from such outside engagements was to be his in addition to the stated salary. Plaintiff considered this opportunity as one especially attractive to him. Defendant had full knowledge of all the foregoing facts.

On October 13, 1930, plaintiff, having received a telegram from Purdue University offering him the position and requiring immediate acceptance or rejection thereof, at once called an officer of defendant over the long-distance telephone informing him of the offer and the necessity on his part of making immediate response thereto. Defendant's officer agreed that if plaintiff would reject the Purdue offer and also agree to purchase the home of defendant's power superintendent, it would give plaintiff permanent employment at a salary of $600 per month. Relying thereon, plaintiff rejected the Purdue offer and immediately thereafter moved to Grand Rapids and there entered upon the performance of his duties under this arrangement. He later entered into a contract for the purchase of the superintendent's home. Appropriate to note is the fact that these negotiations were entirely oral and over the long-distance telephone, plaintiff being at Minneapolis and defendant's officer at Grand Rapids. The only writing between the parties is a letter written on October 14, 1930, reading thus:

Blandin Paper Co., Grand Rapids, Minn.

Attention: Mr. C. K. Andrews.

Gentlemen: In accordance with our conversation yesterday when our agreement was settled regarding my position with your company, I have wired Purdue rejecting their offer. Under the circumstances it was impossible for us to get together on a written agreement: I had to wire Purdue at once. However, I am making this move on the assumption that there will be no difficulty in working out our agreement when I get up to Grand Rapids.

Propositions like the one Purdue made are very rare and I am turning it down since I feel that the opportunities with you for applying my past experience are very attractive, the essential consideration being, however, that the job will be a permanent one.

According to the understanding we have, I am to take over Mr. Kull's duties as Power Superintendent and serve also as Mechanical Engineer for your plant, supervising the mechanical construction and maintenance work and other mechanical technical matters. Mr. Kull is to remain for long enough period, about six months, to permit me to get my work organized and get acquainted with the details of his work. If the proposed new construction work is started within that time it may develop that Mr. Kull may remain until that is completed after which he will leave and I take over his duties. As an accommodation to him when he leaves town I am to purchase his house.

My salary is to be six hundred dollars ($600.00) per month and you are to pay my moving expenses to Grand Rapids.

Very truly yours,

RS/m R. Skagerberg.

Plaintiff rendered the services for which he was thus engaged "dutifully, faithfully and to the complete satisfaction of the defendant and was paid the agreed salary, except as to a voluntary reduction, up to September 1, 1932," when, so the complaint alleges, he was "wrongfully, unlawfully and wilfully" discharged from further employment, although "ready, willing and able to perform." By reason of the alleged breach of contract he claims to have suffered general damages in the amount of $25,000, and for this he prays judgment.

From what has been stated it is clear that the issue raised by the demurrer is simply this: Do the allegations set forth in the complaint show anything more than employment of plaintiff by defendant subject to termination at the will of either party?

1. The words "permanent employment" have a well-established meaning in the law. The general rule is well stated in 18 R.C.L. p. 509, § 20: "In case the parties to a contract of service expressly agree that the employment shall be 'permanent' the law implies, not that the engagement shall be continuous or for any definite period, but that the term being indefinite the hiring is merely at will."...

2. The difficult question presented is whether the allegations set forth in the complaint bring this case within an exception to the rule stated. We find in 18 R.C.L. p. 510, the following statement: "Under some circumstances, however, 'permanent' employment will be held to contemplate a continuous engagement to endure as long as the employer shall be engaged in business and have work for the employee to do and the latter shall perform the service satisfactorily. This seems to be the established rule in case the employee purchases the employment with a valuable consideration outside the services which he renders from day to day."

Plaintiff cites and relies upon [several cases.] In *Carnig v. Carr,* 46 N.E. 117 (Mass. 1897), plaintiff had been engaged in business for himself as an enameler. Defendant was a business competitor. Being such, and for his own advantage, defendant persuaded plaintiff to give up his business and sell his stock in trade to him. As consideration, in part at least, for entering into this arrangement, defendant agreed to employ plaintiff permanently at a stated salary, his work for defendant being the same as that in which plaintiff had been engaged. It is clear that what defendant sought and accomplished was to get rid of his competitor in business upon a promise on his part to give plaintiff permanent employment. The resulting situation amounted to the same thing in substance and effect as if plaintiff had purchased his job. Under such circumstances there can be no doubt that the exception to the general rule was properly invoked and applied and furnishes an illustration thereof.

In *Pierce v. Tennessee Coal, Iron & Railroad Co.,* 173 U.S. 1 (1899), plaintiff had received an injury while employed by defendant. To settle the difficulty defendant promised employment to plaintiff at certain stated wages and was also to furnish certain supplies as long as his disability to do full work continued by reason of his injury. In consideration for these promises plaintiff released the company from all liability for damages on account of the injuries which caused his disability. Here, too, it is clear that plaintiff purchased from defendant his employment. There are many such cases.

[The court then discusses several other cases.]

3. Plaintiff maintains that four different items of consideration entered into the contract relied upon (in addition to the promised service to be rendered) namely: (1) The rejection of the Purdue offer; (2) the agreement to purchase the superintendent's house; (3) that plaintiff gave up an established business; and (4) that defendant saved the commission that it otherwise would have to pay engineers on new construction work.

Plaintiff obviously could not accept both the Purdue and the defendant's offer. It was for him to take one or the other. He could not possibly serve both masters.

A man capable of earning $600 per month necessarily must be possessed of both learning and experience in his particular line of endeavor. The fact that he was able to command such salary at the time of entering into defendant's service is convincing proof that there must be more than one person or enterprise seeking his talents and services. If plaintiff had elected to go to Purdue and, after having been there employed the same length of time as he was by defendant, was then discharged, does it follow that he could successfully sue Purdue University upon the same theory that he is here making a basis for liability against defendant? We have found no case fitting into plaintiff's claim in this regard.

What has been said in respect of the Purdue opportunity applies with equal force to the third point raised by plaintiff. His capacity as a specialist in his line of endeavor had built up for him a lucrative practice. That practice he could not take with him when he entered defendant's employment. Is not this exactly what every person having any line of employment must do when he seeks and obtains another? If plaintiff had been engaged in the practice of the law and as such had established a clientele bringing the same income and had later taken on a contract to act for a corporate enterprise at a fixed salary of $600 per month upon the same basis as here, do his counsel think, in virtue of the well-established rules of applicable law, that he would have a lifetime job? Would not counsel have insisted upon a more definite agreement than that relied upon here?...

With regard to purchase of the superintendent's house, note should be made that in plaintiff's letter written the day following the alleged making of the contract ... [i]t is difficult to find anything in this language indicating a consideration for, going to, or in any way benefiting defendant to induce it to enter into such contract. Plaintiff's own statement is that "as an accommodation to him [Kull] when he leaves town I am to purchase his house." How this could be of any material interest to or concern of defendant in view of plaintiff's own letter and stipulation is not apparent. Nowhere in the complaint is there any allegation that the purchase of the house from the superintendent in any way benefited defendant or damaged plaintiff. A man in plaintiff's position would necessarily be interested in acquiring a place of abode upon leaving Minneapolis for Grand Rapids. In the very nature of his requirements, he entered into the purchase for his own use and accommodation rather than for any benefit to or advantage of defendant. Nowhere is there any suggestion that defendant was to furnish him with a place of abode or do anything whatever in respect of finding or providing such.

Lastly, we come to plaintiff's claim that he rendered professional services in the construction work worth much more than his stipulated monthly salary. By referring to his letter, it is obvious that that was one of the things he was to take in hand and upon the basis of payment mentioned in the letter. He received that compensation during the time of his employment. He was paid the stipulated price according to his own version of the agreement.

The order sustaining defendant's demurrer is affirmed.

NOTES

1. *The Consideration Requirement.* Professor Clyde Summers insists that the courts misapply the consideration requirement in employment at will cases:

> Another spurious contractual doctrine, sometimes used as an exception to the mutuality doctrine and sometimes used independently, was that to overcome the presumption that employment for an indefinite term was employment at will the employee must give some additional consideration. Coming to work, even working for a number of years, was not consideration for a promise of future employment. An employee must give something more. Why something more than faithful service was required was never clearly explained. There seemed to be an assumption that because wages for work performed had been paid, the work could not be consideration for a promise of continued employment. As any first semester law students knows, however, one performance can be consideration to support two or even twenty promises. The work performed could be consideration for both the wages paid and the promise of future employment. The requirement of additional consideration was but a device for converting Wood's presumption into a substantive rule so that even an express promise of permanent employment would not bind the employer.
>
> The employment at will doctrine is cast in contract language, but it has no basis in contract law. The courts have not asked the basic contract question — what did the parties intend? Both the overloaded presumption and the superimposed spurious doctrines led the courts away from an inquiry into what the parties, as reasonable persons, understood or intended. It led to the anti-contract incantation that in the absence of a specified term the employment was at will, regardless whether that fit the parties' intent in entering and continuing the employment relationship.

Clyde W. Summers, *The Contract of Employment and the Rights of Individual Employees: Fair Representation and Employment at Will*, 52 FORDHAM L. REV. 1082, 1098-99 (1984).[*]

2. *Mutuality of Obligation.* Related to the consideration requirement is the notion that contracts must have mutual obligations. Courts sometimes used the mutuality doctrine to defeat employee claims against at-will employment. A typical case is *Meadows v. Radio Industries, Inc.*, 222 F.2d 347, 348-49 (7th Cir. 1955), where the employee had claimed that the employer promised to employ him until the project he was working on was completed. The court, applying Illinois law, refused to enforce the promise, reasoning:

> It is well settled in Illinois that whenever a contract is incapable of being enforced against one party, that party is equally incapable of enforcing it against the other.... "Mutuality of obligation means that both parties are bound or neither [is] bound. In other words there must be a valid consideration. Without a valid consideration, a contract cannot be enforced in law or in equity."...
>
> In the present case, a careful examination of the record discloses that there was not the slightest bit of evidence that plaintiff ever agreed that he would continue in the employment of defendant for any specified time. In other words, he had a right to terminate his employment at any time and did not promise to perform for any definite length of time. Therefore, the contract could not have been enforced against him and was lacking in mutuality. Consequently, he cannot enforce it against defendant.

3. *Mutuality of Obligation and the Constitution.* During the *Lochner* era, the Supreme Court raised the doctrine of mutuality to constitutional status. In *Adair v. United States,* 208 U.S. 161 (1908), the Supreme Court declared unconstitutional a federal statute prohibiting an employer from discharging a worker for being a union member. The Court, per Justice Harlan, reasoned:

> The right of a person to sell his labor upon such terms as he deems proper is, in its essence, the same as the right of the purchaser of labor to prescribe the conditions upon which he will accept such labor from the person offering to sell it. So the right of the employee to quit the service of the employer, for whatever reason, is the same as the right of the employer, for whatever reason, to dispense with the services of such employee. It was the legal right of the defendant Adair — however unwise such a course might have been — to discharge Coppage because of his being a member of a labor organization, as it was the legal right of Coppage, if he saw fit to do so — however unwise such a course on his part might have been — to quit the service in which he was engaged, because the defendant employed some persons who

---

[*] Reprinted with permission of Fordham Law Review.

were not members of a labor organization. In all such particulars the employer and the employee have equality of right, and any legislation that disturbs that equality is an arbitrary interference with the liberty of contract which no government can legally justify in a free land.

208 U.S. at 174-75. The Court acknowledged that "if the parties by contract fix the period of service, and prescribe the conditions upon which the contract may be terminated, such contract would control the rights of the parties as between themselves, and for any violation of those provisions the party wronged would have his appropriate civil action." 208 U.S. at 175.

4. *Mutuality of Obligation in Contract Law.* Consider the following:

> The doctrine of mutuality is as spurious contract law as it is misguided constitutional law. Contracts require only exchanged consideration, not mutual obligations. The employee, by coming to work, provides sufficient consideration to make the employer's promise of continued or permanent employment binding. An offer by an employer to employ so long as there is a need and the employee's performance is satisfactory can be viewed as an offer of a unilateral contract, irrevocable after the employee's performance is begun even though there may be no duty of the employee to continue. Mutuality of obligation, particularly in the form of mirrored obligations as required by the courts in these cases, has never been considered essential to make promises binding. The effect of requiring mutuality was to convert the presumption into the substantive rule that unless the employee bound himself to work for a stated term, the employment must be at will. It was impossible for an employee, by accepting employment, to bind the employer to continue the employment so long as the employee was needed and his work was satisfactory.

Clyde W. Summers, *The Contract of Employment and the Rights of Individual Employees: Fair Representation and Employment at Will,* 52 FORDHAM L. REV. 1082, 1098 (1984).

5. *Interpreting Contracts as At Will.* Lest one think that courts no longer strain to interpret a contract as at will, consider *Main v. Skaggs Community Hospital,* 812 S.W.2d 185 (Mo. Ct. App. 1991). The parties signed a written contract allowing the employer or the employee to terminate "with just cause" by giving sixty days' notice. The court held that the just cause limitation did not alter the employee's at-will status, because the contract had no specified duration and purported to grant perpetual employment rights unless the employee's conduct became deficient enough to constitute "just cause." The court condemned such an "obligation in perpetuity."

Chapter 4

CONTRACT EROSIONS OF EMPLOYMENT AT WILL

Many employment contracts are informal. The parties often say little about their expectations down the road, limiting themselves to an understanding of the basic terms of pay and the basic job description. The contracts often are not in writing, and employees often respond to an offer of employment, not by words, but by beginning to work.

After the employee is later terminated, courts are asked to fill the gaps in the contract. The presumption of employment at will can be seen as the courts' attempt to fill the gap: unless the parties state otherwise, the employer can discharge the employee for a good reason, bad reason, or no reason at all.

Courts and scholars have developed two basic methods for filling in contractual gaps. First, courts can attempt to determine how the parties would have decided the issue had they focused on the question. This approach is sometimes characterized as "mimicking the market," for it asks whether the employer values the flexibility in dismissal more than employees value job security, and assumes the parties would have contracted for whichever clause is valued more highly.

The second method attempts to create a default rule whereby the parties are encouraged to reveal their true valuations. Consider a job applicant negotiating the terms of the employment contract: if the presumption is at will, the applicant must indicate that he or she prefers job security. Is it likely that the applicant will do this? What kind of adverse signals would an applicant send by asking detailed questions about how the firm gets rid of marginal employees? On the other hand, if the presumption is dismissal for just cause, the employer must get the employee to waive this presumption if it prefers employment at will. Will the employee be likely to waive a just-cause requirement?

In Section A, we examine cases where the parties have (at least arguably) expressly modified the at-will presumption. As cases like *Skagerberg* indicate, in the heyday of employment at will courts were extremely reluctant to find that the parties had modified the at-will relationship. Courts today seem more willing to do so.

In Section B we examine actions, rather than words, that may alter the at-will relationship. In Section C we look at the issues surrounding statements of job security in employee handbooks. Section D explores how employers might explicitly assert that the relationship is at will.

A. EXPRESS MODIFICATION OF AT-WILL CONTRACTS, WRITTEN AND ORAL

CHIODO v. GENERAL WATERWORKS CORP.

Supreme Court of Utah

413 P.2d 891 (1966)

CROCKETT, JUSTICE.

The plaintiff, Vincent Chiodo, sued for breach of a contract which employed him for a period of ten years as the manager of the defendant, Bear River Telephone Company, when he was discharged after three years. Defendant seeks to justify its action upon the grounds: (1) that plaintiff was guilty of insubordination and insolence to his superior; (2) that he cheated the company in certain payroll practices; and (3) that he was disloyal. Upon trial to the court it found the issues in favor of the plaintiff and rendered judgment for his salary for the remaining seven years, discounted for payment in cash, in the sum of $81,264.99, plus $6,500 owing on a retirement policy. Defendant appeals.

In 1943, the plaintiff acquired the Bear River Telephone Company, located at Tremonton, Utah, which serves principally Box Elder County in the northwest quadrant of the state. Due to the industrial development attendant upon World War II, particularly because of Thiokol Chemical Corporation, there was a rapid increase in population and business in that area. Under the plaintiff's management the [Bear River Telephone Company] prospered and expanded the number of telephones from about 700 to over 5,000. Because of continued increasing demands and inadequate capital, he decided to sell. After negotiations he accepted an offer from defendant General Waterworks to convey to them for shares of that company upon certain conditions. One of them was that they agreed to employ him as manager of Bear River Telephone Company for ten years at a salary of $12,000 per year. The pertinent language of their letter is thus:

> In accordance with the understanding and agreement, which we have arrived at, *your employment by Bear River is to continue for a period of ten years from the date hereof....* Nothing in this letter agreement, however, shall be held to preclude your continuing employment by Bear River after such ten-year period.

Under a contract of employment for a stated term it is to be assumed that the parties intended that the employee would conform to the usual standards expected of an employee, and that he would render honest, faithful and loyal service in accordance with his ability. If there is a wilful and substantial failure to adhere to those standards it would be justifiable cause for the employer to discharge him. The question of moment here is whether the plaintiff's conduct constituted such justifiable cause for his discharge.

Inasmuch as the contract for plaintiff's employment stated nothing with respect to standards of his conduct, nor of his possible discharge, the trial court properly received evidence relating to the negotiations of the parties which resulted in the contract to determine their intent with respect to these questions. Some of these discussions between plaintiff and defendant (its Vice President, A.W. Sanders) had been recorded and were presented in evidence:

> "Mr. Chiodo: I don't want to have this thing [employment contract] come up here with me. I want it tied down so that there's no question about it, *and you decide to fire me, that you're going to pay my $500.00 every two weeks for ten years.*

> "Mr. Sanders: My opinion of this is that we can't fire you for ten years. That is what Hansen [defendant's attorney] tells me....

> "Mr. Chiodo: Yes, but I can't write myself a check for $500.00 on payday if you refuse to sign the check; then what? I'm fired right?

> "Mr. Sanders: No, I'm no attorney, of course, but the attorneys tell me this all your way. We can't do anything....

> "Mr. Sanders: No. As you and I discussed it before, we're going to let you run the property as you see fit."

In an attempt to justify its discharge of the plaintiff the defendant makes these accusations:

Payroll Padding:

(1) That the plaintiff had his adult son, Don Chiodo, on the defendant's payroll while he was working for a construction company in Montana;

(2) That two of plaintiff's sons at various times between July 1961, and December 1962, used other employees of the defendant to do work which the sons had contracted to do for defendant on a fixed-fee-basis, which they received;

(3) That plaintiff improperly had his 14-year-old granddaughter on the payroll and paid her $354.20.

Insubordination:

(1) That the plaintiff refused to obey orders to cancel a policy of insurance on defendant's properties;

(2) That plaintiff told employees of the defendant that certain of defendant's officers were incompetent.

Disloyalty:

That he breached confidence by telling the Public Service Commission of
Utah that General Waterworks was trying to sell the company to Mountain States
Telephone & Telegraph Company; and that he was himself interested in repur-
chasing the company.

It is interesting, almost amazing, at times to see how human minds with their
own interests to serve see pictures as either black or white and fail to discern and
recognize the shadings and the grays. The accusations against plaintiff as stated
by the defendant seem impressive, and there appears to be some truth in each,
but that does not paint the whole picture as it is filled out by the plaintiff's
evidence as to his answers:

Payroll Padding:

(1) The son, Don Chiodo, had worked for defendant during his vacation, had
done extensive night work for it on his own time, for which he had not been
paid. In order to make up for this, the plaintiff had kept him on the defendant's
payroll during a period of nine days while he was in Montana.

(2) The charge that the defendant's employees were used to perform work on
the Don and Gene Chiodo subcontract: Mr. Sanders, the Vice President, who
arranged for the work to be done on the contract, knew and agreed that some of
defendant's employees would have to be used to perform some of the technical
work. The employees who testified stated on cross-examination that they did not
know whether the work done by them was included under the Chiodo's sub-con-
tract or not.

(3) Payment to the 14-year-old granddaughter: The plaintiff had for some
years followed a policy of determining what the mailing of telephone directories
would cost, then permitting employees, including sometimes members of his
family, to have the same amount of money for personally delivering them, which
work was done by the granddaughter and she was compensated for it.

Insubordination:

(1) Plaintiff admits refusing to follow the directive to cancel a policy of insurance covering properties of the defendant. He had purchased the policy on the
basis of bids submitted; under the circumstances felt a moral obligation not to
cancel it; thought it was a good policy, necessary for the protection it afforded;
and that it was within his prerogative as manager to keep it in force. When he
refused to cancel it and so advised the defendant's main office, nothing more
was said about the matter until this action was brought over 20 months later.

(2) What he said about the incompetency of certain of defendant's officers was
true.

Disloyalty:

In informing the Public Service Commission of pending negotiations for sale, he was keeping faith with the Commission because he had assisted in the transfer of the franchise to defendant by making personal assurances that General Waterworks was not purchasing for purposes of speculation, but with bona fide intention of continuing the operation of the defendant company. He felt that the latter's disregard of the representations made justified his advising the Commission and indicating a willingness to repurchase the company himself.

There were other accusations of less consequence, generally similar to those recited above both in character and in explanation, which we need not detail. For the most part they can be characterized as disagreements between defendant's officers and plaintiff which he insists were provoked by their own mistakes and their continual attempts to interfere with his management.

The decisive answer to defendant's arguments about the matters above recited is that the trial court was persuaded in accordance with the plaintiff's contentions. It is true that some of his remarks in discussing the case could be interpreted as reflecting doubt as to his views on certain of the evidence, and as to the standards of honesty and integrity applied to the plaintiff. But the overall view taken appears to be this: that although the plaintiff's conduct may not have been exemplary in all respects, he had been a good manager as evidenced by the fact that the operation of the company had been profitable under his leadership; and that after friction developed between him and other officers of the company as to various aspects of the management, the latter sought to dredge up accusations of misconduct to justify discharging him. But his explanations of whatever irregularities may have existed were sufficiently reasonable and acceptable under the circumstances that the defendant failed to meet its burden of showing justification for his discharge....

Judgment affirmed.

HENRIOD, C.J., and MCDONOUGH, WADE and CALLISTER, JJ., concur.

NOTES

1. *Firing Employees During Definite Term Contracts.* This contract was for a specific term — ten years. Do the negotiations between Chiodo and the Telephone Company indicate they thought Chiodo could be fired, even for cause, during the term? Is it reasonable for a court to imply a clause allowing employers to fire employees for cause during a definite-term contract? If so, does a definite-term contract provide any protection for an employee that a just-cause indefinite-term contract would not? Could Chiodo have been terminated if, during a severe recession, the company was losing money?

2. *Moral Hazard.* If an employee is absolutely protected from discharge regardless of his behavior, is he likely to work hard and honestly? He has little incentive to do so. Economists would call this a "moral hazard" problem. When people are fully insured or protected against a bad event [in this case, little work being done], they have little reason to exert effort to see that the bad event does not take place.

Moral Hazard [handwritten in margin]

Because the employee might shirk if fully protected against discharge for laziness or theft, one would expect that parties who expressly considered the issue would agree that the employee could be fired for cause, even in a definite-term contract. Is this sufficient reason for the law to imply a right to fire for cause when a definite-term contract is silent on the issue? Or should employers be required to obtain an express right-to-fire clause if they agree to hire for a specific term or else suffer the consequences of a shirking employee? This penalty default would encourage employers explicitly to notify employees that they want the right to fire for cause.

3. *Terminations for Business Downturns.* Suppose an employee has a definite-term contract, but the company decides during the term to abolish the position because of adverse business conditions. Does the employee have a breach of contract claim, or does the employer's implied right to terminate for cause include terminations for business downturns? *See Grappone v. City of Miami Beach*, 495 So. 2d 838 (Fla. Ct. App. 1986) (employer bound by its promises); *Helberg v. Community Work & Dev. Ctr. Indus., Inc.*, No. CX-93-958, 1994 WL 1121 (Minn. Ct. App. Jan. 4, 1994) (president who demanded twelve-month contract because of employer's financial hardship is entitled to compensation when discharged after four months).

Does not appear that there is a right to terminate term contract because of business downturn [handwritten in margin]

4. *Statutory Right to Terminate.* The South Dakota legislature has codified the employer's right to terminate for cause during a definite term contract with the following standard:

> An employment even for a specified term may be terminated at any time by the employer for habitual neglect of duty or continued incapacity to perform or any willful breach of duty by the employee in the course of his employment.

S.D. CODIFIED LAWS ANN. § 60-4-5. *See also* CAL. LAB. CODE § 2924.

5. *Meaning of Just Cause.* Just cause as applied in a particular case is a notoriously slippery concept. A rich body of arbitral decisions has developed determining when employers may fire union workers protected by just cause provisions in collective bargaining agreements. Professors Abrams and Nolan have synthesized these decisions with the following criteria:

A. Just cause for discipline exists only when an employee has failed to meet his obligations under the fundamental understanding of the employment relationship. The employee's general obligation is to provide satisfactory work. Satisfactory work has four components:

Substantive [handwritten in margin]

   1. Regular attendance.

2. Obedience to reasonable work rules.

3. A reasonable quality and quantity of work.

4. Avoidance of conduct, either at or away from work, which would interfere with the employer's ability to carry on the business effectively.

B. For there to be just cause, the discipline must further one or more of management's three legitimate interests:

1. Rehabilitation of a potentially satisfactory employee.

2. Deterrence of similar conduct, either by the disciplined employee or by other employees.

3. Protection of the employer's ability to operate the business successfully.

C. The concept of just cause includes certain employee protections that reflect the union's interest in guaranteeing "fairness" in disciplinary situations.

Objective procedures 1. The employee is entitled to industrial due process. This includes:

a. actual or constructive notice of expected standards of conduct and penalties for wrongful conduct;

b. a decision based on facts, determined after an investigation that provides the employee an opportunity to state his case, with union assistance if he desires it;

c. the imposition of discipline in gradually increasing degrees, except in cases involving the most extreme breaches of the fundamental understanding. In particular, discharge may be imposed only when less severe penalties will not protect legitimate management interests, for one of the following reasons: (1) the employee's past record shows that the unsatisfactory conduct will continue, (2) the most stringent form of discipline is needed to protect the system of work rules, or (3) continued employment would inevitably interfere with the successful operation of the business; and

d. proof by management that just cause exists.

2. The employee is entitled to industrial equal protection, which requires like treatment of like cases.

3. The employee is entitled to *individualized treatment*. Distinctive facts in the employee's record or regarding the reason for discipline must be given appropriate weight.

Roger I. Abrams & Dennis R. Nolan, *Toward a Theory of "Just Cause" in Employee Discipline Cases,* 1985 DUKE L.J. 594, 611-12.[*]

6. *Just Cause and High-Level Jobs.* Chiodo was a high-level worker. Should employers be given more latitude when attempting to show just cause for terminating such workers?

---

7. *Employee Quitting During Term.* Should an employee who quits during a definite-term contract be liable for breach of contract? Or should the court imply that the employee may quit for good cause, just as the employer may fire during the term for good cause? In the principal case, did Chiodo agree to work for ten years?

The issue of employee breach arises with schoolteacher contracts, which often are for one year. In *Handicapped Children's Education Board v. Lukaszewski*, 332 N.W.2d 774 (Wis. 1983), a speech therapist signed a contract to teach the following school year in a town forty-five miles from her home. In August, shortly before the school year was to begin, she was offered a teaching job with a twenty percent higher salary in her home town, meaning she no longer had to commute long distances to work. She attempted to resign from her first job, but the School Board sued for breach of contract. The court found her liable for the extra salary the school board paid for a replacement teacher, but indicated she would not have been liable had she resigned for a legitimate medical reason.

HETES v. SCHEFMAN & MILLER LAW OFFICE

Court of Appeals of Michigan
393 N.W.2d 577 (1986)

Before CYNAR, P.J., and WAHLS and E.E. BORRADAILE, JJ.

PER CURIAM.

Plaintiff appeals as of right from a circuit court order granting summary disposition of plaintiff's complaint for breach of an oral employment contract.

Plaintiff was employed as a receptionist for defendant law firm from September, 1983, until May, 1984. Plaintiff did not enter into a written contract. At the time of her hire, the law firm gave plaintiff an office manual which outlined employee duties and responsibilities. The manual did not specify termination procedures. In addition, plaintiff had at least two conversations with representatives of the law firm prior to assuming the receptionist position. Plaintiff testified in her deposition that, in both conversations, she was assured that "I had a job as long as I did a good job."

Plaintiff was discharged from employment on May 9, 1984. The circumstances surrounding her discharge are in dispute. In August, 1984, plaintiff filed a complaint alleging that defendants had breached the employment contract by failing to pay plaintiff's hospitalization benefits and by terminating plaintiff's employment in bad faith and without just cause....

The trial court granted defendants' motion for summary judgment on the basis that plaintiff's deposition testimony established that plaintiff had a "satisfaction" contract and could be terminated at any time without just cause. Plaintiff argues on appeal that the defendants' assurances that she would have a job as long as she "did a good job" constituted an oral promise that she not be discharged except for just cause and that the lower court erred in summarily dismissing her claim....

In *Toussaint v. Blue Cross & Blue Shield of Michigan*, 292 N.W.2d 880, 885 (Mich. 1980), the Supreme Court held that:

[handwritten: L of Michigan]

[handwritten right margin: But see next page]

"1) a provision of an employment contract providing that an employee shall not be discharged except for cause is legally enforceable although the contract is not for a definite term — the term is 'indefinite,' and

"2) such a provision may become part of the contract either by express agreement, oral or written, or as a result of an employee's legitimate expectations grounded in an employer's policy statements."

The oral representations relied upon in *Toussaint* and *Ebling v. Masco Corp.*, its companion case, are almost identical to those given to plaintiff in the present case. Moreover, in both cases, the Court decided that, based on the representations, juries could conclude that the defendant companies had entered into express agreements to discharge Toussaint and Ebling only for cause. We believe that a jury could reach a similar conclusion in the present case.

Here, defendants' representatives orally assured plaintiff that she would remain employed as long as she did a good job. Contrary to the lower court's finding, a jury could reasonably have construed the oral representations as a promise to discharge only for good or just cause. Therefore, the questions of whether plaintiff's contract included a termination for just cause provision and whether she was terminated in breach of the oral contract were for the jury and summary judgment was improperly granted on this basis....

Reversed in part and affirmed in part.

NOTES

1. Satisfaction, Good Faith and Just Cause. An employer's promise that it will provide employment "as long as I am satisfied with your work" is sometimes termed a satisfaction contract. Many courts assume that an employer could never breach such a contract, because the fact of firing shows the employer is no longer satisfied. Is such a contract any different from an at-will contract?

[handwritten right margin: Good Faith & Just Cause Distinguished]

A few courts imply a good-faith obligation on the employer for such a contract, so that the employee might show breach of contract by showing the employer was not "in good faith" dissatisfied with the employee's job performance. In *Hetes*, however, the court interpreted the employer's statement as a promise not to terminate without just cause. The distinction between good faith and just cause is that between a subjective and objective standard.

2. Casual Words of Encouragement. Most employees have received encouraging words from a supervisor like "you have a future with this company," or "keep up the good work and we'll look after you." Under the reasoning of *Hetes*, may such employees have their dismissal reviewed by a jury? *See, e.g., Forman v. BRI Corp.*, 532 F. Supp. 49 (E.D. Pa. 1982) (applying Pennsylvania law) (statement in interview that job was good one in which to "stay and grow," and that employer was concerned applicant would take job and "not stay" was sufficient to overcome presumption of employment at will).

3. *Retreat in Michigan.* In *Rowe v. Montgomery Ward & Co.,* 473 N.W.2d 268 (1991), the Michigan Supreme Court reversed a judgment on a jury verdict of $86,500 for an eight-year salesperson fired for being absent from the store for four hours without explanation. When the salesperson had applied for the job, the sales manager told her that "*generally,* as long as *they* generated sales and were honest [commissioned salespersons] had a job at Wards. [A]bout the only way that you could be terminated would be if you failed to make your draw." When hired, the employee signed a "Rules of Personal Conduct" form that enumerated four reasons for immediate discharge.

In finding for the employer, the Court distinguished *Toussaint,* emphasizing that the *Toussaint* employees had applied for singular, executive job positions, had several interviews with top company officials, and had inquired about job security. The Court also emphasized that in *Rowe* the sales manager's words (italicized above) were couched in general terms. The court also emphasized that nothing in the Rules of Personal Conduct suggested that the enumerated conduct was the only basis for dismissal.

After *Rowe,* can low-level employees like Hetes get to a jury in Michigan?

4. *Firing At-Will Employee for Pretextual Reason.* Suppose the employee concedes she is working under an at-will contract, but claims that the employer's stated reason for firing her (e.g., dishonesty) is false. Must the employer give the employee an opportunity to rebut the charges? *See Prout v. Sears, Roebuck & Co.,* 772 P.2d 288 (Mont. 1989) (yes).

5. *Probationary Periods.* Many employment contracts expressly provide for a short probationary period, during which the employee can be dismissed for any reason. Does such a contract imply that an employee who has survived the probationary period can be dismissed only for cause? Most courts have held that probationary periods are consistent with an implied at-will relationship after probation is over. A few courts have held that a probationary period is evidence that the parties intended greater job protection later. *See, e.g., Washington Welfare Ass'n v. Wheeler,* 496 A.2d 613 (D.C. 1985).

OHANIAN v. AVIS RENT A CAR SYSTEM, INC.

United States Court of Appeals, Second Circuit
779 F.2d 101 (1985)

Before KEARSE and CARDAMONE, CIRCUIT JUDGES, and WYATT, DISTRICT JUDGE.

CARDAMONE, CIRCUIT JUDGE:

Defendant Avis Rent A Car System (Avis) appeals from a judgment entered on a jury verdict in the Eastern District of New York (Weinstein, Ch. J.) awarding $304,693 in damages to plaintiff Robert S. Ohanian for lost wages and pension benefits arising from defendant's breach of a lifetime employment contract made orally to plaintiff.... Avis argues that the alleged oral contract is barred by the statute of frauds, is inadmissible under the parol evidence rule and, in any event, that the evidence is insufficient to establish a promise of lifetime employment. [W]e affirm.

Plaintiff Ohanian began working for Avis in Boston in 1967. Later he was appointed District Sales Manager in New York, and subsequently moved to San Francisco. By 1980 he had become Vice President of Sales for Avis's Western Region. Robert Mahmarian, a former Avis general manager, testified that Ohanian's performance in that region was excellent. During what Mahmarian characterized as "a very bad, depressed economic period," Ohanian's Western Region stood out as the one region that was growing and profitable. According to the witness, Ohanian was directly responsible for this success.

In the fall of 1980, Avis's Northeast Region — the region with the most profit potential — was "dying." Mahmarian and then Avis President Calvano decided that the Northeast Region needed new leadership and Ohanian was the logical candidate. They thought plaintiff should return to New York as Vice President of Sales for the Northeast Region. According to Mahmarian, "nobody anticipated how tough it would be to get the guy." Ohanian was happy in the Western Region, and for several reasons did not want to move. First, he had developed a good "team" in the Western Region; second, he and his family liked the San Francisco area; and third, he was secure in his position where he was doing well and did not want to get involved in the politics of the Avis "World Head-quarters," which was located in the Northeast Region. Mahmarian and Calvano were determined to bring Ohanian east and so they set out to overcome his reluctance. After several phone calls to him, first from then Vice President of Sales McNamara, then from Calvano, and finally Mahmarian, Ohanian was convinced to accept the job in the Northeast Region. In Mahmarian's words, he changed Ohanian's mind

> On the basis of promise, that a good man is a good man, and he has proven his ability, and if it didn't work out and he had to go back out in the field, or back to California, or whatever else, fine. As far as I was concerned, his future was secure in the company, unless — and I always had to qualify — unless he screwed up badly. Then he is on his own, and even then I indicated that at worst he would get his [severance] because there was some degree of responsibility on the part of management, Calvano and myself, in making this man make this change.

Ohanian's concerns about security were met by Mahmarian's assurance that "[u]nless [he] screwed up badly, there is no way [he was] going to get fired ... [he would] never get hurt here in this company." Ohanian accepted the offer and began work in the Northeast Region in early February 1981.

In April 1981 Ohanian told Fred Sharp, Vice President of Personnel, that he needed relocation money that had been promised, but not yet received. Sharp subsequently sent two form letters to Ohanian: one from Sharp to Ohanian and the other, prepared by Avis, from Ohanian to Sharp. The second letter was a form with boxes for Ohanian to check to signify his choice of relocation expense plans. Ohanian checked one of the boxes, signed the form, and returned it to Sharp.

The following language appeared on the form that Ohanian signed and returned:

> I also hereby confirm my understanding that nothing contained herein or in connection with the change in my position with Avis shall be deemed to constitute an obligation on the part of Avis to employ me for any period of time, and both the company and I can terminate my employment at will. There are no other agreements or understandings in respect of my change in position with Avis or the moving of my residence except as is set forth or referred to herein, and in your confirmation letter to me dated April 21, 1981, and the agreements and undertakings set forth therein cannot be modified or altered except by an instrument in writing signed by me and by an executive officer of Avis.

At trial, Ohanian said that he did not believe he read the letter other than to check the relocation plan he desired. He testified that he did not intend this letter to be a contract or to change the terms of his prior agreement with Avis.

Seven months after Ohanian moved to the Northeast Region, he was promoted to National Vice President of Sales and began work at Avis World Headquarters in Garden City, New York. He soon became dissatisfied with this position and in June 1982, pursuant to his request, returned to his former position as Vice President of Sales for the Northeast Region. A month later, on July 27, 1982, at 47 years of age, plaintiff was fired without severance pay. He then instituted this action. Within three months of termination, plaintiff obtained a job as Vice President of Sales for American International Rent A Car. His first year's salary at American International was $50,000 plus a $20,000 bonus. When Ohanian was fired by Avis, his yearly salary was $68,400, and the jury found that he was owed a $17,100 bonus that he had earned before being fired....

The jury returned with a verdict in which it found:

(1) That Ohanian had proven that Avis agreed to employ him until he retired unless he was terminated for just cause;
(2) That Avis had not proven that Ohanian was terminated for just cause;
(3) That Ohanian had proven that he was entitled to lost wages and pension benefits;
(4) That the present value of Ohanian's lost wages was $245,409;
(5) That the present value of Ohanian's lost pension benefits was $59,284;
(7) That Ohanian proved he was entitled to an award representing a $17,100 bonus; and

(8) That Ohanian proved he was entitled to an award representing incidental relocation expenses of $6,000.

....

Avis does not challenge the jury's finding that it had not proved that plaintiff was terminated for just cause. Neither has it appealed the awards for the bonus and relocation expenses. Both parties agree that New York law applies.

Defendant's principal argument is that the oral contract that the jury found existed is barred under the statute of frauds, § 5-701 (subd. a, para. 1) of the General Obligations Law. Section 5-701 provides in relevant part:

> Every agreement, promise or undertaking is void, unless it or some note or memorandum thereof be in writing, and subscribed by the party to be charged therewith, or by his lawful agent, if such agreement, promise or undertaking ... [b]y its terms is not to be performed within one year from the making thereof or the performance of which is not to be completed before the end of a lifetime.

It has long been held that the purpose of the statute is to raise a barrier to fraud when parties attempt to prove certain legal transactions that are deemed to be particularly susceptible to deception, mistake, and perjury. The provision making void any oral contract "not to be performed within one year" is to prevent injustice that might result either from a faulty memory or the absence of witnesses that have died or moved.

The fact that inconsistent theories have been advanced to explain the statute's enactment perhaps sheds light on modern courts' strict construction of it. Parliament enacted An Act for Prevention of Frauds and Perjuries in 1677 that required certain contracts to be evidenced by a signed writing. One theory for its enactment was that evidence of oral contracts tended to be susceptible to perjury and inherently unreliable. *See, e.g., Burns v. McCormick,* 135 N.E. 273, 274 (N.Y. 1922) (Cardozo, J.) (passage of the statute of frauds was necessary because of the "peril of perjury ... latent in the spoken promise"). This view is premised on the theory that an interested plaintiff will testify untruthfully about the existence of an oral contract. Another view derives from the fact that in a seventeenth century jury trial the parties and all others interested in the outcome were incompetent to testify as witnesses. T. Plucknett, A Concise History of the Common Law 55-56 (2d ed. 1936). To overcome that hurdle, so this theory goes, parties desiring legal protection for their transactions had to embody them in documents whose contents and authenticity were easily ascertainable. *Id.* at 56.

Whatever may be the fact with regard to the history of the statute, and whatever may have been the difficulties arising from proof that all sides agree brought about the enactment of the statute of frauds over 300 years ago, it is an anachronism today. The reasons that prompted its passage no longer exist. And, far from serving as a barrier to fraud — in the case of a genuinely aggrieved plaintiff barred from enforcing an oral contract — the statute may actually shield fraud. Note, *The Statute of Frauds as a Bar to an Action in Tort for Fraud*, 53 Fordham L. Rev. 1231, 1232-33 (1985).

In fact, New York courts perhaps also believing that strict application of the statute causes more fraud than it prevents, have tended to construe it warily. The one-year provision has been held not to preclude an oral contract unless there is "not ... the slightest possibility that it can be fully performed within one year." 2 Corbin on Contracts § 444, at 535; *Warner v. Texas and Pacific Railway*, 164 U.S. 418, 434 (1896) ("The question is not what the probable, or expected, or actual performance of the contract was; but whether the contract, according to the reasonable interpretation of its terms, required that it should not be performed within the year."); *D & N Boening, Inc. v. Kirsch Beverages, Inc.*, 472 N.E.2d 992 (N.Y. 1984) ("this court has continued to analyze oral agreements to determine if, according to the parties' terms, there might be any possible means of performance within one year").

It was long ago established that

> [i]t is not the meaning of the statute that the contract must be performed within a year.... [I]f the obligation of the contract is not, by its very terms, or necessary construction, to endure for a longer period than one year, it is a valid agreement, although it may be capable of an indefinite continuance.

Trustees of First Baptist Church v. Brooklyn Fire Ins. Co., 19 N.Y. 305, 307 (1859). Therefore, a contract to continue for longer than a year, that is terminable at the will of the party against whom it is being enforced, is not barred by the statute of frauds because it is capable of being performed within one year. *See North Shore Bottling Co. v. C. Schmidt & Sons, Inc.*, 239 N.E.2d 189 (N.Y. 1968). Similarly, it has been held that a contract which provides that either party may rightfully terminate within the year falls outside the statute. *Blake v. Voigt*, 31 N.E. 256 (N.Y. 1892).

When does an oral contract not to be performed within a year fall within the strictures of the statute? A contract is not "to be performed within a year" if it is terminable within that time only upon the breach of one of the parties. *Boening*, 472 N.E.2d 992. That rule derives from logic because "[p]erformance, if it means anything at all, is 'carrying out the contract by doing what it requires or permits' ... and a breach is the unexcused failure to do so." *Id.* (citing *Blake v. Voigt*, 31 N.E. 256). The distinction is between an oral contract that provides for its own termination at any time on the one hand, and an oral contract that is terminable within a year only upon its breach on the other. The former may be proved by a plaintiff and the latter is barred by the statute.

Avis contends that its oral agreement with Ohanian is barred by the statute of frauds because it was not performable within a year. Avis claims that it could only fire plaintiff if he breached the contract, and breach of a contract is not performance. Defendant further states that an option in plaintiff alone to terminate the contract at will, if there was in fact such an option, also would not remove this agreement from the statute's coverage.

What defendant fails to recognize is that under New York law "just cause" for termination may exist for reasons other than an employee's breach. Thus, for example, in *Weiner v. McGraw-Hill, Inc.,* 443 N.E.2d 441 (N.Y. 1982), the plaintiff was induced to leave his former position to take up employment with defendant McGraw-Hill, in part by an assurance from defendant's representative that "since his company's firm policy was not to terminate employees without 'just cause,' employment by it would, among other things, bring him the advantage of job security." The company handbook describing its dismissal policies stated, "'[t]he company will resort to dismissal for just and sufficient cause only.... However, if the welfare of the company indicates that dismissal is necessary, then that decision is arrived at and carried out forthrightly.'" *Id.* The New York Court of Appeals held that the arguably oral contract in question "whether terminable at will or only for just cause, [was] not one which, 'by its terms,' could not be performed within one year and, therefore, [was] not one which [was] barred." *Id.*

Later, in *Boening,* the court noted that "the reference in [*Weiner*] ... to an agreement terminable 'only for just cause' falling outside the Statute of Frauds is not to be construed as including an agreement where 'just cause' can *only* be the other party's breach." (emphasis added). The *Boening* court recognized therefore that some contracts terminable for "just cause" do not require a breach in order to terminate. In *Boening,* the court determined that the supply contract in question required plaintiff to "conduct its subdistributorship satisfactorily, exerting its best efforts and acting in good faith." Defendant was only allowed to terminate the contract for failure to satisfy those requirements. Since the *only possible cause* for termination was plaintiff's breach, the contract was barred by the statute of frauds.

In the instant case, just cause for dismissing Ohanian would plainly include any breach of the contract, such as drinking on the job or refusing to work, since the agreement contemplates plaintiff giving his best efforts. But, as noted, just cause can be broader than breach and here there may be just cause to dismiss without a breach. To illustrate, under the terms of the contract it would be possible that despite plaintiff's best efforts the results achieved might prove poor because of adverse market conditions. From defendant's standpoint that too would force Avis to make a change in its business strategy, perhaps reducing or closing an operation. That is, there would be just cause for plaintiff's dismissal. But if this is what occurred, it would not constitute a breach of the agreement. Best efforts were contemplated by the parties, results were not. Defendant was anxious to have plaintiff relocate because of his past success, but plaintiff made no guarantee to produce certain results. Thus, this oral contract could have been terminated for just cause within one year, without any breach by plaintiff, and is therefore not barred by the statute of frauds.

Defendant's further claim that a contract does not escape the statute if it is terminable at will only by plaintiff is negated by the fact that the contract provided that plaintiff could be terminated for reasons other than the plaintiff's breach. As just stated, defendant could fire the plaintiff on account of conduct that would not constitute breach of contract. Where either party under the contract may rightfully terminate within a year, the contract is outside the statute.

Defendant next urges that any claims based on the oral agreement between Ohanian and Avis are barred by the parol evidence rule. Avis says that the clear and unambiguous letter of April 21, 1981 was signed by plaintiff, and it contradicts plaintiff's assertion that he was promised lifetime employment and severance on termination. It is, of course, a fundamental principle of contract law "that, where parties have reduced their bargain, or any element of it, to writing, the parol evidence rule applies to prevent its variance by parol evidence." *Laskey v. Rubel Corp.,* 100 N.E.2d 140 (N.Y. 1951).

Avis's argument fails for a very basic reason: the jury found that the April 21st letter did not constitute a contract between it and Ohanian. The trial judge had correctly instructed the jury that if it found the letter to be a contract it could not find for plaintiff, and the jury found for plaintiff. Parol evidence is excluded only when used as an attempt to vary or modify the terms of an existing written contract. *See Kirtley v. Abrams,* 299 F.2d 341, 345 (2d Cir. 1962) (the rule does not preclude a party "from attempting to show that there never was any agreement such as the writing purported to be"); *Whipple v. Brown Brothers Co.,* 121 N.E. 748, 750 (N.Y. 1919) ("One cannot be made to stand on a contract he never intended to make.").

This case is quite unlike *Franzek v. Calspan Corp.,* 434 N.Y.S.2d 288 (Fourth Dep't 1980), upon which defendant relies. In *Franzek* the plaintiff, about to embark on a hazardous "white water" raft ride in the Niagara River, was handed and signed a release form. He later claimed he had not read it. Such failure on his part was held not to raise an issue of fact to relieve plaintiff of its effect when the release was asserted against his claim of injury. But the contrary appears in the present case where there is strong evidence in the record to support the jury's finding that the writing was not intended to be a contract: the letter was on a form; it was sent to Ohanian in response to his request for relocation expenses; and he testified that he did not believe he read the letter other than to check a box indicating the type of relocation reimbursement he wanted. Most significantly, no evidence was presented that suggests that either Ohanian or Sharp, the Avis Vice President who sent the form to plaintiff, intended it to define the terms of Ohanian's employment with Avis.

Avis says that inasmuch as the evidence of an oral promise of lifetime employment was insufficient as a matter of law, that issue should not have gone to the jury. It relies on *Brown v. Safeway Stores, Inc.,* 190 F. Supp. 295 (E.D.N.Y. 1960), as support for this argument. Defendant can draw little solace from *Brown.* In that case the claimed assurances were made in several ways including meetings of a group of employees — the purpose of which was not to discuss length of employment — or during casual conversation. The conversations were not conducted in an atmosphere, as here, of critical one-on-one negotiation regarding the terms of future employment. Further, in *Brown* the district court found as a matter of fact that the alleged promise of lifetime employment was never made. In contrast, in the instant case the evidence was ample to permit the jury to decide whether statements made to Ohanian by defendant were more than casual comments or mere pep talks delivered by management to a group of employees. All of the surrounding circumstances — fully related earlier — were sufficient for the jury in fact to find that there was a promise of lifetime employment to a "star" employee who, it was hoped, would revive a "dying" division of defendant corporation.

Avis argues further that even if a promise of lifetime employment terminable only for just cause is found, evidence of that promise is not sufficiently definite and for that reason cannot be enforced.... Yet, promises of lifetime employment have long been enforced if found to be supported by sufficient consideration. *See* 9 Williston on Contracts § 1017, at 132-35 & nn. 17-19 (3d ed. 1967); 3A Corbin on Contracts § 684, at 229 (1960). Defendant does not contend that Ohanian's consideration for the promise of lifetime employment — his relocation from San Francisco to New York — was inadequate....

WYATT, DISTRICT JUDGE, dissenting:

Believing that the oral lifetime employment contract as claimed by plaintiff is void under the New York Statute of Frauds, I am compelled to dissent....

The "oral employment contract," as claimed by Ohanian in this Court — and at all times since the action began — was a "lifetime employment contract," which he could terminate at any time, but which Avis could terminate only for "just cause." The evidence showed that the words "just cause" were never used. The evidence for plaintiff showed, if believed, that Ohanian was guaranteed his job for life "unless he totally screws up," and that Ohanian was told he would not be fired "unless you screwed up badly." "Just cause" was the legal term selected by counsel for Ohanian as a translation of the words actually used: "totally screws up" and "screwed up badly."...

In the oral contract in suit, Avis had a right to terminate if Ohanian "totally screws up" or "screwed up badly." There is no evidence that these words referred to anything other than a breach by Ohanian of the duties and obligations of an employee, a breach of contract. There is no evidence that the words included a right in Avis to terminate whenever Avis was forced "to make a change in its business strategy" or for reasons other than fault on the part of Ohanian.

The majority opinion recognizes that the promise made by Avis to meet "Ohanian's concerns about security" was: Avis would not fire him unless he "screwed up badly." It then holds, however, that, despite these words, Ohanian could be fired even though he had not done anything in violation of the employment contract. To me, it is inconceivable that Ohanian — demanding *job security* to persuade him to leave California — would agree to leave California for an oral contract which could be terminated by Avis without any breach on his part. To give Avis a right to fire him even though he had not "screwed up badly" or "totally" would deprive Ohanian of the very security on which he was insisting....

The Statute of Frauds does not seem to be an "anachronism" for such cases as that at bar. The oral lifetime employment contract was claimed by Ohanian to have been made in a telephone conversation between him in California and Mahmarian for Avis in New York. The conversation was not recorded; no memoranda were made. The only testimony was, and could only be, that of Ohanian and Mahmarian. Not only was Ohanian a witness hostile to Avis, but, Mahmarian, whose testimony was given by deposition on November 9, 1983, had himself been dismissed by Avis on August 4, 1982, a few days after Ohanian was dismissed, and was presumably hostile to Avis. Thus, Avis was at the mercy of Ohanian and Mahmarian in the sense that no person and no writing was available to confirm or contradict them; they alone had made the claimed oral contract and there was no writing....

Statute of Frauds should Apply

NOTES

1. Irony of Result. Ohanian wins by convincing the court that the contract gave the employer a right to terminate for adverse market conditions. As a precedent, is this a victory for employees or employers?

2. Measuring Damages. The jury in *Ohanian* was instructed to compute lost wages by first multiplying plaintiff's yearly salary by the number of years he would have remained at Avis had he not been fired. The jury was then directed to deduct the amount plaintiff had earned and would earn from other employment. Should the jury have been instructed to consider that Ohanian might have been dismissed during a later business downturn?

3. Narrow Reading of Ohanian. In *Burke v. Benona,* 866 F.2d 532, 538 (2d Cir. 1989), the Second Circuit found a supervisor's promise of a job "for as long as you live" to be void under the Statute of Frauds, rejecting an argument that business conditions could have forced the employer to lay off the employee within a year without breaching the contract:

> The New York cases uniformly hold that implied termination terms are not sufficient to take an oral contract out of the statute [of frauds]. The terms must be express. As we read *Ohanian,* it purports to adhere to this established New York rule.... To the extent that the *Ohanian* panel may have interpreted the "terms" of the *Ohanian* contract more broadly than other judges would have done, the interpretation was peculiar to the facts of that case.

4. Promissory Estoppel. In addition to the Statute of Frauds issues and responses dealt with in *Ohanian,* many courts use a promissory estoppel theory to enforce oral contracts that will last more than a year. If the employee reasonably relied on oral assurances to his detriment, the court will estop the employer from asserting a Statute of Frauds defense.

The many exceptions to the Statute of Frauds have led one set of commentators to predict:

> [T]he statute of frauds [has] little significance in employment litigation.... It is rare that a case will be dismissed on the basis that the agreement, if made, would be unenforceable because it was not performable within one year of when it was made. It appears that most jurisdictions construe the statute so that it rarely, if ever, operates on any employment contract. In the few jurisdictions that apply the statute to these contracts, the pitfalls can often be sidestepped by pleading and proving matters in avoidance of the statute that are inherent in any personal service contract and that make possible the end of employment before the lapse of 12 months.

WILLIAM J. HOLLOWAY & MICHAEL J. LEECH, EMPLOYMENT TERMINATION: RIGHTS AND REMEDIES 25 (2d ed. 1993). *But see* Wior v. Anchor Indus., Inc., 669 N.E.2d 172 (Ind. 1996) (applying Statute of Frauds to oral contract with forty-two-year-old employee for permanent employment until retirement, distinguishing promises of lifetime employment that could end by death within one year).

5. *Requiring Written Agreements.* Why should courts require a written agreement for a two-year term contract, but not require one in a case like *Ohanian*? Should employees who count on job security be expected to get the agreement in writing? Could Hetes have obtained her assurances in writing?

Because of the importance of job security, parties that have actually focused on the issue might be expected to put their agreement in writing. The Statute of Frauds requirement of a writing perhaps can be justified on grounds of requiring what most parties would have wanted had they focused on the issue. On the other hand, employees might have difficulty getting such promises in writing. Under a penalty default model, perhaps courts should enforce oral promises of job security, thereby encouraging employers to put disclaimers in writing if they do not want to provide job security.

6. *Parol Evidence Rule.* The parol evidence rule prohibits a party from using outside evidence to rebut the meaning of a written contract. This rule is frequently invoked when the employee alleges that oral promises of job security were made at the job interview, but he later signed a contract declaring the job to be at will. The *Ohanian* court recognized this principle, but upheld the jury's determination that the relocation expense reimbursement form declaring at-will status was not a contract, thereby allowing consideration of the prior oral evidence of job security.

Frequently, however, an employer makes oral assurances of job security after the employee signs a written contract specifying at-will status. The parol evidence rule does not apply here, because the employee is not denying the validity of the written contract but arguing that the later oral agreement modified the written contract. Some courts, however, may question whether the employee has provided independent consideration for the later promise of job security.

7. *Right to Lay Off.* The basic argument in *Ohanian* is whether Avis had the right to terminate the employee for reasons other than Ohanian's breach of contract. The majority thought the contract allowed Avis to terminate Ohanian if bad conditions at the company required it. Should such a clause be implied in employment contracts like this? What would the parties have wanted? One bit of evidence is that collective bargaining contracts, which invariably incorporate a just-cause standard, usually allow employers to lay off workers when business conditions are bad.

A puzzle with layoffs for bad business conditions is why workers would not prefer to keep their jobs at reduced pay. One reason why workers might agree to layoffs, but not wage cuts, when business conditions are poor comes from the asymmetry of information between the employer and employees. Employees have difficulty assessing whether business conditions are truly bad when the employer claims they are. Even if conditions were good, the employer has an incentive to claim conditions are bad and cut wages, thereby increasing its profits. If its only permissible response to bad conditions is to lay off workers, however, the employer's claim is self-monitoring. If it falsely claims times are bad and lays off employees, it reduces the output of the firm and lowers its own profits. For a formal model using this argument, see Sanford Grossman & Oliver Hart, *Implicit Contracts, Moral Hazard and Unemployment,* 71 AM. ECON. REV. 301 (1981). Does this self-monitoring argument suggest that courts should imply a contractual right of employers to lay off workers when business conditions are bad, absent specific contractual language to the contrary?

B. RELIANCE AND IMPLIED-IN-FACT CONTRACTS

GROUSE v. GROUP HEALTH PLAN, INC.

Supreme Court of Minnesota
306 N.W.2d 114 (1981)

OTIS, JUSTICE.

Plaintiff John Grouse appeals from a judgment in favor of Group Health Plan, Inc., in this action for damages resulting from repudiation of an employment offer. The narrow issue raised is whether the trial court erred by concluding that Grouse's complaint fails to state a claim upon which relief can be granted. In our view, the doctrine of promissory estoppel entitles Grouse to recover and we, therefore, reverse and remand for a new trial on the issue of damages.

The facts relevant to this appeal are essentially undisputed. Grouse, a 1974 graduate of the University of Minnesota School of Pharmacy, was employed in 1975 as a retail pharmacist at Richter Drug in Minneapolis. He worked approximately 41 hours per week earning $7 per hour. Grouse desired employment in a hospital or clinical setting, however, because of the work environment and the increased compensation and benefits. In the summer of 1975 he was advised by the Health Sciences Placement office at the University that Group Health was seeking a pharmacist.

Grouse called Group Health and was told to come in and fill out an application. He did so in September and was, at that time, interviewed by Cyrus Elliott, Group Health's Chief Pharmacist. Approximately 2 weeks later Elliott contacted Grouse and asked him to come in for an interview with Donald Shoberg, Group Health's General Manager. Shoberg explained company policies and procedures as well as salary and benefits. Following this meeting Grouse again spoke with Elliott who told him to be patient, that it was necessary to interview recent graduates before making an offer.

On December 4, 1975, Elliott telephoned Grouse at Richter Drug and offered him a position as a pharmacist at Group Health's St. Louis Park Clinic. Grouse accepted but informed Elliott that 2 weeks' notice to Richter Drug would be necessary. That afternoon Grouse received an offer from a Veteran's Administration Hospital in Virginia which he declined because of Group Health's offer. Elliott called back to confirm that Grouse had resigned.

Sometime in the next few days Elliott mentioned to Shoberg that he had hired, or was thinking of hiring, Grouse. Shoberg told him that company hiring requirements included a favorable written reference, a background check, and approval of the general manager. Elliott contacted two faculty members at the School of Pharmacy who declined to give references. He also contacted an internship employer and several pharmacies where Grouse had done relief work. Their responses were that they had not had enough exposure to Grouse's work to form a judgment as to his capabilities. Elliott did not contact Richter because Grouse's application requested that he not be contacted. Because Elliott was unable to supply a favorable reference for Grouse, Shoberg hired another person to fill the position.

On December 15, 1975 Grouse called Group Health and reported that he was free to begin work. Elliott informed Grouse that someone else had been hired. Grouse complained to the director of Group Health who apologized but took no other action. Grouse experienced difficulty regaining full time employment and suffered wage loss as a result. He commenced this suit to recover damages; the trial judge found that he had not stated an actionable claim.

In our view the principle of contract law applicable here is promissory estoppel. Its effect is to imply a contract in law where none exists in fact. On these facts no contract exists because due to the bilateral power of termination neither party is committed to performance and the promises are, therefore, illusory. The elements of promissory estoppel are stated in Restatement of Contracts § 90 (1932):

> A promise which the promisor should reasonably expect to induce action or forbearance ... on the part of the promisee and which does induce such

action or forbearance is binding if injustice can be avoided only by enforcement of the promise.

Group Health knew that to accept its offer Grouse would have to resign his employment at Richter Drug. Grouse promptly gave notice to Richter Drug and informed Group Health that he had done so when specifically asked by Elliott. Under these circumstances it would be unjust not to hold Group Health to its promise.

The parties focus their arguments on whether an employment contract which is terminable at will can give rise to an action for damages if anticipatorily repudiated. Group Health contends that recognition of a cause of action on these facts would result in the anomalous rule that an employee who is told not to report to work the day before he is scheduled to begin has a remedy while an employee who is discharged after the first day does not. We cannot agree since under appropriate circumstances we believe section 90 would apply even after employment has begun.

When a promise is enforced pursuant to section 90 "[t]he remedy granted for breach may be limited as justice requires." Relief may be limited to damages measured by the promisee's reliance.

The conclusion we reach does not imply that an employer will be liable whenever he discharges an employee whose term of employment is at will. What we do hold is that under the facts of this case the appellant had a right to assume he would be given a good faith opportunity to perform his duties to the satisfaction of respondent once he was on the job. He was not only denied that opportunity but resigned the position he already held in reliance on the firm offer which respondent tendered him. Since, as respondent points out, the prospective employment might have been terminated at any time, the measure of damages is not so much what he would have earned from respondent as what he lost in quitting the job he held and in declining at least one other offer of employment elsewhere.

Reversed and remanded for a new trial on the issue of damages.

VENO v. MEREDITH

Superior Court of Pennsylvania
515 A.2d 571 (1986)

Before CIRILLO, PRESIDENT JUDGE, and CAVANAUGH and TAMILIA, JJ.

CAVANAUGH, JUDGE.

[Veno, the managing editor of The Free Press, was fired by the newspaper's owner for publishing a story criticizing a local judge. Veno filed suit for illegal termination of his employment contract. At the end of Veno's case-in-chief, the trial court issued a nonsuit in favor of the newspaper. Veno appealed.]

... Once again we are asked to decide whether or not an employer had the right to discharge an employee.

In the area of employment relations, Pennsylvania still largely adheres to the "at-will" rule.... The essence of the employment-at-will presumption is that the decision to discharge an employee is best left to the managerial prerogative and generally will not be reviewed in a judicial forum. The other side of the rule is that an employee may resign at any time, for any reason, or for no reason at all. Of course, a discharge may be subject to review in a judicial forum if the employer and employee so agree.

"at-will rule"

overcoming the "at-will presumption"

The most elementary way that the parties can overcome the at-will presumption is by express contract. For example, a contract may be made for a definite term, or it may forbid discharge in the absence of just cause or without first utilizing an internal dispute resolution mechanism. The presumption may also be overcome by implied contract. That is, all of the surrounding circumstances of the hiring may indicate that the parties did not intend the employment to be "at-will."

① ②

Another way that the at-will presumption may be overcome is where the employee gives the employer sufficient consideration in addition to the services for which he was hired. (See our discussion, *infra.*)

③

In short, if there is a dispute over the discharge of an employee, the threshold inquiry is whether or not the employment was at-will. If it was, then the discharge is not reviewable in a judicial forum. An exception is that the discharge will be reviewable in a judicial forum when there is sufficient evidence to suggest that it was against public policy or made with the specific intent to harm the employee. The latter two causes of action are classified as "wrongful discharge" torts in Pennsylvania. They are limited exceptions to the at-will presumption in this Commonwealth and only rarely occasion relief for the discharged employee....

④

Moreover, because of its vitality, courts insist that to contract-away the at-will presumption, much clarity is required. The intention to overcome the presumption will not be unheedingly inferred. This court has recently held that the modification of an "at-will" relationship to one that can never be severed without "just cause" is such a substantial modification that a very clear statement of an intention to so modify is required. Absent this clarity, again, the relationship is "at-will" and a discharge is not reviewable in a judicial forum (absent sufficient evidence of "wrongful discharge")....

Turning to the instant case, appellant alleges that he presented sufficient evidence from which a jury could conclude that his employment was not terminable at-will and that therefore the court erred in granting a nonsuit. He alleges the following facts in support of this contention. In April, 1973, when appellant and his wife purchased a home, his employer, Mr. Meredith co-signed both the disclosure statement and demand note in the sum of $5,400.00. Appellant further testified that Mr. Meredith said to him, "We're both the same age, we're both going to retire together, we're not making a lot now, but we'll make it later on. I want you to raise your children here. I want them to go to the school. I want to retire together." Moreover, appellant turned down other job opportunities throughout his employment, including one from his former employer — an offer he made known to Mr. Meredith.

These facts could not support a recovery for appellant. The statements made by the employer are broad, vague, and do not suggest that the parties contemplated a definite duration for the employment. Such statements generally do not overcome the at-will presumption.

Moreover, the statements have an aspirational quality to them. The law does not attach binding significance to comments which merely evince an employer's hope that the employee will remain in his employ until retirement. In the instant case, there was no express contract limiting the employer's ability to discharge; nor was there a reasonable "understanding" to that effect.

Nor do we find the appellant's refusal to take other jobs as significant to his contention. This forebearance was merely a manifestation of his preference to remain with the Free Press and in no way suggests he had the reasonable belief that he could never be fired except for "just cause."

Appellant also contends that he gave his employer sufficient consideration additional to the services for which he was hired and therefore his employment was not at-will. The alleged consideration consists of the following: that appellant gave up a job with a newspaper and moved his family from Newark to Pennsylvania, and that throughout the years he refused other employment opportunities.

We stated in *Darlington v. General Electric*, 504 A.2d at 315:

> [A] court will find "additional consideration" when an employee affords his employer a substantial benefit other than the services which the employee is hired to perform, or when the employee undergoes a substantial hardship other than the services which he is hired to perform. "If the circumstances are such that a termination of the relation by one party will result in great hardship or loss to the other, as they must have known it would when they made the contract, this is a factor of great weight in inducing a holding that the parties agreed upon a specific period." 3 A. Corbin, Corbin on Contracts § 684 (1960).

When sufficient additional consideration is present, an employee should not be subject to discharge without just cause for a reasonable time. The length of time during which it would be unreasonable to terminate, without just cause, an employee who has given additional consideration should be commensurate with the hardship the employee has endured or the benefit he has bestowed.

Appellant has not presented evidence tending to show that he gave his employer sufficient additional consideration. The detriments alleged are commensurate with those incurred by all manner of salaried professionals. We do not believe that appellant's termination by the Free Press some eight years into his employment over a legitimate difference of opinion constitutes the kind of "great hardship or loss" that Professor Corbin referred to, *supra*. Virtually all terminations result in some hardship and loss to the employee. Instantly, we are not presented with facts to suggest that appellant brought to the employment so substantial a benefit, or incurred so detrimental a hardship in taking the job, that he should be accorded treatment any different from the typical at-will employee.[4]

Order affirmed.

NOTES

1. *Consideration as Interpretation Device.* The *Veno* court suggests that the expenses of moving to a new job could be consideration for an employer's promise of just cause dismissal. Is there an independent promise of just cause, for which moving is consideration, or does the fact of moving itself create an obligation by the employer to give a reasonable time to recoup the costs of moving?

As the Pennsylvania Superior Court explained in *Darlington v. General Elec. Co.,* 504 A.2d 306, 314 (Pa. Super. Ct. 1986):

> The term "consideration" is not used here as it is in the usual contractual context to signify a *validation* device. The term is used, rather, more as an *interpretation* device. When "sufficient additional consideration" is present, courts infer that the parties *intended* that the contract will not be terminable at-will. This inference may be nothing more than a legal fiction because it is possible that in a given case, the parties never truly contemplated how long the employment would last even though additional consideration is present. Even so, the at-will presumption would be overcome. On the other hand, if the parties specifically agreed that the employment would be *at-will,* even though additional consideration were present, we would expect a court to construe the contract according to the parties' stated intention and hold it to be at-will. Thus, we start with the usual at-will presumption which, let us say, has not been overcome by evidence of a contract for a term or for a reasonable length of time. Then, if sufficient additional consideration is present, the law presumes this to be sufficient to rebut the at-will

---

[4] ... Appellant also cites *Lucacher v. Kerson,* 45 A.2d 245 (Pa. Super. Ct. 1946), where an employee was promised "permanent" employment in his new job. In order to take the job, he moved from New York to Philadelphia. Three days into his employment, employee was abruptly discharged. The court allowed recovery and held the contract of "permanent" employment was capable of enforcement due largely to the additional consideration rendered by employee. It is doubtful that the court in *Lucacher* should have enforced the terms of the vague and broad contract which allowed for "permanent" employment. Rather, the court should have ignored the "promise" of permanent employment because of its breadth and vagueness and *inferred* a contract for a reasonable length of time based solely on the sufficient additional consideration. The facts in *Lucacher* are obviously different from those presented instantly. In *Lucacher,* after having moved from New York to Philadelphia in reliance on a promise of a new job, employee was discharged just three days into his employment. Here, in contrast, appellant had been employed for 8 years before he was dismissed. The "reasonable length of time" here has surely passed based on the consideration given.

presumption. Such a contract could not be rightfully terminated at-will but would continue for a reasonable length of time. However, the presumption created by the additional consideration rule could *itself* be rebutted by evidence that the parties specifically contracted for employment at-will.

For an application, see *Cashdollar v. Mercy Hospital*, 595 A.2d 70 (Pa. Super. Ct. 1991) (professional selling house and moving his pregnant wife and child to a different state after quitting secure job paying $82,000 shows "hardships constitut[ing] sufficient additional consideration to rebut the at-will presumption").

2. *Is Reliance Reasonable?* Is it reasonable to incur moving expenses or quit a job in reliance on an offer of at-will employment? Some courts have held no. *See Ferreyra v. E. & J. Gallo Winery*, 41 Cal. Rptr. 819 (Cal. Ct. App. 1964) (Argentinean worker who gave up his job in Argentina and moved his family to United States to become a crew boss of one of Gallo's pruning and irrigation crews did not show sufficient consideration to protect against firing without cause).

Other courts put the issue the other way around. Rather than asking whether an employee should reasonably rely on assurances of an at-will contract, they ask whether an employee who has suffered moving expenses would have done so without some assurances of more than an at-will contract. Thus, in *Miller v. Community Discount Centers*, 228 N.E.2d 113 (Ill. App. Ct. 1967), a job applicant left his family in Toledo, Ohio to move to Chicago after receiving the following letter, which the parties stipulated was the entire agreement between them:

Dear Mr. Miller:

First, let me again extend an official welcome to the Community family; we are certain you have a rewarding and satisfying career ahead of you.

For the record, I should like to confirm the employment arrangements with you. Your beginning salary will be $10,000.00 per year as a Store Management Trainee. Regarding moving expenses, we will pay one-half now and the balance after one year.

Looking forward to seeing you soon.

Sincerely yours,

/s/ Melvin Kent
Director of Personnel

The employee sued when he was dismissed after three months. The court of appeals upheld a trial court judgment for breach of a definite one-year contract, reasoning in part:

Furthermore, we find it inconceivable that a man of plaintiff's age[*] would leave his home to come to Chicago for the mere possibility that he

---

[*] The opinion never reveals the employee's age. What age would make the argument for a definite-term contract most powerful?

would have a permanent position. It was clearly the intention of the parties, by their words, to have this contract be a contract for at least one year and nothing they can say changes that intention of the parties at the time the contract was made.

It was the intention of the parties that this man be hired for a year at least. This is made evident by the reference in the contract in regard to moving expenses. It is clear that if moving expenses are to be paid they are to be paid for coming to Chicago to take a position which would certainly be for a year or more.... This, [it] is to be noted, is a construction of language and not the adoption of a new rule. It merely states that when the moving expenses are mentioned, it is to be construed for one year and not at will.

Consider also *Lanier v. Alenco,* 459 F.2d 689, 692-93 (5th Cir. 1972) (applying Louisiana law). Louisiana is one of the few states without a Statute of Frauds, but Louisiana does require that oral contracts with greater than $500 value be proved by corroborating circumstances. The court upheld a finding of a valid oral contract, emphasizing that the employee had given up a secure job:

Lanier, with a wife and four children, left a secure and well-paying position with General Electric, a position that he had held for eleven years, to join Alenco as a branch sales manager. Like the trial judge, we find it unlikely that Lanier would leave that sort of employment without some substantial representation of a secure position at Alenco. Employment at will does not have much security, particularly when there is testimony in the record from former Alenco employees that Alenco had a history of discharges without cause. Furthermore, it does not appear that Lanier was precipitous in his shift of employment to Alenco, for his negotiations with Shelton took longer than one year.... We conclude that these factors are not, as a matter of law, insufficient "corroborating circumstances" to overturn the trial court's judgment that Lanier and Shelton agreed upon an oral contract of employment for a fixed term of one year at certain salary and commission levels, including "start up" commissions. Lanier's failure to acquiesce to Alenco's "new offer of reimbursement" at reduced salary and commission levels does not constitute "good cause" for discharge under Louisiana law, for such a substantive change in the terms of a contract requires the consent of both parties.

PUGH v. SEE'S CANDIES, INC.

California Court of Appeal
171 Cal. Rptr. 917 (1981)

GRODIN, ASSOCIATE JUSTICE.

After 32 years of employment with See's Candies, Inc., in which he worked his way up the corporate ladder from dishwasher to vice-president in charge of production and member of the board of directors, Wayne Pugh was fired. Asserting that he had been fired in breach of contract and for reasons which offend public policy he sued his former employer seeking compensatory and punitive damages for wrongful termination, and joined as a defendant a labor organization which, he alleged, had conspired in or induced the wrongful conduct. The case went to trial before a jury, and upon conclusion of the plaintiff's case-in-chief the trial court granted defendants' motions for nonsuit, and this appeal followed....

Pugh began working for See's at its Bay Area plant (then in San Francisco) in January 1941 washing pots and pans. From there he was promoted to candy maker, and held that position until the early part of 1942, when he entered the Air Corps. Upon his discharge in 1946 he returned to See's and his former position. After a year he was promoted to the position of production manager in charge of personnel, ordering raw materials, and supervising the production of candy. When, in 1950, See's moved into a larger plant in San Francisco, Pugh had responsibility for laying out the design of the plant, taking bids, and assisting in the construction. While working at this plant, Pugh sought to increase his value to the company by taking three years of night classes in plant layout, economics, and business law. When See's moved its San Francisco plant to its present location in South San Francisco in 1957, Pugh was given responsibilities for the new location similar to those which he undertook in 1950. By this time See's business and its number of production employees had increased substantially, and a new position of assistant production manager was created under Pugh's supervision.

In 1971 Pugh was again promoted, this time as vice-president in charge of production and was placed upon the board of directors of See's Northern California subsidiary, "in recognition of his accomplishments." In 1972 he received a gold watch from See's "in appreciation of 31 years of loyal service."

In May 1973 Pugh travelled with Charles Huggins, then president of See's, and their respective families to Europe on a business trip to visit candy manufacturers and to inspect new equipment. Mr. Huggins returned in early June to attend a board of director's meeting while Pugh and his family remained in Europe on a planned vacation.

Upon Pugh's return from Europe on Sunday, June 25, 1973, he received a message directing him to fly to Los Angeles the next day and meet with Mr. Huggins. Pugh went to Los Angeles expecting to be told of another promotion. The preceding Christmas season had been the most successful in See's history, the Valentine's Day holiday of 1973 set a new sales record for See's, and the March 1973 edition of See's Newsletter, containing two pictures of Pugh, carried congratulations on the increased production.

Instead, upon Pugh's arrival at Mr. Huggins' office, the latter said, "Wayne, come in and sit down. We might as well get right to the point. I have decided your services are no longer required by See's Candies. Read this and sign it." Huggins handed him a letter confirming his termination and directing him to remove that day "only personal papers and possessions from your office," but "absolutely no records, formulas or other material"; and to turn in and account for "all keys, credit cards, et cetera." The letter advised that Pugh would receive unpaid salary, bonuses and accrued vacation through that date, and the full amount of his profit sharing account, but "No severance pay will be granted." Finally, Pugh was directed "not to visit or contact Production Department employees while they are on the job."

The letter contained no reason for Pugh's termination. When Pugh asked Huggins for a reason, he was told only that he should "look deep within [him]self" to find the answer, that "Things were said by people in the trade that have come back to us." Pugh's termination was subsequently announced to the industry in a letter which, again, stated no reasons.

When Pugh first went to work for See's, Ed Peck, then president and general manager, frequently told him: "if you are loyal to (See's) and do a good job, your future is secure." Laurance See, who became president of the company in 1951 and served in that capacity until his death in 1969, had a practice of not terminating administrative personnel except for good cause, and this practice was carried on by his brother, Charles B. See, who succeeded Laurance as president.

During the entire period of his employment, there had been no formal or written criticism of Pugh's work.[1] No complaints were ever raised at the annual meetings which preceded each holiday season, and he was never denied a raise or bonus. He received no notice that there was a problem which needed correction, nor any warning that any disciplinary action was being contemplated.

Pugh's theory as to why he was terminated relates to a contract which See's at that time had with the defendant union....

In 1968 the supplemental [union] agreement contained a new rate classification which permitted See's to pay its seasonal employees at a lower rate. At a company meeting prior to the 1968 negotiations, Pugh had objected to the proposed new seasonal classification on the grounds that it might make it more difficult to recruit seasonal workers, and create unrest among See's regular seasonal workers who had worked previously for other manufacturers at higher rates. Huggins overruled Pugh's objection and (unknown to Pugh) recommended his termination for "lack of cooperation" as to which Pugh's objection formed "part of the reason." His recommendation was not accepted....

In April [1973], Huggins asked Pugh to be part of the negotiating team for the new union contract. Pugh responded that he would like to, but he was bothered by the possibility that See's had a "sweetheart contract" with the union. In

---

[1] Huggins testified that in 1953 there was some personality conflict between Pugh and Huggins' assistant, a Mr. Forrest, on account of which Huggins recommended to Laurance See that Pugh be terminated, but See declined. Huggins again recommended Pugh's termination in 1968, under circumstances to be described in this opinion, and again See declined. It does not appear that Huggins' actions in this regard, or the criticism of Pugh which they implied, were made known to Pugh.

response, someone banged on the table and said, "'You don't know what the hell you are talking about.'" Pugh said, "Well, I think I know what I am talking about. I don't know whether you have a sweetheart contract, but I am telling you if you do, I don't want to be involved because they are immoral, illegal and not in the best interests of my employees." At the trial, Pugh explained that to him a "sweetheart contract" was "a contract whereby one employer would get an unfair competitive advantage over a competitor by getting a lower wage rate, would be one version of it."...

The presumption that an employment contract is intended to be terminable at will is subject, like any presumption, to contrary evidence. This may take the form of an agreement, express or implied, that the relationship will continue for some fixed period of time. Or, and of greater relevance here, it may take the form of an agreement that the employment relationship will continue indefinitely, pending the occurrence of some event such as the employer's dissatisfaction with the employee's services or the existence of some "cause" for termination. Sometimes this latter type of agreement is characterized as a contract for "permanent" employment, but that characterization may be misleading. In one of the earliest California cases on this subject, the Supreme Court interpreted a contract for permanent employment as meaning "that plaintiffs' employment ... was to continue indefinitely, and until one or the other of the parties wish, for some good reason, to sever the relation." *Lord v. Goldberg*, 22 P. 1126 (Cal. 1889).

A contract which limits the power of the employer with respect to the reasons for termination is no less enforceable because it places no equivalent limits upon the power of the employee to quit his employment. "If the requirement of consideration is met, there is no additional requirement of ... equivalence in the values exchanged, or 'mutuality of obligation.'" Rest. 2d Contracts, § 81 (Tent. Draft No. 2, 1965).

Moreover, while it has sometimes been said that a promise for continued employment subject to limitation upon the employer's power of termination must be supported by some "independent consideration," i.e., consideration other than the services to be rendered, such a rule is contrary to the general contract principle that courts should not inquire into the adequacy of consideration.... Thus there is no analytical reason why an employee's promise to render services, or his actual rendition of services over time, may not support an employer's promise both to pay a particular wage (for example) and to refrain from arbitrary dismissal.

The most likely explanation for the "independent consideration" requirement is that it serves an evidentiary function: it is more probable that the parties intended a continuing relationship, with limitations upon the employer's dismissal authority, when the employee has provided some benefit to the employer, or suffers some detriment, beyond the usual rendition of service....

In determining whether there exists an implied-in-fact promise for some form of continued employment courts have considered a variety of factors in addition to the existence of independent consideration. These have included, for example, the personnel policies or practices of the employer, the employee's longevity of service, actions or communications by the employer reflecting assurances of continued employment, and the practices of the industry in which the employee is engaged.

[The court then discusses the implied-in-law covenant of good faith and fair dealing, but says "We need not go that far, however." Results of cases applying that covenant are "equally explicable in traditional contract terms: the employer's conduct gave rise to an implied promise that it would not act arbitrarily in dealing with its employees."]

Here, similarly, there were facts in evidence from which the jury could determine the existence of such an implied promise: the duration of appellant's employment, the commendations and promotions he received, the apparent lack of any direct criticism of his work, the assurances he was given, and the employer's acknowledged policies. While oblique language will not, standing alone, be sufficient to establish agreement, it is appropriate to consider the totality of the parties' relationship: Agreement may be "shown by the acts and conduct of the parties, interpreted in the light of the subject matter and the surrounding circumstances." We therefore conclude that it was error to grant respondents' motions for nonsuit as to See's.

Since this litigation may proceed toward yet uncharted waters, we consider it appropriate to provide some guidance as to the questions which the trial court may confront on remand. We have held that appellant has demonstrated a prima facie case of wrongful termination in violation of his contract of employment. The burden of coming forward with evidence as to the reason for appellant's termination now shifts to the employer. Appellant may attack the employer's offered explanation, either on the ground that it is pretextual (and that the real reason is one prohibited by contract or public policy), or on the ground that it is insufficient to meet the employer's obligations under contract or applicable legal principles. Appellant bears, however, the ultimate burden of proving that he was terminated wrongfully. *Cf. McDonnell Douglas Corp. v. Green* (1973) 411 U.S. 792, 802-807.

By what standard that burden is to be measured will depend, in part, upon what conclusions the jury draws as to the nature of the contract between the parties. The terms "just cause" and "good cause," "as used in a variety of contexts ... have been found to be difficult to define with precision and to be largely relative in their connotation, depending upon the particular circumstances of each case." Essentially, they connote "a fair and honest cause or reason, regulated by good faith on the part of the party exercising the power." Care must be taken, however, not to interfere with the legitimate exercise of managerial discretion. "Good cause" in this context is quite different from the standard applicable in determining the propriety of an employee's termination under a contract for a specified term. And where, as here, the employee occupies a sensitive manage-

rial or confidential position, the employer must of necessity be allowed substantial scope for the exercise of subjective judgment.

Reversed.

RACANELLI, P. J., and NEWSOM, J., concur.

NOTES

1. *Pugh's Fate on Remand.* While *Pugh* is the leading case establishing implied-in-fact good cause contracts for long-tenured employees, Pugh himself did not succeed under the standard. At the second trial, See's Candies presented evidence that it had discharged Pugh for good cause. See's employees, former employees, and business associates testified that Pugh was disrespectful to his superiors and subordinates, disloyal to the company, and uncooperative with other administrative staff. Charles Huggins, president and chief executive officer of See's, testified that his complaints about Pugh spanned almost twenty years and that he had recommended Pugh's termination in 1953 and in 1968. The jury found for the defendant in a general verdict, which was upheld on appeal. *Pugh v. See's Candies, Inc.*, 250 Cal. Rptr. 195 (Cal. Ct. App. 1988).

2. *Longevity of Service.* What is the key fact supporting Pugh's claim? Is it the assurances given to him, or is it simply that he has devoted thirty-two years of his life to this company? If the latter, when should the presumption against arbitrary dismissal begin? In *Cleary v. American Airlines,* 168 Cal. Rptr. 722 (Cal. Ct. App. 1980), the court upheld a claim of an employee dismissed without cause after eighteen years of service, holding: "Termination of employment without legal cause after such a period of time offends the implied-in-law covenant of good faith and fair dealing contained in all contracts including employment contracts." In *Foley v. Interactive Data Corp.,* 765 P.2d 373 (Cal. 1988), the California Supreme Court upheld a *Pugh* claim for an employee with six years and nine months of service.

In *Foley v. Community Oil Co.,* 64 F.R.D. 561 (D.N.H. 1974) (applying New Hampshire law), the employee was both long-term and a recent mover. Foley had worked for thirty-two years when his company was bought by Community Oil. He continued to work for Community Oil for another five years, when it asked him to move from Maine to New Hampshire. Three years after he sold his house and moved with his wife to New Hampshire, he was fired. The court declared that a forty-year employee's "[l]ongevity of service can also give rise to an implied contract right," explaining that "the employee, in providing long-term employment to a single employer substantially diminishes his economic mobility." In what way is the lack of economic mobility relevant to the employee's claim?

3. *Implied Tenure for Public Employees.* A famous pair of due process cases illustrates the centrality of long service in finding implied job tenure for public employees. In *Board of Regents v. Roth,* 408 U.S. 564 (1972), a college terminated without reason an assistant professor at his first teaching job upon com-

Chris McCullock

pletion of his one-year contract. The Supreme Court rejected his due process claim, concluding he had no property interest beyond the one-year job.

In *Perry v. Sindermann*, 408 U.S. 593 (1972), decided the same day, Professor Perry had completed ten one-year contracts in the Texas system and had been a full professor at Odessa Junior College for four years when he was dismissed. The college had no formal tenure system. The Court found he had a property right in his job that could not be taken away without due process. Justice Stewart, writing for the Court, explained that "[a] teacher, like the respondent, who has held his position for a number of years, might be able to show from the circumstances of this service — and from other relevant facts — that he has a legitimate claim of entitlement to job tenure." 408 U.S. at 602.

4. *Defining Good Cause — Good Faith or Just Cause?* When a court finds an implied-in-fact agreement for job security, a remaining issue is how much security to imply. *Pugh* upholds a "good cause" standard, and indicates that it is less stringent than under a definite-term contract. A major question is whether the good-cause standard is closer to subjective good faith or objective just cause.

Suppose, in a *Pugh* situation, the jury finds that the employer had a reasonable belief the employee smoked marijuana on the job in violation of company rules, but the jury also finds that the employee did not, in fact, smoke marijuana. Does the employee win on a claim of breach of the implied-in-fact contract? For a spirited debate on this issue, see *Sanders v. Parker Drilling Co.*, 911 F.2d 191 (9th Cir. 1990), *cert. denied*, 500 U.S. 917 (1991), in which the court held that, under Alaska law, the employer must show that the employee actually engaged in prohibited conduct. Judge Kozinski dissented, warning that the majority reaches "a result so preposterous it would be laughable if it were not so scary." *Id.* at 215.

Alaska law apparently differs from California law on this point, as explored in *Cotran v. Rollins Hudig Hall Int'l, Inc.*, 948 P.2d 412 (Cal. 1998). After two coworkers accused Cotran of sexual harassment, the company conducted twenty-one interviews over two weeks, concluded that the accusations were probably true, and fired him. He filed suit for breach of an implied-in-fact contract not to be fired without good cause. At trial, the court instructed the jury to determine whether Cotran had, in fact, engaged in the alleged sexual harassment. The jury found that Cotran had not and awarded him $1.8 million in compensatory damages. The court of appeals overturned the judgment and the California Supreme Court affirmed, holding that the proper question for the jury was not whether the misconduct had actually occurred, but whether the employer had reasonable grounds for believing it had occurred and acted fairly otherwise.

5. *Good Faith or Just Cause in the Constitution.* The Supreme Court has wrestled with the same issue for public employees with constitutional protection, but has been unable to articulate a clear rule. In *Waters v. Churchill*, 511 U.S. 661 (1994), a supervisor in a public hospital fired a nurse for allegedly making comments that were personal and disruptive. The nurse claimed her comments only criticized the hospital's cross-training policy, which allowed nurses to work in areas without sufficient training. Because the employer was a governmental body subject to the First Amendment, any firing would be subject to the test of *Connick v. Myers*, 461 U.S. 138 (1983), which holds that a governmental employer cannot fire an employee for speaking on a matter of public concern unless the employee's interest in expressing herself is outweighed by any injury the speech could cause to the State's interest in efficient public service by its employees. (*See generally* Chapter 7.) For purposes of the case, the Court assumed that the *Connick* test would forbid the hospital from knowingly firing the nurse for speaking on cross-training, but that the nurse had no claim if she uttered only personal, disruptive comments. The question dividing the Justices was whether the nurse had a claim if she in fact was talking about cross-training but the supervisor thought she was making only comments unprotected by the First Amendment.

Justice O'Connor, writing for four Justices, declared that the *Connick* test should be applied to what the employer thought was said, not to what a fact-finder later determines was actually said. However, the employer must make reasonable efforts to determine the true facts. O'Connor's test could be labeled a reasonable good-faith test.

Justice Scalia, writing for three Justices, rejected any constitutional requirement that the employer must conduct an investigation before firing an employee. He would find that a public employer violated the First Amendment by firing an employee only if the firing was in retaliation for protected speech. His test could be labeled a subjective good-faith test.

Justice Stevens, writing for two Justices, would find the firing impermissible unless a judicial fact-finder determines that the employee in fact made the disparaging remarks. Justice Stevens began his opinion by declaring that "[t]his is a free country," and ended by declaring that freedom of speech requires that, "before firing a public employee for her speech, management get its facts straight." His test might be labeled an objective good-cause test.

6. *Implied-In-Fact Demotion Claims.* Should courts entertain claims that an employer breached an implied-in-fact contract not to demote an employee without cause? Or not to transfer an employee? Or reduce pay? Or discipline? Or change the work schedule? On the one hand, such claims seem doctrinally identical to implied-in-fact termination claims. This is especially so since these claims often blend into termination claims if the employee quits and claims conditions were so intolerable that he was constructively discharged. On the other hand, entertaining all such claims even when the employee does not quit or is not fired might turn courts into super-personnel managers. In *Scott v. Pacific Gas & Electric Co.*, 904 P.2d 834 (Cal. 1995), the California Supreme Court held that an implied agreement not to demote except for good cause may be enforced by demoted employees, rejecting the lower court's theory that courts should not interfere in on-going employment relationships.

7. *Enforcing Life-Cycle Contracts.* Many employees spend most of their *Interesting Policy Point* working life in an internal labor market with a single employer. As with many long-term relationships, an employer and employees have difficulty specifying in advance many of the terms under which they will operate. Of necessity, much of the agreement is implicit rather than explicit. Both the firm and worker make heavy investments in training and recruitment. A problem in such long-term relationships is that neither side can easily terminate it, because of the costs of duplicating these sunk investments. Being locked in can lead to exploitation. The temptation for exploitation is greatly increased when one party has largely completed its investment or promises and the other side has not. A major role for courts might be to enforce the implicit agreements, thereby making them more secure and valuable for both sides.

One common life-cycle model suggests that a firm pays its employees less than they are worth at the beginning of their career with the promise of paying them more than they are worth at the end. This will induce employees to work hard and acquire firm-specific skills, so that both the firm and employees are better off than under an arrangement whereby employees are paid their current worth at all times. The danger with this arrangement, however, is that a firm has an incentive to fire workers nearing the end of their life cycle, when they are paid more than they are currently producing. One way to justify the result in *Pugh* is to suggest that the court is enforcing an implicit life-cycle contract. *See* Stewart J. Schwab, *Life-Cycle Justice: Accommodating Just Cause and Employment At Will*, 92 MICH. L. REV. 8 (1993) (excerpted in Chapter 7).

C. EMPLOYMENT MANUALS

WOOLLEY v. HOFFMANN-LA ROCHE, INC.

Supreme Court of New Jersey
491 A.2d 1257, *modified*, 499 A.2d 515 (1985)

WILENTZ, C.J.

I

The issue before us is whether certain terms in a company's employment manual may contractually bind the company. We hold that absent a clear and prominent disclaimer, an implied promise contained in an employment manual that an employee will be fired only for cause may be enforceable against an employer even when the employment is for an indefinite term and would otherwise be terminable at will.

II

Plaintiff, Richard Woolley, was hired by defendant, Hoffmann-La Roche, Inc., in October 1969, as an Engineering Section Head in defendant's Central Engineering Department at Nutley. There was no written employment contract between plaintiff and defendant. Plaintiff began work in mid-November 1969. Some time in December, plaintiff received and read the personnel manual on which his claims are based.

In 1976, plaintiff was promoted, and in January 1977 he was promoted again, this latter time to Group Leader for the Civil Engineering, the Piping Design, the Plant Layout, and the Standards and Systems Sections. In March 1978, plaintiff was directed to write a report to his supervisors about piping problems in one of defendant's buildings in Nutley. This report was written and submitted to plaintiff's immediate supervisor on April 5, 1978. On May 3, 1978, stating that the General Manager of defendant's Corporate Engineering Department had lost confidence in him, plaintiff's supervisors requested his resignation. Following this, by letter dated May 22, 1978, plaintiff was formally asked for his resignation, to be effective July 15, 1978.

Plaintiff refused to resign. Two weeks later defendant again requested plaintiff's resignation, and told him he would be fired if he did not resign. Plaintiff again declined, and he was fired in July.

Plaintiff filed a complaint alleging breach of contract, intentional infliction of emotional distress, and defamation, but subsequently consented to the dismissal of the latter two claims. The gist of plaintiff's breach of contract claim is that the express and implied promises in defendant's employment manual created a contract under which he could not be fired at will, but rather only for cause, and then only after the procedures outlined in the manual were followed.[1] Plaintiff contends that he was not dismissed for good cause, and that his firing was a breach of contract.

Defendant's motion for summary judgment was granted by the trial court, which held that the employment manual was not contractually binding on defendant, thus allowing defendant to terminate plaintiff's employment at will.[2] The Appellate Division affirmed. We granted certification.

---

[1] According to the provisions of the manual, defendant could, and over the years apparently did, unilaterally change these provisions....

[2] ... It may be of some help to point out some of the manual's general provisions here. It is entitled "Hoffmann-La Roche, Inc. Personnel Policy Manual" and at the bottom of the face page is the notation "issued to: [and then in handwriting] Richard Woolley 12/1/69." The portions of the manual submitted to us consist of eight pages. It describes the employees "covered" by the manual ("all employees of Hoffmann-La Roche"), the manual's purpose ("a practical operating tool in the equitable and efficient administration of our employee relations program"); five of the eight pages are devoted to "termination." In addition to setting forth the purpose and policy of the termination section, it defines "the types of termination" as "layoff," "discharge due to performance," "discharge, disciplinary," "retirement" and "resignation." As one might expect, layoff is a termination caused by lack of work, retirement a termination caused by age, resignation a termination on the initiative of the employee, and discharge due to performance and discharge, disciplinary, are both terminations for cause. There is no category set forth for discharge without cause. The termination section includes "Guidelines for discharge due to performance," consisting of a fairly detailed procedure to be used before an employee may be fired for cause. Preceding these definitions of the five categories of termination is a section on "Policy," the first sentence of

III

Hoffmann-La Roche contends that the formation of the type of contract claimed by plaintiff to exist — Hoffmann-La Roche calls it a permanent employment contract for life — is subject to special contractual requirements: the intent of the parties to create such an undertaking must be clear and definite; in addition to an explicit provision setting forth its duration, the agreement must specifically cover the essential terms of employment — the duties, responsibilities, and compensation of the employee, and the proof of these terms must be clear and convincing; the undertaking must be supported by consideration in addition to the employee's continued work. Woolley claims that the requirements for the formation of such a contract have been met here and that they do not extend as far as Hoffmann-La Roche claims. Further, Woolley argues that this is not a "permanent contract for life," but rather an employment contract of indefinite duration that may be terminated only for good cause and in accordance with the procedure set forth in the personnel policy manual. Both parties agree that the employment contract is one of indefinite duration; Hoffmann-La Roche contends that in New Jersey, when an employment contract is of indefinite duration, the inescapable legal conclusion is that it is an employment at will; Woolley claims that even such a contract — of indefinite duration — may contain provisions requiring that termination be only for cause....

We are thus faced with the question of whether this is the kind of employment contract — a "long-range commitment" — that must be construed as one of indefinite duration and therefore at will ..., or whether ordinary contractual doctrine applies. In either case, the question is whether Hoffmann-La Roche retained the right to fire with or without cause or whether, as Woolley claims, his employment could be terminated only for cause. We believe another question, not explicitly treated below, is involved: should the legal effect of the dissemination of a personnel policy manual by a company with a substantial number of employees be determined solely and strictly by traditional contract doctrine? Is that analysis adequate for the realities of such a workplace?...

V

....

We acknowledge that most of the out-of-state cases demonstrate an unwillingness to give contractual force to company policy manuals that purport to enhance job security. These cases, holding that policy manual provisions do not give rise to any contractual obligation, have to some extent confused policy manuals with individual long-term employment contracts and have applied to the manuals rules appropriate only to the individual employment contract. When there was

---

which provides: "It is the policy of Hoffmann-La Roche to retain to the extent consistent with company requirements, the services of all employees who perform their duties efficiently and effectively."

such an individual contract before them (often consisting of oral assurances or a skeletal written agreement) not specifying a duration or term, courts understandably ruled them to be "at-will" contracts. They did so since they feared that by interpreting a contract of indefinite duration to be terminable only for cause, the courts would be saddling an employer with an employee for many years. In order to insure that the employer intended to accept the burdens of such an unusual "lifetime employment," the courts understandably insisted that the contract and the surrounding circumstances demonstrate unmistakably clear signs of the employer's intent to be bound, leading to the requirements of additional independent consideration and convincing specificity....

Whatever their worth in dealing with individual long-term employment contracts, these requirements, over and above those ordinarily found in contract law, have no relevancy when a policy manual is involved. In that case, there is no individual lifetime employment contract involved, but rather, if there is a contract, it is one for a group of employees — sometimes all of them — for an indefinite term, and here, fairly read, one that may not be terminated by the employer without good cause....

What is before us in this case is not a special contract with a particular employee, but a general agreement covering all employees. There is no reason to treat such a document with hostility.

The trial court viewed the manual as an attempt by Hoffmann-La Roche to avoid a collective bargaining agreement.[6] Implicit is the thought that while the employer viewed a collective bargaining agreement as an intrusion on management prerogatives, it recognized, in addition to the advantages of an employment manual to both sides, that unless this kind of company manual were given to the workforce, collective bargaining, and the agreements that result from collective bargaining, would more likely take place.

A policy manual that provides for job security grants an important, fundamental protection for workers. If such a commitment is indeed made, obviously an employer should be required to honor it. When such a document, purporting to give job security, is distributed by the employer to a workforce, substantial injustice may result if that promise is broken.

We do not believe that Hoffmann-La Roche was attempting to renege on its promise when it fired Woolley. On the contrary, the record strongly suggests that even though it believed its manual did not create any contractually binding agreements, Hoffmann-La Roche nevertheless almost invariably honored it. In effect, it gave employees more than it believed the law required. Its position taken before us is one of principle: while contending it treated Woolley fairly, it maintains it had no legal obligation to do so.

---

[6] The trial court, after noting that if Hoffmann-La Roche had been unionized, Woolley would not be litigating the question of whether the employer had to have good cause to fire him, said "[T]here is no question in my mind that Hoffmann-La Roche offered these good benefits to their employees to steer them away from this kind of specific collective bargaining contract...."

VI

Given the facts before us and the common law of contracts interpreted in the light of sound policy applicable to this modern setting, we conclude that the termination clauses of this company's Personnel Policy Manual, including the procedure required before termination occurs, could be found to be contractually enforceable. Furthermore, we conclude that when an employer of a substantial number of employees circulates a manual that, when fairly read, provides that certain benefits are an incident of the employment (including, especially, job security provisions), the judiciary, instead of "grudgingly" conceding the enforceability of those provisions, should construe them in accordance with the reasonable expectations of the employees.

The employer's contention here is that the distribution of the manual was simply an expression of the company's "philosophy" and therefore free of any possible contractual consequences. The former employee claims it could reasonably be read as an explicit statement of company policies intended to be followed by the company in the same manner as if they were expressed in an agreement signed by both employer and employees. From the analysis that follows we conclude that a jury, properly instructed, could find, in strict contract terms, that the manual constituted an offer; put differently, it could find that this portion of the manual (concerning job security) set forth terms and conditions of employment.

In determining the manual's meaning and effect, we must consider the probable context in which it was disseminated and the environment surrounding its continued existence. The manual, though apparently not distributed to all employees ("in general, distribution will be provided to supervisory personnel ..."), covers all of them. Its terms are of such importance to all employees that in the absence of contradicting evidence, it would seem clear that it was intended by Hoffmann-La Roche that all employees be advised of the benefits it confers.

We take judicial notice of the fact that Hoffmann-La Roche is a substantial company with many employees in New Jersey. The record permits the conclusion that the policy manual represents the most reliable statement of the terms of their employment. At oral argument counsel conceded that it is rare for any employee, except one on the medical staff, to have a special contract. Without minimizing the importance of its specific provisions, the context of the manual's preparation and distribution is, to us, the most persuasive proof that it would be almost inevitable for an employee to regard it as a binding commitment, legally enforceable, concerning the terms and conditions of his employment. Having been employed, like hundreds of his co-employees, without any individual employment contract, by an employer whose good reputation made it so attractive, the employee is given this one document that purports to set forth the terms and conditions of his employment, a document obviously carefully prepared by the company with all of the appearances of corporate legitimacy that one could imagine. If there were any doubt about it (and there would be none in the mind of most employees), the name of the manual dispels it, for it is nothing short of the official policy of the company, it is the Personnel Policy Manual. As every employee knows, when superiors tell you "it's company policy," they mean business.

The mere fact of the manual's distribution suggests its importance. Its change-ability — the uncontroverted ability of management to change its terms — is argued as supporting its non-binding quality, but one might as easily conclude that, given its importance, the employer wanted to keep it up to date, especially to make certain, given this employer's good reputation in labor relations, that the benefits conferred were sufficiently competitive with those available from other employers, including benefits found in collective bargaining agreements. The record suggests that the changes actually made almost always favored the employees.

Given that background, then, unless the language contained in the manual were such that no one could reasonably have thought it was intended to create legally binding obligations, the termination provisions of the policy manual would have to be regarded as an obligation undertaken by the employer. It will not do now for the company to say it did not mean the things it said in its manual to be binding. Our courts will not allow an employer to offer attractive induce-ments and benefits to the workforce and then withdraw them when it chooses, no matter how sincere its belief that they are not enforceable.

Whatever else the manual may deal with ... one of its major provisions deals with the single most important objective of the workforce: job security. The reasons for giving such provisions binding force are particularly persuasive. Wages, promotions, conditions of work, hours of work, all of those take second place to job security, for without that all other benefits are vulnerable....

Job security is the assurance that one's livelihood, one's family's future, will not be destroyed arbitrarily; it can be cut off only "for good cause," fairly deter-mined. Hoffmann-La Roche's commitment here was to what working men and women regard as their most basic advance. It was a commitment that gave workers protection against arbitrary termination.

Many of these workers undoubtedly know little about contracts, and many probably would be unable to analyze the language and terms of the manual. Whatever Hoffmann-La Roche may have intended, that which was read by its employees was a promise not to fire them except for cause.

Under all of these circumstances, therefore, it would be most unrealistic to construe this manual and determine its enforceability as if it were the same as a lifetime contract with but one employee designed to induce him to play on the company's baseball team.[8]

---

[8] The contract arising from the manual is of indefinite duration. It is not the extraordinary "lifetime" contract .... For example, a contract arising from a manual ordinarily may be terminated when the employee's performance is inadequate; when business circumstances require a general reduction in the employment force, the positions eliminated including that of plaintiff; when those same circumstances require the elimination of employees performing a certain function, for instance, for technological reasons, and plaintiff performed such functions; when business

VII

CONSIDERATION

Having concluded that a jury could find the Personnel Policy Manual to constitute an offer, we deal with what most cases deem the major obstacle to construction of the terms as constituting a binding agreement, namely, the requirement under contract law that consideration must be given in exchange for the employer's offer in order to convert that offer into a binding agreement. The cases on this subject deal with such issues as whether there was a promise in return for the employer's promise (the offer contained in the manual constituting, in effect, a promise), or whether there was some benefit or detriment bargained for and in fact conferred or suffered, sufficient to create a unilateral contract; whether the action or inaction, the benefit or the detriment, was done or not done in reliance on the employer's offer or promise; whether the alleged agreement was so lacking in "mutuality" as to be insufficient for contractual purposes — in other words, whether the fundamental requirements of a contract have been met.

We conclude that these job security provisions contained in a personnel policy manual widely distributed among a large workforce are supported by consideration and may therefore be enforced as a binding commitment of the employer.

In order for an offer in the form of a promise to become enforceable, it must be accepted. Acceptance will depend on what the promisor bargained for: he may have bargained for a return promise that, if given, would result in a bilateral contract, both promises becoming enforceable. Or he may have bargained for some action or nonaction that, if given or withheld, would render his promise enforceable as a unilateral contract. In most of the cases involving an employer's personnel policy manual, the document is prepared without any negotiations and is voluntarily distributed to the workforce by the employer. It seeks no return promise from the employees. It is reasonable to interpret it as seeking continued work from the employees, who, in most cases, are free to quit since they are almost always employees at will, not simply in the sense that the employer can fire them without cause, but in the sense that they can quit without breaching any obligation. Thus analyzed, the manual is an offer that seeks the formation of a unilateral contract — the employees' bargained-for action needed to make the offer binding being their continued work when they have no obligation to continue.

bilateral or unilateral contract

---

conditions require a general reduction in salary, a reduction that brings plaintiff's pay below that which he is willing to accept; or when any change, including the cessation of business, requires the elimination of plaintiff's position, an elimination made in good faith in pursuit of legitimate business objectives: all of these terminations, long before the expiration of "lifetime" employment, are ordinarily contemplated in a contract arising from a manual, although the list does not purport to be exhaustive. The essential difference is that the "lifetime" contract purports to protect the employment against any termination; the contract arising from the manual protects the employment only from arbitrary termination.

The unilateral contract analysis is perfectly adequate for that employee who was aware of the manual and who continued to work intending that continuation to be the action in exchange for the employer's promise; it is even more helpful in support of that conclusion if, but for the employer's policy manual, the employee would have quit.[9]

Those solutions seem to be technically correct.... [I]n *Anthony v. Jersey Cent. Power & Light Co.,* 143 A.2d 762 (N.J. Super. Ct. App. Div. 1958), practically every contractual objection that could be made here was disposed of by the Appellate Division in the context of a claim for pension rights by supervisory personnel based on a company manual (entitled "General Rules"). There, the defendant-employer argued that its severance-pay rule was a mere gratuitous promise, not supported by consideration. The court responded, analyzing the promise as an offer of a unilateral contract and the employees' continued services as sufficient acceptance and consideration therefor. To the defendant's argument that there was no evidence of reliance upon its promise, the *Anthony* court responded that reliance was to be presumed under the circumstances. We agree.[10]

VIII

The lack of definiteness concerning the other terms of employment — its duration, wages, precise service to be rendered, hours of work, etc., does not prevent enforcement of a job security provision. The lack of terms (if the complete manual is similarly lacking) can cause problems of interpretation about

---

[9] Third-party-beneficiary doctrines might be used to confer the benefits on all workers; or the employer's offer could be construed as inviting acceptance in the form of continuance of work by merely one worker in order to benefit all.

Similarly, the doctrine of promissory estoppel could be relied on as a rationale for enforcement of an employer's promises in a policy manual or similar document under certain circumstances....

The doctrine of unconscionability of the Uniform Commercial Code is analogous to the employment-at-will rule. The unconscionability doctrine developed to protect the disadvantaged party in a one-sided bargain.

[10] If reliance is not presumed, a strict contractual analysis might protect the rights of some employees and not others. For example, where an employee is not even aware of the existence of the manual, his or her continued work would not ordinarily be thought of as the bargained-for detriment. Similarly, if it is quite clear that those employees who knew of the offer knew that it sought their continued work, but nevertheless continued without the slightest intention of putting forth that action as consideration for the employer's promise, it might not be sufficient to form a contract. In this case there is no proof that plaintiff, Woolley, relied on the policy manual in continuing his work. Furthermore, as the Appellate Division correctly noted, Woolley did "not bargain for" the employer's promise. The implication of the presumption of reliance is that the manual's job security provisions became binding the moment the manual was distributed. Anyone employed before or after became one of the beneficiaries of those provisions of the manual. And if *Toussaint* [*v. Blue Cross & Blue Shield of Mich.,* 292 N.W.2d 880 (Mich. 1980)] is followed, employees neither had to read it, know of its existence, or rely on it to benefit from its provisions any more than employees in a plant that is unionized have to read or rely on a collective-bargaining agreement in order to obtain its benefits.

these other aspects of employment, but not to the point of making the job security term unenforceable. Realistically, the objection has force only when the agreement is regarded as a special one between the employer and an individual employee. There it might be difficult to determine whether there was good cause for termination if one could not determine what it was that the employee was expected to do. That difficulty is one factor that suggests the employer did not intend a lifetime contract with one employee. Here the question of good cause is made considerably easier to deal with in view of the fact that the agreement applies to the entire workforce, and the workforce itself is rather large. Even-handedness and equality of treatment will make the issue in most cases far from complex; the fact that in some cases the "for cause" provision may be difficult to interpret and enforce should not deprive employees in other cases from taking advantage of it. If there is a problem arising from indefiniteness, in any event, it is one caused by the employer. It was the employer who chose to make the termination provisions explicit and clear. If indefiniteness as to other provisions is a problem, it is one of the employer's own making from which it should gain no advantage.

Defendant expresses some concern that our interpretation will encourage lawsuits by disgruntled employees. As we view it, however, if the employer has in fact agreed to provide job security, plaintiffs in lawsuits to enforce that agreement should not be regarded as disgruntled employees, but rather as employees pursuing what is rightfully theirs. The solution is not deprivation of the employees' claim, but enforcement of the employer's agreement. The defendant further contends that its future plans and proposed projects are premised on continuance of the at-will employment status of its workforce. We find this argument unpersuasive. There are many companies whose employees have job security who are quite able to plan their future and implement those plans. If, however, the at-will employment status of the workforce was so important, the employer should not have circulated a document so likely to lead employees into believing they had job security....

X

We are aware that problems that do not ordinarily exist when collective bargaining agreements are involved may arise from the enforcement of employment manuals. Policy manuals may not generally be as comprehensive or definite as typical collective bargaining agreements. Further problems may result from the employer's explicitly reserved right unilaterally to change the manual. We have no doubt that, generally, changes in such a manual, including changes in terms and conditions of employment, are permitted. We express no opinion, however, on whether or to what extent they are permitted when they adversely affect a binding job security provision.

XI

Our opinion need not make employers reluctant to prepare and distribute company policy manuals. Such manuals can be very helpful tools in labor relations, helpful both to employer and employees, and we would regret it if the consequence of this decision were that the constructive aspects of these manuals were in any way diminished. We do not believe that they will, or at least we certainly do not believe that that constructive aspect should be diminished as a result of this opinion.

All that this opinion requires of an employer is that it be fair. It would be unfair to allow an employer to distribute a policy manual that makes the workforce believe that certain promises have been made and then to allow the employer to renege on those promises. What is sought here is basic honesty: if the employer, for whatever reason, does not want the manual to be capable of being construed by the court as a binding contract, there are simple ways to attain that goal. All that need be done is the inclusion in a very prominent position of an appropriate statement that there is no promise of any kind by the employer contained in the manual; that regardless of what the manual says or provides, the employer promises nothing and remains free to change wages and all other working conditions without having to consult anyone and without anyone's agreement; and that the employer continues to have the absolute power to fire anyone with or without good cause.

Reversed and remanded for trial.

NOTES

1. *Reliance.* Many courts require that the employee have relied on the manual before its promises can bind the employer. *See, e.g., Weiner v. McGraw-Hill, Inc.,* 443 N.E.2d 441 (N.Y. 1982), where the court sustained a cause of action where the employee rejected other offers of employment in reliance on a manual's promises of job security, which were incorporated by reference in the job application.

Should reliance be required, or can the employer be said to have benefited from the manual even if the employee did not rely? If the employer does not benefit from the manual, why did it produce one?

Suppose there are two types of job seekers: (1) cautious types who carefully weigh all parts of the employer's compensation package, including job security and other provisions of the employment manual, before accepting employment; and (2) free riders who assume or hope without inquiring that the employer's compensation package is the best available. If an employer offers job security in its manual, cautious types will be willing to accept a lower wage with the firm than they otherwise would. If the employer must pay all workers similarly, this low wage, job security package may be the "market" price.

A rough analogy may be provided by the fraud-on-the-market theory, which the Supreme Court has upheld in securities law. *Basic Inc. v. Levinson,* 485 U.S.

224 (1988). Suppose an investor sells stock the day before a company merges with another, which drives the price up wildly. He complains that he sold at a depressed price because of a fraudulent statement (e.g., "no merger is planned") by corporate insiders. The investor need not show that he was aware of the fraudulent statement.

2. *Usefulness of Meaningless Manuals.* Why would an employer want a manual that is legally meaningless? One possibility is that the manual is primarily addressed to supervisors rather than employees in an attempt to prevent supervisors from making statements inconsistent with basic personnel policy. Another possibility is that the firm is attempting to exploit legally unsophisticated workers by giving the appearance of job security when it knows none really exists.

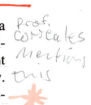

Prof. Gonzales mentions this *

3. *Unions and Employment Law.* If the AFL-CIO were to write an amicus brief in this case, which side should it support? The *Woolley* court suggests that the employer used the employment manual to keep its workforce non-unionized. A legally enforceable manual should provide even greater benefits for workers, giving them even less incentive to unionize. On the other hand, to the extent that the ability to fire at will gives nonunion employers a cost advantage, the *Woolley* holding should reduce the cost disadvantage of unions, perhaps reducing employer opposition to unions. Additionally, of course, can the AFL-CIO publicly support an employer's position against even nonunion workers?

D. DISCLAIMERS

REID v. SEARS, ROEBUCK & CO.

United States Court of Appeals, Sixth Circuit
790 F.2d 453 (1986)

LIVELY, CHIEF JUDGE.

These three appeals were argued separately, but have been consolidated for opinion since all require application of the same body of Michigan law. The three plaintiffs are former employees of Sears who were discharged without a showing of good cause. The plaintiffs brought separate suits in Michigan courts, claiming that their employment contracts with Sears, though for indefinite terms, required Sears to show good cause before they could be discharged. All relied on the seminal decision of the Supreme Court of Michigan in *Toussaint v. Blue Cross & Blue Shield of Michigan,* 408 Mich. 579, 292 N.W.2d 880 (1980). The cases were removed to the United States District Court for the Eastern District of Michigan on the basis of diversity of citizenship. Three judges of the District heard the cases, and each granted summary judgment in favor of Sears.

I

In *Toussaint* the Supreme Court of Michigan recognized the general rule that "in the absence of distinguishing features or provisions or a consideration in addition to the services to be rendered, ... contracts [for permanent employment] are indefinite hirings, terminable at the will of either party." 408 Mich. at 596. The court held, however, that the general rule does not apply when the contract of employment provides that the employee may not be discharged except for cause. Though such a contract is indefinite, the requirement of cause is enforceable. A provision requiring cause for the discharge of an indefinite term employee "may become part of the contract either by express agreement, oral or written, or as a result of an employee's legitimate expectations grounded in an employer's policy statements." *Id.* at 598. The court further held that the jury properly could have found that Toussaint had a legitimate expectation of continued employment on the basis of his employer's written policy statement set forth in a manual of personnel policies.

Toussaint's employer, Blue Cross, and Masco Corporation, the employer of the plaintiff Ebling in a companion case, argued that the rule announced by the Michigan Supreme Court would make it impossible to have a contract of employment that was terminable at the will of either party. The court responded to this argument:

> Employers are most assuredly free to enter into employment contracts terminable at will without assigning cause. We hold only that an employer's express agreement to terminate only for cause, or statements of company policy and procedure to that effect, can give rise to rights enforceable in contract.

Id. at 610. The court further amplified this condition as follows:

> If Blue Cross or Masco had desired, they could have established a company policy of requiring prospective employees to acknowledge that they served at the will or the pleasure of the company and, thus, have avoided the misunderstandings that generated this litigation.

Id. at 612. Footnote 24 states in part:

> Where the employer has not agreed to job security, it can protect itself by entering into a written contract which explicitly provides that the employee serves at the pleasure or at the will of the employer or as long as his services are satisfactory to the employer.

Id. The Supreme Court of Michigan found that neither employer in *Toussaint* had so protected itself and that both had created situations in which the employees had legitimate expectations of continued employment in the absence of a showing of good cause for discharge.

The Supreme Court of Michigan recently described its holding in *Toussaint* as follows:

> In *Toussaint v. Blue Cross & Blue Shield of Michigan,* 408 Mich. 579, 292 N.W.2d 880 (1980), this Court held that an employment contract

providing that an employee would not be terminated except for cause was enforceable although no definite term of employment was stated.

Toussaint makes employment contracts which provide that an employee will not be dismissed except for cause enforceable in the same manner as other contracts. It did not recognize employment as a fundamental right or create a new "special" right. The only right held in *Toussaint* to be enforceable was the right that arose out of the promise not to terminate except for cause.

Employers and employees remain free to provide, or not to provide, for job security. Absent a contractual provision for job security, either the employer or the employee may ordinarily terminate an employment contract at any time for any, or no, reason.

Valentine v. General American Credit, Inc., 420 Mich. 256, 258-59, 362 N.W.2d 628 (1984) (footnote omitted). Justice Charles L. Levin was the author of both the *Toussaint* and the *Valentine* opinions.

II

A

Each of the plaintiffs in the three cases before us had been employed by Sears for more than ten years. Before being hired each had signed an application for employment that provided:

> In consideration of my employment, I agree to conform to the rules and regulations of Sears, Roebuck and Co., and my employment and compensation can be terminated with or without cause, and with or without notice, at any time, at the option of either the Company or myself. I understand that no store manager or representative of Sears, Roebuck and Co., other than the president or vice president of the Company, has any authority to enter into any agreement for employment for any specified period of time or to make any agreement contrary to the foregoing.

It is clear that, though this acknowledgement was obtained long before the ruling in *Toussaint,* Sears attempted to protect itself from claims such as those of these plaintiffs in precisely the manner described by the court in *Toussaint.* However Reid, Serra and Batchelor all contend that they produced evidence from which a jury could have found that Sears created a legitimate expectation of continued employment, and that the district court committed reversible error in granting summary judgment.

B

The plaintiffs rely on certain promises allegedly made to them. Mrs. Reid states that when she first began working full time at Sears her store manager told her, "The job is yours as long as you want it." Ms. Batchelor claims not only that she was told in her job interview that there were "three main reasons" why Sears employees are fired but also that she was told by a former supervisor that he would intervene on her behalf to make sure she was not laid off. Mr. Serra relies on promises of job security from his supervisors. Sears replies that since none of these alleged oral promises came from a president or vice president, they cannot possibly have created a legitimate expectancy in the face of the language contained in the application for employment.

All of the plaintiffs also assert that the Sears employee handbook, "Getting Acquainted with Sears," created an implied contract to discharge only for cause. The handbook provided, at page 23:

HANDBOOK

EMPLOYE RULES

Since you are new to Sears, it is important for you to know what personal conduct is expected of you while on the job. In most instances your own good judgment will tell you what is the right thing to do. However, you should know what specific rules must be followed since violation of these rules may result in termination of your employment.

* Unsatisfactory performance of your job.
* Theft.
* Refusal to follow instructions directly related to the performance of your job (example: insubordination).
* Disorderly conduct; reporting for work under the influence of liquor, drugs or other stimulants, or consumption of such substances while on Company premises.
* Obtaining employment on the basis of false or misleading information.
* Falsifying a timecard by intentionally punching another employe's timecard or intentionally permitting anyone else to punch your timecard.
* Excessive absences or tardiness including absence from your job for two consecutive days without notifying your unit.
* Soliciting or accepting gifts (money or merchandise) in connection with a Company transaction of any kind. Also conducting other than Company business on Company premises without authority.
* Committing, or attempting to commit, deliberate damage to Company property, advocating or taking part in unlawful seizure of, or trespassing on, Company property.

The plaintiffs argue that the effect of this language was to create an implied contract to discharge only for one of the listed causes or for some other good reason.

C

We state briefly the circumstances surrounding the three discharges:

Mary Ann Reid had been employed by Sears for 17 years. In January 1981, the battery was stolen from a car which her son had borrowed from his grandmother, plaintiff's mother. When the son called his father for advice, Mr. Reid agreed to buy a new battery to replace the stolen one, and he did so using his wife's 10% employee discount at Sears. When Mrs. Reid's mother consulted her insurance company, she was told that she could not recover without receipts for the purchase both of the stolen battery and of the replacement. She no longer had the first receipt, and the insurance company would not accept the second because it was in Mr. Reid's name, not hers. To substantiate her mother's insurance claim, Mrs. Reid asked Tom Dunaj, a non-supervisory employee in the automotive department, to make out two new invoices. He did so, although the new invoice for the replacement battery failed to take the employee discount into account. Mr. Everest, the manager of the Grosse Pointe store where Mrs. Reid worked, was contacted by the insurance company when they noticed that the two invoices, though dated two months apart, were numbered consecutively. Upon being questioned, Dunaj and Reid admitted their actions, and both were fired for willful misconduct.

Mrs. Reid

John Serra asserts that, during the year before he was fired, he was under pressure to give older salespeople working under him lower performance evaluations than they deserved. Because of this, he had arranged to transfer to sales. Before the transfer, however, a "bookcheck audit" was performed on the two divisions he was responsible for. A number of items were questioned, and Mr. Serra submitted explanations. One of the questionable bookchecks was for the sale of a lawnmower to Gary Redfern, one of Serra's salesmen. The lawnmower was sold at a sale price after the sale had ended. Mr. Serra's version of the story is that while the lawnmower was on sale, Redfern's father-in-law had received a "raincheck" on the lawnmower, which he intended to buy for Gary. Mr. Serra says that Gary, on questioning, told him that when the lawnmower came in, his father-in-law suggested that he instead give Gary the money so that he could use his 10% discount. Mr. Redfern, however, told company officials, in investigating the matter, that this story was a complete fabrication and that Mr. Serra had simply given him a sale price on the mower. The sale came into question initially because a raincheck sale is supposed to be rung up on the original bookcheck with the sale date on it; this one was recorded on a new bookcheck. Mr. Serra notes that this deviation from policy required his authorization, and that the bookcheck does not bear his signature; the clerk who made the sale said he had Serra's oral authorization. Redfern also told the investigators that Serra had repeatedly authorized the sale of regular merchandise at sale prices. Mr. Serra was fired, and told that he was being discharged for a violation of company policy on "category 57 miscellaneous markdown," i.e., for allowing the sale of merchandise at a promotional price when it was not on sale.

Mr. Serra

On March 20, 1982, while on break, Mary Batchelor went to the cosmetics department of Sears and made some purchases. While she was there, she dropped a bottle of nail polish into her purse. Sears asserts that she intended to steal it; she maintains that the polish must have fallen into her purse inadver-

Ms. Batchelor

tently after she checked its color against her own make-up. She says that when she discovered that she still had the polish she intended to pay for it, but decided to wait until later because her co-worker was so rushed. She went into the locker room, placed her purse in her locker, and put the polish in a separate locker, intending to pay for it later. She contends that employees customarily used the locker for that purpose, though she knew she wasn't supposed to. (A written directive forbidding this practice was sent around to some employees after Ms. Batchelor was fired.) Shortly after leaving the polish in the locker room, Ms. Batchelor was approached and questioned by two security guards. When she returned to work the following Monday morning, she was questioned. Ms. Batchelor maintains that she was badly intimidated by the interrogation. That morning, she wrote out a signed statement which reads:

> I went and paid for three items Droped [sic] nail polish in pocket book Got back to my dept. and I took it out put it in locker. I had started not to pay for it. But could not do so. I was going to get Ann to ring it up but there was a lot of customers at the time.

> Mary Batchelor

At her deposition, Ms. Batchelor stated that she never meant to steal anything. Shortly after the statement was signed, Ms. Batchelor was fired. She alleges that she suffered severe depression.

Each of the three contends he or she was actually fired for reasons other than those which Sears gave. Mrs. Reid asserts that the cash office, where she worked, was soon to need fewer employees, and that her firing fits in with a general pattern at Sears of replacing higher paid full-time employees with lower paid part-timers. Mr. Serra claims he was fired in retaliation for his unwillingness to adjust his employee evaluations to further this policy. Ms. Batchelor maintains that the store was in the midst of a record-setting shoplifting campaign and that catching her redounded to the credit of the store manager....

IV

A

We conclude that summary judgment was proper in all three cases. A contract to discharge only for cause may not be based on "a mere subjective expectancy." The plaintiffs maintain that they had more than a subjective expectancy of continued employment; that the "Employee Rules" created an implied contract to discharge only for cause. The plaintiffs argue that by listing conduct that "may result in the termination of your employment" in the handbook Sears limited its right to discharge employees and that a discharge for any other reason would not be for good cause. They rely principally on *Schipani v. Ford Motor Co.*, 302 N.W.2d 307 (Mich. Ct. App. 1981), in support of this argument. In *Schipani* the employee had signed a written agreement providing:

I understand that my employment is not for any definite term, and may be terminated at any time, without advance notice by either myself or Ford Motor Company.

The plaintiff in *Schipani* argued that he was entitled to continued employment because Ford's literature, policy and practices led him to believe he would be employed to normal retirement age. The Michigan Court of Appeals held that Schipani had demonstrated the existence of a genuine issue of material fact as to whether he reasonably relied on policy statements. *Schipani* is readily distinguishable. The Ford disclaimer did not provide that no employee of Ford other than the president or a vice president of the company could make a contrary agreement.

We do not believe the listing of causes that "may result in the termination of your employment" in the Sears handbook detracted in any way from the language in the application or provided a reasonable basis for the conclusion that the plaintiffs were employed under a "for cause" contract. The fact that certain acts were identified as conduct that might lead to discharge did not indicate that these acts were the exclusive permissible grounds for discharge. Moreover, the Sears handbook had no language similar to that relied upon in *Toussaint*: "to treat employees leaving Blue Cross in a fair and consistent manner *and to release employees for just cause only*." 408 Mich. at 617 (emphasis added). Finally, there was no showing that the handbook had been written or approved by the president or a vice president of Sears.

The feature that distinguishes the present cases from *Toussaint* and all other Michigan decisions relied upon by the plaintiffs is the unequivocal language contained in the application for employment that each of the plaintiffs signed. *Toussaint* makes it clear that an employer can defeat claims that an employee could be discharged only for good cause by "requiring *prospective employees* to acknowledge that they serve[] at the will or pleasure of the company ...." 408 Mich. at 612 (emphasis added). Since the acknowledgement should be obtained from prospective employees, Sears properly included this provision of employment in the application form rather than in some documents to be signed by the employee after he or she was hired.

Every reported district court case involving a claim of unlawful discharge in the face of the language contained in the Sears application has resulted in summary judgment for Sears. *Novosel v. Sears, Roebuck & Co.*, 495 F. Supp. 344 (E.D. Mich. 1980); *Summers v. Sears, Roebuck & Co.*, 549 F. Supp. 1157 (E.D. Mich. 1982); *Ringwelski v. Sears, Roebuck & Co.*, 636 F. Supp. 519 (E.D. Mich. 1985). Further, the Michigan Court of Appeals affirmed summary judgment for Sears in *Eliel v. Sears, Roebuck & Co.*, 387 N.W.2d 842 (Mich. Ct. App. 1985). The court found that Eliel's employment was governed by the terms of the application and that none of the subsequent statements by Sears representatives relied on by the plaintiff was made by the president or a vice president of the company. The Michigan Court of Appeals reached the same conclusion in a case against another employer whose agreement with its employees required an acknowledgement that "my employment and compensation can be terminated, with or without cause, and with or without notice at any time at the option of either the Company or myself...." *Ledl v. Quik Pik Stores,* 349 N.W.2d 529 (Mich. Ct. App. 1984).

B

Mrs. Reid and Ms. Batchelor contend that the "with or without cause" provision of the application never became part of their employment contracts. Ms. Batchelor states that she signed the application one day, was interviewed another day and hired a third day. The district court agreed with her that the application was not a job offer, but found that it was part of the negotiations and became part of the employment contract when Sears did make an offer which Ms. Batchelor accepted. Ms. Batchelor stated in her affidavit that she read poorly and signed the application without understanding that it purported to make her employment at will. Her affidavit did not state that she informed any Sears representative of her difficulty or sought assistance from a company source. We have ruled that the affidavit statement concerning alleged assurances made by unidentified representatives of Sears did not create an issue of fact. Nevertheless, since the application was not mentioned at the subsequent interview or on the day of hiring, Ms. Batchelor argues that its provisions were never incorporated into the contract. Mrs. Reid joins in this argument.

The district court correctly held that Ms. Batchelor was bound by the terms of the application. She had an obligation to seek assistance before she signed if she felt she did not understand the application. The Supreme Court of Michigan so held in *Sponseller v. Kimball,* 246 Mich. 255, 260, 224 N.W. 359 (1929):

> The stability of written instruments demands that a person who executes one shall know of its content or be chargeable with such knowledge. If he cannot read, he should have a reliable person read it to him. His failure to do so is negligence which estops him from voiding the instrument on the ground that he was ignorant of its contents, in the absence of circumstances fairly excusing his failure to inform himself.

The employment contract with the three plaintiffs clearly included the terms of the application. *Toussaint* held that employers can avoid misunderstanding over the term of employment by "requiring prospective employees to acknowledge that they serve[] at the will or pleasure of the company ...." 408 Mich. at 612. Having obtained such an acknowledgement from each of the plaintiffs when they were prospective employees, Sears had done all that was required to create contracts for employment at will. Though *Toussaint* holds that there may be an implied contract that employment may be terminated only for good cause, it does not hold that this may be the case where an express contract makes the term of employment at will. It is well settled in Michigan that there cannot be an implied contract covering the same subject as an express one.

V

[The court then rejected claims for negligent evaluation and intentional infliction of emotional distress.]

JONES, CIRCUIT JUDGE, concurring in part and dissenting in part.

Concurrence & Dissent

I concur in the court's interpretation and application of the *Toussaint* rule. I am troubled, however, by the short shrift given to Ms. Batchelor's claim that, due to her poor reading ability, she could not comprehend the disclaimer and merely signed the job application form in routine manner without realizing its contractual nature. Batchelor presented evidence of her limited education and reading level, and also presented an expert's analysis of the level of reading difficulty of the Sears "contract." The district court rejected her argument summarily, relying on a passage from a 1929 decision that states the general rule of "signer beware." *Sponseller v. Kimball,* 224 N.W. 359 (Mich. 1929).

The general rule is not always applicable, however. When a person signs a document unaware of its contractual nature, courts do not always require or presume the caution and scrutiny ordinarily associated with signing a contract. Although it is established under Michigan law that these employment contracts are not adhesion contracts in which parties are compelled by unequal bargaining power to accept unreasonable terms, it is a different question, I believe, as to whether a valid contract exists when the signer does not comprehend that placing his signature on a form constitutes assent to specific contractual terms.

....

All of the Michigan cases citing *Sponseller* involve situations in which the signers clearly understood that the documents to be signed were legal instruments, and they were therefore negligent in failing to determine precisely the meaning of the contents.... I believe a distinction may be made under Michigan law between comprehending which rights were signed away and comprehending that rights were being signed away at all. This is especially so in the context of employment applications when marginally educated persons in desperate search of economic survival are in the job market coping with skillfully drafted and carefully considered application documents.

I would remand on this issue for further consideration. I therefore respectfully dissent from the portion of the opinion disposing of Batchelor's argument that, because she was unable to comprehend the language, she did not knowingly assent to a contract term regarding at will employment.

NOTES

1. *Prominence of the Disclaimer.* Even if a disclaimer might protect an employer's at-will employment policy, many courts will not allow employers to rely on the disclaimer unless it is conspicuous and obvious to the employees.

Prof. Correntes Mentions this case

For example, in *McDonald v. Mobil Coal Producing, Inc.*, 789 P.2d 866 (Wyo. 1990), *modified on reh'g*, 820 P.2d 986 (Wyo. 1991), the Wyoming Supreme Court held that Mobil's handbook amendment creating a disclaimer was ineffective. The court emphasized that Mobil's disclaimer was not capitalized, was in the same print as the rest of the handbook, and was contained in the general welcoming section of the handbook. *See also Jones v. Central Peninsula Gen. Hosp.*, 779 P.2d 783 (Alaska 1989) (finding one sentence disclaimer in eighty-five page policy manual to be ineffective, because it did not unambiguously and conspicuously inform employees that the manual was not part of their employment contract).

Other courts have held that a "conspicuous" requirement leads to unnecessary confusion. In *Anderson v. Douglas & Lomason Co.*, 540 N.W.2d 277 (Iowa 1995), the court considered a disclaimer appearing on the last page of a fifty-three page handbook, two inches below the preceding language, that read: "This Employee Handbook is not intended to create any contractual rights in favor of you or the Company. The Company reserves the right to change the terms of this handbook at any time." The court refused to consider arguments that the disclaimer was not displayed prominently enough, declaring that a disclaimer should be considered like any other language in the handbook. The court then enforced the disclaimer as unambiguous.

2. *Dangers of Disclaimers*. *Reid* suggests that a prominent disclaimer attached to a no-oral-modification clause might protect employers from employees claiming more than at-will status. Nevertheless, there may be important reasons for employers to forsake the protection. Most importantly, a prominent disclaimer might erode employee confidence that the employer will treat them fairly, causing morale problems among the current workforce and recruiting problems among applicants. This leads to higher turnover, training costs, and unemployment compensation costs. In addition, disclaimers might increase the chance of a successful union organizing effort. *See generally* Julius M. Steiner & Allan M. Dabrow, *The Questionable Value of the Inclusion of Language Confirming Employment-At-Will Status in Company Personnel Documents*, 37 LAB. L.J. 63 (1986).

3. *Modifying Job Security*. The first-generation manual cases, such as *Woolley*, examined whether a manual that purportedly moved from at-will to just-cause could create a binding promise. Second-generation manual cases examine new manuals going in the opposite direction: employees formerly were protected by just cause, but the employer decides to move to employment at will. Assuming the change is prominently displayed, can the company simply issue a new handbook declaring that current employees are now at will? A unilateral-contract theory enforces first-generation manual changes promising just cause by finding adequate consideration in the employees' willingness to continue working. Would unilateral-contract theory similarly enforce second-generation manual changes that reduce benefits, by saying that the worker accepted the new offer of employment by continuing work? A life-cycle model might be more skeptical of harmful changes in the contract late in a worker's career.

In *In re Certified Question (Bankey v. Storer Broadcasting Co.)*, 443 N.W.2d 112 (Mich. 1989), the court held that an employer could revoke promises of job security in a new manual, so long as the employer had not expressly promised never to change the policy and gave reasonable notice of the change. As one commentator has put it, the employer's unilateral offer can be characterized as follows: "I promise I will not dismiss you without cause (or without exhausting specified procedures) unless I change this policy before you are discharged." Kenneth A. Jenero, *Employers Beware: You May Be Bound by the Terms of Your Old Employee Handbooks*, 20 EMPLOYEE RELATIONS L.J. 299, 307 (1994).

Other courts have found that employers could not revoke promises of job security without the employee's consent. For example, in *Doyle v. Holy Cross Hosp.*, 682 N.E.2d 68 (Ill. App. Ct. 1997), the court upheld job security protections promised twenty-five years earlier, despite a later employer policy statement purporting to create an at-will relationship. The court, using a unilateral contract theory, found that a 1971 handbook clearly promised job security, and that the employees accepted the promise by beginning or continuing to work. The 1983 disclaimer, however, was unenforceable, because the employees received no benefit and the employer incurred no detriment from the change. The court rejected the argument that merely coming to work the next day constituted sufficient consideration to enforce the modification to at-will. Otherwise, the only way the employee could maintain his contractual rights would be by refusing to come to work, which would forfeit the very job protections he was attempting to preserve.

This result had been anticipated in *Robinson v. Ada S. McKinley Community Services, Inc.*, 19 F.3d 359 (7th Cir. 1994) (applying Illinois law), where the court held that the employer was bound by the job-security provisions of the old manual, even though the employee continued working for three years after receiving a new manual that disclaimed any contractual intent.

STOP

Chapter 5

TORT EROSIONS OF EMPLOYMENT AT WILL

In this chapter we turn to the inroads on at-will employment made by tort doctrine. One justification for tort law regulation of contractual relationships is to protect third parties. A general goal of this chapter is to see whether employment-law tort cases fit this pattern. In Section A we consider the tort of wrongful discharge in violation of public policy, which also is called the tort of retaliatory discharge or abusive discharge. The third-party rationale fits fairly well. In Section B we examine other torts, particularly intentional infliction of emotional stress. The third-party rationale fares less well, but in some cases the tort is nevertheless compelling.

A. WRONGFUL DISCHARGE IN VIOLATION OF PUBLIC POLICY

NEES v. HOCKS

Supreme Court of Oregon (*en banc*)
536 P.2d 512 (1975)

DENECKE, JUSTICE.

The principal question is whether the plaintiff alleged and proved conduct of the defendants which amounts to a tort of some nature....

The jury found for plaintiff; therefore, we must consider the facts as established by the evidence most favorable to plaintiff. The plaintiff performed clerical duties for defendants. She started work in 1971. In 1972 she was called for jury duty; however, as she informed defendants, she requested and was granted a 12-month postponement because of her honeymoon. On February 2, 1973, plaintiff was again subpoenaed to serve on the jury. She told defendants and they stated that a month was too long for her "to be gone." Defendants gave her a letter which stated defendants could spare plaintiff "for awhile" but not for a month and asked that she be excused. Plaintiff presented this letter to the court clerk and told the clerk that she had been called before and had to be excused, but she would like to serve on jury duty. The clerk told plaintiff she would not be excused. The plaintiff immediately came back to the office and told defendants that she would have to serve a minimum of two weeks' jury duty. She did not tell defendants she had told the court clerk she really wanted to serve.

Plaintiff started her jury duty on February 26, 1973. On March 1, 1973, she received a termination letter from defendants. The letter stated, in part: "Although we asked you to request an excusal from Jury Duty and wrote a letter confirming the Labls [defendants'] position, it has been brought to our attention you, in fact, requested to be placed on Jury Duty." The letter went on to state the defendants also were not otherwise satisfied with plaintiff's work. Based upon other evidence, however, the jury could have found plaintiff was not terminated because of dissatisfaction with the quality of plaintiff's work.

A representative of the firm that employed plaintiff after she was terminated by defendants testified one of the defendants told him plaintiff was terminated because she went on jury duty.

Plaintiff testified she suffered emotional distress because of her termination. She secured employment commencing one week after she finished jury duty for a higher salary than she had received from defendants. The jury awarded plaintiff compensatory and punitive damages.

Plaintiff has labeled the tort she contends she pleaded and proved, "prima facie tort." This is a label used by some courts, particularly New York.... We are of the opinion that the term serves no purpose in Oregon and we will advance the jurisprudence of this state by eliminating it....

This court has not felt unduly restricted by the boundaries of pre-existing common-law remedies. We have not hesitated to create or recognize new torts when confronted with conduct causing injuries which we feel should be compensable....

We recognize, as defendants assert, that, generally, in the absence of a contract or legislation to the contrary, an employer can discharge an employee at any time and for any cause. Conversely, an employee can quit at any time for any cause. Such termination by the employer or employee is not a breach of contract and ordinarily does not create a tortious cause of action. The question to us is, however, are there instances in which the employer's reason or motive for discharging harms or interferes with an important interest of the community and, therefore, justifies compensation to the employee?

Other courts have held that there are such instances. In *Petermann v. International Brotherhood of Teamsters,* 344 P.2d 25 (Cal. Ct. App. 1959), the plaintiff was discharged by his employer for refusing to give perjured testimony before a committee of the legislature. A judgment on the pleadings for the defendant employer was reversed....

In *Frampton v. Central Indiana Gas Company,* 297 N.E.2d 425 (Ind. 1973), the plaintiff employee alleged he was discharged for filing a workmen's compensation claim. The court reversed the order of the trial court dismissing the complaint for failing to state a cause of action.

The same division of the court that decided the *Petermann* case, cited above, in *Becket v. Welton Becket & Associates,* 114 Cal. Rptr. 531 (Cal. Ct. App. 1974), distinguished *Petermann* and held for the employer. In *Becket* plaintiff was employed by a corporate architectural firm. Plaintiff's father, who owned all of the stock in the firm, died and plaintiff was appointed co-executor of his father's estate. Plaintiff also was the largest legatee. Plaintiff as co-executor brought a suit against the firm and his co-executor alleging breach of fiduciary duties, corporate waste and improper usurpation of corporation control. The defendant firm told plaintiff to drop the litigation or they would discharge him. Plaintiff persisted and he was discharged. The court stated there was no statute evidencing any public policy protecting any right of an employee to sue his employer as a fiduciary or in a stockholder's derivative suit.

Our recent decision in *Campbell v. Ford Industries, Inc.,* 513 P.2d 1153 (Or. 1973), probably falls into the same category as the case just discussed. In both the interest of the employee was purely private and not of general public concern. In *Campbell* the plaintiff alleged he was a minority stockholder and employee of the defendant. He alleged he was discharged because he refused to sell his stock to defendant. We held that while he might be able to recover for any injury to his interest as a shareholder, he could not recover for any injury to his interest as an employee.

We conclude that there can be circumstances in which an employer discharges an employee for such a socially undesirable motive that the employer must respond in damages for any injury done. The next question is, does the evidence in this case permit a finding that such circumstances are present? There is evidence from which the jury could have found that the defendants discharged the plaintiff because, after being subpoenaed, and contrary to the defendants' wishes, plaintiff told the clerk she would like to serve and she did serve on jury duty.[2] Therefore, the immediate question can be stated specifically — is the community's interest in having its citizens serve on jury duty so important that an employer, who interferes with that interest by discharging an employee who served on a jury, should be required to compensate his employee for any damages she suffered?

Art. VII, § 3, of the Oregon Constitution provides that jury trial shall be preserved in civil cases. Art. I, § 11, provides a defendant in a criminal case has a right of trial by jury. Art. VII, § 5, provides: "The Legislative Assembly shall so provide that the most competent of the permanent citizens of the county shall be chosen for jurors."

ORS 10.040 provides for certain exemptions from jury duty. ORS 10.050 provides for certain excuses from jury duty including health, age and "(c) When serving as a juror would result in extreme hardship to the person including but not limited to unusual and extraordinary financial hardship." ORS 10.055 provides for deferment of jury duty "for good cause shown" for not more than one year. ORS 10.990 provides that if a juror "without reasonable cause," neglects to attend for jury service the sheriff may impose a fine, not exceeding $20 for each day the juror does not attend.

People v. Vitucci, 199 N.E.2d 78 (Ill. App. Ct. 1964), stated that an employer who discharged an employee who was absent because of jury duty was guilty of

---

[2] If the only evidence was that the defendants would have suffered a substantial hardship if plaintiff served this particular month, defendants requested only a postponement of jury service but the plaintiff nevertheless asked to serve this particular month, we probably would regard the discharge as justifiable.

contempt of court. Massachusetts has a statute making such conduct contemptuous.

These actions by the people, the legislature and the courts clearly indicate that the jury system and jury duty are regarded as high on the scale of American institutions and citizen obligations. If an employer were permitted with impunity to discharge an employee for fulfilling her obligation of jury duty, the jury system would be adversely affected. The will of the community would be thwarted. For these reasons we hold that the defendants are liable for discharging plaintiff because she served on the jury.

[The Court then overturned the award of punitive damages because the cause of action was newly created.]

That part of the judgment awarding $650 compensatory damages is affirmed; that part of the judgment awarding punitive damages in the amount of $3,000 is reversed. The trial court will enter judgment accordingly.

Affirmed in part; reversed in part.

NOTES

1. ***Typology of Wrongful Discharge Cases.*** *Petermann, Frampton,* and *Nees* illustrate the classic fact patterns where courts have upheld lawsuits for wrongful discharge in violation of public policy:

    (1) *Refusing to commit unlawful acts.* The classic example is refusing to commit perjury when the government is investigating the company for wrongdoing.

    (2) *Exercising a statutory right.* The classic example is filing a claim for benefits under the workers' compensation statute.

    (3) *Fulfilling a public obligation.* The classic example is serving on jury duty.

A fourth pattern, (4) *whistleblowing,* occurs when an employee reports the company's unlawful conduct to a supervisor or outside authorities. The following two lead cases deal with this pattern.

2. ***Third-Party Effects.*** A classic tort justification for overriding freedom of contract is that the conduct between contracting parties adversely affects third parties. A contract to murder will not be enforced. Thus, even if the employer and employee have agreed to an at-will contract, the law should not give effect to this contract if it adversely affects third parties. Of the classic categories of wrongful discharge actions, which has the clearest third-party effects? Which is most suspect?

3. ***Pigeonholing Fact Patterns.*** Can the following cases be put in one of the pigeonholes above? If not, should the claim nevertheless be allowed? When the court rejects a possible public policy claim, is the asserted interest largely a private one?

    (a) A bank manager was fired when he attempted to defend himself after a subordinate physically attacked him. *See McLaughlin v. Barclays Am. Corp.,* 382

S.E.2d 836 (N.C. Ct. App.), *cert. denied,* 385 S.E.2d 498 (N.C. 1989) (rejecting claim that employee was wrongfully fired for engaging in his right to self-defense).

(b) An employee is fired for writing a letter to the editor in the local newspaper criticizing management. *See Schultz v. Indus. Coils, Inc.,* 373 N.W.2d 74 (Wis. Ct. App. 1985) (rejecting claim that state constitutional provision declaring that every person may freely speak, write and publish his sentiments on all subjects provides public policy exception).

(c) A gas station attendant is fired for refusing to pump leaded gas into automobile equipped only for unleaded gas, which would violate Federal Clean Air Act. *See Phipps v. Clark Oil & Ref. Corp.,* 396 N.W.2d 588 (Minn. Ct. App. 1986), *aff'd,* 408 N.W.2d 569 (Minn. 1987) (upholding cause of action).

(d) A movie theater employee was fired after he called the police and emptied the theater because he feared there was an intruder in the projection room. *See Girgenti v. Cali-Con, Inc.,* 544 A.2d 655 (Conn. App. Ct. 1988) (claim stated).

(e) An employee scheduled to work at 3:00 p.m. was in a car accident at 1:00 p.m. and taken by ambulance to a hospital, where he was not released until 5:00 p.m. When he was fired for not reporting for work on time, he filed suit, asserting that "it is the public policy of the State of Illinois for injured persons to receive medical attention, particularly in an emergency situation." *See Thomas v. Zamberletti,* 480 N.E.2d 869 (Ill. App. Ct. 1985) (no claim stated). *majority view*

(f) An employee was brutally beaten and raped off-work by her estranged husband. To avoid dealing with the situation, the employer fired her. *See Green v. Bryant,* 887 F. Supp. 798 (E.D. Pa. 1995) (applying Pennsylvania law) (dismissing wrongful discharge claim because no public harm occurred).

(g) A bartender was fired for refusing to serve liquor to a visibly intoxicated patron who was going to drive home. *See Woodson v. AMF Leisureland Ctrs., Inc.,* 842 F.2d 699 (3d Cir. 1988) (applying Pennsylvania law, court recognizes cause of action). *Very small minority opinion*

(h) An employee injured at work filed for and received workers' compensation benefits. When he was able to return to work, he was told he no longer had a job because he had filed a workers' compensation claim. *See Shick v. Shirey,* 691 A.2d 511 (Pa. Super. Ct. 1997) (rejecting reasoning of *Frampton* and finding no public policy violation).

4. *Finding Public Policy.* Some courts have broadly defined public policy. In *Palmateer v. International Harvester Co.,* 421 N.E.2d 876, 878 (Ill. 1981), the Illinois Supreme Court reversed the dismissal of a complaint alleging an employee was fired for reporting a possible crime to law-enforcement authorities, stating:

> There is no precise definition of the term. In general, it can be said that public policy concerns what is right and just and what affects the citizens of

the State collectively. It is to be found in the State's constitution and statutes and, when they are silent, in its judicial decisions.

Accord Pierce v. Ortho Pharmaceutical Corp., 417 A.2d 505, 512 (N.J. 1980) ("In certain instances, a professional code of ethics [such as the Hippocratic Oath] may contain an expression of public policy," but an employee's personal morals do not); *Parnar v. Americana Hotels, Inc.*, 652 P.2d 625, 631 (Haw. 1982) ("Courts should inquire whether the employer's conduct contravenes the letter or purpose of a constitutional, statutory, or regulatory provision or scheme. Prior judicial decisions may also establish the relevant public policy"); *Boyle v. Vista Eyewear, Inc.*, 700 S.W.2d 859, 871 (Mo. Ct. App. 1985) ("'Public policy' is that principle of law which holds that no one can lawfully do that which tends to be injurious to the public or against the public good").

Other courts, however, have refused to accept such a broad definition of public policy, insisting that an employee point to some specific public policy as articulated in a constitution or state statute. A leading case following this narrower definition of public policy is *Gantt v. Sentry Ins.*, 824 P.2d 680, 687-88 (Cal. 1992). In upholding a $1.34 million judgment when a manager was terminated in retaliation for testifying truthfully about an employee's sexual harassment claim in an administrative investigation, the California Supreme Court declared:

> A public policy exception carefully tethered to fundamental policies that are delineated in constitutional or statutory provisions strikes the proper balance among the interests of employers, employees and the public. The employer is bound, at a minimum, to know the fundamental public policies of the state and nation as expressed in their constitutions and statutes; so limited, the public policy exception presents no impediment to employers that operate within the bounds of the law. Employees are protected against employer actions that contravene fundamental state policy. And society's interests are served through a more stable job market, in which its most important policies are safeguarded.

5. *Legal Contortions in Finding Statutory Violations*. Courts are understandably nervous about the nebulousness of a general public policy standard. But a rule that employment terminations only violate public policy if they would violate a specific statute can lead to legal contortions. For example, in *Lucas v. Brown & Root, Inc.*, 736 F.2d 1202 (8th Cir. 1984) (applying Arkansas law), an employee was fired for refusing the sexual advances of her foreman. The court upheld her wrongful discharge claim, finding that, in effect, she was being asked to violate the anti-prostitution statute. Does this mean that in states where prostitution is lawful, such an employee would have no claim? Does focusing on whether the prostitution statute is violated address the real issues involved, or simply find a pigeonhole in which to afford the employee a remedy?

In *Wagenseller v. Scottsdale Mem. Hosp.*, 710 P.2d 1025 (Ariz. 1985), a nurse and her supervisor went on an eight-day rafting trip with employees of other hospitals. The nurse refused to join in a parody of "Moon River," where the group mooned the audience. Her refusal led to strained relations with the supervisor and eventually to her being fired. In support of her wrongful discharge claim, the employee argued that the mooning skit would have violated the indecent exposure statute, which prohibits exposure of the anus or genitalia if the viewer would be offended or alarmed by the act. The court refused to determine whether mooning would actually violate the statute, finding the policy of the statute to be sufficiently implicated:

> We have little expertise in the techniques of mooning. We cannot say as a *Good Grief* matter of law, therefore, whether mooning would always violate the statute by revealing the mooner's anus or genitalia. That question could only be determined, we suppose, by an examination of the facts of each case. We deem such an inquiry unseemly and unnecessary in a civil case. Compelled exposure of the bare buttocks, on pain of termination of employment, is a sufficient violation of the *policy* embodied in the statute to support the action, even if there would have been no technical violation of the statute.

Id. at 1035 n.5.

6. *Federal Law as State Public Policy.* What third-party effects are courts searching for? Must the discharge adversely affect citizens of the state? In its search for public policy, the court in *Nees* pointed to a Massachusetts statute and an Illinois case, as well as the Oregon constitution and statutes. Courts routinely turn to federal law as well, although some cases question whether the search should be so wide-ranging. In *Peterson v. Browning,* 832 P.2d 1280 (Utah 1992), the Utah Supreme Court upheld the claim of a customs officer who claimed he was terminated for refusing to falsify tax documents in violation of federal and Missouri law. The court held that federal or other states' laws could serve as a source of Utah public policy, but warned that not just any violation would suffice: "A plaintiff must establish the connection between the law violated and the public policies of Utah."

Some courts have actually rejected federal law as a source of state public policy. In *Guy v. Travenol Labs.,* 812 F.2d 911 (4th Cir. 1987), the employee claimed retaliatory discharge when he refused to falsify records required by federal food and drug law. The court determined that North Carolina law had no obligation to use its tort system to bolster federal policies. *See also Rachford v. Evergreen Int'l Airlines,* 596 F. Supp. 384 (N.D. Ill. 1984) (Illinois has general interest in air safety, but no interest in enforcing FAA regulations); *Pratt v. Caterpillar Tractor Co.,* 500 N.E.2d 1001 (Ill. App. Ct. 1986) (refusal to engage in conduct prohibited by Federal Corrupt Practices Act implicates no state policy because no harm to state's citizens alleged). At the other extreme, states may be preempted from bolstering some federal policies through wrongful discharge actions. *See Ingersoll-Rand Co. v. McClendon,* 498 U.S. 133 (1990) (ERISA preempts employee's state law wrongful discharge claim that employer fired him to avoid making contributions to his pension fund).

7. Supplementing Legislative Remedies. A court that allows a claim of wrongful discharge in violation of express statutory policy can be seen as supplementing whatever remedies or penalties the legislature has expressly provided in enacting the statute. The general issue of when courts should imply private remedies for individual statutes arises in many fields. In *Cort v. Ash*, 422 U.S. 66 (1975), the Supreme Court articulated three factors for determining whether to recognize a private cause of action for violation of statutes: (1) is the plaintiff one of the class for whose special benefit the statute was enacted; (2) is there any indication of express or implied legislative intent to create or deny a remedy; and (3) would implying a private remedy be consistent with the underlying statutory scheme.

The issue was directly confronted in wrongful discharge law in *Ambroz v. Cornhusker Square, Ltd.*, 416 N.W.2d 510 (Neb. 1987). The Nebraska legislature had enacted a statute regulating when employers could use polygraphs, expressly declaring that violation of the statute was a criminal misdemeanor. An employee brought a wrongful discharge suit, claiming he had been fired after the employer illegally gave him a polygraph test. The court upheld the cause of action, emphasizing that the purpose of the criminal statute was to protect employees such as the plaintiff.

The validity of a wrongful discharge claim was also at issue in *Hodges v. S.C. Toof & Co.*, 833 S.W.2d 896 (Tenn. 1992). The Tennessee legislature had enacted a jury service statute which not only imposed criminal penalties on an employer who fired employees for doing jury duty, but provided that an employee who is fired, demoted or suspended for taking time off to serve jury duty "shall be entitled to reinstatement and reimbursement for lost wages and work benefits caused by such acts of the employer." In *Hodges*, the Tennessee Supreme Court held that an employee fired for serving jury duty was not limited to the damages laid out in the statute and affirmed an award of $200,000 in compensatory damages. The court vacated a punitive damages award of $375,000, but only to make sure the jury had been instructed on and followed the clear and convincing evidence standard necessary for punitive damages. The court expressly held that punitive damages would be allowed if a jury followed the clear and convincing standard. Thus, Tennessee courts will uphold both compensatory and punitive damage awards in jury duty wrongful discharge cases, even though the jury service statute only calls for employee reinstatement and reimbursement for lost wages and benefits.

8. Fired for Obeying. Suppose a supervisor tells an employee to ignore a defect in the company's product. The employee ignores it and is later fired for not bringing the defect to the company's attention. Is this a wrongful discharge in violation of public policy?

In *DeVries v. McNeil Consumer Prods. Co.*, 593 A.2d 819 (N.J. Super. Ct. App. Div. 1991), the court rejected an obeying-orders claim. A drug company received a large shipment of soon-to-be outdated Tylenol. The supervisor instructed a sales representative to give away the Tylenol at doctor's offices she visited for the personal use of the staff. One doctor became outraged and insisted that the company fire DeVries for unprofessional behavior. After being fired, DeVries sued for wrongful discharge "in violation of the public policy supporting the doctrine of equitable estoppel." The court upheld summary judgment against her. Although the discharge may have been unfair, the court reasoned, it implicated only the private interests of the parties. No public policy is served by distributing outdated Tylenol, whether instructed to do so by a supervisor or not.

9. *Backbone to Resist a Faustian Bargain.* Consider the following rationale for providing a tort cause of action to at-will employees:

> Imagine in these cases that the employer explained at the initial job interview, "This job pays extra-high wages because it is potentially dangerous. It may require you to be convicted of perjury, or to be held in contempt of court for refusing jury service, or simply to violate your moral beliefs against enabling drunk drivers. But the value to this company of perjury, or constant attendance, or serving customers, outweighs these high wages; that is why we offer the job." The employee then asks: "What happens if I don't agree to this perjury term, or refusing-jury-service term, or must-serve-drunks term?" "If you refuse the term now," the employer replies, "you won't be hired. If you refuse to perform later, you will be fired." If the employee accepts the job with this understanding, presumably it is because the high wages and other aspects of the job are worth the expected criminal/moral penalties from perjury, or refusing jury service, or serving drunks. Thus, the employer and employee are jointly better off with these conditions than without. But even as valiant a freedom-of-contract buff as Professor Epstein would refuse to enforce such contracts. The rationale is simple. The parties, while furthering their own self-interests, are ignoring the effects of their deal on others. Because the private contract has substantial adverse third-party effects, we refuse to enforce it.
>
> In theory, under this imaginary bargaining story, an employee taking the job agrees to commit perjury, or to refuse jury duty, or to serve drunks. If the employee maintains his end of the bargain, the investigating agency hears perjured testimony, the jury pool lacks a member, and a drunk-driving accident occurs. The employee keeps his job, and no wrongful discharge suit is filed. What the tort of wrongful discharge allows, however, is for the employee to change his mind. He can renege on the Faustian deal without fear of losing the job.
>
> In practice, employers and employees rarely expressly negotiate over job duties that violate the public interest. Even if they did, their agreement rarely would call for civic-minded action by the employee. A public-goods problem exists here. An employee acting in the public interest gets only a small share of the social benefit created. The public-good activity, therefore, will be underproduced unless tort law intervenes. The wrongful discharge

tort gives the employee some backbone to look at the overall social interest. The employee deciding whether to testify against his employer or to take time off to perform jury duty knows that, if he is fired, he will be compensated with tort damages. Of course, compensatory damages at best put him in the same position had he not testified or been a juror (and thereby not been fired). If the employee recognizes that he may not win his lawsuit because of the vagaries of trial, or recognizes that he must generally pay attorney fees out of his damage award, he may rationally decide to commit perjury or to reject jury duty. Perhaps an employee's sense of morality is enough to let him take the plunge. Tort law attempts to tip the balance by adding the possibility of punitive damages.

Stewart J. Schwab, *Wrongful Discharge Law and the Search for Third-Party Effects*, 74 TEX. L. REV. 1952-53 (1996).[*]

ADLER v. AMERICAN STANDARD CORP.

Court of Appeals of Maryland
432 A.2d 464 (1981)

Argued before MURPHY, C. J., and SMITH, DIGGES, ELDRIDGE, COLE, DAVIDSON and RODOWSKY, JJ.

MURPHY, CHIEF JUDGE.

The United States District Court for the District of Maryland ... has certified for our determination the following questions of state law:

(1) Is a cause of action for "abusive discharge" recognized under the substantive law of the State of Maryland?

(2) Do the allegations of the Amended Complaint, if taken as true, state a cause of action for "abusive discharge" under the substantive law of the State of Maryland?

The amended complaint was filed by Gerald Adler against American Standard Corporation (the Corporation) to recover general, special and punitive damages for Adler's claimed "abusive discharge" from his employment with the Corporation. Adler alleged in his complaint that he was employed in March of 1975 as an Assistant General Manager of the Corporation's Commercial Printing Division at a salary of $37,000 per year; that James Kinealy was Vice President and General Manager of the Division and James Sinclair was Vice President in charge of the Corporation's Graphic Arts Group, which encompassed the Commercial Printing Division; and that it was Adler's responsibility to conduct a thorough analysis of the management and operational structure of the Commercial Printing Division and to propose changes which would promote efficiency in management and operations and enhance the accuracy of intra-corpo-

---

[*] Copyright 1996 by the Texas Law Review Association. Reprinted by permission.

rate transmittal of information. The complaint alleged that Adler was "complimented for his efforts by his superiors" and by August 1, 1978 his annual salary had been increased to $60,000. According to further averments of the amended complaint, Adler "discovered numerous inadequacies in the management and operation of the Commercial Printing Division and, also, numerous improper and possibly illegal practices, including:

a. Attempts to treat capital expenditures as expenses.
b. Payment of commercial bribes.
c. Falsification of sales and income information, and alteration of commercial documents to support the falsified information.
d. Misuse of corporate funds by officers for their personal benefit.
e. Manipulation of work-in-process inventory information.
f. Alteration of forecasts in connection with intra-corporate financial reporting."

The amended complaint alleged that on repeated occasions Adler reported his "discoveries" to Kinealy and Sinclair and made recommendations respecting their correction but that Kinealy and Sinclair "consistently failed and refused to give consideration to plaintiff's discoveries and recommendations and, indeed, discouraged further efforts on his part." The complaint alleged that Adler communicated his findings to the Corporation's headquarters personnel on several occasions and "was praised for his candor, was urged to continue his efforts and was assured that his position would not be jeopardized by so doing"; that as a result of Adler's activities Kinealy and Sinclair "became increasingly insecure and suspicious that ... [Adler's] adherence to his stipulated responsibilities compromised their own positions"; that a high-level managerial meeting was scheduled for October 13, 1978, at which headquarters personnel were to be present; that Adler intended at that meeting "to discuss frankly the improprieties which troubled him"; that Kinealy and Sinclair insisted at that time that Adler resign; and that after Adler refused to resign, he received a letter signed by Kinealy and Sinclair on behalf of the Corporation informing him that his employment was terminated "for unsatisfactory performance." The amended complaint alleged that Adler's discharge by the Corporation "was motivated solely by its desire, and the desire of its superior management personnel, to conceal improprieties and illegal activities which plaintiff might have disclosed at the meeting scheduled for October 13, 1978 and on other occasions should he have remained in defendant's employ ... including the payment of commercial bribes and the falsification of corporate records and financial statistics, ... [which were] contrary to the public policy of the State of New York, the State of Maryland and of the United States, and thus constituted an abusive discharge."

The Corporation filed a motion to dismiss Adler's complaint on the ground that it failed to state a cause of action under Maryland law....

Adler concedes that his discharge was not specifically prohibited by any Maryland statute. However, he urges that a judicial exception to the terminable at will doctrine be recognized in Maryland to permit an at will employee, discharged in a manner that contravenes public policy, to maintain a cause of action for abusive or wrongful discharge against his former employer.

3 Courses of action

Jurisdictions that have considered wrongful discharge actions as an exception to the common law terminable at will doctrine have followed essentially three courses of action. Some courts have flatly refused to recognize a cause of action for wrongful discharge, rigidly adhering to the rule that an employer's motivation for discharging an at will employee is irrelevant. Other courts, while declining to recognize a cause of action for wrongful discharge on the facts of the cases before them, have indicated a willingness to adopt a judicial exception to the terminable at will doctrine in a proper case. Still other courts have recognized a cause of action for wrongful discharge, either in tort or in contract, and in doing so have primarily focused upon the employer's motivation for discharging the employee.

[The Court then discusses numerous cases.]

We recognize that modern economic conditions differ significantly from those that existed when the at will rule was first advanced in the latter part of the nineteenth century. According to 1980 census statistics, a majority of American workers do not have the job security provided by collective bargaining agreements or civil service regulations. When terminated without notice, an employee is suddenly faced with an uncertain job future and the difficult prospect of meeting continuing economic obligations. But this circumstance, of itself, hardly warrants adoption of a rule that would forbid termination of at will employees whenever the termination appeared "wrongful" to a court or a jury. On the other hand, an at will employee's interest in job security, particularly when continued employment is threatened not by genuine dissatisfaction with job performance but because the employee has refused to act in an unlawful manner or attempted to perform a statutorily prescribed duty, is deserving of recognition. Equally to be considered is that the employer has an important interest in being able to discharge an at will employee whenever it would be beneficial to his business. Finally, society as a whole has an interest in ensuring that its laws and important public policies are not contravened. Any modification of the at will rule must take into account all of these interests.

As we have indicated, few courts have flatly rejected the notion that the wrongful discharge of an at will employee may give rise to a cause of action for damages. Where courts differ is in determining where the line is to be drawn that separates a wrongful from a legally permissible discharge. This determination depends in large part on whether the public policy allegedly violated is sufficiently clear to provide the basis for a tort or contract action for wrongful discharge.

The common law terminable at will doctrine in Maryland is, of course, subject to modification by judicial decision where this Court finds that it is no longer suitable to the circumstances of our people. Nor have we hesitated to adopt a new cause of action by judicial decision where that course was compelled by changing circumstances. The reasoning of the growing number of jurisdictions that have recognized wrongful discharge as a new cause of action persuades us that, in a proper case, such an action should be adopted in this State. The fundamental issue then is whether Adler's amended complaint, on its face, contains allegations sufficient to state a cause of action for wrongful discharge. To answer this certified question, we must determine from the averments of the complaint whether Adler's discharge contravened some clear mandate of public policy.

Adler points to two sources of public policy. First, he contends that the misconduct of the Corporation's employees involving the payment of commercial bribes and the falsification of corporate records the disclosure of which prompted his discharge was in violation of the criminal law of the State, Md. Code Art. 27, § 174. Second, he urges that practices such as commercial bribery and the falsification of corporate records are so clearly against public policy that he need not identify any statute or rule of law specifically prohibiting such improper and possibly illegal practices. Adler defines "public policy" as that which is "commonly accepted as necessary to the public good" a definition which encompasses more than violations of the criminal laws of the State. Adler maintains that because the allegations of the complaint demonstrate that his discharge by the Corporation was motivated by the latter's desire to prevent his further disclosure of the improper conduct, and to permit its continuation, his discharge was itself a violation of a clear mandate of public policy, giving rise to a cause of action for wrongful discharge.

Adler's reliance upon § 174 is misplaced. The section declares it a misdemeanor for any officer or agent of any corporation

> fraudulently [to] sign, or in any other manner assent to any statement or publication, either for the public or the shareholders thereof, containing untruthful representations of its affairs, assets or liabilities with a view either to enhance or depress the market value of the shares therein, or the value of its corporate obligations, or in any other manner to accomplish any fraud thereby ....

Accepting the averments of Adler's complaint as true, we think they are too general, too conclusory, too vague and lacking in specifics to mount up to a prima facie showing that the claimed misconduct contravened § 174 and hence violated the public policy of this State. Adler's complaint does not assert that the falsification of corporate records was done with an intent to defraud either stockholders or the public at large by enhancing or depressing the market value of the Corporation's shares or other obligations. As a result, the allegations of the complaint do not set forth a violation of the conduct proscribed by § 174. Indeed, during oral argument of the case before us, Adler's counsel was asked whether his complaint was intended to allege the commission of a crime. In response, he stated that he could not say one way or the other whether the claimed misconduct constituted a crime.

Nor do we think that the averments of Adler's complaint otherwise demonstrate a violation of a clear mandate of the public policy of this State. Judge Levine, writing for the Court, in *Md.-Nat'l Cap. P. & P. v. Wash. Nat'l Arena,* 386 A.2d 1216 (Md. 1978), discussed the concept of public policy at length:

> Nearly 150 years ago Lord Truro set forth what has become the classical formulation of the public policy doctrine to which we adhere in Maryland:
>
> > "Public policy is that principle of the law which holds that no subject can lawfully do that which has a tendency to be injurious to the public, or against the public good, which may be termed, as it sometimes has been, the policy of the law, or public policy in relation to the administration of the law." *Egerton v. Earl Brownlow,* 4 H.L. Cas. 1, 196 (1853).
>
> ... But beyond this relatively indeterminate description of the doctrine, jurists to this day have been unable to fashion a truly workable definition of public policy. Not being restricted to the conventional sources of positive law (constitutions, statutes and judicial decisions), judges are frequently called upon to discern the dictates of sound social policy and human welfare based on nothing more than their own personal experience and intellectual capacity.... Inevitably, conceptions of public policy tend to ebb and flow with the tides of public opinion, making it difficult for courts to apply the principle with any degree of certainty.

As indicated, the Court has not confined itself to legislative enactments, prior judicial decisions or administrative regulations when determining the public policy of this State. We have always been aware, however, that recognition of an otherwise undeclared public policy as a basis for a judicial decision involves the application of a very nebulous concept to the facts of a given case, and that declaration of public policy is normally the function of the legislative branch. We have been consistently reluctant, for example, to strike down voluntary contractual arrangements on public policy grounds. As Mr. Justice Sutherland stated for the Supreme Court in *Patton v. United States,* 281 U.S. 276, 306 (1930):

> "The truth is that the theory of public policy embodies a doctrine of vague and variable quality, and, unless deducible in the given circumstances from constitutional or statutory provisions, should be accepted as the basis of a judicial determination, if at all, *only with the utmost circumspection.* The public policy of one generation may not, under changed conditions, be the public policy of another." (Emphasis added).

To recapitulate, Adler's amended complaint alleged that he observed and disclosed the following "improper and possible illegal practices" while employed by the Corporation: attempts to treat capital expenditures as expenses; payment of commercial bribes; falsification of corporate sales and income data and alteration of commercial documents to support the falsified information; misuse of corporate funds by officers for their personal benefit; manipulation of work-in-process inventory information; and alteration of forecasts in connection with intra-corporate financial reporting. The allegations suggest serious misconduct, yet Adler fails to provide any factual details to support the general and conclusory averments of the complaint. Nor does he point to any specific statutory provision, other than Art. 27, § 174, or other existing rule of law that particularly prohibits the claimed misconduct. While Adler suggested before us that the commercial bribery and falsification of corporate records violated the Sherman Act, 15 U.S.C. §§ 1-7 (1973), and the Maryland Antitrust Act, Md. Code (1975, 1980 Cum. Supp.) Commercial Law, §§ 11-201 to -213, his complaint does not recite, with the requisite degree of specificity, the manner in which these statutory enactments were offended so as to constitute a violation of the public policy of this State. The bald allegations of Adler's complaint do not provide a sufficient factual predicate for determining whether any declared mandate of public policy was violated. Adler's undisclosed perception of what constitutes "commercial bribery" or "falsification of corporate documents" is hardly an adequate ground upon which to base a decision that such activities violate the declared or undeclared public policy of this State. The allegations are therefore legally insufficient to state a cause of action for wrongful discharge.

Accordingly, in answer to the first certified question, Maryland does recognize a cause of action for abusive discharge by an employer of an at will employee when the motivation for the discharge contravenes some clear mandate of public policy; and in answer to the second certified question, the allegations of the amended complaint, taken as true, together with all reasonable inferences to be drawn therefrom, do not state a cause of action for abusive discharge.

NOTES

1. *Subsequent Litigation.* Upon returning to federal district court, Adler amended his complaint, now enumerating seventeen federal and state statutes that he claimed the company had violated. The district court denied the employer's motion to dismiss the complaint, specifically rejecting the employer's claim that the employee could not rely on federal law as the source of public policy. 538 F. Supp. 572 (D. Md. 1982). After the trial, the jury awarded Adler $1,232,000 in compensatory damages and $1,000,000 in punitive damages for abusive discharge, as well as $70,000 in compensatory damages and $500,000 in punitive damages for defamation. The district court granted the employer's motion for a judgment notwithstanding the verdict on the defamation claim and on the punitive damage award in the abusive discharge action.

Upon appeal, the court of appeals reversed the employee's judgment for abusive discharge. The court emphasized that there was "no allegation, claim or testimony that Adler threatened to report [illegal] activities to law enforcement agencies or to anyone outside the corporate group," and held that abusive discharge should be limited to "situations involving the actual refusal to engage in illegal activity, or the intention to fulfill a statutorily prescribed duty." 830 F.2d 1303, 1306-07 (4th Cir. 1987).

Judge Butzner, dissenting, emphasized that Adler was fired on the eve of a company meeting where he was not only going to reveal crimes of other corporate officers, but would announce that he would not engage in or condone similar crimes in the future:

> It is Adler's refusal to commit unlawful acts that distinguishes this case from those where whistle blowers, who did no more than accuse other persons of derelictions, were not given protection. Indeed, when a whistle blower is also the person who must decide whether a course of illegal conduct will continue, implicit in his disclosure of the illegality to his superiors is his renunciation of its continuance in the absence of any express intention to the contrary.

830 F.2d at 1308.

2. *Internal Investigations.* Employees are understandably reluctant to finger supervisors during internal company investigations of wrongdoing, for fear that the supervisor will remain in power and retaliate against defectors. Should employees be able to rely on assurances that "no one will lose their job" for answering questions during an investigation? *See Mueller v. Union Pac. R.R.,* 371 N.W.2d 732 (Neb. 1985) (holding that employees fired after an internal investigation had a valid contract claim, even though public policy was too vague for a wrongful discharge tort claim).

3. *Internal Versus External Whistleblowers.* Should it matter whether the employee reports the violation internally to a supervisor or externally to the agency regulating the area at issue? If courts are searching for third-party effects from the discharge, should they be more inclined to protect external whistleblowers? If courts draw such a line, will it unduly encourage whistleblowers to go outside the company rather than attempt to resolve the problem internally?

These issues were discussed in *Belline v. K-Mart Corp.,* 940 F.2d 184 (7th Cir. 1991) (applying Illinois law). An employee was fired after reporting to senior K-Mart officials that his manager let a local Rotary Club obtain some merchandise without completing the proper forms. The majority reversed the grant of summary judgment against the employee, rejecting the argument that wrongful discharge law should not protect internal complaints. "To hold otherwise," the court reasoned, "would be to create perverse incentives by inviting concerned employees to bypass internal channels altogether and immediately summon the police." Judge Easterbrook, in dissent, would have denied the wrongful discharge claim. He emphasized that theft is an *unconsented* taking, so that Illinois has no interest in the outcome independent of K-Mart's.

Other courts have held that internal whistleblowers have no wrongful discharge claim. In *Fox v. MCI Communications Corp*, 931 P.2d 857 (Utah 1997), an employee was fired after reporting to an internal audit committee that other employees were "churning" — making existing customer accounts appear new on the corporate records so they could meet sales quotas and earn higher commissions. The employee alleged the churning was computer-aided fraud in violation of state criminal law. The court rejected her wrongful discharge claim, emphasizing that the company had not asked her to commit a criminal act and that she had not reported anything to outside authorities:

> [I]f an employee reports a criminal violation to an employer, rather than to public authorities, and is fired for making such reports, that does not, in our view, contravene a clear and substantial public policy. In the instant case, the employer did not require plaintiff to engage in a criminal act or to violate her public duty to disclose criminal conduct. The conduct that plaintiff's co-workers engaged in was dishonest, but it did not cause harm to any of MCIT's customers; no customer was overcharged or defrauded as a result of the dishonest practices of MCIT's employees. The churning and creation of "new" accounts, while clearly intended to produce higher pay for the employees, was a practice defendant knew about and, by tolerating it, acquiesced in. For that reason, the corporation was not defrauded.

> Although employees may have a duty to disclose information concerning the employer's business to their employer, that duty ordinarily serves the private interest of the employer, not the public interest. *Foley v. Interactive Data Corp.*, 765 P.2d 373, 380 (Cal. 1988). Nothing in this case affects the public interest in any significant way. The conduct of plaintiff's co-workers may have resulted in increased costs of the corporation's products and services and thereby adversely affected the corporate shareholders to some minor degree, but that does not violate a clear and substantial public policy. Nor would the effect of the increased costs on the corporation's prices result in a violation of a clear and substantial public policy. There are, no doubt, many instances of avoidable inefficiencies that produce higher costs and affect an employer's profits, but, for the most part, those are matters that involve private policy that is more or less regulated by forces in the marketplace, not matters that rise to a level that implicates a clear and substantial public interest.

BALLA v. GAMBRO, INC.

Supreme Court of Illinois
584 N.E.2d 104 (1991)

JUSTICE CLARK delivered the opinion of the court:

The issue in this case is whether in-house counsel should be allowed the remedy of an action for retaliatory discharge.

Appellee, Roger Balla, formerly in-house counsel for Gambro, Inc. (Gambro), filed a retaliatory discharge action against Gambro, its affiliate Gambro Dialysatoren, KG (Gambro Germany), its parent company Gambro Lundia, AB (Gambro Sweden), and the president of Gambro in the circuit court of Cook County (Gambro, Gambro Germany and Gambro Sweden collectively referred to as appellants). Appellee alleged that he was fired in contravention of Illinois public policy and sought damages for the discharge. The trial court dismissed the action on appellants' motion for summary judgment. The appellate court reversed. We granted appellant's petition for leave to appeal and allowed amicus curiae briefs from the American Corporate Counsel Association and Illinois Bar Association.

Gambro is a distributor of kidney dialysis equipment manufactured by Gambro Germany. Among the products distributed by Gambro are dialyzers which filter excess fluid and toxic substances from the blood of patients with no or impaired kidney function. The manufacture and sale of dialyzers is regulated by the United States Food and Drug Administration (FDA); the Federal Food, Drug, and Cosmetic Act; FDA regulations; and the Illinois Food, Drug and Cosmetic Act.

Appellee, Roger J. Balla, is and was at all times throughout this controversy an attorney licensed to practice law in the State of Illinois. On March 17, 1980, appellee executed an employment agreement with Gambro which contained the terms of appellee's employment. Generally, the employment agreement provided that appellee would "be responsible for all legal matters within the company and for personnel within the company's sales office." Appellee held the title of director of administration at Gambro. As director of administration, appellee's specific responsibilities included, inter alia: advising, counseling and representing management on legal matters; establishing and administering personnel policies; coordinating and overseeing corporate activities to assure compliance with applicable laws and regulations, and preventing or minimizing legal or administrative proceedings; and coordinating the activities of the manager of regulatory affairs. Regarding this last responsibility, under Gambro's corporate hierarchy, appellee supervised the manager of regulatory affairs, and the manager reported directly to appellee.

In August 1983, the manager of regulatory affairs for Gambro left the company and appellee assumed the manager's specific duties. Although appellee's original employment agreement was not modified to reflect his new position, his annual compensation was increased and Gambro's corporate organizational chart referred to appellee's positions as "Dir. of Admin./Personnel; General Counsel; Mgr. of Regulatory Affairs." The job description for the position described the manager as an individual "responsible for ensuring awareness of and compliance with federal, state and local laws and regulations affecting the company's operations and products." Requirements for the position were a bachelor of science degree and three to five years in the medical device field plus two years' experience in the area of government regulations. The individual in the position prior to appellee was not an attorney.

In July 1985 Gambro Germany informed Gambro in a letter that certain dialyzers it had manufactured, the clearances of which varied from the package insert, were about to be shipped to Gambro. Referring to these dialyzers, Gambro Germany advised Gambro:

> For acute patients risk is that the acute uremic situation will not be improved in spite of the treatment, giving continuous high levels of potassium, phosphate and urea/creatine. The chronic patient may note the effect as a slow progression of the uremic situation and depending on the interval between medical check-ups the medical risk may not be overlooked.

Appellee told the president of Gambro to reject the shipment because the dialyzers did not comply with FDA regulations. The president notified Gambro Germany of its decision to reject the shipment on July 12, 1985.

However, one week later the president informed Gambro Germany that Gambro would accept the dialyzers and "sell [them] to a unit that is not currently our customer but who buys only on price." Appellee contends that he was not informed by the president of the decision to accept the dialyzers but became aware of it through other Gambro employees. Appellee maintains that he spoke with the president in August regarding the company's decision to accept the dialyzers and told the president that he would do whatever necessary to stop the sale of the dialyzers.

On September 4, 1985, appellee was discharged from Gambro's employment by its president. The following day, appellee reported the shipment of the dialyzers to the FDA. The FDA seized the shipment and determined the product to be "adulterated within the meaning of section 501(h) of the [Federal Act]."

On March 19, 1986, appellee filed a four-count complaint in tort for retaliatory discharge seeking $22 million in damages. Counts III and IV for emotional distress were dismissed from the action, as was the president in an order entered by the trial court on November 5, 1986.

On July 28, 1987, Gambro filed a motion for summary judgment[, which the trial court granted.]

We agree with the trial court that appellee does not have a cause of action against Gambro for retaliatory discharge under the facts of the case at bar. Generally, this court adheres to the proposition that "'an employer may discharge an employee-at-will for any reason or for no reason [at all].'" However, in *Kelsay v.*

Motorola, Inc., 384 N.E.2d 353 (Ill. 1978), this court first recognized the limited and narrow tort of retaliatory discharge. In *Kelsay*, an at-will employee was fired for filing a worker's compensation claim against her employer. After examining the history and purpose behind the Workers' Compensation Act to determine the public policy behind its enactment, this court held that the employee should have a cause of action for retaliatory discharge. This court stressed that if employers could fire employees for filing workers' compensation claims, the public policy behind the enactment of the Workers' Compensation Act would be frustrated.

Subsequently, in *Palmateer v. International Harvester Co.*, 421 N.E.2d 876 (Ill. 1981), this court again examined the tort of retaliatory discharge. In *Palmateer*, an employee was discharged for informing the police of suspected criminal activities of a co-employee, and because he agreed to provide assistance in any investigation and trial of the matter. Based on the public policy favoring the investigation and prosecution of crime, this court held that the employee had a cause of action for retaliatory discharge. Further, we stated:

> "All that is required [to bring a cause of action for retaliatory discharge] is that the employer discharge the employee in retaliation for the employee's activities, and that the discharge be in contravention of a clearly mandated public policy." *Palmateer*, 85 Ill. 2d at 134.

In this case it appears that Gambro discharged appellee, an employee of Gambro, in retaliation for his activities, and this discharge was in contravention of a clearly mandated public policy. Appellee allegedly told the president of Gambro that he would do whatever was necessary to stop the sale of the "misbranded and/or adulterated" dialyzers. In appellee's eyes, the use of these dialyzers could cause death or serious bodily harm to patients. As we have stated before, "there is no public policy more important or more fundamental than the one favoring the effective protection of the lives and property of citizens." (*See Palmateer*, 85 Ill. 2d at 132.) However, in this case, appellee was not just an employee of Gambro, but also general counsel for Gambro.

[I]n *Herbster v. North American Co. for Life & Health Insurance*, 150 Ill. App. 3d 21 (1986), our appellate court held that the plaintiff, an employee and chief legal counsel for the defendant company, did not have a claim for retaliatory discharge against the company due to the presence of the attorney-client relationship. Under the facts of that case, the defendant company allegedly requested the plaintiff to destroy or remove discovery information which had been requested in lawsuits pending against the company. The plaintiff refused arguing that such conduct would constitute fraud and violate several provisions of the Illinois Code of Professional Responsibility. Subsequently, the defendant company discharged the plaintiff.

The appellate court refused to extend the tort of retaliatory discharge to the plaintiff in *Herbster* primarily because of the special relationship between an attorney and client. The court stated:

The mutual trust, exchanges of confidence, reliance on judgment, and personal nature of the attorney-client relationship demonstrate the unique position attorneys occupy in our society. (*Herbster,* 150 Ill. App. 3d at 99.)

The appellate court recited a list of factors which make the attorney-client relationship special such as: the attorney-client privilege regarding confidential communications, the fiduciary duty an attorney owes to a client, the right of the client to terminate the relationship with or without cause, and the fact that a client has exclusive control over the subject matter of the litigation and a client may dismiss or settle a cause of action regardless of the attorney's advice. Thus, in *Herbster,* since the plaintiff's duties pertained strictly to legal matters, the appellate court determined that the plaintiff did not have a claim for retaliatory discharge.

We agree with the conclusion reached in *Herbster* that, generally, in-house counsel do not have a claim under the tort of retaliatory discharge. However, we base our decision as much on the nature and purpose of the tort of retaliatory discharge, as on the effect on the attorney-client relationship that extending the tort would have. In addition, at this time, we caution that our holding is confined by the fact that appellee is and was at all times throughout this controversy an attorney licensed to practice law in the State of Illinois. Appellee is and was subject to the Illinois Code of Professional Responsibility (see the Rules of Professional Conduct which replaced the Code of Professional Responsibility, effective August 1, 1990), adopted by this court. The tort of retaliatory discharge is a limited and narrow exception to the general rule of at-will employment. The tort seeks to achieve "'a proper balance ... among the employer's interest in operating a business efficiently and profitably, the employee's interest in earning a livelihood, and society's interest in seeing its public policies carried out.'" (*Fellhauer,* 142 Ill. 2d at 507, quoting *Palmateer,* 85 Ill. 2d at 129.) Further, as stated in *Palmateer*, "*the foundation of the tort of retaliatory discharge lies in the protection of public policy ....*" (*Emphasis added.*) *Palmateer,* 85 Ill. 2d at 133.

In this case, the public policy to be protected, that of protecting the lives and property of citizens, is adequately safeguarded without extending the tort of retaliatory discharge to in-house counsel. Appellee was required under the Rules of Professional Conduct to report Gambro's intention to sell the "misbranded and/or adulterated" dialyzers. Rule 1.6(b) of the Rules of Professional Conduct reads:

"A lawyer *shall* reveal information about a client to the extent it appears necessary to prevent the client from committing an act that would result in death or serious bodily injury." (Emphasis added.) (134 Ill. 2d R. 1.6(b).)

Appellee alleges, and the FDA's seizure of the dialyzers indicates, that the use of the dialyzers would cause death or serious bodily injury. Thus, under the above-cited rule, appellee was under the mandate of this court to report the sale of these dialyzers.

In his brief to this court, appellee argues that not extending the tort of retaliatory discharge to in-house counsel would present attorneys with a "Hobson's choice." According to appellee, in-house counsel would face two alternatives: either comply with the client/employer's wishes and risk both the loss of a professional license and exposure to criminal sanctions, or decline to comply with client/employer's wishes and risk the loss of a full-time job and the attendant benefits. We disagree. Unlike the employees in *Kelsay* which this court recognized would be left with the difficult decision of choosing between whether to file a workers' compensation claim and risk being fired, or retaining their jobs and losing their right to a remedy (*see Kelsay,* 74 Ill. 2d at 182), in-house counsel plainly are not confronted with such a dilemma. In-house counsel do not have a choice of whether to follow their ethical obligations as attorneys licensed to practice law, or follow the illegal and unethical demands of their clients. In-house counsel must abide by the Rules of Professional Conduct. Appellee had no choice but to report to the FDA Gambro's intention to sell or distribute these dialyzers, and consequently protect the aforementioned public policy.

In addition, we believe that extending the tort of retaliatory discharge to in-house counsel would have an undesirable effect on the attorney-client relationship that exists between these employers and their in-house counsel. Generally, a client may discharge his attorney at any time, with or without cause. This rule applies equally to in-house counsel as it does to outside counsel. Further, this rule "recognizes that the relationship between an attorney and client is based on trust and that the client must have confidence in his attorney in order to ensure that the relationship will function properly." (*Rhoades,* 78 Ill. 2d at 228.) As stated in *Herbster,* "the attorney is placed in the unique position of maintaining a close relationship with a client where the attorney receives secrets, disclosures, and information that otherwise would not be divulged to intimate friends." We believe that if in-house counsel are granted the right to sue their employers for retaliatory discharge, employers might be less willing to be forthright and candid with their in-house counsel. Employers might be hesitant to turn to their in-house counsel for advice regarding potentially questionable corporate conduct knowing that their in-house counsel could use this information in a retaliatory discharge suit.

We recognize that under the Illinois Rules of Professional Conduct, attorneys shall reveal client confidences or secrets in certain situations (*see* 134 Ill. 2d Rules 1.6(a), (b), (c)), and thus one might expect employers/clients to be naturally hesitant to rely on in-house counsel for advice regarding this potentially questionable conduct. However, the danger exists that if in-house counsel are granted a right to sue their employers in tort for retaliatory discharge, employers might further limit their communication with their in-house counsel. As stated in *Upjohn Co. v. United States,* 449 U.S. 383, 389 (1981), regarding the attorney-client privilege:

> "Its purpose is to encourage full and frank communication between attorneys and their clients and thereby promote broader public interests in the observance of law and administration of justice. The privilege recognizes that sound legal advice or advocacy serves public ends and that *such advice or advocacy depends upon the lawyer being fully informed by the client.*" (Emphasis added.)

If extending the tort of retaliatory discharge might have a chilling effect on the communications between the employer/client and the in-house counsel, we believe that it is more wise to refrain from doing so.

Our decision not to extend the tort of retaliatory discharge to in-house counsel also is based on other ethical considerations. Under the Rules of Professional Conduct, appellee was required to withdraw from representing Gambro if continued representation would result in the violation of the Rules of Professional Conduct by which appellee was bound, or if Gambro discharged the appellee. In this case, Gambro did discharge appellee, and according to appellee's claims herein, his continued representation of Gambro would have resulted in a violation of the Rules of Professional Conduct. Appellee argues that such a choice of withdrawal is "simplistic and uncompassionate, and is completely at odds with contemporary realities facing in-house attorneys. These contemporary realities apparently are the economic ramifications of losing his position as in-house counsel. However difficult economically and perhaps emotionally it is for in-house counsel to discontinue representing an employer/client, we refuse to allow in-house counsel to sue their employer/client for damages because they obeyed their ethical obligations. In this case, appellee, in addition to being an employee at Gambro, is first and foremost an attorney bound by the Rules of Professional Conduct. These Rules of Professional Conduct hope to articulate in a concrete fashion certain values and goals such as defending the integrity of the judicial system, promoting the administration of justice and protecting the integrity of the legal profession. An attorney's obligation to follow these Rules of Professional Conduct should not be the foundation for a claim of retaliatory discharge.

We also believe that it would be inappropriate for the employer/client to bear the economic costs and burdens of their in-house counsel's adhering to their ethical obligations under the Rules of Professional Conduct. Presumably, in situations where an in-house counsel obeys his or her ethical obligations and reveals certain information regarding the employer/client, the attorney-client relationship will be irreversibly strained and the client will more than likely discharge its in-house counsel. In this scenario, if we were to grant the in-house counsel the right to sue the client for retaliatory discharge, we would be shifting the burden and costs of obeying the Rules of Professional Conduct from the attorney to the employer/client. The employer/client would be forced to pay damages to its former in-house counsel to essentially mitigate the financial harm the attorney suffered for having to abide by Rules of Professional Conduct. This, we believe, is impermissible for all attorneys know or should know that at certain times in their professional career, they will have to forgo economic gains in order to protect the integrity of the legal profession.

[The Court then reviewed cases from other jurisdiction.]

In light of our decision that in-house counsel generally are not entitled to bring a cause of action for retaliatory discharge against their employer/client, we must consider appellee's argument that he learned of the dialyzers' defect and Gambro's noncompliance with FDA regulations in his role as manager of regulatory affairs at Gambro, and not as corporate counsel. Appellee argues that, if he did learn of Gambro's alleged violation of FDA regulations as manager of regulatory affairs, and acted pursuant to his duties as manager of regulatory affairs, he is merely an "employee" at Gambro and therefore should be entitled to bring a cause of action for retaliatory discharge. The appellate court in this matter agreed with appellee and held that a question of fact exists as to whether "[appellee's] discharge resulted from information he learned as a 'layman' in a nonlegal position."

We disagree. A motion for summary judgment should be granted when the pleadings, depositions, and affidavits reveal that there is no genuine issue as to any material fact and that the moving party is entitled to judgment as a matter of law. In this case, there is no issue of fact as to whether appellee learned of Gambro's violations of FDA regulations as a "layman," as opposed to general counsel for Gambro. After examining the pleadings, exhibits and appellee's deposition testimony, we find that appellee was acting as Gambro's general counsel throughout this ordeal. As noted earlier, at the time of this controversy, appellee not only was acting as general counsel for Gambro, but also was its manager of regulatory affairs. Under the corporate hierarchy at Gambro, the corporate counsel supervised the manager of regulatory affairs. Thus, appellee "supervised" himself in his role as manager of regulatory affairs. More importantly, based on the official job descriptions supplied by Gambro, it is clear that the general counsel and the manager of regulatory affairs performed essentially the same roles with regards to FDA compliance. The job description for the director of administration, which defined the position of general counsel, required appellee to "*coordinate[] and oversee[] corporate activities to assure compliance with applicable laws* and regulations and prevent[] or minimize[] [the] possibility of legal or administrative proceedings." Along the same vein, the job description for manager of regulatory affairs required appellee to "*establish programs and procedures to ensure compliance with applicable FDA laws and regulations.*" Thus, both roles had equivalent duties for assuring compliance with FDA regulations....

Appellee relies on the fact that previous managers of regulatory affairs at Gambro were not attorneys, and the position only required a bachelor of science degree and three to five years' experience in the medical device field as evidence that this position is a nonlegal position. We disagree. Although previous managers evidently were not attorneys, the two roles appellee performed for Gambro were so intertwined and inextricably bound, we fail to see how appellee was not performing his general counsel functions in this matter. As support for our conclusion, we quote from the ABA Formal Opinion No. 328, which addressed the dual role situation appellee confronted:

> "If the second occupation is so law-related that the work of the lawyer in such occupation will involve, inseparably, the practice of law, the lawyer is considered to be engaged in the practice of law while conducting that occupation." (ABA Formal Opinion No. 328, at 65 (June 1972).)

In this case, as the trial court explained, appellee investigated certain facts, applied the law to those investigated facts and reached certain conclusions as to whether these dialyzers complied with the FDA regulations. In that sense, appellee inescapably engaged in the practice of law. Consequently, although appellee may have been the manager of regulatory affairs for Gambro, his discharge resulted from information he learned as general counsel, and from conduct he performed as general counsel.

For the foregoing reasons, the decision of the appellate court is reversed, and the decision of the trial court is affirmed.

Appellate court reversed; circuit court affirmed.

JUSTICE FREEMAN, dissenting:

I respectfully dissent from the decision of my colleagues. In concluding that the plaintiff attorney, serving as corporate in-house counsel, should not be allowed a claim for retaliatory discharge, the majority first reasons that the public policy implicated in this case, i.e., protecting the lives and property of Illinois citizens, is adequately safeguarded by the lawyer's ethical obligation to reveal information about a client as necessary to prevent acts that would result in death or serious bodily harm. I find this reasoning fatally flawed.

The majority so reasons because, as a matter of law, an attorney cannot even contemplate ignoring his ethical obligations in favor of continuing in his employment. I agree with this conclusion "as a matter of law." However, to say that the categorical nature of ethical obligations is sufficient to ensure that the ethical obligations will be satisfied simply ignores reality. Specifically, it ignores that, as unfortunate for society as it may be, attorneys are no less human than nonattorneys and, thus, no less given to the temptation to either ignore or rationalize away their ethical obligations when complying therewith may render them unable to feed and support their families.... I do not believe any useful purpose is served by distinguishing attorneys from ordinary citizens. It is incontrovertible that the law binds all men, kings and paupers alike. An attorney should not be punished simply because he has ethical obligations imposed upon him over and above the general obligation to obey the law which all men have. Nor should a corporate employer be protected simply because the employee it has discharged for "blowing the whistle" happens to be an attorney....

[I]t should be borne in mind that this case involves an attorney discharged from his employment, not one who has voluntarily resigned due to his ethical obligations. I believe the majority's reasoning, in general, and with respect to the question of who should bear the economic burdens of the attorney's loss of job, specifically, would be valid grounds for denying a cause of action to an attorney who voluntarily resigns, rather than is discharged. By focusing upon the immediate economic consequences of the discharge, the majority overlooks the very real possibility that in-house counsel who is discharged, rather than allowed to resign in accordance with his ethical obligations once the employer's persistence in illegal conduct is evident to him, will be stigmatized within the legal profession. That stigma and its apparent consequences, economic and otherwise, in addition to the immediate economic consequences of a discharge, also militate strongly in favor of allowing the attorney a claim for retaliatory discharge....

GENERAL DYNAMICS CORP. v. SUPERIOR COURT

Supreme Court of California
876 P.2d 487 (1994)

[Andrew Rose, an in-house lawyer, was fired after fourteen years of service.] The complaint relied on two main theories of relief. First, it alleged that General Dynamics had by its conduct and other assurances impliedly represented to Rose over the years that he was subject to discharge only for "good cause," a condition that the complaint alleged was not present in the circumstances under which he was fired. Second, the complaint alleged that Rose was actually fired for cumulative reasons, all of which violated fundamental public policies: in part because he spearheaded an investigation into employee drug use at the Pomona plant (an investigation, the complaint alleged, that led to the termination of more than sixty General Dynamics employees), in part because he protested the company's failure to investigate the bugging of the office of the chief of security (allegedly a criminal offense and, since it involved a major defense contractor, a serious breach of national security), and in part as a result of advising General Dynamics officials that the company's salary policy with respect to the compensation paid a certain class of employees might be in violation of the federal Fair Labor Standards Act, possibly exposing the firm to several hundred million dollars in back pay claims.

General Dynamics filed a general demurrer to the complaint, asserting that Rose had failed to state a claim for relief. Because he had been employed as an in-house *attorney*, the company contended, Rose was subject to discharge at any time, "for any reason or for no reason." The trial court overruled the demurrer and the Court of Appeal denied General Dynamics' ensuing petition for a writ of mandate, ruling that, at least at the pleading stage, the complaint was sufficient to survive a general demurrer as to both theories of relief.

[Rose states a cause of action on both theories of relief.] Roses' complaint does not contest the right of General Dynamics to terminate a member of its corporate legal department at any time or for any reason, nor could it. It simply asserts that there is a cost to be paid for such an action under the circumstance alleged in the complaint — either in lost wages and related damages in the case of the implied-in-fact contract claim, or as tort damages in the case of the public policy tort claim....

As the name suggests, an implied-in-fact contract claim as a limitation on an employer's historical at-will power to terminate one of its employees is rooted in the conduct of the parties to the employment relationship itself.... In short, implied-in-fact limitations being a species of contract, no reason appears why an employer that elects to limit its at-will freedom to terminate the employment relationship with in-house counsel should not be held to the terms of its bargain.... In any event, employers who wish to treat their in-house legal personnel differently from other workers have a variety of means to limit the potential for exposure. Without addressing the question in detail, we note that in the case of confidential corporate employees such as attorneys, an employer has wide latitude in determining the circumstances under which it has just or good cause to terminate the relationship. *See, e.g., Pugh v. See's Candies, Inc.* (1988) 203 Cal. App. 3d 743.

We turn next to an evaluation of Rose's claim that he was discharged for multiple reasons, each of which violated a "fundamental polic[y] that [is] delineated in constitutional or statutory provisions" of the law of this state. (*Gantt v. Sentry Insurance* (1992) 1 Cal. 4th 1083, 1095.) Unlike implied-in-fact contract claims, which as discussed above, arise out of the conduct and expectations of the parties to the employment relationship, so-called public policy wrongful discharge claims are pure creatures of law.... [A]lthough the public policy served by the conduct of the aggrieved employee at issue may often be directly protective of the interest in employment itself, the doctrinal foundation of the public policy tort claim is not so much the *plaintiff's* continued interest in employment as the preservation of the *public* interest as it is expressed in multiple forms in the Constitution and statutory law....

This foundational *public* rationale is especially important in the case of the attorney-employee. Perhaps the defining feature of professionals as a class is the extent to which they embody a dual allegiance. On the one hand, an attorney's highest duty is to the welfare and interests of the client. This obligation is channeled, however, by a limiting and specifically *professional* qualification: attorneys are required to conduct themselves *as such*, meaning that they are bound at all events not to transgress a handful of professional ethical norms that distinguish their work from that of the nonattorney....

The case for shielding the in-house attorney — among *all* corporate employees — from retaliation by the employer for either insisting on adhering to mandatory ethical norms of the profession or for refusing to violate them is thus clear. And because their professional work is by definition affected with a public interest, in-house attorneys are even more liable to conflicts between corporate goals and professional norms than their nonattorney colleagues. On this view, then, in-house counsel, forced to choose between the demands of the employer and the requirements of a professional code of ethics have, if anything, an *even more* powerful claim to judicial protection than their nonprofessional colleagues.

[The Court then discusses *Balla v. Gambro* and other cases.]

There is no doubt that the Illinois courts in *Balla* and *Herbster,* grappled conscientiously with the conflicting values presented by cases such as this one. If their reasoning and conclusions can be faulted, it is because one searches in vain for a principled link between the ethical duties of the in-house attorney and the courts' refusal to grant such an employee a tort remedy under conditions that directly implicate those professional obligations. As more than one critic of these opinions has pointed out, both cases appear to reflect not only an unspoken adherence to an anachronistic model of the attorney's place and role in contemporary society, but an inverted view of the consequences of the in-house attorney's essential professional role....

Granted the priest-like license to receive the most intimate and damning disclosures of the client, granted the sanctity of the professional privilege, granted the uniquely influential position attorneys occupy in our society, it is precisely *because of* that role that attorneys should be accorded a retaliatory discharge remedy in those instances in which *mandatory ethical norms* embodied in the Rules of Professional Conduct *collide with illegitimate demands of the employer* and the attorney insists on *adhering to his or her clear professional duty.* It is, after all, the office of the retaliatory discharge tort to vindicate fundamental public policies by encouraging employees to act in ways that advance them. By providing the employee with a remedy in tort damages for resisting socially damaging organizational conduct, the courts mitigate the otherwise considerable economic and cultural pressures on the individual employee to silently conform.

Within their area of professional competence, in-house attorneys, more than other organizational employees, are imbued with ethical constraints on the direction their efforts may legitimately take. Among other strictures on their conduct, they may not be a party to the commission of a crime, destroy evidence or suborn perjury. They are forbidden to do these things by the very ethical codes that define their professional identity. It is a short step from this premise to the conclusion that in-house lawyers ought to have access to a judicial remedy in those instances in which their employment is terminated for adhering to the requirements of just such a mandatory professional duty, either by an *affirmative act* required by the ethical code or statute or by resisting a demand of the employer on the ground that it is unequivocally *barred* by the professional code....

In addition, the emphasis by the *Balla, Herbster* and [other] courts on the "remedy" of the in-house attorney's duty of "withdrawal" strikes us as illusory. Courts do not require nonlawyer employees to quietly surrender their jobs rather than "go along" with an employer's unlawful demands. Indeed, the retaliatory discharge tort claim is designed to encourage and support precisely the *opposite* reaction. Why, then, did the courts in these three cases content themselves with the bland announcement that the only "choice" of an attorney confronted with an employer's demand that he violate his professional oath by committing, say, a criminal act, is to voluntarily withdraw from employment, a course fraught with the possibility of economic catastrophe and professional banishment?

High cost o- resignato

Whatever the reason, the withdrawal "remedy" fails to confront seriously the extraordinarily high cost that resignation entails. More importantly, it is virtually certain that, without the prospect of limited judicial access, in-house attorneys — especially those in mid-career who occupy senior positions — confronted with the dilemma of choosing between adhering to professional ethical norms and surrendering to the employer's unethical demands will almost always find silence the better part of valor. Declining to provide a limited remedy under defined circumstances will thus almost certainly foster a degradation of in-house counsel's professional stature....

[I]n determining whether an in-house attorney has a retaliatory discharge claim against his or her employer, a court must first ask whether the attorney was discharged for following a mandatory ethical obligation prescribed by professional rule or statute. If, for example, in-house counsel is asked to commit a crime, or to engage in an act of moral turpitude that would subject him to disbarment (*see, e.g.*, Bus. & Prof. Code, §§ 6101, 6106 [providing, respectively, for disbarment on conviction of a felony or a misdemeanor involving moral turpitude, and for the "commission of any act involving moral turpitude, dishonesty or corruption"]), and is discharged for refusing to engage in such an act, counsel would have been discharged for adhering to a mandatory ethical obligation; under most circumstances, the attorney would have a retaliatory discharge cause of action against the employer.

If, on the other hand, the conduct in which the attorney has engaged is merely ethically *permissible*, but not *required* by statute or ethical code, then the inquiry facing the court is slightly more complex. Under these circumstances, a court must resolve *two* questions: First, whether the employer's conduct is of the kind that would give rise to a retaliatory discharge action by a *non*-attorney employee under *Gantt v. Sentry Insurance* and related cases; second, the court must determine whether some statute or ethical rule, such as the statutory exceptions to the attorney-client privilege codified in the Evidence Code (*see id.*, §§ 956-958), specifically permits the attorney to depart from the usual requirement of confidentiality with respect to the client-employer and engage in the "nonfiduciary" conduct for which he was terminated.

We emphasize the limited scope of our conclusion that in-house counsel may state a cause of action in tort for retaliatory discharge. The lawyer's high duty of fidelity to the interests of the client work against a tort remedy that is coextensive with that available to the nonattorney employee. Although claims by in-house attorneys are cognate to those we approved in *Foley,* the underlying rationale differs somewhat, being grounded in the attorney's obligation to adhere to ethical norms specific to the profession. The cause of action is thus one designed to support in-house counsel in remaining faithful to those fundamental public policies reflected in the governing ethical code when carrying out professional assignments. Thus, in addition to the limitations on the scope of the retaliatory tort action mentioned above, the concerns expressed by the courts in *Balla* and *Herbster* for the integrity of the fiduciary aspects of the attorney-client relationship impose additional limitations.

First, those values that underlie the professional relationship — the fiduciary qualities of mutual trust and confidence — can be protected from the threat of damage by limiting judicial access to claims grounded in *explicit and unequivocal ethical norms* embodied in the Rules of Professional Responsibility and *statutes*, and claims which are maintainable by the *non*-attorney employee under our decision in *Gantt v. Sentry Insurance*, under circumstances in which the Legislature has manifested a judgment that the principle of professional confidentiality *does not apply.* (*See, e.g.,* Evid. Code, § 956.5 ["*There is no privilege* ... if the lawyer reasonably believes that disclosure of any confidential communication ... is necessary to prevent the client from committing a criminal act that the lawyer believes is likely to result in death or substantial bodily harm." (Italics added).])

Similarly, the in-house attorney who publicly exposes the client's secrets will usually find no sanctuary in the courts. Except in those rare instances when disclosure is explicitly permitted or mandated by an ethics code provision or statute, it is never the business of the lawyer to disclose publicly the secrets of the client. In any event, where the elements of a wrongful discharge in violation of fundamental public policy claim cannot, for reasons peculiar to the particular case, be fully established without breaching the attorney-client privilege, the suit must be dismissed in the interest of preserving the privilege. We underline the fact that such drastic action will seldom if ever be appropriate at the demurrer stage of litigation. Although General Dynamics argues that Rose's claims are barred from disclosure by the lawyer-client privilege, that is an issue that is incapable of resolution in a challenge to the facial sufficiency of the complaint. Indeed, in most wrongful termination suits brought by discharged in-house counsel, whether the attorney-client privilege precludes the plaintiff from recovery will not be resolvable at the demurrer stage. Rather, in the usual case, whether the privilege serves as a bar to the plaintiff's recovery will be litigated and determined in the context of motions for protective orders or to compel further discovery responses, as well as at the time of a motion for summary judgment.

Second, the contours of the statutory attorney-client privilege should continue to be strictly observed. We reject any suggestion that the scope of the privilege should be diluted in the context of in-house counsel and their corporate clients. Members of corporate legal departments are as fully subject to the demands of the privilege as their outside colleagues. It is likely, however, that many of the cases in which house counsel is faced with an ethical dilemma will lie outside the scope of the statutory privilege. Matters involving the commission of a crime or a fraud, or circumstances in which the attorney reasonably believes that disclosure is necessary to prevent the commission of a criminal act likely to result in death or substantial bodily harm, are statutory and well-recognized exceptions to the attorney-client privilege. Although their revelation in the course of a retaliatory discharge suit may do lasting damage to the expectations of the corporate client (or, more likely, a corporate executive) that disclosures to counsel would remain inviolate, a concern for protecting the fiduciary aspects of the relationship in the case of a client who confides in counsel for the purpose of planning a crime or practicing a fraud is misplaced; such disclosures do not violate the privilege.

The Exceptions

Moreover, the trial courts can and should apply an array of ad hoc measures from their equitable arsenal designed to permit the attorney plaintiff to attempt to make the necessary proof while protecting from disclosure client confidences subject to the privilege. The use of sealing and protective orders, limited admissibility of evidence, orders restricting the use of testimony in successive proceedings, and, where appropriate, in camera proceedings, are but some of a number of measures that might usefully be explored by the trial courts as circumstances warrant. We are confident that by taking an aggressive managerial role, judges can minimize the dangers to the legitimate privilege interests the trial of such cases may present.

ad hoc measures

Finally, a handful of subsidiary rules will effectively raise the ante on the in-house attorney contemplating a tort action, thus deterring the incidence of strike suits or claims filed in bad faith. The contested ethical requirement must be clearly established by the ethics code or statutory provision; disagreements over policy are *not* actionable. The plaintiff, of course, bears the burden of establishing the *unequivocal* requirements of the ethical norm at issue and that the employer's conduct was motivated by impermissible considerations under a "but for" standard of causation. The ethical norm at issue must be one that is intended for the protection of the public at large; measures designed solely for the benefit of the attorney or the client will not suffice to support a retaliatory discharge claim. Moreover, an attorney who unsuccessfully pursues a retaliatory discharge suit, and in doing so discloses privileged client confidences, may be subject to State Bar disciplinary proceedings. Finally, of course, the defendant employer is always free to challenge plaintiff's claim by demonstrating the discharge was motivated by reasons other than a demand that counsel engage in conduct amounting to a breach of professional ethical norms....

The judgment of the Court of Appeal is affirmed and the cause is remanded to that court with directions to order further proceedings in accordance with the views expressed herein.

LUCAS, C.J., MOSK, J., KENNARD, J., BAXTER, J., GEORGE, J., and TURNER, J., concurred.

NOTES

1. *Duty or Discretion to Disclose.* Illinois is one of the few states mandating lawyers to disclose information about future acts of clients that will result in death or serious bodily injury. Most lawyer ethics codes permit, but do not require, a lawyer to disclose such information. Most states other than Illinois limit disclosable acts to upcoming crimes or frauds by the client. Some codes expand the scope of permissible disclosure to include substantial financial loss as well as serious bodily injury. *See* RESTATEMENT OF THE LAW GOVERNING LAWYERS §§ 117A, 117B (Proposed Final Draft No. 1, 1996). Is the *Balla* rationale persuasive in a state with a discretionary disclosure rule?

2. *The Independence of In-House Counsel.* The *Balla* court emphasized that lawyers are employed by their clients at will. As the RESTATEMENT OF THE LAW GOVERNING LAWYERS § 44, Comment b, puts it:

> A client may always discharge a lawyer, regardless of whether cause exists for the discharge and regardless of what may have been provided in any contract between them. The client's consent creates the client-lawyer relationship, and withdrawing consent ends it.

Some commentators have argued that the reasons supporting this right do not apply fully to in-house lawyers. In-house lawyers are economically dependent on a single client/employer, who controls their entire compensation, hours, and working conditions. The general concern that unsophisticated clients should not be required to justify their decision to terminate an overreaching outside counsel (even if the contract required just-cause termination) is less relevant for corporations who employ inside counsel. The *General Dynamics* court recognized that corporations could, by their words or actions, agree not to fire their in-house counsel without cause.

On the other hand, creating a cause of action may limit desirable flexibility in replacing top corporate officers such as in-house counsel. It is one thing to allow corporate counsel expressly to negotiate a golden parachute or other contract protection against discharge. It is another to say that an at-will lawyer can threaten an implied-in-fact contract claim or a tort claim upon being fired (and what in-house counsel cannot make some claim about disclosing possible corporate fraud?).

Would an acceptable compromise be to create a tort cause of action that is more restrictive for corporate counsel than other employees? Could the tort be limited to health and safety violations? An actual violation, as opposed to counsel's good-faith belief of a violation? Reporting the violation to outsiders, as opposed to internal whistleblowing? Is the *General Dynamics* distinction between mandatory and permissive disclosures an effort toward compromise?

3. *Exposing Trivial Violations.* Should an employee be protected from discharge for revealing any violation of law? Consider the hypothetical discussed in *Palmateer v. International Harvester Co.,* 421 N.E.2d 876 (Ill. 1981), of an employee fired for reporting to police that a coworker had stolen a $2 screwdriver from the company. Is such a firing a wrongful discharge in violation of public policy? The *Palmateer* majority declared the hypothetical would state a cause of action, reasoning that the company's business judgment about how to handle this personnel problem could not override the legislature's determination that the problem was a crime to be resolved by the criminal justice system.

NOTES ON WHISTLEBLOWER STATUTES

In addition to common law protection of whistleblowers, in recent years both the state and federal governments have enacted numerous statutes to protect employees who expose wrongdoing by their employers. These statutes raise many similar issues to their common law counterparts. *See generally* John D. Feerick, *Toward a Model Whistleblowing Law,* 19 FORDHAM URB. L.J. 585 (1992); Martin H. Malin, *Protecting the Whistleblower From Retaliatory Discharge,* 16 U. MICH. J.L. REF. 277 (1983).

1. *Anti-Retaliation Versus General Whistleblower Statutes.* Specific employment statutes often include an anti-retaliation provision that protects employees who report violations or exercise their rights under the act. For example, section 704 of Title VII of the Civil Rights Act of 1964 (which prohibits race and sex discrimination in employment) declares it to be an unlawful employment practice for an employer to discriminate against an employee "because he has opposed any ... unlawful employment practice, or because he has made a charge, testified, assisted, or participated in any manner in an investigation, proceeding, or hearing under this title." Section 704 has been interpreted to extend even to employees who have filed false and malicious charges with the EEOC. The section prohibits such employer reprisal as firing, suspension, demotion, transfers to undesirable positions, filing a retaliatory lawsuit, or withholding reference letters for employee activity consistent with the legislation. Many state statutes similarly protect employees from retaliation for fulfilling public duties or exercising statutory rights. Examples include protecting employees who file workers' compensation charges, who serve on juries, or who vote or hold political office against the wishes of their employers.

In addition to specific anti-retaliation provisions, nearly half the states have enacted general whistleblower statutes to protect employees who report wrongdoing by their employers. While the line between a specific anti-retaliation statute and a general whistleblower statute is sometimes indistinct, whistleblower statutes usually protect against a wide variety of substantive law violations, rather than focusing on a particular area.

2. *Public Versus Private Employers.* Legislatures have given public employees extensive protection when exposing government wrongdoing. For example, the Whistleblower Protection Act of 1989, Pub. L. No. 101-12, 103 Stat. 16 (codified in scattered sections of title 5, U.S.C.), protects federal employees who expose government violations of law, gross waste of funds, or specific danger to public health or safety. The Act creates an independent Office of Special Coun-

sel, to which employees may turn to vindicate their rights under the statute. About half the states have enacted similar whistleblower statutes to protect public employees. General whistleblower protection of private employees is more limited, but at least eight states, including Michigan, California, Connecticut, and Maine, have enacted such statutes.

   3. *Federal False Claims Act.* This statute was enacted in 1863 to punish contractors who sold defective supplies to the Union army in the Civil War. Congress amended the statute in 1986 to allow the Government to recover triple damages from contractors defrauding the federal government, and to give individual whistleblowers 15-25% of the government recovery. Some spectacular settlements have occurred under the Act. For example, a former financial officer for United Technologies Corporation received $22.5 million for his share in exposing his company's fraudulent billing practices for military helicopters. This whistleblower statute was part of the plot in John Grisham's recent best-selling novel, *The Partner* 163 (1997) (the partner stole from the client's $90 million whistleblower reward of 15% of a $600 million fraud against the government.)

   4. *Scope of the Whistle.* Some states protect employees who report any violation of law. For example, the California whistleblower statute protects employee disclosure of "a violation of state or federal statute, or violation or noncompliance with a state or federal regulation." CAL. LAB. CODE § 1102.5. Other states only protect whistleblowers who report illegal acts that threaten public health and safety. For example, the New York statute protects disclosure to "a supervisor or to a public body" of a violation of law that "creates and presents a substantial and specific danger to the public health or safety." N.Y. LAB. LAW § 740. In such states, the reporting of much white-collar crime is not protected. *See Remba v. Federation Employment & Guidance Serv.*, 559 N.E.2d 655 (N.Y. 1990) (employee fired for reporting fraudulent billing practices not protected by New York whistleblower statute).

   As a further limitation on the scope of the whistle, New York courts have interpreted the statutory reference to "public" safety to imply that the statute does not protect the reporting of activity that threatens the health or safety of only a few individuals. *E.g., Kern v. DePaul Mental Health Servs.*, 529 N.Y.S.2d 265 (N.Y. Sup. Ct. 1988), *aff'd*, 544 N.Y.S.2d 252 (N.Y. App. Div. 1989) (whistleblowing on employer's complacency regarding sexual activity between mentally handicapped residents of a state-run facility not protected by statute, because employer's alleged actions, even if true, did not create the substantial and specific danger required by the statute).

   5. *Internal Versus External Statutory Whistleblowers.* Whistleblower statutes vary widely on whether they protect internal whistleblowers. In *Hejmadi v. AMFAC, Inc.*, 249 Cal. Rptr. 5 (Cal. Ct. App. 1988), the court interpreted California's whistleblower protection statute as protecting only external whistleblowing, dismissing an employee's action for wrongful discharge because he did not complain to a governmental agency.

By contrast, the Maine whistleblower statute expressly requires that whistle-blowers report internally first, if feasible. In the statute's words, the protections do not apply unless the employee has "first brought the alleged violation ... to the attention of a person having supervisory authority with the employer and has allowed the employer a reasonable opportunity to correct that violation...." ME. REV. STAT. ANN. tit. 26, § 833. New Jersey additionally requires that the employee give the employer "written notice" of the alleged violation of law. N.J. STAT. ANN. § 34:19-4.

What if the statute only expressly protects reporting to external authorities, and the employee is fired after reporting the violation to company officials? In *Shores v. Senior Manor Nursing Ctr., Inc.*, 518 N.E.2d 471 (Ill. App. Ct. 1988), a nursing assistant was fired after reporting to her administrator that a fellow nurse was sleeping on the job and otherwise endangering patients. Illinois's Nursing Home Care Reform Act expressly prohibits the discharge of an employee who reports abuse to the Department of Public Health. The court recognized a common law action for wrongful discharge in violation of public policy (the public policy being articulated in the nursing home statute), rejecting the employer's argument that the limited anti-retaliation statute showed the legislature was unconcerned with internal reporting of wrongdoing.

6. *Remedies.* Some whistleblowing statutes, such as New Hampshire's, provide for a hearing before an administrative agency. If the firing was found to violate the statute, the agency may award reinstatement and back pay. Section 11(c) of the federal Occupational Safety and Health Act requires employees who believe they have been retaliated against for filing complaints to complain to the Secretary of Labor. Upon investigation, the Secretary brings a lawsuit on the employee's behalf in federal district court.

Many whistleblowing statutes allow individual causes of action before courts. New York and Connecticut allow only reinstatement with back pay and attorney fees. Pennsylvania and Michigan allow employees to recover "actual" damages. New Jersey empowers courts to also award punitive damages or a civil fine payable to the state treasury.

7. *Warning vs. Asserting Rights.* Section 215(a)(3) of the Fair Labor Standards Act makes it unlawful for an employer to "discharge or in any other manner discriminate against any employee because such employee has filed any complaint ...." Suppose a personnel manager warns that the company is violating the FLSA by not paying certain employees proper overtime compensation. Top management, not liking the advice, fires her. Does the personnel manager have a claim under the FLSA?

In *McKenzie v. Renberg's Inc.*, 94 F.3d 1478 (10th Cir. 1996), the court rejected such a claim, finding that the personnel manager never crossed the line of an at-will employee doing her job to a person lodging a personal complaint. The court declared that to engage in protected activity under [the FLSA's retaliation provision], the employee must step outside his or her role of representing the company and either file (or threaten to file) an action adverse to the employer, actively assist other employees in asserting FLSA rights, or otherwise engage in activities that reasonably could be perceived as directed towards the assertion of rights protected by the FLSA.

Would the personnel manager have had greater success bringing a common law wrongful discharge action, or would she be barred as merely being an internal whistleblower?

8. *Supplanting Common Law.* What is the relationship between whistleblower statutes and common law wrongful discharge actions. Are state laws the exclusive remedy? Do federal statutes preempt common law actions? Must an employee elect remedies?

In *Shuttleworth v. Riverside Osteopathic Hosp.*, 477 N.W.2d 453 (Mich. Ct. App. 1991), the court held that the Michigan Whistleblower Protection Act provides the exclusive remedy for employees fired for reporting an employer's violation of the law. Thus, an employee who failed to file suit within the time limitations of the Act was barred from proceeding under a common law theory of wrongful discharge.

By contrast, in *English v. General Elec. Co.*, 496 U.S. 72 (1990), the Supreme Court held that the whistleblower protection provisions of the federal Energy Reorganization Act did not preempt a common law action for intentional infliction of emotional distress.

Finally, the New York whistleblower statute expressly preserves all available remedies, but provides that "the institution of an action ... shall be deemed a waiver of the rights and remedies available under any other contract, collective bargaining agreement, law, rule or regulation or under the common law." N.Y. LAB. LAW § 740(7).

JOHNSTON v. DEL MAR DISTRIBUTING CO.

Court of Appeals of Texas
776 S.W.2d 768 (1989)

Before NYE, C.J., and BENAVIDES and KENNEDY, JJ.

BENAVIDES, JUSTICE.

Nancy Johnston, appellant, brought suit against her employer, Del Mar Distributing Co., Inc., alleging that her employment had been wrongfully terminated. Del Mar filed a motion for summary judgment in the trial court alleging that appellant's pleadings failed to state a cause of action. After a hearing on the motion, the trial court agreed with Del Mar and granted its motion for summary judgment.

On appeal, appellant ... contends that her pleadings did in fact state a cause of action. We agree. Accordingly, we reverse and remand....

In her petition, appellant alleged that she was employed by Del Mar during the summer of 1987. As a part of her duties, she was required to prepare shipping documents for goods being sent from Del Mar's warehouse located in Corpus Christi, Texas to other cities in Texas. One day, Del Mar instructed appellant to package a semi-automatic weapon (for delivery to a grocery store in Brownsville, Texas) and to label the contents of the package as "fishing gear." Ultimately, the package was to be given to United Parcel Service for shipping. Appellant was required to sign her name to the shipping documents; therefore, she was concerned that her actions might be in violation of some firearm regulation or a regulation of the United Postal Service. Accordingly, she sought the advice of the United States Treasury Department Bureau of Alcohol, Tobacco & Firearms (hereinafter referred to as "the Bureau"). A few days after she contacted the Bureau, appellant was fired. Appellant brought suit for wrongful termination alleging that her employment was terminated solely in retaliation for contacting the Bureau.[3]

Good Grief!

In its motion for summary judgment, Del Mar stated that the facts alleged in appellant's petition would be taken as true. Specifically, it acknowledged that it required appellant to package and ship firearms with labels that did not reflect the package's true contents. It further acknowledged that appellant's employment was terminated when she became concerned about such practices and sought the "advice" of personnel employed by the Bureau.

Del Mar asserted in its motion that, notwithstanding the above described facts, appellant's cause of action was barred by the employment-at-will doctrine. Specifically, Del Mar asserted that since appellant's employment was for an indefinite amount of time, she was an employee-at-will and it had the absolute right to terminate her employment for any reason or no reason at all....

Recently, the Texas Supreme Court, recognizing the need to amend the employment-at-will doctrine, invoked its judicial authority to create a very narrow common law exception to the doctrine. *Sabine Pilot Service, Inc. v. Hauck,* 687 S.W.2d 733, 735 (Tex. 1985). In *Sabine Pilot,* the Texas Supreme Court was faced with a narrow issue for consideration, i.e., whether an allegation by an employee that he or she was discharged for refusing to perform an illegal act stated a cause of action. The Court held that

> public policy, *as expressed in the laws* of this state and the United States which *carry criminal penalties,* requires a very *narrow* exception to the employment-at-will doctrine ... [t]hat *narrow* exception covers *only* the discharge of an employee for the *sole* reason that the employee refused to perform an *illegal act. Id.* (emphasis ours).

---

[3] Appellant's petition can be construed as alleging that she was fired because (1) she inquired into whether her acts were illegal; and (2) she reported suspected violations to a regulatory agency (commonly referred to as "whistleblowing").

....

On appeal, appellant alleges that her petition did state a cause of action pursuant to the public policy exception announced in *Sabine Pilot*. In her brief, appellant contends that since Texas law currently provides that an employee has a cause of action when she is fired for refusing to perform an illegal act, it necessarily follows that an employee states a cause of action where she alleges that she is fired for simply inquiring into whether or not she is committing illegal acts. To hold otherwise, she argues, would have a chilling effect on the public policy exception announced in *Sabine Pilot*. We agree.

It is implicit that in order to refuse to do an illegal act, an employee must either know or suspect that the requested act is illegal. In some cases it will be patently obvious that the act is illegal (murder, robbery, theft, etc.); however, in other cases it may not be so apparent. Since ignorance of the law is no defense to a criminal prosecution, it is reasonable to expect that if an employee has a good faith belief that a required act might be illegal, she will try to find out whether the act is in fact illegal prior to deciding what course of action to take. If an employer is allowed to terminate the employee at this point, the public policy exception announced in *Sabine Pilot* would have little or no effect. To hold otherwise would force an employee, who suspects that a requested act might be illegal, to: (1) subject herself to possible discharge if she attempts to find out if the act is in fact illegal; or (2) remain ignorant, perform the act and, if it turns out to be illegal, face possible criminal sanctions.

We hold that since the law recognizes that it is against public policy to allow an employer to coerce its employee to commit a criminal act in furtherance of its own interest, then it is necessarily inferred that the same public policy prohibits the discharge of an employee who in good faith attempts to find out if the act is illegal. It is important to note that we are not creating a new exception to the employment-at-will doctrine. Rather, we are merely enforcing the narrow public policy exception which was created in *Sabine Pilot*.

Therefore, we find that the *Sabine Pilot* exception necessarily covers a situation where an employee has a good faith belief that her employer has requested her to perform an act which may subject her to criminal penalties. Public policy demands that she be allowed to investigate into whether such actions are legal so that she can determine what course of action to take (i.e., whether or not to perform the act).

Furthermore, it is the opinion of this Court that the question of whether or not the requested act was in fact illegal is irrelevant to the determination of this case. We hold that where a plaintiff's employment is terminated for attempting to find out from a regulatory agency if a requested act is illegal, it is not necessary to prove that the requested act was in fact illegal. A plaintiff must, however, establish that she had a good faith belief that the requested act might be illegal, and that such belief was reasonable. Accordingly, we sustain appellant's third and fourth points of error.

Del Mar also contends, for the first time on appeal, that this case involves a "whistleblower" fact situation because appellant was fired for reporting suspected illegal activity to a police agency.[4] Del Mar asks this Court not to create a "whistleblower" exception to the employment-at-will doctrine since neither the Legislature nor the Supreme Court has created such an exception. Del Mar cites Tex. R. Civ. Stat. Ann. art. 6252-16a, § 2 (Vernon Supp. 1989) in support of its position.

Article 6252-16a, § 2 provides that a governmental employee cannot be fired because she reports suspected illegal activity to a police agency. Del Mar argues that we must exercise judicial restraint since the Legislature had the opportunity to include employees of the private sector, but declined to do so.

It is well-settled in Texas that a motion for summary judgment shall state with specificity the grounds upon which the movant is relying. Any issues that are not specifically before the trial court at the hearing on the motion may not be considered for the first time on appeal.

Since, in the instant case, Del Mar did not specifically assert this issue in its motion for summary judgment, we will not consider it for the first time on appeal.[5]

The judgment of the trial court is reversed and remanded for trial.

NOTES

1. *Who Is a Whistleblower?* A fine line exists between an employee who merely seeks advice on whether she is committing an illegal act and an employee who reports the company's wrongdoing. Is it defensible to allow a wrongful discharge claim in the first case but not the second? Are the third-party effects likely to be any different in the two situations?

2. *Mistaken Whistleblowers.* Johnston was right on the facts, but wrong on the law. She knew what the company had done, but incorrectly thought it was illegal. Most whistleblower statutes, analogous to the *Johnston* case, protect whistleblowers who have a reasonable or good faith belief that the conduct was illegal. For example, Michigan protects reports of violations "unless the employee knows that the report is false." MICH. COMP. LAWS § 15.362. California protects disclosure where the employee "has reasonable cause to believe" a statute has been violated. CAL. LAB. CODE § 1102.5. Maine protects a "good faith" reporting of violations. ME. REV. STAT. ANN. tit. 26, § 833.

---

[4] In its motion for summary judgment, appellee did not make a distinction between an employee who seeks information concerning her own potential criminal activity and an employee who reports the suspected criminal activity of her employer.

[5] Nonetheless, we add that our holdings in the determination of appellant's points of error three and four are not to be construed as creating a whistleblower exception to the employment-at-will doctrine.

New York takes a harsher view, demanding that the company's actions in fact be illegal. *See Remba v. Federation Employment & Guidance Serv.*, 545 N.Y.S.2d 140 (N.Y. App. Div.), *aff'd*, 559 N.E.2d 655 (N.Y. 1989) (to be protected by New York's whistleblower statute, employee must show actual violation of law, as opposed to reasonable belief); *Kern v. DePaul Mental Health Servs.*, 529 N.Y.S.2d 265 (N.Y. Sup. Ct. 1988), *aff'd*, 152 A.D.2d 957 (1989) (employee belief that employer has violated the law is not sufficient).

What if the employee is right on the law but wrong on the facts — he thought the company was doing something that would have been illegal, but in fact the company did not do it? Should such an employee get protection? In *Schriner v. Meginnis Ford Co.*, 421 N.W.2d 755 (Neb. 1988), an auto salesman bought a used car with some 48,000 miles from his employer. When the car developed severe engine damage, the salesman checked with the county clerk's office and was "mistakenly" told that records showed the car had over 100,000 miles. When the salesman reported to the Attorney General's office that his employer might be illegally altering odometers, he was fired. Odometer fraud is a felony in Nebraska. The court recognized that a wrongful discharge action lies "when an at-will employee acts in good faith and upon reasonable cause in reporting his employer's suspected violation of the criminal code." *Id.* at 759. The court upheld summary judgment for the employer, however (two justices dissenting), because the employee had no evidence that the employer had changed the odometer. *This might be an important distinction*

3. Employees Who Don't Know the Law. Suppose a California truck driver is assigned a trailer which he thought could not be operated legally because it had expired registration papers for Illinois and an expired prorated vehicle tag for California. The employer gave the driver a letter stating it accepted complete responsibility for the lack of registration. Nevertheless, the truck driver refused to drive the trailer, was fired, and sued for wrongful discharge in violation of public policy. It was later discovered that an agreement between the two states gave a grace period before a proper California sticker had to be displayed. Therefore, although the employee thought that driving the trailer in this situation was illegal, he was mistaken. Does he have a valid wrongful discharge claim?

The Ninth Circuit faced this issue in *DeSoto v. Yellow Freight Sys., Inc.*, 957 F.2d 655 (9th Cir. 1992). No California case had squarely decided whether a mistaken employee could bring a wrongful discharge claim, but the Ninth Circuit predicted that California courts would deny the action. As the court put it, the employee "was not acting in defense of a public policy of the state of California, but incorrectly asserting his own interpretation of the law."

Additionally, the court noted that operating a trailer without proper registration papers does not implicate fundamental public policy concerns of safety, health or crime prevention. The court saw "the failure to carry registration papers simply as one of the '[m]any statutes [that] impose requirements whose fulfillment does not implicate fundamental public policy concerns,'" quoting *Foley v. Interactive Data Corp.*, 765 P.2d 373, 379 (Cal. 1988) (casebook *infra*).

Thus, even if the employee were correct, he might not have a wrongful discharge claim.

This debate over reasonable belief versus correctness mirrors the problem explored in the Notes following the *Pugh* case in Chapter 4. There, the question was whether the *employer* could fire an employee if it had a reasonable belief of employee wrongdoing, or whether the employer must be correct that the employee engaged in wrongdoing. Here, the focus is whether the *employee* has a tort claim when he or she was fired while acting in good faith, or whether the employee must be correct.

4. *Employers Who Don't Know the Facts*. Suppose an employer mistakenly thinks that an employee called the Occupational Safety and Health Administration or the Department of Labor's Wage and Hour Division to inquire about company violations. The employer fires the employee because of this, although in fact the employee never contacted the agencies. Does the employee have a claim under the anti-retaliation provisions of the statutes or under the common law tort of wrongful discharge in violation of public policy? *See Saffels v. Rice*, 40 F.3d 1546 (8th Cir. 1994) (yes to both claims).

B. INTENTIONAL INFLICTION OF EMOTIONAL DISTRESS

While wrongful discharge in violation of public policy is the most common tort claim an employee brings when fired, other torts are alleged in addition or as alternatives. The most important is the claim of intentional infliction of emotional distress.

In *Harless v. First National Bank*, 289 S.E.2d 692 (W. Va. 1982), the court considered the problem of overlapping torts when the employee suffers great upset when fired in violation of public policy. A bank officer was harassed and eventually fired for reporting to the bank's board of directors that his supervisor had illegally overcharged customers who prepaid loans. On his retaliatory discharge claim, the jury awarded compensatory damages of $20,000 against the bank and $5,000 against the supervisor, and the same amounts in punitive damages. On his intentional infliction of emotional distress claim, the jury awarded compensatory damages of $5,000 against the bank and $20,000 against the supervisor, and the same amounts in punitive damages. Upon review of the retaliatory discharge claim, the Supreme Court upheld the compensatory damage award but reversed the punitive damages award, holding that punitive damages could only be awarded for "wanton, willful or malicious conduct" not present in this case. The court then turned to the emotional distress award.

> The plaintiff's theory of the tort of outrageous conduct related to the same events that make up the retaliatory discharge claim.... The tort of retaliatory discharge differs from the tort of outrageous conduct in several fundamental

aspects. First, a retaliatory discharge begins with an employment relationship between the plaintiff and defendant. Second, the discharge is found actionable not because of any outrageous conduct on the part of the employer but because the discharge contravenes a substantial public policy right exercised by the employee.

On the other hand, a degree of congruency exists in the damages recoverable. We permit recovery for emotional distress arising from a retaliatory discharge which is the same type of injury that the tort of outrageous conduct is designed to cover. Courts have also permitted a recovery of punitive damages on a claim for outrageous conduct. As we have earlier pointed out, a claim for punitive damages may also be available in a retaliatory discharge claim if the defendant's conduct is sufficiently aggravated. In substance then the retaliatory discharge cause of action, depending on the facts, is sufficiently accommodating to include outrageous conduct such that there is no need to permit an independent cause of action for outrageous conduct in a retaliatory discharge case.[22]

In the present case, we do not find the conduct of the Bank or Wilson to have reached the level of outrageous conduct that would support a claim for the tort of outrage. Moreover, in this jurisdiction, a claim for the tort of outrageous conduct is duplicitous to a claim for retaliatory discharge. The damages are essentially the same under both claims since we recognize that if the employer's conduct is outrageous punitive damages may be recovered in a retaliatory discharge suit as well as compensatory damages including an award for emotional distress.

Id. at 705.

AGIS v. HOWARD JOHNSON CO.

Supreme Judicial Court of Massachusetts
355 N.E.2d 315 (1976)

Before REARDON, QUIRICO, BRAUCHER and WILKINS, JJ.

QUIRICO, JUSTICE.

This case raises the issue ... whether a cause of action exists in this Commonwealth for the intentional or reckless infliction of severe emotional distress without resulting bodily injury. Counts 1 and 2 of this action were brought by the plaintiff Debra Agis against the Howard Johnson Company and Roger Dionne, manager of the restaurant in which she was employed, to recover damages for mental anguish and emotional distress allegedly caused by her summary dismissal from such employment. Counts 3 and 4 were brought by her husband,

---

[22] There may be situations where the plaintiff has not been discharged or his termination of employment cannot be fitted into a retaliatory discharge cause of action, yet a cause of action will fall within the tort of outrageous conduct as against his employer.

James Agis, against both defendants for loss of the services, love, affection and companionship of his wife. This case is before us on the plaintiffs' appeal from the dismissal of their complaint.

Briefly, the allegations in the plaintiffs' complaint, which we accept as true for purposes of ruling on this motion, are the following. Debra Agis was employed by the Howard Johnson Company as a waitress in a restaurant known as the Ground Round. On or about May 23, 1975, the defendant Dionne notified all waitresses that a meeting would be held at 3 P.M. that day. At the meeting, he informed the waitresses that "there was some stealing going on," but that the identity of the person or persons responsible was not known, and that, until the person or persons responsible were discovered, he would begin firing all the present waitresses in alphabetical order, starting with the letter "A." Dionne then fired Debra Agis.

Yikes!

The complaint alleges that, as a result of this incident, Mrs. Agis became greatly upset, began to cry, sustained emotional distress, mental anguish, and loss of wages and earnings. It further alleges that the actions of the defendants were reckless, extreme, outrageous and intended to cause emotional distress and anguish. In addition, the complaint states that the defendants knew or should have known that their actions would cause such distress....

The most often cited argument for refusing to extend the cause of action for intentional or reckless infliction of emotional distress to cases where there has been no physical injury is the difficulty of proof and the danger of fraudulent or frivolous claims. There has been a concern that "mental anguish, standing alone, is too subtle and speculative to be measured by any known legal standard," that "mental anguish and its consequences are so intangible and peculiar and vary so much with the individual that they cannot reasonably be anticipated," that a wide door might "be opened not only to fictitious claims but to litigation over trivialities and mere bad manners as well," and that there can be no objective measurement of the extent or the existence of emotional distress. There is a fear that "[i]t is easy to assert a claim of mental anguish and very hard to disprove it." *See also* Magruder, Mental and Emotional Disturbance in the Law of Torts, 49 Harv. L. Rev. 1033 (1936); W. Prosser, Torts § 12 (4th ed. 1971).

Judicial concerns regarding the cause of action

While we are not unconcerned with these problems, we believe that "the problems presented are not ... insuperable" and that "administrative difficulties do not justify the denial of relief for serious invasions of mental and emotional tranquility ...." ...

Furthermore, the distinction between the difficulty which juries may encounter in determining liability and assessing damages where no physical injury occurs and their performance of that same task where there has been resulting physical harm may be greatly overstated. "The jury is ordinarily in a better position ... to determine whether outrageous conduct results in mental distress than whether that distress in turn results in physical injury. From their own experience jurors are aware of the extent and character of the disagreeable emotions that may

juries

result from the defendant's conduct, but a difficult medical question is presented when it must be determined if emotional distress resulted in physical injury.... Greater proof that mental suffering occurred is found in the defendant's conduct designed to bring it about than in physical injury that may or may not have resulted therefrom." *State Rubbish Collectors Ass'n v. Siliznoff,* 240 P.2d 282, 286 (Cal. 1952). We are thus unwilling to deny the existence of this cause of action merely because there may be difficulties of proof. Instead, we believe "the door to recovery should be opened but narrowly and with due caution." *Barnett v. Collection Serv. Co.,* 242 N.W. 25, 28 (Iowa 1932).

In light of what we have said, we hold that one who, by extreme and outrageous conduct and without privilege, causes severe emotional distress to another is subject to liability for such emotional distress even though no bodily harm may result. However, in order for a plaintiff to prevail in a case for liability under this tort, four elements must be established. It must be shown (1) that the actor intended to inflict emotional distress or that he knew or should have known that emotional distress was the likely result of his conduct, Restatement (Second) of Torts sec. 46, comment i (1965); (2) that the conduct was "extreme and outrageous," was "beyond all possible bounds of decency" and was "utterly intolerable in a civilized community," Restatement (Second) of Torts sec. 46, comment d (1965); (3) that the actions of the defendant were the cause of the plaintiff's distress; and (4) that the emotional distress sustained by the plaintiff was "severe" and of a nature "that no reasonable man could be expected to endure it." Restatement (Second) of Torts sec. 46, comment j (1965). These requirements are "aimed at limiting frivolous suits and avoiding litigation in situations where only bad manners and mere hurt feelings are involved," and we believe they are a "realistic safeguard against false claims ...."

Testing the plaintiff Debra Agis's complaint by the rules stated above, we hold that she makes out a cause of action and that her complaint is therefore legally sufficient. While many of her allegations are not particularly well stated, we believe that the "[p]laintiff has alleged facts and circumstances which reasonably could lead the trier of fact to conclude that defendant's conduct was extreme and outrageous, having a severe and traumatic effect upon plaintiff's emotional tranquility." Because reasonable men could differ on these issues, we believe that "it is for the jury, subject to the control of the court," to determine whether there should be liability in this case. While the judge was not in error in dismissing the complaint under the then state of the law, we believe that, in light of what we have said, the judgment must be reversed and the plaintiff Debra Agis must be given an opportunity to prove the allegations which she has made.

[The Court also held that Agis's husband stated a valid claim for loss of consortium as a result of the mental distress and anguish suffered by his wife Debra.]

The judgment entered in the Superior Court dismissing the plaintiffs' complaint is reversed.

NOTES

1. *Backdoor Wrongful Discharge Claims.* If Howard Johnson could have fired Agis — an at-will employee — for a good reason, bad reason, or no reason, why is her firing improper? Indeed, did not Howard Johnson have a business motivation — deterring theft — for the firing? Could Agis have a claim of wrongful discharge in violation of public policy? Does the intentional infliction of emotional distress claim address different or larger concerns, or is it simply a backdoor way to bring a wrongful discharge claim?

2. *Manner of Discharge Claims.* In some situations, at-will employees concede that they cannot challenge the fact of discharge, but complain about the manner of discharge. Is *Agis* such a case?

3. *Third-Party Effects.* Does the infliction of emotional distress hurt anyone besides the plaintiff? If not, the justification for allowing the tort cannot be to regulate third-party effects of contracts. Should the tort nevertheless be allowed? On what theory? Fundamental fairness? Inequality of bargaining power between the parties?

BODEWIG v. K-MART, INC.

Court of Appeals of Oregon
635 P.2d 657 (1981)

Before BUTTLER, P. J., JOSEPH, C. J., and WARREN, J.

BUTTLER, PRESIDING JUDGE.

In this tort action for outrageous conduct, plaintiff seeks damages against her former employer, K-Mart, and a K-Mart customer, Mrs. Golden. Both defendants moved for summary judgment, which the trial court granted. Plaintiff appeals from the resulting final judgments entered. We reverse and remand.

... On the evening of March 29, 1979, plaintiff was working as a part-time checker at K-Mart. Defendant Golden entered plaintiff's checkout lane and plaintiff began to ring up Golden's purchases on the cash register. When plaintiff called out the price on a package of curtains, Golden told plaintiff the price was incorrect because the curtains were on sale. Plaintiff called a domestics department clerk for a price check. That clerk told plaintiff the curtains in question were not on sale. Upon hearing this, Golden left her merchandise on plaintiff's counter and returned with the clerk to the domestics department to find the "sale" curtains.

After Golden left, plaintiff moved Golden's merchandise to the service counter, voided the register slip containing the partial listing of Golden's items and began to check out other customers. Three to ten minutes later, Golden returned to plaintiff's checkstand, where another customer was being served. Golden "looked around" that customer and asked what plaintiff had done with her money. When plaintiff replied, "What money?," Golden said that she had left four five-dollar bills on top of the merchandise she was purchasing before she left with the domestics clerk. Plaintiff told Golden she had not seen any money. Golden continued in a loud, abrupt voice to demand her money from plaintiff and caused a general commotion. Customers and store personnel in the area began to look on curiously.

The K-Mart manager, who had been observing the incident from a nearby service desk, walked over to plaintiff's counter. After a short discussion with Golden, he walked up to plaintiff, pulled out her jacket pockets, looked inside and found nothing. Then he, plaintiff and two or three other store employees conducted a general search of the area for the money. When this effort proved fruitless, the manager explained there was nothing more he could do except check out plaintiff's register. Golden said, "Well, do it." The manager and an assistant manager locked plaintiff's register and took the till and the register receipt to the cash cage. While the register was being checked, Golden continued to glare at plaintiff while plaintiff checked out customers at another register. The register balanced perfectly. When the manager so advised Golden, Golden replied that she still believed plaintiff took her money and continued to "cause commotion" and glare at plaintiff. A further general search of the surrounding area was conducted without success. Golden still would not leave; another employee was trying to calm her down.

The manager then told plaintiff to accompany a female assistant manager into the women's public restroom for the purpose of disrobing in order to prove to Golden that she did not have the money. As plaintiff and the assistant manager walked to the restroom, the manager asked Golden if she wanted to watch the search; Golden replied: "You had better believe I do, it is my money." In the restroom, plaintiff took off all her clothes except her underwear while Golden and the assistant manager watched closely. When plaintiff asked Golden if she needed to take off more, Golden replied that it was not necessary because she could see through plaintiff's underwear anyway.

Plaintiff put on her clothes and started to leave the restroom when the assistant manager asked Golden how much money she had in her purse. Golden replied that she did not know the exact amount, but thought she had between five and six hundred dollars. She did not attempt to count it at that time.

Plaintiff then returned to her checkstand. Golden followed plaintiff to the counter and continued to glare at her as she worked. Finally, the manager told Golden nothing more could be done for her, and after more loud protestations, Golden left the store.

Upon arriving home, Golden counted the money in her purse. She had $560. She called plaintiff's mother, whom she knew casually, and related the entire incident to her, stating that she had told K-Mart that plaintiff had taken her money. She described the strip search to plaintiff's mother and stated that when she was asked if she wanted to watch the strip, she responded, "Damn right." The mother expressed concern that plaintiff would lose her job; Golden said she would call the store and ask them not to let her go. Golden did make that call.

After the conversation with Golden, plaintiff's mother, father and sister went to K-Mart to see if plaintiff was all right and to take her home.

Plaintiff returned to work the next day and was told that the keys to the cash register were lost and she was to work on a register with another employee. That procedure is known as "piggy-backing," and plaintiff had been told three months earlier that the store would no longer "piggy-back" checkers. Plaintiff believed the store was monitoring her by the "piggy-back" procedure; she quit at the end of her scheduled shift that day....

K-Mart contends that the trial court properly granted its motion, because the facts presented do not constitute outrageous conduct as a matter of law. Its principal argument is that plaintiff consented to the strip search, either expressly as its manager stated, or tacitly by not expressly objecting. Plaintiff stated, variously, that she was told or asked by the manager to disrobe, but, whether asked or told, she did not consider that she had a choice. She thought she would lose her job if she refused, and she needed the job. The issue of lack of consent to that search is an issue of fact, but whether it is an issue of material fact depends upon whether, assuming plaintiff's version to be true, the facts are sufficient to submit the case to the jury on the outrageous conduct theory.

... There are at least two versions of the tort [of outrageous conduct]. One is represented by *Turman v. Central Billing Bureau,* 568 P.2d 1382 (Or. 1977), and involves intentional conduct, the very purpose of which is to inflict psychological and emotional distress on the plaintiff. The other is represented by *Rockhill v. Pollard,* 485 P.2d 28 (Or. 1971), where the wrongful purpose was lacking, but "the tortious element can be found in the breach of some obligation, statutory or otherwise, that attaches to defendant's relationship to plaintiff ...." 600 P.2d 398....

Neither the Supreme Court nor this court has been presented with the question of whether the employer-employee relationship falls into that special category. This court, however, has treated the landlord-tenant relationship as a "prime consideration" in evaluating the defendant's conduct. We reached that conclusion because landlords were in a position of authority with respect to tenants and could affect the tenants' interest in the quiet enjoyment of their leasehold. An employer has even more authority over an employee, who, by the nature of the relationship, is subject to the direction and control of the employer and may be discharged for any or no reason, absent an agreement restricting that authority. Clearly, that relationship is not an arm's length one between strangers. Accordingly, we conclude that the relationship between plaintiff and K-Mart was a special relationship, based on which liability may be imposed if K-Mart's conduct, though not deliberately aimed at causing emotional distress, was such that a jury might find it to be beyond the limits of social toleration and reckless of the conduct's predictable effects on plaintiff.

We conclude that a jury could find that the K-Mart manager, a 32-year-old male in charge of the entire store, after concluding that plaintiff did not take the customer's money, put her through the degrading and humiliating experience of submitting to a strip search in order to satisfy the customer, who was not only acting unreasonably, but was creating a commotion in the store; that the manager's conduct exceeded the bounds of social toleration and was in reckless disregard of its predictable effects on plaintiff.

Because there was no special relationship between plaintiff and Golden, the evidence must be such that a jury could find Golden's conduct not only socially intolerable, but that it was deliberately aimed at causing plaintiff emotional distress. Golden contends the evidence does not permit those findings, because she was merely trying to get her money back from plaintiff. To sustain that position, it would be necessary to resolve the disputed facts relating to Golden's conduct in her favor. As in the case against K-Mart, those factual issues are material only if, after resolving them in plaintiff's favor, the evidence would permit a jury to find for plaintiff.

We conclude that the facts, viewed most favorably to plaintiff, would permit a jury to find that Golden's entire course of conduct was intended to embarrass and humiliate plaintiff in order to coerce her into giving Golden $20, whether rightfully hers or not; that Golden did not know how much money she had in her purse, variously stated to be between $300 and $600, made no effort to determine if she was, in fact, missing four five dollar bills until she returned home, at which time she found she was mistaken; that Golden's insistence on a check of plaintiff's cash register, her insistence that plaintiff still had her money after the register checked out perfectly, her eager participation in the strip search of plaintiff and her continuing to stare angrily at plaintiff over an extended period, even after all efforts to find her money failed, would permit a jury to find Golden's conduct deliberately calculated to cause plaintiff emotional distress and exceeded the bounds of social toleration.

A jury could also find in Golden's favor, but the mere fact that her stated ultimate objective was to get her money back is not sufficient to defeat plaintiff's claim.... There are lawful (socially tolerable) ways to collect money from another, and there are unlawful (socially intolerable) ways to do so.

Common to her claims against both defendants is the requirement that plaintiff prove that she suffered severe emotional distress. If the facts presented are believed, plaintiff suffered shock, humiliation and embarrassment, suffering that was not merely transient. Plaintiff characterized herself as a shy, modest person, and said that she had two or three sleepless nights, cried a lot and still gets nervous and upset when she thinks about the incident. Concededly, this element of the tort has been, and still is, troublesome to courts. K-Mart contends there is no objective evidence of the distress, such as medical, economic or social problems. In *Rockhill v. Pollard, supra,* plaintiff became nervous and suffered from sleeplessness and a loss of appetite over a period of about two years. The court said:

"... Defendant belittles these symptoms, but it is the distress which must be severe, not the physical manifestations...." 485 P.2d 28.

Defendant Golden contends that the purpose of requiring proof of severe emotional distress is to guard against fraudulent or frivolous claims and that some degree of transient and trivial distress is a part of the price of living among people. Here, however, it is not unreasonable to expect that a shy, modest, young woman put in plaintiff's position would suffer the effects she claims to have suffered from the incident, and that her distress was more than that which a person might be reasonably expected to pay as the price of living among people.

We cannot say as a matter of law that plaintiff's evidence of severe emotional distress is insufficient to go to a jury. Because neither defendant was entitled to judgment as a matter of law, neither motion for summary judgment should have been granted.

The judgment for each of the defendants is reversed. The case is remanded for trial.

NOTES

1. *The Special Relationship Test.* The court in *Bodewig* emphasizes that employers are in a position of authority over employees. Why does this fact support liability for emotional distress that was not purposeful? Is it that employees have less ability to end an abusive relationship with the employer than they would with a stranger who attempts to abuse them? Or is it because the employer is in a better position than are other defendants to know that the employee is particularly vulnerable to harsh conduct? In this case, for example, was the manager in a better position than was the customer to know the employee was shy and modest? In *Rhodes v. Sun Elec. Corp.,* 121 L.R.R.M. (BNA) 2203 (N.D. Ill. 1985), a corporate manager of legal affairs was accused of theft and eventually fired. The court refused to dismiss her claim of intentional infliction of emotional distress, emphasizing that the employer had special knowledge that the employee was in a weakened emotional and physical state because she had undergone major surgery and was involved in a contested divorce.

2. *Outrageousness in the Workplace.* Most reported decisions deny employees' claims of intentional infliction of emotional distress. In doing so, courts often follow the RESTATEMENT (SECOND) OF TORTS § 46, comment d, in defining the requisite standard. The defendant's conduct must be

> so outrageous in character, and so extreme in degree, as to go beyond all possible bounds of decency, and to be regarded as atrocious, and utterly intolerable in a civilized community. Generally, the case is one in which the recitation of the facts to an average member of the community would arouse his resentment against the actor, and lead him to exclaim, "Outrageous!"

> The liability clearly does not extend to mere insults, indignities, threats, annoyances, petty oppressions, or other trivialities. The rough edges of our society are still in need of a good deal of filing down, and in the meantime plaintiffs must necessarily be expected and required to be hardened to a certain amount of rough language.

The Restatement would allow recovery for gross insults not amounting to extreme outrage only when there is a special relation between the parties. The Restatement recognizes a special relation between public utilities and their customers, and perhaps between landowners and their business or other invitees.

3. *Special or Harsh Relationship.* Court treatment of workplace claims of intentional infliction of emotional distress can be unpredictable. In *Kentucky Fried Chicken National Management Co. v. Weathersby,* 607 A.2d 8 (Md. 1992), the Maryland Court of Appeals affirmed a judgment notwithstanding the verdict after a jury had ruled for the plaintiff in a suit for intentional infliction of emotional distress. The plaintiff was harassed by her supervisor and suspended in front of customers and employees and told that she was being investigated for missing money, and was later demoted to a position under a person she once supervised at a salary cut of $11,000. The plaintiff was eventually hospitalized and was unable to return to work. The court found that this treatment did not satisfy the level of "outrageous conduct" required for the tort. Judge Bell, in dissent, warned that the decision signaled the end of the tort of emotional distress in the workplace:

> The message that comes through in the case, and, I believe, is intended, is that the tort of intentional infliction of emotional distress does not exist in the employer-employee context; the limitations the majority places on the tort are such that it is virtually inconceivable that any employment case will ever qualify.

The Oklahoma Supreme Court conveyed the same skepticism about emotional distress employment claims when it declared that "[t]he salon of Madame Pompadour is not to be likened to the rough-and-tumble atmosphere of the American oil refinery." *Eddy v. Brown,* 715 P.2d 74, 77 (Okla. 1986).

A contrasting case is a Fifth Circuit decision upholding a $3.4 million jury award to an employee for intentional infliction of emotional distress and age discrimination. In *Wilson v. Monarch,* 939 F.2d 1138 (5th Cir. 1991) (applying Texas law), a sixty-year-old vice president was demoted to an entry-level warehouse supervisor with menial and demeaning duties, including sweeping up and cleaning the warehouse cafeteria. This treatment eventually caused the plaintiff to be involuntarily hospitalized with a psychotic manic episode. While the Fifth Circuit expressed "real concern about the consequences of applying the cause of action of intentional infliction of emotional distress to the workplace," it found that the defendant's conduct was "so outrageous that civilized society should not tolerate it." The irresistible questions from Professor Alan Hyde are: who swept up and cleaned the cafeteria before Wilson? Was that intentional infliction of emotional distress? Or does this doctrine, too, only protect senior employees at *Give me a break,* the end of their life cycle who are precipitously demoted — perhaps because their productivity has declined?

4. *Is Minor Abuse Justifiable?* Professor Regina Austin has criticized the Restatement standard for minimizing the seriousness of the abuse that workers — particularly minority or female workers — face in the workplace.

> The approach mandated by Section 46 immediately focuses on whether the employer's or supervisor's coercion was excessive and skips the threshold issue of whether any amount of emotional mistreatment was justified. In this regard, it differs from the 1948 version of the section which required that the defendant show that abuse of the plaintiff was privileged. The legal analysis required by the current version of Section 46 thus allows courts to avoid elaborate explanations for their decisions. Beginning with the assumption that some amount of intentionally inflicted pain is acceptable, they need not and often do not go much beyond quoting the comments to Section 46 and offering several conclusory sentences sprinkled with *Restatement* terminology....
>
> The gist of the story the courts tell about abuse in the workplace can be summarized as follows: Only the extraordinary, the excessive, and the nearly bizarre in the way of supervisory intimidation and humiliation warrant judicial relief through the tort of intentional infliction of emotional distress. All other forms of supervisory conduct that cause workers to experience emotional harm are more or less "trivial" in the terminology of the *Restatement of Torts*. The very ordinariness of such conduct and the ubiquity of the experience of pain at the hands of supervisors are justification enough for the law's refusal to intervene. At the same time, the genesis of the problem makes it largely inescapable. Little can be done about the vagaries of human nature. Moreover, the efficient operation of the workplace depends on employers' having broad privileges with regard to discipline and control of the work force. Thus, abuse is a predicament that is not susceptible to, let alone demanding of, a more thoroughgoing legal remedy.
>
> Rather, the solution lies principally in individual workers shrugging off petty insults. Worker self-reliance and stamina are repeatedly touted in the outrage cases. Courts see toughness and strength as such positive attributes that they simply assume that the capacity to tolerate abuse, and the propriety of dishing it out, vary with the nature of the work, the workplace, and the characteristics of the workers. Males and blue-collar workers, for example, may be subjected to harsher supervision than females or white-collar workers because of the acceptability of sex and class distinctions and the implications of group pride that underlie the disparate treatment.

....

Workers would agree with the law's assessment that supervisory abuse is an ordinary, everyday occurrence in the workplace. They would, however, part company with the courts and commentators when the latter argue that it is so mundane and commonplace that it should escape severe censure. On the contrary, from the workers' perspective, the frequency with which they encounter supervisory mistreatment means that it cannot be warranted or justified in the way the law and the conventional wisdom assert.

Among workers, there is widespread condemnation of close, coercive supervision. It is not acceptable behavior. The hostility to this sort of abusive authority is manifested in the words and actions of workers performing disparate jobs, in disparate workplaces....

... [A]buse can be objectionable to workers because it does not reflect objective assessments of their productivity. Whereas the law assumes that abuse is utilized because workers are not contributing to the enterprise as they should be, workers view abuse as a calculated devaluation of themselves and their work. For example, the clerical employees interviewed by Roberta Goldberg for her book *Organizing Women Office Workers* [1983] objected to the close supervision of their work and time away from their desks because it indicated that they were not trusted. They also complained about low pay because it meant that their work was considered trivial and unimportant. They resented the demeaning terms (like "girl" and "honey") others used in referring to them. They especially objected to being asked to do "menial" domestic chores because it meant that their employers did not take them seriously with regard to the tasks they were hired to perform.

....

Minority and female employees have reason to suspect that the disparagement and mistreatment they receive on the job is motivated by racial prejudice and sexist animosity, not merely by a concern for productivity and profits or by individualized assessments of merit. The young black men investigated by Elijah Anderson for his essay, *Some Observations of Black Youth Employment* [1980], indicated that they were especially oppressed by the distrust and suspicion which pervaded their working environments. Their supervisors and co-workers watched them closely to see if they displayed the inadequacies of the blacks who had preceded them and to prevent them from stealing. Anderson reports that

> it is not uncommon for many black workers to be treated as outsiders ... even though they have been working on the job for a long time. Among black workers who face such problems on a common job, a standing phrase is the "can I help you?" routine.... "When a black arrives at work, some white employee is ready with 'can I help you?'" The blacks interpret this question as a "nice" way of saying "what business do you have here?" ... It appears to be a device of someone who is very concerned about

outsiders committing a crime on the work premises. To be black and young is to be suspect. Black youth understand the nuance here, and they joke about such slights during lunch or breaks. They often gather together on the job for purposes of social defense, telling "horror stories" and communing in what they see as a hostile social and work environment.

The exclusionary treatment about which these workers complain is, of course, not the sort of overt discriminatory behavior that the tort of outrage reaches.

Regina Austin, *Employer Abuse, Worker Resistance, and the Tort of Intentional Infliction of Emotional Distress,* 41 STAN. L. REV. 1, 7, 18, 21-24 (1988).[*]

Chapter 6

GOOD FAITH LIMITATIONS ON EMPLOYMENT AT WILL

FORTUNE v. NATIONAL CASH REGISTER CO.

Supreme Judicial Court of Massachusetts
364 N.E.2d 1251 (1977)

Before HENNESSEY, C. J., and KAPLAN, WILKINS, LIACOS and ABRAMS, JJ.

ABRAMS, JUSTICE.

Orville E. Fortune (Fortune), a former salesman of The National Cash Register Company (NCR), brought a suit to recover certain commissions allegedly due as a result of a sale of cash registers to First National Stores Inc. (First National) in 1968. Counts 1 and 2 of Fortune's amended declaration claimed bonus payments under the parties' written contract of employment. The third count sought recovery in quantum meruit for the reasonable value of Fortune's services relating to the same sales transaction. Judgment on a jury verdict for Fortune was reversed by the Appeals Court, and this court granted leave to obtain further appellate review. We affirm the judgment of the Superior Court. We hold, for the reasons stated herein, there was no error in submitting the issue of "bad faith" termination of an employment at will contract to the jury.

The issues before the court are raised by NCR's motion for directed verdicts. Accordingly, we summarize the evidence most favorable to the plaintiff.

Fortune was employed by NCR under a written "salesman's contract" which was terminable at will, without cause, by either party on written notice. The contract provided that Fortune would receive a weekly salary in a fixed amount plus a bonus for sales made within the "territory" (i.e., customer accounts or stores) assigned to him for "coverage or supervision," whether the sale was made by him or someone else.[2] The amount of the bonus was determined on the basis of "bonus credits," which were computed as a percentage of the price of products sold. Fortune would be paid a percentage of the applicable bonus credit as follows: (1) 75% if the territory was assigned to him at the date of the order, (2) 25% if the territory was assigned to him at the date of delivery and installation, or (3) 100% if the territory was assigned to him at both times. The contract further provided that the "bonus interest" would terminate if shipment of the order was not made within eighteen months from the date of the order unless (1) the territory was assigned to him for coverage at the date of delivery and installation, or (2) special engineering was required to fulfill the contract. In

---

[2] Apparently, NCR's use of a "guaranteed territory" was designed to motivate "the salesman to develop good will for the company and also avoided a damaging rivalry among salesmen."

addition, NCR reserved the right to sell products in the salesman's territory without paying a bonus. However, this right could be exercised only on written notice.

In 1968, Fortune's territory included First National. This account had been part of his territory for the preceding six years; he had been successful in obtaining several orders from First National, including a million dollar order in 1963. Sometime in late 1967, or early 1968, NCR introduced a new model cash register, Class 5. Fortune corresponded with First National in an effort to sell the machine. He also helped to arrange for a demonstration of the Class 5 to executives of First National on October 4, 1968. NCR had a team of men also working on this sale.

... On November 29, 1968, First National signed an order for 2,008 Class 5 machines to be delivered over a four-year period at a purchase price of approximately $5,000,000. Although Fortune did not participate in the negotiation of the terms of the order, his name appeared on the order form in the space entitled "salesman credited." The amount of the bonus credit as shown on the order was $92,079.99.

On January 6, 1969, the first working day of the new year, Fortune found an envelope on his desk at work. It contained a termination notice addressed to his home dated December 2, 1968. Shortly after receiving the notice, Fortune spoke to the Boston branch manager with whom he was friendly. The manager told him, "You are through," but, after considering some of the details necessary for the smooth operation of the First National order, told him to "stay on," and to "(k)eep on doing what you are doing right now." Fortune remained with the company in a position entitled "sales support." In this capacity, he coordinated and expedited delivery of the machines to First National under the November 29 order as well as servicing other accounts.

Commencing in May or June, Fortune began to receive some bonus commissions on the First National order. Having received only 75% of the applicable bonus due on the machines which had been delivered and installed, Fortune spoke with his manager about receiving the full amount of the commission. Fortune was told "to forget about it." Sixty-one years old at that time, and with a son in college, Fortune concluded that it "was a good idea to forget it for the time being."

NCR did pay a systems and installations person the remaining 25% of the bonus commissions due from the First National order although contrary to its usual policy of paying *only* salesmen a bonus....

Approximately eighteen months after receiving the termination notice, Fortune, who had worked for NCR for almost twenty-five years, was asked to retire. When he refused, he was fired in June of 1970. Fortune did not receive any bonus payments on machines which were delivered to First National after this date.

At the close of the plaintiff's case, the defendant moved for a directed verdict, arguing that there was no evidence of any breach of contract, and adding that the existence of a contract barred recovery under the quantum meruit count. Ruling that Fortune could recover if the termination and firing were in bad faith, the trial judge, without specifying on which count, submitted this issue to the jury. NCR then rested and, by agreement of counsel, the case was sent to the jury for special verdicts on two questions:

> "1. Did the Defendant act in bad faith ... when it decided to terminate the Plaintiff's contract as a salesman by letter dated December 2, 1968, delivered on January 6, 1969?
> "2. Did the Defendant act in bad faith ... when the Defendant let the Plaintiff go on June 5, 1970?"

The jury answered both questions affirmatively, and judgment entered in the sum of $45,649.62.

The central issue on appeal is whether this "bad faith" termination constituted a breach of the employment at will contract. Traditionally, an employment contract which is "at will" may be terminated by either side without reason....

The contract at issue is a classic terminable at will employment contract. It is clear that the contract itself reserved to the parties an explicit power to terminate the contract without cause on written notice. It is also clear that under the express terms of the contract Fortune has received all the bonus commissions to which he is entitled. Thus, NCR claims that it did not breach the contract, and that it has no further liability to Fortune.[7] According to a literal reading of the contract, NCR is correct.

However, Fortune argues that, in spite of the literal wording of the contract, he is entitled to a jury determination on NCR's motives in terminating his services under the contract and in finally discharging him. We agree. We hold that NCR's written contract contains an implied covenant of good faith and fair dealing, and a termination not made in good faith constitutes a breach of the contract.

We do not question the general principles that an employer is entitled to be motivated by and to serve its own legitimate business interests; that an employer must have wide latitude in deciding whom it will employ in the face of the uncertainties of the business world; and that an employer needs flexibility in the face of changing circumstances. We recognize the employer's need for a large amount of control over its work force. However, we believe that where, as here, commissions are to be paid for work performed by the employee, the employer's decision to terminate its at will employee should be made in good faith, NCR's right to make decisions in its own interest is not, in our view, unduly hampered by a requirement of adherence to this standard. On occasion some courts have

---

[7] Damages were, by stipulation of the parties, set equal to the unpaid bonus amounts. Thus we need not consider whether other measures of damages might be justified in cases of bad faith termination. Nor do we now decide whether a tort action, with possible punitive damages, might lie in such circumstances. *See, e.g.,* Blades, *Employment at Will vs. Individual Freedom: On Limiting the Abusive Exercise of Employer Power,* 67 Colum. L. Rev. 1404, 1421-1427 (1967).

Some courts use tort; this court uses contract

avoided the rigidity of the "at will" rule by fashioning a remedy in tort.[8] We believe, however, that in this case there is remedy on the express contract.[9] In so holding we are merely recognizing the general requirement in this Commonwealth that parties to contracts and commercial transactions must act in good faith toward one another. Good faith and fair dealing between parties are pervasive requirements in our law; it can be said fairly, that parties to contracts or commercial transactions are bound by this standard. *See* G.L. c. 106, § 1-203 (good faith in contracts under Uniform Commercial Code); G.L. c. 93B, § 4(3)(c) (good faith in motor vehicle franchise termination)....

Recent decisions in other jurisdictions lend support to the proposition that good faith is implied in contracts terminable at will. In a recent employment at will case, *Monge v. Beebe Rubber Co.*, 316 A.2d 549, 552 (N.H. 1974), the plaintiff alleged that her oral contract of employment had been terminated because she refused to date her foreman. The New Hampshire Supreme Court held that "(i)n all employment contracts, whether at will or for a definite term, the employer's interest in running his business as he sees fit must be balanced against the interest of the employee in maintaining his employment, and the public's interest in maintaining a proper balance between the two.... We hold that a termination by the employer of a contract of employment at will which is motivated by bad faith or malice ... constitutes a breach of the employment contract.... Such a rule affords the employee a certain stability of employment and does not interfere with the employer's normal exercise of his right to discharge, which is necessary to permit him to operate his business efficiently and profitably."

We believe that the holding in the *Monge* case merely extends to employment contracts the rule that "'in *every* contract there is an implied covenant that neither party shall do anything which will have the effect of destroying or injuring the right of the other party to receive the fruits of the contract, which means that in *every* contract there exists an implied covenant of good faith and fair dealing.'"

In the instant case, we need not pronounce our adherence to so broad a policy nor need we speculate as to whether the good faith requirement is implicit in every contract for employment at will. It is clear, however, that, on the facts

---

[8] This theory has generally been utilized in order to protect public policy. *See, e.g., Montalvo v. Zamora*, 86 Cal. Rptr. 401 (Cal. Ct. App. 1970) (employee terminated after having an attorney to negotiate a claim that the employer had violated the minimum wage law); *Petermann v. International Bhd. of Teamsters, Local 396*, 344 P.2d 25 (Cal. Ct. App. 1959) (employee discharged for refusing to commit perjury before government commission); *Frampton v. Central Ind. Gas Co.*, 297 N.E.2d 425 (Ind. 1973) (employee fired for filing a workman's compensation claim); *Nees v. Hocks*, 536 P.2d 512 (Or. 1975) (employee fired for performing jury duty in violation of company policy). *Cf. Geary v. United States Steel Corp.*, 319 A.2d 174 (Pa. 1974) (tort remedy not available where employee fired for not following corporate hierarchy procedure in protesting company policy as to safety of a product).

[9] Thus, we do not reach the issues raised by count 3 for quantum meruit recovery.

before us, a finding is warranted that a breach of the contract occurred. Where the principal seeks to deprive the agent of all compensation by terminating the contractual relationship when the agent is on the brink of successfully completing the sale, the principal has acted in bad faith and the ensuing transaction between the principal and the buyer is to be regarded as having been accomplished by the agent. Restatement (Second) of Agency § 454, and Comment a (1958). The same result obtains where the principal attempts to deprive the agent of any portion of a commission due the agent. Courts have often applied this rule to prevent overreaching by employers and the forfeiture by employees of benefits almost earned by the rendering of substantial services. In our view, the Appeals Court erroneously focused only on literal compliance with payment provisions of the contract and failed to consider the issue of bad faith termination.

NCR argues that there was no evidence of bad faith in this case; therefore, the trial judge was required to direct a verdict in any event. We think that the evidence and the reasonable inferences to be drawn therefrom support a jury verdict that the termination of Fortune's twenty-five years of employment as a salesman with NCR the next business day after NCR obtained a $5,000,000 order from First National was motivated by a desire to pay Fortune as little of the bonus credit as it could. The fact that Fortune was willing to work under these circumstances does not constitute a waiver or estoppel; it only shows that NCR had him "at their mercy."

NCR also contends that Fortune cannot complain of his firing in June, 1970, as his employment contract clearly indicated that bonus credits would be paid only for an eighteen-month period following the date of the order. As we have said, the jury could have found that Fortune was stripped of his "salesman" designation in order to disqualify him for the remaining 25% of the commissions due on cash registers delivered prior to the date of his first termination. Similarly, the jury could have found that Fortune was fired so that NCR would avoid paying him any commissions on cash registers delivered after June, 1970....

We think that NCR's conduct in June, 1970 permitted the jury to find bad faith....

Judgment of the Superior Court affirmed.

NOTES

1. ***What Is Good Faith?*** A supervisor fired a nurse for not following an order that was never given. After the firing the supervisor altered the duty sheet to insert a fictitious assignment to justify the discharge. Would these facts support a claim that the employer had discharged the worker in bad faith? *See Hinson v. Cameron,* 742 P.2d 549 (Okla. 1987) (no).

2. Good Faith and Sick Pay. Suppose an employment contract allows employees to accrue sick pay at a rate of one day per month. An office manager at a seven-employee firm was hospitalized for major surgery and took eight weeks' sick pay, which was far more than any employee had ever taken but was within the contract limits. The company, faced with a hardship from the extended absence, terminated her and replaced her with another employee. Did the company violate the covenant of good faith and fair dealing? *See Metcalf v. Intermountain Gas Co.,* 778 P.2d 744 (Idaho 1989) (yes).

3. Good Faith and Public Policy. Footnote 8 of the court's opinion suggests a close relationship between breach of the implied covenant of good faith and fair dealing, and tortious discharge in violation of public policy. Is there a distinction between the cases cited in footnote 8 and *Fortune?* One justification for interfering with private contracts occurs when the parties to the bargain do not consider all the costs of their actions. Arguably, each of the cases in footnote 8 has third-party effects. Are there third-party effects if the court literally enforces the *Fortune* contract?

4. Gap-Filling. Another role of courts in contract cases is to fill the gaps in contracts. A common method for filling a gap is to insert the term that most parties would want, so that most parties can avoid the costs of bargaining for and enforcing the term. Is U.C.C. § 1-203, which implies good faith in all commercial transactions, relevant here? Assuming that most parties to an employment contract prefer employment at will, would they want a good faith clause as well? Or is good faith inconsistent with employment at will?

5. Good Faith and Just Cause. What is the meaning of good faith and fair dealing? In general commercial litigation, the covenant often means that one party cannot deprive the other party of the benefit of the bargain. In the employment context, the covenant has been applied to prohibit an employer from firing an employee shortly before a pension vests. Can the covenant be applied expansively to mean that the employer must have just cause to fire an employee, or is it concerned more with the timing of arbitrary firings?

6. NCR's Motivation. Did NCR have a financial motive in discharging Fortune? On the facts, did denying Fortune his commission increase NCR's profit? Consider Professor Epstein's analysis of the case:

The decision seems wrong in principle. The contractual provisions concerning commissions represent a rough effort to match payment with performance where the labor of more than one individual was necessary to close the sale. The case is not simply one where a strategically timed firing allowed the company to deprive a dismissed employee of the benefits due him upon completion of performance. Indeed, the firm kept none of the commission at all, so that when the case went to the jury, the only issue was whether the company should be called upon to pay the same commission twice. The court in *Fortune* did not try to understand the commission structure that it was prepared to condemn; instead, it made the chronic mistake of thinking that what it intuited to be an unfortunate business outcome invalidated the entire contractual structure. In its enthusiastic meddling in private contracts, the court nowhere suggested an alternative commission structure that would have better served the joint interests of the parties at the time of contract formation. Here, as in so many cases, an unquestioning adherence to the principle of freedom of contract would have yielded results both simpler and superior to those generated after an extensive but flawed judicial examination of the basic terms.

Richard A. Epstein, *In Defense of the Contract at Will,* 51 U. CHI. L. REV. 947, 981-82 (1984).[*] Does Epstein's critique suggest that the courts should never imply a covenant of fair dealing in employment contracts, or simply that the court in *Fortune* misconstrued the covenant?

7. *Opportunism and Reputations.* In *Jordan v. Duff & Phelps, Inc.,* 815 F.2d 429 (7th Cir. 1987), an at-will employee of a close corporation resigned and sold his stock back to the company for book value as required under his compensation plan. The company's chairman accepted his resignation without telling him of a possible merger that would increase his shares' value from $23,000 to over $600,000. When Jordan learned of the merger, he filed a 10b-5 action alleging fraud in the purchase of corporate securities. The majority opinion by Judge Easterbrook reversed a summary judgment for the employer, distinguishing between an employer who is "thoughtless, nasty, and mistaken" from one who engages in "[a]vowedly opportunistic conduct." In his opinion Judge Easterbrook gave a hypothetical variation of the facts: Suppose the employer sent a note to the employee, saying:

> There will be a lucrative merger tomorrow. You have been a wonderful employee, but in order to keep the proceeds of the merger for ourselves, we are letting you go, effective this instant. Here is the $23,000 for your shares.

Judge Easterbrook said the court did not "suppose for a second" that the firm could fire an employee for this reason. Judge Posner, in dissent, noted that "the possibility that corporations will exploit their junior executives ... may well be the least urgent problem facing our nation." Judge Posner argued that junior executives would rather rely on their employer's good will and interest in reputation, and on their own bargaining power, than "pay for contract rights that are difficult and costly to enforce."

[*]Reprinted with permission of the University of Chicago Law Review.

MURPHY v. AMERICAN HOME PRODUCTS CORP.

Court of Appeals of New York
448 N.E.2d 86 (1983)

JONES, JUDGE.

This court has not and does not now recognize a cause of action in tort for abusive or wrongful discharge of an employee; such recognition must await action of the Legislature. Nor does the complaint here state a cause of action for intentional infliction of emotional distress, for prima facie tort, or for breach of contract. These causes of action were, therefore, properly dismissed. Appellant's cause of action based on his claim of age discrimination, however, should be reinstated.

Plaintiff, Joseph Murphy, was first employed by defendant, American Home Products Corp., in 1957. He thereafter served in various accounting positions, eventually attaining the office of assistant treasurer, but he never had a formal contract of employment. On April 18, 1980, when he was 59 years old, he was discharged.

Plaintiff claims that he was fired for two reasons: because of his disclosure to top management of alleged accounting improprieties on the part of corporate personnel and because of his age. As to the first ground, plaintiff asserts that his firing was in retaliation for his revelation to officers and directors of defendant corporation that he had uncovered at least $50 million in illegal account manipulations of secret pension reserves which improperly inflated the company's growth in income and allowed high-ranking officers to reap unwarranted bonuses from a management incentive plan, as well as in retaliation for his own refusal to engage in the alleged accounting improprieties. He contends that the company's internal regulations required him to make the disclosure that he did. He also alleges that his termination was carried out in a humiliating manner....

The complaint set up four causes of action. As his first cause of action, plaintiff alleged that his discharge "was wrongful, malicious and in bad faith" and that defendant was bound "not to dismiss its employees for reasons that are contrary to public policy." In his second cause of action, plaintiff claimed that his dismissal "was intended to and did cause plaintiff severe mental and emotional distress thereby damaging plaintiff." His third claim was based on an allegation that the manner of his termination "was deliberately and viciously insulting, was designed to and did embarrass and humiliate plaintiff and was intended to and did cause plaintiff severe mental and emotional distress thereby damaging plaintiff." In his fourth cause of action, plaintiff asserted that, although his employment contract was of indefinite duration, the law imposes in every employment contract "the requirement that an employer shall deal with each employee fairly and in good faith." On that predicate he alleged that defendant's conduct in stalling his advancement and ultimately firing him for his disclosures "breached the terms of its contract requiring good faith and fair dealing toward plaintiff and damaged plaintiff thereby." Plaintiff demanded compensatory and punitive damages.

With respect to his first cause of action, plaintiff urges that the time has come when the courts of New York should recognize the tort of abusive or wrongful discharge of an at-will employee. To do so would alter our long-settled rule that where an employment is for an indefinite term it is presumed to be a hiring at will which may be freely terminated by either party at any time for any reason or even for no reason. Plaintiff argues that a trend has emerged in the courts of other States to temper what is perceived as the unfairness of the traditional rule by allowing a cause of action in tort to redress abusive discharges. He accurately points out that this tort has elsewhere been recognized to hold employers liable for dismissal of employees in retaliation for employee conduct that is protected by public policy.... Plaintiff would have this court adopt this emerging view. We decline his invitation, being of the opinion that such a significant change in our law is best left to the Legislature.

Those jurisdictions that have modified the traditional at-will rule appear to have been motivated by conclusions that the freedom of contract underpinnings of the rule have become outdated, that individual employees in the modern work force do not have the bargaining power to negotiate security for the jobs on which they have grown to rely, and that the rule yields harsh results for those employees who do not enjoy the benefits of express contractual limitations on the power of dismissal. Whether these conclusions are supportable or whether for other compelling reasons employers should, as a matter of policy, be held liable to at-will employees discharged in circumstances for which no liability has existed at common law, are issues better left to resolution at the hands of the Legislature. In addition to the fundamental question whether such liability should be recognized in New York, of no less practical importance is the definition of its configuration if it is to be recognized.

Both of these aspects of the issue, involving perception and declaration of relevant public policy (the underlying determinative consideration with respect to tort liability in general) are best and more appropriately explored and resolved by the legislative branch of our government. The Legislature has infinitely greater resources and procedural means to discern the public will, to examine the variety of pertinent considerations, to elicit the views of the various segments of the community that would be directly affected and in any event critically interested, and to investigate and anticipate the impact of imposition of such liability. Standards should doubtless be established applicable to the multifarious types of employment and the various circumstances of discharge. If the rule of nonliability for termination of at-will employment is to be tempered, it should be accomplished through a principled statutory scheme, adopted after opportunity for public ventilation, rather than in consequence of judicial resolution of the partisan arguments of individual adversarial litigants.

Additionally, if the rights and obligations under a relationship forged, perhaps some time ago, between employer and employee in reliance on existing legal principles are to be significantly altered, a fitting accommodation of the competing interests to be affected may well dictate that any change should be given prospective effect only, or at least so the Legislature might conclude.

For all the reasons stated, we conclude that recognition in New York State of tort liability for what has become known as abusive or wrongful discharge should await legislative action.[1]

Plaintiff's second cause of action is framed in terms of a claim for intentional infliction of emotional distress. To survive a motion to dismiss, plaintiff's allegations must satisfy the rule set out in Restatement of Torts, Second, ... : "One who by extreme and outrageous conduct intentionally or recklessly causes severe emotional distress to another is subject to liability for such emotional distress" (§ 46, subd. [1]). Comment d to that section notes that: "Liability has been found only where the conduct has been so outrageous in character, and so extreme in degree, as to go beyond all possible bounds of decency, and to be regarded as atrocious, and utterly intolerable in a civilized community." The facts alleged by plaintiff regarding the manner of his termination fall far short of this strict standard. Further, in light of our holding above that there is now no cause of action in tort in New York for abusive or wrongful discharge of an at-will employee, plaintiff should not be allowed to evade that conclusion or to subvert the traditional at-will contract rule by casting his cause of action in terms of a tort of intentional infliction of emotional distress.

Plaintiff's third cause of action was also properly dismissed. If considered, as plaintiff would have us, as intended to allege a prima facie tort it is deficient inasmuch as there is no allegation that his discharge was without economic or social justification. Moreover, we held in *James v. Board of Educ.*, 340 N.E.2d 735 (N.Y. 1975), which also involved the exercise of an unrestricted right to discharge an employee, that: "Plaintiff cannot, by the device of an allegation that the sole reason for the termination of his employment by these public officials acting within the ambit of their authority was to harm him without justification (a contention which could be advanced with respect to almost any such termination), bootstrap himself around a motion addressed to the pleadings." Nor does the conclusory allegation of malice by plaintiff here supply the deficiency. As with the intentional infliction of emotional distress claim, this cause of action cannot be allowed in circumvention of the unavailability of a tort claim for wrongful discharge or the contract rule against liability for discharge of an at-will employee.

---

[1] Employees in New York have already been afforded express statutory protection from firing for engaging in certain protected activities (e.g., Judiciary Law, § 519 (prohibiting discharge of employee due to absence from employment for jury service); [laws barring discharge for opposing unlawful discriminatory practices or for filing a complaint or participating in a proceeding under Human Rights Law or Labor Law])....

Plaintiff's fourth cause of action is for breach of contract. Although he concedes in his complaint that his employment contract was of indefinite duration (inferentially recognizing that, were there no more, under traditional principles his employer might have discharged him at any time), he asserts that in all employment contracts the law implies an obligation on the part of the employer to deal with his employees fairly and in good faith and that a discharge in violation of that implied obligation exposes the employer to liability for breach of contract. Seeking then to apply this proposition to the present case, plaintiff argues in substance that he was required by the terms of his employment to disclose accounting improprieties and that defendant's discharge of him for having done so constituted a failure by the employer to act in good faith and thus a breach of the contract of employment.

No New York case upholding any such broad proposition is cited to us by plaintiff (or identified by our dissenting colleague), and we know of none. New York does recognize that in appropriate circumstances an obligation of good faith and fair dealing on the part of a party to a contract may be implied and, if implied will be enforced. In such instances the implied obligation is in aid and furtherance of other terms of the agreement of the parties. No obligation can be implied, however, which would be inconsistent with other terms of the contractual relationship. Thus, in the case now before us, plaintiff's employment was at will, a relationship in which the law accords the employer an unfettered right to terminate the employment at any time. In the context of such an employment it would be incongruous to say that an inference may be drawn that the employer impliedly agreed to a provision which would be destructive of his right of termination. The parties may by express agreement limit or restrict the employer's right of discharge, but to imply such a limitation from the existence of an unrestricted right would be internally inconsistent. In sum, under New York law as it now stands, absent a constitutionally impermissible purpose, a statutory proscription, or an express limitation in the individual contract of employment, an employer's right at any time to terminate an employment at will remains unimpaired.

Of course, if there were an express limitation on the employer's right of discharge it would be given effect even though the employment contract was of indefinite duration. Thus, in *Weiner v. McGraw-Hill, Inc.,* 443 N.E.2d 441 (N.Y. 1982), cited by plaintiff, we recently held that, on an appropriate evidentiary showing, a limitation on the employer's right to terminate an employment of indefinite duration might be imported from an express provision therefor found in the employer's handbook on personnel policies and procedures. Plaintiff's attempts on this appeal to bring himself within the beneficial scope of that holding must fail, however. There is here no evidence of any such express limitation. Although general references are to be found in his brief in our court to an employer's "manual," no citation is furnished to any provision therein pertinent to the employer's right to terminate his employment, and the alleged manual was not submitted with his affidavit in opposition to the motion to dismiss his complaint.

Accordingly, the fourth cause of action should have been dismissed for failure to state a cause of action.[2]

[The court then held that the courts below improperly dismissed Murphy's age-discrimination claim as barred by the Statute of Limitations.]

MEYER, JUDGE (dissenting in part).

... I agree with the majority that we should not now adopt the tort remedies proposed in those writings, because such remedies are essentially grounded in public policy, the declaration of which is a function of both the Legislature and the courts, because the New York Legislature has not been reticent in the area, and because of the difficulty encountered by the courts adopting such remedies in articulating the exact nature of the public policy which will bring them into play.

... I cannot, however, accept the majority's refusal to follow precedent decisional law recognizing an implied-in-law obligation on the part of the employer not to discharge an employee for doing that which the employment contract obligated him to do or to differentiate between that existing contract obligation and the public policy laden tort of abusive discharge. Plaintiff's complaint alleges that "defendant's internal regulations ... required that plaintiff report any deviation from proper accounting practice to defendant's top management" and that he was dismissed as a result of his doing just that. Because those allegations sufficiently state a cause of action for breach of contract not only under decisions of other States but as a matter of New York law as well, I dissent from the majority's affirmance of the dismissal of the fourth cause of action.

I do not gainsay that *Martin v. New York Life Ins. Co.*, 42 N.E. 416 (N.Y. 1895), however questionable its origin and continued existence, is the New York rule concerning employment contracts of unspecified duration.... But the policy reasons behind refusing to read a durational term into employment contracts do

---

[2] ....

We reject the view of the dissenter that a good faith limitation should now be judicially engrafted on what in New York has been the unfettered right of termination lying at the core of an employment at will. We do so for precisely the reasons which persuade him as well as the other members of the court that we should now refrain from judicial recognition of the tort action for abusive discharge. As the dissenter is at pains to note, there has been much criticism of the traditional conception of the legal obligations and rights which attach to an employment at will. It may well be that in the light of modern economic and social considerations radical changes should be made. As all of us recognize, however, resolution of the critical issues turns on identification and balancing of fundamental components of public policy. Recognition of an implied-in-law obligation of good faith as restricting the employer's right to terminate is as much a part of this matrix as is recognition of the tort action for abusive discharge. We are of the view that this aggregate of rights and obligations should not be approached piecemeal but should be considered in its totality and then resolved by the Legislature.

not require reading out of such contracts the "implied covenant of fair dealing and good faith" which "is implicit in all contracts" and is "a contractual obligation of universal force which underlies all written agreements."

I refer not to the promise that each party will use reasonable efforts to carry out the contract purpose, which may be implied-in-fact from the contract negotiations to establish consideration though the writing be "imperfectly expressed" in that respect, but to the covenant implied by the law that the parties will not "frustrate the contracts into which they have entered" and that one party will "not intentionally and purposely do anything to prevent the other party from carrying out the agreement on his part" or that may hinder or obstruct his doing that which the contract stipulates he should do....

The principle, moreover, is espoused by the Restatement of Contracts, Second (§ 205), which flatly states that "Every contract imposes upon each party a duty of good faith and fair dealing in its performance and its enforcement," and which in Comment e and the Reporter's Notes thereto indicates its application to the "abuse of a power ... to terminate the contract" including "an express power to terminate a contract at will." It is recognized as well in section 1-203 of the Uniform Commercial Code and by Williston, Contracts, which tells us that: "Wherever, therefore, a contract cannot be carried out in the way in which it was obviously expected that it should be carried out without one party or the other performing some act not expressly promised by him, a promise to do that act must be implied." The same reasoning that reads into an output contract the requirement that the manufacturing plant continue to perform in good faith and into the contract of an employee hired to invent that the resulting patent belongs to the employer though no express provision to such effect be contained in the contract requires reading into the contract the present plaintiff alleges a provision that he will not be terminated for doing that which the parties have expressly contracted he shall do.[7] To be borne in mind is the fact that we deal not with a contract which by its expressed term authorizes the employer to terminate without cause, but with one in which, because no durational term has been expressed, the law implies a right of termination. In the latter situation only the strongest of policy reasons can sustain reading the implied right of termination as a limitation upon the express obligation imposed upon the employee.

There is, moreover, no compelling policy reason to read the implied obligation of good faith out of contracts impliedly terminable at will. To do so belies the "universal force" of the good faith obligation which, as we have seen, the law reads into "all contracts." Nor can credence be given the *in terrorem* suggestion

---

[7] Ironically, the employer's implied absolute right to terminate at-will employment for any reason or for no reason had its origin in the necessity of according the employer mutuality with the right of the employee to quit his job at any time. Logically, of course, the same principle of mutuality requires that if, as plaintiff alleges and must prove in order to succeed, defendant's contract with him required him to report to defendant's top management any deviation from proper accounting practice, plaintiff's employment not be terminated because he did so.

that to limit terminable-at-will contracts by good faith will drive industry from New York. That is no more than speculation and hardly appears acceptable in the face of (1) the recognition without apparent industrial exodus of the even more burdensome tort remedy for discharge of at-will employees by such industrial States as California, Connecticut, Illinois, Indiana, Maryland, Massachusetts, Michigan, New Jersey, Pennsylvania and Wisconsin, and (2) the responses reported in Ewing, *What Business Thinks About Employee Rights,* a Harvard Business Review survey of employers reprinted in Individual Rights in the Corporation: A Reader on Employee Rights (Westin & Salisbury eds.), at page 21. The more particularly is this so because collective bargaining "just cause" provisions, which impose a greater burden on employers than does a good faith limitation, have not done so, and because employers can obtain a large measure of protection by expressly reserving in the employment contract the right to terminate without cause....

NOTES

1. *Merits of Murphy's Tort Claim.* If Murphy's claim were to arise in a state that recognized the tort of wrongful discharge against public policy, how would his claim fare? Is the basic tort rationale for interfering with contracts — third-party effects — present in *Murphy*? Even in such a state, would Murphy need an implied covenant of good faith and fair dealing?

2. *Legislative Versus Judicial Action.* Judge Meyer, in dissent, agrees with the majority that the creation of a tort of wrongful discharge should be left to the legislature, but argues that the judiciary need not wait for the legislature to imply a covenant of good faith and fair dealing in employment contracts. Is this distinction between the wrongful discharge tort and the good faith covenant viable?

For a general judicial statement endorsing judicial change of the at-will doctrine, consider the following:

> The employment-at-will rule is not set indelibly in stone. It is a part of the common law, *judicially* created, and within the power of judicial reform. Thus, there is no reason to treat it as though it has the strength of legislation.... "If this were not so, we must succumb to a rule [of *stare decisis*] that a judge should let others 'long dead and unaware of the problems of the age in which he lives, do his thinking for him.'..."

Meeks v. Opp Cotton Mills, 459 So. 2d 814, 816 (Ala. 1984) (Justice Beatty, dissenting).

3. *Defining Good Faith.* In a leading essay on good faith in general contract and commercial law, Professor Robert Summers insists that good faith cannot be defined. As he says,

> [to ask what good faith means] misconceives good faith. Good faith, as judges generally use the term in matters contractual, is best understood as an "excluder" — a phrase with no general meaning or meanings of its own.

Instead, it functions to rule out many different forms of bad faith. It is hard to get this point across to persons used to thinking that every word must have one or more general meanings of its own — must be either unequivocal or ambiguous.

... In most cases the party acting in bad faith frustrates the justified expectations of another.... [T]he ways in which he may do this are numerous and radically diverse. Moreover, whether an aggrieved party's expectations are justified must inevitably vary with attendant circumstances. For these reasons it is not fruitful to try to generalize further. It is easy enough to formulate examples of bad faith and work from them. Besides, any general definition of good faith, if not vacuous, is sure to be unduly restrictive, especially if cast in statutory form.

Robert S. Summers, *"Good Faith" in General Contract Law and the Sales Provisions of the Uniform Commercial Code,* 54 VA. L. REV. 195, 262-63 (1968).[*] Does Summers's argument suggest that common law courts are better able than a legislature to develop a doctrine of good faith in employment contracts?

FOLEY v. INTERACTIVE DATA CORP.

Supreme Court of California (*en banc*)
765 P.2d 373 (1988)

LUCAS, CHIEF JUSTICE.

After Interactive Data Corporation (defendant) fired plaintiff Daniel D. Foley, an executive employee, he filed this action seeking compensatory and punitive damages for wrongful discharge. In his second amended complaint, plaintiff asserted three distinct theories: (1) a tort cause of action alleging a discharge in violation of public policy, (2) a contract cause of action for breach of an implied-in-fact promise to discharge for good cause only, and (3) a cause of action alleging a tortious breach of the implied covenant of good faith and fair dealing. The trial court sustained a demurrer without leave to amend, and entered judgment for defendant.

The Court of Appeal affirmed on the grounds (1) plaintiff alleged no statutorily based breach of public policy sufficient to state a cause of action; (2) plaintiff's claim for breach of the covenant to discharge only for good cause was barred by the statute of frauds; and (3) plaintiff's cause of action based on breach of the covenant of good faith and fair dealing failed because it did not allege necessary longevity of employment or express formal procedures for termination of employees....

We will hold that the Court of Appeal properly found that ... plaintiff failed to allege facts showing a violation of a fundamental public policy. We will also

[*] Reprinted with permission of the Virginia Law Review Association and Fred B. Rothman & Co.

conclude, however, that plaintiff has sufficiently alleged a breach of an "oral" or "implied-in-fact" contract, and that the statute of frauds does not bar his claim so that he may pursue his action in this regard. Finally, we will hold that the covenant of good faith and fair dealing applies to employment contracts and that breach of the covenant may give rise to contract but not tort damages.

Facts

....

Defendant hired plaintiff in June 1976 as an assistant product manager at a starting salary of $18,500. As a condition of employment defendant required plaintiff to sign a "Confidential and Proprietary Information Agreement" whereby he promised not to engage in certain competition with defendant for one year after the termination of his employment for any reason. The agreement also contained a "Disclosure and Assignment of Information" provision that obliged plaintiff to disclose to defendant all computer-related information known to him, including any innovations, inventions or developments pertaining to the computer field for a period of one year following his termination. Finally, the agreement imposed on plaintiff a continuing obligation to assign to defendant all rights to his computer-related inventions or innovations for one year following termination. It did not state any limitation on the grounds for which plaintiff's employment could be terminated.

Over the next six years and nine months, plaintiff received a steady series of salary increases, promotions, bonuses, awards and superior performance evaluations. In 1979 defendant named him consultant manager of the year and in 1981 promoted him to branch manager of its Los Angeles office. His annual salary rose to $56,164 and he received an additional $6,762 merit bonus two days before his discharge in March 1983. He alleges defendant's officers made repeated oral assurances of job security so long as his performance remained adequate.

Plaintiff also alleged that during his employment, defendant maintained written "Termination Guidelines" that set forth express grounds for discharge and a mandatory seven-step pretermination procedure. Plaintiff understood that these guidelines applied not only to employees under plaintiff's supervision, but to him as well. On the basis of these representations, plaintiff alleged that he reasonably believed defendant would not discharge him except for good cause, and therefore he refrained from accepting or pursuing other job opportunities.

The event that led to plaintiff's discharge was a private conversation in January 1983 with his former supervisor, vice president Richard Earnest. During the previous year defendant had hired Robert Kuhne and subsequently named Kuhne to replace Earnest as plaintiff's immediate supervisor. Plaintiff learned that Kuhne was currently under investigation by the Federal Bureau of Investigation for embezzlement from his former employer, Bank of America.[1] Plaintiff reported what he knew about Kuhne to Earnest, because he was "worried about working for Kuhne and having him in a supervisory position ..., in view of Kuhne's suspected criminal conduct." Plaintiff asserted he "made this disclosure in the interest and for the benefit of his employer," allegedly because he believed that because defendant and its parent do business with the financial community on a confidential basis, the company would have a legitimate interest in knowing about a high executive's alleged prior criminal conduct.

In response, Earnest allegedly told plaintiff not to discuss "rumors" and to "forget what he heard" about Kuhne's past. In early March, Kuhne informed plaintiff that defendant had decided to replace him for "performance reasons" and that he could transfer to a position in another division in Waltham, Massachusetts. Plaintiff was told that if he did not accept a transfer, he might be demoted but not fired. One week later, in Waltham, Earnest informed plaintiff he was not doing a good job, and six days later, he notified plaintiff he could continue as branch manager if he "agreed to go on a 'performance plan.' Plaintiff asserts he agreed to consider such an arrangement." The next day, when Kuhne met with plaintiff, purportedly to present him with a written "performance plan" proposal, Kuhne instead informed plaintiff he had the choice of resigning or being fired. Kuhne offered neither a performance plan nor an option to transfer to another position.

Defendant demurred to all three causes of action. After plaintiff filed two amended pleadings, the trial court sustained defendant's demurrer without leave to amend and dismissed all three causes of action. The Court of Appeal affirmed the dismissal as to all three counts. We will explore each claim in turn.

[The Court upheld the dismissal of Foley's claim of tortious discharge in contravention of public policy, reasoning that "[w]hether or not there is a statutory duty requiring an employee to report information relevant to his employer's interest, we do not find a substantial public policy prohibiting an employer from discharging an employee for performing that duty.... When the duty of an employee to disclose information to his employer serves only the private interest of the employer, the rationale underlying the [public policy] cause of action is not implicated."

[The Court reversed the dismissal of Foley's breach of implied contract claim, finding the Statue of Frauds inapplicable because Foley could have quit or been fired for good cause within a year, and holding the allegations sufficient for an implied-in-fact contract on the rationale of *Pugh v. See's Candies, Inc.*, 171 Cal. Rptr. 917 (Cal. Ct. App. 1981).]

---

[1] In September 1983, after plaintiff's discharge, Kuhne pleaded guilty in federal court to a felony count of embezzlement.

We turn now to plaintiff's cause of action for tortious breach of the implied covenant of good faith and fair dealing. [P]laintiff asserts we should recognize tort remedies for such a breach in the context of employment termination.

The distinction between tort and contract is well grounded in common law, and divergent objectives underlie the remedies created in the two areas. Whereas contract actions are created to enforce the intentions of the parties to the agreement, tort law is primarily designed to vindicate "social policy." The covenant of good faith and fair dealing was developed in the contract arena and is aimed at making effective the agreement's promises. Plaintiff asks that we find that the breach of the implied covenant in employment contracts also gives rise to an action seeking an award of tort damages.

In this instance, where an extension of tort remedies is sought for a duty whose breach previously has been compensable by contractual remedies, it is helpful to consider certain principles relevant to contract law. First, predictability about the cost of contractual relationships plays an important role in our commercial system. Moreover, "Courts traditionally have awarded damages for breach of contract to compensate the aggrieved party rather than to punish the breaching party."[25] With these concepts in mind, we turn to analyze the role of the implied covenant of good faith and fair dealing and the propriety of the extension of remedies urged by plaintiff.

"Every contract imposes upon each party a duty of good faith and fair dealing in its performance and its enforcement." (Rest. 2d Contracts, § 205.) This duty has been recognized in the majority of American jurisdictions, the Restatement, and the Uniform Commercial Code. Because the covenant is a contract term, however, compensation for its breach has almost always been limited to contract rather than tort remedies. As to the scope of the covenant, "'[t]he precise nature and extent of the duty imposed by such an implied promise will depend on the contractual purposes.'" Initially, the concept of a duty of good faith developed in contract law as "a kind of 'safety valve' to which judges may turn to fill gaps and qualify or limit rights and duties otherwise arising under rules of law and specific contract language." (Summers, *The General Duty of Good Faith — Its Recognition and Conceptualization* (1982) 67 Cornell L. Rev. 810, 812.) As a contract concept, breach of the duty led to imposition of contract damages determined by the nature of the breach and standard contract principles.

An exception to this general rule has developed in the context of insurance contracts where, for a variety of policy reasons, courts have held that breach of the implied covenant will provide the basis for an action in tort....

---

[25] At times certain breaches of contract have been deemed economically desirable. As the reporter's notes to Restatement Second of Contracts, state, "a breach of contract will result in a gain in 'economic efficiency' if the party contemplating breach evaluates his gains at a higher figure than the value that the other party puts on his losses, and this will be so if the party contemplating breach will gain enough from the breach to have a net benefit even though he compensates the other party for his resulting loss."

In *Egan v. Mutual of Omaha Ins. Co.,* 620 P.2d 141 (Cal. 1979), we described some of the bases for permitting tort recovery for breach of the implied covenant in the insurance context. "The insured in a contract like the one before us does not seek to obtain a commercial advantage by purchasing the policy — rather, he seeks protection against calamity."...

In addition, the *Egan* court emphasized that "the relationship of insurer and insured is inherently unbalanced: the adhesive nature of insurance contracts places the insurer in a superior bargaining position." This emphasis on the "special relationship" of insurer and insured has been echoed in arguments and analysis in subsequent scholarly commentary and cases which urge the availability of tort remedies in the employment context....

In our view, the underlying problem in the line of cases relied on by plaintiff lies in the decisions' uncritical incorporation of the insurance model into the employment context, without careful consideration of the fundamental policies underlying the development of tort and contract law in general or of significant differences between the insurer/insured and employer/employee relationships. When a court enforces the implied covenant it is in essence acting to protect "the interest in having promises performed" (Prosser, Law of Torts (4th ed. 1971) p. 613) — the traditional realm of a contract action — rather than to protect some general duty to society which the law places on an employer without regard to the substance of its contractual obligations to its employee. Thus, in *Tameny v. Atlantic Richfield Co.,* 610 P.2d 1330 (Cal. 1980), as we have explained, the court was careful to draw a distinction between "ex delicto" and "ex contractu" obligations. An allegation of breach of the implied covenant of good faith and fair dealing is an allegation of breach of an "ex contractu" obligation, namely one arising out of the contract itself. The covenant of good faith is read into contracts in order to protect the express covenants or promises of the contract, not to protect some general public policy interest not directly tied to the contract's purposes. The insurance cases thus were a major departure from traditional principles of contract law. We must, therefore, consider with great care claims that extension of the exceptional approach taken in those cases is automatically appropriate if certain hallmarks and similarities can be adduced in another contract setting. With this emphasis on the historical purposes of the covenant of good faith and fair dealing in mind, we turn to consider the bases upon which extension of the insurance model to the employment sphere has been urged.

After review of the various commentators, and independent consideration of the similarities between the two areas, we are not convinced that a "special relationship" analogous to that between insurer and insured should be deemed to exist in the usual employment relationship which would warrant recognition of a tort action for breach of the implied covenant. Even if we were to assume that the special relationship model is an appropriate one to follow in determining whether to expand tort recovery, a breach in the employment context does not place the employee in the same economic dilemma that an insured faces when an insurer in bad faith refuses to pay a claim or to accept a settlement offer within policy limits. When an insurer takes such actions, the insured cannot turn to the marketplace to find another insurance company willing to pay for the loss already incurred. The wrongfully terminated employee, on the other hand, can (and must, in order to mitigate damages) make reasonable efforts to seek alternative employment. Moreover, the role of the employer differs from that of the "quasi-public" insurance company with whom individuals contract specifically in order to obtain protection from potential specified economic harm. The employer does not similarly "sell" protection to its employees; it is not providing a public service. Nor do we find convincing the idea that the employee is necessarily seeking a different kind of financial security than those entering a typical commercial contract. If a small dealer contracts for goods from a large supplier, and those goods are vital to the small dealer's business, a breach by the supplier may have financial significance for individuals employed by the dealer or to the dealer himself. Permitting only contract damages in such a situation has ramifications no different from a similar limitation in the direct employer-employee relationship.

Finally, there is a fundamental difference between insurance and employment relationships. In the insurance relationship, the insurer's and insured's interest are financially at odds. If the insurer pays a claim, it diminishes its fiscal resources. The insured of course has paid for protection and expects to have its losses recompensed. When a claim is paid, money shifts from insurer to insured, or, if appropriate, to a third party claimant. Putting aside already specifically barred improper motives for termination which may be based on both economic and noneconomic considerations,[30] as a general rule it is to the employer's economic benefit to retain good employees. The interests of employer and employee are most frequently in alignment. If there is a job to be done, the employer must still pay someone to do it. This is not to say that there may never be a "bad motive" for discharge not otherwise covered by law. Nevertheless, in terms of abstract employment relationships as contrasted with abstract insurance relationships, there is less inherent relevant tension between the interests of employers and employees than exists between that of insurers and insureds. Thus the need to place disincentives on an employer's conduct in addition to those already imposed by law simply does not rise to the same level as that created by the conflicting interests at stake in the insurance context. Nor is this to say that the Legislature would have no basis for affording employees additional protections.

---

[30] In the employment relationship, the employer is already barred by law from, and the employee can obtain relief for, discriminatory discharges based on age, sex, race, and religion. Similarly, the employee is protected from discrimination based on the exercise of rights under the workers' compensation laws or for engaging in union activities. He can gain relief if he is terminated in order for the employer to avoid payment of certain benefits. The employee may sue in tort for discharges based on breaches of public policy.

It is, however, to say that the need to extend the special relationship model in the form of judicially created relief of the kind sought here is less compelling.

We therefore conclude that the employment relationship is not sufficiently similar to that of insurer and insured to warrant judicial extension of the proposed additional tort remedies in view of the countervailing concerns about economic policy and stability, the traditional separation of tort and contract law, and finally, the numerous protections against improper terminations already afforded employees....

Moreover, it would be difficult if not impossible to formulate a rule that would assure that only "deserving" cases give rise to tort relief. Professor Summers, in his seminal article, described the term "good faith" as used in the duty of good faith imposed in contract law and the Uniform Commercial Code, as an "excluder" phrase which is "without general meaning (or meanings) of its own and serves to exclude a wide range of heterogenous forms of bad faith. In a particular context the phrase takes on specific meaning, but usually this is only by way of contrast with the specific form of bad faith actually or hypothetically ruled out." In a tort action based on an employee's discharge, it is highly likely that each case would involve a dispute as to material facts regarding the subjective intentions of the employer. As a result, these actions could rarely be disposed of at the demurrer or summary judgment stage....

Finally, and of primary significance, we believe that focus on available contract remedies offers the most appropriate method of expanding available relief for wrongful terminations. The expansion of tort remedies in the employment context has potentially enormous consequences for the stability of the business community.

We are not unmindful of the legitimate concerns of employees who fear arbitrary and improper discharges that may have a devastating effect on their economic and social status. Nor are we unaware of or unsympathetic to claims that contract remedies for breaches of contract are insufficient because they do not fully compensate due to their failure to include attorney fees and their restrictions on foreseeable damages. These defects, however, exist generally in contract situations. As discussed above, the variety of possible courses to remedy the problem is well demonstrated in the literature and include increased contract damages, provision for award of attorney fees, establishment of arbitration or other speedier and less expensive dispute resolution, or the tort remedies (the scope of which is also subject to dispute) sought by plaintiff here.

The diversity of possible solutions demonstrates the confusion that occurs when we look outside the realm of contract law in attempting to fashion remedies for a breach of a contract provision. As noted, numerous legislative provisions have imposed obligations on parties to contracts which vindicate significant social policies extraneous to the contract itself. As Justice Kaus observed in his concurring and dissenting opinion in *White v. Western Title Ins. Co.*, 40 Cal. 3d 870, 901, (1985) "our experience ... surely tells us that there are real problems in applying the substitute remedy of a tort recovery — with or without punitive damages — outside the insurance area. In other words, I believe that under all the circumstances, the problem is one for the Legislature ...."

PANELLI, ARGUELLES and EAGLESON, JJ., concur.

DISSENT

BROUSSARD, JUSTICE, concurring and dissenting....

If we must argue analogies, the question is not whether the employment contract differs from an insurance contract in one particular respect, or resembles a commercial contract in another. It is whether, as a whole, the contract of employment more closely resembles an insurance contract or an ordinary commercial contract. The answer is clear. The principal reason we permit tort damages for breach of the covenant of good faith and fair dealing in an insurance contract is that persons do not generally purchase insurance to obtain a commercial advantage, but to secure the peace of mind and security it will provide in protecting against accidental loss. That reason applies equally to the employer-employee relationship. A man or a woman usually does not enter into employment solely for the money; a job is status, reputation, a way of defining one's self-worth and worth in the community. It is also essential to financial security, offering assurance of future income needed to repay present debts and meet future obligations. Without a secure job a worker frequently cannot obtain a retirement pension, and often lacks access to affordable medical insurance. In short, "in a modern industrialized economy employment is central to one's existence and dignity."[6]

The majority then argue that it would be difficult if not impossible to formulate a rule to confine tort relief to "deserving" cases, apparently because the concept of "good faith" is subjective. In fact, a suitable test is simple to describe: an employer acts in bad faith in discharging an employee if and only if he does not believe he has a legal right to discharge the employee.[10]

---

[6] A second significant similarity is that both insurance contracts and employment contracts arise from a context of disparity of bargaining power. Numerous cases have noted this disparity in insurance cases; it has led to the adoption of a general rule that insurance contracts are construed against the insurer. There are fewer cases in the employment context, but here the principle is embodied in a statutory finding that "the individual unorganized worker is helpless to exercise actual liberty of contract and to protect his freedom of labor, and thereby to obtain acceptable terms and conditions of employment." (Lab. Code, § 923.)

[10] Some cases and writers have suggested that the courts should also consider whether the employer acted reasonably. Since the majority abolish the entire cause of action, it is pointless now to decide that question. I would note only that the concept of reasonableness, like that of bad faith, is one familiar to tort law, and not generally considered so unpredictable or subjective as to justify denial of relief for injuries suffered.

KAUFMAN, JUSTICE, concurring and dissenting....

In attempting to emphasize its contractual origins, the majority characterize the covenant of good faith and fair dealing[1] as "a contract term" "aimed at making effective the agreement's promises." That characterization is simply incorrect under the decisions of this court and the authorities on which they relied. It is true that the law implies in every *contract* a duty of good faith and fair dealing. The duty to deal fairly and in good faith with the other party to a contract, however, "is a *duty imposed by law, not one arising from the terms of the contract itself.* In other words, this duty of dealing fairly and in good faith is nonconsensual in origin rather than consensual." While the nature of the obligations imposed by this duty is dependent upon the nature and purpose of the contract and the expectations of the parties, these obligations are not consensual, not agreed to in the contract; they are imposed by law and thus reflect the normative values of society as a whole. The interest which the duty of good faith and fair dealing is designed to preserve and protect is essentially not the parties' interest in having their promises performed, but society's interest in protecting its members from harm on account of nonconsensual conduct.

[The majority's conclusions], in my view, expose an unrealistic if not mythical conception of the employment relationship. They also reveal a misplaced reluctance to define the minimal standards of decency required to govern that relationship. The delineation of such standards is not, as the majority strongly implies, judicial legislation, but rather constitutes this court's fundamental obligation.

It is, at best, naive to believe that the availability of the "marketplace," or that a supposed "alignment of interests," renders the employment relationship less special or less subject to abuse than the relationship between insurer and insured. Indeed, I can think of no relationship in which one party, the employee, places more reliance upon the other, is more dependent upon the other, or is more vulnerable to abuse by the other, than the relationship between employer and employee. And, ironically, the relative imbalance of economic power between employer and employee tends to increase rather than diminish the longer that relationship continues. Whatever bargaining strength and marketability the employee may have at the moment of hiring, diminishes rapidly thereafter. Marketplace? What market is there for the factory worker laid-off after 25 years of labor in the same plant, or for the middle-aged executive fired after 25 years with the same firm?

Financial security? Can anyone seriously dispute that employment is generally sought, at least in part, for financial security and all that that implies: food on the

---

[1] As the commentators have noted, the very term "implied covenant" is misleading, since it "evokes the notion of contract, and therefore the term 'duty' might be more appropriate for treating the violation of good faith and fair dealing as a tort." The Restatement Second of Contracts, section 205, has adopted the language of duty: "Every contract imposes upon each party a duty of good faith and fair dealing in its performance and enforcement."

table, shelter, clothing, medical care, education for one's children. Clearly, no action for breach of the covenant of good faith and fair dealing will lie unless it has first been proved that, expressly or by implication, the employer has given the employee a reasonable expectation of continued employment so long as the employee performs satisfactorily. And that expectation constitutes a far greater and graver security interest than any which inheres in the insurance context. Most of us can live without insurance. Few of us could live without a job.

Peace of mind? One's work obviously involves more than just earning a living. It defines for many people their identity, their sense of self-worth, their sense of belonging. The wrongful and malicious destruction of one's employment is far more certain to result in serious emotional distress than any wrongful denial of an insurance claim....

The majority's implicit fears of judicial activism are unfounded. We overstep no institutional bounds or constitutional constraints in recognizing that a willful and malicious termination of employment is so offensive to community values that it may give rise to tort remedies. On the contrary, such a holding would be entirely consistent with our judicial function, and with the great common law tradition of this court.

[Justice Mosk's dissenting opinion is omitted.]

NOTES

1. *Ex Post and Ex Ante Analysis.* The majority opinion in *Foley* distinguishes the insurance cases (which allow tort damages for breach of good faith) by insisting that the insurer and insured have opposing interests, while employer and employee interests are most frequently in alignment. Is not the court comparing apples and oranges by using an ex post perspective for insurance relationships and an ex ante perspective for employment relationships? Viewed after the calamity occurs (e.g., fire burns the house), the court correctly notes that the insurer loses by paying the insured. But before the calamity occurs, the insured and insurer have a similar interest in providing and obtaining the optimal insurance protection for the premium paid.

2. *A Landmark Decision.* Many view *Foley* as a landmark decision that significantly cuts back on the developing California law on employment termination. A study of 120 wrongful termination jury trials in California between 1980 and 1986 (covering perhaps 65-70% of all such trials in California during that time) revealed that plaintiffs recovered punitive damages in one-third of the trials, with the average punitive award in those forty cases being $523,170. JAMES N. DERTOUZOS ET AL., THE LEGAL AND ECONOMIC CONSEQUENCES OF WRONGFUL TERMINATION 26 (1988). While it is not known how many of these were cases of wrongful discharge in violation of public policy (where punitive damages remain an element of recovery after *Foley*), presumably many were good faith cases that could not be pigeonholed into the public policy tort. *Foley* has dramatically reduced the economic incentive to bring such claims.

Some observers have reported that plaintiff's attorneys in California are more selective in the post-*Foley* era, and are reluctant to take cases for workers earning less than $50,000. Perhaps as a result of this greater selectivity, jury awards have risen. One study found that in 1989-1991, the average verdict awarded to plaintiffs after successful jury trials in California was $1.4 million (nearly triple the pre-*Foley* average award), with an average of almost one verdict of over $1 million per month. Angel Gomez, III, *Case Studies and Trends in Employment Jury Verdicts*, 8 S. CAL. LAB. & EMPLOY. L.Q. 1 (Spring 1992).

3. *Affirmation of Pugh.* Despite the cautious tone of *Foley,* one should not overlook that *Foley* is the first California Supreme Court case upholding the lower court decision that a covenant of good faith and fair dealing exists in every employment contract. It also is the first time the California Supreme Court clearly endorsed the *Pugh* doctrine of implied-in-fact contract rights.

4. *The Tort-Contract Boundary.* *Foley* emphatically declares that employees bringing good-faith claims can receive only contract damages. Employees continue to craft tort claims to avoid the limitations of contract damages. The California Supreme Court has wrestled with the tort-contract boundary in two later cases.

In *Hunter v. Up-Right*, 864 P.2d 88 (Cal. 1993), a welder was falsely told by his supervisor that the company had decided to eliminate his position. After being refused a lesser position within the company, Hunter signed a resignation. When he realized the company had not eliminated his position, Hunter sued for fraud and deceit as well as breach of an implied contract not to dismiss without cause. The Court rejected his attempt to recover tort damages, declaring that a tort recovery is available only "when the plaintiff's fraud damages cannot be said to result from [the] termination itself."

In *Lazar v. Superior Ct. (Rykoff-Sexton, Inc.)*, 909 P.2d 981 (Cal. 1996), the Court distinguished *Foley* and *Hunter* and allowed tort recovery for fraudulent inducement of employment contract. Lazar had been the president of a family-owned company in New York for eighteen years, making $120,000. Rykoff-Sexton persuaded him to move with his family to California to accept a job as general manager for contract design, promising that his job would be secure and would involve significant pay increases. Lazar asked for a written employment contract, but was refused, Rykoff stating that a written contract was unnecessary because "our word is our bond." Lazar began work in May 1990 and was terminated two years later.

Lazar brought a fraud claim, alleging that Rykoff had a company policy limiting salary increases to 2-3% and was planning a merger that would eliminate his position, even while it was promising him large salary increases and job security. The California Supreme Court determined that Lazar made out a good claim of promissory fraud, because he properly alleged (a) misrepresentation; (b) knowledge of falsity; (c) intent to defraud, i.e., to induce reliance; (d) justifiable reliance; and (e) resulting damage. The Court distinguished *Hunter*, asserting that Hunter had failed to show detrimental reliance, because he would have been fired even had he not had been falsely lead to resign. Lazar, by contrast, relied to his detriment on the false promises when he left New York.

These cases illustrate the border war between tort and contract. In *Lazar*, the court recognizes a promissory fraud action, even though the facts show a classic oral contract (complete with all the classic dangers of an oral contract). A tort cause of action avoids parol evidence and statute of frauds problems, allows broader damages, and typically has a different (and shorter) statute of limitations. But the deeper question is whether and when the common law should recognize a tort cause of action that overlaps substantially with a contract cause of action.

5. *Damages in Wrongful Termination Cases.* Wrongfully discharged employees, suing in either tort or contract, can generally recover lost wages, salary, commissions, and fringe benefits. Most courts will allow employees to be compensated for expected reductions in future income as well, if not too speculative. In *Goins v. Ford Motor Co.,* 347 N.W.2d 184 (Mich. Ct. App. 1983), for example, the court upheld a recovery of lost future earnings calculated as the difference between the discharged employee's current salary and the salary of the job he would have received had he not been replaced, multiplied by his forty years' life expectancy, and reduced to present value. It may be more appropriate, however, also to attempt to measure the likelihood that the employee would have later been dismissed for cause, including a termination for business reasons, or have quit. *See* Tyler J. Bowles, *Wrongful Discharge: The Time Horizon of Future Damages and the Economic Basis for Damages*, 4 J. LEGAL ECON. 75 (1994).

Employees suing in tort can additionally recover damages for mental distress, for loss of reputation, and other compensatory damages such as the loss on the sale of a house. If the defendant's conduct is sufficiently outrageous, tort recoveries can also include punitive damages.

6. *Reinstatement in Wrongful Discharge Cases.* Reinstatement is another possible remedy in tort and contract, but courts are reluctant to order reinstatement. As one court put it: "full redress for breach of the contract is available by an award of damages. Additionally, in light of the hostility between the parties, it would be inappropriate to order reinstatement of plaintiff to her employment position." *Zahler v. Niagara County Chapter of N.Y. State Ass'n for Retarded Children,* 491 N.Y.S.2d 880, 881 (N.Y. App. Div. 1985).

The reluctance of courts in wrongful discharge cases to order reinstatement and willingness to award frontpay differs from the relief pattern in Title VII and ADEA discrimination cases and in NLRA cases. In those cases, reinstatement is the preferred remedy and frontpay is given only where reinstatement is impossible or impracticable. To what extent might this difference be explained by the fact that wrongful discharge plaintiffs tend to be high-level employees, and courts are more reluctant to order reinstatement to jobs perceived as requiring a personal relationship between employer and employee? *See* Martha West, *The Case Against Reinstatement in Wrongful Discharge,* 1988 U. ILL. L. REV. 1, 53-54.

7. ***Indirect Costs of Wrongful Termination Litigation.*** A recent study by the Rand Corporation estimated that employer costs of being sued for wrongful discharge are only about 0.1% of total labor costs. This amounts to less than $10 per employee, or $100 per termination. JAMES N. DERTOUZOS & LYNN A. KAROLY, LABOR-MARKET RESPONSES TO EMPLOYER LIABILITY xi (1992).

The indirect costs of litigation may overwhelm the direct costs, as firms attempt to avoid liability by not firing poor performers and being more cautious in hiring. The Rand study found that firms are sizing their workforces as if wrongful termination litigation adds 10% to their wage bill. The authors offer the unpredictability of case outcomes as a possible explanation for this behavior. STOP

Chapter 7

THE FUTURE OF WRONGFUL DISCHARGE LAW

A. A RETURN TO EMPLOYMENT AT WILL

RICHARD A. EPSTEIN, IN DEFENSE OF THE CONTRACT AT WILL, 51 University of Chicago Law Review 947, 951-69 (1984)[*]

There is ... today a widely held view that the contract at will has outlived its usefulness. But this view is mistaken. The contract at will is not ideal for every employment relation. No court or legislature should ever command its use. Nonetheless, there are two ways in which the contract at will should be respected: one deals with entitlements against regulation and the other with presumptions in the event of contractual silence.

First, the parties should be permitted as of right to adopt this form of contract if they so desire. The principle behind this conclusion is that freedom of contract tends both to advance individual autonomy and to promote the efficient operation of labor markets.

Second, the contract at will should be respected as a rule of construction in response to the perennial question of gaps in contract language: what term should be implied in the absence of explicit agreement on the question of duration or grounds for termination? The applicable standard asks two familiar questions: what rule tends to lend predictability to litigation and to advance the joint interests of the parties? On both these points I hope to show that the contract at will represents in most contexts the efficient solution to the employment relation. To be sure, the stakes are lower where the outright prohibition is no longer in the offing. No rule of construction ever has the power of a rule of regulation, since the parties by negotiation can reverse what the law otherwise commands. Nonetheless, bad rules of contract construction have costs that should not be understated, here or elsewhere. The rule of construction is normally chosen because it reflects the dominant practice in a given class of cases and because that practice is itself regarded as making good sense for the standard transactions it governs. It is of course freely waivable by a joint expression of contrary intention. When the law introduces a just-cause requirement, it flies in the face of ordinary understandings and thus rests upon an assumption that just-cause arrangements are in the broad run of cases either more frequent or desirable than the contract at will, though neither is the case. Where this rule of construction is used, therefore, contracting-out will have to take place in the very large number of cases where the parties desire to conform to the norm by entering into a contract at will. Fur-

---

[*] Reprinted with permission of the University of Chicago Law Review.

thermore, it may be difficult to waive the for-cause requirement in fact, even if waiver is formally allowable as a matter of law, because of high standards for "informed" waiver that cannot be met after the fact. By degrees, the original presumption against the contract at will could so gain in strength that a requirement that is waivable in theory could easily become conclusive in fact....

In this area of private-contracting autonomy, there are some exceptions, arising out of the infrequent cases in which discharge of the contract at will is inconsistent with the performance of some public duty or with the protection of some public right. Just as a contract to commit murder should not be enforceable, neither should one to pollute illegally or to commit perjury.[11] But these cases, however difficult in their own right, in no way require abandoning the basic common law presumption in favor of contracts at will. The recent efforts to undermine or abolish the contract at will should be evaluated not in terms of what they *hope* to achieve, whether stated in terms of worker participation, industrial harmony, fundamental fairness, or enlightened employment relations. Instead they should be evaluated for the generally harsh results that they actually produce. They introduce an enormous amount of undesirable complexity into the law of employment relations; they increase the frequency of civil litigation; and over the broad run of cases they work to the disadvantage of both the employers and the employees whose conduct they govern....

The first way to argue for the contract at will is to insist upon the importance of freedom of contract as an end in itself. Freedom of contract is an aspect of individual liberty, every bit as much as freedom of speech, or freedom in the selection of marriage partners or in the adoption of religious beliefs or affiliations. Just as it is regarded as prima facie unjust to abridge these liberties, so too is it presumptively unjust to abridge the economic liberties of individuals. The desire to make one's own choices about employment may be as strong as it is with respect to marriage or participation in religious activities, and it is doubtless more pervasive than the desire to participate in political activity. Indeed for most

---

[11] This problem has arisen where employees at will have refused to perjure themselves on behalf of the employer, *e.g., Petermann v. Teamsters Local 396*, 174 Cal. App. 2d 184, 188-89, 344 P.2d 25, 27-28 (1959) (discharge for refusal to commit perjury held wrongful), or where workers have been dismissed because they have filed workers' compensation claims, *e.g., Frampton v. Central Ind. Gas Co.*, 260 Ind. 249, 252-53, 297 N.E. 2d 425, 428 (1973) (discharge for filing claim held wrongful). It seems clear that any contract to commit perjury should simply be treated as illegal. The workers' compensation case is more difficult both because there is less justification for the coercive character of compensation, since no third-party interests are at stake, and because in all events the worker is entitled to file his claim and will do so if its value exceeds the gains he expects from the employment contract. A common law court cannot, however, attack the soundness of a statutory compensation system, so that this restraint on freedom of contract should be as valid as one imposed for the protection of strangers. At this point the central question concerns the proper remedy. Typically, reinstatement of the plaintiff is ordered, which has the disadvantage of requiring the court to supervise an ongoing relationship. It may well be that the employer should be able to fire the worker, but nonetheless be required to pay damages, preferably fixed by statute, to the worker....

people, their own health and comfort, and that of their families, depend critically upon their ability to earn a living by entering the employment market. If government regulation is inappropriate for personal, religious, or political activities, then what makes it intrinsically desirable for employment relations?...

The strong fairness argument in favor of freedom of contract makes short work of the various for-cause and good-faith restrictions upon private contracts. Yet the argument is incomplete in several respects. In particular, it does not explain why the presumption in the case of silence should be in favor of the contract at will. Nor does it give a descriptive account of why the contract at will is so commonly found in all trades and professions. Nor does the argument meet on their own terms the concerns voiced most frequently by the critics of the contract at will. Thus, the commonplace belief today (at least outside the actual world of business) is that the contract at will is so unfair and one-sided that it cannot be the outcome of a rational set of bargaining processes any more than, to take the extreme case, a contract for total slavery....

In order to rebut this charge, it is necessary to do more than insist that individuals as a general matter know how to govern their own lives. It is also necessary to display the structural strengths of the contract at will that explain why rational people would enter into such a contract, if not all the time, then at least most of it....

From this perspective, then, the task is to explain how and why the at-will contracting arrangement (in sharp contrast to slavery) typically works to the mutual advantage of the parties.... The inquiry into mutual benefit in turn requires an examination of the full range of costs and benefits that arise from collaborative ventures. It is just at this point that the nineteenth-century view is superior to the emerging modern conception. The modern view tends to lay heavy emphasis on the need to control employer abuse. Yet ... the rights under the contract at will are fully bilateral, so that the employee can use the contract as a means to control the firm, just as the firm uses it to control the worker.

The issue for the parties, properly framed, is not how to minimize employer abuse, but rather how to maximize the gain from the relationship, which in part depends upon minimizing the sum of employer and employee abuse. Viewed in this way the private-contracting problem is far more complex. How does each party create incentives for the proper behavior of the other? How does each side insure against certain risks? How do both sides minimize the administrative costs of their contracting practices?...

Begin for the moment with the fears of the firm, for it is the firm's right to maintain at-will power that is now being called into question. In all too many cases, the firm must contend with the recurrent problem of employee theft and with the related problems of unauthorized use of firm equipment and employee kickback arrangements. As the analysis of partnerships shows, however, the proper concerns of the firm are not limited to obvious forms of criminal misconduct. The employee on a fixed wage can, at the margin, capture only a portion of the gain from his labor, and therefore has a tendency to reduce output. The employee who receives a commission equal to half the firm's profit attributable to his labor may work hard, but probably not quite as hard as he would if he received the entire profit from the completed sale, an arrangement that would solve the agency-cost problem only by undoing the firm....

The problem of management then is to identify the forms of social control that are best able to minimize these agency costs.... Internal auditors may help control some forms of abuse, and simple observation by coworkers may well monitor employee activities. (There are some very subtle tradeoffs to be considered when the firm decides whether to use partitions or separate offices for its employees.) Promotions, bonuses, and wages are also critical in shaping the level of employee performance. But the carrot cannot be used to the exclusion of the stick. In order to maintain internal discipline, the firm may have to resort to sanctions against individual employees. It is far easier to use those powers that can be unilaterally exercised: to fire, to demote, to withhold wages, or to reprimand. These devices can visit very powerful losses upon individual employees without the need to resort to legal action, and they permit the firm to monitor employee performance continually in order to identify both strong and weak workers and to compensate them accordingly. The principles here are constant, whether we speak of senior officials or lowly subordinates, and it is for just this reason that the contract at will is found at all levels in private markets....

Thus far, the analysis generally has focused on the position of the employer. Yet for the contract at will to be adopted *ex ante,* it must work for the benefit of workers as well. And indeed it does, for the contract at will also contains powerful limitations on employers' abuses of power. To see the importance of the contract will to the employee, it is useful to distinguish between two cases. In the first, the employer pays a fixed sum of money to the worker and is then free to demand of the employee whatever services he wants for some fixed period of time. In the second case, there is no fixed period of employment. The employer is free to demand whatever he wants of the employee, who in turn is free to withdraw for good reason, bad reason, or no reason at all.

The first arrangement invites abuse by the employer, who can now make enormous demands upon the worker without having to take into account either the worker's disutility during the period of service or the value of the worker's labor at contract termination. A fixed-period contract that leaves the worker's obligations unspecified thereby creates a sharp tension between the parties, since the employer receives all the marginal benefits and the employee bears all the marginal costs.

Matters are very different where the employer makes increased demands under a contract at will. Now the worker can quit whenever the net value of the employment contract turns negative. As with the employer's power to fire or demote, the threat to quit (or at a lower level to come late or leave early) is one that can be exercised without resort to litigation. Furthermore, that threat turns out to be most effective when the employer's opportunistic behavior is the greatest because the situation is one in which the worker has least to lose. To be sure, the worker will not necessarily make a threat whenever the employer insists that the worker accept a less favorable set of contractual terms, for sometimes the changes may be accepted as an uneventful adjustment in the total compensation level attributable to a change in the market price of labor. This point counts, however, only as an additional strength of the contract at will, which allows for small adjustments *in both directions* in ongoing contractual arrangements with a minimum of bother and confusion....

Another reason why employees are often willing to enter into at-will employment contracts stems from the asymmetry of reputational losses. Any party who cheats may well obtain a bad reputation that will induce others to avoid dealing with him. The size of these losses tends to differ systematically between employers and employees — to the advantage of the employee. Thus in the usual situation there are many workers and a single employer. The disparity in number is apt to be greatest in large industrial concerns, where the at-will contract is commonly, if mistakenly, thought to be most unsatisfactory because of the supposed inequality of bargaining power. The employer who decides to act for a bad reason or no reason at all may not face any legal liability under the classical common law rule. But he faces very powerful adverse economic consequences. If coworkers perceive the dismissal as arbitrary, they will take fresh stock of their own prospects, for they can no longer be certain that their faithful performance will ensure their security and advancement. The uncertain prospects created by arbitrary employer behavior is functionally indistinguishable from a reduction in wages unilaterally imposed by the employer. At the margin some workers will look elsewhere, and typically the best workers will have the greatest opportunities. By the same token the large employer has more to gain if he dismisses undesirable employees, for this ordinarily acts as an implicit increase in wages to the other employees, who are no longer burdened with uncooperative or obtuse coworkers....

The reason why these contracts at will are effective is precisely that the employer must always pay an implicit price when he exercises his right to fire. He no longer has the right to compel the employee's service, as the employee can enter the market to find another job. The costs of the employer's decision therefore are borne in large measure by the employer himself, creating an implicit system of coinsurance between employer and employee against employer abuse. Nor, it must be stressed, are the costs to the employer light. It is true that employees who work within a firm acquire specific knowledge about its operation and upon dismissal can transfer only a portion of that knowledge to the new job. Nonetheless, the problem is roughly symmetrical, as the employer must find, select, and train a replacement worker who may not turn out to be better than the first employee. Workers are not fungible, and sorting them out may be difficult: résumés can be misleading, if not fraudulent; references may be only too eager to unload an unsuitable employee; training is expensive; and the new worker may not like the job or may be forced to move out of town. In any case, firms must bear the costs of voluntary turnover by workers who quit, which gives them a frequent reminder of the need to avoid self-inflicted losses. The institutional stability of employment contracts at will can now be explained in part by their legal fragility. The right to fire is exercised only infrequently because the threat of firing is effective....

An examination of the contracting objectives of parties explains why contracts at will are common. The same set of considerations, however, also helps explain why contracts at will are *not* found in all employment contexts, but are instead sometimes displaced by more elaborate contractual mechanisms. The central point is that the contract at will works only where performance on both sides takes place in lockstep progression. This condition will be satisfied where neither side has performed or where the worker's past performance has been matched by appropriate payment from the employer. In these cases the contract at will provides both employer and employee with a simple, informal "bond" against the future misfeasance of the other side: fire or quit. Where the sequence of performance requires one side to perform in full before the other side begins performance, this bonding mechanism will break down because there are no longer two unperformed promises of roughly equal value to stand as security for each other. That is why an employee will have to resort to legal action if the employer simply refuses to pay wages for work that has already been done. It is also why a contract at will cannot handle the question of compensation for job-related personal injuries, for after injury the value of the right to quit no longer balances off the right to fire.

B. RATIONALIZING THE CONTEMPORARY CASES

STEWART J. SCHWAB, LIFE-CYCLE JUSTICE: ACCOMMODATING JUST CAUSE AND EMPLOYMENT AT WILL, 92 Michigan Law Review 8-11, 39-50 (1993)[*]

Snapshot examinations of current unjust dismissal law have led employment law commentators to see only chaos, a set of cases with little internal coherence or rationale. A view of the decisions in their historical sweep causes commentators to see evolution: in the beginning was employment at will, now chaos exists, the natural ending point will be just cause. Most commentators applaud the trend, urge its completion, and bemoan any hesitation or backsliding by the courts. Their continual refrain is that the United States lags behind the rest of the world on this issue. At the other extreme, some conservatives, most prominently Richard Epstein, hearken back to the heyday of employment at will as the ideal state of employment law. Such observers lament every move away from a strict presumption that all employment contracts can be terminated at will by either party.

---

[*] Reprinted with permission of Michigan Law Review Association.

The fundamental problem with these perspectives is that they criticize current law but they do not understand or explain it, except in the crudest way. The just-cause boosters simply applaud every pro-employee decision and decry the others as backsliding responses to conservative political pressures. The at-will zealots simply cheer and boo the other way. Neither perspective appreciates the apparent vacillation of current courts, which erode the at-will presumption without rejecting it.

Current termination law does have an underlying coherence. We should recognize this coherence before we reject the contemporary common law system for either the Model Act's futuristic scheme of arbitrating just cause or a return to the heyday of employment at will. This paper attempts to articulate the coherence of current doctrine. Reacting to the almost uniform polarization on this issue, I argue both positively and normatively for an intermediate position. The current intermediate position of the common law balances two conflicting problems. A career-employment relationship faces two types of opportunism: opportunistic firings by an unfettered employer and shirking by employees with job security. An extreme legal rule can handle either problem alone, but only by ignoring the other. Thus, a legal presumption of employment at will handles the shirking problem well but gives no protection against opportunistic firings. A just-cause regime has the opposite virtue and flaw. The legal challenge is to find an intermediate rule that provides the optimal check against both dangers.

The common law has groped towards such a rule by recognizing that the relative magnitudes of the two problems vary over the life cycle of the worker. The danger of employer opportunism is greatest for late-career workers, and it is also a problem for some beginning-career employees. By contrast, the greater problem at midcareer is shirking. In response, the courts have begun to offer contract protections for workers at the beginning and end of the life cycle, while maintaining a presumption of at-will employment for midcareer employees. In arguing for the wisdom of this approach, I, like the courts, refrain from making a categorical statement that at-will or just-cause employment should never — or should always — be the governing presumption....

1. *Beginning-Career Opportunism*

Employees face a risk of opportunistic termination at the beginning of the life cycle. The risk arises because employees commit irretrievable investments to the relationship before the employer does. Usually the beginning-career cases involve employees who have moved to take a job or quit another job in reliance on a job offer.

[The article then discusses several cases, including *Grouse v. Group Health Plan* and *Veno v. Meredith*.]

We see, then, that courts sometimes allow claims by beginning-career employees who are arbitrarily fired after moving or quitting a prior job. Some courts use a promissory estoppel or reliance theory, some find an implied contract for a reasonable time to allow the employee to recoup his expenses, and some simply use the decision to move or to quit as evidence of an actual definite-term agreement. Regardless of the theory for recovery, one can explain these cases as attempts to regulate opportunistic firings early in the life cycle. Employers have not yet invested in the relationship and thus are not hurt if they arbitrarily dismiss the new employee. This means that the relationship is not self-enforcing, as it is when both parties have incurred sunk costs.

Nevertheless, protection for beginning-career employees is far from universal. Many or even most courts refuse to find that reliance on an at-will job offer is reasonable. In these cases, an employee quits another job or moves to a new job at his own risk.

The ambivalence of courts in this area is understandable. For at least three reasons, the opportunistic termination rationale for protecting employees is weaker in these beginning-career cases than it is later in the life cycle. First, very often the employer also makes substantial investments early in the relationship. Recruiting and training new employees can be a major cost to many firms.

Second, even if recruiting costs are insignificant — as they will be in many cases — so that arbitrarily firing the employee does not penalize the employer, the employer gains nothing from firing a person early in his career. Thus, while employees [*sic*] often suffer no penalty from an arbitrary beginning-career firing, they gain no benefit from them either. This fact distinguishes beginning-career from late-career firings, in which the employer can gain from firing employees whom it pays more than their current output.

A final problem with job protection for new employees is that employers often need a probationary period to sort out hiring mistakes, wherein they can fire employees without explanation or extensive documentation of their reasons. Relevant here is the fact that competitive firms, largely responding to the entry and exit of early-career employees, virtually always contract for at-will dis-missal. Even the Model Employment Termination Act, which calls for general good-cause protection for employees, refuses to protect employees with less than a year of service.

In sum, in many situations employer opportunism against beginning employees is either a trivial threat or outweighed by legitimate needs to maintain employer flexibility. In these situations, courts do not scrutinize the sudden termination. Still, the potential for opportunistic employer offers is real. An employer engages in opportunistic behavior when it hires a better person before training anyone but after the first job applicant has relied on the offer. Courts protect beginning employees from such opportunism.

2. *Late-Career Opportunism*

Late-career employees face the greatest danger of opportunistic firings. At the end of their life cycle, they often earn more than their current productivity. If they do, the employer has a financial incentive to terminate them, even if it violates an implicit promise to allow the employee to reap the rewards of hard work earlier in his career.

The Age Discrimination in Employment Act provides one check against late-career opportunism. By prohibiting employers from firing workers above the age of forty because of their age, the ADEA protects older workers from discharges based upon stereotypes that lead employers to underestimate their productivity. "We need new blood" and "Doe is slowing down a notch" are classic statements that create age discrimination lawsuits.

However, the ADEA may offer only limited protection against the central concern of the life-cycle model — opportunistic firings when salary and forthcoming benefits outweigh current productivity....

Greater protection may come from common law courts, which in recent years have begun policing opportunistic firings of late-career employees. The leading case is *Pugh v. See's Candies, Inc.*, in which a thirty-two-year employee was abruptly fired after working his way up from dishwasher to corporate vice president. The employee never had a clear agreement about job security, although managers had given him encouraging evaluations over the years. The court held that this career pattern, including the length of service and the policies and practices of the company, could establish an implied-in-fact promise against arbitrary dismissal. *Pugh* epitomizes the efficiency-wage story and its end-game dangers. Pugh committed himself to a single firm, worked hard to gain promotions to the promised easy life, but then was terminated. *Pugh* also demonstrates the effect of the arrival of new management on job security. In *Pugh*, new management arrived a year before Pugh's firing. Such major corporate changes may diminish the reputational check on firings of late-career employees.

Length of service is the key element that motivates courts to scrutinize a late-career firing. Most opinions, like *Pugh*, also examine oral statements and the company's general procedures....

Occasionally, an employee faces the danger of beginning-career and late-career opportunism at the same time. This situation occurs when a long-time employee agrees to a job transfer. A prominent example is *Foley v. Community Oil Co.*, in which a thirty-year employee was fired three years after accepting a job transfer to another state. The court's explicit rationale in finding the employee had stated a claim tracks the life-cycle theory. The court first noted that "uprooting and moving a family" could give rise to a contractual claim. The court then declared that "longevity of service can also give rise to an implied contract right." Tracking the lock-in problem with which we have wrestled, the court explained that "the employee, in providing long-term employment to a single employer substantially diminishes his economic mobility."

In sum, one can explain these cases as attempts to monitor and enforce the implicit life-cycle employment contract. Late in an employee's career, the usual checks against opportunistic firings unravel. Courts enter to monitor the bargain. The bargain does not give late-career employees complete job security. They can be dismissed for cause, because otherwise the shirking problems would be immense, but the employer does not prove cause simply by proving that salary exceeds current productivity. That is the typical life-cycle pattern that both sides to career employment anticipate and, ex ante, it is in the interests of both sides.

3. *Midcareer Shirking*

Once the employer has begun to make substantial, asset-specific investments in an employee, the risk of arbitrary firing diminishes. The greater danger of opportunistic behavior — at least, behavior that an appropriate dismissal standard could limit — comes from the employee's side. Because the employer does not want to repeat recruiting and training costs with another employee, the incumbent employee has an opportunity to shirk without fear of dismissal. Shirking at midcareer can occur even if the employer has the right to dismiss at will, but the shirking problem can be exacerbated if the employer must also surmount the hurdle of proving just cause.

This is not to say that the employer cannot exploit the midcareer employee. Indeed, as I emphasized above, being trapped by investments in firm-specific capital and in community roots can make a midcareer employee ripe for exploitation. But the exploitation will not take the form of firing because the employer is making money from the relationship. Rather than fire a midcareer employee, an employer may pay him less than would be called for under a fair division of the gains from the long-term relationship or make his workload or working conditions more onerous. Just cause cannot protect the midcareer employee from these abuses. Better, then, for the law to focus on something it can handle, which is deterrence of shirking by midcareer employees.

The courts seem to have intuited this fact by refusing, in general, to create contract protections against arbitrary terminations for midcareer workers. Midcareer employees have made the fewest contributions to the doctrinal erosion of at-will employment....

In summary, my argument is that the general pattern of good-faith and implied-contract cases reflects an intuitive understanding by the courts that employees are subject to opportunistic discharge at the end, and less consistently at the beginning, of the life cycle. Courts are reluctant, however, to give general protection against arbitrary dismissal to midcareer employees. The economic self-interest of employers should keep such dismissals in check. The greater concern is with employee shirking....

NOTE

Judicial Interference with Social Norms. Even if a life-cycle arrangement is good for the employment relationship, it may be overly costly for the courts to enforce. Professors Rock and Wachter have argued that employers and employees often choose to operate under informal norms (often including the life-cycle model), rather than under more formal contracts or legal rules. If employees and employer so choose, Rock and Wachter contend that the courts should generally leave the parties alone because an important part of the value of norms is their low cost. If the courts start enforcing norms rather than allowing unilateral changes in the relationship, their value is diminished. Edward B. Rock & Michael L. Wachter, *The Enforceability of Norms and the Employment Relationship*, 144 U. PA. L. REV. 1913 (1996).

C. THE LEGISLATIVE FUTURE

Several scholars have argued that the vague, patchwork law of wrongful discharge as created by courts should be superseded by clear legislation. *See* Clyde W. Summers, *Individual Protection Against Unjust Dismissal: Time for a Statute,* 62 VA. L. REV. 481 (1976); Arthur S. Leonard, *A New Common Law of Employment Termination,* 66 N.C. L. REV. 631 (1987); Jack Steiber & Michael Murray, *Protection Against Unjust Discharge: The Need for a Federal Statute,* 16 U. MICH. J.L. REFORM 319 (1983). In 1987, Montana became the first state to pass a comprehensive statute mandating good cause for employment terminations.[*] In 1991, the Commissioners on Uniform State Laws (the same group that promulgated the Uniform Commercial Code), passed a Model Employment Termination Act[**] to serve as a model for legislatures considering just-cause termination statutes. For an excellent overview by the principal draftsperson, see Theodore J. St. Antoine, *The Making of the Model Employment Termination Act,* 69 WASH. L. REV. 361 (1994). Among the many issues these statutes present are the following:

1. *Defining Just Cause.* A major issue is how to define "just cause." At one pole is the objective just-cause standard used in collective bargaining contracts. This standard generally requires objective evidence of actual misconduct before an individual employee can be terminated. Such a definition maximizes the proof problem for employers. At the other pole are cases like *Pugh v. See's Candies, Inc.,* 171 Cal. Rptr. 917, 928 (Cal. Ct. App. 1981), which would require only that the employer have "a fair and honest cause or reason, regulated by good faith on the part of the party exercising the power," and would insist that the decision-maker take care "not to interfere with the legitimate exercise of managerial discretion."

The distinction between just cause and good cause, as it is sometimes put, came to a head in *Sanders v. Parker Drilling Co.,* 911 F.2d 191 (9th Cir. 1990). There, an employer fired several employees (who were found to have an implied protection against discharge without just cause) for smoking marijuana on the job in violation of company rules. The jury, in a special verdict procedure, found the employer's investigation gave it a reasonable belief that the employees had smoked marijuana; but the jury also found that the employees did not, in fact, smoke marijuana. Applying Alaska law, the majority held that just cause

---

[*] The statute appears in the Statutory Appendix.

[**] The Model Act appears in the Statutory Appendix.

required the employer to show that the discharged employees actually engaged in the prohibited conduct, and upheld the trial court's award of approximately one-third of a million dollars to the fired employees. Judge Kozinski, dissenting, would equate just cause with a good faith standard, which would "protect[] the employee from being dismissed based on personal animosity, ill will and any other ulterior motive; and [would] require[] the employer to conduct a reasonable investigation ...."

Both the Montana statute and the Model Act use the term "good cause" rather than "just cause." Just cause is the typical term in collective bargaining contracts. Section 39-2-903(5) of the Montana statute defines good cause this way:

> "Good cause" means reasonable job-related grounds for dismissal based on a failure to satisfactorily perform job duties, disruption of the employer's operation, or other legitimate business reason.

Montana also prohibits discharges in retaliation for the employee's refusal to violate public policy or for reporting a violation of public policy. § 39-2-904(1), as defined in § 39-2-903(7).

The Model Act § 1(4) defines good cause this way:

> "Good cause" means (i) a reasonable basis related to an individual employee for termination of the employee's employment in view of relevant factors and circumstances, which may include the employee's duties, responsibilities, conduct on the job or otherwise, job performance, and employment record, or (ii) the exercise of business judgment in good faith by the employer, including setting its economic or institutional goals and determining methods to achieve those goals, organizing or reorganizing operations, discontinuing, consolidating, or divesting operations or positions or parts of operations or positions, determining the size of its work force and the nature of the positions filled by its work force, and determining and changing standards of performance for positions.

In what ways do these good cause standards differ from a just cause standard? In what ways do they differ from the standard used to judge a discharge under a definite-term contract?

In the following situations, under which statute would you prefer to represent a terminated worker? What are the chances of prevailing?

(a) A worker is fired for failing (or refusing to take) a drug test.

(b) A high-school teacher in a small town is fired for having a child out of wedlock.

(c) A worker who has received several merit and seniority-based wage increases is terminated because his salary is out of line with his productivity.

(d) A worker is fired for being absent because she was engaged in jury duty.

(e) A worker is fired for reporting that the company violated federal financial disclosure laws.

2. *Burden of Proof.* A second issue concerns the burden of proof. The collective bargaining analogue requires that the employer show just cause. Federal anti-discrimination statutes, by contrast, require that the employee persuade the factfinder that discrimination motivated the discharge. The *Pugh* court explicitly adopted the anti-discrimination standard.*

The Montana statute does not specify who has the burden of proof. The Model Act places the burden of proof on the complaining employee (§ 6(e)). It also gives the employer an affirmative defense of showing it would have terminated the employee even in the absence of the impermissible grounds (§ 6(f)). The Model Act has a declaratory judgment procedure by which the employer prior to termination can have the tribunal declare it has good cause to terminate the employee (§ 5(c)). In this declaratory judgment proceeding, the employer has the burden of proof (§ 6(e)).

3. *Courts or Arbitration?* A third issue is whether the tribunal that determines just cause should be a common law court, arbitrator, or something else.** An arbitration system would lower the costs of each adjudicated case, but the lower cost would increase the number of discharges challenged by employees, perhaps increasing total costs of adjudication.

The Montana statute contemplates litigation of termination cases in state court, but it encourages the parties to arbitrate the dispute (§ 39-2-914(1)). If a party offers to arbitrate, the offer is rejected, and the offeror prevails in court, the other side must pay its attorney fees (§ 39-2-914(4)). If the employee wins in arbitration, the employer must pay the arbitrator's fee and all costs (§ 39-2-914(5)).

The Model Termination Act proposes a more thorough system of arbitration (§ 5), although it also proposes variations that would have a state agency (Alternative A) or courts (Alternative B) handle termination disputes.

---

* Indeed, *Pugh* adopted the three-part minuet that the Supreme Court created for Title VII anti-discrimination cases. Citing *McDonnell Douglas Corp. v. Green*, 411 U.S. 792, 802-07 (1973), the *Pugh* court explained that once the employee "has demonstrated a prima facie case of wrongful termination in violation of his contract of employment[, t]he burden of coming forward with evidence as to the reason for [the employee's] termination now shifts to the employer. [The employee] may attack the employer's offered explanation, either on the ground that it is pretextual (and that the real reason is one prohibited by contract or public policy), or on the ground that it is insufficient to meet the employer's obligations under contract or applicable legal principles. [The employee] bears, however, the ultimate burden of proving that he was terminated wrongfully." 171 Cal. Rptr. at 927.

** Professor Bellace suggests that unemployment insurance tribunals should be used to determine wrongful discharge claims. Janice R. Bellace, *A Right of Fair Dismissal: Enforcing a Statutory Guarantee*, 16 U. MICH. J.L. REFORM 207 (1983). As she points out, unemployment insurance panels already decide comparable issues in determining whether a claimant was fired for job-related misconduct, which disqualifies them from benefits.

For an argument that arbitration should be a central feature of any just-cause scheme, consider the following:

WILLIAM B. GOULD, THE IDEA OF THE JOB AS PROPERTY IN CONTEMPORARY AMERICA: THE LEGAL AND COLLECTIVE BARGAINING FRAMEWORK, 1986 Brigham Young University Law Review 885, 908-10[*]

The first basic ingredient should be arbitration, its virtues being speed, economy, and informality. Yet there are problems with the use of this forum since arbitration is an institution which has gained such prominence in the organized sector. One of the most perplexing problems relates to the impartiality of arbitrators. It is one thing to have near unbounded confidence in impartiality where two institutions are contending with one another and arbitrators can expect to deal with both of them in the future. But in wrongful discharge cases, unless unions intervene in a good number of them to represent the unorganized, it is a contest between the individual employee and the employer. Can arbitrators be counted upon to demonstrate the same degree of impartiality where they know that it is unlikely that the individual employee will ever appear before them again — in contrast to dealings with unions and employers where the opposite is likely to be true? No response to this question is completely reassuring. But Canada has now had arbitration for unorganized employees at the federal level for nine years, and there do not seem to be major problems with impartiality. To date, the system in that country seems to be working well.

A virtue of the arbitration system is that it would provide for not only a swift resolution of an unfair dismissal complaint, but also the remedy of reinstatement rather than punitive and compensatory damages. The assumption is that this is what the average worker wants most — especially if the remedy could be obtained quickly. But one problem with this approach is that again, unless the unions become involved, there is no institution which can monitor management attempts to harass and rid itself of the employee who has been foisted upon it through the reinstatement remedy. This may be the reason (aside from common law tradition in Britain) why reinstatement is so apparently infrequent in Europe. Even in this country, a very substantial number of employees do not take the reinstatement remedy offered under The National Labor Relations Act and arbitration — even though an exclusive bargaining agent is on the scene to monitor potential harassment. Accordingly, potential evasion of a reinstatement order is likely to be present in wrongful discharge cases — although this fact may simply argue for a more discriminate and cautious approach to use of the reinstatement remedy in such arbitrations.

A third concern, besides impartiality and reinstatement, relates to the potential avalanche of arbitration cases. Part of the rationale for substituting arbitration for the courts is that more substantial employee access can be obtained. Yet if all

---

[*] Reprinted with permission of Brigham Young University Law Review.

dismissed employees decide to roll the dice and go to arbitration, that system may grind to a halt. In the organized sector, unions sift out grievances which are unmeritorious or less important. No similar entity can play a role under wrongful discharge legislation — although it is interesting to note that the number of Canadian cases at the federal level has recently diminished, not increased.

The answer here would seem to be, as the California State Bar Committee advocates, that mediation and informal discovery be used to diminish the number of cases. The imposition of financial costs equally shared by employee and employer would also help. True, the fifty-fifty sharing will often be unfair to the employee since he or she will have less resources than the corporation. But this system not only will diminish the number of cases that would otherwise go to arbitration, but it also is more fair to the employees than the status quo which, more often than not, employees find too expensive to pursue.

A related concern is the number of arbitrators. Arbitrators acceptable to both labor and management are already in short supply. Whatever the success of statutory mechanisms in reducing the number of cases that proceed to hearings on their merit, the demand for arbitrators will increase substantially if such legislation is passed.

But this is a problem, like the question of impartiality, which affects the development of alternative dispute resolution processes as a general matter. Does anyone believe that if the entire membership of the National Academy of Arbitrators were to vanish from the face of the earth, that most unions and employers would eliminate their arbitration clauses in collective bargaining agreements? While most of us like to see ourselves as indispensable, programs that have been adopted on a limited basis for the training of new arbitrators could go a long way toward filling the supply that will be needed if such legislation is passed.

———————

4. *Remedies*. To obtain employer support for wrongful discharge legislation, statutes generally limit the damages that a wrongfully terminated employee can recover. The tradeoff is similar to the classic one underlying workers' compensation laws: more certain recovery of smaller damages.

The Montana statute calls for an award of lost wages and fringe benefits for a period of four years from the date of discharge, together with interest (§ 39-2-905(1)). Interim earnings must be deducted. The Montana statute allows punitive damages only if the employee establishes "by clear and convincing evidence that the employer engaged in actual fraud or actual malice" (§ 39-2-905(2)). The statute expressly disallows any recovery for pain and suffering, emotional distress, and compensatory damages (§ 39-2-905(3)).

The Model Act contemplates reinstatement and backpay as the prime remedies (§§ 7(b)(1), 7(b)(2)). If reinstatement is not awarded, the Model Act authorizes an award of wages and fringe benefits for up to three years, taking into account such equitable considerations as the employee's length of service with the employer and the reasons for the termination (§ 7(b)(3)). Interim and likely alternative earnings must be deducted from the award. Like the Montana statute, the Model Act expressly prohibits the arbitrator from awarding "damages for pain and suffering, emotional distress, defamation, fraud, or other injury under the common law, punitive damages, compensatory damages, or any other monetary award." (§ 7(d)).

5. *Waiver.* The Montana statute does not apply to employees under collective bargaining contracts or a written contract for a specific term (§ 39-2-912(2)). Similarly, the Model Act does not cover terminations at the end of a written or oral contract "of specified duration related to the completion of a specified task, project, undertaking, or assignment." (§ 4(d)).

The Model Act also allows the parties in writing to waive the good-cause requirement for termination, if the employer agrees that for any termination other than willful misconduct it will pay one month's severance pay for every full year of employment, up to thirty months (§ 4(c)).

The Model Act leaves the term "willful misconduct" undefined. It is a term often used in unemployment insurance law for determining whether a fired employee is ineligible for unemployment insurance. Generally, willful misconduct requires more than employee incompetence.

For what jobs are employers most likely to seek 4(c) waivers? The good-cause requirements will prove most burdensome in jobs in which it is difficult to document good cause. For example, should law firms and other employers of professionals seek 4(c) waivers in their employment contracts?

6. *Who Supports These Laws?* Do the Montana statute and the Model Termination Act clearly favor employees, by giving them general good-cause protection they did not have before? Or are the statutes a grand compromise (similar to workers' compensation statutes), whereby employers give up some defenses and employees give up some claims in exchange for a more streamlined process? What aspects of the law would be supported by employees, employers, or both?

Professor Krueger has empirically estimated the likelihood that unjust-dismissal legislation will be introduced in a state legislature: after controlling for such factors as the amount of union membership in manufacturing and the proportion of Democrats in the state legislature, he found that

> the probability that a state legislature proposes an unjust-dismissal law is increased by 6.7 percentage points if its court system has recognized the good faith exception, by 8.5 percentage points if the public policy exception has been recognized, and by 2.0 percentage points if the implied contract exception has been recognized. Put another way, the probability that a law is proposed is more than quadrupled if these causes of action have been allowed in a state.

Alan B. Krueger, *The Evolution of Unjust-Dismissal Legislation in the United States,* 44 INDUS. & LAB. REL. REV. 644, 655-56 (1991). Does this evidence suggest that legislatures consider wrongful discharge statutes in order to curb expansive court decisions?

D. ARBITRATION OF EMPLOYMENT CLAIMS

One important development in wrongful termination claims, as well as other, statutory employment claims, is shifting disputes to binding arbitration rather than litigation. Arbitration has a long history in labor arbitration contracts, but it remains controversial in nonunion employment disputes.

GILMER v. INTERSTATE/JOHNSON LANE CORP.

Supreme Court of the United States
500 U.S. 20 (1991)

JUSTICE WHITE delivered the opinion of the Court.

The question presented in this case is whether a claim under the Age Discrimination in Employment Act of 1967 (ADEA) can be subjected to compulsory arbitration pursuant to an arbitration agreement in a securities registration application. The Court of Appeals held that it could, and we affirm.

I

Respondent Interstate/Johnson Lane Corporation (Interstate) hired petitioner Robert Gilmer as a Manager of Financial Services in May 1981. As required by his employment, Gilmer registered as a securities representative with several stock exchanges, including the New York Stock Exchange (NYSE). His registration application, entitled "Uniform Application for Securities Industry Registration or Transfer," provided, among other things, that Gilmer "agree[d] to arbitrate any dispute, claim or controversy" arising between him and Interstate "that is required to be arbitrated under the rules, constitutions or by-laws of the organizations with which I register." Of relevance to this case, NYSE Rule 347 provides for arbitration of "[a]ny controversy between a registered representative and any member or member organization arising out of the employment or termination of employment of such registered representative."

Interstate terminated Gilmer's employment in 1987, at which time Gilmer was 62 years of age. After first filing an age discrimination charge with the Equal Employment Opportunity Commission (EEOC), Gilmer subsequently brought suit in the United States District Court for the Western District of North Carolina, alleging that Interstate had discharged him because of his age, in violation of the ADEA. In response to Gilmer's complaint, Interstate filed in the District Court a motion to compel arbitration of the ADEA claim. In its motion, Interstate relied upon the arbitration agreement in Gilmer's registration application, as well as the Federal Arbitration Act (FAA), 9 U.S.C. § 1 *et seq.* The District Court denied Interstate's motion ... [, but the Court of Appeals reversed.]

We granted certiorari to resolve a conflict among the Courts of Appeals regarding the arbitrability of ADEA claims.

II

The FAA was originally enacted in 1925, and then reenacted and codified in 1947 as Title 9 of the United States Code. Its purpose was to reverse the long-standing judicial hostility to arbitration agreements that had existed at English common law and had been adopted by American courts, and to place arbitration agreements upon the same footing as other contracts. Its primary substantive provision states that "[a] written provision in any maritime transaction or a contract evidencing a transaction involving commerce to settle by arbitration a controversy thereafter arising out of such contract or transaction ... shall be valid, irrevocable, and enforceable, save upon such grounds as exist at law or in equity for the revocation of any contract." 9 U.S.C. § 2. The FAA also provides for stays of proceedings in federal district courts when an issue in the proceeding is referable to arbitration, § 3, and for orders compelling arbitration when one party has failed, neglected, or refused to comply with an arbitration agreement, § 4. These provisions manifest a "liberal federal policy favoring arbitration agreements." *Moses H. Cone Memorial Hospital v. Mercury Construction Corp.*, 460 U.S. 1, 24 (1983).[2]

It is by now clear that statutory claims may be the subject of an arbitration agreement, enforceable pursuant to the FAA. Indeed, in recent years we have held enforceable arbitration agreements relating to claims arising under the Sherman Act; § 10(b) of the Securities Exchange Act of 1934; the civil provisions of the Racketeer Influenced and Corrupt Organizations Act (RICO); and § 12(2) of the Securities Act of 1933. *See Mitsubishi Motors Corp. v. Soler Chrysler-Plymouth, Inc.*, 473 U.S. 614 (1985); *Shearson/American Express Inc. v. McMahon*, 482 U.S. 220 (1987); *Rodriguez de Quijas v. Shearson/American*

---

[2] Section 1 of the FAA provides that "nothing herein contained shall apply to contracts of employment of seamen, railroad employees, or any other class of workers engaged in foreign or interstate commerce." 9 U.S.C. § 1. Several *amici curiae* in support of Gilmer argue that that section excludes from the coverage of the FAA all "contracts of employment." Gilmer, however, did not raise the issue in the courts below; it was not addressed there; and it was not among the questions presented in the petition for certiorari. In any event, it would be inappropriate to address the scope of the § 1 exclusion because the arbitration clause being enforced here is not contained in a contract of employment. The FAA requires that the arbitration clause being enforced be in writing. *See* 9 U.S.C. §§ 2, 3. The record before us does not show, and the parties do not contend, that Gilmer's employment agreement with Interstate contained a written arbitration clause. Rather, the arbitration clause at issue is in Gilmer's securities registration application, which is a contract with the securities exchanges, not with Interstate. The lower courts addressing the issue uniformly have concluded that the exclusionary clause in § 1 of the FAA is inapplicable to arbitration clauses contained in such registration applications.... Unlike the dissent, we choose to follow the plain language of the FAA and the weight of authority, and we therefore hold that § 1's exclusionary clause does not apply to Gilmer's arbitration agreement. Consequently, we leave for another day the issue raised by *amici curiae*.

Express, Inc., 490 U.S. 477 (1989). In these cases we recognized that "[b]y agreeing to arbitrate a statutory claim, a party does not forgo the substantive rights afforded by the statute; it only submits to their resolution in an arbitral, rather than a judicial, forum." *Mitsubishi*, 473 U.S. at 628.

Although all statutory claims may not be appropriate for arbitration, "[h]aving made the bargain to arbitrate, the party should be held to it unless Congress itself has evinced an intention to preclude a waiver of judicial remedies for the statutory rights at issue." *Ibid.* In this regard, we note that the burden is on Gilmer to show that Congress intended to preclude a waiver of a judicial forum for ADEA claims. *See McMahon*, 482 U.S. at 227. If such an intention exists, it will be discoverable in the text of the ADEA, its legislative history, or an "inherent conflict" between arbitration and the ADEA's underlying purposes. *See ibid.* Throughout such an inquiry, it should be kept in mind that "questions of arbitrability must be addressed with a healthy regard for the federal policy favoring arbitration." *Moses H. Cone*, 460 U.S. at 24.

III

Gilmer concedes that nothing in the text of the ADEA or its legislative history explicitly precludes arbitration. He argues, however, that compulsory arbitration of ADEA claims pursuant to arbitration agreements would be inconsistent with the statutory framework and purposes of the ADEA. Like the Court of Appeals, we disagree.

A

Congress enacted the ADEA in 1967 "to promote employment of older persons based on their ability rather than age; to prohibit arbitrary age discrimination in employment; [and] to help employers and workers find ways of meeting problems arising from the impact of age on employment." 29 U.S.C. § 621(b). To achieve those goals, the ADEA, among other things, makes it unlawful for an employer "to fail or refuse to hire or to discharge any individual or otherwise discriminate against any individual with respect to his compensation, terms, conditions, of privileges of employment, because of such individual's age." § 623(a)(1). This proscription is enforced both by private suits and by the EEOC. In order for an aggrieved individual to bring suit under the ADEA, he or she must first file a charge with the EEOC and then wait at least 60 days. § 626(d). An individual's right to sue is extinguished, however, if the EEOC institutes an action against the employer. § 626(c)(1). Before the EEOC can bring such an action, though, it must "attempt to eliminate the discriminatory practice or practices alleged, and to effect voluntary compliance with the requirements of this chapter through informal methods of conciliation, conference, and persuasion." § 626(b); *see also* 29 CFR § 1626.15 (1990).

As Gilmer contends, the ADEA is designed not only to address individual grievances, but also to further important social policies. We do not perceive any inherent inconsistency between those policies, however, and enforcing agreements to arbitrate age discrimination claims. It is true that arbitration focuses on specific disputes between the parties involved. The same can be said, however, of judicial resolution of claims. Both of these dispute resolution mechanisms nevertheless also can further broader social purposes. The Sherman Act, the Securities Exchange Act of 1934, RICO, and the Securities Act of 1933 all are designed to advance important public policies, but, as noted above, claims under those statutes are appropriate for arbitration. "[S]o long as the prospective litigant effectively may vindicate [his or her] statutory cause of action in the arbitral forum, the statute will continue to serve both its remedial and deterrent function." *Mitsubishi, supra*, at 637.

We also are unpersuaded by the argument that arbitration will undermine the role of the EEOC in enforcing the ADEA. An individual ADEA claimant subject to an arbitration agreement will still be free to file a charge with the EEOC, even though the claimant is not able to institute a private judicial action. Indeed, Gilmer filed a charge with the EEOC in this case. In any event, the EEOC's role in combating age discrimination is not dependent on the filing of a charge; the agency may receive information concerning alleged violations of the ADEA "from any source," and it has independent authority to investigate age discrimination. *See* 29 CFR §§ 1626.4, 1626.13 (1990). Moreover, nothing in the ADEA indicates that Congress intended that the EEOC be involved in all employment disputes. Such disputes can be settled, for example, without any EEOC involvement.[3] Finally, the mere involvement of an administrative agency in the enforcement of a statute is not sufficient to preclude arbitration. For example, the Securities Exchange Commission is heavily involved in the enforcement of the Securities Exchange Act of 1934 and the Securities Act of 1933, but we have held that claims under both of those statutes may be subject to compulsory arbitration.

Gilmer also argues that compulsory arbitration is improper because it deprives claimants of the judicial forum provided for by the ADEA. Congress, however, did not explicitly preclude arbitration or other nonjudicial resolution of claims, even in its recent amendments to the ADEA. "[I]f Congress intended the substantive protection afforded [by the ADEA] to include protection against waiver of the right to a judicial forum, that intention will be deducible from text or legislative history." *Mitsubishi*, 473 U.S. at 628. Moreover, Gilmer's argument ignores the ADEA's flexible approach to resolution of claims. The EEOC, for example, is directed to pursue "informal methods of conciliation, conference, and persuasion," 29 U.S.C. § 626(b), which suggests that out-of-court dispute resolution, such as arbitration, is consistent with the statutory scheme established

---

[3] In the recently enacted Older Workers Benefit Protection Act, Pub. L. 101-433, 104 Stat. 978, Congress amended the ADEA to provide that "[a]n individual may not waive any right or claim under this Act unless the waiver is knowing and voluntary." *See* § 201. Congress also specified certain conditions that must be met in order for a waiver to be knowing and voluntary. *Ibid.*

by Congress. In addition, arbitration is consistent with Congress' grant of concurrent jurisdiction over ADEA claims to state and federal courts, *see* 29 U.S.C. § 626(c)(1) (allowing suits to be brought "in any court of competent jurisdiction"), because arbitration agreements, "like the provision for concurrent jurisdiction, serve to advance the objective of allowing [claimants] a broader right to select the forum for resolving disputes, whether it be judicial or otherwise." *Rodriguez de Quijas, supra*, at 483.

B

In arguing that arbitration is inconsistent with the ADEA, Gilmer also raises a host of challenges to the adequacy of arbitration procedures. Initially, we note that in our recent arbitration cases we have already rejected most of these arguments as insufficient to preclude arbitration of statutory claims. Such generalized attacks on arbitration "res[t] on suspicion of arbitration as a method of weakening the protections afforded in the substantive law to would-be complainants," and as such, they are "far out of step with our current strong endorsement of the federal statutes favoring this method of resolving disputes." *Rodriguez de Quijas, supra*, at 481. Consequently, we address these arguments only briefly.

Gilmer first speculates that arbitration panels will be biased. However, "[w]e decline to indulge the presumption that the parties and arbitral body conducting a proceeding will be unable or unwilling to retain competent, conscientious and impartial arbitrators." *Mitsubishi, supra*, at 634. In any event, we note that the NYSE arbitration rules, which are applicable to the dispute in this case, provide protections against biased panels. The rules require, for example, that the parties be informed of the employment histories of the arbitrators, and that they be allowed to make further inquiries into the arbitrators' backgrounds. In addition, each party is allowed one peremptory challenge and unlimited challenges for cause. Moreover, the arbitrators are required to disclose "any circumstances which might preclude [them] from rendering an objective and impartial determination." The FAA also protects against bias, by providing that courts may overturn arbitration decisions "[w]here there was evident partiality or corruption in the arbitrators." 9 U.S.C. § 10 (b). There has been no showing in this case that those provisions are inadequate to guard against potential bias.

Gilmer also complains that the discovery allowed in arbitration is more limited than in the federal courts, which he contends will make it difficult to prove discrimination. It is unlikely, however, that age discrimination claims require more extensive discovery than other claims that we have found to be arbitrable, such as RICO and antitrust claims. Moreover, there has been no showing in this case that the NYSE discovery provisions, which allow for document production, information requests, depositions, and subpoenas, will prove insufficient to allow ADEA claimants such as Gilmer a fair opportunity to present their claims. Although those procedures might not be as extensive as in the federal courts, by agreeing to arbitrate, a party "trades the procedures and opportunity for review of the courtroom for the simplicity, informality, and expedition of arbitration." *Mitsubishi, supra*, at 628. Indeed, an important counterweight to the reduced discovery in NYSE arbitration is that arbitrators are not bound by the rules of evidence.

A further alleged deficiency of arbitration is that arbitrators often will not issue written opinions, resulting, Gilmer contends, in a lack of public knowledge of employers' discriminatory policies, an inability to obtain effective appellate review, and a stifling of the development of the law. The NYSE rules, however, do require that all arbitration awards be in writing, and that the awards contain the names of the parties, a summary of the issues in controversy, and a description of the award issued. In addition, the award decisions are made available to the public. Furthermore, judicial decisions addressing ADEA claims will continue to be issued because it is unlikely that all or even most ADEA claimants will be subject to arbitration agreements. Finally, Gilmer's concerns apply equally to settlements of ADEA claims, which, as noted above, are clearly allowed.[4]

It is also argued that arbitration procedures cannot adequately further the purposes of the ADEA because they do not provide for broad equitable relief and class actions. As the court below noted, however, arbitrators do have the power to fashion equitable relief. Indeed, the NYSE rules applicable here do not restrict the types of relief an arbitrator may award, but merely refer to "damages and/or other relief." The NYSE rules also provide for collective proceedings. But "even if the arbitration could not go forward as a class action or class relief could not be granted by the arbitrator, the fact that the [ADEA] provides for the possibility of bringing a collective action does not mean that individual attempts at conciliation were intended to be barred." *Nicholson v. CPC Int'l Inc.*, 877 F.2d 221, 241 (CA3 1989) (Becker, J., dissenting). Finally, it should be remembered that arbitration agreements will not preclude the EEOC from bringing actions seeking class-wide and equitable relief.

C

An additional reason advanced by Gilmer for refusing to enforce arbitration agreements relating to ADEA claims is his contention that there often will be unequal bargaining power between employers and employees. Mere inequality in bargaining power, however, is not a sufficient reason to hold that arbitration agreements are never enforceable in the employment context. Relationships between securities dealers and investors, for example, may involve unequal bargaining power, but we nevertheless held in *Rodriguez de Quijas* and *McMahon*

---

[4] Gilmer also contends that judicial review of arbitration decisions is too limited. We have stated, however, that "although judicial scrutiny of arbitration awards necessarily is limited, such review is sufficient to ensure that arbitrators comply with the requirements of the statute" at issue. *Shearson/American Express Inc. v. McMahon*, 482 U.S. 220, 232 (1987).

that agreements to arbitrate in that context are enforceable. As discussed above, the FAA's purpose was to place arbitration agreements on the same footing as other contracts. Thus, arbitration agreements are enforceable "save upon such grounds as exist at law or in equity for the revocation of any contract." 9 U.S.C. § 2. "Of course, courts should remain attuned to well-supported claims that the agreement to arbitrate resulted from the sort of fraud or overwhelming economic power that would provide grounds 'for the revocation of any contract.'" *Mitsubishi*, 473 U.S. at 627. There is no indication in this case, however, that Gilmer, an experienced businessman, was coerced or defrauded into agreeing to the arbitration clause in his registration application. As with the claimed procedural inadequacies discussed above, this claim of unequal bargaining power is best left for resolution in specific cases.

IV

In addition to the arguments discussed above, Gilmer vigorously asserts that our decision in *Alexander v. Gardner-Denver Co.*, 415 U.S. 36 (1974), and its progeny — *Barrentine v. Arkansas-Best Freight System, Inc.*, 450 U.S. 728 (1981), and *McDonald v. West Branch*, 466 U.S. 284 (1984) — preclude arbitration of employment discrimination claims. Gilmer's reliance on these cases, however, is misplaced.

In *Gardner-Denver*, the issue was whether a discharged employee whose grievance had been arbitrated pursuant to an arbitration clause in a collective-bargaining agreement was precluded from subsequently bringing a Title VII action based upon the conduct that was the subject of the grievance. In holding that the employee was not foreclosed from bringing the Title VII claim, we stressed that an employee's contractual rights under a collective-bargaining agreement are distinct from the employee's statutory Title VII rights:

> "In submitting his grievance to arbitration, an employee seeks to vindicate his contractual right under a collective-bargaining agreement. By contrast, in filing a lawsuit under Title VII, an employee asserts independent statutory rights accorded by Congress. The distinctly separate nature of these contractual and statutory rights is not vitiated merely because both were violated as a result of the same factual occurrence." 415 U.S. at 49-50.

We also noted that a labor arbitrator has authority only to resolve questions of contractual rights. The arbitrator's "task is to effectuate the intent of the parties" and he or she does not have the "general authority to invoke public laws that conflict with the bargain between the parties." *Id.*, at 53. By contrast, "in instituting an action under Title VII, the employee is not seeking review of the arbitrator's decision. Rather, he is asserting a statutory right independent of the arbitration process." *Id.*, at 54. We further expressed concern that in collective-bargaining arbitration "the interests of the individual employee may be subordinated to the collective interests of all employees in the bargaining unit." *Id.,* at 58, n. 19.[5]

Barrentine and *McDonald* similarly involved the issue whether arbitration under a collective-bargaining agreement precluded a subsequent statutory claim. In holding that the statutory claims there were not precluded, we noted, as in *Gardner-Denver*, the difference between contractual rights under a collective-bargaining agreement and individual statutory rights, the potential disparity in interests between a union and an employee, and the limited authority and power of labor arbitrators.

There are several important distinctions between the *Gardner-Denver* line of cases and the case before us. First, those cases did not involve the issue of the enforceability of an agreement to arbitrate statutory claims. Rather, they involved the quite different issue whether arbitration of contract-based claims precluded subsequent judicial resolution of statutory claims. Since the employees there had not agreed to arbitrate their statutory claims, and the labor arbitrators were not authorized to resolve such claims, the arbitration in those cases understandably was held not to preclude subsequent statutory actions. Second, because the arbitration in those cases occurred in the context of a collective-bargaining agreement, the claimants there were represented by their unions in the arbitration proceedings. An important concern therefore was the tension between collective representation and individual statutory rights, a concern not applicable to the present case. Finally, those cases were not decided under the FAA, which, as discussed above, reflects a "liberal federal policy favoring arbitration agreements." *Mitsubishi*, 473 U.S. at 625. Therefore, those cases provide no basis for refusing to enforce Gilmer's agreement to arbitrate his ADEA claim.

V

We conclude that Gilmer has not met his burden of showing that Congress, in enacting the ADEA, intended to preclude arbitration of claims under that Act. Accordingly, the judgment of the Court of Appeals is

Affirmed.

JUSTICE STEVENS, with whom JUSTICE MARSHALL joins, dissenting.
Section 1 of the Federal Arbitration Act (FAA) states:

---

[5] The Court in *Alexander v. Gardner-Denver Co.*, also expressed the view that arbitration was inferior to the judicial process for resolving statutory claims. That "mistrust of the arbitral process," however, has been undermined by our recent arbitration decisions. *McMahon*, 482 U.S. at 231-232. "[W]e are well past the time when judicial suspicion of the desirability of arbitration and of the competence of arbitral tribunals inhibited the development of arbitration as an alternative means of dispute resolution." *Mitsubishi Motors Corp. v. Soler Chrysler-Plymouth, Inc.*, 473 U.S. 614, 626-627 (1985).

"[N]othing herein contained shall apply to contracts of employment of seamen, railroad employees, or any other class of workers engaged in foreign or interstate commerce." 9 U.S.C. § 1.

The Court today, in holding that the FAA compels enforcement of arbitration clauses even when claims of age discrimination are at issue, skirts the antecedent question whether the coverage of the Act even extends to arbitration clauses contained in employment contracts, regardless of the subject matter of the claim at issue. In my opinion, arbitration clauses contained in employment agreements are specifically exempt from coverage of the FAA, and for that reason respondent Interstate/Johnson Lane Corporation cannot, pursuant to the FAA, compel petitioner to submit his claims arising under the Age Discrimination in Employment Act of 1967 to binding arbitration.

Petitioner did not, as the majority correctly notes, raise the issue of the applicability of the FAA to employment contracts at any stage of the proceedings below. Nor did petitioner raise the coverage issue in his petition for writ of certiorari before this Court. It was *amici* who first raised the argument in their briefs in support of petitioner prior to oral argument of the case.

Notwithstanding the apparent waiver of the issue below, I believe that the Court should reach the issue of the coverage of the FAA to employment disputes because resolution of the question is so clearly antecedent to disposition of this case....

When the FAA was passed in 1925, I doubt that any legislator who voted for it expected it to apply to statutory claims, to form contracts between parties of unequal bargaining power, or to the arbitration of disputes arising out of the employment relationship. In recent years, however, the Court "has effectively rewritten the statute," and abandoned its earlier view that statutory claims were not appropriate subjects for arbitration. *See Mitsubishi Motors v. Soler Chrysler-Plymouth, Inc.*, 473 U.S. 614, 646-651 (1985) (Stevens, J., dissenting). Although I remain persuaded that it erred in doing so, the Court has also put to one side any concern about the inequality of bargaining power between an entire industry, on the one hand, and an individual customer or employee, on the other. Until today, however, the Court has not read § 2 of the FAA as broadly encompassing disputes arising out of the employment relationship. I believe this additional extension of the FAA is erroneous. Accordingly, I respectfully dissent.

NOTES

1. *The FAA and Individual Employment Contracts.* The lower courts have overwhelmingly rejected the dissenters' view of Section 1 of the FAA holding that the exception should apply narrowly only to "employment contracts of seamen, railroad workers, and any other class of workers actually engaged in the

movement of goods in interstate commerce in the same way that seamen and railroad workers are." *Asplundh Tree Expert Co. v. Bates*, 71 F.3d 592, 600-01 (6th Cir. 1995). *See also Patterson v. Tenet Healthcare, Inc.*, 113 F.3d 832 (8th Cir. 1997); *Great W. Mtg. Corp. v. Peacock*, 110 F.3d 222 (3d Cir. 1997) (*en banc*). The lower courts have also extended the rationale of *Gilmer* to claims under other discrimination statutes, such as Title VII. *See, e.g., Cole v. Burns Int'l Sec. Servs.*, 105 F.3d 1465 (D.C. Cir. 1997); *Austin v. Owens-Brockway Glass Container, Inc.*, 78 F.3d 875 (4th Cir.), *cert. denied*, 117 S. Ct. 432 (1996).

   2. Rethinking Handbooks? Earlier we saw that one aspect of the demise of employment at will has been the increased willingness of courts to enforce employment manuals. In the employment-at-will context, employees generally want manuals enforced and employers want to avoid their enforcement. But with arbitration provisions, the situation is often reversed. Should employment manuals, or other contractual agreements, be enforced strictly when they require arbitration of disputes and waive access to judicial forums? *See Nelson v. Cyprus Bagdad Copper Corp.*, 119 F.3d 756 (9th Cir. 1997) (employee did not agree to arbitrate dispute and waive judicial forum by signing acknowledgment of receipt of handbook, continuing to work after receiving handbook, or initiating complaint procedure under handbook); *Prudential Ins. Co. v. Lai*, 42 F.3d 1299 (9th Cir. 1994), *cert. denied*, 516 U.S. 812 (1995) (agreement to arbitrate only enforceable when employees knowingly agree to it, thus agreement to arbitrate "any dispute" insufficient to require employees to arbitrate because it did not specifically mention employment or discrimination claims).

   3. Gilmer and Unionized Employees. Most union contracts have arbitration clauses. The majority in *Gilmer* carefully distinguished its holding from *Alexander v. Gardner-Denver Co.*, in which the Court held that arbitration clauses in union contracts generally have no effect on the ability of plaintiffs to pursue statutory employment claims. In applying this distinction, most lower courts have held that plaintiffs can bypass union grievance and arbitration procedures, even though they would be bound to follow them in a non-union context. *See Brisentine v. Stone & Webster Eng'g Corp.*, 117 F.3d 519 (11th Cir. 1997); *Harrison v. Eddy Potash, Inc.*, 112 F.3d 1437 (10th Cir. 1997). *But see Austin v. Owens-Brockway Glass Container, Inc.*, 78 F.3d 875 (4th Cir. 1996) (applying *Gilmer* even though arbitration clause was in collective bargaining agreement). As a result, non-union plaintiffs may be bound by a grievance and arbitration procedure even though they may have had limited influence in designing the procedure, while plaintiffs represented by a union can bypass a procedure that was the product of hard bargaining between the company and union. Do the rationales expressed in *Gilmer* override this concern? Would you expect unions to like, or dislike, the distinction between union and non-union grievance procedures? Would you expect the distinction to affect the procedures provided by non-union employers?

   4. The Spectre of Gilmer. The worst-case scenario for plaintiffs under *Gilmer* is that employers will require all employees to sign arbitration agreements to resolve statutory claims, the arbitration procedures will favor employers in a number of respects (no class actions, limited discovery, etc.), the arbitrators themselves will be more likely to favor employers than courts would be, and the courts will enforce arbitration awards with only a very cursory review of the arbitrator's decision. *Compare, e.g., Cole v. Burns Int'l Sec. Servs.*, 105 F.3d 1465, 1487 (D.C. Cir. 1997) (courts should "review an arbitrator's award to ensure that its resolution of public law issues is correct") *with DiRussa v. Dean Witter Reynolds, Inc.*, 936 F. Supp. 104, 106-07 (S.D.N.Y. 1996) (enforcing arbitrator's award even though clearly contrary to ADEA because error not "obvious and capable of being readily and instantly perceived by the average person qualified to serve as an arbitrator"). *See generally* Katherine Van Wezel Stone, *Mandatory Arbitration of Individual Employment Rights: The Yellow Dog Contract of the 1990s*, 73 DENV. U. L. REV. 1017 (1996).

In addition to these concerns about individual claimants, the EEOC opposes arbitration of discrimination claims because of the harm to the public enforcement effort. In its policy statement on the issue, the EEOC argues that arbitration undercuts the central role of the courts in molding and enforcing the nation's anti-discrimination policy. The courts provide a more public forum than arbitration and, hence, are subject to more "public scrutiny and to system-wide checks and balances designed to ensure uniform expression of and adherence to statutory principles." EEOC Policy Statement on Mandatory Binding Arbitration of Employment Discrimination Disputes as a Condition of Employment, II EEOC Compliance Manual § 603. *Cf.* Owen M. Fiss, *Against Settlement*, 93 YALE L.J. 1073 (1984) (movement to non-judicial forums jeopardizes unique public role played by courts, as exemplified by *Brown v. Board of Education*).

5. *The Promise of Gilmer.* Others see a different future entirely:

> [M]ediation and arbitration of statutory disputes conducted under proper due process safeguards should be encouraged in order to provide expeditious, accessible, inexpensive and fair private enforcement of statutory employment disputes for the 100,000,000 members of the workforce who might not otherwise have ready, effective access to administrative or judicial relief.... [S]uch a system will [also] serve to reduce the delays which now arise out of the huge backlog of cases pending before administrative agencies and courts.

Task Force on Alternative Dispute Resolution in Employment, A Due Process Protocol for Mediation and Arbitration of Statutory Disputes Arising Out of the Employment Relationship (1995). The Task Force's Protocol provides guidelines on important issues, such as the selection and training of arbitrators, the right of representation during arbitration proceedings, discovery, and judicial review. The protocol has been endorsed by the National Academy of Arbitrators, the ABA Labor and Employment Section, and the National Employment Lawyers Association.

RICHARD A. BALES, COMPULSORY ARBITRATION: THE GRAND EXPERIMENT IN EMPLOYMENT 102-13 (1997)[*]

Brown & Root was one of the first major companies in the United States to institute an in-house program for the nonjudicial resolution of employment disputes.... Brown & Root's dispute resolution program demonstrates that compulsory arbitration and employee fairness are not necessarily mutually exclusive.

Brown & Root is a Houston-based company that employs between 25,000 and 30,000 employees, all of whom are nonunion. Its principal products are construction, maintenance, and engineering services....

The company decided to explore alternatives to litigation after a sexual harassment trial in which the company prevailed cost it $450,000 in outside legal fees. During the five years between the alleged harassment and the trial, the litigation profoundly affected the lives and careers of several employees and former employees, including the plaintiff. The financial and human costs associated with such litigation prompted the company to examine alternatives to the litigation system for resolving employment matters....

Just as the Program compels employees to use the Program in lieu of litigation, it also creates a contractual obligation on the part of the company, explicitly amending the at-will employment relationship for that limited effect. Brown & Root can cancel the Program only after giving ten days' notice to employees, and such cancellation does not effect any dispute arising prior to cancellation. Similarly, Brown & Root can amend the Program and its rules at any time, but no such amendment affects any dispute of which the company had notice on the date of amendment.

The Program covers all types of employment disputes, including tort, contract, and statutory claims, as well as claims for equitable relief. It explicitly lists sex, race, religion, national origin, and disability discrimination; sexual harassment; defamation; intentional infliction of emotional distress; and claims related to employee benefits as types of claims to which the Program applies. The Program excludes claims for workers' compensation benefits or unemployment compensation benefits, but includes claims for workers' compensation retaliation. It makes clear to employees that they are still free to contact the EEOC or their state Human Rights Commission about workplace discrimination if they so desire....

Brown & Root employs a full-time Program Administrator to run the dispute resolution program. Employees are encouraged to call this Administrator with questions or to initiate conferences and other internal dispute resolution processes.

In addition to administration, the Program Administrator has benefited the company by providing "upward feedback" about how company employees are

---

being supervised. The Administrator is in a position to recognize which sections of the company have an unusually large number of employee complaints. This recognition allows the Administrator to recommend proactive action, such as removing or retraining supervisors, addressing concerns important to employees, and helping prevent future disputes from occurring. Brown & Root's Associate General Counsel, William Bedman, notes that this has had the unintended consequence of helping the company avoid union attempts to organize the company's employees by helping to resolve problems before they induce employees to seek assistance from a union....

Brown & Root pays for the employees or former employees to consult with and retain attorneys of their choice, provided that their disputes involve legally protected employee rights. Reimbursements for attorneys' fees are paid like benefits under standard medical plans. The employee pays a deductible of $25.00. After the deductible, the employee pays 10 percent of the balance; Brown & Root reimburses the employee for the remainder, up to a maximum of $2,500 per year. The employee is solely responsible for choosing the attorney....

An employee is not required to take advantage of the company's legal representation reimbursement. An employee may, without jeopardizing reimbursement, consult with or hire an attorney before initiating any part of the dispute resolution program; this would be considered an initial consultation that would be reimbursed by Brown & Root....

[The final step, after an open-door meeting, an in-house conference, and outside mediation,] of Brown & Root's dispute resolution program requires employees who have a legal claim against the company to submit that claim to binding arbitration....

If an employee elects not to bring a lawyer to arbitration, Brown & Root also will agree not to bring a lawyer to arbitration. This does not, however, preclude a Brown & Root attorney from working "behind the scenes" to prepare witnesses for the hearing or to draft briefs supporting Brown & Root's argument....

Prior to the arbitration hearing, and on a schedule determined by the arbitrator, each party must produce, both to the arbitrator and to the other parties, the names and addresses of the witnesses it intends to bring to the hearing and any documents it intends to present. The arbitrator has the discretion to determine the form, amount, and frequency of other prehearing discovery. This discovery may take any form permitted by the Federal Rules of Civil Procedure....

At the hearing, witnesses are required to testify under oath. The arbitrator may subpoena witnesses or documents at the request of a party or on the arbitrator's own initiative. Strict conformity to the federal or state rules of evidence is not required; as with arbitration in the labor and commercial context, the arbitrator is "the sole judge of the relevance, materiality, and admissibility of evidence offered." A witness may testify by affidavit, but such testimony is only given "such weight as the arbitrator deems it is entitled to after consideration of any objection made to its admission." The award must be in writing and signed by the arbitrator. The arbitrator is required to write a summary of the reasons for the decision if so requested by the parties in either the request for arbitration or the answering statement.

The arbitrator's authority is limited to the resolution of legal disputes between the parties. The arbitrator is bound by, and is required to apply, all applicable law, including that related to the allocation of the burdens of proof as well as substantive law. The arbitrator does not have the authority either to abridge or enlarge substantive rights available under existing law. The arbitrator has the authority to order any relief that a party could obtain from court, including injunctive and other equitable relief, and all forms of damages, including punitive damages. However, the arbitrator, at his or her discretion, may allow an employee a reasonable attorneys' fee as part of the award, regardless of the employee's right to request an attorneys' fee under existing law. This award must be reduced by any amounts which have been paid by the Legal Expense Reimbursement Program. There is no provision permitting the arbitrator to award attorneys' fees to Brown & Root under circumstances in which existing law does not give the company the right to request such fees.

[In the first three years, the Brown & Root program] handled approximately 1,529 employment disputes. Nearly half involved the termination of an employee's employment. Of the disputes that did not involve termination, approximately 10 percent concerned wage and benefits issues. Fewer than 10 percent involved an allegation that the employee had been discriminated against or harassed because of his or her membership in a class protected by federal civil rights laws. The remainder involved conflicts with supervisors and coworkers; morale; job assignments; retaliation; health, safety, and injury issues; and complaints about the hiring process.

The median amount of time taken to resolve each dispute is slightly less than three weeks; the mean is a little more than six and one-half weeks. Forty-one percent of the disputes were resolved within one week of the employee's initial complaint; approximately 65 percent were resolved within four weeks. The longest any dispute took was slightly more than two years; only twenty-one took more than one year. This represents a marked contrast to litigation, which easily can take half a decade or more.

Of the 1,529 disputes filed thus far, approximately 45 percent have been resolved by Program staff, approximately 20 percent have been resolved by an Advisor, 2.5 percent have been resolved through in-house mediation, and only approximately 6 percent had to be referred to outside mediation or arbitration (several of these, however, settled before mediation/arbitration). Approximately 8.5 percent have been resolved in some other manner and approximately 7.5 percent remain pending. In the remaining 10.5 percent of disputes, the employee decided not to pursue the matter further.

In the first two years (the only period for which these particular statistics are available), only eighty employees have requested reimbursement for legal expenses. During this time, Brown & Root paid approximately $85,000 in employees' legal fees. The relatively low number of employees requesting reimbursement reflects the fact that employees seldom decided to hire an attorney to represent them in their dispute. Employees elected to proceed without the use of legal counsel in two-thirds of the arbitrations that have occurred....

Not surprisingly, Brown & Root has had far fewer employment lawsuits filed against it than it did prior to implementing the Program. Before implementation, the company averaged approximately fifteen to twenty lawsuits per year; in the first three and one-half years following implementation, Brown & Root was sued in court a total of fifteen times. In twelve of those suits, the employee voluntarily elected to dismiss the suit and to submit the claim to arbitration....

The number of disputes filed by Brown & Root's employees after the program was implemented — approximately five hundred per year — is commensurate with the number of annual complaints that Brown & Root received through its internal channels before implementation of the Program. Similarly, the company's settlement rate and its annual budget for those settlements did not change significantly after implementing the Program. Neither did its budget for paying arbitration/litigation awards. The company's adjudicatory winning percentage has actually decreased slightly since arbitration was substituted for litigation.

What has changed dramatically is the company's legal budget. Over the three years that the Program has been in place, the company's outside legal fees, plus the costs of administering the Program (including arbitrator and mediator fees, the salaries of the Program's three administrators, the reimbursement program for employees' legal expenses, and the company's outside legal fees in arbitrations where the employee is represented by counsel) is less than half — approximately forty-seven percent — of what the company spent on outside legal fees before the Program was put in place....

The fact that the company's settlement rate, settlement budget, and award budget have remained constant would seem to indicate that the Program is at least as fair to employees as litigating the company's employment disputes would be. The increased success rate for employees in arbitration (as compared to litigation) means that more employees are receiving adjudicatory awards, although the awards of victorious employees are likely to be smaller than in litigation. Though empirically unverifiable, this may mean that employees with meritorious claims, who before could not obtain redress because they were unable to hire a lawyer, or because they ran afoul of the convoluted procedural requirements of the federal antidiscrimination statutes, now are obtaining the redress they deserve. The smaller awards indicate a departure from the "jackpot" litigation system. This means that instead of a very few employees receiving very large awards, awards are distributed more equitably among a larger number of aggrieved employees.

Part III

Employee Privacy

In this Part, we focus on privacy claims of workers. As we shall see, the common law often frames the issue against the backdrop of at-will employment, modified by the public policy exception. While some privacy claims can fit within the public policy exception, many cannot. Some employees attempt to apply the general common law right to privacy to the workplace. Many of the privacy protections, however, have required statutory intervention by the legislature.

We begin, in Chapter 8, with the free speech and privacy claims of government workers. In general, our book covers the employment law of private-sector employees. In the case of privacy, however, the claims of government workers have been developed and have had spill-over effects on private workers, so it is worth studying public-sector developments. In Chapter 9, we examine free speech and privacy claims of private sector workers.

Chapter 8

FREE SPEECH AND PRIVACY PROTECTIONS
OF GOVERNMENT WORKERS

Except for the Thirteenth Amendment, which declares that "neither slavery nor involuntary servitude ... shall exist within the United States," the federal Constitution only regulates state action. The Constitution does not restrict the actions of purely private employers, or give private employees any rights against their employers. The Constitution, particularly in its majestic due process and equal protection clauses, does restrict the actions of the Government as employer. In addition, Congress and state legislatures have given important civil-service protections to government workers.

The Constitution is consistent with at-will employment of government workers. As then state Judge Oliver Wendell Holmes famously put it, in rejecting the constitutional claim of a police officer fired for engaging in political activity, a person "may have a constitutional right to talk politics, but he has no constitutional right to be a policeman." *McAuliffe v. Mayor & City of New Bedford*, 29 N.E. 517 (Mass. 1892). Government employment was regarded as a privilege, which the worker takes "on the terms which are offered to him." *Id.* But just as the common law has eroded the clean principle of employment at will in the private sector, the Supreme Court has found several important Constitutional limitations on an at-will rule for government employees. As Justice Brennan declared in *Keyishian v. Board of Regents*, 385 U.S. 589, 605-06 (1967), "the theory that public employment which may be denied altogether may be subjected to any conditions, regardless of how unreasonable, has been uniformly rejected.... It is too late in the day to doubt that the liberties of religion and expression may be infringed by the denial of or placing of conditions upon a benefit or privilege." The classic analysis in this shift is William Van Alstyne, *The Demise of the Right-Privilege Distinction in Constitutional Law*, 81 HARV. L. REV. 1439 (1968).

The following cases examine three Constitutional protections enjoyed by government workers: (1) protection against discrimination for their political affiliation; (2) protection of free speech rights on issues of public concern; and (3) (weak) protections against allegedly invasive drug tests. The Notes outline some of the statutory protections and regulation of government workers, which in practice are often more significant.

RUTAN v. REPUBLICAN PARTY

United States Supreme Court

497 U.S. 62 (1990)

JUSTICE BRENNAN delivered the opinion of the Court.

To the victor belong only those spoils that may be constitutionally obtained. *Elrod v. Burns*, 427 U.S. 347 (1976), and *Branti v. Finkel*, 445 U.S. 507 (1980), decided that the First Amendment forbids government officials to discharge or threaten to discharge public employees solely for not being supporters of the political party in power, unless party affiliation is an appropriate requirement for the position involved. Today we are asked to decide the constitutionality of several related political patronage practices — whether promotion, transfer, recall, and hiring decisions involving low-level public employees may be constitutionally based on party affiliation and support. We hold that they may not.

I

The petition and cross-petition before us arise from a lawsuit protesting certain employment policies and practices instituted by Governor James Thompson of Illinois. On November 12, 1980, the Governor issued an executive order proclaiming a hiring freeze for every agency, bureau, board, or commission subject to his control. The order prohibits state officials from hiring any employee, filling any vacancy, creating any new position, or taking any similar action. It affects approximately 60,000 state positions. More than 5,000 of these become available each year as a result of resignations, retirements, deaths, expansions, and reorganizations. The order proclaims that "no exceptions" are permitted without the Governor's "express permission after submission of appropriate requests to [his] office." ...

Requests for the Governor's "express permission" have allegedly become routine. Permission has been granted or withheld through an agency expressly created for this purpose, the Governor's Office of Personnel (Governor's Office). Agencies have been screening applicants under Illinois' civil service system, making their personnel choices, and submitting them as requests to be approved or disapproved by the Governor's Office. Among the employment decisions for which approvals have been required are new hires, promotions, transfers, and recalls after layoffs.

By means of the freeze, according to petitioners and cross-respondents, the Governor has been using the Governor's Office to operate a political patronage system to limit state employment and beneficial employment-related decisions to those who are supported by the Republican Party. In reviewing an agency's request that a particular applicant be approved for a particular position, the Governor's Office has looked at whether the applicant voted in Republican primaries in past election years, whether the applicant has provided financial or other support to the Republican Party and its candidates, whether the applicant has promised to join and work for the Republican Party in the future, and whether the applicant has the support of Republican Party officials at state or local levels.

....

II

A

In *Elrod*, we decided that a newly elected Democratic sheriff could not constitutionally engage in the patronage practice of replacing certain office staff with members of his own party "when the existing employees lack or fail to obtain requisite support from, or fail to affiliate with, that party." The plurality explained that conditioning public employment on the provision of support for the favored political party "unquestionably inhibits protected belief and association." It reasoned that conditioning employment on political activity pressures employees to pledge political allegiance to a party with which they prefer not to associate, to work for the election of political candidates they do not support, and to contribute money to be used to further policies with which they do not agree. The latter, the plurality noted, had been recognized by this Court as "tantamount to coerced belief." *Id.*, at 355 (*citing Buckley v. Valeo*, 424 U.S. 1, 19 (1976)). At the same time, employees are constrained from joining, working for, or contributing to the political party and candidates of their own choice." [P]olitical belief and association constitute the core of those activities protected by the First Amendment," the plurality emphasized. Both the plurality and the concurrence drew support from *Perry v. Sindermann*, 408 U.S. 593 (1972), in which this Court held that the State's refusal to renew a teacher's contract because he had been publicly critical of its policies imposed an unconstitutional condition on the receipt of a public benefit.

The Court then decided that the government interests generally asserted in support of patronage fail to justify this burden on First Amendment rights because patronage dismissals are not the least restrictive means for fostering those interests. The plurality acknowledged that a government has a significant interest in ensuring that it has effective and efficient employees. It expressed doubt, however, that "mere difference of political persuasion motivates poor performance" and concluded that, in any case, the government can ensure employee effectiveness and efficiency through the less drastic means of discharging staff members whose work is inadequate. The plurality also found that a government can meet its need for politically loyal employees to implement its policies by the less intrusive measure of dismissing, on political grounds, only those employees in policymaking positions. Finally, although the plurality recognized that preservation of the democratic process "may in some instances justify limitations on First Amendment freedoms," it concluded that the "process functions as well without the practice, perhaps even better." Patronage, it explained, "can result in the entrenchment of one or a few parties to the exclusion of others" and "is a very effective impediment to the associational and speech freedoms which are essential to a meaningful system of democratic government."

Four years later, in *Branti*, we decided that the First Amendment prohibited a newly appointed public defender, who was a Democrat, from discharging assistant public defenders because they did not have the support of the Democratic Party. The Court rejected an attempt to distinguish the case from *Elrod*, deciding that it was immaterial whether the public defender had attempted to coerce employees to change political parties or had only dismissed them on the basis of their private political beliefs. We explained that conditioning continued public employment on an employee's having obtained support from a particular political party violates the First Amendment because of "the coercion of belief that necessarily flows from the knowledge that one must have a sponsor in the dominant party in order to retain one's job." "In sum," we said, "there is no requirement that dismissed employees prove that they, or other employees, have been coerced into changing, either actually or ostensibly, their political allegiance." To prevail, we concluded, public employees need show only that they were discharged because they were not affiliated with or sponsored by the Democratic Party.[5]

B

... Respondents urge us to view *Elrod* and *Branti* as inapplicable because the patronage dismissals at issue in those cases are different in kind from failure to promote, failure to transfer, and failure to recall after layoff. Respondents initially contend that the employee petitioners' and cross-respondents' First Amendment rights have not been infringed because they have no entitlement to promotion, transfer, or rehire. We rejected just such an argument in *Elrod* and *Branti*, as both cases involved state workers who were employees at will with no legal entitlement to continued employment. In *Perry*, 408 U.S. at 596-598, we held explicitly that the plaintiff teacher's lack of a contractual or tenure right to re-employment was immaterial to his First Amendment claim. We explained the viability of his First Amendment claim as follows:

> "For at least a quarter-century, this Court has made clear that even though a person has no 'right' to a valuable governmental benefit and even though the government may deny him the benefit for any number of reasons, *there are some reasons upon which the government may not rely. It may not deny a benefit to a person on a basis that infringes his constitutionally protected*

---

[5] *Branti* also refined the exception created by *Elrod* for certain employees. In *Elrod*, we suggested that policymaking and confidential employees probably could be dismissed on the basis of their political views. In *Branti*, we said that a State demonstrates a compelling interest in infringing First Amendment rights only when it can show that "party affiliation is an appropriate requirement for the effective performance of the public office involved." The scope of this exception does not concern us here as respondents concede that the five employees who brought this suit are not within it.

interests — especially, his interest in freedom of speech. For if the government could deny a benefit to a person because of his constitutionally protected speech or associations, his exercise of those freedoms would in effect be penalized and inhibited. This would allow the government to 'produce a result which [it] could not command directly.' *Speiser v. Randall*, 357 U.S. 513, 526 [(1958)]. Such interference with constitutional rights is impermissible." *Id.*, at 597 (emphasis added).

Likewise, we find the assertion here that the employee petitioners and cross-respondents had no legal entitlement to promotion, transfer, or recall beside the point.

Respondents next argue that the employment decisions at issue here do not violate the First Amendment because the decisions are not punitive, do not in any way adversely affect the terms of employment, and therefore do not chill the exercise of protected belief and association by public employees.[6] This is not credible. Employees who find themselves in dead-end positions due to their political backgrounds are adversely affected. They will feel a significant obligation to support political positions held by their superiors, and to refrain from acting on the political views they actually hold, in order to progress up the career ladder. Employees denied transfers to workplaces reasonably close to their homes until they join and work for the Republican Party will feel a daily pressure from their long commutes to do so. And employees who have been laid off may well feel compelled to engage in whatever political activity is necessary to regain regular paychecks and positions corresponding to their skill and experience.

We find, however, that our conclusions in *Elrod*, and *Branti*, are equally applicable to the patronage practices at issue here. A government's interest in securing effective employees can be met by discharging, demoting, or transferring staff members whose work is deficient. A government's interest in securing employees who will loyally implement its policies can be adequately served by choosing or dismissing certain high-level employees on the basis of their political views....

We therefore determine that promotions, transfers, and recalls after layoffs based on political affiliation or support are an impermissible infringement on the First Amendment rights of public employees. In doing so, we reject the Seventh Circuit's view of the appropriate constitutional standard by which to measure alleged patronage practices in government employment. The Seventh Circuit

---

[6] Respondents' reliance on *Johnson v. Transportation Agency, Santa Clara County*, 480 U.S. 616 (1987), to this effect is misplaced. The question in *Johnson* was whether the Santa Clara County affirmative-action program violated the antidiscrimination requirement of Title VII of the Civil Rights Act of 1964. In that context, we said that the denial of a promotion did not unsettle any legitimate, firmly rooted expectations. We did not dispute, however, that it placed a burden on the person to whom the promotion was denied....

proposed that only those employment decisions that are the "substantial equiva-lent of a dismissal" violate a public employee's rights under the First Amend-ment. We find this test unduly restrictive because it fails to recognize that there are deprivations less harsh than dismissal that nevertheless press state employees and applicants to conform their beliefs and associations to some state-selected orthodoxy....

C

Petitioner James W. Moore presents the closely related question whether patronage hiring violates the First Amendment. Patronage hiring places burdens on free speech and association similar to those imposed by the patronage prac-tices discussed above. A state job is valuable. Like most employment, it provides regular paychecks, health insurance, and other benefits. In addition, there may be openings with the State when business in the private sector is slow. There are also occupations for which the government is a major (or the only) source of employment, such as social workers, elementary school teachers, and prison guards. Thus, denial of a state job is a serious privation.

Nonetheless, respondents contend that the burden imposed is not of constitu-tional magnitude. Decades of decisions by this Court belie such a claim. We premised *Torcaso v. Watkins*, 367 U.S. 488 (1961), on our understanding that loss of a job opportunity for failure to compromise one's convictions states a constitutional claim. We held that Maryland could not refuse an appointee a commission for the position of notary public on the ground that he refused to declare his belief in God, because the required oath "unconstitutionally invades the appellant's freedom of belief and religion." *Id.*, at 496. In *Keyishian v. Board of Regents of Univ. of New York*, 385 U.S. 589, 609-610 (1967), we held a law affecting appointment and retention of teachers invalid because it premised employment on an unconstitutional restriction of political belief and association. In *Elfbrandt v. Russell*, 384 U.S. 11, 19 (1966), we struck down a loyalty oath which was a prerequisite for public employment.

... The Court of Appeals reasoned that "rejecting an employment application does not impose a hardship upon an employee comparable to the loss of [a] job." *Ibid.*, *citing Wygant v. Jackson Bd. of Education*, 476 U.S. 267 (1986) (plurality opinion). Just as we reject the Seventh Circuit's proffered test, we find the Seventh Circuit's reliance on *Wygant* to distinguish hiring from dismissal unavailing. The court cited a passage from the plurality opinion in *Wygant* explaining that school boards attempting to redress past discrimination must choose methods that broadly distribute the disadvantages imposed by affirmative action plans among innocent parties. The plurality said that race-based layoffs placed too great a burden on individual members of the nonminority race, but suggested that discriminatory hiring was permissible, under certain circum-stances, even though it burdened white applicants, because the burden was less intrusive than the loss of an existing job.

Wygant has no application to the question at issue here. The plurality's concern in that case was identifying the least harsh means of remedying past wrongs. It did not question that some remedy was permissible when there was sufficient evidence of past discrimination. In contrast, the Governor of Illinois has not instituted a remedial undertaking. It is unnecessary here to consider whether not being hired is less burdensome than being discharged, because the government is not pressed to do either on the basis of political affiliation. The question in the patronage context is not which penalty is more acute but whether the government, without sufficient justification, is pressuring employees to discontinue the free exercise of their First Amendment rights.

....

JUSTICE STEVENS, concurring.

While I join the Court's opinion, these additional comments are prompted by ... propositions advanced by JUSTICE SCALIA in his dissent. First, he implies that prohibiting imposition of an unconstitutional condition upon eligibility for government employment amounts to adoption of a civil service system....

Denying the Governor of Illinois the power to require every state employee, and every applicant for state employment, to pledge allegiance and service to the political party in power is a far cry from a civil service code. The question in these cases is simply whether a Governor may adopt a rule that would be plainly unconstitutional if enacted by the General Assembly of Illinois.

....

JUSTICE SCALIA, with whom THE CHIEF JUSTICE and JUSTICE KENNEDY join, and with whom JUSTICE O'CONNOR joins as to Parts II and III, dissenting.

Today the Court establishes the constitutional principle that party membership is not a permissible factor in the dispensation of government jobs, except those jobs for the performance of which party affiliation is an "appropriate requirement." It is hard to say precisely (or even generally) what that exception means, but if there is any category of jobs for whose performance party affiliation is not an appropriate requirement, it is the job of being a judge, where partisanship is not only unneeded but positively undesirable. It is, however, rare that a federal administration of one party will appoint a judge from another party. And it has always been rare. *See Marbury v. Madison*, 1 Cranch 137 (1803). Thus, the new principle that the Court today announces will be enforced by a corps of judges (the Members of this Court included) who overwhelmingly owe their office to its violation. Something must be wrong here, and I suggest it is the Court.

The merit principle for government employment is probably the most favored in modern America, having been widely adopted by civil service legislation at both the state and federal levels. But there is another point of view, described in characteristically Jacksonian fashion by an eminent practitioner of the patronage system, George Washington Plunkitt of Tammany Hall:

"I ain't up on sillygisms, but I can give you some arguments that nobody can answer.

"First, this great and glorious country was built up by political parties; second, parties can't hold together if their workers don't get offices when they win; third, if the parties go to pieces, the government they built up must go to pieces, too; fourth, then there'll be hell to pay." W. Riordon, Plunkitt of Tammany Hall 13 (1963).

It may well be that the Good Government Leagues of America were right, and that Plunkitt, James Michael Curley, and their ilk were wrong; but that is not entirely certain. As the merit principle has been extended and its effects increasingly felt; as the Boss Tweeds, the Tammany Halls, the Pendergast Machines, the Byrd Machines, and the Daley Machines have faded into history; we find that political leaders at all levels increasingly complain of the helplessness of elected government, unprotected by "party discipline," before the demands of small and cohesive interest groups.

The choice between patronage and the merit principle — or, to be more realistic about it, the choice between the desirable mix of merit and patronage principles in widely varying federal, state, and local political contexts — is not so clear that I would be prepared, as an original matter, to chisel a single, inflexible prescription into the Constitution. Fourteen years ago, in *Elrod v. Burns*, 427 U.S. 347 (1976), the Court did that. *Elrod* was limited, however, as was the later decision of *Branti v. Finkel*, 445 U.S. 507 (1980), to patronage firings, leaving it to state and federal legislatures to determine when and where political affiliation could be taken into account in hirings and promotions. Today the Court makes its constitutional civil service reform absolute, extending to all decisions regarding government employment. Because the First Amendment has never been thought to require this disposition, which may well have disastrous consequences for our political system, I dissent.

NOTES

1. *Growth of the Non-Partisan Civil Service.* As Justice Scalia notes, the spoils system of political patronage has a long history in this country. *Marbury v. Madison*, 5 U.S. (1 Cranch) 137 (1803), the famous case establishing the power of judicial review, involved political patronage. Andrew Jackson, elected in 1828, explicitly introduced a spoils system into federal appointments to promote political responsiveness. Abraham Lincoln continued the practice with a vengeance, dismissing 1,457 of the 1,639 officers appointed by previous Presidents.

Support for a professional, independent civil service was galvanized by the assassination in 1881 of President James Garfield by a disappointed office seeker. The Pendleton Act, passed two years later, established a bipartisan Civil Service Commission to create competitive examinations as the basis for hiring federal workers. Originally covering only 10 percent of government workers, the "classified" service grew to 70 percent of the government workforce by 1919.

Protections against arbitrary dismissal came later. The 1912 Lloyd-LaFollete Act prohibited a dismissal unless it would promote the "efficiency of the service," a standard that survives today. *See* 5 U.S.C. §§ 7503(a), 7513(a).

The efficiency of the independent bureaucracy was celebrated by Max Weber as "the most rational known means of exercising authority over human beings." 1 MAX WEBER, ECONOMY AND SOCIETY 223 (G. Roth & C. Wittich eds. 1978). Bureaucratic theory justified the apolitical civil service: "a merit-based system, staffed by professional experts and freed from the corrosive influence of politics by formal legal constraints on appointment and tenure, would provide the most efficient, rational tool for achieving the aims of public policy." *Developments in the Law: Public Employment*, 97 HARV. L. REV. 1611, 1629 (1984). *See generally* P. VAN RIPER, HISTORY OF THE UNITED STATES CIVIL SERVICE (1958).

2. *Civil Service Reform Act of 1978.* The elaborate protections given civil servants were increasingly criticized as causing and immunizing indifference or incompetence by government workers. The Watergate scandals showed, paradoxically, that the protections did not prevent manipulation of the civil service for political ends. The criticisms led to the Civil Service Reform Act of 1978, which the Senate Report declared to be "the most comprehensive reform of the Federal work force since passage of the Pendleton Act in 1883."

The CSRA dismantled the Civil Service Commission, which was criticized for combining the roles of manager, prosecutor, judge, and jury of the federal work force. Administrative and managerial functions were given to the Office of Personnel Management. A three-member Merit Systems Protection Board (MSPB) was created to hear appeals of personnel decisions by individual agencies. The MSPB has developed a highly formal, adversarial process modeled on the Federal Rules of Civil Procedure, complete with discovery and subpoena power. The MSPB will uphold an agency's decision to fire a worker if it rests on "substantial evidence," a lesser standard than the preponderance of the evidence. Employees claiming discrimination can get a de novo review of the MSPB's decision in federal district court. Review in all other cases is limited to whether the MSPB's decision was arbitrary or capricious, obtained without required procedures, or unsupported by substantial evidence.

The CSRA also created a new category of approximately 7,000 upper-level federal jobs, the Senior Executive Service. Workers in the SES are evaluated on the basis of "performance," often by political appointees. SES workers have far fewer rights of appeal than ordinary civil servants. In return, merit bonuses are potentially available. The shift toward performance evaluations has led at least one commentator to declare that "the CSRA has sacrificed the goals of merit and political neutrality embedded in the bureaucratic vision that has dominated the development of the civil service in this century to the Jacksonian goal of political responsiveness." *Developments in the Law: Public Employment*, 97 HARV. L. REV. 1611, 1650 (1984).

3. Procedural Requirements for Government Employees with Property Interests in Their Jobs. The Constitution does not give a government worker a property interest in his job. A property interest must come from an independent source, such as a statute, municipal ordinance, or express or implied contract between the parties. For example, in *Perry v. Sindermann*, 408 U.S. 593 (1972), the Court found an implied entitlement to job tenure in a state college teacher who had completed ten one-year contracts.

Once a property interest in a job has been established, the Constitution does regulate the process that is due before the Government may take it away. In *Cleveland Board of Education v. Loudermill*, 470 U.S. 532 (1985), the school board fired a security guard when it discovered that he had falsely claimed on his application that he was not a felon. The guard was a "classified civil servant." By state statute, such an employee could only be dismissed for cause and was entitled to administrative review after a dismissal. The guard filed suit, claiming an entitlement to respond to the charges before being dismissed. The District Court rejected the claim, reasoning that the very statute that created the property interest in the job also defined the procedures by which the government could take the job away. The Supreme Court rejected this "bitter with the sweet" theory. It held that the Constitution entitles government employees who cannot be fired without just cause to notice and an explanation of the charges and an opportunity to respond and be heard before being terminated.

4. Due Process for Lesser Job Sanctions. Are government employees with job tenure entitled to notice and a prior hearing when they are subject to lesser penalties than dismissal — such as demotions or transfer? Judge Posner, among other judges, fears that these procedural due process requirements could swallow state contract law. *See Brown v. Brienan*, 722 F.2d 360 (7th Cir. 1983) (expressing doubt that state employees have constitutional property interest in contractual rights concerning compensatory time off, and holding that no pre-deprivation hearing is required).

RANKIN v. McPHERSON

United States Supreme Court
483 U.S. 378 (1987)

JUSTICE MARSHALL delivered the opinion of the Court.

The issue in this case is whether a clerical employee in a county Constable's office was properly discharged for remarking, after hearing of an attempt on the life of the President, "If they go for him again, I hope they get him."

I

On January 12, 1981, respondent Ardith McPherson was appointed a deputy in the office of the Constable of Harris County, Texas. The Constable is an elected official who functions as a law enforcement officer. At the time of her appointment, McPherson, a black woman, was 19 years old and had attended college for a year, studying secretarial science. Her appointment was conditional for a 90-day probationary period.... Although McPherson's title was "deputy constable," this was the case only because all employees of the Constable's office, regardless of job function, were deputy constables.

She was not a commissioned peace officer, did not wear a uniform, and was not authorized to make arrests or permitted to carry a gun. McPherson's duties were purely clerical. Her work station was a desk at which there was no telephone, in a room to which the public did not have ready access. Her job was to type data from court papers into a computer that maintained an automated record of the status of civil process in the county. Her training consisted of two days of instruction in the operation of her computer terminal.

On March 30, 1981, McPherson and some fellow employees heard on an office radio that there had been an attempt to assassinate the President of the United States. Upon hearing that report, McPherson engaged a co-worker, Lawrence Jackson, who was apparently her boyfriend, in a brief conversation, which according to McPherson's uncontroverted testimony went as follows:

"Q: What did you say?
"A: I said I felt that that would happen sooner or later.
"Q: Okay. And what did Lawrence say?
"A: Lawrence said, yeah, agreeing with me.
"Q: Okay. Now, when you — after Lawrence spoke, then what was your next comment?
"A: Well, we were talking — it's a wonder why they did that. I felt like it would be a black person that did that, because I feel like most of my kind is on welfare and CETA, and they use medicaid, and at the time, I was thinking that's what it was.
"... But then after I said that, and then Lawrence said, yeah, he's cutting back medicaid and food stamps. And I said, yeah, welfare and CETA. I said, shoot, if they go for him again, I hope they get him."

McPherson's last remark was overheard by another Deputy Constable, who, unbeknownst to McPherson, was in the room at the time. The remark was reported to Constable Rankin, who summoned McPherson. McPherson readily admitted that she had made the statement, but testified that she told Rankin, upon being asked if she made the statement, "Yes, but I didn't mean anything by it." After their discussion, Rankin fired McPherson.

McPherson brought suit in the United States District Court for the Southern District of Texas under 42 U.S.C. § 1983, alleging that petitioner Rankin, in discharging her, had violated her constitutional rights under color of state law. She sought reinstatement, backpay, costs and fees, and other equitable relief....

[T]he District Court ... ruled ... that the statements were not protected speech. [T]he Court of Appeals reversed. It held that McPherson's remark had addressed a matter of public concern, requiring that society's interest in McPherson's free-

Nonsense!

dom of speech be weighed against her employer's interest in maintaining efficiency and discipline in the workplace. Performing that balancing, the Court of Appeals concluded that the Government's interest did not outweigh the First Amendment interest in protecting McPherson's speech. Given the nature of McPherson's job and the fact that she was not a law enforcement officer, was not brought by virtue of her job into contact with the public, and did not have access to sensitive information, the Court of Appeals deemed her "duties ... so utterly ministerial and her potential for undermining the office's mission so trivial" as to forbid her dismissal for expression of her political opinions. "However ill-considered Ardith McPherson's opinion was," the Court of Appeals concluded, "it did not make her unfit" for the job she held in Constable Rankin's office....

We granted certiorari, and now affirm.

II

It is clearly established that a State may not discharge an employee on a basis that infringes that employee's constitutionally protected interest in freedom of speech. *Perry v. Sindermann*, 408 U.S. 593, 597 (1972). Even though McPherson was merely a probationary employee, and even if she could have been discharged for any reason or for no reason at all, she may nonetheless be entitled to reinstatement if she was discharged for exercising her freedom of expression.

The determination whether a public employer has properly discharged an employee for engaging in speech requires "a balance between the interests of the [employee], as a citizen, in commenting upon matters of public concern and the interest of the State, as an employer, in promoting the efficiency of the public services it performs through its employees." *Pickering v. Board of Education*, 391 U.S. 563, 568 (1968); *Connick v. Myers*, 461 U.S. 138, 140 (1983). This balancing is necessary in order to accommodate the dual role of the public employer as a provider of public services and as a government entity operating under the constraints of the First Amendment. On the one hand, public employers are employers, concerned with the efficient function of their operations; review of every personnel decision made by a public employer could, in the long run, hamper the performance of public functions. On the other hand, "the threat of dismissal from public employment is ... a potent means of inhibiting speech." *Pickering, supra*, at 574. Vigilance is necessary to ensure that public employers do not use authority over employees to silence discourse, not because it hampers public functions but simply because superiors disagree with the content of employees' speech.

The threshold question in applying this balancing test is whether McPherson's speech may be "fairly characterized as constituting speech on a matter of public concern." *Connick*, 461 U.S., at 146.[7]

---

[7] Even where a public employee's speech does not touch upon a matter of public concern, that speech is not "totally beyond the protection of the First Amendment," *Connick v. Myers*, 461 U.S., at 147, but "absent the most unusual circumstances a federal court is not the appropriate forum in

Considering the statement in context, as *Connick* requires, discloses that it plainly dealt with a matter of public concern. The statement was made in the course of a conversation addressing the policies of the President's administration. It came on the heels of a news bulletin regarding what is certainly a matter of heightened public attention: an attempt on the life of the President. While a statement that amounted to a threat to kill the President would not be protected by the First Amendment, the District Court concluded, and we agree, that McPherson's statement did not amount to a threat punishable under 18 U.S.C. § 871(a) or 18 U.S.C. § 2385, or, indeed, that could properly be criminalized at all.[12] ... The inappropriate or controversial character of a statement is irrelevant to the question whether it deals with a matter of public concern." Debate on public issues should be uninhibited, robust, and wide-open, and ... may well include vehement, caustic, and sometimes unpleasantly sharp attacks on government and public officials." *New York Times Co. v. Sullivan*, 376 U.S. 254, 270 (1964); *see also Bond v. Floyd*, 385 U.S. 116, 136 (1966): "Just as erroneous statements must be protected to give freedom of expression the breathing space it needs to survive, so statements criticizing public policy and the implementation of it must be similarly protected."

Because McPherson's statement addressed a matter of public concern, *Pickering* next requires that we balance McPherson's interest in making her statement against "the interest of the State, as an employer, in promoting the efficiency of the public services it performs through its employees." The State bears a burden of justifying the discharge on legitimate grounds. *Connick*.

In performing the balancing, the statement will not be considered in a vacuum; the manner, time, and place of the employee's expression are relevant, as is the context in which the dispute arose. We have previously recognized as pertinent considerations whether the statement impairs discipline by superiors or harmony among co-workers, has a detrimental impact on close working relationships for which personal loyalty and confidence are necessary, or impedes the performance of the speaker's duties or interferes with the regular operation of the enterprise.

These considerations, and indeed the very nature of the balancing test, make apparent that the state interest element of the test focuses on the effective functioning of the public employer's enterprise. Interference with work, personnel relationships, or the speaker's job performance can detract from the public employer's function; avoiding such interference can be a strong state

---

which to review the wisdom of a personnel decision taken by a public agency allegedly in reaction to the employee's behavior." *Ibid.*

[12] Constable Rankin was evidently unsure of this; he testified that he called the Secret Service to report the incident and suggest that they investigate McPherson. McPherson testified that the Secret Service did, in fact, come to her home:

"Oh, they told me that they thought it was a prank call, but ... they have to investigate any call that they get." ....

interest. From this perspective, however, petitioners fail to demonstrate a state interest that outweighs McPherson's First Amendment rights. While McPherson's statement was made at the workplace, there is no evidence that it interfered with the efficient functioning of the office. The Constable was evidently not afraid that McPherson had disturbed or interrupted other employees — he did not inquire to whom respondent had made the remark and testified that he "was not concerned who she had made it to." In fact, Constable Rankin testified that the possibility of interference with the functions of the Constable's office had not been a consideration in his discharge of respondent and that he did not even inquire whether the remark had disrupted the work of the office. Nor was there any danger that McPherson had discredited the office by making her statement in public. McPherson's speech took place in an area to which there was ordinarily no public access; her remark was evidently made in a private conversation with another employee....

But in weighing the State's interest in discharging an employee based on any claim that the content of a statement made by the employee somehow undermines the mission of the public employer, some attention must be paid to the responsibilities of the employee within the agency. The burden of caution employees bear with respect to the words they speak will vary with the extent of authority and public accountability the employee's role entails. Where, as here, an employee serves no confidential, policymaking, or public contact role, the danger to the agency's successful functioning from that employee's private speech is minimal. We cannot believe that every employee in Constable Rankin's office, whether computer operator, electrician, or file clerk, is equally required, on pain of discharge, to avoid any statement susceptible of being interpreted by the Constable as an indication that the employee may be unworthy of employment in his law enforcement agency. At some point, such concerns are so removed from the effective functioning of the public employer that they cannot prevail over the free speech rights of the public employee.

This is such a case. McPherson's employment-related interaction with the Constable was apparently negligible. Her duties were purely clerical and were limited solely to the civil process function of the Constable's office. There is no indication that she would ever be in a position to further — or indeed to have any involvement with — the minimal law enforcement activity engaged in by the Constable's office. Given the function of the agency, McPherson's position in the office, and the nature of her statement, we are not persuaded that Rankin's interest in discharging her outweighed her rights under the First Amendment.

Because we agree with the Court of Appeals that McPherson's discharge was improper, the judgment of the Court of Appeals is

Affirmed.

JUSTICE POWELL, concurring.

Powell

It is not easy to understand how this case has assumed constitutional dimensions and reached the Supreme Court of the United States. The fact that the case is here, however, illustrates the uniqueness of our Constitution and our system of judicial review: courts at all levels are available and receptive to claims of injustice, large and small, by any and every citizen of this country.

There is no dispute that McPherson's comment was made during a private conversation with a co-worker who happened also to be her boyfriend. She had no intention or expectation that it would be overheard or acted on by others. Given this, I think it is unnecessary to engage in the extensive analysis normally required by *Connick* and *Pickering*. If a statement is on a matter of public concern, as it was here, it will be an unusual case where the employer's legitimate interests will be so great as to justify punishing an employee for this type of private speech that routinely takes place at all levels in the workplace. The risk that a single, offhand comment directed to only one other worker will lower morale, disrupt the work force, or otherwise undermine the mission of the office borders on the fanciful. To the extent that the full constitutional analysis of the competing interests is required, I generally agree with the Court's opinion.

In my view, however, the case is hardly as complex as might be expected in a dispute that now has been considered five separate times by three different federal courts. The undisputed evidence shows that McPherson made an ill-considered — but protected — comment during a private conversation, and the Constable made an instinctive, but intemperate, employment decision on the basis of this speech. I agree that on these facts, McPherson's private speech is protected by the First Amendment.

I join the opinion of the Court.

JUSTICE SCALIA, with whom THE CHIEF JUSTICE, JUSTICE WHITE, and JUSTICE O'CONNOR join, dissenting.

DISSENT

I agree with the proposition, felicitously put by Constable Rankin's counsel, that no law enforcement agency is required by the First Amendment to permit one of its employees to "ride with the cops and cheer for the robbers." ...

That McPherson's statement does not constitute speech on a matter of "public concern" is demonstrated by comparing it with statements that have been found to fit that description in prior decisions involving public employees. McPherson's statement is a far cry from the question by the Assistant District Attorney in *Connick* whether her co-workers "ever [felt] pressured to work in political campaigns," *Connick*, 461 U.S., at 149; from the letter written by the public school teacher in *Pickering* criticizing the Board of Education's proposals for financing school construction, *Pickering, supra*, at 566; from the legislative testimony of a state college teacher in *Perry v. Sindermann*, 408 U.S. 593, 595 (1972), advocating that a particular college be elevated to 4-year status; from the memorandum given by a teacher to a radio station in *Mt. Healthy City Board of*

Not speech on a matter of public concern

Ed. v. Doyle, 429 U.S. 274, 282 (1977), dealing with teacher dress and appearance; and from the complaints about school board policies and practices at issue in *Givhan v. Western Line Consolidated School Dist.*, 439 U.S. 410, 413 (1979). *See Connick, supra*, at 145-146.

McPherson's statement is indeed so different from those that it is only one step removed from statements that we have previously held entitled to no First Amendment protection even in the nonemployment context — including assassination threats against the President (which are illegal under 18 U.S.C. § 871), *see Frohwerk v. United States*, 249 U.S. 204, 206 (1919); "'fighting' words," *Chaplinsky v. New Hampshire*, 315 U.S. 568, 572 (1942); epithets or personal abuse, *Cantwell v. Connecticut*, 310 U.S. 296, 309-310 (1940); and advocacy of force or violence, *Harisiades v. Shaughnessy*, 342 U.S. 580, 591-92 (1952). A statement lying so near the category of completely unprotected speech cannot fairly be viewed as lying within the "heart" of the First Amendment's protection; it lies within that category of speech that can neither be characterized as speech on matters of public concern nor properly subject to criminal penalties. Once McPherson stopped explicitly criticizing the President's policies and expressed a desire that he be assassinated, she crossed the line.

In sum, since Constable Rankin's interest in maintaining both an esprit de corps and a public image consistent with his office's law enforcement duties outweighs any interest his employees may have in expressing on the job a desire that the President be killed, even assuming that such an expression addresses a matter of public concern it is not protected by the First Amendment from suppression. I emphasize once again that that is the issue here — and *not*, as both the Court's opinion and especially the concurrence seem to assume, whether the means used to effect suppression (viz., firing) were excessive. The First Amendment contains no "narrow tailoring" requirement that speech the government is entitled to suppress must be suppressed by the mildest means possible. If Constable Rankin was entitled (as I think any reasonable person would say he was) to admonish McPherson for saying what she did on the job, within hearing of her co-workers, and to warn her that if she did it again a formal censure would be placed in her personnel file, then it follows that he is entitled to rule that particular speech out of bounds in that particular work environment — and that is the end of the First Amendment analysis. The "intemperate" manner of the permissible suppression is an issue for another forum, or at least for a more plausibly relevant provision of the Constitution.

NOTES

1. *Statutory Restrictions on Employee Political Activity.* In 1939, Congress passed "An Act to prevent pernicious political activities," better known as the Hatch Act, 5 U.S.C. §§ 1501-1508, 7321-7327. It severely restricts the permissible political activity of federal civil service workers. State "little Hatch Acts" place similar restrictions on state workers. Controversial from its beginning, the

purpose of the Hatch Act is to ensure that civil servants are politically unbiased and free themselves of political coercion.

The centerpiece of the Hatch Act prohibits covered federal workers from taking an "active part in political management or in political campaigns." 5 U.S.C. § 7324(a)(2). Detailed regulations attempt to distinguish between partisan and nonpartisan activities, active leadership and individual participation, and solicitation versus mere expression of opinion. Since 1978, enforcement of the Hatch Act rests with the Merit Systems Protection Board. For example, the regulations make the following distinctions:

- An employee may register and vote in any election, but may not solicit votes for candidates in partisan elections.
- An employee may actively support candidates in nonpartisan elections or ballot questions not specifically identified with a particular party, but may not take an active role in the campaign of a candidate in a partisan election.
- An employee may privately or publicly express her personal opinion on political matters, but may not address a political gathering in support of or in opposition to a candidate in a partisan election.
- An employee may display political buttons, stickers, and the like, but may not endorse candidates in partisan elections by means of "a political advertisement, a broadcast, campaign[ ] literature, or similar material."
- An employee may belong to a political party or other organization, but may not run for party office or organize a political organization.
- An employee may make financial contributions to political parties, but may not solicit, receive, collect, or disburse funds for partisan political purposes.
- An employee may participate in nonpartisan activities of civic and other nonpolitical organizations, but may not organize or promote fundraising activities for political organizations or for candidates in partisan elections.
- An employee may sign a political petition, but may not initiate or circulate a partisan nominating petition.
- An employee may attend political conventions and other gatherings, but may not serve as a delegate, alternate, or proxy at a convention.
- An employee may run for public office in a nonpartisan election, but may not run for party office or for public office in a partisan election.
- An employee may serve as an election judge or clerk, but may not serve as a recorder, watcher, or other poll officer on behalf of a political party or a candidate in a partisan election.

Developments in the Law: Public Employment, 97 HARV. L. REV. 1611, 1652-53 (1984).[*]

---

[*] Reprinted by permission of the Harvard Law Review Association.

The constitutionality of the Hatch Act was upheld in *United Public Workers v. Mitchell*, 330 U.S. 75 (1947), and reaffirmed in *United States Civil Service Commission v. National Association of Letter Carriers*, 413 U.S. 548 (1973).

2. *Exclusive Statutory Remedies.* The Civil Service Reform Act, as did prior civil service regulations, protects employees who exercise their free speech rights consistently with the Hatch Act. In *Bush v. Lucas*, 462 U.S. 367 (1983), the Court declined to create a separate judicial remedy for a federal employee demoted for exercising his free speech rights, holding that it was inappropriate to interfere with the statute's comprehensive scheme to protect civil servants against arbitrary action by supervisors.

NATIONAL TREASURY EMPLOYEES UNION v. VON RAAB

United States Supreme Court
489 U.S. 656 (1989)

JUSTICE KENNEDY delivered the opinion of the Court.

We granted certiorari to decide whether it violates the Fourth Amendment for the United States Customs Service to require a urinalysis test from employees who seek transfer or promotion to certain positions.

[In 1986, the Commissioner of Customs began a drug-testing program requiring urinalysis tests from Customs employees seeking transfer or promotion to positions having a direct involvement in drug interdiction or requiring the employee to carry firearms or handle classified material.]

The purposes of the program are to deter drug use among those eligible for promotion to sensitive positions within the Service and to prevent the promotion of drug users to those positions. These substantial interests ... present a special need that may justify departure from the ordinary warrant and probable cause requirements....

The Customs Service is our Nation's first line of defense against one of the greatest problems affecting the health and welfare of our population.... The record in this case confirms that, through the adroit selection of source locations, smuggling routes, and increasingly elaborate methods of concealment, drug traffickers have managed to bring into this country increasingly large quantities of illegal drugs. The record also indicates, and it is well known, that drug smugglers do not hesitate to use violence to protect their lucrative trade and avoid apprehension.

Many of the Service's employees are often exposed to this criminal element and to the controlled substances they seek to smuggle into the country. The physical safety of these employees may be threatened, and many may be tempted not only by bribes from the traffickers with whom they deal, but also by their own access to vast sources of valuable contraband seized and controlled by the Service. The Commissioner indicated below that "Customs [o]fficers have been shot, stabbed, run over, dragged by automobiles, and assaulted with blunt objects while performing their duties." At least nine officers have died in the line of duty since 1974. He also noted that Customs officers have been the targets of bribery by drug smugglers on numerous occasions, and several have been removed from the Service for accepting bribes and other integrity violations.

It is readily apparent that the Government has a compelling interest in ensuring that front-line interdiction personnel are physically fit, and have unimpeachable integrity and judgment.... This national interest in self protection could be irreparably damaged if those charged with safeguarding it were, because of their own drug use, unsympathetic to their mission of interdicting narcotics. A drug user's indifference to the Service's basic mission or, even worse, his active complicity with the malefactors, can facilitate importation of sizable drug shipments or block apprehension of dangerous criminals. The public interest demands effective measures to bar drug users from positions directly involving the interdiction of illegal drugs....

Against these valid public interests we must weigh the interference with individual liberty that results from requiring these classes of employees to undergo a urine test. The interference with individual privacy that results from the collection of a urine sample for subsequent chemical analysis could be substantial in some circumstances. We have recognized, however, that the "operational realities of the workplace" may render entirely reasonable certain work-related intrusions by supervisors and co-workers that might be viewed as unreasonable in other contexts. While these operational realities will rarely affect an employee's expectations of privacy with respect to searches of his person, or of personal effects that the employee may bring to the workplace, it is plain that certain forms of public employment may diminish privacy expectations even with respect to such personal searches. Employees of the United States Mint, for example, should expect to be subject to certain routine personal searches when they leave the workplace every day. Similarly, those who join our military or intelligence services may not only be required to give what in other contexts might be viewed as extraordinary assurances of trustworthiness and probity, but also may expect intrusive inquiries into their physical fitness for those special positions.

We think Customs employees who are directly involved in the interdiction of illegal drugs or who are required to carry firearms in the line of duty likewise have a diminished expectation of privacy in respect to the intrusions occasioned by a urine test. Unlike most private citizens or government employees in general, employees involved in drug interdiction reasonably should expect effective inquiry into their fitness and probity. Much the same is true of employees who are required to carry firearms. Because successful performance of their duties depends uniquely on their judgment and dexterity, these employees cannot reasonably expect to keep from the Service personal information that bears directly on their fitness. While reasonable tests designed to elicit this information doubtless infringe some privacy expectations, we do not believe these expectations outweigh the Government's compelling interests in safety and in the integrity of our borders.

Petitioner's Arguments — Without disparaging the importance of the governmental interests that support the suspicionless searches of these employees, petitioners nevertheless contend that the Service's drug testing program is unreasonable in two particulars. First, petitioners argue that the program is unjustified because it is not based on a belief that testing will reveal any drug use by covered employees. In pressing this argument, petitioners point out that the Service's testing scheme was not implemented in response to any perceived drug problem among Customs employees, and that the program actually has not led to the discovery of a significant number of drug users. Counsel for petitioners informed us at oral argument that no more than 5 employees out of 3,600 have tested positive for drugs. Second, petitioners contend that the Service's scheme is not a "sufficiently productive mechanism to justify [its] intrusion upon Fourth Amendment interests," *Delaware v. Prouse*, 440 U.S. 648, 658-659 (1979), because illegal drug users can avoid detection with ease by temporary abstinence or by surreptitious adulteration of their urine specimens. These contentions are unpersuasive.

Petitioners' first contention evinces an unduly narrow view of the context in which the Service's testing program was implemented. Petitioners do not dispute, nor can there be doubt, that drug abuse is one of the most serious problems confronting our society today. There is little reason to believe that American workplaces are immune from this pervasive social problem, as is amply illustrated by our decision in [*Skinner v*]. *Railway Labor Executives'* [*Ass'n*, 489 U.S. 602 (1989)]. *Skinner see p.264* — Detecting drug impairment on the part of employees can be a difficult task, especially where, as here, it is not feasible to subject employees and their work-product to the kind of day-to-day scrutiny that is the norm in more traditional office environments. Indeed, the almost unique mission of the Service gives the Government a compelling interest in ensuring that many of these covered employees do not use drugs even off-duty, for such use creates risks of bribery and blackmail against which the Government is entitled to guard. In light of the extraordinary safety and national security hazards that would attend the promotion of drug users to positions that require the carrying of firearms or the interdiction of controlled substances, the Service's policy of deterring drug users from seeking such promotions cannot be deemed unreasonable.

The mere circumstance that all but a few of the employees tested are entirely innocent of wrongdoing does not impugn the program's validity. The same is likely to be true of householders who are required to submit to suspicionless housing code inspections, *see Camara v. Municipal Court*, 387 U.S. 523 (1967), and of motorists who are stopped at the checkpoints we approved in *United States v. Martinez-Fuerte*, 428 U.S. 543 (1976). The Service's program is designed to prevent the promotion of drug users to sensitive positions as much as it is designed to detect those employees who use drugs. Where, as here, the possible harm against which the Government seeks to guard is substantial, the need to prevent its occurrence furnishes an ample justification for reasonable searches calculated to advance the Government's goal.

We think petitioners' second argument — that the Service's testing program is ineffective because employees may attempt to deceive the test by a brief abstention before the test date, or by adulterating their urine specimens — overstates the case. As the Court of Appeals noted, addicts may be unable to abstain even for a limited period of time, or may be unaware of the "fade-away effect" of certain drugs. More importantly, the avoidance techniques suggested by petitioners are fraught with uncertainty and risks for those employees who venture to attempt them. A particular employee's pattern of elimination for a given drug cannot be predicted with perfect accuracy, and, in any event, this information is not likely to be known or available to the employee. Petitioners' own expert indicated below that the time it takes for particular drugs to become undetectable in urine can vary widely depending on the individual, and may extend for as long as 22 days. Thus, contrary to petitioners' suggestion, no employee reasonably can expect to deceive the test by the simple expedient of abstaining after the test date is assigned. Nor can he expect attempts at adulteration to succeed, in view of the precautions taken by the sample collector to ensure the integrity of the sample. In all the circumstances, we are persuaded that the program bears a close and substantial relation to the Service's goal of deterring drug users from seeking promotion to sensitive positions.

In sum, we believe the Government has demonstrated that its compelling interests in safeguarding our borders and the public safety outweigh the privacy expectations of employees who seek to be promoted to positions that directly involve the interdiction of illegal drugs or that require the incumbent to carry a firearm. We hold that the testing of these employees is reasonable under the Fourth Amendment....

[On the present record, however, we are unable] to assess the reasonableness of the Government's testing program insofar as it covers employees who are required "to handle classified material." We readily agree that the Government has a compelling interest in protecting truly sensitive information from those who, "under compulsion of circumstances or for other reasons, ... might compromise [such] information." *Department of Navy v. Egan*, 484 U.S. 518, 528 (1988). We also agree that employees who seek promotions to positions where they would handle sensitive information can be required to submit to a urine test under the Service's screening program, especially if the positions covered under this category require background investigations, medical examinations, or other intrusions that may be expected to diminish their expectations of privacy in respect of a urinalysis test.

It is not clear, however, whether the category defined by the Service's testing directive encompasses only those Customs employees likely to gain access to sensitive information. Employees who are tested under the Service's scheme include those holding such diverse positions as "Accountant," "Accounting

Technician," "Animal Caretaker," "Attorney (All)," "Baggage Clerk," "Co-op Student (All)," Electric Equipment Repairer," "Mail Clerk/Assistant," and "Messenger." We assume these positions were selected for coverage ... by reason of the incumbent's access to "classified" information, as it is not clear that they would fall under either of the two categories we have already considered. Yet it is not evident that those occupying these positions are likely to gain access to sensitive information, and this apparent discrepancy raises in our minds the questions whether the Service has defined this category of employees more broadly than is necessary to meet the purposes of the Commissioner's directive.

We cannot resolve this ambiguity on the basis of the record before us, [and, therefore, we remand the issue to the Court of Appeals.]

JUSTICE SCALIA, with whom JUSTICE STEVENS joins, dissenting. *The "odd couple"*

I decline to join the Court's opinion in the present case because neither frequency of use nor connection to harm is demonstrated or even likely. In my view the Customs Service rules are a kind of immolation of privacy and human dignity in symbolic opposition to drug use....

The Court's opinion in the present case ... will be searched in vain for real evidence of a real problem that will be solved by urine testing of Customs Service employees.... To paraphrase Churchill, [the Court's opinion] contains much that is obviously true, and much that is relevant; unfortunately, what is obviously true is not relevant, and what is relevant is not obviously true. The only pertinent points, it seems to me, are supported by nothing but speculation, and not very plausible speculation at that. It is not apparent to me that a Customs Service employee who uses drugs is significantly more likely to be bribed by a drug smuggler, any more than a Customs Service employee who wears diamonds is significantly more likely to be bribed by a diamond smuggler — unless, perhaps, the addiction to drugs is so severe, and requires so much money to maintain, that it would be detectable even without benefit of a urine test. Nor is it apparent to me that Customs officers who use drugs will be appreciably less "sympathetic" to their drug-interdiction mission, any more than police officers who exceed the speed limit in their private cars are appreciably less sympathetic to their mission of enforcing the traffic laws. (The only difference is that the Customs officer's individual efforts, if they are irreplaceable, can theoretically affect the availability of his own drug supply — a prospect so remote as to be an absurd basis of motivation.) Nor, finally, is it apparent to me that urine tests will be even marginally more effective in preventing gun-carrying agents from risking "impaired perception and judgment" than is their current knowledge that, if impaired, they may be shot dead in unequal combat with unimpaired smugglers — unless, again, their addiction is so severe that no urine test is needed for detection.

What is absent in the Government's justifications — notably absent, revealingly absent, and as far as I am concerned dispositively absent — is the recitation of even a single instance in which any of the speculated horribles actually occurred: an instance, that is, in which the cause of bribe-taking, or of poor aim, or of unsympathetic law enforcement, or of compromise of classified information, was drug use. Although the Court points out that several employees have in the past been removed from the Service for accepting bribes and other integrity violations, and that at least nine officers have died in the line of duty since 1974, there is no indication whatever that these incidents were related to drug use by Service employees. Perhaps concrete evidence of the severity of a problem is unnecessary when it is so well known that courts can almost take judicial notice of it; but that is surely not the case here. The Commissioner of Customs himself has stated that he "believe[s] that Customs is largely drug-free," that "[t]he extent of illegal drug use by Customs employees was not the reason for establishing this program," and that he "hope[s] and expect[s] to receive reports of very few positive findings through drug screening." The test results have fulfilled those hopes and expectations. According to the Service's counsel, out of 3,600 employees tested, no more than 5 tested positive for drugs....

... I do not believe for a minute that the driving force behind these drug-testing rules was any of the feeble justifications put forward by counsel here and accepted by the Court. The only plausible explanation, in my view, is what the Commissioner himself offered in the concluding sentence of his memorandum to Customs Service employees announcing the program: "Implementation of the drug screening program would set an important example in our country's struggle with this most serious threat to our national health and security." Or as respondent's brief to this Court asserted: "if a law enforcement agency and its employees do not take the law seriously, neither will the public on which the agency's effectiveness depends." What better way to show that the Government is serious about its "war on drugs" than to subject its employees on the front line of that war to this invasion of their privacy and affront to their dignity? To be sure, there is only a slight chance that it will prevent some serious public harm resulting from Service employee drug use, but it will show to the world that the Service is "clean," and — most important of all — will demonstrate the determination of the Government to eliminate this scourge of our society! I think it obvious that this justification is unacceptable; that the impairment of individual liberties cannot be the means of making a point; that symbolism, even symbolism for so worthy a cause as the abolition of unlawful drugs, cannot validate an otherwise unreasonable search....

Those who lose because of the lack of understanding that begot the present exercise in symbolism are not just the Customs Service employees, whose dignity is thus offended, but all of us — who suffer a coarsening of our national manners that ultimately give the Fourth Amendment its content, and who become subject to the administration of federal officials whose respect for our privacy can hardly be greater than the small respect they have been taught to have for their own.

[The dissenting opinion of Justice Marshall, joined by Justice Brennan, is omitted.]

NOTES

1. *Private Railroad Workers.* In *Skinner v. Railway Labor Executives Ass'n,* 489 U.S. 602 (1989), decided by a 7-2 vote the same day as *von Raab,* the Supreme Court found no Fourth Amendment violation for Federal Railroad Administration regulations mandating that private railroads test for drugs or alcohol after major railroad accidents. The record contained evidence that drug and alcohol abuse were substantial problems in the railroad industry and had led to numerous accidents. The Court also upheld regulations that authorized but did not mandate breath or urine tests for employees who violated certain safety rules. The Court found that the "Government's encouragement, endorsement, and participation [in the drug testing] suffice to implicate the Fourth Amendment." Nevertheless, the Court upheld the regulations as reasonable.

2. *Random and Periodic Drug Testing.* The Supreme Court has not yet ruled on the constitutionality of random or periodic drug testing. Lower federal courts are split. *Compare Feliciano v. City of Cleveland,* 661 F. Supp. 578 (N.D. Ohio 1987) (urinalysis of entire class of police academy cadets without individualized suspicion is unreasonable search and seizure) *and American Fed'n of Gov't Employees v. Weinberger,* 651 F. Supp. 726 (S.D. Ga. 1986) (mandatory, periodic urinalysis of civilian police officers is unreasonable search and seizure) *with McDonell v. Hunter,* 809 F.2d 1302 (8th Cir. 1987) (upholding urinalysis of prison guards picked by systematic random selection or upon reasonable suspicion) *and Shoemaker v. Handel,* 795 F.2d 1136 (3d Cir.), *cert. denied,* 479 U.S. 986 (1986) (Racing Commission's daily selection by lot of jockeys for urine testing does not violate Fourth Amendment, given the high degree of regulation in racing industry).

3. *Statutory Drug-Testing Mandates.* Both the executive and legislative branches of the federal government have attempted to promote drug-free workplaces. In 1986 President Reagan signed Executive Order 12,564 calling for executive agency heads to develop plans for a drug-free workplace. Each plan is to include a statement of policy, a counseling and rehabilitation program, supervisory training, treatment referral provisions, and a drug testing program for employees in sensitive positions. In addition, agencies are authorized to test any job applicant and to test employees upon reasonable suspicion of drug use, after an accident or unsafe practice, or to help with rehabilitation or counseling. The order also mandates procedural safeguards.

The Drug-Free Workplace Act of 1988, 41 U.S.C. §§ 701-707, extends beyond government employees to federal contractors and federal grant recipients. To receive a federal contract or grant, employers must certify they will provide a drug-free workplace by notifying employees that illegal drugs are prohibited in the workplace and establishing drug-free awareness programs. The act does not specifically refer to drug testing. An early survey of affected employers found the Act to be largely ineffective. Donald J. Peterson & Douglas Massengill,

Employer Response to the Drug-Free Workplace Act of 1988: A Preliminary Look, LAB. L.J., March 1991, at 144, 149-50.

4. *Public Employee Privacy in General.* The Fourth Amendment protects public employees from unreasonable searches whenever the employee has a reasonable expectation of privacy. In *O'Connor v. Ortega*, 480 U.S. 709 (1987), five Justices concluded that a physician at a government hospital had a reasonable expectation of privacy in his office, and all nine Justices agreed that he had a reasonable expectation of privacy in his desk and file cabinets. For hospital officials lawfully to search his office while investigating charges that he had improperly acquired a computer and had sexually harassed employees, the invasion of this reasonable expectation of privacy had to be outweighed by the government's need for supervision, control, and the efficient operation of the workplace. The Court remanded for a determination of whether this search was justified, but the plurality opinion warned that "public employees' expectations of privacy in their offices, desks, and file cabinets, like similar expectations of employees in the private sector, may be reduced by virtue of actual office practices and procedures, or by legitimate regulation." 480 U.S. at 717 (O'Connor, J.).

Chapter 9

FREE SPEECH AND PRIVACY PROTECTIONS IN THE PRIVATE SECTOR

A. PROTECTIONS WHILE ON THE JOB

In this section, we look at free speech and at-work privacy rights of private-sector workers. A major question will be the extent to which constitutional and statutory protections given public workers spill over to the private sector, or on the other hand the extent to which the at-will paradigm is thought to be inconsistent with free speech and privacy rights.

NOVOSEL v. NATIONWIDE INSURANCE CO.

United States Court of Appeals, Third Circuit

721 F.2d 894 (1983)

Before ADAMS, HUNTER and GARTH, CIRCUIT JUDGES.

ADAMS, CIRCUIT JUDGE.

This appeal presents us with the task of determining under what circumstances a federal court sitting in diversity under Pennsylvania law may intercede in a non-union employment relationship and limit the employer's ability to discharge employees....

Novosel was an employee of Nationwide from December 1966 until November 18, 1981. He had steadily advanced through the company's ranks in a career unmarred by reprimands or disciplinary action. At the time his employment was terminated, he was a district claims manager and one of three candidates for the position of division claims manager.

In late October 1981, a memorandum was circulated through Nationwide's offices soliciting the participation of all employees in an effort to lobby the Pennsylvania House of Representatives. Specifically, employees were instructed to clip, copy, and obtain signatures on coupons bearing the insignia of the Pennsylvania Committee for No-Fault Reform. This Committee was actively supporting the passage of House Bill 1285, the "No-Fault Reform Act," then before the state legislature.

The allegations of the complaint charge that the sole reason for Novosel's discharge was his refusal to participate in the lobbying effort and his privately stated opposition to the company's political stand. Novosel contends that the discharge for refusing to lobby the state legislature on the employer's behalf constituted the tort of wrongful discharge on the grounds it was willful, arbitrary, malicious and in bad faith, and that it was contrary to public policy.... Novosel sought damages, reinstatement and declaratory relief. Nationwide did not file an

267

answer to the complaint; instead it presented a motion to dismiss. Following the submission of briefs on the motion to dismiss, and without benefit of either affidavits or oral argument, the district court granted the motion on January 14, 1983....

The circumstances of the discharge presented by Novosel fall squarely within the range of activity embraced by the emerging tort case law. As one commentator has written:

> The factual pattern alleged in these cases seldom varies. The employee objects to work that the employee believes is violative of state or federal law or otherwise improper; the employee protests to his employer that the work should not be performed; the employee expresses his intention not to assist the employer in the furtherance of such work and/or engages in "self-help" activity outside the work place to halt the work; and the employer discharges the employee for refusal to work or incompatibility with management.

Olsen, *Wrongful Discharge Claims Raised by At Will Employees: A New Legal Concern for Employers*, 32 Lab. L.J. 265, 276 (1981). In a landmark opinion, the Pennsylvania Supreme Court acknowledged that such a situation could give rise to a legal cause of action:

> It may be granted that there are areas of an employee's life in which his employer has no legitimate interest. An intrusion into one of these areas by virtue of the employer's power of discharge might plausibly give rise to a cause of action, particularly where some recognized facet of public policy is threatened. The notion that substantive due process elevates an employer's privilege of hiring and discharging his employees to an absolute constitutional right has long since been discredited.

Geary v. United States Steel Corp., 319 A.2d 174, 180 (Pa. 1974). Under the particular facts of *Geary*, the court held:

> [T]his case does not require us to define in comprehensive fashion the perimeters of this privilege [to employ-at-will], and we decline to do so. We hold only that where the complaint itself discloses a plausible and legitimate reason for terminating an at-will employment relationship and no clear mandate of public policy is violated thereby, an employee at will has no right of action against his employer for wrongful discharge.

319 A.2d at 180.

Applying the logic of *Geary*, we find that Pennsylvania law permits a cause of action for wrongful discharge where the employment termination abridges a significant and recognized public policy. The district court did not consider the question whether an averment of discharge for refusing to support the employer's lobbying efforts is sufficiently violative of such public policy as to state a cause of action. Nationwide, however, now proposes that "the only prohibition on the termination of an employee is that the termination cannot violate a *statutorily* recognized public policy," Brief of Appellee at 5 (emphasis added).

This Court has recognized that the "only Pennsylvania cases applying public policy exceptions have done so where no statutory remedies were available." *Bruffett* [*v. Warner Communications, Inc.*, 692 F.2d 910 (3d Cir. 1982] at 919.... Given that there are no statutory remedies available in the present case and taking into consideration the importance of the political and associational freedoms of the federal and state Constitutions, the absence of a statutory declaration of public policy would appear to be no bar to the existence of a cause of action. Accordingly, a cognizable expression of public policy may be derived in this case from either the First Amendment of the United States Constitution or Article I, Section 7 of the Pennsylvania Constitution.[6]

The key question in considering the tort claim is therefore whether a discharge for disagreement with the employer's legislative agenda or a refusal to lobby the state legislature on the employer's behalf sufficiently implicate a recognized facet of public policy. The definition of a "clearly mandated public policy" as one that "strikes at the heart of a citizen's social right, duties and responsibilities," set forth in *Palmateer v. International Harvester Co.*, 421 N.E.2d 876 (Ill. 1981), appears to provide a workable standard for the tort action. While no Pennsylvania law directly addresses the public policy question at bar, the protection of an employee's freedom of political expression would appear to involve no less compelling a societal interest than the fulfillment of jury service or the filing of a workers' compensation claim.

An extensive case law has developed concerning the protection of constitutional rights, particularly First Amendment rights, of government employees. As the Supreme Court has commented, "[f]or most of this century, the unchallenged dogma was that a public employee had no right to object to conditions placed upon the terms of employment — including those which restricted the exercise of constitutional rights." *Connick v. Myers*, 461 U.S. 138, 143 (1983). The Court in *Connick*, however, also observed the constitutional repudiation of this dogma: "[f]or at least 15 years, it has been settled that a state cannot condition public employment on a basis that infringes the employee's constitutionally protected interest in freedom of expression." *Id.* at 1687, *citing Branti v. Finkel*, 445 U.S. 507, 515-516 (1980); *Perry v. Sindermann*, 408 U.S. 593, 597 (1972); *Pickering v. Board of Education*, 391 U.S. 563 (1968); *Keyishian v. Board of Regents*, 385 U.S. 589, 605-606 (1967).... Thus, there can no longer be any doubt that speech on public issues "has always rested on the highest rung of the hierarchy of First Amendment values." *NAACP v. Claiborne*

---

[6] The relevant portion of Article I, Section 7 of the Pennsylvania Constitution states:

The free communication of thoughts and opinions is one of the invaluable rights of man, and every citizen may freely speak, write and print on any subject, being responsible for the abuse of that liberty.

Hardware Co., 458 U.S. 886 (1982), *quoting Carey v. Brown*, 447 U.S. 455, 467 (1980).[7]

In striking down the use of patronage appointments for federal government employees, the Court further noted that one of its goals was to insure that "employees themselves are to be sufficiently free from improper influences." *CSC v. Letter Carriers*, 413 U.S. 548, 564 (1973). It was not, however, simply the abuse of state authority over public employees that fueled the Court's concern over patronage political appointments; no less central is the fear that the political process would be irremediably distorted. If employers such as federal, state or municipal governments are allowed coercive control of the scope and direction of employee political activities, it is argued, their influence will be geometrically enhanced at the expense of both the individual rights of the employees and the ability of the lone political actor to be effectively heard....

Although Novosel is not a government employee, the public employee cases do not confine themselves to the narrow question of state action. Rather, these cases suggest that an important public policy is in fact implicated wherever the power to hire and fire is utilized to dictate the terms of employee political activities. In dealing with public employees, the cause of action arises directly from the Constitution rather than from common law developments. The protection of important political freedoms, however, goes well beyond the question whether the threat comes from state or private bodies. The inquiry before us is whether the concern for the rights of political expression and association which animated the public employee cases is sufficient to state a public policy under Pennsylvania law. While there are no Pennsylvania cases squarely on this point, we believe that the clear direction of the opinions promulgated by the state's courts suggests that this question be answered in the affirmative.

Having concluded thereby that an important public policy is at stake, we now hold that Novosel's allegations state a claim within the ambit of *Geary* in that Novosel's complaint discloses no plausible and legitimate reason for terminating his employment, and his discharge violates a clear mandate of public policy. The Pennsylvania Supreme Court's rulings ... are thus interpreted to extend to a non-constitutional claim where a corporation conditions employment upon political subordination. This is not the first judicial recognition of the relationship between economic power and the political process:

> [T]he special status of corporations has placed them in a position to control vast amounts of economic power which may, if not regulated, dominate not only the economy but also the very heart of our democracy, the electoral

---

[7] Nor can there be any doubt that the right to petition or not petition the legislature is incorporated within protected speech on public issues. Thus, for example, in limiting the scope of the Sherman Act, the Supreme Court declared, "[t]he right of petition is one of the freedoms protected by the Bill of Rights, and we cannot, of course, lightly impute to Congress an intent to invade these freedoms." *Eastern RR Presidents' Conference v. Noerr Motor Freight, Inc.*, 365 U.S. 127, 138 (1961).

process.... [The desired end] is not one of equalizing the resources of opposing candidates or opposing positions, but rather of preventing institutions which have been permitted to amass wealth as a result of special advantages extended by the State for certain economic purposes from using that wealth to acquire an unfair advantage in the political process....

First National Bank of Boston v. Bellotti, 435 U.S. 765, 809 (1978) (White, J., dissenting).[9]

... [O]n remand the district court should employ the four part inquiry the [Pennsylvania Supreme Court] derived from *Connick* and *Pickering*:

1. Whether, because of the speech, the employer is prevented from efficiently carrying out its responsibilities;
2. Whether the speech impairs the employee's ability to carry out his own responsibilities;
3. Whether the speech interferes with essential and close working relationships;
4. Whether the manner, time and place in which the speech occurs interferes with business operations.

Sacks [*v. Commonwealth of Pennsylvania, Department of Public Welfare*, 465 A.2d 981 (Pa. Sup. Ct. 1983)] at 988.

In weighing these issues, a court should employ the balancing test factors set forth for wrongful discharge cases by the Pennsylvania Superior Court in *Yaindl* [*v. Ingersoll-Rand Co.*, 422 A.2d 611 (Pa. Super. Ct. 1980)]:

(a) the nature of the actor's conduct,
(b) the actor's motive,
(c) the interests of the other with which the actor's conduct interferes,
(d) the interests sought to be advanced by the actor,
(e) the social interests in protecting the freedom of action of the actor and the contractual interests of the other,
(f) the proximity or remoteness of the actor's conduct to the interference, and
(g) the relations between the parties.

....

---

[9] The district court relies heavily upon the majority opinion in *Bellotti* to support the proposition that so long as an employer's actions were "in furtherance of its normal and ordinary business interests," its political activities are beyond court scrutiny. By extending constitutional protection to corporate political activity, the district court precludes any common law tort claim. In our view, this reliance on *Bellotti* obscures the fact that there are two distinct issues present here: 1) whether a corporation may engage in the type of lobbying demonstrated by defendant; and 2) whether the economic power of such corporations (in this case the power to discharge) may be utilized to coerce individual employee assistance to the corporate political agenda. Although *Bellotti* does find that corporate speech is entitled to First Amendment protection, the opinion does not stand for the proposition that corporations in the political arena can neither do any wrong nor be regulated.... At the very least, it does not follow from *Bellotti* that the right of political expression of a corporation enjoys a transcendent constitutional position regardless of other societal or constitutional interests.

Statement of Judge Becker sur the Denial of the
Petition for Rehearing

Because this is a diversity case, the holding of the panel constitutes a mere prediction of the likely course of Pennsylvania law, one subject to revision by the Pennsylvania Supreme Court or the Pennsylvania General Assembly. While this fact would ordinarily render en banc consideration inappropriate, I nonetheless believe that the panel's decision is sufficiently important and sufficiently questionable to call for reconsideration by the en banc Court....

My concern is that the panel has announced an extremely broad "public policy" exception to the law of at-will employment in Pennsylvania that threatens to engulf or "overrule" the holding of the Pennsylvania Supreme Court in *Geary v. U.S. Steel Corp.*, 319 A.2d 174 (Pa. 1974) — an action Pennsylvania itself has apparently shown no inclination to undertake. More specifically, I have three major problems with the panel opinion.

First, the opinion ignores the state action requirement of first amendment jurisprudence, particularly by its repeated, and, in my view, inappropriate citation of public employee cases, and by its implicit assumption that a public policy against government interference with free speech may be readily extended to private actors in voluntary association with another. Second, the opinion could be read to suggest that an explicit contractual provision authorizing an employer to dismiss a lobbyist for failure to undertake lobbying might be unenforceable or subject to a balancing test. Third, the opinion fails to consider other public policy interests, such as the economic interests of the public in efficient corporate performance, the first amendment interests of corporations, and the legitimate interests of a corporation in commanding the loyalty of its employees to pursue its economic well being.

NOTES

1. *Distorting the Legislative Process.* Is the problem with Nationwide's policy that it uses its power at the workplace to "artificially" magnify its clout with the legislature? Is this a third-party cost of at-will employment worthy of regulation by the tort system?

2. *The Public Sector Analogy.* Judge Becker's complaint about relying on public-sector values in deciding private-employment claims is a familiar one, and courts are typically cautious about doing so. But consider the argument of Professor Issacharoff, who finds it natural that public-employment principles will influence private-employment common law:

> One of the key sources for modern developments in employment law has been the public sector, where the Bill of Rights provides a built-in general presumption against parity for relations between the citizenry and the state. Once constitutional doctrine jettisoned the strict rights/privileges distinction and recognized entitlements to certain state benefits, public employment became a natural arena for the pioneering of substantive claims to

employment rights. Since the 1960s, the public sector has been the source of dramatic expansions in employee rights to free expression, due process, and privacy.

Weiler's discussion of the developing common law of wrongful termination overlooks the dramatic expansion of public-sector employment and the critical role that public-sector litigation has played in the development of the common law. Given that only recently has a subject denominated "employment law" emerged independent of "labor law," it is perhaps to be expected that commentators such as Weiler view the common law developments through the comparative prism of union-based labor law.

If we return to the premise of the NLRA, however, the increased impact of the public sector fits with the expectation that the terms and conditions of employment set in the dominant economic sectors would spill over into the rest of the labor market. The public sector has come to rival, if not surpass, the private union sector in setting the terms and conditions of the current labor market. The proportion of the work force employed by government is roughly equal to the union sector. In addition, a substantial number of unionized employees are currently in the public sector, which has a unionization rate almost three times that of the private sector. The relative weight of public sector employment is even greater among professional and managerial employees, precisely the group most likely to initiate private wrongful-discharge claims. Thus, it is not surprising that courts seeking to redress wrongful-discharge claims routinely look to the public sector cases for guidance....

Unfortunately, reference to the public sector case law further exposes the limitations of the current common law developments. Although the public sector cases have developed a doctrinal overview based on the establishment of enforceable property rights for tenured employees, no equivalent development has taken hold in the common law cases. The defining feature of the common law retrenchment on employment at will has been the use of tort and contract doctrines that define employee rights only transactionally, in relation to what a particular employer said or did or promised.

Samuel Issacharoff, *Reconstructing Employment*, 104 HARV. L. REV. 607, 616-17 (1990)[*] (reviewing PAUL C. WEILER, GOVERNING THE WORKPLACE (1990)).

3. Political Autonomy for Workers. *Chavez v. Manville Products Corp.*, 777 P.2d 371 (N.M. 1989), presents a similar situation. There, an employee was fired after complaining when the plant manager sent a mailgram urging their U.S. Senator to support proposed asbestos legislation, and added the employee's name to the telegram without his consent. The trial court held that the firing violated a clear public policy, and the employer did not raise the issue on appeal.

Correales mentions

Louisiana Computing Corp.

Suppose an employee decides to run for local office. Can the employer terminate him? In *Davis v. Louisiana Computing Corp.*, 394 So. 2d 678 (La. Ct. App. 1981), the court upheld a $24,000 jury verdict against a computer company, whose major clients were local governmental agencies, when it fired an employee for becoming a candidate for city council. The court recognized that the "candidacy would antagonize persons who could withdraw business from plaintiff's employer," but found the employee protected by a state statute that prohibited employers with more than twenty employees from preventing any employee from engaging in politics or becoming a candidate for public office. Should the type of job the employee performs be a consideration? What if a newspaper reporter covering the local government decides to run for city council?

The statute was important here. Otherwise an at-will employee could have been fired.

Korb

In *Korb v. Raytheon Corp.*, 574 N.E.2d 370 (Mass. 1991), a defense contractor executive in charge of Washington operations was fired for criticizing increased defense spending at a news conference. The court rejected a claim that the firing interfered with his right to express himself, determining that his statements were directly contrary to the company's financial interests.

TIMEKEEPING SYSTEMS, INC.

National Labor Relations Board

323 NLRB No. 30 (1997)

Protected Concerted Activity Case

By Chairman Gould and Members Browning and Fox.

On November 12, 1996, Administrative Law Judge Bernard Ries issued the attached decision.... The Board has considered the decision and the record in light of the exceptions and briefs and has decided to affirm the judge's rulings, findings, and conclusions and to adopt the recommended Order as modified....

ISSUE

... The sole issue presented is whether Respondent discharged Lawrence Leinweber on December 5, 1995, because of his protected concerted activities and therefore violated Section 8(a)(1) of the [National Labor Relations] Act....

I. THE FACTS

Sect. 8(a)(1) National Labor Relations Act

Respondent is a small Cleveland, Ohio company which manufactures data collection products. The chief operational officer of Respondent is Barry Markwitz.... Larry Leinweber, the Charging Party, 1 of about 23 employees located in two buildings, was hired by Respondent in April 1995 as a "software engineer" who prepared computer programs.

On December 1, Markwitz sent a message to all of Respondent's employees by electronic mail ("e-mail") regarding "proposed plans" for an incentive based bonus system (as to which employees were told to "reply with your comments or stop by to see me. A response to this is required.") and changes in vacation policy ("Your comments are welcome, but not required"). The incorporated memorandum regarding the proposed vacation policy changes, which are our only concern here, stated prefatorily, "Please give me your comments (send me an e-mail or stop in and talk to me) by Tuesday, 12/5." The particular suggested policy changes in which we are interested were to close the offices on December 23 and reopen on January 2 and to adjust the number of paid days off over a 5-year period, the effect of which, Markwitz asserted, was that the employees "actually get more days off each year, compared to our present system."

Markwitz received a number of employee responses regarding his vacation proposals, including one on December 1, by e-mail, from Leinweber. Leinweber's response demonstrated that, in fact, the change referred to above would result in the same number of vacation days per year, and less flexibility as to their use. On December 4, Leinweber, having checked his calculations over the weekend, discovered a minor error, and notified Markwitz by e-mail.

Markwitz did not reply to Leinweber's communications. On December 5, Tom Dutton, a member of the engineering team, sent an e-mail to Markwitz, with copies to other engineering team members (which would include Leinweber), reading, "In response to the proposed vacation plan, I have only one word, GREAT!" Promptly, Leinweber, according to his credible testimony, sent an e-mail to Dutton telling him that the proposed policy did not, in fact, redound to the advantage of the employees.

Also on December 5, Leinweber sent a lengthy e-mail message to all employees, including Markwitz. The message spelled out in detail Leinweber's calculations regarding the result of the proposed vacation policy change. It contained, as well, some flippant and rather grating language.

The salutation was "Greetings Fellow Traveler." In his initial remarks, Leinweber wrote, "The closing statement in Barry's memo: 'The effect of this is that you actually get more days off each year, compared to our present system,' will be proven false." This declaration is reiterated in the final thought of the memo: "Thus, the closing statement in Barry's memo ... is proven false." The paragraph preceding that statement reads, "Assuming anyone actually cares about the company and being productive on the job, if Christmas falls on Tuesday or Wednesday (sic) as it will in 1996 and 1997, respectively, two work weeks of one and two days each will be produced by the proposed plan, and I wouldn't expect these to be any more productive than the fragmented weeks that they replace." In closing, Leinweber asked that the recipient "please send errata to the (sic) Larry."

Also on December 5, after reading the e-mail message from Leinweber, Dutton e-mailed again to Markwitz, and also the engineering team (as shown on the e-mail address), saying in part, "After reading Larry's E-mail(s) of this date[,] I realized I had made a mistake in calculating the vacation days and wish to change my comment from 'GREAT' to 'Not so Great' on the proposed vacation policy." Dutton also noted in his message that the proposals had "generated more E-mail than any other plan in the company."

At the hearing, Markwitz at first admitted that he was "angry that Mr. Leinweber sent his e-mail messages to all employees." He prepared on December 5 a memorandum to Leinweber which was conveyed to him by the engineering team leader. The memo stated that Markwitz was "saddened and disappointed" by Leinweber's e-mail, which was "inappropriate and intentionally provocative" and beneath "someone as talented and intelligent as you are." Markwitz then wrote:

> Our employment manual states: "Certain actions or types of behavior may result in immediate dismissal. These include, but are not limited to: Failure to treat others with courtesy and respect."

Markwitz went on to "direct" Leinweber to write him, by 5 p.m. that day: "In light of the above, why this e-mail message was inappropriate. How sending an e-mail message like this hurts the company. How this matter should have been handled."

Markwitz continued: "If your response is acceptable to me, you will post it by e-mail today to those who received your other message. If you decline to do so, or if your response is unacceptable to me, your employment will be terminated immediately. Otherwise, your employment will continue on a probationary basis for six months, during which time your employment may be terminated at any time and for any reason. Larry, I am very disappointed in you."

At the hearing, Markwitz testified that what upset him about the document was its "tone": it was a "slap in the face" of employees with good attitudes and a "personal attack" upon him. [Leinweber was then fired.]

II. DISCUSSION AND CONCLUSIONS

See. Note. # 2

In *Meyers I*, the Board stated the principles applicable to an alleged discharge for protected concerted activity under Section 8(a)(1) of the Act, and *Meyers II* did not purport to change those principles:[9] Once the activity is found to be concerted, an 8(a)(1) violation will be found if, in addition, the employer knew of the concerted nature of the employee's activity, the concerted activity was protected by the Act, and the adverse employment action at issue (e.g., discharge) was motivated by the employee's protected concerted activity.

Leinweber's e-mailings clearly constituted "concerted" activity ... for the "purpose of mutual aid or protection," as required by Section 7 of the Act. Leinweber's effort to incite the other employees to help him preserve a vacation policy which he believed best served his interests, and perhaps the interests of other employees, unquestionably qualified his communication as being in pursuit of "mutual aid or protection." While the court in *New River Industries, Inc. v. NLRB*, 945 F.2d 1290 (4th Cir. 1991), may have thought, contrary to the Board, that a sarcastic letter was, in Respondent's words, intended "merely to belittle

---

[9] *Meyers Industries*, 268 NLRB 493, 497 (1984), *remanded sub nom. Prill v. NLRB*, 755 NLRB 941 (D.C. Cir. 1987), *on remand, Meyers Industries*, 281 NLRB 882 (1986), *affd. sub nom., Prill v. NLRB*, 835 F.2d 1481 (D.C. Cir.).

management," here there is no doubt that Leinweber had a specific objective in mind for which he hoped to elicit "mutual aid." ...

While I have found that Markwitz was principally aggrieved by the tenor of Leinweber's e-mail and its perceived personal denigration of Markwitz, his December 9 message to employees establishes as well that a component of his anger was caused by the fact that Leinweber had attempted to enlist other employees in his cause. Although the law of "protected concerted activity" does not require the General Counsel to prove that the employer has disciplined an employee because he/she has engaged in concerted activity, but rather only requires that the employer knows that the conduct being disciplined is concerted, the evidence here shows that the concertedness of Leinweber's conduct also very likely infected Markwitz's decision to discharge.[11]

In considering the other elements of a prima facie protected concerted activity case, as outlined in *Meyer I* there is obviously no question that Markwitz was aware of the concerted activity, nor any doubt that it played the principal role in Leinweber's discharge.

The final question raised by the Respondent is whether Leinweber's December 5 message was "protected." Some concerted conduct can be expressed in so intolerable a manner as to lose the protection of Section 7. While the legal description of the sort of behavior which withdraws the protection of the Act from concerted activity has varied, *Dreis & Krump Mfg. Co., Inc. v. NLRB*, 544 F.2d 320, 329 (7th Cir. 1976), ... has often been spotlighted for its statement of the test:

> [C]ommunications occurring during the course of otherwise protected activity remain likewise protected unless found to be 'so violent or of such serious character as to render the employee unfit for further service.'

In applying the foregoing or similar standards, the Board has invoked a forfeiture of the protection of the Act only in cases where the concerted behavior has been truly insubordinate or disruptive of the work process. It has generally been the Board's position that unpleasantries uttered in the course of otherwise protected concerted activity do not strip away the Act's protection. In *Postal Service*, 241 NLRB 389 (1979), a letter characterizing acting supervisors as "a-holes" was not beyond the pale. In *Harris Corp.*, 269 NLRB 733 (1984), a letter describing management with such words as "hypocritical," "despotic," and "tyrannical" was not disqualifying, despite its "boorish, ill-bred, and hostile tone." In *Churchill's Restaurant*, 276 NLRB 775 (1985), where an employer dis-

---

[11] I note that Respondent's employee manual lists as a ground for discharge "Discussing your rate of pay or your compensation arrangement with another employee." This would normally constitute an unfair labor practice, *see, e.g., Radisson Plaza Minneapolis*, 307 NLRB 94 (1992); *Heck's, Inc.*, 293 NLRB 1111, 1113 (1989). However, the complaint contains no such allegation and the General Counsel has not, on brief, sought a finding based on this statement. I shall therefore not address the matter further.

charged an employee who, he believed, was saying that the employer was "prejudiced," which the latter considered an "insult," the remarks were held not "so offensive as to threaten plant discipline." A statement to other employees that the chief executive officer was a "cheap son of a bitch" was considered to be protected concerted activity in *Groves Truck & Trailer*, 281 NLRB 1194, 1195 (1986).

The question of the protected nature of Leinweber's activity is controlled by the latter line of precedents. It is clear from Markwitz's correspondence and testimony that his ultimate decision to discharge Leinweber was based on two aspects of Leinweber's conduct. The major reason was the tone of the letter and the specific remarks about Markwitz. As I have noted previously, it is also evident that Markwitz was displeased by the fact that Weber had communicated the message to the other employees,[13] and that concern entwined with and aggravated, in Markwitz's mind, the first reaction.

Markwitz, like any other employer, wants a friction free working environment. But, as the court of appeals pointed out in *Thor Power Tool*, Section 7 activity may acceptably be accompanied by some "impropriety." And, in *Dreis & Krump Mfg. Co.*, the court of appeals laid down the rather stiff test of whether the questioned activity is "of such serious character as to render the employee unfit for further service." Surely, the words and phrases used by Leinweber in his message were not that egregious. The Leinweber message has arrogant overtones, but the language is less assaultive than the "boorish, ill-bred, and hostile" wording found not to be disqualifying in *Harris Corp.* Indeed, Markwitz was prepared to retain Leinweber if he would submit some sort of apology, which he failed to do. I find that the message itself was not couched in language sufficiently serious to warrant divestment of Section 7 protection....

Finally, although unnecessarily, I address Respondent's contention that "[i]t would be wrong to saddle Respondent for many years into the future with the burden of a reinstated employee the likes of Leinweber." Leinweber is, I concede, a rather unusual person, perhaps one of the new breed of cyberspace pioneers who are attracting public attention, and at the same time — how else can I say it — a bit of a wise guy. Still, in his December 5 e-mail, Markwitz described Leinweber as " talented and intelligent," and he was willing to retain Leinweber after receipt of the offending message if Leinweber would publicly apologize. Markwitz also implored employee Heather Hudson on December 5 to urge Leinweber to write the apology because "he did not want to fire him." I do not gather from this that Markwitz would be totally distraught if he had to rehire Leinweber. In any event, Markwitz's feelings must take second place to the dic-

---

[13] As indicated earlier, Markwitz wrote the employees on December 6 that the "right way" to handle a "grievance, or a question, or a comment, or a complaint" was to speak to him or one of the other managers. This statement is itself probably violative of Sec. 8(a)(1), *see* fn. 11, *supra*, but, for the reasons there given, I will not consider the issue further....

tates of the statute; the employer who was called a "cheap son-of-a-bitch" by an employee in *Groves Truck & Trailer* was probably not entirely pleased either....

[The Board ordered that Leinweber be reinstated with back pay, and that the company post a notice at its facility explaining the violation found and promising not to violate the National Labor Relations Act again.]

NOTES

1. *The NLRA in the Non-Union Workplace.* The National Labor Relations Act is the major statute regulating unions; indeed, the NLRA often is thought to have no relevance to nonunion establishments, except when a union is trying to organize. But § 7 of the NLRA, which defines the rights of employees under the Act, gives employees the right "to engage in other concerted activities for the purpose of ... other mutual aid or protection." As the *Leinweber* case illustrates, § 7 rights are increasingly being applied to workplaces that have no thought of unionizing.

For a thoughtful examination of the NLRA in the nonunion workplace, see Charles J. Morris, *NLRB Protection in the Nonunion Workplace: A Glimpse at a General Theory of Section 7 Conduct*, 137 U. PENN. L. REV. 1673 (1989). Professor Morris emphasizes that Congress protected "pre-organizational" concerted activities by employees in part because they could evolve toward more formalized union activity, thus furthering the overall NLRA policy of "encouraging the practice and procedure of collective bargaining." But employees need not have a conscious goal of forming a union in order to be protected:

> In the early organizational stages of the process that Section 7 describes, employees need not be consciously aware that they are engaged in a concerted act. They need only be involved in an act of association, speech, or petition ("petition," in workplace terminology, being essentially the presentation of a grievance) that reasonably relates to "wages, hours, [or] other terms and conditions of employment." It is important, however, that the employer must not have unreasonably interfered with or denied their opportunity to engage in such activity. If equality of organizational power is to have a meaning consistent with the policy of the statute, then it follows that Section 7 guarantees (1) that employees will have the right to confer among themselves about any of the foregoing matters; (2) that several employees may each voice a common concern about such matters and thereby impliedly engage in concerted activity; (3) that a single employee has the right to turn to one or more fellow employees to seek mutual aid or protection as to such matters; and (4) that a single employee has the right to attempt to initiate an action or seek support, for the benefit of the employees as a group, with respect to such matters, regardless of whether she or he is ultimately successful in that endeavor. The only restrictions the employer

should be able to place on such conduct are those for which there are "legitimate and substantial business justifications."

Id. at 1701-02.

2. *Protected Concerted Activities.* Three inquiries must be satisfied before the NLRA will protect an employee's action.

(1) *Concerted.* The NLRA protects only group activities. Activities by an individual employee solely on his or her own behalf are not covered. In *Meyers I* and *II*, the NLRB held that a truck driver in a nonunion plant who refused to drive his vehicle and who complained to a state regulatory agency about allegedly unsafe brakes was not engaged in concerted activity. The Board in *Meyers II* emphasized that concerted activity "encompasses those circumstances where individual employees seek to initiate or to induce or to prepare for group action, as well as individual employees bringing truly group complaints to the attention of management." But the Board held that invocation of a safety statute cannot be regarded as an extension of concerted activity in any realistic sense. The Board in the *Meyers* cases distinguished *NLRB v. City Disposal System*, 465 U.S. 104 (1984), where the Supreme Court found that a unionized truck driver who refused to drive because of faulty brakes was engaged in concerted activity, because the collective bargaining agreement entitled workers to refuse to operate unsafe equipment. The *Meyers II* Board declared that "invocation of employee contract rights is a continuation of an ongoing process of employee concerted activity, whereas employee invocation of statutory rights is not. We believe that we best effectuate the policies of the Act when we focus our resources on the protection of actions taken pursuant to that process."

(2) *Work-Related Object.* The action must be for mutual aid or protection reasonably related to wages, hours, and other terms and conditions of employment. In *Eastex, Inc. v. NLRB*, 437 U.S. 556 (1978), the Supreme Court gave a broad reading to the phrase. An employer refused to permit employees to circulate a union newsletter on company property during nonworking time that included material criticizing a presidential veto of a minimum wage increase and urging employees to oppose a right-to-work provision in the state constitution. The Supreme Court found this to be an unfair labor practice because the newsletter was for "mutual aid or protection," even though the subject matter was outside the employer's immediate control. The union status of the workers appeared to be irrelevant to the decision.

(3) *Protected.* Even if the employees' act is concerted activity for work-related mutual aid or protection, it may still be unprotected if it is unlawful, violent, in breach of contract, or indefensible. The classic case finding indefensible conduct is *NLRB v. IBEW Local 1129 (Jefferson Standard Broadcasting Co.)*, 346 U.S. 464 (1953), where employees, without referring to an on-going dispute with the union, distributed handbills in the off-hours to the public that disparaged the company's product.

K-MART CORP. STORE NO. 7441 v. TROTTI

Court of Appeals of Texas

Appellee

677 S.W.2d 632 (1984)

Before EVANS, C.J., and COHEN and BULLOCK, JJ.

BULLOCK, JUSTICE.

K-Mart Corporation appeals from a judgment awarding the appellee, Trotti, $8,000.00 in actual damages and $100,000.00 in exemplary damages for invasion of privacy.

We reverse and remand.

The appellee was an employee in the hosiery department at the appellants' store number 7441. Her supervisors had never indicated any dissatisfaction with her work nor any suspicion of her honesty.

The appellants provided their employees with lockers for the storage of personal effects during working hours. There was no assignment of any given locker to any individual employee. The employees could, on request, receive locks for the lockers from the appellants, and if the appellants provided the lock to an employee they would keep either a copy of the lock's combination or a master key for padlocks. Testimony indicated that there was some problem in providing a sufficient number of locks to employees, and, as a result, the store's administrative personnel permitted employees to purchase and use their own locks on the lockers, but in these instances, the appellants did not require the employee to provide the manager with either a combination or duplicate key. The appellee, with appellants' knowledge, used one of these lockers and provided her own combination lock.

On October 31, 1981, the appellee placed her purse in her locker when she arrived for work. She testified that she snapped the lock closed and then pulled on it to make sure it was locked. When she returned to her locker during her afternoon break, she discovered the lock hanging open. Searching through her locker, the appellee further discovered her personal items in her purse in considerable disorder. Nothing was missing from either the locker or the purse. The store manager testified that, in the company of three junior administrators at the store, he had that afternoon searched the lockers because of a suspicion raised by the appellants' security personnel that an unidentified employee, not the appellee, had stolen a watch. The manager and his assistants were also searching for missing price-marking guns. The appellee further testified that, as she left the employee's locker area after discovering her locker open, she heard the manager suggest to his assistants, "Let's get busy again." The manager testified that none of the parties searched through employees' personal effects.

The appellee approached the manager later that day and asked if he had searched employees' lockers and/or her purse. The manager initially denied either kind of search and maintained this denial for approximately one month. At

Store manager searches purse

that time, the manager then admitted having searched the employees' lockers and further mentioned that they had, in fact, searched the appellee's purse, later saying that he meant that they had searched only her locker and not her purse.

The manager testified that during the initial hiring interviews, all prospective employees received verbal notification from personnel supervisors that it was the appellants' policy to conduct ingress-egress searches of employees and also to conduct unannounced searches of lockers. A personnel supervisor and an assistant manager, however, testified that, although locker searches did regularly occur, the personnel supervisors did not apprise prospective employees of this policy....

The appellants requested the trial court to define an "invasion of privacy" as "the intentional intrusion upon the solitude or seclusion of another that is highly offensive to a reasonable person." This is the definition enunciated in *Gill v. Snow,* [644 S.W.2d 222 (Tex. Ct. App. 1982)], and in the Restatement (Second) of Torts, Sec. 652B (1977). The court refused to include the part of the requested instruction, "... that is highly offensive to a reasonable person." The appellants argue that this refusal constituted an abuse of discretion because the Rules of Civil Procedure require such an instruction. Tex. R. Civ. P. 273 and 277. The appellee alleges that the record establishes that the intrusion was highly offensive as a matter of law, and that, therefore, the instruction was unnecessary....

The definition of "invasion of privacy" that the appellant requested is one widely and repeatedly accepted. Although the Texas Supreme Court has not adopted a verbatim rendition of this definition, it is clear that, in Texas, an actionable invasion of privacy by intrusion must consist of an unjustified intrusion of the plaintiff's solitude or seclusion of such magnitude as to cause an ordinary individual to feel severely offended, humiliated, or outraged.

The appellants correctly point out that no Texas case yet reported has ever declined to include a requirement that the intrusion complained of be highly offensive to a reasonable person, and the appellee agrees with this statement. Nevertheless, the appellee urges that since the facts of this case established the highly objectionable nature of the intrusion as a matter of law, the requested instruction was unnecessary, and thus the trial court properly refused to include it.

We disagree with the appellee's contention. The record does indicate the appellee's outrage upon discovering the appellants' activities but fails to demonstrate that there could be no dispute as to the severity of the offensiveness of the intrusion, thereby making it impossible for us to conclude that the facts established the disputed portion of the instruction as a matter of law.

Moreover, we note that the result of accepting this contention would be to raise the legal theory of invasion of privacy from the realm of intentional torts into the sphere of strict liability. It would make any wrongful intrusion actionable, requiring a plaintiff to establish merely that the intrusion occurred and that the plaintiff did not consent to it. Because of the stern form of liability which already stems from an invasion of privacy, discussed *infra,* accepting a definition of invasion of privacy which lacked a standard of high offensiveness would result in fundamentally unfair assessments against defendants who offended unreasonably sensitive plaintiffs, but whose transgressions would not realistically fill either an ordinary person or the general society with any sense of outrage. A business executive, for example, could find himself liable for entering an associate's office without express permission; so could a beautician who opened a co-worker's drawer in order to find some supplies needed for a customer.

We hold that the element of a highly offensive intrusion is a fundamental part of the definition of an invasion of privacy, and that the term "invasion of privacy" is a highly technical, legal term, requiring, under Rule 277, an explanation to the jury. In the instant case, the definition of an invasion of privacy necessarily required the inclusion of the requested standard of offensiveness.

We sustain the appellant's first four points of error, and, since we are ordering a new trial, we find it appropriate to examine the sufficiency of the evidence supporting the jury's finding.

The lockers indisputably were the appellants' property, and in their unlocked state, a jury could reasonably infer that those lockers were subject to legitimate, reasonable searches by the appellants. This would also be true where the employee used a lock provided by the appellants, because in retaining the lock's combination or master key, it could be inferred that the appellants manifested an interest both in maintaining control over the locker and in conducting legitimate, reasonable searches. Where, as in the instant case, however, the employee purchases and uses his own lock on the lockers, with the employer's knowledge, the fact finder is justified in concluding that the employee manifested, and the employer recognized, an expectation that the locker and its contents would be free from intrusion and interference.

In the present case, there is evidence that the appellee locked the locker with her own lock; that when the appellee returned from a break, the lock was lying open; that upon searching her locker, the appellee discovered that someone had rifled her purse; that the appellants' managerial personnel initially denied making the search but subsequently admitted searching her locker and her purse. We find this is far more evidence than a "mere scintilla," and we hold that there is some evidence to support the jury's finding.

... We hold that the weight of the evidence indicates that the appellants' employees came upon a locker with a lock provided by an employee, disregarded the appellee's demonstration of her expectation of privacy, opened and searched the locker, and probably opened and searched her purse as well; and, in so holding, we consider it is immaterial whether the appellee actually securely locked her locker or not. It is sufficient that an employee in this situation, by having placed a lock on the locker at the employee's own expense and with the appellants' consent, has demonstrated a legitimate expectation to a right of privacy in both the locker itself and those personal effects within it. We accordingly overrule appellants' fifth point of error....

The judgment is reversed, and the case is remanded for new trial.

NOTES

1. *Rationale for Privacy Claims.* The privacy cause of action sounds in tort, but has loud contract or relational overtones. A traditional tort rationale — controlling the third party effects of employer actions — is difficult to find. In *Trotti*, the manager testified that all prospective employees were warned about unannounced searches of lockers. If this testimony were believed, would Trotti have a privacy claim? Would her expectation of privacy be reasonable? If she has no claim, is it because the parties implicitly agreed that their relationship would include unannounced locker searches? Is there any reason to think the employer and employee will not agree on the appropriate level of privacy at the workplace?

2. *Employer Response.* After cases like *Trotti*, are workplace policies likely to be more or less respectful of employee privacy? One employer response might be to reduce the expectation of privacy, perhaps by announcing a clear policy of random, unannounced searches. An alternative response might be to monitor supervisors to ensure they respect employee privacy.

3. *Phone Calls and the Wiretapping Statute.* Employees sometimes complain that a supervisor has invaded their privacy by listening to private phone calls made at work. While common law invasion of privacy lawsuits are rare, employees have sought protection from an unlikely-sounding source: Title III of the Omnibus Crime Control and Safe Streets Act of 1968, 18 U.S.C. §§ 2510-2520. Congress focused on law enforcement's battle against organized crime, but the statute more broadly prohibits most electronic surveillance by private persons, including the interception of telephone calls. Employees can bring civil suits to recover actual damages or liquidated damages of the higher of $100 a day or $1,000, plus punitive damages and attorney's fees. The statute excepts, however, listening on an extension phone "in the ordinary course of ... business."

In *Briggs v. American Air Filter Co.*, 630 F.2d 414 (5th Cir. 1980), a supervisor suspected that a sales employee was disclosing confidential information to a former co-worker who ran a competing business, so he listened on an extension and recorded a telephone conversation between the two. The court found this snooping to be within the business extension exception:

> [W]hen an employee's supervisor has particular suspicions about confidential information being disclosed to a business competitor, has warned the employee not to disclose such information, has reason to believe that the employee is continuing to disclose information, and knows that a particular phone call is with an agent of the competitor, it is within the ordinary course of business to listen in on an extension phone for at least as long as the call involves the type of information he fears is being disclosed.

Id. at 420. The court warned, however, that

> it is hard to see how use of an extension telephone to intercept a call involving non-business matters could be "in the ordinary course of business," since such activity is unlikely to further any legitimate business interest. However, interception of calls reasonably suspected to involve non-business matters might be justifiable by an employer who had had difficulty controlling personal use of business equipment through warnings.

Id. at 420 n.8.

Three years later the Eleventh Circuit reversed a summary judgment for an employer who had monitored an employee's incoming call during lunch, where she spoke with a friend about interviewing for another job. The court recognized that the employer had a business interest in learning that an employee might quit, but declared that "[t]he phrase 'in the ordinary course of business' cannot be expanded to mean anything that interests a company." The court held:

> [A] personal call may not be intercepted in the ordinary course of business under the exemption in section 2510(5)(a)(i), except to the extent necessary to guard against unauthorized use of the telephone or to determine whether a call is personal or not. In other words, a personal call may be intercepted in the ordinary course of business to determine its nature but never its contents.

Watkins v. L.M. Berry & Co., 704 F.2d 577, 583 (11th Cir. 1983).

4. *Private Mail.* Should an employee have a valid claim for invasion of privacy when an employer opens mail addressed to the employee at work marked personal? *See Vernars v. Young*, 539 F.2d 966 (3d Cir. 1976) (yes). If so, could employees bring a successful claim against employers who monitor private telephone calls, even without the wiretapping statute? (*Vernars* suggests yes.)

5. *Electronic Monitoring of Performance.* The Office of Technology Assessment estimates that 4 to 6 million office workers are now evaluated with computer-generated statistics. The value to employers is great:

> Computer monitoring of productivity can help [employers] enhance productivity, maintain production standards, spot bottlenecks, and plan personnel and equipment needs. "Service observation," the capability to listen in on telephone conversations between employees and customers, helps them make sure that customers receive correct information and courteous service. Telephone call accounting can be a powerful management tool for allocating telephone costs, checking the correctness of telephone bills, and reducing personal use of employers' telephones. The Federal Government, through a recent audit of call accounting records, found that about 33 percent of off-network long-distance calls on the Federal Telecommunications System were personal calls.

OFFICE OF TECHNOLOGY ASSESSMENT, THE ELECTRONIC SUPERVISOR: NEW TECHNOLOGY, NEW TENSIONS 5 (1987). Supporters of electronic monitoring also praise its objectivity as a method of evaluating workers. It avoids the potential biases and prejudices of subjective evaluations by supervisors.

On the other hand, the intensity and omnipresence of electronic monitoring is intrusive and places great stress on employees:

> Some workers complain that electronic monitoring is intrusive because it is making a constant minute-by-minute record, creating a feeling of "being watched" all the time. This, they say, is quite different from having a human supervisor occasionally checking their work. Privacy can also refer to exercising one's own autonomy; even in routine work, there is some personal variation in work style. Some people work fast for short periods but take lots of breaks, others work fast in the morning and slow in the afternoon. These individual work styles may not matter when the basic unit evaluation is long — say a day or a week. People with widely differing styles might accomplish the same amount of work in a day. However, continuous monitoring offers management more detailed information. If the employer uses the information gathered through monitoring to change the pace or style of work — regulating the number of breaks or requiring people to accomplish as much in the afternoon as in the morning — then the employee loses a certain amount of control over his or her own job.
>
> ....
>
> Two major objections to electronic monitoring of individual performance are allegations that it contributes to employee stress and stress-related illnesses and that it contributes to an atmosphere of distrust in the workplace. While there has been only limited direct research on the stress effects of electronic monitoring, there does seem to be some evidence that it can contribute to stress.

Id. at 8.

Professor Schroeder, giving a devil's advocate argument, dismisses the complaints about electronic supervision by analogizing them to the controversy over radar detectors:

> Indeed, some might claim that objections to the supervisory omnipresence permitted by monitoring devices smack of the controversy over automobile radar detectors. Drivers are supposed to obey the speed limits at all times, not just when they know a police officer is near. Therefore, good citizens have no legitimate interest in owning or using radar detectors. Similarly, "working time is for work." Good employees have no need to know when they are being monitored. Therefore, they have no reason to object to continuous monitoring.

Elinor P. Schroeder, *On Beyond Drug Testing: Employer Monitoring and the Quest for the Perfect Worker*, 36 KAN. L. REV. 869, 882-83 (1988) (footnotes omitted).

In 1986, Congress passed the Electronic Communications Privacy Act, which bans the interception or disclosure of electronic communications. Like the 1968 wiretapping statute, however, it creates an exception for interception done in "the ordinary course of business." The exception allows employers to monitor computer terminals for work performance. Several bills to regulate electronic monitoring have been introduced in Congress and the state legislatures. In addition to requiring employee access to the recorded information, most of the proposed legislation requires employers to notify employees when and how they will be electronically monitored. In particular, some proposals require a beeping tone or a signal light to appear whenever employees are being monitored. Other suggested standards include collecting information weekly rather than daily and on a group rather than individual basis.

6. Government Intervention in the Rat Race. One major issue in any government regulation of electronic monitoring (as of most employment privacy issues) is whether weighing the costs and benefits of electronic monitoring should be left to private employers and employees. If monitoring increases productivity, the employer can compensate workers for the stress and loss of autonomy with higher wages. Employers who engage in overly invasive monitoring will be at a competitive disadvantage by having to pay abnormally high compensating wages or by having difficulty in hiring workers. The argument, then, is that the private marketplace can reach an appropriate decision on the amount of monitoring.

What arguments can be made why government should intervene in this decision? All the costs and benefits of monitoring seem to be borne by employers and employees themselves, so regulating third-party effects is an implausible justification for government intervention.

One possible model is to recognize that, to an extent, workers are in a rat race with each other. Not only are workers interested in their absolute standard of living, but in their relative standard of living as well, for many benefits accrue to being in the top percentile of society. Thus, individuals may well agree to accept high-pressure, high-paying employment in an attempt to get into the upper middle class. To keep up, other employees must likewise join the rat race. But, unless the Lake Wobegon effect operates, not everyone can be in the upper middle class. Thus, everyone rationally accepts high-stress work even though (like in an arms race) we may all be better off by agreeing to less stressful jobs. For a general discussion of this problem, with many examples, see ROBERT H. FRANK, CHOOSING THE RIGHT POND (1985).

7. Smoking in the Workplace. Courts have been practically uniform in denying common law claims by nonsmokers for smokefree workplaces. A noted exception is *Shimp v. New Jersey Bell Telephone Co.*, 368 A.2d 408 (N.J. Super. Ct. Ch. Div. 1976), brought by a secretary who suffered severe allergic reactions

SMOKING

to cigarette smoke. The *Shimp* court, using a theory that an employer has an affirmative common law duty to provide a work area that is free from unsafe conditions, required the employer to forbid smoking in all work areas of the company except the lunch room. Such judicial creativity is in the distinct minority. The later New Jersey case of *Smith v. Blue Cross & Blue Shield*, No. C-3617-81E (N.J. Super. Ct. Ch. Div. Aug. 18, 1983), cautioned that:

> Insofar as the *Shimp* case is read by some as requiring an employer to institute Draconian measures to smoking employees, I think it has to be viewed somewhat skeptically and cautiously. I myself have no problem with the basic concept of *Shimp*, that a safe workplace is required, but I must say that it seems to me that some of the prohibitions contained in the *Shimp* case are too sweeping and go well beyond what is necessary to ensure a safe working place.

In contrast to the courts, legislatures in at least fourteen states and numerous municipalities have enacted statutes to govern smoking in the workplace. Some states, such as New Jersey and Montana, merely require employers to establish and post policies concerning smoking in the workplace, while leaving the employers free to determine the content of the policies. At the other end of the spectrum is Utah, which allows an individual employee to designate his or her immediate work area as nonsmoking and directs employers to give preference to the rights of nonsmoking employees when disputes arise.

At the federal level, the Occupational Safety and Health Administration has issued no standard for smoking in the workplace, and has not claimed that cigarette smoke violates OSHA's general duty clause. OSHA may take a more active role in the future.

Even more dubious is the existence of any legal "right" to smoke at work. Employees have little recourse if their employer declares the workplace to be smokefree. Hawaii and Virginia require a majority vote of affected employees before a work area can be declared smokefree, but most states have no provision concerning smokers' rights in the workplace. Also, while the Americans With Disabilities Act of 1990 may be used by employees who are discriminated against because of an addiction, the Act explicitly allows employers to declare workplaces smokefree.

B. PROTECTIONS FOR ACTIVITIES WHILE AWAY FROM THE JOB

BRUNNER v. AL ATTAR

Appellant

Court of Appeals of Texas

786 S.W.2d 784 (1990)

Before SAM BASS, DUNN and O'CONNOR, JJ.

SAM BASS, JUSTICE.

Brunner appeals from a summary judgment for Farouk Al Attar, Rima Al Attar, and Apollo Paint & Body. We affirm.

Farouk Al Attar and Rima Al Attar are husband and wife, and partners in a general partnership, known as Apollo Paint & Body.... Brunner alleged that Farouk terminated her, because he feared that she would catch and spread the Acquired Immune Deficiency Syndrome (AIDS) to employees. Appellees urged that Brunner was terminated because of her refusal to work during the hours required, her request to be terminated, and her failure, inability and/or refusal to perform the work expected of her.

Brunner stated that she had neither contracted AIDS, nor been infected with the human immunodeficiency virus which causes AIDS.

Appellees moved for summary judgment, alleging that Brunner did not state a cause of action, and could not amend her pleadings to state a cause of action.

Brunner testified by deposition that she was terminated from Apollo Paint & Body because she was a volunteer with the AIDS Foundation. Brunner had told Farouk that she would be volunteering in her free time on Saturdays and Sundays, and in the evenings. Brunner promised that her volunteer work would not interfere with her position at Apollo, and stated that there was no danger to the employees at Apollo Paint & Body, because Brunner could not catch AIDS from the patients' touching, sneezing, or breathing on her. She further stated that the only way to catch AIDS is through sexual contact or blood transfusions. Brunner told Farouk that his customers did not have to know about her volunteer work. Farouk responded by saying that he could not allow Brunner to perform volunteer work at the AIDS Foundation and work at Apollo. Farouk told Brunner that he did not want to place himself, his family, and the office workers in jeopardy. Farouk urged Brunner to resign, and she refused....

In her first point of error, Brunner asserts that this Court should not permit her to be terminated for performing volunteer work for the AIDS Foundation because her termination violates the public policy exception to the employment-at-will doctrine.

Brunner does not allege that her employment was governed by a contract, or that it was for a definite term. The general rule is that employment for an indefinite term may be terminated at will and without cause. In *Sabine Pilot, Inc. v.*

[margin note: volunteered during off-hours]

[margin note: General Rule for indefinite term employment]

Hauck, 687 S.W.2d 733 (Tex. 1985), the Texas Supreme Court recognized a very narrow exception to the judicially-created employment-at-will doctrine. "That narrow exception covers only the discharge of an employee for the sole reason that the employee refused to perform an illegal act."... In *McClendon v. Ingersoll-Rand Co.*, 779 S.W.2d 69, 71 (Tex. 1989),[*] the supreme court announced another judicially-created exception to the employment-at-will doctrine, which permits recovery of lost future wages, mental anguish, and punitive damages, where the "plaintiff proves that the principal reason for his termination was the employer's desire to avoid contributing to or paying benefits under the employee's pension fund."

(margin note: Two TX Supreme Court exceptions to employment at will)

Brunner alleges that she was fired because she refused to quit her volunteer work with the AIDS Foundation; however, she has not alleged that she was terminated for refusing to perform an illegal act, or because her employer wished to avoid paying benefits under her pension fund. Brunner has failed to allege sufficient facts to place her within these two exceptions to the employment-at-will doctrine. *See Jennings v. Minco Technology Labs, Inc.*, 765 S.W.2d 497, 500-502 (Tex. App. — Austin 1989, *writ denied*) (court refused to create an exception to the doctrine on the grounds of public policy, to enable an employee to obtain declaratory and injunctive relief, restraining employer from administering random urinalysis drug tests on employees); *Berry v. Doctor's Health Facilities*, 715 S.W.2d 60, 61, 62-63 (Tex. App. — Dallas 1986, *no writ*) (court declined to create an exception to the employment-at-will doctrine on the grounds of public policy, to encompass a cause of action asserting wrongful termination, because the employee "knew too much" about alleged improprieties within the hospital administration); *Winters v. Houston Chronicle Publishing Company*, 781 S.W.2d 408 (Tex. App. — Houston [1st Dist.] 1989, *writ pending*) (court declined to extend *Sabine Pilot* exception to employment-at-will doctrine, where private employee alleged he was discharged for reporting to management that his upper level managers and supervisors were engaged in circulation fraud, inventory theft, and a "kickback" scheme). This Court cannot create another exception for performing volunteer work at the Houston AIDS Foundation. If such an exception is to be created, that is a matter within the province of the Texas Supreme Court....

The judgment is affirmed.

---

[*] This case was later reversed by the United States Supreme Court in *Ingersoll-Rand Co. v. McClendon*, 498 U.S. 133 (1990), which held that ERISA preempts a state law wrongful discharge claim that an employer fired an employee to avoid contributing to a pension fund.

NOTES

1. *Volunteering as Public Policy.* As this case shows, an employee who is fired for off-work conduct objectionable to the employer has difficulty fitting within one of the standard categories of wrongful discharge in violation of public policy. Texas at this time had not recognized a claim for wrongful discharge for fulfilling a public duty. Would Brunner have had greater success fitting into this pigeonhole?

2. *Employer Interests.* Given the current medical information concerning the communicability of the AIDS virus, did the employer here have a business interest in Brunner's volunteer work at the AIDS clinic? Or is this simply an example of the hysteria surrounding AIDS? Does the employer have a legitimate concern if fellow employees are (irrationally) fearful of working with Brunner?

More generally, should the law police the firing of productive employees for off-work conduct? Are employers likely to do this often, or will they face marketplace penalties for firing productive employees?

3. *Member of Repugnant Group.* May an employer fire an employee who joins the Ku Klux Klan? Does it matter whether other employees refuse to work with the person because of his views? Is such a situation distinguishable from *Brunner*? *Cf. Baltimore Transit Co.*, 47 Lab. Arb. (BNA) 62 (1966) (Duff, Arb.) (Bus operator publicly identified as grand dragon of KKK justifiably terminated for cause when fellow employees threatened wildcat strike).

4. *Night Law School.* In *Scroghan v. Kraftco Corp.*, 551 S.W.2d 811 (Ky. Ct. App. 1977), an at-will employee was fired when he announced that he planned to attend law school at night. The employee brought a suit for wrongful discharge, but the court upheld a summary judgment dismissing the claim, declaring that the employee's "attendance at night school was a private rather than a public concern." The employee had claimed a violation of the public policy in favor of continued education, as embodied in the National Defense Education Act of 1958, 20 U.S.C. § 401.

Was the court correct in asserting that education is a purely private matter? Although the court in *Scroghan* did not rely on this fact, Congress had stopped funding programs under the National Defense Education Act by the time the suit was brought. Does this weaken Scroghan's argument that the statute enunciated a clear public policy? Or does a focus on this obscure federal statute trivialize the claim that higher education of citizens is an important public policy?

Would the claim have been more powerful if characterized as an invasion of personal privacy rather than a violation of public policy? The case illustrates the tension between privacy rights and an insistence on public concern.

5. *Off-Work Conduct and Arbitration.* Arbitrators interpreting union contracts with just-cause provisions rarely uphold discharges for off-work conduct unless the employer can demonstrate a clear detriment to the workplace.

> Arbitrators have long held that what an employee does on his own time and off Company premises is not a proper basis for disciplinary action unless it can be shown that the employee's conduct has an adverse effect on the Company's business or reputation, the morale and well-being of other employees, or the employee's ability to perform his regular duties.

Indian Head, Inc., 71 Lab. Arb. (BNA) 82, 85 (1978) (Rimer, Arb.) (reinstating employee fired for off-work possession of marijuana).

6. *Legal Off-Work Activity.* A few states, including Colorado, Nevada, and North Dakota, have recently enacted statutes prohibiting employers from firing workers for legal off-work activity. N.D. CENT. CODE § 14-02.4-03 reads:

> It is a discriminatory practice for an employer to fail or refuse to hire a person; to discharge an employee; or to accord adverse or unequal treatment to a person or employee with respect to application, hiring, training, apprenticeship, tenure, promotion, upgrading, compensation, layoff, or a term, privilege, or condition of employment, because of ... participation in lawful activity off the employer's premises during nonworking hours.

7. *Off-Duty Smoking.* The push for a smokefree workplace has led some employers to reject job applicants who smoke, whether on or off the job. Employers have a clear business interest in discriminating against smokers. A study of Boston postal workers showed that smokers had 34% higher absenteeism, 29% higher risk of industrial accidents, 40% more occupational injuries, and 55% more disciplinary incidents. The debilitating effects of smoking remained after controlling for age, gender, race, job category, exercise habits, and drug abuse. *See* James Ryan et al., *Occupational Risks Associated With Cigarette Smoking: A Prospective Study*, 82 AM. J. PUB. HEALTH 29 (1992). One scholar reports that "the estimated costs borne by businesses for the average smoker — including health insurance, fire losses, workers' compensation, absenteeism, productivity losses, and health difficulties for nonsmokers — ... today may be as high as $1000 per worker." Mark A. Rothstein, *Refusing to Employ Smokers: Good Public Health or Bad Public Policy?*, 62 NOTRE DAME L. REV. 940, 944-46 (1987).

On the other hand, refusing to hire workers because they smoke at home raises privacy concerns. A 1992 National Consumers League poll found that 79% of workers said a prospective employer has no right to ask whether they smoke off the job. Monitoring whether an employee smokes at home would itself be problematic.

As with other employee privacy issues, including drug testing and polygraphs, public employees with constitutional claims were the first to challenge no-smoking-off-work policies. An early case challenged a public fire department's regulation prohibiting on- and off-duty smoking for firefighter trainees. The Tenth Circuit Court of Appeals, upholding the regulation against a due process challenge, applied a rational relationship test:

We need look no further for a legitimate purpose and rational connection than the Surgeon General's warning on the side of every box of cigarettes sold in this country that cigarette smoking is hazardous to health. Further, we take notice that good health and physical conditioning are essential requirements for firefighters. We also note that firefighters are frequently exposed to smoke inhalation and that it might reasonably be feared that smoking increases this risk. We conclude that these considerations are enough to establish, prima facie, a rational basis for the regulation.

Grusendorf v. City of Okla. City, 816 F.2d 539, 543 (10th Cir. 1987).

Some state legislatures have protected private-employee smokers. In 1991, New Jersey passed a smokers' rights bill, which prohibits employers from making hiring, firing, compensation, or other personnel decisions based on whether a worker or job applicant smokes away from the job, "unless the employer has a rational basis for doing so which is reasonably related to the employment, including the responsibilities of the employee or prospective employee." The law specifically allows employers to offer better options and rates for non-smokers for life and health insurance benefits. Several other states, including Indiana and New Mexico, have also passed smokers' rights laws that restrict the ability of employers to discriminate against smokers.

LUEDTKE v. NABORS ALASKA DRILLING, INC.

Supreme Court of Alaska
768 P.2d 1123 (1989)

Before MATTHEWS, C.J., and RABINOWITZ, BURKE, COMPTON and MOORE, JJ.

COMPTON, JUSTICE.

This case addresses one aspect of drug testing by employers. A private employer, Nabors Alaska Drilling, Inc. (Nabors), established a drug testing program for its employees. Two Nabors employees, Clarence Luedtke and Paul Luedtke, both of whom worked on drilling rigs on the North Slope, refused to submit to urinalysis screening for drug use as required by Nabors. As a result they were fired by Nabors. [Paul Luedtke had earlier given a urine sample during a company physical exam while on a 28-day leave from work, not realizing that the sample would be used to test for drugs. His urine tested positive for cannabinoids. Two weeks later the employer announced a new policy of testing for drug use, and suspended Paul for failing the earlier test. When Paul refused to take subsequent tests required by the employer, he was fired.] The Luedtkes challenge their discharge on the following grounds:

1. Nabors' drug testing program violates the Luedtkes' right to privacy guaranteed by article I, section 22 of the Alaska Constitution;

[handwritten margin note, top: "Ignore this ←"]

[handwritten margin note, left: "Good Arguments to use for Exam analysis. Tick through each of these (and others) when writing answers not just the causes of action generally, not there use in the privacy context"]

2. Nabors' demands violate the covenant of good faith and fair dealing implicit in all employment contracts;

3. Nabors' urinalysis requirement violates the public interest in personal privacy, giving the Luedtkes a cause of action for wrongful discharge; and

4. Nabors' actions give rise to a cause of action under the common law tort of invasion of privacy....

II. *Discussion*

A. *The Right to Privacy*

[handwritten margin note, right: "Origin of Right to privacy"]

The right to privacy is a recent creation of American law. The inception of this right is generally credited to a law review article published in 1890 by Louis Brandeis and his law partner, Samuel Warren. Brandeis & Warren, *The Right to Privacy*, 4 Harv. L. Rev. 193 (1890). Brandeis and Warren observed that in a modern world with increasing population density and advancing technology, the number and types of matters theretofore easily concealed from public purview were rapidly decreasing. They wrote:

> Recent inventions and business methods call attention to the next step which must be taken for the protection of the person, and for securing to the individual what Judge Cooley calls the right "to be let alone." Instantaneous photographs and newspaper enterprise have invaded the sacred precincts of private and domestic life; and numerous mechanical devices threaten to make good the prediction that "what is whispered in the closet shall be proclaimed from the housetops."

Id. at 195 (footnotes omitted). Discussing the few precedential cases in tort law in which courts had afforded remedies for the publication of private letters or unauthorized photographs, Brandeis and Warren drew a common thread they called "privacy." They defined this right as the principle of "inviolate personality."

While the legal grounds of this right were somewhat tenuous in the 1890's, American jurists found the logic of Brandeis and Warren's arguments compelling. The reporters of the first Restatement of Torts included a tort entitled "Interference with Privacy." By 1960, Professor Prosser could write that "the right of privacy, in one form or another, is declared to exist by the overwhelming majority of the American courts." Prosser, *Privacy*, 48 Calif. L. Rev. 383, 386 (1960).... In addition, while Brandeis and Warren were mainly concerned with the publication of private facts, Professor Prosser identified four different manifestations of the right to privacy: intrusion upon the plaintiff's seclusion; public disclosure of embarrassing private facts; publicity which places the plaintiff in a false light; and appropriation, for the defendant's pecuniary advantage, of the plaintiff's name or likeness. Professor Prosser's categories form the framework of the expanded tort of invasion of privacy found in the Restatement (Second) of Torts.

Eventually the right to privacy attained sufficient recognition to be incorporated in several state constitutions. *See* Alaska Const. art. I, § 22 (adopted 1972); Cal. Const. art. I, § 1 (adopted 1972); Haw. Const. art. 1, § 6 (adopted 1978); Mont. Const. art. II, § 10 (adopted 1972).

Interpreting the Constitution of the United States, the United States Supreme Court in 1965 held that a Connecticut statute banning the use of birth control devices by married couples was "repulsive to the notions of privacy surrounding the marriage relationship." *Griswold v. Connecticut,* 381 U.S. 479, 486 (1965). The Supreme Court wrote that "specific guarantees in the Bill of Rights have penumbras, formed by emanations from those guarantees that help give them life and substance. Various guarantees create zones of privacy." Justice Goldberg's concurrence suggested that the right of marital privacy was fundamental to the concept of liberty. Since *Griswold* the Supreme Court has found the federal constitutional right of privacy to apply to a number of other situations. *See Cleveland Bd. of Educ. v. La Fleur*, 414 U.S. 632, 640 (1974) (maternity leave regulations struck down for "penaliz[ing] the pregnant teacher for deciding to bear a child."); *Roe v. Wade*, 410 U.S. 113 (1973) (right of privacy broad enough to encompass a woman's decision whether or not to terminate her pregnancy); *Eisenstadt v. Baird*, 405 U.S. 438 (1972) (regulation which made contraceptives less available to unmarried than married couples invalidated). *But see Bowers v. Hardwick*, 478 U.S. 186 (1986) (due process clause of Fourteenth Amendment does not confer any fundamental right on homosexuals to engage in acts of consensual sodomy).

Thus, the concept of privacy has become pervasive in modern legal thought. But a clear definition of this right, so fundamental to ordered liberty, has eluded both courts and legal scholars. It is the fundamental nature of the concept that leads to such great difficulty in application....

In this case the plaintiffs seek to fit their cases within at least one of four legal frameworks in which the right to privacy has found expression: constitutional law, contract law, tort law, and the emerging mixture of theories known as the public policy exception to the at-will doctrine of employment law.

B. *The Right to Privacy Under the Alaska Constitution*

[The Court held that the right to privacy of the Alaska constitution did not apply to the actions of private parties.]

C. *Wrongful Termination*

[The Court first determined that the Luedtkes were at-will employees.]

The next question we address is whether a public policy exists protecting an employee's right to withhold certain "private" information from his employer. We believe such a policy does exist, and is evidenced in the common law, statutes and constitution of this state.....

Alaska Law

Alaska law clearly evidences strong support for the public interest in employee privacy. First, state statutes support the policy that there are private sectors of employee's lives not subject to direct scrutiny by their employers. For example, employers may not require employees to take polygraph tests as a condition of employment. In addition, AS 18.80.200(a) provides:

> It is determined and declared as a matter of legislative finding that discrimination against an inhabitant of the state because of race, religion, color, national origin, age, sex, marital status, changes in marital status, pregnancy, or parenthood is a matter of public concern and that this discrimination not only threatens the rights and privileges of the inhabitants of the state but also menaces the institutions of the state and threatens peace, order, health, safety and general welfare of the state and its inhabitants.

This policy is implemented by AS 18.80.220, which makes it unlawful for employers to inquire into such topics in connection with prospective employment. This statute demonstrates that in Alaska certain subjects are placed outside the consideration of employers in their relations with employees. The protections of AS 18.80.220 are extensive. This statute has been construed to be broader than federal anti-discrimination law. We believe it evidences the legislature's intent to liberally protect employee rights.

Alaska's Constitution

Second, as previously noted, Alaska's constitution contains a right to privacy clause. While we have held, *supra*, that this clause does not proscribe the private action at issue, it can be viewed by this court as evidence of a public policy supporting privacy. *See Novosel v. Nationwide Ins. Co.*, 721 F.2d at 900 (finding evidence of public policy in free speech clauses of Pennsylvania and United States Constitutions).... Certainly the fact that the citizenry has incorporated the right to privacy into the Alaska Constitution strongly supports the contention that this right "strike[s] at the heart of a citizen's social rights."

Common Law Right to Privacy

Third, there exists a common law right to privacy. The Restatement (Second) of Torts § 652B provides:

> *Intrusion upon Seclusion.* One who intentionally intrudes, physically or otherwise, upon the solitude or seclusion of another or his private affairs or concerns, is subject to liability to the other for invasion of his privacy, if the intrusion would be highly offensive to a reasonable person.

While we have not expressly considered the application of this tort in Alaska, we have recognized its existence. Thus, the citizens' right to be protected against unwarranted intrusions into their private lives has been recognized in the law of Alaska. The constitution protects against governmental intrusion, statutes protect against employer intrusion, and the common law protects against intrusions by other private persons. As a result, there is sufficient evidence to support the conclusion that there exists a public policy protecting spheres of employee conduct into which employers may not intrude. The question then becomes whether

Summary of the above points

Resulting Question

employer monitoring of employee drug use outside the work place is such a prohibited intrusion....

This court discussed, on the one hand, the reasons society protects privacy,
and, on the other hand, the reasons society rightfully intrudes on personal privacy in *Ravin v. State,* 537 P.2d 494 (Alaska 1975). *Ravin* addressed the issue of
whether the state could prohibit the use of marijuana in the home. We held that it
could not. We observed that "the right to privacy amendment to the Alaska Constitution cannot be read so as to make the possession or ingestion of marijuana
itself a fundamental right." Rather, we "recognized the distinctive nature of the
home as a place where the individual's privacy receives special protection."
However, we recognized also that this "fundamental right" was limited to activity which remained in the home. We acknowledged that when an individual
leaves his home and interacts with others, competing rights of others collectively
and as individuals may take precedence:

> Privacy in the home is a fundamental right, under both the federal and
> Alaska constitutions. We do not mean by this that a person may do anything
> at anytime as long as the activity takes place within a person's home. There
> are two important limitations on this facet of the right to privacy. First, we
> agree with the Supreme Court of the United States, which has strictly
> limited the *Stanley*[*] guarantee to possession for purely private,
> noncommercial use in the home. And secondly, we think this right must
> yield when it interferes in a serious manner with the health, safety, rights
> and privileges of others or with the public welfare. No one has an absolute
> right to do things in the privacy of his own home which will affect himself
> or others adversely. Indeed, one aspect of a private matter is that it is
> private, that is, that it does not adversely affect persons beyond the actor,
> and hence is none of their business. When a matter does affect the public,
> directly or indirectly, it loses its wholly private character, and can be made
> to yield when an appropriate public need is demonstrated.

The *Ravin* analysis is analogous to the analysis that should be followed in
cases construing the public policy exception to the at-will employment doctrine.
That is, there is a sphere of activity in every person's life that is closed to scrutiny by others. The boundaries of that sphere are determined by balancing a person's right to privacy against other public policies, such as "the health, safety,
rights and privileges of others." *Ravin,* 537 P.2d at 504.

The Luedtkes claim that whether or not they use marijuana is information
within that protected sphere into which their employer, Nabors, may not intrude.

---

[*] The court is referring here to *Stanley v. Georgia,* 394 U.S. 557 (1969), which held that "mere
private possession of obscene matter cannot constitutionally be made a crime." *Id.* at 559.

Employers can inquire as to employee drug use due to their (abuse) effects and the dangerous nature of work on an oil rig

We disagree. As we have previously observed, marijuana can impair a person's ability to function normally:

> The short-term physiological effects are relatively undisputed. An immediate slight increase in the pulse, decrease in salivation, and a slight reddening of the eyes are usually noted. There is also impairment of psychomotor control.

Ravin, 537 P.2d at 506.

We also observe that work on an oil rig can be very dangerous. We have determined numerous cases involving serious injury or death resulting from accidents on oil drilling rigs. In addition, in Paul's case the trial court expressly considered the dangers of work on oil rigs. It found:

> 13. It is extremely important that the driller be drug free in the performance of his tasks in order to insure the immediate safety of the other personnel on the particular drill rig.
> 14. It is extremely important that the driller be drug free in the performance of his tasks in order to insure the safety and protection of the oil field itself and the oil resource contained within it.

Where the public policy supporting the Luedtkes['] privacy in off-duty activities conflicts with the public policy supporting the protection of the health and safety of other workers, and even the Luedtkes themselves, the health and safety concerns are paramount. As a result, Nabors is justified in determining whether the Luedtkes are possibly impaired on the job by drug usage off the job.

We observe, however, that the employer's prerogative does have limitations.

Limitations

First, the drug test must be conducted at a time reasonably contemporaneous with the employee's work time. The employer's interest is in monitoring drug use that may directly affect employee performance. The employer's interest is not in the broader police function of discovering and controlling the use of illicit drugs in general society. In the context of this case, Nabors could have tested the Luedtkes immediately prior to their departure for the North Slope, or immediately upon their return from the North Slope when the test could be reasonably certain of detecting drugs consumed there. Further, given Nabors' need to control the oil rig community, Nabors could have tested the Luedtkes at any time they were on the North Slope.

Second, an employee must receive notice of the adoption of a drug testing program. By requiring a test, an employer introduces an additional term of employment.[13] An employee should have notice of the additional term so that he may contest it, refuse to accept it and quit, seek to negotiate its conditions, or prepare for the test so that he will not fail it and thereby suffer sanctions.

---

[13] Note that where the employment agreement is at-will, continuing to work after a modification of that agreement is sufficient consideration to support the modification. Thus there is no support for the argument that the Luedtkes' employment contracts could not be modified to provide for drug testing. The question before the court is whether those modifications are reasonable.

These considerations do not apply with regard to the tests both Paul and Clarence refused to take. Paul was given notice of the future tests. He did not take the November 30 test. As a result, Nabors was justified in discharging Paul. Clarence had notice and the opportunity to schedule his test at a reasonable time. However, he refused to take any test. As a result, Nabors was justified in discharging Clarence. Neither discharge violated the implied covenant of good faith and fair dealing.

The question whether Paul's *suspension* breached the covenant of good faith and fair dealing is for the trier of fact. On remand, the trial court should determine whether the covenant has been breached, taking additional evidence if necessary.

D. Common Law Right to Privacy Claims

We recognize that "[t]he [common law] right to be free from harassment and constant intrusion into one's daily affairs is enjoyed by all persons." As previously discussed, that law is delineated in the Restatement (Second) of Torts § 652B, entitled Intrusion upon Seclusion. That section provides: "One who intentionally intrudes ... upon the solitude or seclusion of another or his private affairs or concerns, is subject to liability ... if the intrusion would be highly offensive to a reasonable person."

It is true, as the Luedtkes contend, that publication of the facts obtained is not necessary. Instead, the liability is for the offensive intrusion. However, courts have construed "offensive intrusion" to require either an unreasonable manner of intrusion, or intrusion for an unwarranted purpose. Paul has failed to show either that the manner or reason for testing his urine was unreasonable. During his physical, he voluntarily gave a urine sample for the purpose of testing. Therefore, he cannot complain that urine testing is "highly offensive." Paul can only complain about the purpose of the urine test, that is, to detect drug usage. However, we have held, *supra*, that Nabors was entitled to test its employees for drug usage. As a result, the intrusion was not unwarranted. Paul complains additionally that he was not aware his urine would be tested for drug usage. In this regard we observe that Paul was not aware of any of the tests being performed on his urine sample. Nor did he know the ramifications of those tests. But he did know that whatever the results were they would be reported to Nabors. Therefore, his complaint about a particular test is without merit. We conclude that for these reasons Paul could not maintain an action for invasion of privacy with regard to the urinalysis conducted October 19.

As to the urinalyses Paul and Clarence refused to take, we hold that no cause of action for invasion of privacy arises where the intrusion is prevented from taking place....

MATTHEWS, CHIEF JUSTICE, concurring.

I agree with the majority's conclusion that Nabors was justified in discharging both appellants. Further I agree that on remand the trial court should determine whether Nabors breached the covenant of good faith and fair dealing by suspending Paul Luedtke because he tested positive for using marijuana during a twenty-eight day leave period, without first notifying him that it was against company policy for employees to use marijuana at any time.

The critical element in Paul Luedtke's suspension claim is the alleged failure of Nabors to notify its employees that they were expected to refrain from using marijuana during their weeks on leave. It seems to me that a jury might find, if there was such a failure, that it amounted to conduct which was so unfair as to be a violation of the covenant of good faith and fair dealing. I do not, however, share the view that an employer may not impose as a condition of employment a requirement that its employees refrain from all use of marijuana at all times.

In the private sector, the establishment of employment criteria has traditionally been left to employers, except as to such relatively narrow but important categories as race, religion, gender, and age. So, if an employer wants to impose a condition of continued employment that none of its employees use marijuana at any time, I can see no legal impediment, apart from the possibility that advance notice of the condition may be required.

It may be that the covenant of good faith and fair dealing also requires that any employment criterion have some relationship to a legitimate employer concern. If a relationship is required, it would be easily met in the case of an employer whose policy it is to hire no one who used marijuana or other consciousness altering substances. Safety is a prime concern, as today's majority opinion makes clear. Those who use marijuana off duty are more likely to use or be influenced by marijuana on duty than those who do not use it at all. Moreover, considerations of lost productivity, absenteeism, and medical insurance rates may justify a total abstinence employment criterion. Drug use, including alcohol, has been estimated to cost employers between $60 billion and $100 billion per year. Thus I believe that a private employer could, with proper notice, impose as a condition of employment a requirement that its employees not use marijuana at any time.

NOTES

1. *The Good-Faith Claim on Remand.* Upon remand, Paul Luedtke continued to argue that his November 5th suspension, if not his later discharge on November 30, violated the employer's duty of good faith. The trial court dismissed the claim and imposed Rule 11 sanctions of some $8,500 against Luedtke and his attorney for pursuing a frivolous claim. The Alaska Supreme Court reversed, emphasizing that Luedtke had no prior notice about the drug test, that no other employee was similarly tested, and that the employer immediately suspended Luedtke without offering a retest. The Court held that, as a matter of law, the employer violated the covenant of good faith and fair dealing. Because the company later fired Luedtke lawfully, the Court refused to order reinstatement as a remedy, but declared that Luedtke would be entitled to wages lost between November 5 and November 30, as well as any incidental damages he could prove. *Luedtke v. Nabors Alaska Drilling, Inc.*, 834 P.2d 1220 (Alaska 1992) (*Luedtke II*).

2. *Constitutional Privacy Rights Against Private Action.* Unlike in Alaska, California courts have extended their state constitutional right of privacy to private action. This constitutional right has been used to strike down the drug testing policies of some private employers. *See Semore v. Pool,* 266 Cal. Rptr. 280 (Cal. Ct. App. 1990) (employee fired for refusing to submit to random pupillary eye drug test has an action for wrongful discharge in violation of public policy under state constitutional right to privacy).

Even without an explicit state constitutional basis, the Third Circuit, applying Pennsylvania law, has ruled that a mandatory drug testing program of private employees may violate public policy. *Borse v. Piece Goods Shop, Inc.*, 963 F.2d 611 (3d Cir. 1992). Borse was discharged for refusing to sign a consent form allowing urinalysis. While rejecting the employee's constitutional arguments, the court reversed a summary judgment for the employer on a wrongful discharge suit, stating that "based on our prediction of Pennsylvania law, we hold that dismissing an employee who refused to consent to urinalysis testing ... would violate public policy if the testing tortiously invaded the employee's privacy."

An opposite result was reached by the Sixth Circuit in *Baggs v. Eagle-Picher Industries, Inc.*, 957 F.2d 268 (6th Cir. 1992), which held that private employees could be discharged for refusing to take, or for failing, unannounced drug tests. In rejecting the employees' claim that the drug tests violated Michigan's common law right to privacy, the court found that "a Michigan employer may use intrusive and even objectionable means to obtain employment-related information about an employee."

3. *Privacy as a Public Policy?* Can a privacy claim ever rise to the level of public policy, or by definition are private interests not public? Consider *Luck v. Southern Pacific Transp. Co.*, 267 Cal. Rptr. 618 (Cal. Ct. App.), *cert. denied,* 498 U.S. 939 (1990), where the court upheld a jury verdict that a railroad breached its implied covenant of good faith and fair dealing by firing a computer operator who refused to submit to urinalysis. The employee was pregnant and feared a test that revealed this would harm her career. The court determined that the employer must show a "compelling interest" to justify the intrusion on privacy, a heavier burden than that imposed by a Fourth Amendment privacy analysis, where the privacy intrusion is simply balanced against legitimate governmental interests. Nevertheless, the court refused to find a violation of public policy that would support tort damages:

> A termination that is against public policy must affect a duty which inures to the benefit of the public at large rather than to a particular employer or employee. Past cases recognizing a tort action for termination in violation of

public policy seek to protect the public by protecting an employee who refused to commit a crime, reported criminal activity, or disclosed other illegal, unethical, or unsafe practices. However, even the reporting of improper conduct may not constitute a public policy interest; if, for example, an employee's duty to disclose information to his employer serves only the employer's private interest, the public policy rationale does not apply.... [T]he absence of a distinctly public interest is apparent when we consider that if an employer and employee expressly agreed that the employee had no obligation to, and should not, inform the employer of any adverse information the employee learned about a coworker's background, no public policy would render the agreement void. If the employer and employee could have lawfully made such an agreement, *Foley* [*v. Interactive Data Corp.*] reasoned, it cannot be said that the employer, by discharging an employee on this basis, violated a fundamental duty imposed on all employers for the protection of the public interest.

Measured against the *Foley* standard, Luck did not state a cause of action for wrongful termination in violation of public policy. The right to privacy is, by its very name, a private right, not a public one. The parties could have lawfully agreed that Luck would submit to urinalysis without violating any public interest. Such an agreement between Luck and Southern Pacific would not have been against public policy. Therefore, under *Foley*, there was no violation of public policy.

Judge Poche, dissenting, complained that the majority missed the inherent public policy contained in a constitutional right:

Unless we accept the perfectly logical and defensible position that inalienable personal rights inure by their very nature to the benefit of all Californians and thus to the public benefit, we accord no practical protection to the very rights given the greatest deference by our Constitution. The bizarre outcome of the majority's reasoning is evident here. Barbara Luck has, they acknowledge, an inalienable right to be free from an involuntary intrusion into her privacy by her employer's demand she submit to urinalysis. Had her employer not fired her for refusing the test, she presumably could have obtained injunctive relief from the testing. However, because her employer immediately fired her for insubordination before she could seek such judicial vindication of her rights she is deprived of her job and of any tortious claim for the employer's conduct.

Justice Brotherton put the issue more succinctly when he dissented in *Twigg v. Hercules Corp.*, 406 S.E.2d 52 (W. Va. 1990), from the majority's holding that it is contrary to public policy in West Virginia for an employer to require an employee to submit to drug testing, absent reasonable suspicion of drug usage or where the job involves public safety or the safety of others. He said:

> I dissent to the majority's opinion for one reason: How can an attempt to create a drug-free environment be against the public policy of this State?

For a thoughtful discussion of the tension between privacy claims and the at-will doctrine, see Pauline T. Kim, *Privacy Rights, Public Policy, and the Employment Relationship*, 57 OHIO ST. L.J. 671 (1996).

4. *The Fourth Amendment Analogy.* Courts have drawn sharp distinctions between public employees, protected to some degree by the Fourth Amendment from their governmental employers, and private employees. In one outlying case, *Hennessey v. Coastal Eagle Point Oil Co.,* 6 Indiv. Empl. Rts. Cas. (BNA) 113 (N.J. Super. Ct. 1989), the New Jersey Superior Court upheld a wrongful discharge claim by an employee fired after failing a random drug test. The court relied on cases upholding constitutional claims of public employees against drug testing, insisting that they "pronounced a standard of general public policy regarding drug screening throughout the workplace, which applies to public as well as private employment." The Appellate Division promptly reversed, declaring:

> We are reluctant to utilize constitutional values of privacy as a source of public policy [in a wrongful discharge case] in a private employment context. Application of constitutional values such as individual privacy to private relationships carries the danger that those values will "expand like a gas to fill up the available space."

Hennessey v. Coastal Eagle Point Oil Co., 589 A.2d 170, 176 (N.J. Super. Ct. App. Div. 1991). The New Jersey Supreme Court affirmed the Appellate Division, emphasizing the employee's safety responsibilities, but hinted in dicta that the Constitution could serve as a source of public policy even in the private sector. *Hennessey v. Coastal Eagle Point Oil Co.,* 609 A.2d 11 (N.J. 1992).

5. *Statutory Regulation of Private-Sector Drug Testing.* Many states have legislation regulating drug testing. These include prohibitions against random testing; regulations of applicant screening; requirements of reasonable suspicion, confirmatory tests, and confidentiality of results; and provisions for employee rebuttal. Some statutes seem primarily concerned with employee privacy (*e.g.,* ME. REV. STAT. ANN. tit. 26, § 681 (restricting the permissible circumstances and procedures for testing employees for drugs)), while others attempt to insulate employers from liability if they follow limited restrictions on drug testing (*e.g.,* UTAH CODE ANN. §§ 34-38-1 to -15).

6. *The Employer Interest.* Employers have justified drug testing programs on many grounds, including:

> (1) drug use is illegal and therefore employers have a responsibility to discover employees who may be breaking the law; (2) employees abusing drugs often need substantial sums of money to buy drugs and these employ-

ees are likely to steal from their employee or to accept bribes on the job; (3) employees using drugs are likely to have a reduction in their productivity; (4) maintaining a drug-free workplace is essential to an employer's public image; and (5) drug testing is essential to protect safety and health.

Mark A. Rothstein, *Drug Testing in the Workplace: The Challenge to Employment Relations and Employment Law*, 63 CHI-KENT L. REV. 683, 736 (1987).

Are these concerns valid? Consider the following:

> If the underlying purpose of drug testing is safety, there is no reason why drug testing should be limited to illicit drugs. In terms of the number of people who abuse them and the fatalities, injuries, and property damage caused by their effects in the workplace, alcohol and prescription drugs (often in combination) pose a much greater threat than illicit drugs.

Id. at 740.

Is safety or productivity the true employer motivation in drug testing, or do employers want to be seen as being on the right side in the war on drugs? Several studies have concluded that drug screening is not cost effective for most private employers. *See* Drug Testing: Cost and Effect, Cornell/Smithers Report on Workplace Substance Abuse Policy (1992).

7. Invasive Procedures or Results? Are employees who challenge drug testing more concerned about the invasive or embarrassing procedures used in collecting samples, or that testing is overinclusive in the information it reveals to employers?

Kelley v. Schlumberger, 849 F.2d 41 (1st Cir. 1988) (applying Louisiana law), is one of the few cases upholding a claim that the collection of a urine specimen is overly invasive. There, the Court of Appeals upheld a jury verdict of $1 for violating the employee's right to privacy and $125,000 for negligently inflicted emotional distress. As the court described the claim: "Direct observation of employees urinating was at the core of the plaintiff's complaint. During the trial he described himself as being 'disgusted by the whole idea of someone being paid to look at [his] penis while [he] urinated.'" *But see Fowler v. New York City Dep't of Sanitation*, 704 F. Supp. 1264 (S.D.N.Y. 1989) (upholding urinalysis testing of public employees which required male employees to provide urine samples under the direct observation of female supervisors).

More common is for employees to emphasize the overinclusive results of drug testing. Drug tests not only supply information about illegal drug use but potentially provide employers with data on an employee's ingestion of other legal drugs or present medical conditions. Questionnaires requiring employees to list all drugs they have ingested that might affect the test results, as well as the test itself, can reveal to the employer whether the employee is pregnant, epileptic, diabetic, or taking birth control pills, among other medical facts. In *Capua v. City of Plainfield*, 643 F. Supp. 1507 (D.N.J. 1986), the District Court emphasized these concerns:

[C]ompulsory urinalysis forces plaintiffs to divulge private, personal medical information unrelated to the government's professed interest in discovering illegal drug abuse. Advances in medical technology make it possible to uncover disorders, including epilepsy and diabetes, by analyzing chemical compounds in urine. Plaintiffs have a significant interest in safeguarding the confidentiality of such information whereas the government has no countervailing legitimate need for access to this personal medical data. The dangers of disclosure as a result of telltale urinalysis range from embarrassment to improper use of such information in job assignments, security, and promotion.

Some judges are more skeptical about the privacy claims. For example, Judge Higginbotham wrote in the lower court opinion in *National Treasury Employees Union v. von Raab*, 808 F.2d 1057, 1061 (5th Cir. 1987) (denying stay pending appeal):

The precise privacy interest asserted is elusive, and the plaintiffs are, at best, inexact as to just what that privacy interest is. Finding an objectively reasonable expectation of privacy in urine, a waste product, contains inherent contradictions. The district court found such a right of privacy, but, in fairness, plaintiffs do not rest there. Rather, it appears from the plaintiffs' brief that it is the manner of taking the samples that is said to invade privacy, because outer garments in which a false sample might be hidden must be removed and a person of the same sex remains outside a stall while the applicant urinates. Yet, apart from the partial disrobing (apparently not independently challenged) persons using public toilet facilities experience a similar lack of privacy. The right must then be a perceived indignity in the whole process, a perceived affront to personal identity by the presence in the same room of another while engaging in a private body function.

It is suggested that the testing program rests on a generalized lack of trust and not on a developed suspicion of an individual applicant. Necessarily there is a plain implication that an applicant is part of a group that, given the demands of the job, cannot be trusted to be truthful about drug use. The difficulty is that just such distrust, or equally accurate, care, is behind every background check and every security check; indeed the information gained in tests of urine is not different from that disclosed in medical records, for which consent to examine is a routine part of applications for many sensitive government posts. In short, given the practice of testing and background checks required for so many government jobs, whether any expectations of privacy by these job applicants were objectively reasonable is dubious at best. Certainly, to ride with the cops one ought to expect inquiry, and by the surest means, into whether he is a robber.

8. *The Dilemma of Consent.* Some courts refuse to decide the legality of drug testing programs if the employee refuses to take the test. The employee must make a choice: take the drug test and litigate its invasiveness later or refuse to take the test, retain privacy, but lose the job. In addition to *Luedtke, see Everett v. Napper*, 632 F. Supp. 1481 (N.D. Ga. 1986) (no search under the Fourth Amendment when discharged employees refused to take urinalysis drug test). *But see American Fed'n of Gov't Employees v. Weinberger*, 651 F. Supp. 726 (S.D. Ga. 1986) (advance consent ineffective when the drug testing program is unreasonable search under the Fourth Amendment); *Luck v. Southern Pacific Transportation Co.*, 267 Cal. Rptr. 618 (Cal. Ct. App.), *cert. denied*, 498 U.S. 939 (1990), (right to refuse to submit to urinalysis a privacy interest protected by state constitution).

The issue was posed directly in *Jennings v. Minco Technology Labs*, 765 S.W.2d 497 (Tex. Ct. App. 1989), when an employee sought to enjoin a drug testing plan under which the employer would ask employees on a random basis to give urine samples to be tested, with their consent, for evidence of illegal-drug consumption. Employees would be fired for refusing to give a urine sample. While recognizing the common law right to privacy, the court refused to find that the drug testing program fit within the public policy exception to employment at will. The court continued:

> We cannot accept Jennings's theory for an additional reason. Jennings's employer threatens no *unlawful* invasion of any employee's privacy interest; therefore it threatens no act contrary to the public policy underlying the common-law right of privacy. The company's plan contemplates, rather, that an employee's urine will be taken and tested only if he consents. The plan therefore assumes, respects, and depends upon the central element of the right of privacy and its attendant public policy: the individual's exclusive right to determine the occasion, extent, and conditions under which he will disclose his private affairs to others. This consensual predicate to any test reduces Jennings's argument to her remaining contention.

> Jennings contends finally that she is poor and needs her salary to maintain herself and her family. Consequently, any "consent" she may give, in submitting to urinalysis, will be illusory and not real. For that practical reason, she argues, the company's plan does threaten a non-consensual, and therefore unlawful, invasion of her privacy. We disagree with the theory. A competent person's legal rights and obligations, under the common law governing the making, interpretation, and enforcement of contracts, cannot vary according to his economic circumstances. There cannot be one law of contracts for the rich and another for the poor. We cannot imagine a theory more at war with the basic assumptions held by society and its law. Nothing would introduce greater disorder into both. Because Jennings may not be denied the legal rights others have under the common law of contracts, she may not be given greater rights than they. The law views her economic

circumstances as neutral and irrelevant facts insofar as her contracts are concerned.

RULON-MILLER v. INTERNATIONAL BUSINESS MACHINE CORP.

IBM

California Court of Appeal
208 Cal. Rptr. 524 (1984)

RUSHING, ASSOCIATE JUSTICE.

International Business Machines (IBM) appeals from the judgment entered against it after a jury awarded $100,000 compensatory and $200,000 punitive damages to respondent (Virginia Rulon-Miller) on claims of wrongful discharge and intentional infliction of emotional distress. Rulon-Miller was a low-level marketing manager at IBM in its office products division in San Francisco. Her termination as a marketing manager at IBM came about as a result of an accusation made by her immediate supervisor, defendant Callahan, of a romantic relationship with the manager of a rival office products firm, QYX....

IBM is an employer traditionally thought to provide great security to its employees as well as an environment of openness and dignity. The company is organized into divisions, and each division is, to an extent, independent of others. The company prides itself on providing career opportunities to its employees, and respondent represents a good example of this. She started in 1967 as a receptionist in the Philadelphia Data Center. She was told that "career opportunities are available to [employees] as long as they are performing satisfactorily and are willing to accept new challenges." While she worked at the data center in Philadelphia, she attended night school and earned a baccalaureate degree. She was promoted to equipment scheduler and not long after received her first merit award. The company moved her to Atlanta, Georgia where she spent 15 months as a data processor. She was transferred to the office products division and was assigned the position of "marketing support representative" in San Francisco where she trained users (i.e., customers) of newly-purchased IBM equipment. Respondent was promoted to "product planner" in 1973 where her duties included overseeing the performance of new office products in the marketplace. As a product planner, she moved to Austin, Texas and later to Lexington, Kentucky. Thereafter, at the urging of her managers that she go into sales in the office products division, she enrolled at the IBM sales school in Dallas. After graduation, she was assigned to San Francisco.

[Rulon-Miller continued to receive superb evaluations. In 1978 she was named a marketing manager in the office products branch, which sold typewriters and other office equipment.]

IBM knew about respondent's relationship with Matt Blum well before her appointment as a manager. Respondent met Blum in 1976 when he was an account manager for IBM. That they were dating was widely known within the organization. In 1977 Blum left IBM to join QYX, an IBM competitor, and was transferred to Philadelphia. When Blum returned to San Francisco in the summer of 1978, IBM personnel were aware that he and respondent began dating again. This seemed to present no problems to respondent's superiors, as Callahan confirmed when she was promoted to manager. Respondent testified: "Somewhat in passing, Phil said: I heard the other day you were dating Matt Blum, and I said: Oh. And he said, I don't have any problem with that. You're my number one pick. I just want to assure you that you are my selection." The relationship with Blum was also known to Regional Manager Gary Nelson who agreed with Callahan. Neither Callahan nor Nelson raised any issue of conflict of interest because of the Blum relationship.

Respondent flourished in her management position, and the company, apparently grateful for her efforts, gave her a $4,000 merit raise in 1979 and told her that she was doing a good job. A week later, her manager, Phillip Callahan, left a message that he wanted to see her.

When she walked into Callahan's office he confronted her with the question of whether she was *dating* Matt Blum. She wondered at the relevance of the inquiry and he said the dating constituted a "conflict of interest," and told her to stop dating Blum or lose her job and said she had a "couple of days to a week" to think about it.

The next day Callahan called her in again, told her "he had made up her mind for her," and when she protested, dismissed her.[3] IBM and Callahan claim that he merely "transferred" respondent to another division.

---

[3] Respondent stated the next day she was again summoned to his office where Callahan sat ominously behind a desk cleared of any paperwork, an unusual scenario for any IBM manager.

She further testified: "I walked into Phil's office, and he asked me to shut the door, and he said he was removing me from management effectively immediately. And I said: What?

"And he repeated it. And I was taken aback, I was a little startled, and I think I said: Well, gee, I thought I had a couple of days to a week to think over the situation that we discussed yesterday.

"And he said: I'm making the decision for you.

"And I said: Phil, you've told me that I'm doing a good job. You told me that we are not losing anybody to QYX because I am dating Matt Blum, that we are not losing any equipment to QYX. I just don't understand what bearing dating has to do with my job.

"And he said: We have a conflict of interest....

"I said: Well, what kind of a job would it be?

"And he said: Well, I don't have it, but it will be non-management. You won't be a manager again.

"Pardon me? ...

"And I think I was getting very upset so I think I said something because of that respect for the individual tenet of IBM's that I really believed in I didn't think that he was following what I thought IBM, really did believe in. And he just said: You know, you are removed from management effective immediately.

"And I said: I think you are dismissing me.

"And he said: If you feel that way, give me your I.D. card and your key to the office. I want you to leave the premises immediately.

"And I was just about to burst into tears, and I didn't cry at work, so I basically fled his office.

"I felt he dismissed me."

Respondent's claims of wrongful discharge and intentional infliction of emotional distress were both submitted to the jury....

The initial discussion between Callahan and respondent of her relationship with Blum is important. We must accept the version of the facts most favorable to the respondent herein. When Callahan questioned her relationship with Blum, respondent invoked her right to privacy in her personal life relying on existing IBM policies. A threshold inquiry is thus presented whether respondent could reasonably rely on those policies for job protection. Any conflicting action by the company would be wrongful in that it would constitute a violation of her contract rights.

Under the common law rule codified in Labor Code section 2922, an employment contract of indefinite duration is, in general, terminable at "the will" of either party. This common law rule has been considerably altered by the recognition of the Supreme Court of California that implicit in any such relationship or contract is an underlying principle that requires the parties to deal openly and fairly with one another.... The duty of fair dealing by an employer is, simply stated, a requirement that like cases be treated alike. Implied in this, of course, is that the company, if it has rules and regulations, apply those rules and regulations to its employees as well as affording its employees their protection....

In this case, there is a close question of whether those rules or regulations permit IBM to inquire into the purely personal life of the employee. If so, an attendant question is whether such a policy was applied consistently, particularly as between men and women. The distinction is important because the right of privacy, a constitutional right in California, could be implicated by the IBM inquiry. Much of the testimony below concerned what those policies were. The evidence was conflicting on the meaning of certain IBM policies. We observe ambiguity in the application but not in the intent. The "Watson Memo" (so called because it was signed by a former chairman of IBM) provided as follows:

"TO ALL IBM MANAGERS:

"The line that separates an individual's on-the-job business life from his other life as a private citizen is at times well-defined and at other times indistinct. But the line does exist, and you and I, as managers in IBM, must be able to recognize that line.

"I have seen instances where managers took disciplinary measures against employees for actions or conduct that are not rightfully the company's concern. These managers usually justified their decisions by citing their personal code of ethics and morals or by quoting some fragment of company policy that seemed to support their position. Both arguments proved unjust on close examination. What we need, in every case, is balanced judgment which weighs the needs of the business and the rights of the individual.

"Our primary objective as IBM managers is to further the business of this company by leading our people properly and measuring quantity and quality of work and effectiveness on the job against clearly set standards of responsibility and compensation. This is performance — and performance is, in the final analysis, the one thing that the company can insist on from everyone.

"We have concern with an employee's off-the-job behavior only when it reduces his ability to perform regular job assignments, interferes with the job performance of other employees, or if his outside behavior affects the reputation of the company in a major way. When on-the-job performance is acceptable, I can think of few situations in which outside activities could result in disciplinary action or dismissal.

"When such situations do come to your attention, you should seek the advice and counsel of the next appropriate level of management and the personnel department in determining what action — if any — is called for. Action should be taken only when a legitimate interest of the company is injured or jeopardized. Furthermore the damage must be clear beyond reasonable doubt and not based on hasty decisions about what one person might think is good for the company.

"IBM's first basic belief is respect for the individual, and the essence of this belief is a strict regard for his right to personal privacy. This idea should never be compromised easily or quickly.

"/s/ Tom Watson, Jr."

It is clear that this company policy insures to the employee both the right of privacy and the right to hold a job even though "off-the-job behavior" might not be approved of by the employee's manager.

IBM had adopted policies governing employee conduct. Some of those policies were collected in a document known as the "Performance and Recognition" (PAR) Manual. IBM relies on the following portion of the PAR Manual:

PAR Manual

"A conflict of interest can arise when an employee is involved in activity for personal gain, which for any reason is in conflict with IBM's business interests. Generally speaking, 'moonlighting' is defined as working at some activity for personal gain outside of your IBM job. If you do perform outside work, you have a special responsibility to avoid any conflict with IBM's business interests.

"Obviously, you cannot solicit or perform in competition with IBM product or service offerings. Outside work cannot be performed on IBM time, including 'personal' time off. You cannot use IBM equipment, materials, resources, or 'inside' information for outside work. Nor should you solicit business or clients or perform outside work on IBM premises.

"Employees must be free of any significant investment or association of their own or of their immediate family's [sic], in competitors or suppliers, which might interfere or be thought to interfere with the independent exercise of their judgment in the best interests of IBM."

This policy of IBM is entitled "Gifts" and appears to be directed at "moonlighting" and soliciting outside business or clients on IBM premises. It prohibits "significant investment" in competitors or suppliers of IBM. It also prohibits "association" with such persons "which might interfere or be thought to interfere with the independent exercise of their judgment in the best interests of IBM."

Callahan based his action against respondent on a "conflict of interest." But the record shows that IBM did not interpret this policy to prohibit a romantic relationship. Callahan admitted that there was no company rule or policy requiring an employee to terminate friendships with fellow employees who leave and join competitors.[4] Gary Nelson, Callahan's superior, also confirmed that IBM had no policy against employees socializing with competitors.

This issue was hotly contested with respondent claiming that the "conflict of interest" claim was a pretext for her unjust termination. Whether it was presented a fact question for the jury.

Do the policies reflected in this record give IBM a right to terminate an employee for a conflict of interest? The answer must be yes, but whether respondent's conduct constituted such was for the jury. We observe that while respondent was successful, her primary job did not give her access to sensitive information which could have been useful to competitors. She was, after all, a seller of typewriters and office equipment. Respondent's brief makes much of the concession by IBM that there was no evidence whatever that respondent had given any information or help to IBM's competitor QYX. It really is no concession at all; she did not have the information or help to give. Even so, the question is one of substantial evidence. The evidence is abundant that there was no conflict of interest by respondent.

It does seem clear that an overall policy established by IBM chairman Watson was one of no company interest in the outside activities of an employee so long as the activities did not interfere with the work of the employee. Moreover, in the last analysis, it may be simply a question for the jury to decide whether, in the application of these policies, the right was conferred on IBM to inquire into the personal or romantic relationships its managers had with others. This is an important question because IBM, in attempting to reargue the facts to us, casts this argument in other terms, namely: that it had a right to inquire even if there was no evidence that such a relationship interfered with the discharge of the employee's duties *because* it had the effect of diminishing the morale of the employees answering to the manager. This is the "Caesar's wife" argument; it is merely a recast of the principal argument and asks the same question in different

---

[4] An interesting side issue to this point is that Blum continued to play on an IBM softball team while working for QYX.

terms.[5] The same answer holds in both cases: there being no evidence to support the more direct argument, there is no evidence to support the indirect argument.

Moreover, the record shows that the evidence of rumor was not a basis for any decline in the morale of the employees reporting to respondent. Employees Mary Hrize and Wayne Fyvie, who reported to respondent's manager that she was seen at a tea dance at the Hyatt Regency with Matt Blum and also that she was not living at her residence in Marin, did not believe that those rumors in any way impaired her abilities as a manager. In the initial confrontation between respondent and her superior the assertion of the right to be free of inquiries concerning her personal life was based on substantive direct contract rights she had flowing to her from IBM policies. Further, there is no doubt that the jury could have so found and on this record we must assume that they did so find....

Intentional Infliction of Emotional Distress

The contract rights in an employment agreement or the covenant of good faith and fair dealing gives both employer and employee the right to breach and to respond in damages. Here, however, the question is whether if IBM elected to exercise that right it should also be liable for punitive damages, because of its intentional infliction of emotional distress. The issue is whether the conduct of the marketing manager of IBM was "extreme and outrageous," a question involving the objective facts of what happened in the confrontation between the employee and employer as well as the special susceptibility of suffering of the employee.

General Rule

The general rule is that this tort, in essence, requires the defendant's conduct to be so extreme and outrageous as to go beyond all possible bounds of decency, and to be regarded as atrocious and utterly intolerable in a civilized community....

The jury was entitled to consider the evidence of extreme and outrageous conduct in light of the June 7 exchange followed by Callahan's conduct and pretextual statements, as well as in light of express corporate policy as manifested by the Watson memo. Indeed, the concern of the Watson memo is also a right protected by law. As we earlier noted "the right of privacy is unquestionably a 'fundamental interest of our society'" (*City and County of San Francisco v. Superior Court*, 125 Cal. App. 3d 879, 883.) It is guaranteed to all people by article I, section 1, of the state Constitution. So the question is whether the invasion of plaintiff's privacy rights by her employer, in the setting of this case, constitutes extreme and outrageous conduct. The jury by special verdict so found.

---

[5] What we mean by that is that if you charge that an employee is passing confidential information to a competitor, the question remains whether the charge is true on the evidence available to the person deciding the issue, in this case, the respondent's managers at IBM. If you recast this argument in the form of the "Caesar's wife" argument attempted by IBM, it will be seen that exactly the same question arises, namely, "is it true?" Indeed, the import of the argument is that the rumor, or an unfounded allegation, could serve as a basis for the termination of the employee.

To determine if Callahan's conduct could reach the level of extreme, outrageous, and atrocious conduct, requires detailed examination. First, there was a decided element of deception in Callahan acting as if the relationship with Blum was something new. The evidence was clear he knew of the involvement of respondent and Blum well before her promotion. Second, he acted in flagrant disregard of IBM policies prohibiting him from inquiring into respondent's "off job behavior." By giving respondent "a few days" to think about the choice between job and lover, he implied that if she gave up Blum she could have her job. He then acted without giving her "a few days to think about it" or giving her the right to choose.

So far the conduct is certainly unfair but not atrocious. What brings Callahan's conduct to an actionable level is the way he brought these several elements together in the second meeting with respondent. He said, after calling her in, "I'm making the decision for you." The implications of his statement were richly ambiguous, meaning she could not act or think for herself, or that he was acting in her best interest, or that she persisted in a romantic involvement inconsistent with her job. When she protested, he fired her.

The combination of statements and conduct would under any reasoned view tend to humiliate and degrade respondent. To be denied a right granted to all other employees for conduct unrelated to her work was to degrade her as a person. His unilateral action in purporting to remove any free choice on her part contrary to his earlier assurances also would support a conclusion that his conduct was intended to emphasize that she was powerless to do anything to assert her rights as an IBM employee. And such powerlessness is one of the most debilitating kinds of human oppression. The sum of such evidence clearly supports the jury finding of extreme and outrageous conduct.

Accordingly we conclude that the emotional distress cause of action was amply proved and supports the award of punitive damages.

The judgment is affirmed.

RACANELLI, P.J., and HOLMDAHL, J., concur.

NOTES

1. *Employer Respect for Privacy.* Why did IBM have the policy, described in the Watson memo, of respecting employee privacy rights? Does such a policy make good business sense? Without the memo, would Rulon-Miller have won her case? If not, does this suggest that the default rule is that employees have no right to date whomever they want without fear of discharge?

2. *Dating Cases.* Considerable litigation has surrounded the discharge of workers for relationships or affairs. Most cases, like *Rulon*, involve affairs with co-workers or competitors. Here, employers have at least an arguable interest in the relationship, and most courts have held against employees. In *Patton v. J.C.*

Penney Co., 719 P.2d 854 (Or. 1986), for example, an employee was fired for continuing a "social relationship" with a female co-worker even though he had received a "Merchant of the Year" award during the relationship and the employer had no general policy against socializing between employees. The court rejected a wrongful discharge claim, reasoning that "[i]t may seem harsh that an employer can fire an employe because of dislike of the employe's personal lifestyle, but because the plaintiff cannot show that the actions fit under an exception to the general rule, plaintiff is subject to the traditional doctrine of 'fire at will.'" *Id.* at 857.

In *Trumbauer v. Group Health Coop.*, 635 F. Supp. 543 (W.D. Wash. 1986) (applying Washington law), an employee was fired because of a "brief sexual relationship" with his supervisor several years before being hired. The court granted summary judgment on the wrongful discharge claim because it could find no public policy "against discrimination based on a social relationship." The court rejected the claim that the employer should be estopped from firing for this reason when it knew about the relationship before hiring the employee, because the estoppel argument assumes that the employer must have a valid reason for firing the employee.

In *Rogers v. I.B.M.*, 500 F. Supp. 867 (W.D. Pa. 1980), the supervisor was fired for a relationship with a subordinate that "exceeded normal or reasonable business associations." The court dismissed his claim as well. *See also Salazar v. Furr's, Inc.*, 629 F. Supp. 1403 (D.N.M. 1986) (no claim for abusive discharge where plaintiff was terminated because she was married to an employee of the employer's competitor).

In *Hillenbrand v. City of Evansville*, 457 N.E.2d 236 (Ind. Ct. App. 1983), neither party to the affair was fired, but an employee was fired after unwittingly discovering his boss having an affair with a secretary. Even here, the court dismissed a complaint against being fired because the employee "observed something which he was not supposed to see."

Even when the other party to the relationship is neither a competitor or co-worker, courts are reluctant to second-guess a discharge. In *Staats v. Ohio National Life Insurance Co.*, 620 F. Supp. 118 (W.D. Pa. 1985) (applying Pennsylvania law), the court dismissed a wrongful discharge claim of an employee fired for attending a convention with a person who was not his spouse. The court reasoned that

> though freedom of association is an important social right, and one that ordinarily should not dictate employment decisions, ... the right to "associate with" a non-spouse *at an employer's convention* is hardly the kind of threat to "some recognized facet of public policy" [contemplated by the tort of wrongful discharge].

And in *Karren v. Far West Federal Savings*, 717 P.2d 1271 (Or. Ct. App.), *review denied*, 725 P.2d 1293 (Or. 1986), the court upheld the dismissal of a wrongful discharge claim where a bank loan coordinator was fired for becoming engaged to marry. The court found her claim was "based on a private right which is not related to her role as an employee."

In *Holloway v. Professional Care Centers*, 42 Fair Empl. Prac. Cas. (BNA) 161 (E.D. Mo. 1986), a black nurse's aide was turned down for a promotion as a certified medication technologist in favor of three white applicants, in part because her husband had a reputation as a drug abuser and perhaps would pressure her to obtain drugs for him at work. The court rejected a Title VII claim of race discrimination, finding that the employer could act on possibly inaccurate judgments of the employee's husband so long as it did not base any part of its decision on racial considerations. Would Holloway have had better success with a common law privacy claim? How would you articulate the claim?

One of the few successful cases in this area, besides *Rulon-Miller*, is *Slohoda v. United Parcel Service*, 475 A.2d 618 (N.J. Super. Ct. App. Div. 1984). There the court overturned a summary judgment against a married employee who was fired for having an affair. The court concluded that, if the company would not have fired an unmarried employee in a similar situation, the firing would discriminate on the basis of marital status in violation of state law.

C. POLYGRAPHS AND HONESTY TESTING

1. POLYGRAPH TESTING

The annual economic loss to American business from employee theft may be as high as $25 billion. *See* IRA M. SHEPARD & ROBERT L. DUSTON, THIEVES AT WORK: AN EMPLOYER'S GUIDE TO COMBATING WORKPLACE DISHONESTY 19 (1988). In the 1970s and 1980s, employers increasingly used polygraphs to screen job applicants for honesty and to investigate thefts. The legal response of the states to polygraphs varied widely, and many commentators perceived widespread employer abuse of the polygraph. In 1988 Congress passed the Employee Polygraph Protection Act.

EMPLOYEE POLYGRAPH PROTECTION ACT OF 1988[*]
(Principal Features)

29 U.S.C. §§ 2001-2009

— The Act makes it unlawful for any employer directly or indirectly to require or request any employee or applicant to submit to a lie detector test, or to use the results of any lie detector test (§ 2002).
— The Act provides for civil penalties up to $10,000 and authorizes private civil actions by employees or applicants (§ 2005). One of the largest penalties assessed so far was for $315,000 against a chain of Wendy's restaurants in Kansas City, Missouri.

---

[*]The text of the act is in the statutory appendix.

— The Act exempts from its coverage public employers, national defense and security contractors, security guard firms, and drug manufacturers and distributors (§ 2006). The Senate Report, citing *Texas State Employees Union v. Texas Department of Mental Health & Mental Retardation*, 746 S.W.2d 203 (Tex. 1987), justified the exemption for public employees by asserting that they were protected anyway: "[I]ncreasingly state and federal courts are finding the use of lie detectors on government employees violative of constitutional protections, which do not apply to private employees."

— The Act does not prohibit an employer from requesting an employee to submit to a polygraph test as part of an ongoing investigation involving economic loss or injury to the employer's business, such as theft, embezzlement, or misappropriation, if certain procedures are followed (§§ 2006(d), 2007). The Act gives examinees the right to terminate the test at any time and to be exempted if a medical condition verified by a physician would produce abnormal responses. The examinee may also not be "asked questions in a manner designed to degrade, or needlessly intrude on, such examinee" or asked questions regarding religious, racial, political, sexual, or union beliefs.

— The Act does not preempt more restrictive state laws (§ 2009).

EMPLOYEE POLYGRAPH PROTECTION ACT OF 1988
SENATE REPORT NO. 100-284
(Labor and Human Resources Committee)

The last decade has witnessed an explosive growth in "lie-detector" tests, particularly the polygraph test. Today over two million polygraph tests are administered annually. While the polygraph was originally developed as an adjunct to criminal investigations within the law enforcement community, the vast majority of tests today are used as a screening procedure in private sector employment. These screening tests, either preemployment or random post-employment, account for much of the recent increase in testing of employees, despite the growing consensus of the scientific community about the lack of scientific validity of these examinations. Testimony provided to the Committee by the American Medical Association concluded that the polygraph can provide evidence of deception or honesty in a percentage of people that is statistically only somewhat better than chance. Another witness calculated that a minimum of 400,000 honest workers are wrongfully labeled deceptive, and suffer adverse employment consequences each year....

The standard polygraph has three components. First, a sphygmograph, wrapped around the upper arm, records changes in blood pressure. Second, two pneumograph tubes attached around the upper and lower chest record changes in respiration patterns. Third, two electrodes are attached to the index and second finger of one hand and record changes in the electrical conductivity, as measure by perspiration, of the skin.

Each of these instruments is connected to a pen register, and the physiological changes are recorded simultaneously on a chart. It is the analysis of this chart from which the examiner forms an opinion of honesty or dishonesty, an opinion drawn from the relative changes in these physiological responses to questions asked during the examination.

There is little debate over the ability of these components of the polygraph instrument to accurately register these physiological changes. But there is no evidence to support that these physiological changes recorded during an examination are unique to deception. Anger, fear, anxiety, surprise, shame, embarrassment and resentment are some of the psychological states which can cause identical changes. At best, the polygraph can claim to measure changes indicative of stress; but neither the machine nor the examination can distinguish whether deception or another state of mind caused the stressed response with an acceptable degree of certainty.

Despite the popular perception that the machine is a "lie-detector," most experts agree that it is not. In addition to the charted responses most examiners base their conclusion on the conduct of the examinee, the natural inclinations of the examiner, and on statements made during the examination. Confessions made during the examination are what many examiners claim as proof of the machine's validity. Many of the experts agree that fear of the machine is an essential element necessary to obtain confessions. One noted examiner claimed the polygraph to be "the best confession-getter since the cattle-prod." But it is this intentional use of fear and intimidation which disturbs many of the opponents of the test.

Private sector examination techniques

Most private sector pre-employment examinations utilize a series of relevant-irrelevant questions. A person is asked a series of questions which contain relevant information about the subject matter being tested, which are interspersed among a series of neutral questions. If the physiological reactions are stronger to the relevant questions than to the neutral ones, the person is diagnosed as being deceptive. Conversely, a lack of difference is considered to be an indication of truthfulness.

A second method, the control question technique, is the kind of test most generally used in criminal investigations or in instances which involve a reportable offense. Here, the control questions are deliberately vague, cover a long period of time and involve acts which almost everyone has committed at some time in his or her life. The purpose of this kind of exam is to force an individual to be more concerned with the control questions than with the relevant ones so that the latter will generate a physiological response. The questions are developed, reviewed and refined with the person taking the exam during a lengthy pretest interview....

State regulation

The large increase in the use of polygraph tests in the private sector, and the resulting abuses and complaints have occurred despite an increase in restriction and regulation at the state level.... The statutes and regulations in the states that allow polygraph examinations vary widely regarding the questions that may be asked, the rights of the employees who are tested, and the kind of training required for licensing.

Given the absence of uniform standards, it has been easy for employers and examiners to circumvent state restrictions. For example, applicants for work in a state which prohibits polygraph testing have been asked to submit to polygraph tests in a neighboring state that has more lenient standards. This is especially true in large metropolitan areas which have common borders with one or more states....

The Committee found the reliance placed upon the polygraph machine by private sector employers making employment decisions, in most situations, is misplaced and unwarranted. This is particularly true in the situations involving preemployment and random testing, where there is no scientific evidence of reliability, according to all the credible evidence presented to the Committee. The Committee found no credible study validating the accuracy of the typical examination being given in the private sector. The data suggests that 70% of tests administered are preemployment, another 15% of tests are post-employment random, and only 15% involve polygraph examinations as part of an investigation of a specific incident relating to the employer. Only in this last category did the Committee find some evidence of validity....

While the Committee heard concerns raised about written psychological pre-employment tests used by some employers, there have been few complaints about such tests, and little evidence of abuse. Such tests are not addressed by this legislation.

Exemptions

....

Section 7(d) provides that private employees are not prohibited from requesting a polygraph examination when there has been a specific incident of economic loss or injury to the employer's business, and the predicate conditions are met. The rationale for this limited exemption is based on the fact that there is some scientific evidence of validity in this narrow use of the polygraph examination. This evidence, coupled with the other safeguards in the bill, should dramatically reduce the number of tests administered as well as the number of abuses.

The Committee intends the requirement in section 7(d)(1) of a specific economic loss or injury to the employer's business be narrowly construed. But there are specific incidents, such as check-kiting, money laundering, or the misappropriation of inside or confidential information which might actually result in gain to the employer in the short term, yet are specific incidents of employees which the employer should vigorously investigate. These types of incidents meet the requisite "injury" standard even though resulting in short-term gain, and an employer may request a polygraph examination for these types of specific incidents. Similarly, such instances as theft from property managed by an employer would meet the requisite standard....

The bill would reduce the denial of employment opportunity due to erroneous test results. Estimates provided the Committee varied widely, but probably between 100,000 and 300,000 fewer individuals will be wrongfully denied employment opportunities solely due to the inaccuracy of the testing procedures. The Committee found no evidence that business losses were greater in states where the test is widely used compared to states in which the test is already banned, nor any related difference in consumer prices between these two classifications of states. Therefore the impact on consumers will be negligible. Businesses currently using the tests prohibited under the bill will have to find alternative screening criteria....

Minority Views of Mr. Quayle on S. 1904

Federalism

I am opposed to this bill, not because I have any belief in the validity of the polygraph, but because it would create a new intrusion of Federal law into the employment relationship. Up to now, Federal law has not regulated the employer's hiring and firing decision, except to prohibit unlawful discrimination....

If this Committee considered federal legislation every time there were an abuse in hiring and firing practices, we would find ourselves obsessed with every detail of employment now subject to state regulation or collective bargaining decision....

NOTES

1. *Scope of the Ongoing Investigation Exemption.* Suppose a worker accuses a supervisor of sexual assault when they were alone on a shift, which the supervisor vigorously denies. How should the employer resolve this situation? Could it ask the supervisor to take a polygraph examination, and fire him if he failed the test? Read § 2006(d).

Suppose the employer decides to forego any polygraph exam and simply fires the supervisor on the basis of the worker's accusation. Might the supervisor ask the employer to give him a polygraph test, so that if he passes he can keep his job? Read § 2002.

Suppose an employee is suspected of taking other employees' purses (or breaking into cars in the company parking lot). Can the employer ask the employee to submit to a polygraph test?

Suppose an employer suspects an employee was drunk when he had an accident in a company car while driving to deposit cash in the company account.

Much of the cash is lost. Can the employer give a polygraph test to determine if the employee was drunk or was careless with the money?

2. *Psychological Horrors of Polygraph Testing.* In addition to wrongful discharge, invasion of privacy, and defamation claims, employees have brought claims of intentional infliction of emotional distress. In *Kamrath v. Suburban National Bank,* 363 N.W.2d 108 (Minn. Ct. App. 1985), the court upheld a jury verdict of $60,000 in favor of a bank teller subjected to a polygraph test during the course of a theft investigation. The facts of *Kamrath* illustrate the potential horrors of the polygraph machine:

> Several days after Kamrath took the test, she began to have nightmares about the examination. In the nightmares, which lasted approximately sixteen months, the polygraph test chair turned into an electric chair, and ended with Kamrath's wetting the bed. Her family testified she became more withdrawn, gained weight, and was very tired. She did not seek any counseling or medical treatment.
>
> At the request of Kamrath's counsel, Dr. John Curran, a psychiatrist, met with Kamrath three times in late 1983 and early 1984. Dr. Curran testified that he was initially skeptical that a polygraph test could have such a strong effect on anyone. However, after meeting Kamrath, he decided she suffers from post-traumatic stress syndrome. Dr. David Lykken, a professor of psychiatry and psychology, testified that someone with Kamrath's structured religious socialization, with a strong moral code emphasizing honesty, could react more strongly than an average individual. To Kamrath the mere request of a test was an accusation of dishonesty. The polygraph examiner pressured her to reveal any acts of dishonesty in her life. As a child, Kamrath had stolen change from her father, which she had never admitted to anyone and refused to tell the examiner.

Id. at 110.

The negative psychological effects of polygraph tests are not limited to those with sensitive emotional makeups. As the Senate Report noted, often the prime use of the polygraph is to extract confessions, which requires the examiner and the machine to intimidate the test taker. Consider Professor David Lykken's remarks:

> [P]olygraphic interrogation in the hands of a skillful examiner is a powerful cathartic (emetic?), an effective inducer of confessions. Its confessionary influence may be most effective with the naive and gullible or, among criminals, with the less experienced, less hardened types. In pre-employment or other screening applications, it appears that the majority of ordinary citizens may be led to make damaging admissions in this secular confessional. In criminal investigations, as many as 25% of those cases where suspects are available for questioning may be settled expeditiously by confessions obtained through polygraphy. This aspect of polygraphic interrogation is quite independent of the actual validity of the technique as a detector of

deception. If all polygraphs were stage props it is likely that just as many admissions or confessions would be elicited. Certainly much of the popularity and utility of the polygraph derives from this incidental effect. This may be why so many polygraphers show little interest in research on the actual validity of the various forms of polygraph test; even if its true validity is no better than chance, so long as most people believe in the lie detector or the voice stress analyzer, these tools will continue to elicit admissions and confessions, and that is their principal purpose. Because they are so effective, however, these methods commonly inflict great stress and emotional disturbance on the innocent and guilty alike.

DAVID LYKKEN, A TREMOR IN THE BLOOD 214-15 (1981).[*]

Is the intimidation of the polygraph necessarily a bad thing? Many employers claim the threat of the polygraph itself prevents employees from engaging in counterproductive activity in the first place. Or as President Nixon said when commanding John Ehrlichman to polygraph State and Defense Department employees after a leak of information: "I don't know anything about polygraphs and I don't know how accurate they are but I know they'll scare the hell out of people." *Hearings Before the House Judiciary Committee on the Impeachment of the President*, 93d Cong., 2d Sess., Statement of Information, bk. VII, pt. 2 at 881 (1974).

3. *The Control Question Dilemma.* Many polygraph tests, especially those used during investigations of specific incidents, employ the control question technique:

> [C]ontrol questions are designed to be arousing for nondeceptive subjects. The questions are designed to cause innocent subjects to be doubtful and concerned about whether they have actually told the truth or told a lie. These questions usually probe for past misdeeds of the same general nature as the crime being investigated but they are transgressions that polygraphers suspect most people have "committed" or considered committing in some form. An example of a control question might be, "Before the age of 25, did you ever steal anything from a place you worked?" Control questions are designed to cover a long period of time, which may make the subject even more doubtful about the veracity of answers provided.

OFFICE OF TECHNOLOGY ASSESSMENT, SCIENTIFIC VALIDITY OF POLYGRAPH TESTING: A RESEARCH REVIEW AND EVALUATION — A TECHNICAL MEMORANDUM 19 (1983).

The answers to the control questions are then compared to the answers to relevant questions, which are questions directly pertaining to the incident being investigated. A person is presumed to be lying if he responds more strongly to direct questions than to control questions. But consider the following dilemma:

Under the [Employee Polygraph Protection] Act, questions that are "unnecessarily intrusive" or "degrading" are prohibited. Polygraph examiners may not inquire into irrelevant matters such as religion, racial concerns, politics, sexual preferences, or union sentiments. Yet, while naturally intrusive, control questions and irrelevant questions serve a vital function in developing valid interpretations of exam results. Examiners compare responses to control questions, assumed to be answered truthfully, with responses to relevant questions in order to identify the "guilty" subjects. Thus, assuming acceptance of the reliability of the polygraph, as the Act appears to do under limited circumstances, the control questions become vital to ensuring the polygraph's validity. However, the Act compromises the critical nature of the control questions in favor of limiting the "probing" of what it assumes to be an accurate tool.

Yvonne K. Sening, Note, *Heads or Tails: The Employee Polygraph Protection Act*, 39 CATH. U. L. REV. 235, 262-63 (1989).

Courts in litigating public-employee complaints over invasive control questions have split over the issue. In *Hester v. City of Milledgeville*, 777 F.2d 1492 (11th Cir. 1985), the court upheld the use of control questions for public-employee firefighters, concluding:

The tested Milledgeville firefighters ... were asked whether they had ever done anything which, if discovered, would have resulted in their dismissal or would have discredited the department...

The city's interest in using control questions to improve the accuracy of the polygraph testing is an important one, especially since the testing was directed toward improving the public's safety by ferreting out drug problems in the fire department. At the same time, the specific control questions at issue here constitute only a limited intrusion into the sphere of confidentiality. The questions were general in nature, were asked for a specific, limited purpose, and, although potentially embarrassing, avoided the issues such as those related to marriage, family and sexual relations generally considered to be the most personal....

We emphasize *proper* use. We would have reservations if the city or any governmental unit were to use a subject's response to a control question for any purpose other than comparing the polygraph reading for the control question to the same subject's reaction to a relevant question. There is, however, no indication that the city plans to take disciplinary actions based on the control questions, release the responses to the public, or even make the responses a part of the subjects' employment records. We also note that there might well be a point at which a control question is so embarrassing or specific, or concerns so personal a matter, as to render the question unconstitutional even when asked for a proper purpose.

Id. at 1497 (emphasis in original). In *Truesdale v. University of North Carolina*, 371 S.E.2d 503 (N.C. Ct. App. 1988), the court took a more strident tone in defending control questions. A public university police officer sued after being fired for refusing to take a polygraph examination in which some of the questions would address her sexual practices, preferences and partners. The court rejected her privacy claims, reasoning:

> The control questions which are asked prior to the administering of the actual polygraph examination include questions relating to theft, prior commission of crimes, homosexual activity, sexual arousal by contact with children, unusual sex acts and anti-governmental activity. The actual polygraph questions, which are only thirteen in number, are designed to determine if the applicant was untruthful on the application for employment or in answering the control questions.
>
> Requiring plaintiff to answer questions regarding sexual practices, preferences and partners does not violate her constitutional right to privacy. The control questions address homosexual activity, sexual arousal by viewing children, sexual contact with minors and unusual or unnatural sex acts. There is no fundamental right to engage in homosexual activity. *Bowers v. Hardwick*, 478 U.S. 186 (1986).... The other sexual activities addressed by the control questions are likewise not entitled to protection as a fundamental right. The fundamental rights entitled to protection under the right to privacy, including family relationships, marriage or procreation, bear no resemblance to the right to engage in the activities in question. Thus, the trial court erred in concluding that the polygraph examination violated plaintiff's constitutional right to privacy.

The Texas Supreme Court has been more sympathetic to the plight of employees asked invasive control questions. In *Texas State Employees Union v. Texas Department of Mental Health & Mental Retardation*, 746 S.W.2d 203 (Tex. 1987), it struck down a state agency polygraph policy as violative of privacy rights protected by the Texas Constitution, in part because of the invasive control questions:

> Control questions are not job-related and ordinarily require the disclosure of matters personal to the employee. For example, Department employees testified that they had been asked such questions as: "Do members of your family smoke dope?" "Have you stolen anything in your life or in the last ten years?" "Have you beaten your kids?"

Id. at 204.

2. PAPER-AND-PENCIL HONESTY TESTING

As we shall see in Section D of this Chapter, employers are increasingly unwilling to divulge information about former employees for fear it will provide ammunition for a defamation suit. The explosion in pre-employment polygraph testing arose as reference checking became increasingly ineffective. Now that pre-employment polygraph testing is largely illegal, employers have turned to honesty testing (also called paper-and-pencil testing or integrity testing).

The Department of Labor's final regulations make clear that paper-and-pencil honesty tests are not included in the definition of "lie detector" under the Employee Polygraph Protection Act of 1988. Most state anti-polygraph statutes likewise do not cover paper-and-pencil tests. For example, the Minnesota supreme court interpreted its statute banning a "polygraph, voice stress analysis, or any test purporting to test honesty" as covering only tests that measure physiological changes. *See State by Spannaus v. Century Camera, Inc.*, 309 N.W.2d 735 (Minn. 1981). Only a few states, including Massachusetts and Rhode Island, have statutorily restricted the use of honesty tests. An added consideration is the relatively low cost of honesty tests, which cost perhaps $5 to $20 each to give and score, compared with polygraph testing, which costs from $35 to $50. The upshot has been a dramatic increase in the use of honesty testing in recent years.

Honesty tests purport to measure dishonesty or general counterproductive behavior, which may include such acts as "participating in strikes, coming to work late, and abusing sick leave." OFFICE OF TECHNOLOGY ASSESSMENT, THE USE OF INTEGRITY TESTS FOR PRE-EMPLOYMENT SCREENING 25 (1990). This report concluded, however, that "the research on integrity tests has not yet produced data that clearly supports or dismisses the assertion that these tests can predict honest behavior." *Id.* at 8. Much of the research on honesty tests has so far been conducted by the test makers themselves.

SOROKA v. DAYTON HUDSON CORP. (Target)

Court of Appeal of California

1 Cal. Rptr. 2d 77 (1991)

REARDON, ASSOCIATE JUSTICE.

Appellants Sibi Soroka, Sue Urry and William d'Arcangelo filed a class action challenging respondent Dayton Hudson Corporation's practice of requiring Target Store security officer applicants to pass a psychological screening. The trial court denied Soroka's motion for a preliminary injunction to prohibit the use of this screening pending the outcome of this litigation.... The American Civil Liberties Union (ACLU) filed an amicus brief in support of Soroka's constitutional right to privacy claims. We reverse the trial court's order denying a preliminary injunction and remand the matter to the trial court for further proceedings on class certification.

I. *Facts*

Respondent Dayton Hudson Corporation owns and operates Target Stores throughout California and the United States. Job applicants for store security officer (SSO) positions must, as a condition of employment, take a psychological test that Target calls the "Psychscreen." An SSO's main function is to observe, apprehend and arrest suspected shoplifters. An SSO is not armed, but carries handcuffs and may use force against a suspect in self-defense. Target views good judgment and emotional stability as important SSO job skills. It intends the Psychscreen to screen out SSO applicants who are emotionally unstable, who may put customers or employees in jeopardy, or who will not take direction and follow Target procedures.

The Psychscreen is a combination of the Minnesota Multiphasic Personality Inventory and the California Psychological Inventory. Both of these tests have been used to screen out emotionally unfit applicants for public safety positions such as police officers, correctional officers, pilots, air traffic controllers and nuclear power plant operators.[4] The test is composed of 704 true-false questions. At Target, the test administrator is told to instruct applicants to answer every question.

The test includes questions about an applicant's religious attitudes, such as: "¶ 67. I feel sure that there is only one true religion.... ¶ 201. I have no patience with people who believe there is only one true religion.... ¶ 477. My soul sometimes leaves my body.... ¶ 483. A minister can cure disease by praying and putting his hand on your head.... ¶ 486. Everything is turning out just like the prophets of the Bible said it would.... ¶ 505. I go to church almost every week.... ¶ 506. I believe in the second coming of Christ.... ¶ 516. I believe in a life hereafter.... ¶ 578. I am very religious (more than most people).... ¶ 580. I believe my sins are unpardonable.... ¶ 606. I believe there is a God.... ¶ 688. I believe there is a Devil and a Hell in afterlife."

The test includes questions that might reveal an applicant's sexual orientation, such as: "¶ 137. I wish I were not bothered by thoughts about sex.... ¶ 290. I have never been in trouble because of my sex behavior.... ¶ 339. I have been in trouble one or more times because of my sex behavior.... ¶ 466. My sex life is satisfactory.... ¶ 492. I am very strongly attracted by members of my own sex.... ¶ 496. I have often wished I were a girl. (Or if you are a girl) I have never been sorry that I am a girl.... ¶ 525. I have never indulged in any unusual sex practices.... ¶ 558. I am worried about sex matters.... ¶ 592. I like to talk about sex.... ¶ 640. Many of my dreams are about sex matters."[5]

An SSO's completed test is scored by the consulting psychologist firm of Martin-McAllister. The firm interprets test responses and rates the applicant on five traits: emotional stability, interpersonal style, addiction potential, dependability and reliability, and socialization — i.e., a tendency to follow established

---

[4] We view the duties and responsibilities of these public safety personnel to be substantially different from those of store security officers.

[5] Soroka challenges many different types of questions on appeal. However, we do not find it necessary to consider questions other than those relating to religious beliefs and sexual orientation.

rules. Martin-McAllister sends a form to Target rating the applicant on these five traits and recommending whether to hire the applicant. Hiring decisions are made on the basis of these recommendations, although the recommendations may be overridden. Target does not receive any responses to specific questions. It has never conducted a formal validation study of the Psychscreen, but before it implemented the test, Target tested 17 or 18 of its more successful SSO's.

Appellants Sibi Soroka, Susan Urry and William d'Arcangelo were applicants for SSO positions when they took the Psychscreen. All three were upset by the nature of the Psychscreen questions. Soroka was hired by Target. Urry — a Mormon — and d'Arcangelo were not hired. In August 1989, Soroka filed a charge that use of the Psychscreen discriminated on the basis of race, sex, religion and physical handicap with the Department of Fair Employment and Housing.

Having exhausted their administrative remedies, Soroka, Urry and D'Arcangelo filed a class action against Target in September 1989 to challenge its use of the Psychscreen.... Soroka alleged causes of action for violation of the constitutional right to privacy, invasion of privacy, disclosure of confidential medical information, fraud, negligent misrepresentation, intentional and negligent infliction of emotional distress, violation of the Fair Employment and Housing Act, violation of sections 1101 and 1102 of the Labor Code, and unfair business practices....

In June 1990, Soroka moved for a preliminary injunction to prohibit Target from using the Psychscreen during the pendency of the action. A professional psychologist submitted a declaration opining that use of the test was unjustified and improper, resulting in faulty assessments to the detriment of job applicants. He concluded that its use violated basic professional standards and that it had not been demonstrated to be reliable or valid as an employment evaluation. For example, one of the two tests on which the Psychscreen was based was designed for use only in hospital or clinical settings. Soroka noted that two of Target's experts had previously opined that the Minnesota Multiphasic Personality Inventory was virtually useless as a preemployment screening device. It was also suggested that the Psychscreen resulted in a 61 percent rate of false positives — that is, that more than 6 in 10 qualified applicants for SSO positions were not hired.

Target's experts submitted declarations contesting these conclusions and favoring the use of the Psychscreen as an employment screening device. Some Target officials believed that use of this test has increased the quality and performance of its SSO's. However, others testified that they did not believe that there had been a problem with the reliability of SSO applicants before the Psychscreen was implemented. Target's vice president of loss prevention was unable to link changes in asset protection specifically to use of the Psychscreen. In rebuttal, Soroka's experts were critical of the conclusions of Target's experts. One rebuttal expert noted that some of the intrusive, non-job-related questions had been deleted from a revised form of the test because they were offensive, invasive and added little to the test's validity....

The trial court ... denied Soroka's motion for preliminary injunction....

II. *Preliminary Injunction*

....

1. *The Right to Privacy*

The California Constitution explicitly protects our right to privacy. Article I, section 1 provides: "All people are by nature free and independent and have inalienable rights. Among these are enjoying and defending life and liberty, acquiring, possessing, and protecting property, and pursuing and obtaining safety, happiness, and privacy."

Target concedes that the Psychscreen constitutes an intrusion on the privacy rights of the applicants, although it characterizes this intrusion as a limited one. However, even the constitutional right to privacy does not prohibit all incursion into individual privacy. The parties agree that a violation of the right to privacy may be justified, but disagree about the standard to be used to make this determination. At trial, Target persuaded the court to apply a reasonableness standard because Soroka was an applicant, rather than a Target employee. On appeal, Soroka and the ACLU contend that Target must show more than reasonableness — that it must demonstrate a compelling interest — to justify its use of the Psychscreen.

[margin note: Standards proposed by Soroka and Target]

2. *Applicants vs. Employees*

Soroka and the ACLU contend that job applicants are entitled to the protection of the compelling interest test, just as employees are. The trial court disagreed, employing a reasonableness standard enunciated in a decision of Division Three of this District which distinguished between applicants and employees. (*Wilkinson v. Times Mirror Corp.,* 215 Cal. App. 3d 1034.)

In *Wilkinson,* a book publisher required job applicants to submit to drug urinalysis as part of its preemployment physical examination. The appellate court rejected the applicants' contention that the compelling interest test should apply to determine whether the publisher's invasion of their privacy interests was justified under article I, section 1. Instead, the court fashioned and applied a lesser standard based on whether the challenged conduct was reasonable. When setting this standard, the most persuasive factor for the *Wilkinson* court appears to have been that the plaintiffs were applicants for employment rather than employees. "Any individual who chooses to seek employment necessarily also chooses to disclose certain personal information to prospective employers, such as employment and educational history, and to allow the prospective employer to verify that information." (*Id.,* at 1048.) This applicant-employee distinction was pivotal for the *Wilkinson* court. "Simply put, applicants for jobs ... have a choice; they

[margin note: Wilkinson]

[margin note: Potentially important standard]

may consent to the limited invasion of their privacy resulting from the testing, or may decline both the test and the conditional offer of employment." (*Id.*, at 1049.)

ballot argument

Our review of the ballot argument satisfies us that the voters did not intend to grant less privacy protection to job applicants than to employees. The ballot argument specifically refers to job applicants when it states that Californians "are required to report some information, regardless of our wishes for privacy or our belief that there is no public need for the information. Each time we ... *interview for a job*, ... a dossier is opened and an informational profile is sketched." (Ballot Pamp., Proposed Amends. to Cal. Const. with arguments to voters, Gen. Elec. (Nov. 7, 1972) p. 27, emphasis added.) Thus, the major underpinning of *Wilkinson* is suspect.

Appellate court decisions predating *Wilkinson* have also applied the compelling interest standard in cases involving job applicants. (*See Central Valley Ch. 7th Step Foundation, Inc. v. Younger* (1989) 214 Cal. App. 3d 145, 151, 162-165 [arrest records distributed to public employers].) Target attempts to distinguish these cases as ones involving public, not private, employers, but that is a distinction without a difference in the context of the state constitutional right to privacy. Private and public employers alike are bound by the terms of the privacy provisions of article I, section 1....

In conclusion, we are satisfied that any violation of the right to privacy of job applicants must be justified by a compelling interest. This conclusion is consistent with the voter's expression of intent when they amended article I, section 1 to make privacy an inalienable right and with subsequent decisions of the California Supreme Court.

3. *Nexus Requirement*

Soroka and the ACLU also argue that Target has not demonstrated that its Psychscreen questions are job-related — i.e., that they provide information relevant to the emotional stability of its SSO applicants. Having considered the religious belief and sexual orientation questions carefully, we find this contention equally persuasive.

Although the state right of privacy is broader than the federal right, California courts construing article I, section 1 have looked to federal precedents for guidance. Under the lower federal standard, employees may not be compelled to submit to a violation of their right to privacy unless a clear, direct nexus exists between the nature of the employee's duty and the nature of the violation. We are satisfied that this nexus requirement applies with even greater force under article I, section 1.

Again, we turn to the voter's interpretation of article I, section 1. The ballot argument — the only legislative history for the privacy amendment — specifically states that one purpose of the constitutional right to privacy is to prevent businesses "from collecting ... *unnecessary* information about us ...." (*White v. Davis*, 13 Cal. 3d at 774, emphasis added; *see Wilkinson v. Times Mirror Corp.*,

Legislative History

supra, 215 Cal. App. 3d at 1040.) It also asserts that the right to privacy would "preclude the collection of *extraneous* or *frivolous* information." (Ballot Pamp., Proposed Amends. to Cal. Const. with arguments to voters, Gen. Elec. (Nov. 7, 1972) p. 28, emphasis added.) Thus, the ballot language requires that the information collected be *necessary* to achieve the purpose for which the information has been gathered. This language convinces us that the voters intended that a nexus requirement apply.

The California Supreme Court has also recognized this nexus requirement. When it found that public employees could not be compelled to take a polygraph test, it criticized the questions asked as both highly personal and unrelated to any employment duties. (*See Long Beach City Employees Assn. v. City of Long Beach*, 41 Cal. 3d 937, 945 (1986).) It found that a public employer may require its workers to answer *some* questions, but only those that specifically, directly and narrowly relate to the performance of the employee's official duties. (*Id.*, at 947.) This nexus requirement also finds support in the seminal case from our high court on the right to privacy, which characterizes as one of the principal *[right to privacy case]* mischiefs at which article I, section 1 was directed "the *overbroad* collection ... of unnecessary personal information ...." (*White v. Davis, supra*, 13 Cal. 3d at 775, emphasis added.) If the information Target seeks is not job-related, that collection is overbroad, and the information unnecessary.

Wilkinson attempted to address this nexus requirement but its conclusion is inconsistent with federal law, which affords less protection than that provided by the state constitutional privacy amendment. *Wilkinson* held that an employer has a legitimate interest in not hiring individuals whose drug abuse may render them unable to perform their job responsibilities in a satisfactory manner. Federal courts have held that this sort of generalized justification is not sufficient to justify an infringement of an employee's Fourth Amendment rights. If this justification is insufficient to satisfy a lesser Fourth Amendment test, then it cannot pass muster under the more stringent compelling interest test. *[criticizing Wilkinson]*

4. *Application of Law*

Target concedes that the Psychscreen intrudes on the privacy interests of its job applicants. Having carefully considered *Wilkinson*, we find its reasoning unpersuasive. As it is inconsistent with both the legislative history of article I, section 1 and the case law interpreting that provision, we decline to follow it. Under the legislative history and case law, Target's intrusion into the privacy rights of its SSO applicants must be justified by a compelling interest to withstand constitutional scrutiny. Thus, the trial court abused its discretion by committing an error of law — applying the reasonableness test, rather than the compelling interest test.

While Target unquestionably has an interest in employing emotionally stable persons to be SSO's, testing applicants about their religious beliefs and sexual orientation does not further this interest. To justify the invasion of privacy resulting from use of the Psychscreen, Target must demonstrate a compelling interest and must establish that the test serves a job-related purpose. In its opposition to Soroka's motion for preliminary injunction, Target made no showing that a person's religious beliefs or sexual orientation have any bearing on the emotional stability or on the ability to perform an SSO's job responsibilities. It did no more than to make generalized claims about the Psychscreen's relationship to emotional fitness and to assert that it has seen an overall improvement in SSO quality and performance since it implemented the Psychscreen. This is not sufficient to constitute a compelling interest, nor does it satisfy the nexus requirement. Therefore, Target's inquiry into the religious beliefs and sexual orientation of SSO applicants unjustifiably violates the state constitutional right to privacy. Soroka has established that he is likely to prevail on the merits of his constitutional claims....

B. Statutory Claims

....

1. Fair Employment and Housing Act

Soroka contends that the trial court abused its discretion by concluding that he was unlikely to prevail on his FEHA claims. These claims are based on allegations that the questions require applicants to divulge information about their religious beliefs....

In California, an employer may not refuse to hire a person on the basis of his or her religious beliefs. Likewise, an employer is prohibited from making any non-job-related inquiry that expresses "directly or indirectly, any limitation, specification, or discrimination as to ... religious creed...." (Gov. Code, § 12940, subd. (d).) FEHA guidelines provide that an employer may make any pre-employment inquiry that does not discriminate on a basis enumerated in FEHA. However, inquiries that identify an individual on the basis of religious creed are unlawful unless pursuant to a permissible defense. Job-relatedness is an affirmative defense. A means of selection that is facially neutral but that has an adverse impact on persons on the basis of religious creed is permissible only on a showing that the selection process is sufficiently related to an essential function of the job in question to warrant its use.

The trial court committed an error of law when it found that questions such as "I feel sure that there is only one true religion," "Everything is turning out just like the prophets of the Bible said it would," and "I believe in the second coming of Christ" were not intended to reveal religious beliefs. Clearly, these questions were intended to — and did — inquire about the religious beliefs of Target's SSO applicants. As a matter of law, these questions constitute an inquiry that expresses a "specification [of a] religious creed." (Gov. Code, § 12940, subd. (d).)

Once Soroka established a prima facie case of an impermissible inquiry, the burden of proof shifted to Target to demonstrate that the religious beliefs questions were job-related. As we have already determined, Target has not established that the Psychscreen's questions about religious beliefs have any bearing on that applicant's ability to perform an SSO's job responsibilities. Therefore, Soroka has established the likelihood that he will prevail at trial on this statutory claim.

2. *Labor Code Sections 1101 and 1102*

Soroka also argues that the trial court abused its discretion by concluding that he was unlikely to prevail on his claims based on sections 1101 and 1102 of the Labor Code. The trial court found that Soroka did not establish that the questions asked in the Psychscreen are designed to reveal an applicant's sexual orientation. It also found that Soroka did not establish that Target's hiring decisions are made on the basis of sexual orientation.

Under California law, employers are precluded from making, adopting or enforcing any policy that tends to control or direct the political activities or affiliations of employees. (Lab.Code, § 1101, subd. (b).) Employers are also prohibited from coercing, influencing, or attempting to coerce or influence employees to adopt or follow or refrain from adopting or following any particular line of political activity by threatening a loss of employment. (*Id.*, § 1102.) These statutes have been held to protect applicants as well as employees. (*Gay Law Students Assn. v. Pacific Tel. & Tel. Co.* (1979) 24 Cal.3d 458, 487, fn. 16, 595 P.2d 592.)

Labor Code sections 1101 and 1102 protect an employee's fundamental right to engage in political activity without employer interference. (*Gay Law Students Assn. v. Pacific Tel. & Tel. Co., supra,* 24 Cal.3d at 487.) The "struggle of the homosexual community for equal rights, particularly in the field of employment, must be recognized as a political activity." (*Id.*, at 488.) These statutes also prohibit a private employer from discriminating against an employee on the basis of his or her sexual orientation. (*See* 69 Ops. Cal. Atty. Gen. 80, 82 (1986).)

The trial court committed an error of law when it determined that Psychscreen questions such as "I am very strongly attracted by members of my own sex" were not intended to reveal an applicant's sexual orientation. On its face, this question directly asks an applicant to reveal his or her sexual orientation. One of the five traits that Target uses the Psychscreen to determine is "socialization," which it defines as "the extent to which an individual subscribes to traditional values and mores and feels an obligation to act in accordance with them." Persons who identify themselves as homosexuals may be stigmatized as "willing to defy or violate" these norms, which may in turn result in an invalid test.

As a matter of law, this practice tends to discriminate against those who express a homosexual orientation. (*See* Lab. Code, § 1101.) It also constitutes an attempt to coerce an applicant to refrain from expressing a homosexual orientation by threat of loss of employment. (*See id.*, § 1102.) Therefore, Soroka has established that he is likely to prevail at trial on this statutory basis, as well.

The order denying the preliminary injunction is reversed....

POCHE, ACTING P.J., and PERLEY, J., concur.

NOTES

1. *Settlement*. The *Soroka* case eventually settled for over $2 million. The 2,500 applicants who had taken the invasive test split $1.3 million; $60,000 went to the four named plaintiffs; and the rest went for attorney's fees. *See* 89 Ind. Emp. Rts (BNA) No. 16 (July 20, 1993) and No. 22 (October 12, 1993).

2. *Psychologically Naked*. Professor Finkin finds the *Soroka* case to be a small victory.

> *Soroka*, seemingly a vindication of employee privacy, illustrates how narrow the idea of intrusion is even under a legal regime seemingly more generous than the common law. If the gravamen of the wrong is requiring an employee to answer certain intimate questions, it follows that privacy would not be implicated if the questions were non-intrusive.... This eludes the real privacy issue posed by a psychological assessment: It strips the "test subject" — note the dehumanization inherent in the language — psychologically naked. Unlike an interview, where one confronts a human being whom one can attempt to persuade ..., the individual is rendered helpless, depersonalized, transparent, an object of scientific scrutiny....
>
> This might be justified by the special circumstances of a particular employment, for example, in aviation or atomic energy. But in almost all jurisdictions, so long as members of protected classes are not disproportionately disadvantaged, these devices may be used with impunity, irrespective of the want of professional validation for such use.

Matthew W. Finkin, *Employee Privacy, American Values, and the Law*, 72 CHI.-KENT L. REV. 221 234-35 (1996).

3. *Gay Rights and Political Activity*. While sometimes lost in the constitutional discussion, the *Soroka* court's discussion of the statutory claims is important. It expands on cases holding that California's Labor Code prohibits private employers from interfering with the political activity of employees, concluding that this prohibition includes discrimination on the basis of sexual orientation. Through the ban on interfering with political activity, the court holds as a matter of law that a private employer cannot inquire about sexual orientation.

4. *Privacy Claims of Job Applicants*. *Soroka* required employers to pass the same compelling interest test before invading the privacy of job applicants as well as incumbent employees. This ruling probably does not survive *Loder v. City of Glendale*, 927 P.2d 1200 (Cal. 1997). The city of Glendale required all applicants for new jobs and current employees seeking promotions to pass a drug and alcohol test. The Court held that the federal Constitution prohibited the drug test for incumbents, but held that the federal and state Constitutions permitted the drug test for job applicants. It reasoned that the employer has a greater need to conduct suspicionless drug tests on applicants, and that the drug test was a lesser invasion of privacy on applicants than incumbents:

> [A]n employer generally need not resort to suspicionless drug testing to determine whether a current employee is likely to be absent from work or less productive or effective as a result of current drug or alcohol abuse: an employer can observe the employee at work, evaluate his or her work product and safety record, and check employment records to determine whether the employee has been excessively absent or late. If a current employee's performance and work record provides some basis for suspecting that the employee presently is abusing drugs or alcohol, the employer will have an individualized basis for requesting that the particular employee undergo drug testing, and current employees whose performance provides no reason to suspect that they currently are using drugs or abusing alcohol will not be compelled to sustain the intrusion on their privacy inherent in mandatory urinalysis testing....

> When deciding whether to hire a job applicant, however, an employer has not had a similar opportunity to observe the applicant over a period of time. Although the employer can request information regarding the applicant's performance in past jobs or in nonemployment settings, an employer reasonably may lack total confidence in the reliability of information supplied by a former employer or other references. And although an employer will, of course, obtain the opportunity to make its own observations after it has hired the applicant, the hiring of a new employee frequently represents a considerable investment on the part of an employer, often involving the training of the new employee. Furthermore, once an applicant is hired, any attempt by the employer to dismiss the employee generally will entail additional expenses, including those relating to the hiring of a replacement. In view of these considerations, we believe that an employer has a greater need for, and interest in, conducting suspicionless drug testing of job applicants than it does in conducting such testing of current employees.

> Turning to the degree of the intrusion on reasonable expectations of privacy imposed by the city's drug testing program, we believe that the intrusion on privacy is significantly diminished because the drug testing urinalysis in this case was administered as part of a preemployment medical examination that the job applicant, in any event, would have been required to undergo.... Plaintiff in this case, however, has not contended that the city's examination procedure is unlawful insofar as it requires all job applicants who have been offered employment to submit to a medical examination as a condition of their hiring, and plaintiff has not cited, and our independent research has not revealed, any authority suggesting it is

impermissible for an employer to require all job applicants to submit to medical examinations without regard to the nature of the position in question.

927 P.2d at 1223-24.

DISSENT

Justice Kennard, dissenting, disputed the basic distinction between applicants and incumbents. First, he questioned "whether the government's purely economic considerations ... can ever be sufficient 'to overcome the interests in vindicating human dignity' embodied in the constitutionally guaranteed right of privacy." Further, hiring applicants on a probationary basis would be an alternative, less intrusive means of determining whether an individual's performance is affected by substance abuse. Justice Kennard granted that the alternative "may impose certain costs on the employer," but declared that such costs would be partially offset by the greater accuracy of on-the-job observation.

Policy

Despite Justice Kennard's hesitations, greater judicial scrutiny of drug testing of incumbent employees may make sense under the internal labor markets model. Job applicants have not established roots with the company or made firm-specific investments, and thus are freer to reject invasive applications. Employers have more power to exploit existing employees, who because of their job specific capital have much more to lose if they refuse to consent to invasive testing.

UNIONS

Labor law regulation of unionized employees also distinguishes between drug testing of job applicants and incumbent employees. Drug and alcohol testing of current employees is a mandatory subject of bargaining, thus requiring employers to bargain with the union before implementing a drug testing program. *Johnson-Bateman Co. v. International Ass'n of Machinists, Local 1047*, 295 N.L.R.B. 26 (1989). Employers are free to test job applicants without consulting the union, however, because applicants are not employees within the meaning of the collective bargaining obligations of the NLRA. *Cowles Media Co. v. Newspaper Guild, Local 2*, 295 N.L.R.B. 63 (1989).

MMPI

5. *The MMPI.* One of the two tests upon which Psychscreen is based is the Minnesota Multiphasic Personality Inventory-2. This is a well-known and well-validated personality test originally designed to identify psychopathology in mental patients.

As Target pointed out to the court, the employer does not see the job applicant's answers to individual questions. Rather, it receives a checklist from the testing company summarizing the applicant's personality. These checklists have never been independently validated. Typical checklists highlight the validity and acceptability of the MMPI profile (e.g., denied common, trivial moral faults), serious psychological-emotional problems (e.g., overconcern about own health, potential medical absence and disability problems), stability and judgment (e.g., potential for overreactions and loss of judgment under stress), self-control and anger control (e.g., could be dangerous to others), and work factors (e.g., problems in handling criticism; rationalizer). *See* JAMES N. BUTCHER, NEW DEVELOPMENTS IN THE USE OF THE MMPI 189 (1979).

Unlike most honesty tests, the MMPI demonstrates extremely low rates of false positive error — less than one percent of persons diagnosed by the test as ill are free of psychopathology. It suffers from high rates of false negative error, however, which can lead to the mistaken hiring of individuals who are not psychologically suited for the job. This is an inversion of the usual public policy concern with false positives. *See* Office of Technology Assessment, The Use of Integrity Tests for Pre-Employment Screening 39 n.47 (1990).

Very Accurate in some respects

6. *Fakability.* As veterans of many standardized tests, law students might think it particularly easy to know how to answer honesty questions if one wants the job. Will dishonest job applicants simply fake their answers? An American Psychological Association study suggests not:

> A common reaction to paper-and-pencil honesty tests is one of incredulity that they should work at all. Most of the questions seem quite transparent, and it seems obvious to many observers that job applicants would not willingly report undesirable behaviors that would ruin their chances for employment; surely they would lie. Although we would not like to discourage continued research on dissimulation, faking may not be as great a problem as most people fear. Some applicants may not regard the tests as very important, and hence are not motivated to lie to any great extent; others may think they can "outsmart" the tests by admitting to various transgressions. Still others may believe that companies can and will check up on what they say and therefore they should be truthful. Finally, at a more theoretical level, we know that people tend to assume that others are much the same as themselves; to the extent to which less honest applicants succumb to this "false consensus" effect, they will assume that their anti-social attitudes and behaviors are quite normal, and therefore they can express them freely.

LEWIS R. GOLDBERG ET AL., QUESTIONNAIRES USED IN THE PREDICTION OF TRUSTWORTHINESS IN PRE-EMPLOYMENT SELECTION DECISIONS: AN A.P.A. TASK FORCE REPORT 12-13 (1991).

Also consider the following experiment about honesty tests, which suggests that job applicants do not fake answers even when they could:

> Two common employer concerns about pre-employment honesty testing were addressed: fakability and the test taker's reaction to such tests. Students, 84% with work experience in industries where honesty tests are common, took an honesty test under one of three instructional sets: respond honestly, fake good, and respond as if applying for a job. While subjects instructed to fake good could easily do so, the scores of subjects responding as job applicants more closely resembled those of subjects instructed to

respond honestly. Strong negative reactions to honesty tests were not found; rather, most subjects felt that such tests were appropriate.

Ann Marie Ryan & Paul R. Sackett, *Pre-Employment Honesty Testing: Fakability, Reactions of Test Takers, and Company Image*, 1 J. BUS. & PSYCH. 248 (1987).

7. *Dangers of Misclassification.* While no one is pleased when they fail a test they should have passed, the dangers of false positives[*] in (dis)honesty testing may be particularly severe.

> [M]isclassification of honest individuals is particularly onerous. First, honesty and integrity are highly value-laden concepts that cut to the core of basic concepts of morality. Identifying an individual as "at risk to commit dishonest acts" almost certainly carries a greater stigma than does the classification of an individual in other terms, e.g., relatively low cognitive abilities: the latter may channel the individual toward certain kinds of jobs not requiring those specific cognitive skills, but there are virtually no jobs for which dishonesty would be either required or desired.

Office of Technology Assessment, *supra at* p. 12. A broader question is whether "honesty" is indeed a fixed personality trait, or depends on the situation. Some have argued that one's honesty depends on the situation:

> [T]here is disagreement among psychologists as to whether honesty is an individual trait or whether it is situationally determined. Some psychologists believe that honesty or dishonesty is more a function of the climate created by management than an individual's personality. If honesty is in fact situationally determined, this suggests that problems with dishonesty could be addressed more effectively by management practices that support (encourage and reward) honest behavior.

Carolyn Wiley & Docia L. Rudly, *Managerial Issues and Responsibilities in the Use of Integrity Tests*, 42 LAB. L.J. 152, 154 (1991).

On the other hand, if dishonesty is an immutable trait then employees cannot learn to be honest. "Individuals who perform poorly on honesty tests could, presumably, seek professional counseling or somehow change their thinking. But the question is whether genuine changes in underlying character would be reflected in subsequent tests: for example, the answer to a question like "did you ever steal" would be the same despite an individual's successful transformation into an honest person. On a math test, however, an individual who has mastered a skill since failing the first test would, presumably, answer the relevant ques-

---

[*] The term "false positive" is confusing here because the term "honesty" testing is a misnomer. Like drug tests, honesty tests attempt to uncover bad traits in employees. For both types of tests, standard terminology calls a falsely accused person a false positive. A drug user or dishonest employee who escapes detection is a false negative. In a skills test that employees want to pass, a false positive would be an unskilled employee that somehow passed the test.

tions more successfully on subsequent attempts." Office of Technology Assessment, *supra at* p. 13.

Some have found the very scientific cast of honesty tests to be troubling:

> [I]ntegrity tests carry a scientific imprimatur — they are marketed with literature proclaiming their "experimental validation" — therefore substantially intensifying an individual's burden of proving that misclassification has occurred. Thus, while a virtue of the tests is their attempt to reduce the prevalence of subjective biases that might contaminate other screening and selection processes, the result can be more severe for individuals who are misclassified.

Office of Technology Assessment, *supra at* p. 14.

8. *Test Accuracy and the Base Rate Problem.* A major factor in the debate over polygraph and honesty testing is the accuracy of tests. Reliable estimates are difficult to obtain. The OTA reviewed five studies that compared honesty test scores for retail employees and whether they were detected for theft. The results showed that, for employees detected for theft, the tests labeled 50% to 95% as dishonest. [Not labeling a dishonest person as dishonest is sometimes called a false negative.] Of the (presumably honest) employees not detected for theft, the tests labeled between 35% and 84% as honest. [Labeling an honest person as dishonest is sometimes called a false positive.] This suggests a wide range in the accuracy of honesty tests.

Often overlooked in this debate is a greater problem in many contexts — the low base rate. If most people in the population to be tested are honest, even very accurate tests will falsely label people as dishonest more often than they correctly label them dishonest. False positives become a serious problem. *See generally* Kevin R. Murphy, *Detecting Infrequent Deception,* 72 J. APPLIED PSYCHOLOGY 611 (1987).

To see this, let us take the most generous results described above. Let us suppose that 95% of all dishonest test-takers will fail the honesty test. (This figure is sometimes called the sensitivity rate.) Let us suppose that 84% of honest test-takers will pass the honesty test. (This figure is sometimes called the selectivity rate.)

Most policymakers should not be directly interested in either of these numbers. Rather, the concern should be with the likelihood that one who fails a test is nevertheless honest. These are the innocent persons who will not receive the job because of the test. This number depends, however, not only on the sensitivity and selectivity rates of the test, but also on the base rate of dishonest people who will be given the test.

Suppose, as is plausible in an honesty test given to all job applicants (and consistent with the findings of the OTA study), that only 5% of the applicants are dishonest. Then, if 1,000 job applicants are given the test, we would expect the results shown in Table 9-1.

Table 9-1
EXPECTED RESULTS OF HONESTY TESTS
Sensitivity Rate = 95%, Selectivity Rate = 84%
Base Rate of Dishonest Test-takers = 5%

	TEST LABELS HONEST	TEST LABELS DISHONEST	TOTAL NUMBER
HONEST APPLICANTS	798	152 (false positives)	950
DISHONEST APPLICANTS	3 (false negatives)	47	50
TOTAL	801	199	1,000

The fairness issue, which focuses on the false positives, is stark. If the employer rejects all applicants failing the honesty test, over $^3/_4$ of rejected applicants ($^{152}/_{199}$) will be honest. This result obtains not because the test is inaccurate (we assumed a 95% sensitivity rate and 84% selectivity rate) but because so few applicants are dishonest.

On the other hand, the chart also reveals the incentives many employers have in using honesty tests for job applicants. If the employer did not screen for honesty, the chance of hiring a dishonest person is 5% (the base rate of dishonesty). If the employer only hires test passers, the chance of hiring a dishonest person is only $^3/_{801}$, or 0.4%. In many situations, employers will be more concerned about hiring dishonest persons (false negatives) than rejecting honest persons (false positives). This is likely when an employer has many applications for job openings and honesty is important relative to other skills. It is no surprise, then, that retail trade employers were major users of polygraphs for job applicants, and continue to use honesty testing today, even though such tests exclude many qualified applicants.

If the base rate were as high as 50%, by contrast, the test seems much fairer. In that case, assuming the same selectivity and sensitivity rates as before, the test would label 555 of every 1,000 test-takers as dishonest. Of these 555, only 80 (17%), would actually be honest.

For example, suppose an employer only gives an honesty test upon reasonable (50/50) suspicion that the employee had stolen property. This would create a base rate of 50%, in that half of the test-takers would in fact be dishonest. If an employer fired every employee in such a case who failed the test, only 17% of the fired employees would be fired unfairly. The changing base rate may explain why Congress, in prohibiting most uses of the polygraph, allowed employers to use a polygraph to investigate economic losses.

9. *Genetic Screening.* Another type of employee testing — one with a specter of science run amok — is genetic screening. Using blood samples, the screening process can identify individuals who are genetically predisposed to diseases such as sickle cell anemia, Tay Sachs and cystic fibrosis. Employers use this information to evaluate health insurance costs and to bar especially sensitive employees from positions with dangerous substances. Due to its high costs, only a few employers (mostly in the chemical industry) currently genetically test their employees. As the price declines, personnel directors may be more prone to use the tests in the future.

As of October 1997, fourteen states had laws protecting against genetic discrimination in the workplace. Wisconsin, for example, forbids employers from using genetic tests to affect terms of employment, but expressly allows the employer, with the employee's written consent, to use a genetic test to investigate a worker's compensation claim or to determine the employee's susceptibility to a potentially toxic substance. WIS. STAT. § 111.372.

One reason for banning genetic discrimination is its disparate impact along racial and ethnic lines, an impact that could also violate Title VII if not job related. In addition, genetic screening by employers raises similar issues to those from drug and alcohol testing. In particular, many people are concerned with the invasion of privacy and the accuracy of genetic testing in predicting harm. The American Medical Association's Council on Ethical and Judicial Affairs declared that genetic tests alone "do not have sufficient predictive value to be relied on as a basis for excluding workers." *Use of Genetic Testing by Employers,* 266 JAMA 1827, 1830 (1991).

The only federal statute directly addressing genetic discrimination is the 1996 Health Insurance Portability and Accountability Act (analyzed in Chapter 19). **HIPAA** HIPAA prohibits group health plans from using any health-related factor, including genetic information, as a basis for denying or limiting eligibility for coverage or for charging an individual more for coverage. ERISA §§ 701(b)(1)(B), 702(a)(1)(F).

The Americans with Disabilities Act (analyzed in Chapter 14) may also limit **ADA** the employer's use of genetic tests. In 1995, the Equal Employment Opportunity Commission issued an enforcement guideline advising that an employer who **Interesting** makes an employment decision based on genetic information regards that individual as having a disability within the meaning of the ADA. II EEOC COMPLIANCE MANUAL § 902. Others have argued that the ADA covers only past or present disabilities, rather than potential future disabilities that genetic screening is designed to detect. *Cf. Runnebaum v. Nationsbank of Maryland,* 123 F.3d 156 (4th Cir. 1997) (*en banc*) (asymptomatic person infected with HIV virus is not an individual with a disability under the ADA). *But cf. Abbott v. Bragdon,* 107 F.3d 934 (1st Cir.), *cert. granted in part,* 118 S. Ct. 554 (1997) (asymptomatic person infected with HIV virus is an individual with a disability).

NOTE ON NEGLIGENT HIRING

Suppose an employer hires an applicant despite questionable results on a psychological test. Might the employer face liability if the employee harms someone? The following case explores this issue.

ISSUE

THATCHER v. BRENNAN   *Negligent Hiring*

United States District Court, S.D. Mississippi

657 F. Supp. 6 (1986)

Tom S. Lee, District Judge.

....

The plaintiff brought this action against Bert Brennan and Mead Johnson, jointly and severally, following an altercation between the plaintiff and Brennan which occurred on May 21, 1984. The alleged liability of Mead Johnson is predicated upon two theories: (1) respondeat superior and (2) negligent hiring. Mead Johnson has moved for summary judgment on both theories....

Respondeat Superior

On May 21, 1984, Bert Brennan was an employee of Mead Johnson, having been hired February 8, 1982. As a medical sales specialist, Brennan was responsible for the sale of Mead Johnson pharmaceutical products, primarily through physician specifications. Although he lived in Covington, Louisiana, Brennan's sales territory included Hinds County, Mississippi. He was required by Mead Johnson to be in Jackson, Mississippi at least once every five weeks to make calls on physicians. Due to the travel required, Brennan was provided an automobile by his employer and was reimbursed for his travel expenses, including the expenses for his trips to Jackson.

On the morning of May 21, 1984, Brennan had made some physician sales calls in New Orleans, Louisiana. About 12:30 or 1:00 p.m., he left his home in Louisiana and drove to Jackson. Upon arrival, Brennan checked into a hotel, got some paper work "squared away," and then drove to the post office to mail it. Upon leaving the post office, Brennan turned his automobile right onto a street in front of Thatcher, and a disagreement began, which continued until the cars stopped and a fight took place in the parking lot of a jewelry store. After this incident, which occurred about 5:45 p.m., Brennan returned to his motel. For purposes of this motion, Mead Johnson has admitted that Brennan instigated the altercation without provocation from the plaintiff.

The paper work which Brennan mailed consisted of physician call cards and a sample inventory. The parties disagree as to whether Brennan was in fact *required* to mail these papers. Mead Johnson claims that these items could have been mailed at some other time and/or place, whereas the plaintiff asserts that Brennan was required by Mead Johnson to mail the call cards daily. The court is of the opinion that this is immaterial since, whether required or not, Brennan did mail the papers and, in doing so, was performing his work as a Mead Johnson sales representative.

When Brennan left the post office, he was returning to his hotel where he had planned to make dinner arrangements with a doctor friend. As such social interaction with physicians is encouraged by Mead Johnson, it may be reasonably inferred that Brennan was returning to the hotel to perform business-related activities. Nevertheless, the parties agree that while Brennan was in Jackson, he was not required by Mead Johnson to follow any specific schedule or agenda. Importantly, it is also agreed between the parties that nothing about Brennan's altercation promoted the sale of pharmaceuticals for Mead Johnson.

It is clear in Mississippi that an employer may be held liable for the intentional acts of its employees if the employer either authorized the act prior to or ratified the act after its commission, or the act was committed within the scope of employment. Since there is nothing to indicate that Mead Johnson either authorized or ratified Brennan's intentional assault and battery upon Thatcher, Brennan must have been acting within the scope of his employment in order for Mead Johnson to be held liable.

In *Loper v. Yazoo and M.V.R. Co.*, 145 So. 743 (Miss. 1933), the Mississippi Supreme Court recognized that the phrase "scope of employment" which is used to determine an employer's liability for the acts of its employees has no fixed legal or technical meaning. Instead, the court has enunciated various tests for determining whether particular conduct of an employee is within the scope of employment. These tests include, for example,

(1) Whether the employee's conduct is "so unlike that authorized that it is substantially different";

(2) Whether the act complained of is committed in the prosecution of the employer's business and within the scope of the employee's authority;

(3) Whether such act is in the furtherance of the business of the master and as an incident to the performance of the duties of the character or kind which he was employed to perform; and

(4) Whether the act was done in the course of and as a means of accomplishing the purposes of the employment and, therefore, in furtherance of the master's business.

These "tests" provide some guidance, but often a fine line separates those acts which are within and those which are without the scope of employment. It has been noted that

> The most difficult questions arise where the servant, for strictly personal reasons and not in furtherance of his employment, loses his temper and attacks the plaintiff in a quarrel which arises out of the employment — as where, for example, a truck driver collides with the plaintiff, and an altercation follows. Here, unless some non-delegable duty can be found, the older rule denied recovery, and this is still the holding of the majority of the decisions. There has been a tendency in the later cases, however, to allow recovery on the ground that the employment has provided a peculiar opportunity and even incentive for such loss of temper[.]

Prosser and Keeton, The Law of Torts, 465-66 (5th ed. 1984).

... In the instant case, Brennan was authorized, expected, and even required to drive an automobile as part of his employment. However, he was not authorized to assault other persons, and there is nothing in the previous relationship between Brennan and Mead Johnson which would indicate that such conduct was acceptable. Moreover, the act is not one which is commonly performed by Mead Johnson sales personnel, nor can it be said to be a "normal" method of selling, or similar to acts which Brennan was authorized to perform. The most that can be said is that the assault was within the "time and place" of employment. The "purpose" of the assault was not to further any of Mead Johnson's interests but, rather, was intended to satisfy Brennan's purely personal objectives....

Negligent Hiring

The plaintiff has also asserted a claim against Mead Johnson on the basis of negligent hiring. He contends that Mead Johnson either knew or should have known of Brennan's alleged propensity for violence but nevertheless employed Brennan, placed him in contact with residents of Hinds County and directed him to travel the streets of Jackson for the purpose of selling pharmaceutical products "even though he has violent and malicious personality traits."

... [T]he court concludes that in this case plaintiff must prove that (1) Brennan had a propensity for violence, (2) Mead Johnson knew or should have known of such propensity, and (3) Mead Johnson, in disregard for the rights of those persons with whom Brennan could reasonably be expected to come into contact, hired Brennan, either negligently or with callous disregard for the rights of such persons.

... The plaintiff herein has failed to demonstrate any propensity for, or likelihood of, violence on the part of Brennan and has further failed to produce sufficient evidence that Mead Johnson knew, or had reason to know, of any such propensity for violence. The only evidence of actual violent conduct by Brennan is the affray between him and the plaintiff which is the subject of this action. Plaintiff has directed the court's attention to no other incident, either preceding or following his being hired by Mead Johnson, which would tend to show that Brennan was a violent or vicious individual. Instead, plaintiff asserts that the results of a personality inventory test and an adaptability test taken by Brennan reveal his propensity for violence.

These tests were administered to Brennan by Mead Johnson personnel prior to his being hired in February 1982. An evaluation of the test results led Mead Johnson's personnel employees to the following conclusion:

> Bert has the potential to be a moody, opinionated and headstrong and early in his life might even have been considered spoiled or immature
> .... Bert is a person of high aggression....

Overall profile appears to be significantly different from the temperament profile of most sales candidates we see. It appears to reflect a young person undergoing a great deal of emotional and personal stress and turmoil.

Plaintiff contends on the sole basis of this evaluation that Brennan, as a person of "high aggression," did indeed have a propensity for violence, and that Mead Johnson had knowledge of this propensity as a result of its own analysis of Brennan's personality inventory tests.

The plaintiff has supplied the court with an analysis of the test results by a clinical psychologist, J. Donald Matherne, Ph.D. Dr. Matherne states that upon review of the information provided him, it is "quite apparent that ... Wilbert Brennan, manifests evidence of very serious emotional and personality instability." He further states that the "test findings clearly indicate an individual lacking in self-control, socialization skills and responsibility," and that Mead Johnson apparently hired Wilbert Brennan with full knowledge of his propensity for aggression as well as his propensity for violent behavior. He further opines that Wilbert Brennan should not have been employed by Mead Johnson as a pharmaceutical sales representative since "one would predict with a high degree of clinical probability that this individual would have manifested, within a period of time, significant adjustment problems, work inefficiency and problems involving self control." The court is of the opinion that the test results alone did not provide a sufficient basis to put Mead Johnson on notice of any purported violent tendencies of Brennan. While Brennan may have been accurately evaluated as a person of "high aggression," the term "aggression" is not synonymous with "violent."

The tests in question were administered in late 1981, and the evaluation by Mead Johnson personnel was rendered in January 1982. The altercation between Thatcher and Brennan did not occur until May 1984, after Brennan was hired, and during this two-year period there is no evidence that Brennan demonstrated any violent behavior whatsoever. One who is volatile and malicious and who has a propensity for violence would presumably have manifested such aberrant traits over a two-year period. Yet, during the interim between the time that Brennan was hired and the date of the altercation with Thatcher, there were no incidents of violent behavior. Therefore, even assuming Mead Johnson, at the time it hired Brennan, could have reasonably concluded on the basis of the tests that Brennan had a potential for violence, the total lack of evidence of any violent conduct by Brennan over the succeeding two years certainly belies any claim of negligent hiring under the circumstances of this case.

Accordingly, it is ordered that the motion for summary judgment of defendant Mead Johnson is granted.

NOTES

Important Points

1. *Theories of Employer Liability.* Under the doctrine of *respondeat superior*, employers are held strictly liable for the torts of employees acting within the scope of their duties. *Respondeat superior* does not usually apply when an employee assaults a third person or otherwise acts beyond the scope of his duties. In such a case, the injured third party must show that the actions of the employer itself make it liable for the injury. Usually this is attempted by showing that the employer was negligent in hiring, training, or retaining the employee. Thus, negligent hiring claims usually arise when an employee assaults some third party.

2. *Criminal Record of Employees.* The fact situation in the Mead Johnson case (negligent processing of the company's internal information) is relatively rare. A more common negligent hiring claim is that the employer did not sufficiently check references or the background of an applicant, particularly whether the applicant had a criminal record that might indicate a likelihood to assault third parties. In *Malorney v. B&L Motor Freight, Inc.*, 496 N.E.2d 1086 (Ill. App. Ct. 1986), for example, a hitchhiker raped by a truck driver survived a summary judgment motion and was allowed to proceed to trial on the claim that the company had hired the truck driver despite the fact that he had been convicted of violent sex crimes.

Malorney

What should the company in *B&L Motor Freight* have done? If it had asked the rapist's former employer, would that employer have told the truth? If the former employer had lied or given a bland reference, could the rape victim sue it as well? *See Randi W. v. Muroc Joint Unified School District*, 929 P.2d 582 (Cal. 1997) (employers giving good references with affirmative misrepresentations can be liable to third parties).

3. *Negligent Failure to Test.* One response of employers to cases like *Thatcher* is not to give personality tests. But the failure to test employees can lead to lawsuits as well. In *Southern Bell Telephone & Telegraph Co. v. Sharara*, 302 S.E.2d 129 (Ga. Ct. App. 1983), a telephone company employee physically attacked a woman after installing a phone in her home. The victim sued Southern Bell for negligence in hiring or retaining the attacker. She argued that the company should have given periodic psychological tests to employees who enter customers' homes. The trial court agreed that this claim could survive summary judgment, but the court of appeals reversed. In concurrence, Judge Deen wrote:

Southern Bell Telephone

> While concurring fully with the majority opinion, it might be added the better practice, in cases as here, would be for installer-repairman employees who are required to enter into homes of customers be more closely checked, observed, screened and interviewed by employers as to any outward manifestation of dangerous propensities relating to aggression or violence. We know of no requirement of compulsory psychological periodic blanket testing and counseling of all of one's employees. In fact, were this to be done by employers, without the employees' consent, serious First

Amendment individual rights of privacy and other employee constitutional and civil rights might be at issue.

Even an owner of a dog is not liable for an injury to another unless knowledge of prior propensities or a penchant to bite or attack by the dog exists. The same type theory or a form of negligent entrustment obtains here with respect to hiring or retaining an employee without any prior knowledge of overaggressiveness, violent or criminal propensities or tendencies. Unless there exists present knowledge by the employer (owner) of prior propensities, aggression and violence (to bite), there can be no liability.

In psychological interviews seeking to pinpoint the origin and sources of negative, antisocial, violent propensities of aggression of humans, most alleged experts usually concentrate in only two areas: Nature (instinctivism — heredity — innateness) or Nurture (behaviorism — environment — society). While nature-nurture norms may well influence what happens to us, the criminal law of Georgia recognizes a third area it considers of prime importance, that is, a consideration of and the presumption of voluntary free will and the resulting responsibility of paying the penalty for our wrongful criminal acts committed. Many times psychological testing by alleged experts obscures and ignores any reference to the latter area since the voluntary free will of humans is considered and thought by many as unpredictable and, therefore, empirically unscientific. The law presumes, on the other hand, that all humans know right from wrong, as to their acts committed; therefore, the latter area of voluntary will under our criminal code needs to be again emphasized, that the actor is to blame, in all psychological counseling as to aggression, and the former two nature-nurture norms need to be deemphasized, as they suggest someone else is to blame other than the actor. Concentrating only on nature and nurture norms in psychological testing is counter productive to encouraging all citizens in upholding restrictions that certain conduct is wrong as set forth in our juvenile and criminal code and in the reduction of criminal acts of violence and aggression.

Id. at 132-33.

4. *Negligent Hiring in the Public Sector.* After a high-speed car chase, Jill Brown was caught and thrown to the ground by a deputy sheriff, suffering injuries that required four knee operations. The deputy sheriff was the great-nephew of the sheriff, and had a known propensity for violence. Brown sued the county under 42 U.S.C. § 1983, claiming that the inadequate hiring standards amounted to deliberate indifference to her constitutional right against excessive violence by law enforcement officials. The Fifth Circuit upheld a $872,500 jury verdict for Brown, but the Supreme Court reversed in a 5-4 decision. *Board of County Comm'rs v. Brown*, 117 S. Ct. 1382 (1997). Justice O'Connor, writing for the majority, declared that the evidence was insufficient to go to the jury because the causal connection between the negligence and the harm was too weak: The use of excessive force was not a "plainly obvious" consequence of the decision to hire, even though the officer was an extremely poor deputy candidate.

D. EMPLOYER REFERENCES — DEFAMATION AND OTHER TORTS

In addition to claims of improper intrusion into one's private sphere, another category of privacy claims addresses the public disclosure of private facts. In the employment context, such claims often arise when personnel records are shown to others. For example, in *Bratt v. IBM Corp.*, 785 F.2d 352 (1st Cir. 1986), a supervisor recommended that an employee see a psychiatrist under contract with IBM. The psychiatrist later discussed her examination with several IBM managers. Balancing "the employer's legitimate business interest in disseminating the information against the nature and substantiality of the intrusion," the court upheld the employee's privacy claim.

A harsher view was taken in *Eddy v. Brown*, 715 P.2d 74 (Okla. 1986). There, the court rejected a privacy claim when a supervisor had told a "limited number" of co-workers that Eddy had been seeing a psychiatrist. The court rejected an intrusion upon privacy claim because the psychiatric visits were part of Eddy's employment medical records, and "hence of legitimate concern to his supervisor." The court rejected a claim of unreasonable publicity of private facts because only a small group of co-workers were made privy to Eddy's private affairs, while the tort requires disclosure to the general public.

Closely related to concerns of public disclosure of private facts is the tort of defamation. Employees often bring defamation claims when the reasons for a firing are made public. As the following cases illustrate, this complicated tort has common law roots that have been modified in part by constitutional law. THE RESTATEMENT (SECOND) OF TORTS § 558 lays out the standard requirements for defamation:

> To create liability for defamation there must be:
>
> (a) a false and defamatory statement concerning another;
> (b) an unprivileged publication to a third party;
> (c) fault amounting at least to negligence on the part of the publisher; and
> (d) either actionability of the statement irrespective of special harm or the existence of special harm caused by the publication.

ELBESHBESHY v. FRANKLIN INSTITUTE

United States District Court, E.D. Pennsylvania

618 F. Supp. 170 (1985)

BECHTLE, DISTRICT JUDGE.

Presently before the court is the motion for partial summary judgment of defendant The Franklin Institute. For the reasons stated herein, defendant's motion will be denied.

Plaintiff was employed by defendant in its nuclear structural mechanics unit from January 3, 1984 to April 17, 1984. Plaintiff's job description involved a technical aspect of drafting proposals after plaintiff reviewed the plans for nuclear power plants submitted by architects and engineers to the Nuclear Regulatory Commission, and a marketing aspect of submitting the proposals to the Nuclear Regulatory Commission. Plaintiff drafted two proposals, one concerning "overcooling transient" and one concerning "hydrogen blanketing." Plaintiff's proposals were reviewed by plaintiff's supervisor, Dr. Vu Con ("Dr. Con") and by Dr. Con's supervisor, Dr. Salvatore Carfagno ("Dr. Carfagno"). Dr. Con believed that the proposals contained substantive shortcomings. Plaintiff did not agree with Dr. Con's assessment. Dr. Carfagno did not express an opinion with respect to the substantive quality of plaintiff's work, but he did decide that the working relationship between Dr. Con and plaintiff was not pleasant.

On April 17, 1984, defendant terminated plaintiff's employment. The reason given for the termination in plaintiff's employment record was plaintiff's "lack of cooperation."...

Defendant argues first that its statement was not defamatory. A defamatory statement is one which tends "to harm the reputation of another as to lower him in the estimation of the community or to deter third persons from associating or dealing with him." *Thomas M. Merton Center v. Rockwell Int'l Corp.*, 442 A.2d 213 (Pa. 1981), *cert. denied*, 457 U.S. 1134 (1982), citing Restatement (Second) of Torts § 559 (1977).

In the circumstances of the instant case, at this stage of the proceedings, the court believes that the assertion in plaintiff's employment record that plaintiff was terminated for "lack of cooperation" could be defamatory. It is not unreasonable that the assertion, standing alone, might lead members of the community and third persons to reasonably believe that plaintiff's nature was irremediably insubordinate, obnoxious, and antagonistic. Such a conclusion is especially likely where plaintiff was terminated after only three and a half months of employment. Additionally, the assertion that plaintiff was terminated because plaintiff lacked cooperation is quite different from an assertion that plaintiff was terminated due to a personality conflict between plaintiff and Dr. Con, or because he was not qualified to perform the work for which he was employed. It is one thing to say that plaintiff could not fit into the organization of the defendant, but it is very different to say that plaintiff cannot get along with management and disrupts the harmony of the workplace. Persons who are said to be disruptive, insubordinate, obnoxious, and antagonistic are persons with whom third persons tend not to want to deal or associate and whom members of the community tend to hold in low esteem.

Second, defendant argues that the statement that the reason behind plaintiff's termination was "lack of cooperation" was not published. Publication occurs, however, when the defamer communicates the statement to one other person, even if that one other person is the defamer's agent. Restatement (Second) of

Torts § 577, comment c (1977). Since plaintiff presented evidence that the statement was communicated to Dr. Con, Dr. Carfagno, and members of defendant's personnel department, the publication element may be satisfied here.

Third, defendant argues that plaintiff's claim for defamation is barred by defendant's qualified privilege to evaluate the job performance of its employees. Plaintiff, however, presented some evidence that plaintiff was terminated for reasons of professional jealousy. Accordingly, the court holds that a genuine issue as to a material fact exists here as to whether defendant acted with malice or abused its privilege....

In conclusion, the court will deny defendant's motion for partial summary judgment.

NOTES

1. *Libel and Slander.* Traditionally, slander is oral defamation and libel is written defamation. Employers are often charged with both. The importance of the common law distinction is that plaintiffs cannot recover for slander without proving special damages, unless the statement is slander per se. In general, special damages are not needed to support a libel claim. Some states, however, further distinguish between libel per se, where the statement is defamatory on its face, and libel per quod, where the factfinder must look to facts beyond the statement itself to determine if it is defamatory. In these states, a libel per quod claim also requires a showing of special damages. Special damages are pecuniary losses directly caused by the reaction of others to the defamatory statement.

In practice, these distinctions are less important in the employment context than in other areas for two reasons. First, defamed employees often can show special damages, if the defamation causes them to lose a job opportunity. Second, oral statements damaging to one's business, trade, or profession are considered slander per se, for which recovery is possible without proving special damages. RESTATEMENT (SECOND) OF TORTS § 573 comment b explicitly declares that this slander per se rule "is equally applicable to artisans, mechanics and workmen generally, whether skilled or unskilled."

2. *Defamatory Acts.* Suppose an employer, eager to avoid a defamation claim, gives no explanation when firing an employee. Might this in itself be defamatory, in that it tends to harm the employee's reputation? In *Tyler v. Macks Stores*, 272 S.E.2d 633 (S.C. 1980), an employee and his manager were fired following a polygraph test. The court held that these acts supported a defamation claim sufficient to reach the jury, because they might have given "fellow employees and others the feeling that he had been discharged for some wrongful activity." *Accord, Berg v. Consolidated Freightways*, 421 A.2d 831 (Pa. Super. Ct. 1980) (firing employee in midst of criminal investigation into theft at work valid basis for slander suit).

3. *Publication*. *Elbeshbeshy* applies the majority rule that the publication element of defamation is satisfied even if the statement never goes outside the company, as long as a third person hears or reads it. *Accord Luttrell v. United Tel. Sys.*, 683 P.2d 1292 (Kan. Ct. App. 1984) (employer sufficiently protected by qualified privilege). Several courts have ruled, however, that intracorporate defamation is simply the corporation talking to itself and cannot be a publication. *See, e.g., Monahan v. Sims*, 294 S.E.2d 548 (Ga. Ct. App. 1982).

As with other acts of its agents, a corporation is liable for the defamatory statements of its employees made while acting within the scope of their authority. In *Tacket v. General Motors Corp.*, 836 F.2d 1042 (7th Cir. 1987) (applying Indiana law) (per Easterbrook, J.), an unknown person painted a small sign saying "TACKET TACKET WHAT A RACKET" on a factory wall. The sign was possibly defamatory because it reinforced rumors that Tacket, the night superintendent of the plant, had improperly subcontracted work to himself. The company painted over the sign after seven or eight months. The court, following RESTATEMENT § 577(2), held that a reasonable juror could conclude that the company intentionally and unreasonably failed to remove the sign and thereby published a defamatory statement. It therefore reversed a directed verdict for the employer.

On remand, Tacket prevailed at trial and was awarded $100,000 in damages. The judgment was reversed on appeal because Tacket had shown only psychological injury, and not the pecuniary damages required under Indiana defamation law. *Tacket v. General Motors Corp.*, 937 F.2d 1201 (7th Cir. 1991).

4. *Self-Publication*. Suppose a personnel director falsely fires an employee for gross insubordination, but tells no one other than the fired employee of the reason. Still, it is foreseeable that prospective employers will ask the employee why he was discharged, and he will be compelled to lie or publish the defamation. Should the employee have a defamation claim against the employer? *See Lewis v. Equitable Life Assur. Soc'y*, 389 N.W.2d 876 (Minn. 1986) (recognizing doctrine of compelled self-publication on these facts).

The self-publication doctrine has had a mixed reception by courts and legislatures. In *Olivieri v. Rodriguez*, 122 F.3d 406 (7th Cir. 1997), a probationary police officer was discharged without a hearing for sexual harassment. He alleged harm even though there was no evidence the reason for the discharge was disclosed to anyone other than the plaintiff:

> The doctrine [of compelled self-defamation] is inconsistent with the fundamental principle of mitigation of damages.... The principle of self-defamation ... would encourage Olivieri to apply for a job to every police force in the nation, in order to magnify his damages; and to blurt out to each of them the ground of this discharge in the most lurid terms, to the same end.

Id. at 408-09.

In the legislatures, a 1987 Minnesota statute, enacted in response to *Lewis*, requires employers to provide a written, truthful reason for the termination at the employee's request, and prohibits a defamation action based on this statement. MINN. STAT. ANN. § 181.933. Colorado also enacted a statute in response to a case recognizing the doctrine of compelled self-publication; the statute eliminated the doctrine altogether. *See Churchey v. Adolph Coors Co.*, 759 P.2d 1336 (Colo. 1988); COLO. REV. STAT. ANN. § 13-25-125.5 (effective 1989). *See generally* Markita D. Cooper, *Between a Rock and a Hard Case: Time for a New Doctrine of Compelled Self-Publication*, 72 NOTRE DAME L. REV. 373 (1997) (urging a restructured claim that would require plaintiffs to show egregious employer conduct, an inquiry by a prospective employer, and efforts by plaintiff to mitigate damages by explaining the circumstances of the termination).

ZINDA v. LOUISIANA PACIFIC CORP.

Supreme Court of Wisconsin

440 N.W.2d 548 (1989)

BABLITCH, JUSTICE.

Allan D. "Rick" Zinda (Zinda) brought both a defamation and invasion of privacy action against his former employer, Louisiana Pacific Corporation (Louisiana Pacific), based on a statement concerning his discharge which was published in a company newsletter....

The essential facts are undisputed. Approximately two years prior to his employment with Louisiana Pacific, Zinda was injured as a result of falling through "waferboard" on the roof of a garage he was constructing at his home. Zinda sustained numerous injuries, including a broken rib, a broken bone in the back, and a broken heel.

In connection with his application for employment with Louisiana Pacific in 1983, Zinda completed a standard application form as well as a medical history form. In the "personal health history" portion of the medical form, Zinda provided the following answers:

> Upper Back Trouble — No.
> Middle Back Trouble — No.
> Low Back Trouble — No.
> Back Injury or Disability — No
> Fracture or Broken Bone — No.
> Back X-ray — No.

In explaining a "yes" answer regarding previous hospitalizations and surgery, Zinda wrote: "[W]hen I was 15 years old for Hay Fever, Tonsil, Appendits [*sic*], and fall off roof." Later, during a pre-employment interview, Zinda clarified that he had previously fallen off a roof and broken some bones including his ribs and a heel, but that he had no present problems. Zinda signed both forms acknowledging that all answers were true and that any false statements or misrepresentations would result in immediate discharge, regardless of when such facts were discovered.

Approximately one year later, Zinda filed a products liability action against Louisiana Pacific, alleging that it negligently manufactured the "waferboard" involved in his fall off the roof. The complaint asserted that Zinda had suffered permanent disabilities as a result of the injuries, and sought substantial compensatory and punitive damages.

The complaint was served on the personnel manager of the Louisiana Pacific plant who compared the allegations against the answers Zinda gave on his application forms. Apparently concluding that Zinda had intentionally withheld adverse information concerning his physical condition, the personnel manager notified Zinda that his employment was suspended pending an investigation into possible fraud regarding his employment forms. Approximately three weeks later, Louisiana Pacific terminated Zinda's employment.

Subsequently, Louisiana Pacific published a notice regarding Zinda's termination on the seventh page of the plant newspaper, the "Waferboard Press," under the following heading:

COMINGS AND GOINGS

5/1/84	Death	Leland Thysen	
5/10/84	Voluntary Quit	Jeff Aiken	Back to Railroad
5/14/84	Hire	Paul Lueck	Electrician
5/25/84	Terminate	Al Christner	Falsification of Emp. forms
5/27/84	Hire	Bill Nordback	A crew
5/29/84	Hire	Dennis Voight	B crew
5/29/84	Terminate	Larry Radzak	Theft
5/29/84	Terminate	Al Zinda	Falsification of Emp. forms
5/31/84	Hire	Mike Hoskins	Panel Saw
5/31/84	Voluntary Quit	Mike Laronge	Personal reasons
5/31/84	Hire	Jeff Walker	C crew

Approximately 160 copies of the newsletter were distributed to employees by placement in the lunchroom. Employees were not restricted from taking the newsletter home, and employees regularly took the newsletters out of the workplace. Testimony indicates that a copy reached the local hospital, where Zinda's wife worked, and two of her co-workers read the reference to Zinda's termination.

Zinda amended his complaint to include allegations of defamation, invasion of privacy, and wrongful discharge. Louisiana Pacific answered, raising conditional privilege as a defense, asserting that it had no liability for good faith communications to employees concerning the reasons for the discharge of another employee.

The circuit court granted summary judgment dismissing Zinda's claim for wrongful discharge. Zinda then voluntarily dismissed the products liability

claim. The defamation and invasion of privacy claims were tried to a jury....
Regarding the defamation and invasion of privacy claims, the trial court refused
without explanation to submit Louisiana Pacific's requested instruction on conditional privilege.

The jury returned a verdict awarding $50,000.00 for defamation as well as
$50,000.00 for invasion of privacy. The trial court denied all post verdict
motions and granted judgment on the verdict....

We turn first to the issue of liability for defamation. We conclude that the
information published in the company newsletter was conditionally privileged as
a communication of common interest concerning the employer-employee relationship. We further conclude that although the privilege may be lost if abused, a
jury question was presented in this case as to whether the information was
excessively published.

A communication is defamatory if it tends to harm the reputation of another so
as to lower him in the estimation of the community or deter third persons from
associating or dealing with him. If the statements are capable of a nondefamatory
as well as a defamatory meaning, then a jury question is presented as to how the
statement was understood by its recipients.

However, not all defamations are actionable. Some defamations fall within a
class of conduct which the law terms privileged. The defense of privilege has
developed under the public policy that certain conduct which would otherwise be
actionable may escape liability because the defendant is acting in furtherance of
some interest of societal importance, which is entitled to protection even at the
expense of uncompensated harm to the plaintiff.

Privileged defamations may be either absolute or conditional. Absolute privileges give complete protection without any inquiry into the defendant's motives.
This privilege has been extended to judicial officers, legislative proceedings, and
to certain governmental executive officers.

The arguments in this case, however, are concerned only with conditional
privilege. In the area of conditional privilege, we have endorsed the language of
the Restatement of Torts. The Restatement recognizes the existence of a conditional privilege in a number of different situations. Among these are statements
made on a subject matter in which the person making the statement and the person to whom it is made have a legitimate common interest.

Section 596 of the Restatement 2d of Torts defines the "common interest"
privilege:

> An occasion makes a publication conditionally privileged if the circum-
> stances lead any one of several persons having a common interest in a par-
> ticular subject matter correctly or reasonably to believe that there is infor-
> mation that another sharing the common interest is entitled to know.

The common interest privilege is based on the policy that one is entitled to
learn from his associates what is being done in a matter in which he or she has an
interest in common. Thus, defamatory statements are privileged which are made

in furtherance of common property, business, or professional interests. The Restatement extends such privilege to "partners, fellow officers of a corporation for profit, fellow shareholders, and fellow servants...." *See id.*, Comment d. at 597.

The common interest privilege is particularly germane to the employer-employee relationship. We have applied a conditional privilege to various communications between employers and persons having a common interest in the employee's conduct. For instance, in *Hett v. Ploetz*, 121 N.W.2d 270 (Wis. 1963), a defamatory letter of reference from an ex-employer to a prospective employer was held to be entitled to a conditional privilege. We stated that the prospective employer has an interest in receiving information concerning the character and qualifications of the former employee, and the ex-employer has an interest in giving such information in good faith to insure that he may receive an honest evaluation when he hires new employees.

Similarly, in *Johnson v. Rudolph Wurlitzer Co.*, 222 N.W. 451, 454 (Wis. 1928), we held that a conditional privilege applied to defamatory statements by a store manager to other employees in the office about an alleged embezzlement involving a fellow employee. We stated that because of their employment, the employees had a common interest in discovering the source of the shortage that was being investigated.

We conclude that the common interest privilege attaches to the employer-employee relationship in this case. Employees have a legitimate interest in knowing the reasons a fellow employee was discharged. Conversely, an employer has an interest in maintaining morale and quieting rumors which may disrupt business. Here, Louisiana Pacific's personnel manager testified that at the time of Zinda's termination, the plant had been going through a rather extensive retooling and reprocessing. During that time, normal crews had been broken apart and there were prevailing rumors that Louisiana Pacific was laying off employees. The company believed for this reason that it would be the best policy to immediately suppress rumors by being completely honest concerning employees who were no longer with the company.

Moreover, we conclude that truthfulness and integrity in the employment application process is an important common interest. An employer who asks questions such as those involved here is entitled to receive an honest answer, and reasonable communication in a plant newsletter concerning terminations for misrepresentations discourages other employees from engaging in similar conduct. In addition, the employees have an interest in knowing how the rules are enforced, and the type of conduct that may result in their discharge from employment. Accordingly, Louisiana Pacific's communication to its employees concerning Zinda's discharge was entitled to a conditional privilege.

However, conditional privilege is not absolute and may be forfeited if the privilege is abused. The Restatement 2d of Torts lists five conditions which may constitute an abuse of the privilege, and the occurrence of any one causes the loss of the privilege. The privilege may be abused: (1) because of the defendant's knowledge or reckless disregard as to the falsity of the defamatory matter; (2) because the defamatory matter is published for some purpose other than that for which the particular privilege is given; (3) because the publication is made to some person not reasonably believed to be necessary for the accomplishment of the purpose of the particular privilege; (4) because the publication includes defamatory matter not reasonably believed to be necessary to accomplish the purpose for which the occasion is privileged; or (5) the publication includes unprivileged matter as well as privileged matter.

Zinda insists that any privilege which may have existed in this case was abused as a matter of law by excessive publication under condition (3). Essentially, Zinda argues that Louisiana Pacific made no attempt to restrict the publication to persons with a common interest in his termination. Zinda alludes to testimony elicited on cross-examination which purportedly indicates that the personnel manager had knowledge that employees routinely took the newsletters home. Furthermore, Zinda asserts that the content of the newsletter encouraged its removal from the plant.

We disagree that Louisiana Pacific abused its privilege as a matter of law. The question whether a conditional privilege has been abused is a factual question for the jury, unless the facts are such that only one conclusion can be reasonably drawn. Restatement 2d, Torts, sec. 619 (2), Comment b. at 316.

Contrary to Zinda's insistence, the evidence alluded to does not necessarily lead to the conclusion that Louisiana Pacific excessively published the statement concerning Zinda's discharge. Once it is determined by the court that the defamatory communication was made on an occasion of conditional privilege, the burden shifts to the plaintiff to affirmatively prove abuse. Here, despite allegations of widespread distribution throughout the community, Zinda's proof at trial was limited to the testimony of two unprivileged women who read the reference to Zinda's termination at the hospital where his wife worked.

An employer is entitled to use a method of publication that involves an incidental communication to persons not within the scope of the privilege. Often the only practical means of communicating defamatory information involves a probability or even a certainty that it will reach persons whose knowledge of it is of no value in accomplishing the purpose for which the privilege is given. In *Walters* [*v. Sentinel Co.*, 169 N.W. 564 (Wis. 1918)], this court stated that if "a newspaper, published primarily for a given constituency, such as county or state, church or lodge, have a small circulation outside such constituency, it is not deprived of its privilege in the discussion of matters of concern to its constituency because of such incidental outside circulation."

As previously discussed, Louisiana Pacific had an interest in informing each and every one of its employees about the subject of Zinda's discharge.[2] We

---

[2] To the extent that Zinda implies that the allegedly defamatory matter was indiscriminately taken home by the employees and communicated to various family members, we agree with courts

cannot as a matter of law consider the communication in this case an unreasonable means to accomplish this purpose. Testimony indicates that the company attempted to correlate the number of copies printed to the number of employees in the plant. These copies were circulated only in the lunchroom, over the course of several days, so that every workshift would have an opportunity to read the newsletter. Thus, despite the company's alleged knowledge that employees often took the newsletter home, a jury could conclude that the great bulk of its readers had a direct and legitimate interest in the information regarding Zinda's termination, and that the outside communication was reasonably believed to be necessary to communicate the privileged information. Accordingly, the privilege was not abused as a matter of law, and it was error to refuse the requested instruction.

[The court then reversed and remanded the privacy judgment, holding that a claim for public disclosure of private facts, like a defamation claim, had a defense of conditional privilege.]

NOTE

Absolute Privilege. Parties and witnesses to judicial proceedings are absolutely privileged to publish defamatory statements, even if with malice they knowingly say something false. *See* RESTATEMENT (SECOND) OF TORTS §§ 587, 588. Several states have extended the privilege to administrative proceedings, including unemployment compensation hearings. In those states, an employer can testify at an unemployment compensation hearing about the reason for discharge without fear of a defamation suit. *See Volte v. First Fed. Sav. & Loan Ass'n*, 422 N.W.2d 834 (S.D. 1988).

SIGAL CONSTRUCTION CORP. v. STANBURY

District of Columbia Court of Appeals
586 A.2d 1204 (1991)

Before FERREN, BELSON, and FARRELL, ASSOCIATE JUDGES.

FERREN, ASSOCIATE JUDGE:
In this defamation case, a jury awarded appellee, Kenneth S. Stanbury, $370,440 against his former employer, appellant Sigal Construction Corporation. The jury found that a Sigal project manager, Paul Littman, had slandered Stanbury while giving an employment reference to another construction company after Sigal had terminated Stanbury's employment. The trial court denied Sigal's motion for judgment notwithstanding the verdict or for a new trial. The court, however, granted a remittitur ordering Stanbury to accept $250,000 or a new trial

---

of other jurisdictions which have held that defamatory communications made to family members are ordinarily subject to a conditional privilege.

for damages. Stanbury accepted the $250,000. Sigal appeals the trial court's denial of its motion for judgment notwithstanding the verdict ....

Stanbury worked as a project manager for Sigal from May 1984 to June 1985. According to Sigal's personnel manager, Pamela Heiber, Sigal terminated Stanbury's employment because he "was not doing his job correctly." Sigal, however, told Stanbury he was let go for "lack of work or reduction in work." According to Heiber, "[w]e felt sympathy for Ken because of his age in life" (he was 63 when Sigal terminated his employment). Stanbury contacted Ray Stevens, a previous employer and Regional Manager at Daniel Construction, to find out whether any work was available. Some time later, Stevens called Stanbury about employment as a project manager on the Pentagon City project. Stanbury was eventually offered the job subject to approval by the owner of the project, Lincoln Properties.

William Janes, a Lincoln Properties general partner, had responsibility for investigating Stanbury's employment references. Janes called David Orr, a former Sigal project executive, who suggested that Janes contact Paul Littman, a current Sigal project executive. Janes did so, and Littman later memorialized the conversation:

> [Janes] claimed David [Orr] had told him not to hire Ken [Stanbury] and asked me what I thought. I told him.
> 1) Ken seemed detail oriented to the point of losing sight of the big picture.
> 2) He had a lot of knowledge and experience on big jobs.
> 3) With a large staff might be a very competent P.M. [project manager].
> 4) Obviously he no longer worked for us and that might say enough.
> These paraphrase what I said nearly word for word.

At trial, Littman acknowledged and Stanbury confirmed that Littman had made these statements without having supervised, evaluated, read an evaluation of, or even worked with Stanbury (other than seeing Stanbury in the halls at the office). According to them both, their contact was entirely casual. More specifically, Stanbury testified without contradiction that he had talked to Littman only once during Stanbury's fourteen months with Sigal, and that this conversation was a general discussion about Stanbury's previous job. According to Littman, in evaluating Stanbury for Janes he relied entirely on the "general impression [he] had developed" from "hearing people talk about [Stanbury's] work at the job," perhaps at "casual luncheons" or "project executive meetings" or "over a beer on a Friday afternoon." Littman did nothing to verify the second-hand knowledge he had acquired about Stanbury. At trial, he could recall no facts or work-related incidents that would support the impressions he reported to Janes. When asked where his information about one of Stanbury's projects came from, Littman testified that "[t]here aren't any real specific instances I can point to. I think it was a general opinion I had just developed in the year or two [Stanbury] had been there." Littman thought that his opinion "possibly" came from "hearing people talk about [Stanbury's] work or job."

In contrast with Littman's acknowledgments at trial that his information about Stanbury was limited to vague hearsay, Janes testified at trial that Littman appeared to have knowledge of Stanbury's performance — indeed, that Littman told Janes he had worked with Stanbury on a project. Janes further testified that he could not recall whether Littman had acknowledged never supervising or seeing an evaluation of Stanbury. Littman's trial testimony substantially corroborated Janes' account of his interaction with Littman. Littman testified that Janes knew Littman was a project executive (who would supervise a project manager), that Stanbury was a project manager, and that Littman did not tell Janes he had never supervised, worked with, evaluated, or read an evaluation of Stanbury even though Littman knew Janes wanted to speak with someone who had "interact[ed]" with Stanbury. Littman also testified that, although he lacked explicit authority from Sigal to provide employment references, it was common in the construction industry for someone in his position to do so. Although the impact of Littman's statements on Janes was disputed at trial, Daniel Construction did not hire Stanbury for the Pentagon City project or for any other project. According to Stanbury, Stevens told him that Daniel Construction had not hired him because Lincoln Properties would not approve him. Stanbury further testified that, according to Stevens, Lincoln Properties (presumably Janes) had made "serious negative comments" about Stanbury and that Daniel Construction would have hired him but for Lincoln Properties' disapproval. Stanbury concluded, after further contacts, that Daniel Construction would not consider him for other projects because of Lincoln Properties' negative impression attributable to Littman's comments....

Sigal first challenges the trial court's refusal to grant a judgment n.o.v. on the ground that the court erroneously characterized Littman's statements as purported facts, not opinions. This argument is attributable to *Gertz v. Robert Welch, Inc.*, 418 U.S. 323 (1974), where the Supreme Court stated in dictum:

> Under the First Amendment there is no such thing as a false idea. However pernicious an opinion may seem, we depend for its correction not on the conscience of judges and juries but on the competition of other ideas. But there is no constitutional value in false statements of fact.

Thereafter, a majority of the federal circuit courts of appeal have interpreted the *Gertz* dictum to mean that statements of fact can be actionable defamation; statements of opinion cannot. This court has joined the trend.

Recently, however, in *Milkovich v. Lorain Journal Co.*, 110 S. Ct. 2695 (1990), the Supreme Court ruled that freedom of expression "is adequately secured by existing constitutional doctrine without creation of an artificial dichotomy between 'opinion' and fact." *Id.*, 110 S. Ct. at 2706. The Court said, in effect, that the lower courts had misinterpreted the *Gertz* dictum:

> Read in context, ... the fair meaning of the passage is to equate the word "opinion" in the second sentence with the word "idea" in the first sentence.

Under this view, the language was merely a reiteration of Justice Holmes' classic "marketplace of ideas" concept. (Citation omitted.)

Thus we do not think this passage from *Gertz* was intended to create a wholesale defamation exemption for anything that might be labeled "opinion." (Citation omitted.) Not only would such an interpretation be contrary to the tenor and context of the passage, but it would also ignore the fact that *expressions of "opinion" may often imply an assertion of objective fact.*

Id., 110 S. Ct. at 2705 (emphasis added; citation omitted)....

Accordingly, while reserving a place for non-actionable "figurative or hyperbolic language" that could not reasonably be understood as a defamatory statement, the Court concluded that the perceived distinction between "opinion" and "fact" was an "artificial dichotomy," which did not advance constitutional analysis. Rather, according to *Milkovich*, any statement — even one expressed as an "opinion" — can amount to actionable defamation, unprotected by the First Amendment, if it reasonably implies a false assertion of fact and the statement is made with the level of fault required for recovery, respectively, by public figures or officials or by private figures.

This case, however, was tried, and appellate briefs were filed, on the premise that the opinion/fact dichotomy derived from *Gertz* and ensuing cases was the applicable law.... Because we conclude (as elaborated below) that Littman's statements about Stanbury were sufficiently factual under the pre-*Milkovich* standard to preclude constitutional protection as "opinion," we need not decide whether *Milkovich* applies. We therefore turn to the *Gertz* caselaw....

[W]e conclude that — viewed (as they must be) in the light most favorable to Stanbury — Littman's statements were expressions of fact, not of constitutionally protected opinion. We look, first, at context. Littman told Janes that Stanbury was "detail oriented ... to the point of losing sight of the big picture."[10] The context of this statement was an interview intended to help Janes (and thus Lincoln Properties) determine Stanbury's suitability for employment. In commenting on Stanbury's work habits, Littman must have known, or at least should have known, that Janes would interpret his statements as factual evaluations of Stanbury's approach to managing a construction project; otherwise, the information would have been meaningless in the context that had generated Janes' inquiry.

Furthermore, in considering the entire context of the statements — an employment reference — we note that, in the very conversation in which Littman made the allegedly defamatory remarks, he made several undisputed factual statements to Janes about Stanbury's history as a project manager, as well

---

[10] The trial court ruled that "detail oriented," standing alone, was too vague to constitute a defamatory statement of fact but that it became defamatory when combined with Littman's statement about the "big picture."

as a remark that "he no longer worked for us and that might say enough."[12] These remarks add still additional evidence to support the conclusion that Littman stated actionable facts, not protected opinion. Finally, the fact that Stanbury was not hired, apparently because of Littman's statements, could reasonably be taken as evidence of a factual content to the statements.

[Additionally], Littman's statements can be said to have implied "undisclosed defamatory facts." Stanbury testified, without contradiction, that "not seeing the big picture" meant in the construction trade that he did not perform his job properly, could not recognize unusual problems, and thus could not determine what is necessary to correct such problems so that the project would be properly completed on time. Stanbury also testified that "seeing the big picture" was critical to the job of project manager:

> It is important because unless you can visualize the whole project and determine whether it is normal or if it is unusual, and if it is unusual how it is unusual, what has to be done to fix it, it can serious[ly] affect your final completion and your cost ...[.] [T]he project manager is the planner and the person that is responsible for the job, and he is the one that has to visualize and make the decisions.

Moreover, Littman's own testimony buttressed Stanbury's interpretation. Littman said he meant "as an outside observer that the project wasn't going well, and that in the end that was the big picture." Thus, a reasonable juror could find that Littman's statements to Janes implied undisclosed factual data.

[A third] criterion is the verifiability of the statements. Both parties introduced evidence to support either the truth or the falsity of Littman's statements. This evidence made clear that whether Stanbury was too detail oriented to complete the project properly and on time could be objectively evaluated and thus verified. Sigal has proffered no alternative meaning for Littman's statement, either in the trial court or on appeal, that would suggest the words were subjective or vague. We agree with the trial court:

> While [Sigal] asserts that the meaning of the statement may vary from individual to individual, there was no evidence produced by [Sigal] which suggested that the statement made in the context in which it was made, meant anything different than what Plaintiff sought to prove it meant.

In fact, Janes — the person to whom the statement was made, and who was in the best position to interpret what it meant — testified that he derived from Littman's comments specific information concerning Stanbury's work....

---

[12] In addition to his editorial comment about Stanbury's termination of employment, Littman testified he told Janes that Stanbury had a lot of experience on big jobs and that with a large staff Stanbury might be competent. The trial court ruled that these three "statements in the surrounding context would signal to the average reader that the statements uttered by Littman were assertions of fact."

Given the context in which Littman aired his comments about Stanbury, and judged in their entirety, we conclude the statements were assertions of fact within the meaning of *Gertz* and *Myers*, not constitutionally protected opinions.

Although Littman's statements were actionable assertions of "fact," not constitutionally protected "opinion," Stanbury had the burden of proving Sigal (through Littman) was negligent, including the fact that Littman's statements were false. The trial court accordingly gave the jury a negligence instruction. Sigal does not contest, on appeal, either that the statements were false or were negligently made. Sigal does contend, however — and Stanbury does not dispute — that Littman's negligent statements were subject to a "qualified privilege."...

Once the privilege applies, the plaintiff has the burden of proving the defendant has abused, and thus lost, it. To defeat the privilege, a plaintiff must prove the defendant acted with "common law malice." Such malice implies a greater level of ill will than the mind-set reflected by mere negligence....

There was sufficient evidence at trial, viewed in the light most favorable to Stanbury, from which a reasonable jury could find by clear and convincing evidence that Littman and Sigal had abused the qualified privilege under Virginia law by acting with "such gross indifference or recklessness as to amount to wanton and willful disregard of the rights of" Stanbury. Littman testified, and Stanbury's testimony confirmed, that Littman had never supervised, worked with, evaluated, or read an evaluation of Stanbury. Moreover, Littman testified that he had not received information from anyone in particular, let alone anyone who had had a work-related relationship with Stanbury. Littman's sources for his statements to Janes were observations in the company's halls and general office contacts with unnamed third parties, perhaps at "casual lunches" or "project executive meetings" or "over beer on a Friday afternoon." But he could recall none of the conversations or otherwise provide any concrete support for his statements, whether first-hand information or hearsay. Littman admitted that he had no facts to support any of his statements to Janes and that he had never sought to verify the information before giving his evaluation. Littman also testified that he knew Janes wanted to speak with someone who had "interacted" with Stanbury at Sigal, and yet Littman further testified that he did not tell Janes he had never done so. Nor did Littman tell Janes the altogether vague sources of his statements. To make matters worse, according to Janes testimony, Littman told Janes that he had worked with Stanbury on a project.

In short, this is a case of pure "rumor" or "gossip" or "scuttlebutt" conveyed as fact, without any disclaimer or explanation, coupled with Littman's erroneously leading the prospective employer to believe he had worked on a project with Stanbury. Reviewing the evidence in the light most favorable to Stanbury, as we must, we cannot say there was no record basis for the jury to find by clear and convincing evidence that Littman made the statements to Janes with gross indifference or recklessness amounting to wanton and willful disregard of Stanbury's rights under Virginia law.

In sustaining the conclusion that Sigal (through Littman) abused the qualified privilege, we do not mean to imply that employers are at serious risk when providing employment references in the normal course of business. Nor are we suggesting that employers, when providing such references, may not rely on information from the employee's co-workers, even when hearsay. Our analysis here is limited to an office gossip situation where the recommender (1) has conveyed information which cannot be traced to anyone with personal knowledge of the employee whose reputation is at stake, (2) has not qualified his statements by disclosing the nebulous source of his information, and (3) has led the prospective employer to believe he has worked on a project with the employee and thus has first-hand information....

Affirmed.

NOTES

1. *Employer Policies on References.*

No area of employment law frustrates managers and personnel departments more than employee references. [A] corporate security survey found that 50 percent of human resources, loss prevention, and legal professionals feel that employers' refusals to share important information about job applicants hamper workplace crime control, and many think this is a serious impediment to such efforts. Another 1985 study of 258 human resource executives ... found that 74 percent provide only job titles and dates of employment to other employers seeking employment references. Only 14 percent said they would "comment candidly." That study concluded, "[i]ronically, while nearly all prospective employers try to verify resume information, many of the same people will not provide this information to other companies."

IRA M. SHEPARD & ROBERT L. DUSTON, THIEVES AT WORK: AN EMPLOYER'S GUIDE TO COMBATING WORKPLACE DISHONESTY 245 (1988).

2. *Encouraging the Flow of Reference Information.* A free rider problem may exist with references. The risks that a candidly negative reference will be found defamatory fall on the old employer, while the benefits accrue to the interviewing employer. As a result, a policy of refusing to give references may be wise for each individual employer, even though it would harm the public interest by limiting the flow of valuable information about prospective employees.

In the past decade, about half the states have responded to this problem by enacting statutes designed to provide employers with qualified immunity from defamation liability when providing reference information. One curious feature of these "immunity" statutes is that, in general, they tend to re-state the common law defamation standards that were in place before the statutes were enacted. *See* OKLA STAT. tit. 40, § 61 (enacted in 1995) (employer immune unless knowledge of falsity, malice, or reckless disregard of truth); TENN. CODE ANN. § 50-1-105 (enacted in 1995) (similar). Sometimes the statutes even cut in the other direction and increase the possibility of a defamation suit, for example, by requiring employers to provide copies of references to employees. *See* COLO. REV. STAT. § 8-2-114(b); IND. CODE § 22-5-3-1(c).

Ironically, however, these curious statutes may achieve the Legislatures' goal of encouraging employers to provide references. Professors Paetzold and Willborn contend that employers are refusing to give references based on an irrational or highly biased fear of defamation liability. Paetzold and Willborn found that, over the past two decades as more and more employers refused to give references because of fear of liability, their actual exposure to that type of liability declined. They speculate that employer perceptions have been based on reports of large defamation awards made by juries, which are widely reported, rather than on a full sample of cases in which most are dismissed and even large jury awards tend to be greatly reduced through remittur or on appeal. Ramona L. Paetzold & Steven L. Willborn, *Employer (Ir)rationality and the Demise of Employment References,* 30 AM. BUS. L.J. 123 (1992). If this is true, the "immunity" statutes may increase reference-giving by correcting employer misperceptions about their exposure to defamation liability, even if they do not change the actual liability standard at all.

3. *Constitutional Overlay.* The Supreme Court has limited the scope of defamation actions that place an unconstitutional chill on free speech. As applied to employment cases, the constitutional limitations are unclear. One question is whether the employee must prove the employer was negligent in making the defamatory statement. At common law, defamation was a strict liability tort, in that a speaker could be liable for publishing a defamatory statement even if he could not reasonably have known it was false. In *New York Times Co. v. Sullivan,* 376 U.S. 254 (1964), the Court held that public officials could maintain a defamation action only by proving "actual malice" — that the speaker had knowledge the statement was false or acted with reckless disregard of whether or not it was false. In *Gertz v. Robert Welch, Inc.,* 418 U.S. 323 (1974), the Court held that, in defamation suits by a private individual against a media defendant, states cannot impose liability without fault, and cannot impose presumed or punitive damages without a showing of knowledge of falsity or reckless disregard for the truth.

Most employment defamation claims, however, involve neither public officials or figures nor media defendants. The Court has not definitively declared whether a private plaintiff suing a nonmedia defendant must show any kind of fault. In *Dun & Bradstreet, Inc. v. Greenmoss Builders, Inc.,* 472 U.S. 749 (1985), five justices said that the *Gertz* requirement on presumed or punitive damages — no recovery without malice — should extend to non-media defendants. But whether liability against non-media defendants requires fault remains unclear. As set out at the beginning of this section, the RESTATEMENT — extrapolating from *Gertz* — requires a showing of negligence in all actions.

Related to the issue of whether negligence is required is the standard for showing whether the employer abused its conditional privilege. *Stanbury* (which included negligence as part of the employee's basic case) reflects the standard view that the employee must show by clear and convincing evidence that the employer abused its privilege by acting recklessly. If the employee need only show negligence, the conditional privilege would add no protection. In those states that do not require negligence as an element of the basic tort of defamation, however, a lower standard may apply. In those states, perhaps it is sufficient for the employee to show that the employer abused the conditional privilege by proving negligence.

4. *Bad References as Breach of Contract.* Often, employees are asked to resign rather than be fired, and one reason for them to do so is that a resignation provides an opportunity to negotiate a contract specifying the reasons the employer will give for the resignation. Discrimination and other lawsuits that are settled often contain similar agreements, in which the employee agrees to go quietly in return for cash and an agreement that the employer will give only good or neutral references. To what degree should such contracts be enforceable?

A limited-reference agreement was held to be enforceable in *Resnik v. Blue Cross & Blue Shield*, 912 S.W.2d 567 (Mo. Ct. App. 1995). Upon termination, the parties agreed that "reference inquiries ... will be limited to name, job title, and dates of employment only." The court held that a jury could find that a bad reference was given, breaching the agreement, from circumstantial evidence including a telephone call from a prospective employer lasting forty-five minutes.

On the other hand, an agreement was held non-enforceable on the painful facts of *Picton v. Anderson Union High School District*, 57 Cal. Rptr. 2d 829 (Cal. Ct. App. 1996). A teacher settled charges of sexual misconduct towards students, including rape, by resigning in exchange for a withdrawal of all accusations and an agreement not to disclose the real reason for the separation. The rape victim agreed to the settlement. The school district then broke the agreement, sending documents to the state commission on teacher credentialing. The court rejected the teacher's breach of contract suit, holding that the Education Code and regulations made it illegal for the school district to agree to suppress the facts of discharge. The court also rejected a defamation claim, finding that communications to the commission were absolutely privileged. The court also rejected the teacher's claims of fraudulent inducement of contract as falling within the improper breach of contract claim. Finally, the court rejected claims of wrongful discharge, civil conspiracy, tortious interference with prospective economic advantage, and intentional and negligent infliction of emotional distress, because the part of the agreement whereby the parties agreed to release all claims was legally binding on the teacher. Had the employer been a private employer not subject to the Education Code — say a nursery school or YMCA — would the court have reached the same result on grounds of public policy?

5. *Good References as Torts.* In *Randi W. v. Muroc Joint Unified School District*, 929 P.2d 582 (Cal. 1997), a school district wrote a positive reference for an employee, even though it had forced him to resign because of sexual misconduct allegations. Based in part on the reference, the employee was hired by another school district as an administrator. In that position, he sexually assaulted a thirteen-year-old student. The student sued the school district for the positive reference on fraud and negligent misrepresentation theories. The California Supreme Court held that employers giving good references may be liable if they make affirmative misrepresentations that present a foreseeable and substantial risk of physical harm to third parties.

The Court declared that the school district would not have been liable if it had not provided any reference at all, but "having volunteered [positive] information, [the school district was] obliged to complete the picture by disclosing material facts regarding [the employee's] sexual improprieties." *Id* at 592.

6. *Waiving Defamation Claims.* Suppose a prospective employer, wanting candid references, asks a job applicant to sign a release waiving any possible defamation claims against prior employers who may serve as references. Can this contract shield prior employers from defamation claims against the applicant who fails to get a job? *See Cox v. Nasche*, 70 F.3d 1030 (9th Cir. 1995) (applying Alaskan law) (holding that signed release confers absolute privilege upon prior employers in defamation suit). *See also* RESTATEMENT (SECOND) OF TORTS § 583 ("the consent of another to the publication of defamatory matter concerning him is a complete defense to his action for defamation"). *But see Kellums v. Freight Sales Ctrs., Inc.*, 467 So. 2d 816 (Fla. Dist. Ct. App. 1985) (holding that a release waives claims of invasion of privacy or tortious interference with business relations, but does not waive claims against defamatory statements made "knowingly and maliciously," because a party cannot absolve itself by contract of an intentional or "quasi-intentional" tort claim).

Part IV

Employee Duties and Promises

Most of this book examines legal restrictions on employers. These include the common law limitations on wrongful discharge and the invasion of privacy, and the statutory prohibitions against discrimination on the basis of race, sex, age, religion, and disability. Later chapters will deal with government regulation of employers in regard to wages, pensions, and safety in the workplace.

In this Part, by contrast, we look at the legal regulation of employees. Under the common law of master and servant, an employee owes a duty of loyalty to the employer. Usually, employers use self-help when harmed by an employee. Employees not earning their wages are simply fired. Except in a case of embezzlement or the like, an employer rarely takes legal action against the employee. The harm is usually not worth it. The major exceptions are when ex-employees reveal trade secrets or otherwise compete against the employer.

In prior chapters, the event that triggered legal scrutiny was a firing. The employer ended a relationship that the employee wanted to continue. In this Part, the triggering event is a quit. The employee ends a relationship the employer wants to continue, and typically begins competing against the former employer. Chapter 10 examines the common law regulation of employee competition in the absence of specific contractual language protecting employers. Chapter 11 examines legal enforcement of contractual provisions limiting employee quits. Chapter 12 turns to the specific legal problems arising from employee inventions.

Chapter 10
TRADE SECRETS AND DUTY OF LOYALTY

JET COURIER SERVICE v. MULEI

Supreme Court of Colorado, *en banc*
771 P.2d 486 (1989)

LOHR, JUSTICE.

....

I

Jet is an air courier company engaged principally in supplying a specialized transportation service to customer banks. Jet provides air and incidental ground courier service to carry canceled checks between banks to facilitate rapid processing of those checks through the banking system. Shortened processing time enables the banks at which the checks are cashed to make use of the funds sooner. Because the sums involved are large, substantial amounts of daily interest are at stake. As a result, the ability to assure speedy deliveries is essential to compete effectively in the air courier business.

In 1981 Jet was an established family-owned corporation headed by Donald W. Wright. The principal offices of the corporation were in Cincinnati, Ohio. Jet had no office in Denver. Anthony Mulei at that time was working in Denver for another air courier service in a management capacity. Mulei had worked in the air courier business for a number of years and was very familiar with it. He had numerous business connections in the banking industry in Denver and other cities. On February 18, 1981, Wright and Mulei agreed that Mulei would come to work for Jet and would open a Denver office and manage Jet's Western Zone operations from that office. They orally agreed that Mulei would be vice president and general manager for the Western Zone and would have autonomy in matters such as the solicitation of business, the operation of the business, and personnel policies. The parties further agreed that Mulei would be paid $36,000 per year, plus a bonus of ten percent of the net profits of the Western Zone, to be calculated and paid every three months. Based in part on Mulei's business relationships with several regional banks, Wright and Mulei expected that Mulei would be able to expand Jet's business.

Late in 1981 Wright sent Mulei a written employment agreement containing the same terms as the oral agreement with the addition of a noncompetition covenant whereby Mulei would agree not to compete with Jet for two years after termination of his employment, without any geographic restriction. Mulei signed the written agreement. At some time before this litigation commenced, Wright also signed the agreement on behalf of Jet.

367

Mulei performed services as agreed and was successful in significantly increasing the business of Jet in the Western Zone as well as other areas of the United States. Although Jet regularly paid Mulei his monthly salary, and paid him additional sums from time to time totaling $31,000 over the period of his employment, Jet never computed or paid the quarterly bonuses in the manner contemplated by the contract. From time to time Mulei requested payments and accountings but was not successful in obtaining them.

Mulei became progressively dissatisfied with his inability to resolve the bonus issue and with what he believed to be intrusions into his promised areas of autonomy in personnel and operational matters. Toward the end of 1982 he began to look for other work in the air courier field and sought legal advice concerning the validity of the noncompetition covenant in his employment contract.

In the course of seeking other employment opportunities and while still employed by Jet, Mulei began to investigate setting up another air courier company that would compete with Jet in the air courier business. In January 1983, Mulei spoke with John Towner, a Kansas air charter operator who was in the business of supplying certain air transportation services, about going into business together. In February 1983, Mulei met with Towner and two Jet employees to discuss setting up this new business and obtaining customers.

On February 27, 1983, Mulei, while still employed by Jet and on Jet business in Phoenix, talked to two of Jet's customer banks to inform them he would be leaving Jet in mid-March and to tell them he "would try to give them the same service." He engaged in similar discussions with two bank customers of Jet in Dallas while still employed by Jet. Early in March 1983, Mulei met with representatives of three of Jet's Denver customers, First Interstate Bank of Denver, Central Bank of Denver, and United Bank of Denver, and discussed the new air courier company that Mulei and Towner were forming. Mulei told the United Bank of Denver float manager that "if they wished to give us [ACT] the business," then ACT would be able to serve them without any break in the service, and that ACT would be able to take over their business and fully satisfy their air courier service needs. Mulei further told United Bank of Denver that "by minimizing expenses, I would be in a position, sometime later, to reduce cost." Mulei had similar conversations with representatives of First Interstate Bank of Denver.

Prior to the termination of Mulei's employment by Jet on March 10, 1983, Mulei met with nine pilots who were flying for Jet to discuss his formation of ACT. Before his termination, Mulei also met with Jet's Denver office staff and with its ground couriers to discuss potential future employment with ACT. Mulei offered Jet's office staff better working conditions, including health and dental insurance and part ownership of ACT, if they were to join ACT. Mulei did not inform Wright of any of these activities with respect to Jet customers, contractors or employees.

ACT was incorporated on February 28, 1983. Mulei was elected president at the first shareholders meeting. On behalf of Jet, Wright fired Mulei on March 10, 1983, when Wright first learned of Mulei's organization of a competing enterprise. On that same day Mulei caused ACT to become operational and compete with Jet.[6] Five Denver banks that had been Jet customers became ACT customers at that time. Additionally, when Mulei was fired, three of the four other employees in Jet's Denver office also left Jet and joined ACT. All of Jet's ground carriers in Denver immediately left Jet and joined ACT. All nine of Jet's pilots in Denver either quit or were fired. Jet was able to maintain its Denver operations only through a rapid and massive transfer of resources, including chartered aircraft and ground couriers, from Jet's other offices....

II

The court of appeals affirmed the trial court's conclusion that Mulei did not breach his duty of loyalty to Jet by his activities prior to the time he was fired by Jet. Specifically, the court of appeals concluded that Mulei did not breach his duty of loyalty either by meeting with Jet's customers to discuss ACT's future operating plans or by meeting with Jet's employees to discuss future employment opportunities with ACT. We conclude that the court of appeals applied improper legal standards in reviewing the trial court's conclusions as to what actions constitute a breach of an employee's duty of loyalty to his employer....

Section 387 of the Restatement (Second) of Agency provides that "[u]nless otherwise agreed, an agent is subject to a duty to his principal to act solely for the benefit of the principal in all matters connected with his agency." Rest. (2d) Agency § 387 (1957).... Underlying the duty of loyalty arising out of the employment relationship is the policy consideration that commercial competition must be conducted through honesty and fair dealing. "Fairness dictates that an employee not be permitted to exploit the trust of his employer so as to obtain an unfair advantage in competing with the employer in a matter concerning the latter's business." *Maryland Metals, Inc. v. Metzner*, 382 A.2d 564, 568 (Md. 1978).

Thus, one facet of the duty of loyalty is an agent's "duty not to compete with the principal concerning the subject matter of his agency." Rest. (2d) Agency § 393. A limiting consideration in delineating the scope of an agent's duty not to compete is society's interest in fostering free and vigorous economic competition. In attempting to accommodate the competing policy considerations of honesty and fair dealing on the one hand and free and vigorous economic competition on the other, courts have recognized "a privilege in favor of employees

---

[6] Mulei had intended to make ACT operational on March 14 at the beginning of a business week. Mulei advanced the date to March 10 when Wright "prematurely" learned of Mulei's activities in setting up a competing business and discharged him from his employment with Jet. Activity on March 10 was frenzied. Mulei ran ACT from a Denver hotel room and attempted to obtain the business of Jet's bank customers and to assure them that ACT could provide uninterrupted quality service. At the same time, Wright brought in personnel from Cincinnati and other cities and attempted to keep the Denver office operational and to persuade Jet's customers to continue to obtain air courier service from Jet.

which enables them to prepare or make arrangements to compete with their employers prior to leaving the employ of their prospective rivals without fear of incurring liability for breach of their fiduciary duty of loyalty." *Maryland Metals,* 382 A.2d at 569. Previous decisions have acknowledged that "the line separating mere preparation from active competition may be difficult to discern in some cases." *Id.* at 569 n.3. Thus, "[i]t is the nature of [the employee's] preparations which is significant" in determining whether a breach has occurred. *Bancroft-Whitney Co. v. Glen,* 411 P.2d 921, 935 (Cal. 1966).

Given the employee's duty of loyalty to and duty not to compete with his employer and the employee's corresponding privilege to make preparations to compete after termination of his employment, the issue here is whether Mulei's pre-termination meetings with Jet's customers and his co-employees to discuss ACT's future operations constituted violations of his duty of loyalty or whether these meetings were merely legally permissible preparations to compete.

A

We first apply the principles outlined above to determine whether the court of appeals erred in concluding that Mulei's meetings with Jet's customers did not breach Mulei's duty of loyalty....

... While still employed by Jet, Mulei was subject to a duty of loyalty to act solely for the benefit of Jet in all matters connected with his employment. Jet was entitled to receive Mulei's undivided loyalty. The fact that ACT did not commence operations and begin competing with Jet until after Mulei's departure from Jet is not dispositive. Instead, the key inquiry is whether Mulei's meetings amounted to solicitation, which would be a breach of his duty of loyalty. Generally, under his privilege to make preparations to compete after the termination of his employment, an employee may advise current customers that he will be leaving his current employment. However, any pre-termination solicitation of those customers for a new competing business violates an employee's duty of loyalty. Accordingly, we conclude that the court of appeals and the trial court applied an unduly narrow legal standard in holding that Mulei's pre-termination customer meetings were not a breach of Mulei's duty of loyalty simply because ACT did not commence competing with Jet until after Mulei had been discharged.

[The Court then remanded for a retrial on whether Mulei's conversations with some of Jet's customers violated his duty of loyalty to Jet.]

B

We next consider whether the court of appeals erred in concluding that Mulei's meetings with Jet employees did not breach his duty of loyalty. An employee's duty of loyalty applies to the solicitation of co-employees, as well as to the solicitation of customers, during the time the soliciting employee works for his employer. Generally, an employee breaches his duty of loyalty if prior to the termination of his own employment, he solicits his co-employees to join him in his new competing enterprise.

In the case now before us, the court of appeals affirmed the trial court's conclusion that Mulei did not breach his duty of loyalty by meeting with other Jet employees prior to the termination of his own employment with Jet. In concluding that there was no breach of Mulei's duty of loyalty, the court of appeals relied on its previous decision in *Electrolux Corp. v. Lawson,* 654 P.2d 340 (Colo. App. 1982). The court of appeals cited *Electrolux* for the proposition that an employee will not be liable for a breach of his duty of loyalty unless he causes co-employees to breach a contract. We disagree with this proposition, and we again conclude that the court of appeals and the trial court applied an unduly restrictive legal standard in determining whether Mulei's pre-termination discussions with co-employees breached his duty of loyalty.

In *Electrolux,* an Electrolux branch manager solicited a number of his co-workers to join him in a new distributorship he was opening. Six of the co-workers then left Electrolux to join the new firm. The court of appeals read the Restatement (Second) of Agency § 393 comment e as imposing liability for breach of an employee's duty not to compete only when "he causes his fellow employees to breach a contract." 654 P.2d at 341. Because the Electrolux workers' employment contracts were terminable at will, their resignations did not constitute a breach of their employment contracts. Thus, reasoned the court of appeals, since there was no breach of any employment contracts there was no breach of the manager's duty not to compete.

Comment e to section 393 of the Restatement notes that the "limits of proper conduct with reference to securing the services of fellow employees are not well marked." The comment goes on to state that an "employee is subject to liability if, before or after leaving the employment, he causes fellow employees to break their contracts with the employer." Rest. (2d) Agency § 393 comment e. However, the Restatement neither implies nor explicitly states, as did the court of appeals in *Electrolux* and *Mulei,* that causing co-employees to break their contracts is the only instance where an employee will be liable for breaching his duty of loyalty by soliciting co-employees. For instance, the Restatement notes that "a court may find that it is a breach of duty for a number of the key officers or employees to agree to leave their employment simultaneously and without giving the employer an opportunity to hire and train replacements." *Id.*

The distinction between breaching contracts terminable at will and those not terminable at will is the standard applied in the Restatement (Second) of Torts for determining liability for the tort of intentional interference with contractual relations. *See Memorial Gardens, Inc. v. Olympian Sales & Management Consultants, Inc.,* 690 P.2d 207, 210-11 (Colo. 1984) (noting that the Restatement (Second) of Torts "provides less protection for contracts terminable at will because an interference with a contract terminable at will is an interference with a future expectancy, not a legal right"). However, we conclude that the distinction between contracts terminable at will and those not terminable at will is not dispositive in a breach of duty of loyalty analysis. Although inducing another to breach a contract terminable at will may not lead to liability for tortious interference with contractual relations under the Restatement (Second) of Torts, it does not follow that the same standard is dispositive of whether an employee breached his duty of loyalty by soliciting co-employees to leave their employ and join a new enterprise.

To adopt the holding of the court of appeals would be to conclude that the scope of an employee's duty of loyalty with respect to solicitation of co-employees is limited to his duty to refrain from tortious interference with his employer's contractual relations with the co-employees. The court of appeals' holding thus fails to apply applicable principles of agency law and finds liability only for a breach of duties imposed by tort law. This result is readily apparent in the court of appeals' opinion in the present case, which applied the same terminable-at-will analysis to both Jet's breach of duty of loyalty counterclaim and its counterclaim for tortious interference with contractual relations. Such an analytical approach is fundamentally inconsistent with the broad duty of loyalty imposed on an agent/employee by the principles of agency law as stated in the Restatement. By virtue of the agency relationship, the duty of loyalty and non-competition placed on the agent is necessarily greater than the duty imposed on all persons by tort law to refrain from wrongful interference with contract relations.

[W]e conclude that a court should focus on the following factors in determining whether an employee's actions amount to impermissible solicitation of co-workers. A court should consider the nature of the employment relationship, the impact or potential impact of the employee's actions on the employer's operations, and the extent of any benefits promised or inducements made to co-workers to obtain their services for the new competing enterprise. No single factor is dispositive; instead, a court must examine the nature of an employee's preparations to compete to determine if they amount to impermissible solicitation. Additionally, an employee's solicitation of co-workers need not be successful in order to establish a breach of his duty of loyalty....

Again, based on the trial court's findings and the record before us, we are unable to determine whether Mulei's pre-termination meetings with his Jet co-employees were permissible preparations for competition or whether these actions constituted solicitation of co-employees that amounted to a breach of his duty of loyalty. Accordingly, this case must be returned to the trial court for retrial for the additional purpose of determining whether under the standards of an employee's duty of loyalty set forth in this opinion, Mulei's pre-termination meetings with Jet co-employees amounted to impermissible solicitation in violation of his duty of loyalty.

C

The trial court concluded that Mulei did not violate any duty of loyalty to Jet in part because he "continued to operate the Western Zone on a profitable, efficient and service-oriented basis." Mulei now contends that this finding regarding his profitable operation of Jet's Western Zone precludes a determination that he breached any duty of loyalty to Jet. We disagree....

... The key inquiry in determining whether Mulei breached his duty of loyalty is not whether Jet's Western Zone was profitable. Instead, the focus is on whether Mulei acted solely for Jet's benefit in all matters connected with his employment, and whether Mulei competed with Jet during his employment, giving due regard to Mulei's right to make preparations to compete. Accordingly, the fact that Mulei operated Jet's Western Zone efficiently and profitably does not preclude a determination that he breached his duty of loyalty to Jet by his pre-termination actions.

D

Neither does the fact that Jet failed to make the agreed-upon quarterly bonus payments excuse Mulei from being subject to a duty of loyalty to Jet....

Assuming, without deciding, that Jet's nonpayment amounted to a material breach of Mulei's employment agreement, then Mulei had the option of renouncing his authority and leaving Jet's employ. However, there is no evidence in the record indicating that Mulei renounced his authority; instead, the record shows he continued to act for Jet and to operate the Western Zone despite Jet's failure to make the quarterly bonus payments. If the trial court finds on retrial that Mulei did not renounce his agency/employment relation with Jet, then he had a duty to continue that relationship and a corresponding duty of loyalty. Thus, Jet's breach of the employment agreement would not excuse Mulei from being subject to a continuing duty of loyalty to act solely for Jet's benefit in all matters connected with his employment until the time his employment with Jet was terminated on March 10, 1983.

III

[The Court then held that Mulei would not be entitled to any compensation or bonus payments for the period in which he was disloyal.]

The general rule is that an employee is not entitled to any compensation for services performed during the period he engaged in activities constituting a breach of his duty of loyalty even though part of these services may have been properly performed....

However, if Mulei breached any duty of loyalty, he could still recover compensation for services properly rendered during periods in which no such breach occurred and for which compensation is apportioned in his employment agreement.

Mulei's employment contract provided that his salary was to be paid on a monthly basis, and that his bonus was to be calculated and paid on a quarterly basis. Applying the principles outlined above, if on retrial the trial court concludes that Mulei breached his duty of loyalty to Jet, then Mulei would be entitled to compensation for services properly performed during periods in which no such breach occurred and for which compensation is apportioned in the employment agreement. Moreover, under this apportionment approach, Mulei would not be entitled to any salary compensation for any month during which he engaged in acts breaching his duty of loyalty, nor would he be entitled to any bonus payments for any quarter during which he engaged in acts breaching his duty of loyalty.

compensation rule applied

NOTES

1. *Irrelevance of Contract.* Some six months after starting work, Mulei signed an employment agreement in which he agreed not to compete with Jet for two years after termination of his employment. Would the court's analysis have differed had he not signed this agreement?

2. *Corporate Opportunities.* In addition to the duty of loyalty that constrains all employees, high-level fiduciaries of a corporation are constrained by the related principle of corporate opportunity. This principle prohibits a corporation's directors, officers, and controlling shareholders from usurping a corporate opportunity for themselves. A corporate opportunity has been defined as "a business opportunity in which the corporation has an *interest* or *expectancy* or which is *essential* to the corporation." ROBERT C. CLARK, CORPORATE LAW § 7.2.1 (1986). A broader definition would include as corporate opportunities "any business opportunities that are within the subject corporation's line of business." *Id.* at § 7.2.2. A fiduciary can defend his action on the grounds that the corporation was financially or legally unable to take the opportunity, rejected or abandoned the opportunity, or had approved of the fiduciary's action. Dean Clark has urged a greater express recognition of differences between public versus closely held corporations, with the corporate-opportunity doctrine being used more forcefully to restrict fiduciaries of public corporations.

CORPORATE OPPORTUNITIES

If Mulei is treated as an officer of Jet Courier Service, would the corporate-opportunity principle be an additional ground preventing him from grabbing the Jet Courier business for himself? What if Mulei acquired a competing business?

SCHULENBURG v. SIGNATROL, INC.

Supreme Court of Illinois
212 N.E.2d 865 (1965)

SOLFISBURG, JUSTICE.

....

In 1932 the plaintiff Edward J. Schulenburg, Sr., went to work for Sangamo Electric Company at Springfield, Illinois, as head of its flasher and timer division and held that position until 1945 when he purchased all of the assets of the flasher and timer division for the sum of $2,718.61. However, this amount is unimportant for since that time many blueprints, plans, specifications and drawings have been revised or added over the years by the plaintiff to perfect the flasher. In fact, there now are approximately 15,000 drawings of various types. He moved the operation to Danville, Illinois, under the name of Time-O-Matic Company. Defendant J. W. Sutphin had been an employee of Sangamo and when he returned from military service in 1945 he was employed by Time-O-Matic until January, 1959, when he and the plaintiff Schulenburg had a disagreement of policy concerning the operation of the company and he resigned. Signatrol, Inc. was organized by defendant Sutphin in March, 1959, to manufacture and sell flashers.

The defendant Bachman had been employed by Time-O-Matic since 1947, designing special equipment and assisting in sales work. Bachman left Time-O-Matic in the middle of March, 1959, after a disagreement with Schulenburg and joined the new corporation with Sutphin. The defendants McNamara and Walker had also been employees of Time-O-Matic for several years, McNamara as purchasing agent and Walker in the engineering department. Both of them asked Sutphin whether they could join his organization and in April, 1959, McNamara left Time-O-Matic and joined Signatrol as its purchasing agent and the following June, Walker also joined Signatrol.

The flashers produced by the plaintiffs are not patented nor is there any contention that the flasher itself or the method of assembling the flasher is a trade secret. Indeed, neither the plaintiffs nor defendants are true manufacturers, but actually buy the motors, gears, side plates, switches and other parts which they assemble. Many of these parts are regular catalogue items furnished by suppliers and can be ordered by anyone. For that matter, anyone may legally duplicate the plaintiffs' product and go into business in competition with the plaintiffs in the manufacture and sale of electric flashers.

Plaintiffs allege, however, that their manufacturing "know-how" is a trade secret which was imparted in confidence to defendants while employees and that such secret has been used by them in manufacturing a competing product. Defendants deny utilization by them of any such secret, in fact they deny its very existence. The trial and appellate courts held that the information, measurements, designs and material specifications contained on plaintiffs' blueprints or drawings and used in the manufacturing process qualified as a trade secret. They further found that defendants copied or memorized the information contained on these blueprints and drew on such knowledge in making up their own blueprints to be used in the manufacture of their product.

The trial judge in his memorandum opinion stated the issues involved in the following language:

> [The defendants' product] was very similar to the product of the plaintiffs. However, similarity of products is not the controlling test which is determinative of the issues in this case, but is a factor to be considered. The ques-

tion of infringement of patents is not involved. The real question is whether or not the individual defendants, or some of them, either traced, copied or reproduced Time-O-Matic plans, drawings, prints, designs, or carried away in their minds information as to the same so that they could reproduce them from their memory, provided further that such information was such as would be classed as a 'trade secret'. The determinative question here is, how did the defendants go about reproducing the plaintiffs' flasher? Did they violate the confidence reposed by their employer by appropriating, in an unlawful manner, the trade secrets of the plaintiffs?

The trial judge has correctly stated the issues involved, and, of course, there is another issue in this appeal, and that is whether the injunctive relief granted was appropriate.

The trial and the appellate courts concluded that the manufacturing "know-how" contained in the plaintiffs' blueprints and drawings were trade secrets in view of the fact that they were kept confidential and that plaintiffs considered such as secret and attempted reasonably to keep it so.... Several of the more salient findings of the trial court are:

The Defendants insist that they made their drawings directly from the parts themselves by measuring, except when they drew them from their memory of Time-O-Matic's drawings. However, their expert witness, Dale Beck, a skilled engineer, looked with considerable askance (*sic*) upon the ability of any engineer to make accurate drawings of many of the delicate parts merely by measurements of the parts. This was particularly true as to those parts where the measurements were to a 10/1000 of an inch. And to come up with the identical measurement, tolerances, etc., as appear upon Time-O-Matic drawings were (*sic*) almost impossible.

There is a marked similarity between the drawings and sketches of Signatrol and those of Time-O-Matic, in other respects. The data is too often too alike to be just accidental. The placement of the data on the drawing is almost universally the same.

The likenesses and similarities occur so often, with such exactness, that it seems most unlikely that they should so occur, if, as claimed by defendants all their drawings were made from the torn down flasher parts, and without reference to any drawings or sketches or specifications of Time-O-Matic.

It is to be observed that at no time did the Defendants seek to produce a new and improved flasher. They advanced no 'new novel' improvements. They only sought to reproduce the identical basic flasher of the Plaintiffs.

From the character of the Defendants' own evidence, their admissions, the very nature of their procedure in entering into this competing business, their evasive attitude, one cannot but conclude that here was a carefully designed scheme and plan to reproduce from their employer's trade secrets, the product of their employer. This conclusion is emphasized by Sutphin's testimony that he anticipated he would be sued. He had sought the advice of an attorney, then anticipating a suit he preserved a large number of his sketches. Why would he anticipate being sued, if he only intended to copy the product from the product itself, and did not intend to resort to the use of his employer's trade secrets?

....

The trial judge also stated "it is of the very essence of things to see to it that the stringent and clamorous voice of self interest does not drown out the still, small voice of duty and conscience."

After having considered the entire record in the trial court, including the transcript of the evidence, and the trial judge's opinion, we have determined, as did the appellate court, that the evidence supported the findings of the trial court. The controlling definition of a trade secret in Illinois is supplied by *Victor Chemical Works v. Iliff*, 299 Ill. 532, 540, where this court said that it is a secret *plan* or process, tool, mechanism or compound known only to its owner and those of his employees to whom it is necessary to confide it. The initial requirement that the plan, tool, etc., be regarded as a secret has been found to exist by both the trial and appellate courts herein. There is ample evidence in the record to support these findings, and they should not be disturbed here. The more difficult question presented to this court is whether, notwithstanding the fact that the parties treated the information contained in the blueprints as containing confidential material, it nevertheless does not amount to a trade secret....

The defendants cite *Sears, Roebuck & Co. v. Stiffel Co.*, 376 U.S. 225 (1964), and *Compco Corp. v. Day-Brite Lighting*, 376 U.S. 234 (1964), for the proposition "that no state may, by laws dealing with unfair competition, impose damages or enjoin the copying, manufacturing and sale of an article which is protected by neither a Federal patent nor a copyright." In a proper case, we would concur with this statement. However, a reading of *Sears* and *Compco* clearly indicates that they are inapposite here. There, the defendants had copied the plaintiffs' unpatentable products by legal means. No problem concerning trade secrets was present. Plaintiffs here readily concede that their finished products may be copied by legal means (such as acquiring one of the finished products and measuring and analyzing it, until a copy can be produced), but maintain that employees in positions of confidence may not surreptitiously copy plaintiffs' blueprints while in their employ and subsequently use them to establish a competing business. *Sears* has in fact been distinguished on this very basis, in *Servo Corporation of America v. General Electric Co.*, 337 F.2d 716 (4th Cir. 1964). It was there held that one could not take advantage of a confidential relationship and pirate another's trade secrets without responding in damages — even though the finished product was unpatentable and could be copied by legal means. It is readily apparent that the *Sears* and *Compco* cases do not cover a situation of industrial espionage by employees who plan to organize a competing company and thereafter do that very thing.

A holding that the confidential information contained in the blueprints does not constitute a trade secret would be incompatible with the practical problems inherent in attempting to copy a product from examination of the product itself. The measurements, tolerances, quality of material, etc., cannot ordinarily be discovered by these means without expensive and time-consuming analyses. Plaintiffs have gone through this process by trial and error and have preserved the information thus acquired in working drawings and blueprints. Defendants, however, have chosen to capitalize upon their positions of trust — to clandestinely acquire the blueprints and reproduce them exactly. There is evidence in the record indicating that when some of defendant's drawings are superimposed over plaintiffs' corresponding ones, they match exactly — even to the lettering thereon. Better evidence of copying would be hard to obtain. In fact, defendants have even copied some of plaintiffs' mistakes.

It is clear that an employee may take with him, at the termination of his employment, general skills and knowledge acquired during his tenure with the former employer. It is equally clear that the same employee may not take with him confidential particularized plans or processes developed by his employer and disclosed to him while the employer-employee relationship exists, which are unknown to others in the industry and which give the employer advantage over his competitors. The facts and circumstances in a particular case sometimes necessitate the drawing of a fine line of distinction in determining which rule should properly apply. Suffice it to say that the facts and circumstances indicated herein fall well within the contemplation of the latter rule.

It should, moreover, make no difference whether the information contained in the blueprints, if it qualified as a trade secret (which in our judgment it does), has been pilfered by tracing the blueprints themselves, as some testimony herein indicates, or has been memorized by someone with a photographic memory, or has been committed to memory by constant exposure to the prints while in the employ of plaintiffs. This record is replete with evidence leading to but one conclusion: that these defendants have surreptitiously taken the particularized information contained in plaintiffs' blueprints and have employed it to establish a competing business. Even today's "morals of the market place" are more demanding than this, and should not be relaxed by this court. The determinations of the trial and appellate courts on the trade secret question are affirmed.

The bothersome aspect of the trial and appellate court decisions is the scope of the injunction that has been issued. It does not restrict its application as to time or geographical area. Defendants have, in effect, been put out of business for all time, everywhere. This clearly is not necessary to make plaintiffs whole as it is conceded by them that their products may legally be copied by competitors. Since defendants might have reproduced plaintiffs' flasher in this fashion, it is difficult to justify prohibition of such reproduction for a period of time longer than that required to duplicate the product by lawful means. The record contains no indication of the time so required, but such fact should be readily ascertainable since a Minnesota firm apparently did legally copy plaintiffs' product.

Accordingly, we believe that the injunction should have been limited in duration to the period of time reasonably required for defendants to legally produce such copies. Since the original injunction has been stayed pending the determination of this appeal, we believe that justice will be served upon remand by an order of the trial court ordering the enforcement of the original injunction pending a prompt determination of the period of time required for the reproduction of the flashers by lawful means. The injunction should then be modified to terminate upon the expiration of such time period.

The trial and appellate court determinations on the trade secret issue are affirmed and the cause is remanded to the trial court with instructions to consider the question of damages and modification of the injunction in accordance with the views expressed herein.

NOTES

1. *Memorized Customer Lists.* One recurring trade-secrets pattern involves customer lists. In general, the common law allows ex-employees to contact customers of their old employer. As one court put it: "an employee's recollection of information pertaining to specific needs and business habits of particular customers is not confidential." *Walter Karl, Inc. v. Wood*, 528 N.Y.S.2d 94, 98 (App. Div. 1988). On the other hand, courts will find a violation of the duty of loyalty if the employer can show the customer list was developed at great expense over a period of years and could not be replicated without great expense. *See Allen v. Johar, Inc.*, 823 S.W.2d 824 (Ark. 1992) (enjoining employee from using memorized customer list).

2. *Limited Injunctions and Deterrence.* The court limits the injunction to the time it would have taken the defendants to reproduce the flashers by lawful means. Professor Kitch has criticized this limited remedy:

> For the last 100 years, courts have routinely enjoined a defendant proven to have wrongfully appropriated a trade secret from using the secret in perpetuity. Recently, however, defendants have persuaded some courts that the period of the injunction should not exceed the time that it would have taken the defendant to engineer the secret independently. The trade secret remedy, they have argued, should only make the plaintiff whole, not put him in a better position than he otherwise would have been. The older, still widely followed practice had a punitive element; the defendant ended up worse off than if there had been no theft. In an assumed model in which most thefts are detected, a pure compensation remedy makes sense. But where most thefts are not likely to be detected, a disproportionate remedy makes sense if the courts' objective is to reduce the amount of trade secret theft.

Edmund W. Kitch, *The Law and Economics of Rights in Valuable Information,* 9 J. LEGAL STUD. 683, 693 (1980).

3. *Federal Statutory Law.* In 1996, Congress turned the misappropriation of trade secrets into a federal criminal offense. Economic Espionage Act of 1996, 18 U.S.C. § 1831 *et seq.* The Act protects a wider range of information than most state statutes. "Trade secret" is defined to include:

> all forms and types of financial, business, scientific, technical, economic, or engineering information, including patterns, plans, compilations, program devices, formulas, designs, prototypes, methods, techniques, processes, procedures, programs, or codes, whether tangible or intangible, and whether or how stored, compiled, or memorialized physically, electronically, graphically, photographically, or in writing if —
> (A) the owner thereof has taken reasonable measures to keep such information secret; and
> (B) the information derives independent economic value, actual or potential, from not being generally known to, and not being readily ascertainable through proper means by, the public....

18 U.S.C. § 1839(3). The Act provides significant penalties. Misappropriations that benefit foreign governments can result in fines of up to $500,000 or imprisonment for up to fifteen years (or, for organizations, fines of up to $10 million). Misappropriations for commercial purposes can result in imprisonment for up to ten years (or, for organizations, fines of up to $5 million). In the first reported application of the Act, two defendants were charged with allegedly trying to purchase the formulae and manufacturing processes for the anti-cancer drug "Taxol" owned by the Bristol-Myers Squibb Company. *United States v. Hsu*, 982 F. Supp. 1022 (E.D. Pa. 1997) (granting a protective order).

Chapter 11

ENFORCEMENT OF NONCOMPETITION CLAUSES

Many employers are not content to rely on the common law of trade secrets or duty of loyalty to protect their investment in workers. One alternative is to extract a promise that the employee will work for the employer for a specified period. Such a definite-term contract cannot be a complete solution, however, because courts will not specifically enforce a promise to work. In addition to the practical problem of judicially monitoring whether the employee is adequately performing the court-mandated work, compelling someone to work may violate the thirteenth amendment's prohibition of involuntary servitude. *See Beverly Glen Music, Inc. v. Warner Communications, Inc.*, 224 Cal. Rptr. 260 (Cal. Ct. App. 1986) (thirteenth amendment prohibits specific enforcement of singer's contract). *Cf. Bailey v. Alabama*, 219 U.S. 219 (1911) (thirteenth amendment prohibits criminal remedies for breaches of promise to work).

Instead, employers often negotiate noncompetition clauses whereby employees promise not to compete against the employer if they leave. Such clauses indirectly protect employer's investments in training their workers and revealing trade secrets to them. The employer's interest is easy to see. A 1979 survey of Los Angeles employers, for example, found that recruitment and initial training costs ranged from over $2,000 for each office worker, to over $3,500 for production workers, to over $10,000 for salary-exempt workers. On the other hand, employers can use noncompetition clauses opportunistically to exploit workers. To understand the dynamics more fully, we need to examine how workers and firms invest in human capital and how noncompetition clauses protect these investments. The following article provides a framework for thinking about these issues.

PAUL H. RUBIN & PETER SHEDD, HUMAN CAPITAL AND COVENANTS NOT TO COMPETE, 10 Journal Of Legal Studies 93 (1981)[*]

In his seminal work on human capital, Gary Becker has distinguished between "general" and "specific" on the job training.[2] "General training is useful in many firms besides those providing it."[3] "Training that increased productivity more in

[*] Copyright 1981 by The University of Chicago. Reprinted with permission of the Journal of Legal Studies and the University of Chicago Press.

[2] GARY S. BECKER, HUMAN CAPITAL (1964).

[3] *Id.* at 11.

firms providing it will be called specific training."[4] The concept of human capital has been one of the most fruitful innovations in recent economic theory; moreover, on the job training is empirically very important in explaining observed patterns of earnings....

Specific human capital and general human capital are the polar opposites in markets for types of training. If training is specific, there is only one firm that can employ the trained worker. After training, the worker is worth more to this firm than to any other potential employer. The employer, knowing this, will pay the worker more than any other employer in order to retain the worker and recoup his investment. However, to pay this higher wage, the employer will require the worker to pay for part of the specific training. Employers and workers will thus share the cost and the gain from specific training. In the case of general training, the trained worker faces a competitive market with many bidders for his talent. The employer, knowing that he will be required to pay the full market price for the trained worker, will not pay for any training. Conversely, the worker, knowing that he will receive the full value of his training, will be willing to pay for it.

In both of these market structures, prices are determinate. Both parties to labor transactions can be certain about the future value of training and can plan their investments accordingly. There is no uncertainty in either case, except for the normal uncertainty about future changes in demand or technology. Training in both cases will be efficient, in the sense that money will be spent on training to the point where the cost of the training will be equal to the present value. No mention has been made of labor contracts because they would have no relevance in the market structures considered. If training is truly specific, the employer needs no assurance that the worker will continue to work for him, for there is no other market in which the employer can sell his skill. If training is truly general, the employee knows that he can recoup his investment by quitting the current employer and going to work for any of a number of other firms. A long-term contract has no value to either party.

Thus, in the two cases analyzed by Becker, there is no need for any contractual term limiting the future market behavior of the worker; market forces will generate solutions without contracts. But in fact many employment contracts do contain clauses limiting the future behavior of employees, and such contracts are common sources of legal dispute. Thus, there must be some aspects of real-world labor markets that Becker's analysis does not fully capture.... [T]he lacuna in the Becker analysis is in terms of types of general training. In particular, there are some types of general training for which the worker will not pay. Assume, for example, that it takes a firm one day to teach a worker the details of a trade secret valuable to many other firms and worth $100,000. The value of the information is so great that the worker cannot pay for it by accepting reduced wages. Moreover, because of difficulties in borrowing with human capital as collateral,

---

[4] *Id.* at 18.

there may be no other way for the worker to finance the acquisition of human capital with sufficiently high value. If the worker borrows the money needed to finance the acquisition of the capital, the lender has as security for his loan only the human capital of the worker. However, the inability of the worker to sign a binding contract, which creates the difficulty for the employer, also creates the same problem for the lender. Human capital cannot serve as collateral for loans because of the impossibility of compelling specific performance. In this circumstance, the firm would want the worker to sign a noncompetition clause, for such a clause would indicate that the worker could not use the training acquired elsewhere. Covenants not to compete would be signed by workers who receive general training with value sufficiently high so that the worker could not finance the acquisition of this training by accepting reduced wages.

why noncompetition clauses are needed

Once the worker has received this training, however, an incentive for opportunistic behavior is created. The worker has an incentive to violate the contract and profit from his training — either by going to work for himself or by going to work for another firm, which will pay him a premium because of the value of his training. In this situation, the worker is attempting to appropriate for himself the value of training for which he did not pay. If workers were able to do this, the incentive for firms to invest in acquiring valuable information would be greatly reduced, for firms would not be able to protect valuable information. We are specifically dealing here with cases where information cannot be protected by patent and trade secrets are therefore used.

Another inefficiency could be created if firms were not able to require contractually workers not to use valuable information elsewhere. If information were not protected by contract, firms might spend resources in other ways to protect this information .... For example, if a secret process requires three steps, there are two methods of maintaining secrecy. One allows one employee to undertake all three steps but binds him by contract not to use the acquired information elsewhere. An alternative is to teach each of three employees only one of the three steps, so that no one employee will know enough to compete with the firm. It is possible, however, that the production process will be more costly if the second method of protection is used. (If not, then the second method would always be used, and the law is irrelevant.) Thus, if the noncompetition clause is not binding, firms will be forced to use more costly methods of production in some circumstances in order to protect their proprietary information.

... [F]irms may also have an incentive to behave opportunistically and may try to pay workers less than the full value of their marginal product, even after adjusting for human-capital investments.

Assume that the courts will enforce all covenants not to compete in labor contracts. Some types of employment relationships will involve both types of general training — general training for which the worker will pay in the normal manner, by accepting reduced wages, and general training for which the worker cannot pay because of its high value. If the worker signs a covenant, he would be unable to use any of the training in other jobs. Presumably, the employer would then be forced to finance all of the investment, since it would all be specific. If the worker then left this place of employment, some of his training would be valuable to many firms and its use would not cost the original employer anything. Yet the worker would be constrained from using his training. Not using general training (absent trade secrets) thus imposes a cost. The covenant not to compete should therefore ideally apply only to those types of training involving trade secrets of the employer.

It may, however, be difficult or impossible to draft a contract with sufficient specificity to include only the training that the employer desires to protect. The employer may not know in advance for exactly what sort of work a particular employee is best suited, and thus may not be able to specify contractually which information is to be protected. Moreover, the details of trade secrets often cannot be written down; the secret may consist of a series of actions involving a particular process. Even when the secret can be written down in a contract, the writing itself will seriously compromise the secrecy of information. The contract not to compete will thus necessarily involve some ambiguity. The employer may have an incentive to behave opportunistically and underpay the worker relative to the value of that part of the general training financed by the worker if the employer believes that the covenant will reduce the worker's mobility. It would therefore be inefficient to enforce all restrictive covenants, just as it would be inefficient to enforce none of them. In such circumstances, the courts, in enforcing covenants not to compete, may serve a useful function. Specifically, in disputes about the term of contracts, the courts may attempt to determine just what sorts of information the parties expected to be included in the covenant and to enforce the contract accordingly. This is consistent with the view that, in the case of ambiguous contracts, the role of the courts is in general to determine what the parties would have done had they predicted the apparently unforeseen circumstance.

In summary, we have the following situation. Workers will be unable to pay the full value of some training they receive from firms and will therefore sign contracts with clauses banning the workers from competing with former employers. Once the contracts are signed and the workers trained, both workers and employers may have incentives to behave opportunistically: employees to attempt to violate the contracts and sell the information acquired, and employers to underpay workers for general training for which the workers themselves have paid. If the courts are to be economically efficient in enforcement of contracts with these clauses, they must attempt to separate the two types of behavior.

NOTE

Statutory Balancing. Most states use the common law to regulate the opportunistic behavior that noncompetition clauses create. Louisiana had attempted to balance the competing interests by statute, by banning noncompetition clauses except to protect training expenses. *See* LA. REV. STAT. ANN. § 23:921 (repealed 1989):

> No employer shall require or direct any employee to enter into any contract whereby the employee agrees not to engage in any competing business for himself, or as the employee of another, upon the termination of his contract of employment with such employer, and all such contracts, or provisions thereof containing such agreement shall be null and unenforceable in any court, provided that in those cases where the employer incurs an expense in the training of the employee or incurs an expense in the advertisement of the business that the employer is engaged in, then in that event it shall be permissible for the employer and employee to enter into a voluntary contract and agreement whereby the employee is permitted to agree and bind himself that at the termination of his or her employment that said employee will not enter into the same business that employer is engaged over the same route or in the same territory for a period of two years.

In 1989, the Louisiana legislature replaced the statute with one that allowed noncompetition clauses for specified parishes or municipalities for a period of two years after termination of employment. LA. REV. STAT. ANN. § 23:921C.

REM METALS CORP. v. LOGAN

Supreme Court of Oregon
565 P.2d 1080 (1977)

Before TONGUE, LINDE and CAMPBELL, JJ.

TONGUE, JUSTICE.

This is a suit in equity to enforce "noncompetition" provisions of two employment agreements between plaintiff and defendant, who had been employed by plaintiff as a welder of precision titanium castings. Defendant appeals from a decree enjoining him from engaging in such work for a period of six months in Oregon for Precision Castparts Corporation, a competitor of plaintiff. We reverse.

The primary question presented for decision in this case, according to plaintiff Rem, is whether, as an employer, it had a sufficient "protectible interest" in the skills and knowledge of defendant as a skilled craftsman engaged as a repair welder of precision titanium castings, so as to justify enforcement of such a "noncompetition" agreement as a "reasonable restraint" upon defendant.

The titanium castings on which defendant Logan worked as a repair welder were produced by his employer, the plaintiff, under contract with Pratt & Whitney Aircraft Division for use as bearing housings for jet aircraft engines under exceedingly strict specifications. Only three companies are engaged in the production of such castings for Pratt & Whitney. These include plaintiff, Precision Castparts (its principal competitor) and Misco of Michigan (a smaller company).

In the process of the production of such castings any defects are repaired by welding performed by skilled welders who are "certified" by Pratt & Whitney inspectors as being sufficiently skilled to be entrusted with this important work. There was also some evidence that titanium is a "rare" or "reactive" metal and is difficult to weld.

Defendant was one of two or three "certified" welders employed by plaintiff and was plaintiff's best welder, with a proficiency rating of 98.3 per cent. Other welders rated below 95 per cent. There was testimony, however, that three other welders had been able to become sufficiently qualified so as to be "certified" for Pratt & Whitney work after 20 hours of training and that during 1966 seven of plaintiff's welders (including defendant) were so "certified."

Defendant Logan had been previously employed by Wah Chang Corporation, where he learned to weld electrodes of titanium. He was employed by plaintiff in 1969 and subsequently signed two employment contracts, as did nearly all Rem employees, including provisions to the effect that for a period of one year after termination he would not engage in any business in competition with Rem within the United States, "whether as principal, agent, employer, consultant or otherwise."

In 1972 defendant was transferred to the welding department. He testified that he became "certified" in "less than two weeks," and that no one gave him "any instruction before he took the certification test" for the welding of titanium.

Plaintiff offered testimony describing its training program for welders. When asked whether Rem had any "trade secrets in the welding department that are not generally known in the industry," that witness answered that "Rem was able to do a better job," to ship ahead of its schedules, and with fewer "rejects" from Pratt & Whitney than its competitors, so that "there is something we must be doing that our competitors are not doing." Rem's president testified that defendant received job training at Rem and "extensive written procedures prepared by Rem" which enable him to weld titanium castings. He also testified, however, that it was nevertheless not surprising that defendant Logan was able to become "certified" within "a matter of a few days," as testified by Logan.

Rem's supervisor of welding testified that:

> I don't think it's a matter of disclosing inasmuch as it is its instructional nature. If a welder's in the tank doing the work, we're qualifying it and giving what instructions we are capable of.

There was also testimony by another former Rem titanium welder, since employed by Precision Castparts, that he observed no differences in the welding procedures and techniques at Rem and at PCP except that Rem uses a "vacuum tank," while PCP uses a "plastic bubble," both of which are standard techniques.

On September 18, 1976, defendant Logan, after being refused a wage increase of 50 cents per hour by Rem, went to work at that increased rate for Precision

Castparts. Plaintiff offered evidence that, as a result, it was unable for a period of two weeks to ship castings worth approximately $25,000 to Pratt & Whitney and that it then had difficulty in maintaining its shipping schedules of such titanium castings because it did not have welders who were "able to complete the weld repair cycle in a satisfactory manner." It appears, however, that Rem was then able to train two welders who "shortly thereafter were able to pass the qualification test of Pratt & Whitney." Plaintiff's witnesses also testified to their concern over Rem's continued ability to compete with Precision Castparts, its principal competitor, which by then had 14 or 15 titanium welders, including defendant Logan.[2]

It would serve no useful purpose to discuss at length the many authorities on the subject of the enforcement ability of noncompetition provisions in employment contracts. The general rule, as adopted for application in such cases in Oregon in *Eldridge v. Johnston,* 245 P.2d 239 (Or. 1952), is as follows:

> Three things are essential to the validity of a contract in restraint of trade: (1) it must be partial or restricted in its operation in respect either to time or place; (2) it must be on some good consideration; and (3) it must be reasonable, that is, *it should afford only a fair protection to the interests of the party in whose favor it is made,* and must not be so large in its operation as to interfere with the interests of the public.... (Emphasis added.)

As also stated in *North Pacific Lbr. v. Moore,* 551 P.2d 431 (Or. 1976):

> To be entitled to the protection which a noncompetition covenant purports to provide, the employer must show that he has a 'legitimate interest' entitled to protection....

In our judgment, this case falls within the rule as stated in Blake, *Employee Agreements Not to Compete,* 73 Harv. L. Rev. 625, 652 (1960), as follows:

> ... It has been uniformly held that general knowledge, skill, or facility acquired through training or experience while working for an employer appertain exclusively to the employee. The fact that they were acquired or developed during the employment does not, by itself, give the employer a sufficient interest to support a restraining covenant, even though the on-the-job training has been extensive and costly. In the absence of special circumstances the risk of future competition from the employee falls upon the employer and cannot be shifted, even though the possible damages is greatly increased by experience gained in the course of the employment."

To the same effect, although under different facts, it was held in *McCombs v. McClelland,* 354 P.2d 311 (Or. 1960) that:

---

[2] It also appears that Precision Castparts is "underwriting" the cost of Mr. Logan's defense.

... The fact that defendant may have gained considerable experience while in plaintiff's employ is not grounds for injunctive relief. An employer cannot by contract prevent his employee upon termination of the employment from using skill and intelligence acquired or increased and improved through experience or through instruction received in the course of employment ...."

We recognize, however, as does Blake, *supra* (at 653), that on any given set of facts it may be difficult to "draw a line" between "training in the general skills and knowledge of the trade, and training which imparts information pertaining especially to the employer's business" and that this is the "central problem" in such cases. In other words, as stated by Blake, *supra* (at 647):

... Its objective is not to prevent the competitive use of the unique personal qualities of the employee — either during or after the employment — but to prevent competitive use, for a time, of information or relationships which pertain peculiarly to the employer and which the employee acquired in the course of the employment....[6]

In such a case, however, the burden of proof is upon the employer to establish the existence of "trade secrets," "information or relationships which pertain peculiarly to the employer," or other "special circumstances" sufficient to justify the enforcement of such a restrictive covenant.

Based upon our examination of this record, which we review de novo, and under the facts and circumstances of this case, we hold that this employer failed to sustain that burden of proof. Although defendant received training and experience while employed by plaintiff which developed his skill as a repair welder of titanium castings, plaintiff did not, in our judgment, establish by sufficient and credible evidence "special circumstances" of such a nature as to entitle Rem to demand the enforcement upon this defendant by injunction of this "noncompetition" clause as a "reasonable restraint."

For these reasons, the decree of the trial court is reversed.

NOTES

1. *General Training and Exceptional Talent. Rem Metals* is a classic example of an employer who provides general training that makes an employee valuable to other employers as well. The court applied the rule that recouping the costs of general training or preventing competition is insufficient to justify a non-competition clause. That Logan was the most talented welder in the company seems irrelevant. The Becker model of human capital predicts that Logan would receive lower wages than he otherwise would during his general training. The

---

[6] As stated in *Sarkes Tarzian, Inc. v. Audio Devices, Inc.,* 166 F. Supp. 250, 265 (S.D. Cal. 1958): "... Trade secrets must be 'the particular secrets of the employer as distinguished from the general secrets of the trade in which he is engaged' ...."

training was so short, however, that this prediction would be difficult to test here.

Occasionally, courts find that an employer has a protectible interest in employees whose services are special, unique or extraordinary. For example, when the soul singer James Brown breached his agreement with King Records "not to perform for the purpose of making phonographic records with any person other than us," by recording on the Mercury label, a New York court enforced the covenant because of Brown's special, unique and extraordinary skills. *King Records, Inc. v. Brown*, 252 N.Y.S.2d 988 (N.Y. App. Div. 1964). *See also Matuszak v. Houston Oilers, Inc.*, 515 S.W.2d 725 (Tex. Civ. App. 1974) (upholding preliminary injunction preventing a number-one draft choice from defecting to rival football league, in part because of player's uniqueness). *But see* 6A ARTHUR L. CORBIN, CORBIN ON CONTRACTS § 1391B (Supp. 1991) ("Princeton could not have enjoined Albert Einstein from leaving to take a position at Harvard just because he was famous and his scientific writings enhanced Princeton's reputation").

2. *Recovering Training Expenses.* Suppose a truck driver signs a three-year employment contract in which he agrees to pay $1,500 to reimburse the employer for training expenses if he quits during the term. Is this contract distinguishable from the one in *Rem Metals? See Becker v. Blair*, 361 N.W.2d 434 (Minn. Ct. App. 1985) (enforcing promise as part of fixed-term employment contract rather than a "restrictive employment covenant"). *See also New York State United Teachers v. Thompson*, 459 F. Supp. 677 (N.D.N.Y. 1978) (employer has cause of action for breach of contract when teacher refuses to return to job after educational leave of absence); *Milwaukee Area Joint Apprenticeship Training Comm. v. Howell*, 67 F.3d 1333 (7th Cir. 1995) (finding no violation of ERISA or state law regulating restrictive covenants when an apprenticeship program costing over $10,000 requires participants to accept employment with contributing employers or repay the costs).

3. *Parol Evidence and Consideration.* The various contract-law doctrines regulating enforceability often pose problems in noncompetition cases, as they do in employment termination cases. For example, should oral promises not to compete be enforceable? *See Metcalfe Investments, Inc. v. Garrison*, 919 P.2d 1356 (Alaska 1996) (an employee's oral promise to refrain from using customer lists in a new business for an unlimited period of time not subject to statute of frauds and therefore enforceable). What about the argument that noncompetition clauses signed after the employee begins work are unenforceable because the employer has given no extra consideration for the promise? *Compare CRC — Pipeline Int'l, Inc. v. Myers*, 927 S.W.2d 259 (Tex. 1996) (noncompetition covenant made by at-will employee unenforceable as illusory), *with Curtis 1000, Inc. v. Suess*, 24 F.3d 941 (7th Cir. 1994) (holding that at-will employment can support valid noncompetition clause because employee gets an "expectation of continued employment," even if expectation not legally enforceable).

4. *Suing the Second Employer.* An employer whose employee violates a non-competition clause is not limited to suing that employee, but may also sue the subsequent employer. In *United Labs., Inc. v. Kuykendall,* 403 S.E.2d 104 (N.C. Ct. App. 1991), the second employer promised a job applicant that it would pay legal costs for any lawsuit by the first employer based upon a noncompetition clause. In a subsequent lawsuit, the original employer recovered $11,700 against the employee for breach of contract and over $145,000 in compensatory and punitive damages against the second employer on theories of interference with restrictive covenants and unfair trade practices.

A British White Paper proposed an alternative method of protecting employers against the loss of their employees to competitors. Under the plan, former employers could reclaim at least part of the cost of training if a worker left within a certain period. The costs of training and the length of service required would be set out in the contracts of employment. While questions were raised by both Conservatives and Labour concerning the practicality of the proposal, a Labour employment spokesperson said the plan was "at least an acknowledgement that training could not be left to market forces." Diane Summers, *UK May Introduce Transfer Fees for Poached Workers,* LONDON FINANCIAL TIMES, Feb. 10, 1992, at 12.

KARPINSKI v. INGRASCI

Court of Appeals of New York
268 N.E.2d 751 (1971)

FULD, CHIEF JUDGE.

This appeal requires us to determine whether a covenant by a professional man not to compete with his employer is enforceable and, if it is, to what extent.

The plaintiff, Dr. Karpinski, an oral surgeon, had been carrying on his practice alone in Auburn — in Cayuga County — for many years. In 1953, he decided to expand and, since nearly all of an oral surgeon's business stems from referrals, he embarked upon a plan to "cultivate connections" among dentists in the four nearby Counties of Tompkins, Seneca, Cortland and Ontario. The plan was successful, and by 1962 twenty per cent of his practice consisted of treating patients referred to him by dentists located in those counties. In that year, after a number of those dentists had told him that some of their patients found it difficult to travel from their homes to Auburn, the plaintiff decided to open a second office in centrally-located Ithaca. He began looking for an assistant and, in the course of his search, met the defendant, Dr. Ingrasci, who was just completing his training in oral surgery at the Buffalo General Hospital and was desirous of entering private practice. Dr. Ingrasci manifested an interest in becoming associated with Dr. Karpinski and, after a number of discussions, they reached an understanding; the defendant was to live in Ithaca, a locale with which he had no prior familiarity, and there work as an employee of the plaintiff.

A contract, reflecting the agreement, was signed by the defendant in June, 1962. It was for three years and, shortly after its execution, the defendant started working in the office which the plaintiff rented and fully equipped at his own expense. The provision of the contract with which we are concerned is a covenant by the defendant not to compete with the plaintiff. More particularly, it recited that the defendant

> promises and covenants that while this agreement is in effect and forever thereafter, he will never practice dentistry and/or Oral Surgery in Cayuga, Cortland, Seneca, Tompkins or Ontario counties except: (a) In association with the [plaintiff] or (b) If the [plaintiff] terminates the agreement and employs another oral surgeon.

The Contract

In addition, the defendant agreed, "in consideration of the ... terms of employment, and of the experience gained while working with" the plaintiff, to execute a $40,000 promissory note to the plaintiff, to become payable if the defendant left the plaintiff and practiced "dentistry and/or Oral Surgery" in the five enumerated counties.[1]

When the contract expired, the two men engaged in extended discussions as to the nature of their continued association — as employer and employee or as partners. Unable to reach an accord, the defendant, in February, 1968, left the plaintiff's employ and opened his own office for the practice of oral surgery in Ithaca a week later. The dentists in the area thereupon began referring their patients to the defendant rather than to the plaintiff, and in two months the latter's practice from the Ithaca area dwindled to almost nothing and he closed the office in that city. In point of fact, the record discloses that about 90% of the defendant's present practice comes from referrals from dentists in the counties specified in the restrictive covenant, the very same dentists who had been referring patients to the plaintiff's Ithaca office when the defendant was working there.[2]

The plaintiff, alleging a breach of the restrictive covenant, seeks not only an injunction to enforce it but also a judgment of $40,000 on the note. The Supreme Court, after a nonjury trial, decided in favor of the plaintiff and granted him both an injunction and damages as requested. On appeal, however, the Appellate Division reversed the resulting judgment and dismissed the complaint; it was that court's view that the covenant was void and unenforceable on the ground that its restriction against the practice of both dentistry *and* oral surgery was impermissibly broad.

---

[1] Either party was privileged to terminate the agreement on 60 days' notice within the three-year period and, if the plaintiff were to do so, the contract recited, the defendant was released from the restrictive covenant and the note.

[2] There are two other oral surgeons, in addition to the plaintiff and the defendant, serving the Ithaca area.

There can be no doubt that the defendant violated the terms of the covenant when he opened his own office in Ithaca. But the mere fact of breach does not, in and of itself, resolve the case. Since there are "powerful considerations of public policy which militate against sanctioning the loss of a man's livelihood," the courts will subject a covenant by an employee not to compete with his former employer to an "overriding limitation of 'reasonableness.'" Such covenants by physicians are, if reasonable in scope, generally given effect. "It is a firmly established doctrine," it has been noted, "that a member of one of the learned professions, upon becoming assistant to another member thereof, may, upon a sufficient consideration, bind himself not to engage in the practice of his profession upon the termination of his contract of employment, within a reasonable territorial extent, as such an agreement is not in restraint of trade or against public policy."

Each case must, of course, depend, to a great extent, upon its own facts. It may well be that, in some instances, a restriction not to conduct a profession or a business in two counties or even in one, may exceed permissible limits. But, in the case before us, having in mind the character and size of the counties involved, the area restriction imposed is manifestly reasonable. The five small rural counties which it encompasses comprise the very area from which the plaintiff obtained his patients and in which the defendant would be in direct competition with him. Thus, the covenant's coverage coincides precisely with "the territory over which the practice extends," and this is proper and permissible. In brief, the plaintiff made no attempt to extend his influence beyond the area from which he drew his patients, the defendant being perfectly free to practice as he chooses outside the five specified counties.

Nor may the covenant be declared invalid because it is unlimited as to time, forever restricting the defendant from competing with the plaintiff. It is settled that such a covenant will not be stricken merely because it "contains no time limit or is expressly made unlimited as to time." "According to the weight of authority as applied to contracts by physicians, surgeons and others of kindred profession ... relief for violation of these contracts will not be denied merely because the agreement is unlimited as to time, where as to area the restraint is limited and reasonable." In the present case, the defendant opened an office in Ithaca, in competition with the plaintiff, just one week after his employment had come to an end. Under the circumstances presented, we thoroughly agree with the trial judge that it is clear that nearly all of the defendant's practice was, and would be, directly attributable to his association with his former employer.

This brings us to the most troublesome part of the restriction imposed upon the defendant. By the terms of the contract, he agreed not to practice "dentistry and/or Oral Surgery" in competition with the plaintiff. Since the plaintiff practices only "oral surgery," and it was for the practice of that limited type of "dentistry" that he had employed the defendant, the Appellate Division concluded that the plaintiff went beyond permissible limits when he obtained from the defendant the covenant that he would not engage in any "dentistry" whatsoever. The restriction, *as formulated,* is, as the Appellate Division concluded, too broad; it is not reasonable for a man to be excluded from a profession for which he has been trained when he does not compete with his former employer by practicing it.

The plaintiff seeks to justify the breadth of the covenant by urging that, if it had restricted only the defendant's practice of oral surgery and permitted him to practice "dentistry" — that is, to hold himself out as a dentist generally — the defendant would have been permitted, under the Education Law, to do all the work which an oral surgeon could. We have no sympathy with this argument; the plaintiff was not privileged to prevent the defendant from working in an area of dentistry in which he would not be in competition with him. The plaintiff would have all the protection he needs if the restriction were to be limited to the practice of oral surgery, and this poses the question as to the court's power to "sever" the impermissible from the valid and uphold the covenant to the extent that it is reasonable.

... As Professor Blake put it (73 Harv. L. Rev., at pp. 674-675), "If in balancing the equities the court decides that his [the employee's] activity would fit within the scope of a reasonable prohibition, it is apt to make use of the tool of severance, paring an unreasonable restraint down to appropriate size and enforcing it." In short, ... "we find it just and equitable to protect appellant [employer] by injunction to the extent necessary to accomplish the basic purpose of the contract insofar as such contract is reasonable." Accordingly, since his practice is solely as an oral surgeon, the plaintiff gains all the injunctive protection to which he is entitled if effect be given only to that part of the covenant which prohibits the defendant from practicing oral surgery.

The question arises, however, whether injunctive relief is precluded by the fact that the defendant's promissory note for $40,000 was to become payable if he breached the agreement not to compete. We believe not. The mere inclusion in a covenant of a liquidated damages provision does not automatically bar the grant of an injunction. As this court wrote in the *Diamond Match Co.* case (106 N.Y., at p. 486, 13 N.E., at p. 424), "It is a question of intention, to be deduced from the whole instrument and the circumstances; and if it appear that the performance of the covenant was intended, and not merely the payment of damages in case of a breach, the covenant will be enforced." The covenant under consideration in this case may not reasonably be read to render "the liquidated damages provision ... the sole remedy." On the other hand, it would be grossly unfair to grant the plaintiff, in addition to an injunction, the full amount of damages ($40,000) which the parties apparently contemplated for a total breach of the covenant, since the injunction will halt any further violation. The proper approach is that taken in *Wirth* (265 N.Y. 214, 192 N.E. 297). The court, there faced with a similar situation, granted the injunction sought and, instead of awarding the amount of liquidated damages specified, remitted the matter for determination of the *actual* damages suffered during the period of the breach.

The hardship necessarily imposed on the defendant must be borne by him in view of the plaintiff's rightful interest in protecting the valuable practice of oral surgery which he built up over the course of many years. The defendant is, of course, privileged to practice "dentistry" generally in Ithaca or continue to practice "oral surgery" anywhere in the United States outside of the five small rural counties enumerated. The covenant, part of a contract carefully negotiated with no indication of fraud or overbearing on either side, must be enforced, insofar as it reasonably and validly may, according to its terms. In sum, then, the plaintiff is entitled to an injunction barring the defendant from practicing oral surgery in the five specified counties and to damages actually suffered by him in the period during which the defendant conducted such a practice in Ithaca after leaving the plaintiff's employ.

NOTES

1. *Lifetime and Worldwide Bans.* Enforcing a lifetime ban, even with a limited geographic restriction, is highly unusual. Courts seem increasingly receptive, however, to arguments that the increasing geographic scope of competition justifies nationwide or even worldwide bans. *See Briggs v. R.R. Donnelley & Sons,* 446 F. Supp. 153 (D. Mass. 1978) (do-not-compete clause with no explicit geographic term enforced to prohibit contacts with customers worldwide).

2. *Court Decrees and Reality.* More than twenty years after the court injunction, Dr. Ingrasci continued to advertise in the Ithaca Yellow Pages a practice limited to oral surgery. How can this be explained? Suppose an oral surgery practice in Ithaca was worth more to Dr. Ingrasci than it cost Dr. Karpinski. If so, both dentists would be better off if Ingrasci paid Karpinski to waive the injunction. This may be an example of the Coase Theorem's assertion that, if transaction costs are sufficiently low, initial legal entitlements will not affect the final outcome.

A major argument against noncompetition clauses is that, by restricting employees from changing employers, they prevent workers from moving to jobs where they would be most productive. Does the Ingrasci "reality" noted above undermine this argument? Professor Kitch has argued that it does:

> [T]he parties to the transaction can always retransact. If an employee has a higher valued activity in some other employment, he can offer a payment to his employer to obtain release from his contract, as is done in professional sports.... The question is not whether there will be competition but whether such contracts would serve a useful purpose in permitting firms to capture the returns from investments in human capital and, thus, create the appropriate incentives to make such investments.

Edmund W. Kitch, *The Law and Economics of Rights in Valuable Information,* 9 J. LEGAL STUD. 683, 688 (1980).

3. *Vagaries in a Reasonableness Inquiry.* The court in *Karpinski* emphasizes that each case must depend upon its own facts. This makes it difficult for lawyers to advise their clients on whether a do-not-compete clause will be enforceable. For a vivid illustration of this, compare the following cases which involve the same employer suing on nearly identical noncompetition agreements. *Compare Welcome Wagon, Inc. v. Morris,* 224 F.2d 693 (4th Cir. 1955) (refusing to enforce five-year nationwide noncompetition agreement when defendant locates in same city), *and Briggs v. Boston,* 15 F. Supp. 763 (N.D. Iowa 1936) (same), *with Welcome Wagon Int'l, Inc. v. Pender,* 120 S.E.2d 739 (N.C. 1961) (enforcing five-year noncompetition agreement when defendant locates in same city), *Briggs v. Butler,* 45 N.E.2d 757 (Ohio 1942) (same), *and Briggs v. Glover,* 3 N.Y.S.2d 979 (N.Y. Sup. Ct. 1939) (same).

4. *Protecting a Monopoly Position.* What is the significance of footnote 2's statement that two other oral surgeons practiced in Ithaca? If Karpinski and Ingrasci were the only oral surgeons in the area, should the case come out differently? Would the residents of Ithaca then face a monopoly, if the noncompetition clause was enforced?

In deciding whether to enforce a noncompetition clause, courts usually weigh the employer's interest against the employee's burden. Sometimes a direct appeal to the public interest is involved. For example, suppose the *Karpinski* case involved small-town doctors rather than dentists, and no other doctors serviced the town. In this situation, should the court enforce the noncompetition clause?

In *Iredell Digestive Disease Clinic v. Petrozza,* 373 S.E.2d 449 (N.C. Ct. App. 1988), *aff'd,* 377 S.E.2d 750 (N.C. 1989), a noncompetition clause forbade a gastroenterologist from working for three years within a twenty-mile radius of a rural clinic. The court refused to enforce the clause, despite its limited geographical and time restrictions, emphasizing the importance of patients having freedom to choose between personal physicians and that the defendant was the only practitioner capable of performing certain emergency services. *See also Dick v. Geist,* 693 P.2d 1133 (Idaho Ct. App. 1985), which refused to enforce a covenant that would have prevented the region's only neonatologist from continuing to work in the area. The court made no reference to the covenant's monopolistic effects, instead emphasizing the serious adverse public health implications of forcing the doctor to leave the area.

5. *Lawyers and Noncompetition Clauses.* ABA MODEL RULES OF PROFESSIONAL CONDUCT Rule 5.6 prohibits a lawyer from making a partnership or employment agreement restricting his or her right to practice law after the relationship ends. The principal rationale is that such restrictions may infringe on the ability of clients to choose their lawyers. In *Howard v. Babcock,* 863 P.2d 150 (Cal. 1993), the California Supreme Court upheld a law firm partnership agreement that allowed the firm to withhold funds from a departing partner who intends to compete in the same market. The Court argued that the agreement left the partner free to "practice at a price" while compensating the firm for the loss of clients, and thus did not restrict the practice of law. The Court observed that a revolution in the practice of law now requires economic interests of the law firm to be protected as they are in other business enterprises. Justice Kennard, dissenting, refused to admit "that a new reality in the practice of law justifies its erosion of legal ethical standards." *Id.* at 161.

6. *Enforcing Noncompetition Covenant Against Fired Employee.* In *Karpinski,* the parties failed to agree on a new contract when the definite-term contract expired. Should this affect the analysis? Suppose an employee is fired, with or without just cause. Should an otherwise valid noncompetition clause be enforceable in this situation? *Compare Wark v. Ervin Press Corp.,* 48 F.2d 152 (7th Cir. 1931) (enforcing noncompetition clause against fired employee) *and Robert S. Weiss & Assoc. v. Wiederlight,* 546 A.2d 216 (Conn. 1988) ("the reasonableness of a restrictive covenant of employment does not turn on whether the employee subject to the covenant left his position voluntarily or was dismissed by the employer") *with Ma & Pa, Inc. v. Kelly,* 342 N.W.2d 500 (Iowa 1984) (termination is factor opposing injunction) *and Insulation Corp. v. Brobston,* 667 A.2d 729, (Pa. Super. Ct. 1995) (refusing to enforce noncompetition clause against employee fired for poor performance because such a bad worker cannot pose the same competitive threat as one who voluntarily joins another business).

7. *Contracting Beyond the Common Law.* As we saw in the previous chapter, the common law duty of loyalty prevents employers from exploiting trade secrets after leaving work, even in the absence of a noncompetition promise. Some courts and commentators have suggested that noncompetition clauses cannot go beyond the common law in restricting employees. For example, in *Curtis 1000 Inc. v. Suess,* 24 F.3d 941 (7th Cir. 1994), a salesman had signed a covenant promising not to call on any former customers for two years after leaving his employer. The court refused to issue a preliminary injunction, finding that Illinois law limited the interests that a noncompete clause may protect to trade secrets, confidential information, and relations with "near permanent" customers of the employer. *See also Reed, Roberts Assocs. v. Strauman,* 353 N.E.2d 590 (N.Y. 1976) (requiring existence of trade secrets or a unique skill for the enforcement of a non-solicitation promise). Why would an employer want a contract clause if it cannot exceed the restriction the employer already has under the common law?

8. *Trimming Overbroad Clauses.* Courts have developed three responses to an overly broad noncompetition clause. Some will rewrite an offensive clause. For example, in *Dean Van Horn Consulting Assocs. v. Wold,* 395 N.W.2d 405 (Minn. Ct. App. 1986), the court reduced a three-year noncompetition clause to one year and enjoined the employee from competing with his former employer for one year. Others adopt a "blue pencil" rule, enforcing the reasonable parts of the clause if they are grammatically separable from the invalid parts. *See Timenterial, Inc. v. Dagata,* 277 A.2d 512 (Conn. Super. Ct. 1971). Finally, some courts refuse to sever objectionable portions or rewrite the covenant, reasoning that this would encourage employers to write "truly ominous covenants" knowing that courts would pare them down if found overbroad. *White v. Fletcher/Mayo/Assocs.*, 303 S.E.2d 746 (Ga. 1983). *See also CAE Vanguard, Inc. v. Newman*, 518 N.W.2d 652 (Neb. 1997).

STOP

FRANCKLYN v. GUILFORD PACKING CO.

United States Court of Appeals, Ninth Circuit
695 F.2d 1158 (1983)

Before WRIGHT, SKOPIL and ALARCON, CIRCUIT JUDGES.

ALARCON, CIRCUIT JUDGE:

....

Guilford [Packing Company] has been in the fishing and fish processing business for a number of years. Francklyn was hired to harvest clams on beds leased by Guilford. Francklyn was paid on a piecework basis, and he was required to deliver all of his catch to Guilford. Guilford also owned the boat and harvester that Francklyn used in harvesting the clams. Although Francklyn's work schedule was flexible, Guilford expected him to harvest clams when the tide and weather permitted. In the interim periods Francklyn was to maintain the boat and harvester in good repair. At the end of each clamming season, Francklyn returned the boat and harvester to Guilford. The district court found that the arrangement between Guilford and Francklyn also contemplated that Francklyn would be making modifications to the clam harvester in an attempt to improve its performance; Guilford also agreed to reimburse Francklyn for expenses incurred in modifying the harvester.

Francklyn became dissatisfied with the operation of Guilford's harvester. Over a two-year period, while employed by Guilford, he perfected and completed a modified version of the harvester which he used on Guilford's clam boat, the LITTLE JERK. The district court found that much or all the early work in modifying the harvester was done at the Guilford Packing Company plant, with the company's tools. The district court also found that pursuant to their agreement, Guilford reimbursed Francklyn for all materials used to modify the harvester for which Francklyn asked payment, although at some point Francklyn unilaterally determined not to seek further reimbursement.

In 1969, Francklyn obtained a patent for the modified harvester. Francklyn told Wilbur Harms (appellee and officer of Guilford) that Guilford could use his harvester without paying royalties on the "Little Jerk or any other clam boat you may have...." The parties agree that Francklyn gave Guilford a royalty-free license to the harvester used on the LITTLE JERK.

In 1972, Guilford retired this boat and harvester. Subsequently, Guilford manufactured a second harvester, based on the Francklyn invention, and used it on a different boat, the SIDEWINDER. Francklyn now claims that Guilford's manufacture and use of this second harvester infringed his patent.

In 1968, ... Carr built a harvester which was owned by the partnership of Lowman and Carr. It is undisputed that the harvester infringed Francklyn's patented invention. In October, 1969, Francklyn sent Lowman a notice of infringement. Lowman and Carr consulted a patent attorney who advised them that Francklyn's patent was invalid and that even if it was valid, Guilford had a shop right to the patent. The attorney also advised Lowman and Carr that Guilford could utilize its shop right by buying the harvester from Lowman and Carr and leasing it back to them. Lowman and Carr then sold the harvester to Guilford and Guilford leased it back to them. Lowman continued to use the device in harvesting clams for Guilford. In February, 1975, Francklyn served Lowman with a second notice of infringement. Thereafter, this action was filed.

The district court found that Guilford and its officers had a shop right to Francklyn's invention.... The district court [also determined] that neither Lowman nor Guilford infringed Francklyn's patent when they entered into the sale and leaseback transaction ....

Francklyn contends that Guilford could not acquire shop rights in his invention because he was not an employee of Guilford's. In our view, this reflects too narrow a view of the nature of a shop right.

This court has indicated that while a shop right generally arises out of an employer-employee relationship, it is not necessarily limited to such a relationship. *Kierulff v. Metropolitan Stevedore Co.,* 315 F.2d 839, 842 (9th Cir. 1963) (*quoting Gate-Way, Inc. v. Hillgren,* 82 F. Supp. 546, 555 (S.D. Cal. 1949), *aff'd per curiam,* 181 F.2d 1010 (9th Cir. 1950)). The full nature of the parties' relationship must be examined to determine whether a shop right exists, not merely whether that relationship is characterized as an employment or as an independent contractual arrangement.

As this court noted in *Kierulff,* the doctrine of the shop right is of equitable origin:

> The principle involved is that where an inventor or owner of an invention *acquiesces* in the use of the invention by another, particularly where he *induces* and *assists* in such use without demand for compensation or other notice of restriction of the right to continue, he will be deemed to have vested the user with an irrevocable, equitable license to use the invention.

Kierulff v. Metropolitan Stevedore Co., 315 F.2d at 841 (*quoting Gate-Way, Inc. v. Hillgren,* 82 F. Supp. at 555) (emphasis added).

In this case, the factual findings made by the district court fully support the conclusion that Guilford acquired a shop right to Francklyn's invention broad enough to cover its manufacture and use of the second harvester. First, the district court found that Francklyn knew, after his patent was issued, that Guilford was utilizing his harvester on the SIDEWINDER; nevertheless, Francklyn did not seek royalties from Guilford or otherwise attempt to enforce his patent against it until he instituted this suit in 1975. Such a finding clearly supports the conclusion that Francklyn knowingly acquiesced in Guilford's manufacture and use of a copy of his invention on the SIDEWINDER.

Moreover, the findings of the district court support the conclusion that Francklyn induced Guilford to manufacture and use a copy of his invention on the SIDEWINDER. Francklyn testified at trial that he told Wilbur Harms "you will also be able to use the LITTLE JERK or any other clam boat that you may have free of any royalties as long as my patent is valid." Francklyn's testimony certainly supports the district court's finding that "Francklyn offered Guilford Packing Company free use of the LITTLE JERK or any other clam boat with the harvesting rig for the life of his patent without payment of royalties." The district court also found that "Francklyn consistently told Wilbur and Richmond Harms that they could operate using the patented invention without payment of royalties." These findings, supported by credible evidence, are not clearly erroneous, and fully support the ruling below. On the basis of both Francklyn's statements and his silence, Guilford could certainly have reasonably inferred, and apparently did infer, that Francklyn consented to its manufacture and use of his invention on the SIDEWINDER. Under these facts, the finding of a shop right was clearly correct.

Francklyn also argues that under *United States v. Dubilier Condenser Corp.*, 289 U.S. 178 (1933), he is entitled as a matter of law to a finding that Guilford did not have a shop right in his invention. Again, we disagree.

According to *Dubilier* a shop right may arise where the conception and perfection of the invention occurs during the hours of employment and is accomplished while working with the employer's tools and appliances. Here, the evidence adduced at trial supports the conclusion that Francklyn tested and perfected the modified harvester during his hours of work. Francklyn argues that the modifications were made on his own time, and not during his hours of employment, i.e., when he was actually harvesting clams. However, as noted earlier, the work agreement between Francklyn and Guilford contemplated that Francklyn would be making modifications to the harvester in an attempt to improve its performance; the time Francklyn spent modifying the harvester can therefore reasonably be considered as part of his work time. As Francklyn candidly stated at trial, "if it hadn't been for him [Wilbur Harms] I would never have had the opportunity to develop what I developed on the boat in the first place because I would never have had the job to do it." It is also apparent that Francklyn tested the modified harvester while he was harvesting clams for Guilford.

Francklyn also contends that the second aspect of the *Dubilier* test has not been met, since modifications to the harvester were not done with Guilford's materials or appliances. He bases his argument on the fact that the modifications took place at his boat house rather than at Guilford's factory, and that he used his own tools. The district court, however, found that early work on the modification of the harvester took place at Guilford's factory, with Guilford's tools. Moreover, Guilford presented evidence, and the district court found, that Guilford agreed to underwrite all expenses incurred by Francklyn in his modifications of the harvester. Indeed, Francklyn testified that during a May 27, 1975 deposition he had stated that "Mr. Harms told me that if I did anything to the machine [harvester], worked on it, he said that he would pay for the materials that I used and in hopes that we could come up with something that would make it work better, which he did up to a certain point." Francklyn thus conceded that Harms had offered to pay for materials, and that he had been reimbursed for at least a portion of his expenses. The court found that Francklyn unilaterally chose not to seek reimbursement for most of his expenses. Under these circumstances, Guilford's offer to pay for the expenses incurred in the modification of the harvester substantially complies with *Dubilier*'s requirement that the employer supply materials and appliances necessary to perfect the inventions.

We conclude that the district court correctly found that Guilford had a shop right that Francklyn's invention was broad enough to cover its manufacture and use of invention.

We must next decide whether a third party such as Lowman can avoid paying royalties to an inventor by selling an infringing device to the holder of a shop right, such as Guilford, and then leasing the device back from the holder of the right. We hold that a third party cannot evade liability for patent infringement pursuant to such a transaction.

The court below found that the harvester manufactured and used by Lowman applied the teachings of claims 3 and 6 of Francklyn's patent. The parties do not dispute this finding. Moreover, both prior and subsequent to the sale of the harvester to Guilford, Lowman had used that harvester to gather clams to sell to various fish processing plants, including Guilford's. It is therefore clear that Lowman's manufacture and use of this harvester would constitute an infringement of Francklyn's patent unless otherwise privileged. The issue, then, is whether Lowman can evade liability for infringement by entering into a sale and lease back transaction with Guilford, the holder of a shop right to Francklyn's invention. We hold that he cannot.

As noted above, Guilford's shop right was broad enough to encompass the manufacture of Francklyn's invention. The sale and lease back of the device manufactured by Lowman, however, was an attempt by Guilford to assign its shop right to manufacture Francklyn's invention to Lowman. This it cannot do. It is a well established principle that shop right is personal to the employer; it cannot be assigned or transferred by contract to a third person.

The agreement between Guilford and Lowman could not affect Lowman's duty to pay royalties or damages to Francklyn for his infringement of Francklyn's patented invention. Guilford and Lowman could not contract between themselves to abrogate Lowman's duty to pay royalties to Francklyn.

We conclude that Guilford had a shop right to Francklyn's invention. That right is personal to Guilford. It cannot be transferred to Lowman to give him a defense to a claim of patent infringement based on his manufacture and use of a product which is a copy of Francklyn's invention.

INGERSOLL-RAND CO. v. CIAVATTA

Supreme Court of New Jersey
542 A.2d 879 (1988)

GARIBALDI, J.

....

Ingersoll-Rand is engaged in the research, development, manufacture, and sale of products for use in various heavy industries. It does business through more than thirty divisions, which are organized into eleven business groups that cover a broad range of technology, including air compressors, construction equipment, mining machinery, oil field products, and tools. Ingersoll-Rand's sales exceed $2 billion and the company dedicates approximately 3.5% to 4.0% of its revenues, or $70-80 million, to research and development.

Historically, one of the dangers of underground mining is the potential collapse of a mine's rock roof. Several methods and devices have been employed to stabilize the strata of rock layers in the roof of a mine. In 1973, Dr. James Scott, a Professor of Mining Engineering at the University of Missouri, conceived of the friction stabilizer roof support system and communicated with Ingersoll-Rand regarding the development of this concept. Ingersoll-Rand, working with Dr. Scott, expended substantial sums on the research and development of the product. On December 2, 1975, the United States Patent Office issued the first patent for Dr. Scott's friction stabilizer. Dr. Scott subsequently assigned the patent to Ingersoll-Rand. In February 1977 Ingersoll-Rand began marketing its stabilizer under an agreement with Dr. Scott....

The split set stabilizer has been a very successful product for Ingersoll-Rand. It represented over half of all stabilizer units sold in the United States for metal and non-metal mines, with over one million units sold in 1984. Ingersoll-Rand controls over ninety percent of the submarket for friction stabilizers. Ingersoll-Rand has never reduced the price of the split set below list in response to competition; and prior to 1983, when the defendant's company, Safeguard Energy Products, Inc., entered the market, only one other competitor was in the submarket: Atlas Copco Corporation. The design of Atlas Copco's friction stabilizer is identical to a configuration of the Ingersoll-Rand stabilizer sketched by Dr. Walter McGahan of Ingersoll-Rand Research on December 10, 1978. Friction stabilizers, however, do compete with other methods of roof stabilization.

Defendant, Armand Ciavatta, is a 57-year-old engineer. He was graduated from the Rhode Island School of Design in 1953 with a Bachelor of Science degree in machine design. Subsequently, he took classes in mining, tunneling, and heavy construction engineering as well as graduate business classes. Since 1950, Ciavatta has held a number of technical engineering positions involving a variety of engineering principles ....

Ciavatta joined the Millers Falls Division of Ingersoll-Rand as Director of Engineering and Quality Control in 1972. From 1972 to 1974, Ciavatta was responsible for quality control and materials management in the production of hand and electric tools. In the fall of 1974, the company terminated his employment in the Millers Falls Division, at which time he became Program Manager with Ingersoll-Rand Research, Inc. As a condition of his employment with Ingersoll-Rand Research, he executed an "Agreement Relating to Proprietary Matter" (Proprietary Agreement) in which he agreed, in pertinent part:

> 1. To assign and I hereby do assign, to the COMPANY, its successors and assigns, my entire right, title and interest in and to all inventions, copyrights and/or designs I have made or may hereafter make, conceive, develop or perfect, either solely or jointly with others either
>
> (a) during the period of such employment, if such inventions, copyrights and/or designs are related, directly or indirectly, to the business of, or to the research or development work of the COMPANY or its affiliates, or
>
> (b) with the use of the time, materials or facilities of the COMPANY or any of its affiliates, or
>
> (c) within one year after termination of such employment if conceived as a result of and is attributable to work done during such employment and relates to a method, substance, machine, article of manufacture or improvements therein within the scope of the business of the COMPANY or any of its affiliates.

Additionally, in Paragraph 4 of the Agreement, Ciavatta agreed:

> 4. Not to divulge, either during my employment or thereafter to any person, agency, firm or corporation, any secret, confidential or other proprietary information of the COMPANY or any of its affiliates which I may obtain through my employment without first obtaining written permission from the COMPANY.

Ciavatta signed this Agreement on October 1, 1974, and at that time he had read and understood its terms.

While employed by Ingersoll-Rand Research as a Program Manager from October 1974 through March 1978, Ciavatta worked on a variety of development projects, other than those relevant to this litigation, including a tunneling device and the development of coal haulage machinery. As a result of his participation in these development projects, Ciavatta became interested in underground mining and read extensively the industry literature on the subject. From 1974 to 1978, Ciavatta never was formally involved in or assigned to research or development relevant to the friction stabilizer. Nevertheless, Dr. McGahan, the Director of Research, encouraged the research staff to be creative, to discuss ideas for projects or potential projects beyond those to which they had been assigned. These ideas were to be submitted on disclosure forms. Through 1975, Ciavatta submitted thirteen patent disclosures to his employer for mining technology and instrumentation. Five of the thirteen proposals were for devices to support or stabilize roofs of underground mines. Four of the five invention disclosures were not friction stabilizers, but one was an improvement to Ingersoll-Rand's split-set. Ciavatta's work during this period was his first exposure to mining support equipment. Ingersoll-Rand chose not to pursue any of his concepts. Thereafter, defendant claims, he lost his motivation to invent and did not originate any additional concepts while employed by Ingersoll-Rand.

In March 1978, the company transferred Ciavatta to the Split Set Division of Ingersoll-Rand Equipment Corp. While there, he served as Manufacturing Manager and Quality Control Manager. Ingersoll-Rand does not fabricate the stabilizer in any of its plants. Rather, it contracts with two vendors who manufacture the Split Set roof stabilizers, which Ingersoll-Rand then sells to the mining industry. As manager of manufacturing, it was Ciavatta's position to administer the manufacturing program. His responsibilities in that post included supervising the manufacture, production, quality control, and distribution of Ingersoll-Rand's Split Set roof stabilizers. During this period, the company did not employ Ciavatta to design, invent, or modify the basic configuration of its Split Set roof stabilizer, and in fact he did not do so. Ciavatta did, however, have access to Ingersoll-Rand's manufacturing drawings, materials, and specifications. Ingersoll-Rand considers all of that information confidential, although the information had been published in industry trade publications. At the Ingersoll-Rand Research Center the company maintains a security system in order to ensure the confidentiality of its information. Drawings are stamped proprietary, visitors are escorted while in the Ingersoll-Rand Research Center, vendors must sign proprietary information agreements, and all employees must enter into a Proprietary Master Agreement similar to that at issue in this case.

In the spring of 1979, as a result of certain quality control problems, Ciavatta stopped certain shipments of the stabilizer and recommended that the vendors modify their production process. Ciavatta's superior countermanded this directive and directed the vendors to make their scheduled shipments. Subsequently, in June of that year, Ingersoll-Rand terminated Ciavatta's employment. Ciavatta claims that the company did not offer any explanation for his termination; the company claims it terminated his employment because of unsatisfactory performance and his poor relations with fellow employees.

After his termination, Ciavatta circulated more than one hundred resumes seeking employment with other engineering firms. From February to July 1980, he briefly obtained employment as general manager of a bankrupt company located in Michigan.

Ciavatta asserts, and the trial court found, that he first conceived of the invention in dispute in the summer of 1979 while unemployed and off the Ingersoll-Rand payroll. Apparently, he was installing a light fixture in his home when he first conceived of his invention, an elliptical metal tube designed to stabilize the roofs of mines. While searching for employment following his discharge from Ingersoll-Rand, Ciavatta intermittently worked on his design. He completed his first sketch of the stabilizing device on August 25, 1979, approximately two months after Ingersoll-Rand fired him. Ciavatta's stabilizer differs from Ingersoll-Rand's in two respects: its tubular portion is closed rather than split, and the tube is elliptical in shape.

As he continued to develop the stabilizing device, Ciavatta consulted a patent attorney to determine his rights with regard to the device. At his attorney's request, Ciavatta obtained a copy of the Ingersoll-Rand employee Proprietary Agreement he had signed when beginning his employment with Ingersoll-Rand Research. He did not inform Ingersoll-Rand of his activities with respect to his roof support system. By letter dated October 24, 1979, his attorney advised Ciavatta that "this invention is yours and Ingersoll has no enforceable claim thereto."

After his brief employment with the bankrupt company in Michigan, Ciavatta returned to his work on the stabilizing device and began refining the system in a more systematic manner. Although still looking for employment, he "started to go through significantly more calculations," and obtained sample tubing to run experimental tests. In March 1980, nine months after his termination, Ciavatta filed for a United States patent on the device and was awarded U.S. Patent No. 4316677 in February 1982. Subsequently, in March 1982, Ciavatta received a second patent, U.S. Patent No. 4322183, which involved an improvement to the roof stabilizer protected by Ciavatta's first patent.

In July 1980, Ciavatta prepared a business plan and solicited venture capital from a number of firms, including Kerr McGee Co. and United Nuclear Corp. These financing efforts failed, however, and Ciavatta used his life savings and borrowed over $125,000 from his brother and a bank to take his invention to the marketplace. Ciavatta exhibited his now-patented invention at a trade show in October 1982, and sales of his product then began. He made his first sale in January 1983. Sales for 1983 totalled approximately $30,000. By the time that the trial of this case commenced in June 1985 his total sales approximated $270,000. Ciavatta's stabilizer sells for approximately 15% less than Ingersoll-Rand's stabilizer. The trial court observed "[t]he market place has begun to accept defendant's product and his device appears to be a competitive threat to plaintiff's device."

The parties disagree on when Ingersoll-Rand learned of Ciavatta's invention. The company acknowledges that it had learned of the model for his invention by December 1981 or early 1982. In July 1982, Ciavatta received a letter from Ingersoll-Rand's patent counsel requesting that he assign his patent to the company. Ciavatta communicated to Ingersoll-Rand that his lawyer had advised him that he was not obligated to assign his patent to his former employer. Simultaneously, Ingersoll-Rand employees prepared several internal memoranda analyzing the feasibility of Ciavatta's product and its potential competitive impact. Ingersoll-Rand, now aware of the challenge posed by Ciavatta's invention, began to consider competitive responses to the introduction of the invention in the market.

In September 1983, after Ciavatta had sold his product to several Ingersoll-Rand customers, the company decided to lower the price of its split set stabilizer and to commence this lawsuit....

The issue of Ciavatta's liability for breach of contract was tried without a jury. Ingersoll-Rand attempted to prove that Ciavatta had stolen his invention and that he had relied on Ingersoll-Rand's trade secrets or other confidential information in conceiving his product. Ciavatta argued that the "holdover" clause is unenforceable in the absence of a finding that the invention was based on the employer's trade secrets or other confidential information ....

[The trial court found that Ciavatta did not pirate any trade secrets or confidential information in conceiving his invention, but nevertheless enforced the agreement. The trial court] articulated a general reasonableness test and determined that the balance tilted in favor of Ingersoll-Rand because Ciavatta's "knowledge of the underground mining industry was based entirely on his employment experience with Ingersoll-Rand," and he had been "enriched" by the company's non-confidential ideas and by his access to Ingersoll-Rand's "information, experience, expertise and ideas and the creative interaction gleaned from his employment with the company." The court also determined that Ciavatta's engineering experience was so diverse that "assignment of this specific invention did not unreasonably preclude realistic employment opportunities in other fields."...

The Appellate Division accepted the trial court's factual determination but reversed the judgment....

II

Paragraph 1(c) of Ciavatta's Proprietary Agreement with Ingersoll-Rand comprises a one-year so-called "holdover" agreement under which the employee promises to assign his or her "entire right, title and interest" in any invention he or she creates during a one-year period following termination of employment if that invention is "conceived as a result of and is attributable to work done during such employment." The central question presented in this case is the enforceability of that covenant.

The common law regards an invention as the property of the inventor who conceived, developed, and perfected it. The Supreme Judicial Court of Massachusetts accurately summarized the common-law position in *National Development Co. v. Gray,* 55 N.E.2d 783, 786 (Mass. 1944):

> One by merely entering an employment requiring the performance of services of a noninventive nature does not lose his rights to any inventions that he may make during the employment ... and this is true even if the patent is for an improvement upon a device or process used by the employer or is of such great practical value as to supersede the devices or processes with which the employee became familiar during his employment.... The law looks upon an invention as the property of the one who conceived, devel-

oped and perfected it, and establishes, protects and enforces the inventor's rights in his invention unless he has contracted away those rights.

Thus, employment alone does not require an inventor to assign a patent to his employer. Absent a specific agreement, an employed inventor's rights and duties with respect to an invention or concept arise from the inventor's employment status when he actually designed the invention. *See* Note, "Patent Ownership: An Employer's Right to His Employee's Invention," 58 Notre Dame L. Rev. 863, 866 (1983).

Generally, where an employer hires an employee to design a specific invention or solve a specific problem, the employee has a duty to assign the resulting patent. Where the employee is not hired specifically to design or invent, but nevertheless conceives of a device during working hours with the use of the employer's materials and equipment, the employer is granted an irrevocable but non-exclusive right to use the invention under the "shop right rule." A shop right is an employer's royalty or fee, a non-exclusive and non-transferable license to use an employee's patented invention.

Since the common-law doctrines are vague and ambiguous in defining the rights of employers and employees in employees' inventions, most employers use written contracts to allocate invention rights. Such contracts requiring an employee to assign to the employer inventions designed or conceived during the period of employment are valid.

The contractual allocation of invention rights between employers and employees is especially critical given the fact that 80% to 90% of all inventions in the United States are made by employed inventors. *See* Rights of Employed Inventors, 1982: Hearings on H.R. 4732 and H.R. 6635 Before the House Subcomm. on Courts, Civil Liberties, and the Administration of Justice, 97th Cong., 2d Sess. 1 (1982) (remarks of Rep. Kastenmeier) (quoting Patent Office report stating that 84% of the U.S. patents go to corporate assignees). The United States is not alone in this regard. In West Germany, 60% to 75% of all inventions come from employed inventors; in France the figure is 70% to 75%. In both countries, 90% of all useful inventions are made by employees. Commission of the European Communities, "Comparative Study of Employees' Inventions Law in the Member States of the European Communities," 2 Collective Studies, Labour Law Series 9 (1977).

Most large, technologically advanced companies today require their employees by contract to assign their patents to their employers. Courts, however, will not enforce invention assignment contracts that unreasonably obligate an employee in each and every instance to transfer the ownership of the employee's invention to the employer. Additionally, several states have recently adopted legislation that delimits employer-employee invention assignment agreements. Those statutes restrict the instances in which employers may compel the assignment of employee inventions. *See* Minn. Stat. Ann. §§ 181.78 (1980); N.C. Gen. Stat. §§ 66-57.1 to 57-2 (1981); Wash. Rev. Code Ann. § 49.44.140 (1987); Cal. Lab.

Code § 2870 (West 1987). All of these statutes provide that any employee invention assignment agreement that purports to give employers greater rights than they have under the statute is against public policy and, consequently, unenforceable.

In the instant case, the contract involves the assignment of future or post-employment inventions. Contractual provisions requiring assignment of post-employment inventions are commonly referred to as "trailer" or "holdover" clauses. The public policy issues involved in the enforceability of these holdover clauses reflect the dichotomy of our views on the rights of an inventor and rights of an employer. Our society has long recognized the intensely personal nature of an invention and the importance of providing stimulation and encouragement to inventors. Some commentators believe that the existing patent system does not present sufficient motivation to an employee-inventor. These commentators allege that the United States is in danger of losing its position as technology leader of the world. They cite for support that America is experiencing a declining patent balance and is less patent-productive than many foreign countries. More and more United States patents are not issued to United States citizens and companies but to foreigners. Interestingly, Japan, which began tying employed inventors' compensation to the market value of the invention in 1959, has witnessed a dramatic increase in the number of inventions generated by employed inventors. Stipp, "Inventors Are Seeking Bigger Share of Gains from Their Successes," Wall St. J., Sept. 9, 1982, at 1, col. 6.

To encourage an inventor's creativity, courts have held that on terminating his employment, an inventor has the right to use the general skills and knowledge gained through the prior employment. Nonetheless, it is acknowledged that the inventive process is increasingly being supported and subsidized by corporations and governments. It is becoming a more collective research process, the collective product of corporate and government research laboratories instead of the identifiable work of one or two individuals. Stedman, "Rights and Responsibilities of the Employed Inventor," 45 Ind. L.J. 254 (1974). Employers, therefore, have the right to protect their trade secrets, confidential information, and customer relations. Thus, employees and employers both have significant interests warranting judicial attention.

In view of the competing interests involved in holdover agreements, courts have not held them void per se. Rather, the courts apply a test of reasonableness. Moreover, courts strictly construe contractual provisions that require assignment of post-employment inventions; they must be fair, reasonable, and just. Generally, a clause is unreasonable if it: (1) extends beyond any apparent protection that the employer reasonably requires; (2) prevents the inventor from seeking other employment; or (3) adversely impacts on the public.

New Jersey courts previously have not specifically addressed the enforceability of a "holdover" clause. We have, however, addressed the enforceability of analogous employee noncompetition contracts. We find that our determination of the enforceability of those post-contracts is applicable to our determination in this case of the enforceability of "holdover" clauses.

In [*Solari Industries, Inc. v. Malady*, 264 A.2d 53 (N.J. 1970), and *Whitmyer Bros., Inc. v. Doyle*, 274 A.2d 577 (N.J. 1971)] we articulated a three-part test to determine the validity of a noncompetition covenant in an employment contract. Under those cases, a court will find a noncompetition covenant reasonable if it "simply protects the legitimate interests of the employer, imposes no undue hardship on the employee and is not injurious to the public." *Solari* and *Whitmyer* both recognize as legitimate the employer's interest in protecting trade secrets, confidential information, and customer relations. Since adopting the three-part *Solari/Whitmyer* test, New Jersey courts have addressed similar questions with respect to lawyers, *Dwyer v. Jung*, 133 N.J. Super. 343 (Ch. Div.), *aff'd*, 137 N.J. Super. 135 (App. Div. 1975) (restrictive covenants among attorneys are per se unreasonable); doctors, *Karlin v. Weinberg*, 77 N.J. 408 (1978) (rejecting per se rule of unenforceability with respect to physicians); accountants, *Mailman, Ross, Toyes, & Shapiro v. Edelson*, 183 N.J. Super. 434 (Ch. Div. 1982) (accounting firm alleged insufficient encroachments on business interests to warrant enforcement of covenant); and management and consulting firms, *A.T. Hudson & Co., Inc. v. Donovan*, 216 N.J. Super. 426 (App. Div. 1987) (enforcing two-year restriction because employer has legitimate interest in protecting his customer relationships).

[The Court then discussed several cases from various jurisdictions.]

Regardless of the results reached in the individual cases, all courts recognize the competing interests at stake. That is, the question of the enforceability of holdover covenants clearly presents the interest of the employee in enjoying the benefits of his or her own creation, on the one hand, and the interest of the employer in protecting confidential information, trade secrets, and, more generally, its time and expenditures in training and imparting skills and knowledge to its paid work force, on the other. Moreover, courts recognize that the public has an enormously strong interest in both fostering ingenuity and innovation of the inventor and maintaining adequate protection and incentives to corporations to undertake long-range and extremely costly research and development programs.

IV

The cases thus support the enforceability of holdover agreements if they are reasonable. In assessing the reasonableness of holdover agreements, this Court will follow the *Solari/Whitmyer* test of reasonableness. By applying the reasonableness test, the judicial analysis of holdover agreements will parallel the judicial analysis of contracts requiring an employee to assign to the employer inventions made or conceived of by an employee *during* his or her employment. We have held such contracts to be enforceable when reasonable. Likewise, we will enforce holdover agreements to the same extent that we will enforce similar post-employment restrictive agreements, giving employers "that limited measure of relief within the terms of the noncompetitive agreement which would be reasonably necessary to protect his 'legitimate interests,' would cause 'no undue hardship' on the employee, and would 'not impair the public interest.'" *Whitmyer*, 274 A.2d at 582; *Solari*, 264 A.2d at 61.

The first two parts of the *Solari/Whitmyer* test focus on the protection of the legitimate interests of the employer and the extent of the hardship on the employee. Plainly, the court must balance these competing interests. In cases where the employer's interests are strong, such as cases involving trade secrets or confidential information, a court will enforce a restrictive agreement. Conversely, in cases where the employer's interests do not rise to the level of a proprietary interest deserving of judicial protection, a court will conclude that a restrictive agreement merely stifles competition and therefore is unenforceable. Courts also recognize that knowledge, skill, expertise, and information acquired by an employee during his employment become part of the employee's person. "They belong to him as an individual for the transaction of any business in which he may engage, just the same as any part of the skill, knowledge and information received by him before entering the employment." von Kalinowski, "Key Employees and Trade Secrets," 47 Va. L. Rev. 583, 586 (1961). An employee can use those skills in any business or profession he may choose, including a competitive business with his former employer. Courts will not enforce a restrictive agreement merely to aid the employer in extinguishing competition, albeit competition from a former employee. Ultimately, the consuming public would suffer from judicial nurturing of such naked restraints on competition.

At the same time, we recognize that employers have a right to protect their trade secrets and other confidential information. Initially, of course, employers can rely on the patent laws and their common law derivatives as a foundation for protecting their patented goods and trade secrets.[4] Beyond such protections, employers may protect themselves contractually from the misappropriation of other company information by former employees. Through contract, an employer may protect its legitimate interest in preventing employees from using the thoughts and ideas generated by the employee and fellow workers while being paid by and using the resources of the employer to invent a product that directly competes with the employer's product.

---

[4] We note that plaintiff does not directly attack defendant's patents or claim infringement of its own. Further, we find no basis for overturning the factual findings made by the trial court. The trial court made two specific factual findings on this issue:

(g) There is no evidence that defendant pirated trade secrets or utilized confidential information.

(h) There is no evidence that plaintiff's friction stabilizer involved trade secrets. The principles involved in the stabilizer's functioning had been freely discussed by Dr. Scott [the inventor of the friction stabilizer] and others. The specifications and methods of manufacture are easily discoverable.

Most courts have limited the legitimate protectable interests of an employer "to trade secrets and other proprietary information ... and customer relations." *See, e.g., Solari; Whitmyer*. The rationale offered for such a limitation is the broad definition of trade secret and other confidential information. There is no exact definition of a trade secret. Generally, cases rely on the broad definition of trade secret found in the Restatement of Torts § 757 comment b (1939):

> b. *Definition of trade secret*. A trade secret may consist of any formula, pattern, device or compilation of information which is used in one's business, and which gives him an opportunity to obtain an advantage over competitors who do not know or use it. It may be a formula for a chemical compound, a process of manufacturing, treating or preserving materials, a pattern for a machine or other device, or a list of customers.

The Restatement also lists six factors to determine whether a given idea or information is a trade secret: (1) the extent to which the information is known outside of the business; (2) the extent to which it is known by employees and others involved in the business; (3) the extent of measures taken by the owner to guard the secrecy of the information; (4) the value of the information to the business and to its competitors; (5) the amount of effort or money expended in developing the information; and (6) the ease or difficulty with which the information could be properly acquired or duplicated by others. Restatement of Torts § 757 comment b. In sum, a trade secret need not be novel, inventive, or patentable, and may be a device that is clearly anticipated in the prior art or one that is merely a mechanical improvement that a good mechanic can make. However, it may not be part of the general knowledge or information of an industry or a matter of public knowledge.

Ciavatta urges that holdover agreements also should be enforced only when the former employee has used the trade secrets or confidential information of the employer in developing his post-termination invention. Since it is undisputed that he did not do so in inventing his stabilizer, he argues, paragraph 1(c), the holdover clause, should not be enforced against him.

Ingersoll-Rand, however, argues that it is inequitable to limit an employer's "protectable interest" solely to trade secrets and other confidential information. Today, large corporations maintain at great expense modern research and development programs that involve synergistic processes. Such "think tanks" require the free and open exchange of new ideas among the members of a research staff using the employer's body of accumulated information and experiences. This creative process receives its impetus and inspiration from the assimilation of an employer's advanced knowledge and a spontaneous interaction among colleagues, co-employees, and superiors. Ingersoll-Rand argues that it maintains this creative atmosphere in its research and development effort at great expense and that it should be allowed to protect itself against a former employee who invents a unique, competing concept attributable to such brainstorming. Ingersoll-Rand contends that such creative brainstorming enriched Ciavatta and led to his invention and therefore that paragraph 1(c) of the proprietary agreement should be enforced.

We agree with Ingersoll-Rand that the protection afforded by holdover agreements such as the one executed by the parties in this lawsuit may under certain circumstances exceed the limitation of trade secrets and confidential information. We recognize that employers may have legitimate interests in protecting information that is not a trade secret or proprietary information, but highly specialized, current information not generally known in the industry, created and stimulated by the research environment furnished by the employer, to which the employee has been "exposed" and "enriched" solely due to his employment. We do not attempt to define the exact parameters of that protectable interest.

We expect courts to construe narrowly this interest, which will be deemed part of the "reasonableness" equation. The line between such information, trade secrets, and the general skills and knowledge of a highly sophisticated employee will be very difficult to draw, and the employer will have the burden to do so. Nevertheless, we do not hesitate to recognize what appears to us a business reality that modern day employers are in need of some protection against the use or disclosure of valuable information regarding the employer's business, which information is passed on to certain employees confidentially by virtue of the positions those employees hold in the employer's enterprise. *See* Stedman, "Rights and Responsibilities of the Employed Inventor," 45 Ind. L.J. 254, 259 (1970).

Courts, however, must be aware that holdover agreements impose restrictions on employees. Such agreements clearly limit an employee's employment opportunities and in many instances probably interfere with an employee securing a position in which he could most effectively use his skills, at the same time depriving society of a more productive worker. How restrictive the clause is on a particular employee depends, of course, on the facts and circumstances of the case. Indeed, in many instances, the employee may have little choice but to sign a holdover agreement in order to secure employment. Conversely, some very talented or experienced individuals, pursued by several corporations, may bargain for highly lucrative positions in exchange for their promise to be bound by a holdover agreement. Accordingly, courts must evaluate the reasonableness of holdover agreements in light of the individual circumstances of the employer and employee. Courts must balance the employer's need for protection and the hardship on the employee that may result.

The third prong of the *Solari/Whitmyer* test relates to the public interest. Throughout this opinion, we have analyzed the relevant competing public interests. We reiterate that the public has a clear interest in safeguarding fair commercial practices and in protecting employers from theft or piracy of trade secrets, confidential information, or, more generally, knowledge and technique in which the employer may be said to have a proprietary interest. The public has an equally clear and strong interest in fostering creativity and invention and in encouraging technological improvement and design enhancement of all goods in the marketplace. The competing public interests are also evident from the current debate raging in the scientific community about the effect of secrecy in scientific research arising from increased ties between scientists, commercial enterprises, and the government, and the effect of such secrecy on the long term progress of scientific programs and innovations.

In sum, we conclude that holdover agreements are enforceable when reasonable, and that in determining if the post-termination restriction is reasonable, we will apply the three-prong test of *Solari/Whitmyer*. Thus, resolution of each case will depend on its own facts and circumstances. Courts must not go too far in construing holdover agreements to insulate employers from competition from former employees. That courts should not be overly zealous in protecting employers should not, however, dissuade a court from analyzing the reasonableness of a holdover covenant or from enforcing it where it is reasonable. Thus, here, we must balance the interests of Ingersoll-Rand and Ciavatta on the basis of the facts to determine whether the enforcement of the holdover agreement in this instance would be reasonable.

VI

We conclude that on the facts of this case, Ingersoll-Rand is not entitled to an assignment of the patent on Ciavatta's friction stabilizer. We find that Ingersoll-Rand has not substantiated that Ciavatta invented his friction stabilizer in violation of his contractual obligation under the holdover clause. Ingersoll-Rand has not established that Ciavatta "conceived" of his invention as a result of his employment at Ingersoll-Rand. The facts convince us that the holdover clause does not apply here however liberally we are willing to construe the protection afforded employers by such clauses. Furthermore, we also find that enforcement of the holdover agreement in this case would be unreasonable even if the contract by its terms applied to Ciavatta's invention.

The record shows that Armand Ciavatta was not hired to invent or to work on design improvements or other variations of the split set friction stabilizer. He was not directed by his employer into its research and development department, and even though Ciavatta himself submitted numerous product ideas to Ingersoll-Rand, the company never developed any of those ideas. Indeed, Ciavatta testified that as a result of plaintiffs' rejection of his submitted ideas, he was discouraged from creating or using his ingenuity to develop new ideas or suggest adaptations to existing Ingersoll-Rand products. Ingersoll-Rand did not assign Ciavatta to a "think tank" division in which he would likely have encountered on a daily basis the ideas of fellow Ingersoll-Rand personnel regarding how the split set stabilizer could be improved or how a more desirable alternative stabilizer might be designed.

More importantly, the information needed to invent the split set stabilizer is not that unique type of information that we would deem protectable even under our expanded definition of a protectable interest. All of the specifications and capabilities of the Ingersoll-Rand split set stabilizer were widely publicized throughout industry and trade publications. In fact, the general design of Atlas Copco's friction stabilizer, the leading competitor of the Ingersoll-Rand stabilizer, is identical to the general design of the Ingersoll-Rand product. Moreover, Ingersoll-Rand openly advertised the characteristics of its split set product. The uses of the product were well known throughout the mining industry as were the names of the particular users of the product. Production cost figures and pricing schedules were known in the industry as well. Furthermore, the technology behind the split set was no mystery; there was trial testimony that the technology behind the production of the split set was over fifty years old. Thus, it is clear that Ingersoll-Rand has done little to guard the details of its friction stabilizer or maintain a secretive atmosphere surrounding corporate development and marketing of the product. Instead, the company deliberately created and perpetuated an open, public posture in the mining industry submarket in which it operated and in which it enjoyed a commanding market share. Matters of general knowledge throughout an industry cannot be claimed as secrets nor as "unique information" derived as a result of current, ongoing research of the employer.

Ciavatta did not develop his stabilizer on the basis of valuable information about the Ingersoll-Rand product imparted to him because he held a special position with the company. His departure from Ingersoll-Rand and subsequent invention and development of his own competing product do not suggest that he purposefully left to develop a competing product on the basis of the knowledge he gained from his employment. We do not hold that the manner of an employee's departure is dispositive. It is a factor that the court should consider, however, and, in this case, that factor weighs heavily in defendant's favor. Ciavatta was fired from Ingersoll-Rand and testified that he conceived of his invention while installing a light fixture at his home some months after he was terminated. Thereafter, he performed further, independent calculations to test and refine his concept. He worked intermittently on the product as he searched for employment. He developed the product based on his general skill, expertise, and knowledge. While Ciavatta employed certain skills and knowledge he undoubtedly gained during his employment by Ingersoll-Rand, his invention was not the result of any research currently being done by the company or any company research in which he personally was involved. Indeed, the technology Ciavatta employed was developed over fifty years ago and well known in the industry. Nor did he use any of Ingersoll-Rand's capital or materials in the development of his invention. When his attempts to lure capital failed, he borrowed and used his own savings to get the small business started.

These facts lead us to believe that the factors of the *Solari/Whitmyer* balancing test weigh heavily in favor of defendant, even assuming that paragraph 1(c) applies. Although we specifically hold today that reasonable holdover agreements may be enforceable, we decline to enforce the agreement between Ingersoll-Rand and Ciavatta because, as it relates to the patented invention in dispute, the restriction is unreasonable under *Solari/Whitmyer*.[6] We recognize that employers may have a protectable interest in certain proprietary information that former employees may use to invent competing products. We also recognize that the range of the employer's proprietary information that may be protected by contract may narrowly exceed the specific types of information covered by the law of trade secrets and confidential information. Here, however, when we apply the reasonableness test of *Solari/Whitmyer,* we conclude that enforcement of the holdover agreement would work an undue hardship on defendant. Thus, we conclude that the restraint in this specific case is unreasonable and hence unenforceable.

Accordingly, we affirm the judgment of the Appellate Division.

NOTES

1. *Works of Authorship*. Under the federal Copyright Act of 1976, 17 U.S.C. § 201(b), an employer is presumed to be the author of any work made for hire:

> In the case of a work made for hire, the employer or other person for whom the work was prepared is considered the author for purposes of this title, and unless the parties have expressly agreed otherwise in a written instrument signed by them, owns all the rights comprised in the copyright.

The Supreme Court addressed § 201(b) in *Community for Creative Non-Violence v. Reid,* 490 U.S. 730 (1989). A nonprofit organization sponsored a nativity scene of contemporary homeless people for the annual Christmastime Pageant of Peace in Washington, D.C. The group hired James Earl Reid to build the sculpture, called "Third World America." Reid donated his labor to the project. C.C.N.V. built a pedestal for the statue and made several suggestions which Reid incorporated into his work. After the pageant was completed, the parties could not agree what should be done with the statue, and each party then filed a copyright claim. The case eventually reached the Supreme Court.

The Supreme Court held that federal common law of agency, rather than state law, should be used to determine whether the creator of a copyrighted work is an

---

[6] As an aid to employer's drafting future holdover agreements, we emphasize the following language of Paragraph 1(c) that applies the agreement to "inventions, copyrights and/or designs ... if conceived as a result of and is attributable to work done during such employment and *relates to a method, substance, machine, article of manufacture or improvements therein within the scope of the business of the COMPANY or any of its affiliates*." (emphasis added). Ingersoll-Rand has thirty divisions worldwide, so arguably the clause could apply to activities outside the scope of Ciavatta's employment but within the scope of any of those numerous divisions. We caution employers that such language appears to be overly broad, and, hence, would be unenforceable.

employee. It found that Reid was an independent contractor rather than an employee, and that "Third World America" thus was not a "work made for hire" within the meaning of 17 U.S.C. § 201(b). The Court remanded the case for a determination of whether C.C.N.V. and Reid prepared the work "with the intention that their contributions be merged into inseparable or interdependent parts of a unitary whole," in which case the "joint work" doctrine would apply.

2. *Independent Contractors and Works for Hire.* Suppose a corporation hires independent computer programmers to create software for its workplace. Even if the corporation closely supervises the development of the program, the independent contractors are the authors and owners of the copyright. Unless they have waived their rights by contract, they have the right to make modifications and sell the software to others. This is an example where workers have greater rights as independent contractors than as employees. *See generally* Charles D. Ossola, *"Joint Work" Theory Raises New Questions on Authors' Rights*, NATIONAL L.J. S10 (Jan. 18, 1993).

Part V
Prohibitions on Status Discrimination

Chapter 13

POLICY RATIONALES FOR PROHIBITIONS ON STATUS DISCRIMINATION

A. TRADITIONAL ANALYSIS

PAUL BREST, THE SUPREME COURT 1975 TERM — FOREWORD: IN DEFENSE OF THE ANTIDISCRIMINATION PRINCIPLE, 90 Harvard Law Review 1, 6-11 (1976)[*]

Stated most simply, the antidiscrimination principle disfavors race-dependent decisions and conduct — at least when they selectively disadvantage the members of a minority group. By race-dependent, I mean decisions and conduct (hereafter, simply decisions) that would have been different but for the race of those benefited or disadvantaged by them. Race-dependent decisions may take several forms, including overt racial classifications on the face of statutes and covert decisions by officials.

A. *Rationales for the Antidiscrimination Principle*

The antidiscrimination principle guards against certain defects in the *process* by which race-dependent decisions are made and also against certain harmful *results* of race-dependent decisions. Restricting the principle to a unitary purpose vitiates its moral force and requires the use of sophisticated reasoning to explain applications that seem self-evident.

1. *Defects of Process.* — The antidiscrimination principle is designed to prevent both irrational and unfair infliction of injury.

Race-dependent decisions are irrational insofar as they reflect the assumption that members of one race are less worthy than other people. Not all such decisions are necessarily irrational, however. For example, if black laborers tend to be absent from work more often than their white counterparts — for whatever reason — it is not irrational for an employer to prefer white applicants for the job.... Regulations and decisions based on statistical generalizations are commonplace in all developed societies and essential to their functioning....

In short, the mere fact that most blacks are industrious ... does not make the employer's or the Government's decision irrational. Indeed, if all race-dependent decisions were irrational, there would be no need for an anti-discrimination principle, for it would suffice to apply the widely held moral, constitutional, and practice principle that forbids treating persons irrationally. The antidiscrimination principle fills a special need because — as even a glance at history indicates — race-dependent decisions that are rational and purport to be

---

[*] Copyright © 1976 by The Harvard Law Review Association. Reprinted with permission.

based solely on legitimate considerations are likely in fact to rest on assumptions of the differential worth of racial groups or on the related phenomenon of racially selective sympathy and indifference[, by which] I mean the unconscious failure to extend to a minority the same recognition of humanity, and hence the same sympathy and care, given as a matter of course to one's own group....

2. *Harmful Results.* — A second and independent rationale for the anti-discrimination principle is the prevention of the harms which may result from race-dependent decisions. Often, the most obvious harm is the denial of the opportunity to secure a desired benefit — a job, a night's lodging at a motel, a vote. But this does not completely describe the consequences of race-dependent decisionmaking. Decisions based on assumptions of intrinsic worth and selective indifference inflict psychological injury by stigmatizing their victims as inferior. Moreover, because acts of discrimination tend to occur in pervasive patterns, their victims suffer especially frustrating, cumulative and debilitating injuries....

Racial generalizations usually inflict psychic injury whether or not they are in fact premised on assumptions of differential moral worth. Although all of us recognize that institutional decisions must depend on generalizations based on objective characteristics of persons and things rather than on individualized judgments, we nonetheless tend to feel unfairly treated when disadvantaged by a generalization that is not true as applied to us. Generalizations based on immutable personal traits such as race or sex are especially frustrating because we can do nothing to escape their operation. These generalizations are still more pernicious, for they are often premised on the supposed correlation between the inherited characteristic and the undesirable voluntary behavior of those who possess the characteristic — for example, blacks are less industrious, trustworthy or clean than whites. Because the behavior is voluntary, and hence the proper object of moral condemnation, individuals as to whom the generalization is inaccurate may justifiably feel that the decisionmaker has passed moral judgment on them.

The psychological injury inflicted by generalizations based on race is compounded by the frustrating and cumulative nature of their material injuries.... A person who is denied one opportunity because he or she is short or overweight will find other opportunities, for in our society height and weight do not often serve as the bases for generalizations determining who will receive benefits. By contrast, at least until very recently, a black was not denied *an* opportunity because of his or her race, but denied virtually *all* desirable opportunities. As door after door is shut in one's face, the individual acts of discrimination combine into a systematic and grossly inequitable frustration of opportunity.

The cumulative disadvantage caused by the use of race as a proxy even for legitimate characteristics provides an independent ground for disfavoring non-benign race-dependent decisions regardless of the integrity of the process by which they were made. To the unprejudiced employer who would prefer white applicants to blacks solely for reasons of efficiency, the antidiscrimination principle says in effect: "If you were the only one to do this, we would permit you to make efficient generalizations based on race. But so many other firms might employ similar generalizations that black individuals would suffer great cumulative harms. And, in the absence of an overriding justification, this cannot be permitted."

OWEN M. FISS, A THEORY OF FAIR EMPLOYMENT LAWS, 38 University of Chicago Law Review 235, 237-43, 290-310 (1971)[*]

Laws prohibiting racial discrimination in employment are inextricably linked to the goal of securing for Negroes a position of "equality." There are, however, two senses to "equality" in this context. One is equal treatment. Individual Negroes should be treated "equally" by employers in the sense that their race should be "ignored," that is, not held against them. This sense of equality focuses on the starting positions in a race: If color is not a criterion for employment, blacks will be on equal footing with whites. The second sense of equality — "equal achievement" — looks to the outcome of the race. It relates to the actual distribution of jobs among racial classes and is concerned with both the quantity and the quality (measured, for example, by pay level and social status) of the jobs. Jobs should be distributed so that the relative economic position of Negroes — as a class — is improved, so that the economic position of Negroes is approximately equal to that of whites....

These two senses of equality are linked in fair employment laws, but it is not clear which is the goal of the law. Under one interpretation, the aim of a fair employment law is to secure equal treatment, and although equal treatment might alter the actual distribution of jobs and lead to equal achievement, such a result would be only incidental. Under an alternative interpretation, the aim is equal achievement, and the guarantee of equal treatment — the antidiscrimination prohibition — is the chosen method for equalizing the distribution of jobs among racial classes.

The distinction between these two views of the aim of the law is of little moment if it can be assumed that equal treatment will lead to equal achievement. But the assumption may be incorrect. It is conceivable, and indeed, likely, that even if color is not given any weight in employment decisions, and in that sense equal treatment obtained, substantial inequalities by race in the distribution of jobs will persist in the immediate and foreseeable future [because of the unfortunate legacy of slavery and Jim Crow]....

1. *The Equal-Treatment Concept: Responding to a Particularized Wrong.* An employment decision is analyzable primarily as a decision to allocate a scarce opportunity — a job. The paradigm situation is one in which several individuals are competing for a limited number of opportunities. A choice among these individuals is required, and the question arises as to the appropriate criteria for that choice. A choice made on the basis of an improper criterion — classified by the

---

law as "invidious" or "arbitrary" — is viewed as a particularized wrong. The rejected individual is not being treated fairly.

Two attributes of the racial criterion account for the sense of unfairness engendered by its use as the basis of an employment decision. The first is that an individual's race is not considered an accurate predictor of his productivity. Fair employment laws reflect a rejection of any views of innate inferiority and also a commitment to the principle that the choice among individuals for scarce opportunities should be on the basis of the individual's merit....

The second attribute is the absence of individual control. To judge an individual on the basis of his race is to judge him on the basis of his membership in a class where that membership is truly predetermined.... Individual control is a value because it provides the prospect for upward mobility, an important incentive to self-improvement and efficient performance. Further, it is valuable because it rationalizes, and thus makes more tolerable, the unequal distribution of status and wealth among people in the society: failure is the individual's own fault....

In identifying these two attributes of race — unrelatedness to productivity and the absence of individual control — I do not mean to suggest that either attribute by itself would be sufficient to generate unfairness.... Instead, the suggestion is that both these attributes, unrelatedness to productivity and the absence of individual control, are inherent in race, and that together they account for the unfairness.[11] ...

Because of these attributes — unrelated to productivity and beyond individual control — allocating an employment opportunity on the basis of race constitutes a particularized wrong.... The particularized wrong — the unfair treatment — exists independently of ... consequences to the individual [such as loss of income and adverse psychological reactions], and is perceived without regard to an actual measurement of the consequences. It arises from the attributes of race, not from the consequences to the individual [or, indeed to society itself]....

---

[11] Criteria other than race may, of course, be both unrelated to productivity and beyond individual control. When these criteria are used as a basis for allocating a scarce employment opportunity, unfair treatment or a particularized wrong occurs in much the same way as when race is used. Some of these criteria, such as sex and national origin, are frequently included in the reach of fair employment laws; others, such as eye color, are not. The selection among this universe of allegedly arbitrary criteria for inclusion within the reach of the fair employment laws depends on various factors: the size and power of the victim group within the total constituency; political strategies; some estimation as to whether conduct based on those criteria is sufficiently widespread and so firmly rooted as to warrant coercive intervention by the law; differences in the degree of unfairness; and, whether interfering with conduct based on these criteria would also serve other permissible purposes. The usual absence of some of these arbitrary criteria, such as eye color, from the reach of the fair employment laws may be due simply to these factors. One cannot argue from their absence that there is no unfairness in using race as a basis of allocating an employment opportunity, and that the aim of the prohibition against racial discrimination is not to express legal disapproval of the unfair treatment inherent in judging an individual on the basis of his race and to provide sanctions and remedies to respond to such particularized wrongs....

2. *The Evaluation of Facially Innocent Criteria.* The choice among individuals competing for a particular employment opportunity is often made on the basis of criteria that are allegedly applied to both Negroes and whites — facially innocent criteria. For example, ... [g]raduation from high school or the absence of an arrest record may be required of all new employees....

[These types of criteria present concern because they can be used by employers to evade the antidiscrimination principle, because they seem unfair to blacks, and because they impede the goal of improving the relative economic position of blacks, but they also present] a stubborn analytic problem: how can an employment decision *based* on the individual's nonperformance under a facially innocent criterion be deemed to be an employment decision *based* on the individual's race? A desire to evade is not sufficient to establish a violation; it still remains to be determined that the employer chose his employees on the basis of race....

One approach to the analytic problem emphasizes the employer's motive for choosing the criterion. The central causal concepts of the antidiscrimination prohibition, such as "based on," "because of," and "on the grounds of," are given a psychological gloss. They are thought to refer to the employer's state of mind. The theory is that if the employer chose the seemingly innocent criterion not to further his business interests but merely to satisfy his taste for discrimination (or that of his customers or workers), then the employment decision adversely affecting Negroes is not based on the innocent criterion but instead on race. Race is the "real" basis of the job allocation.

Perhaps, as a matter of semantics, it is possible to give the causal concepts such a psychological gloss. Even so, there are problems with this approach. One set of problems stems from the difficulties of proof.... [A] facially innocent criterion, by its very nature, always permits an assertion that it was chosen for legitimate business reasons, unrelated to a desire to exclude blacks....

Another set of problems stems from the failure of the psychological approach to deal adequately with the situation where the employer's choice of criteria is based on motivation related to efficiency or to a mixed motive — race and efficiency. In these instances, the court may be able to make an independent assessment of the employer's alleged non-racial reasons for his choice and find that these reasons are not "sufficient," leading to the conclusion that only a desire to exclude blacks could "rationally" or "objectively" explain the use of the criterion. But it is hardly a solution to the analytic problem to give the causal terms a psychological gloss and then "presume" as a matter of law that whenever, in the court's judgment, the use of the criteria cannot be justified on efficiency grounds, the "motivation" of the employer was a racial one. The bootstrap quality of that reasoning is apparent....

Finally, and perhaps most importantly, the psychological approach is inadequate because it incorrectly conceives the nature of the regulatory device. Antidiscrimination prohibitions try to regulate by prohibiting the use of a criterion (race), and generally a violation of the prohibition does not turn on the motives or reason for the choice of the criterion.... [An] employer violates the prohibition when he judges people on the basis of race, regardless of whether the employer chose that particular criterion, in whole or in part, because he wants to save the administrative costs of screening applicants (and uses race as symptomatic of poor education), because he hates blacks (and wants to screen out as many as possible), or because he wants to please his customers or his workers (who simply wish to maximize their wealth by limiting the supply of labor or preserving their competitive edge). The conduct that is regulated is the use of the criterion — judging people on the basis of the criterion — and the reasons or motives for the choice of the criterion are irrelevant under the theory and structure of fair employment laws....

Another approach to this analytic problem, and one that seems more satisfactory, focuses on the criterion itself. The theory is that the seemingly innocent criterion is the functional equivalent of "race."... There are two steps necessary to establish functional equivalence. The first is a determination that the criterion, like race, has or is likely to have an adverse differential impact on Negroes: the use of the criterion is more likely to limit the employment opportunities of Negroes as a class than those of whites.... The second step ... is to drain nonperformance under the criterion of any normative power: failure to satisfy the particular criterion could no more justify the adverse employment decision than could "race." This second step requires that the two attributes of race that make it an inappropriate basis for allocating jobs — unrelatedness to productivity and absence of individual control — also be attributes of the criterion in question....

Even assuming that the theory of functional equivalence "overcomes" the analytic problem in a manner consistent with the structure of the anti-discrimination prohibition, the question of the role it should play in the enforcement of the law remains. Part of the answer to that question depends on the importance attached to such values as improving the relative economic position of blacks, insuring fair treatment in employment decisions, and preventing evasion. For example, the stronger the commitment to the value of improving the relative economic position of blacks (the equal-achievement goal), the rougher the approximation one will accept in establishing the equivalence. Indeed, that commitment may lead one even to forget the analytic problem altogether.[71] However, the role of the functional equivalence theory in enforcing fair employment laws may also turn on an awareness of certain conceptual and evidentiary difficulties in applying the theory — in establishing that a facially

---

[71] ...The theory of functional equivalence might also be responsive to the problems posed by the fact that [Title VII] did not become effective until July 2, 1965. (Elsewhere the theory might be responsive to statutes of limitations.) Without such a theory it would have been difficult or impossible to reach the clear discriminatory employment practices occurring before the effective date of the law, and that are perpetuated by the use — after the effective date — of such criteria as seniority and nepotism. This cannot ordinarily explain a concern with the use of other facially innocent criteria, such as aptitude tests or high school graduation....

innocent criterion is the equivalent of race and determining the appropriate remedy once that equivalence is established....

In order to establish a functional equivalence, it [must] be determined that the criterion, like race, is unrelated to productivity.... One difficulty involved in evaluating [facially neutral] criteria stems from the fact that the concept of predictiveness is a relative one.... The theory is that it is almost as poor a predictor as race, but there is no absolute or *a priori* measure of a "poor" predictor. A further complication arises because the relation of a criterion to productivity is not simply a function of its accuracy as a predictor. It may pay to use a poor predictor if the costs of administering or developing alternative predictors would exceed the value of the increase in productivity that would result from an increase in the accuracy of the predictor. Thus, whether the criterion is conducive to productivity turns on four complex and interrelated judgments: (a) the accuracy of the predictor in question; (b) the accuracy that can be obtained by alternative means of predicting (either ones that are currently available or ones that can be developed); (c) the costs of developing better predictors; and (d) the costs of administering the alternative predictors....

Once it is established that the seemingly innocent criterion is almost as unrelated to productivity as race, there remains, of course, the task of determining whether the individual is responsible for his failure to satisfy the criterion. Lack of individual control is one of the attributes of race that accounts for the unfairness inherent in its use as a basis of allocating scarce employment opportunities. It should also be required to establish functional equivalence ... and for this purpose past discrimination against the racial class is relevant. Past discrimination may have impaired the individual's ability to satisfy the criteria and has put the victims at a competitive disadvantage as compared to whites. For example, discrimination in the public educational system or exclusion from company training programs may be the explanation for poor performance on a test.... [T]he court must attempt to reconstruct the past and, perhaps more importantly, must distinguish between the past wrongs that are an inevitable part of the socialization or development process and those that are of such unique, systematic character as to relieve the individual of responsibility for his nonperformance while holding most others responsible for their nonperformance....

The difficulties inherent in making the judgments and the individualized nature of any conclusion of functional equivalence suggest that the rational law enforcement policy is to save this analysis for exceptional cases.... A properly selective use of the theory of functional equivalence would preclude the wholesale legitimation of all facially innocent criteria and keep some pressure on employers to develop criteria that are not near-cousins of race. At the same time it would minimize the societal costs involved in using this theory.

NOTE

Criticism of the Traditional View. On libertarian grounds, Professor Richard Epstein has called for repeal of the employment discrimination laws:

> [T]he difficulties [with antidiscrimination laws are] fundamental. The root difficulty [is that they] maintain that a qualified norm of forced association is better than a strong norm of freedom of association. It is dangerous to assume that whatever conduct is thought to be wise or enlightened can and should be forced on society by the public speaking with one voice. There is little understanding of why the proscribed differences might matter, and little appreciation of the enormous political risks that come with concentrating power over employment decisions in the hands of a bureaucracy that operates under its own set of expansionist imperatives. There is also a failure to understand that the first question that should be asked in any public debate is *who* shall decide, not *what* should be decided. On the question of association, the right answer is the private persons who may (or may not) wish to associate, and not the government or the public at large. But having given the wrong collective answer to the "who" question, we find the "what" question receiving an extended elaboration that has resulted in the extensive and disruptive coercive structure that is civil rights enforcement today.... [M]y study of the employment discrimination laws has persuaded me of the bedrock social importance of the principles of individual autonomy and freedom of association. Their negation through the modern civil rights law has led to a dangerous form of government coercion that in the end threatens to do more than strangle the operation of labor and employment markets. The modern civil rights laws are a new form of imperialism that threatens the political liberty and intellectual freedom of us all.

RICHARD A. EPSTEIN, FORBIDDEN GROUNDS: THE CASE AGAINST EMPLOYMENT DISCRIMINATION LAWS 505 (1992) (emphasis in original). As you might expect, Professor Epstein's views have been heavily criticized. *See* Marion Crain, *Rationalizing Inequality: An Antifeminist Defense of the "Free" Market*, 61 GEO. WASH. L. REV. 556 (1993) (book review); J. Hoult Verkerke, *Free to Search*, 105 HARV. L. REV. 2080 (1992) (book review).

B. ECONOMIC ANALYSIS

GARY S. BECKER, THE ECONOMICS OF DISCRIMINATION 11, 153-54 (2d ed. 1971)[*]

I have attempted to [develop] a theory of discrimination [that] can be applied to "discrimination" and "nepotism" in all their diverse forms, whether the discrimination be against Negroes, Jews, women, or persons with "unpleasant" personalities or whether the nepotism be in favor of blood relative, countrymen,

---

[*] Copyright © 1971 by The University of Chicago. Reprinted with permission.

or classmates, since they have in common the use of non-monetary considerations in deciding whether to hire, work with, or buy from an individual or
group....

Individuals[, under the framework proposed here,] are assumed to act as if
they have "tastes for discrimination," and these tastes are the most important
immediate cause of actual discrimination. When an employer discriminates
against employees, he acts as if he incurs non-pecuniary, psychic costs of production by employing them; when an employee discriminates against fellow
employees or employers, he acts as if he incurs non-pecuniary, psychic costs of
employment by working with them; when a consumer discriminates against
products, he acts as if he incurs non-pecuniary, psychic costs of consumption by
consuming them.

It is desirable to formulate these non-pecuniary costs or tastes in a way that is
sufficiently specific to yield quantitative empirical insights and sufficiently general to incorporate new information as it becomes available. Both these desid-
erata are satisfied by the concept of a "discrimination coefficient." The discrimination coefficient of an employer against an employee measures the value placed
on the non-pecuniary cost of employing him, since it represents the percentage
difference between the money and the true or net wage rate "paid" to him. If π is
the money wage rate paid, then $\pi (1 + d)$ is the net wage rate, with d being the
discrimination coefficient. Likewise, the discrimination coefficient of other
employees against this employee measure[s] the value placed on the non-
pecuniary costs of working with him, since it represents the percentage difference between the money and the net wage rates received for working with him;
and the discrimination coefficient of a consumer measures the value placed on
the non-pecuniary costs of buying a product (partly) produced or sold by him,
since it represents the percentage difference between the money and the net price
paid for this product.

WILLIAM M. LANDES, THE ECONOMICS OF FAIR EMPLOYMENT LAWS, 76 Journal of Political Economy 507, 508-12 (1968)[*]

State fair employment laws explicitly make it a violation for firms and unions
to (1) refuse employment or discharge a non-white because of his race (referred
to as the "segregation provision") or (2) discriminate in terms and compensation
of employment against non-whites for firms and unions that employ both whites
and non-whites (referred to as the "wage differential provision").[4] Provision (1)
is necessarily ineffectual without provision (2). In the absence of (2) a firm
would comply with the law if it offered a qualified non-white employment at a

---

[*] Copyright © 1968 by the University of Chicago Press. Reprinted with permission.

[4] These two provisions, which are the key ones in all state statutes, apply more generally to
persons discriminated against on grounds of race, creed, color, or national origin. Some states also
prohibit discrimination because of age or sex....

wage equal to zero or a small fraction of the white wage. Clearly, the non-white would choose not to work in this firm, and hence compliance with the law would not have altered market behavior. For provision (1) to have any effect, there must be a minimum wage below which a firm cannot offer employment to a qualified non-white without violating the law. Provision (2) defines this minimum as equal to the white wage....

[T]he passage of a fair employment law adds an expected cost to firms and unions that are violating either the segregation or wage differential provision of the law, and induces a substitution away from discriminatory behavior. The magnitude of the expected cost equals the cost of violating the fair employment law if one is caught (e.g., adverse publicity, costly litigation, possible fines and imprisonment) times the probability of apprehension. The net effect of these expected costs is to increase the market demand for non-whites relative to whites, which leads to a rise in the ratio of non-white to white wages and a fall in market discrimination against non-whites. This proposition can be demonstrated in the following examples where either employers [or] employees ... have a taste for discrimination against non-whites, and where non-white and white workers have equal marginal products.[5]

1. *Employer Discrimination*

In the absence of a fair employment law, non-whites, to obtain employment, must offer their services at lower wages than equally able whites in order to compensate employers for their tastes for discrimination. The resulting market wage differential will depend on the magnitude of these tastes, their variance among employers, and the proportion of non-white to white workers. To illustrate, if the proportion is low, non-whites can find employment with firms that have small tastes for discrimination and the ratio of non-white to white wages would approximate one. As the proportion rises, non-whites must seek employment in firms with more intense tastes for discrimination, and these firms require a larger money wage differential to offset their tastes. Thus, non-white to white wages fall as the proportion of non-whites rises.... The smaller the variance in tastes among employers, the less responsive are relative wages to a change in the proportion of non-whites.... Given [the white-non-white wage] differential [that results from employer tastes, their variance, and the proportion of non-white workers], firms can be divided into three groups, depending on the magnitude of their discrimination tastes: segregated non-white (SN) firms employ only non-whites as their tastes are more than compensated by the market white-non-white wage differential; integrated (I) firms employ both whites and non-whites as their tastes are exactly offset by the wage differential; and segregated white

---

[5] The concept of a taste for discrimination or discrimination coefficient was developed by Becker.... It is assumed throughout the theoretical discussion that whites and non-whites are perfect substitutes in production. This assumption is consistent with fair employment legislation, for such laws try to assure equal employment opportunity for people of roughly equal economic capabilities.

(SW) firms employ only whites since the wage differential is insufficient to overcome their tastes.[7]

The enactment of a fair employment law adds an expected cost to SW firms for violating the segregation provision, and to I firms for violating the wage differential provision.[8] SW firms must choose between voluntary compliance with the law, which involves the employment of non-whites at wages equal to the white wage, or continued violation. They are more likely to prefer voluntary compliance the smaller its losses (i.e., psyche income losses from foregoing one's tastes for discrimination) compared to the expected losses from violation. Losses from voluntary compliance will be smaller the fewer non-whites an SW firm must hire to avoid possible penalties from enforcement, the smaller the firm's taste for discrimination, and the lower the wage it must pay to non-whites. Expected losses from violation are greater the greater the probability of being caught and the larger the losses if one is caught. In addition, attitudes toward risk ... are relevant because the choice between voluntary compliance and violation is analogous to the choice between a loss with certainty and a risky prospect involving the chance of no loss or a loss greater than the certain loss.[9] Other things the same, the more risk averse the firm, the less likely it will choose violation.

If I firms respond to the wage differential violation by dismissing non-white workers, which is the traditional interpretation of "equal pay" legislation, they incur expected losses from violating the segregation prohibition. An alternative response that allows I firms initially to maintain their pre-fair employment income is the dismissal of whites and the employment of only non-whites at the original non-white wage. However, shifts in the supply of whites and non-whites to I firms that result from the compliance of SW firms can alter the decision of I firms to employ only non-whites. Non-whites are attracted away from I (as well as SN) firms by higher wages in SW firms, and, at the same time, SW firms will release some whites as they substitute non-whites. This produces a rise in non-white wages and a fall in white wages to I firms, which in turn act as an incentive for some I firms to employ only whites in violation of the segregation provi-

---

[7] SW firms are more common than might be suggested from their definition. They include firms that hire non-whites in menial jobs but refuse to employ qualified non-whites (i.e., perfect substitutes for whites) in more skilled jobs.

[8] SN firms do not violate the law. They cannot be accused of discriminating in employment against whites, as they are willing to hire whites at the same money wage as non-whites. Whites, however, refuse employment in these firms because money wages are higher elsewhere. Since SN firms employ only non-whites, the provision of the law regarding wage differentials within firms is not relevant.

[9] Losses from voluntary compliance must be less than losses from being apprehended, because the latter include not only the former losses (for the firm caught must now comply with the law and employ non-whites) but also possible fines, litigation, and the monetary equivalent of adverse publicity.

sion. The determinants of this choice include the same factors that bear upon the decision of SW firms, in addition to the changes in white and non-white wages. The greater these changes, the more likely I firms will prefer all whites.[11]

To summarize, one predicts that a fair employment law will cause an increase in the average non-white to white ratio for a given proportion of non-whites to whites.... The more SW firms that comply, the greater will be the increase in non-white to white money wages....

2. *Employee Discrimination*

Tastes for discrimination among white employees who are perfect substitutes in production for non-whites result in segregation but not wage discrimination. Since whites must be compensated for working with non-whites, a profit maximizing employer never hires both whites and non-whites together. He employs only non-whites if their wages are less than the white wage, and only whites if their wages are less than the non-white wage. For both groups to find employment in segregated firms their wages must be equal.

A fair employment law alters this condition. Although there is no market discrimination against non-whites, these laws penalize segregated white firms.[12] Previously all-white firms would no longer employ whites because white wages, as viewed by employers, are greater than the wages of equally productive non-whites by an amount equal to the expected costs of violating the segregation provision per worker. These firms shift their demand to non-whites. White wages fall and non-white wages rise, and the change in wages acts as an incentive for some firms to employ only whites. The reduction in white wages required to compensate firms for bearing the expected costs of violation will be greater the greater these expected costs and the more risk averse the firms.

Integration would take place if some whites receive a disutility from associating with non-whites less than the resulting difference between non-white and white wages. These whites would choose to work with non-whites at a wage equal to the non-white wage rather than accept a lower wage in all-white firms. This in turn reduces the supply of whites to segregated white firms, increases the supply of workers to non-white firms, and lowers the ratio of non-white to white wages (which is still greater than one). In the extreme case, if the expected losses from violation per worker are greater than the monetary equivalent of the taste for discrimination of whites with the most intense tastes, all whites would prefer to work in integrated firms in preference to compensating employers for maintaining segregation. Every firm would then integrate, and whites and non-whites

---

[11] These wage changes may be sufficient to induce some previously all-non-white firms (SN) to employ only whites.

[12] Firms that employ only non-whites are not violating the segregation provision, as they are willing to employ whites at the same wage as non-whites. However, whites prefer employment in all-white firms.

would receive equal money wages. In all other cases, fair employment laws result in an increase in the ratio of non-white to white average wages.

JOHN J. DONOHUE III, FURTHER THOUGHTS ON EMPLOYMENT DISCRIMINATION LEGISLATION: A REPLY TO JUDGE POSNER, 136 University of Pennsylvania Law Review 523, 531-33 (1987)[*]

Many analysts have found [Becker's] model appealing and have emphasized its prediction that the free market will eliminate discriminatory employers. [E]mployment discrimination[, however,] could have a different genesis, in which the disciplinary role of the market as the ally of the victims of discrimination is absent.... [A] "reluctance by employers to employ blacks at the same wage as whites" may be the product of "statistical discrimination," in which discrimination against, for example, blacks is not the result of racial animus, but rather stems from a realization that, for whatever reasons, black workers are on average less productive than white workers. If this generalization is accurate, and if it is costly to ascertain individual abilities, then statistical discrimination, unlike Beckerian discrimination, may be profit-maximizing....

[T]he [statistical discrimination] model assumes that employers discriminate against blacks because knowledge of race conveys useful information. Even though employers realize that such generalizations are not universally true, it may still be profitable for firms to act as if they were rather than to expend resources to determine which blacks have higher than average productivity or which whites have lower than average productivity. At first glance, it might seem that statistical discrimination will necessarily be efficient whenever it is profit-maximizing. Nonetheless, it is possible that discrimination could be profit-maximizing for the firm, yet inefficient for society as a whole.

The basic argument is that statistical discrimination will distort the incentives for individuals to invest in human capital since they will simply be treated as the average member of their class whether or not they make such investments. By divorcing an employee's individual productivity from the wage that the employee receives, statistical discrimination introduces inefficiencies into the human capital investment decisions of workers. If the concomitant costs are large, statistical discrimination may be harmful from a social perspective, although beneficial to individual employers.[34] By discouraging workers from investing in their own human capital, society is deprived of all of the benefits that flow from these investments. Therefore, while we should recognize that, unlike animus-based discrimination, statistical discrimination is presumably

---

[*] Copyright © 1987 by University of Pennsylvania Law Review. Reprinted with permission.

[34] See Lundberg & Startz, *Private Discrimination and Social Intervention in Competitive Labor Markets,* 73 Am. Econ. Rev. 340, 346-47 (1983); Schwab, *Is Statistical Discrimination Efficient?,* 76 Am. Econ. Rev. 228, 233 (1986).

profit-maximizing, a *full* cost-benefit analysis of Title VII would include the benefits from proscribing statistical discrimination as well as the costs....[37]

C. CRITICAL LEGAL STUDIES ANALYSIS

ALAN DAVID FREEMAN, LEGITIMIZING RACIAL DISCRIMINATION THROUGH ANTIDISCRIMINATION LAW: A CRITICAL REVIEW OF SUPREME COURT DOCTRINE, 62 Minnesota Law Review 1049, 1052-57 (1978)[*]

The concept of "racial discrimination" may be approached from the perspective of either its victim or its perpetrator. From the victim's perspective, racial discrimination describes those conditions of actual social existence as a member of a perpetual underclass. This perspective includes both the objective conditions of life — lack of jobs, lack of money, lack of housing — and the consciousness associated with those objective conditions — lack of choice and lack of human individuality in being forever perceived as a member of a group rather than as an individual. The perpetrator perspective sees racial discrimination not as conditions, but as actions, or series of actions, inflicted on the victim by the perpetrator. The focus is more on what particular perpetrators have done or are doing to some victims than it is on the overall life situation of the victim class.

The victim, or "condition," conception of racial discrimination suggests that the problem will not be solved until the conditions associated with it have been eliminated. To remedy the condition of racial discrimination would demand affirmative efforts to change the condition. The remedial dimension of the perpetrator perspective, however, is negative. The task is merely to neutralize the inappropriate conduct of the perpetrator.

In its core concept of the "violation," antidiscrimination law is hopelessly embedded in the perpetrator perspective. Its central tenet, the "antidiscrimination principle," is the prohibition of race-dependent decisions that disadvantage members of minority groups,[17] and its principal task has been to select from the maze of human behaviors those particular practices that violate the principle, outlaw the identified practices, and neutralize their specific effects. Antidiscrimination law has thus been ultimately indifferent to the condition of the victim; its demands are satisfied if it can be said that the "violation" has been remedied.

The perpetrator perspective presupposes a world composed of atomistic individuals whose actions are outside of and apart from the social fabric and without

---

[37] Even if when viewed in isolation the costs from prohibiting statistical discrimination appeared to exceed the benefits, there may still be a basis for prohibiting it on efficiency grounds. This might be the case if allowing statistical discrimination defenses by employers substantially increased the [number of errors] in Title VII cases alleging animus-based discrimination....

[*] Copyright © 1978 by Alan David Freeman. Reprinted with permission.

[17] The best summary and explanation is Brest, *The Supreme Court, 1975 Term — Foreword: In Defense of the Antidiscrimination Principle,* 90 Harv. L. Rev. 1 (1976).

historical continuity. From this perspective, the law views racial discrimination not as a social phenomenon, but merely as the misguided conduct of particular actions. It is a world where, but for the conduct of these misguided ones, the system of equality of opportunity would work to provide a distribution of the good things in life without racial disparities and where deprivations that did correlate with race would be "deserved" by those deprived on grounds of insufficient "merit." It is a world where such things as "vested rights," "objective selection systems," and "adventitious decisions" (all of which serve to prevent victims from experiencing any change in conditions) are matters of fate, having nothing to do with the problem of racial discrimination.

Central to the perpetrator perspective are the twin notions of "fault" and "causation." Under the fault idea, the task of antidiscrimination law is to separate from the masses of society those blameworthy individuals who are violating the otherwise shared norm. The fault idea is reflected in the assertion that only "intentional" discrimination violates the antidiscrimination principle. In its pure form, intentional discrimination is conduct accompanied by a purposeful desire to produce discriminatory results. One can thus evade responsibility for ostensibly discriminatory conduct by showing that the action was taken for a good reason, or for no reason at all.

The fault concept gives rise to a complacency about one's own moral status; it creates a class of "innocents," who need not feel any personal responsibility for the conditions associated with discrimination, and who therefore feel great resentment when called upon to bear any burdens in connection with remedying violations. This resentment accounts for much of the ferocity surrounding the debate about so-called "reverse" discrimination, for being called on to bear burdens ordinarily imposed only upon the guilty involves an apparently unjustified stigmatization of those led by the fault notion to believe in their own innocence.

Operating along with fault, the causation requirement serves to distinguish from the totality of conditions that a victim perceives to be associated with discrimination those that the law will address. These dual requirements place on the victim the nearly impossible burden of isolating the particular conditions of discrimination produced by and mechanically linked to the behavior of an identified blameworthy perpetrator, regardless of whether other conditions of discrimination, caused by other perpetrators, would have to be remedied for the outcome of the case to make any difference at all. The causation principle makes it clear that some objective instances of discrimination are to be regarded as mere accidents, or "caused," if at all, by the behavior of ancestral demons whose responsibility cannot follow their successors in interest over time. The causation principle also operates to place beyond the law discriminatory conduct (action taken with a purpose to discriminate under the fault principle) that is not linked to any discernible "discriminatory effect."

The perpetrator perspective has been and still is the only formal conception of a violation in antidiscrimination law. Strict adherence to that form, however, would have made even illusory progress in the quest for racial justice impossible. The challenge for the law, therefore, was to develop, through the usual legal techniques of verbal manipulation, ways of breaking out of the formal constraints of the perpetrator perspective while maintaining ostensible adherence to the form itself. This was done by separating violation from remedy, and doing through remedy what was inappropriate in cases involving only identification of violations. But since one of the principal tenets of the perpetrator perspective is that remedy and violation must be coextensive, it was necessary to state that tenet and violate it at the same time, no mean task even for masters of verbal gamesmanship. For a while, the remedial doctrines seemingly undermined the hegemony of the perpetrator form, threatening to replace it with a victim perspective. [*Griggs v. Duke Power Co.*,[18] which eliminated the fault requirement and muddied the causation issue, is the principal case during this era.] In the end, however, [as *Griggs* has been increasingly limited and marginalized,] form triumphed, and the perpetrator perspective, always dominant in identifying violations, was firmly reasserted in the context of remedies as well.

D. FEMINIST ANALYSIS

CATHARINE A. MacKINNON, SEXUAL HARASSMENT OF WORKING WOMEN: A CASE OF SEX DISCRIMINATION 101-02, 117-18, 225-31 (1979)[*]

[Two conceptual approaches to issues of sex discrimination exist.] The first ... implicitly conceives of the social situation of the sexes as an expression of a pattern of sex differences. I term this the *differences* approach.... The second approach implicitly conceives of the social situation of the sexes as unequal, rather than merely — or even basically — different. I term this the *inequality* approach....

A rule or practice is discriminatory, in the inequality approach, if it participates in the systemic social deprivation of one sex because of sex. The only question for litigation is whether the policy or practice in question integrally contributes to the maintenance of an underclass or a deprived position because of gender status. The disadvantage which constitutes the injury of discrimination is not the failure to be treated "without regard to" one's sex; that is the injury of arbitrary differentiation. The unfairness lies in being deprived *because of* being a woman or a man, a deprivation given meaning in the social context of the dominance or preference of one sex over the other. The social problem addressed is not the failure to ignore woman's essential sameness with man, but the recognition of womanhood to women's comparative disadvantage. In this approach, few reasons, not even biological ones, can justify the institutionalized disadvantage of women. Comparability of sex characteristics is not required

---

[18] 401 U.S. 424 (1971)

[*] Copyright © 1978 by Yale University Press. Reprinted with permission.

because policies are proscribed which transform women's sex-based differences from men into social and economic deprivations. All that is required are comparatively unequal results.

Under the inequality approach, variables as to which women and men are not comparable, such as pregnancy and sexuality, would be among the *first* to trigger suspicion and scrutiny, rather than the last; they would not be exceptions to the rule. From the inequality perspective the question [in the *Gilbert*[9] case, where the employer's health plan covered virtually all health needs except pregnancy] would be: is not the structure of the job market, which accommodates the physical needs, life cycle, and family expectations of men but not of women, integral to women's inferior employment status? What can then justify a policy that makes pregnancy, a condition unique and common to women as a gender, into a disadvantage in employment? The affirmative form of the argument is that the health needs of women workers should be accommodated equally with those of men....

In the differences approach, a differentiation is based on sex when it can be shown that a person of the opposite sex in the same position is not treated the same. This requires that a person of the opposite sex can reasonably be in a comparable position. A clear example is *Phillips v. Martin-Marietta,* in which mothers but not fathers of preschool children were excluded from applying for jobs. Lacking evidence of "bias against women as such," the Supreme Court prohibited "one hiring policy for women and another for men — each having preschool age children."[10] ...

The logic of the inequality approach, by contrast, requires no comparability of situation, only that a rule or practice disproportionately burden one sex because of sex. Under the facts of *Phillips v. Martin-Marietta,* suppose the lower court had found that family obligations presented a greater job conflict for mothers than for fathers of preschool children. In this approach, the differential hiring rule would still be discriminatory because it would reinforce the traditionally disproportionate burden of parenthood on women. As it was, the court suggested that such a finding on remand might support a Bona Fide Occupational Qualification (BFOQ) for men for the job, over Justice Marshall's concurring protest. But this was a correct result under the court's differences approach. Mothers of preschool children *are* less "qualified" for jobs than fathers, if the "qualifications" related to the job include freedom from child care obligations, and fathers who apply are not so burdened. In effect, this is no less true if each mother's qualifications are *individually* considered than if her application is flatly barred by a BFOQ, although the former gives individual women a chance to be exceptional, so is, of course, preferable. In the differences perspective, dissimilar circumstances can legitimately ground sex-unequal results, even if the

---

[9] *General Elec. Co. v. Gilbert,* 429 U.S. 125 (1976).

[10] 400 U.S. 542 (1971)....

situated differences are themselves the product of a sexist distribution of social responsibilities.

If its logic is dissected, the differences approach implicitly grounds a conception of sex upon a conception of biology. The inequality framework emphasizes the grounding of sex in the *social* meaning of biology. Translated into doctrinal terms, under the differences approach, the closer a variable comes to sexual biology, or to those social differences which are seen to be biologically necessary, the less a differentiation will tend to qualify as "gender as such." This is the opposite of the result one would expect for a doctrine that ostensibly *prohibits* different treatment of two groups that are defined by the biology of sex....

According to an inequality approach, the differences conception of the injustice of discrimination fails to grasp the nature of the problem it is trying to solve. Due to the fact that the society defines and treats women as a group, as a distinct and subordinate category of being on the apparent basis of biological femaleness, this treatment will shape the actual characteristics, personalities, circumstances, qualifications, even many of the physical qualities and attributes of individuals of both sexes. To the extent the law allows sex-based differences to be a reason for considering that differential outcomes are not sex-based, it will allow the very factors the law against discrimination exists to prohibit to be the reason not to prohibit them.

Illustrations of the divergence between the two approaches, and of the deep incoherence of the differences approach, exist throughout sex discrimination adjudications of the issue of sex-basis.... *Rafford v. Randle Eastern Ambulance* presents a striking example of this reasoning, holding that the discharge of pregnant women and bearded men does not violate Title VII because "only women become pregnant, and only men grow beards."[17] This observation is intended to indicate that the differentiation is *not* sex-based because "in neither instance are similarly situated persons of the opposite sex favored." Only too true: there *are* no similarly situated persons of the opposite sex, precisely because of the sex difference.

[The treatment of justifications for group detriment also illustrates divergence between the two approaches. Under the differences approach, disparate treatment by sex can be justified if] a job legitimately requires one sex[, if the difference in treatment] derive[s] from a "factual basis, as opposed to a commonly held stereotype" and [if] the qualification [is] "*necessary* to the business ..., not merely tangential" or convenient....

In the inequality approach, by contrast, there are no justifications for group detriment. Most issues are resolved [by determining] whether the deprivation is based upon the social meaning of the sex difference, that is, whether it inures to the systematic disadvantage of one sex. The entire notion that a detrimental differentiation based on sex can be "justified," in the inequality framework, amounts to recognizing the potential validity of the inferiority of one sex to the

---

[17] 348 F. Supp. 316, 320 (S.D. Fla. 1972).

other. The mistake of this type of analysis has been to confound differences with detriments. Treatment that recognizes or benefits differences, injuring no one, has never been the issue. Detriments supposedly corresponding to sex differences — usually women's differences from the male standard — have been. To justify sex-based detriments enshrines as an exception to the law requiring equal treatment the very incidents of social inferiority the law proposes to change. Not a case of the exception swallowing the rule, this is a matter of translating the legal mandate of equality into a doctrine that allows social inequality to be a limiting condition upon its own delivery.

DEBORAH L. RHODE, JUSTICE AND GENDER 81-85, 120-24 (1989)[*]

American [discrimination] analysis developed largely within an Aristotelian tradition that defines equality as similar treatment for those similarly situated. Under this approach, discrimination presents no legal difficulties if the groups differ in ways relevant to a valid regulatory objective. During the 1970s and 1980s increasing challenges to gender classifications underscored the theoretical and practical limitations of this approach. On a theoretical level, it verges on tautology. It allows different treatment for those who are different with respect to legitimate purposes, but offers no criteria for determining which differences matter and what counts as legitimate. On a practical level, the focus on difference has failed adequately to raise, let alone resolve, the problems it seeks to address....

Although discourses of difference must sometimes have a place, they should begin, not end, analysis. As deconstructionists remind us, women are always already the same and different: the same in their humanity, different in their anatomy. Whichever category we privilege in our legal discourse, the other will always be waiting to disrupt it. By constantly presenting gender issues in difference-oriented frameworks, conventional legal discourse implicitly biases analysis. To pronounce women either the same or different allows men to remain the standard of analysis.

Significant progress toward gender equality will require moving beyond the sameness-difference dilemma. We must insist not just on equal treatment but on woman's treatment as an equal. Such a strategy will require substantial changes in our legal paradigms and social priorities. The alternative framework offered here shifts emphasis from gender differences to gender disadvantages.... This framework is responsive to two enduring strands of feminist jurisprudence: approaches that stress women's fundamental equality with men and those that demand accommodation of women's differences from men. A disadvantage approach also incorporates the insights though not the formulation of the dominance-oriented paradigm that critics such as Catharine MacKinnon have advocated.

[A] disadvantage framework is concerned not with differences but with its consequences. The legitimacy of sex-based treatment does not depend on whether the sexes are differently situated. Rather, analysis turns on whether legal recognition of gender distinctions is more likely to reduce or to reinforce gender disparities in political power, social status, and economic security. This alternative model focuses not only on the rationality of means and legitimacy of ends in governmental policies. It demands also that such policies include a substantive commitment to gender equality.

What that commitment requires in particular legal settings cannot be resolved in the abstract. Rather, it demands close attention to context, and to the complexity of women's interests. While this approach shares the concerns of feminist theories phrased in terms of gender dominance, it relies for most purposes on an alternative formulation that can command greater support in legal settings.

Although they differ in other respects, dominance frameworks generally begin with two central premises. The first is that the "relation between the sexes is organized so that men may dominate and women must submit." A second premise, accepted in varying degrees, is that this relation constitutes the most fundamental social hierarchy across time and culture, and that all male-female interactions reflect its structure. From such a perspective, traditional legal doctrine may have talked in terms of gender difference, but only as a means of legitimating gender dominance. As MacKinnon puts it, differences are "inequality's *post hoc* excuse for itself. They are the outcome presented as origin."[5]

This framework has been important to the development of feminist theory and politics in several respects. By emphasizing the subordination that women encounter as women, it offers a sense of shared identity and a powerful rationale for common action. Such an approach makes clear that the discrimination individuals experience is not an isolated instance of irrational prejudice or anachronistic stereotypes, but part of a systematic social hierarchy. By stressing the cumulative significance of gender differentiation, this paradigm demands focus on fundamental causes. In this sense, it deepens our understanding of sex-based dynamics and of the strategies necessary to change them.

Yet the sources of this theory's strengths are also the sources of its limitations. A we/they world view sharpens our perceptions of women's inequalities but only by obscuring other critical dynamics. As a foundation for an alternative legal framework, dominance paradigms are too often theoretically reductive and strategically counterproductive. A top-down analysis presents a limited view of relations both within and between gender groups. Part of the difficulty stems from the paradox common to most feminist theory and practice. Feminism gains its power from the claim to speak on behalf of women and to identify common

---

[5] *See* MacKinnon, *Feminism Unmodified,* pp. 3, 32-45 [1987].

values, perceptions, and interests growing out of women's experience. Yet that experience also teaches that gender is mediated by other patterns of inequality involving race, class, age, ethnicity, and sexual orientation. On a descriptive level, dominance-oriented paradigms that divide the world solely along gender lines ignore the ways that common biological constraints are experienced differently by different groups of women. On a prescriptive level, no theory adequate to challenge gender subordination can avoid addressing the other forms of inequality with which it intersects.

If dominance cannot capture the complexity of women's experience in relation to each other, it is also limited in its account of women's relation to men. Hierarchical analyses often discuss power in undefined ways and understate the influence women can exercise individually and collectively. Power is a contested concept, and in legal settings its meaning needs to be explored rather than assumed.

Even if one passes over these conceptual questions and proceeds with some commonsense understanding of central theoretical terms, dominance frameworks remain more problematic than their advocates often acknowledge. Dynamics of age, class, race, ethnicity, and sexual orientation can be as powerful as gender in ordering social relations. To take an obvious example, a wealthy woman's relations with her young sons or nonwhite male domestic staff do not fit easily within perspectives that stress only gender hierarchies.... Gender dominance is too crude a label for the mutual dependencies and complex power dynamics that characterize certain male-female relations.

For legal purposes, these limitations in dominance approaches pose both strategic and substantive difficulties. As a practical matter, most individuals, including those who exercise lawmaking authority in this society, do not perceive themselves as oppressor and oppressed. To dismiss their perceptions simply as the product of "false consciousness" is to ignore critical questions about the process by which such labels are attached and altered. It is not sufficient to maintain, as dominance approaches generally do, that the public's failure to perceive the extent gender inequalities is itself a product of such inequalities. If that is the case, the crucial question becomes how best to challenge such patterns under current social conditions and perceptions. For legal settings, the answer is likely to require frameworks that can command greater consensus than those cast in terms of oppression....

This is not to suggest that disadvantage is always a preferable paradigm or to overstate its potential in recasting legal analysis. For some theoretical, political, and legal purposes, dominance remains a crucial organizing principle; one does not, for example, speak of rape or pornography as questions of disadvantage. What again bears emphasis is the importance of contextual analysis. Rather than framing the issue as either/or — disadvantage vs. dominance — we should focus on issues of when and why. Each paradigm has its place. Not all historical patterns or contemporary issues fit tidily under any single scheme. The choice of formulation is less important than the conceptual commitment that both imply. Underlying each approach is a sensitivity to patterns of inequality that conventional legal traditions have failed to address....

[The controversy over maternity leave policies] highlights limitations in prevailing difference or dominance-oriented approaches to gender issues.

Defenders of maternity protections generally begin from the premise that working men and women are different with respect to reproduction. Although a no-leave policy creates hardships for both sexes concerning the disabilities they share, it places an additional burden on female employees. [Distinguishing between childbearing and child-rearing, some feminist defenders of maternity protections] argue that gender-specific childbirth policies are appropriate, while gender-specific parental policies are not. From this premise, many commentators draw two further conclusions: that the absence of disability leaves has a disparate impact on women in violation of Title VII; and that states or employers may respond to this disproportionate effect through policies requiring job reinstatement after pregnancy.

This rationale for preferential treatment rests on arguments of both principle and prudence. As a matter of principle, pregnancy should not have to seem the same as male disabilities in order to gain adequate protection.... From a prudential perspective, as long as policymakers fail to require adequate protection for all workers, partial coverage can be a useful interim strategy. As was true with protective legislation in the early twentieth century, a "women and children first" approach can lay the groundwork for broader gender-neutral regulation.

[Preferential maternity leave policies, however, also pose risks: They may retard the development of more comprehensive approaches to address the tensions between work and childcare; reinforce the sexual division of childcare responsibilities and, indeed, slow the assumption by men of their fair share of those responsibilities; and create the perception among employers that women cost more to employ.]

The complexity of this issue underscores the need to move beyond the dichotomies in which it has generally emerged. As in other contexts, a sameness-difference approach is ultimately unilluminating. Women are both the same and different. They are different in their needs at childbirth but the same in their needs for broader medical, child-rearing, and care-taking policies. To determine which side of the sameness-difference dichotomy to emphasize in legal contexts requires some other analytic tool.

A dominance-oriented framework is inadequate for that role. By inviting analysis in terms of zero-sum transfers from "us to them," it may misconstrue the problem and misconceive the solution. Women and men have neither monolithic nor competing interests. As was true earlier in the century, female employees experience and value the tradeoffs of preferential protections differently, depending on their own particular circumstances. Men have lined up on both sides of the maternity-leave debate, and it is possible to view either their support or opposition as an expression of patriarchal interests. Some conservative male legislators have supported special maternity leave requirements to help women who assume "traditional roles in the family, and in society." Other male employers and politicians have opposed such requirements as an unduly expensive accommodation to women's personal choices and an inappropriate "interference" with market processes. The theory is that if a female employee places high priority on maternity or disability policies, she can go to work for an organization that offers them.

Yet to suppose that employees can effectively restructure workplace practices by "voting with their feet" is to ignore the history that necessitated a vast array of governmental regulation, including safety requirements, maximum-hour legislation, and antidiscrimination mandates. Fearing covert discrimination, many job applicants may not convey concerns about parental policy when seeking employment. Nor will they always anticipate future disability needs when applying for a particular position. To oppose state "interference" with the market is to ignore the effects of noninterference on family relationships. The absence of adequate care taking policies in the United States diminishes opportunities for both sexes, as children, as parents, and as elderly dependents.

For issues such as preferential treatment, the advantage of focusing on disadvantage is that it can acknowledge complexity and encourage contextual inquiry. It can avoid entrapment in unproductive disputes over male motivation or female "difference." Rather, attention can center on identifying strategies most likely to promote gender equality in a given set of social, political, and economic circumstances. From a disadvantage-oriented perspective, the preferable approach is to press for the broadest possible maternal, parental, and medical coverage for all workers. Sex-neutral strategies pose the least risk of entrenching stereotypes or encouraging covert discrimination and offer the widest range of protections for disadvantaged groups. The distinctive consequences of pregnancy should not be overlooked, but neither should they be overemphasized. More employers provide job-protected childbirth leaves than other forms of assistance that are equally critical to workers and their dependents. Pregnancy-related policies affect most women workers for relatively brief intervals. The absence of broader disability, health, child-rearing, and caretaking policies remains a chronic problem for the vast majority of employees, male and female, throughout their working lives.

Chapter 14

LEGAL MODELS OF DISCRIMINATION

Employment discrimination is prohibited by a large number of laws. At the federal level, Title VII of the Civil Rights Act of 1964 is the central statute. It prohibits discrimination because of race, color, religion, sex, and national origin. But a number of other federal statutes also exist. Some provide protection against other forms of status discrimination, such as age discrimination or discrimination against persons with disabilities, while others provide protections that overlap with Title VII's protections in substance, but differ in procedure and remedy. These include the Americans with Disabilities Act of 1990; the Age Discrimination in Employment Act; the Equal Pay Act of 1963; the Civil Rights Act of 1866, 42 U.S.C. 1981; and the Ku Klux Klan Act of 1871, 42 U.S.C. § 1983. In addition to these federal statutes, literally hundreds of state and local laws exist, often increasing the types of status that are protected and the number of employers covered and always providing their own procedures and remedies.

Despite this multitude of laws, only three basic models exist for proving status discrimination. The three models — disparate treatment, disparate impact, and reasonable accommodation — rely on different underlying theories and impose different burdens of proof on employers and employees, but together they define the range of what is legally cognizable as status discrimination in this country.

A. DISPARATE TREATMENT

1. INDIVIDUAL DISPARATE TREATMENT

McDONNELL DOUGLAS CORP. v. GREEN

United States Supreme Court
411 U.S. 792 (1973)

MR. JUSTICE POWELL delivered the opinion of the Court.

The case before us raises significant questions as to the proper order and nature of proof in actions under Title VII of the Civil Rights Act of 1964.

Petitioner, McDonnell Douglas Corp., is an aerospace and aircraft manufacturer headquartered in St. Louis, Missouri, where it employs over 30,000 people. Respondent, a black citizen of St. Louis, worked for petitioner as a mechanic and laboratory technician from 1956 until August 28, 1964 when he was laid off in the course of a general reduction in petitioner's work force.

Respondent, a long-time activist in the civil rights movement, protested vigorously that his discharge and the general hiring practices of petitioner were racially motivated. As part of this protest, respondent and other members of the Congress on Racial Equality illegally stalled their cars on the main roads leading to petitioner's plant for the purpose of blocking access to it at the time of the

445

morning shift change. The District Judge described the plan for, and respondent's participation in, the "stall-in" as follows:

> "[F]ive teams, each consisting of four cars would 'tie up' five main access roads into McDonnell at the time of the morning rush hour. The drivers of the cars were instructed to line up next to each other completely blocking the intersections or roads. The drivers were also instructed to stop their cars, turn off the engines, pull the emergency brake, raise all windows, lock the doors, and remain in their cars until the police arrived. The plan was to have the cars remain in position for one hour.
>
> "Acting under the 'stall in' plan, plaintiff [respondent in the present action] drove his car onto Brown Road, a McDonnell access road, at approximately 7:00 a.m., at the start of the morning rush hour. Plaintiff was aware of the traffic problems that would result. He stopped his car with the intent to block traffic. The police arrived shortly and requested plaintiff to move his car. He refused to move his car voluntarily. Plaintiff's car was towed away by the police, and he was arrested for obstructing traffic. Plaintiff pleaded guilty to the charge of obstructing traffic and was fined." 318 F. Supp. 846, 849.

On July 2, 1965, a "lock-in" took place wherein a chain and padlock were placed on the front door of a building to prevent the occupants, certain of petitioner's employees, from leaving. Though respondent apparently knew beforehand of the "lock-in," the full extent of his involvement remains uncertain.

 Some three weeks following the "lock-in," on July 25, 1965, petitioner publicly advertised for qualified mechanics, respondent's trade, and respondent promptly applied for re-employment. Petitioner turned down respondent, basing its rejection on respondent's participation in the "stall-in" and "lock-in." Shortly thereafter, respondent filed a formal complaint with the Equal Employment Opportunity Commission, claiming that petitioner had refused to rehire him because of his race....

The critical issue before us concerns the order and allocation of proof in a private, non-class action challenging employment discrimination.... The broad, overriding interest [protected by Title VII and] shared by employer, employee, and consumer, is efficient and trustworthy workmanship assured through fair and racially neutral employment and personnel decisions. In the implementation of such decisions, it is abundantly clear that Title VII tolerates no racial discrimination, subtle or otherwise.

In this case respondent, the complainant below, charges that he was denied employment "because of his involvement in civil rights activities" and "because of his race and color." Petitioner denied discrimination of any kind, asserting that its failure to re-employ respondent was based upon and justified by his participation in the unlawful conduct against it. Thus, the issue at the trial on remand is framed by those opposing factual contentions....

The complainant in a Title VII trial must carry the initial burden under the statute of establishing a prima facie case of racial discrimination. This may be done by showing (i) that he belongs to a racial minority; (ii) that he applied and was qualified for a job for which the employer was seeking applicants; (iii) that, despite his qualifications, he was rejected; and (iv) that, after his rejection, the position remained open and the employer continued to seek applicants from persons of complainant's qualifications.[13] In the instant case, we agree with the Court of Appeals that respondent proved a prima facie case. Petitioner sought mechanics, respondent's trade, and continued to do so after respondent's rejection. Petitioner, moreover, does not dispute respondent's qualifications[14] and acknowledges that his past work performance in petitioner's employ was "satisfactory."

The burden then must shift to the employer to articulate some legitimate, nondiscriminatory reason for the employee's rejection. We need not attempt in the instant case to detail every matter which fairly could be recognized as a reasonable basis for a refusal to hire. Here petitioner has assigned respondent's participation in unlawful conduct against it as the cause for his rejection. We think that this suffices to discharge petitioner's burden of proof at this stage and to meet respondent's prima facie case of discrimination.

The Court of Appeals intimated, however, that petitioner's stated reason for refusing to rehire respondent was a "subjective" rather than objective criterion which "carr[ies] little weight in rebutting charges of discrimination." This was among the statements which caused the dissenting judge to read the opinion as taking "the position that such unlawful acts as Green committed against McDonnell would not legally entitle McDonnell to refuse to hire him, even though no racial motivation was involved...." Regardless of whether this was the intended import of the opinion, we think the court below seriously underestimated the rebuttal weight to which petitioner's reasons were entitled. Respondent admittedly had taken part in a carefully planned "stall-in," designed to tie up access to and egress from petitioner's plant at a peak traffic hour. Nothing in Title VII compels an employer to absolve and rehire one who has engaged in such deliberate, unlawful activity against it....[17]

---

[13] The facts necessarily will vary in Title VII cases, and the specification above of the prima facie proof required from respondent is not necessarily applicable in every respect to differing factual situations.

[14] We note that the issue of what may properly be used to test qualifications for employment is not present in this case. Where employers have instituted employment tests and qualifications with an exclusionary effect on minority applicants, such requirements must be "shown to bear a demonstrable relationship to successful performance of the jobs" for which they were used, *Griggs v. Duke Power Co.,* 401 U.S. 424, 431 (1971).

[17] The unlawful activity in this case was directed specifically against petitioner. We need not consider or decide here whether, or under what circumstances, unlawful activity not directed against the particular employer may be a legitimate justification for refusing to hire.

Petitioner's reason for rejection thus suffices to meet the prima facie case, but the inquiry must not end here. While Title VII does not, without more, compel rehiring of respondent, neither does it permit petitioner to use respondent's conduct as a pretext for the sort of discrimination prohibited by § 703(a)(1). On remand, respondent must, as the Court of Appeals recognized, be afforded a fair opportunity to show that petitioner's stated reason for respondent's rejection was in fact pretext. Especially relevant to such a showing would be evidence that white employees involved in acts against petitioner of comparable seriousness to the "stall-in" were nevertheless retained or rehired. Petitioner may justifiably refuse to rehire one who was engaged in unlawful, disruptive acts against it, but only if this criterion is applied alike to members of all races.

Other evidence that may be relevant to any showing of pretext includes facts as to the petitioner's treatment of respondent during his prior term of employment; petitioner's reaction, if any, to respondent's legitimate civil rights activities; and petitioner's general policy and practice with respect to minority employment. On the latter point, statistics as to petitioner's employment policy and practice may be helpful to a determination of whether petitioner's refusal to rehire respondent in this case conformed to a general pattern of discrimination against blacks.[19] In short, on the retrial respondent must be given a full and fair opportunity to demonstrate by competent evidence that the presumptively valid reasons for his rejection were in fact a coverup for a racially discriminatory decision....

In sum, respondent should have been allowed to pursue his claim under § 703(a)(1). If the evidence on retrial is substantially in accord with that before us in this case, we think that respondent carried his burden of establishing a prima facie case of racial discrimination and that petitioner successfully rebutted that case. But this does not end the matter. On retrial, respondent must be afforded a fair opportunity to demonstrate that petitioner's assigned reason for refusing to re-employ was a pretext or discriminatory in its application. If the District Judge so finds, he must order a prompt and appropriate remedy. In the absence of such a finding, petitioner's refusal to rehire must stand.

NOTE

Sharpening the Inquiry. In *Texas Department of Community Affairs v. Burdine,* 450 U.S. 248, 253-56 (1981), the Supreme Court discussed the underlying rationale of the *McDonnell Douglas* framework for analyzing individual disparate treatment cases:

Burdine

---

[19] The District Court may, for example, determine, after reasonable discovery that "the [racial] composition of defendant's labor force is itself reflective of restrictive or exclusionary practices." We caution that such general determinations, while helpful, may not be in and of themselves controlling as to an individualized hiring decision, particularly in the presence of an otherwise justifiable reason for refusing to rehire.

The burden of establishing a prima facie case of disparate treatment is not onerous. The plaintiff must prove by a preponderance of the evidence that she applied for an available position for which she was qualified, but was rejected under circumstances which give rise to an inference of unlawful discrimination. The prima facie case serves an important function in the litigation: it eliminates the most common nondiscriminatory reasons for the plaintiff's rejection, [lack of qualifications and no job vacancy]. Establishment of the prima facie case in effect creates a presumption that the employer unlawfully discriminated against the employee. If the trier of fact believes the plaintiff's evidence, and if the employer is silent in the face of the presumption, the court must enter judgment for the plaintiff because no issue of fact remains in the case.[7]

The burden that shifts to the defendant, therefore, is to rebut the presumption of discrimination by producing evidence that the plaintiff was rejected, or someone else was preferred, for a legitimate, nondiscriminatory reason. The defendant need not persuade the court that it was actually motivated by the proffered reasons. It is sufficient if the defendant's evidence raises a genuine issue of fact as to whether it discriminated against the plaintiff.[8] To accomplish this, the defendant must clearly set forth, through the introduction of admissible evidence, the reasons for the plaintiff's rejection. The explanation provided must be legally sufficient to justify a judgment for the defendant. If the defendant carries this burden of production, the presumption raised by the prima facie case is rebutted, and the factual inquiry proceeds to a new level of specificity. Placing this burden of production on the defendant thus serves simultaneously to meet the plaintiff's prima facie case by presenting a legitimate reason for the action and to frame the factual issue with sufficient clarity so that the plaintiff will have a full and fair opportunity to demonstrate pretext. The sufficiency of the defendant's evidence should be evaluated by the extent to which it fulfills these functions.

The plaintiff retains the burden of persuasion. She now must have the opportunity to demonstrate that the proffered reason was not the true reason for the employment decision. This burden now merges with the ultimate

---

[7] The phrase "prima facie case" not only may denote the establishment of a legally mandatory, rebuttable presumption, but also may be used by courts to describe the plaintiff's burden of producing enough evidence to permit the trier of fact to infer the fact at issue. *McDonnell Douglas* should have made it apparent that in the Title VII context we use "prima facie case" in the former sense.

[8] This evidentiary relationship between the presumption created by a prima facie case and the consequential burden of production placed on the defendant is a traditional feature of the common law.... Usually, assessing the burden of production helps the judge determine whether the litigants have created an issue of fact to be decided by the jury. In a Title VII case, the allocation of burdens and the creation of a presumption by the establishment of a prima facie case is intended progressively to sharpen the inquiry into the elusive factual question of intentional discrimination.

burden of persuading the court that she has been the victim of intentional discrimination. She may succeed in this either directly, by persuading the court that a discriminatory reason more likely motivated the employer, or indirectly, by showing that the employer's proffered explanation is unworthy of credence.

I think this bit gets overruled

ST. MARY'S HONOR CENTER v. HICKS

United States Supreme Court
509 U.S. 502 (1993)

JUSTICE SCALIA delivered the opinion of the Court, in which CHIEF JUSTICE REHNQUIST and JUSTICES O'CONNOR, KENNEDY and THOMAS joined.

Issue

We granted certiorari to determine whether, in a suit against an employer alleging intentional racial discrimination in violation of § 703(a)(1) of Title VII of the Civil Rights Act of 1964, the trier of fact's rejection of the employer's asserted reasons for its actions mandates a finding for the plaintiff.

I

Petitioner St. Mary's Honor Center (St. Mary's) is a halfway house operated by the Missouri Department of Corrections and Human Resources (MDCHR). Respondent Melvin Hicks, a black man, was hired as a correctional officer at St. Mary's in August 1978 and was promoted to shift commander, one of six supervisory positions, in February 1980.

In 1983 MDCHR conducted an investigation of the administration of St. Mary's, which resulted in extensive supervisory changes in January 1984. Respondent retained his position, but John Powell became the new chief of custody (respondent's immediate supervisor) and petitioner Steve Long the new superintendent. Prior to these personnel changes respondent had enjoyed a satisfactory employment record, but soon thereafter became the subject of repeated, and increasingly severe, disciplinary actions. He was suspended for five days for violations of institutional rules by his subordinates on March 3, 1984. He received a letter of reprimand for alleged failure to conduct an adequate investigation of a brawl between inmates that occurred during his shift on March 21. He was later demoted from shift commander to correctional officer for his failure to ensure that his subordinates entered their use of a St. Mary's vehicle into the official log book on March 19, 1984. Finally, on June 7, 1984, he was discharged for threatening Powell during an exchange of heated words on April 19....

II

With the goal of "progressively ... sharpen[ing] the inquiry into the elusive factual question of intentional discrimination," *Texas Dept. of Community Affairs v. Burdine*, 450 U.S. 248, 255 n. 8 (1981), our opinion in *McDonnell Douglas Corp. v. Green*, 411 U.S. 792 (1973), established an allocation of the burden of production and an order for the presentation of proof in Title VII dis- *Rule from* criminatory-treatment cases. The plaintiff in such a case, we said, must first *McDonell* establish, by a preponderance of the evidence, a "prima facie" case of racial dis- *Douglas Comm.* crimination. Petitioners do not challenge the District Court's finding that *v. Green* respondent satisfied the minimal requirements of such a prima facie case (set out *applied* in *McDonnell Douglas*) by proving (1) that he is black, (2) that he was qualified for the position of shift commander, (3) that he was demoted from that position and ultimately discharged, and (4) that the position remained open and was ultimately filled by a white man.

Under the *McDonnell Douglas* scheme, "[e]stablishment of the prima facie case in effect creates a presumption that the employer unlawfully discriminated against the employee." *Burdine, supra,* at 254. To establish a "presumption" is to say that a finding of the predicate fact (here, the prima facie case) produces "a required conclusion in the absence of explanation" (here, the finding of unlawful discrimination). 1 D. Louisell & C. Mueller, Federal Evidence § 67, p. 536 (1977). Thus, the *McDonnell Douglas* presumption places upon the defendant the burden of producing an explanation to rebut the prima facie case — *i.e.,* the burden of "producing evidence" that the adverse employment actions were taken "for a legitimate, nondiscriminatory reason." *Burdine,* 450 U.S., at 254. "[T]he defendant must clearly set forth, through the introduction of admissible evidence," reasons for its actions which, *if believed by the trier of fact,* would support a finding that unlawful discrimination was not the cause of the employment action. *Id.,* at 254-255, and n. 8. It is important to note, however, that although the *McDonnell Douglas* presumption shifts the burden of *production* to the defendant, "[t]he ultimate burden of persuading the trier of fact that the defendant intentionally discriminated against the plaintiff remains at all times with the plaintiff," *id.,* at 253. In this regard it operates like all presumptions, as described in Rule 301 of the Federal Rules of Evidence:

> "In all civil actions and proceedings not otherwise provided for by Act of Congress or by these rules, a presumption imposes on the party against whom it is directed the burden of going forward with evidence to rebut or meet the presumption, but does not shift to such party the burden of proof in the sense of the risk of nonpersuasion, which remains throughout the trial upon the party on whom it was originally cast."

Respondent does not challenge the District Court's finding that petitioners sustained their burden of production by introducing evidence of two legitimate, nondiscriminatory reasons for their actions: the severity and the accumulation of rules violations committed by respondent. Our cases make clear that at that point the shifted burden of production became irrelevant: "If the defendant carries this burden of production, the presumption raised by the prima facie case is rebutted," *Burdine,* 450 U.S., at 255, and "drops from the case," *id.,* at 255, n. 10. The plaintiff then has "the full and fair opportunity to demonstrate," through presentation of his own case and through cross-examination of the defendant's witnesses, "that the proffered reason was not the true reason for the employment decision," *id.*, at 256, and that race was. He retains that "ultimate burden of persuading the [trier of fact] that [he] has been the victim of intentional discrimination." *Ibid.*

The District Court, acting as trier of fact in this bench trial, found that the reasons petitioners gave were not the real reasons for respondent's demotion and discharge. It found that respondent was the only supervisor disciplined for violations committed by his subordinates; that similar and even more serious violations committed by respondent's coworkers were either disregarded or treated more leniently; and that Powell manufactured the final verbal confrontation in order to provoke respondent into threatening him. It nonetheless held that respondent had failed to carry his ultimate burden of proving that his race was the determining factor in petitioners' decision first to demote and then to dismiss him.[2] In short, the District Court concluded that "although [respondent] has proven the existence of a crusade to terminate him, he has not proven that the crusade was racially rather than personally motivated."

The Court of Appeals set this determination aside on the ground that "[o]nce [respondent] proved all of [petitioners'] proffered reasons for the adverse employment actions to be pretextual, [respondent] was entitled to judgment as a matter of law." 970 F.2d, at 492. The Court of Appeals reasoned:

> "Because all of defendants' proffered reasons were discredited, defendants were in a position of having offered no legitimate reason for their actions. In other words, defendants were in no better position than if they had remained silent, offering no rebuttal to an established inference that they had unlawfully discriminated against plaintiff on the basis of his race." *Ibid.*

That is not so. By producing *evidence* (whether ultimately persuasive or not) of nondiscriminatory reasons, petitioners sustained their burden of production, and thus placed themselves in a "better position than if they had remained silent."

In the nature of things, the determination that a defendant has met its burden of production (and has thus rebutted any legal presumption of intentional discrimination) can involve no credibility assessment. For the burden-of-production determination necessarily *precedes* the credibility-assessment stage. At the close of the defendant's case, the court is asked to decide whether an issue of fact remains for the trier of fact to determine. None does if, on the evidence presented, (1) any rational person would have to find the existence of facts constituting a prima facie case, and (2) the defendant has failed to meet its burden of production — *i.e.*, has failed to introduce evidence which, *taken as true*, would

---

[2] Various considerations led it to this conclusion, including the fact that two blacks sat on the disciplinary review board that recommended disciplining respondent, that respondent's black subordinates who actually committed the violations were not disciplined, and that "the number of black employees at St. Mary's remained constant." 756 F. Supp. 1244, 1252 (E.D. Mo. 1991).

permit the conclusion that there was a nondiscriminatory reason for the adverse action. In that event, the court must award judgment to the plaintiff as a matter of law under Federal Rule of Civil Procedure 50(a)(1) (in the case of jury trials) or Federal Rule of Civil Procedure 52(c) (in the case of bench trials). If the defendant has failed to sustain its burden but reasonable minds could differ as to whether a preponderance of the evidence establishes the facts of a prima facie case, then a question of fact does remain, which the trier of fact will be called upon to answer.[3]

If, on the other hand, the defendant has succeeded in carrying its burden of production, the *McDonnell Douglas* framework — with its presumptions and burdens — is no longer relevant. To resurrect it later, after the trier of fact has determined that what was "produced" to meet the burden of production is not credible, flies in the face of our holding in *Burdine* that to rebut the presumption "[t]he defendant need not persuade the court that it was actually motivated by the proffered reasons." 450 U.S., at 254. The presumption, having fulfilled its role of forcing the defendant to come forward with some response, simply drops out of the picture. The defendant's "production" (whatever its persuasive effect) having been made, the trier of fact proceeds to decide the ultimate question: whether plaintiff has proven "that the defendant intentionally discriminated against [him]" because of his race, *id.*, at 253. The factfinder's disbelief of the reasons put forward by the defendant (particularly if disbelief is accompanied by a suspicion of mendacity) may, together with the elements of the prima facie case, suffice to show intentional discrimination. Thus, rejection of the defendant's proffered reasons, will *permit* the trier of fact to infer the ultimate fact of intentional discrimination,[4] and the Court of Appeals was correct when it noted that, upon

---

[3] If the finder of fact answers affirmatively — if it finds that the prima facie case is supported by a preponderance of the evidence — it *must* find the existence of the presumed fact of unlawful discrimination and *must*, therefore, render a verdict for the plaintiff. Thus, the *effect* of failing to produce evidence to rebut the *McDonnell Douglas* presumption is not felt until the prima facie case has been *established*, either as a matter of law (because the plaintiff's facts are uncontested) or by the factfinder's determination that the plaintiff's facts are supported by a preponderance of the evidence. It is thus technically accurate to describe the sequence as we did in *Burdine*: "First, the plaintiff has the burden of proving by the preponderance of the evidence a prima facie case of discrimination. Second, if the plaintiff succeeds in proving the prima facie case, the burden shifts to the defendant to articulate some legitimate, nondiscriminatory reason for the employee's rejection." 450 U.S., at 252-253 (internal quotation omitted). As a practical matter, however, and in the real-life sequence of a trial, the defendant *feels* the "burden" not when the plaintiff's prima facie case is *proved*, but as soon as evidence of it is *introduced*. The defendant then knows that its failure to introduce evidence of a nondiscriminatory reason will cause judgment to go against it *unless* the plaintiff's prima facie case is held to be inadequate in law or fails to convince the factfinder. It is this practical coercion which causes the *McDonnell Douglas* presumption to function as a means of "arranging the presentation of evidence," *Watson v. Fort Worth Bank & Trust*, 487 U.S. 977, 986 (1988).

[4] Contrary to the dissent's confusion-producing analysis, there is nothing whatever inconsistent between this statement and our later statements that (1) the plaintiff must show "*both* that the

such rejection, "[n]o additional proof of discrimination is *required*," 970 F.2d, at 493 (emphasis added). But the Court of Appeals' holding that rejection of the defendant's proffered reasons *compels* judgment for the plaintiff disregards the fundamental principle of Rule 301 that a presumption does not shift the burden of proof, and ignores our repeated admonition that the Title VII plaintiff at all times bears the "ultimate burden of persuasion."

III

Only one unfamiliar with our case-law will be upset by the dissent's alarum that we are today setting aside "settled precedent," "two decades of stable law in this Court," "a framework carefully crafted in precedents as old as 20 years," which "Congress is [aware]" of and has implicitly approved.... We mean to answer the dissent's accusations in detail, by examining our cases, but at the outset it is worth noting the utter implausibility that we would ever have held what the dissent says we held.

As we have described, Title VII renders it unlawful "for an employer ... to fail or refuse to hire or to discharge any individual, or otherwise to discriminate against any individual with respect to his compensation, terms, conditions, or privileges of employment, because of such individual's race, color, religion, sex, or national origin." 42 U.S.C. § 2000e-2(a)(1). Here (in the context of the now-permissible jury trials for Title VII causes of action) is what the dissent asserts we have held to be a proper assessment of liability for violation of this law: Assume that 40% of a business' work force are members of a particular minority group, a group which comprises only 10% of the relevant labor market. An applicant, who is a member of that group, applies for an opening for which he is minimally qualified, but is rejected by a hiring officer of that *same minority group*, and the search to fill the opening continues. The rejected applicant files suit for racial discrimination under Title VII, and before the suit comes to trial, the supervisor who conducted the company's hiring is fired. Under *McDonnell Douglas*, the plaintiff has a prima facie case, and under the dissent's interpretation of our law not only must the company come forward with some explanation for the refusal to hire (which it will have to try to confirm out of the mouth of its now antagonistic former employee), but the jury must be instructed that, if they find that explanation to be *incorrect*, they must assess damages against the company, *whether or not they believe the company was guilty of racial discrimination*. The disproportionate minority makeup of the company's work force and the fact that its hiring officer was of the same minority group as the plaintiff will be irrelevant, because the plaintiff's case can be proved "indirectly by showing that the employer's proffered explanation is unworthy of

---

reason was false, *and* that discrimination was the real reason," and (2) "it is not enough ... to *dis*believe the employer." Even though (as we say here) rejection of the defendant's proffered reasons is enough at law to *sustain* a finding of discrimination, *there must be a finding of discrimination*.

credence."[5] Surely nothing short of inescapable prior *holdings* (the dissent does not pretend there are any) should make one assume that this is the law we have created.

We have no authority to impose liability upon an employer for alleged discriminatory employment practices unless an appropriate factfinder determines, according to proper procedures, *that the employer has unlawfully discriminated.* We may, according to traditional practice, establish certain modes and orders of proof, including an initial rebuttable presumption of the sort we described earlier in this opinion, which we believe *McDonnell Douglas* represents. But nothing in law would permit us to substitute for the required finding that the employer's action was the product of unlawful discrimination, the much different (and much lesser) finding that the employer's explanation of its action was not believable. The dissent's position amounts to precisely this, *unless* what is required to establish the *McDonnell Douglas* prima facie case is a degree of proof so high that it would, in absence of rebuttal, require a directed verdict for the plaintiff (for in that case proving the employer's rebuttal noncredible would leave the plaintiff's directed-verdict case in place, and compel a judgment in his favor). Quite obviously, however, what is required to establish the *McDonnell Douglas* prima facie case is infinitely less than what a directed verdict demands. The dissent is thus left with a position that has no support in the statute, no support in the reason of the matter, no support in any holding of this Court (that is not even contended), and support, if at all, only in the dicta of this Court's opinions. It is to those that we now turn — begrudgingly, since we think it generally undesirable, where holdings of the Court are not at issue, to dissect the sentences of the United States Reports as though they were the United States Code.

[Justice Scalia then closely analyzes *McDonnell Douglas, Burdine* and *United States Postal Service Board of Governors v. Aikens*, 460 U.S. 711 (1983), and concludes that, although some difficulties exist, the majority's holding is more consistent with their language and intent than the dissent's view.]

IV

We turn, finally, to the dire practical consequences that the respondents and the dissent claim our decision today will produce. What appears to trouble the

---

[5] The dissent has no response to this (not at all unrealistic) hypothetical, except to assert that *surely* the employer must have "personnel records" to which it can resort to demonstrate the reason for the failure to hire. The notion that every reasonable employer keeps "personnel records" on people who never became personnel, showing *why* they did not become personnel (*i.e.,* in what respects all other people who were hired were better) seems to us highly fanciful — or for the sake of American business we hope it is. But more fundamentally, the dissent's response misses the point. Even if such "personnel records" *do* exist, it is a mockery of justice to say that if the jury believes the reason they set forth is probably not the "true" one, all the other utterly compelling evidence that discrimination was *not* the reason will then be excluded from the jury's consideration.

dissent more than anything is that, in its view, our rule is adopted "for the benefit
of employers who have been found to have given false evidence in a court of
law," whom we "favo[r]" by "exempting them from responsibility for lies." As
we shall explain, our rule in no way gives special favor to those employers
whose evidence is disbelieved. But initially we must point out that there is no
justification for assuming (as the dissent repeatedly does) that those employers
whose evidence is disbelieved are perjurers and liars. Even if these were typically cases in which an individual defendant's sworn assertion regarding a
physical occurrence was pitted against an individual plaintiff's sworn assertion
regarding the same physical occurrence, surely it would be imprudent to call the
party whose assertion is (by a mere preponderance of the evidence) disbelieved,
a perjurer and a liar. And in these Title VII cases, the defendant is ordinarily *not*
an individual but a company, which must rely upon the statement of an employee
— often a relatively low-level employee — as to the central fact; and that central
fact is *not* a physical occurrence, but rather that employee's state of mind. To say
that the company which in good faith introduces such testimony, or even the testifying employee himself, becomes a liar and a perjurer when the testimony is
not believed, is nothing short of absurd.

Undoubtedly some employers (or at least their employees) will be lying. But
even if we could readily identify these perjurers, what an extraordinary notion,
that we "exempt them from responsibility for their lies" unless we enter Title VII
judgments for the plaintiffs! Title VII is not a cause of action for perjury; we
have other civil and criminal remedies for that. The dissent's notion of judg-
ment-for-lying is seen to be not even a fair and even-handed punishment for vice,
when one realizes how strangely selective it is: the employer is free to lie to its
heart's content about whether the plaintiff ever applied for a job, about how long
he worked, how much he made — indeed, about anything and everything *except*
the reason for the adverse employment action. And the plaintiff is permitted to
lie about absolutely *everything* without losing a verdict he otherwise deserves.
This is not a major, or even a sensible, blow against fibbery.

The respondent's argument based upon the employer's supposed lying is a
more modest one: "A defendant which unsuccessfully offers a 'phony reason'
logically cannot be in a better legal position [i.e., the position of having overcome the presumption from the plaintiff's prima facie case] than a defendant
who remains silent, and offers no reasons at all for its conduct." But there is no
anomaly in that, once one recognizes that the *McDonnell Douglas* presumption
is a *procedural* device, designed only to establish an order of proof and production. The books are full of procedural rules that place the perjurer (initially, at
least) in a better position than the truthful litigant who makes no response at all.
A defendant who fails to answer a complaint will, on motion, suffer a default
judgment that a deceitful response could have avoided. Fed. Rule Civ. Proc.
55(a). A defendant whose answer fails to contest critical averments in the complaint will, on motion, suffer a judgment on the pleadings that untruthful denials
could have avoided. Rule 12(c). And a defendant who fails to submit affidavits

creating a genuine issue of fact in response to a motion for summary judgment will suffer a dismissal that false affidavits could have avoided. Rule 56(e). In all of those cases, as under the *McDonnell Douglas* framework, perjury may purchase the defendant a chance at the factfinder — though there, as here, it also carries substantial risks, see Rules 11 and 56(g).

The dissent repeatedly raises a procedural objection that is impressive only to one who mistakes the basic nature of the *McDonnell Douglas* procedure. It asserts that "the Court now holds that the further enquiry [i.e., the inquiry that follows the employer's response to the prima facie case] is wide open, not limited at all by the scope of the employer's proffered explanation." The plaintiff cannot be expected to refute "reasons not articulated by the employer, but discerned in the record by the factfinder." He should not "be saddled with the tremendous disadvantage of having to confront, not the defined task of proving the employer's stated reasons to be false, but the amorphous requirement of disproving all possible nondiscriminatory reasons that a factfinder might find lurking in the record." "Under the scheme announced today, any conceivable explanation for the employer's actions that might be suggested by the evidence, however unrelated to the employer's articulated reasons, must be addressed by [the plaintiff]." These statements imply that the employer's "proffered explanation," his "stated reasons," his "articulated reasons," somehow exist *apart from the record* — in some pleading, or perhaps in some formal, nontestimonial statement made on behalf of the defendant to the factfinder. ("Your honor, pursuant to *McDonnell Douglas* the defendant hereby formally asserts, as its reason for the dismissal at issue here, incompetence of the employee.") Of course it does not work like that. The reasons the defendant sets forth are set forth "through the introduction of admissible evidence." *Burdine*, 450 U.S., at 255. In other words, the defendant's "articulated reasons" *themselves* are to be found "lurking in the record." It thus makes no sense to contemplate "the employer who is caught in a lie, but succeeds in *injecting* into the trial an *unarticulated* reason for its actions." There is a "lurking-in-the-record" problem, but it exists not for us but for the dissent. *If*, after the employer has met its preliminary burden, the plaintiff need not prove discrimination (and therefore need not disprove *all* other reasons suggested, no matter how vaguely, in the record) there must be some device for determining which particular portions of the record represent "articulated reasons" set forth with sufficient clarity to satisfy *McDonnell Douglas* — since it is only *that* evidence which the plaintiff must refute. But of course our *McDonnell Douglas* framework makes no provision for such a determination, which would have to be made not at the close of the trial but in *medias res*, since otherwise the plaintiff would not know what evidence to offer. It makes no sense....

The judgment of the Court of Appeals is reversed, and the case is remanded for further proceedings consistent with this opinion.

It is so ordered.

DISSENT

JUSTICE SOUTER, with whom JUSTICE WHITE, JUSTICE BLACKMUN, and JUSTICE STEVENS join, dissenting.

... The Court today decides to abandon the settled law that sets out [the *McDonnell Douglas*] structure for trying disparate-treatment Title VII cases, only to adopt a scheme that will be unfair to plaintiffs, unworkable in practice, and inexplicable in forgiving employers who present false evidence in court.

The majority's scheme greatly disfavors Title VII plaintiffs without the good luck to have direct evidence of discriminatory intent. The Court repeats the truism that the plaintiff has the "ultimate burden" of proving discrimination, without ever facing the practical question of how the plaintiff without such direct evidence can meet this burden. *Burdine* provides the answer, telling us that such a plaintiff may succeed in meeting his ultimate burden of proving discrimination "indirectly by showing that the employer's proffered explanation is unworthy of credence." 450 U.S., at 256. The possibility of some practical procedure for addressing what *Burdine* calls indirect proof is crucial to the success of most Title VII claims, for the simple reason that employers who discriminate are not likely to announce their discriminatory motive. And yet, under the majority's scheme, a victim of discrimination lacking direct evidence will now be saddled with the tremendous disadvantage of having to confront, not the defined task of proving the employer's stated reasons to be false, but the amorphous requirement of disproving all possible nondiscriminatory reasons that a factfinder might find lurking in the record. In the Court's own words, the plaintiff must "disprove *all* other reasons suggested, no matter how vaguely, in the record." ...

But see p. 457

The Court fails to explain, moreover, ... why proof that the employer's articulated reasons are "unpersuasive, or even obviously contrived," falls short.... Unless *McDonnell Douglas*'s command to structure and limit the case as the employer chooses is to be rendered meaningless, we should not look beyond the employer's lie by assuming the possible existence of other reasons the employer might have proffered without lying. By telling the factfinder to keep digging in cases where the plaintiff's proof of pretext turns on showing the employer's reasons to be unworthy of credence, the majority rejects the very point of the *McDonnell Douglas* rule requiring the scope of the factual enquiry to be limited, albeit in a manner chosen by the employer. What is more, the Court is throwing out the rule for the benefit of employers who have been found to have given false evidence in a court of law. There is simply no justification for favoring these employers by exempting them from responsibility for lies.[11] It may indeed be

---

[11] Although the majority chides me for referring to employers who offer false evidence in court as "liars," it was the first to place such employers in the company of perjurers. In any event, it is hardly "absurd" to say that an individual is lying when the factfinder does not believe his testimony, whether he is testifying on his own behalf or as the agent of a corporation. Factfinders constantly must decide whether explanations offered in court are true, and when they conclude, by a preponderance of the evidence, that a proffered explanation is false, it is not unfair to call that

459

true that such employers have nondiscriminatory reasons for their actions, but ones so shameful that they wish to conceal them. One can understand human frailty and the natural desire to conceal it, however, without finding in it a justification to dispense with an orderly procedure for getting at "the elusive factual question of intentional discrimination." *Burdine*, 450 U.S., at 255, n. 8.

With no justification in the employer's favor, the consequences to actual and potential Title VII litigants stand out sharply.... Under the scheme announced today, any conceivable explanation for the employer's actions that might be suggested by the evidence, however unrelated to the employer's articulated reasons, must be addressed by a plaintiff who does not wish to risk losing. Since the Court does not say whether a trial court may limit the introduction of evidence at trial to what is relevant to the employer's articulated reasons, and since the employer can win on the possibility of an unstated reason, the scope of admissible evidence at trial presumably includes any evidence potentially relevant to "the ultimate question" of discrimination, unlimited by the employer's stated reasons. If so, Title VII trials promise to be tedious affairs.... [P]retrial discovery will become more extensive and wide-ranging (if the plaintiff can afford it), for a much wider set of facts could prove to be both relevant and important at trial. The majority's scheme, therefore, will promote longer trials and more pre-trial discovery, threatening increased expense and delay in Title VII litigation for both plaintiffs and defendants, and increased burdens on the judiciary.

In addition to its unfairness and impracticality, the Court's new scheme, on its own terms, produces some remarkable results. Contrary to the assumption underlying the *McDonnell Douglas* framework, that employers will have "*some reason*" for their hiring and firing decisions, the majority assumes that some employers will be unable to discover the reasons for their own personnel actions. Under the majority's scheme, however, such employers, when faced with proof of a prima facie case of discrimination, still must carry the burden of producing evidence that a challenged employment action was taken for a nondiscriminatory reason. Thus, if an employer claims it cannot produce any evidence of a nondiscriminatory reason for a personnel decision,[12] and the trier of fact concludes

---

explanation a lie. To label it "perjury," a criminal concept, would be jumping the gun, but only the majority has employed that term.

[12] The Court is unrealistically concerned about the rare case in which an employer cannot easily turn to one of its employees for an explanation of a personnel decision. Most companies, of course, keep personnel records, and such records generally are admissible under Rule 803(6) of the Federal Rules of Evidence. Even those employers who do not keep records of their decisions will have other means of discovering the likely reasons for a personnel action by, for example, interviewing co-workers, examining employment records, and identifying standard personnel policies. The majority's scheme rewards employers who decide, in this atypical situation, to invent rather than to investigate. This concern drives the majority to point to the hypothetical case of the employer with a disproportionately high percentage of minority workers who would nonetheless lose a Title VII racial discrimination case by giving an untrue reason for a challenged personnel action. What the majority does not tell us, however, is why such an employer must rely solely on an "antagonistic

that the plaintiff has proven his prima facie case, the court must enter judgment for the plaintiff. The majority's scheme therefore leads to the perverse result that employers who fail to discover nondiscriminatory reasons for their own decisions to hire and fire employees not only will benefit from lying,[13] but must lie, to defend successfully against a disparate-treatment action. By offering false evidence of a nondiscriminatory reason, such an employer can rebut the presumption raised by the plaintiff's prima facie case, and then hope that the factfinder will conclude that the employer may have acted for a reason unknown rather than for a discriminatory reason. I know of no other scheme for structuring a legal action that, on its own terms, requires a party to lie in order to prevail....

The enhancement of a Title VII plaintiff's burden wrought by the Court's opinion is exemplified in this case. Melvin Hicks was denied any opportunity, much less a full and fair one, to demonstrate that the supposedly nondiscriminatory explanation for his demotion and termination, the personal animosity of his immediate supervisor, was unworthy of credence. In fact, the District Court did not find that personal animosity (which it failed to recognize might be racially motivated) was the true reason for the actions St. Mary's took; it adduced this reason simply as a possibility in explaining that Hicks had failed to prove "that the crusade [to terminate him] was racially rather than personally motivated." It is hardly surprising that Hicks failed to prove anything about this supposed personal crusade, since St. Mary's never articulated such an explanation for Hicks's discharge, and since the person who allegedly conducted this crusade denied at trial any personal difficulties between himself and Hicks. While the majority may well be troubled about the unfair treatment of Hicks in this instance and thus remands for review of whether the District Court's factual conclusions were clearly erroneous, the majority provides Hicks with no opportunity to produce evidence showing that the District Court's hypothesized expla-

---

former employee," rather than on its own personnel records, among other things, to establish the credible, nondiscriminatory reason it almost certainly must have had, given the facts assumed. The majority claims it would be a "mockery of justice" to allow recovery against an employer who presents "compelling evidence" of nondiscrimination simply because the jury believes a reason given in a personnel record "is probably not the 'true' one." But prior to drawing such a conclusion, the jury would consider all of the "compelling evidence" as at least circumstantial evidence for the truth of the nondiscriminatory explanation, because the employer would be able to argue that it would not lie to avoid a discrimination charge when its general behavior had been so demonstrably meritorious. If the jury still found that the plaintiff had carried his burden to show untruth, the untruth must have been a real whopper, or else the "compelling evidence" must not have been very compelling. In either event, justice need not worry too much about mockery.

[13] As the majority readily admits, its scheme places any employer who lies in a better position than the employer who says nothing. Under *McDonnell Douglas* and *Burdine*, an employer caught in a lie will lose on the merits, subjecting himself to liability not only for damages, but also for the prevailing plaintiff's attorney's fees, including, presumably, fees for the extra time spent to show pretext. Under the majority's scheme, the employer who is caught in a lie, but succeeds in injecting into the trial an unarticulated reason for its actions, will win its case and walk away rewarded for its falsehoods.

nation, first articulated six months after trial, is unworthy of credence. Whether Melvin Hicks wins or loses on remand, many plaintiffs in a like position will surely lose under the scheme adopted by the Court today, unless they possess both prescience and resources beyond what this Court has previously required Title VII litigants to employ.

Because I see no reason why Title VII interpretation should be driven by concern for employers who are too ashamed to be honest in court, at the expense of victims of discrimination who do not happen to have direct evidence of discriminatory intent, I respectfully dissent.

NOTE

Refinement or Abandonment? Hicks purports merely to refine the proof structure established by *McDonnell Douglas* and its progeny. The case, however, has caused some to question whether the proof structure should be retained at all:

> [My review of *Hicks* suggests] that it would be better to abandon *McDonnell Douglas-Burdine* than to repair it. Abandoning *McDonnell Douglas-Burdine* would leave courts with a less structured approach to disparate treatment cases, in which the only question would be whether the plaintiff had proved intentional discrimination by a preponderance of the evidence, both direct and circumstantial. It is not only intellectual honesty that would be gained from abandoning *McDonnell Douglas-Burdine*. There is also a possibility that abandoning *McDonnell Douglas-Burdine* will draw the attention of the courts ... to the substantive problem that *McDonnell Douglas-Burdine* tried, but failed, to answer in procedural terms: the problem of proving — rather than preaching — the reality of discrimination to the unconverted, on the level of the individual case....
>
> My main hesitation in advocating the dismantling of the *McDonnell Douglas-Burdine* proof structure concerns [the symbolic dimension]. What would it mean to declare, after all this time, that there are no preferential rules for individual discrimination cases — that the law will evaluate these discrimination claims like any other civil claims, with no societal thumb on the scale? But, to answer a question with a question, what is the symbolic significance of acting as though there are preferential standards for disparate treatment cases when, in fact, after *Hicks*, there are none? The claim that we have "special" rules for intentional discrimination creates a false "sense of closure" — a false belief that the law has already taken extraordinary steps to assist Title VII plaintiffs. Perhaps it is better to let the cold winds of litigation blow. At least the cold air will be clear.

[handwritten annotation: Deborah Malamud]

Deborah C. Malamud, *The Last Minuet: Disparate Treatment After Hicks*, 93 MICH. L. REV. 2229, 2237-38, 2324 (1995) (footnotes omitted).*

PRICE WATERHOUSE v. HOPKINS

United States Supreme Court
490 U.S. 228 (1989)

JUSTICE BRENNAN announced the judgment of the Court and delivered an opinion, in which JUSTICE MARSHALL, JUSTICE BLACKMUN, and JUSTICE STEVENS join.

Ann Hopkins had worked at Price Waterhouse[, a nationwide professional accounting partnership,] for five years when the partners in [her] office proposed her as a candidate for partnership. Of the 662 partners at the firm at that time, 7 were women. Of the 88 persons proposed for partnership that year, only 1 — Hopkins — was a woman. Forty-seven of these candidates were admitted to the partnership, 21 were rejected, and 20 — including Hopkins — were "held" for reconsideration the following year....[1]

In a jointly prepared statement supporting her candidacy, the partners in Hopkins' office showcased her successful 2-year effort to secure a $25 million contract with the Department of State, labeling it "an outstanding performance" and one that Hopkins carried out "virtually at the partner level."... Judge Gesell[, the District Court judge,] specifically found that ... "[n]one of the other partnership candidates at Price Waterhouse that year had a comparable record in terms of successfully securing major contracts for the partnership."

The partners in Hopkins' office praised her character as well as her accomplishments, describing her in their joint statement as "an outstanding professional" who had a "deft touch," a "strong character, independence and integrity." Clients appear to have agreed with these assessments. At trial, one official from the State Department described her as "extremely competent, intelligent," "strong and forthright, very productive, energetic and creative."...

On too many occasions, however, Hopkins' aggressiveness apparently spilled over into abrasiveness. Staff members seem to have borne the brunt of Hopkins' brusqueness.... Although later evaluations indicate an improvement, Hopkins' perceived shortcomings in this important area eventually doomed her bid for partnership. Virtually all of the partners' negative remarks about Hopkins — even those of partners supporting her — had to do with her "interpersonal skills." Both "[s]upporters and opponents of her candidacy," stressed Judge

---

* Reprinted with permission of the Michigan Law Review and the author.

[1] Before the time for reconsideration came, two of the partners in Hopkins' office withdrew their support for her, and the office informed her that she would not be reconsidered for partnership. Hopkins then resigned. Price Waterhouse does not challenge the Court of Appeals' conclusion that the refusal to repropose her for partnership amounted to a constructive discharge.

Gesell, "indicated that she was sometimes overly aggressive, unduly harsh, difficult to work with and impatient with staff."

There were clear signs, though, that some of the partners reacted negatively to Hopkins' personality because she was a woman. One partner described her as "macho"; another suggested that she "overcompensated for being a woman"; a third advised her to take "a course at charm school." Several partners criticized her use of profanity; in response, one partner suggested that those partners objected to her swearing only "because it's a lady using foul language." Another supporter explained that Hopkins "ha[d] matured from a tough-talking somewhat masculine hard-nosed mgr to an authoritative, formidable, but much more appealing lady ptr candidate." But it was the man who ... bore responsibility for explaining to Hopkins the reasons for the Policy Board's decision to place her candidacy on hold who delivered the coup de grace: in order to improve her chances for partnership, Thomas Beyer advised, Hopkins should "walk more femininely, talk more femininely, dress more femininely, wear make-up, have her hair styled, and wear jewelry."

Dr. Susan Fiske, a social psychologist and Associate Professor of Psychology at Carnegie-Mellon University, testified at trial that the partnership selection process at Price Waterhouse was likely influenced by sex stereotyping. Her testimony focused not only on the overtly sex-based comments of partners but also on gender-neutral remarks, made by partners who knew Hopkins only slightly, that were intensely critical of her. One partner, for example, baldly stated that Hopkins was "universally disliked" by staff, and another described her as "consistently annoying and irritating"; yet these were people who had had very little contact with Hopkins. According to Fiske, Hopkins' uniqueness (as the only woman in the pool of candidates) and the subjectivity of the evaluations made it likely that sharply critical remarks such as these were the product of sex stereotyping — although Fiske admitted that she could not say with certainty whether any particular comment was the result of stereotyping....

Judge Gesell found that Price Waterhouse legitimately emphasized interpersonal skills in its partnership decisions, and also found that the firm had not fabricated its complaints about Hopkins' interpersonal skills as a pretext for discrimination.... The judge went on to decide, however, that some of the partners' remarks about Hopkins stemmed from an impermissibly cabined view of the proper behavior of women, and that Price Waterhouse had done nothing to disavow reliance on such comments. He held that Price Waterhouse had unlawfully discriminated against Hopkins on the basis of sex by consciously giving credence and effect to partners' comments that resulted from sex stereotyping. Noting that Price Waterhouse could avoid equitable relief by proving by clear and convincing evidence that it would have placed Hopkins' candidacy on hold even absent this discrimination, the judge decided that the firm had not carried this heavy burden.

The Court of Appeals affirmed the District Court's ultimate conclusion, but departed from its analysis in one particular: it held that even if a plaintiff proves that discrimination played a role in an employment decision, the defendant will not be found liable if it proves, by clear and convincing evidence, that it would have made the same decision in the absence of discrimination. Under this approach, an employer is not deemed to have violated Title VII if it proves that it would have made the same decision in the absence of an impermissible motive, whereas under the District Court's approach, the employer's proof in that respect only avoids equitable relief. We decide today that the Court of Appeals had the better approach, but that both courts erred in requiring the employer to make its proof by clear and convincing evidence.

II

The specification of the standard of causation under Title VII is a decision about the kind of conduct that violates that statute. According to Price Waterhouse, an employer violates Title VII only if it gives decisive consideration to an employee's gender, race, national origin, or religion in making a decision that affects that employee. On Price Waterhouse's theory, even if a plaintiff shows that her gender played a part in an employment decision, it is still her burden to show that the decision would have been different if the employer had not discriminated. In Hopkins' view, on the other hand, an employer violates the statute whenever it allows one of these attributes to play any part in an employment decision. Once a plaintiff shows that this occurred, according to Hopkins, the employer's proof that it would have made the same decision in the absence of discrimination can serve to limit equitable relief but not to avoid a finding of liability. We conclude that, as often happens, the truth lies somewhere in-between.

A

In passing Title VII, Congress made the simple but momentous announcement that sex, race, religion, and national origin are not relevant to the selection, evaluation, or compensation of employees. Yet, the statute does not purport to limit the other qualities and characteristics that employers *may* take into account in making employment decisions. The converse, therefore, of "for cause" legislation, Title VII eliminates certain bases for distinguishing among employees while otherwise preserving employers' freedom of choice. This balance between employee rights and employer prerogatives turns out to be decisive in the case before us.

Congress' intent to forbid employers to take gender into account in making employment decisions appears on the face of the statute. In now-familiar language, the statute forbids an employer to "fail or refuse to hire or to discharge any individual, or otherwise to discriminate with respect to his compensation, terms, conditions, or privileges of employment," or to "limit, segregate, or classify his employees or applicants for employment in any way which would deprive or tend to deprive any individual of employment opportunities or otherwise adversely affect his status as an employee, *because of* such individual's ... sex." [Title VII, §§ 703(a)(1), (2)] (emphasis added). We take these words to mean that gender must be irrelevant to employment decisions. To construe the words "because of" as colloquial shorthand for "but-for causation," as does Price Waterhouse, is to misunderstand them.

But-for causation is a hypothetical construct. In determining whether a particular factor was a but-for cause of a given event, we begin by assuming that that factor was present at the time of the event, and then ask whether, even if that factor had been absent, the event nevertheless would have transpired in the same way. The present, active tense of the operative verbs of § 703(a)(1) ("to fail or refuse"), in contrast, turns our attention to the actual moment of the event in question, the adverse employment decision. The critical inquiry, the one commanded by the words of § 703(a)(1), is whether gender was a factor in the employment decision *at the moment it was made.* Moreover, since we know that the words "because of" do not mean *"solely* because of,"[7] we also know that Title VII meant to condemn even those decisions based on a mixture of legitimate and illegitimate considerations. When, therefore, an employer considers both gender and legitimate factors at the time of making a decision, that decision was "because of" sex and the other, legitimate considerations — even if we may say later, in the context of litigation, that the decision would have been the same if gender had not been taken into account.

To attribute this meaning to the words "because of" does not, as the dissent asserts, divest them of causal significance. A simple example illustrates the point. Suppose two physical forces act upon and move an object, and suppose that either force acting alone would have moved the object. As the dissent would have it, *neither* physical force was a "cause" of the motion unless we can show that but for one or both of them, the object would not have moved; apparently both forces were simply "in the air" unless we can identify at least one of them as a but-for cause of the object's movement. Events that are causally overdetermined, in other words, may not have any "cause" at all. This cannot be so.

We need not leave our common sense at the doorstep when we interpret a statute. It is difficult for us to imagine that, in the simple words "because of," Congress meant to obligate a plaintiff to identify the precise causal role played by legitimate and illegitimate motivations in the employment decision she challenges. We conclude, instead, that Congress meant to obligate her to prove that the employer relied upon sex-based considerations in coming to its decision....

To say that an employer may not take gender into account is not, however, the end of the matter, for that describes only one aspect of Title VII. The other important aspect of the statute is its preservation of an employer's remaining

---

[7] Congress specifically rejected an amendment that would have placed the word "solely" in front of the words "because of." 110 Cong. Rec. 2728, 13837 (1964).

freedom of choice. We conclude that the preservation of this freedom means that an employer shall not be liable if it can prove that, even if it had not taken gender into account, it would have come to the same decision regarding a particular person....

The central point is this: while an employer may not take gender into account in making an employment decision (except in those very narrow circumstances in which gender is a BFOQ), it is free to decide against a woman for other reasons. We think these principles require that, once a plaintiff in a Title VII case shows that gender played a motivating part in an employment decision, the defendant may avoid a finding of liability[10] only by proving that it would have made the same decision even if it had not allowed gender to play such a role. This balance of burdens is the direct result of Title VII's balance of rights.

Our holding casts no shadow on *Burdine,* in which we decided that, even after a plaintiff has made out a prima facie case of discrimination under Title VII, the burden of persuasion does not shift to the employer to show that its stated legitimate reason for the employment decision was the true reason. We stress, first, that neither court below shifted the burden of persuasion to Price Waterhouse on this question, and in fact, the District Court found that Hopkins had not shown that the firm's stated reason for its decision was pretextual. Moreover, since we hold that the plaintiff retains the burden of persuasion on the issue whether gender played a part in the employment decision, the situation before us is not the one of "shifting burdens" that we addressed in *Burdine.* Instead, the employer's burden is most appropriately deemed an affirmative defense: the plaintiff must persuade the factfinder on one point, and then the employer, if it wishes to prevail, must persuade it on another.

Price Waterhouse's claim that the employer does not bear any burden of proof (if it bears one at all) until the plaintiff has shown "substantial evidence that Price Waterhouse's explanation for failing to promote Hopkins was not the 'true reason' for its action" merely restates its argument that the plaintiff in a mixed-motives case must squeeze her proof into *Burdine*'s framework. Where a decision was the product of a mixture of legitimate and illegitimate motives, however, it simply makes no sense to ask whether the legitimate reason was "*the* 'true reason'" (emphasis added) for the decision — which is the question asked by *Burdine*.[12] Oblivious to this last point, the dissent would insist that *Burdine*'s

---

[10] Hopkins argues that once she made this showing, she was entitled to a finding that Price Waterhouse had discriminated against her on the basis of sex; as a consequence, she says, the partnership's proof could only limit the relief she received. [The Court rejected this argument and said no liability would result if the employer could carry its burden. This portion of the decision was overturned by Congress in the Civil Rights Act of 1991. See note 2 following the case.]

[12] Nothing in this opinion should be taken to suggest that a case must be correctly labeled as either a "pretext" case or a "mixed-motives" case from the beginning in the District Court; indeed, we expect that plaintiffs often will allege, in the alternative, that their cases are both. Discovery often will be necessary before the plaintiff can know whether both legitimate and illegitimate considerations played a part in the decision against her. At some point in the proceedings, of

framework perform work that it was never intended to perform. It would require a plaintiff who challenges an adverse employment decision in which both legitimate and illegitimate considerations played a part to pretend that the decision, in fact, stemmed from a single source — for the premise of *Burdine* is that *either* a legitimate *or* an illegitimate set of considerations led to the challenged decision. To say that *Burdine*'s evidentiary scheme will not help us decide a case admittedly involving *both* kinds of considerations is not to cast aspersions on the utility of that scheme in the circumstances for which it was designed....

C

In saying that gender played a motivating part in an employment decision, we mean that, if we asked the employer at the moment of the decision what its reasons were and if we received a truthful response, one of those reasons would be that the applicant or employee was a woman. In the specific context of sex stereotyping, an employer who acts on the basis of a belief that a woman cannot be aggressive, or that she must not be, has acted on the basis of gender....

Remarks at work that are based on sex stereotypes do not inevitably prove that gender played a part in a particular employment decision. The plaintiff must show that the employer actually relied on her gender in making its decision. In making this showing, stereotyped remarks can certainly be *evidence* that gender played a part....

As to the employer's proof, in most cases, the employer should be able to present some objective evidence as to its probable decision in the absence of an impermissible motive.[14] Moreover, proving "'that the same decision would have been justified ... is not the same as proving that the same decision would have been made.'" An employer may not, in other words, prevail in a mixed-motives case by offering a legitimate and sufficient reason for its decision if that reason did not motivate it at the time of the decision. Finally, an employer may not meet its burden in such a case by merely showing that at the time of the decision it was motivated only in part by a legitimate reason. The very premise of a mixed-motives case is that a legitimate reason was present.... The employer instead must show that its legitimate reason, standing alone, would have induced it to make the same decision.

---

course, the District Court must decide whether a particular case involves mixed motives. If the plaintiff fails to satisfy the factfinder that it is more likely than not that a forbidden characteristic played a part in the employment decision, then she may prevail only if she proves, following *Burdine,* that the employer's stated reason for its decision is pretextual....

[14] JUSTICE WHITE's suggestion that the employer's own testimony as to the probable decision in the absence of discrimination is due special credence where the court has, contrary to the employer's testimony, found that an illegitimate factor played a part in the decision, is baffling.

III

The courts below held that an employer who has allowed a discriminatory impulse to play a motivating part in an employment decision must prove by clear and convincing evidence that it would have made the same decision in the absence of discrimination. We are persuaded that the better rule is that the employer must make this showing by a preponderance of the evidence. Conventional rules of civil litigation generally apply in Title VII cases and one of these rules is that parties to civil litigation need only prove their case by a preponderance of the evidence....

preponderance of the evidence

IV

The District Court found that sex stereotyping "was permitted to play a part" in the evaluation of Hopkins as a candidate for partnership. Price Waterhouse disputes both that stereotyping occurred and that it played any part in the decision to place Hopkins' candidacy on hold. In the firm's view, in other words, the District Court's factual conclusions are clearly erroneous. We do not agree.

In finding that some of the partners' comments reflected sex stereotyping, the District Court relied in part on Dr. Fiske's expert testimony.... We are not inclined to accept petitioner's belated and unsubstantiated characterization of Dr. Fiske's testimony as "gossamer evidence" based only on "intuitive hunches" and of her detection of sex stereotyping as "intuitively divined." Nor are we disposed to adopt the dissent's dismissive attitude toward Dr. Fiske's field of study and toward her own professional integrity.

Indeed, we are tempted to say that Dr. Fiske's expert testimony was merely icing on Hopkins' cake. It takes no special training to discern sex stereotyping in a description of an aggressive female employee as requiring "a course at charm school." Nor, turning to Thomas Beyer's memorable advice to Hopkins, does it require expertise in psychology to know that, if an employee's flawed "interpersonal skills" can be corrected by a soft-hued suit or a new shade of lipstick, perhaps it is the employee's sex and not her interpersonal skills that has drawn the criticism....

V

We hold that when a plaintiff in a Title VII case proves that her gender played a motivating part in an employment decision, the defendant may avoid a finding of liability only by proving by a preponderance of the evidence that it would have made the same decision even if it had not taken the plaintiff's gender into account. Because the courts below erred by deciding that the defendant must make this proof by clear and convincing evidence, we reverse the Court of Appeals' judgment against Price Waterhouse on liability and remand the case to that court for further proceedings.

Holding

It is so ordered.

JUSTICE WHITE, concurring in the judgment....

I concur in the judgment reversing this case in part and remanding. With respect to the employer's burden, however, the plurality seems to require, at least in most cases, that the employer submit objective evidence that the same result would have occurred absent the unlawful motivation. In my view, however, there is no special requirement that the employer carry its burden by objective evidence. In a mixed-motives case, where the legitimate motive found would have been ample grounds for the action taken, and the employer credibly testifies that the action would have been taken for the legitimate reasons alone, this should be ample proof....

JUSTICE O'CONNOR, concurring in the judgment....

[T]he rule we adopt today is at least a change in direction from some of our prior precedents.... *McDonnell Douglas* and *Burdine* assumed that the plaintiff would bear the burden of persuasion [throughout a disparate treatment case] and we clearly depart from that framework today. Such a departure requires justification, and its outlines should be carefully drawn.

First, *McDonnell Douglas* itself dealt with a situation where the plaintiff presented no direct evidence that the employer had relied on a forbidden factor under Title VII in making an employment decision. The prima facie case established there was ... based only on the statistical probability that when a number of potential causes for an employment decision are eliminated an inference arises that an illegitimate factor was in fact the motivation behind the decision. In the face of this inferential proof, the employer's burden was deemed to be only one of production.... I do not think that the employer is entitled to the same presumption of good faith where there is direct evidence that it has placed substantial reliance on factors whose consideration is forbidden by Title VII....

Second, the facts of this case ... convince me that the evidentiary standard I propose is necessary to make real [Title VII's] promise of [non-discrimination.] In this case, the District Court found that a number of the evaluations of Ann Hopkins submitted by partners in the firm overtly referred to her failure to conform to certain gender stereotypes as a factor militating against her election to the partnership[; that the] evaluations were given "great weight" by the decisionmakers at Price Waterhouse[; and] that the partner responsible for informing Hopkins of the factors which caused her candidacy to be placed on hold indicated that her "professional" problems would be solved if she would "walk more femininely, talk more femininely, wear make-up, have her hair styled, and wear jewelry." As the Court of Appeals characterized it, Ann Hopkins proved that Price Waterhouse "permitt[ed] stereotypical attitudes towards women to play a significant, though unquantifiable, role in its decision not to invite her to become a partner."

At this point Ann Hopkins had taken her proof as far as it could go.... It is as if Ann Hopkins were sitting in the hall outside the room where partnership decisions were being made. As the partners filed in to consider her candidacy, she heard several of them make sexist remarks in discussing her suitability for partnership. As the decisionmakers exited the room, she was *told* by one of those privy to the decisionmaking process that her gender was a major reason for the rejection of her partnership bid. If ... "[p]resumptions shifting the burden of proof are often created to reflect judicial evaluations of probabilities and to conform with a party's superior access to the proof," one would be hard pressed to think of a situation where it would be more appropriate to require the defendant to show that its decision would have been justified by wholly legitimate concerns....

Moreover, there is mounting evidence in the decisions of the lower courts that respondent here is not alone in her inability to pinpoint discrimination as the precise cause of her injury, despite having shown that it played a significant role in the decisional process.... Particularly in the context of the professional world, where decisions are often made by collegial bodies on the basis of largely subjective criteria, requiring the plaintiff to prove that *any* one factor was the definitive cause of the decisionmakers' action may be tantamount to declaring Title VII inapplicable to such decisions....

In my view, in order to justify shifting the burden on the issue of causation to the defendant, a disparate treatment plaintiff must show by direct evidence that an illegitimate criterion was a substantial factor in the decision.... Requiring that the plaintiff demonstrate that an illegitimate factor played a substantial role in the employment decision identifies those employment situations where the deterrent purpose of Title VII is most clearly implicated. As an evidentiary matter, where a plaintiff has made this type of strong showing of illicit motivation, the factfinder is entitled to presume that the employer's discriminatory animus made a difference to the outcome, absent proof to the contrary from the employer. Where a disparate treatment plaintiff has made such a showing, the burden then rests with the employer to convince the trier of fact that it is more likely than not that the decision would have been the same absent consideration of the illegitimate factor. The employer need not isolate the sole cause for the decision; rather it must demonstrate that with the illegitimate factor removed from the calculus, sufficient business reasons would have induced it to take the same employment action....

Thus, stray remarks in the workplace, while perhaps probative of sexual harassment, cannot justify requiring the employer to prove that its hiring or promotion decisions were based on legitimate criteria. Nor can statements by non-decisionmakers, or statements by decisionmakers unrelated to the decisional process itself, suffice to satisfy the plaintiff's burden in this regard. In addition, in my view testimony such as Dr. Fiske's in this case, standing alone, would not justify shifting the burden of persuasion to the employer. Race and gender always "play a role" in an employment decision in the benign sense that these are human characteristics of which decisionmakers are aware and about which they may comment in a perfectly neutral and nondiscriminatory fashion. For example, in the context of this case, a mere reference to "a lady candidate" might show that gender "played a role" in the decision, but by no means could support a rational factfinder's inference that the decision was made "because of" sex. What is required is what Ann Hopkins showed here: direct evidence that decisionmakers placed substantial negative reliance on an illegitimate criterion in reaching their decision....

JUSTICE KENNEDY, with whom the CHIEF JUSTICE and JUSTICE SCALIA join, dissenting.

Today the Court manipulates existing and complex rules for employment discrimination cases in a way certain to result in confusion. Continued adherence to the evidentiary scheme established in *McDonnell Douglas Corp. v. Green,* 411 U.S. 792 (1973) and *Texas Dept. of Community Affairs v. Burdine,* 450 U.S. 248 (1981), is a wiser course than creation of more disarray in an area of the law already difficult for the bench and bar, and so I must dissent....

The plurality begins by noting the quite unremarkable fact that Title VII is written in the present tense.... This observation, however, tells us nothing of particular relevance to Title VII or the cause of action it creates. I am unaware of any federal prohibitory statute that is written in the past tense. Every liability determination, including the novel one constructed by the plurality, necessarily is concerned with the examination of a past event.[1] The plurality's analysis of verb tense serves only to divert attention from the causation requirement that is made part of the statute by the "because of" phrase. That phrase, I respectfully submit, embodies a rather simple concept that the plurality labors to ignore.[2] ...

I would adhere to [the] established evidentiary framework [of *McDonnell Douglas* and *Burdine*], which provides the appropriate standard for this and other individual disparate-treatment cases.... The Court's attempt at refinement provides limited practical benefits at the cost of confusion and complexity, with the attendant risk that the trier of fact will misapprehend the controlling legal principles and reach an incorrect decision....

The potential benefits of the new approach, in my view, are overstated. First, the Court makes clear that the *Price Waterhouse* scheme is applicable only in

---

[1] The plurality's description of its own standard is both hypothetical and retrospective. The inquiry seeks to determine whether "if we asked the employer at the moment of decision what its reasons were and if we received a truthful response, one of those reasons would be that the applicant or employee was a woman."

[2] The plurality's discussion of overdetermined causes only highlights the error of its insistence that but-for is not the substantive standard of causation under Title VII. The opinion discusses the situation where two physical forces move an object, and either force acting alone would have moved the object. Translated to the context of Title VII, this situation would arise where an employer took an adverse action in reliance both on sex and on legitimate reasons, and *either* the illegitimate or the legitimate reason standing alone would have produced the action. If this state of affairs is proved to the factfinder, there will be no liability under the plurality's own test, for the same decision would have been made had the illegitimate reason never been considered.

those cases where the plaintiff has produced direct and substantial proof that an impermissible motive was relied upon in making the decision at issue. The burden shift properly will be found to apply in only a limited number of employment discrimination cases. The application of the new scheme, furthermore, will make a difference only in a smaller subset of cases....

Although the *Price Waterhouse* system is not for every case, almost every plaintiff is certain to ask for a *Price Waterhouse* instruction, perhaps on the basis of "stray remarks" or other evidence of discriminatory animus. Trial and appellate courts will therefore be saddled with the task of developing standards for determining when to apply the burden shift. One of their new tasks will be the generation of a jurisprudence of the meaning of "substantial factor." Courts will also be required to make the often subtle and difficult distinction between "direct" and "indirect" or "circumstantial" evidence. Lower courts long have had difficulty applying *McDonnell Douglas* and *Burdine*. Addition of a second burden-shifting mechanism, the application of which itself depends on assessment of credibility and a determination whether evidence is sufficiently direct and substantial, is not likely to lend clarity to the process....

I do not believe the minor refinement in Title VII procedures accomplished by today's holding can justify the difficulties that will accompany it.... Although the employer does not bear the burden of persuasion under *Burdine*, it must offer clear and reasonably specific reasons for the contested decision, and has every incentive to persuade the trier of fact that the decision was lawful. Further, the suggestion that the employer should bear the burden of persuasion due to superior access to evidence has little force in the Title VII context, where the liberal discovery rules available to all litigants are supplemented by EEOC investigatory files. In sum, the *Burdine* framework provides a "sensible, orderly way to evaluate the evidence in light of common experience as it bears on the critical question of discrimination," and it should continue to govern the order of proof in Title VII disparate-treatment cases....

NOTES

1. *Life After the Supreme Court.* On remand, the District Court found that Price Waterhouse did not carry its burden of proving it would have reached the same decision in the absence of discrimination. Consequently, it found for Hopkins and ordered the firm to make her a partner and pay her $371,000 in backpay. *Hopkins v. Price Waterhouse*, 737 F. Supp. 1202 (D.D.C.), *aff'd*, 920 F.2d 967 (D.C. Cir. 1990). Hopkins accepted the partnership position. She reports that occasionally young staff members have asked her for advice about how to become partner. She replies that "I'd be happy to help, but I don't think [you'd] want to do it the way I did." Amy Saltzman, *Life After the Lawsuit*, U.S. NEWS & WORLD REPORT, Aug. 19, 1996, at 42.

2. *The Civil Rights Act of 1991.* In the Civil Rights Act of 1991, Congress adopted the plurality's position on two issues that divided the Court and overturned another position on which the Court was unanimous. First, the Act added section 703(m) to Title VII, which says that an unlawful employment practice is established when a complaining party demonstrates that sex was a "motivating factor" in an employment decision, thus adopting Brennan's articulation of the plaintiff's initial burden rather than O'Connor's "direct evidence that sex was a substantial factor" articulation. Second, the Act added section 706(g)(2)(B), which says that the employer's burden is to prove that it "would have taken the same action in the absence of the impermissible motivating factor." This amendment also closer approximates Brennan's articulation of the employer's burden than O'Connor's. Third, the Act overturned the unanimous position of the Court that employers are not liable at all when they meet their burden of demonstrating that they would have reached the same result anyway. Sections 706(g)(2)(B)(i) and (ii) say that, in that situation, courts may award declaratory relief, injunctive relief (other than relief that benefits the particular plaintiff, such as backpay or an order to hire), and attorney's fees and costs.

3. *After-Acquired Evidence.* In *Hopkins*, the Court considered how to evaluate a case when the employer may have been influenced by both legitimate and illegitimate factors at the time the decision was made. In *McKennon v. Nashville Banner Publishing Co.*, 513 U.S. 352 (1995), the Supreme Court considered what should happen when the timing is different. In *McKennon*, the employer fired the plaintiff because of her age. During discovery, however, the employer learned that the plaintiff had engaged in misconduct at work that would have resulted in her immediate discharge had the employer known about it at the time.

A unanimous Court held that after-acquired evidence of wrongdoing can be a defense, but only if the employer can establish that it "was of such severity that the employee in fact would have been terminated on those grounds alone if the employer had known of it at the time of the discharge." *Id.* at 362-63. The defense operates not as a complete bar, but as a limitation on the relief available:

> The proper boundaries of remedial relief in [these] cases must be addressed by the judicial system in the ordinary course of further decisions, for the factual permutations and the equitable considerations they raise will vary from case to case. We do conclude that here, and as a general rule in cases of this type, neither reinstatement nor front pay is an appropriate remedy. It would be both inequitable and pointless to order the reinstatement of someone the employer would have terminated, and will terminate, in any event and upon lawful grounds.
>
> The proper measure of backpay presents a more difficult problem.... The beginning point in the trial court's formulation of a remedy should be calculation of backpay from the date of the unlawful discharge to the date the new information was discovered. In determining the appropriate order for relief, the court can consider taking into further account extraordinary equitable circumstances that affect the legitimate interests of either party.

Id. at 361-62.

The Court worried that employers might "as a routine matter undertake extensive discovery into an employee's background or performance" in an attempt to establish the defense, but indicated that the availability of attorney's fees and Rule 11 sanctions would be sufficient to "deter most abuses." *Id*. at 363.

2. SYSTEMIC DISPARATE TREATMENT

HAZELWOOD SCHOOL DISTRICT v. UNITED STATES

United States Supreme Court
433 U.S. 299 (1977)

MR. JUSTICE STEWART delivered the opinion of the Court.

The petitioner Hazelwood School District covers 78 square miles in the northern part of St. Louis County, Mo. In 1973 the Attorney General brought this lawsuit against Hazelwood and various of its officials, alleging that they were engaged in a "pattern or practice" of employment discrimination in violation of Title VII of the Civil Rights Act of 1964....

Hazelwood was formed from 13 rural school districts between 1949 and 1951 by a process of annexation. By the 1967-1968 school year, 17,550 students were enrolled in the district, of whom only 59 were Negro; the number of Negro pupils increased to 576 of 25,166 in 1972-1973, a total of just over 2%.

From the beginning, Hazelwood followed relatively unstructured procedures in hiring its teachers. [An application file was kept and when an opening occurred, 3 to 10 applicants would be selected for interviews, generally those who had submitted applications most recently.]

Interviews were conducted by a department chairman, program coordinator, or the principal at the school where the teaching vacancy existed. [E]ach school principal possessed virtually unlimited discretion in hiring teachers for his school. The only general guidance given to the principals was to hire the "most competent" person available, and such intangibles as "personality, disposition, appearance, poise, voice, articulation, and ability to deal with people" counted heavily. The principal's choice was routinely honored by Hazelwood's Superintendent and the Board of Education.

In the early 1960's Hazelwood found it necessary to recruit new teachers, and for that purpose members of its staff visited a number of colleges and universities in Missouri and bordering States. All the institutions visited were predominantly white, and Hazelwood did not seriously recruit at either of the two predominantly Negro four-year colleges in Missouri.[4] As a buyer's market began to develop for public school teachers, Hazelwood curtailed its recruiting efforts. For the 1971-1972 school year, 3,127 persons applied for only 234 teaching

---

[4] One of those two schools was never visited even though it was located in nearby St. Louis. The second was briefly visited on one occasion, but no potential applicant was interviewed.

vacancies; for the 1972-1973 school year, there were 2,373 applications for 282 vacancies. A number of the applicants who were not hired were Negroes.

Hazelwood hired its first Negro teacher in 1969. The number of Negro faculty members gradually increased in successive years: 6 of 957 in the 1970 school year; 16 of 1,107 by the end of the 1972 school year; 22 of 1,231 in the 1973 school year. By comparison, according to 1970 census figures, of more than 19,000 teachers employed in that year in the St. Louis area, 15.4% were Negro. That percentage figure included the St. Louis City School District, which in recent years has followed a policy of attempting to maintain a 50% Negro teaching staff. Apart from that school district, 5.7% of the teachers in the county were Negro in 1970....

Drawing upon these historic facts, the Government mounted its "pattern or practice" attack in the District Court upon four different fronts. It adduced evidence of (1) a history of alleged racially discriminatory practices, (2) statistical disparities in hiring, (3) the standardless and largely subjective hiring procedures, and (4) specific instances of alleged discrimination against 55 unsuccessful Negro applicants for teaching jobs. Hazelwood offered virtually no additional evidence in response, relying instead on evidence introduced by the Government, perceived deficiencies in the Government's case, and its own officially promulgated policy "to hire all teachers on the basis of training, preparation and recommendations, regardless of race, color or creed."

The District Court ruled that the Government had failed to establish a pattern or practice of discrimination. The court was unpersuaded by the alleged history of discrimination, noting that no dual school system had ever existed in Hazelwood. The statistics showing that relatively small numbers of Negroes were employed as teachers were found nonprobative, on the ground that the percentage of Negro pupils in Hazelwood was similarly small. The court found nothing illegal or suspect in the teacher-hiring procedures that Hazelwood had followed. Finally, the court reviewed the evidence in the 55 cases of alleged individual discrimination, and after stating that the burden of proving intentional discrimination was on the Government, it found that this burden had not been sustained in a single instance. Hence, the court entered judgment for the defendants.

The Court of Appeals for the Eighth Circuit reversed.... We granted certiorari ....

This Court's recent consideration in *International Brotherhood of Teamsters v. United States,* 431 U.S. 324 (1977), of the role of statistics in pattern-or-practice suits under Title VII provides substantial guidance in evaluating the arguments advanced by the petitioners. In that case we stated that it is the Government's burden to "establish by a preponderance of the evidence that racial discrimination was the [employer's] standard operating procedure, the regular rather than the unusual practice." We also noted that statistics can be an important source of proof in employment discrimination cases, since "absent explanation, it is ordinarily to be expected that nondiscriminatory hiring practices will in time result in a work force more or less representative of the racial and ethnic composition of the population in the community from which employees are hired. Evidence of long-lasting and gross disparity between the composition of a work force and that of the general population thus may be significant even though § 703(j) makes clear that Title VII imposes no requirement that a work force mirror the general population." *Id.,* at 340 n.20.

Where gross statistical disparities can be shown, they alone may in a proper case constitute prima facie proof of a pattern or practice of discrimination. *Teamsters, supra,* 431 U.S. at 339.

There can be no doubt, in light of the *Teamsters* case, that the District Court's comparison of Hazelwood's teacher work force to its student population fundamentally misconceived the role of statistics in employment discrimination cases. The Court of Appeals was correct in the view that a proper comparison was between the racial composition of Hazelwood's teaching staff and the racial composition of the qualified public school teacher population in the relevant labor market.[13] The percentage of Negroes on Hazelwood's teaching staff in 1972-1973 was 1.4% and in 1973-1974 it was 1.8%. By contrast, the percentage of qualified Negro teachers in the area was, according to the 1970 census, at least 5.7%.[14] Although these differences were on their face substantial, the Court

---

[13] In *Teamsters,* the comparison between the percentage of Negroes on the employer's work force and the percentage in the general areawide population was highly probative, because the job skill there involved — the ability to drive a truck — is one that many persons possess or can fairly readily acquire. When special qualifications are required to fill particular jobs, comparisons to the general population (rather than to the smaller group of individuals who possess the necessary qualifications) may have little probative value. The comparative statistics introduced by the Government in the District Court, however, were properly limited to public school teachers....

Although the petitioners concede as a general matter the probative force of the comparative work-force statistics, they object to the Court of Appeals' heavy reliance on these data on the ground that applicant-flow data, showing the actual percentage of white and Negro applicants for teaching positions at Hazelwood, would be firmer proof.... [T]here was no clear evidence of such statistics. We leave it to the District Court on remand to determine whether competent proof of those data can be adduced. If so, it would, of course, be very relevant.

[14] As is discussed below, the Government contends that a comparative figure of 15.4%, rather than 5.7%, is the appropriate one. But even assuming, *arguendo,* that the 5.7% figure urged by the petitioners is correct, the disparity between that figure and the percentage of Negroes on Hazelwood's teaching staff would be more than fourfold for the 1972-1973 school year, and threefold for the 1973-1974 school year. A precise method of measuring the significance of such statistical disparities was explained in *Castaneda v. Partida,* 430 U.S. 482, 496-497, n.17. It involves calculation of the "standard deviation" as a measure of predicted fluctuations from the expected value of a sample. Using the 5.7% figure as the basis for calculating the expected value, the expected number of Negroes on the Hazelwood teaching staff would be roughly 63 in 1972-1973 and 70 in 1973-1974. The observed number in those years was 16 and 22, respectively. The difference between the observed and expected values was more than six standard deviations in 1972-1973 and more than five standard deviations in 1973-1974. The Court in *Castaneda* noted

of Appeals erred in substituting its judgment for that of the District Court and holding that the Government had conclusively proved its "pattern or practice" lawsuit.

The Court of Appeals totally disregarded the possibility that this prima facie statistical proof in the record might at the trial court level be rebutted by statistics dealing with Hazelwood's hiring after it became subject to Title VII. Racial discrimination by public employers was not made illegal under Title VII until March 24, 1972. A public employer who from that date forward made all its employment decisions in a wholly nondiscriminatory way would not violate Title VII even if it had formerly maintained an all-white work force by purposefully excluding Negroes.[15] For this reason, the Court cautioned in the *Teamsters* opinion that once a prima facie case has been established by statistical workforce disparities, the employer must be given an opportunity to show that "the claimed discriminatory pattern is a product of pre-Act hiring rather than unlawful post-Act discrimination." 431 U.S., at 360.

The record in this case showed that for the 1972-1973 school year, Hazelwood hired 282 new teachers, 10 [of] whom (3.5%) were Negroes; for the following school year it hired 123 new teachers, 5 of whom (4.1%) were Negroes. Over the two-year period, Negroes constituted a total of 15 of the 405 new teachers hired (3.7%). Although the Court of Appeals briefly mentioned these data in reciting the facts, it wholly ignored them in discussing whether the Government had shown a pattern or practice of discrimination. And it gave no consideration at all to the possibility that post-Act data as to the number of Negroes hired compared to the total number of Negro applicants might tell a totally different story.

What the hiring figures prove obviously depends upon the figures to which they are compared. The Court of Appeals accepted the Government's argument that the relevant comparison was to the labor market area of St. Louis County and the city of St. Louis, in which, according to the 1970 census, 15.4% of all teachers were Negro. The propriety of that comparison was vigorously disputed by the petitioners, who urged that because the city of St. Louis has made special attempts to maintain a 50% Negro teaching staff, inclusion of that school district in the relevant market area distorts the comparison. Were that argument accepted, the percentage of Negro teachers in the relevant labor market area (St.

---

that "[a]s a general rule for such large samples, if the difference between the expected value and the observed number is greater than two or three standard deviations," then the hypothesis that teachers were hired without regard to race would be suspect. 430 U.S., at 497 n.17.

[15] This is not to say that evidence of pre-Act discrimination can never have any probative force. Proof that an employer engaged in racial discrimination prior to the effective date of Title VII might in some circumstances support the inference that such discrimination continued, particularly where relevant aspects of the decisionmaking process had undergone little change. And, of course, a public employer even before the extension of Title VII in 1972 was subject to the command of the Fourteenth Amendment not to engage in purposeful racial discrimination.

Louis County alone) as shown in the 1970 census would be 5.7% rather than 15.4%.

The difference between these figures may well be important; the disparity between 3.7% (the percentage of Negro teachers hired by Hazelwood in 1972-1973 and 1973-1974) and 5.7% may be sufficiently small to weaken the Government's other proof, while the disparity between 3.7% and 15.4% may be sufficiently large to reinforce it.[17] In determining which of the two figures or, very possibly, what intermediate figure provides the most accurate basis for comparison to the hiring figures at Hazelwood, it will be necessary to evaluate such considerations as (i) whether the racially based hiring policies of the St. Louis City School District were in effect as far back as 1970, the year in which the census figures were taken; (ii) to what extent those policies have changed the racial composition of that district's teaching staff from what it would otherwise have been; (iii) to what extent St. Louis' recruitment policies have diverted to the city, teachers who might otherwise have applied to Hazelwood; (iv) to what extent Negro teachers employed by the city would prefer employment in other districts such as Hazelwood; and (v) what the experience in other school districts in St. Louis County indicates about the validity of excluding the City School District from the relevant labor market.

It is thus clear that a determination of the appropriate comparative figures in this case will depend upon further evaluation by the trial court. As this Court admonished in *Teamsters*: "[S]tatistics ... come in infinite variety.... [T]heir usefulness depends on all of the surrounding facts and circumstances." 431 U.S., at 340. Only the trial court is in a position to make the appropriate determination after further findings. And only after such a determination is made can a foundation be established for deciding whether or not Hazelwood engaged in a pat-

---

[17] Indeed, under the statistical methodology explained in *Castaneda,* [*supra* note 14,] the difference between using 15.4% and 5.7% as the areawide figure would be significant. If the 15.4% figure is taken as the basis for comparison, the expected number of Negro teachers hired by Hazelwood in 1972-1973 would be 43 (rather than the actual figure of 10) of a total of 282, a difference of more than five standard deviations; the expected number of 1973-1974 would be 19 (rather than the actual figure 5) of a total of 123, a difference of more than three standard deviations. For the two years combined, the difference between the observed number of 15 Negro teachers hired (of a total of 405) would vary from the expected number of 62 by more than six standard deviations. Because a fluctuation of more than two or three standard deviations would undercut the hypothesis that decisions were being made randomly with respect to race, each of these statistical comparisons would reinforce rather than rebut the Government's other proof. If, however, the 5.7% areawide figure is used, the expected number of Negro teachers hired in 1972-1973 would be roughly 16, less than two standard deviations from the observed number of 10; for 1973-1974, the expected value would be roughly seven, less than one standard deviation from the observed value of 5; and for the two years combined, the expected value of 23 would be less than two standard deviations from the observed total of 15.

These observations are not intended to suggest that precise calculations of statistical significance are necessary in employing statistical proof, but merely to highlight the importance of the choice of the relevant labor market area.

tern or practice of racial discrimination in its employment practices in violation of the law.

We hold, therefore, that the Court of Appeals erred in disregarding the post-Act hiring statistics in the record, and that it should have remanded the case to the District Court for further findings as to the relevant labor market area and for an ultimate determination of whether Hazelwood engaged in a pattern or practice of employment discrimination after March 24, 1972. Accordingly, the judgment is vacated, and the case is remanded to the District Court for further proceedings consistent with this opinion.

It is so ordered.

MR. JUSTICE WHITE, concurring in [the opinion.]

I join the Court's opinion ... but with reservations with respect to the relative neglect of applicant pool data in finding a prima facie case of employment discrimination and heavy reliance on the disparity between the areawide percentage of black public school teachers and the percentage of blacks on Hazelwood's teaching staff. Since the issue is whether Hazelwood discriminated against blacks in hiring after Title VII became applicable to it in 1972, perhaps the Government should have looked initially to Hazelwood's hiring practices in the 1972-1973 and 1973-1974 academic years with respect to the available applicant pool, rather than to history and to comparative workforce statistics from other school districts. Indeed, there is evidence in the record suggesting that Hazelwood, with a black enrollment of only 2%, hired a higher percentage of black applicants than of white applicants for these two years. The Court's opinion, of course, permits Hazelwood to introduce applicant pool data on remand in order to rebut the prima facie case of a discriminatory pattern or practice. This may be the only fair and realistic allocation of the evidence burden, but arguably the United States should have been required to adduce evidence as to the applicant pool before it was entitled to its prima facie presumption. At least it might have been required to present some defensible ground for believing that the racial composition of Hazelwood's applicant pool was roughly the same as that for the school districts in the general area, before relying on comparative work-force data to establish its prima facie case.

[MR. JUSTICE BRENNAN also filed a concurring opinion.]

MR. JUSTICE STEVENS, dissenting.

The basic framework in a pattern-or-practice suit brought by the Government under Title VII of the Civil Rights Act of 1964 is the same as that in any other lawsuit. The plaintiff has the burden of proving a prima facie case; if he does so, the burden of rebutting that case shifts to the defendant. In this case, since neither party complains that any relevant evidence was excluded, our task is to decide (1) whether the Government's evidence established a prima facie case;

and (2), if so, whether the remaining evidence is sufficient to carry Hazelwood's burden of rebutting that prima facie case.

The first question is clearly answered by the Government's statistical evidence, its historical evidence, and its evidence relating to specific acts of discrimination.

One-third of the teachers hired by Hazelwood resided in the city of St. Louis at the time of their initial employment.... [I]t was therefore appropriate to treat the city, as well as the county, as part of the relevant labor market. In that market, 15% of the teachers were black. In the Hazelwood District at the time of trial less than 2% of the teachers were black. An even more telling statistic is that after Title VII became applicable to it, only 3.7% of the new teachers hired by Hazelwood were black. Proof of these gross disparities was in itself sufficient to make out a prima facie case of discrimination.

But this disregards the applicant pool

As a matter of history, Hazelwood employed no black teachers until 1969. Both before and after the 1972 amendment making the statute applicable to public school districts, petitioner used a standardless and largely subjective hiring procedure. Since "relevant aspects of the decisionmaking process had undergone little change," it is proper to infer that the pre-Act policy of preferring white teachers continued to influence Hazelwood's hiring practices.[3]

But they hired more and more black teachers every year

The inference of discrimination was corroborated by post-Act evidence that Hazelwood had refused to hire 16 qualified black applicants for racial reasons. Taking the Government's evidence as a whole, there can be no doubt about the sufficiency of its prima facie case....

Hazelwood "offered virtually no additional evidence in response." It challenges the Government's statistical analysis by claiming that the city of St. Louis should be excluded from the relevant market and pointing out that only 5.7% of the teachers in the county (excluding the city) were black. It further argues that the city's policy of trying to maintain a 50% black teaching staff diverted teachers from the county to the city. There are two separate reasons why these arguments are insufficient: they are not supported by the evidence; even if true, they do not overcome the Government's case.

The petitioners offered no evidence concerning wage differentials, commuting problems, or the relative advantages of teaching in an inner-city school as opposed to a suburban school. Without any such evidence in the record, it is difficult to understand why the simple fact that the city was the source of a third of Hazelwood's faculty should not be sufficient to demonstrate that it is a part of the relevant market....

But even if it were proper to exclude the city of St. Louis from the market, the statistical evidence would still tend to prove discrimination. With the city excluded, 5.7% of the teachers in the remaining market were black. On the basis

---

[3] ... Since Hazelwood's hiring before 1972 was so clearly discriminatory, there is some irony in its claim that "Hazelwood continued [after 1972] to select its teachers on the same careful basis that it had relied on before in staffing its growing system." Brief for Petitioners 29-30.

of a random selection, one would therefore expect 5.7% of the 405 teachers hired by Hazelwood in the 1972-1973 and 1973-1974 school years to have been black. But instead of 23 black teachers, Hazelwood hired only 15, less than two-thirds of the expected number. Without the benefit of expert testimony, I would hesitate to infer that the disparity between 23 and 15 is great enough, in itself, to prove discrimination.[5] It is perfectly clear, however, that whatever probative force this disparity has, it tends to prove discrimination and does absolutely nothing in the way of carrying Hazelwood's burden of overcoming the Government's prima facie case.

Absolute precision in the analysis of market data is too much to expect. We may fairly assume that a nondiscriminatory selection process would have resulted in the hiring of somewhere between the 15% suggested by the Government and the 5.7% suggested by petitioners, or perhaps 30 or 40 black teachers, instead of the 15 actually hired.[6] On that assumption, the Court of Appeals' determination that there were 16 individual cases of discriminatory refusal to hire black applicants in the post-1972 period seems remarkably accurate.

In sum, the Government is entitled to prevail on the present record. It proved a prima facie case, which Hazelwood failed to rebut. [We should not] burden a busy federal court with another trial.... It is always possible to imagine more evidence which could have been offered, but at some point litigation must come to an end.

NOTES

1. *The Inexorable Zero.* In *Teamsters v. United States,* 431 U.S. 324 (1977), the government challenged an employer's record of hiring blacks and Spanish-surnamed persons to positions as line drivers. The employer's actual record of hiring these minorities approached "the inexorable zero": 0.4% of the line drivers were black and 0.3% were Spanish-surnamed. The Court compared that record in the line driver position to the proportion of minorities employed by the company overall (5% for blacks and 4% for Spanish-surnamed persons) and to the proportion of minorities in the areas from which the company hired (in Atlanta, for example, 22% of the metropolitan area and 51% of the city proper was black). In addition to the statistical evidence, the government presented over forty specific instances of discrimination. The Court held that this evidence was sufficient to support a finding of systemic disparate treatment discrimination.

---

[5] After I had drafted this opinion, one of my law clerks advised me that, given the size of the two-year sample, there is only about a 5% likelihood that a disparity this large would be produced by a random selection from the labor pool. If his calculation (which was made using the method described in H. Blalock, Social Statistics 151-173 (1972)) is correct, it is easy to understand why Hazelwood offered no expert testimony.

[6] Some of the other school districts in the county have a 10% ratio of blacks on their faculties.

2. *The Analytical Framework.* *Hazelwood* discusses the three analytical steps in a systemic disparate treatment case. First, the *actual treatment* of the plaintiff group must be determined. In *Hazelwood,* how many black teachers were employed by the school district? Second, the *ideal treatment* of the group — the treatment one would expect in the absence of discrimination — must be determined. In the absence of discrimination, how many black teachers would you expect to see? And third, the actual and ideal treatment must be compared to determine whether any difference is large enough to create an inference of discrimination.

3. *Actual Treatment.* Assume that you represent a rejected female candidate for a tenure-track position on the law school faculty who is claiming that the law school engages in systemic disparate treatment discrimination when hiring faculty. How would you determine the actual treatment of women by the law school? What time frame would you use? What law school employees would you include? Would you include a head law librarian who is a tenured member of the faculty, but who does not teach? How about clinical faculty who have a separate tenure track with different hiring and promotion criteria? Visiting faculty? Legal writing instructors? Adjuncts?

4. *Ideal Treatment.* *Hazelwood* and *Teamsters* identify different pools that can be used to determine ideal treatment. *Teamsters* used the employer's hiring statistics for other positions and general population statistics as indicators of ideal treatment, while one issue in *Hazelwood* was whether the proportion of black teachers in St. Louis City and County or just in the County alone should be used. Justice White argued that the proportion of blacks who *applied* to teach at Hazelwood should be used instead of more general population statistics.

In *Local 28, Sheet Metal Workers' International Ass'n v. EEOC,* 478 U.S. 421 (1986), the Supreme Court accepted a very precise figure (29.23%) as the ideal treatment for a union alleged to have discriminated against black and Hispanic applicants to an apprenticeship program designed to teach sheet metal skills. The expert who produced the precise figure later described her process for determining the ideal treatment:

> Defining a labor pool involves identifying all persons who are ready, willing and able to perform the duties required by the hiring (or admitting) organization. One of the first decisions to make is what the geographic boundaries of the labor pool should be. Having drawn these borders, the analyst may take into account characteristics such as age, labor-force status, education and experience in order to separate those who belong in the labor pool for the given position from those who do not.
>
> It is reasonable, and therefore conventional, to assume that the relevant labor market for low- to middle-level jobs is fairly local, while the labor market for high-level jobs is national or, perhaps, regional in scope....
>
> Given the characteristics of the positions under analysis, I decided that the relevant labor pool was a fairly local one, and I considered the New York

SMSA [standard metropolitan statistical area] together with several nearby New Jersey SMSAs to be the best measure of it. The defendants' expert agreed that the labor pool was relatively local, and the area he used to define it closely approximated the SMSAs I used....

We did disagree, however, on whether some counties within the defined boundaries should be given more weight than others. I saw no reason to do so. After all, Manhattan was no farther from the general area of the union's work activity than Suffolk County; the Bronx was no farther than Essex County. Hence, I applied no weighting scheme in calculating the combined SMSAs' availability rate. The defendants' expert, on the other hand, argued that some counties should be given greater weight than others in the calculation of the minority availability rate. Moreover, he argued that each county's weight in the calculation should depend on the portion of the union's journeymen membership residing there.

The effect of applying such a weighting scheme was to depress seriously the estimated proportion of minorities in the labor pool. Since the membership of the sheet metal workers' union was largely white, and since the sheet metal workers lived in counties with relatively low minority populations, the counties given the heaviest weights in the opposing expert's availability-rate calculation were the counties with the lowest minority availability rates....

The next question concerned the age dimensions of the pool. Including only those over 25 would have biased the estimated minority availability rate downward. None of the locals allowed individuals over 25 into their apprentice programs.... (Because the age distribution of minorities and non-minorities tends to differ, the choice of the relevant labor pool's age dimensions is seldom neutral in its effect on the calculated minority availability rate.)

A third issue was the labor-force status and occupational dimensions of the relevant labor pool. After defining the pool in terms of its geographical and age dimension, the expert must decide whether everyone in the specified area and age interval should be included in the labor pool, or whether only some portion of this population should be included. This decision must be made on the same basis as the prior ones: The relevant labor pool should be defined so as to include all those ready, willing and able to perform the duties required by the hiring (or admitting) organization and to exclude those who are not.

Economists generally exclude from the relevant pool those classified by the Census Bureau as not in the labor force because individuals so classified have reported themselves as not seeking work. They are not "ready" and "willing," although, for all we know, they are "able." Since it is inaccurate to include those who report themselves as unavailable for work in the labor pool used to calculate the availability rate, only labor-force statistics, not population counts, should be used for such a calculation.

Nor is it sufficiently accurate to use the entire labor force in the specified area and age interval. Some degree of occupational specificity is generally necessary as an indicator of ability and willingness to perform the duties of the position in question. For example, bank tellers do not belong in the relevant labor pool for financial analysts. While they might be ready and willing to do the job, they would generally not be able; they lack the necessary skills. On the other hand, corporate lawyers don't belong in the relevant labor pool for paralegals. While they have the skills for the jobs, they have superior opportunities available to them and would not, in general, supply themselves to it; though "able," they would not generally be "ready" and "willing."

 In line with these considerations, I defined the labor pool as consisting only of persons in the labor force. I also chose to specify occupational boundaries narrow enough to exclude those who were not likely to supply themselves as apprentices in sheet metal work and broad enough to include those who might reasonably do so. The category of blue-collar workers satisfied these conditions.

Including the entire population in the area and age group previously specified would have included individuals who were not ready, willing and able to work. Including only sheet metal workers would also have been inappropriate [because, since] minorities were a much smaller proportion of sheet metal workers than of blue-collar workers as a group[, it would have] seriously biased the estimated minority availability rate downward.

The district court accepted a labor-pool specification that included blue-collar workers in the labor force, and only these workers.

Harriet Zellner, *Defining Labor Pools Proves No Easy Task*, NAT'L L.J., Oct. 27, 1986, at 15, 42-43.*

How would you determine the ideal treatment figure in our law school hypothetical?

5. *Analyzing the Difference Between Actual and Ideal Treatment.* As *Hazelwood* indicates, statistics are often used to determine whether the difference between actual and ideal treatment is large enough to be probative of discriminatory intent. The binomial distribution formula discussed by the Court tells us how often one would expect to see the actual treatment (or worse) if random selections were made from the ideal treatment pool. In *Hazelwood,* how often would blacks constitute 3.7% or less of the new hires if the employer hired randomly with respect to race from a pool consisting of 15% black persons? The less probable the actual treatment, the more likely it resulted from discrimination. The "two or three standard deviations" rule announced by the Court means that the difference between actual and ideal treatment will be recognized

---

*Reprinted with the permission of *The National Law Journal,* copyright 1986. The New York Law Publishing Company.

as probative of discrimination if the actual treatment would be seen less than about 1% to 5% of the time.

The binomial distribution formula is:

$$Z = \frac{A - NP}{\sqrt{NP(1 - P)}}$$

Do we need to know this?

where   Z = number of standard deviations
          A = actual number of blacks hired (actual treatment)
          N = total number of people hired   } (N times P is the
          P = proportion of blacks in population   } ideal treatment)

Applying the formula to *Hazelwood,* and still assuming that the 15% ideal treatment figure is right, A would equal 15 (the actual number of black teachers hired during the relevant time period), N would equal 405 (the total number of teachers hired), and P would equal 15%. Doing the math, as the Court did in *Hazelwood,* n.17, would indicate that the actual treatment was more than six standard deviations from the ideal treatment, a sufficient difference to be probative of discrimination.

Although this type of analysis is well accepted in systemic disparate treatment cases, significant questions remain about its appropriateness. *See* David H. Kaye, *Is Proof of Statistical Significance Relevant?,* 61 WASH. L. REV. 1333 (1986); Ramona Paetzold, *Problems With Statistical Significance in Employment Discrimination Litigation,* 26 NEW ENG. L. REV. 395 (1991).

6. *Individual Relief.* A finding of systemic discrimination creates a presumption that the employer has discriminated against individual members of the protected class. Consequently, individual class members who can show that they were "potential victims" (for example, that they unsuccessfully applied for a job with the employer) are entitled to individual relief, unless the employer can demonstrate that it did not discriminate against them. *Teamsters v. United States,* 431 U.S. 324, 362 (1977). If a systemic case could be made out in *Hazelwood,* for example, an individual black applicant who could prove that she unsuccessfully applied for a teaching position with Hazelwood during the relevant time period would be presumptively entitled to individual relief such as backpay. The employer could avoid this liability only if it could demonstrate that it did not discriminate against this particular individual — by proving, for example, that there were no job openings at the time, that the applicant was not qualified, or that there was no discrimination for other reasons.

Determining the appropriate remedy after a finding of systemic discrimination is especially problematic in situations where the individual victims can either no longer be identified or no longer desire employment with the discriminating employer. This issue will be discussed later when we discuss remedies. *See* Chapter 15, Section C, *infra.*

7. *Jurisprudential Foundations and Systemic Disparate Treatment Discrimination.* If the Hazelwood School District is found to have violated Title VII because it hired only 3.7% black teachers from a pool consisting of 15% black teachers, are we certain that Brest's antidiscrimination principle has been violated? How certain ought we to be before we find a Title VII violation?

How useful would the systemic disparate treatment theory have been to a woman challenging a law firm's refusal to hire her as a lawyer in Illinois in 1872? *Bradwell v. Illinois,* 83 U.S. (16 Wall.) 130 (1872) (upholding refusal to admit woman to bar because of her sex). To a woman seeking employment as a bartender in Michigan in 1948? *Goesaert v. Cleary,* 335 U.S. 464 (1948) (upholding statute prohibiting women from being licensed as bartenders). Consider Professor Catharine MacKinnon's argument:

> The women that [traditional discrimination doctrine] benefits ... are the least of sex discrimination's victims. When they are denied a man's chance, it looks the most like sex bias. The more unequal society gets, the fewer such women are permitted to exist. The more unequal society gets, the less likely this sex equality doctrine is to be able to do anything about it, because unequal power creates both the appearance and the reality of sex differences along the same lines as it creates sex inequalities.

CATHARINE A. MACKINNON, TOWARD A FEMINIST THEORY OF THE STATE 225 (1989).

3. THE BONA FIDE OCCUPATIONAL QUALIFICATION DEFENSE

The antidiscrimination statutes do not prohibit every instance of employer disparate treatment discrimination. This section will consider one of the two major exceptions to the general rule of nondiscrimination: employers may rely on suspect criteria when they are very closely related to ability to do the job, the so-called bona fide occupational qualification (BFOQ) defense. The other major exception (affirmative action programs) will be considered later in Chapter 15, Section C.

WESTERN AIR LINES, INC. v. CRISWELL

United States Supreme Court
472 U.S. 400 (1985)

JUSTICE STEVENS delivered the opinion of the Court.

The petitioner, Western Air Lines, Inc., requires that its flight engineers retire at age 60. Although the Age Discrimination in Employment Act of 1967 (ADEA) generally prohibits mandatory retirement, ... the Act provides an exception "where age is a bona fide occupational qualification [BFOQ] reasonably necessary to the normal operation of the particular business." [ADEA, § 4(f)(1).] A jury concluded that Western's mandatory retirement rule did not qualify as a BFOQ even though it purportedly was adopted for safety reasons. The question here is whether the jury was properly instructed on the elements of the BFOQ defense. *ISSUE*

I

In its commercial airline operations, Western operates a variety of aircraft, including the Boeing 727 and the McDonnell-Douglas DC-10. These aircraft require three crew members in the cockpit: a captain, a first officer, and a flight engineer. "The 'captain' is the pilot and controls the aircraft. He is responsible for all phases of its operation. The 'first officer' is the copilot and assists the captain. The 'flight engineer' usually monitors a side-facing instrument panel. He does not operate the flight controls unless the captain and the first officer become incapacitated."

A regulation of the Federal Aviation Administration (FAA) prohibits any person from serving as a pilot or first officer on a commercial flight "if that person has reached his 60th birthday."... At the same time, the FAA has refused to establish a mandatory retirement age for flight engineers.... *FAA Regs.*

In 1978, respondents Criswell and Starley were captains operating DC-10s for Western. Both men celebrated their 60th birthdays in July 1978. Under the collective-bargaining agreement in effect between Western and the union, cockpit crew members could obtain open positions by bidding in order of seniority. In order to avoid mandatory retirement under the FAA's under-age-60 rule for pilots, Criswell and Starley applied for reassignment as flight engineers. Western denied both requests.... [R]espondent Ron, a career flight engineer, was also retired in 1978 after his 60th birthday. *FACTS*

Criswell, Starley, and Ron brought this action against Western contending that the under-age-60 qualification for the position of flight engineer violated the ADEA. In the District Court, Western defended, in part, on the theory that the age-60 rule is a BFOQ "reasonably necessary" to the safe operation of the airline....

As the District Court summarized, the evidence at trial established that the flight engineer's "normal duties are less critical to the safety of flight than those of a pilot." The flight engineer, however, does have critical functions in emergency situations and, of course, might cause considerable disruption in the event of his own medical emergency.

The actual capabilities of persons over age 60, and the ability to detect disease or a precipitous decline in their faculties, were the subject of conflicting medical testimony. Western's expert witness, a former FAA Deputy Federal Air Surgeon, was especially concerned about the possibility of a "cardiovascular event" such as a heart attack. He testified that "with advancing age the likelihood of onset of disease increases and that in persons over age 60 it could not be predicted whether and when such diseases would occur."

The plaintiffs' experts, on the other hand, testified that physiological deterioration is caused by disease, not aging, and that "it was feasible to determine on the basis of individual medical examinations whether flight deck crew members, including those over age 60, were physically qualified to continue to fly."...

III

Usery

In *Usery v. Tamiami Trail Tours, Inc.,* 531 F.2d 224 (1976), the Court of Appeals for the Fifth Circuit was called upon to evaluate the merits of a BFOQ defense to a claim of age discrimination. Tamiami Trail Tours, Inc., had a policy of refusing to hire persons over-age-40 as intercity bus drivers. At trial, the bus company introduced testimony supporting its theory that the hiring policy was a BFOQ based upon safety considerations — the need to employ persons who have a low risk of accidents. In evaluating this contention, the Court of Appeals drew on its Title VII precedents, and concluded that two inquiries were relevant.

First, the court recognized that some job qualifications may be so peripheral to the central mission of the employer's business that *no* age discrimination can be "reasonably *necessary* to the normal operation of the particular business."[18] [ADEA, § 4(f)(1).] The bus company justified the age qualification for hiring its drivers on safety considerations, but the court concluded that this claim was to be evaluated under an objective standard:

> [T]he job qualifications which the employer invokes to justify his discrimination must be *reasonably necessary* to the essence of his business — here, the *safe* transportation of bus passengers from one point to another. The greater the safety factor, measured by the likelihood of harm and the probable severity of that harm in case of an accident, the more stringent may be the job qualifications designed to insure safe driving.

This inquiry "adjusts to the safety factor" by ensuring that the employer's restrictive job qualifications are "reasonably necessary" to further the overriding interest in public safety. In *Tamiami,* the court noted that no one had seriously challenged the bus company's safety justification for hiring drivers with a low risk of having accidents.

Second, the court recognized that the ADEA requires that age qualifications be something more than "convenient" or "reasonable"; they must be "reasonably necessary ... to the particular business," and this is only so when the employer is compelled to rely on age as a proxy for the safety-related job qualifications vali-

---

[18] *Diaz v. Pan American World Airways, Inc.,* 442 F.2d 385 (CA5), *cert. denied,* 404 U.S. 950 (1971), provided authority for this proposition. In *Diaz* the court had rejected Pan American's claim that a female-only qualification for the position of in-flight cabin attendant was a BFOQ under Title VII. The District Court had upheld the qualification as a BFOQ finding that the airline's passengers preferred the "pleasant environment" and the "cosmetic effect" provided by female attendants, and that most men were unable to perform effectively the "non-mechanical functions" of the job. The Court of Appeals rejected the BFOQ defense concluding that these considerations "are tangential to the essence of the business involved."

dated in the first inquiry.[19] This showing could be made in two ways. The employer could establish that it "'had reasonable cause to believe, that is, a factual basis for believing, that all or substantially all [persons over the age qualifications] would be unable to perform safely and efficiently the duties of the job involved.'" In *Tamiami,* the employer did not seek to justify its hiring qualification under this standard.

Alternatively, the employer could establish that age was a legitimate proxy for the safety-related job qualifications by proving that it is "'impossible or highly impractical'" to deal with the older employees on an individualized basis. "One method by which the employer can carry this burden is to establish that some members of the discriminated-against class possess a trait precluding safe and efficient job performance that cannot be ascertained by means other than knowledge of the applicant's membership in the class." In *Tamiami,* the medical evidence on this point was conflicting, but the District Court had found that individual examinations could not determine which individuals over the age of 40 would be unable to operate the buses safely. The Court of Appeals found that this finding of fact was not "clearly erroneous," and affirmed the District Court's judgment for the bus company on the BFOQ defense....

Every Court of Appeals that has confronted a BFOQ defense based on safety considerations has analyzed the problem consistently with the *Tamiami* standard. An EEOC regulation embraces the same criteria. Considering the narrow language of the BFOQ exception, the parallel treatment of such questions under Title VII, and the uniform application of the standard by the federal courts, the EEOC, and Congress, we conclude that this two-part inquiry properly identifies the relevant considerations for resolving a BFOQ defense to an age-based qualification purportedly justified by considerations of safety.

IV

In this Court, Western ... acknowledges that the *Tamiami* standard identifies the relevant general inquiries that must be made in evaluating the BFOQ defense. However, Western claims that in several respects the instructions given below were insufficiently protective of public safety....

---

[19] *Weeks v. Southern Bell Telephone & Telegraph Co.,* 408 F.2d 228 (CA5 1969), provided authority for this proposition. In *Weeks* the court rejected Southern Bell's claim that a male-only qualification for the position of switchman was a BFOQ under Title VII. Southern Bell argued, and the District Court had found, that the job was "strenuous," but the court observed that that "finding is extremely vague." The court rejected the BFOQ defense concluding that "using these class stereotypes denies desirable positions to a great many women perfectly capable of performing the duties involved." Moreover, the employer had made no showing that it was "impossible or highly impractical to deal with women on an individualized basis."

Reasonably Necessary Job Qualifications

Western relied on two different kinds of job qualifications to justify its mandatory retirement policy. First, it argued that flight engineers should have a low risk of incapacitation or psychological and physiological deterioration. At this vague level of analysis respondents have not seriously disputed — nor could they — that the qualification of good health for a vital crew member is reasonably necessary to the essence of the airline's operations. Instead, they have argued that age is not a necessary proxy for that qualification.

On a more specific level, Western argues that flight engineers must meet the same stringent qualifications as pilots, and that it was therefore quite logical to extend to flight engineers the FAA's age-60 retirement rule for pilots. Although the FAA's rule for pilots, adopted for safety reasons, is relevant evidence in the airline's BFOQ defense, it is not to be accorded conclusive weight. The extent to which the rule is probative varies with the weight of the evidence supporting its safety rationale and "the congruity between the ... occupations at issue." In this case, the evidence clearly established that the FAA, Western, and other airlines all recognized that the qualifications for a flight engineer were less rigorous than those required for a pilot.[28]

In the absence of persuasive evidence supporting its position, Western nevertheless argues that the jury should have been instructed to defer to "Western's selection of job qualifications for the position of [flight engineer] that are reasonable in light of the safety risks." This proposal is plainly at odds with Congress' decision, in adopting the ADEA, to subject such management decisions to a test of objective justification in a court of law. The BFOQ standard adopted in the statute is one of "reasonable necessity," not reasonableness.

In adopting that standard, Congress did not ignore the public interest in safety. That interest is adequately reflected in instructions that track the language of the statute. When an employer establishes that a job qualification has been carefully formulated to respond to documented concerns for public safety, it will not be overly burdensome to persuade a trier of fact that the qualification is "reasonably necessary" to safe operation of the business. The uncertainty implicit in the concept of managing safety risks always makes it "reasonably necessary" to err on the side of caution in a close case. The employer cannot be expected to establish the risk of an airline accident "to a certainty, for certainty would require running the risk until a tragic accident would prove that the judgment was sound." *Usery v. Tamiami Trail Tours, Inc.*, 531 F.2d, at 238. When the employer's argument has a credible basis in the record, it is difficult to believe that a jury of laypersons — many of whom no doubt have flown or could expect to fly on com-

---

[28] As the Court of Appeals noted, the "jury heard testimony that Western itself allows a captain under the age of sixty who cannot, for health reasons, continue to fly as a captain or co-pilot to downbid to a position as second officer. [In addition,] half the pilots flying in the United States are flying for major airlines which do not require second officers to retire at the age of sixty, and ... there are over 200 such second officers currently flying on wide-bodied aircraft."

mercial air carriers — would not defer in a close case to the airline's judgment. Since the instructions in this case would not have prevented the airline from raising this contention to the jury in closing argument, we are satisfied that the verdict is a consequence of a defect in Western's proof rather than a defect in the trial court's instructions....

Age as a Proxy for Job Qualifications

Western contended below that the ADEA only requires that the employer establish "a rational basis in fact" for believing that identification of those persons lacking suitable qualifications cannot occur on an individualized basis. This "rational basis in fact" standard would have been tantamount to an instruction to return a verdict in the defendant's favor. Because that standard conveys a meaning that is significantly different from that conveyed by the statutory phrase "reasonably necessary," it was correctly rejected by the trial court.

Western argues that a "rational basis" standard should be adopted because medical disputes can never be proved "to a certainty" and because juries should not be permitted "to resolve bona fide conflicts among medical experts respecting the adequacy of individualized testing." The jury, however, need not be convinced beyond all doubt that medical testing is impossible, but only that the proposition is true "on a preponderance of the evidence." Moreover, Western's attack on the wisdom of assigning the resolution of complex questions to 12 laypersons is inconsistent with the structure of the ADEA. Congress expressly decided that problems involving age discrimination in employment should be resolved on a "case-by-case basis" by proof to a jury.

The "rational basis" standard is also inconsistent with the preference for individual evaluation expressed in the language and legislative history of the ADEA.[36] Under the Act, employers are to evaluate employees between the ages of 40 and 70[*] on their merits and not their age. In the BFOQ defense, Congress provided a limited exception to this general principle, but required that employers validate any discrimination as "reasonably necessary to the normal operation of the particular business." It might well be "rational" to require mandatory retirement at *any* age less than 70, but that result would not comply with Congress' direction that employers must justify the rationale for the age chosen. Unless an employer can establish a substantial basis for believing that all or nearly all employees above an age lack the qualifications required for the position, the age selected for mandatory retirement less than 70 must be an age at which it is highly impractical for the employer to insure by individual testing that its employees will have the necessary qualifications for the job....

---

[36] Indeed, under a "rational basis" standard a jury might well consider that its "inquiry is at an end" with an expert witness' articulation of any "plausible reaso[n]" for the employer's decision.

[*] Subsequent to this case, in 1986, the ADEA was amended to expand its protections beyond age 70. As a result, the ADEA currently protects covered employees from age 40 until death.

Result Given These Facts

When an employee covered by the Act is able to point to reputable businesses in the same industry that choose to eschew reliance on mandatory retirement earlier than age 70, when the employer itself relies on individualized testing in similar circumstances, and when the administrative agency with primary responsibility for maintaining airline safety has determined that individualized testing is not impractical for the relevant position, the employer's attempt to justify its decision on the basis of the contrary opinion of experts — solicited for the purposes of litigation — is hardly convincing on any objective standard short of complete deference. Even in cases involving public safety, the ADEA plainly does not permit the trier of fact to give complete deference to the employer's decision.

The judgment of the Court of Appeals is

Affirmed.

JUSTICE POWELL took no part in the decision of this case.

NOTES

1. *Uses and Limits of the BFOQ Defense.* The BFOQ defense applies only when an employer explicitly relies on an otherwise prohibited status to make an employment decision. In *Criswell*, for example, the employer explicitly relied on age (a prohibited status) to decide who was eligible for flight engineer positions. As a practical matter, the BFOQ defense does not arise in cases in which the existence of discrimination is in issue. An employer, for example, would be hard put to prove that only males could do a particular job, while at the same time claiming that sex was not a factor in its hiring decisions.

Discrimination on the basis of race or color cannot be justified using the BFOQ defense. *See* Title VII, § 703(e). In practice, most BFOQ cases involve either age or sex discrimination.

2. *The Essence of the Job.* The basic rationale for the BFOQ defense becomes most apparent through extreme examples — employers who need sperm or egg donors or wet nurses. Determining the relevance of sex to the essence of the job in such cases is not hard. Obviously, the problems occur at other points on the continuum. How persuasive would you find the following justification by an employer who refused to hire female guards in a male, maximum-security penitentiary?

> The likelihood that inmates [all of whom are deprived of a normal heterosexual environment and some of whom have criminally assaulted women in the past] would assault a woman because she was a woman would pose a real threat not only to the victim of the assault but also to the basic control of the penitentiary and protection of its inmates and the other security personnel. The employee's very womanhood would thus directly undermine her

capacity to provide the security that is the essence of a correctional counselor's responsibility.

Dothard v. Rawlinson, 433 U.S. 321, 336 (1977) (prison permitted to hire only males).

3. *Customer Preferences.* Many of the difficult cases involve the preferences of customers for employees of a particular sex or age. In one of the early cases, relied on in *Criswell, supra,* n.18, a court rejected the claim by an airline that its practice of hiring only female stewardesses was justified because of the preferences of airline passengers. *Diaz v. Pan Am. World Airways, Inc., supra.* But to what extent should employers be allowed to rely on customer preferences:

Customer Preference and BFOQ

Diaz v. Pan Am.

close ties to job performance

(a) When there is a close tie to job performance? *Compare Fernandez v. Wynn Oil Co.,* 653 F.2d 1273 (9th Cir. 1981) (reluctance of Latin American and Southeast Asian customers to conduct business with women did not justify company's failure to promote woman to international marketing position) *with EEOC v. University of Tex. Health Science Ctr.,* 710 F.2d 1091 (5th Cir. 1983) (employer could hire only people under age forty-five as campus police officers because they are better able to deal with students).

Note this split

Customer Privacy

(b) When privacy interests of the customer are present? *Compare Fesel v. Masonic Home of Del., Inc.,* 447 F. Supp. 1346 (D. Del. 1978), *aff'd,* 591 F.2d 1334 (3d Cir. 1979) (employer refusal to assign male nursing aides to attend to female nursing home residents justified by BFOQ because of privacy interests of residents) *with Spragg v. Shore Care,* 679 A.2d 685 (N.J. Super. Ct. App. Div. 1996) (upholding jury verdict that BFOQ did not justify policy of assigning male home health aides to male patients only, despite privacy interests of female patients).

Note this split

Authenticity

(c) When a protected status relates to authenticity? *See* EEOC's Sex Discrimination Guidelines, 29 C.F.R. § 1604.2 (sex can be a BFOQ if "necessary for the purpose of authenticity or genuineness ... e.g., for an actor or actress"). *Cf. Cook v. Babbitt,* 819 F. Supp. 1, 16 (D.D.C. 1993) (if asserted, interest in authenticity may have justified policy of excluding women from portraying soldiers in Civil War reenactments).

Customer's adamant preference

(d) When customers are especially adamant about their preferences? *Kern v. Dynalectron Corp.,* 577 F. Supp. 1196 (N.D. Tex. 1983), *aff'd,* 746 F.2d 810 (5th Cir. 1984) (employer requirement that pilots be Moslem justified by BFOQ because pilots were required to fly to Mecca in Saudi Arabia where non-Moslem pilots, if caught, are beheaded).

employer claim of sensitivity to customers

(e) When employers claim they need to be especially sensitive to customer preferences? *Ferrill v. Parker Group, Inc.,* 967 F. Supp. 472 (N.D. Ala. 1997) (Title VII violated when company making "get out the vote" calls for political candidates matched white callers to white voters and black callers to black voters); *Wilson v. Southwest Airlines Co.,* 517 F. Supp. 292 (N.D. Tex. 1981) (no BFOQ for female flight attendants even though company claims they were an important part of its marketing strategy).

4. *"Protecting" Women from Harm.* Applying the BFOQ also becomes problematic when employers exclude a protected class for "good" reasons that do not relate to ability to do the job. In *UAW v. Johnson Controls,* 499 U.S. 187 (1991), for example, the employer barred all women, except those whose infertility was medically documented, from jobs involving exposure to lead at levels that might be dangerous to fetuses. The Court held that the BFOQ defense did not apply; it only permits employers to discriminate against women who are unable to perform their job duties. Here the women could perform their job duties, albeit at some added risk to their fetuses should they become pregnant.

5. *BFOQ, Statistical Discrimination, and Professor MacKinnon.* One interpretation of the BFOQ defense is that it permits statistical discrimination only if a very strong correlation exists between protected status and ability to do the job. In all other circumstances, statistical discrimination is prohibited, following Donohue's argument that, although it is profit-maximizing for employers, it is inefficient from a broader societal perspective because it reduces incentives for protected group members to invest in their human capital. Are there other ways of dealing with this societal inefficiency that would not impose such high costs on employers?

Professor MacKinnon is very critical of the BFOQ defense, arguing that distinctions that depend on biological differences between men and women should be especially suspect under the discrimination laws. How would Professor MacKinnon treat an employer's refusal to hire a man as a wet nurse or a woman as a sperm donor?

B. DISPARATE IMPACT

GRIGGS v. DUKE POWER CO.

United States Supreme Court
401 U.S. 424 (1971)

Mr. Chief Justice Burger delivered the opinion of the Court.

We granted the writ in this case to resolve the question whether an employer is prohibited by the Civil Rights Act of 1964, Title VII, from requiring a high school education or passing of a standardized general intelligence test as a condition of employment in or transfer to jobs when (a) neither standard is shown to be significantly related to successful job performance, (b) both requirements operate to disqualify Negroes at a substantially higher rate than white applicants, and (c) the jobs in question formerly had been filled only by white employees as part of a longstanding practice of giving preference to whites.

Congress provided, in Title VII of the Civil Rights Act of 1964, for class actions for enforcement of provisions of the Act and this proceeding was brought by a group of incumbent Negro employees against Duke Power Company. All the petitioners are employed at the Company's Dan River Steam Station, a power generating facility located at Draper, North Carolina. At the time this action was instituted, the Company had 95 employees at the Dan River Station, 14 of whom were Negroes; 13 of these are petitioners here.

The District Court found that prior to July 2, 1965, the effective date of the Civil Rights Act of 1964, the Company openly discriminated on the basis of race in the hiring and assigning of employees at its Dan River plant. The plant was organized into five operating departments: (1) Labor, (2) Coal Handling, (3) Operations, (4) Maintenance, and (5) Laboratory and Test. Negroes were employed only in the Labor Department where the highest paying jobs paid less than the lowest paying jobs in the other four "operating" departments in which only whites were employed. Promotions were normally made within each department on the basis of job seniority. Transferees into a department usually began in the lowest position.

In 1955 the Company instituted a policy of requiring a high school education for initial assignment to any department except Labor, and for transfer from the Coal Handling to any "inside" department (Operations, Maintenance, or Laboratory). When the Company abandoned its policy of restricting Negroes to the Labor Department in 1965, completion of high school also was made a prerequisite to transfer from Labor to any other department. From the time the high school requirement was instituted to the time of trial, however, white employees hired before the time of the high school education requirement continued to perform satisfactorily and achieve promotions in the "operating" departments. Findings on this score are not challenged.

The Company added a further requirement for new employees on July 2, 1965, the date on which Title VII became effective. To qualify for placement in any but the Labor Department it became necessary to register satisfactory scores on two professionally prepared aptitude tests, as well as to have a high school education. Completion of high school alone continued to render employees eligible for transfer to the four desirable departments from which Negroes had been excluded if the incumbent had been employed prior to the time of the new requirement. In September 1965 the Company began to permit incumbent employees who lacked a high school education to qualify for transfer from Labor or Coal Handling to an "inside" job by passing two tests — the Wonderlic Personnel Test, which purports to measure general intelligence, and the Bennett Mechanical Comprehension Test. Neither was directed or intended to measure the ability to learn to perform a particular job or category of jobs. The requisite scores used for both initial hiring and transfer approximated the national median for high school graduates.[3] ...

The objective of Congress in the enactment of Title VII is plain from the language of the statute. It was to achieve equality of employment opportunities and remove barriers that have operated in the past to favor an identifiable group of

---

[3] The test standards are thus more stringent than the high school requirement, since they would screen out approximately half of all high school graduates.

white employees over other employees. Under the Act, practices, procedures, or tests neutral on their face, and even neutral in terms of intent, cannot be maintained if they operate to "freeze" the status quo of prior discriminatory employment practices.

The Court of Appeals' opinion, and the partial dissent, agreed that, on the record in the present case, "whites register far better on the Company's alternative requirements" than Negroes.[6] This consequence would appear to be directly traceable to race. Basic intelligence must have the means of articulation to manifest itself fairly in a testing process. Because they are Negroes, petitioners have long received inferior education in segregated schools.... Congress did not intend by Title VII, however, to guarantee a job to every person regardless of qualifications. In short, the Act does not command that any person be hired simply because he was formerly the subject of discrimination, or because he is a member of a minority group. Discriminatory preference for any group, minority or majority, is precisely and only what Congress has proscribed. What is required by Congress is the removal of artificial, arbitrary, and unnecessary barriers to employment when the barriers operate invidiously to discriminate on the basis of racial or other impermissible classification.

Congress has now provided that tests or criteria for employment or promotion may not provide equality of opportunity merely in the sense of the fabled offer of milk to the stork and the fox. On the contrary, Congress has now required that the posture and condition of the job-seeker be taken into account. It has — to resort again to the fable — provided that the vessel in which the milk is proffered be one all seekers can use. The Act proscribes not only overt discrimination but also practices that are fair in form, but discriminatory in operation. The touchstone is business necessity. If an employment practice which operates to exclude Negroes cannot be shown to be related to job performance, the practice is prohibited.

On the record before us, neither the high school completion requirement nor the general intelligence test is shown to bear a demonstrable relationship to successful performance of the jobs for which it was used. Both were adopted, as the Court of Appeals noted, without meaningful study of their relationship to job-performance ability. Rather, a vice president of the Company testified, the requirements were instituted on the Company's judgment that they generally would improve the overall quality of the work force. The evidence, however, shows that employees who have not completed high school or taken the tests have continued to perform satisfactorily and make progress in departments for which the high school and test criteria are now used....

---

[6] In North Carolina, 1960 census statistics show that, while 34% of white males had completed high school, only 12% of Negro males had done so. Similarly, with respect to standardized tests, the EEOC in one case found that use of a battery of tests, including the Wonderlic and Bennett tests used by the Company in the instant case, resulted in 58% of whites passing the tests, as compared with only 6% of the blacks.

The Court of Appeals held that the Company had adopted the diploma and test requirements without any "intention to discriminate against Negro employees." We do not suggest that either the District Court or the Court of Appeals erred in examining the employer's intent; but good intent or absence of discriminatory intent does not redeem employment procedures or testing mechanisms that operate as "built-in headwinds" for minority groups and are unrelated to measuring job capability.

The Company's lack of discriminatory intent is suggested by special efforts to help the undereducated employees through Company financing of two-thirds the cost of tuition for high school training. But Congress directed the thrust of the Act to the consequences of employment practices, not simply the motivation. More than that, Congress has placed on the employer the burden of showing that any given requirement must have a manifest relationship to the employment in question....

Nothing in the Act precludes the use of testing or measuring procedures; obviously they are useful. What Congress has forbidden is giving these devices and mechanisms controlling force unless they are demonstrably a reasonable measure of job performance. Congress has not commanded that the less qualified be preferred over the better qualified simply because of minority origins. Far from disparaging job qualifications as such, Congress has made such qualifications the controlling factor, so that race, religion, nationality, and sex become irrelevant. What Congress has commanded is that any tests used must measure the person for the job and not the person in the abstract.

The judgment of the Court of Appeals is, as to that portion of the judgment appealed from, reversed.

MR. JUSTICE BRENNAN took no part in the consideration or decision of this case.

NOTES

1. *The Elements of a Disparate Impact Claim.* *Griggs* presents the basic elements of a disparate impact claim: 1) identification of a facially neutral factor used to make an employment decision; 2) proof that the factor has a disparate impact on a protected group; and 3) proof that the factor is not justified by business necessity. Subsequent cases articulated a final element: Where a factor with a disparate impact *is* justified by business necessity, a plaintiff can still prevail by demonstrating that "other selection processes that have a lesser discriminatory effect could also suitably serve the employer's business needs." *Watson v. Fort Worth Bank & Trust*, 487 U.S. 977, 1006 (1988) (Blackmun, J., concurring). *See Albemarle Paper Co. v. Moody*, 422 U.S. 405, 425 (1975).

2. *How Disparate Must the Impact Be?* The EEOC has proposed a rough-and-ready rule for determining how large the disparate effect must be to be probative of illegal discrimination:

The "four-fifths" rule [handwritten margin note]

A selection rate for any race, sex, or ethnic group which is less than four-fifths ($^4/_5$) (or eighty percent) of the rate for the group with the highest rate will generally be regarded by the Federal enforcement agencies as evidence of adverse impact, while a greater than four-fifths rate will not be regarded by the Federal enforcement agencies as evidence of adverse impact. 29 C.F.R. § 1607.4(D).

Using the four-fifths rule, how disparate was the impact of the high school diploma requirement in *Griggs*?

Although the four-fifths rule is attractive because it is easy to apply, some have argued that more sophisticated statistical analyses should be used. *See* Anthony E. Boardman & Aidan R. Vining, *The Role of Probative Statistics in Employment Discrimination Cases,* LAW & CONTEMP. PROBS., Autumn 1983, at 189; Elaine W. Shoben, *Differential Pass-Fail Rates in Employment Testing: Statistical Proof Under Title VII,* 91 HARV. L. REV. 793 (1978). *But see* Paul Meier et al., *What Happened in Hazelwood: Statistics, Employment Discrimination and the 80% Rule,* 1984 AM. B. FOUND. RES. J. 139 (four-fifths rule is superior to other statistical models).

3. Business Necessity. As one might expect, the courts have not been consistent, either in their articulation of the standard of business necessity or in their application of the standard(s). Consider, for example, two cases in which courts considered the legitimacy of a rule that the employer would not employ spouses of current employees. Both cases found that the rule had a disparate impact on women and both discussed the same types of business justifications (problems with supervision and scheduling, morale problems with other employees, etc.), but the courts reached different results. In *Yuhas v. Libbey-Owens-Ford Co.,* 562 F.2d 496, 500 (7th Cir. 1977), *cert. denied,* 435 U.S. 934 (1978), the court found that the no-spouse rule was justified by business necessity, because it "plausibly improves the work environment and because it does not penalize women on the basis of their environmental or genetic background," while in *EEOC v. Rath Packing Co.,* 787 F.2d 318, 332 (8th Cir.), *cert. denied,* 479 U.S. 910 (1986), the court found that the rule was *not* justified by business necessity, because it was not "essential" for eliminating a "concrete and demonstrable" problem. The Civil Rights Act of 1991, discussed below, provides a uniform articulation of the standard of business necessity (the challenged practice must be "job related" and "consistent with business necessity"), but the problems of application, of course, remain.

Civil Rights Act of 1991 (Business Necessity) [handwritten margin note]

Even if a good business reason for using a criterion exists, the criterion may violate Title VII if the plaintiff can prove "that other tests or selection devices, without a similarly undesirable racial effect, would also serve the employer's legitimate [business] interest.... Such a showing would be evidence that the employer was using its tests merely as a 'pretext' for discrimination." *Albemarle Paper Co. v. Moody,* 422 U.S. 405, 425 (1975). The following section on the Civil Rights Act of 1991 also discusses this part of a disparate impact claim.

4. *The Seniority Exception.* Seniority systems often have a disparate impact on African-Americans and women. Seniority systems, by their very nature, tend to allocate benefits such as wages and vacation time disproportionately to workers with longer job tenures. As a result, where employers have only recently begun to hire blacks and women in significant numbers, seniority systems tend to allocate benefits disproportionately to white male employees who have more years of work experience.

Title VII, however, exempts seniority systems from the normal operation of the disparate impact model. Section 703(h) provides that:

> it shall not be an unlawful employment practice for an employer to apply different standards of compensation, or different terms, conditions or privileges of employment pursuant to a bona fide seniority ... system, ... provided that such differences are not the result of an intention to discriminate because of race, color, religion, sex or national origin....

Thus, seniority systems violate Title VII only if plaintiffs can prove that the employer uses the system intentionally to discriminate. *Teamsters v. United States,* 431 U.S. 324, 348-56 (1977). The principal issues under section 703(h) are what constitutes a seniority system entitled to the section's protection, *California Brewers Ass'n v. Bryant,* 444 U.S. 598 (1980), and how one proves that an employer is intentionally using a seniority system to discriminate. Mark S. Brodin, *Role of Fault and Motive in Defining Discrimination: The Seniority Question Under Title VII,* 62 N.C. L. REV. 943 (1984).

5. *Jurisprudential Foundations of the Disparate Impact Model.* Professor Fiss argues that disparate impact discrimination is improper because it is the "functional equivalent" of race discrimination — criteria susceptible to this model of discrimination adversely affect protected group members disproportionately and, like race, are unrelated to productivity and not subject to individual control. The courts, however, have been reluctant to engage in the last inquiry, holding many criteria improper despite some degree of individual responsibility. *See Green v. Missouri Pac. R.R.,* 549 F.2d 1158 (8th Cir. 1977) (criminal conviction records); *Johnson v. Pike Corp. of Am.,* 332 F. Supp. 490 (C.D. Cal. 1971) (garnishment records). Under Fiss's theory, should the high school diploma requirement in *Griggs* have been upheld? What about a rule that prohibits the hiring of persons with illegitimate children? *Davis v. American Nat'l Bank of Tex.,* 12 F.E.P. Cases 1052 (N.D. Tex. 1971) (improper).

Professor MacKinnon appears to support the disparate impact model of discrimination. How would her articulation of such a case differ from the articulation in *Griggs* and its progeny?

CIVIL RIGHTS ACT OF 1991

The Civil Rights Act of 1991 made a number of changes to Title VII intended to clarify the burdens of proof and other issues under the disparate impact model of discrimination. In this respect, the Act was largely a response to a 1989 decision of the Supreme Court, *Wards Cove Packing Co. v. Atonio*, 490 U.S. 642.

On the first element of a disparate impact case — identifying a facially neutral factor used by an employer — *Wards Cove* held that plaintiffs have the burden of isolating the *particular* factor that causes a disparate impact. Thus, plaintiffs could not present a prima facie case by demonstrating that, considered together, a group of factors used by an employer to make hiring decisions (for example, a college degree requirement, adequate performance on a written test, and a successful interview) had a disparate impact on black applicants. Rather, the plaintiffs would have to prove that one (or more) of the factors had a disparate impact.

The Civil Rights Act of 1991 eased this burden a bit. Plaintiffs are generally required to prove that a particular employment practice has a disparate impact. Thus, generally they will have to show that either the college degree requirement, performance on the written test, or the interview had a disparate impact. But if plaintiffs cannot do that, the Act provides them with another alternative. If plaintiffs can prove that the elements of an employer's decisionmaking process are not capable of separation for analysis, the process can be treated as one employment practice. Thus, if plaintiffs could demonstrate that the three elements could not be separated for analysis (perhaps because the employer did not keep adequate records of their separate effects), the plaintiffs could establish a prima facie case by demonstrating that the elements together had a disparate impact. Title VII, § 703(k)(1)(B).

Wards Cove also changed the general understanding of who bears the burden of proving business necessity. Before *Wards Cove,* it was widely understood that, once the plaintiff proved that a factor had a disparate impact, the burdens of production and persuasion shifted to the employer to prove business necessity. *Wards Cove* said that was incorrect. The employer had the burden of *producing evidence* of a business justification, but the burden of persuasion remained on the plaintiff to prove that the factor was not justified by business necessity. Earlier Supreme Court cases that seemed to suggest otherwise, the Court said, had simply been misunderstood. The Civil Rights Act of 1991 reversed that portion of *Wards Cove*. Employers bear the burden of production and persuasion at the business necessity stage of a disparate impact case. §§ 701(m), 703(k)(1)(A)(i).

The standard for proving business necessity was another issue addressed by the Court in *Wards Cove*. Although the Court had articulated the standard in different ways in the past,* the *Wards Cove* articulation made it marginally easier for employer practices to be justified. A practice is justified, the Court said, if a "reasoned review" indicates that it "serves, in a significant way, the legitimate goals of the employer." The Court made clear that the practice need not be "essential" or "indispensable" to job performance. 490 U.S. at 659.

The Civil Rights Act of 1991 provided the first legislative articulation of the standard: The employer must demonstrate that "the challenged practice is job related for the position and consistent with business necessity." § 703(k)(1)(A)(i). This standard is not clearly more favorable to plaintiffs than the *Wards Cove* standard, and it is unlikely that it will be more informative than the judicial attempts to define business necessity, but at least the courts are now all interpreting the same language when they struggle with the issue.

Finally, the Court in *Wards Cove* discussed the plaintiff's opportunity to prevail by proving that other employment practices could serve the employer's business interests as well as the suspect criterion, without producing as severe an adverse impact. The Court said that factors such as the cost of the alternative practice were relevant to determining whether it could further the employer's business interests as well, and that courts should "proceed with care" before requiring employers to use alternative practices because courts are less competent than employers to restructure business practices. 490 U.S. at 661. The Civil Rights Act of 1991 inserted a curious provision into Title VII on this issue; section 703(k)(1)(C) says that this stage of a disparate impact case shall be "in accordance with the law as it existed on June 4, 1989," the day before *Wards Cove* was decided. Since *Wards Cove* did not reverse any prior cases on this issue, but instead cited several prior cases as support for its statements, the new section may have very little effect.**

---

* The standards ranged from "essential to safe and efficient job performance," in *Dothard v. Rawlinson,* 433 U.S. 321, 331 n.14 (1977), to a "manifest relationship to the employment" in *Griggs,* 401 U.S. at 432, to simply "job-related" in *New York Transit Auth. v. Beazer,* 440 U.S. 568, 587 (1979).

** Another section of the Civil Rights Act of 1991 ensures that the section cannot be informed by legislative history. Section 105(b) of the Act reads:

No statements other than the interpretive memorandum appearing at Vol. 137 Congressional Record S 15276 ... shall be considered legislative history of, or relied upon in any way as legislative history in construing or applying, any provision of this Act that relates to *Wards Cove*....

The interpretive memorandum says nothing about the alternative business practice phase of a disparate impact case.

NOTES

Conn v. Teal

1. *The Bottom Line Defense ... or Offense.* In *Connecticut v. Teal*, 457 U.S. 440 (1982), the employer decided who would receive promotions by considering the results of a written examination, past work experience, recommendations from supervisors, and seniority. Plaintiffs proved that the written examination had a disparate impact on black candidates; a significantly higher proportion of black than white candidates failed the examination. The employer, however, proved that black candidates were *more* likely than whites to receive promotions. Thus, although one component of the process — the exam — had a disparate impact on blacks, the overall process did not. The employer argued that the statistics on the overall results — the "bottom line" statistics — should be a defense to the plaintiff's disparate impact claim directed at the examination. The Court rejected that argument.

In *Wards Cove,* the Court expanded *Teal,* using a mutuality argument to hold that bottom line statistics cannot be used offensively either: "Just as an employer cannot escape liability under Title VII by demonstrating that, 'at the bottom line,' his work force is racially balanced ..., a Title VII plaintiff does not make out a case of disparate impact simply by showing that, 'at the bottom line,' there is racial *imbalance* in the work force." 490 U.S. at 656-57 (emphasis in original). As indicated in the text above, the requirement of *Teal* and *Wards Cove* that analysis focus on the effects of a *particular* employment practice, rather than on the combined effects of several practices was codified (with slight modification) in the Civil Rights Act of 1991. *See* Title VII, § 703(k)(1).

This requirement raises several difficult issues. Most obviously, it requires that determinations be made about what is and is not a "particular employment practice." If an employer requires employees to be at least 5 feet, 2 inches tall and weigh at least 120 pounds, is there one particular employment practice, or two? Intuition would indicate two (a height requirement and a weight requirement), but the legislative history of the Civil Rights Act of 1991 indicates that there is only one because the two are "functionally integrated" to measure strength. The distinction is very hazy at the margins. The distinction can also be extremely important because the independent effect of separate practices does not bear any necessary relationship to the combined effect of the practices. It is entirely possible, for example, that no practice considered individually has a disparate impact on a protected group, but that the practices in combination have a severe adverse impact. On the other hand, it is also possible that each practice considered individually has an adverse impact, but that the practices in combination do not. For many examples and suggestions on how to analyze these situations, *see* Ramona L. Paetzold & Steven L. Willborn, *Deconstructing Disparate Impact: A View of the Model Through New Lenses*, 74 N.C. L. Rev. 325 (1996).

2. *The Relationship Between Systemic Disparate Treatment and Disparate Impact.* Suppose an employer receives applications from 1,000 prospective

employees, 200 of whom are black persons. The applicant pool provides the best available evidence of the treatment one would expect in the absence of discrimination. The employer hires 200 of the applicants, including twenty black employees. Can a rejected black applicant present a prima facie case of systemic disparate treatment discrimination?

The employer rebuts by showing that it requires applicants to have a college diploma to be considered for the jobs in issue, which eliminated 100 of the black applicants but none of the white applicants from consideration. Has the employer successfully rebutted the systemic disparate treatment claim? Could the rejected black applicant now use the disparate impact model to challenge the employer's practices?

What if the employer rebutted instead by showing that it requires a college diploma, five years of experience, a good job reference, and a passing score on a written examination to be hired and those factors combined eliminated 100 of the black applicants, but none of the white applicants? How would this change your analysis of the disparate impact claim?

3. *The Nineteenth Century Civil Rights Acts.* The disparate impact model cannot be used to establish liability under the nineteenth century civil rights acts, 42 U.S.C. §§ 1981 & 1983. *See General Bldg. Contrs. Ass'n v. Pennsylvania,* 458 U.S. 375 (1982).* The disparate treatment model must be used instead.

Section 1981 prohibits racial discrimination in making and enforcing contracts. Since employment is a contractual relationship, employers who engage in intentional racial discrimination may violate section 1981. All employers except the federal government (even employers too small to be covered by Title VII) are covered by section 1981. About 86% of establishments (employing 14-22% of all workers) have fewer than fifteen employees and thus are covered by section 1981 but not Title VII. *See* Theodore Eisenberg & Stewart Schwab, *The Importance of Section 1981*, 73 CORNELL L. REV. 596, 602 & n.42 (1988). Eleventh Amendment immunity, however, significantly complicates the coverage of state instrumentalities. *See* CHARLES A. SULLIVAN ET AL., EMPLOYMENT DISCRIMINATION §§ 21.1, 23.5 (2d ed. 1988).

Section 1983 provides a cause of action against every person who under color of state law deprives another person of rights secured by the Constitution or federal laws. Thus, section 1983 may provide an independent cause of action against *public* employers that engage in status discrimination.

Sections 1981 and 1983 have long been considered important components of the web of federal laws prohibiting status discrimination primarily because of

---

*Section 1983 protects rights that are found in the Constitution and other federal laws. Consequently, the disparate impact theory would be available in a section 1983 action if the underlying law permitted liability based on that theory. In status discrimination cases, however, section 1983 is generally used to enforce the equal protection clause, which requires a showing of discriminatory intent. *Washington v. Davis,* 426 U.S. 229 (1976).

their procedural and remedial advantages. Compensatory damages (such as damages for pain and suffering) are available under sections 1981 and 1983, as are punitive damages. The availability of legal damages also means that jury trials are available under these laws. Until enactment of the Civil Rights Act of 1991, these types of damages and jury trials were not available under Title VII and, even after the Act, compensatory damages are capped for Title VII claims but not for claims under sections 1981 and 1983. The nineteenth century civil rights acts are also valued by plaintiffs because they differ from Title VII in their coverage, statutes of limitations, and procedural exhaustion requirements.

C. REASONABLE ACCOMMODATION

The reasonable accommodation model applies to discrimination against individuals with disabilities under the Americans with Disabilities Act (ADA) and the Rehabilitation Act and to religious discrimination under Title VII. Our focus here will be on disability discrimination. In general terms, the model requires employers to make reasonable accommodations to individuals with disabilities if the individuals can perform the essential functions of the job with the accommodations. Employers, however, need not make any accommodations that would impose an undue hardship on the employer.

The reasonable accommodation model requires more of employers than the disparate treatment and impact models. All the models require employers to refrain from discriminating against protected persons when they can be as productive as others, but only the reasonable accommodation model requires employers to take affirmative (and sometimes costly) steps to assist protected persons who would not be as productive as others without the extra measures. Another way of thinking about this is that the treatment and impact models permit employers to consider applicants and employees as presented — if an applicant is not as qualified as another applicant or cannot meet justifiable job requirements, the models do not limit the employer's ability to reject the applicant. The reasonable accommodation model, in contrast, requires the employer to consider what steps it can reasonably take to enhance the ability of applicants and employees to be productive or meet justifiable job requirements — if a disabled applicant cannot meet a justifiable job requirement without some accommodation, the model requires the employer to consider what it can do to enable the applicant to meet the requirement.

In this section, the first case will introduce you to the analysis used to determine who fits within the protected class (that is, who is an individual with a disability) and whether the person is qualified to do the job. The following cases will explore the nature and extent of the duty of reasonable accommodation.

SCHOOL BOARD v. ARLINE

United States Supreme Court
480 U.S. 273 (1987)

[handwritten: Defining who has a disability and determining if they are qualified for the job]

JUSTICE BRENNAN delivered the opinion of the Court.

Section 504 of the Rehabilitation Act of 1973, 29 U.S.C. § 794 (Act), prohibits a federally funded state program from discriminating against a handicapped individual solely by reason of his or her handicap. This case presents the questions whether a person afflicted with tuberculosis, a contagious disease, may be considered a "handicapped individual" within the meaning of § 504 of the Act, *[handwritten: ISSUE]* and, if so, whether such an individual is "otherwise qualified" to teach elementary school.

I

From 1966 until 1979, respondent Gene Arline taught elementary school in Nassau County, Florida. She was discharged in 1979 after suffering a third relapse of tuberculosis within two years. After she was denied relief in state administrative proceedings, she brought suit in federal court, alleging that the School Board's decision to dismiss her because of her tuberculosis violated § 504 of the Act....

Arline was [first] hospitalized for tuberculosis in 1957. For the next twenty years, Arline's disease was in remission. Then, in 1977, a culture revealed that tuberculosis was again active in her system; cultures taken in March 1978 and in November 1978 were also positive....

After both her second relapse, in the Spring of 1978, and her third relapse in November 1978, the School Board [in Nassau County] suspended Arline with pay for the remainder of the school year. At the end of the 1978-1979 school year, the School Board held a hearing, after which it discharged Arline, "not because she had done anything wrong," but because of the "continued reoccurrence [sic] of tuberculosis."...

The District Court held ... that although there was "[n]o question that she suf- *[handwritten: District Court]* fers a handicap," Arline was nevertheless not "a handicapped person under the terms of [the] statute." The court found it "difficult ... to conceive that Congress intended contagious diseases to be included within the definition of a handicapped person." The court then went on to state that, "even assuming" that a person with a contagious disease could be deemed a handicapped person, Arline was not "qualified" to teach elementary school.

The Court of Appeals reversed, holding that "persons with contagious diseases *[handwritten: Court of Appeals]* are within the coverage of section 504".... The court remanded the case "for further findings as to whether the risks of infection precluded Mrs. Arline from being 'otherwise qualified' for her job and, if so, whether it was possible to make some reasonable accommodation for her in that teaching position" or in some other position. We granted certiorari and now affirm.

II

....

Section 504 of the Rehabilitation Act reads in pertinent part:

The Rehabilitation Act

> "No otherwise qualified handicapped individual in the United States ... shall, solely by reason of his handicap, be excluded from participation in, be denied the benefits of, or be subjected to discrimination under any program or activity receiving Federal financial assistance...." 29 U.S.C. § 794.

In 1974 Congress expanded the definition of "handicapped individual" for use in § 504 to read as follows:

> "[A]ny person who (i) has a physical or mental impairment which substantially limits one or more of such person's major life activities, (ii) has a record of such an impairment, or (iii) is regarded as having such an impairment." 29 U.S.C. § 706(7)(B).

The amended definition reflected Congress' concern with protecting the handicapped against discrimination stemming not only from simple prejudice, but from "archaic attitudes and laws" and from "the fact that the American people are simply unfamiliar with and insensitive to the difficulties confront[ing] individuals with handicaps." To combat the effects of erroneous but nevertheless prevalent perceptions about the handicapped, Congress expanded the definition of "handicapped individual" so as to preclude discrimination against "[a] person who has a record of, or is regarded as having, an impairment [but who] may at present have no actual incapacity at all."

In determining whether a particular individual is handicapped as defined by the Act, the regulations promulgated by the Department of Health and Human Services are of significant assistance ... because they define two critical terms used in the statutory definition of handicapped individual. "Physical impairment" is defined as follows:

Health & Human Services Regs

> "[A]ny physiological disorder or condition, cosmetic disfigurement, or anatomical loss affecting one or more of the following body systems: neurological; musculoskeletal; special sense organs; respiratory, including speech organs; cardiovascular; reproductive, digestive, genitourinary; hemic and lymphatic; skin; and endocrine." 45 CFR § 84.3(j)(2)(i) (1985).

In addition, the regulations define "major life activities" as:

> "functions such as caring for one's self, performing manual tasks, walking, seeing, hearing, speaking, breathing, learning, and working." § 84.3(j)(2)(ii).

III

Within this statutory and regulatory framework, then, we must consider whether Arline can be considered a handicapped individual.... Arline suffered tuberculosis "in an acute form in such a degree that it affected her respiratory system," and was hospitalized for this condition. Arline thus had a physical impairment as that term is defined by the regulations, since she had a "physiological disorder or condition ... affecting [her] ... respiratory [system]." 45 CFR § 84.3(j)(2)(i) (1985). This impairment was serious enough to require hospitalization, a fact more than sufficient to establish that one or more of her major life activities were substantially limited by her impairment. Thus, Arline's hospitalization for tuberculosis in 1957 suffices to establish that she has a "record of ... impairment" within the meaning of 29 U.S.C. § 706(7)(B)(ii), and is therefore a handicapped individual.

Petitioners concede that a contagious disease may constitute a handicapping condition to the extent that it leaves a person with "diminished physical or mental capabilities," and concede that Arline's hospitalization for tuberculosis in 1957 demonstrates that she has a record of a physical impairment. Petitioners maintain, however, Arline's record of impairment is irrelevant in this case, since the School Board dismissed Arline not because of her diminished physical capabilities, but because of the threat that her relapses of tuberculosis posed to the health of others.

We do not agree with petitioners that, in defining a handicapped individual under § 504, the contagious effects of a disease can be meaningfully distinguished from the disease's physical effects on a claimant in a case such as this. Arline's contagiousness and her physical impairment each resulted from the same underlying condition, tuberculosis. It would be unfair to allow an employer to seize upon the distinction between the effects of a disease on others and the effects of a disease on a patient and use that distinction to justify discriminatory treatment.[7]

Nothing in the legislative history of § 504 suggests that Congress intended such a result. That history demonstrates that Congress was as concerned about the effect of an impairment on others as it was about its effect on the individual. Congress extended coverage to those individuals who are simply "regarded as having" a physical or mental impairment. The Senate Report provides as an example of a person who would be covered under this subsection "a person with some kind of visible physical impairment which in fact does not substantially

---

[7] The United States argues that it is possible for a person to be simply a carrier of a disease, that is, to be capable of spreading a disease without having a "physical impairment" or suffering from any other symptoms associated with the disease. The United States contends that this is true in the case of some carriers of the Acquired Immune Deficiency Syndrome (AIDS) virus. From this premise the United States concludes that discrimination solely on the basis of contagiousness is never discrimination on the basis of a handicap. The argument is misplaced in this case, because the handicap here, tuberculosis, gave rise both to a physical impairment and to contagiousness. This case does not present, and we therefore do not reach, the questions whether a carrier of a contagious disease such as AIDS could be considered to have a physical impairment, or whether such a person could be considered, solely on the basis of contagiousness, a handicapped person as defined by the Act.

limit that person's functioning." Such an impairment might not diminish a person's physical or mental capabilities, but could nevertheless substantially limit that person's ability to work as a result of the negative reactions of others to the impairment.[10]

Allowing discrimination based on the contagious effects of a physical impairment would be inconsistent with the basic purpose of § 504, which is to ensure that handicapped individuals are not denied jobs or other benefits because of the prejudiced attitudes or the ignorance of others. By amending the definition of "handicapped individual" to include not only those who are actually physically impaired, but also those who are regarded as impaired and who, as a result, are substantially limited in a major life activity, Congress acknowledged that society's accumulated myths and fears about disability and disease are as handicapping as are the physical limitations that flow from actual impairment. Few aspects of a handicap give rise to the same level of public fear and misapprehension as contagiousness. Even those who suffer or have recovered from such noninfectious diseases as epilepsy or cancer have faced discrimination based on the irrational fear that they might be contagious. The Act is carefully structured to replace such reflexive reactions to actual or perceived handicaps with actions based on reasoned and medically sound judgments: the definition of "handicapped individual" is broad, but only those individuals who are both handicapped *and* otherwise qualified are eligible for relief. The fact that *some* persons who have contagious diseases may pose a serious health threat to others under certain circumstances does not justify excluding from the coverage of the Act *all* persons with actual or perceived contagious diseases. Such exclusion would mean that those accused of being contagious would never have the opportunity to have their condition evaluated in light of medical evidence and a determination made as to whether they were "otherwise qualified." Rather, they would be vulnerable to discrimination on the basis of mythology — precisely the type of injury Congress sought to prevent. We conclude that the fact that a

---

[10] The Department of Health and Human Services regulations, which include among the conditions illustrative of physical impairments covered by the Act "cosmetic disfigurement," lend further support to Arline's position that the effects of one's impairment on others is as relevant to a determination of whether one is handicapped as is the physical effect of one's handicap on oneself. 45 CFR § 84.3(j)(2)(i)(A) (1985). At oral argument, the Solicitor General took the position that a condition such as cosmetic disfigurement could not substantially limit a major life activity within the meaning of the statute, because the only major life activity that it would affect would be the ability to work. The Solicitor General recognized that "working" was one of the major life activities listed in the regulations, but said that to argue that a condition that impaired *only* the ability to work was a handicapping condition was to make "a totally circular argument which lifts itself by its bootstraps." The argument is not circular, however, but direct. Congress plainly intended the Act to cover persons with a physical or mental impairment (whether actual, past, or perceived) that substantially limited one's ability to work....

person with a record of a physical impairment is also contagious does not suffice to remove that person from coverage under § 504.[15]

She's within the protected class

IV

The remaining question is whether Arline is otherwise qualified for the job of elementary school teacher. To answer this question in most cases, the District Court will need to conduct an individualized inquiry and make appropriate findings of fact. Such an inquiry is essential if § 504 is to achieve its goal of protecting handicapped individuals from deprivations based on prejudice, stereotypes, or unfounded fear, while giving appropriate weight to such legitimate concerns of grantees as avoiding exposing others to significant health and safety risks.[16] The basic factors to be considered in conducting this inquiry are well established.[17] In the context of the employment of a person handicapped with a contagious disease, we agree with *amicus* American Medical Association that this inquiry should include:

Individual Inquiry required

> "[findings of] facts, based on reasonable medical judgments given the state of medical knowledge, about (a) the nature of the risk (how the disease is transmitted), (b) the duration of the risk (how long is the carrier infectious), (c) the severity of the risk (what is the potential harm to third parties) and (d) the probabilities the disease will be transmitted and will cause varying degrees of harm." Brief for American Medical Association as *Amicus Curiae* 19.

---

[15] [T]here [is no] reason to think that today's decision will extend the Act beyond manageable bounds. Construing § 504 not to exclude those with contagious diseases will complement rather than complicate state efforts to enforce public health laws. [C]ourts may reasonably be expected normally to defer to the judgments of public health officials in determining whether an individual is otherwise qualified unless those judgments are medically unsupportable. Conforming employment decisions with medically reasonable judgments can hardly be thought to threaten the States' regulation of communicable diseases. Indeed, because the Act requires employers to respond rationally to those handicapped by a contagious disease, the Act will assist local health officials by helping remove an important obstacle to preventing the spread of infectious diseases: the individual's reluctance to report his or her condition....

[16] A person who poses a significant risk of communicating an infectious disease to others in the workplace will not be otherwise qualified for his or her job if reasonable accommodation will not eliminate that risk. The Act would not require a school board to place a teacher with active, contagious tuberculosis in a classroom with elementary school children.

[17] ... In the employment context, an otherwise qualified person is one who can perform "the essential functions" of the job in question. When a handicapped person is not able to perform the essential functions of the job, the court must also consider whether any "reasonable accommodation" by the employer would enable the handicapped person to perform those functions. Accommodation is not reasonable if it either imposes "undue financial and administrative burdens" on a grantee or requires "a fundamental alteration in the nature of [the] program."

In making these findings, courts normally should defer to the reasonable medical judgments of public health officials.[18] The next step in the "otherwise-qualified" inquiry is for the court to evaluate, in light of these medical findings, whether the employer could reasonably accommodate the employee under the established standards for that inquiry.

Because of the paucity of factual findings by the District Court, we, like the Court of Appeals, are unable at this stage of the proceedings to resolve whether Arline is "otherwise qualified" for her job. The District Court made no findings as to the duration and severity of Arline's condition, nor as to the probability that she would transmit the disease. Nor did the court determine whether Arline was contagious at the time she was discharged, or whether the School Board could have reasonably accommodated her.[19] ...

We remand the case to the District Court to determine whether Arline is otherwise qualified for her position. The judgment of the Court of Appeals is

Affirmed.

NOTES

1. *The ADA and the Rehabilitation Act*. The drafters of the ADA relied heavily on the experience under the Rehabilitation Act. Most of the central concepts of the ADA were borrowed from the Rehabilitation Act and its regulations, including the three-part definition of disability and the notions of reasonable accommodation and undue hardship. On substantive issues, the courts rely on cases under the two statutes almost interchangeably.

The two Acts differ mainly in coverage and procedure. The Rehabilitation Act applies only to a narrow range of employers (the federal government, federal contractors, and recipients of federal funds) and its enforcement mechanisms are complex and limited. The ADA's coverage extends to all employers with fifteen or more employees and it incorporates the enforcement provisions of Title VII. ADA §§ 101(4), 107(a).

2. *The Definition of Disability*. Using the three-part definition of disability, consider whether the following people are individuals with disabilities:

(a) An applicant for a flight attendant position who exceeds the airline's weight limitations because he is an avid bodybuilder. *Tudyman v. United Airlines,* 608 F. Supp. 739 (D.C. Cal. 1984) (no). What if the applicant were simply overweight? *Andrews v. Ohio,* 104 F.3d 803 (6th Cir. 1997) (no). What if the applicant were severely overweight? *Cook v. Rhode Island,* 10 F.3d 17 (1st Cir. 1993) (upholding jury verdict that morbidly obese person is an individual with a

---

[18] This case does not present, and we do not address, the question whether courts should also defer to the reasonable medical judgments of private physicians on which an employer has relied.

[19] Employers have an affirmative obligation to make a reasonable accommodation for a handicapped employee. Although they are not required to find another job for an employee who is not qualified for the job he or she was doing, they cannot deny an employee alternative employment opportunities reasonably available under the employer's existing policies.

disability). *See* Lisa E. Key, *Voluntary Disabilities and the ADA: A Reasonable Interpretation of "Reasonable Accommodation,"* 48 HASTINGS L.J. 75 (1996).

(b) A postal employee who had to miss work seven times over the past two years because of back problems, but who otherwise was able to perform the duties of a letter carrier, including heavy lifting, prolonged standing, and walking six to eight miles at a time. *Compare Diaz v. United States Postal Serv.,* 658 F. Supp. 484 (E.D. Cal. 1987) (no) *with Perez v. Philadelphia Hous. Auth.,* 677 F. Supp. 357 (E.D. Pa. 1987), *aff'd,* 841 F.2d 1120 (3d Cir. 1988) (implies yes).

(c) A utility systems operator with acrophobia who is discharged because he is unable to climb stairs and ladders to perform repairs and maintenance, but whose life otherwise is unaffected by his condition. *Forrisi v. Bowen,* 794 F.2d 931 (4th Cir. 1986) (no).

(d) A left-handed postal employee who is required to deliver mail right-handed. Medical testimony indicates that requiring the employee to use his right hand will cause muscle strain, emotional upset, awkwardness, and slower performance times. *De la Torres v. Bolger,* 781 F.2d 1134 (5th Cir. 1986) (no). *But see* STANLEY COREN, THE LEFT-HANDER SYNDROME (1992) (left-handedness is a sign of damage to left hemisphere of brain).

(e) A person infected with the HIV virus, but who is currently asymptomatic. *Compare Abbott v. Bragdon,* 107 F.3d 934 (1st Cir.), *cert. granted,* 118 S. Ct. 554 (1997) *and Gates v. Rowland,* 39 F.3d 1439 (9th Cir. 1994) (yes) *with Runnebaum v. Nationsbank of Md.,* 123 F.3d 156 (4th Cir. 1997) (en banc) (6-5 decision with one concurrence) (no).

(f) A housekeeper at an upscale ski resort who has no upper teeth and refuses to wear her dentures because they hurt? *Hodgdon v. Mt. Mansfield Co.,* 624 A.2d 1122 (Vt. 1992) (yes).

(g) A person who has a condition which is not itself disabling, but which requires treatment that may significantly interfere with a major life activity. For example, a person with hypercholesterolemia (too much cholesterol in the blood), which requires a complete blood transfusion every month. *Christian v. St. Anthony Med. Ctr.,* 117 F.3d 1051 (7th Cir. 1997) (yes).

3. *Exclusions From the ADA's Definition of Disability.* The ADA also contains specific exclusions from its definition of disability including homosexuality, transvestism, and compulsive gambling. *See* §§ 508, 511. Some of the exclusions merely confirm what almost certainly would have been the result under the general definition of disability, *Blackwell v. United States Dep't of Treasury,* 830 F.2d 1183 (D.C. Cir. 1987) (homosexuality not a disability under general definition of Rehabilitation Act), but others narrow the scope of the general definition. *Blackwell v. United States Dep't of Treasury,* 639 F. Supp. 289 (D.D.C. 1986) (transvestism is a disability under the general definition of the Rehabilitation Act).

The ADA (and the Rehabilitation Act) also exclude from coverage *current* users of illegal drugs; former users who are rehabilitated are covered. ADA

§§ 104, 510; Rehabilitation Act § 8(C). Employers have expressed some concern with this distinction: "Rehabilitated could mean someone who's been off drugs for a year, a month, two days, or someone who just decided this morning not to use drugs anymore." William Current, Director, Institute for a Drug-Free Workplace, 251 DAILY LAB. REP. C-1 (Dec. 31, 1991). *But see Shafer v. Preston Mem. Hosp. Corp.*, 107 F.3d 274 (4th Cir. 1997) (use of drugs one month before discharge constitutes "current" use); *McDaniel v. Mississippi Baptist Med. Ctr.*, 877 F. Supp. 321 (S.D. Miss.), *aff'd*, 74 F.3d 1238 (5th Cir. 1995) (rehabilitated means that the person has been in recovery long enough to be stable).

   4. *Discrimination Based on Sexual Orientation*. Federal law provides very little protection to gays and lesbians. Sexual orientation is not a disability covered by the ADA and the Rehabilitation Act; Title VII's general ban on sex discrimination does not apply to this type of discrimination, *DeSantis v. Pacific Tel. & Tel. Co.*, 608 F.2d 327 (9th Cir. 1979); and distinctions based on sexual orientation receive the lowest level of scrutiny under the Equal Protection Clause. *High Tech Gays v. Defense Indus. Sec. Clearance Office*, 895 F.2d 563 (9th Cir. 1990). *But cf. Romer v. Evans*, 517 U.S. 620 (1996) (state constitutional provision prohibiting any state action intended to protect gays or lesbians struck down under the Equal Protection Clause's rational basis test).

   Many state and local discrimination laws, however, provide protections. Employment discrimination based on sexual orientation is prohibited by state statute in nine states and by local ordinance in over 100 counties and municipalities. For a general discussion, *see Developments in the Law — Sexual Orientation and the Law*, 102 HARV. L. REV. 1508 (1989).

   5. *Pre-employment Inquiries About Disabilities*. The ADA prohibits pre-employment medical examinations and, indeed, all pre-employment inquiries about disabilities. § 102(c). Medical examinations are permissible *after* a conditional offer of employment is made, but only if certain conditions are met. § 102(c)(3). In practice, these provisions mean that employers will first learn of their duty to accommodate either when applicants disclose that they may have difficulty in performing job duties or after a conditional offer of employment is made.

VANDE ZANDE v. STATE OF WISCONSIN DEPARTMENT OF ADMINISTRATION

United States Court of Appeals, 7th Circuit
44 F.3d 538 (1995)

POSNER, Chief Judge.

   In 1990, Congress passed the Americans with Disabilities Act. The stated purpose is "to provide a clear and comprehensive national mandate for the elimination of discrimination against individuals with disabilities," said by Congress to be 43 million in number and growing. §§ 12101(a), (b)(1). "Disability" is broadly defined. It includes not only "a physical or mental impairment that substantially limits one or more of the major life activities of [the disabled] individual," but also the state of "being regarded as having such an impairment." §§ 12102(2)(A), (C). The latter definition, although at first glance peculiar, actually makes a better fit with the elaborate preamble to the Act, in which people who have physical or mental impairments are compared to victims of racial and other invidious discrimination. Many such impairments are not in fact disabling but are believed to be so, and the people having them may be denied employment or otherwise shunned as a consequence. Such people, objectively capable of performing as well as the unimpaired, are analogous to capable workers discriminated against because of their skin color or some other vocationally irrelevant characteristic. (The Act is not limited to employment discrimination, but such discrimination, addressed by Subchapter I of the Act, is the only kind at issue in this case and we limit our discussion accordingly.)

The more problematic case is that of an individual who has a vocationally relevant disability — an impairment such as blindness or paralysis that limits a major human capability, such as seeing or walking. In the common case in which such an impairment interferes with the individual's ability to perform up to the standards of the workplace, or increases the cost of employing him, hiring and firing decisions based on the impairment are not "discriminatory" in a sense closely analogous to employment discrimination on racial grounds. The draftsmen of the Act knew this. But they were unwilling to confine the concept of disability discrimination to cases in which the disability is irrelevant to the performance of the disabled person's job. Instead, they defined "discrimination" to include an employer's "not making reasonable accommodations to the known physical or mental limitations of an otherwise qualified individual with a disability who is an applicant or employee, unless ... [the employer] can demonstrate that the accommodation would impose an undue hardship on the operation of the ... [employer's] business." § 12112(b)(5)(A).

The term "reasonable accommodations" is not a legal novelty, even if we ignore its use (arguably with a different meaning, however) in the provision of Title VII forbidding religious discrimination in employment. 42 U.S.C. § 2000e(j); *see Trans World Airlines, Inc. v. Hardison*, 432 U.S. 63, 84-85 (1977). It is one of a number of provisions in the employment subchapter that were borrowed from regulations issued by the Equal Employment Opportunity Commission in implementation of the Rehabilitation Act of 1973. *See* 29 C.F.R. § 1613.704. Indeed, to a great extent the employment provisions of the new Act merely generalize to the economy as a whole the duties, including that of reasonable accommodation, that the regulations under the Rehabilitation Act imposed on federal agencies and federal contractors. We can therefore look to the decisions interpreting those regulations for clues to the meaning of the same terms in the new law.

It is plain enough what "accommodation" means. The employer must be willing to consider making changes in its ordinary work rules, facilities, terms, and conditions in order to enable a disabled individual to work. The difficult term is "reasonable." The plaintiff in our case, a paraplegic, argues in effect that the term just means apt or efficacious. An accommodation is reasonable, she believes, when it is tailored to the particular individual's disability. A ramp or lift is thus a reasonable accommodation for a person who like this plaintiff is confined to a wheelchair. Considerations of cost do not enter into the term as the plaintiff would have us construe it. Cost is, she argues, the domain of "undue hardship" (another term borrowed from the regulations under the Rehabilitation Act) — a safe harbor for an employer that can show that it would go broke or suffer other excruciating financial distress were it compelled to make a reasonable accommodation in the sense of one effective in enabling the disabled person to overcome the vocational effects of the disability.

These are questionable interpretations both of "reasonable" and of "undue hardship." To "accommodate" a disability is to make some change that will enable the disabled person to work. An unrelated, inefficacious change would not be an accommodation of the disability at all. So "reasonable" may be intended to qualify (in the sense of weaken) "accommodation," in just the same way that if one requires a "reasonable effort" of someone this means less than the maximum possible effort, or in law that the duty of "reasonable care," the cornerstone of the law of negligence, requires something less than the maximum possible care. It is understood in that law that in deciding what care is reasonable the court considers the cost of increased care. (This is explicit in Judge Learned Hand's famous formula for negligence. *United States v. Carroll Towing Co.*, 159 F.2d 169, 173 (2d Cir.1947).) Similar reasoning could be used to flesh out the meaning of the word "reasonable" in the term "reasonable accommodations." It would not follow that the costs and benefits of altering a workplace to enable a disabled person to work would always have to be quantified, or even that an accommodation would have to be deemed unreasonable if the cost exceeded the benefit however slightly. But, at the very least, the cost could not be disproportionate to the benefit. Even if an employer is so large or wealthy — or, like the principal defendant in this case, is a state, which can raise taxes in order to finance any accommodations that it must make to disabled employees — that it may not be able to plead "undue hardship," it would not be required to expend enormous sums in order to bring about a trivial improvement in the life of a disabled employee. If the nation's employers have potentially unlimited financial obligations to 43 million disabled persons, the Americans with Disabilities Act will have imposed an indirect tax potentially greater than the national debt. We do not find an intention to bring about such a radical result in either the language of the Act or its history. The preamble actually "markets" the Act as a cost saver, pointing to "billions of dollars in unnecessary expenses resulting from dependency and nonproductivity." § 12101(a)(9). The savings will be illusory if

Plaintiff's claim

employers are required to expend many more billions in accommodation than will be saved by enabling disabled people to work.

The concept of reasonable accommodation is at the heart of this case. The plaintiff sought a number of accommodations to her paraplegia that were turned down. The principal defendant as we have said is a state, which does not argue that the plaintiff's proposals were rejected because accepting them would have imposed undue hardship on the state or because they would not have done her any good. The district judge nevertheless granted summary judgment for the defendants on the ground that the evidence obtained in discovery, construed as favorably to the plaintiff as the record permitted, showed that they had gone as far to accommodate the plaintiff's demands as reasonableness, in a sense distinct from either aptness or hardship — a sense based, rather, on considerations of cost and proportionality — required. 851 F. Supp. 353 (W.D. Wis. 1994). On this analysis, the function of the "undue hardship" safe harbor, like the "failing company" defense to antitrust liability (on which see *International Shoe Co. v. FTC*, 280 U.S. 291, 302, (1930); 4 Phillip Areeda & Donald F. Turner, *Antitrust Law* ¶¶ 924-31 (1980)), is to excuse compliance by a firm that is financially distressed, even though the cost of the accommodation to the firm might be less than the benefit to disabled employees.

This interpretation of "undue hardship" is not inevitable — in fact probably is incorrect. It is a defined term in the Americans with Disabilities Act, and the definition is "an action requiring significant difficulty or expense." 42 U.S.C. § 12111(10)(A). The financial condition of the employer is only one consideration in determining whether an accommodation otherwise reasonable would impose an undue hardship. *See* 42 U.S.C. §§ 12111(10)(B)(ii), (iii). The legislative history equates "undue hardship" to "unduly costly." These are terms of relation. We must ask, "undue" in relation to what? Presumably (given the statutory definition and the legislative history) in relation to the benefits of the accommodation to the disabled worker as well as to the employer's resources.

So it seems that costs enter at two points in the analysis of claims to an accommodation to a disability. The employee must show that the accommodation is reasonable in the sense both of efficacious and of proportional to costs. Even if this prima facie showing is made, the employer has an opportunity to prove that upon more careful consideration the costs are excessive in relation either to the benefits of the accommodation or to the employer's financial survival or health. In a classic negligence case, the idiosyncrasies of the particular employer are irrelevant. Having above-average costs, or being in a precarious financial situation, is not a defense to negligence. *Vaughan v. Menlove*, 3 Bing. (N.C.) 468, 132 Eng. Rep. 490 (Comm. Pl. 1837). One interpretation of "undue hardship" is that it permits an employer to escape liability if he can carry the burden of proving that a disability accommodation reasonable for a normal employer would break him.

Lori Vande Zande, aged 35, is paralyzed from the waist down as a result of a tumor of the spinal cord. Her paralysis makes her prone to develop pressure ulcers, treatment of which often requires that she stay at home for several weeks. The defendants and the amici curiae argue that there is no duty of reasonable accommodation of pressure ulcers because they do not fit the statutory definition of a disability. Intermittent, episodic impairments are not disabilities, the standard example being a broken leg. But an intermittent impairment that is a characteristic manifestation of an admitted disability is, we believe, a part of the underlying disability and hence a condition that the employer must reasonably accommodate. Often the disabling aspect of a disability is, precisely, an intermittent manifestation of the disability, rather than the underlying impairment. The AIDS virus progressively destroys the infected person's immune system. The consequence is a series of opportunistic diseases which (so far as relevant to the disabilities law) often prevent the individual from working. If they are not part of the disability, then people with AIDS do not have a disability, which seems to us a very odd interpretation of the law, and one expressly rejected in the regulations. We hold that Vande Zande's pressure ulcers are a part of her disability, and therefore a part of what the State of Wisconsin had a duty to accommodate — reasonably.

Vande Zande worked for the housing division of the state's department of administration for three years, beginning in January 1990. The housing division supervises the state's public housing programs. Her job was that of a program assistant, and involved preparing public information materials, planning meetings, interpreting regulations, typing, mailing, filing, and copying. In short, her tasks were of a clerical, secretarial, and administrative-assistant character. In order to enable her to do this work, the defendants, as she acknowledges, "made numerous accommodations relating to the plaintiff's disability." As examples, in her words, "they paid the landlord to have bathrooms modified and to have a step ramped; they bought special adjustable furniture for the plaintiff; they ordered and paid for one-half of the cost of a cot that the plaintiff needed for daily personal care at work; they sometimes adjusted the plaintiff's schedule to perform backup telephone duties to accommodate the plaintiff's medical appointments; they made changes to the plans for a locker room in the new state office building; and they agreed to provide some of the specific accommodations the plaintiff requested in her October 5, 1992 Reasonable Accommodation Request."

But she complains that the defendants did not go far enough in two principal respects. One concerns a period of eight weeks when a bout of pressure ulcers forced her to stay home. She wanted to work full time at home and believed that she would be able to do so if the division would provide her with a desktop computer at home (though she already had a laptop). Her supervisor refused, and told her that he probably would have only 15 to 20 hours of work for her to do at home per week and that she would have to make up the difference between that and a full work week out of her sick leave or vacation leave. In the event, she was able to work all but 16.5 hours in the eight-week period. She took 16.5 hours of sick leave to make up the difference. As a result, she incurred no loss of income, but did lose sick leave that she could have carried forward indefinitely. She now works for another agency of the State of Wisconsin, but any unused sick leave in her employment by the housing division would have accompanied her to her new job. Restoration of the 16.5 hours of lost sick leave is one form of relief that she seeks in this suit.

She argues that a jury might have found that a reasonable accommodation required the housing division either to give her the desktop computer or to excuse her from having to dig into her sick leave to get paid for the hours in which, in the absence of the computer, she was unable to do her work at home. No jury, however, could in our view be permitted to stretch the concept of "reasonable accommodation" so far. Most jobs in organizations public or private involve team work under supervision rather than solitary unsupervised work, and team work under supervision generally cannot be performed at home without a substantial reduction in the quality of the employee's performance. This will no doubt change as communications technology advances, but is the situation today. Generally, therefore, an employer is not required to accommodate a disability by allowing the disabled worker to work, by himself, without supervision, at home. This is the majority view, illustrated by *Tyndall v. National Education Centers, Inc.*, 31 F.3d 209, 213-14 (4th Cir. 1994), and *Law v. United States Postal Service*, 852 F.2d 1278 (Fed. Cir. 1988) (per curiam). The District of Columbia Circuit disagrees. *Langon v. Dept. of Health & Human Services*, 959 F.2d 1053, 1060-61 (D.C. Cir. 1992); *Carr v. Reno*, 23 F.3d 525, 530 (D.C. Cir. 1994). But we think the majority view is correct. An employer is not required to allow disabled workers to work at home, where their productivity inevitably would be greatly reduced. No doubt to this as to any generalization about so complex and varied an activity as employment there are exceptions, but it would take a very extraordinary case for the employee to be able to create a triable issue of the employer's failure to allow the employee to work at home.

And if the employer, because it is a government agency and therefore is not under intense competitive pressure to minimize its labor costs or maximize the value of its output, or for some other reason, bends over backwards to accommodate a disabled worker — goes further than the law requires — by allowing the worker to work at home, it must not be punished for its generosity by being deemed to have conceded the reasonableness of so far-reaching an accommodation. That would hurt rather than help disabled workers. Wisconsin's housing division was not required by the Americans with Disabilities Act to allow Vande Zande to work at home; even more clearly it was not required to install a computer in her home so that she could avoid using up 16.5 hours of sick leave. It is conjectural that she will ever need those 16.5 hours; the expected cost of the loss must, therefore, surely be slight. An accommodation that allows a disabled worker to work at home, at full pay, subject only to a slight loss of sick leave that may never be needed, hence never missed, is, we hold, reasonable as a matter of law....

2nd Complaint

Her second complaint has to do with the kitchenettes in the housing division's building, which are for the use of employees during lunch and coffee breaks. Both the sink and the counter in each of the kitchenettes were 36 inches high, which is too high for a person in a wheelchair. The building was under construction, and the kitchenettes not yet built, when the plaintiff complained about this feature of the design. But the defendants refused to alter the design to lower the sink and counter to 34 inches, the height convenient for a person in a wheelchair. Construction of the building had begun before the effective date of the Americans with Disabilities Act, and Vande Zande does not argue that the failure to include 34-inch sinks and counters in the design of the building violated the Act. She could not argue that; the Act is not retroactive. But she argues that once she brought the problem to the attention of her supervisors, they were obliged to lower the sink and counter, at least on the floor on which her office was located but possibly on the other floors in the building as well, since she might be moved to another floor. All that the defendants were willing to do was to install a shelf 34 inches high in the kitchenette area on Vande Zande's floor. That took care of the counter problem. As for the sink, the defendants took the position that since the plumbing was already in place it would be too costly to lower the sink and that the plaintiff could use the bathroom sink, which is 34 inches high.

Apparently it would have cost only about $150 to lower the sink on Vande Zande's floor; to lower it on all the floors might have cost as much as $2,000, though possibly less. Given the proximity of the bathroom sink, Vande Zande can hardly complain that the inaccessibility of the kitchenette sink interfered with her ability to work or with her physical comfort. Her argument rather is that forcing her to use the bathroom sink for activities (such as washing out her coffee cup) for which the other employees could use the kitchenette sink stigmatized her as different and inferior; she seeks an award of compensatory damages for the resulting emotional distress. We may assume without having to decide that emotional as well as physical barriers to the integration of disabled persons into the workforce are relevant in determining the reasonableness of an accommodation. But we do not think an employer has a duty to expend even modest amounts of money to bring about an absolute identity in working conditions between disabled and nondisabled workers. The creation of such a duty would be the inevitable consequence of deeming a failure to achieve identical conditions "stigmatizing." That is merely an epithet. We conclude that access to a particular sink, when access to an equivalent sink, conveniently located, is provided, is not a legal duty of an employer. The duty of reasonable accommodation is satisfied when the employer does what is necessary to enable the disabled worker to work in reasonable comfort.

In addition...

In addition to making these specific complaints of failure of reasonable accommodation, Vande Zande argues that the defendants displayed a "pattern of insensitivity or discrimination." She relies on a number of minor incidents, such as her supervisor's response, "Cut me some slack," to her complaint on the first day on which the housing division moved into the new building that the bathrooms lacked adequate supplies. He meant that it would take a few days to iron out the bugs inevitable in any major move. It was clearly a reasonable request in the circumstances; and given all the accommodations that Vande Zande acknowledges the defendants made to her disability, a "pattern of insensitivity or discrimination" is hard to discern. But the more fundamental point is that there is no separate offense under the Americans with Disabilities Act called engaging in a pattern of insensitivity or discrimination. The word "pattern" does not appear in the employment subchapter, and the Act is not modeled on RICO. As in other cases of discrimination, a plaintiff can ask the trier of fact to draw an inference of discrimination from a pattern of behavior when each individual act making up that pattern might have an innocent explanation. The whole can be greater than the sum of the parts. But in this case all we have in the way of a pattern is that the employer made a number of reasonable and some more than reasonable — unnecessary — accommodations, and turned down only requests for unreasonable accommodations. From such a pattern no inference of unlawful discrimination can be drawn.

Affirmed.

NOTES

1. *The Procedural Aspect of Reasonable Accommodation*. The evolving concept of reasonable accommodation has a procedural component, as well as a substantive one. Employers have an obligation to explore accommodation possibilities with individuals with disabilities and those individuals, in turn, have a correlative duty to aid in this exploration. *See Bultemeyer v. Fort Wayne Community Sch.,* 100 F.3d 1281 (7th Cir. 1996) (employer not entitled to summary judgment because it failed to explore accommodation possibilities adequately); *Taylor v. Principal Fin. Group,* 93 F.3d 155 (5th Cir.), *cert. denied,* 117 S. Ct. 586 (1996) (employee has obligation to identify disability and suggest accommodations); *Beck v. University of Wis. Bd. of Regents,* 75 F.3d 1130 (7th Cir. 1996) (employer did not fail to accommodate employee reasonably where breakdown in process for determining appropriate accommodation occurred because employee failed to cooperate).

The precise effect of the procedural aspect of reasonable accommodation is difficult to determine, however, because the employer's *substantive* duty of accommodation rarely depends on the individual's accommodation preferences. Where a number of reasonable accommodations exist, for example, an employer need not select the one most preferred by the individual. *See Hankins v. The Gap, Inc.,* 84 F.3d 797 (6th Cir. 1996). At the same time, an employer may not satisfy its duty to accommodate merely by providing the accommodation requested by the individual. *See Feliberty v. Kemper Corp.,* 98 F.3d 274 (7th Cir.

1996) (employer's proffered accommodation is not reasonable merely because it fulfills employee's request).

2. *The Evolving Concept of Reasonable Accommodation.* The courts continue to struggle with the concept of reasonable accommodation. Consider the following issues:

(a) How should a court evaluate reasonableness where an employer has made a number of expensive accommodations for other individuals with disabilities? Should a court hold that an employer is refusing to make reasonable accommodations if it refuses to make similar accommodations for the current plaintiff? Or should the court evaluate reasonableness based on the lesser accommodations that are being made by other, similarly situated employers? *See Myers v. Hose*, 50 F.3d 278 (4th Cir. 1995) (employer's duty to accommodate should not be expanded because employer expansively accommodated other employees).

(b) How should a court evaluate reasonableness where a requested accommodation conflicts with a collective bargaining agreement? *See Shea v. Tisch*, 870 F.2d 786 (1st Cir. 1989) (employer need not accommodate by reassigning in abrogation of seniority rights under a collective bargaining agreement); *Daubert v. United States Postal Serv.*, 733 F.2d 1367 (10th Cir. 1984) (same).

(c) Should the concept of reasonableness include a floor to the types of accommodations required, as well as a ceiling? That is, should an employer be able to resist making minor accommodations requested by an individual with disabilities by arguing that the accommodations are too trivial to be reasonably required? *See Vande Zande, supra.*

BARTH v. GELB

United States Courts of Appeals, D.C. Circuit

2 F.3d 1180 (1993), *cert. denied*, 511 U.S. 1030 (1994)

BUCKLEY, Circuit Judge:

Donald Barth, a severe diabetic, appeals a judgment in favor of his employer, the Voice of America (VOA), on his claim that the VOA illegally discriminated on the basis of handicap by failing to clear him for service at the VOA's overseas radio relay stations. The district court found that the agency was justified in denying Mr. Barth an overseas assignment because the special arrangements required to accommodate his medical condition would have imposed an undue burden on its operations. Mr. Barth's principal challenge is directed to the court's allocation to him of the ultimate burden of proof on that issue. Because a claim of undue burden is an affirmative defense in actions under the Rehabilitation Act of 1973, we find that the burden of proving it should have been placed on the VOA. But because we also find that this error was harmless, we affirm the district court's judgment.

I. BACKGROUND

Donald Barth is a Washington-based computer specialist and employee of the VOA who decided he wanted a change in assignments and a chance to see the world. Accordingly, in 1988, he applied for admittance into the permanent Foreign Service, out of which engineering positions at the VOA's twelve overseas radio relay stations are staffed. Mr. Barth passed all requirements for admittance into the Service, except that he failed a State Department medical clearance examination designed to assess his availability for worldwide service. Mr. Barth suffers from an advanced and degenerative form of diabetes requiring the care of a skilled endocrinologist to control the diabetes, plus an array of other specialists (in ophthalmology, for example) to control its complications. The State Department found that Mr. Barth could not serve worldwide, but only in locations with advanced medical facilities.

After the denial of the medical clearance, Mr. Barth requested a medical waiver from the VOA. His particular suggestion was that the VOA grant a limited waiver restricting his assignments to posts with suitable medical facilities. After protracted deliberations, the VOA denied Mr. Barth's waiver request without a written statement of reasons. Upon exhausting his administrative remedies, Mr. Barth brought suit under the Rehabilitation Act of 1973, as amended, 29 U.S.C. § 701-796i (1988), asking the court to order his assignment to a suitable overseas relay station position and to award him backpay.

After a four-day bench trial, the district court found that Mr. Barth's diabetic condition was the sole reason for his exclusion from the VOA's Overseas Radio Relay Station Program and that, although the waiver panel had not recorded its findings, it had focused on whether a reasonable accommodation could be made to his handicap. The court noted that the entire corps of American overseas relay station engineers consists of only seventy persons divided among the twelve stations, most of which were located in remote, sparsely populated areas. It found that Mr. Barth "could function at only three or four posts" and that

> [t]he thin staffing at each post required flexibility of assignment, put a premium on workers not subject to serious health risks, and offered few options for initial assignment of Mr. Barth. Accepting applicants who could basically only work at a few non-hardship posts would be considered unfair to other Specialists and detrimental to morale and success of the program.

The court concluded "as a matter of law" that accommodating Mr. Barth by limiting his assignments would "place an undue burden on the VOA program," and it granted judgment in favor of the agency. This appeal followed.

II. ANALYSIS

A. The Burden of Proof ...

> Section 505(a)(1) [of the Rehabilitation Act] states, in relevant part:

> The remedies, procedures, and rights set forth in section 717 of the Civil Rights Act of 1964 (42 U.S.C. § 2000e-16) ... shall be available, with respect to any complaint under section 791 of this title, to any employee or applicant for employment aggrieved by the final disposition of such complaint....

29 U.S.C. § 794a(a)(1). Section 717 prohibits discrimination on the basis of race, color, religion, sex, or national origin. Yet, although religious discrimination is a closer analog to handicap discrimination than either race or sex discrimination, courts focusing on this language have tended to look to the allocations of the burdens of proof developed for Title VII race and sex discrimination complaints in shaping rules under the Rehabilitation Act. Thus, courts allocating burdens of proof under the Rehabilitation Act have been prone to adapt and employ the familiar principles of *McDonnell Douglas* as elaborated by *Burdine.*

Burdine places on the plaintiff an initial burden of producing sufficient evidence to support a prima facie case of discrimination. If the plaintiff establishes a prima facie case, the burden shifts to the defendant, which must then produce evidence of an articulable non-discriminatory reason for the challenged action. If the defendant produces such a reason, the plaintiff then bears the ultimate burden of persuading the trier of fact that the reason was pretextual and that intentional discrimination had in fact occurred. *Burdine*, 450 U.S. at 252-56.

The allocation of the burdens of production in the first two steps is designed to "sharpen the inquiry" into an "elusive" fact — an employer's discriminatory motivation. *Id.* at 255 n. 8. Because of the difficulties inherent in establishing such motivation, the Supreme Court placed only a modest initial burden on a Title VII plaintiff; namely, that he establish that although qualified for an available position, he was "rejected under circumstances which give rise to an inference of unlawful discrimination." *Id.* at 253. Once this burden is met, it becomes necessary for the employer to produce admissible evidence of legitimate reasons for the plaintiff's rejection, thus "fram[ing] the factual issue with sufficient clarity so that the plaintiff will have a full and fair opportunity to demonstrate pretext." *Id.* at 255-56. Such a demonstration having been made, it remains the plaintiff's ultimate burden to show that he was in fact the victim of intentional discrimination. *Id.* at 253; *St. Mary's Honor Ctr. v. Hicks*, 509 U.S. 502, 511-12 (1993). In short, the requirement of only a minimal prima facie showing strips the defendant of the ability to remain silent as to its motive while recognizing the plaintiff's ultimate obligation to prove that motive's illegality.

An individual bringing an action under section 501 of the Rehabilitation Act, however, may face a quite different situation from that faced by plaintiffs charging racial discrimination under Title VII. Unlike a person's race, an employer may legitimately take a handicap into consideration in determining whether an applicant or employee is qualified for a particular position. Thus, while an agency would never admit to basing an employment decision on race, agencies frequently acknowledge that they have taken a person's handicap into consideration. Under such circumstances, the ultimate purpose of *Burdine's* requirements is typically achieved from the outset.

It is apparent, then, that the *Burdine* test is not equally applicable to all cases brought under section 501. To illustrate this point, we describe three of the various categories of handicap discrimination cases that may be brought under that section. The first is one in which the employing agency asserts that it refused a job application, or denied an employee a promotion or discharged him, for reasons unrelated to the person's handicap. A second category involves suits in which the employer challenges a plaintiff's claim that he is a "qualified handicapped person" who, with "reasonable accommodation, can perform the essential functions of the position in question." 29 C.F.R. § 1613.702(f). In these cases, the agency will usually contend that no reasonable accommodation is available. In a third category we have those cases, such as the one before us, in which the employing agency offers the affirmative defense of "undue hardship on the operation of its program." 29 C.F.R. § 1613.704(a). This last may at times merge with the second, however, as indicated by the regulation's reference to "the nature and the cost" of a proposed accommodation as an example of "undue hardship." *Id.* § 1613.704(c)(3).

The first of these categories involves the sort of inquiry into subjective facts — the employing agency's true motivation — that the *Burdine* three-step approach was designed to address. But in the last two categories, the fact that the plaintiff's handicap was taken into explicit account in the agency's employment or personnel decision is acknowledged. These cases deal with objective claims that may be tested through the application of traditional burdens of proof. In the second category, for example, a plaintiff must establish that (a) he is handicapped but, (b) with reasonable accommodation (which he must describe), he is (c) able to perform "the essential functions" of the position he holds or seeks. As in the usual case, it would then be up to the employing agency to refute that evidence. The burden, however, remains with the plaintiff to prove his case by a preponderance of the evidence.

In the third category, the agency invokes the affirmative defense of "undue hardship," an inquiry for which the regulations provide three factors for consideration: (1) The overall size of the agency's program with respect to the number of employees, number and type of facilities and size of budget; (2) the type of agency operation, including the composition and structure of the agency's work force; and (3) the nature and the cost of the accommodation. 29 C.F.R. § 1613.704(c). In such a case (as in any other in which an affirmative defense is raised) the agency has the burden of proving the undue hardship.

As a general matter, a reasonable accommodation is one employing a *method of accommodation* that is reasonable in the run of cases, whereas the undue hardship inquiry focuses on the hardships imposed by the plaintiff's preferred accommodation in the context of the particular agency's operations. As noted earlier, a grey area will arise where a proposed accommodation is so costly or of such a nature that it would impose an undue burden on the employer's operations. Thus, an accommodation would be both unreasonable and impose an undue burden "if it either imposes undue financial and administrative burdens on [an agency] or requires a fundamental alteration in the nature of [its] program." *School Bd. of Nassau County v. Arline*, 480 U.S. 273, 287 n. 17 (1987) (internal quotation marks and citations omitted)....

In this case, the issue has been joined in a manner that places us squarely within the third category described above. Therefore, the district court erred in two respects on the question of burdens of proof: Because the VOA acknowledged that it had refused Mr. Barth's application on account of his handicap, the court should not have invoked the *Burdine* three-step scheme; and, more to the point, it wrongly assigned the burden of persuasion on the undue hardship issue to Mr. Barth instead of the agency.

The VOA does not claim that limiting Mr. Barth's overseas assignments to posts at which adequate medical facilities are available would be unreasonable in the abstract. Rather, it asserts that the requested accommodation would result in undue hardship as a result of considerations peculiar to its operation; essentially, its need for flexibility in the difficult task of rotating a small number of radio engineering specialists among twelve far-flung relay stations, most of them "hardship posts," while trying to maintain the efficiency of its operation. The VOA notes that its non-hardship posts, the only ones at which Mr. Barth would be eligible to serve, function as short-term havens for its specialists. Yet, given the "thin staffing" of VOA posts, every transfer from, say, Liberia to Munich, Germany, implies the need for another transfer in the opposite direction. Mr. Barth, however, would be medically disqualified for such transfers, thereby imposing additional burdens on the remaining engineers. For these and other operational reasons, the VOA maintains that its staffing problems would be greatly compounded by admitting someone into the Service who from the outset had Mr. Barth's serious limitations on assignability.

The accommodation Mr. Barth seeks is assignment to one of three or four "non-hardship" posts in the VOA radio relay system. As the VOA admits that it restricts the assignments of certain of its current radio specialists for medical and family reasons, there can be no claim that such an accommodation would mark a "fundamental alteration" in the nature of the VOA's program. The agency argues instead that permanently assigning Mr. Barth to non-hardship postings would impose, in these particular circumstances, undue hardship on the VOA. This is an affirmative defense that the VOA had the burden of proving. The issue to be resolved, then, is whether it has met that burden. But because the district court erred in assigning the ultimate burden of proof to Mr. Barth, we must also decide whether that error was harmless....

Mr. Barth does not claim that the Government failed to produce evidence of undue hardship. Therefore, the only conceivable prejudice from the district court's error is the possibility that its misallocation of the ultimate burden of proof affected the outcome of the case. For this to occur, the evidence presented would have to be in sufficient balance so that the outcome would depend on who had the burden.

Here, the district court examined the administrative record and concluded that the VOA's decision that Mr. Barth's handicap could not be reasonably accommodated "was proper and consistent with the requirements of the Rehabilitation Act." The court observed that "[t]he thin staffing at each post required flexibility of assignment, put a premium on workers not subject to serious health risks, and offered few options for initial assignment of Mr. Barth." It found that "at the time he sought waiver Mr. Barth could function only at three or four posts." Mr. Barth does not challenge the court's findings. To the contrary, he complains that

> the government attempts to characterize this as a fact-bound appeal, claiming appellant has asserted that the District Court's findings are 'clearly erroneous.' The government must have read a different brief, for we have no quarrel here with the facts as found by the district court.

Our examination of the records satisfies us that the VOA introduced sufficient evidence to support a claim of undue hardship by virtue of the loss of essential operational flexibility that would have resulted from an attempt to accommodate Mr. Barth's medical needs. And because Mr. Barth does not challenge the district court's findings of fact, we must accept those findings as true. Viewing the evidence through the lens of those findings, we conclude that it was not so closely balanced that the court's error in assigning the burden of persuasion to Mr. Barth would have affected the outcome.

B. Mr. Barth's Other Claims

Mr. Barth asserts that the district court has made two "significant legal errors," in addition to the misallocation of the burden of proof, "each of which alone justifies reversal." He maintains, first, that the court erred in allowing the VOA to refuse to offer an accommodation to an applicant for employment that it has extended to current employees. Mr. Barth notes that the VOA has made special accommodations for employees who have incurred medical problems while on duty overseas or whose children have particular educational needs. From this, he argues that (1) if such limitations on the assignment of an existing employee do not create an undue hardship, similar restrictions on the assignment of an applicant will not do so; and (2) if the VOA restricts the assignments of a current employee for medical or family reasons, it must be equally willing to restrict the assignment of a handicapped applicant.

These arguments overlook the benefits that agencies derive from accommodating the special needs of existing employees, which they do not gain from serving those of applicants. A willingness to accommodate incumbent employees increases the likelihood that they — and their knowhow — will be retained by the employing agency. It will also contribute to employee morale and, presumably, to productivity. Thus there is economic logic as well as moral truth behind the intuition that distinguishes between "family" and "stranger" and the level of obligation owed to each. Robert Frost captured that intuition in his poem, "The Death of the Hired Man":

> Home is the place where, when you have to go there,
> They have to take you in.

The Poetry of Robert Frost at 38 (Edward C. Lathem ed., 1967). Mr. Barth may knock at the door, but he is not family, and his handicap does not give him the right to be treated as such. An agency is entitled both to take the measure of the burden imposed by an accommodation net of its benefits and to take account of the duty of care, whether legal or not, that is owed employees who develop problems while on the job. Accordingly, we decline to find that the disparate treatment Mr. Barth complains of constitutes handicap discrimination within the meaning of the Act.

In his second claim of legal error, Mr. Barth argues that the district court improperly accepted "speculative assertions of impaired management flexibility and employee morale." He contends that an agency "must establish 'undue hardship' through objective evidence, not mere supposition, of the actual impact of any proposed accommodation on specific aspects of its program." He supports this argument with statements from Title VII religious discrimination cases. *See EEOC v. Townley Engineering & Mfg. Co.*, 859 F.2d 610, 615 (9th Cir. 1988); *Brown v. General Motors Corp.*, 601 F.2d 956, 961 (8th Cir. 1979); *Draper v. United States Pipe & Foundry Co.*, 527 F.2d 515, 520 (6th Cir. 1975). We, however, find nothing in these cases more remarkable than the proposition that evidence becomes less persuasive as it becomes more speculative.

Mr. Barth also contends that even if the VOA had offered admissible evidence of an adverse effect on employee morale, it was inappropriate to take that factor into account. For support, he relies on cases holding, for example, that racial animus may not be used to defend race-based policies or practices. *See, e.g., Palmore v. Sidoti*, 466 U.S. 429, 433 (1984) (holding that community hostility to mixed-race marriages does not excuse a policy that disadvantages mixed-race couples in disputes over child custody).

This argument, however, confuses animus against the handicapped with the morale effects of a particular means of accommodating them. Consider an extreme example: An agency is asked to accommodate an employee with extra-sensitive eyes by moving operations underground. It seems clear that in considering this request, the agency could not properly take into account the other workers' animus against the handicapped or their resentment over the handicapped's protected legal status. But this does not mean the agency must ignore the probable effects of subterranean working conditions on the morale of other employees, however pure of heart.

An element of the undue hardship calculus cited in the EEOC regulation is the relationship between the number of employees and the size of the agency's program. 29 C.F.R. § 1613.704(c). This factor is relevant, we presume, precisely because the degree of the imposition of a particular accommodation on non-handicapped employees as a group, and the effects of such impositions on a small work force, are legitimate concerns under the Rehabilitation Act.

III. CONCLUSION

For the foregoing reasons, the judgment of the district court is

Affirmed.

NOTES

1. *The Uneasy Status of Undue Hardship*. *Barth* briefly discusses the relationship between reasonable accommodation and undue hardship. Analytically, the relationship is problematic. The undue hardship issue is reached only after an accommodation has been proven to be reasonable. But how can a *reasonable* accommodation ever impose an undue hardship? Wouldn't the accommodation be unreasonable if it imposed an undue hardship? But that interpretation would read the undue hardship stage of the analysis out of the statute, which violates standard canons of statutory construction. *Barth* is one of the few cases attempting to deal with this analytical problem.

2. *Interaction Between Models of Discrimination*. *Barth* and other courts are only beginning to explore the relationship between the reasonable accommodation model and the other models of discrimination. Some courts apply the *McDonnell Douglas* model as part of the reasonable accommodation analysis; others do not. *See Muller v. Hotsy Corp.*, 917 F. Supp. 1389, 1409-10 (N.D. Iowa 1996) (listing both types of cases). Some courts say that the mixed-motives model is applicable in ADA cases; others imply that it is not. *Compare McNely v. Ocala Star-Banner Corp.*, 99 F.3d 1068 (11th Cir. 1996), *cert. denied*, 117 S. Ct. 1819 (1997) (mixed-motives model applies to ADA cases) *with Doe v. University of Maryland Med. Sys.*, 50 F.3d 1261 (4th Cir. 1995) (plaintiff must show that disability was sole cause of adverse decision). The ADA has language incorporating the disparate impact model of discrimination, but how it would apply to disability cases is largely unexplored. ADA § 102(b)(6).

These issues are basic to analysis of disability claims. Consider, for example, an employer deciding between two equally qualified candidates for a position, one who has no disabilities and another with a disability who can perform the essential functions of the position with an accommodation requiring a one-time expense of $250. The reasonable accommodation model would clearly require the employer to make the accommodation for the disabled candidate. But the model does not incorporate any type of analysis for comparing the two candidates for the position. Can the employer consider the cost of the accommodation in deciding between the two candidates? Or must the employer ignore that cost in comparing the candidates? *See Muller, supra* (reasoning in dicta that employer violates the ADA by deciding between two employees with disabilities based on the relative costs of accommodating the disabilities). The other models of discrimination, in large part, are designed to facilitate this type of comparison between candidates. The courts are likely to rely on those models to supplement the reasonable accommodation model, but the process of exploring the precise relationship between the models is only beginning.

NELSON v. THORNBURGH

United States District Court, E.D. Pennsylvania
567 F. Supp. 369 (1983), *aff'd,* 732 F.2d 146 (3d Cir. 1984),
cert. denied, 469 U.S. 1188 (1985)

LOUIS H. POLLAK, DISTRICT JUDGE.

Plaintiffs Martin Nelson, Paula Buntele and Thomas Mobley are income maintenance workers ("IMWs") employed by the Department of Public Welfare ("DPW") of the Commonwealth of Pennsylvania, and assigned to neighborhood offices of the Philadelphia County Board of Assistance ("PCBA")....

Plaintiffs are blind. Because their job entails extensive paperwork, they are unable to perform their duties satisfactorily without the aid of a reader. Plaintiffs have therefore hired readers on a part-time basis. With the assistance of these readers, plaintiffs meet the requirements of their position as well as their sighted colleagues.

Plaintiffs, up to now, have borne the expense of these readers, despite requests by plaintiffs and the Office of Civil Rights of the Department of Health and Human Services that DPW assume this cost. Plaintiffs claim in this lawsuit that DPW's refusal to accommodate them by providing readers or, in the alternative, mechanical devices capable of helping them accomplish the reading functions, constitutes "discrimination" within the meaning of section 504 of the Rehabilitation Act of 1973....

DPW is a department of the Commonwealth of Pennsylvania, charged with administering the federal and state programs, such as cash assistance, food stamps and medical assistance, designed to aid those in need....

The IMW is, as a rule, the only point of contact between the individual recipient and the massive apparatus of the state and federal welfare system.... The central function of the job is ... the determination of the client's initial and continued eligibility for federal and state benefits[, primarily through the use of] computerized standard forms.... The standard forms are designed to maximize efficient processing of benefits and minimize mistakes by making it easier to control the IMWs' discretion and keep the client files uniform.

The principal form used by the IMW in the interview with the client is the "743."... The IMW elicits from the client all the information required by the five-page form, which includes everything relating to the client's financial, vocational and family situation that could conceivably bear upon the question of eligibility. DPW's normal procedure calls for the IMW to copy this information by hand on the appropriate block of the 743 form. Depending on the client's situation, the IMW may also have to fill out other forms, such as a food stamp application worksheet or a child support form. During the interview, the IMW often will have to review documents provided by the client. Some documents, such as rent receipts, are used to verify the client's address; others, such as medical reports, are used to evaluate the client's medical fitness for work, an important component of the eligibility requirement.

After a form is completed, the IMW hands it to the client for review. If the information is correct, the client signs the form. The typical IMW spends about half the day conducting interviews.

After the client leaves the office, the IMW makes the determination of eligibility for benefits. To do this, the IMW consults the DPW Income Maintenance Manual ("the Manual"). The Manual is over one thousand pages long, and filled with regulations, procedures, charts and tables. New materials are added to the Manual almost daily, reflecting changes in the amount of aid or the policies affecting its distribution....

After determining eligibility under these programs, the IMW fills out an instruction sheet encoding the decision on the amount of benefits, and sends it with the 743 to the clerical department. The clerical staff then enters all the data into the central computer....

The IMW must also be prepared to handle client emergencies by being able to calm distraught clients, replace lost checks, or track down bureaucratic error.

Changes in the last ten years have operated to limit the range of discretion associated with the IMW position. Yet the IMW remains a professional-level position, with significant responsibilities. The capacity to read without aid is certainly helpful in carrying out the duties of the job, as are the abilities to hear or to move about without help. The essential qualifications for this career, however, are dedication to the work, sufficient judgment and life-experience to enable one accurately to assess the legitimate needs of clients, and the ability to work effectively under the pressure of competing demands from clients and supervisors.

The Blind IMW

With the aid of readers, plaintiffs perform their job as well as sighted IMWs. By employing readers on a part-time basis, plaintiffs have earned fully satisfactory evaluations from their supervisors.

The experience of plaintiff Martin Nelson as a blind IMW is typical of the other plaintiffs.... He currently uses his reader an average of 32.5 hours per week.

Mr. Nelson pays his reader $3.80 per hour, spending approximately $480 per month for reader salary, or about $5,100 per year. Mr. Nelson earns $21,379 in salary, plus fringe benefits of about $4,000. Plaintiffs are able to afford a reader on their salary because they receive $316 per month in Supplemental Security Income (SSI). They receive SSI benefits to help defray work-related expenses that result from their blindness. That portion of the reader expenses not covered by SSI is paid out of salary, and is tax deductible....

When conducting a client interview, Mr. Nelson uses his reader to fill out the forms according to his instructions and to read aloud any documents the client may have brought in. Mr. Nelson takes notes of the interview in braille, with a slate and stylus.[8] After the form is completed, Mr. Nelson confirms that the information given is accurately inscribed, and then has the client sign the form. Mr. Nelson later has his reader review specific sections of the Manual in order to determine eligibility....

[Another of the plaintiffs,] Mr. Mobley, by varying the routine slightly, has been able to reduce significantly ... his demand for a reader.... Mr. Mobley schedules his interviews with clients for the afternoons. Like Mr. Nelson, he takes notes on a slate and stylus. But Mr. Mobley's reader is not present during interviews. His reader works mornings, helping Mr. Mobley to fill in the 743 and the instruction sheet for the previous day's interviews. The client returns sometime during that day, or soon thereafter, to verify and sign the completed form. By following this procedure, Mr. Mobley needs a reader for only four hours per day.

Types of Accommodation

Three expert witnesses testified concerning the methods and costs of accommodating the plaintiffs to enable them to perform the essential functions of their job....

The experts' testimony, in sum, suggested four types of accommodation DPW could pursue: (1) The first may more accurately be called an "alternative technique" than an accommodation, for it involves relatively costless adjustments in the agency's procedures. One such technique would be to braille the forms to make them easier for a blind IMW to follow and explain to a reader. Another such technique would be to allow blind IMWs to require clients to return the next day to sign the face sheet of the 743, enabling the IMWs to conduct interviews without the presence of a reader, as Mr. Mobley already does.

---

[8] A slate is a small sheet of hinged metal inscribed with a series of dots, corresponding to the braille alphabet. After inserting paper into the slate, a piercing tool known as a stylus is used to punch the raised dots onto the paper and thus encode information.

(2) A second type of accommodation would be to print the thousand-page manual in braille. The cost of brailling fifty copies of the Manual — enough for blind IMWs throughout the state — would be approximately $34,000.

(3) A third type of accommodation is technological: DPW could purchase one of a number of kinds of new machines that combine microchip technology and braille. The most promising of these inventions is the Versabraille. The Versabraille is a portable mini-computer that uses a standard cassette to store and retrieve information in braille.... The blind IMW could use the Versabraille to encode all the information gathered from a client interview by plugging in the name of the client as the chapter, and the specific information — say eligibility for foodstamps — as a page. The blind IMW could later "read back" the information by recalling the name of the client and "foodstamps," and touching the display....

Each Versabraille would cost at most $7,000, plus $700 for a printer. A maintenance contract would cost another $700 per year. Because they already know braille, the plaintiffs in this case could learn to use Versabraille in two or three days.

The Versabraille would substantially reduce the need for a reader but it would not eliminate it entirely. Handwritten documents would still require reading, as would mail and material not produced by or entered into the DPW computer.

(4) The fourth type of accommodation is providing a reader.

The Cost of Reasonable Accommodation

Of the four types of accommodation referred to above, the provision of readers is required to enable a blind IMW to perform the essential functions of the position. But a full-time reader is not required, because it is not necessary to have a reader in attendance while determination ... interviews are being conducted. Those interviews consume approximately half of a working day. If the PCBA were to permit each blind IMW to function as Mr. Mobley does, a blind IMW could gather client information one day and, on the following day, use the reader to prepare the form, with client verification on that day or soon thereafter. By using this method a blind IMW could perform the essential functions of the job by using a reader four hours a day or less. During the rest of the day, a person capable of serving as a reader should be "on call" on an emergency basis.... [The cost of this accommodation would be] roughly $6,638 per year for each plaintiff.

Adoption of the first two types of accommodations — changing agency procedures and brailling the Manual — could enhance the efficiency and productivity of readers, and thus lower the cost of accommodation. Investment in the third type of accommodation — new technology and most particularly the Versabraille — could also be expected to lower the cost of accommodation by significantly reducing the blind IMW's dependence on the availability of readers. None of these accommodations, however, would eliminate entirely the need for readers.

Assuming accommodation is found to be required as a matter of law, it will be up to defendants to determine whether readers alone would be utilized or whether use would also be made of one or more of the other types of accommodation. If defendants were to employ other accommodations in addition to readers, the governing principle would be that the aggregate remedial package would, as to each plaintiff, be as effective as providing each of the plaintiffs with (a) daily access to a reader for half of the working day, and (b) emergency access to a reader as required during the other half of the working day.

Discussion

[Two] issues are raised by plaintiffs' claims. The first is whether plaintiffs are "otherwise qualified" within the meaning of section 504. If they are, next to be decided would be whether the accommodation required to enable plaintiffs to perform the essential functions of their job — half-time readers or their equivalent — would be reasonable, or whether it would instead impose an undue hardship on DPW and the PCBA....

Section 504 prohibits only "otherwise qualified" individuals from being discriminated against by reason of handicap. Plaintiffs contend that they are "otherwise qualified" because, with accommodation, they are able to perform all the job functions associated with the IMW position. Defendants respond by arguing the following syllogism: plaintiffs are "otherwise qualified" only if they possess all the abilities necessary to perform their job; that one of the most important abilities for the IMW to possess is the ability to read; that plaintiffs cannot read; and therefore that plaintiffs are not "otherwise qualified."

The legislative history of the Rehabilitation Act does not explain the Congressional intent in choosing the phrase "otherwise qualified." However, the Supreme Court, in *Southeastern Community College v. Davis,* 442 U.S. 397 (1979), has closely examined the meaning of the phrase.... It therefore provides an appropriate starting place for analysis of the issues posed in the present controversy.

Francis Davis suffered from a hearing disorder. By wearing a hearing aid, she was able to detect the presence of sounds almost as well as a person with normal hearing, but still had trouble locating the source of the sounds or discriminating among them sufficiently to understand spoken speech. She therefore had to rely primarily on her lipreading skills for oral communication.

Ms. Davis hoped to be trained as a registered nurse. To achieve that ambition, she enrolled during the 1973-74 academic year in Southeastern Community College's Parallel Program: a program designed to fulfill the prerequisites for the College's Associate Degree Nursing Program. Upon completing the Parallel Program, however, Ms. Davis was refused entry into the nursing program. The decision, made after considerable deliberation, was based on plaintiff's handicap.

Ms. Davis brought suit under section 504. The district court, after a hearing, analyzed her claim first by defining "otherwise qualified" in this context to mean "otherwise able to function sufficiently in the position sought in spite of the handicap, if proper training and facilities are suitable and available." The court then found that Ms. Davis would pose a potential danger as a student or registered nurse because a patient or doctor might be unable to secure her attention and be quickly understood in a medical emergency. Because Ms. Davis could not under certain circumstances perform her functions safely, she could not perform them sufficiently. Therefore, she was not "otherwise qualified," and judgment was entered for the defendant.

The Court of Appeals for the Fourth Circuit reversed[, but the Supreme] Court endorsed the district court's view of the meaning of "otherwise qualified": "An otherwise qualified person is one who is able to meet all of a program's requirements in spite of his handicap." Because plaintiff could not meet these requirements, she was not "otherwise qualified."

Justice Powell's opinion then went on to consider whether the nursing program requirements might be modified to accommodate Ms. Davis. The Court first noted that even the most radical alteration in the program would avail Ms. Davis little, for while the paramount concern for patient safety demanded that Ms. Davis be closely supervised in her practical training, such supervision would frustrate the program's goal of encouraging the assumption of responsibility. Moreover, the Court found that section 504 requires no "affirmative action" — that is, no modifications "in existing programs beyond those necessary to eliminate discrimination against otherwise qualified individuals." The Court then acknowledged the fineness of the line it was drawing "between a lawful refusal to extend affirmative action and illegal discrimination against handicapped persons." The Court explained:

> It is possible to envision situations where an insistence on continuing past requirements and practices might arbitrarily deprive genuinely qualified handicapped persons of the opportunity to participate in a covered program. Technological advances can be expected to enhance opportunities to rehabilitate the handicapped or otherwise to qualify them for some useful employment. Such advances also may enable attainment of these goals without imposing undue financial and administrative burdens upon a State. Thus, situations may arise where a refusal to modify an existing program might become unreasonable and discriminatory.

[In applying *Davis*, it is helpful to distinguish] four types of barriers to equality in the employment area. Two types of barriers — social bias and disparate impact from neutral standards[17] — are common to any member of a disfavored group. Two other types of barriers, however, are unique to the handi-

---

[17] An example of a neutral-standards barrier is a rule against allowing dogs into a federal courthouse, which would operate to impair a blind lawyer relying on a seeing-eye dog. *See also Majors v. Housing Authority,* 652 F.2d 454 (5th Cir. 1981) (housing project may have to permit exception to "no pet" rule for woman with acute psychological dependency on her dog).

Barriers

capped, for these barriers result from the nature of the handicap in combination with the requirements of the position in question. One type is "surmountable impairment barriers," referring to barriers to job performance that can be fully overcome by accommodation. The other is "insurmountable employment barriers," where the handicap itself prevents the individual from fulfilling the essential requirements of the position.

Davis presents an example of an insurmountable employment barrier, because the ability to hear is an essential requirement for a nurse in order to insure patient safety. Thus *Davis* at least stands for the proposition that an individual facing an insurmountable barrier is not "otherwise qualified" within the meaning of section 504.[18]

Davis also teaches that an individual facing a surmountable employment barrier is not "otherwise qualified" if accommodation would require a substantial modification in the requirements of the position, or would result in an undue administrative or financial burden upon the federally assisted program sought to be charged pursuant to section 504. The Court characterized accommodations which it considered excessive as "affirmative action."

This case

There is no claim in the present case that accommodation of these plaintiffs would entail substantial modifications of the requirements of the position, or impose a new administrative burden on DPW. The claim is simply that the accommodation called for would cost too much. Thus, the arguments over "otherwise qualified," "reasonable accommodation," "undue burden" and "affirmative action" all collapse into one issue: would the cost of providing half-time readers be greater than the Act demands? . . .

The HHS regulations that bear on the issue . . . define a "qualified handicapped person" as one who "with reasonable accommodation, can perform the essential functions of the job in question." [45 C.F.R.] § 84.3(k)(1). As examples of reasonable accommodations, the regulations include: "job restructuring, part-time or modified work schedules, acquisition or modification of equipment or devices, *the provision of readers* or interpreters, and other similar actions." *Id.* at § 84.12(b)(2) (emphasis added).

The recipient must make such accommodations unless it "can demonstrate that the accommodation would impose an undue hardship on the operation of its program." *Id.* at § 84.12(a). The regulations do not spell out precisely how that showing can be made, but they do list the following "factors to be considered" in the determination of undue hardship:

Good points

[18] Two recent cases in this court have relied on this strand of *Davis* in ruling that plaintiffs do not fit within the definition of "otherwise qualified." In *Strathie v. Department of Transportation,* 547 F. Supp. 1367 (E.D. Pa. 1982), Judge Ditter ruled that a hearing-impaired school bus driver was not otherwise qualified within the meaning of the Act, because his inability to localize sounds meant that he could not perform two necessary functions of his position: insuring control over and safety for the riders. In *Bey v. Bolger,* 540 F. Supp. 910 (E.D. Pa. 1982), Judge Bechtle held that plaintiff, who suffered from uncontrolled hypertension and cardio-vascular disease, could not safely perform even light duties with the Postal Service without endangering his health and safety.

(1) The overall size of the recipient's program with respect to number of employees, number and type of facilities, and size of budget;

(2) The type of the recipient's operation, including the composition and structure of the recipient's workforce; and

(3) The nature and cost of the accommodation needed.

Id. at § 84.12(c)(1-3). In addition, Appendix A to the regulations illustrates how these factors should be applied in determining whether the recipient of federal funds has discharged the burden of showing undue hardship:

> The weight given to each of these factors in making the determination as to whether an accommodation constitutes undue hardship will vary depending on the facts of a particular situation. *Thus, a small day-care center might not be required to expend more than a nominal sum, such as that necessary to equip a telephone for use by a secretary with impaired hearing, but a large school district might be required to make available a teacher's aide to a blind applicant for a teaching job. Further, it might be considered reasonable to require a state welfare agency to accommodate a deaf employee by providing an interpreter while it would constitute an undue hardship to impose that requirement on a provider of foster home care services.*

Appendix A — Analysis of Final Regulations, 45 C.F.R. § 84 at 300 (emphasis added).

Applying the regulations to the facts of this case reveals that the answer called for by the regulations is clear. "[T]he provision of readers" is an express HHS example of reasonable accommodation. Moreover, in view of DPW's $300,000,000 administrative budget, the modest cost of providing half-time readers, and the ease of adopting that accommodation without any disruption of DPW's services, it is apparent that DPW has not met its burden of showing undue hardship. To be sure, DPW's financial resources are limited. But there is no principled way of distinguishing DPW on this basis from the large school district employing an aide for a blind teacher, or from the state welfare agency providing an interpreter for a deaf employee.

I conclude that accommodating plaintiffs to enable them to perform the essential functions of their position is consistent with the mandates of section 504.... I am not unmindful of the very real budgetary constraints under which the DPW and PCBA operate, and recognize that accommodation of these plaintiffs will impose some further dollar burden upon an already overtaxed system of delivery of welfare benefits. But the additional dollar burden is a minute fraction of the DPW/PCBA personnel budgets. Moreover, in enacting section 504, Congress recognized that failure to accommodate handicapped individuals also imposes real costs upon American society and the American economy. But for the fortuitous availability of supplemental benefits from the federal government — benefits which heretofore have enabled plaintiffs to hire and pay readers on their own — these plaintiffs, despite their education, experience and commitment, would have been barred by their handicap from the position of IMW, where they now serve as examples of how handicaps can be overcome. When one considers the social costs which would flow from the exclusion of persons such as plaintiffs from the pursuit of their profession, the modest cost of accommodation — a cost which seems likely to diminish, as technology advances and proliferates — seems, by comparison, quite small.

NOTES

1. *The Costs of Accommodation.* The accommodations required in *Nelson* were fairly expensive, but that is unusual. Most accommodations tend to be inexpensive. A study of Sears, Roebuck, and Co. found that between 1993 and 1996, seventy-two percent of the company's accommodations for individuals with disabilities required no cost, twenty-seven percent cost less than $500, and only one percent cost more than $500. The average cost of an accommodation was $45. By comparison, the average cost of replacing an employee who was not accommodated was $1,800 to $2,400. Peter David Blanck, *Transcending Title I of the Americans With Disabilities Act: A Report on Sears, Roebuck and Co.*, 20 MENTAL & PHYSICAL DISABILITY L. REP. 278 (1996).

2. *Reasonable Accommodation under Title VII.* The accommodations required for religious beliefs and practices under Title VII are more limited than the accommodations required under the ADA and the Rehabilitation Act. In *Trans World Airlines v. Hardison,* 432 U.S. 63 (1977), for example, the Supreme Court indicated that "undue hardship" in Title VII really means "very small inconvenience."

In *Hardison,* the plaintiff's religious tenets required that he refrain from work from sunset on Friday until sunset on Saturday. TWA eventually discharged the plaintiff for failing to work during his scheduled shifts during those times. The Supreme Court held that TWA had not violated Title VII because both of the possible accommodations in the case would have imposed an "undue hardship." One accommodation that TWA could have made would have been to circumvent the seniority system and schedule another employee to work during the time Hardison's religious tenets prevented him from working. The Court held that TWA was not required to make that accommodation, because it would be anomalous under a statute prohibiting religious discrimination to deprive another employee of her shift preference because she did not adhere to a religion with a Saturday Sabbath. Thus, narrowly read, *Hardison* means that employers need not make accommodations if they would result in any interference with a seniority system. More broadly read, *Hardison* may mean that accommodations need not be made if they would result in any interference with the preferences of other employees. TWA could also have accommodated Hardison by encouraging other employees to work on Hardison's shift by paying them overtime. The Court held, however, that anything more than a "de minimis cost" is an undue hardship.

Thus, that accommodation was not required by Title VII either. In a later case, the Supreme Court indicated that if two or more reasonable accommodations are possible, employers need not select the one that is most favorable to the employee; employers meet their obligation by offering *any* reasonable accommodation. *Ansonia Bd. of Educ. v. Philbrook,* 479 U.S. 60 (1986).

Do you think the courts apply a less stringent version of the reasonable accommodation model to religious discrimination because they perceive that problem to be less serious than discrimination against persons with disabilities? Or are there other reasons? *See Protos v. Volkswagen of Am., Inc.,* 797 F.2d 129 (3d Cir.), *cert. denied,* 479 U.S. 972 (1986) (religious accommodation requirement does not violate First Amendment).

3. *Facilities Requirements.* The ADA also requires employers (and others) to take steps to increase the accessibility of their facilities to persons with disabilities. New construction and alterations must be "readily accessible to and usable by individuals with disabilities." § 303. Detailed regulations have been promulgated to define "readily accessible." 39 C.F.R. pt. 1191, Appendix. For existing facilities, employers must take all "readily achievable" steps to remove barriers to access. § 302(2)(A)(iv), (v). Readily achievable means "easily accomplished and able to be carried out without much difficulty or expense." § 301(9). Examples of readily achievable steps in the legislative history of the ADA include: coming to the door to receive or return dry cleaning; allowing a disabled patron to be served beverages at a table even though nondisabled persons having only drinks are required to drink at an inaccessible bar; and rotating movies between the first floor accessible theater and a second floor inaccessible theater and notifying the public of the rotation.

Chapter 15

APPLYING THE LEGAL MODELS
OF DISCRIMINATION

A. SEX DISCRIMINATION

1. PREGNANCY

The Supreme Court's first discussion of pregnancy discrimination under Title VII provided clear notice that it would pose special problems. In *General Electric Co. v. Gilbert*, 429 U.S. 125 (1976), the Court considered an employer-sponsored disability plan that excluded from coverage disabilities arising from pregnancy. The Court held that discrimination because of pregnancy was not sex discrimination within the meaning of Title VII:

> The lack of identity between [pregnancy] and gender as such becomes clear upon the most cursory analysis. The program divides potential recipients into two groups — pregnant women and nonpregnant persons. While the first group is exclusively female, the second includes members of both sexes.

Id. at 135 (*quoting Geduldig v. Aiello*, 417 U.S. 484 (1974)). Congress reacted to the *Gilbert* case by enacting the Pregnancy Discrimination Act of 1978 (PDA). The PDA inserted language into Title VII which says, in essence, that sex discrimination under Title VII includes discrimination based on pregnancy. Title VII § 701(k), 42 U.S.C. § 2000e(k).

CALIFORNIA FEDERAL SAVINGS & LOAN ASSOCIATION
v. GUERRA

United States Supreme Court
479 U.S. 272 (1987)

JUSTICE MARSHALL delivered the opinion of the Court.

The question presented is whether Title VII of the Civil Rights Act of 1964, as amended by the Pregnancy Discrimination Act of 1978, pre-empts a state statute that requires employers to provide leave and reinstatement to employees disabled by pregnancy.

I

California's Fair Employment and Housing Act (FEHA) is a comprehensive statute that prohibits discrimination in employment and housing. In September 1978, California amended the FEHA to proscribe certain forms of employment discrimination on the basis of pregnancy. Cal. Gov't Code Ann. § 12945(b)(2)

(West 1980).[1] Subdivision (b)(2) — the provision at issue here — is the only portion of the statute that applies to employers subject to Title VII. It requires these employers to provide female employees an unpaid pregnancy disability leave of up to four months. Respondent Fair Employment and Housing Commission, the state agency authorized to interpret the FEHA, has construed § 12945(b)(2) to require California employers to reinstate an employee returning from such pregnancy leave to the job she previously held, unless it is no longer available due to business necessity. In the latter case, the employer must make a reasonable, good faith effort to place the employee in a substantially similar job. The statute does not compel employers to provide paid leave to pregnant employees. Accordingly, the only benefit pregnant workers actually derive from § 12945(b)(2) is a qualified right to reinstatement....

II

Lillian Garland was employed by [California Federal Savings and Loan Association (Cal Fed)] as a receptionist for several years. In January 1982, she took a pregnancy disability leave. When she was able to return to work in April of that year, Garland notified Cal Fed, but was informed that her job had been filled and that there were no receptionist or similar positions available. Garland filed a complaint with respondent Department of Fair Employment and Housing, which issued an administrative accusation against Cal Fed on her behalf. [Before that case could proceed to hearing,] Cal Fed ... brought this action in the United States District Court for the Central District of California. [It] sought a declaration that § 12945(b)(2) is inconsistent with and pre-empted by Title VII and an injunction against [its] enforcement. The District Court granted petitioners' motion for summary judgment [stating] that "California employers who comply with state law are subject to reverse discrimination suits under Title VII brought by temporarily disabled males who do not receive the same treatment as female employees disabled by pregnancy...." On this basis, the District Court held that "[§ 12945(b)(2) is] preempted by Title VII...."

III

A

In two sections of the 1964 Civil Rights Act, §§ 708 and 1104, Congress has indicated that state laws will be pre-empted only if they actually conflict with federal law. Section 708 of Title VII provides:

---

[1] Section 12945(b)(2) provides, in relevant part:

"It shall be an unlawful employment practice ...:

"(b) For an employer to refuse to allow a female employee affected by pregnancy, childbirth, or related medical conditions ...

"(2) To take a leave on account of pregnancy for a reasonable period of time; provided, such period shall not exceed four months.... Reasonable period of time means that period during which the female employee is disabled on account of pregnancy, childbirth, or related medical conditions...."

> Nothing in this title shall be deemed to exempt or relieve any person from any liability, duty, penalty, or punishment provided by any present or future law of any State or political subdivision of a State, other than any such law which purports to require or permit the doing of any act which would be an unlawful employment practice under this title.

Section 1104 of Title XI, applicable to all titles of the Civil Rights Act, establishes the following standard for pre-emption:

> Nothing contained in any title of this Act shall be construed as indicating an intent on the part of Congress to occupy the field in which any such title operates to the exclusion of State laws on the same subject matter, nor shall any provision of this Act be construed as invalidating any provision of State law unless such provision is inconsistent with any of the purposes of this Act, or any provision thereof....

Sections 708 and 1104 severely limit Title VII's pre-emptive effect. Instead of pre-empting state fair employment laws, § 708 "simply left them where they were before the enactment of title VII." *Shaw v. Delta Air Lines, Inc.,* [463 U.S. 85, 103 n.24 (1983).] Similarly, § 1104 was intended primarily to "assert the intention of Congress to preserve existing civil rights laws." 110 Cong. Rec. 2788 (1964) (remarks of Rep. Meader). The narrow scope of pre-emption available under §§ 708 and 1104 reflects the importance Congress attached to state antidiscrimination laws in achieving Title VII's goal of equal employment opportunity....

In order to decide whether the California statute requires or permits employers to violate Title VII, as amended by the [Pregnancy Discrimination Act of 1978 (PDA),] or is inconsistent with the purposes of the statute, we must determine whether the PDA prohibits the States from requiring employers to provide reinstatement to pregnant workers, regardless of their policy for disabled workers generally.

B

Petitioners argue [first] that the second clause of the PDA forbids an employer to treat pregnant employees any differently than other disabled employees. Because "[t]he purpose of Congress is the ultimate touchstone" of the pre-emption inquiry, however, we must examine the PDA's language against the background of its legislative history and historical context....

It is well established that the PDA was passed in reaction to this Court's decision in *General Electric Co. v. Gilbert,* 429 U.S. 125 (1976). "When Congress amended Title VII in 1978, it unambiguously expressed its disapproval of both the holding and the reasoning of the Court in the *Gilbert* decision." By adding pregnancy to the definition of sex discrimination prohibited by Title VII, the first clause of the PDA reflects Congress' disapproval of the reasoning in *Gilbert.* Rather than imposing a limitation on the remedial purpose of the PDA, we believe that the second clause was intended to overrule the holding in *Gilbert* and to illustrate how discrimination against pregnancy is to be remedied. *Cf.* [*Newport News Shipbuilding & Dry Dock Co. v. EEOC*, 462 U.S. 669, 678, n.14 (1983)] ("The meaning of the first clause is not limited by the specific language in the second clause, which explains the application of the general principle to women employees"). Accordingly, subject to certain limitations,[17] we agree with the Court of Appeals' conclusion that Congress intended the PDA to be "a floor beneath which pregnancy disability benefits may not drop — not a ceiling above which they may not rise."

The context in which Congress considered the issue of pregnancy discrimination supports this view of the PDA. Congress had before it extensive evidence of discrimination *against* pregnancy, particularly in disability and health insurance programs like those challenged in *Gilbert*.... The reports, debates, and hearings make abundantly clear that Congress intended the PDA to provide relief for working women and to end discrimination against pregnant workers. In contrast to the thorough account of discrimination against pregnant workers, the legislative history is devoid of any discussion of preferential treatment of pregnancy, beyond acknowledgments of the existence of state statutes providing for such preferential treatment. Opposition to the PDA came from those concerned with the cost of including pregnancy in health and disability benefit plans and the application of the bill to abortion, not from those who favored special accommodation of pregnancy.

In support of their argument that the PDA prohibits employment practices that favor pregnant women, petitioners ... cite statements in the legislative history to the effect that the PDA does not *require* employers to extend any benefits to pregnant women that they do not already provide to other disabled employees.... We do not interpret these references to support petitioners' construction of the statute. On the contrary, if Congress had intended to *prohibit* preferential treatment, it would have been the height of understatement to say only that the legislation would not *require* such conduct. It is hardly conceivable that Congress would have extensively discussed only its intent not to require preferential treatment if in fact it had intended to prohibit such treatment.

We also find it significant that Congress was aware of state laws similar to California's but apparently did not consider them inconsistent with the PDA. In the debates and reports on the bill, Congress repeatedly acknowledged the existence of state antidiscrimination laws that prohibit sex discrimination on the basis of pregnancy. Two of the States mentioned then required employers to provide reasonable leave to pregnant workers. After citing these state laws, Congress failed to evince the requisite "clear and manifest purpose" to supersede them. To the contrary, both the House and Senate Reports suggest that these laws would continue to have effect under the PDA....

---

[17] For example, a State could not mandate special treatment of pregnant workers based on stereotypes or generalizations about their needs and abilities. *See infra.*

Section 12945(b)(2) [and Title VII share the common goal of promoting] equal employment opportunity. By requiring employers to reinstate women after a reasonable pregnancy disability leave, § 12945(b)(2) ensures that they will not lose their jobs on account of pregnancy disability.... By "taking pregnancy into account," California's pregnancy disability leave statute allows women, as well as men, to have families without losing their jobs.

We emphasize the limited nature of the benefits § 12945(b)(2) provides. The statute is narrowly drawn to cover only the period of *actual physical disability* on account of pregnancy, childbirth, or related medical conditions. Accordingly, unlike the protective labor legislation prevalent earlier in this century,[28] § 12945(b)(2) does not reflect archaic or stereotypical notions about pregnancy and the abilities of pregnant workers. A statute based on such stereotypical assumptions would, of course, be inconsistent with Title VII's goal of equal employment opportunity.

C

Moreover, even if we agreed with petitioners' construction of the PDA, we would nonetheless reject their argument that the California statute requires employers to violate Title VII. Section 12945(b)(2) does not prevent employers from complying with both the federal law (as petitioners construe it) and the state law.... Section 12945(b)(2) does not compel California employers to treat pregnant workers better than other disabled employees; it merely establishes benefits that employers must, at a minimum, provide to pregnant workers. Employers are free to give comparable benefits to other disabled employees, thereby treating "women affected by pregnancy" no better than "other persons not so affected but similar in their ability or inability to work."...

Petitioners argue that "extension" of the state statute to cover other employees would be inappropriate in the absence of a clear indication that this is what the California Legislature intended. They cite cases in which this Court has declined to rewrite underinclusive state statutes found to violate the Equal Protection Clause. This argument is beside the point. Extension is a remedial option to be exercised by a court once a statute is found to be invalid.[31]

---

[28] In the constitutional context, we have invalidated on equal protection grounds statutes designed "to exclude or 'protect' members of one gender because they are presumed to suffer from an inherent handicap or to be innately inferior." *Mississippi University for Women v. Hogan,* 458 U.S. 718, 725 (1982).

[31] We recognize that, *in cases where a state statute is otherwise invalid,* the Court must look to the intent of the state legislature to determine whether to extend benefits or nullify the statute. By arguing that extension would be inappropriate in this case, however, and citing this as a basis for pre-emption, the dissent simply ignores the prerequisite of invalidity.

IV

Thus, petitioners' facial challenge to § 12945(b)(2) fails. The statute is not pre-empted by Title VII, as amended by the PDA, because it is not inconsistent with the purposes of the federal statute, nor does it require the doing of an act which is unlawful under Title VII.[32]

[Justice Stevens joined all but Part III-A of the Court's opinion. In a concurring opinion, he agreed with Justice Marshall that the PDA permitted preferential treatment of pregnancy, but thought it was not necessary to decide issues relating to the effect of § 1104 on preemption.]

[Justice Scalia filed an opinion concurring in the judgment. Since § 12945(b)(2) did not prohibit equal treatment of similarly situated nonpregnant persons, he would have held only that the California statute was not preempted because of § 708 of Title VII.]

JUSTICE WHITE, with whom THE CHIEF JUSTICE AND JUSTICE POWELL join, dissenting.

I disagree with the Court that § 12945(b)(2) is not pre-empted by the Pregnancy Discrimination Act of 1978 (PDA) and § 708 of Title VII....

The second clause [of § 701(k) of Title VII] could not be clearer: it mandates that pregnant employees "shall be treated the same for all employment-related purposes" as nonpregnant employees similarly situated with respect to their ability or inability to work. This language leaves no room for preferential treatment of pregnant workers....

Contrary to the mandate of the PDA, California law requires every employer to have a disability leave policy for pregnancy even if it has none for any other disability. An employer complies with California law if it has a leave policy for pregnancy but denies it for every other disability. On its face, § 12945(b)(2) is in square conflict with the PDA and is therefore pre-empted. Because the California law permits employers to single out pregnancy for preferential treatment and therefore to violate Title VII, it is not saved by § 708 which limits pre-emption of state laws to those that require or permit an employer to commit an unfair employment practice.[1]

The majority nevertheless would save the California law on two grounds. First, it holds that the PDA does not require disability from pregnancy to be

---

[32] Because we conclude that in enacting the PDA Congress did not intend to prohibit all favorable treatment of pregnancy, we need not decide and therefore do not address the question whether § 12945(b)(2) could be upheld as a legislative response to leave policies that have a disparate impact on pregnant workers.

[1] The same clear language preventing preferential treatment based on pregnancy forecloses respondents' argument that the California provision can be upheld as a legislative response to leave policies that have a disparate impact on pregnant workers. Whatever remedies Title VII would otherwise provide for victims of disparate impact, Congress expressly ordered pregnancy to be treated in the same manner as other disabilities.

treated the same as other disabilities; instead, it forbids less favorable, but permits more favorable, benefits for pregnancy disability. The express command of the PDA is unambiguously to the contrary....

The Court's second, and equally strange, ground is that even if the PDA does prohibit special benefits for pregnant women, an employer may still comply with both the California law and the PDA: it can adopt the specified leave policies for pregnancy and at the same time afford similar benefits for all other disabilities. This is untenable. California surely had no intent to require employers to provide general disability leave benefits. It intended to prefer pregnancy and went no farther. Extension of these benefits to the entire work force would be a dramatic increase in the scope of the state law and would impose a significantly greater burden on California employers. That is the province of the California Legislature....

In sum, preferential treatment of pregnant workers is prohibited by Title VII, as amended by the PDA. Section 12945(b)(2) of the California Gov't Code, which extends preferential benefits for pregnancy, is therefore pre-empted.

NOTES

1. *The Limitations of § 701(k)*. The basic rule of § 701(k) is that employers must treat pregnancy as they treat other types of temporary disabilities. The limitations of the basic rule are apparent. If an employer can prove that it would refuse to hire *any* applicant who needed to take a leave of absence shortly after beginning work, it can refuse to hire a woman applicant *because* she is pregnant. *Ahmad v. Loyal Am. Life Ins. Co.*, 767 F. Supp. 1114 (S.D. Ala. 1991); *Marafino v. St. Louis Cty. Circuit Ct.*, 707 F.2d 1005 (8th Cir. 1983). If an employer's practice is to discharge employees if they require a leave of more than one week, the employer can discharge women who require longer leaves after giving birth to children. These types of practices would be likely to have a disparate impact on women. Should a Title VII violation be found on that basis? *See* note 32 of the majority opinion and note 1 of Justice White's dissent; *Compare Troupe v. May Dep't Stores Co.*, 20 F.3d 734, 738 (7th Cir. 1994) ("Employers can treat pregnant women just as badly as they treat similarly affected but nonpregnant employees") *with EEOC v. Warshawsky & Co.*, 768 F. Supp. 647 (N.D. Ill. 1991) (policy prohibiting sick leave during first year of employment improper). *See also Chambers v. Omaha Girls Club*, 834 F.2d 697 (8th Cir. 1987) (discharge of black woman because she became pregnant not a violation of Title VII; employer rule prohibiting employment of single persons who become pregnant or cause pregnancy justified by employer's interest in providing role models for youth); *Fleming v. Ayers & Assocs.*, 948 F.2d 993 (6th Cir. 1991) (discharge of mother of sick newborn to avoid paying health care costs of baby not a violation of Title VII); *Piantanida v. Wyman Ctr., Inc.*, 116 F.3d 340 (8th Cir. 1997) (PDA protects only pregnancy; discrimination because of plaintiff's status as a "new mom" not protected).

2. *The Limits of Guerra.* The majority in *Guerra* says that § 701(k) provides a floor but not a ceiling for pregnancy-related benefits. The Third Circuit, however, has limited that language to benefits relating to the period of actual physical disability on account of pregnancy and childbirth. Thus, a provision in a collective bargaining contract which allowed only women to take a one-year unpaid leave of absence after childbirth was found to constitute sex discrimination against men in violation of Title VII because it extended benefits beyond the period of actual physical disability. *Schafer v. Board of Pub. Educ.,* 903 F.2d 243 (3d Cir. 1990).

3. *Unpaid Leaves as a Response.* The federal government and many states have reacted to the limited protections of the Pregnancy Discrimination Act by enacting statutes that require employers to provide unpaid leaves of absence upon the birth or adoption of a child or in the event of a family illness. *See* Family and Medical Leave Act (FMLA) (discussed in Chapter 16). Are these statutes a good idea? Consider several arguments:

   1) The statutes are sex-neutral in that they permit workers of either sex to take a leave, but women will use the opportunity much more often than men which will tend to perpetuate the sexual division of labor.

   2) The statutes provide only for *unpaid* leaves and, as a result, will assist only women who need assistance the least — upper-class women. (Compare the directive on maternity leave in the European Community which requires member states to provide at least fourteen weeks of *paid* maternity leave. Council Directive 92/85, 1992 O.J. (L348) 1.)

   3) The statutes are important to the advancement of women in the workplace because they permit women to retain their seniority and with it their higher pay and job status. *See* INSTITUTE FOR WOMEN'S POLICY RESEARCH, IMPROVING EMPLOYMENT OPPORTUNITIES FOR WOMEN WORKERS: AN ASSESSMENT OF THE TENURE, ECONOMIC AND LEGAL IMPACT OF THE PREGNANCY DISCRIMINATION ACT OF 1978 (1992) (PDA had greater impact than affirmative action on women's progress in workplace because it resulted in longer job tenure and higher wages for women).

2. SEXUAL HARASSMENT

ELLISON v. BRADY

United States Court of Appeals, Ninth Circuit

924 F.2d 872 (1991)

BEEZER, CIRCUIT JUDGE: ...

Kerry Ellison worked as a revenue agent for the Internal Revenue Service in San Mateo, California. During her initial training in 1984 she met Sterling Gray, another trainee, who was also assigned to the San Mateo office. The two co-workers never became friends, and they did not work closely together.

Gray's desk was twenty feet from Ellison's desk, two rows behind and one row over. Revenue agents in the San Mateo office often went to lunch in groups. In June of 1986 when no one else was in the office, Gray asked Ellison to lunch. She accepted. Gray had to pick up his son's forgotten lunch, so they stopped by Gray's house. He gave Ellison a tour of his house.

Ellison alleges that after the June lunch Gray started to pester her with unnecessary questions and hang around her desk. On October 9, 1986, Gray asked Ellison out for a drink after work. She declined, but she suggested that they have lunch the following week. She did not want to have lunch alone with him, and she tried to stay away from the office during lunch time. One day during the following week, Gray uncharacteristically dressed in a three-piece suit and asked Ellison out for lunch. Again, she did not accept.

On October 22, 1986 Gray handed Ellison a note he wrote on a telephone message slip which read:

> I cried over you last night and I'm totally drained today. I have never been in such constant term oil (*sic*). Thank you for talking with me. I could not stand to feel your hatred for another day.

When Ellison realized that Gray wrote the note, she became shocked and frightened and left the room. Gray followed her into the hallway and demanded that she talk to him, but she left the building.

Ellison later showed the note to Bonnie Miller, who supervised both Ellison and Gray. Miller said "this is sexual harassment." Ellison asked Miller not to do anything about it. She wanted to try to handle it herself. Ellison asked a male co-worker to talk to Gray, to tell him that she was not interested in him and to leave her alone. The next day, Thursday, Gray called in sick.

Ellison did not work on Friday, and on the following Monday, she started four weeks of training in St. Louis, Missouri. Gray mailed her a card and a typed, single-spaced, three-page letter. She describes this letter as "twenty times, a hundred times weirder" than the prior note. Gray wrote, in part:

> I know that you are worth knowing with or without sex.... Leaving aside the hassles and disasters of recent weeks. I have enjoyed you so much over these past few months. Watching you. Experiencing you from O so far away. Admiring your style and elan.... Don't you think it odd that two people who have never even talked together, alone, are striking off such intense sparks ... I will [write] another letter in the near future.[1]

Explaining her reaction, Ellison stated: "I just thought he was crazy. I thought he was nuts. I didn't know what he would do next. I was frightened."

---

[1] In the middle of the long letter Gray did say "I am obligated to you so much that if you want me to leave you alone I will.... If you want me to forget you entirely, I can not do that."

She immediately telephoned Miller. Ellison told her supervisor that she was frightened and really upset. She requested that Miller transfer either her or Gray because she would not be comfortable working in the same office with him. Miller asked Ellison to send a copy of the card and letter to San Mateo.

Miller then telephoned her supervisor, Joe Benton, and discussed the problem. That same day she had a counseling session with Gray. She informed him that he was entitled to union representation. During this meeting, she told Gray to leave Ellison alone.

At Benton's request, Miller apprised the labor relations department of the situation. She also reminded Gray many times over the next few weeks that he must not contact Ellison in any way. Gray subsequently transferred to the San Francisco office on November 24, 1986. Ellison returned from St. Louis in late November and did not discuss the matter further with Miller.

After three weeks in San Francisco, Gray filed union grievances requesting a return to the San Mateo office. The IRS and the union settled the grievances in Gray's favor, agreeing to allow him to transfer back to the San Mateo office provided that he spend four more months in San Francisco and promise not to bother Ellison. On January 28, 1987, Ellison first learned of Gray's request in a letter from Miller explaining that Gray would return to the San Mateo office. The letter indicated that management decided to resolve Ellison's problem with a six-month separation, and that it would take additional action if the problem recurred.

After receiving the letter, Ellison was "frantic." She filed a formal complaint alleging sexual harassment on January 30, 1987 with the IRS. She also obtained permission to transfer to San Francisco temporarily when Gray returned.

Gray sought joint counseling. He wrote Ellison another letter which still sought to maintain the idea that he and Ellison had some type of relationship....

Ellison filed a complaint in September of 1987 in federal district court. The court granted the government's motion for summary judgment on the ground that Ellison had failed to state a prima facie case of sexual harassment due to a hostile working environment. Ellison appeals.

II

....

Courts have recognized different forms of sexual harassment. In "quid pro quo" cases, employers condition employment benefits on sexual favors. In "hostile environment" cases, employees work in offensive or abusive environments. This case ... involves a hostile environment claim.

The Supreme Court in *Meritor* [*Savings Bank v. Vinson,* 477 U.S. 57 (1986)] held that Michelle Vinson's working conditions constituted a hostile environment in violation of Title VII's prohibition of sex discrimination. Vinson's supervisor made repeated demands for sexual favors, usually at work, both during and after business hours. Vinson initially refused her employer's sexual advances, but eventually acceded because she feared losing her job. They had intercourse over forty times. She additionally testified that he "fondled her in front of other employees, followed her into the women's restroom when she went there alone, exposed himself to her, and even forcibly raped her on several occasions." The Court had no difficulty finding this environment hostile.

Since *Meritor*, we have not often reached the merits of a hostile environment sexual harassment claim. In *Jordan v. Clark*, 847 F.2d 1368, 1373 (9th Cir. 1988), *cert. denied sub nom., Jordan v. Hodel*, 488 U.S. 1006 (1989), we explained that a hostile environment exists when an employee can show (1) that he or she was subjected to sexual advances, requests for sexual favors, or other verbal or physical conduct of a sexual nature,[5] (2) that this conduct was unwelcome, and (3) that the conduct was sufficiently severe or pervasive to alter the conditions of the victim's employment and create an abusive working environment.

We had another opportunity to examine a hostile working environment claim of sexual harassment in *E.E.O.C. v. Hacienda Hotel*, 881 F.2d 1504 (9th Cir. 1989). In that case the district court found a hostile working environment where the hotel's male chief of engineering frequently made sexual comments and sexual advances to the maids, and where a female supervisor called her female employees "dog[s]" and "whore[s]."... [W]e agreed that the conduct was sufficiently severe and pervasive to alter the conditions of employment and create a hostile working environment.

III

The parties ask us to determine if Gray's conduct, as alleged by Ellison, was sufficiently severe or pervasive to alter the conditions of Ellison's employment and create an abusive working environment. The district court, with little Ninth Circuit case law to look to for guidance, held that Ellison did not state a prima facie case of sexual harassment due to a hostile working environment. It believed that Gray's conduct was "isolated and genuinely trivial." We disagree....

The Supreme Court [in *Meritor*] cautioned ... that not all harassment affects a "term, condition, or privilege" of employment within the meaning of Title VII. For example, the "mere utterance of an ethnic or racial epithet which engenders offensive feelings in an employee" is not, by itself, actionable under Title VII. To state a claim under Title VII, sexual harassment "must be sufficiently severe or pervasive to alter the conditions of the victim's employment and create an abusive working environment."...

---

[5] Here, the government argues that Gray's conduct was not of a sexual nature. The three-page letter, however, makes several references to sex and constitutes verbal conduct of a sexual nature. We need not and do not decide whether a party can state a cause of action for a sexually discriminatory working environment under Title VII when the conduct in question is not sexual. *See Andrews v. City of Philadelphia*, 895 F.2d 1469, 1485 (3d Cir. 1990) (conduct need not be sexual); *Hall v. Gus Construction Co.*, 842 F.2d 1010, 1014 (8th Cir. 1988) (conduct need not be sexual).

Although *Meritor* and our previous cases establish the framework for the resolution of hostile environment cases, they do not dictate the outcome of this case. Gray's conduct falls somewhere between forcible rape and the mere utterance of an epithet. His conduct was not as pervasive as the sexual comments and sexual advances in *Hacienda Hotel,* which we held created an unlawfully hostile working environment.

The government asks us to apply the reasoning of other courts which have declined to find Title VII violations on more egregious facts. In *Scott v. Sears, Roebuck & Co.,* 798 F.2d 210, 212 (7th Cir. 1986), the Seventh Circuit analyzed a female employee's working conditions for sexual harassment. It noted that she was repeatedly propositioned and winked at by her supervisor. When she asked for assistance, he asked "what will I get for it?" Co-workers slapped her buttocks and commented that she must moan and groan during sex. The court examined the evidence to see if "the demeaning conduct and sexual stereotyping cause[d] such anxiety and debilitation to the plaintiff that working conditions were 'poisoned' within the meaning of Title VII." The court did not consider the environment sufficiently hostile.

Similarly, in *Rabidue v. Osceola Refining Co.,* 805 F.2d 611 (6th Cir. 1986), *cert. denied,* 481 U.S. 1041 (1987), the Sixth Circuit refused to find a hostile environment where the workplace contained posters of naked and partially dressed women, and where a male employee customarily called women "whores," "cunt," "pussy," and "tits," referred to plaintiff as "fat ass," and specifically stated, "All that bitch needs is a good lay." Over a strong dissent, the majority held that the sexist remarks and the pin-up posters had only a de minimis effect and did not seriously affect the plaintiff's psychological well-being.

We do not agree with the standards set forth in *Scott* and *Rabidue,*[6] and we choose not to follow those decisions. Neither *Scott*'s search for "anxiety and debilitation" sufficient to "poison" a working environment nor *Rabidue*'s requirement that a plaintiff's psychological well-being be "seriously affected" follows directly from language in *Meritor.* It is the harasser's conduct which must be pervasive or severe, not the alteration in the conditions of employment. Surely, employees need not endure sexual harassment until their psychological well-being is seriously affected to the extent that they suffer anxiety and debilitation. Although an isolated epithet by itself fails to support a cause of action for

---

[6] We note that the Sixth Circuit has called *Rabidue* into question in at least two subsequent opinions. In *Yates v. Avco Corp.,* 819 F.2d 630, 637 (6th Cir. 1987), a panel of the Sixth Circuit expressly adopted one of the main arguments in the *Rabidue* dissent, that sexual harassment actions should be viewed from the victim's perspective. In *Davis v. Monsanto Chemical Co.,* 858 F.2d 345, 350 (6th Cir. 1988), *cert. denied,* 490 U.S. 1110 (1989), the Sixth Circuit once again criticized *Rabidue*'s limited reading of Title VII. *See also Andrews v. City of Philadelphia,* 895 F.2d 1469, 1485 (3d Cir. 1990) (explicitly rejecting *Rabidue* and holding that derogatory language directed at women and pornographic pictures of women serve as evidence of a hostile working environment).

a hostile environment, Title VII's protection of employees from sex discrimination comes into play long before the point where victims of sexual harassment require psychiatric assistance.

We have closely examined *Meritor* and our previous cases, and we believe that Gray's conduct was sufficiently severe and pervasive to alter the conditions of Ellison's employment and create an abusive working environment. We first note that the required showing of severity or seriousness of the harassing conduct varies inversely with the pervasiveness or frequency of the conduct. For example, in *Vance v. Southern Bell Telephone and Telegraph Co.*, 863 F.2d 1503, 1510 (11th Cir. 1989), the court held that two incidents in which a noose was found hung over an employee's work station were sufficiently severe to constitute a jury question on a racially hostile environment.

Next, we believe that in evaluating the severity and pervasiveness of sexual harassment, we should focus on the perspective of the victim. If we only examined whether a reasonable person would engage in allegedly harassing conduct, we would run the risk of reinforcing the prevailing level of discrimination. Harassers could continue to harass merely because a particular discriminatory practice was common, and victims of harassment would have no remedy.

We therefore prefer to analyze harassment from the victim's perspective. A complete understanding of the victim's view requires, among other things, an analysis of the different perspectives of men and women. Conduct that many men consider unobjectionable may offend many women. *See, e.g., Lipsett v. University of Puerto Rico*, 864 F.2d 881, 898 (1st Cir. 1988) ("A male supervisor might believe, for example, that it is legitimate for him to tell a female subordinate that she has a 'great figure' or 'nice legs.' The female subordinate, however, may find such comments offensive"). *See also* Ehrenreich, *Pluralist Myths and Powerless Men: The Ideology of Reasonableness in Sexual Harassment Law*, 99 Yale L.J. 1177, 1207-1208 (1990) (men tend to view some forms of sexual harassment as "harmless social interactions to which only overly-sensitive women would object"); Abrams, *Gender Discrimination and the Transformation of Workplace Norms*, 42 Vand. L. Rev. 1183, 1203 (1989) (the characteristically male view depicts sexual harassment as comparatively harmless amusement).

We realize that there is a broad range of viewpoints among women as a group, but we believe that many women share common concerns which men do not necessarily share. For example, because women are disproportionately victims of rape and sexual assault, women have a stronger incentive to be concerned with sexual behavior. Women who are victims of mild forms of sexual harassment may understandably worry whether a harasser's conduct is merely a prelude to violent sexual assault. Men, who are rarely victims of sexual assault, may view sexual conduct in a vacuum without a full appreciation of the social setting or the underlying threat of violence that a woman may perceive.

In order to shield employers from having to accommodate the idiosyncratic concerns of the rare hyper-sensitive employee, we hold that a female plaintiff states a prima facie case of hostile environment sexual harassment when she alleges conduct which a reasonable woman[11] would consider sufficiently severe or pervasive to alter the conditions of employment and create an abusive working environment.[12]

We adopt the perspective of a reasonable woman primarily because we believe that a sex-blind reasonable person standard tends to be male-biased and tends to systematically ignore the experiences of women. The reasonable woman standard does not establish a higher level of protection for women than men. Instead, a gender-conscious examination of sexual harassment enables women to participate in the workplace on an equal footing with men. By acknowledging and not trivializing the effects of sexual harassment on reasonable women, courts can work towards ensuring that neither men nor women will have to "run a gauntlet of sexual abuse in return for the privilege of being allowed to work and make a living."

We note that the reasonable victim standard we adopt today classifies conduct as unlawful sexual harassment even when harassers do not realize that their conduct creates a hostile working environment. Well-intentioned compliments by co-workers or supervisors can form the basis of a sexual harassment cause of action if a reasonable victim of the same sex as the plaintiff would consider the comments sufficiently severe or pervasive to alter a condition of employment and create an abusive working environment.[13] That is because Title VII is not a fault-based tort scheme. "Title VII is aimed at the consequences or effects of an employment practice and not at the ... motivation" of co-workers or employers. *Griggs v. Duke Power Co.,* 401 U.S. 424 (1971). To avoid liability under Title VII, employers may have to educate and sensitize their workforce to eliminate conduct which a reasonable victim would consider unlawful sexual harassment.

The facts of this case illustrate the importance of considering the victim's perspective. Analyzing the facts from the alleged harasser's viewpoint, Gray could be portrayed as a modern-day Cyrano de Bergerac wishing no more than to woo Ellison with his words. There is no evidence that Gray harbored ill will toward Ellison. He even offered in his "love letter" to leave her alone if she wished. Examined in this light, it is not difficult to see why the district court characterized Gray's conduct as isolated and trivial.

---

[11] Of course, where male employees allege that co-workers engage in conduct which creates a hostile environment, the appropriate victim's perspective would be that of a reasonable man.

[12] We realize that the reasonable woman standard will not address conduct which some women find offensive. Conduct considered harmless by many today may be considered discriminatory in the future. Fortunately, the reasonableness inquiry which we adopt today is not static. As the views of reasonable women change, so too does the Title VII standard of acceptable behavior.

[13] If sexual comments or sexual advances are in fact welcomed by the recipient, they, of course, do not constitute sexual harassment. Title VII's prohibition of sex discrimination in employment does not require a totally desexualized work place.

Ellison, however, did not consider the acts to be trivial. Gray's first note shocked and frightened her. After receiving the three-page letter, she became really upset and frightened again. She immediately requested that she or Gray be transferred. Her supervisor's prompt response suggests that she too did not consider the conduct trivial. When Ellison learned that Gray arranged to return to San Mateo, she immediately asked to transfer, and she immediately filed an official complaint.

We cannot say as a matter of law that Ellison's reaction was idiosyncratic or hyper-sensitive. We believe that a reasonable woman could have had a similar reaction. After receiving the first bizarre note from Gray, a person she barely knew, Ellison asked a co-worker to tell Gray to leave her alone. Despite her request, Gray sent her a long, passionate, disturbing letter. He told her he had been "watching" and "experiencing" her; he made repeated references to sex; he said he would write again. Ellison had no way of knowing what Gray would do next. A reasonable woman could consider Gray's conduct, as alleged by Ellison, sufficiently severe and pervasive to alter a condition of employment and create an abusive working environment....

We hope that over time both men and women will learn what conduct offends reasonable members of the other sex. When employers and employees internalize the standard of workplace conduct we establish today, the current gap in perception between the sexes will be bridged.

IV

We next must determine what remedial actions by employers shield them from liability under Title VII for sexual harassment by co-workers. The Supreme Court in *Meritor* did not address employer liability for sexual harassment by co-workers. In that case, the Court discussed employer liability for a hostile environment created by a supervisor.

The Court's discussion was brief, and it declined to issue a definitive rule. On one hand, it held that employers are not strictly liable for sexual harassment by supervisors. On the other hand, it stated that employers can be liable for sexual harassment without actual notice of the alleged discriminatory conduct. It agreed with the EEOC that courts should look to agency principles to determine liability....

The Fourth Circuit has required that a remedy be "reasonably calculated to end the harassment." *Katz v. Dole,* 709 F.2d 251, 256 (4th Cir. 1983). It has held that an employer properly remedied sexual harassment by fully investigating the allegations, issuing written warnings to refrain from discriminatory conduct, and warning the offender that a subsequent infraction will result in suspension.

Similarly, in *Barrett v. Omaha National Bank,* 726 F.2d 424, 427 (8th Cir. 1984), the Eighth Circuit held that an employer properly remedied a hostile working environment by fully investigating, reprimanding a harasser for grossly inappropriate conduct, placing the offender on probation for ninety days, and warning the offender that any further misconduct would result in discharge. The court concluded that Title VII does not require employers to fire all harassers.

We too believe that remedies should be "reasonably calculated to end the harassment." An employer's remedy should persuade individual harassers to discontinue unlawful conduct. We do not think that all harassment warrants dismissal, rather, remedies should be "assessed proportionately to the seriousness of the offense." Employers should impose sufficient penalties to assure a workplace free from sexual harassment. In essence, then, we think that the reasonableness of an employer's remedy will depend on its ability to stop harassment by the person who engaged in harassment.[17] In evaluating the adequacy of the remedy, the court may also take into account the remedy's ability to persuade potential harassers to refrain from unlawful conduct....

Here, Ellison's employer argues that it complied with its statutory obligation to provide a workplace free from sexual harassment. It promptly investigated Ellison's allegation. When Ellison returned to San Mateo from her training in St. Louis, Gray was no longer working in San Mateo. When Gray returned to San Mateo, the government granted Ellison's request to transfer temporarily to San Francisco.

We decline to accept the government's argument that its decision to return Gray to San Mateo did not create a hostile environment for Ellison because the government granted Ellison's request for a temporary transfer to San Francisco. Ellison preferred to work in San Mateo over San Francisco. We strongly believe that the victim of sexual harassment should not be punished for the conduct of the harasser. We wholeheartedly agree with the EEOC that a victim of sexual harassment should not have to work in a less desirable location as a result of an employer's remedy for sexual harassment.

Ellison maintains that the government's remedy was insufficient because it did not discipline Gray and because it allowed Gray to return to San Mateo after only a six-month separation. Even though the hostile environment had been eliminated when Gray began working in San Francisco, we cannot say that the government's response was reasonable under Title VII. The record on appeal suggests that Ellison's employer did not express strong disapproval of Gray's conduct, did not reprimand Gray, did not put him on probation, and did not inform him that repeated harassment would result in suspension or termination. Apparently, Gray's employer only told him to stop harassing Ellison. Title VII requires more than a mere request to refrain from discriminatory conduct. Employers send the wrong message to potential harassers when they do not

---

[17] We do not think that the appropriate inquiry is what a reasonable employer would do to remedy the sexual harassment. *Contra Brooms v. Regal Tube Co.*, 881 F.2d 412, 421 (7th Cir. 1989). Although employers are statutorily obligated to provide a workplace free from sexual harassment, they may be reluctant, for business reasons, to punish high ranking and highly productive employees for sexual harassment. In addition, asking what a reasonable employer would do runs the risk of reinforcing any prevailing level of discrimination by employers and fails to focus directly on the best way to eliminate sexual harassment from the workplace.

discipline employees for sexual harassment. If Ellison can prove on remand that Gray knew or should have known that his conduct was unlawful and that the government failed to take even the mildest form of disciplinary action, the district court should hold that the government's initial remedy was insufficient under Title VII. At this point, genuine issues of material fact remain concerning whether the government properly disciplined Gray.

Ellison further maintains that her employer's decision to allow Gray to transfer back to the San Mateo office after a six-month cooling-off period rendered the government's remedy insufficient. She argues that Gray's *mere presence* would create a hostile working environment.

We believe that in some cases the mere presence of an employee who has engaged in particularly severe or pervasive harassment can create a hostile working environment. To avoid liability under Title VII for failing to remedy a hostile environment, employers may even have to remove employees from the workplace if their mere presence would render the working environment hostile.[19] Once again, we examine whether the mere presence of a harasser would create a hostile environment from the perspective of a reasonable woman....

Given the scant record on appeal, we cannot determine whether a reasonable woman could conclude that Gray's mere presence at San Mateo six months after the alleged harassment would create an abusive environment. Although we are aware of the severity of Gray's conduct (which we do not consider to be as serious as some other forms of harassment), we do not know how often Ellison and Gray would have to interact at San Mateo.

Moreover, it is not clear to us that the six-month cooling-off period was reasonably calculated to end the harassment or assessed proportionately to the seriousness of Gray's conduct.... We do know that the IRS did not request Ellison's input or even inform her of the proceedings before agreeing to let Gray return to San Mateo. This failure to even attempt to determine what impact Gray's return would have on Ellison shows an insufficient regard for the victim's interest in avoiding a hostile working environment. On remand, the district court should fully explore the facts concerning the government's decision to return Gray to San Mateo....

---

[19] If harassers are not removed from the workplace when their mere presence creates a hostile nvironment, employers have not fully remedied the harassment. When employers cannot schedule harassers to work at another location or during different hours, employers may have to dismiss employees whose mere presence creates a hostile environment. We acknowledge that in rare instances dismissal may be necessary when harassers did not realize that their conduct was unlawful. However, we think that only in very, very few cases will harassers be unaware that their conduct is unlawful when that conduct is so serious that a reasonable victim would thereafter consider the harasser's mere presence sexual harassment. In those few instances, we think it only proper to conclude that the harasser should have known that his or her conduct was unlawful. In order to avoid the loss of well-intentioned productive employees, employers must educate and sensitize their workforce.

[Stephens, District Judge, filed a dissenting opinion.]

NOTES

1. *Sexual Harassment and the Models of Discrimination.* Sexual harassment cases are difficult, in part, because they do not fit easily within the disparate treatment and impact models of discrimination. Sometimes the models are useful in explaining and predicting results; at other times, they are not. For example, consider:

(a) Should a woman who is *not* subjected to sexual harassment have a claim if a promotion is given to another woman who submits to sexual advances? *King v. Palmer,* 778 F.2d 878 (D.C. Cir. 1985); *Priest v. Rotary,* 634 F. Supp. 571 (N.D. Cal. 1986) (yes). What if the person denied the promotion were a man? *DeCintio v. Westchester Cty. Med. Ctr.,* 807 F.2d 304 (2d Cir. 1986), *cert. denied,* 484 U.S. 825 (1987) (no).

(b) The courts have consistently held that Title VII's sex discrimination provisions do not protect people who are discriminated against because of their sexual orientation. *DeSantis v. Pacific Tel. & Tel. Co.,* 608 F.2d 327 (9th Cir. 1979). Should people who are subjected to homosexual advances at work be able to bring sexual harassment claims? *EEOC v. Walden Book Co.,* 885 F. Supp. 1100 (M.D. Tenn. 1995); *Joyner v. AAA Cooper Transp.,* 597 F. Supp. 537 (M.D. Ala. 1983), *aff'd,* 749 F.2d 732 (11th Cir. 1984) (yes). What about people who are harassed at work because of their homosexuality? *Compare Garcia v. Elf Atochem N.A.,* 28 F.3d 446 (5th Cir. 1994) *and Goluszek v. H.P. Smith,* 697 F. Supp. 1452 (N.D. Ill. 1988) (no) *with Doe v. City of Belleville,* 119 F.3d 563 (7th Cir. 1997) (yes).

(c) Should conduct that would be sexual harassment if it were directed only at women still violate Title VII if it is directed at both men and women equally? *Compare Rowinsky v. Bryan Indep. Sch. Dist.,* 80 F.3d 1006 (5th Cir.), *cert. denied,* 117 S. Ct. 165 (1996) (no) *with Steiner v. Showboat Oper. Co.,* 25 F.3d 1459 (9th Cir. 1994), *cert. denied,* 513 U.S. 1082 (1995) (yes).

(d) Is Title VII violated if a male sexually harasses another male? *Oncale v. Sundowner Offshore Servs., Inc.,* 83 F.3d 118 (5th Cir. 1996), *cert. granted,* 117 S. Ct. 2430 (1997) (no). What if a female sexually harasses another female? *Nogueras v. University of Puerto Rico,* 890 F. Supp. 60 (D.P.R. 1995) (yes).

Some have argued that courts in sexual harassment cases have rejected the treatment and impact theories and adopted instead Professor MacKinnon's dominance theory. Cass R. Sunstein, *Feminism and Legal Theory,* 101 HARV. L. REV. 826, 829 (1988). Does that theory do a better job of explaining these cases?

2. *Evidence of Sexual Harassment.* Should there be any limits on the types of evidence used to prove sexual harassment? Should women be able to rely on the presence of nude pinups in the workplace to support their claims? *Robinson v. Jacksonville Shipyards, Inc.,* 760 F. Supp. 1486 (M.D. Fla. 1991) (yes). Should they be able to point to sexist advertising of the employer's product which alleg-

edly fosters harassment in the workplace? *Haston v. Stroh Brewing Co.,* No. C1-91-12990 (Minn. Dist. Ct., filed Nov. 8, 1991) (no). Do these types of evidence raise First Amendment concerns? *See* Cynthia L. Estlund, *Freedom of Expression in the Workplace and the Problem of Discriminatory Harassment,* 75 TEX. L. REV. 687 (1997).

On the other side of the ledger, should an employer be able to defend by arguing that a woman's claim of *unwelcome* sexual comments was not credible because she had appeared as a nude centerfold in a magazine? *Burns v. McGregor Elec. Indus.,* 807 F. Supp. 506 (N.D. Iowa 1992), *rev'd,* 989 F.2d 959 (8th Cir. 1993) (district court said plaintiff not credible; court of appeals reversed). Or that the claim of sexual advances itself was not credible because of the woman's appearance?:

> The Court notes that at the time of the alleged sexual advance, [the complainant] Young wore little or no make up and her hair was not colored in any way. Considering the appearance of [the alleged harasser] Davidson's wife (D. Ex. 10), it is obvious that Young's appearance at the time was not attractive to Davidson.

Young v. Mariner Corp., 56 Empl. Prac. Dec. (CCH) ¶ 40,814 at 67,282 n.1 (N.D. Ala. 1991) (finding for employer). *See Meritor Sav. Bank v. Vinson,* 477 U.S. 57, 68-69 (1986) (evidence of complainant's sexually provocative dress and sexual fantasies not *per se* inadmissible*).

A recent amendment to Rule 412 of the Federal Rules of Evidence limits the use of evidence of victim sexual behavior and sexual predisposition in sexual harassment cases. The amendment prohibits the introduction of such evidence unless the proponent can demonstrate that "its probative value substantially outweighs the danger of harm to any victim and of unfair prejudice to any party." FED. R. EVID. 412(b)(2). The notes of the Advisory Committee on the amendment indicate that the rule should generally exclude evidence of the victim's mode of dress, speech, or life-style and should also limit discovery of evidence of sexual behavior and sexual predisposition.

3. *Employer Liability.* In Title VII cases other than hostile environment sexual harassment cases (including *quid pro quo* harassment cases), employers are strictly liable under the doctrine of respondeat superior. It does not matter whether the employer knew about the discrimination, should have known, or took steps to correct it. But in hostile environment cases, as *Ellison* indicates, employers are only subject to "notice" liability: They are liable only if they knew about the harassment or should have known and, even then, only if they failed to take immediate and effective steps to remedy the situation.

This liability scheme raises a number of difficult issues. For example, when does an employer threat or action rise to the level of *quid pro quo* harassment? *Compare Gary v. Long,* 59 F.3d 1391, 1396 (D.C. Cir.), *cert. denied,* 116 S. Ct. 569 (1995) ("saber rattling alone" is insufficient; supervisor must actually wield authority to subject victim to adverse job consequences) *with Nichols v. Frank*, 42 F.3d 503, 513 (9th Cir. 1994) (supervisor's "intertwining" of request for sexual favors with discussion of job benefits or detriments constitutes *quid pro quo* discrimination). And what constitutes proper notice to an employer? *See Davis v. City of Sioux City*, 115 F.3d 1365 (8th Cir. 1997) (harassment by high-level supervisor insufficient to impute knowledge to employer); *Van Zant v. KLM Royal Dutch Airlines*, 80 F.3d 708 (2d Cir. 1996) (notice to line supervisor insufficient to impute knowledge to company because he was "too low in the hierarchy"). *See generally Jansen v. Packaging Corp. of America*, 123 F.3d 490 (7th Cir. 1997) (en banc), *cert. granted in part*, 118 S. Ct. 876 (1998) (nine separate opinions discussing standards of liability in harassment cases); *Faragher v. City of Boca Raton*, 111 F.3d 1530 (11th Cir.) (en banc), *cert. granted*, 118 S. Ct. 438 (1997) (four separate opinions discussing whether city was responsible for hostile environment harassment).

The liability scheme has been severely criticized. Some contend that the different standard of liability for hostile environment cases indicates that the "courts simply perceive this form of harassment as less serious than [other forms of discrimination]." Susan R. Estrich, *Sex at Work*, 43 STAN. L. REV. 813, 856 (1991). Others mount a more far-reaching attack and suggest fundamental changes to the liability scheme for all types of employment discrimination:

> I reject the commonly invoked distinctions between quid pro quo and hostile environment harassment, between harassment and discriminatory decisions, and between supervisor and coworker conduct. Instead, employers should be strictly liable for systemic discrimination and subject to conditional notice liability for individual claims of discrimination. The proposed notice liability regime requires employers to adopt internal complaint procedures that reduce the cost victims must bear when they give notice of discriminatory conduct. It also gives victims an incentive to share their private information about potential discrimination. Once employers have notice, the postnotice standard of care requires them to provide rightful place relief and pay the attorneys' fees of prevailing claimants.

J. Hoult Verkerke, *Notice Liability in Employment Discrimination Law*, 81 VA. L. REV. 273, 279 (1995).

4. *Damages.* Prior to the Civil Rights Act of 1991, the damages available under Title VII for sexual harassment were inadequate — Title VII did not authorize compensatory or punitive damages. As a result, plaintiffs would often join their Title VII claims with claims under state contract or tort law, which provided opportunities *and* raised new sets of issues. *See Moffett v. Gene B. Glick Co.*, 621 F. Supp. 244 (N.D. Ind. 1985) (plaintiff entitled to $66,640 in compensatory damages and $15,000 in punitive damages under state law); *Brooms v. Regal Tube Co.*, 881 F.2d 412 (7th Cir. 1989) (state claims dismissed because of exclusivity of workers' compensation remedy). The Civil Rights Act of 1991 amended Title VII to permit compensatory and punitive damages (up to certain limits) which eases, but does not eliminate, the problem with remedies in sexual harassment cases. When employers are found liable for sexual harassment, should they be allowed to sue the harassing supervisor (or other employee) for indemnity? *Biggs v. Surrey Broadcasting Co.,* 811 P.2d 111 (Okla. Ct. App. 1991) (yes).

HARRIS v. FORKLIFT SYSTEMS, INC.

United States Supreme Court
510 U.S. 17 (1993)

JUSTICE O'CONNOR, delivered the opinion for a unanimous Court.

In this case we consider the definition of a discriminatorily "abusive work environment" (also known as a "hostile work environment") under Title VII of the Civil Rights Act of 1964.

I

Teresa Harris worked as a manager at Forklift Systems, Inc., an equipment rental company, from April 1985 until October 1987. Charles Hardy was Forklift's president.

The Magistrate found that, throughout Harris' time at Forklift, Hardy often insulted her because of her gender and often made her the target of unwanted sexual innuendos. Hardy told Harris on several occasions, in the presence of other employees, "You're a woman, what do you know" and "We need a man as the rental manager"; at least once, he told her she was "a dumb ass woman." Again in front of others, he suggested that the two of them "go to the Holiday Inn to negotiate [Harris'] raise." Hardy occasionally asked Harris and other female employees to get coins from his front pants pocket. He threw objects on the ground in front of Harris and other women, and asked them to pick the objects up. He made sexual innuendos about Harris' and other women's clothing.

In mid-August 1987, Harris complained to Hardy about his conduct. Hardy said he was surprised that Harris was offended, claimed he was only joking, and apologized. He also promised he would stop, and based on this assurance Harris stayed on the job. But in early September, Hardy began anew: While Harris was arranging a deal with one of Forklift's customers, he asked her, again in front of other employees, "What did you do, promise the guy ... some [sex] Saturday night?" On October 1, Harris collected her paycheck and quit.

Harris then sued Forklift, claiming that Hardy's conduct had created an abusive work environment for her because of her gender. The United States District Court for the Middle District of Tennessee, adopting the report and recommendation of the Magistrate, found this to be "a close case," but held that Hardy's conduct did not create an abusive environment. The court found that some of Hardy's comments "offended [Harris], and would offend the reasonable woman," but that they were not

> "so severe as to be expected to seriously affect [Harris'] psychological well-being. A reasonable woman manager under like circumstances would have been offended by Hardy, but his conduct would not have risen to the level of interfering with that person's work performance.
>
> "Neither do I believe that [Harris] was subjectively so offended that she suffered injury.... Although Hardy may at times have genuinely offended [Harris], I do not believe that he created a working environment so poisoned as to be intimidating or abusive to [Harris]." ...

We granted certiorari to resolve a conflict among the Circuits on whether conduct, to be actionable as "abusive work environment" harassment (no *quid pro quo* harassment issue is present here), must "seriously affect [an employee's] psychological well-being" or lead the plaintiff to "suffe[r] injury."

II

Title VII of the Civil Rights Act of 1964 makes it "an unlawful employment practice for an employer ... to discriminate against any individual with respect to his compensation, terms, conditions, or privileges of employment, because of such individual's race, color, religion, sex, or national origin." 42 U.S.C. § 2000e-2(a)(1). As we made clear in *Meritor Savings Bank v. Vinson*, 477 U.S. 57 (1986), this language "is not limited to 'economic' or 'tangible' discrimination. The phrase 'terms, conditions, or privileges of employment' evinces a congressional intent 'to strike at the entire spectrum of disparate treatment of men and women' in employment," which includes requiring people to work in a discriminatorily hostile or abusive environment. *Id.*, at 64. When the workplace is permeated with "discriminatory intimidation, ridicule, and insult," 477 U.S., at 65, that is "sufficiently severe or pervasive to alter the conditions of the victim's employment and create an abusive working environment," *id.*, at 67, Title VII is violated.

This standard, which we reaffirm today, takes a middle path between making actionable any conduct that is merely offensive and requiring the conduct to cause a tangible psychological injury. As we pointed out in *Meritor*, "mere utterance of an ... epithet which engenders offensive feelings in a employee" does not sufficiently affect the conditions of employment to implicate Title VII. Conduct that is not severe or pervasive enough to create an objectively hostile or abusive work environment — an environment that a reasonable person would find hostile or abusive — is beyond Title VII's purview. Likewise, if the victim does not subjectively perceive the environment to be abusive, the conduct has not actually altered the conditions of the victim's employment, and there is no Title VII violation.

But Title VII comes into play before the harassing conduct leads to a nervous breakdown. A discriminatorily abusive work environment, even one that does not seriously affect employees' psychological well-being, can and often will detract from employees' job performance, discourage employees from remaining on the job, or keep them from advancing in their careers. Moreover, even without regard to these tangible effects, the very fact that the discriminatory conduct was so severe or pervasive that it created a work environment abusive to employees because of their race, gender, religion, or national origin offends Title VII's broad rule of workplace equality. The appalling conduct alleged in *Meritor*, and the reference in that case to environments "so heavily polluted with discrimination as to destroy completely the emotional and psychological stability of minority group workers," merely present some especially egregious examples of harassment. They do not mark the boundary of what is actionable.

We therefore believe the District Court erred in relying on whether the conduct "seriously affect[ed] plaintiff's psychological well-being" or led her to "suffe[r] injury." Such an inquiry may needlessly focus the factfinder's attention on concrete psychological harm, an element Title VII does not require. Certainly Title VII bars conduct that would seriously affect a reasonable person's psychological well-being, but the statute is not limited to such conduct. So long as the environment would reasonably be perceived, and is perceived, as hostile or abusive, there is no need for it also to be psychologically injurious.

This is not, and by its nature cannot be, a mathematically precise test. We need not answer today all the potential questions it raises, nor specifically address the EEOC's new regulations on this subject, *see* 58 Fed. Reg. 51266 (1993) (proposed 29 CFR §§ 1609.1, 1609.2) [Editors' note: The proposed regulations attracted substantial opposition and were later withdrawn]; *see also* 29 CFR § 1604.11 (1993). But we can say that whether an environment is "hostile" or "abusive" can be determined only by looking at all the circumstances. These may include the frequency of the discriminatory conduct; its severity; whether it is physically threatening or humiliating, or a mere offensive utterance; and whether it unreasonably interferes with an employee's work performance. The effect on the employee's psychological well-being is, of course, relevant to determining whether the plaintiff actually found the environment abusive. But while psychological harm, like any other relevant factor, may be taken into account, no single factor is required.

III

Forklift, while conceding that a requirement that the conduct seriously affect psychological well-being is unfounded, argues that the District Court nonetheless correctly applied the *Meritor* standard. We disagree. Though the District Court did conclude that the work environment was not "intimidating or abusive to [Harris]," it did so only after finding that the conduct was not "so severe as to be expected to seriously affect plaintiff's psychological well-being," and that Harris was not "subjectively so offended that she suffered injury." The District Court's application of these incorrect standards may well have influenced its ultimate conclusion, especially given that the court found this to be a "close case."

We therefore reverse the judgment of the Court of Appeals, and remand the case for further proceedings consistent with this opinion.

So ordered.

JUSTICE SCALIA, concurring.

Meritor Savings Bank v. Vinson, 477 U.S. 57 (1986), held that Title VII prohibits sexual harassment that takes the form of a hostile work environment. The Court stated that sexual harassment is actionable if it is "sufficiently severe or pervasive 'to alter the conditions of [the victim's] employment and create an abusive work environment.'" *Id.*, at 67. Today's opinion elaborates that the challenged conduct must be severe or pervasive enough "to create an objectively hostile or abusive work environment — an environment that a reasonable person would find hostile or abusive."

"Abusive" (or "hostile," which in this context I take to mean the same thing) does not seem to me a very clear standard — and I do not think clarity is at all increased by adding the adverb "objectively" or by appealing to a "reasonable person's" notion of what the vague word means. Today's opinion does list a number of factors that contribute to abusiveness, but since it neither says how much of each is necessary (an impossible task) nor identifies any single factor as determinative, it thereby adds little certitude. As a practical matter, today's holding lets virtually unguided juries decide whether sex-related conduct engaged in (or permitted by) an employer is egregious enough to warrant an award of damages. One might say that what constitutes "negligence" (a traditional jury question) is not much more clear and certain than what constitutes "abusiveness." Perhaps so. But the class of plaintiffs seeking to recover for negligence is limited to those who have suffered harm, whereas under this statute "abusiveness" is to be the test of whether legal harm has been suffered, opening more expansive vistas of litigation.

Be that as it may, I know of no alternative to the course the Court today has taken. One of the factors mentioned in the Court's nonexhaustive list — whether the conduct unreasonably interferes with an employee's work performance — would, if it were made an absolute test, provide greater guidance to juries and employers. But I see no basis for such a limitation in the language of the statute. Accepting *Meritor*'s interpretation of the term "conditions of employment" as the law, the test is not whether work has been impaired, but whether working conditions have been discriminatorily altered. I know of no test more faithful to the inherently vague statutory language than the one the Court today adopts. For these reasons, I join the opinion of the Court.

JUSTICE GINSBURG, concurring.

Today the Court reaffirms the holding of *Meritor Savings Bank v. Vinson*, 477 U.S. 57, 66 (1986): "[A] plaintiff may establish a violation of Title VII by proving that discrimination based on sex has created a hostile or abusive work environment." The critical issue, Title VII's text indicates, is whether members of one sex are exposed to disadvantageous terms or conditions of employment to which members of the other sex are not exposed. *See* 42 U.S.C. § 2000e-2(a)(1) (declaring that it is unlawful to discriminate with respect to, *inter alia*, "terms" or "conditions" of employment). As the Equal Employment Opportunity Commission emphasized, the adjudicator's inquiry should center, dominantly, on whether the discriminatory conduct has unreasonably interfered with the plaintiff's work performance. To show such interference, "the plaintiff need not prove that his or her tangible productivity has declined as a result of the harassment." *Davis v. Monsanto Chemical Co.*, 858 F.2d 345, 349 (6th Cir. 1988). It suffices to prove that a reasonable person subjected to the discriminatory conduct would find, as the plaintiff did, that the harassment so altered working conditions as to "ma[k]e it more difficult to do the job." *Davis* concerned race-based discrimination, but that difference does not alter the analysis; except in the rare case in which a bona fide occupational qualification is shown, *see Automobile Workers v. Johnson Controls, Inc.*, 499 U.S. 187, 200-207 (1991), Title VII declares discriminatory practices based on race, gender, religion, or national origin equally unlawful.[*]

The Court's opinion, which I join, seems to me in harmony with the view expressed in this concurring statement.

NOTES

1. *The Fate of the Reasonable Woman Standard.* The Court did not make any holding on the reasonable woman standard, but it did hint. The Court's unanimous opinion pointedly used the reasonable person standard twice. And Justice Ginsburg, who is likely to be one of the more liberal members of the Court on this issue, also used that standard in her concurring opinion. If the Court were squarely faced with a choice between the reasonable woman and reasonable person standards, the odds would have to heavily favor the latter. Nevertheless, cases subsequent to *Harris* indicate that not all Courts are inclined to follow the hints. *Compare Steiner v. Showboat Oper. Co.*, 25 F.3d 1459 (9th Cir. 1994), *cert. denied*, 513 U.S. 1082 (1995) (applying reasonable woman standard) *with DeAngelis v. El Paso Mun. Police Officers Ass'n*, 51 F.3d 591 (5th Cir.), *cert. denied*, 116 S. Ct. 473 (1995) (applying reasonable person standard).

2. *Does the Reasonable Woman Standard Matter?* The reasonable person standard is flexible and, hence, may permit gender to be considered as one factor in determining the reactions of a reasonable person. Thus, the reasonable woman

---

[*] Indeed, even under the Court's equal protection jurisprudence, which requires "an exceedingly persuasive justification" for a gender-based classification, *Kirchberg v. Feenstra*, 450 U.S. 455, 461 (1981), it remains an open question whether "classifications based upon gender are inherently suspect." *See Mississippi Univ. for Women v. Hogan*, 458 U.S. 718, 724, and n.9 (1982).

standard requires an instruction that "the jury should consider the events from the perspective of a reasonable woman," while the reasonable person standard may permit an instruction that "the jury should consider the events from the perspective of a reasonable person of the plaintiff's gender." For a discussion, *see Radtke v. Everett*, 501 N.W.2d 155 (Mich. 1993) (holding that the reasonable person standard is to be applied under the Michigan Civil Rights Act).

3. *The Hardy and the Susceptible. Harris* requires plaintiffs to prove that the work environment is both objectively and subjectively hostile. Thus, if the environment would not have been hostile to a reasonable person (or woman), a particularly susceptible plaintiff would fail to make out a claim even if she suffered severe personal injury. At the other end of the spectrum, even if a reasonable person (or woman) would have considered the environment to be quite hostile, a particularly hardy plaintiff would fail if she could not prove that she personally perceived the environment to be hostile.

4. *Too Far ... Or Not Far Enough.* Has sexual harassment doctrine gone too far? Consider the following:

> Some of the best creative work ever to come out of offices *I've* worked in ... has been produced by teams of men *and* women showing off for each other, getting the best from each other's brains, enjoying each others' *company* as well as their work. There is synergy — is that the word? — there's ... electricity ... excitement ... lucky management! Mostly the sexual tension doesn't lead anywhere. If it does ... an affair ensues ... the participants are smart enough to keep it hushed up. Nobody wants to work around two people in *love* ... yuccck! Many office affairs have led to marriage, of course; the ones that haven't have frequently at least provided *pleasure* without hurting the P & L.
>
> I think we should come down hard on the bullies and creeps but not go stamping out sexual *chemistry* at work.

Helen Gurley Brown, *At Work, Sexual Electricity Sparks Creativity,* WALL ST. J., Oct. 29, 1991.[*]

Or, has sexual harassment doctrine not gone far enough? Consider the following:

> As things stand now, we protect the right of a few to have "consensual" sex in the workplace ... at the cost of exposing the overwhelming majority to oppression and indignity at work. Is the benefit to the few so great as to outweigh the costs to so many more? I think not. For my part, I would have no objection to rules which prohibited men and women from sexual relations in the workplace, at least with those who worked directly for them. Men and women could, of course, violate the rule; but the power to complain, once in the hands of the less powerful, might well "chill" sexual relations by evening the balance of power between the two....

---

[*] Reprinted with permission.

[This change, or even less drastic ones I have proposed in this article, would] require employers to take responsibility for their workplaces, to ensure that they are no more dangerous to a woman's psyche than to her body.

Susan R. Estrich, *Sex at Work,* 43 STAN. L. REV. 813, 860-61 (1991).[*]

B. AGE DISCRIMINATION

AUNGST v. WESTINGHOUSE ELECTRIC CORP.

United States Court of Appeals, Seventh Circuit

937 F.2d 1216 (1991)

MANION, CIRCUIT JUDGE.

Engineer Robert D. Aungst, a 35-year Westinghouse employee, was terminated in 1983 during a reduction in force (RIF). He brought this action under the Age Discrimination in Employment Act (ADEA) alleging that Westinghouse ... terminated him because of his age....

Aungst graduated in 1948 from Pittsburgh's Carnegie Institute of Technology with a bachelor's degree in electrical engineering, and immediately went to work for Westinghouse....

Aungst worked with capacitor units, which are used by utilities in the transmission and distribution of electric power. Although he briefly worked with protective devices in 1949, that same year he was permanently assigned to the capacitor section and began designing capacitor units. He eventually found his niche in designing the "Autotrol," a particular kind of capacitor. Autotrol is a Westinghouse trade name for a polemounted capacitor unit. Autotrols are one of the least complicated forms of capacitor, and Aungst apparently mastered their design quickly. As he continued designing Autotrols year after year, he became comfortable with the nickname "Mr. Autotrol." His very infrequent forays into working on more complicated capacitor units were not always successful.

Aungst was a customer order Autotrol engineer, which meant that he assembled existing devices and components into a design that met customer specifications. By contrast, fundamental development or design engineers hypothesized, created and tested new uses for capacitors....

Pursuant to a 1983 company-wide reorganization, the Westinghouse Bloomington facility was ordered to make a 10 percent across the board reduction in "managed costs," thus requiring substantial reductions in its staff of 155 salaried employees. The Bloomington plant was restructured by William Westlake, the plant and division manager. He named Frank Frederick, formerly manager of the marketing department, to manage the new capacitor department, and Frederick was ordered to make staff reductions in both his old and new departments. In the marketing department, Frederick decided to terminate two employees who were each under 30 years old. In the capacitor department Frederick selected Aungst for termination.... Frederick claims to have wanted more versatility in the department; he concluded that although Aungst's work performance with Autotrols was good, he was the least versatile and creative engineer in the department, and his tasks were the easiest to perform. He also was aware that Aungst had more problems with employees on the shop floor than other engineers. Aungst was 60 years old at the time of his termination. Overall, during the Westinghouse RIF of December 1983, 15 employees were terminated. Eight were in the ADEA's protected age group (between age 40 and 70), seven were not.

Frederick chose Tom Wilkinson, also a 60-year-old engineer with an even longer tenure at Westinghouse and a higher salary than Aungst, to replace Aungst in responding to Autotrol orders. Wilkinson also continued to perform his other engineering responsibilities.... John Warkentin, 51, backed Wilkinson up on Autotrol orders. Warkentin's old job in another division was eliminated during the RIF, so Frederick brought him into the new capacitor department, where he spent about half his time on customer order engineering, including Autotrols. Two younger engineers were retained by Frederick: Steve Seaton, 27, and Joe Kile, 25. Both were fundamental development or design engineers, and neither worked on Autotrols.

Frederick made a number of other employment decisions during the reorganization, some of which resulted in older employees being retained over younger employees. The net result was this: prior to the reorganization, eight of 12 engineers in the capacitor department were in the ADEA's protected age group; after the reorganization, 11 of 14 were in the protected age group. (The capacitor department had been one of six divisions in the Transmission and Distribution Business Unit. Those six divisions were combined into three divisions during the reorganization, which explains why the new capacitor department had two more members despite the reduction in force.) ...

A jury determined that Westinghouse willfully discriminated against Aungst by choosing him for the RIF. Aungst appeals from the district court's decision to grant Westinghouse's JNOV motion....

Under the ADEA, it is unlawful "for an employer ... to fail or refuse to hire or to discharge any individual or otherwise discriminate against an individual ... because of such individual's age." [ADEA § 623(a)].... "[A] terminated plaintiff's ultimate burden in an age discrimination case is to prove that he was discharged because of his age." But Aungst must clear another hurdle in this case — he must also prove that the decision by Westinghouse to unlawfully terminate him was made "willfully." That is because Aungst concededly did not bring this claim within two years of the firing; the ADEA provides that an action "may be commenced within two years after the cause of action accrued ... except that a cause of action arising out of a willful violation may be commenced within three years after the cause of action accrued...." [ADEA § 626(e)(1); Portal-to-Portal Act § 255.] ...[*]

Aungst contends that he put forth sufficient evidence to support the jury's verdict of willful discrimination. Westinghouse concedes that Aungst made out a prima facie case of age discrimination under the burden-shifting method of proof for Title VII cases described in *McDonnell Douglas Corp. v. Green,* 411 U.S. 792 (1973), and later applied to ADEA cases. Aungst proved that he: 1) was within the protected class; 2) was performing his job to the employer's satisfaction; 3) was terminated; and 4) others not in the protected age group were treated more favorably.

This shifted the burden of production to Westinghouse to show a legitimate, non-discriminatory reason for Aungst's termination. Once a plaintiff proves a prima facie case, "a rebuttable presumption of discrimination arises and the burden shifts to the [employer] to articulate a legitimate non-discriminatory reason for the discharge. This burden, however, is merely a burden of production ... that is not difficult to satisfy." Westinghouse offers several lawful reasons for the termination, while pointing out that the firing occurred only because of a reduction in force. First, Westinghouse argues that Aungst was replaced by someone his own age, and that the only younger engineers retained were performing work that Aungst did not do and could not have done, even with retraining. Second, due to the RIF, Westinghouse was forced to make do with fewer engineers, and needed more versatility. Westinghouse argues that Aungst, who worked almost exclusively in Autotrol production for many years, was the least versatile engineer.

Given the explanation produced by Westinghouse, Aungst now had to "prove by a preponderance of the evidence that the reasons offered by [Westinghouse] were not its true reasons but were merely a pretext for discrimination." Aungst was required to disprove each of these "specific explanations" for Westinghouse's actions. Further, "in cases of corporate reorganization a plaintiff must come forward with 'additional direct, circumstantial, or statistical evidence that age was a factor in his termination....'" "[A]n ADEA plaintiff who has been terminated amidst a corporate reorganization carries a greater burden of supporting charges of discrimination than an employee who was not terminated for similar reasons."...

Because there is no "smoking gun" evidence that Frederick willfully fired Aungst because of his age, Aungst must rely on the indirect method of proof to show pretext. In essence, he must disprove Westinghouse's primary reason for

---

[*] The time limit for filing a court action under the ADEA has changed since this case was decided. The two- or three-year statute of limitations based on the Portal-to-Portal Act no longer applies. Instead, the time periods for filing an action generally follow the Title VII limits: plaintiffs may file a court action any time later than sixty days after filing a charge with the E.E.O.C. and, if one exists, the state fair employment practices agency. The action must be filed no later than ninety days after receiving a right-to-sue letter from the E.E.O.C. ADEA §§ 7(d) & (e).

choosing him for the RIF — lack of versatility. Under the three-part analysis from *LaMontagne [v. American Convenience Products, Inc.,* 750 F.2d 1405 (7th Cir. 1984)], Aungst must show that Frederick was not really concerned with versatility, or that if he was, Aungst was fired for reasons other than lack of versatility. If lack of versatility was the actual reason, Aungst must show that lack of versatility should not have caused Aungst to be chosen for the RIF. In other words, after Westinghouse met its burden of producing reasons for the discharge, the burden of proof remained with Aungst, but now he needed to do more than merely restate his prima facie case. He needed to come up with some evidence to disprove the legitimate explanations offered by Westinghouse....

Aungst presents no evidence to counter Frederick's lengthy testimony regarding the need for versatility, or to show that Aungst was actually fired for reasons unrelated to versatility.... Frederick's testimony established that: 1) versatility was his most important criterion for decisionmaking; 2) he thought Aungst was the least versatile engineer; 3) Aungst worked in customer order engineering, and the two younger engineers [who were retained] were in a completely separate section [in the same department] doing separate work; and 4) he did not think Aungst had any experience doing fuse design or fundamental development. Other testimony and documentary evidence established that when Aungst departed, his Autotrol work in the customer order section was divided among two engineers within the ADEA's protected age group, both of whom performed other work and were more versatile than Aungst. Further, Aungst's superiors testified that they did not believe he had the expertise to do more complicated work, and that even with further training, he would not have been able to do the work performed by Seaton and Kile. Aungst himself testified that he had never done fuse design, and had not worked on capacitor unit design since 1963.

Aungst had the burden to counter Westinghouse's "specific explanations" for its decision in a manner that showed these factors were mere pretext for age discrimination. Not only did he not meet that basic burden, he certainly did not meet the "greater burden" of specific evidence of pretext required in a reorganization or RIF case. Aungst testified that he could have performed fundamental development or fuse design work, but a plaintiff's self-serving testimony regarding his own ability is "insufficient to contradict an employer's negative assessment of that ability." Aungst also introduced evidence of: a merit pay increase shortly before his termination; Performance Management System charts that described his good work performance; and a letter of recommendation written by his former boss to help him in an application for a teaching position. However, none of these pieces of evidence responds to Westinghouse's reasons for terminating him — the need for versatility in the context of a reduction in force. Westinghouse never argued that Aungst was an incompetent Autotrol engineer; to the contrary, his work performance and experience in that narrow area were generally considered an asset....

Finally, and significantly, Aungst does not come close to meeting the higher standard necessary for a willful violation of the ADEA — that Westinghouse "knew or showed reckless disregard for the matter of whether its conduct was prohibited by the ADEA." An employer's conduct is not "willful" when the employer acts reasonably in determining its legal obligations, or even when it acts unreasonably, so long as its conduct is not reckless. Willfulness usually means "conduct that is not merely negligent." Frederick was the sole decision-maker, so Aungst needed to show Frederick's intent to recklessly flaunt the ADEA's requirements. Yet, as we have already discussed, the uncontroverted evidence shows that: Frederick divided Aungst's work between two engineers who were within the ADEA's protected class; the average age of engineers in the capacitor department went up after the reorganization; Frederick made a number of other employment decisions that benefited older employees over younger employees; and, Frederick, who began working with the engineering capacitor department in 1980, was not aware that Aungst had ever done development work, and did not believe Aungst could work with fuse design or fundamental development. There is no evidence from which the jury could conclude that Frederick willfully violated the ADEA in selecting Aungst for the RIF.... Even assuming that Aungst could prove that Westinghouse unlawfully terminated him because of his age, he would *not* win this case. That is because Aungst has failed to present *any* evidence that Frederick sought to willfully fire him because of his age, in reckless defiance of the ADEA. Age discrimination is not necessarily willful, and plaintiffs who wait until nearly three years beyond the alleged discrimination should be warned that the statute requires more evidence, specifically relating to the intent and knowledge of the employer, in order to prove that an ADEA violation was willful. Aungst had no evidence of that sort here.

Aungst appears to have been a reliable, loyal employee of Westinghouse for 35 years. But the ADEA is not a tenure statute; a plaintiff must show that his age was the cause of his termination. "[T]he age discrimination law does not protect an older employee from being fired without good cause. It protects him from being fired because of his age."... Aungst failed to provide any evidence to counter Westinghouse's reasons for choosing him for the RIF....

We agree with [District] Judge Noland's conclusion that "no jury could reasonably conclude that age was a determining factor in the decision to terminate Aungst's employment." The district court therefore correctly granted JNOV for Westinghouse....

CUDAHY, CIRCUIT JUDGE, dissenting.

In setting aside a jury verdict the evidence must be viewed in the light most favorable to the party prevailing before the jury. It seems to me the majority opinion places great weight on the testimony of Frank Frederick, who apparently selected Aungst for elimination, and no weight at all on the testimony of Aungst, which is characterized as "self-serving." The jury may well have exactly reversed the order of reliance and hence reached a different conclusion. It also may have believed, consistent with the district court's instructions, that the decision regarding Aungst's termination was influenced by executives outside the capacitor department: thus the jury may have deemed critical the EEO officer's confession to feeling a "moral obligation" to the company's younger employees, or the fact that out of the seven engineers terminated in the Bloomington plant's RIF, six were within ADEA's protection.

The heavy reliance placed on "versatility" by Westinghouse's argument and by the majority here seems to me misplaced. "Versatile" may be virtually a synonym for "young." It is not infrequently the case that long-term employees tend to become specialized, doing primarily the things that they do best and doing them with the encouragement of their employer. Indeed in this case Aungst worked in capacitor unit design (the discipline one of his younger successors was learning) for fourteen years before the company began limiting his assignments to autotrol design. New employees, on the other hand, have been exposed to many facets of the work. They may be uniformly capable of undertaking a wide array of tasks — all perhaps with an equal degree of inexperience. Aungst received substantial increases in pay and excellent ratings on his work — right up to the time he was let go. "Versatility" apparently became an issue only when the RIF arrived or perhaps when litigation threatened. Admittedly, the requirement of willfulness makes this a very close case,[1] but I would let the jury verdict stand.

NOTES

1. *Age Discrimination and the Life Cycle Model.* The life cycle model helps to explain the special vulnerabilities of older workers. Under the life cycle model, workers at the end of their careers receive wages in excess of their marginal productivity. This is not a gift by the employer, but a deferred payment for earlier periods when marginal productivity exceeded wages. This pattern, however, exposes older workers to distinct risks:

> The primary risk is that an employer under financial stress may come to see an expensive senior employee as an unaffordable luxury, regardless of implicit contractual obligations.... [A second risk] directly tied to the first is that if an employee were to lose her employment, there would be a strong disincentive to any subsequent employer hiring her.... An older employee already at (or near) the end stage of the employment cycle would present an unduly expensive investment for a new employer. The employer would have to invest in firm-specific training of the older worker, the worker would

---

[1] I find telling, however, the trial judge's first opinion — issued in denying the defendant's motion for summary judgment on the discrimination count — that Westinghouse's repeated offers of early retirement to Aungst (beginning before the company hired the two younger, inexperienced engineers) were probative of willfulness.

expect a high wage, and the older employee might be retiring within a few years. For an employer to hire an older employee at the wage such an employee would normally command within the firm's employment scale simply would be economically irrational. Further, because a reduction in pay to a level approximating productivity would appear to be a dignitary affront to the employee and would be potentially disruptive within the firm, the life-cycle wage pattern has the predictable effect of freezing unemployed older workers out of the job market altogether.

Samuel Issacharoff & Erica Worth, *Is Age Discrimination Really Age Discrimination?: The ADEA's Unnatural Solution*, 72 N.Y.U. L. REV. 780, 791-92 (1997).

   2. *Disparate Impact Discrimination Under the ADEA*. The courts of appeal are split on whether the disparate impact model of discrimination is available in ADEA cases. *See, e.g., Ellis v. United Airlines, Inc.*, 73 F.3d 999 (10th Cir.), *cert. denied*, 116 S. Ct. (1996) (not available); *Mangold v. California Pub. Utils. Comm'n*, 67 F.3d 1470 (9th Cir. 1995) (available). The legal argument that it may not be is based on § 623(f)(1), which says that the Act does not apply where differentials are based on "reasonable factors other than age." The argument is that, since disparate impact cases begin by identifying a "neutral" (that is, non-age) factor, disparate impact claims are not permitted because, by definition, they are based on "factors other than age." The Supreme Court has not yet ruled on the issue, but Chief Justice (then Justice) Rehnquist has indicated in a dissent to a denial of certiorari that he thinks the disparate impact model should not be available under the ADEA. *Markham v. Geller*, 451 U.S. 945 (1981).

   3. *Sexual Harassment and Age Discrimination*. Should employer attempts to deal with allegations of sexual harassment be given special deference in age discrimination cases? In *Elrod v. Sears, Roebuck & Co.*, 939 F.2d 1466 (11th Cir. 1991), the plaintiff was discharged and replaced with a younger worker. The plaintiff claimed age discrimination and won a jury verdict. The employer claimed the plaintiff was discharged because of allegations of sexual harassment. The Court of Appeals affirmed a JNOV for the employer:

> We can assume for purposes of this opinion that [the female] employees [alleging harassment] were lying through their teeth. The inquiry of the ADEA is limited to whether [the company] *believed* that Elrod was guilty of harassment, and if so, whether this belief was the reason behind Elrod's discharge....
>
>   Elrod may have convinced the jury that the allegations against him were untrue, but he certainly did not present evidence that Sears' asserted belief in those allegations was unworthy of credence.

Id. at 1470-71.

KARLEN v. CITY COLLEGES

United States Court of Appeals, Seventh Circuit
837 F.2d 314, *cert. denied,* 486 U.S. 1044 (1988)

POSNER, CIRCUIT JUDGE.

Three professors brought suit under the Age Discrimination in Employment Act complaining that the Early Retirement Program of the City Colleges of Chicago, adopted in 1982 as part of a collective bargaining agreement with a local union of the American Federation of Teachers, discriminates against persons over 65. All three plaintiffs were between 65 and 69 when they brought the suit. Two had retired — one at 65, the other at 67. The third, who had been 64 when the Early Retirement Program was adopted, was still employed by the Colleges when the district judge granted summary judgment for the defendants and dismissed the case.

[Beginning in the early 1980s,] the Colleges [became] concerned with the high average age of the faculty members in many of their departments — the interaction of the tenure system with declining enrollments and budgets had resulted in there being few openings for new teachers — and had been trying to devise an early-retirement program. [In 1981,] the City Colleges began drafting the Early Retirement Program at issue in this case. In trying to "sell" the Program, the Chancellor of the City Colleges explained that its main purpose was "to realize financial savings by replacing older faculty members earning a higher salary with younger faculty members at the lower end of the salary schedule." Such replacement would not only save money but also promote the "infusion of new views, ... because you couldn't force oldtimers to go out and get more courses in the more recent things in their own field." There was also talk of bringing in "new blood" (an expression that we suspect will soon disappear from the employers' lexicon as awareness of the menace of age discrimination litigation seeps through the employer community), and, as part of this process, of making room for women and members of minority groups; most tenured faculty members were white and male.

The Early Retirement Program is open to any faculty member between 55 and 69 years of age who has been continuously employed full-time for at least ten years. The size of the pension that a faculty member who takes early retirement is entitled to is a function of his highest four years' salary plus his years of service. About this aspect of the Program the plaintiffs have no complaint — for the excellent reason that the size of the pension is keyed not to age but, as we have said, to salary and length of service. The plaintiffs complain about two other features of the Program, which are keyed to age. The first relates to accumulated sick pay. A faculty member who is between the ages of 55 and 58 when he takes early retirement is entitled to receive, in addition to his pension, a lump sum equal to 50 percent of his accumulated sick pay, valued at his base salary rate in his final year of service. The percentage rises to 60 percent for 59-year-olds and 80 percent for 60- to 64-year-olds, then plunges to 45 percent for 65- to

70-year-olds. Retirement is mandatory at 70. Not until 1994 does the Age Discrimination in Employment Act eliminate mandatory retirement for academic employees.

The second feature of the Early Retirement Program of which the plaintiffs complain is that while faculty members who retire between the ages of 55 and 64 continue to be covered by the Colleges' group insurance policy (which includes life, health, dental, vision, homeowner's, and automobile insurance) until they reach the age of 70, those who retire at age 65 or later cease, upon retirement, to be covered. Although they can continue to buy this insurance at the rates in the Colleges' policy, they are out the premiums, which covered employees do not pay.

The combined effect of the two challenged features of the Early Retirement Program on these plaintiffs is substantial. One of the plaintiffs would have received an extra $23,857 in sick-pay distribution had he retired at 64; and a faculty member who retires at 65 rather than 64 has to pay $22,430 in insurance premiums to retain his coverage until 70....

The question of the proper treatment of early-retirement programs is the most difficult question under the Age Discrimination in Employment Act. The purpose of such programs often is to ease out older employees, whether because they cost the employer more in salary or fringe benefits, or have gone stale, or are blocking advancement for the ambitious young. Often, therefore, the discussions leading up to the adoption of such programs will generate evidence of age discrimination. Yet the discrimination seems to be in favor of rather than against older employees, by giving them an additional option and one prized by many older employees. Nor can it seriously be argued that the concept of early retirement for workers over a specified age stigmatizes such workers, as would a program designed to change not the age but the racial composition of the work force by allowing blacks but not whites to retire early. Entitlement to early retirement is a valued perquisite of age — an additional option available only to the older worker and only slightly tarnished by the knowledge that sometimes employers offer it because they want to ease out older workers. These considerations led us to hold recently that a worker who elects early retirement cannot turn around and sue his employer unless he can show that he was forced to take early retirement by an explicit or implicit threat to fire (or otherwise punish) him because of his age if he did not. *Henn v. National Geographic Society,* 819 F.2d 824 [(7th Cir.), *cert. denied,* 484 U.S. 964 (1987)].

This case requires us to consider what at first glance may seem a completely different aspect of early retirement: the complaint not of the worker who elected early retirement but of the worker who, having declined it, believes he is being punished for his decision. Actually these two situations are the same. Whether a worker takes early retirement because he fears he will be discriminated against on account of his age if he does not, or refuses to take early retirement and indeed is then discriminated against on account of his age, his rights under the Age Discrimination in Employment Act have been violated.

There is, however, a real and not merely formal difference between this case and *Henn.* In *Henn,* all employees over 55 were offered a severance bonus equal to a full-year's salary if they retired within two months after the offer was made. There was no discrimination within the group eligible for early retirement; the amount of an employee's early-retirement benefits was not keyed to his age. Of course, everyone in the eligible group who rejected the offer suffered in the sense that if he retired later on he would not get the bonus. But no one suffered because of his age except employees under 55, who were not eligible for the program (more about them shortly). A 56 year old who declined to retire was no better off than a 64 year old who declined to retire; both lost the same thing, a year's bonus. The offer was more attractive, it is true, the nearer one was to leaving; but ordinarily that would be the older worker. A person who plans to retire at 65, and at age 64 is offered a chance to retire with a full-year salary as severance pay, will leap at the chance. But an early retirement plan that treats you better the older you are is not suspect under the Age Discrimination in Employment Act. Title VII protects whites and men as well as blacks and women, but the Age Discrimination in Employment Act does not protect the young as well as the old, or even, we think, the younger *against* the older. The protected zone begins at age 40, but if on that account workers 40 or older but younger than the age of eligibility for early retirement could complain — workers 40 to 54 in *Henn* — early retirement plans would effectively be outlawed, and that was not the intent of the framers of the Age Discrimination in Employment Act. The *reductio ad absurdum* of the reasoning which views early retirement plans with suspicion would be to view permitting workers to retire when they reach the age of 65 as a form of discrimination against workers aged 40 to 64. Then the employer could be confident of escaping liability under the Age Discrimination in Employment Act only by allowing retirement at age 40!

In the present case, however, there is discrimination against the older worker. Everyone between 55 and 69 is eligible for early retirement, but those between 64 and 69 — an older age group — are disfavored relative to the younger employees in the eligible group. If the City Colleges said to their faculty, at age 65 you lose your free parking space (or dental insurance, or any other fringe benefit), they would be guilty, prima facie, of age discrimination. Early-retirement benefits are another fringe benefit — and they plummet at age 65.

There may be good reasons for them to plummet, but the reasons are relevant not to the prima facie case of discrimination but to the defense in section 4(f)(2) of the Act, for "any bona fide employee benefit plan such as a retirement, pension, or insurance plan, which is not a subterfuge to evade the purposes of [the Age Discrimination in Employment Act]." The defense has two elements, and the defendants have the burden of production and of persuasion on both. They must show that the features of the Early Retirement Program of which the plaintiffs complain are (1) part of a bona fide employee benefit plan, and (2) not a subterfuge....

The record compiled in the summary judgment proceeding is adequate to establish (1). The Early Retirement Program, to which the challenged features are integral, is part of the overall retirement plan — a genuine retirement plan — that the City Colleges negotiated with the teachers' union and embodied in their collective bargaining agreement. The hard question is whether the challenged features constitute a subterfuge, that is, are designed to discriminate against faculty members 65 or older.

Nothing in the Age Discrimination in Employment Act forbids an employer to vary employee benefits according to the cost to the employer; and if, because older workers cost more, the result of the employer's economizing efforts is disadvantageous to older workers, that is simply how the cookie crumbles. In *Metz v. Transit Mix, Inc.*, 828 F.2d 1202, 1208-11 (7th Cir. 1987), this court carved an exception to this principle for the case where the older worker's higher cost is due solely to his having received pay increases based on seniority. We do not interpret *Metz* to forbid employers to take into account a higher cost for an older employee that may be due to the higher life-insurance premiums for insuring the lives of older people. But where, as in the present case, the employer uses age — not cost, or years of service, or salary — as the basis for varying retirement benefits, he had better be able to prove a close correlation between age and cost if he wants to shelter in the safe harbor of section 4(f)(2). Otherwise the inference of age discrimination will be strong — certainly strong enough to defeat a motion for summary judgment by the party having the burden of persuasion, that is, the defendant. The City Colleges tried to prove that the age grading in the Early Retirement Program faithfully reflects the pattern of costs; we must decide whether they succeeded to the level required to deprive the plaintiffs of a trial.

Regarding the sick-leave benefit — which, remember, drops from 80 percent at age 64 to 45 percent at age 65 — the Colleges make two arguments. The first is that sick leave not credited to the lump-sum distribution is credited to length of service and therefore goes to increase the pension component of the retirement benefits. The argument is fine in principle, but there are no figures in the record showing the trade-off between the lump-sum distribution of unused sick leave and the crediting of a fraction of that leave to years of service instead. The second argument is that the older a worker is, the more sick leave he will have accumulated and therefore the greater his distribution will be even if it is fixed at a lower percentage of his final base pay (which anyway will ordinarily be higher than that of a younger worker). This argument ignores two points. The first is that older workers may use more of their sick leave than younger ones, because health problems increase with age. The second and more important point is that sick-leave entitlement is a function of years of service — not age. The Colleges reply that age and length of service are highly correlated, but a document put in evidence by the plaintiffs belies this by showing large discrepancies between age

and length of service. Moreover, if the purpose of grading the sick-leave distribution by age is to recognize the greater accumulation of unused sick leave by
workers long on service, why don't the Colleges make the percentages vary with
length of service, rather than use age as a crude proxy? And why the big drop at
age 65? The record does not answer these questions.

Regarding the cut-off of insurance coverage at age 65, the Colleges are on
solider ground in arguing that there is a correlation between age and cost. Insurance premiums are frequently tied to age, life insurance being only the most
dramatic example. However, there is no evidence in the record concerning the
Colleges' cost of insurance under its group policies except for life insurance —
which indeed is about 50 percent higher for a 69-year-old faculty member than a
64-year-old one, but is only 8 percent higher for a 65 year old than for a 64 year
old. And even if it were 50 percent higher for the 65 year old, that would argue
for cutting his coverage by 50 percent, not by 100 percent. It is doubtful that the
premium costs of the other forms of insurance in the Colleges' package rise as
rapidly with age, and some (e.g., homeowner's) may not rise at all. The cost of
health insurance actually falls, because Medicare kicks in at age 65 and the coverage of the group policy is concomitantly reduced.

A feature common to both the sick-pay and insurance components of the Early
Retirement Plan is the sharp drop in benefits at age 65.... [The Colleges] argue
that in order to induce early retirement of faculty members in the 65-69 year
bracket they have to make 65 a breaking point. They say that if the decline in
benefits with age were gradual, as it would have to be to reflect accurately the
changing cost of the retirement package, no one would retire before 70. The
small annual decline in sick-pay distribution and in insurance coverage would be
more than offset by the growth in the pension component of the retirement
package as a result of salary raises and additional years of service. So the purpose of the Early Retirement Program — to induce early retirement — would be
defeated.

This strikes us as a damaging admission rather than a powerful defense. To
withhold benefits from older persons in order to induce them to retire seems
precisely the form of discrimination at which the Age Discrimination in
Employment Act is aimed. Rather than offering a carrot to all workers 55 years
and older, as in the *Henn* case, the City Colleges are offering the whole carrot to
workers 55 to 64 and taking back half for workers 65 to 69. The reason is that
the Colleges want to induce workers to retire by 65. In effect they have two early
retirement programs; a munificent one for workers 55 to 64 and a chintzy one for
workers 65 to 69. It may be that retirees in the second group cost the Colleges
more than retirees in the first group, but the difference in cost seems much
smaller than the difference in retirement benefits; indeed, there may be no net
difference in cost.

As far as the record discloses, the Colleges could achieve all of the lawful
objectives of their Early Retirement Program by tying the sick-pay distribution to
salary and years of service and the insurance coverage to the actual difference in

premium costs that is due to the age of the employee. If so, this is further evidence that the actual Program is a subterfuge, designed to get rid of faculty members when they reach 65.

We sympathize not only with the plight of the City Colleges in an era of declining enrollments and financial stringency, but also with the plight of young academics who cannot find decent teaching jobs because tenured faculty refuse to retire, and with the concerns of those who believe that the quality of American higher education is endangered by the prospect of faculty gerontocracies protected by the Age Discrimination in Employment Act. However, the colleges and universities lobbied hard with Congress against the raising of the minimum mandatory retirement age to 70 (and its elimination altogether, effective in 1994), and they are a powerful lobby. They lost, and they cannot be allowed by indirection to reinstate what was for so long the age-65 mandatory retirement norm.

Whether that is what the City Colleges were trying to do here is a question that must abide the trial that the plaintiffs were erroneously denied. We hold only that the evidence submitted by the defendants in support of their motion for summary judgment does not establish that a reasonable jury could not find that the Early Retirement Program is a subterfuge and therefore violates the Age Discrimination in Employment Act.

Reversed and remanded.

NOTES

1. *Older Workers Benefit Protection Act.* After the principal case, the Supreme Court held that the ADEA did not directly prohibit age discrimination in employee benefit plans, such as retirement, pension, and insurance plans. Discrimination in benefit plans was prohibited only if it was intended to further discrimination in some non-benefit aspect of the employment relationship. *Public Employees Ret. Sys. v. Betts,* 492 U.S. 158 (1989). Congress, however, reversed that decision when it enacted the Older Workers Benefit Protection Act (OWBPA) in 1990. In that Act, Congress clarified that the ADEA *did* apply to employee benefit plans and that the "equal benefit or equal cost" principle discussed in *Karlen* applies to such plans. The Act also provided criteria for evaluating the legality of early retirement programs: the programs must be voluntary (the Act provided notice requirements intended to ensure voluntariness, § 626) and they must be "consistent with the relevant ... purposes of [the ADEA]." § 623(f)(2)(B)(ii). The *Karlen* case was cited with approval in the legislative history of the Act.

2. *Early Retirement Programs.* *Karlen* indicates that an early retirement program which makes an offer of benefits only to employees up to a certain age (age sixty-five in *Karlen*) is unlikely to pass muster under the ADEA, because it discriminates against workers older than the cutoff age. The legislative history of the Older Workers Benefit Protection Act reaffirms that position. But this poses a problem for employers. If employees can receive the benefits *whenever* they retire (over a certain age), the benefits do not provide much of an incentive to retire *early*. So what are employers to do?

One option suggested by the legislative history of the Older Workers Benefit Protection Act is to offer the extra benefits only for a "window" period — workers over age fifty-five will receive *x* extra benefits if they retire between January 1 and May 1 of this year. Would such a temporally-conditioned incentive violate the ADEA? Professor Harper thinks that it does not, but it should: "The only practical way to prevent employers from using retirement incentives to effect the termination of particular workers selected on the basis of age ... is to prohibit age-based incentives from being temporally or otherwise conditioned." Michael C. Harper, *Age-Based Exit Incentives, Coercion, and the Prospective Waiver of ADEA Rights: The Failure of the Older Workers Benefit Protection Act*, 79 VA. L. REV. 1271, 1329 (1993).

Alternatively, employers might eschew early retirement programs altogether. If the size of the work force needs to be reduced, employers might simply discharge employees. Would an employer violate the ADEA if it reduced the size of its work force by discharging the highest paid employees? *See Bay v. Times Mirror Magazines, Inc.*, 936 F.2d 112 (2d Cir. 1991) (no). *See* Steven J. Kaminshine, *The Cost of Older Workers, Disparate Impact, and the Age Discrimination in Employment Act*, 42 FLA. L. REV. 229 (1990).

3. *Waiver of ADEA Rights*. Early retirement incentive plans pose a fairly significant risk of ADEA claims. One employer response to this risk has been to obtain waivers of ADEA claims from employees accepting the retirement offer. The OWBPA specifies several minimum conditions which must be satisfied for these waivers to be effective, for example, the agreement must advise the employee to consult with an attorney and must provide as consideration something "in addition to anything of value to which the [employee] is already entitled." ADEA § 7(f)(1)(A)-(H). If an employee accepts a hefty retirement bonus as an incentive to retire, but the waiver agreement fails to meet all the OWBPA requirements, should the employee be able to keep the money and sue? Or should the employee be required to return the bonus before being allowed to forward an ADEA claim? *Oubre v. Entergy Operations, Inc.*, 118 S. Ct. 838 (1998) (employee can keep the money and sue).

4. *Retirement and the Life Cycle Model*. The life cycle model predicts that employees will receive wages in excess of marginal productivity at the end of their careers. Prior to the ADEA, that period had a finite endpoint: Employers could require employees to retire at a certain age, usually 65. When the 1986 amendments to the ADEA eliminated mandatory retirement, employers turned to retirement incentive programs to try to limit the period, but OWBPA's changes made implementing such programs more costly and risky. Viewed in this light, the ADEA and OWBPA changes are problematic. In the short run, current employees at the end of their careers will receive a windfall. When they entered into their employment, they expected the beneficial final period to end at age 65. Now it can continue indefinitely, unless the employer provides extra benefits to induce retirement. In the long run, the changes threaten the life cycle model. Employers will be less willing to enter into such arrangements if the costs at the final stage cannot be predicted. If that occurs, obviously, the benefits of the life cycle employment arrangement, such as reduced employer monitoring and a gradually upward-sloping salary path, would be lost. *See* Samuel Issacharoff & Erica Worth, *Is Age Discrimination Really Age Discrimination?: The ADEA's Unnatural Solution*, 72 N.Y.U. L. REV. 780 (1997); Erica Worth, Note, *In Defense of Targeted ERIPs: Understanding the Interaction of Life-Cycle Employment and Early Retirement Incentive Plans*, 74 TEX. L. REV. 411 (1995).

C. AFFIRMATIVE ACTION AND THE PROBLEMS OF REMEDIES

JOHNSON v. TRANSPORTATION AGENCY

United States Supreme Court
480 U.S. 616 (1987)

JUSTICE BRENNAN delivered the opinion of the Court.

Respondent, Transportation Agency of Santa Clara County, California, unilaterally promulgated an Affirmative Action Plan applicable, *inter alia,* to promotions of employees. In selecting applicants for the promotional position of road dispatcher, the Agency, pursuant to the Plan, passed over petitioner Paul Johnson, a male employee, and promoted a female employee applicant, Diane Joyce. The question for decision is whether in making the promotion the Agency impermissibly took into account the sex of the applicants in violation of Title VII of the Civil Rights Act of 1964....[2]

I

In December 1978, the Santa Clara County Transit District Board of Supervisors adopted an Affirmative Action Plan (Plan) for the County Transportation Agency. The Plan ... provides that, in making promotions to positions within a traditionally segregated job classification in which women have been significantly underrepresented, the Agency is authorized to consider as one factor the sex of a qualified applicant.

In reviewing the composition of its work force, the Agency noted in its Plan that women were represented in numbers far less than their proportion of the

---

[2] No constitutional issue was either raised or addressed in the litigation below. We therefore decide in this case only the issue of the prohibitory scope of Title VII. Of course, where the issue is properly raised, public employers must justify the adoption and implementation of a voluntary affirmative action plan under the Equal Protection Clause. *See Wygant v. Jackson Board of Education,* 476 U.S. 267 (1986).

county labor force in both the Agency as a whole and in five of seven job categories. Specifically, while women constituted 36.4% of the area labor market, they composed only 22.4% of Agency employees. Furthermore, women working at the Agency were concentrated largely in EEOC job categories traditionally held by women: women made up 76% of Office and Clerical Workers, but only 7.1% of Agency Officials and Administrators, 8.6% of Professionals, 9.7% of Technicians, and 22% of Service and Maintenance workers. As for the job classification relevant to this case, none of the 238 Skilled Craft Worker positions was held by a woman....

The Agency stated that its Plan was intended to achieve "a statistically measurable yearly improvement in hiring, training and promotion of minorities and women throughout the Agency in all major job classifications where they are underrepresented." As a benchmark by which to evaluate progress, the Agency stated that its long-term goal was to attain a work force whose composition reflected the proportion of minorities and women in the area labor force. Thus, for the Skilled Craft category in which the road dispatcher position at issue here was classified, the Agency's aspiration was that eventually about 36% of the jobs would be occupied by women....

The Plan acknowledged that a number of factors might make it unrealistic to rely on the Agency's long-term goals in evaluating the Agency's progress in expanding job opportunities for minorities and women. Among the factors identified were low turnover rates in some classifications, the fact that some jobs involved heavy labor, the small number of positions within some job categories, the limited number of entry positions leading to the Technical and Skilled Craft classifications, and the limited number of minorities and women qualified for positions requiring specialized training and experience....

The Agency's Plan thus set aside no specific number of positions for minorities or women, but authorized the consideration of ethnicity or sex as a factor when evaluating qualified candidates for jobs in which members of such groups were poorly represented. One such job was the road dispatcher position that is the subject of the dispute in this case.

On December 12, 1979, the Agency announced a vacancy for the promotional position of road dispatcher in the Agency's Roads Division. Dispatchers assign road crews, equipment, and materials, and maintain records pertaining to road maintenance jobs....

Twelve County employees applied for the promotion, including Joyce and Johnson. Joyce had worked for the County since 1970, serving as an account clerk until 1975. She had applied for a road dispatcher position in 1974, but was deemed ineligible because she had not served as a road maintenance worker. In 1975, Joyce transferred from a senior account clerk position to a road maintenance worker position, becoming the first woman to fill such a job. During her four years in that position, she occasionally worked out of class as a road dispatcher.

Petitioner Johnson began with the county in 1967 as a road yard clerk, after private employment that included working as a supervisor and dispatcher. He had also unsuccessfully applied for the road dispatcher opening in 1974. In 1977, his clerical position was downgraded, and he sought and received a transfer to the position of road maintenance worker. He also occasionally worked out of class as a dispatcher while performing that job.

Nine of the applicants, including Joyce and Johnson, were deemed qualified for the job, and were interviewed by a two-person board. Seven of the applicants scored above 70 on this interview, which meant that they were certified as eligible for selection by the appointing authority. The scores awarded ranged from 70 to 80. Johnson was tied for second with score of 75, while Joyce ranked next with a score of 73....

[James Graebner was Director of the Agency and authorized to select any of the seven persons deemed eligible.] After deliberation, Graebner concluded that the promotion should be given to Joyce. As he testified: "I tried to look at the whole picture, the combination of her qualifications and Mr. Johnson's qualifications, their test scores, their expertise, their background, affirmative action matters, things like that ... I believe it was a combination of all those."

[Petitioner Johnson then commenced this action.]

II

As a preliminary matter, we note that petitioner bears the burden of establishing the invalidity of the Agency's Plan. Only last term in *Wygant v. Jackson Board of Education,* 476 U.S. 267, 277-78 (1986), we held that "[t]he ultimate burden remains with the employees to demonstrate the unconstitutionality of an affirmative-action program," and we see no basis for a different rule regarding a plan's alleged violation of Title VII. This case also fits readily within the analytical framework set forth in *McDonnell Douglas Corp. v. Green,* 411 U.S. 792 (1973). Once a plaintiff establishes a prima facie case that race or sex has been taken into account in an employer's employment decision, the burden shifts to the employer to articulate a nondiscriminatory rationale for its decision. The existence of an affirmative action plan provides such a rationale. If such a plan is articulated as the basis for the employer's decision, the burden shifts to the plaintiff to prove that the employer's justification is pretextual and the plan is invalid. As a practical matter, of course, an employer will generally seek to avoid a charge of pretext by presenting evidence in support of its plan. That does not mean, however, as petitioner suggests, that reliance on an affirmative action plan is to be treated as an affirmative defense requiring the employer to carry the burden of proving the validity of the plan. The burden of proving its invalidity remains on the plaintiff.

The assessment of the legality of the Agency Plan must be guided by our decision in [*Steelworkers v.*] *Weber,* 443 U.S. 193 (1979). In that case, the Court addressed the question whether the employer violated Title VII by adopting a voluntary affirmative action plan designed to "eliminate manifest racial imbalances in traditionally segregated job categories." The respondent employee in that case challenged the employer's denial of his application for a position in a newly established craft training program, contending that the employer's selection process impermissibly took into account the race of the applicants. The selection process was guided by an affirmative action plan, which provided that 50% of the new trainees were to be black until the percentage of black skilled craftworkers in the employer's plant approximated the percentage of blacks in the local labor force. Adoption of the plan had been prompted by the fact that only 5 of 273, or 1.83%, of skilled craftworkers at the plant were black, even though the work force in the area was approximately 39% black. Because of the historical exclusion of blacks from craft positions, the employer regarded its former policy of hiring trained outsiders as inadequate to redress the imbalance in its work force.

We upheld the employer's decision to select less senior black applicants over the white respondent, for we found that taking race into account was consistent with Title VII's objective of "break[ing] down old patterns of racial segregation and hierarchy." As we stated:

> "It would be ironic indeed if a law triggered by a Nation's concern over centuries of racial injustice and intended to improve the lot of those who had 'been excluded from the American dream for so long' constituted the first legislative prohibition of all voluntary, private, race-conscious efforts to abolish traditional patterns of racial segregation and hierarchy." *Id.*, at 204 (quoting remarks of Sen. Humphrey, 110 Cong. Rec. 6552 (1964)).

We noted that the plan did not "unnecessarily trammel the interests of the white employees," since it did not require "the discharge of white workers and their replacement with new black hirees." Nor did the plan create "an absolute bar to the advancement of white employees," since half of those trained in the new program were to be white. Finally, we observed that the plan was a temporary measure, not designed to maintain racial balance, but to "eliminate a manifest racial imbalance." As JUSTICE BLACKMUN's concurrence made clear, *Weber* held that an employer seeking to justify the adoption of a plan need not point to its own prior discriminatory practices, nor even to evidence of an "arguable violation" on its part. Rather, it need point only to a "conspicuous ... imbalance in traditionally segregated job categories." Our decision was grounded in the recognition that voluntary employer action can play a crucial role in furthering Title VII's purpose of eliminating the effects of discrimination in the workplace, and that Title VII should not be read to thwart such efforts.[8]

---

[8] JUSTICE SCALIA's suggestion that an affirmative action program may be adopted only to redress an employer's past discrimination was rejected in *Steelworkers v. Weber* because the prospect of liability created by such an admission would create a significant disincentive for voluntary action. As JUSTICE BLACKMUN's concurrence in that case pointed out, such a standard would "plac[e] voluntary compliance with Title VII in profound jeopardy. The only way for the employer and the

In reviewing the employment decision at issue in this case, we must first examine whether that decision was made pursuant to a plan prompted by concerns similar to those of the employer in *Weber*. Next, we must determine whether the effect of the plan on males and non-minorities is comparable to the effect of the plan in that case.

The first issue is therefore whether consideration of the sex of applicants for Skilled Craft jobs was justified by the existence of a "manifest imbalance" that reflected underrepresentation of women in "traditionally segregated job categories." In determining whether an imbalance exists that would justify taking sex or race into account, a comparison of the percentage of minorities or women in the employer's work force with the percentage in the area labor market or general population is appropriate in analyzing jobs that require no special expertise, see *Teamsters*, or training programs designed to provide expertise, *see Weber*. Where a job requires special training, however, the comparison should be with those in the labor force who possess the relevant qualifications. See *Hazelwood*. The requirement that the "manifest imbalance" relate to a "traditionally segregated job category" provides assurance both that sex or race will be taken into account in a manner consistent with Title VII's purpose of eliminating the effects of employment discrimination, and that the interests of those employees not benefiting from the plan will not be unduly infringed.

A manifest imbalance need not be such that it would support a prima facie case against the employer, as suggested in JUSTICE O'CONNOR's concurrence, since we do not regard as identical the constraints of Title VII and the federal constitution on voluntarily adopted affirmative action plans. Application of the "prima facie" standard in Title VII cases would be inconsistent with *Weber*'s focus on statistical imbalance,[10] and could inappropriately create a significant

---

union to keep their footing on the 'tightrope' it creates would be to eschew all forms of voluntary affirmative action."...

Contrary to JUSTICE SCALIA's contention, our decision last term in ... *Sheet Metal Workers v. EEOC*, 478 U.S. 421 (1986), provide[s] no support for a standard more restrictive than that enunciated in *Weber*.... In *Sheet Metal Workers*, the issue we addressed was the scope of judicial remedial authority under Title VII, authority that has not been exercised in this case. JUSTICE SCALIA's suggestion that employers should be able to do no more voluntarily than courts can order as remedies ignores the fundamental difference between volitional private behavior and the exercise of coercion by the State. Plainly, "Congress' concern that federal courts not impose unwanted obligations on employers and unions," reflects a desire to preserve a relatively large domain for voluntary employer action.

[10] The difference between the "manifest imbalance" and "prima facie" standards is illuminated by *Weber*. Had the Court in that case been concerned with past discrimination by the employer, it would have focused on discrimination in hiring skilled, not unskilled, workers, since only the scarcity of the former in Kaiser's work force would have made it vulnerable to a Title VII suit. In order to make out a prima facie case on such a claim, a plaintiff would be required to compare the percentage of black skilled workers in the Kaiser work force with the percentage of black skilled craft workers in the area labor market.

disincentive for employers to adopt an affirmative action plan. See *Weber,* [443 U.S.,] at 204 (Title VII intended as a "catalyst" for employer efforts to eliminate vestiges of discrimination). A corporation concerned with maximizing return on investment, for instance, is hardly likely to adopt a plan if in order to do so it must compile evidence that could be used to subject it to a colorable Title VII suit.[11]

It is clear that the decision to hire Joyce was made pursuant to an Agency plan that directed that sex or race be taken into account for the purpose of remedying underrepresentation. The Agency Plan acknowledged the "limited opportunities that have existed in the past," for women to find employment in certain job classifications "where women have not been traditionally employed in significant numbers." As a result, observed the Plan, women were concentrated in traditionally female jobs in the Agency, and represented a lower percentage in other job classifications than would be expected if such traditional segregation had not occurred. Specifically, 9 of the 10 Para-Professionals and 110 of the 145 Office and Clerical Workers were women. By contrast, women were only 2 of the 28 Officials and Administrators, 5 of the 58 Professionals, 12 of the 124 Technicians, none of the Skilled Craft Workers, and 1 — who was Joyce — of the 110 Road Maintenance Workers. The Plan sought to remedy these imbalances through "hiring, training and promotion of ... women throughout the Agency in all major job classifications where they are underrepresented."...

As the Agency Plan recognized, women were most egregiously underrepresented in the Skilled Craft job category, since *none* of the 238 positions was occupied by a woman.... The promotion of Joyce thus satisfies the first requirement enunciated in *Weber,* since it was undertaken to further an affirmative action plan designed to eliminate Agency work force imbalances in traditionally segregated job categories.

Weber obviously did not make such a comparison. Instead, it focused on the disparity between the percentage of black skilled craft workers in Kaiser's ranks and the percentage of blacks in the area labor force. Such an approach reflected a recognition that the proportion of black craft workers in the local labor force was likely as miniscule as the proportion in Kaiser's work force. The Court realized that the lack of imbalance between these figures would mean that employers in precisely those industries in which discrimination has been most effective would be precluded from adopting training programs to increase the percentage of qualified minorities. Thus, in cases such as *Weber,* where the employment decision at issue involves the selection of unskilled persons for a training program, the "manifest imbalance" standard permits comparison with the general labor force. By contrast, the "prima facie" standard would require comparison with the percentage of minorities or women qualified for the job for which the trainees are being trained, a standard that would have invalidated the plan in *Weber* itself.

[11] In some cases, of course, the manifest imbalance may be sufficiently egregious to establish a prima facie case. However, as long as there is a manifest imbalance, an employer may adopt a plan even where the disparity is not so striking, without being required to introduce the non-statistical evidence of past discrimination that would be demanded by the "prima facie" standard. Of course, when there is sufficient evidence to meet the more stringent "prima facie" standard, be it statistical, non-statistical, or a combination of the two, the employer is free to adopt an affirmative action plan.

We next consider whether the Agency Plan unnecessarily trammeled the rights of male employees or created an absolute bar to their advancement. In contrast to the plan in *Weber,* which provided that 50% of the positions in the craft training program were exclusively for blacks, and to the consent decree upheld last term in *Firefighters v. Cleveland,* 478 U.S. 501 (1986), which required the promotion of specific numbers of minorities, the Plan sets aside no positions for women. The Plan expressly states that "[t]he 'goals' established for each Division should not be construed as 'quotas' that must be met." Rather, the Plan merely authorizes that consideration be given to affirmative action concerns when evaluating qualified applicants. As the Agency Director testified, the sex of Joyce was but one of numerous factors he took into account in arriving at his decision. The Plan thus resembles the "Harvard Plan" approvingly noted by JUSTICE POWELL in *University of California Regents v. Bakke,* 438 U.S. 265, 316-319 (1978), which considers race along with other criteria in determining admission to the college.... Similarly, the Agency Plan requires women to compete with all other qualified applicants. *No* persons are automatically excluded from consideration; *all* are able to have their qualifications weighed against those of other applicants.

In addition, petitioner had no absolute entitlement to the road dispatcher position. Seven of the applicants were classified as qualified and eligible, and the Agency Director was authorized to promote any of the seven. Thus, denial of the promotion unsettled no legitimate firmly rooted expectation on the part of the petitioner. Furthermore, while the petitioner in this case was denied a promotion, he retained his employment with the Agency, at the same salary and with the same seniority, and remained eligible for other promotions.[15]

Finally, the Agency's Plan was intended to *attain* a balanced work force, not to maintain one. The Plan contains ten references to the Agency's desire to "attain" such a balance, but no reference whatsoever to a goal of maintaining it....

The Agency acknowledged the difficulties that it would confront in remedying the imbalance in its work force, and it anticipated only gradual increases in the representation of minorities and women. It is thus unsurprising that the Plan contains no explicit end date, for the Agency's flexible, case-by-case approach was not expected to yield success in a brief period of time. Express assurance that a program is only temporary may be necessary if the program actually sets aside positions according to specific numbers. This is necessary both to minimize the effect of the program on other employees, and to ensure that the plan's goals "[are] not being used simply to achieve and maintain ... balance, but rather

---

[15] Furthermore, from 1978 to 1982 Skilled Craft jobs in the Agency increased from 238 to 349.... Of the 111 new Skilled Craft jobs during this period, 105, or almost 95%, went to men.... While this degree of employment expansion by an employer is by no means essential to a plan's validity, it underscores the fact that the Plan in this case in no way significantly restricts the employment prospects of such persons....

as a benchmark against which" the employer may measure its progress in eliminating the underrepresentation of minorities and women. In this case, however, substantial evidence shows that the Agency has sought to take a moderate, gradual approach to eliminating the imbalance in its work force, one which establishes realistic guidance for employment decisions, and which visits minimal intrusion on the legitimate expectations of other employees. Given this fact, as well as the Agency's express commitment to "attain" a balanced work force, there is ample assurance that the Agency does not seek to use its Plan to maintain a permanent racial and sexual balance.

III

... We therefore hold that the Agency appropriately took into account as one factor the sex of Diane Joyce in determining that she should be promoted to the road dispatcher position. The decision to do so was made pursuant to an affirmative action plan that represents a moderate, flexible, case-by-case approach to effecting a gradual improvement in the representation of minorities and women in the Agency's work force. Such a plan is fully consistent with Title VII, for it embodies the contribution that voluntary employer action can make in eliminating the vestiges of discrimination in the workplace. Accordingly, the judgment of the Court of Appeals is

Affirmed.

JUSTICE STEVENS, concurring.
While I join the Court's opinion, I write separately to explain my view of this case's position in our evolving antidiscrimination law and to emphasize that the opinion does not establish the permissible outer limits of voluntary programs undertaken by employers to benefit disadvantaged groups....
The logic of antidiscrimination legislation requires that judicial constructions of Title VII leave "breathing room" for employer initiatives to benefit members of minority groups.... As construed in *Weber* and in *Firefighters,* the statute does not absolutely prohibit preferential hiring in favor of minorities; it was merely intended to protect historically disadvantaged groups *against* discrimination and not to hamper managerial efforts to benefit members of disadvantaged groups that are consistent with that paramount purpose....
Whether a voluntary decision of the kind made by respondent would ever be prohibited by Title VII is a question we need not answer until it is squarely presented. Given the interpretation of the statute the Court adopted in *Weber,* I see no reason why the employer has any duty, prior to granting a preference to a qualified minority employee, to determine whether his past conduct might constitute an arguable violation of Title VII. Indeed, in some instances the employer may find it more helpful to focus on the future. [Employers might give the following forward-looking justifications for affirmative action programs: improving their services to black constituencies, averting racial tension over the

allocation of jobs in a community, or increasing the diversity of a work force, to name but a few examples.]

The Court today does not foreclose other voluntary decisions based in part on a qualified employee's membership in a disadvantaged group. Accordingly, I concur.

JUSTICE O'CONNOR, concurring in the judgment....

In my view, the proper initial inquiry in evaluating the legality of an affirmative action plan by a public employer under Title VII is no different from that required by the Equal Protection Clause. In either case, consistent with the congressional intent to provide some measure of protection to the interests of the employer's nonminority employees, the employer must have had a firm basis for believing that remedial action was required. An employer would have such a firm basis if it can point to a statistical disparity sufficient to support a prima facie claim under Title VII by the employee beneficiaries of the affirmative action plan of a pattern or practice claim of discrimination....

While employers must have a firm basis for concluding that remedial action is necessary, neither *Wygant* nor *Weber* places a burden on employers to prove that they actually discriminated against women or minorities.... [A] contemporaneous finding of discrimination should not be required because it would discourage voluntary efforts to remedy apparent discrimination. A requirement that an employer actually prove that it had discriminated in the past would also unduly discourage voluntary efforts to remedy apparent discrimination.... Evidence sufficient for a prima facie Title VII pattern or practice claim against the employer itself suggests that the absence of women or minorities in a work force cannot be explained by general societal discrimination alone and that remedial action is appropriate....

In this case, I am ... satisfied that the respondent had a firm basis for adopting an affirmative action program. Although the District Court found no discrimination against women in fact, at the time the affirmative action plan was adopted, there were *no* women in its skilled craft positions. The petitioner concedes that women constituted approximately 5% of the local labor pool of skilled craft workers in 1970. Thus, when compared to the percentage of women in the qualified work force, the statistical disparity would have been sufficient for a prima facie Title VII case brought by unsuccessful women job applicants.... Accordingly, I concur in the judgment of the Court.

JUSTICE SCALIA, with whom THE CHIEF JUSTICE joins, and with whom JUSTICE WHITE joins in Parts I and II, dissenting....

The most significant proposition of law established by today's decision is that racial or sexual discrimination is permitted under Title VII when it is intended to overcome the effect, not of the employer's own discrimination, but of societal attitudes that have limited the entry of certain races, or of a particular sex, into certain jobs.... [T]his holding ... contradict[s] a decision of this Court rendered only last Term. *Wygant v. Jackson Board of Education,* 476 U.S. 267 (1986), held that the objective of remedying societal discrimination cannot prevent remedial affirmative action from violating the Equal Protection Clause. Because, therefore, those justifications (e.g., the remedying of past societal wrongs) that are inadequate to insulate discriminatory action from the racial discrimination prohibitions of the Constitution are also inadequate to insulate it from the racial discrimination prohibitions of Title VII; and because the portions of Title VII at issue here treat race and sex equivalently; *Wygant,* which dealt with race discrimination, is fully applicable precedent, and is squarely inconsistent with today's decision.[4]

[The majority also argues that the Plan does not "unnecessarily trammel" the interests of male and nonminority employees.] The majority emphasizes, as though it is meaningful, that "*No* persons are automatically excluded from consideration; *all* are able to have their qualifications weighed against those of other applicants." One is reminded of the exchange from Shakespeare's King Henry the Fourth, Part I:

> "GLENDOWER: I can call Spirits from the vasty Deep."
> "HOTSPUR: Why, so can I, or so can any man. But will they come when you do call for them?" Act III, Scene I, lines 53-55.

Johnson was indeed entitled to have his qualifications weighed against those of other applicants — but more to the point, he was virtually assured that, after the weighing, if there was any minimally qualified applicant from one of the favored groups, he would be rejected....

[I]n many contexts[, the practical effect of today's decision will be to *require*] employers, public as well as private, to engage in intentional discrimination on the basis of race or sex. This Court's prior interpretations of Title VII, especially

---

[4] JUSTICE O'CONNOR's concurrence at least makes an attempt to bring this term into accord with last. Under her reading of Title VII, an employer may discriminate affirmatively, so to speak, if he has a "firm basis" for believing that he might be guilty of (nonaffirmative) discrimination under the Act, and if his action is designed to remedy that suspected prior discrimination. This is something of a half-way house between leaving employers scot-free to discriminate against disfavored groups, as the majority opinion does, and prohibiting discrimination, as do the words of Title VII. In the present case, although the District Court found that in fact no sex discrimination existed, JUSTICE O'CONNOR would find a "firm basis" for the agency's *belief* that sex discrimination existed in the "inexorable zero": the complete absence, prior to Diane Joyce, of any women in the Agency's skilled positions. There are two problems with this: First, even positing a "firm basis" for the Agency's belief in prior discrimination, ... the plan was patently not *designed to remedy* that prior discrimination, but rather to establish a sexually representative work force. Second, even an absolute zero is not "inexorable." While it may inexorably provide "firm basis" for belief in the mind of an outside observer, it cannot conclusively establish such a belief *on the employer's part,* since he may be aware of the particular reasons that account for the zero.... The question is in any event one of fact, which, if it were indeed relevant to the outcome, would require a remand to the District Court rather than an affirmance.

the decision in *Griggs v. Duke Power Co.,* 401 U.S. 424 (1971), subject employers to a potential Title VII suit whenever there is a noticeable imbalance in the representation of minorities or women in the employer's work force. Even the employer who is confident of ultimately prevailing in such a suit must contemplate the expense and adverse publicity of a trial, because the extent of the imbalance, and the "job relatedness" of his selection criteria, are questions of fact to be explored through rebuttal and counter-rebuttal of a "prima facie case" consisting of no more than the showing that the employer's selection process "selects those from the protected class at a 'significantly' lesser rate than their counterparts." If, however, employers are free to discriminate through affirmative action, without fear of "reverse discrimination" suits by their non-minority or male victims, they are offered a threshold defense against Title VII liability premised on numerical disparities. Thus, after today's decision the *failure* to engage in reverse discrimination is economic folly, and arguably a breach of duty to shareholders or taxpayers, wherever the cost of anticipated Title VII litigation exceeds the cost of hiring less capable (though still minimally capable) workers. (This situation is more likely to obtain, of course, with respect to the least skilled jobs — perversely creating an incentive to discriminate against precisely those members of the nonfavored groups *least* likely to have profited from societal discrimination in the past.) It is predictable, moreover, that this incentive will be greatly magnified by economic pressures brought to bear by government contracting agencies upon employers who refuse to discriminate in the fashion we have now approved. A statute designed to establish a color-blind and gender-blind workplace has thus been converted into a powerful engine of racism and sexism, not merely *permitting* intentional race- and sex-based discrimination, but often making it, through operation of the legal system, practically compelled.

NOTES

1. *A Framework for Thinking About Remedies.* Discrimination remedies, and remedies generally, can be thought of as mechanisms for shifting losses from injured parties to parties legally responsible for the losses. For this loss-shifting model to apply easily, one needs to be able to 1) identify the injured party; 2) isolate and quantify the loss; and 3) identify the responsible party to whom the loss should be shifted. Remedies in discrimination cases are difficult, because it is not uncommon for one or more of the elements needed to apply the loss-shifting model to be missing. Indeed, one of the reasons *Johnson* is a difficult case is that *none* of the elements are satisfied. Consider the following variations:

(a) A black plaintiff proves that an employer would have hired him except for his race. The courts, except in rare circumstances, award the plaintiff backpay; require the employer to hire the plaintiff (or at least to make an offer); and require the employer to grant to the plaintiff the seniority the plaintiff would have had had he been hired initially. The backpay award is easy to justify using the loss-shifting model; the award simply shifts the wage loss caused by the employer's discriminatory refusal to hire from the injured party (the black plaintiff) to the responsible party (the employer). Retroactive seniority, although well-accepted, is more difficult to justify, because the loss (seniority) is not shifted to the employer, but to the employer's current employees, whose seniority expectations are diminished because of the remedy. The obligation to hire the black plaintiff is also well-accepted, even though it may shift losses to people other than the responsible party; assuming the employer hires the plaintiff instead of someone else, that someone else is bearing a portion of the cost of the remedy. *See Albemarle Paper Co. v. Moody,* 422 U.S. 405 (1975) (backpay an appropriate remedy); *Franks v. Bowman Transp. Co.,* 424 U.S. 747 (1976) (retroactive seniority an appropriate remedy).

(b) A union discriminatorily denies blacks admission to an apprenticeship program. Using the systemic disparate treatment model, the court determines that forty-five more blacks would have been admitted to the program had the union not discriminated. One hundred and eighty blacks prove that they applied for and were denied admission. How should the remedy be structured? *See Hameed v. Iron Workers, Local 396,* 637 F.2d 506 (8th Cir. 1980) (attempt to determine which blacks would have been hired; if not possible, estimate total wage loss caused by failure to admit forty-five blacks and require employer to pay that amount to 180 black applicants on pro rata basis). *Compare EEOC v. Enterprise Ass'n Steamfitters Local 638,* 542 F.2d 579 (2d Cir. 1976), *cert. denied,* 430 U.S. 911 (1977) (backpay denied to black applicants because their injuries too remote and speculative).

(c) The Alabama Department of Public Safety discriminated against blacks who applied to be state troopers and against blacks who applied for promotions. The discrimination continued even after a court ordered it to stop. Eventually, the court ordered the Department to promote one black trooper for each white trooper promoted, provided qualified black applicants were available, until blacks constituted 25% (the proportion of blacks in the relevant labor market) of the persons in a rank. Using the loss-shifting model, why is this a problematic remedy? The Supreme Court has held that this type of remedy is appropriate, provided that the discrimination against which it is addressed is long-standing and egregious and that the remedy is temporary and flexible and does not have too adverse an effect on non-minority interests. *United States v. Paradise,* 480 U.S. 149 (1987) (case the problem is based on); *Local 28, Sheet Metal Workers' Int'l Ass'n v. EEOC,* 478 U.S. 421 (1986).

2. *Affirmative Action and the Constitution.* *Johnson* involved a public employer, but no constitutional issues were raised. Constitutional analysis requires consideration of the same two general sets of issues considered in *Johnson* — is the employer's preference justified and narrowly tailored? — but it may heighten the level of scrutiny. *See Adarand Constrs., Inc. v. Pena,* 515 U.S. 200 (1995) (strict scrutiny to be applied to race-based preferences); *Associated Gen. Contractors of Cal., Inc. v. San Francisco,* 813 F.2d 922 (9th Cir.

1987) (striking down racial preferences under strict scrutiny, while upholding gender preference under intermediate scrutiny).

TAXMAN v. BOARD OF EDUCATION

United States Court of Appeals, Third Circuit (*en banc*)
91 F.3d 1547 (3d Cir. 1996), *cert. granted*, 117 S. Ct. 2506,
cert. dismissed, 118 S. Ct. 595 (1997)

MANSMANN, Circuit Judge....

In 1975, the Board of Education of the Township of Piscataway, New Jersey, developed an affirmative action policy applicable to employment decisions.... In 1983 the Board also adopted a one page "Policy", entitled "Affirmative Action — Employment Practices." It is not clear from the record whether the "Policy" superseded or simply added to the "Program," nor does it matter for purposes of this appeal.

The 1975 document states that the purpose of the Program is "to provide equal educational opportunity for students and equal employment opportunity for employees and prospective employees," and "to make a concentrated effort to attract ... minority personnel for all positions so that their qualifications can be evaluated along with other candidates." The 1983 document states that its purpose is to "ensure[ ] equal employment opportunity ... and prohibit [ ] discrimination in employment because of [, *inter alia*,] race...."

The operative language regarding the means by which affirmative-action goals are to be furthered is identical in the two documents. "In all cases, the most qualified candidate will be recommended for appointment. However, when candidates appear to be of equal qualification, candidates meeting the criteria of the affirmative action program will be recommended." The phrase "candidates meeting the criteria of the affirmative action program" refers to members of racial, national origin or gender groups identified as minorities for statistical reporting purposes by the New Jersey State Department of Education, including Blacks. The 1983 document also clarifies that the affirmative action program applies to "every aspect of employment including ... layoffs...."

The Board's affirmative action policy did not have "any remedial purpose"; it was not adopted "with the intention of remedying the results of any prior discrimination or identified underrepresentation of minorities within the Piscataway Public School System." At all relevant times, Black teachers were neither "underrepresented" nor "underutilized" in the Piscataway School District work force. Indeed, statistics in 1976 and 1985 showed that the percentage of Black employees in the job category which included teachers exceeded the percentage of Blacks in the available work force.

In May, 1989, the Board accepted a recommendation from the Superintendent of Schools to reduce the teaching staff in the Business Department at Piscataway High School by one. At that time, two of the teachers in the department were of equal seniority, both having begun their employment with the Board on the same day nine years earlier. One of those teachers was intervenor plaintiff Sharon Taxman, who is White, and the other was Debra Williams, who is Black. Williams was the only minority teacher among the faculty of the Business Department.

Decisions regarding layoffs by New Jersey school boards are highly circumscribed by state law; nontenured faculty must be laid off first, and layoffs among tenured teachers in the affected subject area or grade level must proceed in reverse order of seniority. Seniority for this purpose is calculated according to specific guidelines set by state law. Thus, local boards lack discretion to choose between employees for layoff, except in the rare instance of a tie in seniority between the two or more employees eligible to fill the last remaining position.

The Board determined that it was facing just such a rare circumstance in deciding between Taxman and Williams. In prior decisions involving the layoff of employees with equal seniority, the Board had broken the tie through "a random process which included drawing numbers out of a container, drawing lots or having a lottery."[4] In none of those instances, however, had the employees involved been of different races.

In light of the unique posture of the layoff decision, Superintendent of Schools Burton Edelchick recommended to the Board that the affirmative action plan be invoked in order to determine which teacher to retain. Superintendent Edelchick made this recommendation "because he believed Ms. Williams and Ms. Taxman were tied in seniority, were equally qualified, and because Ms. Williams was the only Black teacher in the Business Education Department."

While the Board recognized that it was not bound to apply the affirmative action policy, it made a discretionary decision to invoke the policy to break the tie between Williams and Taxman. As a result, the Board "voted to terminate the employment of Sharon Taxman, effective June 30, 1988...."

At his deposition Theodore H. Kruse, the Board's President, explained his vote to apply the affirmative action policy as follows:

A.   Basically I think because I had been aware that the student body and the community which is our responsibility, the schools of the community, is really quite diverse and there — I have a general feeling during my tenure on the board that it was valuable for the students to see in the various employment roles a wide range of background, and that it was also valuable to the work force and in particular to the teaching staff that they have — they see that in each other.

---

[4] The dissent of Chief Judge Sloviter characterizes the use of a random process as "a solution that could be expected of the state's gaming tables." We take issue with this characterization, noting that those wiser than we have advised that "the lot puts an end to disputes and is decisive in a controversy between the mighty." *Proverbs* 18:18 (New American). Furthermore, the use of a random process is not something which the court has imposed upon the Board but is instead a mechanism adopted by the Board itself in reaching a decision in prior employment matters.

Asked to articulate the "educational objective" served by retaining Williams rather than Taxman, Kruse stated:

A. In my own personal perspective I believe by retaining Mrs. Williams it was sending a very clear message that we feel that our staff should be culturally diverse, our student population is culturally diverse and there is a distinct advantage to students, to all students, to be made — come into contact with people of different cultures, different background, so that they are more aware, more tolerant, more accepting, more understanding of people of all background.

Q. What do you mean by the phrase you used, culturally diverse?

A. Someone other than — different than yourself. And we have, our student population and our community has people of all different background, ethnic background, religious background, cultural background, and it's important that our school district encourage awareness and acceptance and tolerance and, therefore, I personally think it's important that our staff reflect that too.

[The District Court granted a summary judgment for Taxman on liability and held a trial on damages. The Court awarded Taxman $134,015 in damages for backpay and interest and a jury awarded her an additional $10,000 for emotional suffering.]

II.

In relevant part, Title VII makes it unlawful for an employer "to discriminate against any individual with respect to his compensation, terms, conditions, or privileges of employment" or "to limit, segregate, or classify his employees ... in any way which would deprive or tend to deprive any individual of employment opportunities or otherwise affect his status as an employee" on the basis of "race, color, religion, sex, or national origin." For a time, the Supreme Court construed this language as absolutely prohibiting discrimination in employment, neither requiring nor permitting any preference for any group.

In 1979, however, the Court interpreted the statute's "antidiscriminatory strategy" in a "fundamentally different way", holding in the seminal case of *United Steelworkers v. Weber*, 443 U.S. 193 (1979), that Title VII's prohibition against racial discrimination does not condemn all voluntary race-conscious affirmative action plans. [The Court then provided a description and analysis of the *Weber* and *Johnson v. Transportation Agency* cases.]

III.

We analyze Taxman's claim of employment discrimination under the approach set forth in *McDonnell Douglas v. Green*, 411 U.S. 792 (1973). Once a plaintiff establishes a prima facie case, the burden of production shifts to the employer to show a legitimate nondiscriminatory reason for the decision; an affirmative action plan may be one such reason. *Johnson v. Transportation Agency, Santa Clara County*, 480 U.S. 616 (1987). When the employer satisfies this requirement, the burden of production shifts back to the employee to show that the asserted nondiscriminatory reason is a pretext and that the affirmative action plan is invalid.

For summary judgment purposes, the parties do not dispute that Taxman has established a prima facie case or that the Board's decision to terminate her was based on its affirmative action policy. The dispositive liability issue, therefore, is the validity of the Board's policy under Title VII.

IV.

....

A.

Title VII was enacted to further two primary goals: to end discrimination on the basis of race, color, religion, sex or national origin, thereby guaranteeing equal opportunity in the workplace, and to remedy the segregation and underrepresentation of minorities that discrimination has caused in our Nation's work force.

Title VII's first purpose is set forth in section 2000e-2's several prohibitions, which expressly denounce the discrimination which Congress sought to end. 42 U.S.C. § 2000e-2(a)-(d), (l); *McDonnell Douglas*, 411 U.S. at 800 ("The language of Title VII makes plain the purpose of Congress to assure equality of employment opportunities and to eliminate those discriminatory practices and devices which have fostered racially stratified job environments to the disadvantage of minority citizens.")....

Title VII's second purpose, ending the segregative effects of discrimination, is revealed in the congressional debate surrounding the statute's enactment. In *Weber,* the Court carefully catalogued the comments made by the proponents of Title VII which demonstrate the Act's remedial concerns. *Weber*, 443 U.S. at 202-04. By way of illustration, we cite Senator Clark's remarks to the Senate:

> The rate of Negro unemployment has gone up consistently as compared with white unemployment for the past 15 years. This is a social malaise and a social situation which we should not tolerate. That is one of the principal reasons why the bill should pass.

Id. (quoting 110 Cong. Rec. at 7220) (statement of Sen. Clark)....

The significance of this second corrective purpose cannot be overstated. It is only because Title VII was written to eradicate not only discrimination per se but the *consequences* of prior discrimination as well, that racial preferences in the form of affirmative action can co-exist with the Act's antidiscrimination mandate.

Thus, based on our analysis of Title VII's two goals, we are convinced that unless an affirmative action plan has a remedial purpose, it cannot be said to mirror the purposes of the statute, and, therefore, cannot satisfy the first prong of the *Weber* test.

We see this case as one involving straightforward statutory interpretation controlled by the text and legislative history of Title VII as interpreted in *Weber* and *Johnson*. The statute on its face provides that race cannot be a factor in employer decisions about hires, promotions, and layoffs, and the legislative history demonstrates that barring considerations of race from the workplace was Congress' primary objective. If exceptions to this bar are to be made, they must be made on the basis of what Congress has said. The affirmative action plans at issue in *Weber* and *Johnson* were sustained only because the Supreme Court, examining those plans in light of congressional intent, found a secondary congressional objective in Title VII that had to be accommodated — i.e., the elimination of the effects of past discrimination in the workplace. Here, there is no congressional recognition of diversity as a Title VII objective requiring accommodation.

Accordingly, it is beyond cavil that the Board, by invoking its affirmative action policy to lay off Sharon Taxman, violated the terms of Title VII. While the Court in *Weber* and *Johnson* permitted some deviation from the antidiscrimination mandate of the statute in order to erase the effects of past discrimination, these rulings do not open the door to additional non-remedial deviations. Here, as in *Weber* and *Johnson*, the Board must justify its deviation from the statutory mandate based on positive legislative history, not on its idea of what is appropriate.

B.

The Board recognizes that there is no positive legislative history supporting its goal of promoting racial diversity "for education's sake", and concedes that there is no caselaw approving such a purpose to support an affirmative action plan under Title VII. "[T]he Board would have [us] infer the propriety of this purpose from fragments of other authority."...

We find the Board's reliance on Fourteenth Amendment caselaw misplaced.... We are acutely aware, as is the Board, that the federal courts have never decided a "pure" Title VII case where racial diversity for education's sake was advanced as the sole justification for a race-based decision. The Board argues that in deciding just such a case, we should look to the Supreme Court's endorsement of diversity as a goal in the Equal Protection context. This argument, however, is based upon a faulty premise....

We are ... unpersuaded by the Board's contention that Equal Protection cases arising in an education context support upholding the Board's purpose in a Title VII action. These Equal Protection cases, unlike the case at hand, involved corrective efforts to confront racial segregation or chronic minority under-representation in the schools. In this context, we are not at all surprised that the goal of diversity was raised. While we wholeheartedly endorse any statements in these cases extolling the educational value of exposing students to persons of diverse races and backgrounds, given the framework in which they were made, we cannot accept them as authority for the conclusion that the Board's non-remedial racial diversity goal is a permissible basis for affirmative action under Title VII. *See, e.g., Wygant [v. Jackson Board of Education]*, 476 U.S. at 267 [(1986)] (Marshall, J., dissenting) (noting that the racially-conscious layoff provision at issue was aimed at preserving the faculty integration achieved by the Jackson, Michigan Public Schools in the early 1970s through affirmative action; minority representation went from 3.9% in 1969 to 8.8% in 1971); *Columbus Board of Education v. Penick*, 443 U.S. 449, 467 (1979) (condemning intentional segregation and the creation of racially-identifiable schools practiced by the Columbus, Ohio Board of Education); *Regents of the University of California v. Bakke*, 438 U.S. 265 (1978) (Powell, J., announcing the judgment of the Court) (observing that the 1968 class of the Medical School of the University of California at Davis contained three Asians, no Blacks, no Mexican-Americans and no American Indians).

More specifically, two Supreme Court cases upon which the Board relies, *Bakke*, 438 U.S. at 265, and *Metro Broadcasting Inc. v. FCC*, 497 U.S. 547 (1990), are inapposite. *Bakke* involved a rejected White applicant's challenge under the Constitution and Title VI of the Civil Rights Act of 1964 to a special admissions program instituted by the Medical School of the University of California at Davis which essentially set aside 16 places for minority candidates. Justice Powell, whose vote was necessary both to establish the validity of considering race in admission decisions and to invalidate the racial quota before the Court, was of the opinion that the attainment of a "diverse student body" is a constitutionally permissible goal for an institution of higher education....

[However,] *Bakke*'s factual and legal setting, as well as the diversity that universities aspire to in their student bodies, are, in our view, so different from the facts, relevant law and the racial diversity purpose involved in this case that we find little in *Bakke* to guide us.

Likewise, statements regarding the value of programming diversity made by the Court in *Metro Broadcasting* when it upheld two minority preference policies adopted by the Federal Communications Commission have no application here. The diversity interest the Court found sufficient under the Constitution to support a racial classification had nothing whatsoever to do with the concerns that underlie Title VII. Citing *Bakke*, the Court concluded that "[j]ust as a 'diverse student body' contributing to a 'robust exchange of ideas' is a 'constitutionally permissible goal' on which a race-conscious university admissions program may be predicated, the diversity of views and information on the airwaves serves important First Amendment values." *Id.* at 568.

Finally, we turn to the Board's argument that the diversity goal underlying its application of the affirmative action policy was endorsed in Justice O'Connor's concurring opinion in *Wygant* and in Justice Stevens' concurring opinion in *Johnson*. We find that these statements are slender reeds indeed and any bearing that they may have in the situation presented here is minimal. While Justice O'Connor did refer favorably to *Bakke* and the notion of racial diversity in institutions of higher learning [in] *Wygant*, just one year later in *Johnson*, a Title VII case, she rejected Justice Steven's expansive view of the purposes that may underlie affirmative action, stating: "[C]ontrary to the intimations in Justice Stevens' concurrence, this Court did not approve preferences for minorities 'for any reason that might seem sensible from a business or social point of view.'" As for Justice Stevens' concurrence in *Johnson*, while he clearly pondered the idea of "forward-looking" affirmative action where employers do not focus on "purg[ing] their own past sins of discrimination", his comments are not controlling.

V.

Since we have not found anything in the Board's arguments to convince us that this case requires examination beyond statutory interpretation, we return to the point at which we started: the language of Title VII itself and the two cases reviewing affirmative action plans in light of that statute. Our analysis of the statute and the caselaw convinces us that a non-remedial affirmative action plan cannot form the basis for deviating from the antidiscrimination mandate of Title VII.

The Board admits that it did not act to remedy the effects of past employment discrimination. The parties have stipulated that neither the Board's adoption of its affirmative action policy nor its subsequent decision to apply it in choosing between Taxman and Williams was intended to remedy the results of any prior discrimination or identified underrepresentation of Blacks within the Piscataway School District's teacher workforce as a whole. Nor does the Board contend that its action here was directed at remedying any *de jure* or *de facto* segregation. Even though the Board's race-conscious action was taken to avoid what could have been an all-White faculty within the Business Department, the Board concedes that Blacks are not underrepresented in its teaching workforce as a whole or even in the Piscataway High School.

Rather, the Board's sole purpose in applying its affirmative action policy in this case was to obtain an educational benefit which it believed would result from a racially diverse faculty. While the benefits flowing from diversity in the educational context are significant indeed, we are constrained to hold, as did the district court, that inasmuch as "the Board does not even attempt to show that its affirmative action plan was adopted to remedy past discrimination or as the result of a manifest imbalance in the employment of minorities," the Board has failed to satisfy the first prong of the *Weber* test.

We turn next to the second prong of the *Weber* analysis. This second prong requires that we determine whether the Board's policy "unnecessarily trammel[s] ... [nonminority] interests...." Under this requirement, too, the Board's policy is deficient.

We begin by noting the policy's utter lack of definition and structure. While it is not for us to decide how much diversity in a high school facility is "enough," the Board cannot abdicate its responsibility to define "racial diversity" and to determine what degree of racial diversity in the Piscataway School is sufficient.... The affirmative action plans that have met with the Supreme Court's approval under Title VII had objectives, as well as benchmarks which served to evaluate progress, guide the employment decisions at issue and assure the grant of only those minority preferences necessary to further the plans' purpose. By contrast, the Board's policy, devoid of goals and standards, is governed entirely by the Board's whim, leaving the Board free, if it so chooses, to grant racial preferences that do not promote even the policy's claimed purpose. Indeed, under the terms of this policy, the Board, in pursuit of a "racially diverse" work force, could use affirmative action to discriminate against those whom Title VII was enacted to protect. Such a policy unnecessarily trammels the interests of nonminority employees.

Moreover, both *Weber* and *Johnson* unequivocally provide that valid affirmative action plans are "temporary" measures that seek to "attain", not "maintain" a "permanent racial ... balance." The Board's policy, adopted in 1975, is an established fixture of unlimited duration, to be resurrected from time to time whenever the Board believes that the ratio between Blacks and Whites in any Piscataway School is skewed. On this basis alone, the policy contravenes *Weber*'s teaching.

Finally, we are convinced that the harm imposed upon a nonminority employee by the loss of his or her job is so substantial and the cost so severe that the Board's goal of racial diversity, even if legitimate under Title VII, may not be pursued in this particular fashion. This is especially true where, as here, the nonminority employee is tenured. In *Weber* and *Johnson*, when considering whether nonminorities were unduly encumbered by affirmative action, the Court found it significant that they retained their employment. We, therefore, adopt the plurality's pronouncement in Wygant that "[w]hile hiring goals impose a diffuse burden, often foreclosing only one of several opportunities, layoffs impose the entire burden of achieving racial equality on particular individuals, often resulting in serious disruption of their lives. That burden is too intrusive." *Wygant*, 476 U.S. at 283.

Accordingly, we conclude that under the second prong of the Weber test, the Board's affirmative action policy violates Title VII. In addition to containing an impermissible purpose, the policy "unnecessarily trammel[s] the interests of the [nonminority] employees."...

VII.

Having found the Board liable under Title VII, we turn our attention to the issue of damages, addressing first the district court's order that Taxman be awarded one hundred percent backpay for the entire period of her layoff. The Board argues that where a backpay award is appropriate, the court's goal should be to restore "the conditions and relationships that would have been had there been no" unlawful discrimination. According to the Board, the district court's award of one hundred percent backpay was plainly unfair. Had it not invoked the affirmative action plan, the Board would have followed its usual procedure, using a coin toss or other random process to break the seniority tie between Williams and Taxman. Taxman, therefore, would have stood no more than a fifty percent chance of keeping her job had there been no unlawful discrimination.

We disagree. In deciding backpay issues, a district court has wide latitude to "locate 'a just result'" and to further the "make whole remedy of Title VII in light of the circumstances of a particular case." *Albemarle Paper Co. v. Moody*, 422 U.S. 405 (1975). While Taxman cannot be returned to the position that she held prior to her layoff — one of virtually precise equality with Williams in terms of the factors relevant to the decision — she can be returned to a position of financial equality with Williams through a one hundred percent backpay award. We are convinced that this award most closely approximates the conditions that would have prevailed in the absence of discrimination.

We find an additional basis for our holding in the analysis set forth in *Price Waterhouse v. Hopkins*, 490 U.S. 228 (1989). In that case, the Supreme Court held that where an employee proves that discrimination played a role in an employment decision, the employer will not be found "liable if it can prove that, even if it had not taken [race] into account it would have come to the same decision regarding a particular person." Here, Taxman has clearly established that the Board is liable and that she was not paid during the relevant period. Under the logic of *Hopkins*, the Board cannot avoid a one hundred percent backpay award unless it can establish, by a preponderance of the evidence, that Taxman would have received some lesser amount had the Board not taken race into account. This, of course, the Board cannot do.

Given the law and the circumstances presented in this case, we are convinced that the district court's analysis with respect to backpay reflects the sound exercise of judicial discretion and we will affirm the award....

VIII.

While we have rejected the argument that the Board's non-remedial application of the affirmative action policy is consistent with the language and intent of Title VII, we do not reject in principle the diversity goal articulated by the Board. Indeed, we recognize that the differences among us underlie the richness and strength of our Nation. Our disposition of this matter, however, rests squarely on the foundation of Title VII. Although we applaud the goal of racial diversity, we cannot agree that Title VII permits an employer to advance that goal through non-remedial discriminatory measures.

SLOVITER, Chief Judge, dissenting, with whom Judges LEWIS and McKEE join.

In the law, as in other professions, it is often how the question is framed that determines the answer that is received. Although the divisive issue of affirmative action continues on this country's political agenda, I do not see this appeal as raising a broad legal referendum on affirmative action policies. Indeed, it is questionable whether this case is about affirmative action at all, as that term has come to be generally understood — i.e. preference based on race or gender of one deemed "less qualified" over one deemed "more qualified."...

Instead, the narrow question posed by this appeal can be restated as whether Title VII requires a New Jersey school or school board, which is faced with deciding which of two equally qualified teachers should be laid off, to make its decision through a coin toss or lottery, a solution that could be expected of the state's gaming tables, or whether Title VII permits the school board to factor into the decision its bona fide belief, based on its experience with secondary schools, that students derive educational benefit by having a Black faculty member in an otherwise all-White department. Because I believe that the area of discretion left to employers in educational institutions by Title VII encompasses the School Board's action in this case, I respectfully dissent.

The posture in which the legal issue in this case is presented is so stripped of extraneous factors that it could well serve as the question for a law school moot court. I emphasize at the outset issues that this case does not present. We need not decide whether it is permissible for a school to lay off a more qualified employee in favor of a less qualified employee on the basis of race, because that did not happen here. Nor need we consider what requirements Title VII may impose on unwilling employers, or how much racial diversity in a high school faculty may be "enough."...

II.

It was the Board's decision to include the desire for a racially diverse faculty among the various factors entering into its discretionary decision that the majority of this court brands a Title VII violation as a matter of law. *No* Supreme Court case compels that anomalous result. Notwithstanding the majority's literal construction of the language of Title VII, no Supreme Court case has ever interpreted the statute to preclude consideration of race or sex for the purpose of insuring diversity in the classroom as *one of many* factors in an employment decision, the situation presented here. Moreover, in the only two instances in which the Supreme Court examined under Title VII, without the added scrutiny imposed by the Equal Protection Clause, affirmative action plans voluntarily adopted by employers that gave preference to race or sex as a determinative factor, the Court upheld both plans....

The majority presents *Weber* and *Johnson* as if their significance lies in the obstacle course they purportedly establish for any employer adopting an affirmative action program. But ... the significance of each of those cases is that the Supreme Court sustained the affirmative action plans presented, and in doing so deviated from the literal interpretation of Title VII precluding use of race or gender in any employment action.... [I]t does not follow as a matter of logic that because the two affirmative action plans in *Weber* and *Johnson* which sought to remedy imbalances caused by past discrimination withstood Title VII scrutiny, every affirmative action plan that pursues some purpose other than correcting a manifest imbalance or remedying past discrimination will run afoul of Title VII. Indeed, the Court in *Weber* explicitly cautioned that its holding in that case should not be read to define the outer boundaries of the area of discretion left to employers by Title VII for the voluntary adoption of affirmative action measures. The Court stated:

> We need not today define in detail the line of demarcation between permissible and impermissible affirmative action plans. It suffices to hold that the challenged Kaiser-USWA affirmative action plan falls on the permissible side of the line. The purposes of the plan mirror those of the statute. Both were designed to break down old patterns of racial segregation and hierarchy. Both were structured to "open employment opportunities for Negroes in occupations which have been traditionally closed to them."

Weber, 443 U.S. at 208 (Blackmun, J., concurring) (noting that Kaiser plan "is a moderate one" and that "the Court's opinion does not foreclose other forms of affirmative action")....

It is "ironic indeed" that the promotion of racial diversity in the classroom, which has formed so central a role in this country's struggle to eliminate the causes and consequences of racial discrimination, is today held to be at odds with the very Act that was triggered by our "Nation's concern over centuries of racial injustice." *Weber*, 443 U.S. at 204. Nor does it seem plausible that the drafters of Title VII intended it to be interpreted so as to require a local school district to resort to a lottery to determine which of two qualified teachers to retain, rather than employ the School Board's own educational policy undertaken to insure students an opportunity to learn from a teacher who was a member of the very group whose treatment motivated Congress to enact Title VII in the first place. In my view, the Board's purpose of obtaining the educational benefit to be derived from a racially diverse faculty is entirely consistent with the purposes animating Title VII and the Civil Rights Act of 1964....

I therefore respectfully disagree with the majority, both in its construction of *Weber* and *Johnson* as leaving no doors open for any action that takes race into consideration in an employment situation other than to remedy past discrimination and the consequential racial imbalance in the workforce, and in what appears to be its limited view of the purposes of Title VII. I would hold that a school board's bona fide decision to obtain the educational benefit to be derived from a racially diverse faculty is a permissible basis for its voluntary affirmative action under Title VII scrutiny.

III.

It is undeniable that, in the abstract, a layoff imposes a far greater burden on the affected employee than a denial of promotion or even a failure to hire. In this case, however, it cannot be said with any certainty that Taxman would have avoided the layoff had the Board's decision not been race-conscious. If a random selection had been made, Taxman would have had no more than a fifty-percent chance of not being laid off. Thus, this was not a situation where Taxman had a "legitimate and firmly rooted expectation" of no layoff. *Johnson*, 480 U.S. at 638.

This differs from the situation of an employee who is next in line for a promotion by the objective factor of seniority. Taxman's qualifications were merely equal to those of her competitor for this purpose. In *Johnson* the Court held that because there were six other employees who also met the qualifications for the job, Johnson had no "entitlement" or "legitimate firmly rooted expectation" in the promotion, even though he had scored higher than the others on the qualifying test. Moreover, just as the plaintiff in *Johnson* remained eligible for promotion in the future, Taxman retained recall rights after her layoff, and did in fact regain her job....

In the situation before us, I see ample basis from which to deduce an effort to minimize the effect of the Board's affirmative action policy on non-minority employees. One such aspect is the discretionary nature of the policy. The Board is free not to apply the policy, even to break a tie. Also significant is the infrequency with which the Board has resorted to the policy. Although it may be of little comfort to Taxman, the fact that this is the first time in the twenty years since the policy was adopted that it has been applied to a layoff decision demonstrates the minimum impact on White teachers as a whole. And since, by its own terms, it only applies in the rare instances in which two candidates are of different races but equal qualifications and the department in question is not already diverse, it is likely that it will continue to be infrequently applied....

I return to the question raised at the outset: whether Title VII requires that the Board toss a coin to make the layoff selection between equally situated employees. In his opinion for the majority in *Weber*, Justice Brennan noted the distinction made by Congress between *requiring* and *permitting* affirmative action by employers. He deemed it important that, while Congress explicitly provided that Title VII should not be interpreted to *require* any employer to grant preferential treatment to a group because of its race, Congress never stated that Title VII should not be interpreted to *permit* certain voluntary efforts.

In this case, the majority gives too little consideration to the tie-breaking method that its holding will impose on the Board. It points to no language in Title VII to suggest that a lottery is required as the solution to a layoff decision in preference to a reasoned decision by members of the School Board, some of whom are experienced educators, that the race of a faculty member has a relevant educational significance if the department would otherwise be all White. While it may seem fairer to some, I see nothing in Title VII that requires use of a lottery.

Because I cannot say that faculty diversity is not a permissible purpose to support the race-conscious decision made here and because the Board's action was not overly intrusive on Taxman's rights, I would reverse the grant of summary judgment for Taxman under Title VII and direct that summary judgment be granted to the School Board.[1]

NOTES

1. *The Final Resolution.* The *Taxman* case was settled after the Supreme Court had granted certiorari. Sharon Taxman received $433,500. The settlement was quite unusual because it was made possible when the Black Leadership Forum agreed to contribute $308,500 (or about 70% of the total amount) towards the settlement. The School Board paid the rest. The Black Leadership Forum is a coalition of national civil rights organizations which includes the Urban League, the NAACP, and the Rainbow Coalition.

2. *Law Schools and Affirmative Action.* Law schools, for better or worse, have been on the front line in the affirmative action debate. The University of Texas's admissions procedures, which granted preferences to blacks and Mexican-Americans, were ruled unconstitutional in *Hopwood v. Texas*, 78 F.3d 932 (5th Cir.), *cert. denied*, 116 S. Ct. 2581 (1996). In California, the Board of Regents ended affirmative action, in part because of Proposition 209 (the California Civil Rights Initiative), and the first results of that action were seen in law school admissions. At the U.C.L.A. Law School, the number of blacks accepted fell about 80% between 1996 and 1997, from 104 students to 21. Only eight eventually enrolled. At Berkeley, the number of blacks admitted fell from 74 students to 15, and only one eventually enrolled. An empirical analysis has con-

---

[1] Because I think the school board is not liable I will not dwell on the issue of damages. I note simply that there is much logic to the Board's argument that Taxman should be awarded fifty percent rather than one hundred percent of the backpay she would have received had she not been laid off. The record shows that, had the Board not based its decision on race, it would have chosen between Taxman and Williams by means of a coin toss or lottery. Since in such circumstances Taxman would have stood only a fifty-percent chance of retaining her job, a fifty-percent backpay award most accurately "recreate[s] the conditions and relationships that would have been had there been no" consideration of race.

firmed that limits on affirmative action efforts would sharply limit the number of minority law students. Professor Wightman found 1) that "numbers only" policies will sharply limit the number of minority students, and 2) that using substitutes for race and ethnicity, such as socioeconomic status, would not be effective in maintaining the current diversity of law schools. Linda F. Wightman, *The Threat to Diversity in Legal Education: An Empirical Analysis of the Consequences of Abandoning Race as a Factor in Law School Admission Decisions*, 72 N.Y.U. L. REV. 1 (1997).

3. *Diversity*. Scholars who generally support affirmative action have begun to question the diversity rationale:

> I have two recommendations for those who favor affirmative action. First, institutions with affirmative action plans should be open about them or scrap them. If the burdens that an honest affirmative action program imposes on its beneficiaries are too great to bear, the correct response is not to prevaricate, but to try something new. Second, the pro-affirmative action crowd needs to own up to the weakness of "diversity" as a defense of most affirmative action plans. Everyone knows that in most cases a true diversity of perspectives and backgrounds is not really being pursued. (Why no preferences for fundamentalist Christians or for neo-Nazis?)
>
> The purpose of affirmative action is to bring our nation's institutions more blacks, more Hispanics, more Native Americans, more women, sometimes more Asians, and so on — period. Pleading diversity of backgrounds merely invites heightened scrutiny into the true objectives behind affirmative action. This heightened scrutiny would quite properly reveal the existence of a race- or group-related purpose, rather than a genuine interest in achieving a representative diversity of perspectives. In fact, the true, core objective of race-based affirmative action is nothing other than helping blacks. Friends of affirmative action, if there are any left, should acknowledge this objective, and they should embrace it — in the name of justice.

Jed Rubenfeld, *Affirmative Action*, 107 YALE L.J. 427, 471-72 (1997). *See also* Deborah C. Malamud, *Affirmative Action, Diversity, and the Black Middle Class*, 68 U. COLO. L. REV. 939 (1997) (arguing that diversity rationale is "highly problematic" and ought to be augmented with an economic justice rationale).

4. *Symbolism*. Affirmative action is controversial, not only because of its real-world consequences, but also because of its symbolism:

> [A]ffirmative action has meant racial progress for two generations of African Americans. That is its symbolic significance. The dramatic act of eliminating it now carries with it an undeniably negative message to and about its potential beneficiaries. Our original decision to adopt affirmative action as the lynchpin of American race policy may have been wrong. It may have been right, but for reasons that were not the basis for the original decision.

But too much time has gone by, too many reasonable expectations have been built upon it, to change courses now.

Deborah C. Malamud, *Values, Symbols, and Facts in the Affirmative Action Debate*, 95 MICH. L. REV. 1668, 1712 (1997).

D. ENFORCING THE FEDERAL DISCRIMINATION LAWS

The procedures and remedies for enforcing the federal discrimination laws are complex. One reason for the complexity is that the laws rely to a great extent on private enforcement by persons alleging discrimination, and yet a very significant public interest exists in ensuring that the laws are enforced adequately and fairly. Providing adequate incentives for private parties to enforce the laws and determining the appropriate relationship between private enforcers and public enforcement agencies has not been easy. Another reason for the complexity is that the federal discrimination laws are, as a general matter, not preemptive. As a result, an employee alleging sex discrimination in Any City, USA, may be able to proceed under a private arbitration agreement, a local ordinance, a state statute, and a federal law, all of which have different procedures for enforcing the same basic substantive protection. Coordinating these overlapping procedures has resulted in considerable complexity.

Three basic procedural models exist for enforcing the federal discrimination laws. One model is provided by Title VII and is used for claims arising under that act and under the Americans with Disabilities Act. A second model is provided by the Fair Labor Standards Act and is used for Equal Pay Act claims and, in a modified form, for claims under the Age Discrimination in Employment Act. A third model is used to enforce the nineteenth century civil rights acts.

Under Title VII, the federal procedure begins when an employee files a charge with the Equal Employment Opportunity Commission. If no recognized state or local agency exists for dealing with the particular type of discrimination alleged, the employee must file the charge within 180 days of the alleged discrimination. If a state or local agency exists, a charge must be filed with it at least sixty days before the charge is filed with the EEOC; the EEOC filing must occur within 300 days of the alleged discrimination. (The EEOC has worksharing agreements with most state and local agencies which mean, in practice, that only one charge needs to be filed.) The EEOC notifies the employer of the charge and begins an investigation. If, after the investigation, the EEOC finds no reasonable cause to believe discrimination occurred, the agency issues a right-to-sue letter to the charging party which authorizes the party to file a court action. The employee must file the court action within ninety days of receiving the right-to-sue letter. If the EEOC determines that there is reasonable cause to believe that discrimination has occurred, the agency begins a process of conciliation. If conciliation is unsuccessful, the EEOC once again issues a right-to-sue letter which authorizes the charging party to file a court action within ninety days. If appropriate, the charging party may file the action as a class action pursuant to FED. R. CIV. P. 23. The remedies under Title VII include injunctions, backpay, compensatory and punitive damages (for intentional discrimination only),[*] and attorneys' fees. The EEOC (and the Attorney General for public employers) also have the authority to file court actions on behalf of aggrieved employees.

The second enforcement model is provided by the Fair Labor Standards Act for enforcing the Equal Pay Act and, with some modifications, the Age Discrimination in Employment Act. Aggrieved persons may file a court action under these statutes, even if they have not earlier filed charges with an administrative agency. The time limit for filing a court action is normally two years from the time the discrimination occurred, although it is extended to three years for willful violations. (The Supreme Court defined "willful" in *McLaughlin v. Richland Shoe Co.,* 486 U.S. 128 (1988). *See* Chapter 16, Section B.[**] The FLSA permits class actions, but the procedure is less favorable to plaintiffs than the normal FED. R. CIV. P. 23 class action procedure; under the FLSA, persons can be included in a class action only if they affirmatively opt in to the class by filing a notice with the court. Successful plaintiffs may obtain an injunction, backpay, an amount equal to backpay in liquidated damages, and attorneys' fees.

The third enforcement model consists of the procedures for enforcing the nineteenth century civil rights acts. Sections 1981 and 1983 impose no procedural prerequisites to filing an action in court. Plaintiffs may seek injunctive relief, backpay, compensatory and punitive damages, and attorneys' fees. The compensatory and punitive damages are not limited in amount under sections 1981 and 1983 as they are under Title VII. The acts do not contain their own statutes of limitation, so the most analogous state statute applies — generally the limitation for personal injury tort actions.

NOTES

1. *Alternative Enforcement Schemes.* Congress had a broad array of options available to it when it was deciding how to enforce Title VII and the other statutes prohibiting status discrimination:

---

[*] Until 1991, compensatory and punitive damages were unavailable under Title VII. In the Civil Rights Act of 1991, Congress amended Title VII to permit compensatory and punitive damages for amounts up to $50,000 (for employers with 100 or fewer employees) gradually increasing to a cap of $300,000 (for employers with more than 500 employees).

[**] The ADEA does not follow the normal FLSA procedure on charge-filing requirements and the statute of limitations. Under the ADEA, as amended by the Civil Rights Act of 1991, employees must file charges with the EEOC, and the time limits for filing charges mirror those of Title VII (180 or 300 days). Instead of the two- or three-year statute of limitations, the outer time limit for filing court actions under the ADEA is ninety days after being notified by the EEOC that its processing has been completed. Under the Equal Pay Act, aggrieved persons *may* file a charge with the EEOC, even though they are not required to do so. They may do so if, for example, they think conciliation may be helpful or they would like the EEOC to file suit on their behalf.

(a) Congress could have established an administrative agency with the sole authority to prosecute claims arising under the statute. As under the National Labor Relations Act and the Occupational Safety and Health Act, employees or unions could have been permitted to file charges with the agency, but the agency would have had the authority to decide which charges to pursue and would have been the prosecutor.

(b) Congress could have relied on private enforcement alone, authorizing only persons alleging discrimination to sue, and could have implemented either the American rule (parties bear their own costs) or the British rule (loser pays other side's costs) for allocating the costs of suit, including attorneys' fees.

(c) Congress could have relied principally on private enforcement and encouraged such enforcement with a rule that permitted successful plaintiffs (but not successful defendants) to recover their attorneys' fees, while also authorizing government agencies to participate in the enforcement process and to file suit themselves. (This, of course, is a short description of the enforcement structure for Title VII and the ADA.)

Consider the pros and cons of these enforcement options on factors such as the types of suits that are likely to be brought, the amounts expended by the parties on attorneys' fees, the incidence of the costs of enforcement, the likely effects on primary behavior (how much discrimination occurs), and the influence of the government on the shape and direction of antidiscrimination policy.

2. *Attorneys' Fees Provisions.* All of the major federal civil rights statutes have provisions that permit prevailing parties to recover their attorneys' fees. The provisions are generally interpreted to permit plaintiffs to recover their attorneys' fees whenever they prevail, while permitting defendants to recover their fees only if the suit was frivolous, unreasonable, or groundless. *Christiansburg Garment Co. v. EEOC,* 434 U.S. 412 (1978).

Attorneys' fees provisions raise a number of implementation issues, such as:

a) Who is entitled to recover attorneys' fees? *See Kay v. Ehrler,* 499 U.S. 432 (1991) (attorney representing himself in a case not entitled to attorneys' fees).

b) What does it mean to be a "prevailing party"? *See Hewitt v. Helms,* 482 U.S. 755 (1987) (plaintiff who establishes violation, but does not obtain any relief or change the defendant's behavior toward him, is not a prevailing party); *Maher v. Gagne,* 448 U.S. 122 (1980) (plaintiff who obtains consent decree but no judicial determination of discrimination was a prevailing party).

c) How should courts determine the amount of the fees? *See Pennsylvania v. Delaware Valley Citizens' Council,* 478 U.S. 546 (1986) (base fees on "lodestar" amount, determined by multiplying hours by a reasonable hourly rate, and adjustments based on other relevant factors such as the risk of loss); *City of Burlington v. Dague,* 505 U.S. 557 (1992) (not permissible to adjust lodestar amount because of contingency fee arrangement).

3. *Multiple Forums.* Discrimination claims can be heard in a number of different forums, which raises issues about the relationship between the forums. The relationship between private arbitration of discrimination claims and judicial resolution presents one set of issues. Until 1991, the courts had granted little deference to decisions by arbitrators on discrimination issues. *See Alexander v. Gardner-Denver Co.,* 415 U.S. 36 (1974). In *Gilmer v. Interstate/Johnson Lane Corp.,* 500 U.S. 20 (1991), however, the Supreme Court distinguished the prior cases in holding that a plaintiff could be bound by his agreement to arbitrate an age discrimination claim. The *Gilmer* holding has also been applied to other types of discrimination claims, such as Title VII claims. *See, e.g., Patterson v. Tenet Healthcare, Inc.,* 113 F.3d 832 (8th Cir. 1997); *Austin v. Owens-Brockway Glass Container, Inc.,* 78 F.3d 875 (4th Cir.), *cert. denied,* 117 S. Ct. 432 (1996). *Gilmer* is discussed in detail in Chapter 7.

In addition to the *Gilmer* issue of the relationship between arbitral and federal forums, the courts have also had to deal with the relationship between state and federal forums. The Supreme Court has held that state administrative proceedings alone do not have preclusive effect in a subsequent case in federal court under Title VII or the ADEA, but could have preclusive effect under sections 1981 and 1983. State *court* decisions, however, can be used to preclude subsequent federal court litigation under all of these statutes. *Kremer v. Chemical Constr. Corp.,* 456 U.S. 461 (1982) (Title VII); *Astoria Fed. Sav. & Loan Ass'n v. Solimino,* 501 U.S. 104 (1991) (ADEA); *University of Tenn. v. Elliott,* 478 U.S. 788 (1986) (Sections 1981 and 1983). These cases and *Gilmer* indicate that familiarity with these types of procedural rules are an important component of strategy in litigating employment discrimination claims.

4. *Changes in the Volume and Nature of Litigation.* The volume of employment discrimination litigation has increased significantly over the years. Less than 350 cases were filed in fiscal year 1970; over 7,500 cases were filed in 1989. Professors Donohue and Siegelman attribute the increase to a number of factors, including long-term increases in the rate of unemployment; growth in the population of workers eligible to sue; changes in the law that expanded coverage; the movement of protected workers into better jobs; and the increased integration of the workforce.

The nature of employment discrimination litigation has also changed over time. In 1966, charges alleging discrimination in hiring outnumbered charges alleging discrimination in firing by two to one. By 1985, the ratio had reversed dramatically; charges alleging firing discrimination outnumbered hiring discrimination charges by six to one. This change may create perverse incentives for employers:

> Absent any law prohibiting discrimination, [an] employer will make his hiring decision by comparing the value of the applicant's output if hired with the economic and psychological costs of hiring her. If the first quantity

is larger than the second, the employer will decide to hire; otherwise, he will reject the applicant.

When discrimination is illegal, the employer must also take into account the potential costs of rejecting the applicant. These costs include the possible litigation costs if the applicant decided to sue and the damage award if the suit is successful, all weighted by their respective probabilities of occurrence.

The equation becomes more complicated when the possibility of discriminatory firing suits is introduced. A worker who is not hired in the first place is obviously in no position to bring a future firing suit. Thus, an employer must consider the *increase* in expected costs when he hires a female or minority worker, because some probability exists that the worker will be fired and will sue.... With the enormous increase in discharge cases, the probability that a worker will bring a discriminatory firing suit is now substantially higher than the probability that a worker will bring a failure to hire suit. Consequently, antidiscrimination laws may actually provide employers a (small) net disincentive to hire women and minorities.

John J. Donohue, III & Peter Siegelman, *The Changing Nature of Employment Discrimination Litigation,* 43 STAN. L. REV. 983, 1024 (1991). *See also* Ian Ayres & Peter Siegelman, *The Q-Word as Red Herring: Why Disparate Impact Liability Does Not Induce Hiring Quotas,* 74 TEX. L. REV. 1847 (1996) (analyzing the effect of the changed ratio of hiring to firing cases on the disparate impact model of discrimination); Steven L. Willborn, *The Non-Evolution of Enforcement Under the ADA: Discharge Cases and the Hiring Problem, in* EMPLOYMENT, DISABILITY, AND THE AMERICANS WITH DISABILITIES ACT: ISSUES IN LAW, PUBLIC POLICY, AND RESEARCH (Peter David Blanck ed., forthcoming 1999) (analyzing the more severe hiring to discharge ratio of 10 to 1 under the Americans with Disabilities Act).

Part VI
Regulation of Compensation

Chapter 16

WAGES AND HOURS LEGISLATION

A. THE HISTORY OF WAGE AND HOUR REGULATION IN THE UNITED STATES

LOCHNER v. NEW YORK

United States Supreme Court
198 U.S. 45 (1905)

MR. JUSTICE PECKHAM ... delivered the opinion of the court.

The indictment charges ... that the plaintiff in error ... wrongfully and unlawfully required and permitted an employé working for him to work more than sixty hours in one week.[*]... The mandate of the statute, that "no employee shall be required or permitted to work," is the substantial equivalent of an enactment that "no employé shall contract or agree to work," more than ten hours per day, and as there is no provision for special emergencies the statute is mandatory in all cases. It is not an act merely fixing the number of hours which shall constitute a legal day's work, but an absolute prohibition upon the employer permitting, under any circumstances, more than ten hours' work to be done in his establishment. The employé may desire to earn the extra money which would arise from his working more than the prescribed time, but this statute forbids the employer from permitting the employé to earn it.

The statute necessarily interferes with the right of contract between the employer and employés, concerning the number of hours in which the latter may labor in the bakery of the employer. The general right to make a contract in relation to his business is part of the liberty of the individual protected by the Fourteenth Amendment of the Federal Constitution. Under that provision no State can deprive any person of life, liberty or property without due process of law. The right to purchase or to sell labor is part of the liberty protected by this amendment, unless there are circumstances which exclude the right. There are, however, certain powers, existing in the sovereignty of each State in the Union, somewhat vaguely termed police powers, the exact description and limitation of which have not been attempted by the courts. Those powers, broadly stated, and without, at present, any attempt at a more specific limitation, relate to the safety,

---

[*] The section of the New York statute under which the indictment was found reads as follows:

§ 110. *Hours of labor in bakeries and confectionery establishments.* No employé shall be required or permitted to work in a biscuit, bread or cake bakery or confectionery establishment more than sixty hours in any one week, or more than ten hours in any one day, unless for the purpose of making a shorter work day on the last day of the week; nor more hours in any one week than will make an average of ten hours per day for the number of days during such week in which such employé shall work.

health, morals, and general welfare of the public. Both property and liberty are held on such reasonable conditions as may be imposed by the governing power of the State in the exercise of those powers, and with such conditions the Fourteenth Amendment was not designed to interfere.

The State, therefore, has power to prevent the individual from making certain kinds of contracts, and in regard to them the Federal Constitution offers no protection. If the contract be one which the State, in the legitimate exercise of its police power, has the right to prohibit, it is not prevented from prohibiting it by the Fourteenth Amendment. Contracts in violation of a statute, either of the Federal or state government, or a contract to let one's property for immoral purposes, or to do any other unlawful act, could obtain no protection from the Federal Constitution, as coming under the liberty of person or of free contract. Therefore, when the State, by its legislature, in the assumed exercise of its police powers, has passed an act which seriously limits the right to labor or the right of contract in regard to their means of livelihood between persons who are *sui juris* (both employer and employé), it becomes of great importance to determine which shall prevail — the right of the individual to labor for such time as he may choose, or the right of the State to prevent the individual from laboring or from entering into any contract to labor, beyond a certain time prescribed by the State.

This court has recognized the existence and upheld the exercise of the police powers of the States in many cases which might fairly be considered as border ones, and it has, in the course of its determination of questions regarding the asserted invalidity of such statutes, on the ground of their violation of the rights secured by the Federal Constitution, been guided by rules of a very liberal nature, the application of which has resulted, in numerous instances, in upholding the validity of state statutes thus assailed. Among the later cases where the state law has been upheld by this court is that of *Holden v. Hardy,* 169 U.S. 366 [1898]. A provision in the act of the legislature of Utah was there under consideration, the act limiting the employment of workmen in all underground mines or workings, to eight hours per day, "except in cases of emergency, where life or property is in imminent danger." It also limited the hours of labor in smelting and other institutions for the reduction or refining of ores or metals to eight hours per day, except in like cases of emergency. The act was held to be a valid exercise of the police powers of the State. It was held that the kind of employment, mining, smelting, etc., and the character of the employés in such kinds of labor, were such as to make it reasonable and proper for the state to interfere to prevent the employés from being constrained by the rules laid down by the proprietors in regard to labor....

It will be observed that, even with regard to that class of labor, the Utah statute provided for cases of emergency wherein the provisions of the statute would not apply. The statute now before this court has no emergency clause in it, and, if the statute is valid, there are no circumstances and no emergencies under which the slightest violation of the provisions of the act would be innocent. There is nothing in *Holden v. Hardy* which covers the case now before us....

It must, of course, be conceded that there is a limit to the valid exercise of the police power by the State. There is no dispute concerning this general proposition. Otherwise the Fourteenth Amendment would have no efficacy and the legislatures of the States would have unbounded power, and it would be enough to say that any piece of legislation was enacted to conserve the morals, the health, or the safety of the people; such legislation would be valid, no matter how absolutely without foundation the claim might be. The claim of the police power would be a mere pretext, — become another and delusive name for the supreme sovereignty of the State to be exercised free from constitutional restraint. This is not contended for. In every case that comes before this court, therefore, where legislation of this character is concerned, and where the protection of the Federal Constitution is sought, the question necessarily arises: Is this a fair, reasonable, and appropriate exercise of the police power of the State, or is it an unreasonable, unnecessary, and arbitrary interference with the right of the individual to his personal liberty, or to enter into those contracts in relation to labor which may seem to him appropriate or necessary for the support of himself and his family? Of course the liberty of contract relating to labor includes both parties to it. The one has as much right to purchase as the other to sell labor....

The question whether this act is valid as a labor law, pure and simple, may be dismissed in a few words. There is no reasonable ground for interfering with the liberty of person or the right of free contract, by determining the hours of labor, in the occupation of a baker. There is no contention that bakers as a class are not equal in intelligence and capacity to men in other trades or manual occupations, or that they are not able to assert their rights and care for themselves without the protecting arm of the State, interfering with their independence of judgment and of action. They are in no sense wards of the State. Viewed in the light of a purely labor law, with no reference whatever to the question of health, we think that a law like the one before us involves neither the safety, the morals, nor the welfare, of the public, and that the interest of the public is not in the slightest degree affected by such an act. The law must be upheld, if at all, as a law pertaining to the health of the individual engaged in the occupation of a baker. It does not affect any other portion of the public than those who are engaged in that occupation. Clean and wholesome bread does not depend upon whether the baker works but ten hours per day or only sixty hours a week. The limitation of the hours of labor does not come within the police power on that ground....

We think the limit of the police power has been reached and passed in this case. There is, in our judgment, no reasonable foundation for holding this to be necessary or appropriate as a health law to safeguard the public health, or the health of the individuals who are following the trade of a baker. If this statute be valid, and if, therefore, a proper case is made out in which to deny the right of an individual, *sui juris,* as employer or employé, to make contracts for the labor of the latter under the protection of the provisions of the Federal Constitution, there would seem to be no length to which legislation of this nature might not go....

We think that there can be no fair doubt that the trade of a baker, in and of itself, is not an unhealthy one to that degree which would authorize the legislature to interfere with the right to labor, and with the right of free contract on the part of the individual, either as employer or employé. In looking through statistics regarding all trades and occupations, it may be true that the trade of a baker does not appear to be as healthy as some other trades, and is also vastly more healthy than still others. To the common understanding the trade of a baker has never been regarded as an unhealthy one. Very likely physicians would not recommend the exercise of that or of any other trade as a remedy for ill health. Some occupations are more healthy than others, but we think there are none which might not come under the power of the legislature to supervise and control the hours of working therein, if the mere fact that the occupation is not absolutely and perfectly healthy is to confer that right upon the legislative department of the government. It might be safely affirmed that almost all occupations more or less affect the health. There must be more than the mere fact of the possible existence of some small amount of unhealthiness to warrant legislative interference with liberty. It is unfortunately true that labor, even in any department, may possibly carry with it the seeds of unhealthiness. But are we all, on that account, at the mercy of legislative majorities? A printer, a tinsmith, a locksmith, a carpenter, a cabinetmaker, a dry goods clerk, a bank's, a lawyer's, or a physician's clerk, or a clerk in almost any kind of business, would all come under the power of the legislature, on this assumption. No trade, no occupation, no mode of earning one's living, could escape this all-pervading power, and the acts of the legislature in limiting the hours of labor in all employments would be valid, although such limitation might seriously cripple the ability of the laborer to support himself and his family....

It is also urged, pursuing the same line of argument, that it is to the interest of the State that its population should be strong and robust, and therefore any legislation which may be said to tend to make people healthy must be valid as health laws, enacted under the police power. If this be a valid argument and a justification for this kind of legislation, it follows that the protection of the Federal Constitution from undue interference with liberty of person and freedom of contract is visionary, wherever the law is sought to be justified as a valid exercise of the police power. Scarcely any law but might find shelter under such assumptions, and conduct, properly so called, as well as contract, would come under the restrictive sway of the legislature. Not only the hours of employés, but the hours of employers, could be regulated, and doctors, lawyers, scientists, all professional men, as well as athletes and artisans, could be forbidden to fatigue their brains and bodies by prolonged hours of exercise, lest the fighting strength of the State be impaired. We mention these extreme cases because the contention is extreme. We do not believe in the soundness of the views which uphold this law. On the contrary, we think that such a law as this, although passed in the assumed exercise of the police power, and as relating to the public health, or the health of the employés named, is not within that power, and is invalid. The act is not, within any fair meaning of the term, a health law, but is an illegal interference with the rights of individuals, both employers and employés, to make contracts regarding labor upon such terms as they may think best, or which they may agree upon with the other parties to such contracts. Statutes of the nature of that under review, limiting the hours in which grown and intelligent men may labor to earn their living, are mere meddlesome interferences with the rights of the individual, and they are not saved from condemnation by the claim that they are passed in the exercise of the police power and upon the subject of the health of the individual whose rights are interfered with, unless there be some fair ground, reasonable in and of itself, to say that there is material danger to the public health, or to the health of the employés, if the hours of labor are not curtailed. If this be not clearly the case, the individuals whose rights are thus made the subject of legislative interference are under the protection of the Federal Constitution regarding their liberty of contract as well as of person; and the legislature of the State has no power to limit their right as proposed in this statute. All that it could properly do has been done by it with regard to the conduct of bakeries, as provided for in the other sections of the act, above set forth. These several sections provide for the inspection of the premises where the bakery is carried on, with regard to furnishing proper wash rooms and waterclosets, apart from the bake room, also with regard to providing proper drainage, plumbing, and painting; the sections, in addition, provide for the height of the ceiling, the cementing or tiling of floors, where necessary in the opinion of the factory inspector, and for other things of that nature; alterations are also provided for, and are to be made where necessary in the opinion of the inspector, in order to comply with the provisions of the statute. These various sections may be wise and valid regulations, and they certainly go to the full extent of providing for the cleanliness and the healthiness, so far as possible, of the quarters in which bakeries are to be conducted. Adding to all these requirements a prohibition to enter into any contract of labor in a bakery for more than a certain number of hours a week is, in our judgment, so wholly beside the matter of a proper, reasonable and fair provision as to run counter to that liberty of person and of free contract provided for in the Federal Constitution.

It was further urged on the argument that restricting the hours of labor in the case of bakers was valid because it tended to cleanliness on the part of the workers, as a man was more apt to be cleanly when not overworked, and if cleanly then his "output" was also more likely to be so. What has already been said applies with equal force to this contention. We do not admit the reasoning to be sufficient to justify the claimed right of such interference.... In our judgment it is not possible in fact to discover the connection between the number of hours a baker may work in the bakery and the healthful quality of the bread made by the workman. The connection, if any exist, is too shadowy and thin to build any argument for the interference of the legislature. If the man works ten hours a day it is all right, but if ten and a half or eleven his health is in danger and his bread may be unhealthy, and, therefore, he shall not be permitted to do it. This, we think, is unreasonable and entirely arbitrary. When assertions such as we have adverted to become necessary in order to give, if possible, a plausible foundation for the contention that the law is a "health law," it gives rise to at least a suspicion that there was some other motive dominating the legislature than the purpose to subserve the public health or welfare....

It is impossible for us to shut our eyes to the fact that ... laws of this character, while passed under what is claimed to be the police power for the purpose of protecting the public health or welfare, are, in reality, passed from other motives. We are justified in saying so when, from the character of the law and the subject upon which it legislates, it is apparent that the public health or welfare bears but the most remote relation to the law. The purpose of a statute must be determined from the natural and legal effect of the language employed; and whether it is or is not repugnant to the Constitution of the United States must be determined from the natural effect of such statutes when put into operation, and not from their proclaimed purpose....

It is manifest to us that the limitation of the hours of labor as provided for in this section of the statute under which the indictment was found, and the plaintiff in error convicted, has no such direct relation to, and no such substantial effect upon, the health of the employé, as to justify us in regarding the section as really a health law. It seems to us that the real object and purpose were simply to regulate the hours of labor between the master and his employés (all being men, *sui juris*), in a private business, not dangerous in any degree to morals, or in any real and substantial degree to the health of the employés. Under such circumstances the freedom of master and employé to contract with each other in relation to their employment, and in defining the same, cannot be prohibited or interfered with, without violating the Federal Constitution....

Reversed.

MR. JUSTICE HARLAN, with whom MR. JUSTICE WHITE and MR. JUSTICE DAY concurred, dissenting.

[I] take it to be firmly established that what is called the liberty of contract may, within certain limits, be subjected to regulations designed and calculated to promote the general welfare or to guard the public health, the public morals or the public safety....

It is plain that [the] statute [in question] was enacted in order to protect the physical well-being of those who work in bakery and confectionery establishments. It may be that the statute had its origin, in part, in the belief that employers and employés in such establishments were not upon an equal footing, and that the necessities of the latter often compelled them to submit to such exactions as unduly taxed their strength. Be this as it may, the statute must be taken as expressing the belief of the people of New York that, as a general rule, and in the case of the average man, labor in excess of sixty hours during a week in such establishments may endanger the health of those who thus labor. Whether or not this be wise legislation it is not the province of the court to inquire. Under our systems of government the courts are not concerned with the wisdom or policy of legislation. So that in determining the question of power to interfere with liberty of contract, the court may inquire whether the means devised by the State are germane to an end which may be lawfully accomplished and have a real or substantial relation to the protection of health, as involved in the daily work of the persons, male and female, engaged in bakery and confectionery establishments. But when this inquiry is entered upon I find it impossible, in view of common experience, to say that there is here no real or substantial relation between the means employed by the State and the end sought to be accomplished by its legislation....

Professor Hirt in his treatise on the "Diseases of the Workers" has said: "The labor of the bakers is among the hardest and most laborious imaginable.... It is hard, very hard work, not only because it requires a great deal of physical exertion in an overheated workshop and during unreasonably long hours, but more so because of the erratic demands of the public, compelling the baker to perform the greater part of his work at night, thus depriving him of an opportunity to enjoy the necessary rest and sleep, a fact which is highly injurious to his health." Another writer says: "The constant inhaling of flour dust causes inflammation of the lungs and of the bronchial tubes. The eyes also suffer through this dust, which is responsible for the many cases of running eyes among the bakers. The long hours of toil to which all bakers are subjected produce rheumatism, cramps, and swollen legs. The intense heat in the workshops induces the workers to resort to cooling drinks, which together with their habit of exposing the greater part of their bodies to the change in the atmosphere, is another source of a number of diseases of various organs. Nearly all bakers are pale-faced and of more delicate health than the workers of other crafts, which is chiefly due to their hard work and their irregular and unnatural mode of living, whereby the power of resistance against disease is greatly diminished. The average age of a baker is below that of other workmen; they seldom live over their fiftieth year, most of them dying between the ages of forty and fifty. During periods of epidemic diseases the bakers are generally the first to succumb to the disease, and the number swept away during such periods far exceeds the number of other crafts in comparison to the men employed in the respective industries. When, in 1720, the plague visited the city of Marseilles, France, every baker in the city succumbed to the epidemic, which caused considerable excitement in the neighboring cities and resulted in measures for the sanitary protection of the bakers."...

Statistics show that the average daily working time among workingmen in different countries is, in Australia, 8 hours; in Great Britain, 9; in the United States, 9¾; in Denmark, 9¾; in Norway, 10; Sweden, France, and Switzerland, 10½; Germany, 10¼; Belgium, Italy, and Austria, 11; and in Russia, 12 hours.

We judicially know that the question of the number of hours during which a workman should continuously labor has been, for a long period, and is yet, a subject of serious consideration among civilized peoples, and by those having special knowledge of the laws of health. Suppose the statute prohibited labor in bakery and confectionery establishments in excess of eighteen hours each day. No one, I take it, could dispute the power of the State to enact such a statute. But the statute before us does not embrace extreme or exceptional cases. It may be said to occupy a middle ground in respect of the hours of labor. What is the true ground for the State to take between legitimate protection, by legislation, of the public health and liberty of contract is not a question easily solved, nor one in respect of which there is or can be absolute certainty....

We also judicially know that the number of hours that should constitute a day's labor in particular occupations involving the physical strength and safety of workmen has been the subject of enactments by Congress and by nearly all of the States. Many, if not most, of those enactments fix eight hours as the proper basis of a day's labor.

I do not stop to consider whether any particular view of this economic question presents the sounder theory. What the precise facts are it may be difficult to say. It is enough for the determination of this case, and it is enough for this court to know, that the question is one about which there is room for debate and for an honest difference of opinion. There are many reasons of a weighty, substantial character, based upon the experience of mankind, in support of the theory that, all things considered, more than ten hours' steady work each day, from week to week, in a bakery or confectionery establishment, may endanger the health and shorten the lives of the workmen, thereby diminishing their physical and mental capacity to serve the State, and to provide for those dependent upon them.

If such reasons exist that ought to be the end of this case, for the State is not amenable to the judiciary, in respect of its legislative enactments, unless such enactments are plainly, palpably, beyond all question, inconsistent with the Constitution of the United States. We are not to presume that the State of New York has acted in bad faith. Nor can we assume that its legislature acted without due deliberation, or that it did not determine this question upon the fullest attainable information and for the common good. We cannot say that the State has acted without reason nor ought we to proceed upon the theory that its action is a mere sham. Our duty, I submit, is to sustain the statute as not being in conflict with the Federal Constitution, for the reason — and such is an all-sufficient reason — it is not shown to be plainly and palpably inconsistent with that instrument. Let the State alone in the management of its purely domestic affairs, so long as it does not appear beyond all question that it has violated the Federal Constitution. This view necessarily results from the principle that the health and safety of the people of a State are primarily for the State to guard and protect....

MR. JUSTICE HOLMES dissenting....

This case is decided upon an economic theory which a large part of the country does not entertain. If it were a question whether I agreed with that theory, I should desire to study it further and long before making up my mind. But I do not conceive that to be my duty, because I strongly believe that my agreement or disagreement has nothing to do with the right of a majority to embody their opinions in law. It is settled by various decisions of this court that state constitutions and state laws may regulate life in many ways which we as legislators might think as injudicious or if you like as tyrannical as this, and which equally with this interfere with the liberty to contract. Sunday laws and usury laws are ancient examples. A more modern one is the prohibition of lotteries. The liberty of the citizen to do as he likes so long as he does not interfere with the liberty of others to do the same, which has been a shibboleth for some well-known writers, is interfered with by school laws, by the Post Office, by every state or municipal institution which takes his money for purposes thought desirable, whether he likes it or not. The Fourteenth Amendment does not enact Mr. Herbert Spencer's *Social Statics*. [We have upheld a number of laws that cut down on the liberty to contract.] Some of these laws embody convictions or prejudices which judges are likely to share. Some may not. But a constitution is not intended to embody a particular economic theory, whether of paternalism and the organic relation of the citizen to the State or of *laissez faire*. It is made for people of fundamentally differing views, and the accident of our finding certain opinions natural and familiar or novel and even shocking ought not to conclude our judgment upon the question whether statutes embodying them conflict with the Constitution of the United States.

General propositions do not decide concrete cases. The decision will depend on a judgment or intuition more subtle than any articulate major premise. But I think that the proposition just stated, if it is accepted, will carry us far toward the end. Every opinion tends to become a law. I think that the word liberty in the Fourteenth Amendment is perverted when it is held to prevent the natural outcome of a dominant opinion, unless it can be said that a rational and fair man necessarily would admit that the statute proposed would infringe fundamental principles as they have been understood by the traditions of our people and our law. It does not need research to show that no such sweeping condemnation can be passed upon the statute before us. A reasonable man might think it a proper measure on the score of health. Men whom I certainly could not pronounce unreasonable would uphold it as a first instalment of a general regulation of the hours of work. Whether in the latter aspect it would be open to the charge of inequality I think it unnecessary to discuss.

NOTES

1. *Early Wage and Hour Laws.* Laws regulating wages and hours have a long lineage in America, dating back to restrictions on *maximum* wages in the Massachusetts Bay Colony in 1630. Legislation setting maximum hours of work was in place in a number of states by the mid-nineteenth century, while minimum wage legislation made its first appearance in this country after the turn of the twentieth century.

The first maximum hours laws in the United States all limited a day's work to ten hours. The early laws, however, all permitted the statutory limit on hours to be waived by contract, and none of the laws contained enforcement provisions. The language of the first act, the New Hampshire law, is illustrative:

> In all contracts for or relating to labor, ten hours of actual labor shall be taken to be a day's work, unless otherwise agreed by the parties; and no person shall be required or holden to perform more than ten hours labor in any one day, except in pursuance of an express contract requiring a greater time.

New Hampshire Laws, 1847, ch. 488, § 1.

Forty years later, when states began to enact non-waivable and enforceable limits on hours of work, the first rumblings of the *Lochner* era began to be felt. In 1891 in Nebraska, for example, the Populist legislature enacted a law that set the legal work day at eight hours, enforced by a provision that required employers to pay double the time paid for the previous hour for each hour worked over eight hours (that is, double time for the ninth hour, quadruple time for the tenth hour, and so on). In one of the first volleys of the *Lochner* era, the Nebraska Supreme Court held the statute to be unconstitutional. *Low v. Rees Printing Co.*, 59 N.W. 362 (Neb. 1894).

2. *The Effects and Demise of Lochner.* The *Lochner* era extended into the mid-1930s. The Supreme Court struck down nearly two hundred state statutes during that time. But *Lochner* was by no means a complete bar to state regulation — many statutes were also upheld. The Court regularly upheld statutes regulating the labor of women and children and hours of labor for employees in dangerous occupations. Thus, in *Muller v. Oregon,* 208 U.S. 412 (1908), the Court upheld a statute limiting the working hours of women, saying that it "is impossible to close one's eyes to the fact that she still looks to her brother and depends on him." *Id.* at 422. And the Court occasionally upheld other labor statutes. In *Bunting v. Oregon,* 243 U.S. 426 (1917), for example, the Court, without even mentioning *Lochner,* applied a deferential standard to uphold an Oregon statute that limited hours of work in manufacturing establishments to thirteen hours per day and that required premium pay for all work over ten hours. During the *Lochner* era, then, the courts engaged in probing inquiries into the bases of state regulation, but the results of the inquiries were by no means preordained.

The demise of *Lochner* resulted in a deferential standard. State statutes would almost always be upheld in the face of a challenge under the due process clause:

> So far as the requirement of due process is concerned, and in the absence of other constitutional restriction, a state is free to adopt whatever economic policy may reasonably be deemed to promote public welfare, and to enforce that policy by legislation adapted to its purpose. The courts are without authority either to declare such policy, or, when it is declared by the legislature, to override it. If the laws are seen to have a reasonable relation to a proper legislative purpose, and are neither arbitrary nor discriminatory, the requirements of due process are satisfied.... With the wisdom of the policy adopted, with the adequacy or practicability of the law enacted to forward it, the courts are both incompetent and unauthorized to deal.

Nebbia v. New York, 291 U.S. 502, 537 (1934) (upholding a New York statute authorizing an agency to establish minimum milk prices).

3. Courts and Labor Statutes. Whatever its shortcomings, *Lochner* is an important example of an enduring issue: How intensely should courts review labor statutes? In 1938, not long after the demise of *Lochner,* the Supreme Court made what is still undoubtedly its most important statement on the standard of review that was to replace *Lochner.* The Court said that courts should ordinarily presume that statutes were constitutional, but then in a footnote went on to say:

> There may be a narrower scope for operation of the presumption of constitutionality when legislation appears on its face to be within a specific prohibition of the Constitution, such as those of the first ten amendments....
>
> It is unnecessary to consider now whether legislation which restricts those political processes which can ordinarily be expected to bring about repeal of undesirable legislation, is to be subjected to more exacting judicial scrutiny under the general prohibitions of the Fourteenth Amendment than are most other types of legislation....
>
> Nor need we inquire whether similar considerations enter into the review of statutes directed at particular religions, or national or racial minorities: whether prejudice against discrete and insular minorities may be a special condition, which tends seriously to curtail the operation of those political processes ordinarily to be relied upon to protect minorities, and which may call for a correspondingly more searching judicial inquiry.

United States v. Carolene Prods. Co., 304 U.S. 144, 152-53 n.4 (1938).

Using these standards, should the courts today defer even to truly unreasonable legislation? Should a court, for example, uphold a statute that established two hours as the maximum length of the workday? And how should the courts respond to racial and sexual classifications in statutes that are intended to *help* disadvantaged groups? For example, should a court uphold a statute, enacted in an attempt to increase the ability of women and minorities to find jobs, which establishes eight hours as the maximum length of the workday for white males only?

JONATHAN GROSSMAN, FAIR LABOR STANDARDS ACT OF 1938: MAXIMUM STRUGGLE FOR A MINIMUM WAGE, 101 Monthly Labor Review 22, 22-29 (1978)

New Deal promise. In 1933, under the "New Deal" program, Roosevelt's advisers developed a National Industrial Recovery Act (NRA).[4] The act suspended antitrust laws so that industries could enforce fair-trade codes resulting in less competition and higher wages. On signing the bill, the President stated: "History will probably record the National Industrial Recovery Act as the most important and far-reaching legislation ever enacted by the American Congress." The law was popular, and one family in Darby, Penn., christened a newborn daughter Nira to honor it.

As an early step of the NRA, Roosevelt promulgated a President's Reemployment Agreement "to raise wages, create employment, and thus restore business." Employers signed more than 2.3 million agreements, covering 16.3 million employees. Signers agreed to a workweek between 35 and 40 hours and a minimum wage of $12 to $15 a week and undertook, with some exceptions, not to employ youths under 16 years of age. Employers who signed the agreement displayed a "badge of honor," a blue eagle over the motto "We do our part." Patriotic Americans were expected to buy only from "Blue Eagle" business concerns.

In the meantime, various industries developed more complete codes. The Cotton Textile Code was the first of these and one of the most important. It provided for a 40-hour workweek, set a minimum weekly wage of $13 in the North and $12 in the South, and abolished child labor. The President said this code made him "happier than any other one thing ... since I have come to Washington, for the code abolished child labor in the textile industry." He added: "After years of fruitless effort and discussion, this ancient atrocity went out in a day."

A crushing blow. On "Black Monday," May 27, 1935, the Supreme Court disarmed the NRA as the major depression-fighting weapon of the New Deal. The 1935 case of [*A.L.A. Schechter Poultry Corp. v. United States,* 295 U.S. 495,] tested the constitutionality of the NRA by questioning a code to improve the sordid conditions under which chickens were slaughtered and sold to retail kosher butchers. All nine justices agreed that the act was an unconstitutional delegation of government power to private interests. Even the liberal Benjamin Cardozo thought it was "delegation running riot." Though the "sick chicken" decision seems an absurd case upon which to decide the fate of so sweeping a policy, it

---

[4] The proper initials for the Law are NIRA. The initials for the National Recovery Administration created by the act are NRA. Following a common practice, the initials NRA are used here for both the law and the administration.

invalidated not only the restrictive trade practices set by the NRA-authorized codes, but the codes' progressive labor provisions as well.

As if to head off further attempts at labor reform, the Supreme Court, in a series of decisions, invalidated both State and Federal labor laws. Most notorious was the 1936 case of Joseph Tipaldo.[5] The manager of a Brooklyn, N.Y., laundry, Tipaldo had been paying nine laundry women only $10 a week, in violation of the New York State minimum wage law. When forced to pay his workers $14.88, Tipaldo coerced them to kick back the difference. When Tipaldo was jailed on charges of violating the State law, forgery, and conspiracy, his lawyers sought a writ of habeas corpus on grounds the New York law was unconstitutional. The Supreme Court, by a 5-to-4 majority, voided the law as a violation of liberty of contract.

The *Tipaldo* decision was among the most unpopular ever rendered by the Supreme Court. Even bitter foes of President Roosevelt and the New Deal criticized the Court. Ex-President Herbert Hoover said the Court had gone to extremes. Conservative Republican Congressman Hamilton Fish called it a "new Dred Scott decision" condemning 3 million women and children to economic slavery.

A switch in time.... When Roosevelt won the 1936 election by 523 electoral votes to 8, he interpreted his landslide victory as support for the New Deal and was determined to overcome the obstacle of Supreme Court opposition as soon as possible. In February 1937, he struck back at the "nine old men" of the Bench: He proposed to "pack" the Court by adding up to six extra judges, one for each judge who did not retire at age 70. Roosevelt further voiced his disappointment with the Court at the victory dinner for his second inauguration, saying if the "three-horse team [of the executive, legislative, and judicial branches] pulls as one, the field will be ploughed," but that "the field will not be ploughed if one horse lies down in the traces or plunges off in another direction."

However, Roosevelt's metaphorical maverick fell in step. On "White Monday," March 29, 1937, the Court reversed its course when it decided the case of *West Coast Hotel Company v. Parrish* [, 300 U.S. 379]. Elsie Parrish, a former chambermaid at the Cascadian Hotel in Wenatchee, Wash., sued for $216.19 in back wages, charging that the hotel had paid her less than the State minimum wage. In an unexpected turnaround, Justice Owen Roberts voted with the four-man liberal minority to uphold the Washington minimum wage law.

As other close decisions continued to validate social and economic legislation, support for Roosevelt's Court "reorganization" faded. Meanwhile, Justice Roberts felt called upon to deny that he had switched sides to ward off Roosevelt's court-packing plan. He claimed valid legal distinctions between the *Tipaldo* case and the *Parrish* case. Nevertheless, many historians subscribe to the contemporary view of Roberts' vote, that "a switch in time saved nine."

---

[5] *Morehead v. Tipaldo*, 298 U.S. 587 (1936).

Back to the drawing board

Justice Roberts' "Big Switch" is an important event in American legal history. It is also a turning point in American social history, for it marked a new legal attitude toward labor standards. To be sure, validating a single State law was a far cry from upholding general Federal legislation, but the *Parrish* decision encouraged advocates of fair labor standards to work all the harder to develop a bill that might be upheld by the Supreme Court.

An ardent advocate. No top government official worked more ardently to develop legislation to help underpaid workers and exploited child laborers than Secretary of Labor Frances Perkins. Almost all her working life, Perkins fought for pro-labor legislation....

When, in 1933, President Roosevelt asked Frances Perkins to become Secretary of Labor, she told him that she would accept if she could advocate a law to put a floor under wages and a ceiling over hours of work and to abolish abuses of child labor. When Roosevelt heartily agreed, Perkins asked him, "Have you considered that to launch such a program ... might be considered unconstitutional?" Roosevelt retorted, "Well, we can work out something when the time comes."

During the constitutional crisis over the NRA, Secretary Perkins asked lawyers at the Department of Labor to draw up two wage-hour and child-labor bills which might survive Supreme Court review. She then told Roosevelt, "I have something up my sleeve.... I've got two bills ... locked in the lower left-hand drawer of my desk against an emergency." Roosevelt laughed and said, "There's New England caution for you.... You're pretty unconstitutional, aren't you?"

Earlier Government groundwork. One of the bills that Perkins had "locked" in the bottom drawer of her desk was used before the 1937 "Big Switch." The bill proposed using the purchasing power of the Government as an instrument for improving labor standards....

The Roosevelt-Perkins ... initiative resulted in the Public Contracts Act of 1936 (Walsh-Healey)[, which] required most government contractors to adopt an 8-hour day and a 40-hour week, to employ only those over 16 years of age if they were boys or 18 years of age if they were girls, and to pay a "prevailing minimum wage" to be determined by the Secretary of Labor.... Though limited to government supply contracts and weakened by amendments and court interpretations, the Walsh-Healey Public Contracts Act was hailed as a token of good faith by the Federal Government — that it intended to lead the way to better pay and working conditions.

A broader bill is born

President Roosevelt had postponed action on a fair labor standards law because of his fight to "pack" the Court. After the "switch in time," when he felt the time was ripe, he asked Frances Perkins, "What happened to that nice unconstitutional bill you had tucked away?"

The bill — the second that Perkins had "tucked" away — was a general fair labor standards act. To cope with the danger of judicial review, Perkins' lawyers had taken several constitutional approaches so that, if one or two legal principles were invalidated, the bill might still be accepted. The bill provided for minimum-wage boards which would determine, after public hearing and consideration of cost-of-living figures from the Bureau of Labor Statistics, whether wages in particular industries were below subsistence levels....

An early form of the bill being readied for Congress affected only wages and hours. To that version Roosevelt added a child-labor provision based on the political judgment that adding a clause banning goods in interstate commerce produced by children under 16 years of age would increase the chance of getting a wage-hour measure through both Houses, because child-labor limitations were popular in Congress.

Congress — round I

On May 24, 1937, President Roosevelt sent the bill to Congress with a message that America should be able to give "all our able-bodied working men and women a fair day's pay for a fair day's work." He continued: "A self-supporting and self-respecting democracy can plead no justification for the existence of child labor, no economic reason for chiseling workers' wages or stretching workers' hours." Though States had the right to set standards within their own borders, he said, goods produced under "conditions that do not meet rudimentary standards of decency should be regarded as contraband and ought not to be allowed to pollute the channels of interstate trade." He asked Congress to pass applicable legislation "at this session."...

Organized labor supported the bill but was split on how strong it should be.... William Green of the American Federation of Labor (AFL) and John L. Lewis of the Congress of Industrial Organizations (CIO), on one of the rare occasions when they agreed, both favored a bill which would limit labor standards to low-paid and essentially unorganized workers. Based on some past experiences, many union leaders feared that a minimum wage might become a maximum and that wage boards would intervene in areas which they wanted reserved for labor-management negotiations. They were satisfied when the bill was amended to exclude work covered by collective bargaining.

The weakened bill passed the Senate July 31, 1937, by a vote of 56 to 28 and would have easily passed the House if it had been put to a vote. But a coalition of Republicans and conservative Democrats bottled it up in the House Rules Committee. After a long hot summer, Congress adjourned without House action on fair labor standards.

Congress — round II

An angry President Roosevelt decided to press again for passage of the ... bill. Having lost popularity and split the Democratic Party in his battle to "pack" the Supreme Court, Roosevelt felt that attacking abuses of child labor and sweatshop wages and hours was a popular cause that might reunite the party. A wage-hour, child-labor law promised to be a happy marriage of high idealism and practical politics.

On October 12, 1937, Roosevelt called a special session of Congress to convene on November 15. The public interest, he said, required immediate Congressional action: "The exploitation of child labor and the undercutting of wages and the stretching of the hours of the poorest paid workers in periods of business recession has a serious effect on buying power."

Despite White House and business pressure, the conservative alliance of Republicans and Southern Democrats that controlled the House Rules Committee refused to discharge the bill as it stood. Congresswoman Mary Norton of New Jersey, now chairing the House Labor Committee, made a valiant attempt to shake the bill loose. Many representatives had told her that they agreed with the principles of the bill but that they objected to a five-man wage board with broad powers. Therefore, Norton told the House of Representatives that the Labor Committee would offer an amendment to change the administration of the bill from a five-man board to an administrator under the Department of Labor.... [B]y December 2, the bill's supporters had rounded up enough signers to give the petition the 218 signatures necessary to bring the bill to a vote on the House floor.

With victory within grasp, the bill became a battleground in the war raging between the AFL and the CIO. The AFL accused the Roosevelt Administration of favoring industrial over craft unions and opposed wage-board determination of labor standards for specific industries. Accordingly, the AFL fought for a substitute bill with a flat 40-cent-an-hour minimum wage and a maximum 40-hour week.

In the ensuing confusion, shortly before the Christmas holiday of 1937, the House by a vote of 218 to 198 unexpectedly sent the bill back to the Labor Committee. In her memoir of President Roosevelt, Frances Perkins wrote:

> This was the first time that a major administration bill had been defeated on the floor of the House. The press took the view that this was the death knell of wage-hour legislation as well as a decisive blow to the President's prestige.

Roosevelt tries again

Again, Roosevelt returned to the fray. In his annual message to Congress on January 3, 1938, he said he was seeking "legislation to end starvation wages and intolerable hours." He paid deference to the South by saying that "no reasonable person seeks a complete uniformity in wages." He also made peace overtures to business by pointing out that he was forgoing "drastic" change, and he appeased organized labor, saying that "more desirable wages are and should continue to be the product of collective bargaining."

The day following Roosevelt's message, Representative Lister Hill, a strong Roosevelt supporter, won an Alabama election primary for the Senate by an

almost 2-to-1 majority over an anti-New Deal congressman. The victory was significant because much of the opposition to wage-hour laws came from Southern
congressmen. In February, a national public opinion poll showed that 67 percent
of the populace favored the wage-hour law, with even the South showing a substantial plurality of support for higher standards.

Reworking the bill. In the meantime, Department of Labor lawyers worked on
a new bill. Privately, Roosevelt had told Perkins that the length and complexity
of the bill caused some of its difficulties. "Can't it be boiled down to two
pages?" he asked. Lawyers trying to simplify the bill faced the problem that,
although legal language makes legislation difficult to understand, bills written in
simple English are often difficult for the courts to enforce. And because the
wage-hour, child-labor bill had been drafted with the Supreme Court in mind,
Solicitor of Labor Gerard Reilly could not meet the President's two-page goal;
however, he succeeded in cutting the bill from 40 to 10 pages.

In late January 1938, Reilly and Perkins brought the revision to President
Roosevelt. He approved it, and the new bill went to Congress....

Norton appointed Representative Robert Ramspeck of Georgia to head a subcommittee to bridge the gap between various proposals. The subcommittee's
efforts resulted in the Ramspeck compromise which Perkins felt "contained the
bare essentials she could support." The compromise retained the 40-cent minimum hourly wage and the 40-hour maximum workweek. It did not provide for an
administrator as had the previous bill which had been voted back to committee
by the House. Instead, the compromise allowed for a five-member wage board
which would be less powerful than those proposed by the [original] bill.

Congress — The final round

The House Labor Committee voted down the Ramspeck compromise, but, by a
10-to-4 vote, approved an even more "barebones" bill presented by Norton. Her
bill, following the AFL proposal, provided for a 40-cent hourly minimum wage,
replaced the wage boards proposed by the Ramspeck compromise with an
administrator and advising commission, and allowed for procedures for investigation into certain cases....

Braving the floor battle. Proponents of the wage-hour, child-labor bill pressed
the attack. They continued to point to "horror stories." One Congressman quoted
a magazine article entitled "All Work and No Pay" which told how, in a company that paid wages in scrip for use in the company store, pay envelopes contained nothing for a full week's work after the deduction of store charges.

The most bitter controversy raged over labor standards in the South. "There
are in the State of Georgia," one Indiana Congressman declaimed, "canning factories working ... women 10 hours a day for $4.50 a week. Can the canning fac-
tories of Indiana and Connecticut or New York continue to exist and meet such
competitive labor costs?" Southern Congressmen, in turn, challenged the
Northern "monopolists" who hypocritically "loll on their tongues" words like

"slave labor" and "sweatshops" and support bills which sentence Southern industry to death. Some Southern employers told the Department of Labor that they could not live with a 25-cent-an-hour minimum wage. They would have to fire all their people, they said. Adapting a biblical quotation, Representative John McClellan of Arkansas rhetorically asked, "What profiteth the laborer of the South if he gain the enactment of a wage and hour law — 40 cents per hour and 40 hours per week — if he then lose the opportunity to work?"

Partly because of Southern protests, provisions of the act were altered so that the minimum wage was reduced to 25 cents an hour for the first year of the act. Southerners gained additional concessions, such as a requirement that wage administrators consider lower costs of living and higher freight rates in the South before recommending wages above the minimum.

Though the revised bill had reduced substantially the administrative machinery provided for in earlier drafts, several Congressmen singled out Secretary Perkins for personal attack. One Perkins detractor noted that, although Congress had "overwhelmingly rebelled" against delegation of power,

> We delegate to Madam Perkins the authority and power to 'issue an order declaring such industry to be an industry affecting commerce.' Now section 9 is ... one of the 'snooping' sections of the bill. Imagine the feeling of the merchant or the industry up in your district when a 'designated representative' ... of Mme. Perkins 'enter[s] and inspect[s] such places and such records.' ... I know no previous law going quite so far.

A resulting compromise modified the authority of the administrator in the Department of Labor.

The bill was voted upon May 24, 1938, with a 314-to-97 majority. After the House had passed the bill, the Senate-House Conference Committee made still more changes to reconcile differences. During the legislative battles over fair labor standards, members of Congress had proposed 72 amendments. Almost every change sought exemptions, narrowed coverage, lowered standards, weakened administration, limited investigation, or in some other way worked to weaken the bill.

The surviving proposal as approved by the conference committee finally passed the House on June [14], 1938, by a vote of 291 to 89. Shortly thereafter, the Senate approved it without a record of the votes. Congress then sent the bill to the President. On June 25, 1938, the President signed the Fair Labor Standards Act to become effective on October 24, 1938....

The Fair Labor Standards Act of 1938 marked a turning point in American social policy. It substituted for the "rugged individualism" of an earlier era a social responsibility of the Federal Government toward American wage earners. Referring to the FLSA the night before signing the bill into law, President Roosevelt declared that, "Except perhaps for the Social Security Act, it is the most far-reaching, the most far-sighted program for the benefit of workers ever adopted."

NOTES

1. *Regional Effects.* Grossman recounts regional differences in the reactions to the Fair Labor Standards Act proposals. On the ultimate vote in the House, representatives from former Confederate states provided 40% of the votes against the bill, but only 16% of the votes for the bill. Although the motivations were undoubtedly more complex, in broad terms, as the excerpt indicates, the North supported the bill to protect its industries from "unfair" low-wage competition, while the South opposed it because of fears that jobs would be lost.

These concerns are by no means outdated. The United States in recent years has found itself on both sides of the debate. Under the North American Free Trade Agreement (NAFTA), the United States is a relatively low-wage competitor to Canada and a relatively high-wage competitor to Mexico. The European Community has also struggled with the issue as it attempts to reconcile the interests of states with hourly compensation costs that, in 1994, ranged from $4.62 per hour in Portugal to $27.36 per hour in Germany.

How is one to evaluate these conflicting concerns? Consider two arguments:

(a) *Labor Migration.* The wage differences between the North and the South result from imbalances in the supply of and demand for labor in the two regions. In the absence of a minimum wage, the two markets will balance out fairly quickly. The lower wages in the South will cause workers to leave for higher paying jobs elsewhere and will induce outside employers to enter the region in search of lower wage costs. Those two forces will increase wages in the South. In the North the opposite is occurring: Workers are arriving from the South and employers are leaving. Wages will go down. Eventually, labor and capital will end up where they can be most productive. A minimum wage law should not be enacted; it would only slow this natural correction process.

(b) *Social Costs and Lost Jobs.* Low-wage employers do not pay for all the costs of the labor they employ. They do not, for example, pay enough for adequate medical care, so either society must step in and pay or the workers must simply do without. Minimum wage laws should be enacted to force employers to pay enough to cover all of these social costs; employers should not be permitted to externalize these costs to society or to workers. If some employers cannot bear these costs (if instead of raising wages to the new minimum, some employers go out of business and jobs are lost), society is better off without those jobs. They are jobs that were not valuable enough to bear all the costs of the workers needed to perform them. Society benefits when the capital of these employers is redirected to support more productive enterprises.

2. *Union Attitudes.* The attitude of unions to the Fair Labor Standards Act is not without its own complexities. On the one hand, a minimum wage law should make it more difficult for unions to organize low-paid workers. The law provides these workers with a wage increase without the need to pay any union dues. On the other hand, a minimum wage law might make it easier for unions to negotiate higher wages for the employees it already represents. Employers with whom the unions are negotiating should be less resistant to wage increases if they know that their non-union competitors have to pay at least the minimum wage. Why do you think the AFL was concerned about wage boards that would determine labor standards by industry?

B. THE FAIR LABOR STANDARDS ACT

More than a half century after its initial enactment, and after numerous amendments, the Fair Labor Standards Act (FLSA) is still the centerpiece of this country's wage and hour laws. The Act has three principal substantive obligations. First, it establishes a minimum wage. The current minimum wage is $5.15 per hour, although a lower subminimum wage of $4.25 per hour can be paid to some workers. Second, the Act requires premium pay for overtime work — work over forty hours in any week must be paid at a rate one-and-one-half times the regular rate of pay. And third, the Act restricts the ability of employers to employ children. Although exceptions exist, as a general matter, employers may not hire children at all until they are fourteen years old, and various restrictions are placed on their employment until they are eighteen years old.[*]

This section will begin by discussing each of these substantive obligations. The minimum wage, maximum hour, and child labor provisions of the FLSA are each intended to pursue broad social objectives, so for each we will talk first about what those objectives are, how the Act is structured to address them, and the promise and limitations of the FLSA in achieving them. Then we will talk about the difficult implementation problems raised by the obligations in practice.

We will then discuss the coverage of the FLSA. In common with most of the laws we discuss in this book, the FLSA applies only when there is an employer-employee relationship. Even when there is an employer-employee relationship, however, the FLSA does not cover all employers, nor does it cover all of the employees of covered employers. We will discuss issues raised by these additional coverage limitations. Throughout we focus on policy issues: Why is coverage limited? Why not cover all employers and employees? What are the consequences of limited coverage?

Finally, we will talk about enforcement issues under the FLSA. We will discuss how the Act is enforced and focus on whether the enforcement scheme is effective. Most people think that it is not. We will talk about why that is and what could be done about it.

---

[*] The Fair Labor Standards Act also requires equal pay for men and women performing the same work. That important substantive obligation, incorporated into the FLSA by the Equal Pay Act of 1963, is better viewed as a non-discrimination obligation than as a wage-and-hour requirement.

1. SUBSTANTIVE OBLIGATIONS OF THE FLSA

a. Minimum Wages

> The minimum wage today is no longer a living wage.... [It must be increased] if we are to succeed in our national efforts to encourage the poor, the disadvantaged, the young, and the unemployed to achieve a larger measure of self reliance. The reward of fair wages for a job well done is the foundation upon which this nation has built its fortune.

> — H.R. REP. NO. 101-260, 101st Cong., 1st Sess. 14-15 (1989).

> A [$7.00] industrial minimum wage would go a long way toward perpetuating the family farm.

> — ROBERT EVENSON, ORAL TRADITION.*

The minimum wage provisions of the FLSA are intended to address the problems of poverty faced by the working poor, to insure that they can earn a wage that will allow them to live a decent life. The difficulty is that a minimum wage may also mean that some working poor will lose their jobs and be forced back onto the family farm, or worse. In this section, we will first describe the minimum wage provisions of the FLSA and then evaluate them by considering both the people who might be helped by the laws and the people who might be hurt.

The minimum wage, as its name implies, sets a level below which wages cannot fall. The minimum wage in nominal terms has gradually increased over time, from 25 cents an hour when the Act was first enacted in 1938 to $5.15 an hour today. In *real* terms, however, the minimum has gone up and down. Generally, it has been between 45% and 55% of the average hourly earnings in manufacturing. When the minimum wage has reached the low end of the range in real terms, Congress has amended the Act to increase the minimum. When Congress acted to increase the minimum in 1989, the real level of the minimum wage was at its all-time low — 33% of average hourly earnings in manufacturing.

The $5.15 per hour minimum wage does not apply to all workers. Some workers are not covered by the minimum wage provisions of the Act. (We will discuss coverage of the FLSA later in this chapter.) When it was first enacted, the minimum wage provisions of the FLSA covered about 43% of nonsupervisory employees; today they cover about 88%. In addition, the Act permits young workers to be paid a subminimum wage of $4.25 per hour. Workers under twenty-years-old may be paid the subminimum wage for their first ninety days of employment.

To begin our evaluation of the minimum wage, consider Figure 16-1, which presents a model of the labor market for unskilled workers. Because the minimum wage provisions of the FLSA do not cover all employees, the market is

---

* Cited in Finis Welch, *Minimum Wage Legislation in the United States, in* EVALUATING THE LABOR-MARKET EFFECTS OF SOCIAL PROGRAMS 1 (Orley Ashenfelter & James Blum eds., 1976) (the amount of the minimum wage has been increased to correct for inflation).

divided into two sectors, one covered by a minimum wage law and one not covered. Employees can move back and forth between the sectors seeking higher wages. In the absence of a minimum wage law, wages and employment would be at equilibrium, W_E and E_E respectively. Wages should be about the same in both sectors; otherwise, employees would shift from the lower-paying sector to the other.

Figure 16-1. The Effects of a Minimum Wage Law

(a) Covered Sector   (b) Uncovered Sector

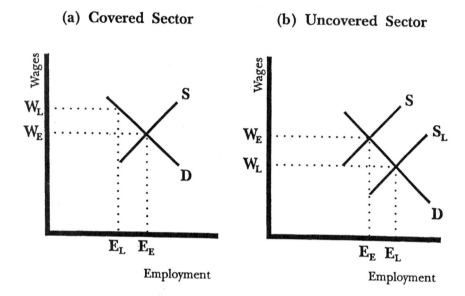

Now assume the existence of a minimum wage of W_L in the covered sector. To have any effect, the minimum wage must be higher than the equilibrium wage. If it were lower, employers would continue to pay the equilibrium wage and no one would benefit from the law or be hurt by it — the law would simply be irrelevant. As illustrated by Figure 16-1(a), higher wages in the covered sector will have one of two effects on workers in that sector. First, they may keep their jobs and earn the higher wages or, second, because the higher wages result in less demand for workers, they may lose their jobs.

Workers who lose their jobs in the covered sector would have some options. First, they could move to the uncovered sector. As Figure 16-1(b) illustrates, that would mean that the supply of workers to that sector would increase (the new supply curve is S_L). As a result, employment opportunities in the uncovered sector would increase, but the wages would be lower than they would have been in the absence of a minimum wage law. Second, workers who lose their jobs in the covered sector could decide to wait for a job opening to occur in the higher-paying covered sector. That would mean that the unemployment rate would increase. Or third, workers could drop out of the labor market and do other things. They might, for example, return to school.

In theory, then, the minimum wage provisions of the FLSA help some people and hurt others. The people who are helped are the workers in the covered sector who keep their jobs and, as a result, earn higher wages. The people who are hurt are the workers who lose their jobs in the covered sector.[*] They may take jobs in the uncovered sector that pay lower wages because of the minimum wage, suffer periods of unemployment, or be forced to pursue activities outside of the labor market that they would not pursue otherwise.

Given these types of possible gains and losses, how does one evaluate the minimum wage provisions of the FLSA? One approach is simply to attempt to add up the gains and losses and see which is greater. The Congressional Budget Office (CBO) did that for one of the proposals that eventually resulted in the 1989 amendments to the FLSA. It determined that the proposal would help low-wage workers because the extra earnings received by those who would receive higher wages would exceed the losses caused by lower employment. *Minimum Wage Legislation,* 68 CONG. DIG. 131, 135 (1989).

The CBO approach, however, does not do a very good job of evaluating the effectiveness of the minimum wage as an aid to the working poor. To do that, we would want to know more about who was helped and who was hurt. Consider two possible minimum wage workers: (1) the teenage son of one of your professors working part-time at a fast food restaurant, and (2) a single mother of three working full-time as a salesperson. If all of the workers who are helped by the minimum wage fall into the first category and all who are hurt fall into the second, we might reject the minimum wage as appropriate public policy even if the CBO conclusions about the effect of the minimum wage overall were correct. If the reverse were true, we might favor the minimum wage even if the losses overall were greater than the gains.

The real world, as usual, does not present clear choices. On the overall balance of gains and losses, some economists believe that modest increases in the minimum wage may not result in any employment losses at all or, indeed, may actually increase employment. DAVID CARD & ALAN B. KRUEGER, MYTH AND MEASUREMENT: THE NEW ECONOMICS OF THE MINIMUM WAGE (1995). If this is true, the overall balance of gains and losses would strongly support a minimum wage and we should seriously re-evaluate the standard economic model that predicts employment losses. This is a controversial view, however. Most economists still believe that the minimum wage produces employment losses consistent with the standard model, although with sharp disagreement about the

---

[*] The minimum wage would also help and hurt other workers more indirectly. The minimum wage, for example, might help a worker who would earn slightly more than the minimum wage even without a law. A minimum wage is likely to have a ripple effect which would increase her wages a bit to maintain a differential between her wages and the wages of minimum wage workers. Similarly, the minimum wage may hurt other workers indirectly. Workers in the uncovered sector when the minimum wage law is enacted, for example, will find their real wages lowered because of the increased supply of workers to the sector.

magnitude and distribution of the losses. For a good review of the issues, *see* Daniel Shaviro, *The Minimum Wage, the Earned Income Tax Credit, and Optimal Subsidy Policy,* 64 U. CHI. L. REV. 405 (1997).

On the issue of who is helped, it is clear that the minimum wage is a fairly blunt anti-poverty instrument: Most of the people who are helped by the law are not poor. In the mid-1980s, 70% of minimum wage workers were in families whose income was 150% or more of the poverty line. A major reason for this was that most minimum wage workers lived in households in which there was more than one worker. Only 19% of minimum wage workers were in families with incomes below the poverty line. Ralph E. Smith & Bruce Vavrichek, *The Minimum Wage: Its Relation to Incomes and Poverty,* MONTHLY LAB. REV., June 1987, at 24. Whether this modest help to poor workers and poor families justifies the minimum wage depends significantly on the extent and distribution of any employment losses. As indicated above, however, that is still a very contested issue.

NOTES

1. *The Youth Subminimum Wage.* The youth subminimum wage is a response to the adverse employment effects of the minimum wage on young workers. Young workers, since they are the least skilled even in the pool of low-wage workers, bear a disproportionate share of any adverse employment effects of increases in the minimum wage. By one estimate, teenage employment declines one to three percent for every 10% increase in the minimum wage. Charles Brown et al., *The Effect of the Minimum Wage on Employment and Unemployment,* 20 J. ECON. LIT. 487, 501 (1982). The subminimum wage, which can be paid only to workers under twenty years of age, should ease those effects to some extent. Do you think it is a good idea? Consider the following argument:

> One of the goals of the minimum wage is to reduce youth employment. The youth subminimum wage interferes with that goal and, as a result, is bad public policy for two reasons. First, the subminimum wage will mean that teenage workers will get jobs that otherwise would go to adults. Since only 13% of teenage minimum wage workers are poor, compared with 22% of adult minimum wage workers, the subminimum wage blunts even more the ability of the minimum wage to reduce poverty. Second, the subminimum wage means that more youth will get low-paying jobs that provide relatively poor training. That is something we should discourage, not encourage. Teenagers would be better off going to school to train for better jobs, and they *do* go to school when increases in the minimum wage limit their ability to get jobs.

Is this argument countered by Section 206(g)(2) of the FLSA which prohibits employers from displacing other workers in favor of those eligible for the subminimum wage?

2. *Reductions in Employment.* A uniform national minimum wage is unlikely to have the same effects across the country:

> [I]n the long run some of the reduction in employment may result from a reduction in the number of firms in the market rather than from changes in the number of workers employed by each firm. Such cases might occur where the firms in question competed in the product market with firms in other labor markets paying wages higher than [the minimum wage] for superior labor. The minimum wage would then raise wages in the low-wage market without improving the quality of its labor. If the firms in question had been competing on even terms before the minimum-wage law, they would now be at a disadvantage and might have to move out of the local labor market or go out of business.

DANIEL S. HAMERMESH & ALBERT REES, THE ECONOMICS OF WORK AND PAY 105-06 (3d ed. 1984). Thus, a minimum wage might cause employment losses in one area of the country, while another area of the country was experiencing gains.

These uneven employment losses could be avoided if areas of the country with high-quality labor had a higher minimum wage than other areas of the country. Several states do have minimum wage laws that provide for higher minimum wages than the FLSA. The FLSA does not preempt such laws. 29 U.S.C. § 218. Are these laws an attempt to avoid the uneven employment losses which may be caused by the FLSA?

3. *Another Look at Reductions in Employment.* Wages are only one part of an employee's compensation package. In return for their work, employees might also receive a variety of fringe benefits (such as health insurance or contributions to a pension plan) or valuable on-the-job training. Employment losses would be minimized if employers responded to increases in the minimum wage by reducing other parts of the compensation package. If this occurs, and some researchers have found that it does, should legislatures be more hesitant to pass minimum wage laws?

Or perhaps we should not be concerned about employment losses at all:

> [B]y downplaying the number of jobs destroyed by a statutory minimum wage, proponents unwittingly undermine the most cogent grounds for supporting it — namely, that the jobs it destroys are low-wage and unproductive.... Thus the appropriate response to the argument that the minimum wage hurts the very people it is supposed to protect is: the minimum wage helps those marginal workers by forcing their inefficient employers either to rationalize or to be driven out of business by more efficient competitors paying higher wages.

Marc Linder, *The Minimum Wage as Industrial Policy: A Forgotten Role,* 16 J. LEGIS. 151, 155-56 (1990).

4. *Alternatives to the Minimum Wage.* If minimum wages are such a blunt anti-poverty tool, should we try something else? Consider these alternatives:

Wage Subsidies. Wage subsidies would be a direct way to increase wages. Heads of low-wage families, for example, might be entitled to a governmental pay subsidy that would be equal to half the difference between their actual wage and a decent wage, say eight dollars per hour. Thus, someone who was earning six dollars per hour would get a wage subsidy of one dollar per hour. "In principle, a wage subsidy could be an ideal tool. It could be carefully targeted to just those persons in families who need their wages boosted. It would increase the rewards of work and, if anything, it would increase employment, rather than diminish it, as raising the minimum wage could do." DAVID ELLWOOD, POOR SUPPORT: POVERTY IN THE AMERICAN FAMILY 113 (1988).

The Earned Income Tax Credit (EITC). Under the EITC, individuals with low earnings receive tax credits for each dollar they earn. If the tax credits exceed tax liability, the credits are treated as overpayments so they can be received in cash as a refund. Under current law, the tax credit can be as high as $3,656 — an individual with two or more children may receive a 40% tax credit on earnings up to $9,140. At higher income levels, the tax credit phases out — for the individual with two children, the credit is reduced by 21 cents for every dollar earned over $11,930 so that it is completed phased out when the individual earns $29,290. (These amounts vary depending on family size; amounts are indexed for inflation.) I.R.C. § 32. The EITC could be expanded to do more, for example, by making it more generous for individuals without children (the maximum credit for these individuals is $332), by increasing the earnings on which the credit is paid, or by slowing the phase-out.

"The EITC helps the working poor while mainly avoiding the conundrums. The rewards of work are increased, not diminished. Benefits go only to those with an earned income.... And employers would have no reason to change their hiring practices.... Moreover, the EITC [can] be adjusted to vary according to the size of a family so that the biggest raise in pay would go to families with the most children and the greatest need." *Id.* at 115-116. *See also* Daniel Shaviro, *The Minimum Wage, the Earned Income Tax Credit, and Optimal Subsidy Policy,* 64 U. CHI. L. REV. 405 (1997) (arguing that the EITC is much better than the minimum wage for both progressive redistribution and encouraging workforce participation among the poor).

With these advantages over the minimum wage, why do you think these alternatives are less central to governmental policy on low-wage workers? *See* Analytical Perspectives, Budget of the United States Government, Fiscal Year 1998, 74-75 (1997) (in 1997, the EITC cost the federal government $27 billion).

5. *Other Federal Wage Statutes.* Although the Fair Labor Standards Act is the most important federal wage statute, a number of other laws impose minimum wage obligations on entities that are performing work for the federal government. The most important of these other laws are the Davis-Bacon Act, 40 U.S.C. §§ 276a to 276a-5, which applies to contracts in excess of $2,000 for work on federal buildings or other public works; the Walsh-Healey Public Contracts Act, 41 U.S.C. §§ 35-45, which applies to employers that provide materials, supplies, and equipment to the United States under contracts exceeding $10,000; and the Service Contract Act, 41 U.S.C. §§ 351-358, which applies to contracts in excess of $2,500 to provide services to the federal government. These statutes all require contracting entities to pay workers, as a minimum, the prevailing wage in the locality.

b. Premium Pay for Overtime Hours

Remember, the long struggle for the 8-hour day was not a struggle for 8 hours of work. It was a struggle for 16 hours away from work.

—Maurice Sugar
General Counsel, UAW[*]

Because most factory workers are working ... longer hours, they have been able to maintain their spendable earnings and to save.

—N. Arnold Tolles
Bureau of Labor Statistics[**]

The FLSA requires employers to pay premium pay when employees work more than forty hours in any workweek. Employers are required to pay for overtime hours at a rate one-and-one-half times the "regular" rate of pay. (Problems with determining the regular rate of pay — and hence the overtime rate — will be discussed later.) The FLSA does not impose any limitation on the number of hours adult employees can work — it only requires that they be paid at a higher rate if they work more than forty hours per week.

The overtime provisions of the FLSA were primarily intended to spread work — to reduce unemployment by encouraging employers to hire more workers, rather than to add hours, when they need additional labor. Secondarily, the provisions were intended to protect individual employees from employers who might require them to work unreasonably long hours — or at least to compensate such employees for the burdens of the long hours.

Consider the work-spreading argument first. Say that an employer has forty employees and needs forty extra hours to be worked each week. The employer needs to decide whether to have each of its forty current employees work an extra hour each week or whether it should hire an additional worker. Because of the overtime provisions of the FLSA, the employer would have to pay its current

---

[*] *The Truth About "Portal to Portal,"* 7 LAW. GUILD REV. 23, 35 (1947).
[**] *Spendable Earnings of Factory Workers, 1941-43,* 58 MONTHLY LAB. REV. 477, 478 (1944).

employees one-and-one-half times their regular rate of pay for the extra forty hours. An additional worker could be paid at the regular rate. Thus, the premium pay requirement should result in an extra employee being hired more often than would occur without the requirement.

So why do employers *ever* have employees work overtime? The principal answer is that even though employers can pay a new employee less for the extra hours, the new employee may be more expensive overall. An employer would have to advertise for, hire and train a new employee and may incur extra expenses for benefits such as health insurance. If current employees did the work, they obviously would not have to be hired again and their health insurance costs would not go up. Indeed, many of the costs of employees are quasi-fixed in this sense — once an employee is hired they do not increase as the number of hours worked increases. An employer may have employees work overtime because the quasi-fixed costs of hiring a new employee are greater than the amount of the wage premium that needs to be paid to current employees.

Is the overtime premium effective at spreading work? As usual, it is hard to tell. Say that because of the overtime premium, an employer hires a new employee to do additional work rather than having current employees work overtime. At first glance, this would seem to further the work-spreading goal of the FLSA. But if the new employee was a moonlighter, the goal would not be furthered. Instead of spreading work, the overtime premium would mean only that employees work long hours for two or more employers rather than for a single employer.

The work-spreading goal may also be frustrated in another way. The overtime premium encourages work-spreading by increasing the cost of overtime. The goal is furthered when employers, because of the extra cost of overtime, decide to hire additional employees instead. But employers have other common responses when the cost of labor increases. They may decide to spend money on labor-saving machines so they do not need the additional hours *or* the additional workers. Or they may decide that at the increased cost, the additional labor simply is not justified. To the extent employers respond to the increased cost of overtime in these ways, the overtime premium would not spread work very well: Less work would exist to spread.

The overtime provisions of the FLSA also are intended to protect the leisure time of workers, to encourage employers to allow them sixteen hours away from work each day. But some workers, obviously, might prefer to work more than forty hours per week, even at straight-time rates, especially during economic periods when real wage levels are not increasing and they must increase their hours to increase their earnings. Why limit the ability of these workers to work the number of hours they would prefer?

One response is that the FLSA is necessary to protect the health of workers. In the absence of the FLSA, workers may injure their health by agreeing to work too many hours. Workers may work too much because they do not have full information about the long-term health consequences of working long hours.

Even if they had that information, they would work too much if they discounted the future too much. That is, they may be too willing to sacrifice future health and productivity for current income. And even if they had full information and discounted the future properly, they may work too much because many of the costs of bad health can be externalized. The state will absorb much of the cost of poor health, both by subsidizing health care and by subsidizing disabled workers. Thus, the FLSA may be necessary to correct for these types of market failures.

NOTES

1. *Changes in Quasi-Fixed Costs.* In the last three decades, fringe benefits have approximately doubled as a proportion of total compensation. Many of these costs (such as the costs for health insurance) are quasi-fixed in the sense that they are per employee costs that do not increase as hours of work increase. Thus, the FLSA is probably not as effective in spreading work today as it was before the relative increases in quasi-fixed costs: One-and-one-half times the regular rate of pay is a lower proportion of total compensation today than it was three decades ago. Proposals have been made periodically in Congress to address this problem by increasing the premium for overtime work to double the regular rate of pay.

2. *The History of Hours and Overtime Premiums.* During the *Lochner* era, legislation that attempted to limit the number of working hours for broad categories of workers was generally struck down as unconstitutional. Nevertheless, during that time, the hours actually worked by employees were going down quite dramatically, from an average of fifty-nine hours per week in 1900, to fifty hours per week before the onset of the depression, to thirty-eight hours per week in 1937 shortly before the FLSA was enacted. DAVID R. ROEDIGER & PHILLIP S. FONER, OUR OWN TIME: A HISTORY OF AMERICAN LABOR AND THE WORKING DAY x (1989). Similarly, overtime premiums were offered by many employers during the 1920s. Does this information mean that the FLSA was unnecessary because the labor market was capable of achieving the goals of the FLSA on its own?

3. *Women and Overtime Hours.* Men work more overtime hours than women, so restrictions on overtime do not have the same effect on men and women. Would you expect the following groups to support, oppose, or be neutral to restrictions on overtime hours: (1) social conservatives who believe that women should not work outside the home, and (2) people who want to support and encourage the trend towards more working women?

c. Restrictions on the Use of Child Labor

> Stooped over a row of squash, ... Alfedo Diaz, aged fourteen, is helping his parents bring in the last of an October harvest they have "sharecropped" for a local grower. The pickings are slim. Together, they hope to earn $50 this day. In adjoining patches of squash, other families are working too. Soon they will all move to winter strawberries.

"I don't think I'll be able to return to school until the strawberries are in," Alfedo says, not stopping to look up. "Maybe then, in a month or so." In truth, he hasn't been to school for eight months. Likely he will never go back. His parents, Jesus and Clementina, are in their late fifties and say they need him to work. "We are too old to work alone," Diaz says, watching his son. "We cannot make the money we need to live if we do not have help."

—THE BOSTON GLOBE
   April 22, 1990

The FLSA limits the use of "oppressive" child labor. What is oppressive under the Act and Department of Labor regulations depends on the age of the child. First, it is oppressive to employ children under age fourteen at all, unless they fall within one of a few, narrow exceptions. Children as young as ten, however, can work under the exceptions. Second, children who are fourteen and fifteen years old may work, but there are limits both on the types of occupations in which they can engage and in the number of hours they can work. When school is in session, these children can work no more than three hours per day and no more than eighteen hours per week. When school is not in session, they can work up to eight hours per day and forty hours per week. The work must be performed between 7 a.m. and 7 p.m., except in the summer (June 1 to Labor Day) when evening work can extend to 9 p.m. Third, children who are sixteen and seventeen years old may work under the same FLSA minimum-wage and maximum-hour conditions as adults, except that they are prohibited from working in occupations that have been determined to be hazardous by the Secretary of Labor. To date, the Secretary has found seventeen occupations to be hazardous. At eighteen years of age, employees are regarded as adults under the FLSA.

The child labor provisions of the FLSA, obviously, are intended in part to protect the interests of children. Portions of the FLSA (most predominantly the prohibition on work in hazardous occupations) are intended to protect the physical safety of children. Prior to the FLSA, there was certainly cause for concern:

It is a sorry but indisputable fact that where children are employed, the most unhealthful work is generally given them. In ... cotton and woolen mills, where large number of children are employed, clouds of lint-dust fill the lungs and menace the health.... In bottle factories ... the atmosphere is constantly charged with microscopic particles of glass. In the wood-working industries ... the air is laden with fine sawdust. Children employed in soap and soap-powder factories work, many of them, in clouds of alkaline dust which inflames the eyelids and nostrils.... In the coal-mines the breaker boys breathe air that is heavy and thick with particles of coal, and their lungs become black in consequence. In the manufacture of felt hats, little girls are often employed at the machines which tear the fur from the skins of rabbits and other animals. Recently, I stood and watched a young girl working at such a machine; she wore a newspaper pinned over her head and a handkerchief tied over her mouth. She was white with dust from head to feet, and when she stooped to pick anything from the floor the dust would fall from her paper headcovering in little heaps. About seven feet from the mouth of the machine was a window through which poured thick volumes of dust as it was belched out from the machine. I placed a sheet of paper on the inner sill of the window and in twenty minutes it was covered with a layer of fine dust, half an inch deep. Yet that girl works midway between the window and the machine, in the very centre of the volume of dust, sixty hours a week. These are a few of the occupations in which the dangers arise from the forced inhalation of dust.

JOHN SPARGO, THE BITTER CRY OF THE CHILDREN 175-80 (1907).

Today, the FLSA's importance and effectiveness in protecting the physical safety of children is less clear. The Occupational Safety and Health Act and related safety laws (which will be discussed later in this volume) have made work safer for *all* workers, so the need for special protection for young workers has declined. Moreover, the FLSA's effectiveness in protecting children who are at risk of physical injury is questionable. Over 90% of FLSA child labor violations are in the trade and service industries, among the safest of the eight major industrial groups, while agriculture, the most dangerous industry, especially for children, is largely unregulated by the Act.[*] *See* 29 U.S.C. § 213(c).

The child labor provisions of the FLSA are also intended to protect the interests of children by promoting education. The rationale is that if their work opportunities are limited, children will be more likely to attend and do well in school. Once again, this was unquestionably a forceful rationale at the beginning and middle of this century when child factory workers generally did not go to school at all and, as a result, were three to four times more likely to be illiterate than other children. Alexander J. McKelway, *The Needs of the Cotton Mill Operatives*, in CHILDREN AND YOUTH IN AMERICA, Vol. II, at 659-61 (Robert Bremner ed., 1971). But is it still a forceful rationale today? Modern research indicates that a potential conflict between work and education still exists, but its nature has changed. Today, children who work usually go to school, too. But children who work a lot (twenty hours per week or more) tend to earn lower grades, cheat more frequently, skip school more often, and use drugs and alcohol more frequently. Laurence Steinberg, *Beyond the Classroom: Why School Reform Has Failed and What Parents Need to Do* 163-73 (1996). About half of all high school seniors who work, and about one-third of all juniors who work, spend more than twenty hours per week on the job. *Id.* at 170. Thus, while the

---

[*] For the eight major industrial groups, the death rates per 100,000 workers for the decade 1980-89 were agriculture (51), mining and quarrying (45), construction (35), transportation and utilities (28), government (9), manufacturing (6), services (6), and trade (5). NATIONAL SAFETY COUNCIL, ACCIDENT FACTS 37 (1990). When adjusted for time spent working, the accident rate for children ages 5 to 14 working in agriculture is more than double the accident rate for any other age group. Cheryl Tevis & Charlene Finck, *We Kill Too Many Farm Kids*, SUCCESSFUL FARMING, Mid-Feb. 1989, at 18A, 18B.

issue is still relevant, the ability of the FLSA to address current problems created by potential conflicts between work and school is suspect.

Finally the child labor restrictions are intended to protect the interests of adults. By limiting the supply of workers, the FLSA should increase the pay of adults and may increase the number of jobs available to them.

NOTES

1. *The History of Federal Child Labor Legislation.* Early attempts to deal with child labor at the federal level were not able to survive the searching judicial inquiries of the *Lochner* era. The Child Labor Act of 1916, 39 Stat. 675, would have prevented interstate commerce in the products of child labor, but it was ruled unconstitutional by the Supreme Court in *Hammer v. Dagenhart,* 247 U.S. 251 (1918), because it intruded too deeply into a matter reserved for state and local control. Congress tried again by imposing a 10% tax on all products of child labor, Child Labor Tax Act, 40 Stat. 1148 (1918), but the Supreme Court struck that statute down, too, holding that it exceeded the federal taxing power. *Child Labor Tax Case,* 259 U.S. 20 (1922). Congress then approved and submitted to the states a constitutional amendment which would have authorized it to regulate child labor, 43 Stat. 670 (1924), but the proposal met with resounding disapproval by the states. The roadblock to federal legislation was removed with the demise of *Lochner.* In *United States v. Darby,* 312 U.S. 100 (1941), the Supreme Court upheld the constitutionality of the Fair Labor Standards Act, expressly overruling *Hammer v. Dagenhart* in the process.

2. *Child Labor and Free Trade.* Child labor is an international issue. The International Labor Organization estimates that 120 million children worldwide work full-time, with at least 40 million of them working in hazardous conditions. Free trade agreements, such as the General Agreement on Tariffs and Trade (GATT), ensure that the products of this labor can flow easily to markets worldwide. The combination of low-wage labor (often including child labor) and free trade has produced dramatic changes in some industries. In textiles, for example, the number of workers in several developing countries increased significantly between 1970 and 1990 (for example, Malaysia, up 600%; Bangladesh, up 416%; and Indonesia, up 334%), while decreasing significantly in more industrialized countries (for example, Finland, down 73%; Germany, down 55%; and the United States, down 31%).

The United States has been vigorous in attempting to have international trade organizations, such as the World Trade Organization (WTO), study the relationship between trade and core labor standards. *See* 19 U.S.C. § 3551 (President required to seek establishment of working party in the WTO to examine worker rights). The United States' efforts to date, however, have been largely unsuccessful. Many other countries view these initiatives skeptically. They suspect that the initiatives may be intended primarily to protect U.S. workers from competition, rather than foreign children from exploitation, and they fear that, if implemented, the initiatives would compromise the principal comparative advantage of developing countries, low-wage labor. These views are shared by many developing countries, such as Malaysia and Indonesia, and even by some industrialized countries, most notably the United Kingdom.

3. *Are Child Labor Laws Necessary at All?* Consider the following argument:

> The child labor laws are superfluous. Everything that they try to accomplish is already covered by other laws. They try to protect the physical safety of children, encourage them to go to school, and protect the jobs and wages of adults. But all of those purposes are already adequately dealt with through safety and health laws, compulsory education laws, and minimum wage laws. But the child labor laws are worse than superfluous. They also interfere with the good judgment of parents in raising their children. Parents know best whether their children can do better by going to school or working, or combining the two in some way, but child labor laws limit the options available to parents and their children.

Convinced?

d. Problems With Implementing the Substantive Obligations

Implementation of the minimum wage and maximum hour provisions of the FLSA requires two basic types of information: wages and hours. How much does the employee make and how many hours does she work? When employers pay strictly by the hour for normal shifts, for example by establishing a wage rate of $10.00 per hour for an 8-to-5 job, implementation is usually quite easy. The base wage rate in our example is greater than the minimum wage requirement of $5.15 per hour and the employee must be paid $15.00 per hour for any hours worked in excess of 40 each week (that is, at a rate one-and-one-half times the "regular" rate). But any variation from this simple pattern may cause problems, and most employers vary in one way or another. Should time when an employer requires an employee to be on call and available for work, but when the employee is not actually working, be considered work time? Should bonuses or incentive pay be added into the regular rate of pay? What if an employer pays less than the minimum wage but allows the employee free use of a company car — should the car be treated as wages and, if so, what is it worth? The possible variations are almost infinite. This section will be a brief introduction to some of the implementation issues raised by the FLSA.

BRIGHT V. HOUSTON NORTHWEST MEDICAL CENTER SURVIVOR, INC.

United States Court of Appeals, Fifth Circuit (*en banc*)
934 F.2d 671 (1991), *cert. denied,* 502 U.S. 1036 (1992)

GARWOOD, CIRCUIT JUDGE: ...

This is a former employee's suit for overtime compensation under section 7(a)(1) of the Fair Labor Standards Act (FLSA), 29 U.S.C. § 207(a)(1). The question presented is whether "on-call" time the employee spent at home, or at other locations of his choosing substantially removed from his employer's place of business, is ... working time in instances where the employee was not actually "called." [The district court granted Northwest's motion for summary judgment. A divided panel of this court reversed and remanded for trial. 888 F.2d 1059 (5th Cir. 1989). Upon reconsideration en banc, this court now affirms the district court decision.]

Bright went to work for Northwest at its hospital in Houston in April 1981 as a biomedical equipment repair technician, and remained in that employment until late January 1983 when, for reasons wholly unrelated to any matters at issue here, he was in effect fired.... [Beginning in February 1982, Bright] was required to wear an electronic paging device or "beeper" [during his off-duty hours] and to be "on call" to come to the hospital to make emergency repairs on biomedical equipment....

Bright was not compensated for his on-call time, and knew this was the arrangement....[2] During the "on-call" time, if Bright were called, and came to the hospital, he was compensated by four hours compensatory time at his then regular hourly rate (which apparently was some $9 or $10 per hour) for each such call.... This case does not involve any claim respecting entitlement to compensation (overtime or otherwise) for time that Bright actually spent pursuant to a call from Northwest received while he was on call.

It is undisputed that during the on-call time at issue Bright was not required to, and did not, remain at or about the hospital or any premises of or designated by his employer. He was free to go wherever and do whatever he wanted, subject *only* to the following three restrictions: (1) he must not be intoxicated or impaired to the degree that he could not work on medical equipment if called to the hospital, although total abstinence was not required (as it was during the daily workshift); (2) he must always be reachable by the beeper; (3) and he must be able to arrive at the hospital within, in Bright's words, "approximately twenty minutes" from the time he was reached on the beeper.... On deposition Bright admitted while on call he not only stayed at home and watched television and the like, but also engaged in other activities away from home, including his "normal

---

[2] Bright was told that efforts were being made to have a future hospital budget contain provision for some unspecified character of compensation in respect to his on-call and beeper status; but it was clear that this would only apply to periods after such a budget were approved (and would not be "retroactive"); as Bright knew all along, no such budget was ever approved.

shopping" (including supermarket and mall shopping) and "occasionally" going out to restaurants to eat.... Bright also testified on deposition that he was "called" on "average" two times during the working week (Monday through Friday) and "ordinarily two to three times" on the weekend.

At issue here is whether the time Bright spent on call, but uncalled on, is working time under section [207 of the FLSA. The two leading Supreme Court cases on the issue, *Armour & Co. v. Wantock,* 323 U.S. 126 (1944) and *Skidmore v. Swift & Co.,* 323 U.S. 134 (1944)] clearly stand for the proposition that, in a proper setting, on-call time may be working time for purposes of section [207]....

In *Armour* the plaintiffs were firemen who worked a regular 8:00 a.m. to 5:00 p.m. shift, and then were on call at the employer's premises from 5:00 p.m. until 8:00 a.m. of the following day, after which they had 24 wholly unrestricted hours, and then repeated the cycle. The Court observed that

> "[t]he litigation concerns the time [5:00 p.m. to 8:00 a.m.] during which these men were required to be on the employer's premises, to some extent amenable to the employer's discipline, subject to call, but not engaged in any specific work. The Company provided cooking equipment, beds, radios, and facilities for cards and amusements with which the men slept, ate, or entertained themselves pretty much as they chose. They were not, however, at liberty to leave the premises except that, by permission of the watchman, they might go to a nearby restaurant for their evening meal." [323 U.S. at 128.]

Armour sustained the district court's determination, which had been affirmed by the Seventh Circuit, that all this time (apart from hours presumably devoted to sleeping or eating, a matter that the plaintiffs did not appeal) was working time.[6]

Bright's case is wholly different from *Armour* and *Skidmore* and similar cases in that Bright did not have to remain on or about his employer's place of business, or some location designated by his employer, but was free to be at his home or at any place or places he chose, without advising his employer, subject only to the restrictions that he be reachable by beeper, not be intoxicated, and be able to

---

[6] In *Skidmore* the facts were similar, and the district court, which this Court had affirmed, concluded that "the time plaintiffs spent in the [employer's] fire hall subject to call to answer fire alarms does not constitute hours worked." [323 U.S. at 136.] The Supreme Court reversed and remanded for reconsideration because the lower court determination apparently rested on the erroneous notion that "waiting time may not be work." [323 U.S. at 140. *Skidmore* differed from *Armour* in several respects.] In *Armour* there was no agreement or payment for on-call time actually spent answering an alarm (although in the suit the employer did not contest liability for such alarm answering time); but in *Skidmore* there was agreed compensation in case the employees received such a call. Further, in *Skidmore* the men apparently did not have to remain strictly on the employer's premises, so long as they were "within hailing distance" thereof, while no such accommodation appears to have been present in *Armour.*

arrive at the hospital in "approximately" twenty minutes.[7] Bright was not only able to carry on his normal personal activities at his own home, but could also do normal shopping, eating at restaurants, and the like, as he chose.

To hold that Bright's on-call time was working time would be inconsistent with several of our own prior decisions, as well as those in other circuits, which have determined that considerably more restrictive on-call status did not result in work time.

In *Brock* [*v. El Paso Natural Gas Co.*, 826 F.2d 369 (5th Cir. 1987)], we ... reversed ... a district court bench trial finding that "on call" time was compensable overtime. There, the employee claimants lived relatively near their employer's pumping stations where their regular work day was 7:30 a.m. to 4:00 p.m. However, during the nonworking hours of 4:00 p.m. to 7:30 a.m. every day, one employee was required to remain "on call"; this required the employee to remain at his home where he could hear an alarm; if it went off, he would go to the station to correct the problem. We noted that "[o]therwise, the on-call employee is free to eat, sleep, entertain guests, watch television, or engage in any other personal recreational activity, alone or with his family, as long as he is within hailing distance of the alarm and the station." *Id.* at 370 (footnote omitted). The employees were compensated for this time only in instances where they were actually called. We held that as a matter of law the on-call time was not work time for purposes of the FLSA.

In *Halferty* [*v. Pulse Drug Co.*, 864 F.2d 1185 (5th Cir. 1989)], we again [reversed] the district court's finding that the on-call time was compensable overtime.... There, the employee time in question was spent at home from 5:00 p.m. to 8:00 a.m. to be available for telephone calls as an ambulance dispatcher. We stated that in these cases "the critical issue ... is whether the employee can use the time effectively for his or her own purposes." *Id.* at 1189. We held that as a matter of law the plaintiff there could use the time effectively for her own purposes and that she was hence not entitled to recover, stating:

> "The facts show that Halferty could visit friends, entertain guests, sleep, watch television, do laundry, and babysit. We, therefore, conclude that she could use the time for her own purposes and that she is not entitled to compensation for her idle time...." *Id.*

We noted that "[e]mployees who have received compensation for idle time generally have had almost no freedom at all." *Id.* at 1190. And, we cited and relied

---

[7] The administrative interpretations reflect the difference in kind between situations where the on-call employee has to remain at or about the employer's place of business and those where the on-call employee can be at home or other accessible places of his choosing. *See* 29 CFR § 785.17:

> "An employee who is required to remain on call on the employer's premises or so close thereto that he cannot use the time effectively for his own purposes is working while 'on call.' An employee who is not required to remain on the employer's premises but is merely required to leave word at his home or with company officials where he may be reached is not working while on call."...

on, among other cases, ... *Pilkenton v. Appalachian Regional Hospitals, Inc.,* 336 F. Supp. 334 (W.D. Va. 1971)....

In *Pilkenton,* the on-call employees had beepers and had to remain within an "approximately twenty minutes" drive from their employer's hospital during their on-call time. That time was held noncompensable (except for instances where they were called).

Also to be considered are our decisions in *Allen v. Atlantic Richfield Co.,* 724 F.2d 1131 (5th Cir. 1984), and *Rousseau* [*v. Teledyne Movible Offshore, Inc.,* 805 F.2d 1245 (5th Cir. 1986)]. In *Allen,* guards at a plant under strike from early January to the end of March were required to remain at the plant twenty-four hours a day, during twelve of which they were on duty, and during the other twelve they "were free to sleep, eat at no expense, watch movies, play pool or cards, exercise, read, or listen to music...." 724 F.2d at 1137. They were not compensated for this off-duty time (except that if, in an emergency, they were called to work during the off-duty time they were paid for that work). We upheld a verdict for the defendant that this off-duty time was not compensable.

In *Rousseau,* the claimant employees worked on derrick barges for seven-day shifts, twelve hours each day; during the other "off" twelve hours, however, they were required to remain on the barges and to be available for emergency work. They were compensated only for the time they actually worked, not for any of the twelve-hour waiting time (except for such actual work as they might do during that time) spent on the barges. [We affirmed the district court's decision that the waiting time was not working time,] relying on the statement in the district court's opinion that "[t]he stipulated facts and evidence show that during their off duty time on the barges, the plaintiffs were free to sleep, eat, watch television, watch VCR movies, play pingpong or cards, read, listen to music, etc." *Id.* at 1248.

As noted, we have described "the critical issue" in cases of this kind as being "whether the employee can use the [on-call] time effectively for his or her own purposes." *Halferty,* 864 F.2d at 1189. This does not imply that the employee must have substantially the same flexibility or freedom as he would if not on call, else all or almost all on-call time would be working time, a proposition that the settled case law and the administrative guidelines clearly reject. Only in the very rarest of situations, if ever, would there be any point in an employee being on call if he could not be reached by his employer so as to shortly thereafter — generally at least a significant time before the next regular workshift could take care of the matter — be able to perform a needed service, usually at some particular location.

Within such accepted confines, Bright was clearly able to use his on-call time effectively for his own personal purposes. Indeed, it is evident that he was *much more* able to do so than the employees in the above discussed cases whose on-call time was held to be nonworking time. Unlike the employees in *Brock* (restricted to home or plant), *Halferty* (restricted to home), *Rousseau* (restricted to barge), and *Allen* (restricted to plant), Bright was not restricted to any one or a few fixed locations, but could go virtually anywhere within approximately twenty minutes of the hospital.... Within that limit, anything was permissible, except excessive alcohol consumption. An approximately twenty minute radius was involved in *Pilkenton*.... We have found no unreversed decision holding compensable on-call time that afforded even nearly as much freedom for personal use as did Bright's. Had the twenty to thirty minute "leash" been longer, Bright would, of course, have been able to do *more* things, but that does not mean that within the applicable restrictions he could not effectively use the on-call time wholly for his own private purposes. Millions of employees go for weeks at a time without traveling more than seventeen miles from their place of employment.

The panel majority did not disagree with our prior decisions. Rather, it placed crucial reliance on the fact that Bright throughout the nearly one year in issue never had any relief from his on-call status during his nonworking hours. The panel majority states that Bright's case "differs from ... other cases in one important respect: Bright ... never had any reprieve from on-call duties," *Bright,* 888 F.2d at 1061; "the restrictions only applied to the workers in *Rousseau* for seven days at a time," which it described as "the critical fact," *id.* at 1063; *Allen* was distinguished because "of critical importance is the fact that the arrangement was a temporary one, lasting only the length of the strike," *id.* (footnote omitted). In essence, the panel majority inferentially conceded that for any given day or week of on-call time, Bright was as free to use the time for his own purposes as were the employees in the above-cited cases where the time was held nonworking. But the panel majority claims that a different result should apply here because Bright's arrangement lasted nearly a year.

We are aware of no authority that supports this theory, and we decline to adopt it.... [T]he FLSA is structured on a workweek basis. Section [207,] at issue here, requires time and a half pay "for a workweek longer than forty hours." What Bright was or was not free to do in the last week in September is wholly irrelevant to whether he worked any overtime in the first week of that month. As we said in *Halferty,* the issue "is whether the employee can use the time effectively for his or her own purposes," and that must be decided, under the statutory framework, on the basis of each workweek at the most.

We do not deny the obvious truth that the long continued aspect of Bright's on-call status made his job highly undesirable and arguably somewhat oppressive. Clearly, it would have been vastly more pleasant from Bright's point of view had he only been on call the first week of every month, for example. But the FLSA's overtime provisions are more narrowly focused than being simply directed at requiring extra compensation for oppressive or confining conditions of employment. A Texan working 8:30 p.m. to 3:00 a.m. six days a week (thirty-nine hours), fifty-two weeks a year, at a remote Alaska location has a most restrictive and oppressive job that as a practical matter prevents, *inter alia,* vacations, visiting relatives, and attending live operatic performances or major league sporting events, but it seems obvious that the FLSA overtime provisions provide no relief for those oppressive and confining conditions. Bright's job was oppressive and confining in many of the same ways, but it, too, did not involve more than forty hours work a week.[8]

The district court properly granted summary judgment for Northwest, and that judgment is accordingly

Affirmed.

JERRE S. WILLIAMS, CIRCUIT JUDGE, with whom JOHNSON, CIRCUIT JUDGE, joins, dissenting:

I dissent from the decision of the en banc court in this case.... The facts as stated in the opinion for the Court are accurate insofar as they go. They need supplementation by way of emphasis. The panel opinion and this dissent are grounded wholly on the circumstance which must be accepted as true that for a period of approximately eleven months from February 1982 until January 1983, employee Bright's life was significantly circumscribed by his employer without compensation. There was no relief by way of other employees sharing the duties so that Bright would have periods of being free from the restrictions. There were no free weekends, there was no vacation, there were no free days or nights. This is the core issue in the case....

I do not go into detail to comment upon the cases discussed and treated as controlling by the majority opinion of the en banc court. None of them control. Every single one of them, without exception, involves a situation where the employer had more than one employee sharing the oppressive schedule or there was some other means of "covering the employee" so that the employee was not committed and under serious limitations without respite over a substantial period of time....

The nearest case to the facts of this case has to do with the employee Pilkenton, who was on a schedule with virtually the identical restrictions as Bright. *Pilkenton v. Appalachian Regional Hosps., Inc.,* 336 F. Supp. 334 (W.D. Va. 1971). But in *Pilkenton* another employee shared the on-call duty so that each employee was freed of the duty and personal limitations for half of his or her overall time. Thus, the employees were not being held on a permanent 20 minute leash.

At the end, the opinion for the Court falls back, as it must, upon the proposition that Bright was in the same situation as someone holding a job in a remote part of Alaska where, after an eight hour day, the use of his or her own time obviously is limited. This reliance is wholly foreign to the thrust of the Fair Labor Standards Act. Admittedly, there are jobs which because of location are in isolated areas. That is in the nature of the jobs. But the isolation is not the result

---

[8] Except in instances, not at issue here, where the extra work was compensated consistently with section [207].

of an employer's direction requiring employee on-call availability during off-duty hours. The employer has nothing to do with the restricted recreational and living accommodations in an isolated job. That is not an on-call situation at all. In contrast, here it is the employer who is enforcing a unique restriction upon a particular employee as part of the particular on-call work assignment. This is of the essence of the thrust of potential work time under the Fair Labor Standards Act.

This distinction can be seen more clearly if in an extreme case the employer directed a particular employee permanently to remain behind on the hospital campus for an hour each day after the workshift was over in case some problem arose about the changeover from one shift to another. The employee would be free to read a book, watch television, walk around the grounds, but would be required to remain on the grounds for an hour in case the employee was needed. It would be exceedingly difficult to hold that that particular hour was not work time. It would be an additional on-call restriction for the benefit of the employer placed upon the employee for an extra hour every day but without compensation.

Bright's case, of course, is not that extreme in its restriction. But it is not a remote location case caused by the nature of the work applicable to all jobs. It is an on-call isolation case caused by the employer's own orders defining the particular work assignment. Thus, we are left, as the panel opinion said, with the circumstance in which Bright "was not far removed from a prisoner serving a sentence under slightly relaxed house arrest terms. He never could go to downtown Houston, he never could go to Galveston and see the ocean. He never could go to a baseball or football game in the Astrodome. An out of town event, even a visit to relatives or friends in San Antonio or Austin, was totally out of the question." *Bright,* 888 F.2d at 1064. Further, the employer had a relatively simple and humane means of avoiding this restriction which was akin to and rather close to house arrest. The remedy is found in every single one of the cases cited by the majority opinion and relied upon by the majority opinion. The employer could have set up a system under which this onerous restrictive duty could be shared or certain periods of relief could be afforded.

Finally, the opinion for the Court asserts that all overtime issues under the statute must be based upon a week by week analysis.... While the FLSA calls for the calculation of the payment of overtime on a weekly basis, it does not require that each individual week be a wholly separate entity in determining whether an employee is working or not.

In *Allen v. Atlantic Richfield Co.,* 724 F.2d 1131 (5th Cir. 1981) (cited in the en banc opinion), we considered a case in which security personnel because of a strike were required to remain on the grounds of the industrial establishment for 24 hours every day for a period of what was apparently the first few weeks of an eleven week strike. Later, arrangements were made during the strike to rotate the 24 hour duty. The jury found that the security employees were not working during this period when they were off duty although they were required to remain at the plant. We upheld the jury verdict.

We can draw two authoritative conclusions from our decision in this case. First, the opinion makes no reference to a week by week limitation but instead assumed that the entire time during which the 24 hour requirement was in effect was relevant to the work time issue. Second, the case shows that we can and should trust juries in these cases to deny bonanzas to unfounded claims of extra work. The jury found no additional work time in that relatively short period of a few weeks involved in *Allen.*

Bright may not be able to prove to a jury that he was entitled to any additional work time credit.... But I dissent because this is not a case for summary judgment. A trial is necessary to assess the facts of this case.... There is a total absence of any authority which goes even close to the extreme presented to us as to the permanent, unrelenting, restrictions placed upon Bright's time by his employer. Thus, it was error to affirm the summary judgment of the district court. Bright is entitled to a jury trial on the facts presented to us. The well-established requirement of the Fair Labor Standards Act that on-call time can constitute work time requires this result and prompts this dissent.

NOTES

1. *Should Bright Move to Kansas?* In *Renfro v. City of Emporia,* 948 F.2d 1529 (10th Cir. 1991), *cert. dismissed,* 503 U.S. 915 (1992), the court affirmed a summary judgment requiring the city to pay overtime and liquidated damages to firefighters for on-call time. In *Renfro,* firefighters were regularly required to be on call for 24-hour periods. While on call, the city required the firefighters to carry a pager and be able to return to work within twenty minutes of being called. They were paid only when called and were called on average three to five times per 24-hour period. Firefighters were able to trade their on-call duties with other firefighters and, while on call, firefighters had "participated in sports activities, socialized with friends and relatives, attended business meetings, gone shopping, gone out to eat, babysitted, and performed maintenance or other activities around their home." *Id.* at 1532. Indeed, one-third of the firefighters were able to maintain second jobs despite the uncertainties created by the on-call time.

2. *Pay for On-Call Time.* On-call time presents a problem under the Fair Labor Standards Act in part because of the dichotomous nature of work time under the Act: Either an employee is or is not working. The firefighters in *Renfro* were awarded overtime pay and liquidated damages for all of their on-call hours. One firefighter, for example, was awarded $122,000 in backpay and liquidated damages. In contrast, Bright was found not to be working during his on-call time, so he was entitled to nothing for his inconveniences. Neither outcome seems quite right.

3. *How Should Employers Respond?* Employers have two primary ways of responding to the problem of on-call time. First, they can attempt to structure the on-call time so that it is not work time that is compensable under the Act. *Bright* and *Renfro* provide some clues on how to do that — longer response time, limiting the number of calls to work, and so forth. Second, employers can attempt to adjust wages so that treating the on-call time as compensable is not too burdensome. That is, by reducing the regular hourly rate, the employer may be able to offset most of the cost of treating the on-call time as compensable. Do you think an employer should be able to pay a lower rate for on-call time than for regular work time? *See Townsend v. Mercy Hosp.,* 862 F.2d 1009 (3d Cir. 1988) (yes, under certain conditions).

4. *The Broader Issue of Compensable Time.* The issue of what hours are compensable under the FLSA reaches far beyond on-call time. Is time during coffee breaks compensable? How about meal periods? Time spent walking from the timeclock to the area where the work is actually performed? Driving to work? Driving from home to a customer's business to perform emergency services? The possible circumstances are virtually endless. The regulations, which merely seem to be endless, answer many of the questions. (The answers to the questions above, for example, are yes, no, no, no, and yes.)

The Portal-to-Portal Act of 1947 was enacted primarily in response to these types of issues. Although it is known only to labor law specialists today, the Act was a major political issue when it was enacted. For a good history, *see* Marc Linder, *Class Struggle at the Door: The Origins of the Portal-to-Portal Act of 1947,* 39 BUFF. L. REV. 53 (1991).

Perhaps the most interesting question here is not how these issues are resolved (for example, is time spent on coffee breaks compensable or not?), but rather why they are important at all. Let us say that the rule on coffee breaks changes — before, time spent on coffee breaks was not compensable, now it is. Why might that change be important? Consider the following argument:

> For most employees, the change in the coffee break rule will not result in any long-term increase in their income. Employers will merely lower the base wage rate (or other parts of the compensation package) to compensate for the extra compensable time. But the change will be important for minimum wage workers. Since employers cannot lower the base wage rate for these workers, the change would result in an increase in income. The increase, however, may also cause some employment losses for minimum wage workers.

MARSHALL v. SAM DELL'S DODGE CORP.

United States District Court, N.D. New York
451 F. Supp. 294 (1978)

PORT, SENIOR DISTRICT JUDGE.

Defendant Sam Dell's Dodge Corp. is an automobile dealership in Syracuse, New York.... The hours and wages of 117 salespersons who were employed at Sam Dell's Dodge ... are at issue....

The defendants paid their salespeople under a series of rather complex plans. Total compensation included combinations of base pay, commissions, and bonuses.... The plans varied from time to time but can be summarized as follows. Each salesperson received base pay of $56.00 per week for most of the period covered by this action. The base pay was received free and clear without regard to sales made. Commissions were paid on the sales of just about everything, new cars, used cars, trucks, accessories and finance agreements. At times the commissions were fixed amounts paid for the sale of each new car. For used cars and, more recently, for new cars the commissions were a percentage of either the sales price or the dealer's profits. On top of commissions, salespersons were paid bonuses as an incentive for increased sales. For selling four or more cars during one week, a salesperson would receive a weekly bonus in the next pay check. If he or she sold over 20 cars during one month, a monthly bonus would be received at the end of that month. Similarly, annual bonuses were paid for the sale of over a given number of cars during a calendar year. For a good salesperson, these bonuses could be substantial compared to the base pay.

Some salesmen testified, however, that they would stagger receipt of their commissions so as to spread out or average their income during the year. In this way, they would not get a disproportionately large pay check after a highly successful selling week. Nevertheless, there were some weeks during each year when each salesperson received only the base salary $56.00 ... and failed to earn any commissions or bonuses.

Many of the salespeople were furnished by defendants with demonstrator cars or "demos." Primarily, these cars were used in connection with the salespersons' duties at Sam Dell's Dodge Corp.... Salespeople used them for demonstration rides for their customers.... Salespersons were permitted to drive the cars for personal use when not working; however, they were specifically told that the cars were not for their families.... The value of the use of the "demos" was never included on the employee's W-2 tax statements or the employer's pay records. After April, 1976, defendants' pay plans indicated that a Form 1099 would be given to each employee listing the value of the "demo" car at $20.00 each month. However, defendants failed to introduce any evidence that the 1099 Forms were ever provided.

The bulk of the testimony received at trial concerned the number of hours worked each week by the sales staff. Defendants' showroom and car lots, referred to throughout the trial as the "store" were open six days a week. On Mondays, Tuesdays and Thursdays, the store was open from 9:00 A.M. to 9:30 P.M. Wednesdays, Fridays and Saturdays the store was open from 9:00 A.M. to 6:30 P.M. Thus, defendants' posted operating time for the store totaled 66 hours per week....

The average workweek for defendants' salespersons ... was 55 hours. The store was open 66 hours each week but eliminating $1\frac{1}{2}$ hours each for early departure, ... four hours for lunch, two for dinner, and another two for personal time leaves a 55 hour workweek.

This is not a precise figure. It is my inference based on the evidence I regarded as credible. The deductions from the scheduled workweek are probably generous to the defendants; certainly they cannot be considered niggardly toward an employer whose deliberately contrived time records made precision impossible.

Despite the fact that defendants encouraged their employees to work long hours, defendants kept time records which grossly understated the number of hours actually worked. While the sales staff was working, on the average, a 55 hour or more week, defendants required their employees to sign time slips which purported to show that the employees were working only 36 hours per week.

The defendants' practice of knowingly maintaining inaccurate time records which greatly understated the number of hours worked by their sales personnel [means that] the violations of the Act were willful.

III. *Conclusions of Law and Discussion*

A. *The Workweek Is the Relevant Pay Period*

Defendants' salespersons worked on the average 55 hours per week. For weeks during which they made no sales and, therefore, earned no commissions or bonuses, they would receive only the base pay [of] $56 per week which was less than the minimum wage. [The minimum wage ranged from $1.60 to $2.65 per hour during the relevant time period.] Plaintiff contends that, by not paying the guaranteed minimum wage for each hour worked in each week, defendants violated section [206] of the Act. Defendants concede that they paid their employees only $56 in some weeks and that simple multiplication of the required minimum wage times the hours worked in those weeks exceeds the amounts paid. They contend, however, that some period other than the week should be used in assessing compliance with the minimum wage requirements of the Act....

The defendants herein established, by their own practice, the workweek as the customary pay period. Their salespersons were paid each week for earnings which accrued during that week. While car sales may be seasonal, defendants' pay practice ... was regular. Having established the week as the applicable pay period, defendants cannot now argue that any other time period measures compliance with the Act.

Further support for this conclusion comes from the Secretary's own interpretations of section [206] of the Act. "Section [206(b)] of the Act ... is applicable on a workweek basis and *requires payment* of the prescribed minimum wages to each employee who 'in any workweek' is employed in a covered enterprise." Likewise, the Secretary's regulations implementing section [207] of the Act base compliance on the workweek. "The Act takes a single workweek as its standard and does not permit averaging of hours over two or more weeks." 29

C.F.R. § 778.104.[9] Clearly, the Secretary's interpretations of the Act, although not binding on the court, are entitled to great weight.

The Supreme Court has emphasized the importance of paying an employee's minimum wage on a weekly basis. In considering the rationale behind the liquidated damages provision of the Act, 29 U.S.C. § 216(b), the Court noted that

> failure to pay the statutory minimum on time may be ... detrimental to maintenance of the minimum standard of living "necessary for health, efficiency and general well-being of workers".... Employees receiving less than the statutory minimum are not likely to have sufficient resources to maintain their well-being and efficiency until such sums are paid at a future date.

Brooklyn Savings Bank v. O'Neil, 324 U.S. 697, 707-08 (1945). The defendants may see this rationale as applicable only to workers with annual incomes in the minimum wage range. However, in the period with which we are dealing even the better paid salesman with a family would be hard pressed if he were obliged to suffer a few weeks at less than minimum wages. Plaintiff has shown that at least four of defendants' salesmen failed to receive the minimum wage during periods of nine to twelve consecutive weeks. This is the precise danger which the Fair Labor Standards Act sought to meet....

In this case the relevant period for analyzing compliance with section [206] of the Act is the workweek. Regardless of the total pay received by an employee, the Act requires that each employee receive, each week, an amount equal to the minimum wage times the number of hours worked. Defendants have, therefore, violated section [206] of the Act by paying less than minimum wage to certain employees in certain weeks. However, because of the nature of defendants' pay plans, it is necessary to inquire whether compensation other than the weekly pay check can be allocated among the various workweeks.

B. *Bonuses*

In addition to their base salary and commissions, defendants' salespersons received weekly, monthly and annual bonuses. The bonuses served as an incentive plan for higher sales and were paid if a salesperson sold over a given number of vehicles during any week, month or year....

[T]he payment of bonuses can only be considered in connection with the minimum wages for the week in which they are paid. Under the facts in this case,

---

[9] This regulation is part of the Secretary's regulations concerning overtime compensation. *See* 29 C.F.R. §§ 778.0-778.603. The workweek is clearly the relevant time period for measuring overtime, since maximum hours are defined in relation to a single week. *See* 29 U.S.C. § 207(a). Arguably the significance of the workweek is not as strong in relation to minimum wage, as long as the employee ultimately receives minimum wage for the hours worked. However, since the courts have noted the importance of the workweek, even when calculating minimum wage, see, e.g., *Brooklyn Savings Bank v. O'Neil,* 324 U.S. 697 (1945), the cited regulation is relevant to the case at bar. This conclusion is buttressed by defendants' own practice of paying their employees weekly.

any other recognition of the bonus payments would obviously be a deferred payment of wages which could not be credited against the minimum wage requirement for any prior week. That is not to say that circumstances other than these present here may not arise which would require different treatment.

C. *Demonstrator Cars*

Although they did not argue the question in their briefs, defendants introduced evidence suggesting that they compensated their salespersons by providing them with demonstrator cars or "demos." The reasonable cost of facilities customarily furnished to employees may be considered part of their wages. 29 C.F.R. § 531.30. However facilities which are "primarily for the benefit or convenience of the employer" do not qualify as wages. 29 C.F.R. § 531.32(c).

Defendants' employees were given "demos" and were permitted to drive them for personal use when not working; their family members were forbidden from driving the cars. The evidence suggested that mileage accumulated by the salespeople when driving for personal use was not insignificant when compared with business use. Nevertheless, it is plain that these "demos" were furnished primarily for the benefit of defendants. Clearly, the cars were valuable and necessary tools.

> It is obvious that a salesman of an automobile should have an automobile in his possession at all times that would be one of those products that his employer was engaged in selling. The very nature of his duties as a car salesman would require his possession and use of an automobile, even on personal business, and that the business of his employer would suffer if this were not the case.

Brennan v. Modern Chevrolet Co., 363 F. Supp. 327, 333 (N.D. Tex. 1973), *aff'd,* 491 F.2d 1271 (5th Cir. 1974). Furthermore, neither defendants nor their employees treated the cars as wages. Although a sum was deducted from each pay check for insurance, the value of the use of the cars was not indicated on defendants' pay records. Nor did the W-2 tax statements reflect the value of the use of the "demos" furnished.

In *Brennan v. Modern Chevrolet Co.,* the district court conceded that personal use of the cars accounted for 90% of the mileage accumulated. Still, because of the primary benefit to the employer, the cars were not wages. The reasoning ... applies at least as strongly to the facts of the instant case. Under the circumstances, the value of the demonstrator cars cannot be counted as wages....

E. *Unpaid Minimum Wages*

Defendants' salespersons are due unpaid minimum wages in amounts to be calculated by the parties in accordance with this Memorandum-Decision and Order.

Defendants must pay minimum wages due from June 21, 1973 until the present. The basic minimum wage which defendants were obligated to pay their salespersons can be calculated by multiplying the applicable statutory hourly minimum wage by the number of hours worked during each week. The number of hours worked by each employee ... was 55 hours per week....

The amount of back wages due to the salespersons is the deficiency between the minimum wage and the amount of pay received in each week that pay fell short of the minimum. Two adjustments must be made to this calculation: Vacation time must be considered, and interest added.

Where defendants' pay records indicate a vacation, the employee is entitled to no recovery for that period. Interest at the lawful rate in effect at the time in New York State is payable from the date of each deficiency on the amount found due. *Hodgson v. Wheaton Glass Co.,* 446 F.2d 527, 535 (3d Cir. 1971)....

NOTES

1. *FLSA Calculus.* The actual minimum wage rate varied during the time of this lawsuit, but for our purposes, let's say the rate was $2.00/hour. Also, to keep things simple, let's ignore interest payments. According to the Court, how much should Employee A recover for the month of February (covering four weeks) when she received the normal base salary each week ($56) plus a bonus at the end of the month of $400? (Note: The Court found that employees worked 55 hours per week.) If the facts were the same except that furniture was sold rather than cars, would the employer have been in compliance with the FLSA if it had paid Employee A that amount? *See* 29 U.S.C. § 213(b)(10) (sellers of automobiles exempt from overtime provisions).

2. *Demonstrator Cars as Wages.* The FLSA recognizes that wages can be paid in forms other than money; wages are defined by the Act to include the reasonable cost of providing "board, lodging, or other facilities." 29 U.S.C. § 203(m). In-kind payments, however, can be included in wages for FLSA purposes only if they are primarily for the benefit or convenience of the employee, are accepted voluntarily by the employee, and are of a kind customarily furnished by the employer or by other employers engaged in similar activities. Why are there such limitations on treating in-kind payments as wages? Was the Court right in holding that the demonstrator cars were primarily for the benefit of the employer and, therefore, not to be considered as wages? Why might some employees want cars to be treated as wages?

3. *Employer Response.* How would you expect Sam Dell's Dodge to pay its sales force in the future?

DUNLOP v. GRAY-GOTO, INC.

United States Court of Appeals, Tenth Circuit
528 F.2d 792 (1976)

McWILLIAMS, CIRCUIT JUDGE.

This is a Fair Labor Standards case. The trial court ... found that though certain employees of the defendant had worked overtime for which no overtime premium was paid, the defendant had nonetheless not violated the overtime requirements of the Act because the defendant had paid its employees certain fringe benefits, including paid vacations and holidays, and biannual bonuses, the value of which equalled or exceeded the amount of overtime compensation otherwise due under the Act. These so-called fringe benefits the trial court allowed to be "set off" against unpaid overtime compensation otherwise due defendant's employees. In so holding the trial court relied on its finding that the defendant and its employees had expressly agreed that such fringe benefits would take the place of overtime pay....

Our study of the matter leads us to conclude that the trial court erred in finding that the so-called fringe benefits could be deemed as the equivalent of overtime pay....

29 U.S.C. § 207(a) provides that an employee who works in interstate commerce in excess of 40 hours per week shall for the excess hours be paid at a rate no less than "one and one-half times the regular rate at which he is employed." Perhaps the primary purpose of the overtime compensation requirement is to "spread employment" by putting pressure on the employer through the overtime pay requirement. A secondary purpose is to compensate an employee in a specific manner "for the strain of working longer than forty hours." *Bay Ridge Co. v. Aaron,* 334 U.S. 446, 470 (1948).

29 U.S.C. § 207(e) defines what "regular rate" of pay is by stating that such term "include(s) all remuneration for employment paid to, or on behalf of, the employee...." That same section goes on to declare that seven categories of employer payments are not to be taken into consideration in determining what an employee's "regular rate" of pay is. 29 U.S.C. § 207(h) provides that the extra compensation described in subsections (5), (6), and (7) in 29 U.S.C. § 207(e) "shall be creditable toward overtime compensation payable pursuant to this section." Implicit therein is that the extra compensation described in subsections (1), (2), (3) and (4) is not to be credited towards overtime payments required by the Act.

The fringe benefits as found by the trial court are "in the form of paid vacations, six holidays with pay each year, biannual bonuses, and the extension of benefits of a group life, health and accident insurance program." Paid vacations and pay for holidays would appear to be included in subsection (2) of 29 U.S.C. § 207(e), which refers to "payments made for occasional periods when no work is performed due to vacation, holiday...." The bonuses would appear to fall into subsection (1) of 29 U.S.C. § 207(e), which refers to "payments in the nature of gifts made at Christmas time or other special occasions, as a reward for service...." The "insurance benefits" found by the trial court would appear to fall within subsection (4) of 29 U.S.C. § 207(e), which refers to "life, accident (and) health insurance or similar benefits for employees." So, under 29 U.S.C. § 207(e) the fringe benefits found by the trial court are not to be included in ascertaining an employee's "regular rate" of pay. At the same time, however, as we read 29 U.S.C. § 207(h) such benefits as were found here by the trial court may not be credited toward overtime compensation due under the Act.

Our holding that the fringe benefits with which we are here concerned may not be credited against overtime pay required by the Act would appear to be in accord with the general case law on the subject.... In *Rigopoulos v. Kervan,* 140 F.2d 506, 507 (2d Cir. 1943) the Second Circuit stated that 29 U.S.C. § 207 "plainly contemplates that overtime compensation shall be paid in the course of employment and not accumulated beyond the regular pay day." And in *Brennan v. Heard,* 491 F.2d 1, 4 (5th Cir. 1974) the Fifth Circuit observed that "[s]et-offs against back pay awards deprive the employee of the 'cash in hand' contemplated by the Act...."

The trial court laid particular emphasis on its finding that in the instant case the employees involved and the defendant employer had an express understanding before any employer-employee relationship was ever entered into that there would be no overtime pay for hours worked in excess of forty hours per week, and that in lieu thereof they would receive the fringe benefits above referred to. In our view any such private agreement or understanding between the parties cannot circumvent the overtime pay requirements of the Act. In this regard see *Brooklyn Bank v. O'Neil,* 324 U.S. 697, 704 (1945) where the Supreme Court held that "[w]here a private right is granted in the public interest to effectuate a legislative policy, waiver of a right so charged or colored with public interest will not be allowed when it would thwart the legislative policy which it was designed to effectuate." *See also Mitchell v. Greinetz,* 235 F.2d 621 (10th Cir. 1956) where we held that waiver of statutory wages under the Fair Labor Standards Act is not permissible. It is on this basis then that we conclude that the trial court erred in permitting fringe benefits to be set off against overtime pay otherwise due.

NOTES

1. FLSA Calculus II. Consider our furniture retailer again. The employer agrees to pay employees $10/hour for non-overtime hours, $15/hour for overtime hours, and a $100 bonus if the employee sells more than $5,000 worth of furniture in a week. Employee A works 50 hours in a week and sells $7,500 worth of furniture. The employer pays her $650 — $10/hour for the first 40 hours ($400), $15/hour for the next 10 hours ($150), and the $100 bonus for selling more than $5,000 worth of furniture. Why has the employer violated the FLSA? What can the employer do if it wants to retain its incentive bonus and yet limit its weekly wage bill for productive employees to about $650?

2. *Compensatory Time Off in Lieu of Overtime Pay.* In the public sector, employers can do part of what Gray-Goto attempted to do. Section 207(o) of the FLSA permits public employers to provide compensatory time off instead of overtime pay, if several conditions are met. For example, the arrangement must be set forth in an agreement arrived at before the overtime work is performed, the employee must receive one-and-one-half hours of compensatory time off for each overtime hour worked, an employee cannot accrue more than a certain number of compensatory hours (240 hours for most employees), and employers must grant employee requests to use their compensatory time unless it would "unduly disrupt" the workplace. Bills are regularly introduced in Congress to extend to all employees the option of receive compensatory time off instead of overtime pay.

3. *The FLSA as a Response to Onerous Work Conditions?* Tew works as a meat market manager for Food Lion, a grocery store. Food Lion has a scheduling system which minimizes overtime hours and performance standards which are very difficult to meet by working only during scheduled work time. As a result, Tew decides to work overtime "off the clock" to avoid discipline for substandard performance, even though Food Lion also has a firm policy against working "off the clock." Later, Tew leaves his employment with Food Lion and files a lawsuit to recover unpaid overtime compensation for the "off the clock" hours. Should he be able to recover? If so, should Food Lion be successful on a counterclaim against Tew for violation of his employment contract (in which he agreed to abide by all company rules) or for violation of his fiduciary duties as manager of the meat market? *Lyle v. Food Lion, Inc.,* 954 F.2d 984 (4th Cir. 1992) (Tew recovers; counterclaims dismissed).

2. COVERAGE

Congress clearly intended coverage under the Fair Labor Standards Act to be broad, and so it is. *See Powell v. United States Cartridge Co.,* 339 U.S. 497, 516 (1950) ("Breadth of coverage was vital to [the Act's] mission"). Broad coverage, however, is merely a guiding principle. In its details, the Act presents three general types of coverage issues.

First, the Act only applies when there is an employer-employee relationship. We have already discussed that issue through the *Lauritzen* case in Chapter 2.

Second, the Act only applies to certain employees. An employee is covered only if she is personally engaged in commerce (individual coverage) or if she works for an enterprise that is engaged in commerce (enterprise coverage). Individual employees are covered if they are engaged in interstate or foreign commerce or in the production of goods for commerce. Although individual coverage is not as broad as the commerce clause might permit, the coverage is nevertheless very broad and the distinctions, as you might expect, are quite fine-grained. For example, employees providing water or seeds to a farmer who is intending to sell his crops in interstate commerce are sufficiently engaged in commerce to be covered by the Act (because the water and seeds become a part of the product in commerce), but employees providing fertilizer to the farmer are not sufficiently engaged in commerce to be covered (because the fertilizer becomes a part of the soil, rather than the product in commerce). For this and other examples, *see* 29 C.F.R. § 776, 776.19(b)(4). Even if employees are not covered individually, they may be covered if their employer (or, more precisely, their enterprise) is covered. The enterprise coverage rules are discussed in the *Arnheim & Neely* case below.

Third, the Act has many exemptions from coverage. Thus, even if employees are engaged in commerce and, hence, fall within the general coverage of the Act, they may not be entitled to the Act's protections because they fit within one of the exemptions. The *Dalheim* case below considers one of the most important exemptions, the exemption for executive, administrative and professional employees.

BRENNAN v. ARNHEIM & NEELY, INC.

United States Supreme Court
410 U.S. 512 (1973)

MR. JUSTICE STEWART delivered the opinion of the Court.

This case began when the Secretary of Labor sued the respondent real estate management company for alleged violations of the Fair Labor Standards Act of 1938, as amended. The Secretary sought an injunction against future violations of the minimum wage, overtime, and recordkeeping provisions of the Act, as well as back wages for the affected employees. An employee is entitled to the benefits of the minimum wage and maximum hours provisions of the Act, if he is, *inter alia,* "employed in an enterprise engaged in commerce or in the production of goods for commerce...." 29 U.S.C. §§ 206(a), 207(a).

As stipulated in the District Court, the respondent company manages eight commercial office buildings and one apartment complex in the Pittsburgh area. With the exception of a minor ownership interest in one of the buildings, the respondent does not own these properties. Its services are provided according to management contracts entered into with the owners. Under these contracts, the respondent obtains tenants for the buildings, negotiates and signs leases, institutes whatever legal actions are necessary with respect to these leases, and generally manages and maintains the properties. The respondent collects rental payments on behalf of the owners, and deposits them in separate bank accounts for each building. These accounts, net of management expenses and the respondent's fees, belong to the owners of the properties. Payments are periodically made from the accounts to these owners.

The respondent's services with respect to the supervisory, maintenance, and janitorial staffs of the buildings are similarly extensive. The respondent conducts the hiring, firing, payroll operations, and job supervision of those employed in the buildings. It also fixes hours of work, and negotiates rates of pay and fringe benefits — subject to the approval of the owners. The respondent engages in collective bargaining on behalf of the owners where the building employees are unionized....

The concept of "enterprise" under the Fair Labor Standards Act came into being with the 1961 amendments, which substantially broadened the coverage of the Act. Rather than confining the protections of the Act to employees who were themselves "engaged in commerce or in the production of goods for commerce," 29 U.S.C. §§ 206(a), 207(a), the new amendments brought those "employed in an enterprise engaged in commerce" within the ambit of the minimum wage and maximum hours provisions. The Congress defined "enterprise engaged in commerce" to include a dollar volume limitation. [Currently, enterprises with an annual gross volume of sales made or business done of less than $500,000 are not covered.[*]] The presence of this dollar-volume cutoff for coverage under the Act, in turn, places importance on the Act's definition of "enterprise."

The term "enterprise" is defined by the statute as follows:

> "'Enterprise' means the related activities performed (either through unified operation or common control) by any person or persons for a common business purpose, and includes all such activities *whether performed in one or more establishments* or by one or more corporate or other organizational units...." 29 U.S.C. § 203(r) (emphasis added).

Specific exemptions are noted, making clear that exclusive-dealership arrangements, collective-purchasing pools, franchises, and leases of business premises from large commercial landlords do not create "enterprises" within the meaning of the Act.

The District Court correctly identified the three main elements of the statutory definition of "enterprise": related activities, unified operation or common control, and common business purpose. We believe the Court of Appeals erred in holding that the aggregate management activities of the respondent failed to meet these statutory criteria. Once the respondent is recognized to be the employer of all of the building employees, it follows quite simply that it is a single enterprise under the Act. The respondent is, after all, but one company. Its activities in all of the buildings are virtually identical, and are plainly "related" in the sense that Congress intended. As the Senate report accompanying the 1961 amendments indicated: "Within the meaning of this term, activities are 'related' when they are the same or similar...." S. Rep. No. 145, 87th Cong., 1st Sess., 41. The respon-

---

[*] Hospitals, public agencies, schools, and institutions for the resident care of the sick, aged and mentally ill are covered even if the dollar volume of their business is less than $500,000. 29 U.S.C. §§ 203(s)(1)(B) & (C).

dent's activities, similarly, are performed "either through unified operation or common control." The respondent is a fully integrated management company directing operations at all nine buildings from its central office. For purposes of determining whether it is an "enterprise" under the Act, it is irrelevant that the relationship between the respondent and the owners is one of agency; that separate bank accounts are maintained for each building; and that the risk of loss and the chance of gain on capital investment belong to the owners, not the respondent. All that is required under the statutory definition is that the respondent's own activities be related and under common control or unified operation, as they plainly are.

In its analysis of this problem, the Court of Appeals placed great weight on the fact that the building owners have no relationship with one another, and have no common business purpose. This is true, but beside the point, for the owners are not defendants in this action and it is not their activities that are under examination. As Judge Winter wrote in the conflicting case from the Fourth Circuit, "It is defendants' activities at each building which must be held together by a common business purpose, not all the activities of all owners of apartment projects." *Shultz v. Falk,* [439 F.2d 340, 346 (4th Cir.), *cert. denied,* 404 U.S. 827 (1971)]. In the present case, the respondent's activities at the several locations are tied together by the common business purpose of managing commercial properties for profit. The fact that the buildings are separate establishments is specifically made irrelevant by § [203(r)]....

The Court of Appeals [also indicated] that the building owners should not be brought under the Act simply because they dealt with a large real estate management company. This is true, but also beside the point, since we deal here with that large management company as a party and, for purposes of this case, as an employer of the employees in question. We do not hold, nor could we in this case, that the individual building owners in *their* capacity as employers[5] are to be aggregated to create some abstract "enterprise" for purposes of the Fair Labor Standards Act.

It is argued that such a straightforward application of the statutory criteria to the respondent's business ignores the significance of the dollar volume limitation included in the § [203(s)] definition of "[e]nterprise engaged in commerce or in the production of goods for commerce." The Court of Appeals cited evidence in the legislative history of the 1961 amendments that indicates a purpose to exempt small businesses from the obligations of the Act. If the individual building owners are engaged in enterprises too small to come within the reach of the Fair Labor Standards Act, reasoned the Court of Appeals, it would be "anomalous" to treat them as a single enterprise subject to the Act "merely

---

[5] As both the District Court and the Court of Appeals noted, the statutory concept of "employer" is "any person acting directly or indirectly in the interest of an employer in relation to an employee...." 29 U.S.C. § 203(d). This definition was held to be broad enough that there might be "several simultaneous 'employers.'" 444 F.2d, at 611-612.

because they hire a rental agent who manages other buildings." Once again, however, the response to this argument is that it is the respondent management company not the individual building owners, that has been held in this case to be an "employer" of all the affected "employees." Furthermore, the proper measure of the respondent's size has been held to be the gross rentals produced by properties under its management. It is true that one purpose of the dollar-volume limitation in the statutory definition of "enterprise" is the exemption of small businesses, but this respondent is not such a business under these holdings of the Court of Appeals.[7] ...

We hold that the District Court was correct in aggregating all of the respondent's management activities as a single "enterprise." Accordingly, the judgment of the Court of Appeals is reversed and the case is remanded to the Court of Appeals for further proceedings consistent with this opinion.

[Justice White dissented.]

NOTES

1. *The Building Owners.* The Court emphasizes that the focus should be on the management company and not on the owners of the buildings. The employees, however, are paid from the owners' bank accounts. If you are a building owner who would fall under the FLSA dollar volume limitation, how would you react to this decision?

2. *Exempting Small Employers.* The dollar volume limitation means that the employees of smaller companies may not be covered by the FLSA. On average, however, smaller companies pay lower wages than larger companies. Why is FLSA coverage more limited for smaller employers when their employees are more likely to need the protections of the Act? Why not just cover all employers?

3. *Coverage of State and Local Government Employees.* The Supreme Court has ruled three times (twice reversing earlier decisions) on the issue of whether Congress has authority under the Commerce Clause to extend FLSA coverage to employees of state and local government. The latest result is that Congress does have such authority. *Garcia v. San Antonio Metro. Transit Auth.,* 469 U.S. 528 (1985). The vote in that case, however, was 5-4, with Justices Brennan and Marshall in the majority and with Justice Rehnquist warning in dissent that he was confident that the view that coverage was unconstitutional would "in time again command the support of a majority of this Court." *Id.* at 580. Nevertheless, for now, state and local government employees are covered.

---

[7] It is stipulated that in all relevant years, the annual gross rental income collected by the respondent exceeded $1,000,000. [The Supreme Court subsequently held that the proper measure of the size of a real estate management company is commissions received, rather than gross rentals. *Falk v. Brennan,* 414 U.S. 190 (1973).]

Unlike other employees, however, state and local employees may not be able to sue in federal court to seek money damages under the FLSA. In *Seminole Tribe of Fla. v. Florida*, 517 U.S. 44 (1996), the Supreme Court held, in another context, that the Eleventh Amendment limits the ability of Congress to authorize suits against States in federal court. The Courts have begun to apply *Seminole Tribe* to dismiss federal court actions filed against State defendants for money damages under the FLSA. *See Moad v. Arkansas State Police Dep't*, 111 F.3d 585 (8th Cir. 1997); *Wilson-Jones v. Caviness*, 99 F.3d 203 (6th Cir. 1996). The Eleventh Amendment, however, does not abrogate the substantive obligation of States to comply with the FLSA and it does not prohibit 1) actions for injunctive relief in federal court; 2) actions for money damages in state court; or 3) actions by the federal government on behalf of employees seeking money damages in federal court. *Id.* at 211.

DALHEIM v. KDFW-TV

United States Court of Appeals, Fifth Circuit
918 F.2d 1220 (1990)

ALVIN B. RUBIN, CIRCUIT JUDGE:

A television station appeals a judgment of the district court holding it liable for violations of the Fair Labor Standards Act (FLSA) by failing to compensate its general-assignment reporters, news producers, directors, and assignment editors for overtime work. Because we find that the district court properly applied the applicable statute and regulations, and because we find that the record supports the district court's conclusion that the employees involved in this case are not exempt under § [213(a)(1)] of the FLSA as bona fide executive, administrative, or professional employees, we affirm....

Plaintiffs are nineteen present and former general-assignment reporters, producers, directors, and assignment editors employed in the news and programming departments of television station KDFW-TV (KDFW).... The news and programming departments are responsible for producing KDFW's local news broadcasts and its public affairs programming.

KDFW's general-assignment reporters usually receive a new coverage assignment each day. The assignment manager or an assignment editor tells the reporter the story to be covered, what she is expected to "shoot," and the intended angle or focus of the story. After the reporter interviews the persons that she or another KDFW employee has arranged to interview, she obtains pertinent video footage, and then writes and records the text of the story, subject to review by the producer. Some reporters help assemble the video and text narration; others rely on a video editor to put the final package together. General-assignment reporters are only infrequently assigned to do a series of reports focusing on a single topic or related topics. Successful reporters usually have a pleasant physical appearance and a strong and appealing voice, and are able to present themselves as credible and knowledgeable.

Producers are responsible for determining the content of the ten-to-twelve minute news portion of KDFW's thirty-minute newscast. They participate in meetings to decide which stories and story angles will be covered; they also decide the amount of time to be given a particular story, the sequence in which stories will be aired, and when to take commercial breaks. Producers have the authority to revise reporters' stories. All of the producers' actions are subject to approval by the executive producer.

Directors review the script for the newscast in order to prepare technical instructions for "calling" the show. The director decides which camera to use and on which machine to run videotaped segments or preproduction graphics. During the broadcast, the director cues the various technical personnel, telling them precisely when to perform their assigned tasks. The overall appearance of KDFW's newscasts, however, is prescribed by station management. The director therefore has no discretion concerning lighting, camera-shot blocking, closing-shot style, or the sequence of opening and closing graphics. KDFW's directors also direct some public affairs programming, which have no prescribed format but involve only simple camera work and a basic set. In addition, KDFW's directors screen commercials to be aired by the station to ensure that they meet the standards set by KDFW's parent, Times Mirror Corporation.

Assignment editors are primarily responsible for pairing reporters with both photographers and videotape editors. They also monitor the wire services, police and fire department scanners, newspapers, and press releases for story ideas that conform to KDFW's general guidelines. Assignment editors have no authority to decide the stories to be covered, but they may reassign reporters if they learn of a story requiring immediate action. Assignment editors operate under the supervision of the assignment manager....

Section [207] of the FLSA requires employers to pay overtime to employees who work more than forty hours per week. Section [213(a)(1)] exempts from the maximum hour provision employees occupying "bona fide executive, administrative, or professional" positions. That same section empowers the Secretary of Labor to define by regulation the terms "executive," "administrative," and "professional." She has done so at 29 C.F.R. § 541.0 et seq., setting out "long" tests for employees earning more than $155 per week but less than $250 per week, which include specific criteria, and "short" tests, described in less detail, for employees earning more than $250 per week. In addition, the Secretary has issued interpretations of those regulations, which are codified at 29 C.F.R. § 541.100 et seq. The § [213(a)(1)] exemptions are "construed narrowly against the employer seeking to assert them," and the employer bears the burden of proving that employees are exempt.

The short test for the executive exemption requires that an employee's "primary duty" consist of the "management of the enterprise" in which she is employed "or a customarily recognized subdivision thereof." In addition, the executive employee's work must include "the customary and regular direction of the work" of two or more employees. The regulations define an exempt administrative employee as one whose "primary duty" consists of "office or nonmanual work directly related to management policies or general business operations" that "includes work requiring the exercise of discretion and independent judgment." The exemption for creative professionals requires that the employee's "primary duty" consist of work that is "original and creative in character in a recognized field of artistic endeavor," the result of which depends "primarily on the invention, imagination, or talent of the employee." *Id.* § 541.3(a)(2)....

Each of the three exemptions claimed by KDFW requires the district court to [decide] what constitutes the employees' "primary duty." KDFW claims that the district court in this case misconstrued the concept of "primary duty" as used in the regulations to mean duties that occupy "a major part, or over fifty percent, of an employee's time."...

We agree with KDFW that an employee's "primary duty" cannot be ascertained by applying a simple "clock" standard that contrasts the amount of time each day an employee spends on exempt and nonexempt work. Section 541.103 of the interpretations defines "primary duty" with respect to all three exemptions. It provides that, while "[i]n the ordinary case it may be taken as a good rule of thumb that primary duty means the major part, or over 50 percent, of the employee's time[,] time alone ... is not the sole test." Exempt work may be an employee's primary duty even though such work occupies less than half her time "if the other pertinent factors support such a conclusion." Precisely what those factors are depends upon which exemption is being claimed, but for each the essence of the test is to determine the employee's chief or principal duty. At least under the short tests,[35] the employee's primary duty will usually be what she does that is of principal value to the employer, not the collateral tasks that she may also perform, even if they consume more than half her time.

We cannot agree, however, with KDFW's contention that the district court misconstrued the concept of primary duty.... After examining the district court's opinion and reviewing the record, we are convinced that the district court did not base its decision solely on the amount of time KDFW's employees spend at various tasks. Instead, the district court's opinion evidences a careful assessment of the nature of each of the job classifications that KDFW claims is exempt. In determining the employees' primary duties, the district court did not act as a judicial punch clock. The district court painstakingly catalogued the tasks performed by each type of employee, and related how each task contributes to producing a KDFW newscast. Accordingly, we find no error.

---

[35] Unlike the short tests, the long tests specifically limit the amount of time an employee may spend on nonexempt work and still qualify for the exemption. 29 C.F.R. §§ 541.1(e), 541.2(d), 541.3(d).

A. *KDFW's General-Assignment Reporters*

KDFW argues that its general-assignment reporters are exempt artistic professionals. Under the regulations, KDFW must prove that the reporter's "primary duty" consists of work that is "original and creative in character in a recognized field of artistic endeavor," the result of which depends "primarily on the invention, imagination, or talent of the employee."

The regulations and interpretations at issue here, §§ 541.3(a)(2) and 541.303(e) and (f), have not changed in any material respect since 1949, long before broadcast journalism evolved into its modern form.[*] To apply the Secre-

---

[*] 29 C.F.R. § 541.3(a)(2) provides that to be exempt as creative professionals, the primary duties of employees must consist of:

> Work that is original and creative in character in a recognized field of artistic endeavor (as opposed to work which can be produced by a person endowed with general manual or intellectual ability and training), and the result of which depends primarily on the invention, imagination, or talent of the employee.

29 C.F.R. §§ 541.303(e) & (f) discuss application of that standard to radio and television announcers and newspaper writers:

> (e)(1) The determination of the exempt or nonexempt status of radio and television announcers as professional employees has been relatively difficult because of the merging of the artistic aspects of the job with the commercial. There is considerable variation in the type of work performed by various announcers, ranging from predominantly routine to predominantly exempt work. The wide variation in earnings as between individual announcers, from the highly paid "name" announcer on a national network ... to the staff announcer paid a comparatively small salary in a small station, indicates not only great differences in personality, voice and manner, but also in some inherent special ability or talent which, while extremely difficult to define, is nevertheless real.
>
> (2) The duties which many announcers are called upon to perform include: Functioning as a master of ceremonies; playing dramatic, comedy, or straight parts in a program; interviewing; ... and acting as a narrator and commentator. Such work is generally exempt. Work such as giving station identification and time signals, announcing the names of programs, and similar routine work is nonexempt work. In the field of radio entertainment ... the status of an employee as a bona fide professional under § 541.3 is in large part dependent upon whether his duties are original and creative in character, and whether they require invention, imagination or talent. The determination ... must be based upon his individual duties and the amount of exempt and nonexempt work performed, as well as his compensation.
>
> (f) The field of journalism also employs many exempt as well as many nonexempt employees under the same or similar job titles....
>
> (1) Exemption for newspaper writers as professional employees is normally available only under the provisions for professional employees of the "artistic" type. Newspaper writing of the exempt type must, therefore, be "predominantly original and creative in character." Only writing which is analytical, interpretative or highly individualized is considered to be creative in nature. [Examples include] editorial writers, columnists, critics, and "top-flight" writers of analytical and interpretative articles.
>
> (2) The reporting of news, the rewriting of stories received from various sources, or the routine editorial work of a newspaper is not predominantly original and creative in character ... and must be considered as nonexempt work. Thus, a reporter or news writer ordinarily collects facts about news events by investigation, interview, or personal observation and

tary's interpretation literally to the plaintiffs would be to assume that those occupations exist today as they did forty years ago. No one disputes that the technological revolution that has swept this society into the so-called Information Age has rendered that assumption untenable. The question is what role, if any, § 541.303(e) and (f) may have in determining the exempt status of modern broadcast journalists.

KDFW argues that the district court gave the interpretation undue weight, thus blinding itself to the realities of modern broadcast journalism. Rather than focusing on the "essential nature" of reporters' duties, KDFW contends, the district court "pigeonholed" reporters according to standards that are decades out of date. Amicus National Association of Broadcasters (NAB) goes even further, contending that the Secretary's interpretation is based on "erroneous, outmoded assumptions about journalism and journalists," and that "[i]nsofar as the District Court took these 1940 assumptions about print journalists and applied them to the present-day duties of KDFW television reporters, [it] erred as a matter of law."...

The district court committed no such error in this case. We have already noted that the inquiry into an employee's exempt status is fact specific. To the extent that a district court finds in the interpretations an analogy useful in deciding the case before it, it may rely on the interpretations as persuasive evidence of both Congress's legislative and the Secretary's regulatory intent. At the same time, should a district court find the concepts expressed inapposite to the facts before it, the court is free to engage in its own application of § [213(a)(1)] and the pertinent regulations....

In reality, KDFW's and NAB's attempt to debunk the analogy between the interpretation's portrayal of broadcasting and journalism as they existed in the 1940s and broadcast journalism as it exists today is a veiled attack on the district court's findings of fact. KDFW makes much of the recognition in § 541.303(e) that a television announcer's "presence" — that "inherent special ability or talent which, while difficult to define, is nevertheless real" — is an important consideration in determining her exempt status. KDFW claims that it is this intangible element, along with the reporter's daily responsibility for melding language and visual images into an informative and memorable presentation, that gives reporters' work its essential creative character.

In the abstract, KDFW's argument has some appeal. We need not go outside the record to recognize, as the district court recognized, that television journalism is undoubtedly a medium capable of bearing original and creative expression, and that the medium's very nature as a fusion of discrete and disparate elements marks a fundamental difference between journalism on television and in print.

---

writes stories reporting these events for publication, or submits the facts to a rewrite man or other editorial employees for story preparation. Such work is nonexempt work.

The Secretary's interpretations make it abundantly clear that § 541.3(a)(2) was intended to distinguish between those persons whose work is creative in nature from those who work in a medium capable of bearing creative expression, but whose duties are nevertheless functional in nature. The factual inquiry in this case was directed precisely at determining on which side of that line KDFW's reporters stand. The district court found that, at KDFW, the emphasis was on "good reporting, in the aggregate," and not on individual reporters with the "presence" to draw an audience. The district court found that the process by which reporters meld sound and pictures relies not upon the reporter's creativity, but upon her skill, diligence, and intelligence. More importantly, the district court found that "[r]eporters are told the story that the station intends they cover, what they are expected to shoot, and the intended angle or focus of the story."

In essence, the district court found that KDFW failed to prove that the work constituting its reporters' primary duty is original or creative in character. The district court recognized, and we think correctly, that general-assignment reporters may be exempt creative professionals, and that KDFW's reporters did, from time to time, do original and creative work. Nevertheless, at KDFW, the approach reporters take to their day-to-day work is in large part dictated by management, and the stories they daily produce are neither analytic nor interpretive nor original. In neither form nor substance does a reporter's work "depend[] primarily on [her] invention, imagination, or talent." Those inferences, while not compelled by the evidence, are certainly supported by it. Based on those inferences and the underlying historical facts, which we review only for clear error, we think the legal conclusion that reporters are nonexempt follows as a matter of course. We therefore conclude that the district court did not err in holding that KDFW's general-assignment reporters are not exempt professionals.

B. *KDFW's News Producers*

KDFW argues that its news producers are exempt either as creative professionals, administrators, executives, or a combination thereof. We address each argument in turn.

1. *Producers as Creative Professionals.* — KDFW does not press this argument much, for good reason. The district court found that KDFW failed to prove that the work producers do in rewriting reporters' copy and in formatting the newscast are products of their "invention, imagination, and talent." Rather, producers perform their work within a well-defined framework of management policies and editorial convention. To the extent that they exercise discretion, it is governed more by skill and experience than by originality and creativity. Because the district court's findings are supported by the record, we find no error.

2. *Producers as Administrators.* — The argument KDFW pursues most vigorously with respect to producers is that they are exempt administrative employees. Section 541.2 of the regulations requires that an exempt administrator perform (1) office or nonmanual work (2) that is directly related to the employer's man-

agement policies or general business operations and (3) involves the exercise of discretion and independent judgment. The Secretary's interpretation, § 541.205(a), defines the "directly related" prong by distinguishing between what it calls "the administrative operations of a business" and "production." Administrative operations include such duties as "advising the management, planning, negotiating, representing the company, purchasing, promoting sales, and business research and control." Work may also be "directly related" if it is of "substantial importance" to the business operations of the enterprise in that it involves "major assignments in conducting the operations of the business, or ... affects business operations to a substantial degree." KDFW argues that the district court erred in finding that producers' work failed the "directly related" requirement because it is neither related to the administrative operations of KDFW, nor is it of "substantial importance" to the enterprise....

KDFW first asserts that the district court erroneously applied the distinction between "administrative work" and "production" drawn in § 541.205(a) to the work of producers. The concept of "production," claims KDFW, applies only to "blue collar manufacturing employees." White collar employees such as producers cannot be involved in production; therefore, their work is directly related to general business operations.

That argument makes little sense. Section 541.205(a) is not concerned with distinguishing between white collar and blue collar employees, or between service industries and manufacturing industries. The distinction § 541.205(a) draws is between those employees whose primary duty is administering the business affairs of the enterprise from those whose primary duty is producing the commodity or commodities, whether goods or services, that the enterprise exists to produce and market....

KDFW claims that applying the § 541.205 distinction between production and administration in the white-collar setting would be contrary to the decisions in previous cases in which employees involved in what would be "production" under our definition were nevertheless held to be exempt administrators. Those cases fail to support KDFW's position. *Cobb v. Finest Foods, Inc.,* [755 F.2d 1148 (5th Cir. 1985) (per curiam)], which KDFW claims involved a chef whose primary duty was "producing" food, actually involved a chef whose primary duty was managing the hot food section of a contract food service operation. In contrast to the producers at KDFW, the chef had no direct on-the-job supervision; had a great deal of discretion in setting his own work schedule; trained, supervised, and set the work schedules for a number of employees; and planned the menus. In both *Adams v. St. Johns River Shipbuilding Co.,* [69 F. Supp. 989 (S.D. Fl.), *rev'd on other grounds,* 164 F.2d 1012 (5th Cir. 1947)] and *Donovan v. Reno Builders Exchange, Inc.,* [100 Lab. Cas. (CCH) ¶ 34,516 (D. Nev. 1984)], which KDFW claims involved editors whose primary duties were "producing" periodicals, actually involved editors who were in charge of editing and publishing his or her respective periodical (though the editor in *Adams* was subject to wartime censorship). The courts accordingly found that their duties were "directly related to management policies or general business operations," as each was primarily responsible for the success or failure of the venture.

That is not the case with KDFW's news producers. Their responsibilities begin and end with the ten-to-twelve minute portion of the newscast they are working on. They are not responsible for setting business policy, planning the long- or short-term objectives of the news department, promoting the newscast, negotiating salary or benefits with other department personnel, or any of the other types of "administrative" tasks noted in § 541.205(b). The district court determined, based on the facts before it, that "[t]he duties of a producer clearly relate to the production of a KDFW news department product and not to defendant's administrative operations." That determination was not erroneous.

KDFW next asserts that the district court erred in holding that producers' work does not consist of carrying out "major assignments" of "substantial importance" to KDFW's business.... The only record evidence KDFW points to in support of its contention that producers' work is of "substantial importance," other than the evidence of what producers do, is that KDFW operates in the nation's eighth largest television market, and that local news is an important source of revenue for the station. The "importance" of producers' work we are left to infer is that, if a producer performs poorly, KDFW's bottom line might suffer.

As a matter of law, that is insufficient to establish the direct relationship required.... The Secretary's interpretations specifically recognize that the fact that a worker's poor performance may have a significant profit-and-loss impact is not enough to make that worker an exempt administrator. "An employee's job can even be 'indispensable' and still not be of the necessary 'substantial importance' to meet the 'directly related' element." In assessing whether an employee's work is of substantial importance, it is necessary yet again to look to "the nature of the work, not its ultimate consequence." The nature of producers' work, the district court found, is the application of "techniques, procedures, repetitious experience, and specific standards" to the formatting of a newscast. KDFW was obliged to demonstrate how work of that nature is so important to KDFW that it should be deemed "directly related" to business operations. It did not do so. Indeed, the evidence shows that the work one would think of as being "substantially important" — such as setting news department policy and designing the uniform "look" of the newscast — is done by employees who seem clearly to be exempt administrators: the executive producer and the news director, for example. We therefore conclude that the district court did not err in holding that producers are not exempt administrators.

3. *Producers as Executives.* — On appeal, KDFW argues that producers are exempt executives only in the context of arguing for a combination exemption. We address the issue briefly here as a prelude to the discussion of combination exemptions below.

To qualify for an executive exemption under the short test, an employee's primary duty must consist of the "management of the enterprise" in which she is employed "or a customarily recognized subdivision thereof." In addition, the employee must customarily and regularly direct the work of two or more employees. The district court found that management was not the producers' primary duty, and that producers do not customarily direct the work of two or more employees.

We agree with the district court. The evidence establishes that, while the producer plays an important role in coordinating and formatting a portion of the newscast, the other members of the ensemble — that is, the reporters, technicians, assignment editors, and so on — are actually supervised by other management personnel. Producers perform none of the executive duties contemplated by the regulations, such as training, supervising, disciplining, and evaluating employees.... Producers, therefore, do not "manage," and are not exempt executives.

4. *The Combination Exemption.* — KDFW argues that the district court erred as a matter of law by failing to consider whether producers qualify for a combination exemption under § 541.600. Section 541.600 allows the "tacking" of exemptions only where (1) an employee performs more than one type of work that would be exempt except that (2) neither type of work alone can be termed the employee's primary duty, but (3) all of the putatively exempt work taken together constitutes the employee's primary duty. That is not the case here. The district court found that the producers at KDFW do *no* exempt work. This is not a case in which the producers do some administrative work and some executive work. Producers do neither administrative work nor executive work. Only the *reporters* do some exempt work, though that work is not their primary duty. Obviously, an employer cannot tack various nonexempt duties and hope to create an exemption. As KDFW failed to prove that its producers do any exempt work, there was no need for the district court to consider a combination exemption. There was no error.

C. *KDFW's Directors and Assignment Editors*

For the same reasons it asserts with respect to its producers, KDFW claims that the district court erred in concluding that its directors and assignment editors are not exempt either as executives or administrators or a combination thereof. KDFW's arguments with respect to directors and assignment editors thus fail for the reasons set out above. First, the evidence wholly fails to establish that the work of either directors or assignment editors is "directly related" to management policies or business operations, as required by § 541.2. Second, the evidence does not demonstrate that either directors or assignment editors "manage" anything, as required by § 541.1. KDFW's directors are, as the district court found, highly skilled coordinators, but they are not managers. Assignment editors have no real authority, and participate in no decisions of consequence.

Finally, because neither directors nor assignment editors do any exempt work, the district court did not err in failing to consider a combination exemption under § 541.600.

For the reasons stated above, the judgment of the district court is

Affirmed.

NOTES

1. *The Salary Test*. To fit within the exemption for executive, administrative, and professional employees, an employee must both perform certain duties and be paid a salary. The principal case discusses the duties test. The salary test can also be problematic. Do employees meet the salary test if they are generally paid a salary, but their pay is docked for working less than eight hours in a day or for disciplinary reasons? *Martin v. Malcolm Pirnie, Inc.*, 949 F.2d 611 (2d Cir. 1991), *cert. denied*, 506 U.S. 905 (1992) (no). What if no employee's pay has ever been docked, but the employer has a clear policy saying that such deductions will be made? *Auer v. Robbins*, 117 S. Ct. 905 (1997) (salary test not met). What if employees are paid a salary, but receive an hourly supplement for overtime hours? *Compare Abshire v. County of Kern*, 908 F.2d 483 (9th Cir. 1990), *cert. denied,* 498 U.S. 1068 (1991) (salary test not met) *with York v. Wichita Falls,* 944 F.2d 236 (5th Cir. 1991) (salary test met).

2. *Exemptions From Coverage*. Executive, administrative, and professional employees are exempted from coverage under the minimum wage and overtime provisions of the FLSA, but are still covered by the equal pay and child labor provisions. The FLSA contains a number of other exemptions that apply to one or more of the Act's requirements. *See* 29 U.S.C. §§ 207, 213. It is easier to see a rationale for some of the exemptions than for others. The basic question once again, however, is why not simply cover all employees?

The exemptions, rather than limits on individual employee and enterprise coverage, account for the bulk of the uncovered sector. In 1988, of the approximately 110 million wage and salary earners in the United States, about 8 million were not covered by the FLSA because of coverage limits and 28 million were not covered because of the exemptions (including 21 million under the exemption for executive, administrative, and professional employees).

The uncovered sector, however, might be defined more broadly to include, in addition, those employees who are *effectively* uncovered — employees who are uncovered because the enforcement mechanisms of the Act do not result in a high level of compliance. That is the subject of the next section.

3. ENFORCEMENT

The FLSA can be enforced by employees themselves, the Secretary of Labor, or the Attorney General.

Under section 216(b) of the Act, employees can file suit in federal or state court to enforce their rights to minimum wages and overtime compensation.

Employees can also seek redress if employers retaliate against them for attempting to enforce their rights under the FLSA. Employees can file suit just on their own behalf or they can file class actions. The class action mechanism, however, is less favorable to plaintiffs than the one under the Federal Rules of Civil Procedure because under the FLSA employees must affirmatively opt-in to the class by filing a consent with the court. Under the Federal Rules, if a class is recognized, employees are generally included in the class unless they affirmatively opt-out.

The Secretary of Labor can also enforce the Act on behalf of employees under sections 216(c) and 217. Section 216(c) authorizes the Secretary to file a wage suit on behalf of employees that is quite analogous (but not identical) to the suit employees can file on their own behalf under section 216(b). The Secretary also has the authority to file an action seeking an injunction under section 217.

If the suit by either employees themselves or the Secretary of Labor is successful, the statute authorizes recovery of any unpaid minimum wages and/or overtime compensation and of an equal amount in liquidated damages. Under the Portal-to-Portal Act, however, a court may refuse to award liquidated damages if the employer can demonstrate that the violation was in good faith and that it had reasonable grounds for believing that its actions were not a violation of the FLSA. 29 U.S.C § 260. Employees who win FLSA suits, but not the Secretary, are also entitled to an award of attorneys' fees. Finally, for repeated or willful violations of the minimum wage or overtime provisions, the Secretary is authorized to assess civil penalties, subject to administrative review, of up to $1,000 per violation. 29 U.S.C. § 217(e).

For child labor violations, the Secretary of Labor is authorized (1) to file suits seeking an injunction under section 217 and (2) to assess civil penalties of up to $10,000 for each violation under section 216(e). Civil penalties, once again, are subject to administrative review.

Finally, the Attorney General is authorized to file criminal actions for FLSA violations. The authority is very rarely exercised.

To aid enforcement, the FLSA requires employers to maintain adequate records of their wages and hours. Failure to comply with the recordkeeping requirements of the FLSA is an independent violation of the Act.

The time limits for filing FLSA suits are governed by the Portal-to-Portal Act, § 255(a), as interpreted by the following case.

McLAUGHLIN v. RICHLAND SHOE CO.

United States Supreme Court
486 U.S. 128 (1988)

JUSTICE STEVENS delivered the opinion of the Court.

The question presented concerns the meaning of the word "willful" as used in the statute of limitations applicable to civil actions to enforce the Fair Labor

Standards Act (FLSA). The statute provides that such actions must be commenced within two years "except that a cause of action arising out of a willful violation may be commenced within three years after the cause of action accrued." [Portal-to-Portal Act,] 29 U.S.C. § 255(a).

Respondent, a manufacturer of shoes and boots, employed seven mechanics to maintain and repair its equipment. In 1984, the Secretary of Labor (Secretary) filed a complaint alleging that "in many work weeks" respondent had failed to pay those employees the overtime compensation required by the FLSA. As an affirmative defense, respondent pleaded the 2-year statute of limitations. The District Court found, however, that the 3-year exception applied because respondent's violations were willful, and entered judgment requiring respondent to pay a total of $11,084.26, plus interest, to the seven employees.

In resolving the question of willfulness, the District Court followed Fifth Circuit decisions that had developed the so-called *Jiffy June* standard. The District Court explained:

> The Fifth Circuit has held that an action is willful when "there is substantial evidence in the record to support a finding that the employer knew or suspected that his actions might violate the FLSA. Stated most simply, we think the test should be: Did the employer know the FLSA was in the picture?" *Coleman v. Jiffy June Farms, Inc.,* 458 F.2d 1139, 1142 (5th Cir. 1971)[, *cert. denied,* 409 U.S. 948 (1972)].
>
> This standard requires nothing more than that the employer has an awareness of the possible application of the FLSA. "An employer acts willfully and subjects himself to the three year liability if he knows, or has reason to know, that his conduct is governed by the FLSA."...

II

Because no limitations period was provided in the original 1938 enactment of the FLSA, civil actions brought thereunder were governed by state statutes of limitations. In the Portal-to-Portal Act of 1947, 29 U.S.C. §§ 216, 251-262, however, as part of its response to this Court's expansive reading of the FLSA, Congress enacted the 2-year statute to place a limit on employers' exposure to unanticipated contingent liabilities.[7] As originally enacted, the 2-year limitations period drew no distinction between willful and nonwillful violations.

In 1965, the Secretary proposed a number of amendments to expand the coverage of the FLSA, including a proposal to replace the 2-year statute of limitations with a 3-year statute. The proposal was not adopted, but in 1966, for reasons that are not explained in the legislative history, Congress enacted the 3-year exception for willful violations.

---

[7] The Portal-to-Portal Act also made the award of liquidated damages discretionary rather than mandatory and authorized exemptions for certain types of wage plans....

The fact that Congress did not simply extend the limitations period to three years, but instead adopted a two-tiered statute of limitations, makes it obvious that Congress intended to draw a significant distinction between ordinary violations and willful violations. It is equally obvious to us that the *Jiffy June* standard of willfulness — a standard that merely requires that an employer knew that the FLSA "was in the picture" — virtually obliterates any distinction between willful and nonwillful violations. As we said in *Trans World Airlines, Inc. v. Thurston,* [469 U.S. 111, 128 (1985)], "it would be virtually impossible for an employer to show that he was unaware of the Act and its potential applicability." Under the *Jiffy June* standard, the normal 2-year statute of limitations would seem to apply only to ignorant employers, surely not a state of affairs intended by Congress.[9]

In common usage the word "willful" is considered synonymous with such words as "voluntary," "deliberate," and "intentional." *See* Roget's International Thesaurus § 622.7, p. 479; § 653.9, p. 501 (4th ed. 1977). The word "willful" is widely used in the law, and, although it has not by any means been given a perfectly consistent interpretation, it is generally understood to refer to conduct that is not merely negligent. The standard of willfulness that was adopted in *Thurston* — that the employer either knew or showed reckless disregard for the matter of whether its conduct was prohibited by the statute — is surely a fair reading of the plain language of the Act....

We also reject the intermediate alternative espoused by the Secretary for the first time in this Court.... [S]he argues that we should announce a two-step standard that would deem an FLSA violation willful "if the employer, recognizing it might be covered by the FLSA, acted without a reasonable basis for believing that it was complying with the statute." This proposal differs from *Jiffy June* because it would apparently make the issue in most cases turn on whether the employer sought legal advice concerning its pay practices. It would, however, permit a finding of willfulness to be based on nothing more than negligence, or, perhaps, on a completely good-faith but incorrect assumption that a pay plan complied with the FLSA in all respects. We believe the Secretary's new proposal, like the discredited *Jiffy June* standard, fails to give effect to the plain language of the statute of limitations.[13]

---

[9] The ease with which the *Jiffy June* standard can be met is exemplified in this case. As the District Court wrote: "[T]he vice president and general manager of the defendant was aware that the FLSA existed and that it governed overtime systems such as that used for the Richland mechanics.... Thus, although Isenberg did not state that he thought that the system used was contrary to the provisions of the FLSA, he did state that he knew that the FLSA applied. I believe that this admission is sufficient to satisfy the liberal willfulness requirement of the FLSA." *Donovan v. Richland Shoe Co.,* 623 F. Supp. 667, 671 (E.D. Pa. 1985).

[13] We recognize that there is some language in *Trans World Airlines v. Thurston,* 469 U.S. 111 (1985), not necessary to our holding, that would seem to permit a finding of unreasonableness to suffice as proof of knowing or reckless disregard, and thus that would render petitioner's standard an appropriate statement of the law. Our decision today should clarify this point: If an employer

Ordinary violations of the FLSA are subject to the general 2-year statute of limitations. To obtain the benefit of the 3-year exception, the Secretary must prove that the employer's conduct was willful as that term is defined in both *Thurston* and this opinion.

The judgment of the Court of Appeals is

Affirmed.

JUSTICE MARSHALL, with whom JUSTICE BRENNAN and JUSTICE BLACKMUN join, dissenting.

The Court today imports into a limitations provision of the Fair Labor Standards Act (FLSA) the "knowing or reckless" definition of "willful" that we previously adopted in construing a liquidated damages provision of the Age Discrimination in Employment Act of 1967, 29 U.S.C. § 621 et seq. (ADEA). In doing so, the Court departs from our traditional contextual approach to the definition of the term "willful," ignores significant differences between the relevant provisions of the two Acts, and fails to accommodate the remedial purpose of civil actions under the FLSA. For these reasons, I would accept the slightly more expansive definition of "willful" urged by the Secretary of Labor.... Under this latter standard, a violation of the FLSA is "willful" and therefore subjects an employer to a 3-year rather than a 2-year statute of limitations if the employer knew that there was an appreciable possibility that it was covered by the Act and failed to take steps reasonably calculated to resolve the doubt.

I have no quarrel with the opinion of the Court to the extent that it rejects the "in the picture" standard of willfulness elaborated in *Coleman v. Jiffy June Farms, Inc.,* 458 F.2d 1139, 1142 (CA5 1971), *cert. denied,* 409 U.S. 948 (1972). As the Court succinctly explains, by permitting a finding of willful violation every time an employer knew that the FLSA was "in the picture," the *Jiffy June* standard "virtually obliterates any distinction between willful and non-willful violations."...

The Court seems to rely in part on "common usage" of the word "willful" in adopting the "knowing or reckless" standard. The Court fails to acknowledge, however, that the dictionary includes a wide variety of definitions of "willful," ranging from "malicious" to "not accidental," and including precisely the intermediate definition urged by the Secretary — under which an act is willful if it is "done without ground for believing it is lawful." Black's Law Dictionary 1434 (5th ed. 1979). By refusing to recognize the various meanings that the term "willful" has come to bear in different legal settings, the Court today departs from our previous contextual approach to defining that term. [Since *Spies v.*

---

acts reasonably in determining its legal obligation, its action cannot be deemed willful under either petitioner's test or under the standard we set forth. If an employer acts unreasonably, but not recklessly, in determining its legal obligation, then, although its action would be considered willful under petitioner's test, it should not be so considered under *Thurston* or the identical standard we approve today.

United States, 317 U.S. 492, 497 (1943),] we consistently have looked to the statutory context in which the word appears in order to determine its proper meaning. The Court's apparent abandonment of this approach in favor of a non-existent "plain language" definition of "willful," is unprecedented and unwise.

Had the Court properly applied the traditional contextual approach, I believe it would have adopted the willfulness standard urged by the Secretary. Such an approach would have revealed that the definition of "willful" adopted previously in the context of the ADEA in *Trans World Airlines, Inc. v. Thurston* does not transplant easily to the context of the FLSA. In *Thurston,* this Court explicitly acknowledged that its choice of the "knowing or reckless" definition of "willful" was influenced by the "punitive" nature of the double damages that flow from a finding of willfulness under the ADEA. In the instant case, a finding of willfulness leads not to a punitive sanction, but merely to an extended period during which an unlawfully underpaid employee may recover compensatory damages. What is at stake here is the applicability of the remedial provisions of the FLSA in the first instance. Perhaps recognizing this crucial distinction, the Court in *Thurston* expressly left open the possibility that the "knowing or reckless" definition of "willful" adopted for the ADEA might not be appropriate for the FLSA statute of limitations. The answer that the Court provides today may have an attractive tidiness, but it fails to recognize the contextual differences that call for different standards of willfulness in varying provisions of the two Acts.[*] As a result, the Court has adopted a definition of "willful" that is improperly narrow in light of its effect on the remedial scope of the FLSA.

Just how narrow that definition is remains to be seen. It is not entirely clear that the "knowing or reckless" definition of willfulness adopted by the Court will differ significantly in practical application from the approach that I would adopt. Employers who know that there is an appreciable possibility that the FLSA covers their operations but fail to take reasonable measures to resolve their doubts may well be deemed "reckless" in many cases under the *Thurston* standard. Although it is difficult to foretell, it appears to me unlikely that a large number of FLSA defendants will fall into the narrow category of employers who "unreasonably" but not "recklessly" fail to apprise themselves of the requirements of the Act. See *ante,* n. 13. Despite the potentially small significance of our different interpretations, however, I cannot agree with the Court's approach to or resolution of the willfulness issue in this case. I therefore respectfully dissent.

---

[*] The Court bases its adoption of the *Thurston* standard of willfulness on the fear that the Secretary's alternative standard, like the *Jiffy June* standard, would undermine Congress's two-tiered liability scheme by permitting a finding of willfulness on a showing of "nothing more than negligence." This fear is ungrounded. In order for a violation to be "willful" under the Secretary's standard, an employer must operate in the face of a known risk that the FLSA covers its operation, without taking reasonable steps to ensure its compliance. This state of mind is sufficiently different from mere negligence to maintain the two-tiered structure of the FLSA.

NOTES

1. *The Effect of Time Limits.* Since most FLSA violations are continuous, time limits under the Act usually serve not to terminate the right to sue as they do in other areas, but rather to measure the period of damages. After *McLaughlin,* employers who violate the FLSA will generally be liable for damages for a period of time that begins two years before the lawsuit is commenced; before *McLaughlin,* under the *Jiffy June* standard, employers were generally liable for a period of time beginning three years before the lawsuit was commenced.

2. *Liquidated Damages and Willfulness. McLaughlin* adopts the definition of "willfulness" used by the Supreme Court in a previous case, *Thurston,* to determine whether liquidated damages were available under the Age Discrimination in Employment Act (ADEA). The standards for obtaining liquidated damages under the FLSA, however, are different from the standards under the ADEA. Under the FLSA, employees are entitled to liquidated damages unless the employer can show that its actions were in good faith and that it had reasonable grounds for believing it was not violating the FLSA. Portal-to-Portal Act, 29 U.S.C. § 260.

RONALD G. EHRENBERG & PAUL L. SCHUMANN, COMPLIANCE WITH THE OVERTIME PAY PROVISIONS OF THE FAIR LABOR STANDARDS ACT, 25 Journal of Law & Economics 159, 164-66 (1982)[*]

What are the factors that influence the probability that an individual who is working overtime and subject to the overtime pay provisions of the FLSA will be observed *not* being paid a premium of at least time and a half, as the FLSA calls for?...

From the perspective of the employer, the benefits from noncompliance are the savings that accrue from his failing to pay workers working overtime a premium of at least time and a half. The costs to the employer of noncompliance include the costs of any increased employee turnover that may result from failure to pay legally required premium payments. These costs are likely to be higher for skilled workers than they are for unskilled workers and for workers that the employer expects (wants) to have long job tenure with the firm than they are for workers with short expected job tenure.

The costs of noncompliance also include any costs that would result if an employer is caught violating the overtime pay provisions; these costs are determined both by the probability of being caught if a violation occurs and by the expected penalty once a violation is identified. The resources available ... to enforce the provisions of the FLSA are minimal, and only rarely does the agency

---

institute investigations on its own. More typically, investigations result from alleged violations being reported by employees who feel that they have not been paid in accordance with the provisions of the act. This suggests that the costs of noncompliance that an employer perceives he faces will increase as his perception that an employee will report a violation increases.[13] It also increases with his perception that such a report will be investigated.

Finally, the costs an employer perceives as associated with noncompliance depend upon the expected penalty once a violation is judged to have occurred. Since ... the typical settlement involves repayment of substantially *less* than 100 percent of the funds that are owed, the incentives for firms to comply with the legislation are not very high. [In addition, o]ther factors, such as the desire not to violate government legislation, clearly are important.

From the perspective of employees, the costs of noncompliance include the loss of premium pay they would suffer if the employer failed to pay them an overtime premium of at least time and a half.... The benefits include the possibility that a lower "price" for overtime hours would induce an employer to expand his usage of overtime hours. If an employer's demand for overtime hours is elastic with respect to the overtime rate, an employee's total labor earnings would be higher if the employer fails to comply with the legislation. In this case noncompliance would yield net benefits to the employee if the increased earnings are sufficient to compensate him for his reduction in leisure hours. Of course, employees also have preferences with respect to the avoidance of violations of government legislation that must be taken into account in the analysis.

NOTES

1. *Estimates of Noncompliance.* Most studies of compliance with the FLSA have reported problems. Ehrenberg and Schumann estimated that at least 10% of employees who worked overtime and were clearly covered by the Act did not receive *any* premium pay for their overtime hours. For employees where coverage was less clear (e.g., employees of small employers), they estimated that 20-25% failed to receive any premium pay for overtime. Similar problems with noncompliance have been found for the other substantive obligations of the FLSA. *See* GOVERNMENT ACCOUNTING OFFICE, CHILD LABOR: INCREASES IN DETECTED CHILD LABOR VIOLATIONS THROUGHOUT THE UNITED STATES

---

[13] Employees, of course must make their own calculations of the benefits and costs to them of reporting noncompliance. While the obvious benefits include the possibility of receiving premium pay for future overtime and back pay to compensate them for their failure to receive overtime premium pay in the past, the costs include the possibility that the employer will use less overtime in the future and/or that he might attempt to retaliate against the "informers" (if he can identify them) by denying them wage increases or promotion opportunities or by laying them off or firing them for cause.

(1990); Brigitte H. Sellekaerts & Stephen W. Welch, *An Econometric Analysis of Minimum Wage Noncompliance,* 23 INDUS. REL. L.J. 244 (1984).

2. *Increasing Compliance.* Within Ehrenberg and Schumann's framework, how would you evaluate the following legal changes in terms of their ability to increase compliance with the overtime provisions of the FLSA: (1) increasing the premium for overtime hours from one-and-one-half times the regular rate to double the regular rate; (2) increasing the maximum civil penalty from $1,000 per violation to $10,000 per violation and making it available for every violation, rather than just for repeated or willful violations; (3) increasing the amount of liquidated damages from an amount equal to backpay to an amount double backpay?

3. *Compliance With Child Labor Laws.* The child labor provisions present special enforcement problems. In contrast to the minimum wage and overtime provisions, there is often no nongovernmental person with an interest in enforcing the provisions: the child, the child's parents, and the employer all want the child to be able to work. Thus, the probability of being caught is lower for child labor violations. Prompted by GAO findings that child labor violations increased 145% between 1983 and 1989, Congress increased the maximum civil penalty for child labor violations to $10,000 in 1990 from the $1,000 maximum that had been in place since 1974. Other proposals that have surfaced in Congress to enhance enforcement include increasing potential criminal liability when children are injured or killed while employed in violation of the child labor provisions (five years in prison for a first offense and ten years for a second when children are injured; ten years for a first offense and twenty years for a second when children are killed) and permitting families to file personal injury actions against businesses when children are seriously hurt or killed. *See* Jeremy S. Sosin, Note, *The Price of Killing a Child: Is the Fair Labor Standards Act Strong Enough to Protect Children in Today's Workplace?,* 31 VAL. U. L. REV. 1181 (1997) (proposing a federal civil cause of action when children are injured or killed while working in violation of the FLSA).

4. *Resolving FLSA Claims Through Private Arbitration.* In 1981, the Supreme Court held that arbitration of FLSA claims pursuant to a collective bargaining agreement would not bar subsequent litigation of those claims in court. *Barrentine v. Arkansas-Best Freight Sys.,* 450 U.S. 728 (1981). As a result, few employers would agree to private arbitration of FLSA claims because it gave employees two bites at the apple — once in arbitration and, if the employee lost there, again in court. In *Gilmer v. Interstate/Johnson Lane Corp.,* 500 U.S. 20 (1991), however, the Supreme Court limited *Barrentine* and opened the door once again to private arbitration of FLSA claims, as well as other statutory claims. As a result, private arbitration of FLSA claims is once again a viable possibility. *See Kaehner v. Dickinson & Co.,* 84 F.3d 316 (9th Cir. 1996) (plaintiff required to submit FLSA dispute to arbitration).

C. THE FAMILY AND MEDICAL LEAVE ACT

The Family and Medical Leave Act, enacted in 1993, is another federal law regulating hours. It requires employers with fifty or more employees to give twelve weeks of unpaid, job-protected leave each year to workers who miss work because of their own serious health condition or because they must care for a newly born or adopted child or for a spouse, child or parent with a serious health condition.* The fifty-employee requirement means that the FMLA covers only five percent of U.S. businesses, but those businesses employ more than half the private sector workforce.

The following case illustrates some of the issues involved when the employee needs sick leave for herself and for her child.

REICH v. MIDWEST PLASTIC ENGINEERING, INC.

United States District Court, W.D. Michigan
66 Empl. Prac. Dec. (CCH) ¶ 43.701 (1995)

BELL, J.

....

I

A

The Department of Labor (DOL) has brought this action on behalf of Lori Van Dosen. Defendant Midwest Plastic Engineering, Inc. (Midwest) hired Ms. Van Dosen on July 26, 1988, and she was a full-time employee from that time until November 29, 1993, when Midwest terminated her employment.

The events immediately leading up to Midwest's termination of Ms. Van Dosen's employment began on Wednesday, November 3, 1993, at a time when she was approximately 25-26 weeks pregnant. After she received a telephone call informing her that her oldest child, Andrea, who was six years old at the time, was ill, Ms. Van Dosen left work early with the permission of her supervisor, Scott Long, to care for Andrea. That evening, Ms. Van Dosen's fiance (now husband), James Mitschelen, took Andrea to Howe Medical Center in Howe, Indiana, where Dr. T.A. Pechin diagnosed her as having chicken pox. Several days later, Ms. Van Dosen's second child, Brittney, who was four years old at that time, also developed chicken pox. Brittney's illness did not necessitate a visit to the doctor.

Ms. Van Dosen called Mr. Long on November 4, 5, 8, and 9, 1993, to tell him that she would not be at work because she had a sick child. But she did return to work on November 10, and worked the remainder of that workweek. Mr. Long daily informed Ms. Van Dosen that she needed to bring in a doctor's slip in order for the four workdays of November 4-9 to be excused, but she failed to do

---

*The Statutory Appendix contains the text of the FMLA.

so on any of the days of November 10-12. Therefore, Midwest treated those absences as unexcused.

On account of these absences, Midwest prepared a written Letter of Reprimand for absenteeism which Mr. Long planned to give to Ms. Van Dosen on Monday, November 15. Notably, the Letter specifically stated that Midwest would not terminate Ms. Van Dosen's employment at that time but that it was intended as a final warning to her.

But Mr. Long was unable to give the Letter of Reprimand to Ms. Van Dosen on November 15 because she did not appear for work on that day. She called in to work either that morning or the evening before and left a message that she had been to the emergency room of a hospital on Sunday, November 14, that she believed that she too had contracted chicken pox, and that she would be going to her doctor that day. Indeed, Dr. Kerry M. Keaffaber of Howe Medical Center examined Ms. Van Dosen on November 15 and confirmed that she too had chicken pox. Dr. Keaffaber prescribed the medication Zovirax for Ms. Van Dosen, which was intended to lessen the likelihood of her developing varicella pneumonia, a relatively common and dangerous complication of chicken pox in pregnant women.

On the morning of November 16, Ms. Van Dosen again called in to work. During that call, she told Mr. Long that she had chicken pox and that she would try to bring a doctor's slip to him by Thursday, November 18. But by Wednesday, November 17, Ms. Van Dosen's condition had worsened, and she was suffering from nausea, vomiting, and dehydration. That day, she was admitted to the emergency room of Vencor Hospital in LaGrange, Indiana, where she was kept overnight and received intravenous fluids. She was released on Thursday, November 18.

It appears that Ms. Van Dosen did not call in to work on November 17, 18, or 19. But on November 19, Mr. Mitschelen went to Midwest's facility to pick up her paycheck. Mr. Long told Mr. Mitschelen to have Ms. Van Dosen call him immediately. But for whatever reason, Ms. Van Dosen did not call in on November 19, or on November 22-24, on which days she also did not come in to work. It is unclear from the evidence before the Court at this time whether Midwest had notice of the fact the Ms. Van Dosen had been hospitalized on November 17 and 18.

Dr. Keaffaber again saw Ms. Van Dosen on November 22. The notes from that visit indicate that her chicken pox were "better". Following that visit, Dr. Keaffaber believed that Ms. Van Dosen would be able to return to work on Monday, November 29. It does not appear that Midwest was aware of either of these impressions of Dr. Keaffaber.

On Saturday, November 27, Ms. Van Dosen went to Howe Medical Center to get a doctor's slip for her absences from and including November 15. In accordance with the center's policy, a slip was filled out by a nurse and signed by Dr. Pechin. Because Ms. Van Dosen indicated that she still did not feel well, the slip excused her absences through Wednesday, December 1.

Midwest's facility reopened on Monday, November 29, following a four-day Thanksgiving weekend vacation. Ms. Van Dosen intended to stop by to present her doctor's slip to Mr. Long on her way home from the grocery store, but she forgot to take the slip with her. When she returned home to get the slip, she listened to a message which Mr. Long had left on her answering machine while she had been out. She immediately called Mr. Long back and, despite the fact that she told him that she had a doctor's slip, he informed her that her employment had been terminated that morning.

At the time Midwest terminated Ms. Van Dosen's employment, its employee handbook did not mention the FMLA. With regard to sick leave, the handbook provided:

> Employees must notify their supervisor of the time and reason for the leave, in advance or as soon as practical, if they are going to take sick leave. A physician's notice is required if the employee is absent for more than two consecutive days.

With regard to absenteeism, the handbook provided:

> Unexcused absences result when an employee fails to notify Midwest Plastic Engineering, Inc. as required, or is absent from work on a scheduled workday when the employee has insufficient cause to be absent. Three (3) unexcused absences in any twelve (12) month period are grounds for immediate dismissal.

> Absences for illness are sometimes unavoidable. If an employee is absent because of illness for more than three (3) scheduled workdays in a row, or more than four (4) days in a calendar month, a doctor's slip stating the employee was ill and is now able to return to work will be required. A doctor's slip may be required for any illness at the discretion of the Supervisor.

Ms. Van Dosen signed a DOL complaint form on December 15, 1993, which was received by the DOL on January 7, 1994. After an investigation by the DOL, the DOL filed its complaint in this matter on August 5, 1994, the first anniversary of the effective date of the Act. The single-count complaint alleges that the defendants have violated Sections 104 and 105 of the Act, and seeks an injunction enjoining the defendants from further violating those sections, compensatory damages and interest thereon, and other equitable relief including reinstatement.

B

Section 107 of the Act authorizes the Secretary of Labor, among others, to initiate a civil action on behalf of an employee whose employer has violated Section 105 of the Act. 29 U.S.C. § 2617(b). Section 105 prohibits covered employers from "interfering with, restraining, or denying the exercise of or the attempt to exercise, any right provided under" the Act. 29 U.S.C. § 2615(a)(1). The right under the Act invoked in this case is the eligible employee's right to be restored to her former position, or an equivalent position, following the employee's qualifying leave. *See* 29 U.S.C. § 2614(a)(1).

Whether leave qualifies for the protection of Section 104(a)(1) is controlled by Section 102. That section provides that an eligible employee shall be entitled to a total of 12 workweeks of leave during any 12-month period for one or more of the following:

> ....
> (D) Because of a serious health condition that makes the employee unable to perform the functions of the position of such employee.

29 U.S.C. § 2612(1). The Act defines "serious health condition" as "an illness, injury, impairment, or physical or mental condition that involve — (A) inpatient care in a hospital, hospice, or residential medical care facility; or (B) continuing treatment by a health care provider." 29 U.S.C. § 2611(11). Pursuant to authority granted him by 29 U.S.C. § 2654, the Secretary of Labor has promulgated regulations further defining what is a "serious health condition": "inpatient care" requires an overnight stay, and "continuing treatment" includes where the employee "is treated two or more times for the injury or illness by a health care provider." 29 C.F.R. § 825.114(a)(1), (b)(1).

The Act itself is silent regarding the notice which an employee must provide to her employer when the leave is not foreseeable. The regulations, however, provide that "when the need for leave ... is not foreseeable, an employee should give notice to the employer of the need for FMLA leave as soon as practicable." 29 C.F.R. § 825.303(a). "'As soon as practicable' means as soon as both possible and practical, taking into account all of the facts and circumstances in the individual case." 29 C.F.R. § 825.302(b). The regulations further provide:

> (c) An employee shall provide at least verbal notice sufficient to make the employer aware that the employee needs FMLA-qualifying leave, and the anticipated timing and duration of the leave. The employee need not expressly assert rights under the FMLA, but may only state that leave is needed for an expected birth or adoption, for example. The employer should inquire further of the employee if it is necessary to have more information about whether FMLA leave is being sought by the employee, and obtain the necessary details of the leave to be taken. In the case of medical conditions, the employer may find it necessary to inquire further to determine if the leave is because of a serious health condition and may request medical certification to support the need for such leave (*see* § 825.305).

29 C.F.R. § 825.302(c). The regulations are silent, however, regarding the effect of an employee's failure to provide adequate notice of an unforeseen serious health condition.

Once an employee has notified her employer of her need for leave, the employer has the option of requiring that the requested leave be certified by a health care provider. 29 U.S.C. § 2613(a). The employer's request for certification must be in writing. 29 C.F.R. § 825.305(a). Once the employer has made a written request for certification supporting an employee's leave request, the employee must generally provide the certification within the time frame requested by the employer, which time frame may not be less than fifteen days. *Id.* The regulations contain several other relevant requirements related to certifications. First, the employer must generally request certification, "in the case of unforeseen leave, soon after the leave commences." 29 C.F.R. § 825.305(b). Second, "at the time the employer requests certification, the employer must also advise an employee of the anticipated consequences of an employee's failure to provide adequate certification." 29 C.F.R. § 825.305(c). And third, an employee's failure to provide requested certification in a timely manner allows the employer to deny FMLA leave. 29 C.F.R. § 825.312(b).

Where an employer has violated Section 105 of the Act, the employee is entitled to compensatory damages equal to the amount of any wages, salary, employment benefits, or other compensation which she was denied or lost as a result of the violation, interest on the compensatory damages, and, unless the court concludes that the employer acted in good faith and reasonably believed that it had not violated the Act, liquidated damages equal to the sum of the amount of the compensatory damages and the interest thereon. 29 U.S.C. § 2617(a)(1).

Two other section of the Act are relevant in this case. The first is Section 401 which provides that "the rights established for employees under this Act or any amendment made by this Act shall not be diminished by any collective bargaining agreement or any employment benefit program or plan." 29 U.S.C. § 2652(b). Any provision in such a program or plan which would diminish an employee's rights under the Act is superseded by the Act. 29 C.F.R. § 825.700(a).

The second is Section 109 which requires an employer "to post, and keep posted, in conspicuous places on the premises of the employer ... a notice, to be prepared and approved by the Secretary, setting forth excerpts from, or summaries of, the pertinent provisions of" the Act. 29 U.S.C. § 2619(a). The Act provides for a civil fine for an employer's failure to comply with this posting requirement, 29 U.S.C. § 2619(b), and the regulations estop such an employer from taking adverse action against an employee who fails "to furnish the employer with advance notice of a need to take FMLA leave", 29 C.F.R. § 825.300(b). The regulations add a second notice requirement for employers who have any written guidance to employees concerning employee benefits or leave rights: Such employers must include in their handbooks information concerning FMLA entitlements and employee obligations under the FMLA. 29 C.F.R. § 825.301(a).

II

The parties' motions seek summary judgment pursuant to Rule 56 of the Federal Rules of Civil Procedure....

III

It is undisputed that Midwest is an "employer" within the meaning of the Act, inasmuch as it "engaged in commerce or in any industry or activity affecting commerce" and "employed 50 or more employees for each working day during each of 20 or more calendar workweeks in" 1993 or 1992. *See* 29 U.S.C. § 2611(4). The DOL also alleges that Defendant Dennis E. Baker (Baker) is also an "employer" for the purpose of this case. The first issue which the Court considers, therefore, is whether Baker is an "employer" within the meaning of the Act.

Section 101 of the Act provides that "the term 'employer' ... includes ... any person who acts, directly or indirectly, in the interest of an employer to any of the employees of such employer...." 29 U.S.C. § 2611(4)(A). This definition is similar to a part of the definition of "employer" in the Fair Labor Standards Act (FLSA). The FLSA includes within the meaning of "employer" "any person acting directly or indirectly in the interest of an employer in relation to an employee...." 29 U.S.C. § 203(d). Because of the similarity between these definitions, the Court will look to the FLSA and its case law in determining whether Baker is an employer for the purposes of the FMLA.

"The FLSA contemplates there being several simultaneous employers who may be responsible for compliance with the FLSA." *Dole v. Elliott Travel & Tours, Inc.*, 942 F.2d 962, 965 (6th Cir. 1991) (*citing* Falk v. Brennan, 414 U.S. 190, 195 (1973)). "In deciding whether a party is an employer, 'economic reality' controls rather than common law concepts of agency." *Id.* (*citing Goldberg v. Whitaker House Cooperative*, 366 U.S. 28, 33 (1961)). "'The overwhelming weight of authority is that a corporate officer with operational control of a corporation's covered enterprise is an employer along with the corporation, jointly and severally liable under the FLSA for unpaid wages.'" *Id.* (*quoting Donovan v. Agnew*, 712 F.2d 1509, 1511 (1st Cir. 1983)).

In *Dole*, the court considered whether the individual defendant, Jared Schubiner, was jointly and severally liable with the corporate defendant, Elliott Travel & Tours. The court concluded that he was:

> The economic realities of this case indicate that Schubiner was an employer within the meaning of the FLSA, and he is chargeable with personal liability for failure to comply with the FLSA. Schubiner was the chief corporate officer, had a significant ownership interest in the corporation, and had control over significant aspects of the corporation's day-to-day functions.... To be classified as an employer, it is not required that a party have exclusive control of a corporation's day-to-day functions. The party need only have

"operational control of significant aspects of the corporation's day to day functions."

Id. at 966 (*quoting Donovan*, 712 F.2d at 1514).

In the instant case, Baker and his wife are the sole owners, the sole directors, and the sole officers of Midwest. Baker is the President of Midwest, and has testified that he "oversee[s] the general day-to-day operation of the company...." Baker's assertion that he oversees the general day-to-day operation of Midwest is substantiated by his more precise description of his specific duties and responsibilities. Accordingly, guided by the factors identified in *Dole* as being relevant in an FLSA case, the Court concludes that Baker is an employer for the purposes of the FMLA.

IV

Next, the Court considers the adequacy of Ms. Van Dosen's notice of her intent to take leave which qualified as FMLA leave. Since Ms. Van Dosen's case of chicken pox was unforeseen, Ms. Van Dosen was required to give Midwest notice of her intent to take leave which qualified as FMLA leave "as soon as practicable under the facts and circumstances of" her case. *See* 29 C.F.R. § 825.303(a).

The question of the adequacy of her notice is further complicated by at least two other provisions in the regulations. The first is 29 C.F.R. § 825.302(c), which implies that Ms. Van Dosen need not have framed her leave request in terms of the Act and places the burden on the employer to get further information, if necessary, to determine whether the leave results from a serious health condition to which the FMLA applies. The second provision is 29 C.F.R. § 825.303(b), which required Ms. Van Dosen to provide her employer with additional information regarding her leave "when it [could have] readily been accomplished as a practical matter".

The evidence before the Court at this time that involves the issue of the adequacy of Ms. Van Dosen's notice to the defendants includes her November 15 telephone message, her November 16 and 29 conversations with Mr. Long, and Mr. Mitschelen's conversation with Mr. Long on November 19. In light of the fact-intensive nature of this issue, the Court will reserve judgment on this issue pending full factual development of this issue at trial. Indeed, several questions related to this issue remain unanswered with sufficient certainty at this time. The first is whether Ms. Van Dosen provided sufficient information regarding her condition to the defendants to put them on notice that her leave qualified as FMLA leave. The second, which presumes that the first question be answered in the negative, is whether she provided sufficient information to shift the burden to the defendants to inquire further to determine if her leave qualified as FMLA leave. A third involves the effect, if any, of 29 C.F.R. § 825.309(a), which provides in part: "An employer may require an employee on FMLA leave to report periodically on the employee's status and intent to return to work."

V

While this case will proceed to trial on the issue of whether Ms. Van Dosen provided adequate notice of her intent to take leave which was FMLA-qualifying leave, with regard to several other issues the Court concludes that there exists no genuine issue as to any material fact and that one or the other of the parties is entitled to partial judgment as a matter of law on these issues.

A

The first of these issues involves the DOL's allegations that the defendants have violated the Act and the regulations by Midwest's alleged failing to post notices concerning the FMLA and by its failing to include information concerning the FMLA in its employee handbook. The Court concludes that the defendants are entitled to partial summary judgment on this issue.

In its complaint, the DOL makes no mention of Section 109 of the Act or of the alleged failure properly to post notices, nor does the complaint seek the imposition of a civil money penalty pursuant to that section. Therefore, the Court concludes that these alleged failures are irrelevant in this case. Midwest's alleged failure to post notices in its facility would have been relevant only if Ms. Van Dosen had been required to provide advance notice of her intent to take leave. *See* 29 C.F.R. § 825.300(b). Moreover, the Court is satisfied that the defendants have satisfied this obligation by their posting of notices in Midwest's two main breakrooms in August or September 1993.

Similarly, neither the Act nor the regulations provide that Midwest's failure to refer to the Act in its employee handbook has any effect in a case such as this, and the Court is unwilling to impose a penalty against the defendants for this failure. In reaching this decision, the Court is particularly mindful of the facts that Ms. Van Dosen is presumed to have had actual notice of the Act's requirements as to notice by her as the result of the defendants' proper posting of the employer's notice, *see* 29 C.F.R. § 825.304(c), and that Midwest updated its employee handbook to include information on the Act in February 1994, merely six months after the effective date of Section 109.

B

With regard to the issue whether Ms. Van Dosen's medical condition was a "serious health condition" within the meaning of the Act, Midwest argues that it was not. Her visits to her physician on November 15 and 22, Midwest contends, were routine prenatal visits and therefore she was not under the "continuing treatment" of a health care provider under 29 C.F.R. § 825.114(b)(1), since her only unscheduled visit to a health care provider occurred when she went to the hospital on November 17. Midwest further contends that her hospital stay does not make her illness a serious medical condition since Dr. Keaffaber stated during his deposition that the problems for which she was admitted to the hospital could be indicative of pneumonia, even though she never actually had pneumonia.

The Court rejects both of these arguments. With regard to Midwest's former argument, the Court concludes that Ms. Van Dosen was clearly under the continuing treatment of a health care provider, within the meaning of the Act, because she was treated for chicken pox on three separate occasions. *See* 29 C.F.R. § 825.114(b)(1). The first was her visit to Dr. Keaffaber on November 15. Regardless of whether this visit was a scheduled prenatal visit, Dr. Keaffaber treated her chicken pox as is clearly demonstrated by the facts that she was diagnosed as having chicken pox and that she was prescribed medication for that condition. The second time she was treated for chicken pox involved her overnight stay at the hospital. The third was her visit to Dr. Keaffaber on November 22. That she was treated for chicken pox during this visit is evident from Dr. Keaffaber's notation in the hospital records regarding a follow-up visit on "Monday or Tuesday", as well as from the notes from the November 22 visit in which Dr. Keaffaber indicated that her condition was better.

Furthermore, there is no genuine issue as to the fact that Ms. Van Dosen was admitted into the hospital and retained overnight as a direct result of her having chicken pox. This fact alone sufficiently establishes that Ms. Van Dosen's condition constituted a "serious health condition". *See* 29 C.F.R. § 825.114(a)(1). Whether she contracted the most serious condition that she could have contracted is irrelevant, since her medical care provider determined that she should be held overnight.

Accordingly, the Court will grant partial summary judgment in favor of the DOL on the issue whether Ms. Van Dosen's medical condition was a "serious health condition" within the meaning of the Act.

C

Next, the Court considers the defendants' argument that they are not liable in this case since Ms. Van Dosen failed to provide certification upon Midwest's request. The Court rejects this argument for several reasons, and therefore will grant partial summary judgment in favor of the DOL on this issue as well. First, Midwest's request for certification, which it made after the DOL filed this action, was not timely made. *See* 29 C.F.R. § 825.305(b).

Second, the requirement in Midwest's employee handbook that an employee provide a doctor's slip in certain circumstances does not satisfy the request for certification requirement since it did not advise Ms. Van Dosen of the anticipated consequences of her failure to provide adequate certification. *See* 29 C.F.R. § 825.305(c). Moreover, the handbook requirement would be inadequate because Midwest must have permitted Ms. Van Dosen at least fifteen days to provide the certification. *See* 29 C.F.R. § 825.305(a). Since her medical condition did not arise until November 15, therefore, Midwest must have allowed her until at least November 30 to provide the requested certification. Ms. Van Dosen was prepared to submit her doctor's slip, which presumably would have satisfied the certification requirement, on November 29, but did not do so only because Midwest terminated her employment on that date.

Even if the Court were to construe Mr. Long's demand for a doctor's slip as a request for certification, this request was inadequate since it was not in writing. *See* 29 C.F.R. § 825.305(a).

D

Finally, the Court considers the defendants' contention that whether Ms. Van Dosen's leave was leave which was protected by the Act is immaterial inasmuch as Midwest had the right to terminate her employment as of Monday, November 15. *Cf.* 29 C.F.R. § 825.216(a). While the Court agrees that Midwest had the right to terminate Ms. Van Dosen's employment on November 15 due to her failure to present a doctor's slip for her absences between November 4 and 9,[2] the fact is, as evidenced by the Letter of Reprimand that Midwest had prepared to give Ms. Van Dosen, that Midwest had decided not to terminate her employment on account of the November 4-9 unexcused absences. Therefore, the Court must conclude that Midwest's termination of Ms. Van Dosen's employment on November 29 was the direct result of her "unexcused" absences between November 15 and 29, and that Midwest would not have terminated her employment but for those absences.

The defendants also argue that, with regard to Ms. Van Dosen's absences between November 15 and 29, Midwest had a sufficient independent basis for terminating her employment inasmuch as she failed to provide the notices and doctor's slip required by its employee handbook. Initially, the Court notes that Midwest's employee handbook did not clearly require that Ms. Van Dosen call in on any particular days. But more significantly, and even if the handbook did so require, the Court concludes that, provided that her leave is otherwise protected by the Act, such a provision would be more restrictive than the notice requirement in the Act and would therefore be superseded by the Act. *See* 29 U.S.C. § 2652(b); 29 C.F.R. § 825.700(a).

For these reasons, the Court will grant partial summary judgment in favor of the DOL on the issue whether Midwest had a sufficient independent basis for terminating Ms. Van Dosen's employment.

. . . .

NOTES

1. *Inadequate Notice of FMLA Leave.* The district court in this case later held a bench trial and concluded that Ms. Van Dosen failed to provide adequate notice of her need to take FMLA-qualifying leave and also failed to report peri-

---

[2] Unlike Ms. Van Dosen's absences which resulted from her own case of chicken pox, her absences related to her daughters' cases of chicken pox were not due to a serious medical condition since the girls did not receive inpatient care and only Andrea visited a health care provider, and then only on one occasion.

odically about her status. It therefore entered final judgment for the employer. In its opinion, the court distinguished the issue of serious medical condition from the issue of adequate notice with the following hypothetical:

> [Suppose two] employees were involved in separate car accidents on Sunday. The first employee incurred substantial injuries as a result of his accident which necessitated his being hospitalized for several weeks. The second employee sustained no injuries in his accident. Neither employee came to work on Monday, the first because he was in the hospital and the second because he decided to go fishing. Each employee called the employer on Monday morning and reported that he would not be at work that day and that he had been involved in a car accident on Sunday. Under the Act and the regulations, the first employee clearly had a "serious health condition", and the second clearly did not. But neither employee provided the employer with adequate notice of his need for FMLA-leave, [because] neither employee informed the employer of his condition with sufficient detail to make it evident to the employer that the absence was protected as FMLA-qualifying leave — a person who is involved in a car accident does not necessarily incur a serious health condition. [T]he first employee should have stated that he had been hospitalized as the result of the accident. Such a statement by the employee would have informed his employer of his condition with sufficient detail to make it evident that the requested leave was protected as FMLA-qualifying leave. An employer should not have to speculate as to the nature of an employee's condition.

Reich v. Midwest Plastic Eng'g, Inc., 1995 U.S. Dist. LEXIS 12130, at *10-*12 (W.D. Mich. July 26, 1995).

2. *The FMLA and COBRA*. Section 104(c) of the FMLA requires employers to maintain the health benefits of employees on leave. Some employees, such as those who want to care for their baby for more than twelve weeks or who never recover from an illness, do not return to work after going on FMLA leave. The FMLA allows employers to recover the employer-paid portion of the premium from these employees.

FMLA leave ends when the employee announces he or she will not return to work. This last day of FMLA leave is a qualifying event for COBRA, entitling the employee to continue in the employer's group-health plan for (generally) eighteen additional months as long as the employee pays the entire premium. An employee is entitled to COBRA coverage even if the employee failed to pay the employee portion of premiums during the FMLA leave, and the employer cannot condition COBRA continuation coverage on the employee's reimbursing the employer for premiums the employer paid to maintain coverage during the FMLA leave. *See* Effect of the Family and Medical Leave Act on COBRA Continuation Coverage, I.R.S. Notice 94-103, 1994-2 C.B. 569.

3. *The FMLA and the ADA.* The Americans with Disabilities Act requires employers with fifteen or more employees to provide reasonable accommodations for workers with disabilities unless that would create an "undue hardship." ADA § 102(5)(A). The FMLA has no "undue hardship" defense, but only mandates unpaid leave. Assuming both statutes apply, sometimes the ADA is more protective and sometimes the FMLA provides greater protection.

For example, suppose a person with a disability requires a period of leave to recover from an operation related to the disability. The ADA does not require the employer to provide the leave if this would create an undue hardship, but the FMLA would require the leave. On the other hand, the FMLA limits leave to twelve weeks, while the ADA would require the employer to give an indefinite amount of leave if this accommodation were reasonable and would not cause an undue hardship.

The FMLA and ADA also differ in coverage of family members. The ADA prohibits employers from discriminating against an employee because they have a relationship with someone with a disability, ADA § 102(b)(4), but only requires reasonable accommodation of employees or job applicants with a disability. Thus, for example, the ADA does not require an employer to give an employee leave to care for a family member with AIDS, even if that could be done without undue hardship. The FMLA does mandate such leave, even if an undue hardship is created.

4. *Stress.* Suppose an employee complains of stress caused by an overbearing supervisor, and feels he must take time off work. What statutes come into play? One possibility is the Americans with Disabilities Act. However, if the stress comes solely from a particular boss, the condition probably is not an impairment substantially affecting a major life activity, as required by the ADA. *See Weiler v. Household Fin. Corp.*, 101 F.3d 519 (7th Cir. 1996). Another possibility is the FMLA. Suppose the employee gets a letter from a certified social worker attesting to his need for leave. This is probably evidence of "a serious health condition" from a "health care provider," which entitles the employee to twelve weeks unpaid leave. The case also raises issues under workers' compensation. If the stress can be seen as an injury arising out of and in the course of employment, the employee may be entitled to medical expenses and partial pay during his time off. *See* Chapter 21.

5. *FMLA and the Poor.* The FMLA imposes costs on employers and so probably reduces wages. The Act mandates only unpaid leave, and thus only benefits workers who can afford to take time off work without pay. Professor Hylton has argued that the working poor get no benefits from the FMLA but may share in its costs. If so, the Act may protect those who are best able to bargain on their own behalf, and leave unprotected those in the weakest bargaining position. *See* Maria O'Brien Hylton, *"Parental" Leaves and Poor Women: Paying the Price for Time Off*, 52 U. PITT. L. REV. 475 (1991).

A 1995 survey of leave-takers conducted by the Survey Research Center of the University of Michigan supports Professor Hylton's claims that most unpaid leave is taken by well-off groups. It found that most leave-takers are between thirty-five and forty-nine years old, that most have had at least some college education, and that 75% are non-Hispanic whites. In addition, 58% of leave-takers are women.

D. WAGE PAYMENT LAWS

BECKWITH v. UNITED PARCEL SERVICE

United States Court of Appeals, First Circuit

889 F.2d 344 (1989)

COFFIN, SENIOR CIRCUIT JUDGE....

Plaintiff Daniel Beckwith, a driver for appellant United Parcel Service, was terminated for gross negligence for violating UPS delivery policies and causing substantial loss of merchandise.[1] In a meeting with his UPS supervisors and his union representative, Beckwith offered to pay back the losses he caused if UPS would reinstate him. UPS agreed, and the parties entered into a written payroll deduction agreement providing that $50 per week would be deducted from Beckwith's paycheck until a total of $7,814 was repaid.[2] The weekly deductions began in April 1986.

About eighteen months later, Beckwith filed this action claiming that payroll deduction agreements such as the one he signed are prohibited by Maine law, and that UPS therefore was required to return to him the total amount deducted from his paychecks. Beckwith relied on 26 M.R.S.A. § 629, which states in pertinent part:

> No person, firm or corporation shall require or permit any person as a condition of securing or retaining employment to work without monetary compensation or when having an agreement, verbal, written or implied that a part of such compensation should be returned to the person, firm or corporation for any reason other than for the payment of a loan, debt or advance made to the person....
>
> For purposes of this subchapter, the word "debt" means a benefit to the employee. Debt does not include items incurred by the employee in the course of the employee's work ..., such as cash shortages, inventory shortages ..., damages to the employer's property in any form or any merchandise purchased by a customer.
>
> An employer shall be liable to the employees for the amount returned to the employer as prohibited in this section.

---

[1] Plaintiff apparently released packages in circumstances not permitted by UPS policies. This resulted in the misdelivery of approximately $8,000 worth of computer equipment and approximately $1,400 worth of other merchandise, including video equipment. This merchandise was never recovered by UPS or its intended recipients.

[2] UPS agreed to forgive the other losses caused by Beckwith's violations.

Beckwith also sought liquidated damages, interest and attorney's fees under 26 M.R.S.A. § 626-A....

The district court [held that Beckwith was entitled to the return of the withheld money, but] rejected Beckwith's claim for liquidated damages and attorney's fees, concluding that the Maine legislature intended to limit an employee's remedy under § 629 to recoupment of the deducted wages....

[Section 629] does not prohibit *all* voluntary agreements between employers and employees for the reimbursement of employee debts. In our view, it simply bars the use of one method, payroll deductions, for doing so. We recognize that § 629 does not explicitly refer to pay withholding agreements. We believe, however, that the statute's reference to the *return of monetary compensation for work* is intended to refer to a direct payment to the employer from one's wages rather than to any payment at all. It is unlikely that the legislature would have chosen these specific words if its purpose was to prohibit employers entirely from securing agreements for the payment of debts caused by an employee's admitted negligence. *Cf. Male v. Acme Markets, Inc.*, 264 A.2d 245 (N.J. Super. Ct. App. Div. 1970) (declining to construe New Jersey statute prohibiting wage withholding to bar voluntary reimbursement of funds).[6]

The legislature undoubtedly viewed the payroll deduction as harmful and unfair because it deprives the worker of wages earned before he has had a chance to decide on a given payday how best to allocate his available resources. With a payroll deduction, an employee suffering an unexpected financial crisis loses the flexibility to pay his debt a little late so that he has enough money for that week's food. In addition, if funds are withheld automatically, the employee who seeks to challenge a particular deduction — for example, because he thinks the debt already is repaid — would nevertheless first lose access to his money....

[T]he district court ruled that the wage withholding agreement was "null and void" and unenforceable against Beckwith. In its reply brief to us, UPS argues for the first time that only the payroll deduction provision should be invalidated and that the remainder of the agreement should be held enforceable. UPS claims that it has not urged this approach previously because Beckwith had not previously argued that it was only the payroll deduction provision that violated § 629. It apparently has been UPS's assumption that *any* agreement to pay back employment-related losses incurred by employees is barred by the statute if made a condition of employment.

We decline to consider whether the agreement is severable. It was UPS's obligation to argue to the district court that some remedy short of invalidating the agreement would satisfy Maine law. Although its failure to do so stems from

---

[6] Thus, § 629 would not foreclose an employee from agreeing, as a condition for reinstatement, to reimburse his employer for damages caused at a specified rate per month — so long as the amount of reimbursement does not come directly out of the employee's paycheck. Of course, any agreement that required the equivalent of a payroll deduction would be invalid. An employer could not, for example, require an employee to pay $50 per week as a condition of receiving his "full" paycheck.

mistaken assumptions about the scope of § 629, UPS had adequate notice of the theory that the *wage withholding* provision, and not the payback agreement itself, violated Maine law. Beckwith's complaint alleged that "[t]he actions of Defendant *in withholding weekly sums from Plaintiff's pay* are in violation of 26 M.R.S.A. § 629." (Emphasis added.)... The district court's opinion also suggests a focus on the payroll deduction element of the agreement: "The facts here do not fit within any of the section 629 exceptions permitting *paycheck deductions* as a condition of employment."

The company was not deceived by Beckwith's arguments, but merely taken unawares. In these circumstances, we see no reason to depart from the well-established principle that issues not raised below will not be considered on appeal. We therefore affirm the judgment of the district court invalidating the wage withholding agreement.

[The Court also affirmed the district court's remedy which required UPS to return to Beckwith the amount wrongly withheld from his pay, but denied Beckwith's request for liquidated damages and attorney's fees.]

NOTES

1. *Recovering Losses.* Employers generally can sue to recover losses caused by an employee's negligence or dishonesty. RESTATEMENT OF AGENCY 2D, § 401. *But see Fried v. Aftec, Inc.,* 587 A.2d 290 (N.J. Super. Ct. App. Div. 1991). (employer can recover for dishonesty, but not for negligence or ineptness; employer's remedy for the latter concerns is to fire the employee). Thus, UPS could have sued Beckwith to recover its losses. Wage payment laws, however, generally restrict UPS's ability to recover its losses more directly by withholding the lost amounts from Beckwith's check. This restriction in wage payment laws furthers both procedural and substantive goals. Procedurally, it is intended to force UPS to sue if it wants to recover to ensure that Beckwith has a fair opportunity to defend against the alleged negligence or dishonesty. Substantively, the restriction is intended to limit the ability of employers to shift to employees costs that should be the employer's responsibility, such as losses from bad checks or robberies.

2. *When Employees Want Losses Withheld From Their Checks.* As *Beckwith* illustrates, sometimes employees *want* to be able to guarantee payments for losses: Beckwith was going to lose his job unless he could guarantee payment in some way. Even without the interest in his job, Beckwith may have preferred a private settlement to a public lawsuit seeking recovery.

Could UPS and Beckwith have agreed:

(1) That UPS would pay Beckwith with two checks each week, one for $50 and the other for the rest of Beckwith's pay, and that upon receipt Beckwith would immediately endorse the $50 check to UPS? *Male v. Acme Mkts.,* 264 A.2d 245 (N.J. Super. Ct. App. Div. 1970) (no).

(2) That Beckwith would make a $50 payment each week until the lost amount was repaid? *Compare id.* (implies no) *with Stoll v. Goodnight Corp.,* 469 So. 2d 1072 (La. Ct. App. 1985) (yes).

(3) That Beckwith would be reemployed at a rate of pay $50 per week less than he had been paid previously with an understanding that his pay would be increased after the amount saved in wage payments equalled the losses? *Salter v. Freight Sales Co.,* 357 N.W.2d 38 (Iowa Ct. App. 1984) (no).

Concern about the voluntariness of employee agreements to repay is a principal reason that the wage payment cases generally make it difficult for an employer to seek to recover losses without filing a lawsuit against the employee. In *Stoll v. Goodnight Corp., supra,* for example, a travel agent agreed to repay the employer in installments for a $778 bad check she had accepted. She had not been negligent in accepting the check, but agreed to the repayment because she understood that she would lose her job if she refused. Two weeks after the repayment was completed, she was fired. No violation of the wage payment statute was found, in part because she had voluntarily agreed to make the repayment.

3. *Other Common Provisions in Wage Payment Laws.* Wage payment laws vary considerably across the states. Most require wage payments to be made in cash or by check (rather than in scrip, for example) and to be made periodically (such as every week or month). Most statutes also regulate the payment of wages upon termination of employment, requiring payment within a certain period of time after the relationship is ended. Often, the period is shorter when the employee is discharged than it is when the employee quits. Most statutes also impose restrictions on the assignment of wages. For example, some states prohibit assignments, while others require the employer and the worker's spouse to consent to any assignment. Many states also impose restrictions on the garnishment of wages and restrict the ability of employers to discharge workers for having their wages garnished. The federal government has also regulated garnishment. Consumer Credit Protection Act, 15 U.S.C. §§ 1673-1674 (limiting the amount that can be garnished and prohibiting discharge for one garnishment). The statutory supplement contains examples of state wage payment laws on each of these topics.

Chapter 17

UNEMPLOYMENT AND UNEMPLOYMENT INSURANCE

A. SKETCHES OF THE UNEMPLOYED

KATHERINE NEWMAN, FALLING FROM GRACE: THE EXPERIENCE OF DOWNWARD MOBILITY IN THE AMERICAN MIDDLE CLASS 1-7 (1988)[*]

David Patterson was a practical man. All his life ... he had made rational decisions about the future. David had a talent for music, but he studied business. He had a flare for advertising, but he pursued a job in the computer industry. He wore his rationality proudly. Having steered clear of personal indulgence, he had a lot to show for his efforts: a beautiful home, two luxury cars, a country club membership, a rewarding executive job, and a comfortable, stable family....

When David's boss left frantic messages with the secretary, asking him to stay late one Friday afternoon, his stomach began to flutter. Only the previous week David had pored over the company's financial statements. Things weren't looking too good, but it never occurred to him that the crisis would reach his level. He was, after all, the director of an entire division, a position he had been promoted to only two years before. But when David saw the pained look on the boss's face, he knew his head had found its way to the chopping block....

Wasting no time, he set to work on the want ads every morning. He called all his friends in the business to let them know he was looking, and he sent his resume` out to the "headhunters" — the executive firms that match openings to people. David was sure, in the beginning, that it wouldn't be long before a new position opened up. He had some savings put aside to cushion the family in the meanwhile. He was not worried. By the third month of looking, he was a bit nervous. Six fruitless months down the line he was in a full-fledged panic. Nothing was coming through. The message machine he had bought the day after losing his job was perpetually blank.

After nine months, David and his wife Julia were at a crossroads. Their savings eroded, they could not keep up the mortgage payments on their four-bedroom neocolonial house. Julia had gone back to work after a two-year hiatus, but her earnings were a fraction of what David's had been. His unemployment compensation together with her paycheck never amounted to more than 25 percent of the income they had had in the old days. The house, their pride and joy and the repository of virtually all their savings, went up for sale.... But their asking price was too high to attract many qualified buyers. Finally it was sold for a song.

---

[*]Reprinted with permission of Katherine S. Newman.

Broke and distressed beyond imagining, the family found a small apartment in a modest section of a nearby town. David continued to look for an executive job, but the massive downturn of the mid-1980s in the computer industry virtually ensured that his search would bear no fruit.... David could not get past the personnel offices of firms in other industries. He was not given the chance to show how flexible he could be, how transferable his managerial experience was to firms outside the computer field....

David could recite the litany of problems in the computer business so familiar to insiders. He could understand completely why his division, located at the market research end of the company, had been targeted as "nonessential" to its survival. In the beginning he told himself that his personal situation could be explained logically. Market forces had put pressure on the company, and it responded, as any rational actor in a competitive capitalist economy would, by cost cutting, aiming first at those activities that were most remote from the nuts and bolts of production and sales. Indeed, had David been at the helm, he argued, he would have made the same decision. For David Patterson is no rebel. He is a true believer in the American way of doing business. Up until now, it had satisfied his every ambition. Hence there was no reason to question its fundamental premise: In economics, as in life, the strong survive and the weak fall by the wayside.

But after months of insecurity, depression, and shaking fear, the economic causes of his personal problems began to fade from view. All David could think about was, What is wrong with me? Why doesn't anyone call me? What have I done wrong? ... With failure closing in from all directions the answer came back "It must be me." The ups and downs of the computer industry and the national economy were forgotten. David's character took center stage as the villain in his own downfall.

H.G. KAUFMAN, PROFESSIONALS IN SEARCH OF WORK: COPING WITH THE STRESS OF JOB LOSS AND UNDEREMPLOYMENT 53-55 (1982)[*]

[T]he degree of stress created by job loss is comparable to that of other losses in life, such as divorce and the death of a spouse or a close friend. The epidemiological evidence also indicates that joblessness has a widespread impact on mental and physical health. The rise in unemployment has been associated with subsequent increases in mental hospitalization, suicides, murders, and alcoholism. Infant mortality and deaths from stroke, heart, and kidney diseases have also risen following periods of high unemployment. Stress created during recession periods appears quite pervasive, affecting not only the unemployed, but also those who are still working.

There does not seem to be any doubt that work is much more central to the identity of professionals than of other workers. Therefore, since work becomes a greater potential source of both frustration and satisfaction for professionals, they would be more likely to experience severe stress as a result of unemployment than would other workers. Furthermore, jobless professionals have consistently been found to exhibit significantly more stress than their colleagues who remain employed, with perhaps as many as two-fifths experiencing psychological impairment extreme enough to require mental assistance. Those professionals who are affected by unemployment stress are likely to manifest at least some of the following psychological changes and symptoms:

1. Low self-esteem.
2. High anxiety.
3. Anomie.
4. Self-blame.
5. Depression.
6. Social isolation.
7. Anger and resentment.
8. Aggression toward others.
9. Psychosomatic disorders.
10. Occupational rigidity.
11. Professional obsolescence.
12. Low motivation to work.
13. Low achievement motivation.
14. External locus of control.
15. Helplessness.
16. Premature death from suicide or illness.

A factor analysis revealed that the unemployed professional may undergo stress which is either general in nature or more specific, involving symptoms of psychopathology or work inhibition. It is likely that those who exhibit the more extreme psychopathological characteristics would be more prone to experience intrapunative symptoms manifested by psychosomatic disorders and even premature death from either stress-induced illness or suicide. In fact, failure in the work role for males precipitates the basic suicide syndrome. Applied to job loss, this syndrome involves failure in a work role to which one is strongly committed, followed by occupational rigidity or inability to change roles, feelings of shame, and finally, social isolation as a defense to protect oneself against such feelings. Although job loss and other types of failure in the work role are apparently the most important cause of male suicides, clearly most unemployed professionals do not resort to this self-destructive path in dealing with their failure. Responses such as withdrawal and work inhibition are much more likely to occur, but as defense mechanisms these become highly dysfunctional in dealing with the problem of finding a job.

There is some evidence that unemployment can have an "ecological" effect on the whole family. Wives of unemployed men have been found to experience psychophysiological stress accompanying that of their husbands. Older children particularly may also suffer psychological effects, such as a loss of self-esteem as a result of their father being out of work. Furthermore, the stress created by unemployment has been identified as the highest risk factor predisposing parents to child abuse.

The drastic psychological changes that some professionals experience as a result of job loss may be explained as resulting from the need to bring their cognitions about themselves into balance and thereby reduce cognitive inconsistencies. Accordingly, a reduction in the motivation to work would reflect an attempt to lower one's level of aspiration to be more congruent with a diminished self-esteem. Nevertheless, despite their devalued self-esteem, professionals for whom work remains an important part of their identity appear to maintain a high motivation to return to work for restoration of their self-esteem.

The reactions of many professionals to unemployment can also be understood in terms of a societal model in which an environment that devalues self-esteem and diminishes the individual's control can result in low levels of achievement and satisfaction, in addition to aggression toward oneself and others. Widespread unemployment creates just such an environment and it is the resulting loss of self-esteem and the emergence of helplessness that appears to be central to the psychological consequences of joblessness among professionals. This helps explain why unemployment has been found to be the best economic predictor of mental health, whereas inflation appears totally unrelated.

B. THE UNEMPLOYMENT INSURANCE PROGRAM

Unemployment insurance in the United States is provided by a unique blend of federal and state government programs, created during the Great Depression with a fascinating constitutional history. It is a major government transfer program, accounting in recession years for some 15% of all government transfer payments to individuals. In 1939, its first full year of operation, the UI system paid a half-billion dollars in benefits. Over a half century later, in 1993, UI programs paid almost $22 billion to 7.8 million unemployed workers. They collected $21 billion from employers, thus nearly breaking even, and imposed an average tax rate of 0.9% on total wages. 1993 was a year of moderate unemployment, 7%. At other points in the business cycle, UI benefits can greatly exceed current UI taxes. In 1983, for example, when unemployment was 10.1%, UI paid regular benefits of over $20 billion to nearly 10 million workers, plus another $8 billion in extended benefits. Federal and state tax collections were about $18 billion in 1983. At other times, UI programs run a surplus.

1. HISTORY AND FINANCIAL STRUCTURE OF UNEMPLOYMENT INSURANCE

In 1932, Wisconsin became the first state to enact an unemployment insurance program, and it remained the only state program prior to passage of federal laws in 1935. The "principal obstacle" to state UI legislation, declared the House Ways and Means Committee in 1935, was that the payroll tax used to finance the system would put the enacting state's employers at a competitive disadvantage. With some 25% of the workforce unemployed, a national mandatory unemployment insurance program soon became a major priority of the New Deal. In particular, Frances Perkins, Roosevelt's Secretary of Labor, placed a high priority on unemployment insurance. One concern, however, was that the Supreme Court would strike down any nationally administered system.

There is a story, perhaps apocryphal, that Supreme Court Justice Louis Brandeis whispered to Perkins at a dinner party, "use the taxing power." (Brandeis's daughter was an administrator of Wisconsin's UI program, and Brandeis was clearly a proponent of a nationwide UI program.) Whether Brandeis was the catalyst or not, in the summer of 1934 the Commission on Economic Security, chaired by Perkins, drafted an unemployment insurance program as part of the Social Security Act that used the federal taxing power to skirt the Supreme Court threat. The federal tax would "encourage" states to adopt an unemployment insurance program. One advantage of the tax approach, thought the drafters, was that even if the Supreme Court struck down the federal law, the state programs would be up and running.

Under the Social Security Act of 1935, as amended, the federal government imposes an employer payroll tax on every covered employee. Currently, the tax is 6.2% of the first $7,000 in wages.[*] However, if the employer operates in a state with a qualified state unemployment insurance program, the federal government offsets the federal tax with any state taxes the employer has paid up to 5.4%. The federal tax credit is not simply a wash. If the state has an approved UI plan that charges some employers less than 5.4% for good experience, they still get credit for the entire 5.4%. Additionally, the federal government uses part of the remaining 0.8% federal tax to fund the administrative costs of state plans.

The incentive for employers to lobby their state government to create a qualified UI program was tremendous. Without a qualified state program, employers would pay a substantial federal tax that would give their state's workers no bene-

---

[*] The original Social Security Act of 1935 taxed all wages of covered workers. This decision was consistent with the goal of imposing a uniform tax throughout the country so no state would have an advantage over another. In the 1939 amendments, Congress limited the tax base to the first $3,000 of wages, a ceiling that exceeded the annual wages of 98% of workers. The federal tax rate at the time was 3%. The FUTA tax base has not kept pace with the rise in payrolls. Today, with the $7,000 federal base (and somewhat higher state bases), only about 40% of total payroll is subject to the tax. Had the 1939 ceiling been continually indexed for wage growth, the current ceiling would be over $42,000 instead of $7,000.

fits. With a state program, employers would pay the same or lower taxes and their workers would receive benefits. By 1937, all states had enacted unemployment insurance laws. In 1937, in *Steward Machine Co. v. Davis,* 301 U.S. 548, the Supreme Court upheld the constitutionality of the UI taxing scheme.

Initially, federal law had modest requirements for a state program to "qualify" for the tax credit. States had to pay benefits through public employment offices (rather than, say, the mails). State administrators had to be hired on a merit basis rather than through political patronage. States were required to deposit all UI tax receipts in the unemployment trust fund in the United States Treasury and could withdraw funds only to pay benefits. States could not deny benefits because a claimant refused a job that (1) was vacant because of a strike; (2) paid less than the prevailing wage; or (3) required membership in a company union or prohibited membership in a "bona fide" labor union.

Nevertheless, the federal program informally created a more uniform pattern than these modest requirements might suggest. The Social Security Board[*] drafted model guidelines in 1936 for states that wanted to be sure they enacted a qualified program. The Board also issued opinion letters on such issues as methods of experience rating. In the early days, Federal grants to states for administration were based on detailed, line-item budgets submitted by the states.

The result is that all state UI programs have significant common elements, with considerable variations among states at the margins. In every state, eligibility depends on earning a certain amount, working a certain number of weeks, or some combination, during a preceding base period. These eligibility requirements are intended to measure the worker's prior attachment to the work force. In most states, claimants must wait a week before collecting benefits. Full-time workers typically are eligible for twenty-six weeks of benefits. Benefits typically are 50% of weekly wages up to a statutory maximum. Most states set their cap as one-half to two-thirds of the average weekly wages in the state. Because of the cap on benefits, on average UI benefits replace only one-third of prior wages. Thirteen states give additional benefits for dependents, generally $10 or less per week. The smallest minimum benefit is $5 in Hawaii; the largest maximum is $382 in Massachusetts.

On the tax side, as of 1995, forty-two states have adopted tax bases higher than the $7,000 federal base, ranging as high as Hawaii's $25,500. Because states attempt to charge higher taxes to those employers with frequent layoffs, tax rates vary widely among employers. In 1993, minimum tax rates ranged from zero percent in seven states to a high of 2.5% in New York. Pennsylvania charges the highest maximum rate — 10.5% of taxable payroll. Overall state taxes were 2.5% of taxable payroll, or 0.9% of total payroll. The average UI tax burden varies widely between states, however. It ranges from 0.5 to 5.3% of taxable payroll, or 0.2 to 2.1% of total payroll. *See* Advisory Council on Unemployment

---

[*] The federal regulatory authority for unemployment insurance was later shifted to the Unemployment Insurance Service of the Department of Labor.

Compensation, Unemployment Insurance in the United States: Benefits, Financing, Coverage 74 (1995).

In 1996, 8 million unemployed workers received UI benefits. Their average weekly benefit was $189 and the average duration was 14.9 weeks. One-third of the recipients exhausted their regular benefits. The average total benefits was roughly $2,800. All these figures vary widely with the business cycle.

Since 1969, the federal unemployment trust fund has been treated as part of the federal budget. Thus, whenever benefits paid exceed UI taxes received (the usual situation in a recession), the UI program adds to the federal budget deficit. In 1982, for example, the unemployment trust fund added almost $7.5 billion to the federal deficit, an increase in the deficit of 6.2%. In 1987, by contrast, the UI fund reduced the deficit by $7.3 billion, keeping the deficit from being 4.6% higher than it was. Importantly, any changes in eligibility and coverage will also affect the federal budget. In part because of UI's inclusion in the federal budget, Congress has become more active in recent decades in amending the UI system. The 1980 National Commission on Unemployment Compensation was formed by both houses of Congress and the President to re-examine the federal-state unemployment insurance system, and unanimously recommended removing UI from the federal unified budget. As Wilbur Cohen, the Chair of the NCUC explained, "[t]he [congressional] emphasis on cost cutting indicates lack of understanding of the intended countercyclical nature of the UI program which is aimed at having an excess of benefits over income during periods of higher-than-normal unemployment." Cohen, *Reflections on the Work of the National Commission on Unemployment Compensation,* 59 U. DETROIT J. URB. L. 486, 496 (1982).

In a series of amendments in the 1970s, Congress greatly expanded the coverage of UI. One major addition was the coverage of state and local government employees. Congress was not so bold as to impose a federal tax on local school boards. Instead, one of the conditions for a qualifying state plan is that it must cover state and local government workers, even though the FUTA tax only covers private-sector employees. Further, states must permit governmental entities (and nonprofit organizations) to finance benefit costs by reimbursing the Trust Fund rather than by paying state taxes. Today, UI programs cover all employers that have at least one employee for at least twenty weeks of the year, or with a payroll of at least $1,500 in any calendar quarter. As a result of these program extensions, coverage of wage and salary workers rose from 65% in 1970 to nearly 98% today.

In 1970, Congress also established a permanent extended benefit program, which grants claimants who exhaust their regular state benefits an additional thirteen weeks of benefits. The extended benefit program is triggered whenever state insured unemployment rates reach specified high levels. The extended benefit program is jointly funded by federal and state payroll taxes.

In addition to the regular UI program and the extended benefit program, in the nine major recessions since World War II, Congress has enacted temporary supplemental programs for unemployed workers. Unlike the regular and extended programs, these temporary programs are funded from general federal revenues.

The expanded coverage created financial difficulties in the UI programs of several states for the first time since World War II. This has led to congressional battles to force states to tighten eligibility requirements. In recent years, Congress has dramatically increased the number of requirements for an approved state program qualifying for the federal tax credit offset. For example, state programs must deny benefits to illegal aliens, to professional athletes between seasons, and to schoolteachers between terms. State programs must offset benefits by the amount of pension benefits a claimant receives and the amount of child support he owes. State agencies must give wage records to welfare agencies determining eligibility of needy families. State programs must disqualify ex-service members who declined the option to reenlist.

2. CAUSES OF UNEMPLOYMENT AND THE ROLE OF UI

One of the most unpleasant consequences of a free-market economy is that some persons desiring work cannot find it. The causes of unemployment are several. Economies periodically have recessions where consumer demand and production falls, leading to cyclical unemployment. Even in a full-employment economy, some workers will be between jobs and therefore unemployed. Information about job vacancies is limited, and it simply takes time for workers to find appropriate jobs. Some frictional unemployment, as this has been called, is perhaps inevitable. Unemployment insurance, by subsidizing job search costs, can extend the length of frictional unemployment. To help reduce this friction, many states tie their UI programs to a state employment service. UI claimants are required to register with the employment service, which serves as a job bank and reference service.

More serious is structural unemployment, which arises from a geographic or skill mismatch between workers and available jobs. Structural unemployment is an acute problem when a major employer in a community goes out of business. Many workers, particularly older workers, are unwilling or unable to learn new skills or relocate to new jobs. Many young workers, particularly those with little education, likewise face structural unemployment, in that appropriate jobs simply do not exist. The federal government has initiated many job training programs, such as the Job Training Partnership Act of 1982, in an attempt to combat structural unemployment. Unemployment insurance programs seem less effective in helping workers combat structural unemployment. Indeed, in recent years several states have disqualified participants in training programs from UI benefits, on the ground they are not currently available for work.

Another type of unemployment has been termed wait unemployment. Many unemployed workers are on temporary layoff and do not actively look for other work, preferring to wait for a recall. Such workers generally are covered by unemployment insurance, and in most states are not subject to the usual requirement that UI claimants actively search for work. We deal more fully with the effect of UI benefits on wait unemployment below.

A continual debate centers on whether unemployment insurance should attempt to combat or alleviate these various forms of unemployment. The general policy has been for unemployment insurance to be a limited response to the problem of unemployment. In the main, unemployment insurance is designed to provide temporary, partial wage replacement to experienced workers who become unemployed through no fault of their own. Teenagers who have trouble finding a first job, homemakers returning to the job market, and the long-term unemployed who have exhausted UI benefits are simply not served by unemployment insurance programs. For a justification of this limited aim of UI, consider the following article.

JOSEPH M. BECKER, THE LOCATION OF FINANCIAL RESPONSIBILITY IN UNEMPLOYMENT INSURANCE, 59 University of Detroit Journal of Urban Law 509, 541-43 (1982)[*]

To the extent that unemployment insurance in the United States is an extension of the wage system it has all the disadvantages of the wage system. It does not, for example, provide a close fit of benefits to proved individual need. The best it can do is to approximate average presumed need. Neither does it attempt to alter the worker, by retraining or relocating him, to improve his job prospects. The best it can do is maintain his income for a time while he finds a job for himself. On the other hand, unemployment insurance has all the advantages of the wage system, especially the advantage that the unemployed claim their benefits with a sense of dignity and freedom that attaches to an earned reward. President Roosevelt insisted from the beginning that the proposed system have this characteristic, and in so doing he had clearly reflected the temper of the American people.

All economic agents attempt to escape the discipline of the market. In unemployment insurance, such attempts have been made throughout its life and presumably will continue to be made. But in addition to this obvious and continuous pressure for change, two additional pressures in recent years have appeared. The pressures, which take the form of proposals to link unemployment insurance with other programs, stem from the two disadvantages of the unemployment insurance program mentioned above. One pressure comes from the side of the war on poverty. There have been many proposals to modify the provisions of unemployment insurance so as to perform some of the functions that would

[*]Reprinted with permission of the University of Detroit Journal of Urban Law.

otherwise have to be performed by welfare programs. There is also pressure from the side of the new manpower programs. The grand strategy of manpower planning calls on unemployment insurance to attempt more than merely maintaining the income of the job seeker.

In my judgment, unemployment insurance would be wise to avoid this Scylla and Charybdis — to keep its skirts clear of the welfare programs and to discourage the enthusiastic embrace of the manpower programs. That conclusion is based on two characteristics of the unemployment insurance program — its distinctive clientele and its high degree of success. The clientele of the unemployment insurance system is a uniquely significant group which should not be lumped with other groups, but should be kept in a distinct program where it can be handled according to its own specific character. The clientele of unemployment insurance consists of the core of the labor force, the regularly employed. In modern society, the regular members of the labor force are a crucial social group. Economically, the prosperity of the country depends upon how effectively this group functions. Politically, the stability of the country turns on how satisfied this group is. There is nothing that can bring down a government faster than dissatisfaction among this group.

This distinctive group differs from the clientele of the other Social Security programs by being more closely intertwined in the competitive market process. Unemployment insurance pays benefits to potential workers — rather than to widows, children, the aged, the sick, the disabled, the retired and all others normally unable to support themselves by the work they do. Where the other Social Security programs operate like Red Cross units behind the lines, unemployment insurance operates somewhat like a troop unit at the front and has implications for the general economic issues of wages, industrial discipline, productivity, unemployment, and inflation. A symbol of this market character of unemployment insurance is to be seen in the fact that unemployment insurance is not administered by the Department of Health and Human Services, as are the other Social Security programs, but is administered by the Department of Labor. Unemployment benefits are inescapably related to the competitive market.

The second characteristic of unemployment insurance is simply its success. Unemployment insurance is an immense program that has been immensely successful. Not completely successful, of course, but as public programs go it has had an admirable track record. It would be difficult to point to another public program that has a better record. Neither the welfare programs to the left of unemployment insurance nor the manpower programs to the right can compare with unemployment insurance in point of success. Granted, unemployment insurance has a simpler and easier task than have the other social programs; but that in itself is an additional reason for limiting unemployment insurance to the performance of its own proper function.

———————

As Professor Becker emphasizes, the architects of unemployment insurance programs have tried hard not to have UI considered a welfare program. Most importantly, there is no means testing for benefits: whether income from other family members is $10,000 or $100,000, job losers are equally entitled to UI benefits. As Table 17-1 shows, most UI recipients are prime-age white males. One reason individuals with these characteristics receive UI benefits disproportionately is that they are also disproportionately represented in the civilian labor force.

Table 17-1

Demographic Characteristics of Unemployed Persons and UI Recipients, Calendar Year 1994 (in percents)

| Characteristic | Distribution of | | | Percent of Unemployed Receiving UI Benefits[a] |
	Civilian Labor Force (1)	Total Unemployed (2)	UI Claimants (3)	(4)
Age				
16 to 34	43	60	38	21
35 to 54	45	32	45	47
55 and over	12	8	12	51
N.A.[b]			5	
Gender				
Men	54	55	57	35
Women	46	45	40	30
N.A.[b]			3	
Race				
White	85	74	65	30
Black/Hispanic	11	21	26	41
Other	4	5	5	32
N.A.[b]			5	

[a] Data from fourth quarter only.

[b] "N.A." indicates data not available.

Sources: Advisory Council on Unemployment Insurance, Defining Federal and State Roles in Unemployment Insurance (1996); United States Department of Labor, Unemployment Insurance Service, Division of Actuarial Services, UI Data Summary (March 1997); United States Department of Labor, Unemployment Insurance Service, Data Retrieval Request (ran Feb. 20, 1998).

Only one-third of all unemployed receive unemployment benefits, as shown by Table 17-2. The majority of unemployed workers are ineligible for UI benefits, because they did not have a job before becoming unemployed or because they voluntarily quit their job. Most job losers are eligible for UI benefits, unless they were fired for job-related misconduct or have exhausted their period of benefits. Even among job losers, only two-thirds receive benefits.

Table 17-2

Reasons for Unemployment
1996

Reason for Unemployment	No. of Workers	% of All Unemployed
New Entrants to the Labor Force (not eligible for UI)	580,000	8%
Reentrants (generally not eligible)	2,512,000	35%
Job Leavers (generally not eligible)	774,000	11%
Job Losers (generally eligible)	3,370,000	46%
Total Unemployment	7,236,000	100%
Workers Receiving UI Benefits	2,238,700	33%

Source: Data downloaded from Department of Labor Web Page.

One disturbing trend is the recent drop in the percentage of unemployed persons who receive UI benefits. As late as the 1960s nearly 43% of the unemployed claimed UI benefits. At least three trends have been identified as contributing to the sharp drop: (1) a decline in unemployment from manufacturing industries, where claimants generally are more knowledgeable about claiming benefits; (2) federal policy changes, including the taxation of UI benefits, the required offset of pension and Social Security benefits, and less generous extended benefit programs; and (3) changes in state laws and practices to tighten eligibility. *See generally* WALTER CORSON & WALTER NICHOLSON, AN EXAMINATION OF DECLINING UI CLAIMS DURING THE 1980S (1988).

a. UI and Job Search Behavior

Many studies have shown that unemployment insurance actually increases unemployment. An unemployed worker receiving UI benefits has an income cushion that reduces the urgency of finding another job. This rise in unemployment is not necessarily a loss for society. By allowing workers to prolong their job search, UI benefits enable workers to reject poor jobs and wait for a better job match that increases their productivity. One study of this tradeoff, using late 1960s census survey data of older men who were laid off and changed employers, concluded that raising the UI benefit rate from 40% to 50% of income would prolong unemployment by 1.5 weeks, but would increase post-unemployment wages by 7%. Ronald G. Ehrenberg & Ronald L. Oaxaca, *Unemployment Insurance, Duration of Unemployment, and Subsequent Wage Gain,* 66 AM.

ECON. REV. 754 (1976). This job search effect did not apply for men who returned to their previous employer or who quit voluntarily. Older women responded similarly but less dramatically to increases in UI benefits. Younger workers increased the length of unemployment slightly when UI benefits were increased, but did not receive higher post-unemployment wages as a result.

Spillover effects influence the job search even of workers ineligible for UI. Estimates suggest that, because covered workers stay unemployed longer than they otherwise would, uncovered job seekers (typically new entrants and re-entrants to the labor force) find work faster than they would in an economy without unemployment insurance.

b. Experience Rating and Employer Layoff Behavior

An important feature of unemployment insurance is its imperfect experience rating. The system tries to force individual employers to recognize the costs to the system of terminating a worker by increasing the tax rate of those employers whose employees frequently receive UI benefits. But the experience rating is imperfect, meaning that an employer's tax payments do not go up by the full amount of the benefits its terminated employees receive. The following excerpt sketches the methods of experience rating, and explains why it is imperfect.

ADVISORY COUNCIL ON UNEMPLOYMENT COMPENSATION, UNEMPLOYMENT INSURANCE IN THE UNITED STATES 73-82 (1995)

The fundamental method of financing the U.S. system of Unemployment Insurance has been a contentious issue since the system was established. During the debates in the 1930s that shaped the basic structure of the system, some argued that it should be funded through an "experience-rated" tax that imposes the highest tax rates on employers that generate the most cost to the system. Others argued that the system should be financed by a flat tax on employers.

Proponents of experience rating eventually prevailed. They argued that experience rating had the following three fundamental advantages, which are still offered today as reasons for its continuance: (1) the encouragement of stable employment, (2) the attribution of the costs of unemployment insurance benefits to the employer responsible for the unemployment, and (3) the creation of an incentive for employers to participate actively in policing the UI program.

Despite these apparent advantages, the United States is the only nation that chooses to finance its UI system through an experience-rated tax. As a result, experience rating has come under close scrutiny and has been the subject of on-going debate. To some, experience rating is the root problem with the UI system, in that its strict allocation of costs tends to limit benefits as employers seek to minimize their costs. To others, experience rating is an essential component in making unemployment benefits one of the costs of doing business.

....

SYSTEMS OF EXPERIENCE RATING

Over the years, states' experience rating provisions have become increasingly varied and complex. Although these systems vary substantially in many ways, the incentives that they create are generally similar. Under each of these methods, employers are ranked annually against one another and are assigned a specific tax rate based on that ranking, with employers who generate more costs to the system assigned a higher rate.

In all states, employers pay an assigned UI tax rate on the amount of their taxable wages, which are those annual wages for each employee that fall below a prescribed base level. The actual ranges of employer tax rates ... vary substantially from state to state. In the 1993 tax year, the states' minimum tax rate varied from 0 percent (in 7 states) to a high of 2.5 percent in New York. The maximum tax rate on taxable wages varied from 5.4 percent (in 13 states) to a high of 10.5 percent in Pennsylvania. As a result of the range in tax rates and taxable wage bases, taxes paid range from zero for some employers to more than $900 per worker for other employers. Within a state, the entire schedule of tax rates is often adjusted up or down, depending on the balance in the state trust fund.

In general, the states' current systems of experience rating can be classified in one of four categories: reserve ratio, benefit ratio, benefit-wage ratio, and payroll decline....

Reserve Ratio

The reserve ratio formula, which is used by 33 states, is the most common method of experience rating. An account is established for each employer; contributions are credit to the account and benefits paid to former employees are charged against the account. The balance is carried over from year to year for the duration of the employer's activity.

The reserve ratio is defined as the account's balance relative to the employer's annual taxable payroll. The higher an employer's reserve ratio, the lower the assigned tax rate. Conversely, the lower an employer's reserve ratio (which can be negative), the higher the assigned tax rate.

Benefit Ratio

The benefit ratio formula is used by 17 states to experience rate UI benefits. Under this formula, firms pay taxes in proportion to the ratio of *benefits* paid relative to taxable wages, without directly taking contributions into account. Because this ratio uses only the most recent 3 years of data to assign tax rates, the benefit ratio formula is more short term in its focus than is the reserve ratio formula, which incorporates the entire life span of an employer's account. [The benefit-wage ratio formula is now used by only two states — Oklahoma and Delaware. The payroll decline method is now used only by Alaska.]

FACTORS AFFECTING THE DEGREE OF EXPERIENCE RATING

The degree to which an experience rating system succeeds in assigning UI benefit costs to the employer who generates an individual cost depends on the details of the system. If a number of provisions allow assignable UI costs to be paid for by entities other than the responsible employer, then the degree of overall experience rating in the system declines....

Noncharged Benefits

All states provide that, in some circumstances, certain benefits paid are not charged to the account of an individual employer, but instead are shared among all UI taxpayers. The purpose of adopting a noncharging provision is often to reduce employer opposition to a particular kind of benefit. Common forms of noncharged benefits include these: (1) payments to workers who quit their last job, (2) dependents' benefits, (3) payments to workers who are enrolled in approved training, (4) erroneous benefit payments that are not recovered, and (5) the state share of the Extended Benefits program. Differences among the states in the use of noncharged benefits are substantial, ranging in 1993 from 1 percent in the District of Columbia to 32 percent in Washington.

Ineffectively Charged Benefits

Ineffectively charged benefits develop when an individual employer's tax rate is too low to cover the benefits paid to that employer's former employees, which happens when employers are at a state's maximum tax rate. Under these circumstances, benefits charged against the employer neither draw on accumulated past taxes nor trigger additional current taxes. Such ineffective charges become a drain to the system which must be made up in some way through taxes paid by other employers.

During 1993, average ineffective charges in the United States ranged from less than 1 percent in Montana to 39 percent in Oklahoma. As expected, the average maximum tax rate was higher in states with fewer ineffective charges. Among the 10 states with the lowest ineffective charges, the average maximum tax rate was 6.7 percent. The 10 states with the highest ineffective charges had an average maximum tax rate of 6.0 percent.

At the end of each fiscal year, several states also automatically reduce the size of an employer's negative balance to a maximum percentage of the employer's payroll. As a result, employers at those states' maximum tax rates routinely benefit from outright tax forgiveness. In those states, employers with large negative balances are never required to make tax payments on those balances, and their costs are shifted permanently to other employers.

716	CH. 17: UNEMPLOYMENT AND UNEMPLOYMENT INSURANCE

Inactive Charges

Inactive charges result when an employer goes out of business and, therefore, stops paying payroll taxes. Benefits collected by former employees result in inactive charges, which also reduce the degree of experience rating in the system.

Changes in the State Taxable Wage Base

Some states change the level of their taxable wage bases relatively frequently. The impact of such changes on the degree of experience rating is complex [but often can result in less perfect experience rating]....

It is by changing the *distribution* of employer tax rates across the tax schedule in a state, that a change in the taxable wage base most directly affects the degree of experience rating in a state. This distribution varies greatly across states. Raising the taxable wage base *reduces* the degree of experience rating to the extent that it moves more employers down to the minimum tax rate. Raising the taxable wage base *increases* the degree of experience rating for employers who were at the maximum tax rate prior to the increase, but below the maximum rate after the increase. (The reason for this is that these employers then have to contribute a higher percentage toward costs attributed to them.) Without detailed information on the distribution of employers at the minimum and maximum tax rates on a state-by-state basis, therefore, it is difficult to determine in advance the overall extent to which an increase in the taxable wage base would raise or lower the overall degree of experience rating.

Benefit Charging for Multiple Employers

States differ as to how they charge benefits to employers' accounts when there are multiple employers. Only nine states charge the most recent or principal employer exclusively. This is a particularly effective mechanism for preserving the degree to which the funding of the system is experience-rated.

To illustrate the influence of UI on the employer's decision to lay off workers, consider the examples outlined in Table 17-3.

Table 17-3

Firm A — Constant Wage/Employment Strategy

Per Worker amounts	Quarter 1	Quarter 2	Quarter 3	Quarter 4	Total
(1) Quarterly Gross Profit (all costs but wages)	$180	$20	$20	$180	$400
(2) Wages	$100	$100	$100	$100	$400
(3) Net Profit	+ $80	- $80	- $80	+ $80	$0

Firm B — Layoff Strategy Using UI Benefits

(1) Quarterly Gross Profit (all costs but wages)	$180	$0 (on layoff)	$0 (on layoff)	$180	$360
(2) Wages	$140	0 (on layoff)	0 (on layoff)	$140	$280
(3) UI Benefits	$0 (at work)	$70	$70	$0 (at work)	$140
(4) Extra UI Costs	$0	$20	$20	$0	$40
(5) Net Profit	+ $40	- $20	- $20	+ $40	$40

Both firms face the same fluctuating revenues and fixed costs. Firm A responds with a constant wage and employment strategy, smoothing the income pattern for its workers. (Another strategy would be to maintain employment but alternate wages from $180 to $20 depending on revenues, but workers probably prefer a steadier stream.)

Firm B adopts a high wage, temporary layoff strategy. Firm B workers receive high wages of $140 when working, but are laid off when demand for the product declines. When laid off, workers receive UI benefits of $70 (half their wage) for two quarters. Because of imperfect experience rating, however, the costs to the firm of temporarily laying off workers is only $20. In effect, other firms and their workers are subsidizing Firm B and its workers $50 for each period of lay-off. The firm can share this subsidy with its workers, making Firm B and its workers better off than Firm A and its workers. Overall, society loses from Firm B's strategy because it loses the $20 per worker extra output when workers are laid off.

Considerable empirical evidence confirms that the UI system causes about one-half of all temporary layoff unemployment. Temporary layoffs, in turn, comprise about half of all the persons classified as unemployed job losers. The use of temporary layoffs in manufacturing is even higher, with about 75% of those laid off returning to their original employers. *See* Martin Feldstein, *The Effect of Unemployment Insurance on Temporary Layoff Unemployment,* 68 AM. ECON. REV. 834 (1978). The challenge for the system is to discourage excessive use of temporary layoffs while fulfilling worthwhile goals of income support and job search.

Until 1987, UI benefits were not fully taxable income, which increased the incentive for employers to adopt a high wage, temporary layoff policy. Using the example of Table 17-3, Firm A workers would have $400 of total income, all taxable, while Firm B workers would have $420 of total income, but only $280 would be fully taxable. In an influential article, Martin Feldstein pointed out the perverse incentives this had on unemployment. Feldstein, *Unemployment Compensation: Adverse Incentives and Distributional Anomalies,* 27 NAT'L TAX J. 231 (1974). In response, Congress phased out the tax-exempt status of UI benefits. Since 1987, the federal government has taxed all unemployment benefits as ordinary income. Many states also subject UI benefits to state taxes.

Imperfect experience rating creates distortions between industries as well. Industries with stable employment pay far more into the system than they take out. For example, in the construction industry, where layoffs are common, workers receive $1.66 in UI benefits for every $1 construction employers pay in UI taxes. On the other hand, workers in finance, insurance, and real estate receive only 40 cents for every $1 paid in taxes by employers. Manufacturing employees receive slightly more ($1.07) for every dollar their employers contribute to the system. Donald R. Deere, *Unemployment Insurance and Employment,* 9 J. LAB. ECON. 307 (1991).

3. WORK SEARCH REQUIREMENTS

All states require that UI claimants actively search for work and accept suitable employment when found. A classic statement of the requirement comes from *Fly v. Industrial Commission,* 359 S.W.2d 481 (Mo. Ct. App. 1962):

> Claimant is not entitled to draw pay because she lost her job. The compensation is payable because she can't get another one. She must really and sincerely look for the job, not wait for the job to seek her out. Nor will a lackadaisical, half-hearted, or occasional effort suffice.

States differ in how they scrutinize the job search of claimants. Many states have customized search requirements, whereby agency staff assess the claimant's occupation and local labor-market conditions and assign the claimant a specific number of employer contacts to make (usually between zero and five per week). Often, claimants must come to the unemployment office weekly or biweekly to receive their benefits check, and at the same time fill out a form listing employers they have contacted and other steps taken to find a job. Whether such scrutiny is effective is questionable. One study showed that, out of every 10,000 claims for UI benefits, only two were denied for refusing suitable work.

The job search issue is most difficult for workers on layoff who hope to return to their employer. Unemployed workers with a definite recall date generally are eligible for UI benefits without actively searching for another job. Major problems arise when the recall is more speculative, as the following case illustrates.

KNOX v. UNEMPLOYMENT COMPENSATION BOARD OF REVIEW

Commonwealth Court of Pennsylvania
315 A.2d 915 (1974)

KRAMER, JUDGE.

This is an appeal by William J. Knox, Jr. (Knox) from an order of the Unemployment Compensation Board of Review (Board) which affirmed the referee's denial of benefits to Knox.

Knox had been employed by H. K. Porter Company (Porter) for 17 years when he was laid off due to the permanent closing of the plant in which he worked. Knox applied for and received unemployment compensation for approximately two and one-half months. His unemployment compensation was terminated after the following incident. Knox was given a job referral by the local office of the Bureau of Employment Security. The job referral was for a position similar to his former employment with Porter and paid approximately the same wage. Knox accepted the referral and reported to the personnel office of the prospective employer for an interview. During the interview, Knox mentioned that he might be recalled by the successor to Porter's plant and that he would return to work there if recalled. As a result, he was not hired.

Section 402(a) of the Unemployment Compensation Law is the applicable controlling statutory provision. It reads:

> An employe shall be ineligible for compensation for any week — (a) in which his unemployment is due to failure, *without good cause,* either to apply for suitable work at such time and in such manner as the department may prescribe, or to accept suitable work when offered to him by the employment office or by any employer, irrespective of whether or not such work is in 'employment' as defined in this act: Provided, That such employer notifies the employment office of such offer within three (3) days after the making thereof. (Emphasis added.)

The words "good cause" found in Section 402(a) have been interpreted to be synonymous with "good faith." In his brief, Knox concedes that conduct which discourages a prospective employer from employing a claimant evidences a lack of good faith and constitutes proper grounds for denying benefits under Section 402(a). He urges, however, that such conduct must indicate that the claimant would be irresponsible, lackadaisical or unreliable, whereas he merely was being honest. While we sympathize with Knox, we cannot agree.

In *Paisley v. Commonwealth of Pennsylvania, Unemployment Compensation Board of Review,* 315 A.2d 908, 908-909 (Pa. Commw. Ct. 1974), we stated:

> The law on this matter is clear that a claimant cannot attach such conditions to his acceptance of work as to render himself unavailable for suitable work. "A claimant is required at all times to be ready, able, and willing to accept suitable employment, temporary or full time.... But one may render himself unavailable for work by conditions and limitations as to employment. Willingness to be employed conditionally does not necessarily meet the test of availability. The determination of availability is largely a question of fact for the Board." *Pinto Unemployment Compensation Case,* 79 A.2d 802, 803 (Pa. Super. Ct. 1951). The statement by a claimant to a prospective employer that he expects to be recalled to his former job at an indefinite time in the future and that he intends to return when recalled limits the claimant's availability for work so as to render him ineligible for benefits....

Knox's desire to protect his 17 years of seniority is understandable, but, nonetheless, he presented the prospective employer with an unacceptable condition of employment.

Our scope of review in unemployment cases is limited, absent fraud, to questions of law and whether or not the findings of the Board are supported by the evidence. The Board's findings in this case are supported by the evidence and we find no error of law. Therefore, ... the order of the Unemployment Compensation Board of Review denying benefits to William J. Knox, Jr., is hereby affirmed.

NOTES

1. *Lying in Good Faith.* Knox went through the hoops of a job search, but honestly told prospective employers that he planned to return to his former employer if recalled. This statement obviously makes him less desirable to other employers: why should they incur the time and expense of hiring someone who is likely to leave soon? The court declares that such statements, even if honest, indicate a lack of good faith. To meet the good faith job search standard, must Knox lie during job interviews?

2. *UI Benefits and Temporary Layoffs.* From the claimant's perspective, denying benefits because he wants to preserve his seventeen years' job seniority at his former job seems harsh. But is this tight standard justifiable to discourage employers from excessive use of temporary layoffs?

3. *Definite Recall Dates.* UI claimants with a definite recall date usually are not required to search for other work. In Michigan, for example, an unemployed person can receive UI benefits without seeking work if the employer promptly "notifies the commission in writing that ... work is expected to be available for the individual within a declared number of days, not to exceed 45 calendar days following the last day the individual worked." If the employer does not notify the commission, the seeking-work requirement can nevertheless be waived "if an individual is on a short-term layoff with a definite return to work date which is not later than 15 consecutive calendar days beginning with the first day of scheduled unemployment resulting from the layoff." Rule 216(3) of the Michigan Employment Security Act.

4. *Work Search Rules.* A telephone survey of some 2,500 former UI claimants in ten states attempted to see whether UI recipients looked harder for work in states with stricter work-search rules:

> Our analysis of the effects of work-search rules on the work-search behavior of claimants tends to provide the expected pattern of results. Claimants from states whose work-search rules are strict are generally more likely to search for work, devote more hours to work search, and contact more employers than is true of claimants from moderately strict and lenient states. Conversely, claimants from states whose work-search rules are lenient are the least likely to search, devote the fewest hours to work search, and contact the fewest number of employers. Thus, it would appear that differences in the work-search rules, or perhaps the overall work-search policy or climate, of states do influence the work-search behavior of claimants.
>
> An unexpected pattern of results emerges when we divide the sample into those claimants who expected to be recalled to their former jobs and those who did not. The results for the latter group of claimants, who are typically the primary job searchers, do not consistently show the expected relationship between the strictness of work-search rules and work-search behavior. Instead, the pattern found for the entire sample appears to be due to the effects of work-search rules on the behavior of claimants who regard themselves as job-attached. It may be that claimants who are not job-attached are sufficiently self-motivated to search fairly rigorously regardless of state rules, but those who expect to be recalled are likely to fail to search rigorously unless they are compelled to do so by state rules....
>
> The analysis of the effects of work-search rules on the job-finding success of claimants produces the unexpected result that claimants from states whose work-search rules are the strictest are less successful at leaving the UI rolls and becoming reemployed. In addition, once they become reemployed, claimants from states whose work-search rules are strict are less likely to work full time, less likely to work for their former employers, and more likely to earn less than claimants from states whose rules are moderate or lenient.
>
> These results appear to stem from the more serious labor-market problems found in the sample states whose work-search rules are strict. We could not control completely for these economic differences, and it seems that the

effects of economic conditions on job-finding success dominate the effects of work-search rules.

WALTER CORSON, STUART KERACHSKY & ELLEN E. KISKER, WORK SEARCH AMONG UNEMPLOYMENT INSURANCE CLAIMANTS: AN INVESTIGATION OF SOME EFFECTS OF STATE RULES AND ENFORCEMENT 164-66 (1987).

5. *Available for Work Requirement.* Suppose the claimant has difficulty searching for work because of problems finding a reliable babysitter. Should she be considered unavailable for work and therefore denied unemployment benefits? *See In re Paula Williams,* 574 N.Y.S.2d 416 (N.Y. App. Div. 1991) (yes).

C. DISQUALIFICATIONS FROM UI BENEFITS

The general premise of unemployment insurance is that workers who lose their jobs through no fault of their own should receive governmental assistance to tide them over while looking for a new job. The corollary is that workers who voluntarily quit their jobs without good cause, or who were terminated for willful misconduct, are generally disqualified from benefits.

Disqualified is a term of art in unemployment insurance. In many states, a disqualified worker receives no benefits for the entire spell of unemployment. The Department of Labor, however, urges states to disqualify workers only for the length of time the average worker in an ordinary labor market needs to find suitable work, which is generally about six weeks. Unemployment spells longer than this average are thought to be due to market forces beyond the worker's control, rather than due to the disqualifying act. Many states have followed this recommendation and grant reduced or postponed benefits to workers who voluntarily quit or are fired for misconduct.

Determining whether a worker should be disqualified for UI benefits raises many of the same issues prominent in wrongful discharge or discrimination lawsuits. Indeed, a UI hearing is the prime forum where low-status, low-paid workers bring such claims. These workers are unlikely to hire a lawyer and file a lawsuit over the employer's action, because monetary damages are likely to be modest. But such workers do want UI benefits while they search for another job, and often represent themselves in appealing a denial of benefits. In New York, for example, lawyers can only charge $500 to represent a UI claimant, and the agency must approve in advance the amount charged. The following cases illustrate the range of issues that can arise:

(1) *Harassment Based on Sexual Orientation*: A hair stylist quit his job after being harassed by the owner of the salon because he was gay. Should this be a voluntary quit, disqualifying him from UI benefits? *See Hanke v. Safari Hair Adventure,* 512 N.W.2d 614 (Minn. Ct. App. 1994) (reversing denial of benefits).

(2) *Public Safety/Internal Whistleblower*: A hospital hired a hystotechnician to prepare tissue samples for microscopic analysis by pathologists. She refused to perform gross-cutting on tissue from live patients because she feared her limited

training would impair the accuracy of the diagnosis, which in turn would risk the patient's life or health. Eventually the hospital fired her for incompetence and insubordination. Should she receive UI benefits because her termination was due to her sincere (but perhaps misguided) concern for public safety? *See Amador v. Unemployment Ins. Appeals Bd.*, 677 P.2d 224 (Cal. 1984) (reversing denial of benefits).

(3) *Drug Testing*: An engineering company employee doing work for a nuclear power plant was fired for refusing to submit to a random drug test. Should he receive UI benefits, perhaps on a privacy rationale? *See Moore v. Unemployment Comp. Bd. of Review*, 578 A.2d 606 (Pa. Commw. Ct. 1990) (upholding denial of benefits). *But see Glide Lumber Prods. Co. v. Employment Div.*, 741 P.2d 907 (Or. Ct. App. 1987) (refusing drug test is not disqualifying misconduct for UI purposes). *See also Grace Drilling Co. v. Novotny*, 811 P.2d 907 (Okla. Ct. App. 1991) (off-duty marijuana use resulting in positive drug test in violation of employer's rule was not misconduct to disqualify employee from receiving unemployment compensation).

(4) *Free Speech Toward Employer*: A machinist and union shop steward was fired when he threatened to publish a newsletter criticizing management policies and calling the corporation "brain dead." Should he receive UI benefits? *See Meehan v. Lull Corp.*, 466 N.W.2d 14 (Minn. Ct. App. 1991) (reversing denial of UI benefits because mere statement of intended misconduct is not disqualifying "willful or wanton" conduct).

(5) *Free Speech Toward Co-Worker*: An employee was fired for uttering anti-Semitic epithets at a Jewish co-worker. Should he receive UI benefits? *See Opara v. Carnegie Textile Co.*, 498 N.E.2d 485 (Ohio Ct. App. 1985) (no; employer justified in discharge).

(6) *Smoking on the Job*: A sixty-five-year-old life-long smoker quit her job when the employer changed its policy to permit smoking only outside the building. Should she receive UI benefits? *See Quinn, Gent, Buseck & Leemhuis v. Unemployment Comp. Bd.*, 606 A.2d 1300 (Pa. Commw. Ct. 1992) (reversing an award of benefits because employee could have quit smoking or gone outside to smoke).

(7) *Honesty Testing*: An employee was fired after refusing to take the Reid psychiatric profile pertaining to employee honesty. Is he eligible for UI benefits? *See Heins v. Commonwealth*, 534 A.2d 592 (Pa. Commw. Ct. 1987) (upholding denial of benefits because employer's request to take test was reasonable).

(8) *Off-Work Conduct*: A male biology teacher at a Catholic school was fired for living with a divorced woman. Should he be eligible for UI benefits? *See Bishop Carroll High Sch. v. Unemployment Comp. Bd. of Review*, 557 A.2d 1141 (Pa. Commw. Ct. 1989) (by 4-3 vote, court reversed award of UI benefits).

(9) *Drinking Off the Job*: A worker accepts employment with a firm that has a rule prohibiting employees from using tobacco, alcohol, or drugs at any time, on or off work. The employee is fired after confessing that he several times con-

sumed alcohol off work. Should he receive UI benefits? *See Best Lock Corp. v. Review Bd.,* 572 N.E.2d 520 (Ind. Ct. App. 1991) (affirming award of benefits because employer had failed to prove its rule was reasonable).

NOTE

UI Benefits and Wrongful Discharge Damages. The general rule of damages in a wrongful discharge suit is that the plaintiff must mitigate losses by seeking employment. Wages actually earned, and wages that could have been earned with reasonable diligence, are deducted from any award. Income from collateral sources, such as UI benefits, however, is not deducted from the award. *See generally* HOWARD A. SPECTER & MATTHEW W. FINKIN, INDIVIDUAL EMPLOYMENT LAW AND LITIGATION § 15.08, at 310 (1989).

———————

As the cases above indicate, UI disqualification issues arise in a variety of contexts. In the following cases, we focus on how women are treated by the UI system.

1. VOLUNTARY QUITS

WIMBERLY v. LABOR & INDUSTRIAL RELATIONS COMMISSION

United States Supreme Court
479 U.S. 511 (1987)

JUSTICE O'CONNOR delivered the opinion of the Court.

The Missouri Supreme Court concluded that the Federal Unemployment Tax Act, 26 U.S.C. § 3304(a)(12), does not prohibit a State from disqualifying unemployment compensation claimants who leave their jobs because of pregnancy, when the State imposes the same disqualification on all claimants who leave their jobs for a reason not causally connected to their work or their employer. We granted certiorari because the court's decision conflicts with that of the Court of Appeals for the Fourth Circuit in *Brown v. Porcher,* 660 F.2d 1001 (1981), *cert. denied,* 459 U.S. 1150 (1983), on a question of practical significance in the administration of state unemployment compensation laws.

I

In August 1980, after having been employed by the J.C. Penney Company for approximately three years, petitioner requested a leave of absence on account of her pregnancy. Pursuant to its established policy, the J.C. Penney Company granted petitioner a "leave without guarantee of reinstatement," meaning that petitioner would be rehired only if a position was available when petitioner was ready to return to work. Petitioner's child was born on November 5, 1980. On

December 1, 1980, when petitioner notified J.C. Penney that she wished to return to work, she was told that there were no positions open.

Petitioner then filed a claim for unemployment benefits. The claim was denied by the Division of Employment Security (Division) pursuant to Mo. Rev. Stat. § 288.050.1(1) (Supp. 1984), which disqualifies a claimant who "has left his work voluntarily without good cause attributable to his work or to his employer." A deputy for the Division determined that petitioner had "quit because of pregnancy," and therefore had left work "voluntarily and without good cause attributable to [her] work or to [her] employer." Petitioner appealed the decision to the Division's appeals tribunal, which, after a full evidentiary hearing, entered findings of fact and conclusions of law affirming the deputy's decision. The Labor and Industrial Relations Commission denied petitioner's petition for review.

Petitioner then sought review in the Circuit Court of Jackson County, Missouri. The court concluded that § 288.050.1(1) was inconsistent with 26 U.S.C. § 3304(a)(12) as construed in *Brown v. Porcher, supra,* and therefore could not be enforced. Following *Brown,* the Circuit Court held that § 3304(a)(12) "banned the use of pregnancy or its termination as an excuse for denying benefits to otherwise eligible women," and accordingly reversed the Commission's decision and remanded for entry of an award. The Missouri Court of Appeals affirmed. Although the Court of Appeals expressed "reservations concerning the soundness of the ruling in *Brown,*" it felt constrained to follow the Fourth Circuit's construction of § 3304(a)(12).

The Missouri Supreme Court reversed, with three judges dissenting. The court held that previous state appellate decisions had correctly interpreted Mo. Rev. Stat. § 288.050.1(1) (Supp. 1984) as disqualifying all claimants who, like petitioner, leave work "for reasons that, while perhaps legitimate and necessary from a personal standpoint, were not causally connected to the claimant's work or employer." 688 S.W.2d, at 346. Rejecting the notion that it was bound by *Brown v. Porcher, supra,* the court determined that § 288.050.1(1) was consistent with the federal statute. The court held that the plain language of § 3304(a)(12) only prohibits state laws from singling out pregnancy for unfavorable treatment. The Missouri scheme does not conflict with this requirement, the court found, because the state law does not expressly refer to pregnancy; rather, benefits are denied only when claimants leave work for reasons not attributable to the employer or connected with the work. The court noted that the Department of Labor, the agency charged with enforcing the statute, consistently has viewed § 3304(a)(12) as prohibiting discrimination rather than mandating preferential treatment. We now affirm.

II

The Federal Unemployment Tax Act (Act), 26 U.S.C. § 3301 et seq., envisions a cooperative federal-state program of benefits to unemployed workers. The Act establishes certain minimum federal standards that a State must satisfy in order for a State to participate in the program. *See* 26 U.S.C. § 3304(a). The standard at issue in this case, § 3304(a)(12), mandates that "no person shall be denied compensation under such State law solely on the basis of pregnancy or termination of pregnancy."

Apart from the minimum standards reflected in § 3304(a), the Act leaves to state discretion the rules governing the administration of unemployment compensation programs. State programs, therefore, vary in their treatment of the distribution of unemployment benefits, although all require a claimant to satisfy some version of a three-part test. First, all States require claimants to earn a specified amount of wages or to work a specified number of weeks in covered employment during a 1-year base period in order to be entitled to receive benefits. Second, all States require claimants to be "eligible" for benefits, that is, they must be able to work and available for work. Third, claimants who satisfy these requirements may be "disqualified" for reasons set forth in state law. The most common reasons for disqualification under state unemployment compensation laws are voluntarily leaving the job without good cause, being discharged for misconduct, and refusing suitable work. *See* Note, *Denial of Unemployment Benefits to Otherwise Eligible Women on the Basis of Pregnancy: Section 3304(a)(12) of the Federal Unemployment Tax Act,* 82 Mich. L. Rev. 1925, 1928-1929 (1984).

The treatment of pregnancy-related terminations is a matter of considerable disparity among the States. Most States regard leave on account of pregnancy as a voluntary termination for good cause. Some of these States have specific statutory provisions enumerating pregnancy-motivated termination as good cause for leaving a job, while others, by judicial or administrative decision, treat pregnancy as encompassed within larger categories of good cause such as illness or compelling personal reasons. A few States, however, like Missouri, have chosen to define "leaving for good cause" narrowly. In these States, all persons who leave their jobs are disqualified from receiving benefits unless they leave for reasons directly attributable to the work or to the employer.

Petitioner does not dispute that the Missouri scheme treats pregnant women the same as all other persons who leave for reasons not causally connected to their work or their employer, including those suffering from other types of temporary disabilities. She contends, however, that § 3304(a)(12) is not simply an antidiscrimination statute, but rather that it mandates preferential treatment for women who leave work because of pregnancy. According to petitioner, § 3304(a)(12) affirmatively requires States to provide unemployment benefits to women who leave work because of pregnancy when they are next available and able to work, regardless of the State's treatment of other similarly situated claimants.

Contrary to petitioner's assertions, the plain import of the language of § 3304(a)(12) is that Congress intended only to prohibit States from singling out pregnancy for unfavorable treatment. The text of the statute provides that compensation shall not be denied under state law "solely on the basis of pregnancy." The focus of this language is on the basis for the State's decision, not the claimant's reason for leaving her job. Thus, a State could not decide to deny benefits to pregnant women while at the same time allowing benefits to persons who are in other respects similarly situated: the "sole basis" for such a decision would be on account of pregnancy. On the other hand, if a State adopts a neutral rule that incidentally disqualifies pregnant or formerly pregnant claimants as part of a larger group, the neutral application of that rule cannot readily be characterized as a decision made "solely on the basis of pregnancy." For example, under Missouri law, all persons who leave work for reasons not causally connected to the work or the employer are disqualified from receiving benefits. To apply this law, it is not necessary to know that petitioner left because of pregnancy: all that is relevant is that she stopped work for a reason bearing no causal connection to her work or her employer. Because the State's decision could have been made without ever knowing that petitioner had been pregnant, pregnancy was not the "sole basis" for the decision under a natural reading of § 3304(a)(12)'s language.

We have, on other occasions, construed language similar to that in § 3304(a)(12) as prohibiting disadvantageous treatment, rather than as mandating preferential treatment. In *Monroe v. Standard Oil Co.,* 452 U.S. 549 (1981), for example, the Court considered 38 U.S.C. § 2021(b)(3), a provision of the Vietnam Era Veterans' Readjustment Assistance Act of 1974, which provides that a person "shall not be denied retention in employment ... because of any obligation" as a member of the Nation's Reserve Forces. The *Monroe* Court concluded that the intent of the provision was to afford reservists "the same treatment afforded their co-workers without military obligations," 452 U.S., at 560; it did not create an "employer responsibility to provide preferential treatment." *Id.,* at 562. Similarly, in *Southeastern Community College v. Davis,* 442 U.S. 397 (1979), we considered § 504 of the Rehabilitation Act of 1973, 29 U.S.C. § 794, which provides that an "otherwise qualified handicapped individual" shall not be excluded from a federally funded program "solely by reason of his handicap." We concluded that the statutory language was only intended to "eliminate discrimination against otherwise qualified individuals," and generally did not mandate "affirmative efforts to overcome the disabilities caused by handicaps." 442 U.S., at 410.

Even petitioner concedes that § 3304(a)(12) does not prohibit States from denying benefits to pregnant or formerly pregnant women who fail to satisfy neutral eligibility requirements such as ability to work and availability for work. Nevertheless, she contends that the statute prohibits the application to pregnant women of neutral *disqualification* provisions. But the statute's plain language will not support the distinction petitioner attempts to draw. The statute does not extend only to disqualification rules. It applies, by its own terms, to any decision to deny compensation. In both instances, the scope of the statutory mandate is the same: the State cannot single out pregnancy for disadvantageous treatment, but it is not compelled to afford preferential treatment.

The legislative history cited by petitioner does not support her view that § 3304(a)(12) mandates preferential treatment for women on account of pregnancy.

[The Court then examines wording changes in the drafting process and discussions in the House Report of various state statutes.]

The Senate Report also focuses exclusively on state rules that single out pregnant women for disadvantageous treatment. In *Turner v. Department of Employment Security,* [423 U.S. 44 (1975)], this Court struck down on due process grounds a Utah statute providing that a woman was disqualified for 12 weeks before the expected date of childbirth and for 6 weeks after childbirth, even if she left work for reasons unrelated to pregnancy. The Senate Report used the provision at issue in *Turner* as representative of the kind of rule that § 3304(a)(12) was intended to prohibit:

> "In a number of States, an individual whose unemployment is related to pregnancy is barred from receiving any unemployment benefits. In 1975 the Supreme Court found a *provision of this type* in the Utah unemployment compensation statute to be unconstitutional.... A number of other States have similar provisions although most appear to involve somewhat shorter periods of disqualification." S. Rep. No. 94-1265, at 19, 21 (emphasis added).

In short, petitioner can point to nothing in the Committee Reports, or elsewhere in the statute's legislative history, that evidences congressional intent to mandate preferential treatment for women on account of pregnancy. There is no hint that Congress disapproved of, much less intended to prohibit, a neutral rule such as Missouri's. Indeed, the legislative history shows that Congress was focused only on the issue addressed by the plain language of § 3304(a)(12): prohibiting rules that single out pregnant women or formerly pregnant women for disadvantageous treatment....

Because § 3304(a)(12) does not require States to afford preferential treatment to women on account of pregnancy, the judgment of the Missouri Supreme Court is affirmed.

It is so ordered.

JUSTICE BLACKMUN took no part in the decision of this case.

NOTE

Family and Medical Leave Act. The Family and Medical Leave Act of 1993, passed after this case was decided, now gives workers like Wimberly the right to take twelve weeks unpaid leave because of pregnancy and childbirth. The FMLA would not have helped Wimberly, however, because she took more than twelve weeks leave.

MacGREGOR v. UNEMPLOYMENT INSURANCE APPEALS BOARD

Supreme Court of California
689 P.2d 453 (1984)

REYNOSO, JUSTICE.

When a worker leaves her employment to accompany her "nonmarital partner" to another state in order to maintain the familial relationship they have established with their child does she voluntarily leave work with good cause within the meaning of the statute governing eligibility for unemployment insurance benefits? We left open the possibility that a claimant might show good cause in such circumstances when we decided *Norman v. Unemployment Insurance Appeals Board,* 663 P.2d 904 (Cal. 1983) less than two years ago. We now hold that Patricia MacGregor has established that her quitting was motivated by the need to preserve the family she had established with her nonmarital partner and their child, and that this need constituted good cause for her voluntary departure from work. We therefore affirm the judgment of the Santa Clara County Superior Court ordering the Unemployment Insurance Appeals Board to reconsider its decision and to award benefits to plaintiff if she meets other eligibility requirements.

Plaintiff Patricia MacGregor worked as a waitress at the Ramada Inn in Santa Clara, California from July 7, 1978, through December 31, 1979. On January 1, 1980, she began a six-month pregnancy leave of absence. According to the terms of her leave, she was to return to work in June of 1980.

MacGregor was engaged to and lived with Dick Bailey, the father of her expected child. Their daughter Leanna was born February 29, 1980. The three continued to live together as a family. Bailey acknowledged that he was Leanna's father.

In April, Bailey decided the family should move to New York to live with and care for his 76-year-old father. At the time, his father was under medical care for a variety of serious ailments and anticipated surgery later that summer. Because of his ill health he no longer wished to live alone. No relatives lived nearby and Bailey was the only child. Bailey's father asked if Bailey, MacGregor and their daughter would come to live with and care for him. In May MacGregor informed her employer that she would not be returning to work.

MacGregor, Bailey and their daughter moved into Bailey's father's home in June. When MacGregor was unable to find work, she applied for unemployment insurance benefits. Her claim was referred to the California Employment Development Department (Department), which determined that she had quit voluntarily without good cause and was thus ineligible for benefits. (Unemp. Ins. Code, § 1256.)

MacGregor appealed this decision. A hearing was conducted before a referee in Massena, New York. The transcript was referred to the Department where it was considered by an administrative law judge. The judge determined MacGrègor had left her most recent work voluntarily without good cause and was thus disqualified from receiving benefits. Although the judge found evidence in the record indicating that Bailey had to return to New York to care for his father who was ill, the judge concluded that "it [was] not apparent why it was essential for the claimant to follow." Since there was no marriage, no plans to marry at a certain future date, and no assurance the relationship would continue for any particular period of time, the judge found there was no family unit to be preserved.

MacGregor again appealed. The California Unemployment Insurance Appeals Board (Board) adopted as its own the administrative law judge's decision and statement of facts and reasons. Plaintiff then sought a writ of mandate from the Santa Clara Superior Court pursuant to Code of Civil Procedure section 1094.5.

After considering the record of the administrative proceeding, the superior court found plaintiff had good cause for leaving her employment. The court found as facts that MacGregor had lived with Bailey for three years, that she and Bailey had established a family unit with their child, that Bailey had decided to move to New York, and that plaintiff had chosen to leave her employment and relocate to New York in order to maintain and preserve their family unit. The court concluded that these underlying facts established good cause for plaintiff's quitting pursuant to section 1256 and that she was therefore entitled to receive benefits if otherwise qualified.

The court issued a peremptory writ of mandate directing the Board to set aside its decision and to reconsider its action in light of the court's findings of fact and conclusions of law. The Board appealed. While the Board's appeal was pending, this court decided *Norman v. Unemployment Insurance Appeals Board, supra.*

In *Norman* we discussed the meaning of "good cause" under section 1256. Section 1256 provides that "an individual is disqualified for unemployment compensation benefits if the director finds that he or she left his or her most recent work voluntarily without good cause or that he or she has been discharged for misconduct connected with his or her most recent work ...."

Whether or not there is "good cause" within the meaning of section 1256 is a question of law which must be answered in relation to the particular facts of each case. Good cause may exist for reasons which are personal and not connected to the employment situation, but those reasons must be imperative and compelling in nature. Several Courts of Appeal have defined "good cause" as used in section 1256 to mean "such a cause as justifies an employee's voluntarily leaving the ranks of the employed; ... such a cause as would, in a similar situation, reasonably motivate the average able-bodied and qualified worker to give up his or her employment with its certain wage rewards in order to enter the ranks of the unemployed." (*Evenson v. Unemployment Ins. Appeals Bd., supra,* 62 Cal. App. 3d at p. 1016; *Zorrero v. Unemployment Ins. Appeals Bd.* (1975) 47 Cal. App. 3d 434 [120 Cal. Rptr. 855].)

Precedent decisions of the Board have long recognized that the circumstances attendant upon a worker's decision to leave employment in order to accompany a spouse and family to a new home may be so compelling as to constitute good cause for quitting within section 1256. Thus, in *In re Dipre* (Cal. Unemp. Ins. App. Bd. Precedent Benefit Dec. No. P-B-230 (1976)), a husband had decided to return to a former home in Pennsylvania after his wife informed him that she planned to leave California with their three minor children and make her home in Pennsylvania regardless of his desires. The Board determined that the husband acted under compelling circumstances. His decision to leave employment in order to preserve his marriage and the family unit was a reasonable one, which constituted good cause under section 1256.

In 1982 the Legislature added the fourth paragraph to section 1256 which recognizes that the desire to preserve a marital relationship, or a relationship in which marriage is imminent, may constitute good cause within the meaning of the statute.[3] The Legislature explicitly stated that the amendment was intended to overturn the Court of Appeal decision in *Norman v. Unemployment Insurance Appeals Board* (which had found good cause based on a nonmarital relationship) and to "endorse the policy of the Employment Development Department, as expressed in its regulations, which distinguishes persons who are married or whose marriage is imminent from others in determining whether a person has left his or her most recent work without good cause ...."

The Court of Appeal's decision in *Norman* was vacated when this court granted a hearing. This court's opinion issued subsequent to the amendment of section 1256. While not specifically addressing or construing the newly enacted statutory presumption, the opinion did reach a result consistent with the statute. We found that a claimant who had left California to preserve her relationship with the man she planned to marry had not established good cause. The record contained no indication that the couple's marriage was imminent and lacked sufficient indications of the need to preserve a permanent and lasting familial relationship. Citing a line of appellate decisions declining to equate nonmarital relationships with marriage for all purposes, the *Norman* opinion concluded that "[the] Legislature's decision to give weight to marital relationships in the determination of 'good cause' supports public policy encouraging marriage and is a reasonable method of alleviating otherwise difficult problems of proof." (34 Cal. 3d at p. 8.) "The inevitable questions would include issues such as the factors deemed relevant, the length of the relationship, the parties' eventual plans as to marriage, and the sincerity of their beliefs as to whether they should ever marry." (*Id.*, at p. 10.)

---

[3] The fourth paragraph of section 1256 provides: "An individual may be deemed to have left his or her most recent work with good cause if he or she leaves employment to accompany his or her spouse to a place from which it is impractical to commute to the employment."

Nevertheless, this court explained there was nothing about Norman's lack of a legally recognized marriage which *precluded* her from receiving benefits if she could establish that compelling circumstances made her voluntary leaving "akin to involuntary departure." (*Ibid.*) Using a hypothetical which foresaw the claim now before us, the *Norman* court suggested that some significant factor in addition to the nonmarital relationship might provide the necessary compelling circumstance: "Thus, for example, where there are children of a nonformalized relationship, and an employee leaves his or her position to be with a nonmarital loved one and their children, good cause might be shown." (*Ibid.*)

It is apparent from the *Norman* decision's treatment of the subject that the presumption which attaches to a couple that is legally married is not the exclusive means of demonstrating good cause based on compelling family circumstances. Regulations of the Department itself recognize the "existing or prospective marital status of the claimant" as but one of three kinds of domestic obligations which might compel a person to leave work with good cause.[4]

....

The evidence here amply supports the trial court's findings that MacGregor had "established a family unit consisting of herself, her fiancé and their child" and that she "chose to relocate to New York with her fiancé and their child in order to maintain and preserve their family unit." The record shows that MacGregor and Bailey had maintained a common household for over two years prior to the birth of their daughter. When the child was born the parents received her into that home and gave her Bailey's surname. It is clear that both MacGregor and Bailey intend to and do provide a stable and secure home for their daughter....

Leanna was only two months old when Bailey decided his father's illness required him to move to New York. The need for MacGregor to follow — which the administrative law judge could not fathom — is in our view manifest. The intimate nature of the family bond among these three individuals would have been forever altered had MacGregor decided that she, or she and Leanna, should not accompany Bailey to New York.

---

[4] The parties agree that the regulations, which became effective May 18, 1980, are not controlling in this case. They nevertheless provide guidance as to the kinds of familial obligations that the board generally considers compelling. In addition to obligations arising out of the existing or prospective marital status of the claimant, legal or moral obligations relating to the health, care, or welfare of the claimant's family, or to the exercise of parental control over a claimant who is an unemancipated minor may also give rise to a voluntary leaving with good cause. Family is broadly defined to include "the spouse of the claimant, or any parent, child, brother, sister, grandparent, grandchild, son-in-law, or daughter-in-law, of the claimant or of the claimant's spouse, including step, foster, and adoptive relationships, or any guardian or person with whom the claimant has assumed reciprocal rights, duties, and liabilities of a parent-child, or a grandparent-grandchild relationship, whether or not the same live in a common household." Compelling circumstances may be found where a minor child of the claimant requires care and supervision and there is no reasonable alternative and where there is a need to preserve family unity.

The Board's arguments here, like the administrative decisions below, focus on the lack of a legal marriage relationship between plaintiff and Bailey. The Board urges that leaving work to join a spouse should be deemed good cause only where there is a marriage to be preserved. This rule, according to the Board, is consistent with the public policy favoring marriage and with laws which afford special benefits and protections to that institution. The rule would also avoid the difficulties and dangers which would accompany a requirement that administrative agencies and the courts make individualized determination of the "true nature" of intimate personal relationships.

This court considered similar arguments in *Norman v. Unemployment Ins. Appeals Bd., supra,* 34 Cal. 3d 1. There, although we declined to find good cause based solely on a nonmarital relationship in which marriage was not imminent, we explicitly declined to hold that a legal marriage is a prerequisite for establishing good cause where other indices of compelling familial obligations exist. Today we reaffirm the principle that the lack of a legally recognized marriage does not prevent a claimant from demonstrating that compelling familial obligations provided good cause for leaving employment.[5]

The state's policy in favor of maintaining secure and stable relationships between parents and children is equally as strong as its interest in preserving the institution of marriage. The Legislature has declared that the rights and obligations of parents and children exist regardless of the marital status of the parents. The purposes of the conciliation statutes relied on by the Board include the protection of the rights of children as well as the protection of the institution of matrimony. The courts have recognized the family as a basic unit of our society.

The problems of proof which concerned this court in the *Norman* case are not substantial in this situation where the basis for the familial relationship is clear and objectively verifiable. Plaintiff and her fiancé share a home with their natural child. Both have acknowledged the child as theirs and have assumed the responsibilities of providing for her care and support, as well as the benefits of her company and companionship.

The Board asserts that a claimant who leaves employment to accompany a spouse to a different locality must show that the spouse was forced to establish the new domicile by "compelling circumstances" which would constitute good cause. Prior decisions of the Board recognize, however, that even if one spouse's reason for relocating appears arbitrary, the importance of preserving the marital or familial relationship may provide good cause for the other spouse's decision to follow.

In this case the decisions of the administrative law judge and the Board conceded that Bailey had a good reason for relocating: the care of his elderly and ill father. This would constitute a compelling circumstance under the Department's

---

[5] In light of this decision we need not resolve plaintiff's contention that a nonmarital rule unconstitutionally infringes her right of privacy in the matters of marriage and reproduction.

own regulations. The trial court found as matters of fact that Bailey made the decision to move and that plaintiff chose to go with him in order to preserve their family unit. The court's findings are supported by substantial, credible and competent evidence. The conclusion that MacGregor had "such a cause as would, in a similar situation, reasonably motivate the average able-bodied and qualified worker to give up his or her employment with its certain wage rewards in order to enter the ranks of the unemployed" is entirely consistent with the laws and public policies of the State of California.

As the record clearly supports the trial court's finding that plaintiff had good cause for leaving work, the judgment is affirmed.

NOTES

1. Statutory Definition of Family. Other state courts have interpreted "family" obligations more narrowly. In *Davis v. Employment Security Dep't*, 737 P.2d 1262 (Wash. 1987), the court declared it would take "immediate family" literally. The court saw no fundamental right to live in a meretricious relationship, and held it not to be good cause for UI purposes to move in order to continue such a relationship.

2. Constitutional Issues. By deciding for the UI claimant on statutory grounds, the Court avoided the lurking constitutional issue. In *Austin v. Berryman*, 878 F.2d 786 (4th Cir.) (en banc), *cert. denied*, 493 U.S. 941 (1989), the Fourth Circuit was forced to face similar constitutional claims in light of a Virginia UI statute (since repealed) that expressly declared "the voluntary leaving of work with an employer to accompany or to join his or her spouse in a new locality" is not good cause for leaving work. The claimant testified she quit work to follow her husband (who had moved some 150 miles to take care of his elderly mother), because her religion commanded that she follow her husband wherever he might go. The court unanimously rejected her claim that the denial of UI benefits infringed her fundamental marital rights protected by the Fourteenth Amendment. In a subsequent opinion, the court rejected her equal protection claim. *Austin v. Berryman*, 955 F.2d 223, *cert. denied*, 505 U.S. 1206 (1992). The claimant showed that 86.8% of persons disqualified from UI for quitting to accompany a spouse were women. The court found this insufficient to prove that the statute had a gender-based discriminatory purpose.

The court also rejected, four judges dissenting, her claim that the denial of UI benefits burdened her first amendment right to the free exercise of her religion. In doing so, the court distinguished several Supreme Court decisions that upheld free exercise claims by workers who were terminated for being unable to work for religious reasons. *See Frazee v. Illinois Dep't of Emp. Sec.*, 489 U.S. 829 (1989) (denial of UI benefits unconstitutionally burdens free exercise of religion when unemployment due to claimant's refusal to work on his Sabbath); *Thomas v. Review Bd.*, 450 U.S. 707 (1981) (same result when worker dismissed for refusing to help build military tanks for religious reasons). The Fourth Circuit found those cases to turn on a conflict between the circumstances of work and the employee's religious beliefs, whereas here the proximate cause of Austin's unemployment was geographic distance, not religious beliefs.

2. WILLFUL MISCONDUCT

McCOURTNEY v. IMPRIMIS TECHNOLOGY, INC.

Court of Appeals of Minnesota
465 N.W.2d 721 (1991)

Considered and decided by KALITOWSKI, P.J., and SHORT and POPOVICH, JJ.

KALITOWSKI, JUDGE.

Relator Diane McCourtney seeks review of a decision by the Commissioner of Jobs and Training which denied her claim for unemployment compensation benefits. McCourtney argues her persistent absences due to a sick baby did not constitute disqualifying misconduct. McCourtney also challenges the Commissioner's decision on equal protection grounds. Respondent employer Imprimis Technology, Inc. has moved to strike portions of McCourtney's brief. We grant the motion to strike, but decline to impose sanctions. We reverse the Commissioner's decision denying benefits.

Facts

McCourtney was employed by Imprimis as a full-time accounts payable clerk for over 10½ years. McCourtney's ending salary was $1,360 per month. Her scheduled hours were 6:30 a.m. to 3:00 p.m. Monday through Friday. McCourtney was an excellent employee, and until January 1990 she had no attendance problems.

On September 30, 1989, McCourtney gave birth to an infant who suffered from numerous illnesses. The baby's father and other members of McCourtney's family were unable to assist her with child care.

Due to her baby's illnesses, McCourtney was frequently absent from work between January and May 1990. She was absent 71% of the time between January 1 and February 25; 36% of the time between February 25 and March 11; 31% of the time between March 12 and March 25; and 13% of the time between March 26 and April 8. Between April 9 and April 12 she was absent for four straight days, and during that same two-week pay period, she missed another eight hours. When she missed 10½ hours of work the following week, she was suspended pending termination. Imprimis issued McCourtney two written warnings before finally discharging her for excessive absenteeism.

McCourtney does not challenge her employer's right to terminate her due to absenteeism. McCourtney applied for unemployment compensation benefits, but the Department of Jobs and Training denied her claim. McCourtney appealed to a Department referee, who conducted a hearing.

The evidence at the hearing demonstrated 99.9% of McCourtney's absences were due to her sick baby. Although each of McCourtney's absences was excused, Imprimis issued a written warning in February requiring McCourtney to develop a written plan to solve her child care problem.

In response to this warning, McCourtney prepared a memo to her manager, discussing two possible options for care of her baby when she was unable to take him to her regular baby sitter: (1) professional in-home care; and (2) back-up day care facilities. McCourtney agreed to determine what services were available in her community.

McCourtney looked through the yellow pages, contacted Hennepin County, and called family members. She investigated the possibility of hiring a nanny, but could not afford the cost.

McCourtney contacted ten local child care facilities, and discovered that "Tender Care" was the only provider which would care for sick infants on short notice. However, Tender Care could not guarantee a caregiver would always be available, and would not allow McCourtney to interview a caregiver before he or she entered her home. Other problems with Tender Care services included the cost and the caregiver's inflexible starting time.

Following the hearing, the referee concluded McCourtney was discharged for misconduct because she had some control over her absences and her conduct constituted a violation of behavior which Imprimis had a right to expect of its employees. McCourtney appealed, and the Commissioner's representative affirmed the referee's decision. McCourtney filed this writ of certiorari, seeking review of the decision of the Commissioner's representative.

Issue

Do McCourtney's frequent absences constitute misconduct disqualifying her from receiving unemployment compensation benefits?

Analysis

An individual who is discharged for misconduct is disqualified from receiving unemployment compensation benefits. Minn. Stat. § 268.09, subd. 1(b) (Supp. 1989). The Minnesota Supreme Court has adopted the following definition of "misconduct":

> The intended meaning of the term "misconduct" is limited to conduct evincing such wilful or wanton disregard of an employer's interests as is found in deliberate violations or disregard of standards of behavior which the employer has the right to expect of his employee, or in carelessness or negligence of such degree or recurrence as to manifest equal culpability, wrongful intent or evil design, or to show an intentional and substantial disregard of the employer's interests or of the employee's duties and obligations to his employer. On the other hand mere inefficiency, unsatisfactory conduct, failure in good performance as the result of inability or incapacity,

inadvertencies or ordinary negligence in isolated instances, or good-faith errors in judgment or discretion are not to be deemed misconduct.

In re Claim of Tilseth, 204 N.W.2d 644, 646 (Minn. 1973). In *Feia v. St. Cloud State College,* 244 N.W.2d 635 (Minn. 1976), the court summarized the *Tilseth* definition of misconduct as "conduct evincing a willful or wanton disregard for the employer's interests or conduct demonstrating a lack of concern by the employee for her job." *Id.* at 636....

The unemployment compensation statutes are "humanitarian in nature and are liberally construed." *Group Health Plan, Inc. v. Lopez,* 341 N.W.2d 294, 296 (Minn. App. 1983). The intent of the unemployment compensation statutes is to assist those who are unemployed "through no fault of their own." Minn. Stat. § 268.03 (1988). The issue is not whether an employer was justified in discharging an employee, but rather, whether the employee committed "misconduct" disqualifying the employee from receiving benefits.

Each of McCourtney's absences was excused and was due to circumstances beyond her control. *Cf. Winkler v. Park Refuse Service, Inc.,* 361 N.W.2d 120, 124 (Minn. App. 1985) ("Absence from work under circumstances *within the control of the employee* has been determined to be misconduct sufficient to deny benefits.... The critical factor is whether the employee's behavior caused his failure to report to work.") (emphasis added). McCourtney made substantial efforts to find care for her child so she could work. Respondents argue McCourtney could have utilized the services of Tender Care. We disagree. The hours offered by Tender Care personnel were incompatible with McCourtney's work schedule.

In light of McCourtney's good faith efforts, her inability to find care for her child is not "misconduct" within the meaning of Minn. Stat. § 268.09, subd. 1(b). McCourtney's actions were motivated by a willful regard for her child's interests and not a wanton disregard of her employer's interest or lack of concern for her job.

We recognize that in some circumstances misconduct may be demonstrated by excessive absenteeism alone. Where the circumstances do not overwhelmingly demonstrate that an employee's absences are deliberate, willful, or equally culpable, we may also examine the employee's history, conduct, and underlying attitude. While McCourtney's absences were undeniably excessive, her work history and good faith attempts to find care for her child weigh against a determination that her absences demonstrated the culpability required by *Tilseth.*

We conclude that under the specific facts and circumstances of this case, Imprimis has failed to meet its burden of proving McCourtney's actions constitute misconduct as intended by the legislature and further defined by *Tilseth.* Therefore, McCourtney is entitled to unemployment compensation benefits. The economic burden this conclusion places on the employer is a necessary cost of the legislature's humanitarian concern for the welfare of persons unemployed through no fault of their own....

Reversed.

POPOVICH, JUDGE (dissenting).

I respectfully dissent and would affirm the decision of the Commissioner's representative for the following reasons:

1. As the majority recognizes, Diane McCourtney's absences were frequent and excessive. She received two warnings yet her absences continued. We have previously said that excessive absenteeism alone may demonstrate misconduct. *See, e.g., Jones v. Rosemount, Inc.,* 361 N.W.2d 118, 120 (Minn. App. 1985); *McLean v. Plastics, Inc.,* 378 N.W.2d 104, 107 (Minn. App. 1985). I believe McCourtney's frequent absences evidenced a "disregard of standards of behavior which an employer has a right to expect of its employees." *Tilseth v. Midwest Lumber Co.,* 204 N.W.2d 644, 646 (Minn. 1973).

2. Under the majority's analysis, an employer becomes the victim of an employee's personal problems with obtaining child care. An employer is forced to (1) put up with the employee's extensive absences or (2) pay for the resulting unemployment at potentially great expense. I do not believe it was the legislature's intent to force employers into this Catch 22 position. Rather, as respondents point out, other social welfare programs have been developed to handle the child care issue....

NOTES

1. *Goodness of Character.* If this opinion is followed in Minnesota, should all working mothers fired for absenteeism because of child-care problems be eligible for UI benefits? Or is it important that McCourtney, before having children, had been an excellent employee and has a good "underlying attitude" about the problems she is creating for her employer? Should benefit decisions hinge on the Unemployment Commission's determination of an employee's attitude? Is such a criterion manageable for a state agency designed to process thousands of claims quickly and cheaply?

2. *Voluntarily Quit Versus Firings.* Suppose McCourtney, feeling badly about not pulling her weight at work, quit rather than was fired. If she continues to take steps to resolve her child-care problem, should she be eligible for UI benefits?

3. *Work Versus Family.* McCourtney, like many working mothers, faces deep conflict between being a good worker and a good parent. Even the majority's presentation of the issue as whether McCourtney is guilty of "misconduct" illustrates that the UI system emphasizes the difference between working mothers and male workers who rarely are asked to choose between work and family. UI's emphasis on giving benefits only to those fully committed to the labor force again reveals that working men are the model for the system. An award of UI benefits to McCourtney perhaps can be justified by lessening the immediacy of a choice between work and family. UI benefits can give her a financial cushion to sort out her situation.

4. *Uncharged Benefits.* Judge Popovich focuses on the employer's plight, and accuses the majority of putting the employer in a Catch-22 position: put up with the absences, or be charged with UI benefits. One response might be to decouple the alternatives by awarding benefits but not charging them to the employer. McCourtney should receive UI benefits, because she fits squarely within UI's purpose of financially supporting workers who involuntarily lose their jobs and need time to find more suitable work. But the employer's UI taxes should not increase, because it cannot control the problem.

Of course, uncharged benefits are a major cause for imperfect experience rating, which in turn leads to inefficiently high unemployment. Further, are worker's child-care problems really beyond the employer's control? Some firms are much better than others at accommodating the needs of working parents.

5. *Alcoholism and Involuntary Misconduct.* Suppose a worker's alcoholism leads to excessive absences, for which he is fired. In what ways is this situation like McCourtney's? *See City & County of Denver v. Industrial Comm'n,* 756 P.2d 373 (Colo. 1988) (alcoholism is not disqualifying misconduct for UI if condition has progressed to point where it is non-volitional); *Crewe v. United States Office of Personnel Mgt.,* 834 F.2d 140 (8th Cir. 1987) (alcoholism is a disability under the Americans With Disabilities Act).

6. *Typical Bad Employees.* Willful misconduct consists of considerably more than simply being a bad employee. An employee dismissed for incompetence generally will receive unemployment insurance. For example, a truck driver who was dismissed for receiving six traffic violations (five on his own time) in two-and-one-half years, causing the employer's insurer to refuse to insure him, was allowed to receive unemployment insurance. *Eddins v. Chippewa Springs Corp.,* 388 N.W.2d 434 (Minn. Ct. App. 1986). Also eligible for unemployment insurance was an employee who was fired for driving a 10'4" truck through a 10'2" underpass. *Ulysses v. Pennsylvania Unemp. Comp. Bd. of Review,* 524 A.2d 552 (Pa. 1987). However, a truck driver fired for being involved in eight accidents in a period of six months was disqualified from receiving unemployment insurance. *Walton v. Pennsylvania Unemp. Comp. Bd. of Review,* 508 A.2d 380 (Pa. 1986).

JONES v. REVIEW BOARD OF INDIANA EMPLOYMENT SECURITY DIVISION

Court of Appeals of Indiana
399 N.E.2d 844 (1980)

GARRARD, PRESIDING JUDGE.

Appellant Tenner R. Jones appeals from a decision of the Review Board of the Indiana Employment Security Division (Board) which denied her unemployment compensation on the basis that she voluntarily left her employment without good cause in connection with her work.

Jones worked for Marian Hill as a cook from December 12, 1977 through March 24, 1978. When she was offered the position she informed her supervisor that she could only work the hours of 9:00 a.m. to 3:00 p.m. because she had family responsibilities. In March 1978, Jones was told that her hours would be changed to 9:00 a.m. to 6:00 p.m. When Jones protested the change she was told that if she did not work the new hours, someone would be hired that would. *Jones then agreed to accept the change of hours.* The next day, however, Jones informed her supervisor that she could not work the hours because she had four children at home to care for. Jones agreed to continue working until a replacement was found.

Jones contends on appeal that the Board's decision was contrary to law since the reason for termination, a change in her working conditions contrary to an existing employment contract, constituted good cause.

Generally, an employer has the prerogative of setting business hours, working schedules and working conditions in the absence of a specific agreement. However, an employee has the right to place conditions or limitations on his employment. If such conditions are made known to the employer and are agreed to by it, these conditions become contractual working conditions. If the working conditions are unilaterally changed by the employer and the employee chooses to terminate the employment rather than accept the change, the employee will be entitled to unemployment benefits since the reason for termination was a change in work agreed to be performed by the employee. Such reason constitutes good cause. *Wade v. Hurly,* 515 P.2d 491 (Colo. Ct. App. 1973); *Gray v. Dobbs House, Inc.,* 357 N.E.2d 900 (Ind. Ct. App. 1976) (concurring opinion). Likewise, if the employee is discharged for refusal to accept a unilateral change in the agreed upon working conditions, the employee would be entitled to benefits as the discharge would not be for just cause as it is defined in IC 22-4-15-1.[1] However, if the employee chooses to remain in the employment under the changed conditions, the prior agreed upon condition will be deemed to have been abandoned and will no longer be considered part of the working conditions.

---

[1] IC 22-4-15-1 provides in pertinent part,

"Discharge for just cause" as used in this section is defined to include but not be limited to separation initiated by an employer for falsification of an employment application to obtain employment through subterfuge; knowing violation of a reasonable and uniformly enforced rule of an employer; unsatisfactory attendance, if the individual cannot show good cause for absences or tardiness; damaging the employer's property through wilful negligence; refusing to obey instructions; reporting to work under the influence of alcohol or drugs or consuming alcohol or drugs on employer's premises during working hours; conduct endangering safety of self or coworkers; incarceration in jail following conviction of a misdemeanor or felony by a court of competent jurisdiction or for any breach of duty in connection with work which is reasonably owed employer by an employee.

In the case at hand, the record supports a Board determination that Jones agreed to the change in the theretofore agreed upon working conditions. Therefore, she was not entitled to good cause status for terminating her employment because of the change. Additionally we note that leaving employment because of family responsibilities constitutes leaving without good cause. *Gray v. Dobbs House, Inc.*, 357 N.E.2d 900 (Ind. Ct. App. 1976).

Jones also contends that the Board's decision is contrary to law because the evidence before the Board shows conclusively that the termination was not voluntary. Jones characterizes the employer's statements that she would be replaced if she did not work the hours as coercive threats rendering her termination involuntary. We do not agree. While it is apparent that Jones would have been discharged had she failed to work the additional three hours, she was not thereby forced into tendering her resignation. She was able to choose, of her own free will, to remain employed by working the additional three hours as she had agreed to do. Furthermore, the record reveals that the spectre of discharge was not the cause of her termination. Jones' motivation to leave her employment was induced by her parental responsibilities and her husband's demands that she not work the hours.

The decision of the Board denying benefits is affirmed.

NOTES

1. *Work and Parental Responsibilities.* Jones has four children at home. Does the court take seriously the limits of her choices? Could she truly choose, of her own free will, to work the additional three hours? While for many men a shift change from 3 p.m. to 6 p.m. may not be a major change, for many working mothers it is an impossible change.

2. *Fine Lines.* The court suggests that the critical fact was that Jones initially agreed to the shift change, but after discussing it with her husband that night, changed her mind. If she had initially rejected the change, would she be eligible for UI benefits? Is such a fine line defensible?

Other courts are more sympathetic to employees in such situations. For example, an employee with thirteen years' experience agreed to a shift change and later asked to have her lunch break changed to between 2:15 and 2:45 so she could pick up her children from school. The employer refused the request and the employee was eventually fired for absenteeism. The Mississippi Employment Security Commission denied UI benefits on grounds of misconduct, but the Mississippi Supreme Court reversed. *Mississippi Emp. Sec. Comm'n v. Bell*, 584 So. 2d 1270 (Miss. 1991).

D. FEDERAL REGULATION OF PLANT CLOSINGS

When the major plant in a town closes, the community faces mass unemployment. The impact on the community can be extremely severe. The following excerpt summarizes studies on the impact of plant closings on the health of workers and their families.

BARRY BLUESTONE & BENNETT HARRISON, THE DEINDUSTRIALIZATION OF AMERICA 61-72 (1982)[*]

Families who fall victim to brief periods of lost earnings are frequently able to sustain their standards of living through unemployment insurance and savings. Unfortunately for the victims of plant closings, the consequences are often much more severe, ranging from a total depletion of savings to mortgage foreclosures and reliance on public welfare. Families sometimes lose not only their current incomes, but their total accumulated assets as well.

During the Great Depression, the waves of plant closings that spread across the country drove millions of families into poverty. A study completed in 1934 of Connecticut River Valley textile workers showed that two years after the mills closed down, 75 percent of the families affected were living in poverty, compared with 11 percent before the shutdown. More than one in four families was forced to move in order to find lower rents. Some families lost their houses when they fell behind on mortgages. Thirty-five percent reported no new purchases of clothing, and the consumption of other items was reduced significantly.

This experience did not die out with the end of the Depression. A similar fate is faced by workers and their families who suffer permanent layoff today. When the Plainfield, New Jersey, Mack Truck facility shut down in 1960, workers had to reduce their food and clothing consumption substantially, and they turned to borrowing and installment credit for other necessities. Aircraft workers in Hartford County, Connecticut — the jet engine capital of the world — responded to the loss of their jobs in the mid-1970's by sharply reducing their expenditures on food, clothing, and medical care in addition to a long list of "luxury" items such as recreation and house repair. Out of the eighty-one workers interviewed in a study by Rayman and Bluestone, three of these displaced jet engine workers lost their houses to foreclosure. Among participants in the upstate New York study conducted by Aronson and McKersie, 11 percent reported cutting back on housing expenses, 16 percent reduced their food consumption, 31 percent bought less clothing, and 43 percent spent less on recreation. In what could lead to a mortgaging of their families' health, one in seven reduced their expenditures for medical care. These figures are remarkably close to those found in the Hartford County research....

---

[*] Reprinted with permission.

Impacts on Physical and Mental Health

The loss of personal assets places families in an extraordinarily vulnerable position; for when savings run out, people lose the ability to respond to short-run crises. The first unanticipated financial burden that comes along — an unexpected health problem, a casualty or fire loss, or even a minor automobile accident — can easily hurl the family over the brink of economic solvency. The trauma associated with this type of loss extends well beyond the bounds of household money matters.

Medical researchers have found that acute economic distress associated with job loss causes a range of physical and mental health problems, the magnitudes of which are only now being assessed. Simply measuring the direct employment and earnings losses of plant closings therefore tends to seriously underestimate the total drain on families caught in the midst of capital shift.

Dr. Harvey Brenner of Johns Hopkins University, along with Sidney Cobb at Brown University and Stanislav Kasl at Yale University, have done careful studies in this area. Writing in Psychometric Medicine, Kasl and Cobb report high or increased blood pressure (hypertension) and abnormally high cholesterol and blood-sugar levels in blue-collar workers who lost their jobs due to factory closure. These factors are associated with the development of heart disease. Other disorders related to the stress of job loss are ulcers, respiratory diseases, and hyper-allergic reactions. Higher levels of serum glucose, serum pepsinogen, and serum uric acid found in those experiencing job termination relative to levels in a control group of continuously employed workers suggest unduly high propensities to diabetes and gout. Compounding these problems is the fact that economically deprived workers are often forced to curtail normal health care and suffer from poorer nutrition and housing.

The Kasl and Cobb findings are by no means unique. Aronson and McKersie write that two-fifths of their sample reported deterioration in their physical and emotional well-being since their termination. Headaches, upset stomachs, and feelings of depression were the most widely-reported health problems. Aggressive feelings, anxiety, and alcohol abuse were the observed psychological consequences of the Youngstown steel closings. Similar conditions were widely reported among the aircraft workers in the Hartford County study. In most of these cases, the factor of time seems to be essential. Those who need much of it to find another job suffer the most....

Special psychological problems arise when a plant closing occurs in a small community, especially when the establishment was the locality's major employer. Writing about the closing of a plant in southern Appalachia, Walter Strange notes that the people

> lost the central focus which had held the community together — its reason
> for existence — a focus which was held in common as community property,

one which provided not only for economic needs but ... a structural frame-work which gave coherence and cohesion to their lives.

These effects typically lessen or disappear following successful re-employment. Yet, "stressful situations" caused by a plant closing can linger long after the final shutdown has occurred. Moreover, feelings of lost self-esteem, grief, depression, and ill health can lessen the chances of finding reemployment; this failure, in turn, can exacerbate the emotional distress, generating a cycle of destruction. Ultimately a debilitating type of "blaming the victim" syndrome can evolve, causing dislocated workers to feel that the plant closing was their own fault. Strange argues "that those feelings of self-doubt can create fear of establishing a new employment relationship or complicate the adjustment process to a new job." As the sociologist Alfred Slote put it, in his seminal work on job termination:

> The most awful consequence of long-term unemployment is the develop-ment of the attitude, "I couldn't hold a job even if I found one," which trans-forms a man from unemployed to unemployable.

The "Ripple Effects" in the Community

While the impact of disinvestment on individual workers and their families, is probably the correct place to begin any inquiry into the social costs of unregulated deindustrialization, it cannot be the end of such an inquiry. For when mills or department stores or supermarket chains shut down, many other things can happen to a community. These can be extraordinarily costly as they ripple through the economy.

The primary effects are, of course, visited on those closest to the production unit that ceases operations. The unit's own employees lose salaries and wages, pensions, and other fringe benefits; supplier firms lose contracts; and the various levels of government lose corporate income and commercial property tax reve-nue. These in turn result in a series of secondary shocks including decreased retail purchases in the community, a reduction in earnings at supplier plants, and increased unemployment in other sectors. Finally, these events produce tertiary effects in the form of increased demand for public assistance and social services, reduced personal tax receipts, and eventually layoffs in other industries, including the public sector. What begins as a behind-closed-doors company deci-sion to shut down a particular production facility ends up affecting literally everyone in town, including the butcher, the baker, and the candlestick maker. By the time all of these "ripple effects" spread throughout the economy, workers and families far removed from the original plant closing can be affected, often with dramatic consequences.

Some of these ripple (or multiplier) effects are felt immediately, while others take time to work through the economy. Some will dissipate quickly (especially if the local economy is expanding), while others may become a permanent part of the local economic environment. The extent of the impact of any particular closing will depend also on whether the plant or store was a major employer in the area, or an important purchaser of goods and services produced by other area businesses. All of these indirect impacts will be multiplied if a number of closings or cutbacks occur in the area simultaneously....

When the company in the classic "company town" closes down, all of these effects are magnified tremendously. The case of Anaconda, Montana provides a perfect example. Anaconda Copper & Mining Co. had operated a huge copper smelter there for over seventy-five years when the Los Angeles-based Atlantic Richfield Co. (ARCO) acquired it. Two years later, on September 29, 1980, ARCO announced that it was abandoning the smelter, thus eliminating 80 percent of the entire annual payroll in this community of 12,000 people. Needless to say, the announcement sent a Richter scale shock wave through the town.

The action erased 1,000 jobs in Anaconda and 500 more in neighboring Great Falls. The fallout was immediate. In two weeks, new unemployment claims added 691 recipients to the rolls and before long, one in six in the work force was out of work. The food-stamp rolls grew by 190, to 434 families. About 170 workers chose early retirement rather than the $3,500 in severance pay....

In all these ways, the ARCO smelter closing "echoed through the city." By December, the Chamber of Commerce found that thirty-six businesses it surveyed (excluding the railroad) had laid off, on the average, 20 percent of their employees. One fourth of the businesses said they anticipated further layoffs, and one third had canceled expansion plans. Most reported their business had dropped 10-50 percent, despite both the severance payments made by ARCO to its recently "pink-slipped" workers and the various forms of unemployment insurance and public aid supplied to those directly and indirectly affected.

The secondary victims of the smelter closing often had recourse to fewer public and private benefits than the smelter workers themselves. "The businessmen are getting the brunt of it right now," the town's Chevrolet dealer told a Los Angeles Times reporter. "They gave [the smelter workers] $3,500 in severance pay — I got caught with $500,000 in cars."

The physical and emotional trauma associated with this particular closing was also striking. Workers sold their $55,000 houses for $35,000 in order to take jobs elsewhere. Businesses that normally would have provided a comfortable retirement for their owners went bankrupt, leaving them with nothing more than Social Security for their old age. Visits to the Alcohol Service Center increased by 52 percent, and there was a 150-percent increase in the number of persons seeking drug counseling. The patient load at the Mental Health Center jumped 62 percent. To add injury to insult, on the day the smelter closing was announced, the local water company raised its rates. No one in town overlooked the fact that the water company was also owned by ARCO.

With the immense size of some industries like automobile and steel, entire regions behave as though they were company towns. The key losses flowing from the recent automobile layoffs are felt in steel, ferrous castings, aluminum,

746 CH. 17: UNEMPLOYMENT AND UNEMPLOYMENT INSURANCE

synthetic rubber, glass, plastics, textiles, and machine tools. The U.S. Department of Labor (DOL) has estimated that for every 100 jobs in the motor vehicle industry, 105 jobs are wiped out in the direct supplier network.

Economists talk about these indirect losses in terms of "employment multipliers." In this case, the DOL study reveals a multiplier of 2.05, since an initial loss of 100 jobs leads to an eventual total loss of 205. In studies of the automobile industry that were performed by the Transportation Systems Center of the U.S. Department of Transportation, the value of the multiplier was estimated to be even higher — in the range of 2.4 to 3.0.

Our own estimates using the M.I.T. Multiregional Input-Output Model (MRIO) suggests a multiplier in the same range. Beginning with a potential loss of 5,000 jobs in automobile assembly in Michigan, the MRIO permits a measurement of the effect of such a cut on all other industries in the United States on a state-by-state basis. According to this analysis, the original displacement of the assembly workers would eventually affect over 8,000 auto workers in all, as parts suppliers in Michigan and elsewhere eliminate jobs due to reduced orders. Along with Michigan, the midwestern states share the heaviest burden, with Ohio losing over 1,000 auto industry jobs, Indiana another 630, and Illinois and Wisconsin each losing at least 200.

In all, the 8,000 jobs potentially lost nationwide in the automobile industry would ultimately cause a decline in employment among all industries of more than 20,600. In other words, more than 12,000 non-auto industry jobs would be affected. For example, iron-ore miners in Minnesota — probably working in that state's northern "iron range" — will lose their jobs because, with fewer domestic cars produced, there is less need for sheet steel and consequently less demand for iron ore. Indeed, because of the staggering complexity and interrelatedness of the economy, nearly every industry will be touched sooner or later by the layoffs in the Michigan plants. Somewhere in the production chain — either in the direct manufacture of automobiles or, for that matter, in the weaving of the cloth that goes into the upholstery — workers will suffer short work weeks or temporary layoffs. Some will lose their jobs permanently. The biggest losers in this instance are those who work in closely allied industries such as steel, rubber, metalworking machinery, and metal stampings.

Of course, non-manufacturing workers are deeply affected as well. Over 1,000 jobs throughout the nation in transportation and warehousing would potentially disappear as a consequence of the original cutback in automobile assembly operations in Michigan. Nearly 1,800 wholesale and retail trade jobs and over 500 jobs in related business services will be affected. Presumably auto dealers, advertisers, truckers, and accountants will feel the pinch when some Detroit assembly lines close down for good. The same is obviously true when a steel or tire factory shuts down or even a major chain of supermarkets or discount department stores. The employment multipliers will differ from industry to industry depending on how well an industry is integrated into the entire production chain. But no instance of a plant, store, or office shutdown is an island unto itself.

Worker Adjustment and Retraining Notification Act of 1988

In 1988, Congress passed the federal Worker Adjustment and Retraining Notification Act (WARN Act), which requires employers with 100 or more full-time employees to give their workers and local government officials 60 days' advance notice of plant closings or mass layoffs. The key term in the WARN Act is — "employment loss," which is defined as a termination of employment (other than through discharge for cause, voluntary resignation, or retirement), a layoff for more than six months, or a greater than 50% reduction in hours over a six-month period. With this term defined, the WARN Act then requires notice for any plant closing or mass layoff, which it defines as follows:

— A "plant closing" is a temporary or permanent shutdown of a single site that causes an "employment loss" for 50 or more employees during a 30-day period.
— A "mass layoff" is a reduction in force other than a plant closing that causes an "employment loss" during a 30-day period for 50 employees and one-third of the workforce, or for 500 employees even if less than one-third of the workforce.

The WARN Act has two major exceptions. The first is a "faltering company" exception, which applies to plant closings and not layoffs. A faltering company can give less than 60 days' notice if it had been actively seeking new financing to keep the plant open and in good faith believed that notice would jeopardize the negotiations. The second exception is for "unforeseeable business circumstances," and applies both to plant closings and mass layoffs. Such circumstances include a client's sudden and unexpected termination of a major contract, and natural disasters such as floods and earthquakes.

Violators are liable for up to 60 days of backpay and benefits for each employee, as well as attorney fees, and are subject to a civil penalty of $500 per day. At least one district court has held that punitive damages are unavailable under the act. The WARN Act does not preempt employees' rights under state law or union contracts.

Not surprisingly, the WARN Act's requirements have led to complex regulations and disputes over such issues as part-time employees, adequate notice, and the like. The following case demonstrates some of the complexity.

KILDEA v. ELECTRO WIRE PRODUCTS, INC.

United States District Court, E.D. Michigan
792 F. Supp. 1046 (1992)

NEWBLATT, J.

....

This action arises out of defendant's closing of its Owosso, Michigan manufacturing plant on April 2, 1990. In compliance with the Worker Adjustment and Retraining Notification Act ("WARN"), 29 U.S.C. § 2101 et seq., defendant provided notice of the impending plant closing on January 31, 1990. Notice was provided to all active workers, but none of the plaintiffs received notice. Plaintiffs, former employees of defendant at its Owosso plant, had been laid-off at various times prior to January 31, 1990 and were not recalled before the plant closed on April 2, 1990. None of the plaintiffs had been laid-off for more than six months prior to April 2, 1990. In this action, plaintiffs claim that defendant violated the WARN Act by failing to provide them with notice of the plant closing as required by the Act.

Defendant previously has stipulated that it is an "employer" within the meaning of the WARN Act, and, thus, admits that it must comply with the Act. The sole issue involved in this motion is whether plaintiffs can be considered "affected employees" as that term is defined at 29 U.S.C. § 2101(a)(5), and thus may have been entitled to notice preceding the closing of defendant's Owosso plant.

The WARN Act provides that:

> the term "affected employees" means employees who may reasonably be expected to experience an employment loss as a consequence of a proposed plant closing or mass layoff by their employer.

29 U.S.C. § 2101(a)(5). The WARN Act further defines "employment loss" as

> ... (A) an employment termination, other than a discharge for cause, voluntary departure, or retirement, (B) a layoff exceeding 6 months, or (C) a reduction in hours of work of more than 50 percent during each month of any 6-month period.

29 U.S.C. § 2101(a)(6). Section 2102(a) of the WARN Act requires an employer to provide notice of a plant closing at least sixty days prior to such closing. Written notice must be given "to each affected employee." 29 U.S.C. § 2102(a)(1).

In this Court's Memorandum Opinion and Order of August 15, 1991, the Court held that "the standard for 'reasonable expectation of recall' as set forth in *Damron v. Rob Fork Mining Corp.*, 739 F. Supp. 341, 344 (E.D. Ky. 1990) may be utilized to determine the identity of affected employees. *Kildea v. Electro Wire Products, Inc.*, 775 F. Supp. 1014, 1016 n.2 (E.D. Mich. 1991). The Court explained that:

> In *Damron,* the court adopted the Secretary of Labor's suggestion that any "reasonable expectation" test under WARN should parallel that used by the National Labor Relations Board ("NLRB") in interpreting the same phrase in the National Labor Relations Act. The three criteria used by the NLRB in determining whether a "reasonable expectation of recall" exists are: (1) the past experience of the employer; (2) the employer's future plans; and (3) the circumstances of the layoff, including what the employees were told as to the likelihood of recall.

775 F. Supp. at 1016 n.2 (citation omitted).

Subsequently on appeal, the Sixth Circuit affirmed the district court's use of the NLRB's factors to determine whether to consider persons on layoff as employees. *Damron v. Rob Fork Mining Corp.,* 945 F.2d 121, 124 (6th Cir. 1991). In addition to the factors noted previously by this Court, the Court of Appeals added (4) the expected length of the layoff, and (5) industry practice. The appeals court held that the plaintiffs in *Damron,* on layoff for at least eight years, were not on "temporary lay-off." Thus, such workers could not be considered employees and did not require notice of the plant closing. The court limited its discussion to whether the plaintiffs were employees for the purpose of determining whether the defendant was covered by the Act only because that question was resolved in the negative. The court did not rule either way as to whether laid-off workers who did possess a reasonable expectation of recall would be entitled to notice as "affected employees." The court did, however, recognize that the regulations provide that "'[w]orkers on temporary layoff or on leave who have a reasonable expectation of recall are counted as employees.'" If such workers were employees, then logically they could suffer an employment loss. Since such employees have a reasonable expectation of recall, they must be given notice of a plant closing as any other employee.

... The Court concludes that the Sixth Circuit would find that workers on temporary lay-off can and should be considered "affected employees," entitled to notice of an impending plant closing, pursuant to the WARN Act. Defendant's arguments to the contrary are unpersuasive.

Defendant argues that plaintiffs, as laid-off employees, are not to be considered "affected employees" entitled to notice preceding a plant closing. It is defendant's contention that while the definition of "employee" for purposes of determining whether an employer is covered by the act is a broad one, including temporarily laid-off workers, the test for determining which employees are entitled to notice is based upon a more narrow definition of "affected employees." Defendant provides several arguments in support of this contention; none of which sway the Court from its above-stated conclusion.

In determining whether an employer is covered by the WARN Act, "[w]orkers on temporary layoff or on leave who have a reasonable expectation of recall are counted as employees." 20 C.F.R. § 639.3(a)(1). Defendant argues that the inclusion of such laid-off workers does not apply similarly to the determination of which employees are "affected employees" requiring notice. In support of this argument, defendant analyzes the statute and regulations which provide that some workers are included in the coverage determination but are not included among "affected employees." For example, employees in a temporary facility, 29 U.S.C. § 2103(1), and employees involved in a strike or lockout, 29 U.S.C. § 2103(2), are not regarded as "affected employees" to whom notice must be given. These same employees are regarded as employees, however, for purposes of determining whether the employer meets the coverage thresholds specified in 29 U.S.C. §§ 2101(a)(2) and 2102(d). Defendant compares these employees, regarding whom the notice requirement is specifically exempted, with workers on temporary lay-off at the time of the plant closing. Defendant states that the regulations make no reference to workers on lay-off, nor to the reasonable expectation of recall analysis that is used in determining coverage. This assertion, however, is misleading. While the regulations do not specifically mention laid-off workers, they do provide that "[n]otice is required to be given to employees *who may reasonably be expected* to experience an employment loss." 20 C.F.R. § 639.6(b) (emphasis added).

Defendant concludes from its analysis of the regulations that the determination of whether employees are due notice generally includes only those workers who are actively working when a plant closing occurs. Defendant argues that this interpretation is consistent with Congress's intent to limit notice to workers who really need it. That is, to "provide workers and their families some transition time to adjust to the prospective loss of employment." 20 C.F.R. § 639.1. Defendant's argument is flawed in two respects.

First, the fact that the regulations and the statute itself do not mention whether laid-off workers can be "affected employees" does not mean that their classification as such is prohibited. To the contrary, the statute defines an "affected employee" as one "who may reasonably be expected to experience an employment loss as a consequence of a proposed plant closing...." 29 U.S.C. § 2101(a)(5). Workers on lay-off status at the time of a plant closing who possess a reasonable expectation of recall would experience an employment loss because their expectation of recall would be dashed and their employment unequivocally terminated at the time of the plant closing. All employees so situated may reasonably be expected to experience an employment loss in such a situation. The statute provides that certain employees who suffer an employment loss are, nevertheless, not entitled to notice. These are employees working in a temporary facility, 29 U.S.C. § 2103(1), and those either on strike or locked out during a labor dispute at the time the plant is closed, 29 U.S.C. § 2103(2). These employees are actively working but are not entitled to notice. That is because they do not have a reasonable expectation of holding onto their employment. Their future depends upon the disposition of the labor dispute, or upon the indefinite period of time their plant stays open. These employees work under conditions where they are aware of their jobs' future instability and can plan accordingly. By specifically exempting workers in these situations, the statute recognizes that any expectation of continued employment of these workers is *per se* unreasonable. This is not true of workers who believe they are on temporary lay-off. The statute does not exempt an employer from giving notice to temporarily laid-off workers. To the contrary, if they hold a reasonable expectation of recall, the statute anticipates their entitlement to notice. Thus, the fact that the statute is silent with respect to laid-off employees does not preclude them from notice; rather, it affirms the general provision that the employer must serve notice to "each affected employee." 29 U.S.C. § 2102(a)(1).

Second, defendant does not persuade the Court that Congress's intent is best effectuated by not requiring notice to temporarily laid-off workers. As defendant notes, by including such laid-off workers in determining whether the coverage threshold is met, the regulations bolster the WARN Act's remedial purposes by making the Act applicable to the largest possible number of employers. The intent of Congress is served even further, however, if laid-off employees with a reasonable expectation of recall are given notice along with all active workers. By implication, such laid-off employees still consider themselves to be employed. To the same extent that currently active workers require notice and "some transition time to adjust to the prospective loss of employment, to seek and obtain alternative jobs and, if necessary, to enter skill training or retraining that will allow [them] to successfully compete in the job market," 20 C.F.R. § 639.1(a), so too do workers on a lay-off that they reasonably believe to be temporary. Thus, defendant's argument regarding Congress's intent is unpersuasive.

Underlying defendant's argument that laid-off employees cannot be included within the definition of "affected employees" is the precept that any definition of "affected employees" broader than that proposed by defendant must be unconstitutionally vague. Defendant portrays its view as the only way constitutionally to provide a standard for the employer to determine which employees are due notice. This, however, overstates the case. The standard recognized by the Court is not unconstitutionally vague. The burden is upon plaintiffs to prove they had a *reasonable* expectation of recall. If plaintiffs carry this burden, then it was foreseeable to the employer that these plaintiffs should have been given notice of the plant closing.

Finally, the Court finds unpersuasive defendant's argument that employees laid-off prior to the aggregation period could not have suffered an "employment loss" within the aggregation period as a result of the plant closing. Workers who have been laid-off but hold a reasonable expectation of recall when a plant closing occurs suffer their employment loss when the plant is closed. These workers are still employees if they have established a reasonable expectation of recall. They have not, therefore, suffered an employment loss until the plant is closed or they are notified that their lay-off has become permanent. Thus, their employment loss has occurred within the aggregation period. This rationale applies equally to employees laid off for more than six months provided that they can establish that they held a legitimate and reasonable expectation of recall up to the time of the plant closing. Such reasonable expectation of recall establishes not only that they are "affected employees," but also that it was foreseeable to the employer that these employees might reasonably be expected to experience an employment loss as a result of the plant closing.[2]

For the foregoing reasons, defendant's Renewed Motion for Summary Judgment is DENIED. This action shall proceed to trial on the remaining issues as scheduled.

So ordered.

NOTES

1. *Sale of Business.* Should the WARN Act be limited to loss of employment, or should employers be required to give advance notice when a major decision can foreseeably cause a loss of wages or benefits. In *International Alliance of Theatrical & Stage Employees v. Compact Video Services, Inc.*, 50 F.3d 1464 (9th Cir. 1995), a company sold its business to a nonunion entity. Almost all the employees continued working for the new entity, but with lower wages and benefits. The union sued for a violation of the WARN Act, arguing they were effectively laid off without advance notice. In a 2-1 decision, the court held that the sale of the business and a reduction in wages was not a WARN event. If the buying company had laid off workers, it rather than the selling company would be responsible for giving the WARN notice. Judge Ferguson, dissenting, complained that the decision "eviscerates the protections against unprecipitated termination which WARN was enacted to guarantee." *Id.* at 1471.

2. *Details Matter.* Even law firms as employers can fail to comply with WARN Act requirements. The law firm of Lord Day & Lord sent a letter to employees thirty days before closing, explaining in the letter that the firm could not give greater advance notice "since this termination arises from unforeseeable business circumstances." Under the Act, an employer relying on the unforeseeable-business-circumstances exception must give as much notice as practicable and "give a brief statement of the basis for reducing the notification period." In *Grimmer v. Lord Day & Lord*, 937 F. Supp. 255 (S.D.N.Y. 1996), the court held that the letter lacked sufficient detail to qualify for the exception.

---

[2] The result might be different where the lay-off has continued for more than six months, thus satisfying the definition of "employment loss" provided at 29 U.S.C. § 2101(a)(6)(B). Arguably, such employees would have already suffered an "employment loss" and would be precluded from establishing a reasonable expectation of recall. This should not be a per se rule, however. The plaintiffs in such a case should be able to argue that they still possessed a reasonable expectation of recall and were entitled to notice of a plant closing. Nevertheless, this situation is not before the Court in this case.

RONALD G. EHRENBERG & GEORGE H. JAKUBSON, ADVANCE NOTICE PROVISIONS IN PLANT CLOSING LEGISLATION 6-7, 79-80 (1988)[*]

Proponents of plant closing legislation argue that advance notice provisions would ease displaced workers' shock and facilitate their search for alternative sources of employment or training. Such notice also would allow employers, workers and the community to see if ways exist to save the jobs, such as wage concessions, tax concessions, or seeking new ownership, including the possibility of employee ownership. If plants do shut, the maintenance of health insurance would be important for individuals during a period when stress leads to increased incidence of physical and mental ailments. Finally, payments by firms to the communities in which the plants were located would help alleviate the extra demands placed on these communities for social services that the shutdowns cause — demands that arise at the same time local property and sales tax revenue are being reduced.

Opponents of the legislation argue that, in addition to restricting the free mobility of capital, advance notice legislation would have a number of other adverse effects on firms. They claim it would increase worker turnover and decrease productivity, as those productive workers with the best opportunities elsewhere would leave and the morale of remaining workers would suffer. It also would decrease the likelihood that buyers of the plant's product would place new orders, that banks would supply new credit, that suppliers would continue to provide services, and that the firm could sell the plant to potential buyers. Finally, it would depress corporate stock prices. Such a provision, as well as others that directly increase the costs of plant shutdowns, effectively increase the cost of reducing employment and thus should encourage firms *not* to expand operation or to substitute overtime hours for additional employment in states where such laws are in effect.

In evaluating the case for plant closing legislation, it is useful to stress the divergence between private and social costs. Employers currently do not bear the full social costs of plant shutdowns, both because unemployment insurance is imperfectly experience rated and because the costs shutdowns impose on communities are not taken into account by them. As such, imposing a "tax" on plant closings, either in the form of advance notice provisions, severance pay requirements, or maintenance of benefits requirements may make sense; it would have the effect of discouraging the action. These efficiency considerations suggest the need for federal, rather than state-by-state rules, to reduce the possibility that locational decisions by firms would be influenced by "tax price" differences. Critics, however, would stress that such legislation might encourage the flight of jobs overseas.

---

[*]Reprinted with permission of W.E. Upjohn Institute for Employment Research.

[Ehrenberg and Jakubson then analyzed data from the January 1984 Current Population Survey of some 7,300 workers who were permanently displaced from a full-time job due to a plant closing or layoff during 1979-83. Roughly sixty percent of the sample had expected or received advance notice of their displacement. These displacements occurred well before the effective date of the WARN Act, so notice was either voluntarily given, the result of a collective bargaining contract, or in a few instances the result of state law.]

[Overall, some 8 to 15 percent of the displaced workers were able to find another job without any unemployment. Advance notice had a significant effect on the chance of avoiding unemployment, especially for white-collar workers, with those receiving notice being 15 to 30 percent less likely to experience unemployment. However, if the displaced worker experienced a spell of unemployment, advance notice did not help reduce its length. Advance notice had little effect on the wage in subsequent jobs for most groups, although notice may have helped white-collar females earn some 15 percent more than those without advance notice. Finally, Ehrenberg and Jakubson could find no evidence that advance notice led more productive workers to quit or decreased productivity of remaining workers. Ehrenberg and Jakubson conclude:]

Ultimately, given all the evidence presented and cited above, the position one takes towards advance notice legislation will depend heavily on one's preconceptions as to how labor markets function. If one believes labor markets in the main are competitive and operate primarily in an efficient manner, one might argue that the onus is on those who propose government intervention to document empirically what the benefits of the proposed legislation are and to document that its adverse side effects will be small. Given such a view, one might argue that the evidence presented here does not support government intervention; there are too many results whose implications are ambiguous and too many yet unanswered questions.

If, on the other hand, one believes that labor markets in the main are not competitive and/or that important externalities exist when workers are displaced, one will find the results presented here very supportive of some form of intervention, perhaps in the form of advance notice legislation. Such individuals may claim that we have documented at least some private benefits that advance notice seems to produce, without uncovering any evidence of its costs.

It is important when designing an intervention, however, to be clear about the source of public concern. If the major concern is the externality imposed on a local community due to a plant closing or large scale layoff, then public policy should specifically address this concern. Such a concern may argue for advance notice legislation. However, in this case, exemptions should not be based on absolute size, as is the case in the recently enacted Worker Adjustment and Retraining Notification Act, but rather on the basis of size relative to the local labor market. In contrast, if the source of concern is the private costs workers suffer from displacement then severance pay provisions may be a viable alternative and/or addition to advance notice legislation.

Our own position is that given the social costs associated with worker displacement, a strong case appears to exist for a federal policy relating to advance notice. One possibility is for the federal government to encourage advance notice by providing inducements for employers to voluntarily do so. For example, the federal government could reduce the costs to firms of providing such notice by funding a share of the unemployment benefits received by notified workers and/or by reducing the firms' corporate profit tax rates.

Alternatively, federal legislation mandating advance notice of plant closings or permanent layoffs (as has recently been enacted) could be undertaken. Well-designed research is needed, however, to more adequately address issues relating to the macro labor market effects of the legislation, including whether advance notice of impending displacement can serve to help prevent displacement from occurring, as proponents of the legislation often assert. Moreover, since so much of prior research has focused on the potential benefits of advance notice legislation, subsequent studies might also focus on research issues that opponents have been concerned about, namely, those relating to the costs of the legislation.

NOTE

WARN Lacks Enforcement Tools. In enacting the WARN Act, Congress required the General Accounting Office to assess the effectiveness of the Act. In its 1993 report, the GAO found that more than half of the employers who laid off workers were not required under the law to give notice, primarily because the layoff or plant closure did not affect enough workers. Even where layoffs met the WARN triggers, half the employers gave no notice and another 29% gave fewer than sixty days' notice. The GAO concluded that private enforcement in the courts appears not to be working, and suggested that Congress give the Department of Labor the responsibility and authority to enforce the law.

Part VII

Employee Benefits

Employee benefits, defined broadly, are forms of employee compensation other than cash. Although many types of employee benefits exist, they can be classified generally as either deferred compensation or in-kind payments. Deferred compensation consists of payments that are earned now but will not be available to the employee until later. Pensions are the best example. In-kind payments are compensation that is usable in the short-term but provided in a form other than money. Health and life insurance, time off for vacations and holidays, and even government-mandated payments (such as those for unemployment insurance or workers' compensation coverage) fall into this category.

Employee benefits have become such a significant part of the compensation package that the common term for them — fringe benefits — has become anachronistic. As a percentage of wages and salaries, employee benefits have almost doubled in the last generation of employees to their current level of about 42% (Table VII-1). Although inflation had more than a little to do with this, the cost of *employee benefits* in 1995 ($1,429 billion) was substantially greater than *total wages and salaries* in 1975 ($815 billion). U.S. CHAMBER RESEARCH CENTER, EMPLOYEE BENEFITS 40, Table 17 (1996). As a result, large numbers of employees have a significant proportion of their income subject to the special risks posed by this form of compensation.

Table VII-1

Employee Benefits as a Percentage of Wages and Salaries, 1929-1995

	1929	1955	1965	1975	1986	1995
Total Benefits	3.0%	17.0%	21.5%	30.0%	35.5%	41.8%
Pensions	0.2	2.2	2.3	3.6	2.8	6.7
Insurance[a]	0.1	1.1	2.0	3.4	5.6	8.3
Legally Required[b]	0.8	3.3	5.3	8.4	11.1	12.0
Time Not Worked, Bonuses, Etc.[c]	1.9	10.4	11.9	14.6	16.0	14.8

[a] Includes employers' share of health and life insurance (more than 90% is attributable to health insurance).

[b] Includes employers' share of Social Security and Medicare taxes, unemployment compensation, and worker's compensation.

[c] Includes bonuses and profit-sharing payments and paid time for rest periods, vacations, holidays, and sick leave.

Source: Adapted from U.S. Chamber Research Center, Employee Benefits 40, Table 17 (1996).

And there are special risks. Employee benefits significantly increase the complexity of the compensation agreement. Pensions, for example, mean that years, indeed decades, may elapse between the time when work is performed and when payment is made to the employee. Agreement must be reached on who bears the risk of loss and gain during that time, on when pension payments may begin and in what form, and on a host of other matters. Similarly, health insurance requires agreement on literally hundreds of details, such as the types of services to be covered and the precise arrangements for allocating costs. The increased complexity translates into increased risk that there will be misunderstandings, or worse, attempts to gain advantage at the expense of the other party.

The Functions of Employee Benefits

Given the extra risks of employee benefits, why are they an important component of employee compensation? Even without the extra risk, other things being equal, one would expect compensation to be in cash rather than employee benefits. Employers should be neutral between providing an employee $1,000 per year in cash and contributing $1,000 per year for that employee in a pension fund. But employees should prefer cash. With cash, the employee could decide whether to save the money for use at retirement or to use it in other ways; the retirement contribution forces the employee to save it. Any extra risk associated with pensions should increase the preference for cash. Even if ERISA completely eliminates the special risks associated with employee benefits (which of course it does not), employees should prefer cash, other things being equal.

Employee benefits are an important component of compensation because other things are not equal — employee benefits serve several purposes that cannot be met, or cannot be met as well, through cash payments. First and most obviously, employee benefits provide tax advantages. Consider health insurance. If an employee in a 15% tax bracket is paid $1,000 in cash, she ends up with $850 after taxes to use towards the purchase of health insurance. But if the employer provides the same amount in health insurance as an employee benefit, it can be paid for with pretax dollars, so the entire $1,000 is available.

These tax benefits are targeted to employees. The employer is entitled to a $1,000 deduction, whether it pays the employee in cash or provides her with health insurance. The employee, however, is required to declare a cash payment as income and pay taxes on it, but is entitled to exclude from her income, and hence avoid taxes on, monies paid for her health insurance. I.R.C. § 106. Who actually captures the tax benefits, however, is difficult to determine. If an employer offers $1,000 in cash or $875 in health insurance to an employee in a 15% tax bracket who wants health insurance, the employee should prefer the insurance. After taxes, the employee could only purchase $850 of insurance with the $1,000 in cash, but she will get $875 worth of insurance if she accepts the employer's alternative offer. But when the employee takes the insurance rather than the cash, the *employer* captures $125 of the $150 in tax benefits. Thus, employers and employees are likely to share the tax benefits in proportions that are determined by the complex workings of the labor market, rather than by whom the tax code targets as the beneficiary.

For pension payments, the advantage is tax deferral. For our hypothetical employee, a cash payment of $1,000 would be taxed immediately, and investment income on the remaining $850 would be taxed as it was earned. For qualified pension plans, neither the $1,000 nor its income would be taxed until they were withdrawn, usually at retirement. I.R.C. § 402. Table VII-2 illustrates the value of these tax advantages. The table assumes that a fifty-five year old person has $1,000 in wages and wishes to save it for fifteen years for use at retirement at age seventy, and that the market interest rate during the fifteen years is 8%. Several points from the table are worth noting. First, the tax advantages are greater for persons in higher tax brackets. The percent gain over the regular account increases from 18% to 37% as our hypothetical employee moves from the 15% tax bracket to the 28% tax bracket. Second, the tax advantages increase significantly if the retirement tax rate is lower than the tax rate during an employee's working years. The percent gain increases from 37% to 62% when the tax rate falls from 28% in working years to 15% in retirement. Third, and significantly today when tax rates are relatively low by historic standards, a tax advantage may remain even if the tax rate is higher in retirement than during working years. Our hypothetical employee comes out ahead marginally when the tax rate increases from 15% during working years to 28% in retirement. The gain would be greater if the money has been invested for more than fifteen years, if the tax rate had increased sometime prior to retirement, or if the market interest rate had been higher than 8%.

Table VII-2

Tax Advantages of a $1,000 Contribution to a Qualified Retirement Plan

	Tax Rate 15% in Working Years		Tax Rate 28% in Working Years	
	Regular Account	Qualified Plan	Regular Account	Qualified Plan
Wage Payment	$1,000	$1,000	$1,000	$1,000
Tax on Wage	150	0	280	0
Deposit	850	1,000	720	1,000
Value at Withdrawal[a]	2,280	3,172	1,668	3,172
Retirement Tax Rate (No Change)	15%	15%	28%	28%
Tax on Withdrawal	0	476	0	888
Net Withdrawal	2,280	2,696	1,668	2,284
Gain Over Regular Account	—	416	—	616
Percent Gain	—	18%	—	37%
Retirement Tax Rate (Change)	28%	28%	15%	15%
Tax on Withdrawal	0	888	0	476
Net Withdrawal	2,280	2,284	1,668	2,696
Gain	—	4	—	1,028
Percent Gain	—	0%	—	62%

[a] Amounts in a regular account compound at effective (after-tax) rates of 6.80% for taxpayers in the 15% tax bracket and 5.76% for taxpayers in the 28% tax bracket. Amounts in qualified plans compound at 8%.

Source: Adapted from CBO, Tax Policy for Pensions and Other Retirement Saving 3-5 (1987).

The tax advantages available for employee benefits are in place to encourage employers and employees to include benefits in the compensation package. And no one doubts that they work. One study indicated that removing the tax advantages would reduce the demand for pensions by about 39% and the demand for health insurance by about 12%. Since employee benefits are a substitute for wages, the study also indicated that the decrease in pensions and health insurance would be accompanied by a 3.4% increase in wages. STEPHEN A. WOODBURY & WEI-JANG HUANG, THE TAX TREATMENT OF FRINGE BENEFITS 140 (1991).

The increased coverage, however, is costly. The tax advantages provided for employer-provided health benefits resulted in lost tax revenues of $70.5 billion in fiscal year 1997, which made them the costliest category in the tax expenditure budget. The revenues lost because of tax advantages provided to retirement savings programs were nearly as much: $67.4 billion. By comparison, the tax revenues lost because of the deduction for home mortgage interest were $49.8 billion in 1997. ANALYTICAL PERSPECTIVES, BUDGET OF THE UNITED STATES GOVERNMENT, FISCAL YEAR 1998, 73-74 (1997). (Note, however, that because of differences in the nature of the programs and the ways in which the losses are calculated, the figures are only roughly comparable.)

Tax considerations are not the only reason for the increasing prominence of employee benefits. Employee benefits have several additional functions. They may, for example, help employers attract particular employees. Employers that provide child care and have generous parental leave policies may be more successful at attracting and retaining employees with families than employers that pay more in wages. Indeed, employee benefit packages can be used to accomplish goals that might be difficult to pursue directly:

> [S]uppose a firm prefers to hire mature adults, preferably those with children, in the hopes of acquiring a stable, dependable work force. An employer attempting to attract these people by offering them higher wages than single, younger, or much older adults would risk charges of discrimination. Instead, the firm can accomplish the same effect by offering its employees fringe benefits that are of much more value to workers with families than to others. For example, offering *family* coverage under a health insurance plan has the effect of compensating those with families more than others, because single or childless people cannot really take advantage of the full benefit.... Thus, at times fringe benefits allow the firm to give preferential treatment to a group it wants to attract without running afoul of discrimination laws.

ROBERT J. FLANAGAN ET AL., ECONOMICS OF THE EMPLOYMENT RELATIONSHIP 244 (1989).

Similarly, employee benefits, and especially pensions, may enhance the ability of employers to retain employees. To the extent a pension is forfeited if the employee leaves the firm too soon, the pension can be used to encourage employees to stay. When this type of bonding works to increase employee tenure, the costs to employers of recruiting and training employees are reduced. The bonding may also serve employee interests. Employers should be more willing to provide costly training to employees if they can be assured employees will remain with the firm long enough for the firm to recoup its investment. Thus, employees may have more on-the-job training opportunities available to them than they would if pensions were not a compensation option.

Somewhat ironically, pensions may also assist employers in getting rid of employees at the end of their careers. Traditionally, employers have required employees to retire at a certain age, presumably when it was thought that productivity would begin to decline. The Age Discrimination in Employment Act, however, now makes it illegal for employers to *require* employees to retire. Pensions, though, can be used to *encourage* employees to retire. Most directly, pensions can help ensure that an employee's finances permit retirement without undue hardship. More subtly, pension plans can be structured so that the present value of lifetime pension benefits begins to decline with age, so that, in effect, the employee suffers a financial penalty by delaying retirement. In one study, for example, the present value of pension benefits for a thirty-year employee with a $25,000 annual salary was $172,000 if the employee retired ten years before the normal retirement age, $91,000 for retirement at the normal age, and only $26,000 for retirement ten years after the normal age. Edward P. Lazear, *Pensions as Severance Pay, in* FINANCIAL ASPECTS OF THE UNITED STATES PENSION SYSTEM 57, 78 (Zvi Bodie & John B. Shoven eds., 1983).

Finally, employee benefits may be made a part of the compensation package because employers have a comparative advantage in providing them. Economies of scale, for example, may mean that employers are able to do a better job of investing retirement savings than individual employees, so it may make sense to have the savings placed in a pension fund administered by the employer rather than paid out to individual employees in current income. Similarly, some employee benefits present adverse selection problems when individual employees attempt to purchase them. Individuals seeking annuities at retirement, for example, are not likely to be offered generous annuities, because they are in a pool with people who expect to live a long time. Individuals seeking health insurance might be hiding health problems. Employers can ease these types of selectivity biases and, as a result, get better deals than individual employees for annuities, health insurance, and other types of employee benefits.

NOTES

1. *Income Levels, Employee Preferences for Pensions, and the Employer's Decision to Offer Pensions.* For several reasons, employees with higher incomes have a stronger preference for pensions. First, the value of the tax benefits is greater for employees with higher incomes; deferring taxes is worth more for people who are in higher tax brackets. Second, employees with higher incomes are in a better position to set money aside for retirement; they do not need the money as much to pay for current needs. And third, Social Security will replace a lower proportion of the pre-retirement income of high income employees, so they *need* to save more to ensure a retirement at close to the same income level they enjoyed before retirement.

Because of these employee preferences (and employer incentives to respond to them), if the Internal Revenue Code did not provide some restraints, one would expect a very large proportion of the significant tax advantages for retirement savings to flow to people with high incomes. Because of this concern, the I.R.C. contains complicated "antidiscrimination" rules designed to require employers who offer pensions to extend their benefits to employees who are not highly compensated. Generally, for pension plans to be qualified for tax advantages, employers must ensure 1) that non-highly compensated employees participate in plans at a rate that is comparable to the rate of participation for highly compensated employees, and 2) that the ratio of contributions or benefits to salary for the two groups is equal. I.R.C. §§ 401(a)(4), 401(a)(26), 410(b).

Employer decisions about whether to offer pension plans are made more complicated by the antidiscrimination rules:

> From its own income tax viewpoint, the employer is theoretically indifferent to the plan's creation. Whether as a $1,000 wage payment or as a $1,000 contribution to a qualified retirement plan, the employer can deduct the total amount as a business expense. Yet by contributing to the plan, the employer channels a government subsidy to the plan participants. Providing this subsidy is not cost free. Establishment and maintenance of a qualified plan involve significant administrative costs....
>
> At first glance it might appear that, as long as the potential subsidy to an employee exceeded the administrative costs of including the employee in the plan, the employer would choose to include the employee in the plan. This ignores the fact that savings and consumption patterns are not identical across the compensation spectrum....
>
> [Because low-paid employees have lower preferences for retirement savings,] a mere dollar-for-dollar substitution of retirement savings for wages would not maintain their level of satisfaction; wages would have to be increased. For example, an employee who was paid $10,000 before the plan's establishment might demand $9,500 after establishment even though the employer contributes an additional $1,000 to the plan....
>
> [On the other hand, for high-wage employees,] a dollar of retirement contribution is worth more than a dollar of compensation. Thus, such employees would be willing to accept some level of actual wage reduction as a cost of plan participation. For example, an employee who was paid $50,000 before the plan's establishment might only demand a salary of $44,500 if an additional $5,000 is contributed to the retirement plan. The total wage cost to the employer would therefore actually drop from $50,000 to $49,500....
>
> As the [anti]discrimination rules require more in the way of contributions for lower paid employees, the employer's costs increase. For any given employer, the costs may eventually exceed the benefits of covering the highly paid employees. At that point, the employer would decline to establish or continue a retirement plan.

Bruce Wolk, *Discrimination Rules for Qualified Retirement Plans: Good Intentions Confronting Economic Reality,* 70 VA. L. REV. 419, 430-33 (1984).[*]

2. *Antidiscrimination Rules for Health Insurance.* The rationale for antidiscrimination rules also applies to employer-provided health insurance:

> The only justification for leaving employer-provided benefits untaxed [is] that it encourages the use of health insurance ... "so that individuals, particularly lower income employees, will be assured of protection against certain contingencies[, such as sickness,] which are particularly difficult to plan for at low income levels." This justification fail[s] if employers provide tax-free benefits only to their more highly paid employees. There [is little] in tax law to prevent the president of a company from having his company pay only for his medical bills, leaving the other employees to pay for their health insurance and medical care out of after-tax income, if they could.

Daniel M. Fox & Daniel C. Schaffer, *Tax Policy as Social Policy: Cafeteria Plans, 1978-1985,* 12 J. HEALTH POL. POL'Y & L. 609, 611-12 (1987).

Congress addressed this problem in 1986. As part of the Tax Reform Act of 1986, Congress enacted § 89 of the Internal Revenue Code, which provided, as a condition of receiving the tax advantages, that employers not discriminate between highly compensated employees and other employees in providing health benefits. An uproar ensued. Lobbyists for business, and especially small business, argued that the rules were complex, so that compliance would be difficult and expensive, and that the rules would significantly increase the cost of health plans (in large part because they would do what they were intended to do — require more employees, including many part-time employees, to be covered). In 1989, § 89 was retroactively repealed. Narrower nondiscrimination rules currently apply to self-funded health plans and to cafeteria plans. *See* Allen R. Norris, *Discrimination Rules Affecting Health Benefits and Group Term Life Insurance After the Repeal of Section 89,* 16 J. PENSION PLAN. & COMPLIANCE 147 (1990).

3. *Fringe Benefit Coverage and the Cost of Regulation.* Antidiscrimination rules can backfire. Instead of complying by increasing coverage, some employers might decide not to offer a pension or health insurance plan at all because of the increased cost. This is especially true for smaller employers who cannot spread the administrative costs over as many employees. The General Accounting Office has estimated the cost of administering a pension plan to be $40 to $54 per participant for a plan with 10,000 participants and $227 to $455 per participant for a plan with fifteen participants. GAO, EFFECTS OF CHANGING THE TAX TREATMENT OF FRINGE BENEFITS 49 (1992). As a result, only one-quarter of small companies (fewer than 100 employees) offer pension plans, compared to two-thirds of large companies (more than 100 employees).

---

[*]Reprinted with permission.

One of the legitimate fears that lead to the repeal of § 89 was that some employers would drop their health insurance coverage instead of complying. Similar concerns over pensions have resulted in several proposals in Congress to permit small employers to offer simple and easy-to-administer pension plans. The goal is to increase coverage for employees of small employers. The fear is that small employers who currently offer pension plans will convert to the simpler and less adequate plans, leaving employees of those employers worse-off than before.

4. *The Advantages of Taxing Benefits.* The high cost of the tax advantages for employee benefits have caused some to reconsider:

> Current tax treatment of fringe benefits works against tax equity because some workers receive employer-provided, tax-preferred fringe benefits while others do not. In addition, because of this country's progressive tax rate structure, workers in higher tax brackets receive larger tax subsidies for these benefits than other workers. Further, some analysts believe that the tax preferences associated with employer-provided health benefits encourage employee "overspending" for health care.
>
> Taxing fringe benefits could raise substantial revenue and improve tax equity. However, full taxation of these benefits could greatly increase employees' taxable incomes and, consequently, the income taxes they may have to pay.... [F]ull taxation of pension and health benefits on a current-income basis could [also] reduce coverage. If the current tax treatment were changed, coverage of low-wage workers is likely to be more responsive because high-wage workers would tend to purchase coverage even without a tax break. However, some of the revenue generated could be used to target benefits at lower income families.

GAO, EFFECTS OF CHANGING THE TAX TREATMENT OF FRINGE BENEFITS 3 (1992).

ERISA and the Distinction between Pension and Welfare Plans

The Employee Retirement Income Security Act of 1974 (ERISA) is the primary legislative response to the growing importance of employee benefits and their special hazards. The Act is especially important because it has a provision which broadly preempts other regulation in the area. The Act is also exceedingly complex.

ERISA applies to a broad range of employer-provided benefits, including pensions, health insurance, child care, prepaid legal services, and a variety of others. But ERISA makes an important distinction between pension plans and other types of employee benefit programs. ERISA §§ 3(1), (2). Pension plans involve saving for retirement during an employee's work life, followed by distribution of the savings to the employee during retirement. Both periods of time (for saving and for distribution) may be decades long. The other types of employee benefit plans, known as welfare plans, are more short-term in nature. At any point in time, employees either use or do not use the available health care, child care, or legal services, but the benefits do not accumulate over time. Viewed from the employer's perspective, welfare plans are paid for on a pay-as-you-go basis (the revenues and liabilities arise at about the same time), in contrast to pension plans which entail a long-term program of savings and distribution.

The distinction between pension and welfare plans is important, because some of ERISA's provisions apply only to pensions with their long-term promises, while other provisions apply to both types of plans. Only pension plans are subject to ERISA provisions intended to protect employees from the forfeiture of pensions that have been building over a number of years (vesting protections), to ensure that contributions adequate to pay the pensions promised at retirement are made during the working lives of employees, and to provide pension insurance when plans are unable to pay promised pension benefits. ERISA §§ 201-11, 301-08, 4001-02. Both pension and welfare plans are subject to ERISA provisions requiring information about plans to be reported to the government and disclosed to employee-participants, imposing fiduciary responsibilities on those making decisions for the plan, and providing remedies and enforcement mechanisms. ERISA §§ 101-11, 401-14, 501-15.

ERISA is an interesting example of labor regulation, in part because of its indecisiveness. On the one hand, ERISA recognizes the voluntary and contractual nature of employee benefits. ERISA does not require employers to provide even a minimal package of employee benefits, and some of its provisions, such as the reporting and disclosure requirements, are intended to address problems that might interfere with the contracting process. On the other hand, ERISA is skeptical of the contractual regime. When employee benefits are provided, ERISA requires certain provisions to be included in the agreement, regardless of the parties' desires. In this part, we will explore and evaluate ERISA's attempt to protect against perceived abuses within a regime that retains its voluntary, contractual nature.

Chapter 18

A. THE PROBLEM WITH PENSIONS

McNEVIN v. SOLVAY PROCESS CO.

New York Supreme Court, Appellate Division
53 N.Y.S. 98 (1898), *aff'd per curiam,*
60 N.E. 1115 (N.Y. 1901)

FOLLETT, J. This action was begun May 14, 1897, to recover $52.54, alleged to be due from the defendant to the plaintiff as his share of a pension fund established by the defendant for the benefit of a class of its employés.... The plaintiff entered the service of the defendant June 18, 1890, and continued therein until April 6, 1895, when he was discharged. January 1, 1892, the defendant established what is known as a "pension fund" for the benefit of a class of its employés, and at the same time established a set of rules ... providing how the fund should be established, for whose benefit, how administered, and how applied for the benefit of the employés entitled to participate therein.

[The rules established a pension fund "to provide a means of support when by reason of accident, sickness, or advanced age labor must cease." The defendant was under no obligation to put any amounts into the pension fund and, when amounts were put into the fund, the rules provided that they were "gifts" that remained the sole property of the defendant and absolutely subject to its control. Each employé signed a pass book that contained the rules and a pledge by the employé "to faithfully perform the work entrusted to me with a true loyalty to the interests of the company." Amounts credited to the employé's account were written into the pass book. The rules provided that no employé could demand payment of the sum credited to his account, except when the defendant adjudged the account to be payable and that the fund's trustees were authorized to decide all questions concerning the rights of employés "without appeal." The rules said that payments would be made to employés at retirement or when employés were discharged without cause of dissatisfaction. Sums could be taken out of the pension fund only to pay allotments to employés. If an amount credited to an employé was not paid for some reason, the amount would go to an "additional fund" which eventually would be paid out to other employés or their survivors.]

It is conceded that this pension fund has been created voluntarily, and is a gift by the defendant, and the question upon which this case turns is whether, when a sum is credited to an employé on the pass book furnished by the defendant, the employé has a vested right in the sum so credited, or whether, under the terms by which the fund is established, the employé acquires no vested right until the gift is completed by actual payment to the employé. It must be conceded at the outset that a person or a corporation proposing to give a sum for the benefit of any person or any set of persons has the right to fix the terms of his bounty, and provide under what circumstances the gift shall become vested and absolute. Under the regulations established, it seems to me that none of the employés have a vested interest in any part of this fund, even though credited upon their pass books until the gift is completed by actual payment. Until that time it is an inchoate gift. The articles provide that an employé cannot, in any case, demand payment of the sum credited to his account, except when the defendant shall adjudge the account to be payable, in whole or in part, according to the rules and regulations established; and it is also provided that the sums credited shall remain the property of the defendant until actually paid, and that the fund shall be and remain under the sole control of the defendant's trustees, who are authorized to decide all questions concerning it without appeal. In this case the defendant's trustees decided, after a hearing of the plaintiff, that the plaintiff was not, when the action was begun, entitled to payment of any portion of the fund credited to him, and it seems to me that under the terms of the gift this decision is final, unless, within the discretion of the defendant's trustees, it shall be modified in the future. In case it shall be held that this plaintiff had a vested right in the fund credited to his account, it would necessarily follow that it might be reached by his creditors through proceedings supplementary to execution, and thus the very object of creating the fund would be destroyed.... It seems to me that the scheme by which this fund is created is simply a promise on the part of the defendant to give to its employés a certain sum in the future, with an absolute reservation that it may at any time determine not to complete the gift, and, if it does so determine, an employé has no right of action to recover the sum standing to his credit on the books of the pension fund. Whether the disposition and management of this fund may or may not be the subject of control in an equity action, in case it should be alleged and proved that the defendant's trustees were squandering the fund, or were guilty of bad faith in its management, is a question not before the court, this being a simple legal action to recover the sum standing to the plaintiff's credit on the theory that when he left the employment of the defendant he acquired an absolute vested right in the sum credited, which he has the right to recover.

The judgement and order should be reversed, and a new trial granted, with costs to the appellant to abide the event. All concur, except GREEN and WARD, JJ., dissenting.

GREEN, J. (dissenting).... Plaintiff entered defendant's service in June, 1890, being employed by the day, and subject to discharge at the pleasure of his employer. After the expiration of three years he was given a pass book, as provided [by the rules,] in which he was credited with various sums, amounting to $52.54, as allotments made to him from the pension fund, and the same sums were credited to him on the books of the company. In April, 1895, the plaintiff was dismissed from the service of the defendant by its foreman without any explanation being given for the reason of his dismissal, or any cause of dissatisfaction expressed. Afterwards he appeared before the trustees of the fund, and made application for payment of the amount allotted to him on his pass book.... He was subsequently notified that the trustees had voted that they would not pay off his allotment.... In the minutes of the trustees' meeting it was stated that plaintiff was discharged "for shirking," but the truth of this declaration was not supported by any evidence.

The court ... charged the jury, in substance, that the plaintiff was entitled to recover, unless they found that he had ... so negligently performed his services that there existed reasonable cause for dissatisfaction therewith, and reasonable ground for his discharge on account thereof. Exceptions were duly taken by the defendant. The defendant's contention is that ... the trustees are the sole and exclusive judges of the existence and the sufficiency of the cause of dissatisfaction. Indeed, the argument amounts to this: that the plaintiff has conferred upon the trustees an arbitrary power to determine that they are dissatisfied with his services, and to forfeit his rights and interest created by the contract, without assigning any cause whatsoever. In the first place, it should be remarked that the provision ... that sums to be paid are to be deemed gifts, and not transferable, cannot alter or impair the true character of the instrument or its legal effect and operation. A promise, founded upon a valuable consideration inuring to the benefit of a promisor, to pay a sum of money upon specified contingencies, is not a promise to make a gift, even though the parties call it so. To have that effect the agreement must annul the obligation to fulfill the promise, and leave it optional with the promisor. There is no such stipulation in this instrument, and the counsel for the defendant admits what cannot be denied — that it constitutes a contract founded upon a valuable consideration.... And therefore, in ascertaining the rights of the respective parties from the terms in which their understanding is expressed, we must start with the proposition that the plaintiff acquired, by virtue of the agreement, a vested legal interest in the pension fund, or a legal right to compel the defendant to fulfill its obligations; and the question is whether the plaintiff has incurred a forfeiture of such right or interest by reason of the nonperformance or misperformance of an essential obligation imposed upon him by the contract. In the determination of this question it is all important to observe the general principle that in the construction of all contracts under which forfeitures are claimed it is the duty of the court to interpret them strictly, in order to avoid such a result, for a forfeiture is not favored in the law. And though it may have been competent for the employés of the defendant to so contract that their rights in the pension fund shall depend upon the determination of a tribunal of their own choice, and to make the decision final and conclusive, yet, when one of the parties or its representatives are sought to be made the final judge, the courts will not give such a construction to the contract as to have that effect, if it be possible to give any other....

Defendant contends that the provision ... that in no case can the employés demand payment of the sums credited to their account except when the company shall adjudge the same to be payable, must be construed as a condition precedent to the right of recovery, and therefore, as a logical consequence, the trustees are vested with an arbitrary discretion in determining whether any cause of dissatisfaction existed, and the legal sufficiency of such cause. In other words, it is sufficient to say that they feel dissatisfied, and their utterance shall be final and conclusive, although there is no such stipulation contained in the contract. In answer to this it should be observed that ... there must be cause for the dissatisfaction to justify a discharge, ... but there is no provision in that or in any other article that the trustees shall be the sole, final, and exclusive judges of the cause, or that a particular act or omission on the part of the employé constituted a breach of the contract "to faithfully perform the work entrusted to me with a true loyalty to the interests of the company." In short, the plaintiff has not, in express terms, nor by necessary implication, constituted the trustees as a tribunal to determine, absolutely and without appeal to the courts, that he has committed a breach of the contract warranting his discharge, and a forfeiture of all rights conferred by it. There is no stipulation that the defendant may relieve itself of its obligation simply by a statement that the plaintiff has failed to perform his. The language of the instrument does not confer upon the defendant an arbitrary power to declare itself dissatisfied, and thereupon to terminate the contract and declare the forfeiture.

Defendant further contends that the authority conferred upon the trustees to decide all questions concerning the funds without appeal ... renders their determination final and conclusive, and precludes an appeal to judicial tribunals for redress.... The answer to this argument is that the courts will not give such a construction to the contract as to have that effect, if any other construction may reasonably and properly be adopted. Now, it is obvious there are many questions that may arise concerning the funds and their application to which [this] provision ... may properly be applied, and therefore [the] article does not necessarily require that it should be construed as an agreement to make the company the final arbiter upon the question whether the employé has been guilty of a breach of contract. For instance, the trustees may decide that only a portion of the allotment made shall be placed to an employés credit, whenever they judge it necessary as a matter of discipline (article 6); they may purchase an annuity for an employé permanently disabled, in their discretion (article 9); they may retain for a period the moneys due a retiring employé, or one discharged without cause, as security for the agreement not to injure the company after leaving its service (article 11); they shall decide the proportion to be paid to the widow and children of a deceased employé (article 12); they may decide other questions in respect of the additional fund, and so forth. We are therefore of the opinion that the plaintiff has not agreed that the trustees shall be the sole and exclusive arbitrators of his rights under the contract.

Defendant lays stress upon the fact that the company itself will gain nothing by a decision in its favor, since the amount withheld from the plaintiff must be transferred to the additional fund, thereby increasing the amount of that fund to be distributed among the widows and children or relatives of deserving employés.... That is true, but we are unable to perceive that it has any pertinent bearing upon the construction of the contract and its legal effect. The agreement was that, if the plaintiff should be discharged for cause of dissatisfaction, his account should be transferred to the additional fund for the benefit of deserving participants therein; otherwise it must be paid to him. It should be observed, by the way, that the employés have no security or protection against the application by the company of all the funds to the uses and purposes of its business; so that, in case of insolvency, a large part of the funds may be lost to them....

In the absence of any adequate proof of the cause of discharge, or cause of dissatisfaction, it must be held that there is no proof that the plaintiff has violated his agreement by the commission of some act that he ought not to have done, or that he omitted to do something required of him, that justified a dismissal.... [T]he plaintiff has earned the moneys placed to his account, and it was incumbent upon the defendant to show some just cause or reason for depriving him of it. He is not claiming damages as for a breach of a purely executory contract, but is seeking to recover moneys due him upon a contract executed....

It is an important observation to make that an adverse decision to the plaintiff in this case would justify the discharge of employés who may have loyally and faithfully performed their duties to the company for a long period of years simply upon a mere declaration that the company had cause for dissatisfaction, and the employé would be deprived of the moneys that he had fairly earned, without any remedy for their recovery in a court of justice. The cause was fairly and properly tried by the court below upon correct principles, and the judgement and order should be affirmed, with costs.

NOTES

1. *The Gratuity Theory of Pensions.* The majority's theory came to be known as the gratuity theory of pensions: the pension was merely a gift that the employer could grant or withhold at its discretion. This theory meshed well with the early employment at will cases. In one case, for example, an employer induced a thirty-seven year employee to retire by promising that his resignation would not result in a forfeiture of his pension payments. Then the employer refused to pay the pension. The court held for the employer, reasoning that since the employee could be discharged without cause, he could also be induced to retire with any representation. *Abbott v. International Harvester Co.,* 36 Erie Co. L.J. 271 (Pa. Ct. C.P. 1953). Would employers want a regime similar to *Skagerberg* in which the law made it virtually impossible to make binding promises to pay pensions?

2. *The Dissent's Theory.* The dissent sees a contract rather than a gift. The contract, however, said that the trustees were to decide all issues under the contract "without appeal." The dissent avoids that language by construing it strictly against the employer. This approach encourages employers to explain their plans in clear and unambiguous language, but, as the next excerpt illustrates, it does not require the plans to contain any substantive provisions to protect employees against potential problems, nor does it ensure that employees will read and understand their plans.

RALPH NADER & KATE BLACKWELL, YOU AND YOUR PENSION 4-7 (1973)[*]

Charlie Reed thought he was going to get a pension. He went to work when he was twenty-one as a coal miner for Jones & Laughlin Steel Corporation, and after twenty-three years in the mines, he was laid off. He waited for a recall, but none came. Numbers of small mines were closing under the pressures of mechanization, and thousands of miners were looking for work wherever they could find it. Like many others, Reed finally found a job outside the coal industry to keep him and his family going.

Thirteen years later, Reed applied for the pension he thought he had been earning during his twenty-three years in the mines. He found there wasn't one; instead, there was a rule Reed didn't know about: he had to have twenty years of service *within the thirty years preceding his application for benefits.* The rules made no exception for miners who had been laid off.

Reed was incensed. He began looking for other miners in southwestern Pennsylvania who had worked for at least twenty years and then found they weren't eligible for pensions when they retired. He has found 1200 of them.

The pension plan booklet that told Reed he would receive a pension said nothing about the possibility that he might be laid off, or that eligibility rules would disqualify him, or that new technology would leave thousands in the industry without jobs or pensions. Your pension description probably doesn't deal with such possibilities either, but they exist in every line of work for every employee who is counting on getting a pension someday....

If you are inclined to say, "It can't happen to me," meet some of the people who found out it could. They aren't merely the short-term employees who quit after a couple of years or jumped from job to job; many have worked thirty years or more, often for the same company. In fact, many of them are exactly the people you thought pensions were set up to help. Most of them thought so, too.

James Tyler, a construction worker from Lakewood, California, paid his union dues for thirty-one years. He worked under the same union local for a number of years and then was told that in order to take a job six miles from his home, he had to join another local. He did. Later, when he applied for a pension, he found he wasn't eligible. After thirty-one years in the same industry, he didn't have enough years of continuous service under either local. He didn't know that *you may not get a pension if you change unions or even union locals.*

Joseph Mintz, fifty-six, of Buena Park, California, has been in aerospace work for over thirty years and has no pension coming to him. For twenty-seven years he worked for three different companies. At each job, he was laid off before he

---

[*] Reprinted with permission.

had the ten-year minimum service requirement for a pension. One company laid him off after nine years and ten months. He always got another job, but not a pension. He didn't know that *you may not get a pension if you are laid off or change jobs.*

A glass worker was employed for thirty-two years by the same company in Salem, New Jersey. When he was forty-eight, he had a stroke and was forced to quit work. He never received a pension: he had to reach age fifty before he was eligible. He didn't know that *you may not get a pension if you become disabled before a certain age.*

A foundry worker in Cleveland, Ohio, was fifty-one and had worked for the same employer for twenty-one years when the company closed down. By that time, the worker had contracted emphysema and was partially disabled, with little chance for another job. He found he didn't have a chance for a pension either. When the plant closed, the pension plan was terminated without enough money to pay him even part of the benefit he had earned. He didn't know that *you may not get a pension if your company goes out of business or if the plan terminates for any other reason.*

Harry Oakes of St. Paul, Minnesota, worked for a large department store for fifty-two years before he retired at the age of sixty-six. He received his pension benefit for thirteen months. The company went bankrupt and the pension fund — including payments to retirees — was terminated. He didn't know that *you may lose your benefits sometime after you retire if the pension fund terminates.*

The Employee Retirement Income Security Act of 1974

ERISA was the legislative response to the kinds of problems discussed in *McNevin* and in the Nader and Blackwell excerpt. ERISA distinguishes between two basic varieties of pension plans — defined benefit plans and defined contribution plans. ERISA §§ 3(34), (35). In defined benefit plans, employers promise employees a "defined benefit" at retirement. The amount of the benefit is determined by a formula specified by the plan which, in most plans, uses length of service and final salary as variables. For example, the formula may promise an annual benefit equal to .02 (the generosity factor) times years of service times the employee's average salary over her last three years of employment. Thus, if a thirty-year employee had an average salary of $50,000 over her last three years of employment, she would be entitled to an annual pension of $30,000 (.02 x 30 x $50,000). Employees do not have individual accounts established for them in defined benefit plans. Instead, the employer is responsible for making contributions to a trust adequate to ensure that the promised pensions can be paid from the pooled fund. The amount of contributions required will depend on a complex actuarial analysis which takes into consideration factors such as the age and length of service of employees, projections of future salary increases, and the rate of return on plan investments.

In defined contribution plans, employers promise only to pay a defined amount into an account established for each employee. The employer makes no promise about the amount of the employee's benefit at retirement, which will depend entirely on the amounts contributed into her individual account and on her account's investment experience.

Defined benefit and defined contribution plans allocate investment risk differently. Employers offering defined benefit plans have promised a certain benefit at retirement. If the pension fund's investments do poorly, or if the fund is short for other reasons, the employer is liable for the shortfall. On the other hand, if the fund's investments do very well, the employer may be able to reduce its level of contributions to the fund or, even better, recoup the excess. Under defined contribution plans, in contrast, the employer has only promised to make certain contributions into individual employee accounts. If the investment experience is poor, the amounts employees will receive at retirement will go down; if the investment experience is good, employees will receive more in retirement than they initially expected.

Because of these differences between the two types of pension plans, some of ERISA's provisions apply only to defined benefit plans. ERISA, for example, contains a scheme to insure employer promises to pay pension benefits. The scheme, however, does not cover defined contribution plans because, by definition, employers offering that type of plan do not promise any particular pension benefit. Instead, employers merely promise to pay to employees their individual account balances. ERISA § 4021(b)(1). Similarly, ERISA contains provisions designed to require employers to make contributions adequate to fund the promised pension benefits when they become due. Once again, since employers offering defined contribution plans do not promise any particular benefit, but instead only promise to pay to employees the amounts contributed to their accounts plus earnings, ERISA's funding provisions are largely inapplicable to that type of plan. ERISA § 301(a)(8).

Historically, defined benefit plans were the predominant form of pension plan. As recently as 1975, more than two-thirds of pension plan participants were in defined benefit plans (27.2 of 38.4 million participants). By 1985, however, most pension plan participants were in defined contribution plans (33.2 of 62.2 million participants), and this trend has continued. In 1991, 58 percent of pension plan participants were in defined contribution plans. A number of factors contributed to the shift toward defined contribution plans, including economic factors (e.g., the types of firms offering defined benefit plans experienced slow growth in the 1980 and 1990s), legal factors (e.g., compliance with laws is more costly for defined benefit plans), and the preferences of both employers and employees (e.g., defined contribution plans are easier to link with current performance and permit greater employee mobility). DOUGLAS L. KRUSE, PENSION SUBSTITUTION IN THE 1980S: WHY THE SHIFT TOWARD DEFINED CONTRIBUTION PLANS? (National Bureau of Economic Research Working Paper No. 3882, 1991).

NOTE

ERISA and Public Pension Plans. Governmental pension plans are not covered by ERISA. ERISA § 4(b)(1). Governmental pension plans are very large, managing in excess of $1 trillion in assets and pose most of the problems to which ERISA is addressed. Some governmental plans, for example, have vesting schedules which are significantly longer than the ERISA standards and some are quite severely underfunded. National Education Ass'n, Characteristics of 100 Large Public Pension Plans 8, 39-48 (1996) (thirty-seven of the plans had vesting schedules of ten years or longer; nineteen of the plans had assets sufficient to fund 75% or less of their expected pension obligations; the least funded plan had assets sufficient to cover only 13% of its expected liability). *See also, e.g.*, MONT. CODE ANN. §§ 19-17-401, 19-18-602 (1995) (twenty-year vesting period for certain fire fighters). Comprehensive bills modeled after ERISA to regulate public pension plans have been introduced periodically in Congress, but have only served to enrich our library of acronyms. *See, e.g.*, Public Employee Pension Plan Reporting and Accountability Act, H.R. 3127, 99th Cong. (1985) (PEPPRA). Recently, the National Conference of Commissioners on Uniform State Laws promulgated a uniform law to regulate the fiduciary duties and reporting and disclosure obligations of public funds. The proposed act, however, is limited in its scope; it does not, for example, cover vesting or funding issues. Uniform Management of Public Employee Retirement Systems Act (1997). What do you think accounts for the reluctance of the federal government and the Uniform Law Commissioners to deal with the entire range of ERISA issues? What is the value of a uniform law that deals only with fiduciary and disclosure issues?

B. PROTECTING EMPLOYEES FROM FORFEITURE — THE BASICS AND A VARIATION

HUMMELL v. S.E. RYKOFF & CO.

United States Court of Appeals, Ninth Circuit
634 F.2d 446 (1980)

EUGENE A. WRIGHT, CIRCUIT JUDGE:

[R]ykoff established a profit-sharing plan for its employees in 1966. It contained a forfeiture or "bad boy" provision which required forfeiture of all of a participating employee's accrued benefits if he or she became a business competitor with Rykoff within two years after leaving Rykoff.

Congress passed ERISA in 1974. The Act provides minimum vesting standards for employee benefits and defines permissible forfeitures. [ERISA § 203]. One of the primary purposes of the Act is to insure that plan participants do not lose vested benefits because of "unduly restrictive" forfeiture provisions....

Rykoff amended its plan to comply with ERISA. It narrowed the anti-competitive forfeiture provision to provide that if Rykoff learns that any former plan participant is employed by a competitor, the Plan Advisory Committee may direct the plan trustee to forfeit a percentage of the participant's benefits derived from company contributions.... The provision applies only to participants with less than seven years experience with Rykoff. Those with seven years or more are fully vested, regardless of any competitive activity.

Section 9.10 includes a vesting schedule to establish what percentage of a participant's interest derived from Rykoff's contribution is forfeited if he or she engages in competitive work.[*]

Years of Service With Employer	Forfeited % of Interest from Employer
3	80%
4	60
5	40
6	20
7	0

A different vesting schedule applies to benefits of plan participants with less than seven years of service who terminate but do not engage in competitive activity. Section 9.05. Their interests are 100% vested after five years.

Years of Service With Employer	Forfeited % of Interest from Employer
less than 2 years	80%
less than 3 years	60
less than 4 years	40
less than 5 years	20
5 or more years	0

Appellee Burton Hummell (Hummell) terminated his employment with Rykoff after $5\frac{1}{2}$ years of service on September 23, 1976. He left to work for a competitor.

---

[*] *Hummell* arose when ERISA permitted ten-year cliff vesting and fifteen-year graduated vesting. The employer relied on those requirements in drafting its plan and Hummell terminated his employment after eleven years, between the two sets of requirements. The case has been edited to reflect ERISA's current five-year cliff and seven-year graduated vesting requirements. The employer's plan and the timing of Hummell's termination have been changed to reflect the ERISA amendments. The substantive holding of the case remains the same.

On October 21, 1977, the Advisory Committee directed the plan trustee to forfeit 40% (or $28,982.74) of Hummell's accrued benefits because of his post-employment competitive activity. The Committee arrived at the 40% figure by reference to the vesting schedule in Section 9.10.

Hummell appealed the decision to the Advisory Committee and lost. He then sued in district court which granted him summary judgment, holding the forfeiture provision violated ERISA....

ERISA requires private pension plans to provide that an employee's right to his or her normal retirement benefit is nonforfeitable upon the attainment of normal retirement age. [§ 203(a)]. In addition, an employee's rights in his accrued benefit derived from his contributions must be nonforfeitable, [§ 203(a)(1)], and the plan must satisfy one of [the] minimum vesting schedules. [§ 203(a)(2)].

The first alternative vesting schedule provides that an employee with at least five years of service must have "a nonforfeitable right to 100% of [the employee's] accrued benefit derived from employer contributions." [§ 203(a)(2)(A)]. There is no requirement for vesting of any lesser percentage of benefits before the required five years of service.

The schedule in subparagraph (a)(2)(B) provides graduated vesting. An employee ... must have

a nonforfeitable right to a percentage of [the employee's] accrued benefit derived from employer contributions ... determined under the following table:

Years of Service	Nonforfeitable %
3	20
4	40
5	60
6	80
7	100

Permitted forfeitures of accrued benefits from employer contributions are in paragraphs (A)-(D) of [§ 203(a)(3)]. They do not include anticompetitive forfeiture provisions or refer to the forfeitability of benefits which exceed the minimum vesting requirements in [§ 203(a)(2)(A)-(B)].

The legislative history indicates that with these limited exceptions, *vested* employee rights cannot be forfeited for any reason.

The district court construed the statute to prohibit any anticompetitive forfeiture provision.... [T]his interpretation is erroneous.

A Treasury Regulation provides ... ["t]o the extent that rights are not required to be nonforfeitable to satisfy the minimum vesting standards, ... they may be forfeited without regard to the limitations on forfeitability required by this section.["] 26 C.F.R. § 1.411(a)-4.[3]...

We hold ERISA does not prohibit forfeiture of benefits in excess of the minimum vesting requirements in [§ 203].

Our holding that ERISA permits limited forfeitures does not resolve the validity of Rykoff's plan. The question remains whether Rykoff may apply the seven-year graded vesting schedule to employees who violate the anticompetitive clause and the five-year 100% vesting schedule to all other employees.

The statute says that *a plan* must satisfy the requirements of subparagraph [§ 203(a)(2)(A) [or] (B).... It says nothing about applying option (A) to some employees and (B) to others....

A Treasury Regulation says that composite arrangements are permissible as long as the plan satisfies all requirements of *one* vesting option for all of *an employee's* years of service. 26 C.F.R. § 1.411(a)-3(a)(2).

> A plan which, for example, satisfies the [five-year cliff vesting requirements of subparagraph A, but not the seven-year graduated vesting requirements of subparagraph B] for an employee's first four years of service and satisfies the requirements of [sub]paragraph [B but not A] for all his remaining years of service, does not satisfy the requirements of this section....

Taken together, the statute ... and Treasury Regulations indicate that Congress intended to determine forfeitable benefits by referring to the same statutory schedule with which the plan's vesting schedule complies. For example, a plan with a minimum vesting schedule satisfying the five-year 100% option in [§ 203(a)(2)(A)] may forfeit 100% of an employee's employer-derived accrued benefits until the employee completes five years of service. A plan with a vesting schedule satisfying the requirements of [§ 203(a)(2)(B)] may forfeit employer-derived accrued benefits in accordance with the seven-year graded schedule in the statute....

We ... should if possible construe Rykoff's plan to make it legal. Applying our interpretation to Rykoff's plan, we find the forfeiture clause must be altered to comply with ERISA. Rykoff's graduated five-year vesting schedule tracks [§ 203(a)(2)(A)].[7]

The forfeiture provision must be adjusted to apply only to that percentage of the vested contributions that may be forfeited lawfully under [§ 203(a)(2)(A)]. This means employees with less than five years experience who violate the forfeiture provision forfeit 100% of employer contributed accrued benefits. Those with five or more years experience are 100% vested in their benefits.

---

[3] This Treasury Regulation [was] issued under the Internal Revenue Code's requirements for pension plans. ERISA provides they apply to analogous provisions of ERISA.

[7] Although Rykoff's schedule is more liberal than § [203(a)(2)(A)] requires because it allows vesting to accumulate before five years of service, we need not alter it. ERISA's legislative history and the Treasury Regulations indicate a plan may provide a vesting schedule more liberal than the statutory minimum.

Hummell had $5^1/_2$ years of service. Accordingly, he was 100% vested in his benefits and not subject to the anticompetitive forfeiture provision. He is entitled to reinstatement of $28,982.74 to his account....

NOTES

1. *Analyzing Hummell.* At the time he resigned, Hummell had $72,457 attributable to employer contributions in his account. The court found Hummell was entitled to the total amount, despite his violation of the "bad boy" clause. The court's analysis, however, would not always favor employees. For example, if Hummell had left to work for a competitor after $4^1/_2$ years of service, he would not have been entitled to any pension using the court's analysis, but he would have been entitled to 40% of his account balance using a plain reading of the "bad boy" forfeiture provision in the plan. Was the court justified in changing the forfeiture called for by the "bad boy" clause? (Hint: Compare the two Rykoff forfeiture provisions to ERISA's seven-year vesting schedule.)

2. *Public Policy and Nonforfeiture Provisions.* If protecting employees against forfeiture is a good idea, why allow total forfeiture of employer contributions for the first five years or partial forfeiture for the first seven years? Why not require employer contributions to be vested immediately?

ERISA's vesting rules have a high degree of precision — they are specific and relatively easy to apply. One cost of that precision is that compliance with the rules may be a *defense* in situations where the underlying public policy against forfeiture seems to be at risk. In *Phillips v. Alaska Hotel & Restaurant Employees Pension Fund,* 944 F.2d 509 (9th Cir. 1991), *cert. denied,* 504 U.S. 911 (1992), for example, a plan's vesting rules, in combination with a highly transient workforce, operated to exclude 97% of the plan's participants from benefits. The plan, however, complied with ERISA's vesting requirements. Nonvested participants in the plan filed a lawsuit claiming that the plan was not being operated for the sole and exclusive benefit of employees, in violation of ERISA and the Labor Management Relations Act. ERISA § 404(a)(1); LMRA § 302(c)(5). The Court held for the plan, relying in part on the plan's compliance with ERISA's vesting rules.

3. *The Inevitable Complexity of Regulation.* Many avenues exist for attempting to avoid the antiforfeiture provisions of ERISA. A plan, for example, could have a five-year cliff vesting provision and yet guarantee very little if 1) the plan's definition of "years of service" made it very difficult for employees to build up years ("a 'year of service' is a year in which an employee works 5,000 hours") or 2) the plan had benefits accrue significantly only after a long period of service ("benefits will accrue at a rate of $1.00 per year for the first twenty-five years of service and at a rate of $25,000 per year thereafter"). ERISA has many detailed provisions designed to make it difficult to avoid the basic policy of the vesting provisions. It has provisions, for example, which define

"year of service" and others which regulate the rate of benefit accrual. *See* ERISA §§ 203(b), 204.

4. *Anti-discrimination and Section 510.* Section 510 is one of the web of ERISA provisions intended to protect employee access to pension funds:

> It shall be unlawful for any person to discharge, fine, suspend, expel, discipline, or discriminate against a participant or beneficiary for exercising any right to which he is entitled under the provisions of an employee benefit plan [or under Title I of ERISA], *or for the purpose of interfering with the attainment of any right to which such participant may become entitled under the plan [or Title I].*

Section 510 applies most directly to prohibit employers from discharging employees shortly before vesting to avoid pension liabilities. In *Reichman v. Bonsignore, Brignati & Mazzotta P.C.*, 818 F.2d 278 (2d Cir. 1987), for example, the employer was found to have violated section 510 by discharging an employee ten months before her pension rights fully vested. Full vesting would have increased the employee's pension benefits by $60,000. As the next case illustrates, however, applying section 510 is not always an easy task.

NEMETH v. CLARK EQUIPMENT CO.

United States District Court, W.D. Michigan

677 F. Supp. 899 (1987)

ENSLEN, DISTRICT JUDGE.

Clark Equipment Company ("Clark") is a manufacturer of material handling equipment, construction machinery, and components. Until February 1983, Clark operated a construction machinery plant at Benton Harbor, Michigan. Plaintiffs are eighteen (18) former Clark employees who lost their jobs, and their full pensions, when Clark closed its Benton Harbor plant in February, 1983. Each plaintiff's employment was terminated when the plant closed. Clark transferred the production formerly accomplished at Benton Harbor to the two remaining plants in its construction machinery division, located in St. Thomas, Ontario and Asheville, North Carolina.

In 1982 Clark's President and Chief Executive Officer, James Reinhart, determined that Clark was in serious financial trouble.... Reinhart determined that Clark might go bankrupt by the end of 1982 unless the company took drastic steps to reduce its production capacity and overhead costs.

To that end, Clark began to consolidate its operations. In order to determine which plants, if any, to close, Clark conducted a series of plant capacity studies....

The construction machinery division had three plants: Benton Harbor, St. Thomas and Asheville. The company decided it could not close St. Thomas since duty restrictions would prevent it from competing in the Canadian market if it did not manufacture a portion of its product in Canada. The plant capacity study evaluated both Clark's options (eliminate Benton Harbor or eliminate Asheville) against a base case, or "do nothing" scenario. On the basis of this study, Clark decided to close the Benton Harbor plant. It announced this decision to the Benton Harbor workforce in early October, 1982. The plant actually closed in February, 1983.

Plaintiffs claim that Clark chose to close Benton Harbor instead of Asheville because of the increased pension expense Clark would incur if it allowed the Benton Harbor workforce to work until normal retirement age.... The plaintiffs in this case were within months or years of full retirement under [the Benton Harbor Pension Plan]. As a result of the plant closing, each plaintiff lost the right to qualify for full retirement benefits....

Section 510 of ERISA prohibits employer conduct taken against an employee who participates in a pension benefit plan for "the purpose of interfering with the attainment of any right to which such participant may become entitled under the plan."... [T]his prohibition was "aimed primarily at preventing unscrupulous employers from discharging their employees in order to keep them from obtaining vested pension rights." In order to prevail under this section, plaintiffs must prove that the defendant made the decision to discharge them from employment with the specific intent to violate ERISA. *Gavalik v. Continental Can Co.,* 812 F.2d 834, 851 [(3d Cir.), *cert. denied,* 484 U.S. 979 (1987)].

Plaintiffs need not prove that defendant's desire to interfere with their pension benefits was the *sole* reason for their termination. Rather, "§ 510 of ERISA requires no more than proof that the desire to defeat pension eligibility is 'a determinative factor' in the challenged conduct." *Gavalik* at 860. Once the plaintiffs establish that the desire to avoid pension liability was a determining factor in the decision to terminate their employment, the defendant, in order to avoid liability, must prove, "that it would have reached the same conclusion or engaged in the same conduct in any event, i.e., in the absence of the impermissible consideration...." *Id.* at 863. If the employer carries its burden to prove an alternative nondiscriminatory justification, the plaintiffs must then demonstrate that the proffered justification is a mere pretext, or that the discriminatory reason more likely motivated the defendant's action. *Id.* at 853.

In this case, plaintiffs' proof that Clark made the decision to close the Benton Harbor plant in order to prevent plaintiffs from obtaining their full retirement benefits consisted primarily of documents comparing payroll, pension expenses and other costs at the Benton Harbor and Asheville plants. Pension expenses at Benton Harbor would have amounted to $7.005 million over the relevant five (5) year period,[3] while those at Asheville would have come to only $1.096 million. According to plaintiffs' expert, the difference in pension costs, before accounting for union cost-cutting proposals and differences in efficiency

---

[3] Defendant's decision was based on an estimate of costs over the five year period from 1983 to 1987.

between the two plants, amounts to 26.79% of the total difference in direct labor costs between the two plants. The overall difference in operating costs between the two plants was $26.9 million. Pension costs amounted to slightly less than 22% of this difference.[5] Pension costs thus amounted to slightly more than one-fifth of the cost difference between the two plants.

Plaintiffs' offered other evidence to show that Clark's decision to close the Benton Harbor plant was motivated by its desire to prevent plaintiffs from obtaining their full retirement benefits. Ken Ward, a former Clark employee, testified that Paul Schultz, former manager of the Benton Harbor plant, told him that "the pension costs were killing us." This comment was made during discussions about the possibility that Clark would close the plant....

The Court finds that this evidence is sufficient to make out a *prima facie* case of pension discrimination in violation of section 510 of ERISA. Pension expenses were a significant item of cost making Benton Harbor more expensive to operate than Asheville. It is undisputed that the defendants considered these costs in making its decision to close the Benton Harbor plant. The Court cannot say that an expense amounting to more than twenty (20%) percent of the difference in operating expenses between the two plants was not a determining factor in Clark's decision to close the Benton Harbor plant, although obviously it was not the sole reason for that decision. The evidence regarding transfer rights further demonstrates Clark's attempts to consolidate those savings by preventing the older and more senior employees from transferring to the Asheville plant and accruing the years of service necessary to obtain full pension benefits. Clark denied transfers to disabled, medically restricted and laid-off employees even though it had the ability to employ many of these individuals.[9] Even the employees who qualified for transfer had to ... hastily move themselves and their families to North Carolina in order to obtain work. These facts, taken together with plaintiffs' direct evidence, are sufficient to show that Clark's decision was motivated, at least in part, by its desire to avoid paying full retirement benefits to the Benton Harbor workforce.

The Court must now determine whether the defendant met its burden of showing that it had a legitimate, nondiscriminatory reason for its actions. *Gavalik* at 853. The Court finds that Clark has met that burden. Clark produced an enormous amount of documentary evidence to establish its alternative justification for the decision to close Benton Harbor. Clark claims that it based its decision on a number of economic considerations, and that no one item of cost

---

[5] The difference in pension costs between Benton Harbor and Asheville, for the years 1983-1987, ... is $5.909 million. This is 22% of the $26.9 million difference in operating costs.

[9] Defendant employed up to one hundred (100) temporary employees at the Asheville plant. These positions could have been made available to plaintiffs. There was no evidence that Clark was financially unable to fill these positions with permanent employees. In fact, Robert Johnson, employee relations manager at Asheville, testified that Clark hired temporary employees in part to keep the positions open for full-time workers and that Clark did not have enough transferees to fill those slots for at least one year after Benton Harbor closed.

was singled out as the cost responsible for Benton Harbor's closure. Clark argues that it considered only "the bottom line," an elusive accounting concept which defied definition by any witness. For Charles Kiopes, General Manager for Construction Machinery, the bottom line was net gross margin. The plant capacity study showed a $33 million advantage in favor of closing Benton Harbor. James Reinhart and Raymond Pirrone said they also considered other items, including pretax income ($30 million advantage in favor of closing Benton Harbor), return on sales (1.3% advantage), return on assets (2.8% advantage), and operating expenses ($26.9 million advantage). Each Clark witness testified that his decision to recommend closing the Benton Harbor plant was based on a consideration of the entire study, and not solely upon a consideration of pension costs or even of direct labor costs.

While the Court is persuaded by Clark's evidence, it believes that Clark has over stated its case on the law. Clark's first argument is that a plaintiff cannot prevail under section 510 where, "elimination of jobs and termination of benefits were attributable to mounting economic losses, plant closures or winding up of a business." This is simply not the law. ERISA was intended to prevent employers from making employment decisions based upon their desire to avoid pension liability. Whether the defendant's motive is cost-saving or ill-will toward a particular employee, the employer will violate ERISA if it makes an employment decision solely, or even substantially, for the purpose of avoiding pension liability. Pensions cost money; money and "economic losses" are essentially synonymous. Allowing an employer to defend an ERISA claim solely on the ground that its pension program was too expensive to maintain would defeat the purpose of § 510, which is to prohibit employers from making employment decisions based upon pension costs....

Certainly, as defendant points out, plaintiffs must establish that Clark acted with the purpose of interfering with their attainment of benefits under the plan. Plaintiffs may not prevail if the loss of benefits was "a mere consequence of, but not a motivating factor behind a termination of employment." *Baker v. Kaiser Aluminum & Chemical Corp.*, 608 F. Supp. 1315, 1319 (N.D. Cal. 1984). Plaintiffs must show "more than ... that the termination of [their] employment 'meant a monetary savings to defendants,' for otherwise an ERISA violation would automatically occur every time an employer terminated a fully-vested employee...." *Donohue v. Custom Management Corp.*, 634 F. Supp. 1190, 1197 (W.D. Pa. 1986). The "something more" referred to in *Donohue* is the requisite causal link between pension benefits and an adverse employment action. Plaintiffs must prove by a preponderance of the evidence that the defendant's desire to avoid pension liability was a determining factor in motivating the challenged conduct. If plaintiffs establish that they lost work because of their pension benefits, plaintiffs will prevail....

If Clark had made the decision based primarily on the costs of the pension plan, Clark would have acted with the purpose of interfering with plaintiffs' rights under that plan. The resulting loss of benefits would not have been an "incidental" result of the decision to terminate plaintiffs' employment, it would have been the motivating factor behind that decision, the cause of their termination. *Gavalik* at 860. The difficulty for plaintiffs in this case is that Clark's witnesses testified that pension costs were one of many considerations in their decision, and that no single factor standing alone motivated or dominated their decision to close the Benton Harbor plant. Combined with the documentary evidence provided by the defendant, this testimony establishes that the decision to close the Benton Harbor plant was not motivated, or caused, by Clark's consideration of pension costs at that plant.

The defendant next argues that "the 'invidious intent' to interfere with participants' ERISA rights is not found where termination cuts along independently established lines.... Section 510 addresses discriminatory conduct directed against individuals, not actions involving a plan in general such as the winding up of a plant or division."...

Taken to its logical extension, defendant's argument essentially means that an employer violates ERISA only when the employer discharges or otherwise discriminates against a single employee, rather than a class or group of employees. Again, Clark misstates the law.... ERISA does not distinguish between the termination of one employee and the termination of 100 employees. Either action is illegal if taken with the purpose of avoiding pension liability. Rather, ERISA distinguishes between the intent to interfere with vested pension rights and the intent to terminate employment for other, nondiscriminatory reasons. While termination of employees in order to reduce labor costs is not always illegal, ERISA prohibits such actions if the primary reason for high labor costs is pension liability.

Defendant's final argument is that ERISA does not provide a remedy for employees whose pension rights have vested and whose only injury is the "lost opportunity to accrue additional benefits." While Clark correctly points out that some courts have denied ERISA claims where the plaintiff's rights under a pension plan have vested, other courts have held that the question of whether an employee's rights were vested is irrelevant to the § 510 cause of action.

[S]ection 510 would make little sense if given the interpretation defendant urges. Employees whose pensions have vested, but whose right to retire has not yet accrued, often rely more heavily upon the promise of an adequate pension than do their younger, unvested colleagues. Older employees, like the plaintiffs in this case, are virtually unemployable if they lose their current jobs and, even if they could find work, would have a shorter working life in which to accrue new retirement benefits. Younger, unvested employees can find new work more easily than older displaced workers. They have a better chance of working long enough to earn a pension simply because they are younger and have a longer working life in which to accrue these rights. Employers also have a greater incentive to discriminate against older, vested employees since these employees are closer to retirement and the employer is closer to having to pay out the benefits it has promised. The employer can make good its promises to younger employees by investing smaller amounts of money over a longer period of time, thus reducing the strain of pension benefits on employers and reducing the incentive to discriminate against younger employees. For these reasons, section 510 would be essentially unnecessary were it intended to protect only unvested employees. Not only are unvested employees in less need of protection, but employers generally lack incentives to discriminate against them. Vested employees, on the other hand, are often in greater need of the statute's protection and the employer's incentive to violate it is often greatest with respect to those employees....

ERISA protects against employer action taken to prevent the accrual of additional rights or benefits under a qualified plan.... [I]n *Folz v. Marriott Corp.*, 594 F. Supp. 1007 (W.D. Mo. 1984) the court found liability under § 510 where an employer discharged an employee suffering from multiple sclerosis for the purpose of preventing him from using the employer's health insurance benefits. In that case, the court held, "The allegation that an employee was terminated from his employment for the purpose of depriving him of *continued participation* in the employer's ... insurance program states a cognizable claim under section 510 of ERISA."

In this case, plaintiffs make a similar claim. They argue that Clark terminated their employment in order to prevent them from accruing additional years of service and from obtaining full retirement benefits. This is exactly the sort of claim ERISA was intended to redress, as ... *Folz* indicate[s]. If Clark terminated the plaintiffs' employment in order to prevent them from obtaining additional benefits under the pension plan, Clark violated ERISA.

While the Court views defendant's legal arguments with some distaste, it must agree with defendant's interpretation of the evidence in this case. The defendant has shown that it had a legitimate, non-discriminatory reason for terminating the plaintiffs' employment. Each Clark witness testified that he made the decision to recommend closure of the Benton Harbor plant based on a review of all the financial data available. No single item of cost or consideration was given more weight than any other. Direct testimony from at least three witnesses (James Reinhart, Raymond Pirrone and Charles Kiorpes) established that pension benefits were not a significant consideration in the decision....

Plaintiffs' highest credible estimation of the significance of pension benefits was slightly less than 40% of the difference in labor costs between Benton Harbor and Asheville. At most, pension costs amounted to 20% of the total difference in cost between the two plants. Although this is a substantial amount, the Court finds that Clark would have made the decision to close Benton Harbor even if it had ignored the cost of the pension plan altogether. Had Clark eliminated consideration of all pension costs, there would still have been a $19.9 million difference in cost between Benton Harbor and Asheville. Even after adjusting these figures for the union's cost-cutting proposals, a difference in cost of $7.44 per standard hour exists, amounting to a difference of approximately $77,376.00 per employee over five years. These figures, together with the testimony of Clark executives, show that while Clark considered the cost of current pension benefits, and that this cost was substantial, it did not make the difference in Clark's decision to close the Benton Harbor plant.

Clark also successfully rebutted the inference of discrimination arising from its transfer policies. Michael Hanesworth, Clark's General Counsel for Labor Relations, testified that he recommended a restrictive interpretation of the Benton Harbor employees' transfer rights in order to protect both the seniority and the pension rights of workers at the Asheville plant. As a fiduciary for the Asheville workers' pension plan, Hanesworth had to consider the effect of transfers on the financial viability of the Asheville plant's pension plan. As he noted, if large numbers of Benton Harbor employees transferred to Asheville, they would place a great deal of strain on the Asheville pension plan. Since that plan was funded with the assumption that few, if any, employees would collect benefits from it for at least ten years ... the plan would have been imperiled by the unanticipated retirement of workers before that date.

After reviewing the evidence, the Court finds that Clark ... would have made the same decision, even if it had factored pension benefits out of the study entirely, because the evidence showed that Clark was looking for the least costly alternative.... Thus the Court concludes, somewhat reluctantly, that defendants should prevail on the ERISA claim.

NOTES

1. *A Natural Extension or Bad Economics?* On the one hand, *Nemeth* is a natural extension of the antiforfeiture protections of ERISA. When ERISA prohibits an employer from denying pension benefits *for any reason* after five years of service, it seems only fair also to prohibit that employer from firing an employee *specifically to avoid pension liabilities* after four years and eleven months of service. And it would seem to make no difference if the employer avoids the near-future pension liabilities one employee at a time or, as in *Nemeth*, simultaneously to large numbers of employees.

On the other hand, *Nemeth* counsels employers to blind themselves to an important set of costs when they make important decisions. If pension costs are significant enough to affect a decision, *Nemeth* holds that it is a violation of § 510 to consider them. (Ironically, if the costs are too small to matter — or even large, but not large enough to tip the decision — the employer can consider them.) Why do you think employee benefits are privileged over wages in this way? Because benefits, but not wages, are deferred compensation that has already been earned? Because benefits are more difficult to replace than wages?

2. *The Breadth of § 510.* Every time an employer discharges an employee, and often when it takes lesser measures, the employee's pension benefits are affected. If the employee's rights have not yet vested, the discharge may elimi-

nate any right of the employee to recover pension benefits. Even when employee rights have vested, the discharge prevents the accrual of additional benefits. *Nemeth* specifically holds that § 510's protections apply even after employee rights have vested. Indeed, § 510 is not limited to pension benefits. Welfare benefits, such as health insurance, can never vest and, unless the employer restricts itself in some way, can be changed by the employer virtually at will. Nevertheless, § 510's protections apply. *Inter-Modal Rail Employees Ass'n v. Atchison, Topeka & Santa Fe Ry. Co.*, 117 S. Ct. 1513 (1997). Employers, however, can defend against § 510 actions by demonstrating that they have legitimate reasons for their adverse employment actions. Viewed in this way, § 510 seems to require employers to justify every adverse employment action. Is § 510 a general wrongful discharge statute masquerading as a statute protecting pension rights? *See* Terry Collingsworth, *ERISA Section 510 — A Further Limitation on Arbitrary Discharges,* 10 INDUS. REL. L.J. 319 (1988) (yes). *But see Meredith v. Navistar Int'l Transp. Co.,* 935 F.2d 124 (7th Cir. 1991) (no § 510 action where loss of benefits is mere consequence of, as opposed to motivating factor behind, the termination). *Accord Dytrt v. Mountain State Tel. & Tel. Co.,* 921 F.2d 889 (9th Cir. 1990).

Should the *Nemeth* rationale be extended to situations where the employee is not yet a participant in the pension plan? In *Garratt v. Walker,* 121 F.3d 565 (10th Cir. 1997), the employer offered an employee either a $21,000 annual salary with a 15% contribution to a pension plan or a $24,000 annual salary with no pension contribution. The employee demanded a $24,000 annual salary with a 15% pension contribution. When the employer refused, the employee sued arguing that § 510 had been violated because the employer was basing his decision on pension costs. The Court held that § 510 had not been violated because some "rights" to pension benefits are "so speculative and contingent that [they] fall outside the bulwark of § 510." *Id.* at 570.

3. *The Necessity of § 510.* Consider an employee who is deciding whether to accept current wages or a pension promise in return for her services. The employee presumably compares the current wages (W) she could receive to the present value of the anticipated pension (V) times the probability of receiving the pension (p). If $pV > W$, the employee accepts the pension promise in lieu of the wages. If not, she takes the wages.

In a world without § 510, employees would have a broader range of choices with respect to the trade-off between p and V. Employees who prefer a higher V at the cost of a higher risk of forfeiture (a lower p) would accept pensions from employers who did not have a provision equivalent to § 510 in their pension plans. Employees who prefer a lower V and a lower risk of forfeiture could accept pensions under plans with § 510 equivalents. Viewed in this way, § 510 is unnecessary. Employees who do not have § 510-type protections in their pension plans and, because of that, never receive pensions, have not been swindled — instead, they have gambled for higher pension payments and lost. Indeed, § 510 may frustrate the preferences of some employees. Section 510, when it has any effect at all, operates to increase *p*. Thus, employees who would prefer higher pensions, albeit at a higher risk that they might receive nothing, are frustrated.

Convinced?

C. GENDER EQUITY

LORENZEN v. EMPLOYEES RETIREMENT PLAN OF THE SPERRY & HUTCHINSON CO.

United States Court of Appeals, Seventh Circuit
896 F.2d 228 (1990)

POSNER, CIRCUIT JUDGE.

This is a suit under the Employee Retirement Income Security Act of 1974 (ERISA) by the widow of an employee of S & H, claiming that S & H's Retirement Plan, an ERISA plan, violated its fiduciary duties to her husband and herself, causing a loss of retirement benefits. The district judge granted summary judgment for Mrs. Lorenzen, awarding her some $192,000 and the plan appeals....

Warren Lorenzen, a sales manager and long-time employee of S & H, was eligible to retire on February 1, 1987, having turned 65. As he was in the midst of managing a company project, the company requested him to postpone his retirement until July 1, and he agreed. At the same time he decided that when he did retire he would take his retirement benefits as a lump sum, rather than as a series of monthly payments for his life followed by monthly payments half as large to his wife for her life should she outlive him (the "50 percent joint and survivor option," as it was called). The taking of retirement benefits in a lump sum was an option expressly permitted by the plan, provided the spouse executed a written consent form, which Mrs. Lorenzen did. Since death is not retirement, in order to receive any retirement benefit at all, lump sum or annuity, the employee must live to the date of his retirement. If he dies before then, his spouse is entitled to a pre-retirement benefit but it is much smaller than the retirement benefit. On June 15, two weeks before his extended retirement date, Lorenzen suffered cardiac arrest and was hospitalized in grave condition. On June 27, he suffered cardiac arrest again and was plugged into life-support machinery. His condition was believed to be hopeless and his physicians advised Mrs. Lorenzen to request that the machinery be disconnected. She did so, it was disconnected, and Mr. Lorenzen died that day.

The plan documents do not define death, but the parties and the district judge assume that if Mrs. Lorenzen had not requested the removal of the life-support apparatus Mr. Lorenzen would have survived, within the meaning of the plan, until his retirement on July 1. In that event he would have received, pursuant to his earlier election, the lump-sum retirement benefit. Assuming he would then have been taken off life support, the lump sum would have passed to his widow.... And this was the amount the district court ordered the plan to pay her.

The plan argues that since Lorenzen died before he retired, the widow is entitled only to the pre-retirement death benefit — in present-value terms and rounded off, $89,000 versus $192,000. Of course if Lorenzen had received the lump sum, frittered it away at the gaming tables, and then died, Mrs. Lorenzen would be even worse off than she is (it is against this possibility that the spouse is required to sign a consent form, as she did), but the plan has not argued this possibility as a ground for reducing her damages.

In holding for Mrs. Lorenzen the district judge appears to have been moved by the human appeal of her case. This is understandable. To have to decide whether to order the removal of life support from a loved one is painful enough without having to incur an enormous financial penalty in the bargain. The equities are not all on one side, however. (They rarely are; the tension between formal justice and substantive justice is often, and perhaps here, illusory.) Life-support equipment is expensive and, to a considerable degree, futile and degrading. It should not be used to secure retirement benefits. If the parties to retirement plans envisaged such a use, they probably would define death as inability to "live" without life-support machinery — at least if permitted by state law, which might forbid the guardian of a patient even in a hopeless vegetative state to disconnect the patient's life-support machinery. *Cruzan v.* [*Director, Missouri Dept. of Health,* 497 U.S. 261 (1990).] By postponing his retirement Mr. Lorenzen took a risk that if he died his widow would obtain less money than if he retired as soon as he was eligible. But he was compensated for bearing this risk by being paid his full salary (which exceeded his retirement benefit, lump sum or annuity, evaluated on a comparable basis, i.e. as a monthly payment) for a longer time, and by having an expectation of slightly increased retirement benefits, for they rose with the length of time that he was employed, although not steeply. This "compensation" was, to be sure, ex ante rather than ex post — had Lorenzen been gifted with pre-vision he would have retired. But a gamble is not unfair merely because the gambler loses. Nor was the plan unjustly enriched at the Lorenzens' expense. "A pension plan is not 'unjustly enriched' where a pensioner dies early with no benefits payable to his survivor. That eventuality simply offsets cases where a pensioner lives well into old age and more benefits are paid to him than were statistically predictable." Finally, the record contains no evidence of what it would have cost Mrs. Lorenzen to maintain her husband on life-support machinery for an additional three days. It could have been a considerable sum, depending on the scope and terms of his hospital insurance.

Mrs. Lorenzen had no contractual entitlement to retirement benefits — this much is clear — since her husband did not survive until retirement. ERISA, however, requires that a retirement or welfare plan make clear to the participants what the plan's terms and conditions are. [ERISA § 101.] Mrs. Lorenzen claims that the plan did not adequately apprise her husband of the consequences of his electing the lump-sum rather than annuity form of retirement benefits and of his electing to keep on working rather than retire at the earliest possible opportunity.

The first claim is frivolous; regardless of which election Lorenzen would have made if fully informed, his death nullified any retirement benefits to which he and his wife might have been entitled had he lived to retirement. If he had elected the annuity form, then even though Mrs. Lorenzen would have been entitled — had he retired and she outlived him — to an annuity that would out-last his death, this entitlement would have been contingent on his retiring; and before he retired he died.

The second claim is that the plan should have advised Mr. Lorenzen more clearly than it did that if he postponed his retirement he was risking a net loss of benefits, since pre-retirement death benefits were lower than retirement benefits. There was no want of clarity, however. The plan summary explains that "if you should die either before retirement or after retirement but before benefits begin ... your spouse or other beneficiary will receive a benefit.... [I]f you die after age 55 and your legal spouse is your beneficiary, this benefit will be the larger of 40% of the lump sum equivalent of the benefits you have earned under the plan or the amount he or she [i.e., the legal spouse] would receive if you had retired on the day before your death under the 50% joint-and-survivor option." Mr. Lorenzen could have been under no illusion that if he died before his extended retirement date arrived, his widow would receive one hundred percent of his lump-sum retirement benefits rather than 50 percent of his retirement annuity. The risk he took in not retiring as soon as he could was an informed, a calcu-lated, one....

Mrs. Lorenzen [does not] argue that the plan summary was defective for failing to advise participants of the consequences of finding themselves on life-support machinery shortly before the scheduled date of retirement. She is wise not to make that argument, for the law is clear that the plan summary is not required to anticipate every possible idiosyncratic contingency that might affect a particular participant's or beneficiary's status. If it were, the summaries would be choked with detail and hopelessly confusing. Clarity and completeness are competing goods....

The judgment is reversed and the case is remanded with directions to award Mrs. Lorenzen only the pre-retirement death benefit to which she is entitled under her husband's retirement plan....

CUDAHY, CIRCUIT JUDGE, dissenting:

[W]ith respect to the merits, I do not quarrel with the essentials of the majority's analysis.... But I am at a loss to understand some of the majority's proffered justifications for its result. Mr. Lorenzen deferred his retirement for six months for the convenience of his employer. There is nothing to suggest that anyone brought to his or his wife's attention the possibility that she would suffer drastic financial penalties if he happened to die in the interim. Nor certainly is there any indication that he "gambled" six months' additional compensation against his wife's taking the risk of pension loss. The "rational bookmaker's" approach to problems is singularly out of place here.

By the same token there is no evidence that Mrs. Lorenzen knew she would suffer financially if she allowed life supports to be withdrawn from her husband "too soon." The human costs of this kind of decision are so overwhelming, economics is the wrong analysis to bring to the problem. And a cost-benefit study is beside the point. Fate claimed Mr. Lorenzen in a period when he was doing his employer a favor. And fate pressed on Mrs. Lorenzen a tragic choice which, quite by chance from her point of view, resulted in losing half her pension benefit. [District Court] Judge Evans thought these fortuities too cruel and decided the case in favor of the widow. Judge Evans, I believe, stepped back from the remorseless logic of the law with respect both to the time-to-appeal question and to the merits. [However, because I do not believe] that we have jurisdiction to hear the Plan's appeal, ... I ... do not reach the merits of the district court's award.

NOTES

1. *The District Court Decision.* The following excerpt is from Judge Evans' opinion in the *Lorenzen* case:

> Mrs. Lorenzen ... argues that she is entitled to summary judgment awarding her the lump sum payment her husband was entitled to. She contends that neither the plan language nor the spousal consent form adequately informed her of the possible effects of her consent, in violation of [ERISA § 205(c)(3)(A)]. She further contends that the plan is contrary to the intention of Congress in protecting surviving spouses and that the court has power to fashion an equitable remedy to keep within the purpose and intent of ERISA....
>
> The cause of what seems to be a very unfortunate result in this case is not that Delvina Lorenzen consented to a lump sum payment over joint and survivor benefits but that she was not aware that the lump sum payment would not be made unless her husband lived to retire. It is impossible to know what Warren Lorenzen knew on that point. It is clear that none of the letters he received provided him with the information.... [N]either the letters nor the spousal consent form gave any warning that the lump sum payment would be paid only if Mr. Lorenzen lived to his retirement date. This is a poignant situation both because Mr. Lorenzen, apparently out of some loyalty to the company, worked past his normal retirement date, and because his life in all probability could have been sustained until his postponed retirement date.
>
> In this situation, certain of defendants' arguments seem coldhearted. S & H argues that by calling a toll-free number, Mrs. Lorenzen could have found out that she would not collect the lump sum payment if her husband died before retirement. Perhaps. But a woman confronted with a decision to remove her husband from life-support systems probably was not thinking about calling a benefits supervisor, toll free or not....

> I am ... convinced that a person who elects a lump sum benefit (and the spouse who agrees to the election) and then continues to work after his normal retirement day should be informed that if he dies before retirement, his wife is not entitled to the full lump sum....
>
> Had Lorenzen refused to continue to work, he would have retired prior to his death and these problems would not have arisen. Had Mrs. Lorenzen been informed that her husband had to live until he retired in order for the payment to be made, she would not, as she states in her affidavit, have agreed to remove the life-support systems. [Given the complexity of, and indeed contradictions in,] the plan documents, it is extremely unfair to expect Mrs. Lorenzen to have figured out anything about her rights.

Lorenzen v. Employees Ret. Plan of the Sperry & Hutchinson Co., 699 F. Supp. 1367, 1369-71 (W.D. Wis. 1988), *rev'd*, 896 F.2d 228 (7th Cir. 1990).

2. *ERISA's Protection of Spousal Interests When the Participant Dies.* The Retirement Equity Act of 1984 (REAct) amended ERISA to provide two types of protections for spousal interests when a participant dies. When the participant survives until retirement, the default form of benefits is a qualified joint and survivor annuity (QJSA), which usually provides an annuity of x until the death of one spouse and 50% of x thereafter. ERISA § 205(a), (d). This form of benefit can be changed (so the benefit can be paid out as a lump sum or even as a single life annuity for the life of the participant), but only if the spouse consents to the change in writing. § 205(c). In the principal case, Mrs. Lorenzen consented to a change to a lump sum form of benefit. The lump sum figure of $192,000 in the case was equal to what it would have cost to purchase a joint and survivor annuity at the time of Mr. Lorenzen's retirement.

If the participant dies before retirement, the surviving spouse is entitled to a qualified preretirement survivor annuity (QPSA), commencing when the participant would have retired and equal to one-half the amount the participant would have received at retirement (equal, in other words, to the survivor annuity under the QJSA). ERISA § 205(a), (e). The QPSA can also be waived, but once again only with the written consent of the spouse. § 205(c). Mrs. Lorenzen did not waive her preretirement annuity; the $89,000 that Mrs. Lorenzen eventually received in the principal case was the QPSA, converted into a lump sum. If Mrs. Lorenzen had not signed any consents and Mr. Lorenzen had died the day after retiring, approximately what would have been the value of Mrs. Lorenzen's pension?

3. *ERISA's Protection of Spousal Interests Upon Divorce.* ERISA has strong provisions that prevent alienation of interests in pension benefits and that broadly preempt state law that affects pension plans. ERISA §§ 206(d), 514. On anti-alienation, see *Patterson v. Schumate*, 504 U.S. 753 (1992) (anti-alienation provision permitted debtor to exclude $250,000 in pension assets from his bankruptcy estate); *Guidry v. Sheet Metal Workers Nat'l Pension Fund*, 493 U.S. 365 (1990) (anti-alienation provision protected union pension benefits of member who had embezzled $377,000 from the union). On preemption, see *Boggs v. Boggs*, 117 S. Ct. 1754 (1997) (ERISA preempted state community property laws which would have permitted deceased spouse of a participant to make testamentary transfer of interests in a retirement plan); *Ingersoll-Rand Co. v. McClendon*, 498 U.S. 133 (1990) (state-law claim that employee discharged to prevent his pension from vesting was preempted by ERISA).

On divorce, the nonparticipant spouse who wants to claim a portion of the participant spouse's pension benefits is seeking an alienation of pension benefits under state domestic relations law. REAct created exceptions to the anti-alienation and preemption provisions of ERISA that permit pension benefits to be allocated between the spouses at divorce through qualified domestic relations orders (QDROs). ERISA §§ 206(d)(3), 514(b)(7). REAct permits QDROs to provide that the nonparticipant spouse is to be treated as a surviving spouse for purposes of QJSAs and QPSAs (and that subsequent spouses, as a result, would not be considered spouses for those purposes). REAct, however, does not establish that, or anything else, as a default regime; divorcing parties can use the option, or not, and the terms of the QDRO (within certain limitations designed to protect the plan from confusion and conflicting claims) are up to the parties. ERISA, then, provides a procedural framework that permits divorcing parties to divide pensions, but does not deal with the very difficult issue of how pension wealth should be allocated upon divorce.

4. *Adequacy of ERISA's Spousal Protections.* When participants die, pension plans generally provide annuities for surviving spouses (who are usually women) that are only 50% as large as the annuity that would have been provided if the participant had not died. The difference is significant. A survey of pension benefits found that the average thirty-year employee retiring at age sixty-five with a $35,000 salary is able to replace 25.9% of his salary from his pension alone and 70.1% from pension and social security benefits combined. If the participant dies, however, his surviving spouse is able to replace only 13.4% of the salary from pension benefits and only 42.8% from pension and social security benefits combined. William J. Wiatrowski, *New Survey Data on Pension Benefits,* MONTHLY LAB. REV., Aug. 1991, at 8, 17. Should ERISA's QJSA and QPSA provisions require a surviving spouse annuity of more than 50%?

Similarly, ERISA has strong antiforfeiture provisions designed to protect funds for retirement, but spouses are permitted to waive their rights. Are the retirement interests of spouses (usually women) less important?

5. *Protections for Women as Pension Plan Participants. Lorenzen* discusses ERISA protections for the interests of spouses in pensions, interests that are disproportionately held by women. But women, of course, can also have interests at stake as employees/participants. For example, since women live longer than men, when male and female employees make the same contributions into a pension fund while they are working and receive equal annuities at retirement, a disproportionate share of the benefits will go to women. To correct for this, many employers used to require either that women make higher contributions into the fund or that they receive smaller annuities at retirement. The Supreme Court has ruled that both of these practices violate Title VII. *City of Los Angeles, Dep't of Water & Power v. Manhart,* 435 U.S. 702 (1978); *Arizona Governing Comm'n v. Norris,* 463 U.S. 1073 (1983).

Although *Manhart* and *Norris* provide some protections, women are still less likely than men to have pensions, and those with pensions are likely to have lower benefits. According to one study, 31% of retirement age women received or expected to receive a pension compared to 57% for men, while the median monthly pension income for women receiving pensions was $250, compared to $460 for men. John R. Woods, *Retirement-Age Women and Pensions: Findings From the New Beneficiary Survey,* SOC. SECURITY BULL., Dec. 1988, at 5, 7, 13.

The lower pension coverage and benefits for women are caused by several factors. For example, women are paid less than men, they work in industries that are less likely to offer pensions, and they are more likely to work part-time and to interrupt their careers, which makes it more difficult for them to become eligible for and vest in pensions. Are those satisfactory explanations for the disparities between men and women, or should steps be taken to narrow the pension gap? On steps that might be taken, see PRESIDENT'S COMM'N ON PENSION POLICY, COMING OF AGE: TOWARD A RETIREMENT INCOME POLICY (1981) (proposing that all employers be required to provide pensions); OLDER WOMEN'S LEAGUE, THE PATH TO POVERTY: AN ANALYSIS OF WOMEN'S RETIREMENT INCOME (1995) (establish three-year vesting requirement; make private and public pensions portable; require that pension benefits be divided between spouses at divorce, unless a court orders or the parties agree otherwise; and make pro-rated pension benefits available to part-time workers).

D. FIDUCIARY DUTIES

BALLONE v. EASTMAN KODAK CO.

United States Court of Appeals, Second Circuit

109 F.3d 118 (1997)

PARKER, Circuit Judge:

In this case, we are called upon to determine the circumstances in which alleged misrepresentations made by an employer to retirement plan beneficiaries about future plan amendments are actionable under the Employee Retirement Income Security Act ("ERISA"), 29 U.S.C. § 1104(a), which imposes a fiduciary duty on retirement plan administrators. Plaintiffs, all former employees of Eastman Kodak Company who retired between January 1 and July 1, 1991, contend that Kodak made affirmative misrepresentations that led them to believe that no enhanced pension plan would be forthcoming in the months following their retirement. Shortly after Plaintiffs retired, Kodak implemented a pension plan with benefits exceeding those of Plaintiffs' retirement plan. Plaintiffs thereafter brought suit in the United States District Court for the Western District of New

York, alleging, among other things, that Kodak breached its fiduciary duty under ERISA. The district court granted judgment to Kodak on Plaintiffs' claims under § 1104(a), and other related claims, concluding that because Kodak had not "seriously considered" changes to the retirement plan before Plaintiffs retired, Kodak's statements about future plan changes were neither material nor misleading. We conclude that because Kodak allegedly assured Plaintiffs that it had ruled out plan changes for the immediate future, when in fact it had not, the district court erred in determining that the absence of "serious consideration" of plan changes warranted judgment in Kodak's favor. Accordingly, we vacate the judgment of the district court and remand for further proceedings consistent with this opinion.

I. BACKGROUND

A. *Kodak's Consideration of Retirement Plan Amendments*

As the district court found, throughout the 1980s, Kodak had been downsizing to cut costs. The company generally achieved its downsizing goals by offering special voluntary separation programs, known as Limited Separation Enhancements ("LSEs"), which offered severance pay and retraining allowances to targeted employees. Kodak provided these severance packages through its Termination Allowance Plan ("TAP"), which provided up to seventy-eight weeks severance pay depending on the employee's length of service. This program was distinct from Kodak's pension plan, the Kodak Retirement Income Plan ("KRIP").

In 1990, Kodak revised KRIP to eliminate the minimum age requirement for retirement and to provide partial or full pension benefits depending on the employee's age and length of service. Although the district court determined that the amendments were only intended to make the program more competitive in the industry and to respond to tax concerns, it is undisputed that KRIP induced more employees to retire and was therefore helpful to Kodak's downsizing efforts. Accordingly, after Kodak enhanced KRIP, the company essentially eliminated LSE and reduced severance pay under TAP to fifty-two weeks.

The district court found that in 1990 Kodak considered KRIP sufficiently generous that no amendments to the plan would be needed in the future. In the spring of 1991, however, Kodak formed a "downsizing task force" to evaluate and improve upon Kodak's past downsizing process. This included review of its pension and separation plans and review of the criteria used to target employees during downsizing. During this time, the company's earnings decreased eleven percent from fiscal 1990, and its costs increased twenty percent.

In June of 1991, in response to the worsening economic condition of the company, Kodak instructed the heads of the Electronic Imaging Organization ("EIO") and the Commercial Imaging Group ("CIG") to seek ways to cut costs. The company did not specifically instruct them to target employees for downsizing. In July, the heads of the two divisions began to explore downsizing options. The district court found that Kodak discussed many scenarios but developed no specific plan. On July 19, 1991, the benefits manager at Kodak convened a conference call of all division managers regarding various issues relating to the downsizing, but the agenda for the call noted that the need for downsizing had not yet been confirmed.

In mid-July, Kodak's second-quarter earnings statement became available. The statement indicated that Kodak's operating goals were not being met and that Kodak's financial condition had deteriorated further. Accordingly, Kay Whitmore, the chief executive officer and chairman of the board of Kodak, instructed Kodak officials to consider various downsizing scenarios, preferring a voluntary discharge program funded by KRIP assets. He stated that Kodak needed to have a plan in place by mid-August.

The district court found that Whitmore's downsizing mandate was galvanized during a July 22, 1991, meeting between John McCarthy, senior vice-president of Kodak and president of Human Resources, and personnel relations directors of Kodak's various business groups. At the meeting, it became clear that the downsizing would extend beyond EIO and CGI to all of the company. On July 25, McCarthy informed the personnel relations directors that a voluntary downsizing program would be implemented, but it was still unclear which divisions would be targeted. Based on McCarthy's statements at the July 25 meeting, the district court concluded that as of July 25, 1991, Kodak's new retirement plan, the Resource Redeployment and Retirement Program ("RRRP"), was under "serious consideration" by Kodak.

After management meetings on July 28-30, Whitmore concluded that Kodak would have to sever 3000 employees. To this end, he instructed McCarthy to prepare a plan by August 2. It was to be a voluntary severance plan funded out of KRIP assets. The outline of the plan was established by August 2. The Board approved the plan on August 9. On August 12, Kodak announced it to the public. The plan, RRRP, provided full pension benefits to employees with seventy-five points (calculated based on the employee's age plus years in the company), plus fifty-two weeks severance pay, a social security bridge payment, and a $5000 retraining allowance. The severance pay, bridge payment, and retraining allowance were not available to Plaintiffs, who retired under KRIP, the plan RRRP replaced.

B. Alleged Misrepresentations

Plaintiffs allege that during the time Kodak considered downsizing scenarios in 1991 it falsely assured them that no changes to its retirement plan were forthcoming. They allege that Kodak assured them that it would implement no retirement plan enhancements during 1991, that KRIP was a permanent plan for the future and that downsizing would not occur before at least 1992. Kodak allegedly told Plaintiffs that the 1990 KRIP plan would not change in the near future for various specific reasons, including the cost of such an enhanced program, government regulations, and the lack of any immediate need for a future enhanced benefits program. Plaintiffs claim that they left the company shortly before the RRRP benefits became available in August, in reliance on Kodak's statements.

C. *Proceedings Below*

The district court held a bench trial limited to the question of whether Kodak "seriously considered" implementing RRRP at the time it made the alleged misrepresentations. Because the district court found that Kodak did not seriously consider implementing RRRP until July 25, 1991, it held that none of the alleged misstatements made before that date were material.

In limiting the scope of its materiality analysis to the serious consideration issue, the district court relied on *Mullins v. Pfizer, Inc.*, 23 F.3d 663 (2d Cir. 1994), where this Court noted that the more seriously an ERISA plan change is being considered, the more material the misrepresentations become. The district court interpreted *Mullins* to stand for the bright-line rule that, "at a minimum, pension plan changes must be under 'serious consideration' before a plan administrator can be held liable for making material misrepresentations about the plan to participants or beneficiaries."

Because the district court believed that the lack of serious consideration of RRRP by Kodak made any alleged misrepresentations immaterial, it did not examine any of the misrepresentations in detail. The court concluded, however, that because Kodak was not seriously considering future changes until July 25, 1991, any statements to Kodak employees made before that date telling them that Kodak had decided not to change the plan were not deceptive....

II. DISCUSSION

ERISA imposes a fiduciary duty on employers with retirement plans to act "solely in the interest of the participants and beneficiaries." 29 U.S.C. § 1104(a). We held in *Mullins v. Pfizer* that a plan administrator may not make affirmative material misrepresentations about proposed future changes to an employee benefit plan. Such misrepresentations are actionable as a breach of fiduciary duty under ERISA. Here, we consider the contours of that holding....

A. *Materiality*

In ruling that Kodak's alleged misrepresentations were immaterial, the district court erred in attributing talismanic significance to its finding that Kodak's future retirement plan, RRRP, was not under serious consideration at the time Kodak allegedly misled Plaintiffs. Where an ERISA fiduciary makes guarantees regarding future benefits that misrepresent present facts, the misrepresentations are material if they would induce a reasonable person to rely upon them....

Whether a plan is under serious consideration is but one factor in the materiality inquiry....

Our conclusion in *Mullins* that a plan administrator has a fiduciary duty not to make material misrepresentations regarding the availability of future plan benefits is squarely in accord with the Supreme Court's recent decision in *Varity Corp. v. Howe*, 116 S. Ct. 1065 (1996). Although *Varity* did not address the materiality of an employer's misstatements, it established that the scope of the employer's fiduciary duty under ERISA is broad. The Court considered a case where the employer made misrepresentations about the security of its employees' non-pension benefits to induce them to transfer to a division of the company that the employer had created as a dumping ground for its failing businesses. The employees eventually lost their benefits when the division went into receivership. The Court held that "[t]o participate knowingly and significantly in deceiving a plan's beneficiaries in order to save the employer money at the beneficiaries' expense[ ] is not to act 'solely in the interest of the participants and beneficiaries,'" as ERISA requires. *Id.* at 1074.

In *Varity*, the Court applied "common-law trust standards 'bearing in mind the special nature and purpose of employee benefit plans.'" The Court could find "no adequate basis ..., in the statute or otherwise, for any special interpretation that might insulate [the employer], acting as a fiduciary, from the legal consequences of the kind of conduct (intentional misrepresentation) that often creates liability even among strangers." The employer's misrepresentations included "repeated reassurances that benefits would remain 'unchanged,' [a] detailed comparison of [the old and new] benefits, and ... assurances about [the new subsidiary's] 'bright' financial future." The employer made these assurances about the employees' future benefits knowing perfectly well that the new division would likely fail.

Applying these trust-law principles, it is clear that Kodak may not actively misinform its plan beneficiaries about the availability of future retirement benefits to induce them to retire earlier than they otherwise would, regardless of whether or not it is seriously considering future plan changes. Kodak has a duty to deal fairly and honestly with its beneficiaries.

If an employer allegedly makes false assurances about future benefits, the materiality of the misstatements turns primarily on the nature and the context of the assurance. Whether consideration is being given to altering a pension plan at the time the misrepresentation is made is relevant to materiality, for the reasons we stated in *Mullins*, but it is not a prerequisite. Regardless whether the employer is seriously considering altering its retirement plan, the employer's false assurance that future enhancements have been ruled out for some specific period can be decisive in inducing an employee to hasten retirement, rather than delay in the hope of receiving enhanced future benefits. This aspect of the assurance can render it material regardless of whether future changes are under consideration at the time the misstatement is made.

This conclusion follows from the breadth of an ERISA fiduciary's trust obligations under *Varity* and the nature of the materiality inquiry under *Mullins*. It is also consistent with precedent under the securities laws relating to affirmative misrepresentations, to which we looked in *Mullins* for guidance in crafting ERISA materiality rules. Under the securities laws, an assurance about the future that by necessary implication misrepresents present facts is clearly actionable. *See ZVI Trading Corp. Employees' Money Purchase Pension Plan and Trust v. Ross (In re Time Warner Inc. Sec. Litig.)*, 9 F.3d 259, 266 (2d Cir. 1993) (assurances may be actionable if made without a basis in fact). Such statements are material if they would induce reasonable reliance.[2]

Determining the materiality of false assurances like those here alleged is fact-specific and will turn on a number of factors, including: how significantly the statement misrepresents the present status of internal deliberations regarding future plan changes; the special relationship of trust and confidence between the plan fiduciary and beneficiary; whether the employee was aware of other information or statements from the company tending to minimize the importance of the misrepresentation or should have been so aware, taking into consideration the broad trust responsibilities owed by the plan administrator to the employee and the employee's reliance on the plan administrator for truthful information; and the specificity of the assurance. Whereas mere mispredictions are not actionable, false statements about future benefits may be material if couched as a guarantee, especially where, as alleged here, the guarantee is supported by specific statements of fact. *Cf. Malone v. Microdyne Corp.*, 26 F.3d 471, 479 (4th Cir. 1994) (misleading prognostications may be material under the securities laws if they are "supported by specific statements of fact or are worded as guarantees").

A guarantee implies that current facts support it — in this case, that Kodak had made a decision not to implement plan changes in the immediate future for various specific reasons — and if the guarantee necessarily misrepresents such facts it may be materially misleading. Of course, the guarantee must be realistic. In most circumstances, an employee probably cannot rely upon a representation that the employer has decided never to alter its benefits package, for example, because such a statement is too speculative and unbelievable to "mislead a reasonable employee in making an adequately informed decision about if and when to retire." *See Mullins*, 23 F.3d at 669 (internal quotation omitted).

Based on these standards, it is far from clear that Kodak's alleged misrepresentations were not material. Plaintiffs contend that Kodak told them that it definitely would not implement a new retirement program in the near future. If Kodak had not actually made such a decision, this could be a material misrepre-

---

[2] We note the difference between the duty of full disclosure under the securities laws and the disclosure obligations imposed on employers under ERISA. We refer here to securities law precedent only insofar as it is relevant to determining the materiality of affirmative misrepresentations.

sentation since Plaintiffs also allege that they would have delayed retiring if they had known that no such decision had been made. Plaintiffs further allege that Kodak supported these false assurances with various other statements of fact, including the representation that financial considerations precluded the need for a plan for at least another two years and that government regulations prohibited any amendments to the plan. The district court should consider each of the alleged misrepresentations in light of the framework outlined here, to determine if reliance on them was reasonable. "Serious consideration" of plan changes is not the sine qua non of materiality.

B. *Misrepresentation*

The district court determined that Kodak's statements to the effect that "no pension enhancements were forthcoming" were truthful because, at the time Kodak made the statements, it was not seriously considering enhanced future benefits. We disagree. The district court did not examine any of the statements in detail, and therefore failed to consider Plaintiffs' allegations that Kodak stated that it had reached a decision not to amend its pension plan when in fact it had not made such a decision....

Plaintiffs allege that Kodak gave them definite assurances that no new benefits would be forthcoming when it knew that plan changes might well be made in the near future. They also allege that Kodak made various false statements of fact to support the assurances. If these allegations are true, a question which the district court did not address, the statements may well have been misleading. While it is correct, as the district court ruled, that Kodak need not be prescient, an employer does not enjoy carte blanche to make statements that the employer knows to be false, or that have no reasonable basis in fact, simply because the statements concern the future.

Our conclusion is not altered by evidence of a September 6, 1990, issue of the "Kodakery," Kodak's employee newsletter, which informed employees that changing economic conditions could result in further amendment to Kodak's retirement plan. The district court found the newsletter relevant to determining whether Kodak made affirmative misrepresentations. Even if the newsletter's statements were true when made, that would not necessarily prevent other statements, especially later ones, from being misleading. Determining whether any single statement allegedly made by Kodak is an actionable misrepresentation requires considering the statement's meaning in context. The district court should examine all alleged statements within the total mix of information available to Plaintiffs, including the newsletter. The newsletter's statements might be relevant in determining a reasonable interpretation of ambiguous later statements, and thus whether those statements were misrepresentations.

If the court determines that Kodak made misrepresentations regarding future benefits, the availability to Plaintiffs of truthful information countering the misrepresentations will be relevant in determining if they reasonably relied on the misrepresentations. *See* [*Virginia Bandshares, Inc. v.*] *Sandberg*, 501 U.S. 1083, 1097 (1991) ("While a misleading statement will not always lose its deceptive edge simply by joinder with others that are true, the true statements may discredit the other one so obviously that the risk of real deception drops to nil.") (proxy statements). On remand, it will fall to the district court to consider the newsletter in light of the other factors that are relevant to materiality, in accordance with the framework we have outlined in this opinion.

NOTES

1. *Days Later in Oklahoma.* Three days after *Ballone* was decided, the 10th Circuit held that companies do not have any fiduciary duty to disclose information about changes to a retirement incentive program until the changes are under "serious consideration." *Hockett v. Sun Co.*, 109 F.3d 1515 (1997). Paul Hockett was fifty-five years old and thinking of early retirement. He talked with two company representatives about whether an early retirement incentive program would be implemented, but was told nothing even though one of the representatives knew that a program was being contemplated. He retired two months before the program providing enhanced retirement benefits became effective:

> The "serious consideration" requirement is designed to balance "the tension between an employee's right to information and an employer's need to operate on a day-to-day basis." This balancing respects Congress' competing desires, in enacting ERISA, to safeguard employee benefit plans, and yet not make such plans so burdensome or threatening that employers would shy away from offering them. As a practical matter, an employer's "consideration" of an ERISA plan can fall anywhere along a continuum, beginning with the most casual mention of a possible plan change and ending, perhaps, with a formal vote by the Board of Directors. Between these two extremes are many stages of research, analysis, and debate, which only some proposals will survive. "Serious consideration" marks the point on the continuum at which imposing fiduciary-related duties will best serve the competing congressional purposes.

> "[S]erious consideration" of a change in plan benefits does not exist until (1) a specific proposal (2) is being discussed for purposes of implementation (3) by senior management with the authority to implement the change. Until these three factors intersect, misrepresentations regarding future plan changes cannot be material, and thus cannot constitute a breach of fiduciary duty.

> In our view, [this] formulation appropriately narrows the range of instances in which an employer must disclose, in response to employees' inquiries, its tentative intentions regarding an ERISA plan. Employers frequently review retirement and benefit plans as part of ongoing efforts to

succeed in a competitive and volatile marketplace. If any discussion by management regarding possible change to an ERISA plan triggered disclosure duties, the employer could be burdened with providing a constant, ever-changing stream of information to inquisitive plan participants. And, most of such information actually would be useless, if not misleading, to employees, considering that many corporate ideas and strategies never reach maturity, or else metamorphose so dramatically along the way, that early disclosure would be of little value. Furthermore, requiring employers to reveal too soon their internal deliberations to inquiring beneficiaries could seriously "impair the achievement of legitimate business goals" by allowing competitors to know that the employer is considering a labor reduction, a site-change, a merger, or some other strategic move.

Even more importantly, we believe [this] standard protects employees' access to material information without discouraging employers from improving their ERISA plans in the first place. "[C]hanging circumstances, such as the need to reduce labor costs, might require an employer to sweeten its severance package, and an employer should not be forever deterred from giving its employees a better deal merely because it did not clearly indicate to a previous employee that a better deal might one day be proposed." Moreover, employers often decide to "sweeten" an early retirement plan only after the employer has determined that not enough employees are opting to retire under the existing one. "If fiduciaries were required to disclose such a business strategy, it would necessarily fail. Employees simply would not leave if they were informed that improved benefits were planned if workforce reductions were insufficient." Thus, precipitous liability could push employers in the direction of involuntary lay-offs, a common alternative to early retirement inducements. [Our] standard minimizes this possibility.

Id. at 1522-23 (citations omitted).

2. *Who's a Fiduciary?* *Ballone* talks about "Kodak" violating its fiduciary responsibilities by making misrepresentations about its plans. But, as a general matter, employers are not fiduciaries under ERISA, nor is anyone else who does not exercise discretionary authority or control over the management or administration of a plan. § 3(21)(A). Thus, when employers adopt, modify, or terminate plans, they are not acting as fiduciaries analogous to trustees of private trusts, but instead are more analogous to the settlors of private trusts. Consequently, in amending its retirement plan, Kodak was acting as a settlor, not as a fiduciary, and, hence, could not have violated any fiduciary duties. *See Lockheed v. Spink*, 116 S. Ct. 1783, 1789-90 (1996). Similarly, employees of Kodak who had no discretionary authority to manage or administer the retirement plan (for example, the immediate supervisors of the plaintiffs) would not be ERISA fiduciaries. Only those with discretionary authority over the plan (for example, the plan administrator) would be subject to duties or liability under *Ballone*.

Limitations on the definition of who is a fiduciary open up rather obvious strategic possibilities for firms in Kodak's position, but it is not a completely open door. In *Varity Corp. v. Howe*, 116 S. Ct. 1065 (1996), the Court rejected an employer's claim that it was acting only as an employer, and not as a fiduciary, in disseminating misleading information about a plan. The information provided was detailed, it was provided by those within the company who had authority to act as fiduciaries under the plan, and reasonable employees could have thought that the employer was communicating with them in its capacity as plan administrator. An employer who chooses to wear hats as both employer and plan administrator may not be able to take the plan administrator hat off at will.

3. *Liability and Preemption*. *Varity Corp.* made it clear for the first time that individual relief was available for fiduciary violations. *Id.* at 1075-79 (limiting *Massachusetts Mut. Life Ins. Co. v. Russell*, 473 U.S. 134 (1985)). Thus, to the extent a fiduciary violated his duties by misleading the plaintiffs in *Ballone,* they will be able to recover individual damages under ERISA.

The plaintiffs will be in a more difficult position, however, if only non-fiduciaries mislead the plaintiffs. There is no non-fiduciary liability under ERISA. *Mertens v. Hewitt Assocs.*, 508 U.S. 248 (1993); *Reich v. Rowe*, 20 F.3d 25 (1st Cir. 1994). Plaintiffs could attempt to allege state law claims instead, but those claims may be preempted. We will consider preemption issues in the next chapter.

DONOVAN v. BIERWIRTH

United States Court of Appeals, Second Circuit
680 F.2d 263, *cert. denied,* 459 U.S. 1069 (1982)

FRIENDLY, CIRCUIT JUDGE:

This action was brought on October 19, 1981, by the Secretary of Labor (the Secretary) under § 502(e)(1) of the Employee Retirement Income Security Act of 1974 (ERISA) in the District Court for the Eastern District of New York, against John C. Bierwirth, Robert G. Freese and Carl A. Paladino, Trustees of the Grumman Corporation Pension Plan (the Plan). The action stems from the unsuccessful tender offer by LTV Corporation (LTV) in the fall of 1981 for some 70% of the outstanding common stock and convertible securities of Grumman Corporation (Grumman) at $45 per share. At the time of the offer the Plan owned some 525,000 shares of Grumman common stock, which it had acquired in the mid-1970's. As hereafter recounted, the Plan not only declined to tender its stock but purchased an additional 1,158,000 shares at an average price of $38.27 per share, at a total cost of $44,312,380. These acts, the Secretary's complaint alleged, constituted a violation of §§ 404(a) and 406(b) of ERISA....

A number of participants in the Plan were allowed to intervene as defendants; a supporting affidavit of one of the Plan participants alleged that:

[S]pontaneously and within days after this suit was commenced, Grumman employees at all levels and in all departments began to circulate petitions expressing their approval of the trustees' actions, as participants in the Pension Plan. To date, petitions have been signed by approximately 17,000 of the 22,000 employees who are Plan participants and beneficiaries....

The LTV tender offer followed a scenario that has become familiar. On September 21, 1981, in the absence of defendant Bierwirth, Chairman of the Board of Grumman, who was on vacation, Joseph O. Gavin, Jr., President of Grumman, received a telephone call from Paul Thayer, Chairman of the Board and Chief Executive Officer of LTV, inviting him to discuss a possible merger. Gavin rejected the invitation. Evidently unsurprised, LTV, prior to the opening of trading on the New York Stock Exchange on September 23, issued a press release announcing that it was planning to make a cash tender offer at $45 per share for up to 70% of Grumman's common stock and securities representing or convertible into common stock. According to the press release, the offer constituted "the first step in a plan to acquire 100% of the voting equity of the Grumman Corporation." On September 21 and 22 Grumman stock had sold on the New York Stock Exchange at prices ranging between $23^{7}/_{8}$ and $27^{1}/_{4}$ ....

The LTV offer was made on September 24. It was conditioned upon the tender of a minimum of 50.01% of Grumman's common stock and securities representing or convertible into common stock. The withdrawal/proration date was 12:01 A.M. on October 16, 1981; the termination date was 12:01 A.M. on October 23. Bierwirth cut short his vacation and reached the Grumman office at midday on September 24.

Although SEC Rule 14e-2 gave the Grumman board 10 business days from the commencement of the offer to communicate its position, if any, the board lost no time in going into action. It met on September 25. By then the LTV offer had caused the price of Grumman stock to rise to a range of $32^{5}/_{8}$ to $34^{1}/_{4}$. The board had before it a two page letter of Dillon, Read & Co., Inc., which had served Grumman as investment banker, stating in a conclusory fashion that it was "of the opinion that the offer is inadequate from a financial point of view to holders of the Grumman securities." The letter said this conclusion was based on certain information of a business and financial nature regarding Grumman which was either publicly available or furnished to us by Grumman and (on) discussions with the management of Grumman regarding its business and prospects. The letter made no attempt at quantification of these factors, and no representative of Dillon, Read attended the meeting for questioning, although apparently there were some supporting financial materials available. Defendant Robert G. Freese had also prepared some projections which are not in the record. The board unanimously adopted a resolution to oppose the tender offer, and issued a press release to that effect, saying that the board had concluded that "the offer is inadequate, and not in the best interests of Grumman, its shareholders, employees or the United States."

On September 28 Grumman began [an action alleging inadequate disclosure and violation of § 7 of the Clayton Act] which was to lead to the injunction of the tender offer. On the same day defendant Bierwirth, Chairman of the Board of Grumman, sent a letter to the company's shareholders seeking their help in defeating the offer. The letter stated:

> We're very optimistic about our chances of defeating the takeover bid. About a third of all shares are held by Grumman's employee investment and pension plans. These plans are managed by Grummanites who will look long and hard at how well their fellow members would be served by selling off Grumman stock. Much of the rest is owned by Grumman people who, I believe, understand their future is worth more than a quick return on a block of shares.

The reasons given for opposing LTV's offer were the inadequacy of the price and others, relating to the pension fund, set forth in the margin.[3] The letter concluded by announcing that "Grumman's management is totally committed to defeating this takeover attempt," and by pleading "If you own Grumman shares, don't sell out to LTV."

On September 30, at the invitation of George Petrilak, President of the Grumman Retirees Club, Bierwirth met with 300 retirees to discuss the LTV offer. An affidavit of Petrilak avers that "there was great concern expressed by the members as to the possible impact of LTV succeeding in their tender offer upon their pensions," and said that "[t]he overwhelming attitude of the retirees was 'what is good for Grumman is good for retirees.'" The Club purchased an advertisement appearing in Newsday, a Long Island newspaper, on October 13, headed

Grumman retirees protect your pension.

Do not tender your stock to LTV....

The Grumman Pension Plan, established in 1943, is a "defined benefit plan" ... covering both salaried and hourly employees. Initially banking institutions had acted as trustees of the Plan. However, in 1973 Grumman adopted a policy of having officers of Grumman or its affiliates serve as trustees, as permitted by § 408(c)(3) of ERISA. The trustees in the fall of 1981 were Bierwirth; Freese, chief financial officer of Grumman since 1972; and Carl A. Paladino, Treasurer of Grumman Aerospace Corporation since 1969. John Mullan, associate general counsel of Grumman, has served as counsel to the trustees and regularly attended their meetings. Sometime prior to January 1, 1975, the Plan had acquired 525,000 Grumman shares.

---

[3] There's one other factor to keep in mind: your pension fund. It's Grumman's policy to fully fund its employee pension fund. In contrast, LTV's pension fund right now is underfunded by almost a quarter of a billion dollars. Grumman people could lose if the two funds were to be merged.

On September 28 Freese mentioned to Bierwirth that the trustees "are going to have to get together here at some point and decide what [to] do in regard to the holdings of Grumman stock." Bierwirth agreed.... During the next ten days, the three trustees had casual conversations as they happened to meet each other. Nothing was said about the Plan's buying Grumman shares and no financial data were assembled for the meeting. Bierwirth had been informed by Mullan that if LTV succeeded, it could "merge the pension Plan though it may take them some time" and also "could cancel the Plan to the extent that they eliminate the Fund although of course they would retain the corporate obligation to pay," and by unidentified other sources that changing the presumed earnings rate would permit the declaration of some of the fund as surplus and recapture for the corporation.

[T]he Plan trustees' meeting ... was held on October 7.... Mullan made a ten minute presentation dealing with ERISA, pointing out that the trustees' decisions "as far as the Grumman stock was concerned had to be predicated solely upon the best interests of the participants of the Plan." There was then a general discussion of how the trustees felt about LTV, the Dillon, Read opinion letter, and Freese's five year financial projections for Grumman. Elaborating on the discussion of LTV, Freese mentioned concern about the underfunding of "their pension plan," LTV's highly leveraged debt situation which would be aggravated by the need for borrowing to finance the acquisition of Grumman, contingent liability with respect to environmental problems and a large number of pending lawsuits and alleged SEC violations, all of which was revealed in a recent LTV prospectus.... Freese expressed concern that the assumed rate of return used by LTV's pension plan was higher than that used by other companies and that LTV would have trouble making contributions to their pension plan. Bierwirth testified that the trustees "were aware of" a report about Grumman by Lehman Brothers Kuhn Loeb Inc. (Lehman Brothers). This report, dated July 8, 1981, which recommended purchase of Grumman common stock, then selling at $28 per share, projected a 1981-84 earnings progression of $2.75, $5.00, $6.50 and $7.50, and contained financial analysis supporting the estimates....

After a half hour's discussion the trustees voted not to tender the 525,000 Grumman shares held by the Plan. According to Bierwirth the trustees "then discussed whether we should take a second step. If we did not want to tender the stock at $45 a share, should we then consider buying additional shares, the market then being in the 30's?" A merit of such a purchase would be in making it more difficult for LTV to gain control of the pension fund. However, "it was also important that a further investment in Grumman shares be the right thing for us to do." "[A] number of fortuitous events had occurred during the summer and early in September which greatly enhanced the outlook for Grumman" and had made Bierwirth "feel earlier that a further investment in Grumman was desirable and should be recommended to the Trustees come this fall." While it had been "very difficult to accumulate substantial positions in Grumman stock," which ordinarily traded at volumes of 20,000 shares a day, the daily volume of half a million shares induced by the LTV offer made it "possible to accumulate a major position in Grumman stock without affecting the price all that much." Bierwirth was then of the view that "probably a majority of the stock would not be tendered" but could not feel confident about it. He recognized that if the LTV tender offer were abandoned, selling by arbitrageurs would push the price down. Following their discussion of these ideas, the trustees concluded that purchases of Grumman stock up to the maximum of 10% of the value of the Plan's assets permitted by § 407(a)(2) of ERISA would be prudent....

The trustees met briefly on Monday, October 12, and authorized the Plan's purchase of 1,275,000 additional Grumman shares — just short of ERISA's 10% limitation. A press release issued on October 13 stated that use of the authorization would increase the Plan's ownership of Grumman stock from 3.8% to approximately 8% of the outstanding fully diluted shares. The Plan, acting through Dillon, Read, purchased 958,000 shares at an average price of $38.61 per share on October 12 and an additional 200,000 shares on October 13 at an average price of $36.62, for a total cost of $44,312,380.

On the next day, October 14 ... the district court temporarily enjoined the LTV offer, thereby drastically reducing its chances for success. The price of Grumman stock fell on October 15 to a range of $28^1/_4$-$29^1/_2$. After this court affirmed the temporary injunction, the price of Grumman shares was 28-$28^3/_4$; the market value of the newly purchased shares was approximately $32,500,000. As this is written, the price is $26^1/_4$-$26^3/_8$....

IV. *The Legal Standard* ...

Sections 404(a)(1)(A) and (B) impose three different although overlapping standards. A fiduciary must discharge his duties "solely in the interests of the participants and beneficiaries." He must do this "for the exclusive purpose" of providing benefits to them. And he must comply "with the care, skill, prudence, and diligence under the circumstances then prevailing" of the traditional "prudent man."

The trustees urge that the mandates of § 404(a)(1)(A) and (B) must be interpreted in the light of two other sections of ERISA. One is § 408(c)(3) which permits the appointment of officers of the sponsoring corporation as trustees. The other is § 407(a)(3) which, as here applicable, permitted the Plan to acquire Grumman stock having an aggregate fair market value not exceeding 10% of the fair market value of the assets of the Plan. This provision, the trustees point out, was the result of a lengthy debate in which the Department of Labor played an important role; they rely especially on the following passage from its statement to the Senate Finance Committee:

> Especially significant among the expressly allowed transactions is that which permits, in most types of plans, investment of up to ten percent of the fund assets in securities issued by the employer of the employees who are participants in the plan. Since such an employer will often be an adminis-

trator of his plan, or will function as a trustee or in some other fiduciary capacity, this provision creates a limited exception to the listed proscription against self-dealing. The exception is made in recognition of *the symbiotic relationship* existing between the employer and the plan covering his employees. (Emphasis supplied).

Appellants do not contend that these provisions relieve corporate officers or directors who are trustees of a plan of the duties imposed by § 404(a) when dealing with stock of the corporation which is an asset of the Plan. They argue rather that, despite the words "sole" and "exclusive," such officers or directors do not violate their duties by following a course of action with respect to the plan which benefits the corporation as well as the beneficiaries.

We accept the argument but not the conclusion which appellants seem to think follows from it. Although officers of a corporation who are trustees of its pension plan do not violate their duties as trustees by taking action which, after careful and impartial investigation, they reasonably conclude best to promote the interests of participants and beneficiaries simply because it incidentally benefits the corporation or, indeed, themselves, their decisions must be made with an eye single to the interests of the participants and beneficiaries. Restatement of Trusts 2d § 170 (1959). This, in turn, imposes a duty on the trustees to avoid placing themselves in a position where their acts as officers or directors of the corporation will prevent their functioning with the complete loyalty to participants demanded of them as trustees of a pension plan.

There is much to be said for the Secretary's argument that the participation of Bierwirth and Freese in the directors' decision of September 25 press release announcing the unanimous decision of the board to do this on the ground, *inter alia,* of its inadequacy; the sending of Bierwirth's letter of September 28 repeating this and also announcing that the LTV offer was a threat to the pension fund; and the other activities of Bierwirth and Freese in opposing the offer precluded their exercising the detached judgment required of them as trustees of the Plan, and that the only proper course was for the trustees immediately to resign so that a neutral trustee or trustees could be swiftly appointed to serve for the duration of the tender offer. Looking at the matter realistically we find it almost impossible to see how Bierwirth and Freese, after what they had said and done between September 24 and October 7, could have voted to tender or even to sell the Plan's stock, no matter how compelling the evidence for one or the other of those courses might have been.[9] Grumman shareholders who had acted in

---

[9] We are not impressed with the defendants' argument that they, and particularly Bierwirth, had nothing to fear from the LTV offer in light of LTV's announced intention to make Grumman's office the headquarters of its aerospace division and to retain Bierwirth as C.E.O. of that division. No offer was made with respect to Freese or Paladino. Even as to Bierwirth there have been countless instances where, even when a proposal to retain the chief executive of the target was wholly sincere, he will have disappeared within a year or so. Moreover, being C.E.O. of a division of LTV was not the same thing as being C.E.O. of an independent Grumman. The press currently recounts how high corporate executives are equipping themselves with "golden parachutes"

accordance with the company's pleas would have had every reason to consider such action a breach of faith....

The record contains specific instances of the trustees' failure to observe the high standard of duty placed upon them. Bierwirth and Freese should have been immediately aware of the difficult position which they occupied as a result of having decided as directors some of the same questions they would have to decide as trustees, and should have explored where their duty lay. Instead the question of a trustees' meeting was treated quite casually — something to be attended to when the hectic pace of fighting the tender offer would permit. One way for the trustees to inform themselves would have been to solicit the advice of independent counsel; Mullan, a junior Grumman employee, was under disabilities similar to those of the trustees themselves. He could hardly have been expected to tell the trustees that the better course would be to resign or even to suggest investigations which might alter the judgment of total commitment to defeating the LTV offer that management had already expressed. We do not mean by this either that trustees confronted with a difficult decision need always engage independent counsel or that engaging such counsel and following their advice will operate as a complete whitewash which, without more, satisfies ERISA's prudence requirement. But this was, and should have been perceived to be, an unusual situation peculiarly requiring legal advice from someone above the battle.

The trustees also failed to measure up to the standard required of them in failing to do a more thorough job in ascertaining the facts with respect to the LTV pension funds, the unfunded liabilities of which were to be a principal ground for their action, and investigating whether anything could be done to protect the Grumman pension fund in the event of an acquisition of Grumman by LTV. So far as the record shows, the sole knowledge the trustees had of the LTV pension plans came from two portions of the prospectus for the May 28, 1981, LTV stock offering.... The September 28 letter from Bierwirth to Grumman's shareholders drew on the prospectus' statement about unfunded liabilities but eliminated the phrase "which relates primarily to unfunded vested pension liabilities assumed in the purchase of Lykes." The omission of this clause was important because it created the false impression, on the basis of which the trustees could well have acted, that LTV had a single pension fund which had unfunded liabilities in the considerable amount stated. If, as the prospectus foreshadowed and investigation would have confirmed, the unfunded liabilities were principally in pension funds covering hourly employees of LTV's steel operations, the danger of these plans being merged with Grumman's was considerably less than if LTV had a single underfunded pension fund.

---

providing large benefits in the event that the executive is dismissed or even if he quits on his own volition after a takeover.

The trustees' perception of danger would have been reduced yet further had they known that LTV treated a number of the 21 pension plans which it sponsored quite well. For example, the pension plan for salaried Vought employees was extremely well-funded, with an excess of current assets over vested liabilities of approximately $78,000,000. Other Vought plans, including one covering hourly workers, had not been treated so favorably, but nonetheless were in better financial condition than LTV's plans for employees in the steel industry.... Further inquiry in these areas ... might well have changed the trustees' views regarding both the danger presented by LTV's offer to the Plan and their ability to obtain satisfactory protections from LTV for the Plan. In addition, even if the trustees' beliefs regarding the financial condition of LTV's pension plans and LTV's policies towards its plans had been entirely accurate, we see little in the record to indicate that they attempted to determine just what LTV could have done and could not have done to inflict financial harm upon the participants in Grumman's Plan.[14] The trustees easily could have retained an expert on ERISA to advise them on this subject....

An even more telling point against the trustees is their swift movement from a decision not to tender or sell the shares already in the fund to a decision to invest more than $44,000,000 in the purchase of additional Grumman shares up to the 10% maximum permitted by § 407(a)(2) of ERISA. Their argument is that once they had reasonably decided not to tender the shares already in the fund since success of the offer would run counter to the interests of the beneficiaries, it followed that they should do everything else they lawfully could do to thwart the offer. This, however, should have involved a calculation of the risks and benefits involved.... Although Grumman shares may have seemed attractive when selling in the high 20's, with what appeared a good chance of appreciation, they were not necessarily attractive when, under the impetus of the tender offer, they had risen to the high 30's. Moreover, and even more important, in purchasing additional shares when they did, the trustees were buying into what, from their own point of view, was almost certainly a "no-win" situation. If the LTV offer succeeded, the Plan would be left as a minority stockholder in an LTV-controlled Grumman — a point that seems to have received no consideration. If it failed, as the Plan's purchase of additional 8% of the outstanding Grumman stock made more likely, the stock was almost certain to sink to its pre-offer level, as the trustees fully appreciated. Given the trustees' views as to the dim future of an LTV-controlled Grumman, it is thus exceedingly difficult to accept Bierwirth's testimony that the purchase of additional shares was justified from an investment standpoint — or even to conclude that the trustees really believed this. Invest-

---

[14] Counsel for the trustees argue that LTV could have merged the Grumman plan with an LTV plan, appointed new trustees, terminated the Grumman plan, and so forth. ERISA, of course, contains elaborate safeguards to protect employees from the financial consequences of such actions. Counsel for the trustees have not suggested how LTV could have avoided such safeguards, much less that the trustees seriously considered these factors in making their decision at the October 7 meeting.

ment considerations dictated a policy of waiting. If LTV's offer were accepted, the trustees would not want more Grumman shares; if it failed, the shares would be obtainable at prices far below what was paid. Mid-October 1981 was thus the worst possible time for the Plan to buy Grumman stock as an investment.[16] It is almost impossible to believe that the trustees did not realize this and that their motive for purchasing the additional shares was for any purpose other than blocking the LTV offer. Moreover, even if we were to make the dubious assumption that a purchase for this purpose would have been permissible despite all the investment risks that it entailed, the trustees should at least have taken all reasonable steps to make sure the purchase was necessary. As indicated, Bierwirth was under the impression that the necessary 50.01% would not be tendered — an expectation not unnatural in view of the fact that Grumman's investment and pension plans already owned nearly a third of the shares — although he could not be sure. The record gives no explanation why, if additional shares were to be purchased, this could not have been done by Grumman, in some way that would not reduce the number of outstanding shares, with the bank credit Freese had negotiated in part for that very purpose, rather than by the Plan. There is also nothing to indicate that the trustees, or other Grumman officers or directors, had been willing to risk their own funds in buying additional Grumman shares....

We do not join in all of the district judge's pejorative adjectives concerning the trustees. They were caught in a difficult and unusual situation — apparently, so far as shown in the briefs, one that had not arisen before. We accept that they were honestly convinced that acquisition of Grumman by the debt-ridden LTV would mean a less bright future for Grumman and also that an LTV acquisition posed some special dangers to the participants of the Plan.[17]

However, they should have realized that, since their judgment on this score could scarcely be unbiased, at the least they were bound to take every feasible precaution to see that they had carefully considered the other side, to free themselves, if indeed this was humanly possible, from any taint of the quick negative

---

[16] The judge was not bound to accept the trustees' claim that purchases of considerable amounts of Grumman stock could not be made (and that their failure to purchase Grumman stock earlier although their belief in its attractiveness was claimed to go back to the summer of 1981 was thereby explained) on the ground that, with a daily volume of only 20,000 shares, substantial purchases would have greatly increased the price. No expert testified to that effect and no explanation was offered how the Plan had managed to accumulate 525,000 shares when, as Bierwirth stated, the market had been much thinner. Even if we assume that a carefully executed buying program would have somewhat boosted the price, there was no testimony that this would have been anything like the increase of ten points that had resulted from LTV's $45 offer.

[17] These dangers included the low level of pension benefits allegedly maintained by LTV; the fact that while LTV complied only with the minimum funding requirements of ERISA, Grumman contributed the impliedly higher amount of the maximum amount deductible under the IRC; the fact that LTV could merge or terminate the Plan; the near certainty that LTV would appoint new trustees for the Plan; and the danger that, even if it had the best of intentions towards the Grumman Plan, LTV's financial condition might preclude it from treating the Plan favorably.

reaction characteristic of targets of hostile tender offers displayed at the September 24 board meeting, and particularly to consider the huge risks attendant on purchasing additional Grumman shares at a price substantially elevated by the tender offer. We need not decide whether even this would have sufficed; perhaps, after the events of late September, resignation was the only proper course. It is enough that, for the reasons we have indicated ... the district judge was warranted in concluding, on the materials before him, that the trustees had not measured up to the high standards imposed by § 404(a)(1)(A) and (B) of ERISA. How the situation will appear after a trial is a different matter which we cannot now decide.

NOTES

1. *An Eye Single.* The court held that the trustees were to make their decisions with "an eye single to the interests of the participants and beneficiaries." More than three-quarters of the participants and beneficiaries signed petitions *supporting* the trustees' decisions. Why? With this backing from the group to be protected, why didn't the "eye single" standard cause the trustees' decisions to be upheld despite their "no win" financial prospects?

One reading of *Bierwirth* is that it adopted an "eye single with blinders" standard. The trustees were to act with only the interests of participants and beneficiaries in mind, but not with *all* of their interests in mind; their interests in continuing employment were not to be considered. Ironically, this resulted in protection for parties other than the participants and beneficiaries. Since this was a defined benefit plan, Grumman stockholders were the parties primarily interested in the financial prospects of the pension fund; they were the ones who would be liable if the fund ran short.

2. *Social Investing.* Social investing occurs when pension fund trustees make investments based on factors other than investment return. Social investing takes many forms, including investments that involve moral or political issues (such as investments in South Africa or Northern Ireland), investments targeted to improve the economic well-being of a State or region, and investments intended to enhance the non-retirement well-being of participants (such as below-market-rate housing loans).

Bierwirth's "eye single" interpretation of ERISA's fiduciary duties implies that social investing is improper. Investment decisions made primarily to benefit someone in South Africa or someone in the local economy generally conflict with the duty under ERISA to act solely in the interest of participants and beneficiaries. § 404. At the same time, however, social goals may be taken into consideration in making an investment decision if they are "costless" to participants and beneficiaries. If a trustee is presented with two investments with equal risk and return characteristics, the trustee may select one over the other *because* it provides greater social benefits. *See* 29 C.F.R. § 2509.94-1; Uniform Management of Public Employee Retirement Systems Act § 8(a)(5). Do you think that standard provides trustees with sufficient discretion to engage in socially responsible investing? Or too much discretion? *Compare* Joel C. Dobris, *Arguments in Favor of Fiduciary Divestment of "South African" Securities*, 65 NEB. L. REV. 209 (1986) *with* John H. Langbein & Richard A. Posner, *Social Investing and the Law of Trusts*, 79 MICH. L. REV. 72 (1980).

3. *The Standard of Judicial Review.* In *Firestone Tire & Rubber Co. v. Bruch*, 489 U.S. 101 (1989), Firestone sold five of its plants to Occidental. Employees who worked at the plants claimed severance pay benefits when Firestone terminated them, even though they were immediately rehired by Occidental at the same pay and position. Firestone denied the claims and the employees sued. The issue in *Firestone* was what standard should the courts use in reviewing decisions like these? On the one hand, a deferential standard of review, such as the arbitrary and capricious standard, would promote efficient plan administration, discourage litigation, and, hence, encourage employers to provide benefits. On the other hand, the administrators making benefits determinations are often operating under a conflict of interest. In *Firestone*, for example, the administrators making the severance pay determination were company employees who probably owed their primary loyalties to their employer and, since the plan was unfunded, the company stood to gain directly from a denial of benefits. *See* ERISA § 408(c)(3) (specifically permitting employers to appoint officers and employees to fiduciary positions). The Supreme Court held in *Firestone* that the courts should use a *de novo* standard in reviewing benefits decisions made by ERISA fiduciaries, unless the plan provides for a narrower standard of judicial review by giving the fiduciary discretionary authority to make benefit determinations and construe the plan. Since the severance pay plan in *Firestone* did not provide for a narrower standard of review, the Court held that the *de novo* standard applied.

The *Firestone* decision has been harshly criticized, for good reason. *See* John H. Langbein, *The Supreme Court Flunks Trusts,* 1990 SUP. CT. REV. 207 (calling the decision "a crude piece of work" and "doctrinal hash"). The predictable result of *Firestone* has been that plan sponsors have amended their plans to provide for narrower standards of review. But what standard of review should courts apply when the plan provides for a narrower standard, but the fiduciary is operating under some type of conflict? *Firestone* provides no guidance. Lower courts have generally held that a conflict justifies stricter judicial scrutiny. *See Anderson v. Blue Cross/Blue Shield*, 907 F.2d 1072 (11th Cir. 1990); *Callahan v. Rouge Steel Co.*, 941 F.2d 456 (6th Cir. 1991).

4. *Other Protection Against Conflicts.* Do conflicts between the interests of a plan administrator and participants and beneficiaries always mean that a strict standard of judicial review is necessary? Perhaps not. Plan participants and beneficiaries may be adequately protected from nonneutral decisionmakers by factors other than strict standards of judicial review. For example, benefit plan decisions are often made in the context of repeat players involved in long-term relationships. In these circumstances, employers would not want to develop reputations for sharp practices that might reduce morale or, indeed, decrease the value employees place on benefit programs. Similarly, unions are often available as monitors. *See* Daniel Fischel & John H. Langbein, *ERISA's Fundamental Contradiction: The Exclusive Benefit Rule,* 55 U. CHI. L. REV. 1105, 1131-32 (1988). A strict standard of review, such as the *de novo* standard, might be reserved for situations where these types of alternative protections against abuse are not present.

E. PLAN TERMINATIONS

Protecting employees when pension plans are terminated is another component of ERISA's broader goal of preventing forfeiture. ERISA's vesting protections would be meaningless if employers could effectively forfeit employee interests at any time by terminating their plans.

Pension plan terminations fall into two broad categories that raise quite different sorts of legal and policy questions. First, plans may be terminated when assets are insufficient to pay accrued liabilities. The primary issue in these types of terminations is: Who must bear the loss? Employers are responsible in the first instance, but Title IV of ERISA establishes the Pension Benefit Guaranty Corporation (PBGC) as a surety to protect employees from loss when employers cannot meet their obligations. Second, plans may be terminated when there are excess assets in the plan. The primary issue in these types of terminations is: Who is entitled to the excess? The potential claimants, as we shall see, are the employer, the employees, and the government.

1. TERMINATIONS WITH INSUFFICIENT ASSETS

In re DEFOE SHIPBUILDING CO.

United States Court of Appeals, Sixth Circuit
639 F.2d 311 (1981)

MERRITT, CIRCUIT JUDGE.

This case concerns the application of the Employee Retirement Income Security Act (ERISA) upon the termination of a retirement pension plan. The Plan was established in 1970 under a collective bargaining agreement between appellant Defoe Shipbuilding Co. and Local 49 of the Industrial Union of Marine and Shipbuilding Workers of America.... After going out of business and filing for dissolution, Defoe terminated the Plan as of January 1977.

The Plan provided for contributions by Defoe to a Trust Fund at a fixed rate per employee per working hour, and the Fund was administered by a board of administration whose members were appointed by the Union and Defoe. The level of benefits to be paid to participants was fixed initially, but was to be adjusted upon recommendation by an appointed Actuary when his analysis revealed that benefit levels no longer appeared appropriate in relation to the level of contributions. The Plan also contained sections defining the employer's liability:

> In the event of termination of the Plan ... accrued benefits shall be non-forfeitable to the extent funded....

> Deposits by the Company with the Trustee of contributions computed in accordance with Section 1 of this Article [setting forth the contribution schedule] shall be in complete discharge of the Company's financial obligation under this Plan. The Company shall have no liability in respect to payments under the Plan except to pay over to the Trustee such contributions.... Each employee or retired employee ... shall look solely to the Trust Fund for any payments or benefits under the Plan....

Two issues are raised in this appeal: (1) Is the Plan a "defined benefit plan" covered by Title IV, or is it a "defined contribution plan" ... excepted from coverage by [ERISA § 4021(b)(1)]? (2) Are the "nonforfeitable" benefits guaranteed by PBGC to participants according to [§ 4022(a)] limited to the amount of assets present in the Fund at the time of termination of the Plan, or do they include the full level of benefits established in the Plan despite the fact that that level exceeds the assets of the Fund? The second question presents the central issue of this case, because if PBGC makes payments that exceed the assets in the Fund, Defoe may be held liable to PBGC for the insufficiency of the assets to cover payments....

On the first issue, Defoe argues that the Plan is of the defined contribution type. It notes that the employer's contributions to the Plan were fixed by the collective bargaining agreements at a certain amount per employee per working hour. On the other hand, Defoe argues, although rates for calculating the benefits were set in the agreements, the benefits were not defined. This is because they were to be adjusted on occasion according to the recommendations of the Actuary.

This argument misconceives the nature of these two categories of pension plans. The definition of a defined contribution plan, incorporated by reference in [§ 4021(b)(1)] for the purpose of determining exemption from Title IV, is found at [§ 3(34)]:

> The term ... "defined contribution plan" means a pension plan which provides for an individual account for each participant and for benefits based solely upon the amount contributed to the participant's account....

In *Connolly v. PBGC*, 581 F.2d 729 (9th Cir. 1978), *cert. denied*, 440 U.S. 935 (1979), the court, in discussing the same issue, derived from the quoted definition two criteria: a separate account for each participant must exist, and a participant's benefits must be measured solely by the level of funds in his account. The *Connolly* court found that a pension plan very similar to the present one failed to satisfy either criterion, for the employer's contributions were pooled and the participant's benefits defined according to a formula independent of the level of funding.

The Ninth Circuit's development of the definition of "[defined contribution] plans" accurately reflects the meaning of the language and makes sense of the reason why that type of plan is exempt from coverage of Title IV. Because benefits in [defined contribution] plans are based solely upon the amount contributed to the account, such a plan can never be underfunded and there is nothing for PBGC to insure. A participant is entitled to no more than the amount of benefits in his account. We are also persuaded by the application in *Connolly* of the criteria to the plan under consideration. The same reasoning derives the same conclusion in the present case. The Plan is a "defined benefit," not a "defined contribution" plan.

Defoe's argument that the benefits in the Plan are not fixed because they may be adjusted upon recommendation of the Actuary is irrelevant to this issue. A "defined benefit plan" is defined in [§ 3(35)] as "a pension plan other than [a defined contribution] plan...." Since Defoe has failed to demonstrate that the Plan satisfies the criteria for the latter type of plan, it is pointless to argue whether its benefits are fixed. Regardless of the characteristics of the benefits, the Plan must be considered a defined benefit plan in the absence of proof that it is a defined contribution plan.

The second issue concerns the interpretation of [§ 4022(a)], which states that "(PBGC) shall guarantee the payment of all nonforfeitable benefits," thus requiring elucidation of the term "nonforfeitable." Two definitions of that term exist, one at [§ 3(19)], and one specifically established for Title IV by PBGC under its authority to make regulations. 29 C.F.R. § 2605.6(a). The latter definition in effect equates the conditions of nonforfeitability with the requirements for vesting of benefits.

In *Nachman Corp. v. PBGC*, 446 U.S. 359 (1980), the Supreme Court held that regardless of the choice of definition of the term "nonforfeitable," the same conclusion obtains: the full amount of benefits vested in participants of a plan is nonforfeitable, and hence full payment is guaranteed by PBGC. This conclusion was reached despite the existence of a provision limiting the benefits to the amount of assets in the fund, similar to those, quoted *supra,* found in Defoe's Plan. Such a clause was held to be subordinate to the mandate of ERISA, for a contrary conclusion would subvert the fundamental purpose of the Act, i.e., to protect employees upon termination of their plans with insufficient assets.... *Nachman* is decisive in the present case.... The clauses in the Plan limiting Defoe's liability and limiting the benefits to the extent funded are overridden by the provisions in ERISA identifying the nonforfeitable benefits guaranteed by PBGC....

NOTES

1. *ERISA's Plan Termination Insurance Scheme.* *Defoe* presents two of the basic components of the plan termination insurance scheme. First, the scheme covers only defined benefit plans; defined contribution plans are not covered. Second, employers cannot limit their liability under defined benefit plans to the amount of money in the pension fund; they are liable for the promised defined benefit regardless of the amount in the fund even if, as in *Defoe,* the plan explicitly limits employer liability to the amount in the fund.

2. *Employee Monitoring of Pension Promises.* Employers have an option if they want to limit their liability to the amount contributed into the fund — offer a defined contribution plan. Some employees may prefer that employers limit their liability in that way; since employees are absorbing the risk associated with plan investments, they should receive something in return, such as higher wages or larger contributions into the fund.

But if the restriction on limiting liability is so easy to avoid, why have it at all? The answer probably lies in concerns about the ability of employees to monitor pension promises. A defined benefit plan promises each employee a pension extending (and often beginning) decades in the future that will be funded by regular contributions into the fund. Employees are unlikely to have the knowledge and information necessary to evaluate the risk associated with that promise — is the contribution high enough to fund the promised benefits? What is the likely investment experience of the fund? What is the age and experience mix of current employees and what effect will that have on the fund? The restriction on limiting liability protects employees from having to make such difficult risk assessments. And yet, if employers want to limit their liability, they can do so by making a much simpler promise, the basic promise of defined contribution plans — we promise to put this amount into your account, but what amount is there when you retire is your concern. Forcing employers to make that promise to limit their liability leaves employees in a better position to evaluate their risk.

Many employers may also favor the restriction on limiting liability. If employers could limit their liability, some employers might act opportunistically, for example, by promising unrealistically high benefits or skimping on investment expertise for the fund. Since employees cannot monitor the pension promises very well, these employers may gain a competitive advantage over more scrupulous employers. Thus, scrupulous employers may favor the restriction on limiting liability because it makes it less likely that other employers will engage in this type of unfair competition.

PENSION BENEFIT GUARANTY CORP. v. LTV CORP.

United States Supreme Court
496 U.S. 633 (1990)

JUSTICE BLACKMUN delivered the opinion of the Court.

In this case we must determine whether the decision of the Pension Benefit Guaranty Corporation (PBGC) to restore certain pension plans under § 4047 of the Employee Retirement Income Security Act of 1974 (ERISA) was, as the Court of Appeals concluded, arbitrary and capricious or contrary to law, within the meaning of § 706 of the Administrative Procedure Act (APA).

I

Petitioner PBGC is a wholly owned United States Government corporation.... The PBGC administers and enforces Title IV of ERISA. Title IV includes a mandatory Government insurance program that protects the pension benefits of over 30 million private-sector American workers who participate in plans covered by the Title. In enacting Title IV, Congress sought to ensure that employees and their beneficiaries would not be completely "deprived of anticipated retirement benefits by the termination of pension plans before sufficient funds have been accumulated in the plans."

When a plan covered under Title IV terminates with insufficient assets to satisfy its pension obligations to the employees, the PBGC becomes trustee of the plan, taking over the plan's assets and liabilities. The PBGC then uses the plan's assets to cover what it can of the benefit obligations. The PBGC then must add its own funds to ensure payment of most of the remaining "nonforfeitable" benefits, i.e., those benefits to which participants have earned entitlement under the plan terms as of the date of termination. ERISA does place limits on the benefits PBGC may guarantee upon plan termination, however, even if an employee is entitled to greater benefits under the terms of the plan.[*] In addition, benefit increases resulting from plan amendments adopted within five years of the termination are not paid in full. Finally, active plan participants (current employees) cease to earn additional benefits under the plan upon its termination, and lose entitlement to most benefits not yet fully earned as of the date of plan termination.

The cost of the PBGC insurance is borne primarily by employers that maintain ongoing pension plans. Sections 4006 and 4007 of ERISA require these employers to pay annual premiums.[**] The insurance program is also financed by statutory liability imposed on employers who terminate under-funded pension plans. Upon termination, the employer becomes liable to the PBGC for the benefits that the PBGC will pay out. Because the PBGC historically has recovered

---

[*] The maximum monthly pension benefit insured by the PBGC was $2,761.36 in 1997. The amount is inflation-indexed.

[**] The basic premium is $19 per participant. In addition, covered plans must pay a supplemental premium of $9 per participant per $1,000 of unfunded vested benefits.

only a small portion of that liability, Congress repeatedly has been forced to increase the annual premiums. Even with these increases, the PBGC in its most recent Annual Report noted liabilities of $4 billion and assets of only $2.4 billion, leaving a deficit of over $1.5 billion.

As noted above, plan termination is the insurable event under Title IV. Plans may be terminated "voluntarily" by an employer or "involuntarily" by the PBGC. An employer may terminate a plan voluntarily in one of two ways. It may proceed with a "standard termination" only if it has sufficient assets to pay all benefit commitments. A standard termination thus does not implicate PBGC insurance responsibilities. If an employer wishes to terminate a plan whose assets are insufficient to pay all benefits, the employer must demonstrate that it is in financial "distress" as defined in [Section 4041(c) of ERISA]. Neither a standard nor a distress termination by the employer, however, is permitted if termination would violate the terms of an existing collective-bargaining agreement.

The PBGC, though, may terminate a plan "involuntarily," notwithstanding the existence of a collective-bargaining agreement. Section 4042 of ERISA provides that the PBGC may terminate a plan [because, among other reasons, "the] possible long-run loss of the [PBGC] with respect to the plan may reasonably be expected to increase unreasonably if the plan is not terminated."

Termination can be undone by PBGC. Section 4047 of ERISA [permits the PBGC to] "restore the plan to its pretermination status, including, but not limited to, the transfer to the employer or a plan administrator of control of part or all of the remaining assets and liabilities of the plan." When a plan is restored, full benefits are reinstated, and the employer, rather than the PBGC, again is responsible for the plan's unfunded liabilities.

II

This case arose after respondent The LTV Corporation (LTV Corp.) and many of its subsidiaries, including LTV Steel Company Inc., (LTV Steel) (collectively LTV), in July 1986 filed petitions for reorganization under Chapter 11 of the Bankruptcy Code. At that time, LTV Steel was the sponsor of three defined benefit pension plans (the Plans) covered by Title IV of ERISA. Two of the Plans were the products of collective-bargaining negotiations with the United Steelworkers of America. The third was for nonunion salaried employees. Chronically underfunded, the Plans, by late 1986, had unfunded liabilities for promised benefits of almost $2.3 billion. Approximately $2.1 billion of this amount was covered by PBGC insurance.

It is undisputed that one of LTV Corp.'s principal goals in filing the Chapter 11 petitions was the restructuring of LTV Steel's pension obligations, a goal which could be accomplished if the Plans were terminated and responsibility for the unfunded liabilities was placed on the PBGC. LTV Steel then could negotiate with its employees for new pension arrangements. LTV, however, could not voluntarily terminate the Plans because two of them had been negotiated in collective bargaining. LTV therefore sought to have the PBGC terminate the Plans.

To that end, LTV advised the PBGC in 1986 that it could not continue to provide complete funding for the Plans. PBGC estimated that, without continued funding, the Plans' $2.1 billion underfunding could increase by as much as $65 million by December 1987 and by another $63 million by December 1988, unless the Plans were terminated. Moreover, extensive plant shutdowns were anticipated. These shutdowns, if they occurred before the Plans were terminated, would have required the payment of significant "shutdown benefits." The PBGC estimated that such benefits could increase the Plans' liabilities by as much as $300 million to $700 million, of which up to $500 million was covered by PBGC insurance. Confronted with this information, the PBGC, invoking § 4042(a)(4) of ERISA, determined that the Plans should be terminated in order to protect the insurance program from the unreasonable risk of large losses, and commenced termination proceedings in the District Court. With LTV's consent, the Plans were terminated effective January 13, 1987.

Because the Plans' participants lost some benefits as a result of the termination, the Steelworkers filed an adversary action against LTV in the Bankruptcy Court, challenging the termination and seeking an order directing LTV to make up the lost benefits. This action was settled, with LTV and the Steelworkers negotiating an interim collective-bargaining agreement that included new pension arrangements intended to make up benefits that plan participants lost as a result of the termination. New payments to retirees were based explicitly upon "a percentage of the difference between the benefit that was being paid under the Prior Plans and the amount paid by the PBGC." Retired participants were thereby placed in substantially the same positions they would have occupied had the old Plans never been terminated. The new agreements respecting active participants were also designed to replace benefits under the old Plans that were not insured by the PBGC, such as early-retirement benefits and shutdown benefits. With respect to shutdown benefits, LTV stated in Bankruptcy Court that the new benefits totaled "75% of benefits lost as a result of plan termination." With respect to some other kinds of benefits for active participants, the new arrangements provided 100% or more of the lost benefits.

The PBGC objected to these new pension agreements, characterizing them as "follow-on" plans. It defines a follow-on plan as a new benefit arrangement designed to wrap around the insurance benefits provided by the PBGC in such a way as to provide both retirees and active participants substantially the same benefits as they would have received had no termination occurred. The PBGC's policy against follow-on plans stems from the agency's belief that such plans are "abusive" of the insurance program and result in the PBGC's subsidizing an employer's ongoing pension program in a way not contemplated by Title IV....

LTV ignored the PBGC's objections to the new pension arrangements and asked the Bankruptcy Court for permission to fund the follow-on plans. The Bankruptcy Court granted LTV's request. In doing so, however, it noted that the

PBGC "may have legal options or avenues that it can assert administratively ... to implement its policy goals. Nothing done here tonight precludes the PBGC from pursuing these options...."

In early August 1987, the PBGC determined that the financial factors on which it had relied in terminating the Plans had changed significantly. Of particular significance to the PBGC was its belief that the steel industry, including LTV Steel, was experiencing a dramatic turnaround. As a result, the PBGC concluded it no longer faced the imminent risk, central to its original termination decision, of large unfunded liabilities stemming from plant shutdowns.... [B]ased upon LTV's improved financial circumstances and its follow-on plans, ... the PBGC's Executive Director ... decided to restore the Plans [under the PBGC's § 4047 powers]....

LTV refused to comply with the restoration decision. This prompted the PBGC to initiate an enforcement action....

III

A

The Court of Appeals first held that the restoration decision was arbitrary and capricious under § 706(2)(A) [of the Administrative Procedure Act] because the PBGC did not take account of all the areas of law the court deemed relevant to the restoration decision. The court expressed the view that "[b]ecause ERISA, bankruptcy and labor law are all involved in the case at hand, there must be a showing on the administrative record that PBGC, before reaching its decision, considered all of these areas of law, and to the extent possible, honored the policies underlying them." The court concluded that the administrative record did not reflect thorough and explicit consideration by the PBGC of the "policies and goals" of each of the three bodies of law. As the court put it, the PBGC "focused inordinately on ERISA." The Court of Appeals did not hold that the PBGC's decision *actually conflicted* with any provision in the bankruptcy or labor laws.... Rather the court held that because labor and bankruptcy law are "involved in the case at hand," the PBGC had an affirmative obligation, which had not been met, to address them.

The PBGC contends that the Court of Appeals misapplied the general rule that an agency must take into consideration all relevant factors by requiring the agency explicitly to consider and discuss labor and bankruptcy law. We agree.

First, and most important, we do not think that the requirement imposed by the Court of Appeals upon the PBGC can be reconciled with the plain language of § 4047, under which the PBGC is operating in this case. This section gives the PBGC the power to restore terminated plans in any case in which the PBGC determines such action to be "appropriate and consistent with its duties *under this title,* [i.e., Title IV of ERISA]" (emphasis added). The statute does not direct the PBGC to make restoration decisions that further the "public interest" generally, but rather empowers the agency to restore when restoration would further the interests that Title IV of ERISA is designed to protect. Given this specific and unambiguous statutory mandate, we do not think that the PBGC did or could focus "inordinately" on ERISA in making its restoration decision.

Even if Congress' directive to the PBGC had not been so clear, we are not entirely sure that the Court of Appeals' holding makes good sense as a general principle of administrative law. The PBGC points up problems that would arise if federal courts routinely were to require each agency to take explicit account of public policies that derive from federal statutes other than the agency's enabling act. To begin with, there are numerous federal statutes that could be said to embody countless policies. If agency action may be disturbed whenever a reviewing court is able to point to an arguably relevant statutory policy that was not explicitly considered, then a very large number of agency decisions might be open to judicial invalidation.

The Court of Appeals' directive that the PBGC give effect to the "policies and goals" of other statutes, apart from what those statutes actually provide,[7] is questionable for another reason as well. Because the PBGC can claim no expertise in the labor and bankruptcy areas, it may be ill-equipped to undertake the difficult task of discerning and applying the "policies and goals" of those fields....

For these reasons, we believe the Court of Appeals erred in holding that the PBGC's restoration decision was arbitrary and capricious because the agency failed adequately to consider principles and policies of bankruptcy law and labor law.

B

The Court of Appeals also rejected the grounds for restoration that the PBGC *did* assert and discuss. The court found that the first ground the PBGC proffered to support the restoration — its policy against follow-on plans — was contrary to law because there was no indication in the text of the restoration provision, § 4047, or its legislative history that Congress intended the PBGC to use successive benefit plans as a basis for restoration. The PBGC argues that in reaching this conclusion the Court of Appeals departed from traditional principles of statutory interpretation and judicial review of agency construction of statutes. Again, we must agree....

Here, the PBGC has interpreted § 4047 as giving it the power to base restoration decisions on the existence of follow-on plans. Our task ... is to determine whether any clear congressional desire to avoid restoration decisions based on successive pension plans exists, and, if the answer is in the negative, whether the PBGC's policy is based upon a permissible construction of the statute.

---

[7] It is worth noting that the provisions of ERISA itself do take account of other areas of federal law. For example, as noted above, an employer may not voluntarily terminate a plan if to do so would violate the terms of a collective-bargaining agreement.

Turning to the first half of the inquiry, we observe that the text of § 4047 does not evince a clear congressional intent to deprive the PBGC of the ability to base restoration decisions on the existence of follow-on plans. To the contrary, the textual grant of authority to the PBGC embodied in this section is broad. As noted above, the section authorizes the PBGC to restore terminated plans "in any such case in which [the PBGC] determines such action to be appropriate and consistent with its duties under [Title IV of ERISA]." The PBGC's duties consist primarily of furthering the statutory purposes of Title IV identified by Congress. These are:

> "(1) to encourage the continuation and maintenance of voluntary private pension plans for the benefit of their participants;
>
> "(2) to provide for the timely and uninterrupted payment of pension benefits to participants and beneficiaries under plans to which this subchapter applies; and
>
> "(3) to maintain premiums established by [the PBGC] under [ERISA § 4006] at the lowest level consistent with carrying out the obligations of this subchapter." [ERISA § 4002(a)].

On their face, of course, none of these statutorily identified purposes has anything to say about the precise question at issue — the use of follow-on plans as a basis for restoration decisions.

Nor do any of the other traditional tools of statutory construction compel the conclusion that Congress intended that the PBGC not base its restoration decisions on follow-on plans. [The legislative history relied on by the Court of Appeals — a listing of the possible reasons for restoration in the 1974 legislative history that did not mention follow-on plans and the consideration and rejection of an amendment to ERISA in 1987 that would have explicitly permitted the PBGC to rely on follow-on plans — does not meet the "clear congressional intent" standard.]

Having determined that the PBGC's construction is not contrary to clear congressional intent, we still must ascertain whether the agency's policy is based upon a "permissible" construction of the statute, that is, a construction that is "rational and consistent with the statute." Respondents argue that the PBGC's anti-follow-on plan policy is irrational because, as a practical matter, no purpose is served when the PBGC bases a restoration decision on something other than the improved financial health of the employer. According to respondents, "financial improvement [is] both a necessary and a sufficient condition for restoration. The agency's asserted abuse policy ... is *logically irrelevant* to the restoration decision." Brief for Respondents LTV Corp. and LTV Steel 33 (emphasis added). We think not. The PBGC's anti-follow-on policy is premised on the belief, which we find eminently reasonable, that employees will object more strenuously to a company's original decision to terminate a plan (or to take financial steps that make termination likely) if the company cannot use a follow-on plan to put the employees in the same (or a similar) position after termination as they were in before. The availability of a follow-on plan thus would remove a significant check — employee resistance — against termination of a pension plan.

Consequently, follow-on plans may tend to frustrate one of the objectives of ERISA that the PBGC is supposed to accomplish — the "continuation and maintenance of voluntary private pension plans." In addition, follow-on plans have a tendency to increase the PBGC's deficit and increase the insurance premiums all employers must pay, thereby frustrating another related statutory objective — the maintenance of low premiums. In short, the PBGC's construction based upon its conclusion that the existence of follow-on plans will lead to more plan terminations and increased PBGC liabilities is "assuredly a permissible one." Indeed, the judgments about the way the real world works that have gone into the PBGC's anti-follow-on policy are precisely the kind that agencies are better equipped to make than are courts.[8] This practical agency expertise is one of the principal justifications behind deference [to administrative agencies].

None of this is to say that financial improvement will never be relevant to a restoration decision. Indeed, if an employer's financial situation remains so dire that restoration would lead inevitably to immediate retermination, the PBGC may decide not to restore a terminated plan even where the employer has instituted a follow-on plan.[9] For present purposes, however, it is enough for us to decide that where, as here, there is no suggestion that immediate retermination of the plans will be necessary, it is rational for the PBGC to disfavor follow-on plans.

[JUSTICE WHITE, joined by JUSTICE O'CONNOR, wrote an opinion concurring in part and dissenting in part.]

---

[8] JUSTICE STEVENS suggests that the possibility of follow-on plans will make employees "no less likely to object to the financial steps that will lead to [an involuntary] plan termination because they would have no basis for belief that a union will insist on [the adoption of follow-on plans] when, perhaps years later, the PBGC involuntarily terminates the plan." There is no reason to believe, however, that financial decisions that lead to an involuntary termination always or ordinarily occur far in advance of the termination itself. Thus, as JUSTICE STEVENS himself acknowledges with respect to a voluntary termination, "those who could object to [the events resulting in an involuntary termination may also be] reasonably assured of receiving benefits when the insurance is paid." Moreover, even when an involuntary termination does not occur until well after the financial decisions that lead to termination are made, we think the PBGC's apparent belief that employee resistance to those financial decisions will be lessened to some degree by the prospect of follow-on plans after termination is not an unreasonable one.

[9] For example, the PBGC did not restore a fourth LTV plan that had been terminated because, among other things, the plan had insufficient assets to pay benefits when due.

JUSTICE STEVENS, dissenting.

In my opinion, at least with respect to ERISA plans that the PBGC has terminated involuntarily, the use of its restoration power under § 4047 to prohibit "follow-on" plans is contrary to the agency's statutory mandate. Unless there was a sufficient improvement in LTV's financial condition to justify the restoration order, I believe it should be set aside. I, therefore, would remand the case for a determination of whether that ground for the agency decision is adequately supported by the record.

A company that is undergoing reorganization under Chapter 11 of the Bankruptcy Code continues to operate an ongoing business and must have a satisfactory relationship with its work force in order to complete the reorganization process successfully. If its previous pension plans have been involuntarily terminated with the consequence that the PBGC has assumed the responsibility for discharging a significant share of the company's pension obligations, that responsibility by PBGC is an important resource on which the company has a right to rely during the reorganization process. It may use the financial cushion to fund capital investments, to pay current salary, or to satisfy contractual obligations, including the obligation to pay pension benefits. As long as the company uses its best efforts to complete the reorganization (and, incidentally, to reimburse PBGC for payments made to its former employees to the extent required by ERISA),[1] the PBGC does not have any reason to interfere with managerial decisions that the company makes and the bankruptcy court approves. Whether the company's resources are dedicated to current expenditures or capital investments and whether the package of employee benefits that is provided to the work force is composed entirely of wages, vacation pay, and health insurance, on the one hand, or includes additional pension benefits, on the other, should be matters of indifference to the PBGC. Indeed, if it was faithful to the statement of congressional purposes in ERISA, it should favor an alternative that increases the company's use and maintenance of pension plans and that provides for continued payment to existing plan beneficiaries. The follow-on plans, in my opinion, are wholly consistent with the purposes of ERISA.

According to the Court, the PBGC policy is premised on the belief that if the company cannot adopt a follow-on plan, the employees will object more strenuously (1) in the case of a voluntary termination, to the "company's original decision to terminate a plan"; and (2) in the case of an involuntary termination, to the company's decision "to take financial steps that make termination likely." That belief might be justified in the case of a voluntary termination of an ERISA plan.

---

[1] At the time of the termination of the LTV plans, PBGC was entitled to recover only 75 percent of the amounts expended to discharge LTV's pension obligations. The statute has since been amended to authorize a 100 percent recovery. LTV represents that if the restoration order is upheld, and if — as seems highly probable — it is promptly followed by another termination, the PBGC bankruptcy claim will increase from about $2 billion to more than $3 billion. PBGC, of course, does not assert this change as a justification for the restoration order.

Since the follow-on plan would be adopted immediately after plan termination, those who could object to the insurable event are also reasonably assured of receiving benefits when the insurance is paid. That view is wholly unwarranted, however, in the case of an involuntary termination. The insurable event, plan termination, is within the control of the PBGC, which presumably has determined that the company does not have the financial resources to meet its current pension obligations. Even if the company could adopt a follow-on plan, the employees will be no less likely to object to the financial steps that will lead to plan termination because they would have no basis for belief that a union will insist on that course when, perhaps years later, the PBGC involuntarily terminates the plan. The safety that comes from a healthy pension plan will not be overcome by the hope that a future union will remember the interests of its retirees and former employees. Plan restoration in these circumstances is not a legitimate curative to the problem of moral hazard, but rather constitutes punishment of both labor and management for the imprudence of their predecessors.

In the case of an involuntary termination, if a mistake in the financial analysis is made, or if there is a sufficient change in the financial condition of the company to justify a reinstatement of the company's obligation, the PBGC should use its restoration powers. Without such a financial justification, however, there is nothing in the statute to authorize the PBGC's use of that power to prevent a company from creating or maintaining the kind of employee benefit program that the statute was enacted to encourage.

Accordingly, I respectfully dissent.

NOTES

1. *The Limits of Employee Protection.* Employees, obviously, receive some protections from the ERISA pension insurance scheme. But the protections are not absolute. *LTV Corp.* discusses some of the limits: a cap on the total amount of benefits insured, only partial coverage for benefits resulting from recent plan amendments, and no coverage for unvested and unearned benefits.

ERISA also fails to protect employee expectations of an inflation-resistant pension benefit. The promised benefit under a defined benefit plan is usually determined by multiplying a worker's final salary times years of service times a generosity factor (usually between .01 and .02). The final salary component is a rough inflation index. Terminating the plan removes the inflation index.

To illustrate, consider two employees. Both always work for employers with this defined benefit formula: (.02) x (years of service) x (final salary). Both work for twenty years. Employee A works for the same employer for the entire period. Employee B, however, works for one employer for ten years, but then that employer goes bankrupt and the plan is terminated, so Employee B works for a second employer for the remaining ten years. The inflation rate during the entire period is about 8% and wage increases have matched inflation. The salaries of both employees are $20,000 at the end of the first ten years and $40,000 at the end of their work lives. These are the pension benefits for the two employees:

> Employee A
>
> $$(.02) (20) (\$40,000) = \$16,000$$
>
> Employee B
>
> From first employer — $\quad (.02) (10) (\$20,000) = \$ 4,000$
>
> From second employer — $\quad (.02) (10) (\$40,000) = \underline{\$ 8,000}$
>
> Total $\qquad\qquad\qquad\qquad\qquad\qquad \$12,000$

Employee B receives less, because the plan termination deprived her of the inflation-indexing effect of the final salary component of the benefit formula for her first ten years of employment. (Note that this example also illustrates why pensions bond employees to particular firms. The result would be the same if Employee B voluntarily left her first employer after the first ten years.)

2. *Allocating the Costs of Pension Insurance.* As the *LTV Corp.* case indicates, the PBGC can seek to recover any benefits it pays out from the employers whose plans are terminated. If all of the PBGC's expenses could be recovered in that way, the PBGC would provide only short-term insurance; the PBGC's primary role would be as an agency that enforces employer promises to pay pensions. But, of course, the PBGC does more than that. Many of the employers whose plans are terminated cannot pay, so the PBGC also fulfills a long-term insurance function.

The costs of this insurance are imposed in part on all plans covered by the PBGC insurance scheme. The *LTV Corp.* case discusses the current premium structure, which requires higher premiums from plans that pose a higher risk of claims upon the fund (as measured by unfunded vested benefits). Until the Pension Protection Act of 1987, the PBGC premiums did not reflect risk; instead, they were flat rate premiums which ranged over the years from $1 per plan participant in 1974 to $8.50 per plan participant in 1987.

The premiums, however, are significantly lower than the amount necessary to fund the PBGC's potential liabilities. One study estimated that, to provide adequate funding, the basic premium would have to be about double the current premium of $19 per plan participant. Arturo Estrella & Beverly Hirtle, *Estimating the Funding Gap of the Pension Benefit Guaranty Corporation,* 13 FED. RESERVE BANK N.Y. Q. REV. 45 (1988). As a result of the PBGC's underfunding, taxpayers also bear a portion of the risk of the pension insurance program.

3. *Pension Insurance as Union Rent-Seeking?* Consider the following argument about who wins and who loses under ERISA's pension insurance scheme:

The beneficiaries of pension insurance are easy to identify. They are unionized workers in dying industries.... [V]irtually all systematic underfunding in private pension plans occurs in plans covering union workers. These plans also have a significantly higher chance of failing. Based on a sample of plans in the period 1978 to 1983, the probability of failure for plans covering union workers was six times higher than the probability for plans covering nonunion workers.

The data also show that as a result of underfunding and poor financial performance, plans covering union workers receive a disproportionate share of PBGC transfers.... Union workers, who account for roughly one-third of pension participants, are the beneficiaries of 95 percent of all claims against the PBGC....

From an economic perspective, it is possible to explain why pension plans covering union workers might have been systematically underfunded and why they have had unusually high failure rates over the years. Organized as a group through a union, workers pose an economic threat to the shareholders of firms. This is particularly true if the shareholders must invest in specialized durable capital, such as heavy machinery usable only in, say, steel production. Once such an investment is made, union workers can appropriate a portion of the returns to capital by raising their wage demands.

Faced with this dilemma, shareholders would be reluctant to make investments in unionized firms that require large, nontransferable capital expenditures. Production processes involving specialized, durable investments do not make economic sense unless opportunistic behavior by organized workers can be controlled. Before ERISA, the underfunding of pension plans was one such control mechanism. If the union tried to capture some of the returns to capital by raising wages, shareholders could threaten to abandon the firm, thereby imposing large pension losses on workers. By underfunding pensions, the firm gave unionized workers a stake in its long-term viability. The prospect of pension losses upon firm failure helped discipline union wage demands throughout the period of investment....

From this perspective, it is clear why unionized pension participants would support ERISA insurance. By supporting a government regulation that guarantees a portion of pension benefits, unionized workers can extract noncompetitive wages and still collect a substantial portion of their pensions. Some unions that had disregarded the consequences of high-wage policies (failure of the firm and loss of pensions) could now reclaim the pensions they were about to lose; other unions could raise their wage demands without fear of losing their pensions. ERISA offered some unionized workers, on a one-time basis, substantial economic rents....

These transfers are paid for by participants in the vast majority of pension plans that are stable and well funded....

Aside from transferring wealth to some union workers, ERISA's system of pension insurance undermines long-term economic efficiency. The system reduces the incentive of unions in troubled firms or industries to reduce wage demands, making capital investment less attractive than they otherwise would be. At the same time, it allows firms with a higher probability of failure to offer deferred wages, that are paid, in part, by the PBGC. In effect, the government subsidizes wages in failing firms, artificially prolonging the economic life of inefficient firms at the expense of efficient firms.

The system also has adverse effects on pensions.... [N]ew successful firms are discouraged from establishing defined benefit plans because these plans carry an implicit — and growing — liability in the form of future expected taxes to retire the PBGC deficit. Unsuccessful firms are encouraged to switch from defined contribution to defined benefit plans to take advantage of the expected wage subsidy. The current policy thus distorts firms' choices among pension contracts, and at the same time, creates a self-selection problem for the PBGC (that is, the PBGC is likely to find that a disproportionate share of the plans it covers are high risk plans).

Richard A. Ippolito, *Pension Security: Has ERISA Had Any Effect?*, 11 REG.: AEI J. ON GOV'T & SOC'Y 19-20 (1987).[*]

4. *The Rents Are Too Low.* Ippolito sees the unionized workers who receive benefits from ERISA's pension insurance scheme as winners. Others see something else:

In 1977, Harvester had owned Wisconsin Steel for seventy-five years, and the mill made the specially hardened steel for the trucks and machinery that Harvester manufactured. Gradually, Harvester had let the mill run down, and sometime in the mid-seventies, it began looking for a buyer. But no one in the business wanted to buy Wisconsin Steel. Not only was it run down, but there was an even bigger problem: the pension fund was short $65 million.

Wisconsin Steel, in short, was unsalable. Yet Harvester did not want to close it either. If it did so, it would owe the whole $65 million in pensions, plus another $20 million in special shutdown benefits, like severance pay. It almost seemed as if Harvester was trapped into keeping the mill open.... It was the revenge of the weak on the strong. "Shut us down, Mr. Employer, and you die, too."

So Harvester tried to close the mill indirectly. It transferred title to a dummy corporation. Then, when this corporate shell went bankrupt Harvester could say, "Too bad, they're not our pensions now." But Harvester had to have an accomplice. It found one in a small engineering company, Envirodyne, Inc., who knew nothing about steel. Envirodyne was not much of a company, just two yuppies in a garage. But Envirodyne transferred title

---

[*] Reprinted with permission of the American Enterprise Institute, Washington, D.C.

to a subsidiary it created, EDC Holding Company. Then EDC transferred title to a subsidiary it created, WSC Corporation. One corporate shell came after another. It was like a game of Chinese boxes, and when you got to the last box, nothing was in it. Nobody would be paying pensions.

Under our law, a subsidiary can go bankrupt and normally the parent company will not be liable for its debts. So when EDC or WSC went bankrupt, Harvester and even Envirodyne could say they owed nothing. Indeed, Harvester was not even the parent. But Harvester was the biggest creditor and held on through mortgages to everything of value. That was the malign beauty of it all, which I spent seven grudging years admiring. Harvester had dumped all the pension liabilities but kept control of all the assets. It could keep running the mill as if it still owned it.... And the workers, who may have been there twenty to thirty years, would lose their pensions, health insurance, severance pay, etc. Dumb, stupid organized labor would take the fall....

[In addition to losing a good share of their pension benefits, the workers could not get other jobs because they were too "old."] It sounds preposterous to call them old when they were just in their forties or fifties. Yet at that age, in manufacturing, everyone calls them "old."...

Their biggest problem was having to drag around these old, puffy-looking, blue-collar bodies. These bodies were like booby traps. One crack or tear in them, and they would sag like an old bag of sand. These old bodies could cost a new employer thousands in worker comp....

I was astonished at some of the men who were still working at Wisconsin Steel when it closed. I saw (no kidding) amputees, asthmatics, old men with pacemakers, men with arthritis, and many who were missing a finger or two. In some little knots of men at our rallies, it was hard to find a whole hand, I noticed. I used to think, "How had this mill been running at all?"...

The point is, no *new* employer would hire them and have these cripples walking around, lifting and bending and carrying things. Some of them, when the mill closed, were a year or so away from death....

If I seem to exaggerate how used up these men were, remember I saw them *after* the mill closed. A steelworker can shut down just like a steel mill. When a mill shuts down and the furnace goes cold, it can take tens of millions of dollars to get it relit. And you could look at some of these men and know: it would take tens of millions of dollars to get them relit....

Now, on the North Side, when I walk along the beach, I cannot even see South Chicago, except on a clear day. Even then, I just barely see the mills and the smokestacks far, far to the south, and the whole steel industry like a ship slowly sinking into the waves. I think of the men of Wisconsin Steel who are still on it, who could not get off.

It was a shipwreck. And nobody planned it, it just happened.

THOMAS GEOGHEGAN, WHICH SIDE ARE YOU ON? TRYING TO BE FOR LABOR WHEN IT'S FLAT ON ITS BACK 93-120 (1991).[*]

Litigation over the closing of the Wisconsin Steel plant finally ended in 1995 when the employees reached a settlement with Envirodyne for benefits that were not covered by the PBGC. The settlement was for much less than the amounts claimed, but the employees' lawyer said that "[s]peed was becoming an important priority for the plaintiffs in light of the advanced age of many of the former Wisconsin Steel employees." *Former Employees of Wis. Steel Settle Pension Dispute with Environdyne*, Daily Lab. Rep. (BNA), Dec. 13, 1995, at d16. The employees had settled earlier with Harvester (now known as Navistar) and the two Environdyne subsidiaries, EDC and WSC. The PBGC had recovered some of its expenses through a settlement with Envirodyne and a judgement against Harvester (Navistar). For a history of the litigation, see *Lumpkin v. Envirodyne Industries, Inc.*, 933 F.2d 449 (7th Cir. 1991).

2. TERMINATIONS WITH SUFFICIENT ASSETS

DISTRICT 65, UAW v. HARPER & ROW, PUBLISHERS, INC.

United States District Court, S.D. New York

576 F. Supp. 1468 (1983)

KEVIN THOMAS DUFFY, DISTRICT JUDGE:

These two actions arise primarily from a transaction finalized on December 9, 1981 in which Harper & Row, Publishers, Inc. ("Harper & Row") terminated its Retirement Plan, liquidated the fund and recaptured the excess contributions in order to purchase approximately one-third of the outstanding shares of Harper & Row stock from defendant Minneapolis Star & Tribune Company ("MST") after being notified by MST that it intended to sell the stock.

In February 1981, MST notified Harper & Row that it intended to dispose of its entire position in Harper & Row which consisted of 1,017,630 shares of stock. The MST holdings represented one-third of the outstanding shares of Harper & Row stock. After learning of MST's decision to sell its shares of Harper & Row stock, a committee of outside directors was formed by Harper & Row to review the possibility of purchasing the stock from MST. The Board of Directors of Harper & Row engaged Kidder, Peabody & Co. ("Kidder, Peabody"), an investment banking firm, to render a financial opinion regarding the feasibility of purchasing the MST shares.

Harper & Row planned to finance the stock purchase in part by terminating the Harper & Row Publishers, Inc. Retirement Plan. After purchasing annuities to provide for the present value of accrued benefits for all employees covered by the Retirement Plan, Harper & Row anticipated an excess fund of $10.2 million. The balance of the purchase price was to be financed from the sale of real prop-

---

[*] Reprinted with permission.

erty ($5 million), the purchase of Harper & Row stock by the Harper & Row employee profit-sharing plan ($2 million) and loans ($3.1 million).[4]

Harper & Row thereafter commenced negotiations with MST in July 1981 for the purchase of the shares held by MST and in August 1981 a tentative agreement was reached. In August, the Harper & Row stockholders, current employees and retirees were notified about the tentative agreement and a notice of intent to terminate the Retirement Plan was filed with the PBGC. Harper & Row also applied to the Internal Revenue Service ("IRS") for a determination that the termination of the Retirement Plan would not adversely affect its qualified status under the Internal Revenue Code.

On November 6, 1981, the PBGC issued a Notice of Sufficiency pursuant to Employee Retirement Income Security Act ("ERISA") § 4041(b) which stated that the assets of the Plan would be sufficient to satisfy all obligations concerning guaranteed benefits. On November 20, 1981, the IRS issued a determination letter finding that the termination of the Retirement Plan "does not adversely affect its qualification for Federal tax purposes." The Retirement Plan was terminated effective August 31, 1981. In an agreement dated September 15, 1981, Harper & Row agreed to purchase the 1,017,630 shares of stock at the price of $20 per share....

To fund the benefits accrued in the Plan, Harper & Row entered into a contract with Prudential to purchase annuities for the present value of the accrued benefits for those members in the Plan whose accrued benefits had a present value of at least $1,000 and to pay lump-sum amounts to the other participants. The arrangement with Prudential was later amended and those participants with an accrued present value of between $250 and $1,000 could opt to either receive a lump-sum payment or an annuity. As a result of this transaction, approximately $9 million was recaptured by Harper & Row after the retirement fund was liquidated.

Two other transactions are challenged by plaintiffs. Harper & Row's Profit-Sharing Plan purchased 152,588 of the 1,017,633 shares from Harper & Row for approximately $11 5/8 per share for a total of $1.8 million. This purchase occurred after the Profit-Sharing Plan was amended to allow an investment of up to $2 million, but not more than one-half of the Plan assets, in Harper & Row shares. The amended Profit-Sharing Plan provided that the price was to be

---

[4] The financing of the proposed purchase of the MST shares was also outlined in a letter dated June 19, 1981.... The letter stated in part:

> The Company's Retirement Plan, the asset value of which exceeds the value of benefits accrued under it by approximately $5 million, would be terminated. Individual annuities would be purchased for each employee out of the proceeds at prevailing interest rates, which are substantially higher than the funding assumptions used in the existing plan. Because of this differential, as well as the generally low age level of our employees, such annuities could be purchased for approximately $4 million less than the amount currently accrued in the Plan. After purchasing such annuities, the trustee would thus have cash remaining amounting to approximately $9 million.

determined by the average of the bid and asked quotation for Harper & Row shares reported in the over-the-counter market at the close of business on the day preceding the purchase....

Discussion ...

2. *Termination of the Retirement Plan*

The Retirement Plan provides for its termination and outlines the procedure by which the benefits are allocated upon termination. Section 9.01 provides that "[w]hile the plan is intended to be permanent, an Employer may terminate or partially terminate the Plan at any time." The Trust Fund may then be liquidated subject to the approval of the PBGC and IRS....

Acknowledging the right to terminate generally, [District 65 asserts] that under the circumstances in this case by terminating its Plan, Harper & Row violated ERISA's fiduciary standard contained in sections 403(c)(1) and 404(a)(1)(A)-(D).

The standard of conduct expected of fiduciaries under ERISA is as follows:

> Subject to sections 1103(c) and (d), 1342, and 1344 of this title, a fiduciary shall discharge his duties with respect to a plan solely in the interest of the participants and beneficiaries and —
>
> (A) for the exclusive purpose of:
>   (i) providing benefits to participants and their beneficiaries; and
>   (ii) defraying reasonable expenses of administering the plan;
> (B) with the care, skill, prudence, and diligence ... that a prudent man ... would use ...; [and]
> (D) in accordance with the documents and instruments governing the plan insofar as such documents and instruments are consistent with the provisions of this subchapter or subchapter III of this chapter.

ERISA § 404(a)(1). Section 403(c)(1) of ERISA sets forth an additional fiduciary obligation. It provides that the assets of the Plan "shall never inure to the benefit of any employer and shall be held for the exclusive purposes of providing benefits to participants in the plan and their beneficiaries." ERISA § 403(c)(1)....

Plaintiffs allege that with the exception of PBGC the defendants failed to discharge their duties as fiduciaries of the Retirement Plan, the Profit-Sharing Plan and/or the Employee Stock Plan solely in the interest of the participants and beneficiaries. Further, plaintiffs allege that by allowing the assets of the plans to "inure to the benefit of the employer," the fiduciaries have violated ERISA. ERISA § 403(c)(1)....

In opposition to District 65's motion for summary judgment and in support of its own motion, Harper & Row argues that ERISA's fiduciary standard has no application to a decision to terminate its pension plan. For the following reasons, I hold that the decision to terminate the Retirement Plan is exempt from ERISA's fiduciary standards. The termination provisions in the Plan and ERISA appear to be predicated on the voluntary nature of such plans. For example, section 9.01 of the Plan provides that the Plan can be terminated by Harper & Row at any time. Further, the sections in ERISA dealing with fiduciary obligations contain exceptions when the challenged conduct involves termination. ERISA § 403(c)(1) states that "[e]xcept as provided in ... sections 1342 and 1344 of this title (relating to termination of insured plans), the assets of a plan shall never inure to the benefit of any employer...." Additionally, ERISA § 404 contains the qualification that it is "[s]ubject to sections 1103(c) and (d), 1342, and 1344 of this title."...

Thus, the ... plaintiffs erroneously seek to have the fiduciary provisions in ERISA applied to the decision to terminate and the arrangements made as a consequence to that decision. Accordingly, plaintiffs' claims are dismissed for failure to state a cause of action to the extent that a breach of fiduciary duty was alleged to have occurred by reason of Harper & Row's decision to terminate the Retirement Plan.

3. *Reversion of Excess Assets to Harper & Row*

Plaintiffs allege that a breach of ERISA's minimum standards for fiduciaries occurred when the surplus assets reverted to Harper & Row upon the termination of the Plan. For the following reasons, I find that these claims for breach of fiduciary duty must be dismissed insofar as they relate to Harper & Row's right to recapture the surplus assets. I note, however, that the question concerning how much of the assets are "surplus" and how much should have been paid out to beneficiaries is a separate issue. I turn first to Harper & Row's surplus recapture rights.

The Harper & Row Plan and ERISA explicitly provide for the recapture of surplus assets by the employer after a pension plan has been terminated and accrued benefits have been allocated.

ERISA § 4044(d) provides that the "[r]esidual assets of a plan may be distributed to the employer if — (A) all liabilities of the plan to participants and their beneficiaries have been satisfied, (B) the distribution does not contravene any provision of law, and (C) the plan provides for such a distribution in these circumstances."

The first condition requires that the "liabilities of the plan to participants and their beneficiaries have been satisfied." Harper & Row entered into a contract with Prudential under which accrued benefits were paid either in the form of an annuity or a lump-sum payment. The sufficiency of the satisfaction of plan liabilities is challenged by plaintiffs on the ground that the individuals opting for a lump-sum payment and those only entitled to a lump-sum payment received less than they should have as a result of the utilization of a 15 percent interest rate. The interest rate assumed in the computation of the annuities and lump-sum payments will be discussed in the next section.

The second condition is that the distribution of excess assets to Harper & Row does not contravene any provision of law. The recapture of funds by employers who have overfunded plans through actuarial error has been recognized as permissible under ERISA.[9]

The third condition set forth in subdivision (C) of ERISA § 4044(d)(1) is satisfied. Section 9.05 of the Harper & Row Retirement Plan permits a reversion of excess assets to the employer upon the termination of the Plan "if all benefits have been allocated and distributed under this Article and all liabilities of the Plan to affected Members, Former Members and Beneficiaries have been satisfied."

Based on the foregoing, I find that Harper & Row had a right to the surplus assets remaining after the termination of the Plan and distribution of accrued benefits. The amount of a surplus that reverted to Harper & Row, however, is in issue. Plaintiffs contend that Harper & Row reaped a windfall by minimizing the expense of providing the value of the accrued benefits to Plan participants. This issue will be discussed in the next section.

4. Purchase of Annuity Contract

A bid was solicited from Prudential in August, 1981 for the purchase of annuities covering all accrued benefits under Harper & Row's Retirement Plan. A bid was submitted and a contract was entered into for the purchase of a group annuity contract. Under the contract, as amended, those participants in the plan with an accrued present value of $1,000 or more receive an annuity and those with accrued benefits between $250 and $1,000 have the option of receiving either an annuity or a lump-sum payment. Finally, those members with less than $250 accrued benefits will receive a lump sum amount....

The ... complaint contains an allegation that Harper & Row used an interest rate of 15 percent per year to calculate the present value of accrued benefits under the Plan in order to deprive plan participants of the actuarial equivalent of his or her accrued benefit. Harwood's argument is that by "choosing an interest rate which was grossly inflated," Harper & Row "minimized the present value of accrued benefits" and maximized the amount of resulting excess assets. Plaintiffs allege also that Harper & Row breached its fiduciary duties by failing to provide to the plan participants information necessary to make an informed decision of whether to select an annuity or lump-sum payment....

---

[9] The District Court for the District of Columbia stated in *Washington-Baltimore Newspaper Guild Local 35 v. Washington Star Co.,* [555 F. Supp. 257 (1983), *aff'd,* 729 F.2d 863 (D.C. Cir. 1984),] that "[i]n addition to section 4044(d)(1), the common law of trusts provides that an employer can retain such surplus.... These provisions are clearly intended to insure that while an employer is obligated to provide defined benefits to plan participants, the participants should not be able to claim a windfall stemming from the employer's accidental overfunding of a defined benefit plan." 555 F. Supp. at 260....

Thus, plaintiffs ... argue that because a 15 percent interest rate assumption was used to calculate the lump-sum payments for those participants with accrued benefits under the $250 threshold or for those in the middle range who opted for the lump-sum payment, the lump-sum received by those participants was unreasonably small. Plaintiffs allege that the use of a 15 percent interest rate by Harper & Row was unfair to plan participants because they "could not be expected to earn more than about 7 percent, on a long-term basis, on the relatively small amounts paid to them in the form of lump sums."

There are several issues of fact that preclude the granting of the defendants' motions for summary judgment and dismissal on these claims. First, although those participants with accrued benefits between $250 and $1,000 had the option of selecting an annuity based on the 15 percent interest rate or a lump-sum payment, it appears that the information supplied to the Plan participants may have been insufficient to enable them to make an informed decision. Harper & Row released memorandums on January 14, 1982 and April 16, 1982 to all of its employees outlining the relative benefits of annuities and lump-sum payments but failed to disclose the 15 percent interest rate assumption.

Second, an issue of fact exists as to whether the rate of 15 percent was reasonable in light of the market conditions prevailing at the time that the Prudential contract was entered into. In a memorandum to the Retirement Plan Committee dated August 29, 1978, several indices for the determination of the interest rate were explored. For example, the interest rates used in Moody's AAA Bond Index (8.6 percent in 1976) and by PBGC (6 percent) were suggested. The reasons for the rejection by defendants of these lower rates is unclear. The PBGC regulations require that "reasonable actuarial assumptions as to interest and mortality" be used in the valuation of accrued benefits.... Here, only one bid was solicited. Prudential's quotation, therefore, is only one factor which may be of limited usefulness to be used in determining the reasonableness of a 15 percent interest rate assumption. Defendants' motions to dismiss, and for summary judgment on plaintiffs' claims concerning the Prudential contract are denied....

[P]laintiffs' claims for breach of fiduciary duty based on the termination of the Plan and reversion of surplus assets to Harper & Row are dismissed....

NOTES

1. *The Employer's Claim to Excess Assets.* Professor Stein has succinctly stated the employer's claim:

> The employer['s] ... fairness argument ... is based on the essential nature of defined benefit plans: in a defined benefit plan, the employer assumes the investment risk, i.e., if the plan's assets are insufficient to meet the plan's benefit obligations, the employer must make additional contributions to the plan; on the other side of the bargain, the employees only have an interest in receiving the promised benefit — so long as that benefit is paid, the employees have lost nothing.... The argument then is one of symmetry: he

who bears the risk of bad investment performance is entitled to harvest the fruits of a superior investment performance.

Norman P. Stein, *Raiders of the Corporate Pension Plan: The Reversion of Excess Plan Assets to the Employer,* 5 AM. J. TAX POL'Y 117, 154-55 (1986).

2. *The Employee's Interest in Excess Assets.* In *Harper & Row,* the Court cites a case which indicates that employees would receive a windfall if the employer was not permitted to recoup the excess assets. But is that right? The first note after the *LTV* case indicates that terminations deprive employees of an inflation-indexed pension. Economic research indicates that employees expect and pay for indexed pensions. *See* Richard A. Ippolito, *Issues Surrounding Pension Terminations for Reversions,* 5 AM. J. TAX POL'Y 81, 83-87 (1986). Thus, the employee claim is that excess assets should go to employees, because they would permit pensions after termination that are closer to what employees paid for and legitimately expected. But consider the following:

> The great difficulty with this argument is that it begs the question of why so important a term [the implicit term promising indexed benefits] would be left implicit rather than made explicit. The employees, who are often represented in pension negotiations by capable labor unions (such as the UAW in the *Harper & Row* case) would seem to have every incentive to see to it that so important a term of the pension contract be spelled out. The persistent failure to spell out the term suggests that it does not exist.

Daniel R. Fischel & John H. Langbein, *ERISA's Fundamental Contradiction: The Exclusive Benefit Rule,* 55 U. CHI. L. REV. 1105, 1152 n.164 (1988).

3. *The Government's Interest.* The government provides considerable tax subsidies to encourage retirement savings. If employers could terminate plans without paying additional taxes, they could recoup a considerable portion of the tax subsidies, and the purpose of the subsidies — encouraging savings for retirement — would be frustrated. Economists have estimated that the portion of reversions attributable to the tax preferences is probably between 10% and 20%. Ippolito, *supra,* at 89-90.

But terminating plans is not the only way for employers to respond to over-funded plans:

> An employer effectively can realize the value of excess assets not only by terminating the plan and recovering a reversion, but by continuing the plan and reducing its contributions to reflect the excess assets. In fact, an employer who continues a plan will realize a greater financial benefit than the sponsor who terminates a plan, recovers the plan assets, and pays tax. This is because ... the trust corpus [will continue to accrue funds] on a tax-deferred basis. Why isn't this as much, or more, of a problem than an employer recovering the surplus and at least paying some tax on it?

Norman P. Stein, *Raiders of the Corporate Pension Plan: The Reversion of Excess Plan Assets to the Employer,* 5 AM. J. TAX POL'Y 117, 169 (1986).[*]

4. The End of Reversions? Between 1980 and 1987 there was an explosion in voluntary plan terminations. Employers terminated 1,635 plans with reversions of $1 million or more. Employers received 45% of the total assets from these reversions; on average, they received more than $11 million per reversion. Individual employees received, on average, about $12,000 each. Dana M. Muir, Note, *Changing the Rules of the Game: Pension Plan Terminations and Early Retirement Benefits,* 87 MICH. L. REV. 1034, 1036 (1989).

Congress has acted three times to discourage reversions. In the Tax Reform Act of 1986, Congress enacted a 10% nondeductible excise tax on asset reversions. The tax was increased to 15% by the Technical and Miscellaneous Revenue Act of 1988 and to 20% by the Revenue Act of 1990. The 1990 Act also provides for a 50% excise tax, unless employees are provided with a qualified replacement plan or increases in their accrued benefits under the terminated plan. I.R.C. § 4980(d). The evidence suggests that these enactments have significantly discouraged terminations designed to capture excess assets, although terminations for other reasons continue (for example, to switch to a defined contribution plan or for business reasons unrelated to plan funding). AMERICAN ACADEMY OF ACTUARIES, SURVEY OF DEFINED BENEFIT PLAN TERMINATIONS (1992).

F. RETIREMENT SECURITY AND EMPLOYER-SPONSORED PENSIONS

MICHAEL J. GRAETZ, THE TROUBLED MARRIAGE OF RETIREMENT SECURITY AND TAX POLICIES 135
University of Pennsylvania Law Review 851, 852-59 (1987)[**]

Commentators typically describe a tripartite system that enables and encourages the provision of income security for individuals in the years following their retirement from the workforce: Social Security, employer-provided pensions, and individual savings....

An effort to analyze these three aspects of retirement security policy as a unified system is inherently complex. It is difficult to conceive of a wider spectrum of public policy mechanisms intended to implement a single goal. At one extreme is Social Security, a mandatory national public program financed by the federal government's power to tax, fulfilled by the government's power to spend, and explicitly redistributional in both purpose and effect — redistributional both across generations and within the same generation. At the opposite extreme is reliance on individual savings as a source of retirement security, a predominantly

---

private program, with the individual (or the family) composing the relevant unit.... Bridging these two public/private extremes are employer-provided pensions, voluntary private programs encouraged through income tax reductions, regulated by government, both directly and as to the many requirements that must be met to qualify for tax benefits, and backed, at least in a limited way, by an insurance system of national scope. Taken together, then, these three retirement security sources reflect a full spectrum of policy initiatives: a federal social program for all Americans, an individualistic program dependent principally upon familial self-reliance, and a pluralistic communitarian program involving both employers and employees....

At the outset one should describe the goals of retirement security policy in order to measure the success or failure of the current mix of public and private programs and to determine whether these programs comprise a coherent whole in addressing the retirement security problem. The shortfall in income upon retirement is lost income from labor. Thus, while there are no doubt disagreements at the margin, replacement of some significant portion of preretirement wages must be the fundamental goal of retirement security policy. Retirement security also implies that the replacement of preretirement labor income will ensure for the retiree the maintenance of an adequate retirement income that will both protect the elderly from widespread poverty and generally ensure against an abrupt decline in a retiree's lifestyle....

Delineating the retirement security goal as a wage-replacement goal helps to clarify the suitable functions of the various elements of our tripartite retirement security system. Social Security — a completely public program — might serve fully to meet the basic income adequacy goal for poorer workers, contribute substantially toward ensuring an adequate threshold retirement income for moderate income workers, and assist somewhat in post-retirement lifestyle maintenance for all workers. This vision of a public Social Security function would require at least all individuals who have enough earnings to satisfy current basic needs to substitute future for current consumption, for example by taxing current wages in exchange for subsequent wage-replacement retirement benefits. In addition, such a view regards as appropriate the redistributional aspects of Social Security and dismisses the contention that a public social security program should resemble an actuarially sound retirement insurance plan for all workers, even those at the highest income levels. The dominant public role of retirement income security policy should be to ensure post-retirement income adequacy for low- and moderate-income workers.

At the other end of the income scale, private individual savings are most likely to ensure retirement income security for those workers who have earned sufficiently high lifetime wages (or who otherwise have sufficient investment assets) to enable them to use current savings to protect themselves from a substantial decline in living standard upon retirement. The public role in this context should obviously permit, and perhaps facilitate, private savings for retirement, but the individual savings component of retirement security for higher-income workers should be a primarily private matter. Once basic income adequacy during retirement is assured, the government might well remain generally neutral about individual decisions by high-income workers regarding the tradeoff between their own current and future consumption, except to the extent that this tradeoff may affect the tendency of employers to create and maintain pension plans that will benefit low- and moderate-income workers as well.

The appropriate role of the social security and individual savings elements of the tripartite retirement security program thus fits easily within this Article's articulation of retirement security goals. Private pensions present more of a problem. While it is clear that these employer-provided pensions often contribute to basic income adequacy, especially for low- and moderate-income workers, it is not nearly so clear to what extent employer-provided plans should serve to facilitate post-retirement lifestyle maintenance for all workers. Specification of the appropriate role for employer-sponsored pension plans depends both on the overall ambitions of the national retirement security program and on the adequacy of Social Security. The voluntariness of such plans links them to individual savings, while their collective nature with respect to benefits and risks as well as with respect to employer and regulatory limitations on employee choices, suggests a public nature. Dominant reliance on income tax incentives as the public stimulus for employer plans necessarily confounds retirement security and income tax policies....

[T]he necessary function of employer-provided pension plans in bridging the public antipoverty/basic income adequacy function of Social Security and the private lifestyle maintenance function of individual savings creates substantial tensions in the formulation of public policy regarding such plans. Typically, the tensions are manifested by debates over the appropriate conditions that must be met by private pensions in order to qualify for income tax benefits and over the propriety and effects of extending similar benefits to private individual retirement savings plans. Viewing employer pensions as an integral part of a coherent national retirement security policy, however, also requires coordinating the significant features of employer plans with the distribution of the benefits and burdens of both Social Security and the public aspects of individual savings. Ultimately, this raises questions about the ability of voluntary employer plans to fulfill their critical function in national retirement security policy.

NOTES

1. *Bottom-Weighted Replacement Rates.* Social Security benefits are "bottom weighted" to a fairly significant degree. That is, they replace more of the preretirement income of low-paid employees than of high-paid employees. Pension benefits are also bottom weighted, but only to a relatively small degree. As a result, the figure of principal interest to retirees — the replacement rate of the combined programs — is also bottom weighted.

Proportion of Pre-Retirement
Income Replaced By:

Final Annual Salary	Social Security	Private Pension	Combined
Retire at Age 62			
$15,000	34.7%	33.1%	67.8%
25,000	29.0	28.1	57.1
35,000	23.5	27.4	50.8
45,000	18.9	27.4	46.4
Retire at Age 65			
$15,000	44.8%	34.4%	79.2%
25,000	37.8	29.4	67.1
35,000	29.4	28.9	58.4
45,000	23.8	29.0	52.8

Source: Adapted from William J. Wiatrowski, New Survey Data on Pension Benefits, Monthly Lab. Rev., Aug. 1991, at 8, 13 Table 4.

Note: Figures are for full-time employees retiring in 1989 with 30 years of service in medium and large private establishments. The retirement ages reflect the age for early retirement with reduced benefits (62) and for normal retirement with full benefits (65) under the Social Security program.

2. *Integrating Social Security and Pension Benefits.* The tax laws currently permit employers to consider Social Security benefits when determining whether a pension plan discriminates against low-paid employees. I.R.C. §§ 401(a)(5)(C), 401(l). Since Social Security is bottom weighted, the effect of this integration is to permit more pension contributions and/or benefits (along with their tax advantages) to flow to high-paid employees and, hence, to close the gap to a limited extent between the replacement rates for low-paid and high-paid employees.

Chapter 19
EMPLOYER-PROVIDED HEALTH INSURANCE

ERISA applies not only to pension plans, but also to "welfare" plans. The principal distinction between pension plans and welfare plans is that pension plans provide benefits upon retirement, while welfare plans provide benefits for other types of contingencies. Health insurance is the most important of the welfare plans, and we will focus on it. The statutory definition, however, also includes plans that provide disability, life, or unemployment insurance; vacation benefits; apprenticeship or other training programs; day-care centers; scholarship funds; and prepaid legal services. ERISA § 3(1).

Although they are covered by ERISA, welfare plans are only minimally regulated by the Act. As originally enacted, the only provisions of ERISA that applied to welfare plans were the reporting and disclosure requirements, the fiduciary rules, and the enforcement provisions. Later, Congress amended ERISA to deal with some fairly specific problems with health care, such as portability of benefits. Nevertheless, in contrast to the rather comprehensive regulation of pension plans, ERISA's substantive regulation of welfare plans is limited. This is significant, in part, because ERISA contains a very broad preemption provision which largely displaces state and local regulation.

A. ERISA PREEMPTION

ERISA has a very broad preemption provision. Section 514(a) provides that ERISA "supercede[s] any and all State laws insofar as they may now or hereafter relate to any [pension or welfare] plan." There are exceptions from preemption, but they are fairly narrow. The most important exceptions are for state insurance, banking, and securities laws; generally applicable criminal laws; and qualified domestic relations orders. ERISA § 514(b).

The legislative history is also clear that the preemption provision was intended to be broad. The original House and Senate bills would have preempted state laws only to the extent that they related to matters that were *actually regulated* by ERISA (for example, state laws relating to reporting and disclosure requirements and fiduciary standards). State laws on other matters, even though related to pension and welfare plans, would not have been preempted. In conference, however, the bill was changed to include the broad preemption language of section 514. This was emphasized by one of the major sponsors of the legislation, Representative John Dent: "[T]he crowning achievement of this legislation [is] the reservation to Federal authority of the sole power to regulate the field of [pension and welfare] plans. With the preemption of the field, we round out the protection afforded participants by eliminating the threat of conflicting and inconsistent State and local regulations...." 120 Cong. Rec. 29,197 (1974).

Preemption issues are difficult throughout labor and employment law. They are no easier here. Preemption under ERISA, however, poses a special concern because it is combined with ERISA's very limited substantive regulation of welfare plans. The risk is that federal protection of employee interests is or will become inadequate, while at the same time state and local efforts to provide protection will be frustrated because of the broad preemption.

METROPOLITAN LIFE INSURANCE CO. v. MASSACHUSETTS

United States Supreme Court
471 U.S. 724 (1985)

JUSTICE BLACKMUN delivered the opinion of the Court.

A Massachusetts statute requires that specified minimum mental-health-care benefits be provided a Massachusetts resident who is insured under a general insurance policy, an accident or sickness insurance policy, or an employee health-care plan that covers hospital and surgical expenses. The ... question before us in these cases is whether the state statute, as applied to insurance policies purchased by employee health-care plans regulated by the federal Employee Retirement Income Security Act of 1974, is pre-empted by that Act....

I

General health insurance typically is sold as group insurance to an employer or other group. Group insurance presently is subject to extensive state regulation, including regulation of the carrier, regulation of the sale and advertising of the insurance, and regulation of the content of the contracts. Mandated-benefit laws, that require an insurer to provide a certain kind of benefit to cover a specified illness or procedure whenever someone purchases a certain kind of insurance, are a subclass of such content regulation....

The substantive terms of group-health insurance contracts ... have been extensively regulated by the States. For example, the majority of States currently require that coverage for dependents continue beyond any contractually imposed age limitation when the dependent is incapable of self-sustaining employment because of mental or physical handicap; such statutes date back to the early 1960's. And over the last 15 years all 50 States have required that coverage of infants begin at birth, rather than at some time shortly after birth, as had been the prior practice in the unregulated market. Many state statutes require that insurers offer on an optional basis particular kinds of coverage to purchasers. Others require insurers either to offer or mandate that insurance policies include coverage for services rendered by a particular type of health-care provider.

Mandated-benefit statutes, then, are only one variety of a matrix of state laws that regulate the substantive content of health-insurance policies to further state health policy. Massachusetts Gen. Laws Ann., ch. 175, § 47B (West Supp. 1985), is typical of mandated-benefit laws currently in place in the majority of

States.[10] With respect to a Massachusetts resident, it requires any general health-insurance policy that provides hospital and surgical coverage, or any benefit plan that has such coverage, to provide as well a certain minimum of mental-health protection. In particular, § 47B requires that a health-insurance policy provide 60 days of coverage for confinement in a mental hospital, coverage for confinement in a general hospital equal to that provided by the policy for nonmental illness, and certain minimum outpatient benefits.

Section 47B was designed to address problems encountered in treating mental illness in Massachusetts. The Commonwealth determined that its working people needed to be protected against the high cost of treatment for such illness. It also believed that, without insurance, mentally ill workers were often institutionalized in large state mental hospitals, and that mandatory insurance would lead to a higher incidence of more effective treatment in private community mental-health centers.

In addition, the Commonwealth concluded that the voluntary insurance market was not adequately providing mental-health coverage, because of "adverse selection" in mental-health insurance: good insurance risks were not purchasing coverage, and this drove up the price of coverage for those who otherwise might purchase mental-health insurance. The legislature believed that the public interest required that it correct the insurance market in the Commonwealth by mandating minimum-coverage levels, effectively forcing the good-risk individuals to become part of the risk pool, and enabling insurers to price the insurance at an average market rather than a market retracted due to adverse selection. Section 47B, then, was intended to help safeguard the public against the high costs of comprehensive inpatient and outpatient mental-health care, reduce non-psychiatric medical-care expenditures for mentally related illness, shift the delivery of treatment from inpatient to outpatient services, and relieve the Commonwealth of some of the financial burden it otherwise would encounter with respect to mental-health problems.

It is our task in these cases to decide whether such insurance regulation violates or is inconsistent with federal law.

The federal Employee Retirement Income Security Act of 1974 (ERISA), comprehensively regulates employee pension and welfare plans. An employee welfare-benefit plan or welfare plan is defined as one which provides to employees "medical, surgical, or hospital care or benefits, or benefits in the event of sickness, accident, disability [or] death," whether these benefits are provided "through the purchase of insurance or otherwise." § 3(1). Plans may self-insure or they may purchase insurance for their participants. Plans that purchase insur-

---

[10] According to the Health Insurance Association of America, 26 States have promulgated 69 mandated-benefit laws. Different States mandate a great variety of different kinds of insurance coverage. For example, many require alcoholism coverage, while others require certain birth-defect coverage, outpatient kidney-dialysis coverage, or reconstructive surgery for insured mastectomies.

ance — so-called "insured plans" — are directly affected by state laws that regulate the insurance industry....

ERISA ... contains almost no federal regulation of the terms of benefit plans. It does, however, contain a broad pre-emption provision declaring that the statute shall "supersede any and all State laws insofar as they may now or hereafter relate to any employee benefit plan." § 514(a). Appellant Metropolitan ... argues that ERISA pre-empts Massachusetts' mandated-benefit law insofar as § 47B restricts the kinds of insurance policies that benefit plans may purchase.

While § 514(a) of ERISA broadly pre-empts state laws that relate to an employee-benefit plan, that pre-emption is substantially qualified by an "insurance saving clause," § 514(b)(2)(A), which broadly states that, with one exception, nothing in ERISA "shall be construed to exempt or relieve any person from any law of any State which regulates insurance, banking, or securities." The specified exception to the saving clause is found in § 514(b)(2)(B), the so-called "deemer clause," which states that no employee-benefit plan, with certain exceptions not relevant here, "shall be deemed to be an insurance company or other insurer, bank, trust company, or investment company or to be engaged in the business of insurance or banking for purposes of any law of any State purporting to regulate insurance companies, insurance contracts, banks, trust companies, or investment companies." Massachusetts argues that its mandated-benefit law, as applied to insurance companies that sell insurance to benefit plans, is a "law which regulates insurance," and therefore is saved from the effect of the general pre-emption clause of ERISA....

II

Appellants are Metropolitan Life Insurance Company and Travelers Insurance Company (insurers) who are located in New York and Connecticut respectively and who issue group-health policies providing hospital and surgical coverage to plans, or to employers or unions that employ or represent employees residing in Massachusetts. Under the terms of § 47B, both appellants are required to provide minimal mental-health benefits in policies issued to cover Commonwealth residents.

In 1979, the Attorney General of Massachusetts brought suit in Massachusetts Superior Court for declaratory and injunctive relief to enforce § 47B. The Commonwealth asserted that since January 1, 1976, the effective date of § 47B, the insurers had issued policies to group policyholders situated outside Massachusetts that provided for hospital and surgical coverage for certain residents of the Commonwealth. It further asserted that those policies failed to provide Massachusetts-resident beneficiaries the mental-health coverage mandated by § 47B, and that the insurers intended to issue more such policies, believing themselves not bound by § 47B for policies issued outside the Commonwealth. In their answer, the insurers admitted these allegations....

III

"In deciding whether a federal law pre-empts a state statute, our task is to ascertain Congress' intent in enacting the federal statute at issue. 'Pre-emption may be either express or implied, and "is compelled whether Congress' command is explicitly stated in the statute's language or implicitly contained in its structure and purpose."'" The narrow statutory ERISA question presented is whether § 47B is a law "which regulates insurance" within the meaning of § 514(b)(2)(A) and so would not be pre-empted by § 514(a).

A

Section 47B clearly "relate[s] to" welfare plans governed by ERISA so as to fall within the reach of ERISA's pre-emption provision, § 514(a).... The phrase "relate to" [in § 514(a) is] given its broad common-sense meaning, such that a state law "relate[s] to" a benefit plan "in the normal sense of the phrase, if it has a connection with or reference to such a plan." The pre-emption provision was intended to displace all state laws that fall within its sphere, even including state laws that are consistent with ERISA's substantive requirements. "[E]ven indirect state action bearing on private pensions may encroach upon the area of exclusive federal concern."

Though § 47B is not denominated a benefit-plan law, it bears indirectly but substantially on all insured benefit plans, for it requires them to purchase the mental-health benefits specified in the statute when they purchase a certain kind of common insurance policy.... [T]he mandated-benefit law as applied relates to ERISA plans and thus is covered by ERISA's broad pre-emption provision set forth in § 514(a).

B

Nonetheless, the sphere in which § 514(a) operates was explicitly limited by § 514(b)(2). The insurance saving clause preserves any state law "which regulates insurance, banking, or securities." The two pre-emption sections, while clear enough on their faces, perhaps are not a model of legislative drafting, for while the general pre-emption clause broadly pre-empts state law, the saving clause appears broadly to preserve the States' lawmaking power over much of the same regulation. While Congress occasionally decides to return to the States what it has previously taken away, it does not normally do both at the same time.

Fully aware of this statutory complexity, we still have no choice but to "begin with the language employed by Congress and the assumption that the ordinary meaning of that language accurately expresses the legislative purpose." We also must presume that Congress did not intend to pre-empt areas of traditional state regulation.

To state the obvious, § 47B regulates the terms of certain insurance contracts, and so seems to be saved from pre-emption by the saving clause as a law "which regulates insurance." This common-sense view of the matter, moreover, is reinforced by the language of the subsequent subsection of ERISA, the "deemer clause," which states that an employee-benefit plan shall not be deemed to be an insurance company "for purposes of any law of any State purporting to regulate insurance companies, *insurance contracts,* banks, trust companies, or investment companies." § 514(b)(2)(B) (emphasis added). By exempting from the saving clause laws regulating insurance contracts that apply directly to benefit plans, the deemer clause makes explicit Congress' intention to include laws that regulate insurance contracts within the scope of the insurance laws preserved by the saving clause. Unless Congress intended to include laws regulating insurance contracts within the scope of the insurance saving clause, it would have been unnecessary for the deemer clause explicitly to exempt such laws from the saving clause when they are applied directly to benefit plans.

The insurers nonetheless argue that § 47B is in reality a health law that merely operates on insurance contracts to accomplish its end, and that it is not the kind of traditional insurance law intended to be saved by § 514(b)(2)(A). We find this argument unpersuasive.

Initially, nothing in § 514(b)(2)(A), or in the "deemer clause" which modifies it, purports to distinguish between traditional and innovative insurance laws. The presumption is against pre-emption, and we are not inclined to read limitations into federal statutes in order to enlarge their pre-emptive scope. Further, there is no indication in the legislative history that Congress had such a distinction in mind.

Appellants assert that state laws that directly regulate the insurer, and laws that regulate such matters as the way in which insurance may be sold, are traditional laws subject to the clause, while laws that regulate the substantive terms of insurance contracts are recent innovations more properly seen as health laws rather than as insurance laws, which § 514(b)(2)(A) does not save. This distinction reads the saving clause out of ERISA entirely, because laws that regulate only the insurer, or the way in which it may sell insurance, do not "relate to" benefit plans in the first instance. Because they would not be pre-empted by § 514(a), they do not need to be "saved" by § 514(b)(2)(A). There is no indication that Congress could have intended the saving clause to operate only to guard against too expansive readings of the general pre-emption clause that might have included laws wholly unrelated to plans. Appellants' construction, in our view, violates the plain meaning of the statutory language and renders redundant both the saving clause it is construing, as well as the deemer clause which it precedes, and accordingly has little to recommend it.

Moreover, it is both historically and conceptually inaccurate to assert that mandated-benefit laws are not traditional insurance laws. As we have indicated, state laws regulating the substantive terms of insurance contracts were commonplace well before the mid-70's, when Congress considered ERISA. The case law concerning the meaning of the phrase "business of insurance" in the McCarran-Ferguson Act, 15 U.S.C. § 1011 *et seq.,* also strongly supports the conclusion that regulation regarding the substantive terms of insurance contracts falls squarely within the saving clause as laws "which regulate insurance."

Cases interpreting the scope of the McCarran-Ferguson Act have identified three criteria relevant to determining whether a particular practice falls within that Act's reference to the "business of insurance": "*first,* whether the practice has the effect of transferring or spreading a policyholder's risk; *second,* whether the practice is an integral part of the policy relationship between the insurer and the insured; and *third,* whether the practice is limited to entities within the insurance industry." *Union Labor Life Ins. Co. v. Pireno,* 458 U.S. 119 (1982) (emphasis in original). Application of these principles suggests that mandated-benefit laws are state regulation of the "business of insurance."

Section 47B obviously regulates the spreading of risk: as we have indicated, it was intended to effectuate the legislative judgment that the risk of mental-health care should be shared. It is also evident that mandated-benefit laws directly regulate an integral part of the relationship between the insurer and the policyholder by limiting the type of insurance that an insurer may sell to the policyholder. Finally, the third criterion is present here, for mandated-benefit statutes impose requirements only on insurers, with the intent of affecting the relationship between the insurer and the policyholder. Section 47B, then, is the very kind of regulation that this Court has identified as a law that relates to the regulation of the business of insurance as defined in the McCarran-Ferguson Act....

In short, the plain language of the saving clause, its relationship to the other ERISA pre-emption provisions, and the traditional understanding of insurance regulation, all lead us to the conclusion that mandated-benefit laws such as § 47B are saved from pre-emption by the operation of the saving clause.

Nothing in the legislative history of ERISA suggests a different result. There is no discussion in that history of the relationship between the general pre-emption clause and the saving clause, and indeed very little discussion of the saving clause at all. In the early versions of ERISA, the general pre-emption clause pre-empted only those state laws dealing with subjects regulated by ERISA. The clause was significantly broadened at the last minute, well after the saving clause was in its present form, to include all state laws that relate to benefit plans. The change was made with little explanation by the Conference Committee, and there is no indication in the legislative history that Congress was aware of the new prominence given the saving clause in light of the rewritten pre-emption clause, or was aware that the saving clause was in conflict with the general pre-emption provision.[23] There is a complete absence of evidence that Congress intended the

---

[23] The insurance saving clause appeared in its present form in bills introduced in 1970 that led to ERISA. The pre-emption clause apparently was broadened out of a fear that "state professional associations" would otherwise hinder the development of such employee-benefit programs as "prepaid legal service programs." *See* 120 Cong. Rec. 29197 (1974) (remarks of Rep. Dent); *id.,* at 29933 (remarks of Sen. Williams); *id.,* at 29949 (remarks of Sen. Javits). There is no suggestion

narrow reading of the saving clause suggested by appellants here. Appellants do call to our attention a few passing references in the record of the floor debate to the "narrow" exceptions to the pre-emption clause, but these are far too frail a support on which to rest appellants' rather unnatural reading of the clause.

We therefore decline to impose any limitation on the saving clause beyond those Congress imposed in the clause itself and in the "deemer clause" which modifies it. If a state law "regulates insurance," as mandated-benefit laws do, it is not pre-empted....

We are aware that our decision results in a distinction between insured and uninsured plans, leaving the former open to indirect regulation while the latter are not. By so doing we merely give life to a distinction created by Congress in the "deemer clause," a distinction Congress is aware of and one it has chosen not to alter. We also are aware that appellants' construction of the statute would eliminate some of the disuniformities currently facing national plans that enter into local markets to purchase insurance. Such disuniformities, however, are the inevitable result of the congressional decision to "save" local insurance regulation. Arguments as to the wisdom of these policy choices must be directed at Congress....

We hold that Massachusetts' mandated-benefit law is a "law which regulates insurance" and so is not pre-empted by ERISA as it applies to insurance contracts purchased for plans subject to ERISA....

NOTES

1. *State Mandated Benefits Laws.* In *New Jersey Business & Industry Ass'n v. State,* 592 A.2d 660 (N.J. Super. Ct. Law Div. 1991), a provision of the state's Family Leave Act that required employers to continue health insurance coverage while employees were on family leave was held to be preempted by ERISA. The New Jersey legislature could still pursue its goal of health insurance coverage for employees who take family leaves by requiring insurance companies, rather than employers, to include such continuation coverage in their policies, but that

---

that the pre-emption provision was broadened out of any concern about state regulation of insurance contracts, beyond a general concern about "potentially conflicting State laws."

The Conference Committee that was convened to work out differences between the Senate and House versions of ERISA broadened the general pre-emption provision from one that pre-empted state laws only insofar as they regulated the same areas explicitly regulated by ERISA, to one that pre-empts all state laws unless otherwise saved. The change gave the insurance saving clause a much more significant role, as a provision that saved an entire body of law from the sweeping general pre-emption clause. There were no comments on the floor of either Chamber specifically concerning the insurance saving clause, and hardly any concerning the exceptions to the pre-emption clause in general. The change in the pre-emption provision was not disclosed until the Report was filed with Congress 10 days before final action was taken on ERISA. The House conferees filed their Report on August 12, 1974, while the Senate conferees filed their report the following day. ERISA was passed by the House on August 20, and by the Senate on August 22.

option would not cover as many employees and would encourage employers to self-insure to avoid any extra costs associated with the continuation coverage.

2. *The Escape Hatch of Self-Insurance.* Mandated benefits, such as those discussed in *Metropolitan Life,* are common. One study found 735 state laws mandating certain benefits or coverages; one state had thirty-eight separate requirements. John R. Gabel & Gail A. Jensen, *The Price of State-Mandated Benefits*, 26 INQUIRY 419 (1989).

Metropolitan Life permits employers to avoid state regulation by self-insuring, and employers in large numbers have taken advantage of the escape hatch. In 1975, only about 5% of employers self-insured for health insurance. By 1987, more than 50% of employers, covering about 60% of all employees with health insurance, self-insured. John R. Gabel et al., *The Changing World of Group Health Insurance*, 7 HEALTH AFFAIRS 48 (1988). In the last few years, the trend has reversed a bit as employers have moved to managed care plans which traditionally have shifted risk away from employers and onto other entities. Between 1993 and 1995, the proportion of employees in self-insured plans dropped from 60% to 51%. KPMG PEAT MARWICK, ANALYSIS OF THE NUMBER OF WORKERS COVERED BY SELF-INSURED HEALTH PLANS UNDER ERISA — 1993 AND 1995 6 (1996). The health care market continues to evolve, however, and many think that the proportion of employees covered by self-insured plans will begin to increase again soon. *Id.* at 6.

3. *The "Relate to" Requirement.* ERISA only preempts state laws that "relate to" employee benefit plans. ERISA § 514(a). In a recent case, the Supreme Court reduced the potential scope of ERISA preemption by interpreting the "relate to" requirement narrowly. In *New York State Conference of Blue Cross & Blue Shield Plans v. Travelers Insurance Co.*, 514 U.S. 645 (1995), the Court rejected a claim that a New York statute that required hospitals to collect surcharges on hospital expenses related to employee benefit plans. The Court recognized that the surcharges could have an indirect effect on ERISA plans by increasing the cost of medical services provided by the plans, but held that that type of effect was not sufficient to meet the "relate to" requirement. To meet the requirement, a state statute had to have a more direct effect on employee benefit plans, for example, by mandating benefit structures (as in *Metropolitan Life*), requiring a certain type of plan administration, or providing alternative enforcement mechanisms. *See also De Buono v. NYSA-ILA Med. & Clinical Servs. Fund*, 117 S. Ct. 1747 (1997) (state tax on health care facilities does not "relate to" ERISA plan even when applied to a facilities wholly owned and operated by an ERISA plan).

4. *State Laws Regulating Managed Care Organizations.* *Travelers Insurance* opened the door to more state involvement in regulating health care. At least one court has upheld a state statute after *Travelers Insurance* that it had struck down as preempted prior to the case. *BPS Clinical Labs. v. Blue Cross & Blue Shield*, 552 N.W.2d 919 (Mich. Ct. App. 1996), *appeal denied*, 570 N.W.2d 782 (Mich. 1997) (upholding Michigan statute permitting insurance companies and nonprofit health care corporations to enter into purchasing agreements with certain providers).

The states have rushed through the door. In 1996 alone, thirty-three states enacted laws regulating managed care plans. The laws cover a wide range of topics such as access to emergency care, access to specialists, standards of quality care, and disclosure of information. The issue of whether these types of regulations survive ERISA preemption is already creating differences in the circuits. *Compare Stuart Circle Hosp. Corp. v. Aetna Health Mgt.*, 995 F.2d 500 (4th Cir.), *cert. denied*, 510 U.S. 1003 (1993) ("any willing provider" law, which required managed care organizations to accept all health care providers who were willing to meet the organizations' requirements, was not preempted) *with Cigna Healthplan of La., Inc. v. State of Louisiana ex rel. Ieyoub*, 82 F.3d 642 (5th Cir), *cert. denied*, 117 S. Ct. 1266 (1996) ("any willing provider" law preempted).

5. *The "Plan" Requirement.* ERISA only preempts state laws that relate to "employee benefit *plans*." ERISA § 514(a). In the leading case on the plan requirement, the Supreme Court held that a Maine statute requiring employers to make a one-time severance payment to employees after a plant closing was not preempted because it did not establish a plan or require employers to maintain one:

> The requirement of a one-time lump-sum payment triggered by a single event requires no administrative scheme whatsoever to meet the employer's obligation. The employer assumes no responsibility to pay benefits on a regular basis, and thus faces no periodic demands on its assets that create a need for financial coordination and control. Rather, the employer's obligation is predicated on the occurrence of a single contingency that may never materialize. The employer may well never have to pay the severance benefits. To the extent that the obligation to do so arises, satisfaction of that duty involves only making a single set of payments to employees at the time the plant closes. To do little more than write a check hardly constitutes the operation of a benefit plan.

Fort Halifax Packing Co. v. Coyne, 482 U.S. 1, 12 (1987).

In *Curtis v. Nevada Bonding Corp.*, 53 F.3d 1023 (9th Cir. 1995), the employer agreed to provide health insurance for an employee, but never did. The employer reimbursed the employee for some minor medical expenses, but stopped when the employee was diagnosed with cancer. The employee sued alleging breach of contract and fraudulent misrepresentation. The Ninth Circuit held that these state law claims were not preempted by ERISA because the plan requirement was not met. ERISA coverage, the Court said, extends only to arrangements that are sufficiently specific to enable a reasonable person to "ascertain the intended benefits, beneficiaries, source of financing, and procedures for receiving benefits." *Id.* at 1028, *quoting Donovan v. Dillingham*, 688 F.2d 1367, 1373 (11th Cir. 1982). The Court held that a bare promise to provide health insurance was not sufficient to create a "plan" and, hence, that the plaintiff's state law claims were not preempted. Do you think the Court would have interpreted the plan requirement in the same way if ERISA provided viable alternatives to the state law claims? *See Kenney v. Roland Parson Contr'g Corp.*, 28 F.3d 1254, 1258-59 (D.C. Cir. 1994) (plan requirement met where employer deducted money from employee's wages and promised to contribute them to a pension fund, but never did).

B. PREEMPTION AND THE LIMITS OF ERISA ENFORCEMENT

CORCORAN v. UNITED HEALTHCARE, INC.

United States Court of Appeals, Fifth Circuit
965 F.2d 1321, *cert. denied*, 506 U.S. 1033 (1992)

KING, Circuit Judge:

I. BACKGROUND

The basic facts are undisputed. Florence Corcoran, a long-time employee of South Central Bell Telephone Company (Bell), became pregnant in early 1989. In July, her obstetrician, Dr. Jason Collins, recommended that she have complete bed rest during the final months of her pregnancy. Mrs. Corcoran applied to Bell for temporary disability benefits for the remainder of her pregnancy, but the benefits were denied. This prompted Dr. Collins to write to Dr. Theodore J. Borgman, medical consultant for Bell, and explain that Mrs. Corcoran had several medical problems which placed her "in a category of high risk pregnancy." Bell again denied disability benefits.... As Mrs. Corcoran neared her delivery date, Dr. Collins ordered her hospitalized so that he could monitor the fetus around the clock.[1]

Mrs. Corcoran was a member of Bell's Medical Assistance Plan (MAP or "the Plan"). MAP is a self-funded welfare benefit plan which provides medical benefits to eligible Bell employees. It is administered by defendant Blue Cross and Blue Shield of Alabama (Blue Cross) pursuant to an Administrative Services Agreement between Bell and Blue Cross. The parties agree that it is governed by ERISA. Under a portion of the Plan known as the "Quality Care Program" (QCP), participants must obtain advance approval for overnight hospital admissions and certain medical procedures ("pre-certification"), and must obtain approval on a continuing basis once they are admitted to a hospital ("concurrent review"), or plan benefits to which they otherwise would be entitled are reduced.

---

[1] This was the same course of action Dr. Collins had ordered during Mrs. Corcoran's 1988 pregnancy. In that pregnancy, Dr. Collins intervened and performed a successful Caesarean section in the 36th week when the fetus went into distress.

QCP is administered by defendant United HealthCare (United) pursuant to an agreement with Bell. United performs a form of cost-containment service that has commonly become known as "utilization review." The Summary Plan Description (SPD) explains QCP as follows:

> The Quality Care Program (QCP), administered by United HealthCare, Inc., assists you and your covered dependents in securing quality medical care according to the provisions of the Plan while helping reduce risk and expense due to unnecessary hospitalization and surgery. They do this by providing you with information which will permit you (in consultation with your doctor) to evaluate alternatives to surgery and hospitalization when those alternatives are medically appropriate. In addition, QCP will monitor any certified hospital confinement to keep you informed as to whether or not the stay is covered by the Plan.

Two paragraphs below, the SPD contains this statement: *When reading this booklet, remember that all decisions regarding your medical care are up to you and your doctor.* It goes on to explain that when a beneficiary does not contact United or follow its pre-certification decision, a "QCP Penalty" is applied. The penalty involves reduction of benefits by 20 percent for the remainder of the calendar year or until the annual out-of-pocket limit is reached. Moreover, the annual out-of-pocket limit is increased from $1,000 to $1,250 in covered expenses, not including any applicable deductible. According to the QCP Administrative Manual, the QCP penalty is automatically applied when a participant fails to contact United. However, if a participant complies with QCP by contacting United, but does not follow its decision, the penalty may be waived following an internal appeal if the medical facts show that the treatment chosen was appropriate.

A more complete description of QCP and the services provided by United is contained in a separate booklet. Under the heading "WHAT QCP DOES" the booklet explains:

> Whenever your doctor recommends surgery or hospitalization for you or a covered dependent, QCP will provide an independent review of your condition (or your covered dependent's). The purpose of the review is to assess the need for surgery or hospitalization and to determine the appropriate length of stay for a hospitalization, based on nationally accepted medical guidelines. As part of the review process, QCP will discuss with your doctor the appropriateness of the treatments recommended and the availability of alternative types of treatments — or locations for treatment — that are equally effective, involve less risk, and are more cost effective.

The next paragraph is headed "INDEPENDENT, PROFESSIONAL REVIEW" and states:

> United Health Care, an independent professional medical review organization, has been engaged to provide services under QCP. United's

staff includes doctors, nurses, and other medical professionals knowledgeable about the health care delivery system. Together with your doctor, they work to assure that you and your covered family members receive the most appropriate medical care....

In accordance with the QCP portion of the plan, Dr. Collins sought pre-certification from United for Mrs. Corcoran's hospital stay. Despite Dr. Collins's recommendation, United determined that hospitalization was not necessary, and instead authorized 10 hours per day of home nursing care. Mrs. Corcoran entered the hospital on October 3, 1989, but, because United had not pre-certified her stay, she returned home on October 12. On October 25, during a period of time when no nurse was on duty, the fetus went into distress and died.

Mrs. Corcoran and her husband, Wayne, filed a wrongful death action in Louisiana state court alleging that their unborn child died as a result of various acts of negligence committed by Blue Cross and United. Both sought damages for the lost love, society and affection of their unborn child. In addition, Mrs. Corcoran sought damages for the aggravation of a pre-existing depressive condition and the loss of consortium caused by such aggravation, and Mr. Corcoran sought damages for loss of consortium. The defendants removed the action to federal court on grounds that it was pre-empted by ERISA and that there was complete diversity among the parties. [The District Court held that the Corcoran's claims were preempted by ERISA and granted summary judgment for the defendants.]

III. PRE-EMPTION OF THE STATE LAW CAUSE OF ACTION

A. *The Nature of the Corcorans' State Law Claims*

The Corcorans' original petition in state court alleged that acts of negligence committed by Blue Cross and United caused the death of their unborn child. Specifically, they alleged that Blue Cross wrongfully denied appropriate medical care, failed adequately to oversee the medical decisions of United, and failed to provide United with Mrs. Corcoran's complete medical background. They alleged that United wrongfully denied the medical care recommended by Dr. Collins and wrongfully determined that home nursing care was adequate for her condition. It is evident that the Corcorans no longer pursue any theory of recovery against Blue Cross.... We, therefore, analyze solely the question of pre-emption of the claims against United....

The Corcorans based their action against United on Article 2315 of the Louisiana Civil Code, which provides that "[e]very act whatever of man that causes damage to another obliges him by whose fault it happened to repair it." Article 2315 provides parents with a cause of action for the wrongful death of their unborn children and also places liability on health care providers when they fail to live up to the applicable standard of care. Whether Article 2315 permits a negligence suit against a third party provider of utilization review services, however, has yet to be decided by the Louisiana courts. [I]t does not appear to us that Louisiana law clearly forecloses the possibility of recovery against United. Thus, assuming that on these facts the Corcorans might be capable of stating a cause of action for malpractice, our task now is to determine whether such a cause of action is pre-empted by ERISA.

B. *Principles of ERISA Pre-emption*

The central inquiry in determining whether a federal statute pre-empts state law is the intent of Congress. *FMC Corp. v. Holliday*, 498 U.S. 52 (1990). In performing this analysis we begin with any statutory language that expresses an intent to pre-empt, but we look also to the purpose and structure of the statute as a whole.

ERISA contains an explicit pre-emption clause, which provides, in relevant part:

> Except as provided in subsection (b) of this section, the provisions of this subchapter and subchapter III of this chapter shall supersede any and all State laws insofar as they may now or hereafter relate to any employee benefit plan described in section 1003(a)....

ERISA § 514(a).[10] It is by now well-established that the "deliberately expansive" language of this clause is a signal that it is [to] be construed extremely broadly. *See FMC Corp.*, 498 U.S. at 407 ("[t]he pre-emption clause is conspicuous for its breadth"). The key words "relate to" are used in such a way as to expand pre-emption beyond state laws that relate to the specific subjects covered by ERISA, such as reporting, disclosure and fiduciary obligations. Thus, state laws "relate[ ] to" employee benefit plans in a much broader sense — whenever they have "a connection with or reference to such a plan." *Shaw v. Delta Air Lines, Inc.*, 463 U.S. 85, 96-97 (1983). This sweeping pre-emption of state law is consistent with Congress's decision to create a comprehensive, uniform federal scheme for the regulation of employee benefit plans.

The most obvious class of pre-empted state laws are those that are specifically designed to affect ERISA-governed employee benefit plans. *See Mackey v. Lanier Collection Agency & Serv., Inc.*, 486 U.S. 825, 829-30 (1988) (statute explicitly barring garnishment of ERISA plan funds is pre-empted); *Ingersoll-Rand v. McClendon*, 498 U.S. 133, 138-45 (cause of action allowing recovery from employer when discharge is premised upon attempt to avoid contributing to pension plan is pre-empted). But a law is not saved from pre-emption merely because it does not target employee benefit plans. Indeed, much pre-emption litigation involves laws of general application which, when applied in particular settings, can be said to have a connection with or a reference to an ERISA plan. *See Pilot Life [Ins. Co. v. Dedeaux]*, 481 U.S. 41, 47-48 (common law tort and

---

[10] Statutory, decisional and all other forms of state law are included within the scope of the preemption clause. ERISA § 514(c)(1) ("The term 'State law' includes all laws, decisions, rules, regulations, or other State action having the effect of law, of any State"). Section 514(b)(2)(A) exempts certain state laws from pre-emption, but none of these exemptions is applicable here.

contract causes of action seeking damages for improper processing of a claim for benefits under a disability plan are pre-empted); *Shaw*, 463 U.S. at 95-100 (statute interpreted by state court as prohibiting plans from discriminating on the basis of pregnancy is pre-empted). On the other hand, the Court has recognized that not every conceivable cause of action that may be brought against an ERISA-covered plan is pre-empted. "Some state actions may affect employee benefit plans in too tenuous, remote or peripheral a manner to warrant a finding that the law 'relates to' the plan." *Shaw*, 463 U.S. at 100 n. 21. Thus, "run-of-the-mill state-law claims such as unpaid rent, failure to pay creditors, or even torts committed by an ERISA plan" are not pre-empted. *Mackey*, 486 U.S. at 833 (discussing these types of claims in dicta).

C. Pre-emption of the Corcorans' Claims

Initially, we observe that the common law causes of action advanced by the Corcorans are not that species of law "specifically designed" to affect ERISA plans, for the liability rules they seek to invoke neither make explicit reference to nor are premised on the existence of an ERISA plan. Rather, applied in this case against a defendant that provides benefit-related services to an ERISA plan, the generally applicable negligence-based causes of action may have an effect on an ERISA-governed plan. In our view, the pre-emption question devolves into an assessment of the significance of these effects.

1. United's position — it makes benefit determinations, not medical decisions

United's argument in favor of pre-emption is grounded in the notion that the decision it made concerning Mrs. Corcoran was not primarily a medical decision, but instead was a decision made in its capacity as a plan fiduciary about what benefits were authorized under the Plan. All it did, it argues, was determine whether Mrs. Corcoran qualified for the benefits provided by the plan by applying previously established eligibility criteria. The argument's coup de grace is that under well-established precedent, participants may not sue in tort to redress injuries flowing from decisions about what benefits are to be paid under a plan....

In support of its argument, United points to its explanatory booklet and its language stating that the company advises the patient's doctor "what the medical plan will pay for, based on a review of [the patient's] clinical information and nationally accepted medical guidelines for the treatment of [the patient's] condition." It also relies on statements to the effect that the ultimate medical decisions are up to the beneficiary's doctor. It acknowledges at various points that its decision about what benefits would be paid was based on a consideration of medical information, but the thrust of the argument is that it was simply performing commonplace administrative duties akin to claims handling.

Because it was merely performing claims handling functions when it rejected Dr. Collins's request to approve Mrs. Corcoran's hospitalization, United contends, the principles of *Pilot Life* and its progeny squarely foreclose this lawsuit.

In *Pilot Life*, a beneficiary sought damages under various state-law tort and contract theories from the insurance company that determined eligibility for the employer's long term disability benefit plan. The company had paid benefits for two years, but there followed a period during which the company terminated and reinstated the beneficiary several times. The Court made clear, however, that ERISA pre-empts state-law tort and contract actions in which a beneficiary seeks to recover damages for improper processing of a claim for benefits. United suggests that its actions here were analogous to those of the insurance company in *Pilot Life*, and therefore urges us to apply that decision.

2. The Corcorans' position — United makes medical decisions, not benefit determinations

The Corcorans assert that *Pilot Life* and its progeny are inapposite because they are not advancing a claim for improper processing of benefits. Rather, they say, they seek to recover solely for United's erroneous medical decision that Mrs. Corcoran did not require hospitalization during the last month of her pregnancy. This argument, of course, depends on viewing United's action in this case as a medical decision, and not merely an administrative determination about benefit entitlements. Accordingly, the Corcorans, pointing to the statements United makes in the QCP booklet concerning its medical expertise, contend that United exercised medical judgment which is outside the purview of ERISA pre-emption.

The Corcorans suggest that a medical negligence claim is permitted ... because it (1) involves the exercise of traditional state authority and (2) is a law of general application which, although it affects relations between principal ERISA entities in this case, is not designed to affect the ERISA relationship.

3. Our view — United makes medical decisions incident to benefit determinations

We cannot fully agree with either United or the Corcorans. Ultimately, we conclude that United makes medical decisions — indeed, United gives medical advice — but it does so in the context of making a determination about the availability of benefits under the plan. Accordingly, we hold that the Louisiana tort action asserted by the Corcorans for the wrongful death of their child allegedly resulting from United's erroneous medical decision is pre-empted by ERISA.

Turning first to the question of the characterization of United's actions, we note that the QCP booklet and the SPD lend substantial support to the Corcorans' argument that United makes medical decisions. United's own booklet tells beneficiaries that it "assess[es] the need for surgery or hospitalization and ... determine[s] the appropriate length of stay for a hospitalization, based on nationally accepted medical guidelines." United "will discuss with your doctor the appropriateness of the treatments recommended and the availability of alternative types of treatments." Further, "United's staff includes doctors, nurses, and other medical professionals knowledgeable about the health care delivery system. Together with your doctor, they work to assure that you and your covered family members receive the most appropriate medical care." According to the SPD, United will "provid[e] you with information which will permit you (in consultation with your doctor) to evaluate alternatives to surgery and hospitalization when those alternatives are medically appropriate."

United makes much of the disclaimer that decisions about medical care are up to the beneficiary and his or her doctor. While that may be so, and while the disclaimer may support the conclusion that the relationship between United and the beneficiary is not that of doctor-patient, it does not mean that United does not make medical decisions or dispense medical advice. In response, United argues that any such medical determination or advice is made or given in the context of administering the benefits available under the Bell plan. Supporting United's position is the contract between United and Bell, which provides that "[United] shall contact the Participant's physician and based upon the medical evidence and normative data determine whether the Participant should be eligible to receive full plan benefits for the recommended hospitalization and the duration of benefits."

United argues that the decision it makes in this, the prospective context, is no different than the decision an insurer makes in the traditional retrospective context. The question in each case is "what the medical plan will pay for, based on a review of [the beneficiary's] clinical information and nationally accepted medical guidelines for the treatment of [the beneficiary's] condition." *See* QCP Booklet at 4. A prospective decision is, however, different in its impact on the beneficiary than a retrospective decision. In both systems, the beneficiary theoretically knows in advance what treatments the plan will pay for because coverage is spelled out in the plan documents. But in the retrospective system, a beneficiary who embarks on the course of treatment recommended by his or her physician has only a potential risk of disallowance of all or a part of the cost of that treatment, and then only after treatment has been rendered. In contrast, in a prospective system a beneficiary may be squarely presented in advance of treatment with a statement that the insurer will not pay for the proposed course of treatment recommended by his or her doctor and the beneficiary has the potential of recovering the cost of that treatment only if he or she can prevail in a challenge to the insurer's decision. A beneficiary in the latter system would likely be far less inclined to undertake the course of treatment that the insurer has at least preliminarily rejected.

By its very nature, a system of prospective decisionmaking influences the beneficiary's choice among treatment options to a far greater degree than does the theoretical risk of disallowance of a claim facing a beneficiary in a retrospective system. Indeed, the perception among insurers that prospective determinations result in lower health care costs is premised on the likelihood that a beneficiary, faced with the knowledge of specifically what the plan will and will not pay for, will choose the treatment option recommended by the plan in order to avoid risking total or partial disallowance of benefits. When United makes a decision pursuant to QCP, it is making a medical recommendation which — because of the financial ramifications — is more likely to be followed.

Although we disagree with United's position that no part of its actions involves medical decisions, we cannot agree with the Corcorans that no part of United's actions involves benefit determinations. In our view, United makes medical decisions as part and parcel of its mandate to decide what benefits are available under the Bell plan. As the QCP Booklet concisely puts it, United decides "what the medical plan will pay for." When United's actions are viewed from this perspective, it becomes apparent that the Corcorans are attempting to recover for a tort allegedly committed in the course of handling a benefit determination. The nature of the benefit determination is different than the type of decision that was at issue in *Pilot Life*, but it is a benefit determination nonetheless. The principle of *Pilot Life* that ERISA pre-empts state-law claims alleging improper handling of benefit claims is broad enough to cover the cause of action asserted here.

Moreover, allowing the Corcorans' suit to go forward would contravene Congress's goals of "ensur[ing] that plans and plan sponsors would be subject to a uniform body of benefit law" and "minimiz[ing] the administrative and financial burdens of complying with conflicting directives among States or between States and the Federal Government." *Ingersoll-Rand Co.*, 498 U.S. at 142. Thus, statutes that subject plans to inconsistent regulatory schemes in different states, thereby increasing inefficiency and potentially causing the plan to respond by reducing benefit levels, are consistently held pre-empted. *See Alessi v. Raybestos-Manhattan, Inc.*, 451 U.S. 504, 524 (1981) (striking down law which prohibited plans from offsetting benefits by amount of worker compensation payments); *Shaw*, 463 U.S. at 105 n. 25 (striking down law which prohibited plans from discriminating on basis of pregnancy); *FMC Corp.*, 498 U.S. at 60 (striking down law which eliminated plans' right of subrogation from claimant's tort recovery). But in *Ingersoll-Rand*, the Court, in holding pre-empted the Texas common law of wrongful discharge, when applied against an employer who allegedly discharged an employee to avoid contributing to the employee's pension plan, made clear that a state common law cause of action is equally capable of leading to the kind of patchwork scheme of regulation Congress sought to avoid:

> It is foreseeable that state courts, exercising their common law powers, might develop different substantive standards applicable to the same employer conduct, requiring the tailoring of plans and employer conduct to the peculiarities of the law of each jurisdiction. Such an outcome is fundamentally at odds with the goal of uniformity that Congress sought to implement.

498 U.S. at 142. Similarly, although imposing liability on United might have the salutary effect of deterring poor quality medical decisions, there is a significant

risk that state liability rules would be applied differently to the conduct of utilization review companies in different states. The cost of complying with varying substantive standards would increase the cost of providing utilization review services, thereby increasing the cost to health benefit plans of including cost containment features such as the Quality Care Program (or causing them to eliminate this sort of cost containment program altogether) and ultimately decreasing the pool of plan funds available to reimburse participants.[16]

It may be true, as the Corcorans assert, that Louisiana tort law places duties on persons who make medical judgments within the state, and the Louisiana courts may one day recognize that this duty extends to the medical decisions made by utilization review companies. But it is equally true that Congress may pre-empt state-law causes of action which seek to enforce various duties when it determines that such actions would interfere with a carefully constructed scheme of federal regulation. The acknowledged absence of a remedy under ERISA's civil enforcement scheme for medical malpractice committed in connection with a plan benefit determination does not alter our conclusion. While we are not unmindful of the fact that our interpretation of the pre-emption clause leaves a gap in remedies within a statute intended to protect participants in employee benefit plans, the lack of an ERISA remedy does not affect a pre-emption analysis. Congress perhaps could not have predicted the interjection into the ERISA "system" of the medical utilization review process, but it enacted a pre-emption clause so broad and a statute so comprehensive that it would be incompatible with the language, structure and purpose of the statute to allow tort suits against entities so integrally connected with a plan.

IV. EXTRACONTRACTUAL DAMAGES

The Corcorans argue in the alternative that the damages they seek are available as "other appropriate equitable relief" under ERISA § 502(a)(3). That section provides:

---

[16] We find *Independence HMO, Inc. v. Smith*, 733 F. Supp. 983 (E.D. Pa. 1990), cited by the Corcorans, distinguishable on its facts. In *Smith*, the district court did not find pre-empted a state court malpractice action brought against an HMO by one of its members. The plaintiff sought to hold the HMO liable, under a state-law agency theory, for the alleged negligence of a surgeon associated with the HMO. The case appears to support the Corcorans because the plaintiff was attempting to hold an ERISA entity liable for medical decisions. However, the medical decisions at issue do not appear to have been made in connection with a cost containment feature of the plan or any other aspect of the plan which implicated the management of plan assets, but were instead made by a doctor in the course of treatment. We also find *Eurine v. Wyatt Cafeterias*, 1991 WL 207468 (N.D. Tex. 1991), cited in the Corcorans' reply brief, irrelevant to this case. In *Eurine*, an employee of Wyatt Cafeterias sued after she slipped and fell at work. Wyatt had opted out of Texas's workers' compensation scheme, but provided benefits for injured employees pursuant to an ERISA plan. The court held that a tort suit against the employer for its negligence in failing to maintain the floor in a safe condition had nothing to do with the ERISA relationship between the parties, but instead arose from their distinct employer-employee relationship.

(a) A civil action may be brought —

....

(3) by a participant, beneficiary, or fiduciary (A) to enjoin any act or practice which violates any provision of this subchapter or the terms of the plan, or (B) to obtain other appropriate equitable relief (i) to redress such violations or (ii) to enforce any provisions of this subchapter or the terms of the plan;...

Section 502(a)(3) provides for relief apart from an award of benefits due under the terms of a plan. When a beneficiary simply wants what was supposed to have been distributed under the plan, the appropriate remedy is § 502(a)(1)(B). Damages that would give a beneficiary more than he or she is entitled to receive under the strict terms of the plan are typically termed "extracontractual." Section 502(a)(3) by its terms permits beneficiaries to obtain "other appropriate equitable relief" to redress (1) a violation of the substantive provisions of ERISA or (2) a violation of the terms of the plan. Although the Corcorans have neither identified which of these two types of violations they seek to redress nor directed us to the particular section of the Plan or ERISA which they claim was violated, we need not determine this in order to resolve the issue before us. As outlined below, we find that the particular damages the Corcorans seek — money for emotional injuries — would not be an available form of damages under the trust and contract law principles which, the Corcorans urge, should guide our interpretation of ERISA's remedial scheme. Thus, we hold that even under the interpretation of § 502(a)(3) urged by the Corcorans, they may not recover.

[The Court held that the damages sought by the Corcorans — emotional distress damages — were not available as "other appropriate equitable relief" under § 502(a)(3). The Court's rationale was that only trust and contract doctrines were incorporated into ERISA and that neither doctrine permits the kind of emotional distress damages claimed by the Corcorans. Later, the United States Supreme Court agreed with that conclusion, but based its decision on the meaning of the word "equitable" in § 502(a)(3). The limitation to "equitable" relief, the Court held, limits the available relief to that traditionally viewed as equitable, such as an injunction or restitution, and precludes relief traditionally viewed as legal, such as compensatory or punitive damages. *Mertens v. Hewitt Assocs.*, 508 U.S. 248 (1993).]

The result ERISA compels us to reach means that the Corcorans have no remedy, state or federal, for what may have been a serious mistake. This is troubling for several reasons. First, it eliminates an important check on the thousands of medical decisions routinely made in the burgeoning utilization review system. With liability rules generally inapplicable, there is theoretically less deterrence of substandard medical decisionmaking. Moreover, if the cost of compliance with a standard of care (reflected either in the cost of prevention or the cost of paying judgments) need not be factored into utilization review companies' cost of doing business, bad medical judgments will end up being cost-free to the plans that rely on these companies to contain medical costs.[20] ERISA plans, in turn, will have one less incentive to seek out the companies that can deliver both high quality services and reasonable prices.

Second, in any plan benefit determination, there is always some tension between the interest of the beneficiary in obtaining quality medical care and the interest of the plan in preserving the pool of funds available to compensate all beneficiaries. In a prospective review context, with its greatly increased ability to deter the beneficiary (correctly or not) from embarking on a course of treatment recommended by the beneficiary's physician, the tension between interest of the beneficiary and that of the plan is exacerbated. A system which would, at least in some circumstances, compensate the beneficiary who changes course based upon a wrong call for the costs of that call might ease the tension between the conflicting interests of the beneficiary and the plan.

Finally, cost containment features such as the one at issue in this case did not exist when Congress passed ERISA. While we are confident that the result we have reached is faithful to Congress's intent neither to allow state-law causes of action that relate to employee benefit plans nor to provide beneficiaries in the Corcorans' position with a remedy under ERISA, the world of employee benefit plans has hardly remained static since 1974. Fundamental changes such as the widespread institution of utilization review would seem to warrant a reevaluation of ERISA so that it can continue to serve its noble purpose of safeguarding the interests of employees. Our system, of course, allocates this task to Congress, not the courts, and we acknowledge our role today by interpreting ERISA in a manner consistent with the expressed intentions of its creators.

NOTES

1. *State Common Law Actions and ERISA Actions.* Where ERISA fails to provide an effective cause of action, as in *Corcoran*, preemption of state common law actions is obviously a problem for plaintiffs. Even where ERISA provides a cause of action, however, preemption may not be viewed with favor by plaintiffs. ERISA actions have a number of characteristics that make them less attractive to plaintiffs than state common law actions. *See, e.g., Cox v. Keystone Carbon Co.*, 894 F.2d 647, (3d Cir.), *cert. denied*, 498 U.S. 811 (1990) (no right to jury trial in an ERISA suit to recover benefits); *Springer v. Wal-Mart Assocs.' Group Health Plan*, 908 F.2d 897 (11th Cir. 1990) (claimant must exhaust pro-

---

[20] We note that, were the Corcorans able to recover against United under state law, the contract between Bell and United indicates that United would bear the cost. However, the general application of a liability system to utilization review companies would ultimately result in increased costs to plans such as the Bell plan as it became more expensive for companies such as United to do business.

cedures provided by plan prior to bringing ERISA action). On the other hand, ERISA does provide for attorney's fees. ERISA § 502(g).

2. Florence Corcoran's Bad Luck. Florence Corcoran participated in a self-funded plan offered by a private employer, the South Central Bell Telephone Company. As a result, the plan was covered by ERISA. Consider her fate under other arrangements:

(a) If Florence Corcoran had been employed by a government or church employer, rather than South Central Bell Telephone Company, her state law claims would not have been preempted by ERISA. ERISA § 4(b)(1) & (2). *See Garvey v. Rush Prudential HMO, Inc.,* 1996 WL 648720 (N.D. Ill. 1996) (HMO refused to authorize treatment and employee's wife dies; court remands case to state court because employee's governmental plan was not covered by ERISA).

(b) If Florence Corcoran had obtained her coverage from an insurance company, either through an individual policy or through an insured employer plan, her state law claims would not have been preempted. ERISA §§ 4(a), 514(b)(2). *See Wilson v. Blue Cross,* 271 Cal. Rptr. 876 (Ct. App. 1990) (state tort claims considered).

(c) If Florence Corcoran had obtained her coverage under a state program providing health care to low-income persons, her state law claims would not have been preempted. ERISA § 4(a). *See Wickline v. State,* 228 Cal. Rptr. 661 (Ct. App. 1986) (state tort claims considered).

3. The Fiduciary Duties of Health Plans. Patrick Shea made several visits to his long-time family doctor complaining of chest pains, shortness of breath, and dizziness. The doctor knew of Shea's extensive family history of heart disease, but advised against referral to a cardiologist. Shea's symptoms did not improve, so he offered to pay for a visit to a specialist himself. His doctor, however, persuaded him that it was unnecessary. A few months later, Shea died of heart failure.

The doctor was a "preferred" physician under Shea's employer-provided health care plan. "Preferred" physicians were rewarded financially for not making referrals to specialists and penalized if they made too many. Under ERISA, the plan's administrators were fiduciaries required to exercise their duties "solely in the interest of the participants and beneficiaries." ERISA § 404(a)(1). Did the administrators have a fiduciary duty to disclose to Shea the plan's compensation arrangements with preferred physicians? *Shea v. Esensten,* 107 F.3d 625 (8th Cir.), *cert. denied,* 118 S. Ct. 297 (1997) (yes). *But see Weiss v. CIGNA Healthcare, Inc.,* 972 F. Supp. 748 (S.D.N.Y. 1997) (failure to disclose physician compensation arrangements not a fiduciary violation, but rule prohibiting physicians from discussing non-covered treatment options with patients is a violation).

4. Broad Preemption and Equity. *Corcoran* is only one example of the types of inequities that can arise because of ERISA's combination of broad preemption and limited remedies. In contrast to *Corcoran,* sometimes the courts respond to these inequities and narrow the scope of ERISA preemption. In *Mendez-Bellido* *v. Board of Trustees*, 709 F. Supp. 329 (E.D.N.Y. 1989), for example, the first wife of a deceased participant brought suit in state court seeking to disqualify the second wife from receiving pension benefits. The second wife had been convicted of first-degree manslaughter in the death of the participant and state law prohibited a killer from profiting from her crime. Held: No preemption. Consider also the next principal case.

DUKES v. U.S. HEALTHCARE, INC.

United States Court of Appeals, Third Circuit
57 F.3d 350, *cert. denied*, 116 S. Ct. 564 (1995)

STAPLETON, Circuit Judge:

The plaintiffs in these two cases filed suit in state court against health maintenance organizations ("HMOs") organized by U.S. Healthcare, Inc., claiming damages, under various theories, for injuries arising from the medical malpractice of HMO-affiliated hospitals and medical personnel. The defendant HMOs removed both cases to federal court, arguing (1) that the injured person in each case had obtained medical care as a benefit from a welfare-benefit plan governed by the Employee Retirement Income Security Act of 1974 ("ERISA"), (2) that removal is proper under the *Metropolitan Life Insurance Co. v. Taylor*, 481 U.S. 58 (1987), "complete preemption" exception to the "well-pleaded complaint rule," and (3) that the plaintiffs' claims are preempted by § 514(a) of ERISA. The district courts agreed with these contentions and dismissed the plaintiffs' claims against the HMOs. The plaintiffs appeal those rulings and ask that their claims against the HMOs be remanded to state court....

I.

A.

Suffering from various ailments, Darryl Dukes visited his primary care physician, defendant Dr. William W. Banks, M.D., who identified a problem with Darryl's ears. A few days later, Banks performed surgery and prepared a prescription ordering that blood studies be performed. Darryl presented that prescription to the laboratory of Germantown Hospital and Medical Center but the hospital refused to perform the tests. The record does not reveal the reasons for the hospital's refusal.

The next day, Darryl sought treatment from defendant Dr. Edward B. Hosten, M.D. at the Charles R. Drew Mental Health Center, who also ordered a blood test. This time, the test was performed. Darryl's condition nevertheless continued to worsen and he died shortly thereafter. Darryl's blood sugar level was extremely high at the time of his death. That condition allegedly would have or could have been diagnosed through a timely blood test.

Darryl received his medical treatment through the United States Health Care Systems of Pennsylvania, Inc., a federally qualified health maintenance organization organized by U.S. Healthcare. As a qualified HMO under the federal Health Maintenance Organization Act of 1973, 42 U.S.C. §§ 300e-300e-17 (1988), this U.S. Healthcare HMO provides basic and supplemental health services to its members on a pre-paid basis.[1] As is often the case, Darryl received his membership in the HMO through his participation in an ERISA-covered welfare plan sponsored by his employer.

Darryl's wife, Cecilia Dukes, brought suit in state court alleging medical malpractice and other negligence against numerous defendants, including Banks, Hosten, the Germantown Hospital, and the Drew Center. She also brought suit against the HMO, alleging that as the organization through which Darryl received his medical treatment, it was responsible, under a Pennsylvania state law ostensible agency theory (the "agency theory"), for the negligence of the various doctors and other medical-service providers. *See Boyd v. Albert Einstein Medical Ctr.*, 547 A.2d 1229, 1234-35 (Pa. Super. Ct. 1988) (holding that an HMO may be held liable for malpractice under an ostensible agency theory where a patient looks to the HMO for care and the HMO's conduct leads the patient to reasonably believe that he or she is being treated by an employee of the HMO). She alleged further that the HMO failed to exercise reasonable care in selecting, retaining, screening, monitoring, and evaluating the personnel who actually provided the medical services (the "direct negligence theory").

The HMO removed the case to district court pursuant to the *Metropolitan Life* complete-preemption exception to the "well-pleaded complaint rule." [The district court then dismissed the Dukes' claims holding that they "related to" an ERISA plan.]

B.

Ronald and Linda Visconti are the biological parents of Serena Visconti, who was stillborn. During the third trimester of her pregnancy with Serena, Linda apparently developed symptoms typical of preeclampsia. The Viscontis claim that Linda's obstetrician, Dr. Wisniewski, negligently ignored these symptoms and that this negligence caused Serena's death.

Like Darryl Dukes, Linda received her medical treatment through a federally qualified HMO organized by U.S. Healthcare. This HMO was called the Health Maintenance Organization of Pennsylvania/New Jersey. The Viscontis received their membership in the HMO through an ERISA-covered welfare plan.

Ronald Visconti, as administrator of Serena's estate, and Ronald and Linda, in their own right (collectively, "the Viscontis"), brought suit in the Philadelphia County Court of Common Pleas. They attempted to hold the HMO liable for Dr. Wisniewski's malpractice under ostensible and actual agency theories, alleging

---

[1] HMOs often contain costs through a strategy known as "utilization review." Unlike traditional insurance policies, HMOs usually decide whether to reimburse patients for medical care prospectively — through utilization or "pre-certification" review. The HMO may either perform the utilization review itself or assign the task to a third-party contractor. *See Corcoran v. United Healthcare, Inc.*, 965 F.2d 1321, 1323 (5th Cir.), *cert. denied*, 506 U.S. 1033 (1992).

that when Linda became pregnant, the HMO held out Dr. Wisniewski as a competent and qualified participating obstetrician/gynecologist. They also sued the HMO under a direct negligence theory, claiming, among other things, that the HMO was negligent in its selection, employment, and oversight of the medical personnel who performed the actual medical treatment.

The HMO removed the case to federal court [which subsequently held that the Viscontis' claims were preempted by ERISA.]

The *Visconti* and *Dukes* cases have been consolidated on appeal.

II.

The HMOs removed these cases to federal court pursuant to 28 U.S.C. § 1441, alleging that the district courts had original jurisdiction over the claims, because the claims "[arose] under the Constitution, treaties or laws of the United States." § 1441(b); 28 U.S.C. § 1331. To determine whether a claim "arises under" federal law — and thus is removable — we begin with the "well-pleaded complaint rule." *See Metropolitan Life Ins. Co. v. Taylor*, 481 U.S. 58, 63 (1987).

Under the well-pleaded complaint rule, a cause of action "arises under" federal law, and removal is proper, only if a federal question is presented on the face of the plaintiff's properly pleaded complaint. *Franchise Tax Bd. v. Construction Laborers Vacation Trust*, 463 U.S. 1, 9-12 (1983). A federal defense to a plaintiff's state law cause of action ordinarily does not appear on the face of the well-pleaded complaint, and, therefore, usually is insufficient to warrant removal to federal court. *Gully v. First Nat'l Bank*, 299 U.S. 109, 115-18 (1936). Thus, it is well-established that the defense of preemption ordinarily is insufficient justification to permit removal to federal court. *Caterpillar, Inc. v. Williams*, 482 U.S. 386, 398 (1987) ("The fact that a defendant might ultimately prove that a plaintiff's claims are pre-empted under [a federal statute] does not establish that they are removable to federal court.").

The Supreme Court has recognized an exception to the well-pleaded complaint rule — the "complete preemption" exception — under which "Congress may so completely pre-empt a particular area that any civil complaint raising this select group of claims is necessarily federal in character." *Metropolitan Life*, 481 U.S. at 63-64. The complete preemption doctrine applies when

> the pre-emptive force of [the federal statutory provision] is so powerful as to displace entirely any state cause of action [addressed by the federal statute]. Any such suit is purely a creature of federal law, notwithstanding the fact that state law would provide a cause of action in the absence of [the federal provision].

Franchise Tax Bd., 463 U.S. at 23. Claims to enforce a collective-bargaining agreement under § 301 of the Labor Management Relations Act of 1947, 29 U.S.C. § 185, present a typical example of the complete-preemption doctrine at work: In *Avco Corp. v. Aero Lodge No. 735*, 390 U.S. 557 (1968), the Court ruled that any claims to enforce a collective-bargaining agreement — even when phrased as a state law cause of action to enforce a contract — are removable to federal court.

The Supreme Court has determined that Congress intended the complete-preemption doctrine to apply to state law causes of action which fit within the scope of ERISA's civil-enforcement provisions.[2] *Metropolitan Life*, 481 U.S. at 66. It explained:

> [T]he legislative history consistently sets out [Congress's] clear intention to make § 502(a)(1)(B) suits brought by participants or beneficiaries federal questions for the purposes of federal court jurisdiction in like manner as § 301 of [the Labor Management Relations Act of 1947, 29 U.S.C. § 185.] For example, Senator Williams, a sponsor of ERISA, emphasized that the civil enforcement section would enable participants and beneficiaries to bring suit to recover benefits denied contrary to the terms of the plan and that when they did so "[i]t is intended that such actions will be regarded as arising under the laws of the United States, in a similar fashion to those brought under section 301 of the Labor Management Relations Act."

481 U.S. at 66 (citations omitted). Thus, courts have found that the *Metropolitan Life* complete-preemption doctrine permits removal of state law causes of action in a host of different ERISA-related circumstances. *See id.* at 63-67 (holding that state common law causes of action asserting improper processing of a claim for benefits under an employee benefit plan are removable to federal court); *Anderson v. Electronic Data Sys. Corp.*, 11 F.3d 1311, 1314 (5th Cir.) (holding that removal was proper because state law claim alleging that plan fiduciary was demoted and terminated for refusing to violate ERISA fell within § 502(a)(2) & (3)), *cert. denied*, 513 U.S. 808 (1994); *Sofo v. Pan-American Life Ins. Co.*, 13 F.3d 239, 240-41 (7th Cir.1994) (plaintiff's state court rescission claim against a group insurance policy for the policy's refusal to reimburse plaintiff for medical treatment received was properly removed because plaintiff's claim was for a denial of benefits).

That the Supreme Court has recognized a limited exception to the well-pleaded complaint rule for state law claims which fit within the scope of § 502 by no means implies that all claims preempted by ERISA are subject to removal. Instead, as the U.S. Court of Appeals for the Sixth Circuit wrote recently,

---

[2] ERISA's "six carefully integrated civil enforcement provisions" are found in § 502. *Massachusetts Mut. Life Ins. Co. v. Russell*, 473 U.S. 134, 146 (1985). The statutory provision relevant for the purposes of this appeal, § 502(a)(1)(B), states in pertinent part:

> (a) *Persons empowered to bring a civil action*
> A civil action may be brought —
> (1) by a participant or beneficiary —
> ....
> (B) to recover benefits due to him under the terms of his plan, to enforce his rights under the terms of the plan, or to clarify his rights to future benefits under the terms of the plan....

"[r]emoval and preemption are two distinct concepts." *Warner v. Ford Motor Co.*, 46 F.3d 531, 535 (6th Cir. 1995). Section 514 of ERISA defines the scope of ERISA preemption, providing that ERISA "supersede[s] any and all State laws insofar as they may now or hereafter *relate to* any employee benefit plan described in [§ 4(a) of ERISA] and not exempt under [§ 4(b) of ERISA]." (Emphasis added.) The *Metropolitan Life* complete-preemption exception, on the other hand, is concerned with a more limited set of state laws, those which fall within the scope of ERISA's civil enforcement provision, § 502. State law claims which fall outside of the scope of § 502, even if preempted by § 514(a), are still governed by the well-pleaded complaint rule and, therefore, are not removable under the complete-preemption principles established in *Metropolitan Life*.

The difference between preemption and complete preemption is important. When the doctrine of complete preemption does not apply, but the plaintiff's state claim is arguably preempted under § 514(a), the district court, being without removal jurisdiction, cannot resolve the dispute regarding preemption. It lacks power to do anything other than remand to the state court where the preemption issue can be addressed and resolved. *Franchise Tax Bd.*, 463 U.S. at 4, 27-28.

III.

The district courts in these cases found that the plaintiffs' state law claims against the U.S. Healthcare HMOs fall within the scope of § 502(a)(1)(B) and that the *Metropolitan Life* complete-preemption doctrine therefore permits removal.[3] We disagree.

To determine whether the state law claims fall within the scope of § 502(a)(1)(B), we must determine whether those claims, properly construed, are "to recover benefits due ... under the terms of [the] plan, to enforce ... rights under the terms of the plan, or to clarify ... rights to future benefits under the terms of the plan." In making that determination, it would be helpful to have a complete understanding in each case of the relationships among the HMO, the employer, and the other defendants, the nature of the plan benefits, and the rights of participants and beneficiaries under the plan. We are somewhat hampered here because these cases come to us on appeal from orders granting motions to dismiss. Because of this procedural status, the parties have had little chance to develop the records and, accordingly, we know very little about the nature of the plan benefits or about the role — if any — that U.S. Healthcare's HMOs play in the respective ERISA welfare plans.

---

[3] There is no contention that the plaintiffs' state law claims implicate any of ERISA's civil enforcement provisions other than those set out in § 502(a)(1)(B). Accordingly, we direct our discussion to whether the plaintiffs' claims fall within the scope of § 502(a)(1)(B).

We recognize that there are issues in dispute. The plaintiffs and the Department of Labor as amicus curie, for example, claim that the U.S. Healthcare HMOs are separate from the ERISA plans and that the sole benefit that participants and beneficiaries receive from each plan is the plaintiffs' *membership* in the HMOs. In their view, the plaintiffs' claims thus have nothing at all to do with § 502(a)(1)(B) because no one contests that the plaintiffs in fact have received their plan benefits (their membership in the HMO). Instead, under their view, the plaintiffs' claims merely attack the behavior of an entity completely external to the ERISA plan.

U.S. Healthcare, on the other hand, claims that the plan benefits are more than just the plan participants' or beneficiaries' memberships in the respective HMOs; it argues that *the medical care received* is itself the plan benefit. As a corollary to that position, it also disagrees with the plaintiffs' view that the HMOs are completely distinct from the respective ERISA plans, arguing that the HMOs in fact play a role in the delivery of plan benefits. It further maintains that ERISA is implicated because both the plaintiffs' agency claims and their direct negligence claims relate to the quality of the plan benefits and the HMOs' role as the entity that arranges for those benefits for the ERISA plans.

We need not here resolve these disputes about how to characterize the plan benefits or the HMOs' role in the respective ERISA plans. We will assume, without deciding, that the medical care provided (and not merely the plaintiffs' memberships in the respective HMOs) is the plan benefit for the purposes of ERISA. We will also assume that the HMOs, either as a part of or on behalf of the ERISA plans, arrange for the delivery of those plan benefits. We thus assume, for example, that removal jurisdiction would exist if the plaintiffs were alleging that the HMOs refused to provide the services to which membership entitled them.

Given those assumptions, we nevertheless conclude that removal was improper. We are compelled to this conclusion because the plaintiffs' claims, even when construed as U.S. Healthcare suggests, merely attack the *quality* of the benefits they received: The plaintiffs here simply do not claim that the plans erroneously withheld benefits due. Nor do they ask the state courts to enforce their rights under the terms of their respective plans or to clarify their rights to future benefits. As a result, the plaintiffs' claims fall outside of the scope of § 502(a)(1)(B) and these cases must be remanded to the state courts from which they were removed.

A.

Nothing in the complaints indicates that the plaintiffs are complaining about their ERISA welfare plans' failure to provide benefits due under the plan. Dukes does not allege, for example, that the Germantown Hospital refused to perform blood studies on Darryl because the ERISA plan refused to pay for those studies. Similarly, the Viscontis do not contend that Serena's death was due to their welfare plan's refusal to pay for or otherwise provide for medical services. Instead of claiming that the welfare plans in any way withheld some quantum of plan benefits due, the plaintiffs in both cases complain about the low quality of the medical treatment that they actually received and argue that the U.S. Healthcare HMO should be held liable under agency and negligence principles.

We are confident that a claim about the quality of a benefit received is not a claim under § 502(a)(1)(B) to "recover benefits due ... under the terms of [the] plan." To reach that conclusion, "we begin as we do in any exercise of statutory construction with the text of the provision in question, and move on, as need be, to the structure and purpose of the Act in which it occurs." *New York State Conference of Blue Cross & Blue Shield Plans v. Travelers Ins. Co.*, 514 U.S. 645, 654 (1995).

The text lends no support to U.S. Healthcare's argument. On its face, a suit "to recover benefits due ... under the terms of [the] plan" is concerned exclusively with whether or not the benefits due under the plan were actually provided. The statute simply says nothing about the quality of benefits received.

Nor does anything in the legislative history, structure, or purpose of ERISA suggest that Congress viewed § 502(a)(1)(B) as creating a remedy for a participant injured by medical malpractice. When Congress enacted ERISA it was concerned in large part with the various mechanisms and institutions involved in the funding and payment of plan benefits.... We find nothing in the legislative history suggesting that § 502 was intended as a part of a federal scheme to control the quality of the benefits received by plan participants. Quality control of benefits, such as the health care benefits provided here, is a field traditionally occupied by state regulation and we interpret the silence of Congress as reflecting an intent that it remain such....

B.

We also reject the HMOs' attempts to characterize the plaintiffs' state court complaints as attempts to enforce their "rights under the terms of the [respective welfare] plan[s]." That phrase is included, we believe, so as to provide a means of enforcing any contract rights other than the right to benefits, as for example the various plan-created rights of plan participants to benefit-claim and benefit-eligibility procedures. Just as § 502(a)(1)(B) provides the means by which a participant can insist on the promised benefits, so too does it provide the means for insisting on the plan-created rights other than plan benefits.[4]

---

[4] ERISA ordinarily requires that welfare plans set out a description of the rights of the participants and their beneficiaries in a summary plan description ("SPD"). 29 U.S.C. § 1022(b). That requirement is relaxed in situations where the ERISA plan chooses to provide benefits through a qualified HMO. Under 29 C.F.R. § 2520.102-5(a), if health benefits are provided through an HMO, the SPD need not contain the usual description of the rights of participants or beneficiaries, provided the SPD contains a notice stating, among other things, that plan participants will receive membership "in one or more qualified health maintenance organizations," § 2520.102-

The HMOs point to no plan-created right implicated by the plaintiffs' state law medical malpractice claims. The best they can do is assert that the plaintiffs' medical malpractice claims "attempt to define a participant's rights under the plan." We cannot accept that characterization. The plaintiffs are not attempting to define new "rights under the terms of the plan"; instead, they are attempting to assert their already-existing rights under the generally-applicable state law of agency and tort. Inherent in the phrases "rights under the terms of the plan" and "benefits due ... under the terms of [the] plan" is the notion that the plan participants and beneficiaries will receive something to which they would not be otherwise entitled. But patients enjoy the right to be free from medical malpractice regardless of whether or not their medical care is provided through an ERISA plan.

C.

Much of the above analysis also precludes us from concluding that the plaintiffs are asking the state courts to "clarify [their] rights to future benefits under the terms of the plan." As noted, there is no allegation here that the HMOs have withheld plan benefits due. Moreover, nothing in the complaints remotely resembles a request that the court clarify a right to a *future* benefit; instead, the plaintiffs' complaints center on past events.

D.

We recognize that the distinction between the quantity of benefits due under a welfare plan and the quality of those benefits will not always be clear in situations like this where the benefit contracted for is health care services rather than money to pay for such services. There well may be cases in which the quality of a patient's medical care or the skills of the personnel provided to administer that care will be so low that the treatment received simply will not qualify as health care at all. In such a case, it well may be appropriate to conclude that the plan participant or beneficiary has been denied benefits due under the plan. This is not such a case, however. While the *Dukes* complaint alleges that the Germantown Hospital committed malpractice when it decided not to perform certain blood tests, no one would conclude from that malpractice that Germantown Hospital was not acting as a health care provider when it made those decisions. Similarly, while the Viscontis claim that Dr. Wisniewski was incompetent, there

---

5(b)(1), and that upon request each available HMO will provide certain written information, namely

> (i) the nature of services provided to members; (ii) conditions pertaining to eligibility to receive such services (other than general conditions pertaining to eligibility for participation in the plan) and circumstances under which services may be denied; and (iii) the procedures to be followed in obtaining such services, and the procedures available for the review of claims for services which are denied in whole or in part.

§ 2520.102-5(b)(3).

is no indication that he was not performing health care services at the time he allegedly committed the malpractice charged.

We also recognize the possibility that an ERISA plan may describe a benefit in terms that can accurately be described as related to the quality of the service. Thus, for example, a plan might promise that all X-rays would be analyzed by radiologists with a prescribed level of advanced training. A plan participant whose X-ray was analyzed by a physician with less than the prescribed training might well be entitled to enforce the plan's promise through a suit under § 502(a)(1)(B) to secure a denied benefit.

Much of the HMOs' argument in these cases is at root a contention that the employer and the HMO impliedly contracted that the health care services provided would be of acceptable quality and, accordingly, that these damage suits rest on a failure to provide services of acceptable quality. Since we do not have before us the documents reflecting the agreements between the employers and the HMOs, we are not in a position to determine whether such a commitment was implicit in their respective agreements. However, the burden of establishing removal jurisdiction rests with the defendant. Accordingly, the HMO is not in a position to press this argument.

Moreover, we hasten to add that while we have no doubt that all concerned expected the medical services arranged for by the HMOs to be of acceptable quality, this seems to us beside the point. The relevant inquiry is not whether there was an expectation of acceptably competent services, but rather whether there was an agreement to displace the quality standard found in the otherwise applicable law with a contract standard.

It may well be that an employer and an HMO could agree that a quality of health care standard articulated in their contract would replace the standards that would otherwise be supplied by the applicable state law of tort. We express no view on whether an ERISA plan sponsor may thus by contract opt out of state tort law and into a federal law of ERISA contract. We will reserve that issue until a case arises presenting it.[5] Nothing in this record suggests an agreement to displace the otherwise applicable state laws of agency and tort.

IV.

The HMOs take heart in a recent case, *Corcoran v. United Healthcare, Inc.*, 965 F.2d 1321 (5th Cir.), *cert. denied*, 506 U.S. 1033 (1992), in which the U.S. Court of Appeals for the Fifth Circuit held that ERISA preempts a medical malpractice claim against a medical consulting company for decisions it made as the third-party administrator of a welfare plan's "pre-certification" review program.

---

[5] It would seem to Judge Roth that, if a plan were to adopt its own standard of acceptable health care to be made available to beneficiaries, the plan should provide concurrently, through insurance or otherwise, an appropriate remedy to beneficiaries for any failure of the plan care providers to meet that standard or, in the alternative, should inform plan beneficiaries that tort law remedies for medical malpractice would not be available to them under the plan.

We agree with the HMOs that under *Corcoran*, third-party private companies may, in some circumstances, play a role in an ERISA plan and that claims against such companies may fall within the scope of § 502(a). We nevertheless find Corcoran inapposite on the facts and claims alleged in this case.

[The Court then described the facts and procedural history of the *Corcoran* case.]

The U.S. Court of Appeals for the Fifth Circuit ruled that ERISA preempted Corcoran's claim against United and — implicitly, at least — that Corcoran's claims were completely preempted. It explained that while United was in fact giving medical advice, it gave that advice as part of its role of making benefit determinations for the plan. Thus, the court determined that plaintiffs were "attempting to recover for a tort allegedly committed in the course of handling a benefit determination," *id.* at 1332, and that such state law claims are preempted by ERISA.

The HMOs argue that we should read *Corcoran* broadly to hold that medical malpractice claims against an HMO should be removable under *Metropolitan Life* whenever an HMO provides the complained-about medical treatment as a benefit of an ERISA-covered health plan....

The HMOs' reliance on *Corcoran* is misplaced. Although United's decisions in *Corcoran* were in part medical decisions, United, unlike the HMOs here, did not provide, arrange for, or supervise the doctors who provided the actual medical treatment for plan participants. (Blue Cross played that role in *Corcoran*.) Instead, United only performed an administrative function inherent in the "utilization review." The difference between the "utilization review" and the "arranging for medical treatment" roles is crucial for the purposes of § 502(a)(1)(B) because only in a utilization-review role is an entity in a position to deny benefits due under an ERISA welfare plan.[6] 965 F.2d at 1333 n. 16 (noting that ERISA is implicated in "utilization review" decisions but not medical-treatment decisions because only the former are "made in connection with a cost containment plan").

In these cases, the defendant HMOs play two roles, not just one.[7] In addition to the utilization-review role played by United in *Corcoran*, the HMOs also arrange for the actual medical treatment for plan participants. Only this second role is relevant for this appeal, however: on the faces of these complaints there is no allegation that the HMOs somehow should be held liable for any decisions

---

[6] As noted in Part III, we are assuming, without deciding, that the medical care provided (and not merely the plaintiffs' memberships in the respective HMOs) is the plan benefit for the purposes of ERISA. So viewed, when acting in their utilization-review role, the HMOs are making benefit determinations.

[7] There is nothing unusual about this. HMOs often arrange for the medical treatment *and* perform the utilization review (instead of hiring a third party).

they might have made while acting in their utilization-review roles.[8] Stated another way, unlike *Corcoran*, there is no allegation here that the HMOs denied anyone any benefits that they were due under the plan. Instead, the plaintiffs here are attempting to hold the HMOs liable for their role as the arrangers of their decedents' medical treatment.

For this reason, these cases are more like *Lupo v. Human Affairs Int'l, Inc.*, 28 F.3d 269 (2d Cir. 1994). There, an employer had contracted with a psychotherapy service group, Human Affairs International, Inc. ("HAI"), to provide mental health services to its employees in connection with an employee benefit plan governed by ERISA. Lupo, an employee who received psychotherapy services from HAI, sued HAI in a state court for his therapist's professional malpractice, breach of fiduciary duty, and intentional infliction of emotional distress. HAI, like the HMOs here, removed the case to federal court, claiming that ERISA completely preempted Lupo's claims. The district court agreed with HAI, and, accordingly, dismissed Lupo's claim. The U.S. Court of Appeals for the Second Circuit reversed, holding that the district court lacked removal jurisdiction and was thus obligated to remand to the state court. It reached this conclusion because "[o]n their face, none of [Lupo's] claims [bore] any significant resemblance to those described in [§ 502(a)(1)(B)]." 28 F.3d at 272. The situation in the cases at bar is closely analogous. As in *Lupo*, the plaintiffs' claims in these cases do not concern a denial of benefits due or a denial of some other plan-created right. Thus, the claims here, like those in Lupo, bear no significant resemblance to the claims described in § 502(a)(1)(B).

V.

For the foregoing reasons, the district courts' judgments in these cases will be reversed and remanded with instructions to remand the cases to the state courts from which they came. Our holding that the districts courts lack removal jurisdiction, of course, leaves open for resolution by the state courts the issue of whether the plaintiffs' claims are preempted under § 514(a).

NOTES

1. *Who Decides?* The holding in *Dukes* was limited to determining who would decide the case: The state court should hear the case since the complete-preemption doctrine did not apply. Complete preemption, however, is only one of the possible grounds for asserting federal court jurisdiction. *See Jass v. Prudential Health Care Plan, Inc.*, 88 F.3d 1482 (7th Cir. 1996) (district court had jurisdiction over HMO because parties were diverse and, in addition, could have exercised supplemental jurisdiction over state law claims). In general, plaintiffs

---

[8] The only possible exception is Dukes' allegation that the Germantown Hospital refused to perform blood studies on Darryl. Still, on the record before the court, there is no indication that the hospital refused to perform those studies because of the ERISA plan's refusal to pay.

tend to prefer that these kinds of claims be heard in state court, while defendants tend to prefer federal court.

2. Preemption, Even if Not Complete. *Dukes* does not decide whether Section 514 of ERISA preempts the plaintiffs' state law claims. It remands that issue, the "conflict preemption" issue, to the state court. *Dukes,* however, does provide a rationale for non-preemption that has been followed by some lower courts. *See Frappier v. Wishnov,* 678 So. 2d 884 (Fla. Dist. Ct. App. 1996) (claim challenging the quality of care is not preempted); *Tufino v. New York Hotel & Motel Trades Council,* 646 N.Y.S.2d 799 (N.Y. App. Div. 1996) (same).

Dukes was the first case in which the United States Department of Labor filed an amicus brief stating its position on the conflict preemption issue. For the Labor Department's briefs in *Dukes* and other cases, see http://www.dol.gov/dol/pwba. The Labor Department's position is that ERISA preemption turns on two key distinctions. First, claims of benefit denials are preempted, but claims challenging the quality of benefits are not. Claims challenging the quality of benefits do not affect the design, structure, or administration of ERISA plans and, hence, do not "relate to" a plan within the meaning of § 514. Second, claims against an employer's health plan are preempted, but claims against entities, such as HMOs, which contract with the plan to provide services are not. ERISA preemption extends only to employer plans and their promise to pay for health care; it does not extend to service providers who actually provide the care. *Dukes* reflects both of these distinctions.

3. Preemption Strategies. Employers have incentives to expand the scope of ERISA preemption. ERISA preemption provides a shield from significant potential liability (for example, from liability for punitive and compensatory damages). To the extent employers can extend the shield of ERISA to service providers, employers should be able to share in the savings by paying lower rates for health care services provided to employees.

Employers can work with both of the Labor Department's distinctions in their attempt to expand the scope of ERISA's preemption. As *Dukes* mentions, one possibility would be to make the quality of care a part of the design, structure, and administration of the ERISA plan. The plan itself, for example, could promise not only to pay for certain benefits, but to provide quality care. If the plan were structured in this way, the argument would be that any claim about the quality of care would "relate to" the plan and, hence, would be preempted by § 514. Similarly, employers could attempt to muddy the distinction between the ERISA plan and service providers. At the extreme, a large employer could provide health care services, not by contract with an independent HMO, but through an HMO which is wholly owned by the employer. *But cf. De Buono v. NYSA-ILA Med. & Clinical Servs. Fund,* 117 S. Ct. 1747 (1997) (state tax on medical services not preempted even when applied to medical centers owned and operated by ERISA plan).

4. ERISA, Tort Reform, and the Status Quo. *Corcoran* and *Dukes* illustrate that, through ERISA, Congress inadvertently enacted tort reform. For the class of claims covered, ERISA eliminated punitive damages, limited other damages, and made other changes favorable to defendants. Efforts to reverse this part of ERISA and restore more normal tort liability have been unsuccessful. For a recent bill, see Patient Access to Responsible Care Act, H.R. 1415, 105th Cong., 1st Sess. § 4 (1997). At the same time, Congress has tried and failed to enact similar tort reform in other areas. In 1996, for example, Congress passed a products liability bill that would have limited punitive damages and made other changes favorable to defendants. President Clinton vetoed the bill and the veto was not overridden. Common Sense Product Liability Reform Act, H.R. 956, 104th Cong., 2d Sess. (1996). Thus, Congress apparently cannot reverse tort reform where it exists (ERISA), or enact it where it does not (products liability). Is Congress simply undecided about the merits of tort reform? Or are there other explanations? *See* Saul Levmore, *Bicameralism: When Are Two Decisions Better Than One?*, 12 INT'L REV. L. & ECON. 145 (1992) (exploring bicameralism as one constitutional mechanism for preserving the status quo); Herbert Hovenkamp, *Legal Policy and the Endowment Effect*, 20 J. LEGAL STUD. 225 (1991) (exploring tendency of people to value what they have more highly than what they can get).

C. PORTABILITY

Employment is the most common source of health insurance in the United States. In 1995, about 65 percent of the nonelderly population received their coverage through employer health plans as workers, retirees, or dependents. John Sheils & Lisa Alecxih, *Recent Trends in Employer Health Insurance Coverage and Benefits* 2 (American Hospital Ass'n 1996).

One of the problems with employment-based health insurance occurs when workers leave their jobs.[*] In the absence of legal regulation, there is no assurance that these workers and their dependents will be eligible for their old employer's plan and they may not be able to obtain new coverage immediately. A new employer may have a waiting period and, in addition, may exclude pre-existing medical conditions from coverage. Individual health insurance policies may be available, but they also may exclude pre-existing conditions and, in addition, tend to be quite expensive because of adverse selection problems and high administrative costs. Health insurers naturally are suspicious that an individual seeking health coverage is anticipating major health expenses. As a result, premiums for individual policies tend to be high.

---

[*] More generally, these types of problems arise whenever a covered worker or a beneficiary is no longer eligible for coverage under the employer's plan. This may occur for a variety of reasons in addition to leaving a job. Coverage may be lost, for example, if the covered worker suffers a reduction in hours, upon divorce, or when a dependent child is no longer eligible for coverage. *See* ERISA § 603.

This problem with the "portability" of employer-based health insurance is significant. In 1994, about 700,000 Americans lost their health insurance each month because they, or a spouse or parent, lost their job. The median length of a lapse in coverage was about 7 months. *Id.* at 9. Problems with portability, then, contribute to the more general problem: millions of Americans do not have health insurance. In 1995, about 15 percent of the population (or 40 million people) did not have health insurance. *Id.* at 6-8. Lack of portability is also a concern because it may interfere with the ability of workers to move to more productive jobs. If workers fear problems with their health insurance coverage (for example, because they or their dependents have pre-existing conditions), they may be locked into their current jobs. *See* Thomas C. Buchmueller & Robert G. Valletta, *The Effects of Employer-Provided Health Insurance on Worker Mobility*, 49 INDUS. & LAB. REL. REV. 439 (1996) (providing empirical evidence of job lock, especially for women).

Congress has reacted to the portability problem twice. In 1986, Congress required employers who offer group health insurance to continue to provide coverage for eighteen to thirty-six months from the time of an event (such as a death or job termination) that might otherwise result in loss of coverage. ERISA §§ 601-608. This type of coverage is called "COBRA" continuation coverage because it was initially enacted as part of the Consolidated Omnibus Budget Amendment Act of 1986. The basic approach of COBRA is to require continued coverage with the "old" employer to give the employee (or spouse or dependent) time to find new health insurance coverage.

COBRA requires employers with twenty or more employees to provide continuation coverage to "covered employees" and "qualified beneficiaries" after "qualifying events." Qualified beneficiaries include the spouse and dependent children of an employee who is covered by the plan. ERISA § 607(3). The qualifying event for an employee is generally termination (although continuation coverage is not required for terminations for "gross misconduct"); for spouses, the qualifying event is usually death of the employee, divorce, or legal separation; and for dependents, the qualifying event is generally loss of dependency status under the terms of the health plan (for example, by becoming too old to be covered as a dependent child). § 603. Employers are required to notify each covered employee and spouse of their COBRA rights at the commencement of coverage under the plan and when a qualifying event occurs. § 606. The employee or qualifying beneficiary has sixty days after the qualifying event to decide whether to accept COBRA coverage. § 605(1). The plan may require those accepting COBRA coverage to pay a premium, but it may not exceed 102 percent of the premium for active employees. § 602(3).

In 1996, Congress reacted to the portability problem again. This time it enacted the Health Insurance Portability and Accountability Act ("HIPAA"). The basic approach of HIPAA contrasts with that of COBRA. COBRA looked to the old employer as the primary source of insurance to bridge the gap during transition periods. HIPAA looks instead to new employers and the private insurance market. HIPAA limits the ability of new employers and private insurers to deny health insurance coverage to new applicants. For example, it limits the ability to deny coverage because of pre-existing conditions or through waiting periods. Hence, HIPAA deals with the portability problem by making it easier for employees and their dependents to get health insurance from their new employers or from insurance companies.

HIPAA imposes requirements on group health plans offered by employers (regardless of whether they are insured or self-insured), on insurers who offer group insurance, and on insurers who offer health insurance policies to individuals:

- For group health plans, HIPAA has two principal requirements. First, group health plans cannot impose pre-existing conditions limitations on coverage for more than 12 months and even that period must be reduced by periods of "creditable coverage" under other health plans. "Creditable coverage" includes most kinds of health insurance, but excludes any coverage occurring before a break in coverage of 63 days or more. ERISA § 701. Thus, a new employee who was covered under her immediately preceding employer's health plan for eight months would need to satisfy only a four-month limit on coverage with a new employer. However, if she had been without health insurance for 63 or more days (perhaps because she declined to purchase COBRA continuation coverage from her old employer's plan and took more than 62 days to find the new job), the new employer could impose a 12-month waiting period. One implication of this requirement is that "old" employers must provide employees with certifications of their prior health insurance coverage. HIPAA provides for that. § 701(e).

  Second, HIPAA provides that group health plans cannot have eligibility rules (such as waiting periods or requirements for continued eligibility) based on health-related factors, such as physical or mental condition, disability, or medical history. § 702(a). Similarly, a group health plan may not require any individual to pay higher premiums because of any of these health-related factors. § 702(b).

- For insurers who offer group insurance, HIPAA requires insurers operating in the small group market to issue health insurance to all small employers and to accept every eligible individual of those employers. 42 U.S.C. § 300gg-11(a). The small group market covers employers with 2 to 50 employees. § 300gg-91(e)(4). Insurers may deny coverage to small employers only for specified reasons, such as inadequate financial reserves to underwrite additional insurance. § 300gg-11(d)-(f). HIPAA also requires insurers in the large and small group markets to renew policies except for specified reasons, such as nonpayment of premiums or fraud. § 300gg-12.

- For insurers who offer health insurance to individuals, HIPAA requires insurers to issue policies to "eligible individuals" and to renew them. 42 U.S.C. § 300gg-41. "Eligible individuals" are people who have been covered for at least 18 months under a group health plan, who are not eligible for any other group health insurance, and who do not have health insurance. § 300gg-41(b). The policies made available to eligible individuals must be either the two highest-volume individual policies offered by the insurer or two policies that are representative of the policies issued by the insurer. § 300gg-41(c). As with group health plans, HIPAA imposes restrictions on the ability of insurers to limit coverage because of pre-existing conditions. § 300gg-41(a)(1)(B).

COBRA and HIPAA have spawned a veritable snakepit of complicated regulations. One set of issues concerns the terminating employer's responsibilities under COBRA when the worker is covered by a spouse's health insurance plan as well. The following case deals with this issue.

SCHLETT v. AVCO FINANCIAL SERVICES, INC.

United States District Court, N.D. Ohio

950 F. Supp. 823 (1996)

KATZ, District Judge.

This matter is before the Court on Defendant's motion for summary judgment and Plaintiff's cross-motion for partial summary judgment. For the following reasons, Defendant's motion will be granted. Plaintiff's motion will be denied.

I. BACKGROUND

Plaintiff Cheryl Schlett ("Schlett") was hired as a part-time customer service representative by Defendant Avco Financial Services, Inc. ("Avco") on March 24, 1993. At the time of Schlett's hire, Avco employed three full-time employees in its Sandusky, Ohio office; Schlett was the fourth employee.

Avco's company policy prescribes a staffing limit requiring that the office service at least 350 accounts per employee. In June, 1993, the Sandusky office where Schlett worked had 1,398 accounts, two short of the number required to justify four full-time employees. Schlett was converted to full-time employment status, however, because the branch manager needed additional assistance in converting the office to a new computer system.

Schlett learned that she was pregnant in August, 1993, and informed her branch manager of her pregnancy in September, 1993.

Between June, 1993 and December, 1993, the number of accounts in the Sandusky office dropped to 1,236, an average of only 309 accounts per employee. The new computer system was fully implemented by November, 1993.

In December, 1993, district manager James Shake informed Schlett that she would be converted back to part-time status because of the decline in the number of accounts. Since Avco provides health care coverage only for full-time employees, the conversion to part-time status would result in the loss of Schlett's medical benefits. At that time, Shake asked Schlett if she expected Avco to pay for her pregnancy and if she were covered under her husband's group health plan. Schlett informed Shake that she was covered under her husband's policy, but intended to keep dual coverage under both plans.

Schlett was reduced to part-time status effective January 1, 1994. She was provided a COBRA election form on January 7, 1994. At some time around January, 1994, branch manager Irene Phipps called Avco's home office in an unsuccessful attempt to allow Schlett to keep her medical benefits. Schlett attempted to elect COBRA benefits on or about February 24, 1994. Avco denied Schlett's request on the ground that she was ineligible for COBRA benefits because she was already covered by other group health coverage.

On February 17, 1994, Schlett gave birth prematurely. Schlett's son, Plaintiff Samuel Schlett, was in the hospital for two months and incurred medical bills of approximately $130,000. Schlett's husband's medical benefits covered approximately $117,500 of that amount, leaving Plaintiffs personally liable for the remaining $12,500.

Shortly after her son was born, Schlett informed Avco that she did not know whether she would be able to return to work because her son was still in the hospital. In April, 1994, she again informed Avco that she had no idea when she would be able to return to work. Avco terminated Schlett effective April 15, 1994.

Schlett, along with her husband and son, brought suit in this Court on numerous claims arising out of her reduction to part-time status, denial of medical benefits, and termination by Avco. In Counts I and II of her amended complaint, they allege that Avco discriminated against Schlett on the basis of her pregnancy in violation of Title VII of the Civil Rights Act of 1964 and Ohio Rev. Code §§ 4112.02 & 4112.99. In Counts III and IV, they allege that Avco denied Schlett and her son continued medical insurance benefits in violation of ERISA and COBRA.... Defendants have moved for summary judgment on all Counts. The Court discusses the parties' contentions below.

II. *DISCUSSION*

[The Court granted Defendants' motion for summary judgement on Courts I and II. The Court found that Schlett had not presented a prima facie case of pregnancy discrimination. Instead, she was reduced to part-time status because of the downturn in the company's sales volume and was terminated because she did not give a date on which she could return to work.]

Plaintiffs allege that Avco denied Schlett continued medical insurance benefits in violation of ERISA and COBRA. Defendants deny that the denial of continued medical insurance benefits violated ERISA or COBRA. They allege that Schlett was ineligible for the continuing benefits she applied for because she was covered under her husband's health insurance.

1. *Extent of Right to Continued Coverage*

The coverage issue raised by the parties appears to be a question of first impression in this Circuit. ERISA, as amended by COBRA, requires employers to offer beneficiaries of their health plans the right to elect continued coverage, when those benefits would otherwise be lost because of termination or reduction of hours. 29 U.S.C. §§ 1161, 1163(2). The beneficiary's right to continue that coverage ends on the date on which he or she "first becomes, after the date of election, covered under any other group health plan ... 'which does not contain any exclusion or limitation with respect to any preexisting condition of such beneficiary.'" 29 U.S.C. § 1162(2)(D). The Sixth Circuit has never addressed the issue of whether the statutory language authorizes an employer to withhold continuation coverage when the departing employee has dual coverage under her spouse's health insurance plan throughout her employment and therefore has a continuing source of coverage when she becomes ineligible for benefits. Other Circuit Courts have come to different conclusions on that issue.

The Tenth Circuit first addressed the dual coverage issue in *Oakley v. City of Longmont*, 890 F.2d 1128 (10th Cir.1989), *cert. denied*, 494 U.S. 1082 (1990). The statute under which *Oakley* was decided stated that continuation coverage ended on the date on which "the qualified employee first becomes, after the date of election, covered under any other group health plan." 42 U.S.C. § 300bb-2(2)(D)(i) (1988).[2] Oakley suffered a permanent head injury in an automobile collision with a drunk driver, and was subsequently terminated because of his inability to return to work. At the time of Oakley's termination, he was covered both by his employer's health plan and as a dependent under his wife's plan. His employer informed him that he was ineligible for continuation coverage because he was covered by his wife's plan. However, his wife's plan, unlike his own plan, did not cover the costs of his medical treatment.

The Tenth Circuit held that the statute did not provide a basis for terminating coverage. In construing the statutory language, the Court focused on the phrase "after the date of election," and held that the plain meaning of the section could not "be construed to include a spouse's preexisting group plan as a condition to terminate continuation coverage." *Oakley*, 890 F.2d at 1132. The Court went on to explain that:

> Surely the facts of this case illustrate the precise gap in coverage which troubled Congress. Mr. Oakley was terminated because of a catastrophic event which otherwise would have put his family at risk and jeopardized his treatment had the continuation rules not been in effect to maintain his rehabilitation for a limited period of time.

Id. at 1133.

---

[2] Since Oakley was a public employee, his case arose under the Public Health Service Act, rather than ERISA. The continuation coverage provisions of the two laws are identical.

Ten days after the Oakley decision was rendered, Congress amended ERISA's continuation coverage provisions to provide that the right to such continuation coverage ends on the date the employee becomes covered under another group health plan *"which does not contain any exclusion or limitation with respect to any preexisting condition."* 29 U.S.C. § 1162(2)(D)(i) (emphasis added). The House Report accompanying the legislation explained that the amendment was:

> intended to carry out the purpose of the health care continuation rules, which *was to reduce the extent to which certain events, such as the loss of one's job, could create a significant gap in health coverage.* Such a gap in coverage occurs when the new employer group health coverage excludes or limits coverage for a preexisting condition that is covered by the continuation coverage.

H.R.Rep. No. 247, 101st Cong., 1st Sess. 1453 (1989), *reprinted in* 1989 U.S.C.C.A.N. 1906, 2923 (emphasis added).

The Fifth Circuit construed the new statute in *Brock v. Primedica, Inc.*, 904 F.2d 295 (5th Cir.1990), and held that a voluntarily terminated employee who had dual coverage under her husband's health plan was not entitled to continue her benefits under COBRA, as long as she did not suffer a gap in the character of her coverage as the result of her termination. That Circuit based its holding both on the legislative history of the statute at issue, and on *dicta* in the *Oakley* opinion expressing concern about the gap in coverage experienced by that plaintiff. *Id.* at 297.

The provision at issue was next construed by the Eleventh Circuit in *National Cos. Health Benefit Plan v. St. Joseph's Hosp. of Atlanta, Inc.*, 929 F.2d 1558 (11th Cir.1991). That Circuit joined the Fifth Circuit in holding that coverage under a preexisting group health plan terminated the plaintiff's former employer's obligation to provide continuation coverage. It rejected the Tenth Circuit's emphasis on the "becomes, after the date of election" language in the statute, and held that the true issue the Court should address was whether Congress' purpose — employee group health coverage — had been served. Thus, under the Eleventh Circuit's reasoning:

> it is immaterial when the employee obtains other group coverage; the only relevant question is when, after the election date, does that other coverage take effect. In the case of an employee covered by preexisting group health coverage, the terminating event occurs immediately; the first time after the election date that the employee becomes covered by a group health plan other than the employer's plan is the moment after the election date. In effect, such an employee is ineligible for continuation coverage.

Id. at 1570.

The Court went on to hold that an employee with dual coverage may be entitled to continuation coverage if there is a significant gap between the coverage afforded under the employer's plan and the coverage afforded under the pre-existing dual plan.

> This is because, in that situation, the employee is not truly "covered" by the preexisting group health plan ... the employee, despite his other coverage, will be liable personally for substantial medical expenses to his and his family's detriment. Denying continuation coverage in that setting would serve to frustrate, rather than foster, Congress' clear intentions.

Id. at 1571.

The Eighth Circuit decided a claim presenting an analogous issue on different grounds in *McGee v. Funderburg*, 17 F.3d 1122 (8th Cir.1994), but *dicta* in that opinion indicates that the Eighth Circuit would have adopted the "significant gap" position of the Fifth and Eleventh Circuits if resolution of the issue had been necessary to its decision.

Finally, in *Lutheran Hospital of Indiana, Inc. v. Business Men's Assurance Co. of Am.*, 51 F.3d 1308 (7th Cir.1995), the Seventh Circuit, in a 2-1 decision, came down on the side of finding a right to continued coverage even if the employee is already covered under a spouse's health plan. In that case, a gap in coverage between the plaintiff's plan and her husband's dual coverage left the plaintiff personally liable for medical bills of $35,000. Although the Court colorably could have ruled in the plaintiff's favor under a "significant gap" analysis, they expressly declined to do so. Like the Tenth Circuit, they focused on the phrase "*becomes, after* the date of election," and held that "an employee loses the right to continuation coverage only if he or she chooses after the election date to accept coverage under another group health plan." *Id.* at 1312.

Judge Coffey, in dissent, argued that the majority opinion "places more importance on grammar and syntax than on Congress' clear intent in enacting COBRA and its subsequent amendments.... COBRA insurance is not, nor has it ever been intended to provide adjunct or double health insurance coverage for those who are covered under another pre-existing policy." *Id.* at 1315 (Coffey, J. dissenting).

District Courts in other jurisdictions have almost universally adopted the view of the Fifth and Eleventh Circuits. *See, e.g., Geissal v. Moore Medical Corp.*, 927 F. Supp. 352, 358 (E.D. Mo. 1996); *Liberty Life Assurance Co. of Boston v. Toys "R" Us, Inc.*, 901 F. Supp. 556, 564 (E.D.N.Y. 1995). This Court agrees with that view. The purpose of statutory interpretation is to effectuate the legislature's intent, not to engage in an academic sentence-parsing exercise. Congressional intent as to this issue is clear: the purpose of the health care continuation rules is "to reduce the extent to which certain events, such as the loss of one's job, could create a significant gap in health coverage." H.R. Rep. No. 247, 101st Cong., 1st Sess. 1453 (1989), *reprinted in* 1989 U.S.C.C.A.N. 1906, 2923. That legislative policy compels the rule that only a beneficiary whose loss of benefits would result in a significant gap in coverage has a right to continuation coverage.

Since Schlett was covered by her husband's health plan, she has a right to continuation coverage only if, because of a significant gap between the coverage afforded under the Avco plan and the coverage afforded under her husband's plan, she is not truly "covered" by the other health plan. The Court, therefore, addresses the issue of whether there is a significant gap between the two plans.

2. Significant Gap

Plaintiffs allege that there is a significant gap in the relative amounts of coverage offered by the two plans. The insurance provided by Schlett's husband's plan left Plaintiffs personally liable for $12,500. Plaintiffs calculate that they would have incurred no personal liability had double coverage been available.

Plaintiffs have not calculated the amount of personal liability they would have incurred under the Avco plan alone. That plan has a family coinsurance limit of $3,000 each year, and Plaintiffs would have been responsible for premiums of $502/month in order to continue their coverage. Therefore, Plaintiffs, had they been allowed to continue their COBRA benefits, would have incurred expenses of $3,000 plus $502 times the number of months Plaintiffs would have paid for the coverage.

The parties have not indicated in their briefs the time periods over which Samuel Schlett incurred his medical bills, except to say that he was hospitalized until at least mid-April, 1994. Since the Court, on a motion for summary judgment, views the evidence in the light most favorable to the nonmovant, it will assume for purposes of this motion that Samuel Schlett incurred all his medical expenses by the end of April, 1994, and that Plaintiffs would not have kept COBRA benefits beyond that time. Under this extremely conservative estimate, Plaintiffs would have been out of pocket about $5,000 for medical expenses.[3]

$3,000	family cap
$2,008	four months of premiums
$5,008	

Thus, the coverage gap between the Avco plan and Schlett's husband's plan can be at most about $7,500.

a. What Constitutes a Significant Gap?

The parties have taken widely divergent positions on the test the Court should use in determining whether the $7,500 gap is significant. Their positions reflect, to some extent, the unsettled nature of this area of law.

The restrictive test uses the literal language of the statute to limit continuation coverage to only those circumstances when the preexisting plan contains a exclusion or limitation with respect to a preexisting condition of the beneficiary,

---

[3] In fact, Schlett indicates in her deposition that she would have continued her COBRA benefits indefinitely. Had the Court used a more realistic eighteen-month premium payment period, the benefit gap would have disappeared entirely.

see 29 U.S.C. § 1162(2)(D). Defendants urge the Court to adopt this test, and then to engraft onto that limitation a further restriction that the gap at issue result from such exclusion or limitation.

The broader test asks only whether the coverage provided by the preexisting health plan is less comprehensive than the coverage provided under the employer's plan, regardless of the reason for the gap. The Court looks not only at preexisting condition exclusions, but also evaluates the benefits offered, including deductibles, co-payments and coverage caps, with a view to the treatment the beneficiary may foreseeably require. This test is based on the policy behind the statute as reflected in its legislative history, and on the principle that where the alternate plan is less comprehensive, "the employee is not truly 'covered' by the preexisting group health plan ... the employee, despite his other coverage, will be liable personally for substantial medical expenses to his and his family's detriment." *National Cos.*, 929 F.2d at 1571. Plaintiffs urge the Court to adopt the broader test, and then to hold, with the benefit of hindsight, that the $7,000 gap in coverage is significant.

Neither of these extremes represents the modern trend in continuation coverage cases. District Courts addressing the issue in recent years have generally followed the broader test, holding that a significant gap exists when coverage is excluded or limited for certain types of conditions or treatments. However, the policy comparison "must be made without benefit of hindsight. The court must look to the difference in the policies at the time of election." *Daniel v. Master Health Plan, Inc.*, 864 F. Supp. 1399, 1406 (S.D. Ga. 1994) (internal quote and citation omitted), *rev'd in part, vacated in part*, 86 F.3d 1169 (11th Cir. 1996).

[T]he Court finds the modern trend to be the better reasoned approach. The position advocated by Defendants suffers from the same defect that led this Court to reject the rule of the Seventh and Tenth Circuits: it invites the Court to engage in syntactic games, rather than to effectuate Congress' intent of reducing the extent to which the loss of a job can create a significant gap in health coverage. The *post hoc* position advocated by Plaintiffs, on the other hand, subjects the employer to an unacceptable degree of uncertainty as to its legal obligations. The employer determines whether it must offer continuation coverage when the original coverage ceases. Whether such determination was reasonable must be adjudged on the basis of the information available to the employer at the time of decision, rather than being subject to *ex post* second-guessing. Accordingly, the Court holds that a significant gap exists when coverage is excluded or limited for certain types of conditions or treatments, when viewed, at the time of election, in light of the benefits offered, preexisting condition exclusions, and the treatment the beneficiary may foreseeably require.

b. *Was There a Significant Gap?*

The Court must determine, therefore, whether Defendants could reasonably have expected a significant gap to result in Plaintiffs' insurance coverage at the time Schlett was converted to part-time status and lost her benefits. In so doing, the Court views the policies as if a choice had to be made in January, 1994, with Schlett knowing that she was pregnant, but not expecting complications or knowing her future medical costs. So viewed, there is no significant gap in the policies. Both policies covered the medical conditions here involved. The co-insurance limits here at issue do not become relevant until medical bills exceed $33,000, far more than the expected cost of the childbirth. And when the cost of premiums is included in the calculus, the numerical gap disappears almost entirely. It could not be said at the time of COBRA coverage election that there was a significant gap in the two coverages.

3. *Exclusion for Preexisting Conditions*

Plaintiffs also allege that they are entitled to continuation coverage on the ground that Mr. Schlett's preexisting plan contained a preexisting conditions limitation, despite the fact that the limitation did not in any way reduce the benefits payable under the plan on the facts of this case. They argue that since the statute at issue terminates the right to continuation coverage only when the employee becomes covered under another "group health plan which does not contain any exclusion or limitation with respect to any preexisting condition of such beneficiary," 29 U.S.C. § 1162(2)(D)(i), that a group health plan with preexisting conditions limitations can never satisfy the demands of the statute, even when the beneficiary's actual medical expenses are covered under the other plan. Plaintiffs' overly literal interpretation of the statutory language flies in the face of both Congressional purpose and common sense. If the Court were to adopt such a rule, virtually no private health plan would pass muster. Congress' clear intent in passing the statute was to avoid significant gaps in health coverage. The Court notes further that the exclusion, under the statutory language, must relate to a preexisting condition *of the beneficiary*; properly understood, the statute describes only specific instances of preexisting conditions exclusions, not preexisting conditions exclusions in general. The Court holds that before a preexisting conditions exclusion creates a right to continuation coverage, it must exclude or limit coverage for the types of condition or treatment for which the employee requires coverage.

4. *Summary*

Plaintiffs have failed to establish that they are entitled to continuation coverage under the COBRA amendments to ERISA. Accordingly, Defendants' motion for summary judgment on Counts III and IV must be granted.

NOTES

1. *A Significant Gap Between the Circuits.* The Seventh Circuit has harshly criticized "significant gap" analysis. In *Lutheran Hosp. v. Business Men's Assurance Co.*, 51 F.3d 1308 (7th Cir. 1995), the Court's legal argument was that the statutory language supports its position that the timing of the coverage under another policy is determinative: "the employee's right to continuation coverage terminates only when he or she *first* becomes, *after* the election date, *covered* by any other group health plan." *Id.* at 1312 (paraphrasing ERISA § 602(2)(D)). In contrast, significant gap analysis "was invented from whole cloth to fill a void resulting from [the Eleventh Circuit's] misreading of the statute." *Id.* at 1314.

On policy, the Seventh Circuit argued that "the terminated employee — who bears the risk and pays the premium — rather than a court [should be permitted to] determine what is or is not comparable coverage." *Id.* In addition, the Court argued that significant gap analysis is unworkable. In determining whether a gap is significant should a court "depend on the ability of the individual to pay or on the overall scale of their medical expenses?" *Id.* If the gap is to be analyzed at the time of the election, rather than *post hoc*:

> How much information about the patient's physical and financial condition is the court to presume of the employer in making this after-the-fact comparison? Is the court to apply an objective or subjective standard, i.e., is it what the employer knew or what a reasonable employer should have known? How does an employer calculate the gap based on whatever information he is presumed to have? Must an employer use an actuary and medical expert to determine the likely effect of policy differences given the patient's physical condition at the time of the qualifying event?

Id. at 1315. What would the Seventh Circuit have thought about the decision in *Schlett* to analyze the gap based on the information available in early January, when the continuation decision was first presented to the employee (and when she did not know of the impending premature birth), rather than in late February, when the election was actually made (and after her baby had been born prematurely)? The Supreme Court may soon resolve the issue. *Geissal v. Moore Med. Corp.*, 114 F.3d 1458 (8th Cir. 1997), *cert. granted*, 118 S. Ct. 877 (1998).

2. *Help from HIPAA?* *Schlett* arose before HIPAA became effective. Would that Act have helped? HIPAA facilitates transitions from one employer to another by limiting the ability of the new employer to impose waiting periods and pre-existing condition limitations. But, as far as we know, Schlett did not have a new job and was not in a position to seek one. HIPAA also deals with the problems of small employers in getting and keeping health insurance for their employees, but that was not at issue here. Finally, HIPAA attempts to facilitate movement from employers to the private insurance market by requiring insurers to offer individual policies to eligible individuals. Schlett, however, was not an "eligible individual" because she had other health insurance coverage. 42 U.S.C. § 300gg-41(b)(2). Do you think *any* other health insurance coverage should permit an insurer to deny an individual policy, or should the courts follow the *Schlett* line of COBRA cases and look to see whether there is a significant gap in the coverage under the two policies?

3. *The Adverse Selection Phenomenon.* Adverse selection is a common and serious obstacle to attempts to improve access to health insurance. Consider COBRA. In opposing passage of COBRA, employers argued that a disproportionate number of persons electing to continue health plan coverage would be high-risk persons. Healthy persons faced with the sudden loss of income from losing their job may be inclined to forego paying for health insurance. Persons who believe they or their family members may need medical assistance will be more likely to continue coverage, even though they have to pay the premiums themselves. Additionally, the stress caused from loss of employment adds to the likelihood that terminated employees will have health problems. In fact, this adverse selection phenomenon materialized under COBRA. One study found that insurance claims from COBRA continuants exceed the premiums they pay by 350%. Thus, on average, COBRA continuants receive approximately $3,500 in benefits for every $1,000 they pay in premiums. Employers and other employees make up the difference. At the margin, some employers may not offer health insurance at all because of the extra costs.

These adverse selection concerns are also present for the "guaranteed issue" portions of HIPAA. Insurers must issue policies to small employers and to individuals, under certain conditions. Consider HIPAA's guarantee of an individual health insurance policy. Individuals who expect high medical costs will be more likely to accept the policies. If that occurs, the pool of people covered by individual policies will become less healthy overall and, hence, the amount of benefits that must be paid will increase. Insurance companies would then charge more for all individual policies to cover the extra costs, which may mean that some "healthy" individuals decide to drop their policies. (HIPAA does not regulate how much insurers can charge for individual policies.) The magnitude of the adverse selection effect, and the extent to which it might increase costs and the number of "voluntarily" uninsured persons, was a major part of the debate on HIPAA.

Evaluating the effects of adverse selection is complex. The effects, however, may be enhanced if employers engage in strategies made more viable by HIPAA. Consider, for example, an employer with a self-insured plan who knows that two employees will have large and long-term health care expenses. The employer can enjoy considerable savings if it can dump the two employees into the market for individual policies. Although dumping is risky, HIPAA makes the strategy more viable, first, because it requires insurers in the individual market to accept the employees (after exhaustion of their COBRA eligibility) and, second, because it would tend to reduce employee resistance. The strategy, however, could produce devastating adverse selection effects in the market for individual policies. *See* American Academy of Actuaries, *Providing Universal Access in a Voluntary Private-Sector Market* 8 (1996) (prices in the individual market could increase by 60% if self-insured groups dumped high-risk employees into the market).

D. HEALTH CARE COVERAGE FOR INDIVIDUALS WITH DISABILITIES

McGANN v. H & H MUSIC CO.

United States Court of Appeals, Fifth Circuit

946 F.2d 401 (1991), *cert. denied,* 506 U.S. 981 (1992)

GARWOOD, CIRCUIT JUDGE:

Plaintiff-appellant John McGann (McGann) filed this suit under section 510 of the Employee Retirement Income Security Act of 1974 (ERISA), against defendants-appellees H & H Music Company (H & H Music) ... and General American Life Insurance Company (General American) claiming that they discriminated against McGann, an employee of H & H Music, by reducing benefits available to H & H Music's group medical plan beneficiaries for treatment for acquired immune deficiency syndrome (AIDS) and related illnesses. The district court granted defendants' motion for summary judgment on the ground that an employer has an absolute right to alter the terms of medical coverage available to plan beneficiaries. We affirm.

McGann, an employee of H & H Music, discovered that he was afflicted with AIDS in December 1987. Soon thereafter, McGann submitted his first claims for reimbursement under H & H Music's group medical plan ... issued by General American, the plan insurer, and informed his employer that he had AIDS. McGann met with officials of H & H Music in March 1988, at which time they discussed McGann's illness. Before the change in the terms of the plan, it provided for lifetime medical benefits of up to $1,000,000 to all employees.

In July 1988, H & H Music informed its employees that, effective August 1, 1988, changes would be made in their medical coverage. These changes included, but were not limited to, limitation of benefits payable for AIDS-related claims to a lifetime maximum of $5,000.[1] No limitation was placed on any other catastrophic illness. H & H Music became self-insured under the new plan and General American became the plan's administrator. By January 1990, McGann had exhausted the $5,000 limit on coverage for his illness.

In August 1989, McGann sued H & H Music ... and General American under section 510 of ERISA, which provides, in part, as follows:

> It shall be unlawful for any person to discharge, fine, suspend, expel, discipline, or discriminate against a participant or beneficiary for exercising any right to which he is entitled under the provisions of an employee benefit plan, ... or for the purpose of interfering with the attainment of any right to which such participant may become entitled under the plan ....

---

[1] Other changes included increased individual and family deductibles, elimination of coverage for chemical dependency treatment, adoption of a preferred provider plan and increased contribution requirements.

McGann claimed that defendants discriminated against him in violation of
both prohibitions of section 510. He claimed that the provision limiting coverage
for AIDS-related expenses was directed specifically at him in retaliation for
exercising his rights under the medical plan and for the purpose of interfering
with his attainment of a right to which he may become entitled under the plan.

Defendants, conceding the factual allegations of McGann's complaint, moved
for summary judgment. These factual allegations include no assertion that the
reduction of AIDS benefits was intended to deny benefits to McGann for any
reason which would not be applicable to other beneficiaries who might then or
thereafter have AIDS, but rather that the reduction was prompted by the knowledge of McGann's illness, and that McGann was the only beneficiary then
known to have AIDS.[4] On June 26, 1990, the district court granted defendants'
motion....

McGann contends that defendants violated both clauses of section 510 by discriminating against him for two purposes: (1) "for exercising any right to which
[the beneficiary] is entitled," and (2) "for the purpose of interfering with the
attainment of any right to which such participant may become entitled." In order
to preclude summary judgment in defendants' favor, McGann must make a
showing sufficient to establish the existence of a genuine issue of material fact
with respect to each material element on which he would carry the burden of
proof at trial.

At trial, McGann would bear the burden of proving the existence of defendants' specific discriminatory intent as an essential element of either of his
claims. Thus, in order to survive summary judgment McGann must make a
showing sufficient to establish that a genuine issue exists as to defendants' specific intent to retaliate against McGann for filing claims for AIDS-related treatment or to interfere with McGann's attainment of any right to which he may
have become entitled.

Although we assume there was a connection between the benefits reduction
and either McGann's filing of claims or his revelations about his illness, there is
nothing in the record to suggest that defendants' motivation was other than as
they asserted, namely to avoid the expense of paying for AIDS treatment (if not,
indeed, also for other treatment), no more for McGann than for any other present
or future plan beneficiary who might suffer from AIDS. McGann concedes that
the reduction in AIDS benefits will apply equally to all employees filing AIDS-
related claims and that the effect of the reduction will not necessarily be felt only
by him. He fails to allege that the coverage reduction was otherwise specifically
intended to deny him particularly medical coverage except "in effect." He does

---

[4] We assume, for purposes of this appeal that the defendants' knowledge of McGann's illness
was a motivating factor in their decision to reduce coverage for AIDS-related expenses, that this
knowledge was obtained either through McGann's filing of claims or his meetings with defendants,
and that McGann was the only plan beneficiary then known to have AIDS.

not challenge defendants' assertion that their purpose in reducing AIDS benefits was to reduce costs.

Furthermore, McGann has failed to adduce evidence of the existence of "any right to which [he] may become entitled under the plan." The right referred to in the second clause of section 510 is not simply any right to which an employee may conceivably become entitled, but rather any right to which an employee may become entitled pursuant to an existing, enforceable obligation assumed by the employer. "Congress viewed [section 510] as a crucial part of ERISA because, without it, employers would be able to circumvent the provision of *promised* benefits." *Ingersoll-Rand Co. v. McClendon,* 498 U.S. 133, 143 (1990) (emphasis added).

McGann's allegations show no *promised* benefit, for there is nothing to indicate that defendants ever promised that the $1,000,000 coverage limit was permanent. The H & H Music plan expressly provides: "Termination or Amendment of Plan: The Plan Sponsor may terminate or amend the Plan at any time or terminate any benefit under the Plan at any time." There is no allegation or evidence that any oral or written representations were made to McGann that the $1,000,000 coverage limit would never be lowered. Defendants broke no promise to McGann. The continued availability of the $1,000,000 limit was not a right to which McGann may have become entitled for the purposes of section 510.

To adopt McGann's contrary construction of this portion of section 510 would mean that an employer could not effectively reserve the right to amend a medical plan to reduce benefits respecting subsequently incurred medical expenses, as H & H Music did here, because such an amendment would obviously have as a purpose preventing participants from attaining the right to such future benefits as they otherwise might do under the existing plan absent the amendment. But this is plainly not the law, and ERISA does not require such "vesting" of the right to a continued level of the same medical benefits once those are ever included in a welfare plan.

McGann appears to contend that the reduction in AIDS benefits alone supports an inference of specific intent to retaliate against him or to interfere with his future exercise of rights under the plan. McGann characterizes as evidence of an individualized intent to discriminate the fact that AIDS was the only catastrophic illness to which the $5,000 limit was applied and the fact that McGann was the only employee known to have AIDS. He contends that if defendants reduced AIDS coverage because they learned of McGann's illness through his exercising of his rights under the plan by filing claims, the coverage reduction therefore could be "retaliation" for McGann's filing of the claims.[6] Under McGann's

---

[6] We assume that discovery of McGann's condition — and realization of the attendant, long-term costs of caring for McGann — did in fact prompt defendants to reconsider the $1,000,000 limit with respect to AIDS-related expenses and to reduce the limit for future such expenses to $5,000.

theory, any reduction in employee benefits would be impermissibly discriminatory if motivated by a desire to avoid the anticipated costs of continuing to provide coverage for a particular beneficiary. McGann would find an implied promise not to discriminate for this purpose; it is the breaking of this promise that McGann appears to contend constitutes interference with a future entitlement.

McGann cites only one case in which a court has ruled that a change in the terms and conditions of an employee-benefits plan could constitute illegal discrimination under section 510.[7] *Vogel v. Independence Federal Sav. Bank,* 728 F. Supp. 1210 (D. Md. 1990). In *Vogel,* however, the plan change at issue resulted in the plaintiff and only the plaintiff being excluded from coverage. McGann asserts that the *Vogel* court rejected the defendant's contention that mere termination of benefits could not constitute unlawful discrimination under section 510, but in fact the court rejected this claim not because it found that mere termination of coverage could constitute discrimination under section 510, but rather because the termination at issue affected only the beneficiary. Nothing in *Vogel* suggests that the change there had the potential to then or thereafter exclude any present or possible future plan beneficiary other than the plaintiff. *Vogel* therefore provides no support for the proposition that the alteration or termination of a medical plan could alone sustain a section 510 claim. Without necessarily approving of the holding in *Vogel,* we note that it is inapplicable to the instant case. The post-August 1, 1988 $5,000 AIDS coverage limit applies to any and all employees.[8]...

McGann's claim cannot be reconciled with the well-settled principle that Congress did not intend that ERISA circumscribe employers' control over the content of benefits plans they offered to their employees. McGann interprets section 510 to prevent an employer from reducing or eliminating coverage for a particular illness in response to the escalating costs of covering an employee suffering from that illness. Such an interpretation would, in effect, change the terms of H

---

[7] Additionally, McGann relies on three cases involving wrongful termination claims brought under section 510. *Fitzgerald v. Codex Corp.,* 882 F.2d 586 (1st Cir. 1989); *Kross v. Western Electric Co.,* 701 F.2d 1238 (7th Cir. 1983); *Folz v. Marriott Corp.,* 594 F. Supp. 1007 (W.D. Mo. 1984). In none of these cases, however, did the employer alter the terms or conditions of the plan at issue. Nor did any one of the three suggest that the changing of the terms of the plan might constitute a violation of section 510.

[8] [T]he district court stated as one ground for its decision that an employer has an absolute right to alter the terms of an employee benefits plan, barring contractual provisions to the contrary. *See Deeming v. American Standard, Inc.,* 905 F.2d 1124, 1127 (7th Cir. 1990) ("allegation that the employer-employee relationship, and not merely the pension plan, was changed in some discriminatory or wrongful way" is "a fundamental prerequisite to a § 510 action"); *Owens v. Storehouse, Inc.,* 773 F. Supp. 416, 418 (N.D. Ga. 1991) (relying on *Deeming* in rejecting claim that employer violated section 510 by reducing AIDS benefits from $1,000,000 to $25,000 under employee health plan on ground that "§ 510 was designed to protect the 'employment relationship,' not the integrity of specific plans.") We do not find it necessary to decide this question.

& H Music's plan. Instead of making the $1,000,000 limit available for medical expenses on an as-incurred basis only as long as the limit remained in effect, the policy would make the limit *permanently* available for all medical expenses as they might thereafter be incurred because of a single event, such as the contracting of AIDS. Under McGann's theory, defendants would be effectively proscribed from reducing coverage for AIDS once McGann had contracted that illness and filed claims for AIDS-related expenses. If a federal court could prevent an employer from reducing an employee's coverage limits for AIDS treatment once that employee contracted AIDS, the boundaries of judicial involvement in the creation, alteration or termination of ERISA plans would be sorely tested....

Proof of defendants' specific intent to discriminate among plan beneficiaries on grounds not proscribed by section 510 does not enable McGann to avoid summary judgment. ERISA does not broadly prevent an employer from "discriminating" in the creation, alteration or termination of employee benefits plans; thus, evidence of such intentional discrimination cannot alone sustain a claim under section 510. That section does not prohibit welfare plan discrimination between or among categories of diseases. Section 510 does not mandate that if some, or most, or virtually all catastrophic illnesses are covered, AIDS (or any other particular catastrophic illness) must be among them. It does not prohibit an employer from electing not to cover or continue to cover AIDS, while covering or continuing to cover other catastrophic illnesses, even though the employer's decision in this respect may stem from some "prejudice" against AIDS or its victims generally. The same, of course, is true of any other disease and its victims. That sort of "discrimination" is simply not addressed by section 510. Under section 510, the asserted discrimination is illegal only if it is motivated by a desire to retaliate against an employee or to deprive an employee of an existing right to which he may become entitled. The district court's decision to grant summary judgment to defendants therefore was proper. Its judgment is accordingly

Affirmed.

NOTES

1. *The Attractions of Self-Insurance.* Subsequent to *McGann,* the state in which the case arose enacted a statute that prohibits insurers from canceling health insurance policies because an insured has been diagnosed as having the HIV virus or AIDS. TEX. INS. CODE ANN. § 3.70-3A. Even if the statute had been in force at the time, however, it would not have helped McGann. When H & H Music learned of McGann's illness, one of its first steps was to self-insure. Presumably, H & H Music did that to make sure that its actions could not be challenged under state laws regulating insurance companies.

2. *What About HIPAA?* HIPAA has provisions prohibiting group health plans, whether insured or self-insured, from discriminating against individual participants and beneficiaries based on health status. ERISA § 702. Would

HIPAA have helped McGann? Probably not. Section 702 prohibits health-status discrimination only with respect to eligibility rules, such as waiting periods before one can join a plan. § 702(a)(1). The Section specifically denies any intent to infringe on an employer's ability to "establish[] limitations or restrictions on the amount, level, extent, or nature of the benefits or coverage for similarly situated individuals enrolled in the plan." § 702(a)(2)(B). *See* House Conf. Rep. No. 104-736, 104th Cong., 2d Sess. 186-87, *reprinted in* 1996 U.S.C.C.A.N. 1990, 1999-2000 (under provision, employer cannot deny benefits to an individual beneficiary if they are available to others, but it can deny benefits to all beneficiaries even if denial has disparate impact on certain individuals).

McGann also arose before the effective date of the Americans With Disabilities Act. Read the EEOC's guidance on application of the ADA to health insurance below and consider how it might have affected McGann's claim.

EEOC INTERIM ENFORCEMENT GUIDANCE ON THE APPLICATION OF THE ADA TO DISABILITY-BASED DISTINCTIONS IN EMPLOYER-PROVIDED HEALTH INSURANCE, EEOC Notice No. 915.002 (1993)

I. INTRODUCTION

The interplay between the nondiscrimination principles of the ADA and employer provided health insurance, which is predicated on the ability to make health-related distinctions, is both unique and complex. This interplay is, undoubtedly, most complex when a health insurance plan contains distinctions that are based on disability. The purpose of this interim guidance is to assist Commission investigators in analyzing ADA charges which allege that a disability-based distinction in the terms or provisions of an employer provided health insurance plan violates the ADA....

II. BACKGROUND AND LEGAL FRAMEWORK

The ADA provides that it is unlawful for an employer to discriminate on the basis of disability against a qualified individual with a disability in regard to "job application procedures, the hiring, advancement, or discharge of employees, employee compensation, job training, and other terms, conditions, and privileges of employment." 42 U.S.C. § 12112(a). Section 1630.4 of the Commission's regulations implementing the employment provisions of the ADA further provides, in pertinent part, that it is unlawful for an employer to discriminate on the basis of disability against a qualified individual with a disability in regard to "[f]ringe benefits available by virtue of employment, whether or not administered by the [employer]." 29 C.F.R. § 1630.4(f). Employee benefit plans, including health insurance plans provided by an employer to its employees, are a fringe benefit available by virtue of employment. Generally speaking, therefore, the ADA prohibits employers from discriminating on the basis of disability in the provision of health insurance to their employees.

Several consequences result from the application of these statutory provisions. First, disability-based insurance plan distinctions are permitted only if they are within the protective ambit of section 501(c) of the ADA. Second, decisions about the employment of an individual with a disability cannot be motivated by concerns about the impact of the individual's disability on the employer's health insurance plan. Third, employees with disabilities must be accorded "equal access" to whatever health insurance the employer provides to employees without disabilities. Fourth, in view of the statute's "association provision," it would violate the ADA for an employer to make an employment decision about any person, whether or not that person has a disability, because of concerns about the impact on the health insurance plan of the disability of someone else with whom that person has a relationship....

III. DISABILITY-BASED DISTINCTIONS

A. Framework of Analysis

Whenever it is alleged that a health-related term or provision of an employer provided health insurance plan violates the ADA, the first issue is whether the challenged term or provision is, in fact, a disability-based distinction. If the Commission determines that a challenged health insurance plan term or provision is a disability-based distinction, the respondent will be required to prove that that disability-based distinction is within the protective ambit of section 501(c) of the ADA.

In pertinent part, section 501(c) permits employers, insurers, and plan administrators to establish and/or observe the terms of an insured health insurance plan that is "bona fide," based on "underwriting risks, classifying risks, or administering such risks that are based on or not inconsistent with State law," and that is not being used as a "subterfuge" to evade the purposes of the ADA. Section 501(c) likewise permits employers, insurers, and plan administrators to establish and/or observe the terms of a "bona fide" self-insured health insurance plan that is not used as a "subterfuge."

Consequently, if the Commission determines that the challenged term or provision is a disability-based distinction, the respondent will be required to prove that: 1) the health insurance plan is either a bona fide insured health insurance plan that is not inconsistent with state law, or a bona fide self-insured health insurance plan; and 2) the challenged disability-based distinction is not being used as a subterfuge. If the respondent so demonstrates, the Commission will conclude that the challenged disability-based distinction is within the protective ambit of section 501(c) and does not violate the ADA. If, on the other hand, the respondent is unable to make this two-pronged demonstration, the Commission will conclude that the respondent has violated the ADA.

B. What Is a Disability-Based Distinction?

It is important to note that not all health-related plan distinctions discriminate on the basis of disability. Insurance distinctions that are not based on disability, and that are applied equally to all insured employees, do not discriminate on the basis of disability and so do not violate the ADA.

For example, a feature of some employer provided health insurance plans is a distinction between the benefits provided for the treatment of physical conditions on the one hand, and the benefits provided for the treatment of "mental/nervous" conditions on the other. Typically, a lower level of benefits is provided for the treatment of mental/nervous conditions than is provided for the treatment of physical conditions. Similarly, some health insurance plans provide fewer benefits for "eye care" than for other physical conditions. Such broad distinctions, which apply to the treatment of a multitude of dissimilar conditions and which constrain individuals both with and without disabilities, are not distinctions based on disability. Consequently, although such distinctions may have a greater impact on certain individuals with disabilities, they do not intentionally discriminate on the basis of disability and do not violate the ADA.

Blanket pre-existing condition clauses that exclude from the coverage of a health insurance plan the treatment of conditions that pre-date an individual's eligibility for benefits under that plan also are not distinctions based on disability, and do not violate the ADA. Universal limits or exclusions from coverage of all experimental drugs and/or treatments, or of all "elective surgery," are likewise not insurance distinctions based on disability. Similarly, coverage limits on medical procedures that are not exclusively, or nearly exclusively, utilized for the treatment of a particular disability are not distinctions based on disability. Thus, for example, it would not violate the ADA for an employer to limit the number of blood transfusions or X-rays that it will pay for, even though this may have an adverse effect on individuals with certain disabilities.

> Example 1. The R Company health insurance plan limits the benefits provided for the treatment of any physical conditions to a maximum of $25,000 per year. CP, an employee of R, files a charge of discrimination alleging that the $25,000 cap violates the ADA because it is insufficient to cover the cost of treatment for her cancer. The $25,000 cap does not single out a specific disability, discrete group of disabilities, or disability in general. It is therefore not a disability-based distinction. If it is applied equally to all insured employees, it does not violate the ADA.

In contrast, however, health-related insurance distinctions that are based on disability may violate the ADA. A term or provision is "disability-based" if it singles out a particular disability (e.g., deafness, AIDS, schizophrenia), a discrete group of disabilities (e.g., cancers, muscular dystrophies, kidney diseases), or disability in general (e.g., non-coverage of all conditions that substantially limit a major life activity).

As previously noted, employers may establish and/or observe the terms and provisions of a bona fide benefit plan, including terms or provisions based on disability, that are not a "subterfuge to evade the purposes" of the ADA. Such terms and provisions do not violate the ADA. However, disability-based insurance distinctions that are a "subterfuge" do intentionally discriminate on the basis of disability and so violate the ADA.

Example 2. R Company's new self-insured health insurance plan caps benefits for the treatment of all physical conditions, except AIDS, at $100,000 per year. The treatment of AIDS is capped at $5,000 per year. CP, an employee with AIDS enrolled in the health insurance plan, files a charge alleging that the lower AIDS cap violates the ADA. The lower AIDS cap is a disability-based distinction. Accordingly, if R is unable to demonstrate that its health insurance plan is bona fide and that the AIDS cap is not a subterfuge, a violation of the ADA will be found.

Example 3. R Company has a health insurance plan that excludes from coverage treatment for any pre-existing blood disorders for a period of 18 months, but does not exclude the treatment of any other pre-existing conditions.[*] R's pre-existing condition clause only excludes treatment for a discrete group of related disabilities, e.g., hemophilia, leukemia, and is thus a disability-based distinction. CP, an individual with acute leukemia who recently joined R Company and enrolled in its health insurance plan, files a charge of discrimination alleging that the disability-based pre-existing condition clause violates the ADA. If R is unable to demonstrate that its health insurance plan is bona fide and that the disability-specific pre-existing condition clause is not a subterfuge, a violation of the ADA will be found.

It should be noted that the ADA does not provide a "safe harbor" for health insurance plans that were adopted prior to its July 26, 1990 enactment. As the Senate Report states, subterfuge is to be determined "regardless of the date an insurance or employer benefit plan was adopted." Consequently, the challenged disability-based terms and provisions of a pre-ADA health insurance plan will be scrutinized under the same subterfuge standard as are the challenged disability-based terms, provisions, and conditions of post-ADA health insurance plans.

C. The Respondent's Burden of Proof

Once the Commission has determined that a challenged health insurance term or provision constitutes a disability-based distinction, the respondent must prove that the health insurance plan is either a bona fide insured plan that is not inconsistent with state law, or a bona fide self-insured plan. The respondent must also prove that the challenged disability-based distinction is not being used as a sub-

---

[*] This guidance was issued before HIPAA, which generally limits pre-existing condition exclusions to twelve months.

terfuge. Requiring the respondent to bear this burden of proving entitlement to the protection of section 501(c) is consistent with the well-established principle that the burden of proof should rest with the party who has the greatest access to the relevant facts. In the health insurance context, it is the respondent employer (and/or the employer's insurer, if any) who has control of the risk assessment, actuarial, and/or claims data relied upon in adopting the challenged disability-based distinction. Charging party employees have no access to such data, and, generally speaking, have no information about the employer provided health insurance plan beyond that contained in the employer provided health insurance plan description. Consequently, it is the employer who should bear the burden of proving that the challenged disability-based insurance distinction is within the protective ambit of section 501(c).

1. The Health Insurance Plan Is "Bona Fide" and Consistent with Applicable Law

In order to gain the protection of section 501(c) for a challenged disability-based insurance distinction, the respondent must first prove that the health insurance plan in which the challenged distinction is contained is either a bona fide insured health insurance plan that is not inconsistent with state law, or a bona fide self-insured health insurance plan. If the health insurance plan is an insured plan, the respondent will be able to satisfy this requirement by proving that: 1) the health insurance plan is bona fide in that it exists and pays benefits, and its terms have been accurately communicated to eligible employees; and 2) the health insurance plan's terms are not inconsistent with applicable state law as interpreted by the appropriate state authorities. If the health insurance plan is a self-insured plan, the respondent will only be required to prove that the health insurance plan is bona fide in that it exists and pays benefits, and that its terms have been accurately communicated to covered employees.

2. The Disability-Based Distinction Is Not a Subterfuge

The second demonstration that the respondent must make in order to gain the protection of section 501(c) is that the challenged disability-based distinction is not a subterfuge to evade the purposes of the ADA. "Subterfuge" refers to disability-based disparate treatment that is not justified by the risks or costs associated with the disability. Whether a particular challenged disability-based insurance distinction is being used as a subterfuge will be determined on a case by case basis, considering the totality of the circumstances.

The respondent can prove that a challenged disability-based insurance distinction is not a subterfuge in several ways. A non-exclusive list of potential business/insurance justifications follows.

  a. The respondent may prove that it has not engaged in the disability-based disparate treatment alleged. For example, where a charging party has alleged that a benefit cap of a particular catastrophic disability is discriminatory, the respondent may prove that its health insurance plan actually treats all similarly catastrophic conditions in the same way.

b. The respondent may prove that the disparate treatment is justified by legitimate actuarial data, or by actual or reasonably anticipated experience, and that conditions with comparable actuarial data and/or experience are treated in the same fashion. In other words, the respondent may prove that the disability-based disparate treatment is attributable to the application of legitimate risk classification and underwriting procedures to the increased risks (and thus increased cost to the health insurance plan) of the disability, and not to the disability per se.

c. The respondent may prove that the disparate treatment is necessary (i.e., that there is no nondisability-based health insurance plan change that could be made) to ensure that the challenged health insurance plan satisfies the commonly accepted or legally required standards for the fiscal soundness of such an insurance plan. The respondent, for example, may prove that it limited coverage for the treatment of a discrete group of disabilities because continued unlimited coverage would have been so expensive as to cause the health insurance plan to become financially insolvent, and there was no nondisability-based health insurance plan alteration that would have avoided insolvency.

d. The respondent may prove that the challenged insurance practice or activity is necessary (i.e., that there is no nondisability-based change that could be made) to prevent the occurrence of an unacceptable change either in the coverage of the health insurance plan, or in the premiums charged for the health insurance plan. An "unacceptable" change is a drastic increase in premium payments (or in co-payments or deductibles), or a drastic alteration to the scope of coverage or level of benefits provided, that would: 1) make the health insurance plan effectively unavailable to a significant number of other employees, 2) make the health insurance plan so unattractive as to result in significant adverse selection or 3) make the health insurance plan so unattractive that the employer cannot compete in recruiting and maintaining qualified workers due to the superiority of health insurance plans offered by other employers in the community.

e. Where the charging party is challenging the respondent's denial of coverage for a disability-specific treatment, the respondent may prove that this treatment does not provide any benefit (i.e., has no medical value). The respondent, in other words, may prove by reliable scientific evidence that the disability-specific treatment does not cure the condition, slow the degeneration/deterioration or harm attributable to the condition, alleviate the symptoms of the condition, or maintain the current health status of individuals with the disability who receive the treatment....

NOTES

1. *Disability-Based Distinctions*. How helpful do you think the EEOC Guidance is in defining disability-based distinctions? The Guidance says that distinctions based on "discrete groups of disabilities" (such as cancer) are disability based, but "broad" distinctions, which apply to a multitude of dissimilar conditions and which constrain individuals both with and without disabilities (such as mental/nervous conditions), are not disability based. Consider the following:

A. Why doesn't cancer fit into the second category? The term certainly seems to cover a "multitude of dissimilar conditions." Some cancers seem genetic in origin, others environmental. Some cancers manifest themselves in immediate tumor growth, others do not. Doctors who are qualified to provide care for some types of cancers would be quite unqualified to provide care for other types. In addition, many people with cancer do not fit the definition of an individual with disabilities; many men, for example, have prostate cancer for decades without knowing it.

B. How would the EEOC's guidelines apply to an employer that excluded from coverage all immune system disorders (including AIDS)? Would that be a disability-based distinction because it refers to a "discrete group of disabilities"? Or is it a "broad" distinction more analogous to an exclusion for mental/nervous conditions?

2. *The Employer Defenses are Too Permissive*. H & H Music may have been able to prove that its cap on AIDS coverage was not a subterfuge. When *McGann* began, H & H Music was a small employer with an insured plan; subsequently, it converted to a self-insured plan. The company may have attempted to defend under a couple of provisions of the EEOC guidelines, for example, that the change in the plan was necessary to ensure the continued fiscal soundness of the plan or to prevent an unacceptable change in the plan's cost and/or coverage. Would HIPAA have affected H & H Music's ability to establish these defenses? *See* 42 U.S.C. §§ 300gg-11 to 300gg-12 (HIPAA requires insurers in the small-employer market to offer and renew policies, but does not regulate premiums).

3. *The Employer Defenses are Too Restrictive*. High-dose chemotherapy with autologous bone marrow transplant is an accepted treatment for certain cancers, but has only recently been introduced to treat solid tumors, such as breast cancer. It is also very expensive. Can an employer's health plan exclude from coverage the use of this treatment for solid tumors? *Compare Henderson v. Bodine Aluminum, Inc.*, 70 F.3d 958 (8th Cir. 1995) (denial of treatment violated ADA) *with Hilliard v. Bellsouth Med. Assistance Plan*, 918 F. Supp. 1016 (S.D. Miss. 1995) (denial of treatment did not violate ADA). Could an employer defend by demonstrating that the treatment does not provide any benefit? Could any employer ever make that demonstration for an experimental treatment?

E. RETIREE HEALTH CARE

The cost of retiree health benefits has increased faster than the cost of health benefits generally, especially in the older "rust belt" industries, for a number of reasons: the proportion of retired to active employees has increased; the trend towards early retirement increased the proportion of retired employees who were not covered by Medicare; and changes in Medicare coverage shifted costs to corporate plans. Stephen R. Miller et al., *Postretirement Medical Benefit Plans: An Analysis of Funding and Termination Issues,* 12 J. PENSION PLAN. & COMPLIANCE 193 (1986). Employers have reacted to these increasing costs by attempting to reduce their liability for retiree health benefits. Those attempts have not gone unchallenged.

SPRAGUE v. GENERAL MOTORS CORP.

United States Court of Appeals, Sixth Circuit (*en banc*)
133 F.3d 388 (1998)

DAVID A. NELSON, Circuit Judge.

In 1961 General Motors began paying part of the cost of health insurance for its salaried retirees[1] and their surviving spouses. Three years later GM assumed the full cost of basic health insurance for its salaried retirees, and in 1968 it extended this benefit to surviving spouses as well. (In the interest of simplicity, further reference to surviving spouses will generally be omitted.)...

Prior to 1985 the health care benefits were provided through arrangements with private insurers. The insurers issued each covered person a certificate of insurance describing the terms and conditions of the underlying policy.

GM became fully self-insured in 1985. At that time the company prepared a document, entitled "The General Motors Health Care Insurance Program for Salaried Employees," that set forth the terms and conditions of GM's self-insured health care program. The district court found that this document, together with subsequent documents announcing changes in coverage, comprised GM's health care benefits plan from and after 1985.[2]...

GM has long made it a practice to inform its salaried employees and retirees of their health care coverage by providing them booklets containing summaries of the company's health insurance policies and programs. Prior to 1974 GM put out

---

[1] As used here, the term "salaried retirees" signifies non-union GM employees who had been receiving salaries, rather than hourly wages, at the time they retired. All of the plaintiffs are either salaried retirees or the surviving spouses of salaried retirees.

[2] Although the content of the plan was not static, this fact has no relevance here; the district court found, and we agree, that all versions clearly reserved to GM the right of amendment or termination. We shall therefore refer to a single GM "plan," recognizing that this is something of a simplification.

a booklet entitled "The GM Insurance Program for Salaried Employees." After ERISA took effect in 1974 the booklet became "Highlights of Your GM Benefits." Beginning in 1977 GM also issued a booklet called "Your Benefits in Retirement." Each of these publications went through a series of different editions.

A number of the booklets contained language informing plan participants that the health care plan called for GM to pay health insurance costs during retirement:

* "If you retire ... and are eligible to receive retirement benefits under the provisions of the GM Retirement Program for Salaried Employees, you may keep your basic hospital, surgical and medical expense coverages in effect.... GM will pay the full monthly premium or subscription charge for such coverages." The General Motors Insurance Program for Salaried Employees (1968). The 1971 version was nearly identical.

* "Hospital-Medical Coverages: Your basic coverages will be provided at Corporation expense for your lifetime...." Highlights of Your GM Benefits (1974).

* "Your basic health care coverages will be provided at GM's expense for your lifetime...." Your Benefits in Retirement (1977).

* "General Motors pays the full cost of any basic health care coverages that are continued for most retired employees and for eligible surviving spouses and children of deceased retirees." Your Benefits in Retirement (1977).

However, most of the booklets also put plan participants on notice of GM's right to change or terminate the health care plan at any time:

* "General Motors believes wholeheartedly in this Insurance Program for GM men and women, and expects to continue the Program indefinitely. However, GM reserves the right to modify, revoke, suspend, terminate, or change the Program, in whole or in part, at any time...." The General Motors Insurance Program for Salaried Employees (1965, 1968, and 1971).

* "General Motors Corporation reserves the right to amend, change or terminate the Plans and Programs described in this booklet." Your GM Benefits (1985).

* "The Corporation reserves the right to amend, modify, suspend, or terminate its benefit Plans or Programs by action of its Board of Directors." Your Benefits in Retirement (1985).

For more than two decades GM has engaged in systematic reductions in the size of its salaried workforce. In this connection the company has launched special early retirement programs designed to induce salaried workers to retire before reaching normal retirement age. The inducements have included, among other things, offers to provide pension benefits to early retirees at levels not reduced to reflect the longer periods over which such benefits can be expected to accrue. Some of the early retirement programs were company-wide initiatives, while others applied to a particular plant, division, or group of plants or divisions.

Salaried employees who accepted early retirement were often asked to sign documents evincing their acceptance of the terms of the particular program under which they were retiring. From 1974 until 1984 GM utilized a so-called "short form" statement of acceptance.... In 1984 GM adopted the "long form" statement of acceptance.... Both forms had numerous variants, but all stated in essence that the early retiree had "reviewed the benefits applicable" and "accept[ed] them." In return for such benefits, the early retirees agreed to waive certain causes of action they might have had against GM.

Not all early retirees signed a statement of acceptance. Some merely signed a "statement of intent" to retire, while others apparently signed nothing.

In the course of explaining its special early retirement programs, GM made numerous oral and written representations about the health care benefits available to early retirees. Most of the early retirees participated in exit interviews where a particular early retirement program was described. These interviews were conducted by plant supervisors, members of the benefits staff, and others. Many of the early retirees also received documents summarizing applicable retirement benefits. These summaries often informed retirees that their health insurance would be paid by GM for life. Again, however, such documents sometimes put the retirees on notice of GM's right to change benefits. Certain summaries advised, for example, that "General Motors Corp. reserves the right to amend, change or terminate the Programs described."

Some early retirees received individualized letters about early retirement programs. And a small number of early retirees explicitly asked GM representatives about future changes to health care benefits. The answers given, it seems, were accurate — benefits could be changed in the future.

Late in 1987 GM announced that early in the following year significant changes would become effective in health care coverage for both salaried employees and retirees. In the case of plan participants who elected traditional fee-for-service coverage, the changes included an annual deductible of $200 for individuals and $250 for families. Fee-for-service participants were required to make 20% co-payments on medical services, up to an annual maximum co-payment of $500. By reason of these two changes, fee-for-service plan participants could find themselves responsible for paying as much as $700 a year (with individual coverage) or $750 (with family coverage) that would previously have been paid by GM....

The present lawsuit was commenced in August of 1989 by 114 salaried retirees who challenged the legality of the changes to the health care plan that took effect in 1988. The main thrust of the plaintiffs' complaint was that GM had bound itself to provide salaried retirees and their spouses basic health coverage for life, entirely at GM's expense. The right to such coverage vested upon retirement, according to the plaintiffs, so the coverage could never be changed or revoked.

Seven separate causes of action were pleaded: (1) failure to maintain the written plan documentation required by ERISA; (2) violation of the health care plan; (3) breach of fiduciary duty; (4) breach of contract; (5) equitable or promissory estoppel; (6) failure to supply requested information; and (7) failure to comply with the requirements for summary plan descriptions. The named plaintiffs purported to represent a class of some 84,000 similarly-situated individuals, about 50,000 of whom were early retirees and 34,000 of whom were general retirees.[3]

The district court entered partial summary judgment in favor of GM after making the following rulings:

* the plaintiffs' benefits did not vest under the terms of the welfare plan, *Sprague v. General Motors Corp.*, 768 F. Supp. 605, 610-11 (E.D. Mich. 1991) ("*Sprague I*");

* the summary plan descriptions generally put the plaintiffs on notice of GM's right to amend or terminate the plan, *id.*; and

* the plaintiffs had no claim for breach of fiduciary duty, GM not having acted in a fiduciary capacity when amending the plan, *id.* at 612....

Following a lengthy bench trial, the district court made these rulings on the merits:

* GM was found to have made a bilateral contract with each early retiree to vest health care benefits at retirement, *Sprague v. General Motors Corp.*, 843 F. Supp. 266, 299 (E.D. Mich. 1994) ("*Sprague II*");

* these bilateral contracts were held to be enforceable as ERISA plans or as modifications to the general plan, *id.*;

---

[3] The term "early retirees" refers to salaried, non-union employees who agreed to retire between 1974 and 1988 under one of GM's special early retirement programs. The term "general retirees" refers to salaried, non-union employees who "voluntarily retired, either at age 65 or before, and were able to do so without GM's consent, pursuant to the terms of the General Motors Retirement Program for Salaried Employees."

* GM was held not to be estopped from changing the health care benefits of the general retirees, to whom it made no promises to vest benefits, *Sprague v. General Motors Corp.*, 857 F. Supp. 1182, 1188-89 (E.D. Mich. 1994) ("*Sprague III*");

* GM was held to be estopped from changing the health care benefits of the early retirees based on the oral and written representations it made to them, *id.* at 1190-92; and

* GM was enjoined during this appeal from making further adverse changes to the health care benefits of the prevailing plaintiffs, *id.* at 1192-93....

III

A

The plaintiffs' first theory of recovery is that GM committed a breach of the terms of the plan documents when it implemented the changes in 1988. Under the plan documents, according to the plaintiffs, their health care benefits were vested — and having vested, the benefits could not be altered without the plaintiffs' consent....

ERISA distinguishes between pension plans and welfare plans.... Because the plan in question here provided health insurance to its participants, it was a welfare plan.

Welfare plans are specifically exempted from vesting requirements to which pension plans are subject. 29 U.S.C. § 1051(1). Therefore, employers "are generally free under ERISA, for any reason at any time, to adopt, modify, or terminate welfare plans." *Curtiss-Wright Corp. v. Schoonejongen*, 514 U.S. 73, 78 (1995). Employers may vest welfare benefits if they choose to do so, however. *See Inter-Modal Rail Employees Ass'n v. Atchison, Topeka & Santa Fe Ry. Co.*, 117 S. Ct. 1513, 1516 (1997) (an employer may "contractually cede[ ] its freedom" not to vest benefits).

To vest benefits is to render them forever unalterable. Because vesting of welfare plan benefits is not required by law, an employer's commitment to vest such benefits is not to be inferred lightly; the intent to vest "must be found in the plan documents and must be stated in clear and express language." *Wise v. El Paso Natural Gas Co.*, 986 F.2d 929, 937 (5th Cir.), *cert. denied*, 510 U.S. 870 (1993). It is the plaintiffs' burden to prove GM's intent to vest.

The plaintiffs have not seriously disputed that the plan itself permitted GM to amend or terminate benefits. Instead the plaintiffs focus on the plan summaries, which must "be written in a manner calculated to be understood by the average plan participant, and shall be sufficiently accurate and comprehensive to reasonably apprise such participants and beneficiaries of their rights and obligations under the plan." 29 U.S.C. § 1022(a)(1).

In *Edwards v. State Farm Mut. Auto. Ins. Co.*, 851 F.2d 134, 136 (6th Cir. 1988), we held that "statements in a summary plan are binding and if such

statements conflict with those in the plan itself, the summary shall govern."
Application of the *Edwards* principle, the plaintiffs say, compels a judgment in
their favor. We disagree.

The principle announced in *Edwards* was based on ERISA's directive that
plan administrators furnish summary plan descriptions to participants and beneficiaries. This requirement did not become generally effective until 1977. We
could not hold GM liable for violations of a statutory requirement based on
actions taken prior to the effective date of that requirement. If the plaintiffs have
any cause of action based on GM's pre-1977 summaries, it is probably not one
based on ERISA. It appears likely that only the booklets issued in 1977 and
thereafter are relevant to the inquiry. We shall assume that all of the booklets
issued in 1977 or later were intended to serve as summary plan descriptions.

Most of the summary plan descriptions unambiguously reserved GM's right to
amend or terminate the plan. For example:

* "General Motors Corporation reserves the right to amend, change or terminate the Plans and Programs described in this booklet." Your GM Benefits
  (1984).

* "The Corporation reserves the right to amend, modify, suspend, or terminate
  its benefit Plans or Programs by action of its Board of Directors." Your
  Benefits in Retirement (1985).

The plaintiffs counter by pointing out that these summaries also told them that
their health coverage would be paid "at no cost to" them and "for [their] lifetime[s]." Such language, they argue, created an ambiguity within the summaries
that must be resolved by extrinsic evidence.

We have rejected this argument in the past, and we reject it again now. We see
no ambiguity in a summary plan description that tells participants both that the
terms of the current plan entitle them to health insurance at no cost throughout
retirement and that the terms of the current plan are subject to change.

> "To read this summary as saying that the plan can never be changed in such
> a way as to mandate retiree contributions for continued medical coverage is
> to read into the summary something its authors did not put there (a promise
> to provide lifetime 'paid up' medical insurance), while reading out of the
> summary something that clearly was put there (an express reservation of
> right to change the plan)." *Musto* [*v. American Gen. Corp.*], 861 F.2d [897,]
> 906 [(6th Cir. 1988)].

As the Third Circuit explained in a similar case, "the promise made to retirees
was a qualified one: the promise was that retiree medical benefits were for life
provided the company chose not to terminate the plans, pursuant to clauses that
preserved the company's right to terminate the plan under which those benefits
are provided." *Unisys Corp.* [*Retiree Med. Benefits ERISA Litig.*], 58 F.3d [896,]
904 n. 12 [(3rd Cir. 1995)].

Not all of the summaries clearly stated that GM could amend or terminate the plan. But the failure to allude to this power in some of the booklets did not prejudice GM's right, clearly stated in the plan itself, to change the plan's terms.

In the first place, the principle announced in *Edwards* does not apply to silence. An omission from the summary plan description does not, by negative implication, alter the terms of the plan itself. The reason is obvious: by definition, a summary will not include every detail of the thing it summarizes. GM's failure to include in some summaries a notice of its right to change the plan does not trump the clearly-stated right to do so in the plan itself.

In the second place, GM was not required to disclose in the summary plan descriptions that the plaintiffs' benefits were not vested.

ERISA specifies in detail the information that every summary plan description "shall contain." *See* 29 U.S.C. § 1022(b). Among the items a summary must include is "a description of the provisions providing for nonforfeitable pension benefits." Despite having required that summaries inform plan participants about the vesting of benefits under pension plans, Congress did not require such information for welfare plans; neither did the Department of Labor in its ERISA reporting and disclosure regulations. *See* 29 C.F.R. § 2520.102-3(n) (summary plan descriptions shall contain, "*[i]n the case of an employee pension benefit plan*, a description and explanation of the plan provisions for ... vesting") (emphasis added). The absence of a similar requirement for welfare plans was no mistake. ERISA, after all, is a "comprehensive and reticulated statute," and the reporting and disclosure requirements are themselves "comprehensive." *Curtiss-Wright*, 514 U.S. at 83. We decline to apply the judge-made rule of *Edwards* in such a way as to augment the detailed disclosure provisions of the statute.

Neither the GM plan itself nor any of the various summaries of the plan states or even implies that the plaintiffs' benefits were vested. Accordingly, we conclude that the district court acted correctly in granting summary judgment to GM on the plaintiffs' claim that the company violated the terms of its plan.

<h1 style="text-align:center">B</h1>

We turn next to the theory that GM bilaterally contracted with each early retiree to vest benefits. All of the early retirees took retirement under one of the special early retirement programs offered by GM between 1974 and 1988. The early retirees argue that, as the district court held, the statements, promises, and representations GM made to them in connection with these programs, and the documents that they signed, created binding bilateral contracts. The alleged contracts, which supposedly provided for vesting of the early retirees' health care benefits, are said to be enforceable either as modifications to the general plan, or as ERISA plans themselves, or as a matter of federal common law.

ERISA "has an elaborate scheme in place for beneficiaries to learn their rights and obligations at any time, a scheme that is built around reliance on the face of written plan documents." *Curtiss-Wright*, 514 U.S. at 83. To implement this scheme, ERISA requires that every plan "shall be established and maintained pursuant to a written instrument." 29 U.S.C. § 1102(a)(1). ERISA also requires, as we have said, a written summary plan description that will "reasonably apprise ... participants and beneficiaries of their rights and obligations under the plan." 29 U.S.C. § 1022(a).

The writing requirement ensures that "every employee may, on examining the plan documents, determine exactly what his rights and obligations are under the plan." *Curtiss-Wright*, 514 U.S. at 83. And the requirement lends predictability and certainty to employee benefit plans. This serves the interests of both employers and employees.

Our court has consistently refused to recognize oral modifications to written plan documents. "[W]e are quite certain," we have explained, "that Congress, in passing ERISA, did not intend that participants in employee benefit plans should be left to the uncertainties of oral communications in finding out precisely what rights they were given under their plan." *Musto*, 861 F.2d at 909-10. Therefore, the "clear terms of a written employee benefit plan may not be modified or superseded by oral undertakings on the part of the employer." *Id.* at 910. The plaintiffs may not invoke oral statements by GM personnel in order to modify the terms of the written plan.

Neither can we accept the argument that the plan was modified or superseded either by the written "statements of acceptance" signed by some of the named plaintiffs or by the written representations received by some from GM.... None of GM's representations suggested that the plan was being modified. The statements of acceptance, moreover, merely said that the employee "ha[d] reviewed the benefits applicable to [him]" and "accept[ed] them." Far from modifying the terms of the welfare plan, it seems to us, this language incorporated the plan's terms.

The statements of acceptance were not ERISA plans themselves. Every ERISA plan must specify a funding mechanism, must allocate operational and administrative responsibilities, and must state how payments are made to and from the plan. 29 U.S.C. § 1102(b)(1)-(2), (4). While it is at least conceivable that an enforceable ERISA plan might not meet all of these requirements, the alleged bilateral contracts at issue here met none of them. The "statements of acceptance" simply did not purport to be ERISA plans, and we decline to treat them as such.

For us to sanction informal "plans" or plan "amendments" — whether oral or written — would leave the law of employee benefits in a state of uncertainty and would create disincentives for employers to offer benefits in the first place. Such a result is not in the interests of employees generally, and it is certainly not compatible with the goals of ERISA. "Altering a welfare plan on the basis of non-plan documents and communications, absent a particularized showing of conduct tantamount to fraud, would undermine ERISA."

IV

The plaintiffs argue that GM is estopped from enforcing the terms of the written plan against them. After the bench trial, the district court found that GM made no misleading representations to the general retirees. *Sprague III*, 857 F. Supp. at 1188-89. That finding appears unassailable. As to the early retirees, however, the district court ruled that GM was estopped from enforcing the plan because it misrepresented the plan's terms. *Id.* at 1189-92. In this, we believe, the court erred as a matter of law.

We have held that equitable estoppel may be a viable theory in ERISA cases, at least in regard to welfare plans. The elements of an equitable estoppel claim ... are as follows: (1) there must be conduct or language amounting to a representation of material fact; (2) the party to be estopped must be aware of the true facts; (3) the party to be estopped must intend that the representation be acted on, or the party asserting the estoppel must reasonably believe that the party to be estopped so intends; (4) the party asserting the estoppel must be unaware of the true facts; and (5) the party asserting the estoppel must reasonably or justifiably rely on the representation to his detriment.

Principles of estoppel, however, cannot be applied to vary the terms of unambiguous plan documents; estoppel can only be invoked in the context of ambiguous plan provisions. There are at least two reasons for this. First, as we have seen, estoppel requires reasonable or justifiable reliance by the party asserting the estoppel. That party's reliance can seldom, if ever, be reasonable or justifiable if it is inconsistent with the clear and unambiguous terms of plan documents available to or furnished to the party. Second, to allow estoppel to override the clear terms of plan documents would be to enforce something other than the plan documents themselves. That would not be consistent with ERISA.

In the case at bar, we conclude that the plaintiffs' estoppel claims fail as a matter of law. As we have said, GM's plan and most of the summary plan descriptions issued to the plaintiffs over the years unambiguously reserved to GM the right to amend or terminate the plan. In the face of GM's clearly-stated right to amend — a right contained in the plan to which the plaintiffs had access and in many of the summaries they were given — reliance on statements allegedly suggesting the contrary was not, and could not be, reasonable or justifiable, especially when GM never told the plaintiffs that their benefits were vested or fully paid-up.

V

The last theory of recovery, applicable only to the early retirees, is that GM was in breach of the fiduciary duty it owed such retirees as administrator of their welfare plan. The district court dismissed this claim in its entirety, holding that an employer is not a fiduciary when it amends or terminates a plan. *Sprague I,* 768 F. Supp. at 612.

The court's holding was correct as far as it went. GM did not act as a fiduciary in deciding to change its health insurance policies. The plaintiffs argue, however, that the district court misconstrued the breadth of their fiduciary duty claim. The claim, they say, encompassed all of GM's oral and written representations to them in connection with the special early retirement programs. We agree with this interpretation of the complaint....

In *Varity Corp. v. Howe*, 516 U.S. 489 (1996), the Supreme Court held that an employer acted in a fiduciary capacity when making misrepresentations to its employees about their benefit plan. The employer in that case created a new subsidiary to enable the parent to shed some of its debt, knowing that the subsidiary might well fail. The employer induced employees to transfer to the new subsidiary with deliberately misleading assurances that the new subsidiary would be financially successful and that employee benefits plan would be financially sound and would not change.

The Court held that the employer, in making these misrepresentations about the status of the plan, was exercising "discretionary authority" in connection with the plan's "management" or "administration," as those terms are used in § 1002(21)(A). Applying the law of trusts, which it said would inform the fiduciary inquiry, the Court stated that "conveying information about the likely future of plan benefits" was a discretionary act of plan administration. The employer therefore acted in a fiduciary capacity when it misled its employees, and its misrepresentations amounted to a breach of fiduciary duty.

Varity Corp. teaches that GM may have acted in a fiduciary capacity when it explained its retirement program to the early retirees. As a matter of law, however, we do not believe that GM committed a breach of any applicable fiduciary duty. In the first place, GM never told the early retirees that their health care benefits would be fully paid up or vested upon retirement. What GM told many of them, rather, was that their coverage was to be paid by GM for their lifetimes. This was undeniably true under the terms of GM's then-existing plan....

GM's failure, if it may properly be called such, amounted to this: the company did not tell the early retirees at every possible opportunity that which it had told them many times before — namely, that the terms of the plan were subject to change. There is, in our view, a world of difference between the employer's deliberate misleading of employees in *Varity Corp.* and GM's failure to begin every communication to plan participants with a caveat.

In the second place, as we have said, GM was not required to disclose in its summary plan descriptions that the plan was subject to amendment or termination. *See* 29 U.S.C. § 1022(b); 29 C.F.R. § 2520.102-3. It would be strange indeed if ERISA's fiduciary standards could be used to imply a duty to disclose information that ERISA's detailed disclosure provisions do not require to be disclosed. As a matter of statutory construction, a specific statutory provision governs a general one — and here the "comprehensive" disclosure provisions control the broad fiduciary duty standard....

Had an early retiree asked about the possibility of the plan changing, and had he received a misleading answer, or had GM on its own initiative provided misleading information about the future of the plan, or had GM been required by ERISA or its implementing regulations to forecast the future, a different case would have been presented. But we do not think that GM's accurate representations of its current program can reasonably be deemed misleading. GM having given out no inaccurate information, there was no breach of fiduciary duty....

[LIVELY and MERRITT delivered separate opinions concurring in part and dissenting in part.]

BOYCE F. MARTIN, JR., Chief Judge, with whom Judges MOORE and COLE join, dissenting.

The question before this Court is whether General Motors has created a lifetime right to basic health care for its retirees. The *en banc* majority found that former General Motors salaried employees do not have any vested right in free lifetime health care, which they were promised at their retirement. This decision not only makes it more difficult for tens of thousands of retired General Motors employees to receive the health care they thought they deserved, but it also flouts the law. Basically, the *en banc* majority finds no claim. It ignores ambiguities and conflates arguments. I believe that a finer caliber of analysis is necessary. I write to highlight my differences with the *en banc* majority and to point out shortcomings in its analysis....

The facts have been stated repeatedly elsewhere, but they bear a brief recap because they weigh heavily in favor of the plaintiffs. The case involves General Motors's right to change the health care plans of 84,000 retirees. The case involves roughly 34,000 salaried employees who retired in the due course of their General Motors careers. They are the so-called "general retirees." From 1974 to 1988, General Motors offered early retirement incentive packages, and roughly 50,000 employees took early retirement at the inducement of General Motors. They are the so-called "early retirees." Both types of retirees received a variety of information from General Motors regarding employee health insurance.

A quick discussion of the particulars of the written materials General Motors distributed is a necessary predicate for the analysis that follows. The factual recitation will show that General Motors repeatedly promised retirees lifetime health care, in a variety of written materials, and only occasionally included a reservation of its right to change retiree benefits. Among the primary sources of information were booklets entitled "Highlights of Your GM Benefits" ("Your GM Benefits") and "The General Motors Insurance Program for Salaried Employees" ("General Motors Insurance"). All eight of the "Your GM Benefits" and "General Motors Insurance" booklets promised lifetime health benefits at the company's expense for salaried General Motors employees and their spouses, and only four contained any reservation of General Motors's rights to amend the agreement. According to Beach Hall, General Motors's director of health care plans, "Your GM Benefits" booklets were distributed to active salaried employees and published in 1966, 1974, 1977, 1980, and 1985. "General Motors Insurance" booklets also were distributed to active salaried employees and published in 1965, 1968, and 1971. "General Motors Insurance" booklets included a promise that "GM will pay" the health insurance costs of retirees but also noted that "GM reserves the right to modify, revoke, suspend, terminate, or change the Program." "Your GM Benefits" promised health care "at GM's expense for your lifetime" but only the 1985 edition carried any disclaimer or reservation of rights. Therefore, from 1974 to 1985 General Motors distributed employee booklets that promised free lifetime health care and contained no reservation of rights.

General Motors also published "Your Benefits in Retirement" brochures. New versions were issued in 1977, 1980, and 1985. "Your Benefits in Retirement" promised that "[y]our basic health care coverages will be provided at GM's expense for your lifetime," but also noted that "GM health care coverages ... are subject to change in the future." In a sworn declaration, Hall wrote that the 1977 and 1985 booklets were given to salaried retirees. He did not indicate to whom the 1980 books were distributed. There was some indication that "Your Benefits in Retirement" went to active employees, but the record provides no definitive answer. This would have remained a question for the district court to answer on remand. If General Motors's Hall is correct in saying that the booklets were given to employees after they retired, though, the booklets could not have entered the calculus of the employees' decision to retire....

Finally, many early retirees signed "statements of acceptance" in which they acknowledged that they had reviewed the benefits available to them in accepting the offer of early retirement.... In addition, the early retirees received other written and oral representations from General Motors personnel.... The written formulations of General Motors's various promises to the early retirees contained the following descriptions of lifetime health care: "Fully Paid by GM," "paid for by the Corporation for life," "continued at the corporation's expense," "a Corporation paid basis," "Corporation continues to pay full contribution for the retiree, spouse and eligible dependents," "GM paying the full cost," and "at no cost to retiree."

There are several issues in this case — vested rights, estoppel, class certification, fiduciary duty — but the underlying question is clear: Do the retirees have a right to the lifetime free health care General Motors promised them or can General Motors renege on its promise? In finding for General Motors, the *en banc* majority determined that General Motors was not legally bound by its promise. General Motors has profited from distributing a welter of contradictory materials on its health coverage. In light of General Motors's obscurantism, though, it seems paradoxical that General Motors would have some claims dismissed and win others at the summary judgment stage. At the very least, plaintiffs should have the benefit of a trial on some issues to unravel the web of misinformation General Motors has woven. Instead, General Motors profits from

914   CH. 19: EMPLOYER-PROVIDED HEALTH INSURANCE

having a salaried workforce that operated under the assumption it would receive lifetime health care. When the bill came due, though, General Motors was allowed to walk away.

To follow the *en banc* majority's decision, it is heads, General Motors wins; tails, the employees lose. I disagree with this outcome, and believe the district court's final judgment should be affirmed in part and reversed and remanded in part....

I. Vested Rights

A. General Retirees

General Motors repeatedly promised its retirees health care "at GM's expense" and constantly touted "improvements" in its health plan, yet it contends that it did not create a vested right to health care. The *en banc* majority agreed, finding that most of the summary plan descriptions unambiguously reserved General Motors's right to amend the benefits.... It is true under ERISA that employees do not automatically have a vested right to welfare benefits, but it is equally true that a company can create vested rights to such benefits. A vested right is created by "agreement or by private design."

General Motors has created a vested right to health care through its written promises. I, like the *en banc* majority, find no ambiguity in much of the written material, but I do so in favor of the retirees. The steps to that conclusion are easily taken. The first question is whether the "Your GM Benefits" and "General Motors Insurance" booklets were summary plan descriptions as defined by 29 U.S.C. § 1022. If so, the focus shifts to determining what should govern when the summary plan description differs from the plan documents.

The *en banc* majority acknowledges that General Motors's summary booklets were summary plan descriptions....

General Motors's summary plan descriptions suffer from either the internal inconsistency of contradictory terms or the external inconsistency of conflict with underlying formal plan documents. In some of the summary plan descriptions there is no internal ambiguity — the plan guarantees lifetime health care with no disclaimer. This is true of the 1974, 1977, and 1980 "Your GM Benefits" brochures. These summary plan descriptions, however, are at odds with the underlying plan documents, which do include a reservation of rights. In *Edwards v. State Farm Mut. Auto. Ins. Co.*, 851 F.2d 134 (6th Cir. 1988), this Court enunciated a principle for dealing with such discrepancies: "This Circuit has decided that statements in a summary plan are binding and if such statements conflict with those in the plan itself, the summary shall govern." *Id.* at 136. The *Edwards* principle governs pension plans and welfare plans.

From 1974 to 1985 the summary plan descriptions contained no reservation of rights and did carry a guarantee of lifetime health care. The *en banc* majority notes that "Edwards does not apply to silence," and argues that the summaries were silent on General Motors's right to change the plan. This ignores, however, the plain import of statements such as "at GM's expense for your lifetime." Just because the summary does not speak to General Motors's rights in the same language used in the plan does not mean the summaries are silent on the issue. Noting that benefits are "for your lifetime" is tantamount to saying that General Motors cannot change the plan. In addition, the *en banc* majority contends that "[n]either the GM plan itself nor any of the various summaries of the plan states or even implies that the plaintiffs' benefits were vested." Again, lifetime rights are vested rights.

It is true that from 1977 to 1985 "Your Benefits in Retirement" did include reservations of rights clauses. It bears noting, though, that these clauses were the rather tepid statement that benefits "have been changed from time to time through the years and are subject to change in the future." This clause is particularly problematic because General Motors always trumpeted its changes as improvements....

In sum, the district court should have had an opportunity on remand to determine whether the 1974 "Your GM Benefits" booklet was a summary plan document and whether the "Your Benefits in Retirement," in particular the 1980 edition, were distributed only to retirees. If those questions were answered affirmatively, there would be an eleven-year window from 1974 to 1985 in which the summary plan documents, which govern under *Edwards*, contained an unambiguous promise of lifetime health care. For general retirees who retired while these summary plan descriptions were in effect, this uncontradicted promise would be sufficient to vest their rights to lifetime health care. They deserved a chance to prove that in the district court.

B. Early Retirees

The early retirees base their claims for vested rights to health care on the bilateral contracts they signed with General Motors. The *en banc* majority determined that such extra-plan documents carried no weight under ERISA. This Court, however, had left the question of the validity of extra-plan documents open in *Musto v. American Gen. Corp.*, 861 F.2d 897 (6th Cir. 1988). In *Musto* this Court noted: "Whether, under ERISA, employees can ever obtain vested rights in welfare plan benefits on the strength of written representations outside the official plan document is a question we need not decide." *Id.* at 907. I believe the answer should be in the affirmative in this case.

The early retirees' claims are founded on the early retirement agreements they signed and other representations General Motors made to them at retirement. These agreements, they argue, constitute binding, bilateral contracts with General Motors for lifetime health care — a bargained-for agreement. The early retirees not only gave up their jobs, but some also surrendered the right to bring causes of action, including civil rights and age discrimination claims, against the company. They argue that this mutual consideration entitles them to bring a breach of bilateral contract claim. Typically a breach of contract claim falls under state law, and ERISA preempts state law. 29 U.S.C. § 1144(a). Preemption need not sound the death knell for a contract-based claim, though. As the district court recognized, plaintiffs can make claims beyond state law....

"'The legislative history demonstrates that Congress intended federal courts to develop federal common law in fashioning' relief under ERISA." *Massachusetts Mutual Life Insurance Co. v. Russell*, 473 U.S. 134, 156 (1985) (Brennan, J., concurring). These contracts are best enforced under federal common law.

Given that the contracts are enforceable under federal common law, the focus then turns to divining the contracts' terms. The district court in *Sprague II* argued that the agreements were not fully integrated, which opens the door to extrinsic evidence. This extrinsic evidence, as discussed above, includes written materials showing that General Motors personnel used almost virtually every possible permutation of the words "free lifetime health care" when presenting future benefits to employees. The district court in *Sprague II* found enforceable contracts for [some of the] early retirees.... That judgment should have been affirmed.

II. Estoppel

The General Motors retirees are prime candidates for bringing an estoppel claim. General Motors clearly wanted employees, potential employees, retirees, and potential retirees to rely on its boastful presentations of its benefit programs. The 1966 "Your GM Benefits" booklets provides an example of the sort of representations General Motors was making: "Today's General Motors benefits are an important factor in making your life more enjoyable and your future more secure." The brochures in question here undoubtedly were helpful in the recruitment and retention of personnel, and, when the time came, the inducement of certain employees to take early retirement. Yet, when retirees claim that they relied on these representations, General Motors calls such reliance unjustifiable.

The *en banc* majority acknowledges that estoppel can be a viable theory in ERISA cases but makes a misstep in dismissing the early retirees' estoppel claim because there was no reasonable reliance.... Reliance on repeated assurances of free lifetime health care, sometimes couched with timid caveats, from one of the largest corporations in the world was not justifiable in the *en banc* majority's view. The *en banc* majority erred in this determination, and the district court should have been affirmed in finding an estoppel cause of action for the early retirees.

In *Sprague III*, the district court held that any reliance on the part of the general retirees "was inherently unreasonable and unjustified." The *en banc* majority, finding the district court's determination that there were no misleading representations to general retirees "unassailable," does not even deal with the general retirees' estoppel claims. Why could the general retirees not reasonably rely on materials that repeatedly promised them lifetime health care and only occasionally included a reservation of rights? As I have shown, General Motors failed to reserve its rights in the "Your GM Benefits" brochures in effect from 1974 to 1985. In addition, when General Motors did reserve its rights, this reservation was less than clear, particularly when considered in light of General Motors's incessant touting of "improvements" to the plan and General Motors's boasting about "one of the finest and most comprehensive employe (sic) benefit packages in the industry." The issue of the reasonableness of the general retirees' reliance should have been remanded to the district court. The reliance of those who retired from 1974 to 1985 appears eminently justifiable. For other general retirees, there were sufficient representations on the part of General Motors to create a question of material fact as to whether a person justifiably could rely on them....

IV. Fiduciary Duty

The *en banc* majority limits its discussion of fiduciary duty to the early retirees, and acknowledges that "GM may have acted in a fiduciary capacity when it explained its retirement program to the early retirees." The *en banc* majority then finds, however, that General Motors did not breach this duty. "In the first place, GM never told the early retirees that their health care benefits would be fully paid or vested upon retirement. What GM told many of them, rather, was that their coverage was to be paid by GM for their lifetimes." In essence, the *en banc* majority argues that even though General Motors promised free lifetime health care and later forced retirees to pay part of the bill, the initial promise was not misleading.

I disagree, and plaintiffs, both general and early retirees, should have a chance to argue their breach of fiduciary duty claims. It is true that "a company does not act in a fiduciary capacity when deciding to amend or terminate a welfare benefits plan." It is also true, however, that "a fiduciary may not materially mislead those to whom the duties of loyalty and prudence described in 29 U.S.C. § 1104 are owed." Had General Motors never created a right to free lifetime health care, it would be free to amend or even terminate the insurance for retirees. When an employer establishes a right to lifetime health care benefits through vesting, as General Motors has done, the employer loses the unfettered freedom to amend or terminate the plan. General Motors has violated its fiduciary duty, and the district court in *Sprague I* erred in dismissing plaintiffs' fiduciary duty claim.

Conclusion

This is a classic case of corporate shortsightedness. When General Motors was flush with cash and health care costs were low, it was easy to promise employees and retirees lifetime health care. Later, when General Motors was trying to sweeten the pot for early retirees, health care was another incentive to get employees off General Motors's groaning payroll. Of course, many of the executives who promised lifetime health care to early and general retirees are probably long since gone themselves. Rather than pay off those perhaps ill-considered promises, it is easier for the current regime to say those promises never were made. There is the tricky little matter of the paper trail of written assurances of lifetime health care, but General Motors, with the *en banc* majority's assistance, has managed to escape the ramifications of its now-regretted largesse.

The plaintiff class's claims for lifetime health care lie in shambles despite General Motors's repeated assurances of just such coverage. As I survey the wreckage of these claims, I am reminded that ERISA's underlying purpose is "to protect ... the interests of participants in employee benefit plans and their beneficiaries." 29 U.S.C. § 1001(b). ERISA is not a cure-all for disputes between companies and employees over welfare and pension plans, but this case provides a role for ERISA. The *en banc* majority opinion validates General Motors's decision to institute premiums and raise deductibles on retirees' health insurance, but the decision bestows upon General Motors the freedom to eliminate health care coverage completely. Seemingly, any reservation of rights, no matter how weakly worded or unconnected to the grant of rights, will inure a company from having to live up to its obligations in the future. Ultimately, the *en banc* majority puts a new twist on an old aphorism, and what is good for General Motors is not good for the country but rather is bad for its retirees. I therefore respectfully dissent.

NOTES

1. *Reconciling the Irreconcilable.* The conflict in *Sprague* was between language providing for lifetime benefits paid by GM and language permitting the plan to be amended at any time. The Court followed *Musto* in holding that the latter took precedence over the former. In *Musto,* however, the language granting the benefits did not say that the employer would provide them for the life of the employee.

Is there any way to reconcile the two types of provisions in *Sprague*? One possibility would be to argue that because employees forego current wages in return for the promise of lifetime health benefits, employers should not be permitted to renege on the promise after retirement. Prior to retirement, however, when employees can still react to an employer's change in promised retiree health benefits by increasing their wage demands, employers may amend their plans. *Cf. UAW v. Yard-Man, Inc.,* 716 F.2d 1476, 1482 (6th Cir. 1983), *cert. denied,* 465 U.S. 1007 (1984). But that solution has its own problems. One problem relates to the bright line between retired and active workers. If an employer amended its plan today to exclude lifetime health benefits, the suggested rule would guarantee benefits for a thirty-year employee who retired yesterday, but deny benefits to a thirty-year employee due to retire tomorrow. More fundamentally, the suggested analysis assumes that employees rely on the promise of lifetime benefits and accept the corresponding wage reduction. Employees instead may very well discount the promise and rely instead on the provision permitting amendments; if employees did that, they would not accept wage reductions in return for the promise, and the basis for requiring employers to provide the lifetime benefits would disappear.

2. *ERISA's Reporting and Disclosure Requirements.* ERISA's reporting and disclosure requirements apply to both pension and welfare plans. In addition to summary plan descriptions, § 102, plan administrators are required to provide each participant with a summary annual report, § 104(b)(3), and, for pension plans and upon written request, a statement of the participant's accrued benefits and nonforfeitable benefits. § 105(a). Plan administrators must also file summary plan descriptions, plan descriptions, and annual and terminal reports with the Secretary of Labor. § 101(b). The requirements can be enforced through a civil suit under § 502. The suit can seek actual damages, up to $100/day for failing to provide required information to a participant, and/or up to $1,000/day for failing to file an annual report with the Secretary of Labor. § 502(c). In addition, criminal sanctions are available for willful violations. § 501.

Sprague provides an introduction to the types of issues that arise under ERISA's reporting and disclosure provisions:

(a) *Which document controls in the event of a conflict: the plan itself or the summary plan description? Sprague* indicates, as have other courts, that the summary should control, because that is the document employees receive and rely on. *See Pierce v. Security Trust Life Ins. Co.*, 979 F.2d 23 (4th Cir. 1992); *Heidgerd v. Olin Corp.*, 906 F.2d 903 (2d Cir. 1990). The courts, however, have been unwilling to extend the employee notice rationale to documents other than the plan summary. In *Alday v. Container Corp. of America*, 906 F.2d 660 (11th Cir. 1990), *cert. denied*, 498 U.S. 1026 (1991), for example, the company increased the amount retirees had to pay to participate in the company's health plan. The Court held that the change was permissible, because the summary plan description indicated that changes in the plan could be made, even though other documents provided to employees — an employee handbook, letters sent to employees when they neared retirement age, and documents distributed at retirement seminars — did not inform employees of the company's ability to change the retiree health plan. *See also Hicks v. Fleming Co.*, 961 F.2d 537 (5th Cir. 1992) (employee could not rely on document he thought was a summary plan description; "looks like a duck, quacks like a duck" test would discourage employers from providing information to employees); *Gridley v. Cleveland Pneumatic Co.*, 924 F.2d 1310 (3d Cir.), *cert. denied*, 501 U.S. 1232 (1991) (participants not justified in relying on brochure provided by employer).

(b) *How specific does the summary plan description need to be?* Some courts have held that the summary must notify participants of their rights with a high degree of specificity. *See Ruotolo v. Sherwin-Williams Co.*, 622 F. Supp. 546 (1985) (requirements violated where summary indicates all benefits may be lost by working when in fact the plan provided that only 70% of benefits would be lost); *Zittrouer v. Uarco Inc. Group Benefit Plan*, 582 F. Supp. 1471 (N.D. Ga. 1984) (requirements violated where summary failed to disclose one of many exclusions from coverage under a welfare plan providing benefits for stays in extended care facilities). *But see Dzinglski v. Weirton Steel Corp.*, 875 F.2d 1075 (4th Cir.), *cert. denied*, 493 U.S. 919 (1989) (employer consent required for eligibility for early retirement; summary acceptable even though it did not specify reasons employer might grant or withhold consent).

(c) *Is reliance required before an employee can recover for a violation of the disclosure requirements?* Some circuits do not require any reliance to make out a violation, because such a requirement would "undermine the legislative command by imposing technical requirements upon the employee." *Edwards v. State Farm Mut. Auto. Ins. Co.*, 851 F.2d 134, 137 (6th Cir. 1988). *See also Hansen v. Continental Ins. Co.*, 940 F.2d 971 (5th Cir. 1991). Other circuits require plaintiffs to demonstrate some reliance on the SPD before they can recover. *See Branch v. G. Bernd Co.*, 955 F.2d 1574 (11th Cir. 1992); *Maxa v. John Alden Life Ins. Co.*, 972 F.2d 980 (8th Cir. 1992), *cert. denied*, 506 U.S. 1080 (1993); *Bachelder v. Communications Satellite Co.*, 837 F.2d 519 (1st Cir. 1988).

F. PUBLIC POLICY INITIATIVES

Providing health care at a reasonable cost has proven to be a very difficult task in the United States. We spend a significantly higher proportion of our income on the health care system than our industrial competitors. In 1991, for example, we spent 13.2% of our gross domestic product on health care, while Canada, the United Kingdom, and Germany spent 10.0%, 6.6% and 8.5%, respectively. The average for the twenty-four member countries of the Organization for Economic Cooperation and Development (OECD) was 7.9%. George J. Schieber et al., *Health Spending, Delivery, and Outcomes in OECD Countries*, 12 HEALTH AFFAIRS 120, 121 (1993). Per capita, health care expenditures in the United States ($2,868) were more than double the OECD average ($1,305). *Id.* at 122. Our health outcomes, however, are generally no better than those in other countries. *Id.* at 127-29. In part, this is because a high proportion of the United States population does not have any health insurance and, hence, does not enjoy easy access to the health care system. Estimates vary, but 31 to 37 million Americans have no health insurance. Lawrence D. Brown, *The Medically Uninsured: Problems, Policies, and Politics*, 15 J. HEALTH POL. POL'Y & L. 413 (1990). Many of the problems with the health care system, of course, are beyond the scope of a textbook on employment law. At the same time, however, most Americans obtain their health insurance through their employment and most of the initiatives designed to deal with the problems have direct relevance in the workplace. This section will not attempt to provide an overview of health care initiatives. It will, however, provide a brief introduction to current trends in health care reform and some ways of thinking about them.

Until recently, employer-provided health care was relatively unregulated. ERISA itself did not provide much substantive regulation and its broad pre-emption provision provided a fairly broad shield from state laws attempting to regulate employee welfare plans. Two current trends are increasing the level of regulation. First, Congress has begun to enact substantive regulation in particular areas. The Health Insurance Portability and Accountability Act, which has already been discussed, is one example. In addition, Congress recently enacted laws requiring health plans to provide forty-eight-hour hospital stays after child-birth (ninety-six hours for cesarean sections) and requiring that the aggregate and annual limits provided for mental health benefits not exceed those for medical and surgical benefits. Newborns' and Mothers' Health Protection Act, 29 U.S.C. § 1185; Mental Health Parity Act, 29 U.S.C. § 1185a. As this is written, Con-gress is considering similar types of regulation targeted to particular problems. *See* Breast Cancer Patient Protection Act, H.R. 135, 105th Cong., 1st Sess. (1997) (amending ERISA to require 48-hour hospital stay after mastectomies); Children's Health Coverage Act, S. 13, 105th Cong., 1st Sess. (1997) (attempting to reduce the number of uninsured children). Second, the states have been re-invigorated in their attempts to regulate health care. As indicated above, there has been a surge in state initiatives since the Supreme Court signaled that ERISA preemption may not be as broad as previously thought. *New York State Conference of Blue Cross & Blue Shield Plans v. Travelers Ins. Co.*, 514 U.S. 645 (1995).

The general issue raised by these types of initiatives is: What is the appro-priate role for government in regulating employer-provided health care?

LAWRENCE H. SUMMERS, SOME SIMPLE ECONOMICS OF MANDATED BENEFITS, 79 AEA Papers & Proceedings 177, 178-82 (1989)[*]

[The standard efficiency argument militates against requiring employers to provide any type of health insurance benefits,] just as it militates against other government interventions. Imagine that employers can compensate their workers in different ways: with cash, by providing them with insurance, or by giving them consumption goods directly. If employers and employees can negotiate freely over the terms of the compensation package, they will reach a mutually efficient outcome. If a health benefit that would cost an employer $20 to provide is worth $30 to prospective employees, employers could provide the benefit and reduce the employee's salary by between $20 and $30, leaving both better off. Reasoning of this sort demonstrates that benefits will be provided up to the point where an extra $1 spent by employers on benefits is valued by employees at $1.

When is there ever a case for mandating benefits or publicly providing goods that employers could provide their workers? Most obviously, there is the paternalism, or "merit goods," argument that individuals value certain services too little. They may irrationally underestimate the probability of catastrophic health expenses, or of a child's illness that would require a sustained leave. In the pension context, this argument may be especially persuasive since individuals are likely to be especially inept at making intertemporal decisions. A closely related argument involves the idea that society cares more about equal consumption of some merit good commodities than about others.

There are at least two further rationales for mandating benefits that do not assume individual irrationality. First, there may be positive externalities associated with the good — externalities that cannot be captured by either the provider or the recipient. The most obvious example is health insurance. Society cares about preventing the spread of contagious diseases more than any individual does or would take account of....

Much more important is the externality that arises from society's unwillingness or inability to deny care completely to those in desperate need, even if they cannot pay. The Congressional Budget Office estimates that there are 23 million American employees without health insurance. Health insurance for this group would cost about $25 billion. Currently, these uninsured employees incur $15 billion in health care costs for which they do not pay. The costs are borne in part by physicians and other providers of health care, but most of the cost is passed on to other consumers in the form of higher insurance and medical costs.

The externality here is quite large. About 60 percent of the benefit of employer-provided health insurance accrues ultimately to neither employer nor employee. Even with the current tax subsidy to employer-provided health insurance, there might be a further case for government action....

There is a second, perhaps stronger, argument for government intervention in the market for fringe benefits based on adverse selection considerations.... If employees have more information about whether they will need parental leave or face high medical bills than their employers do, then employers that provide these benefits will receive disproportionately more applications from employees who require benefits and so will lose money. The market thus discourages provision of any fringe benefits.

Suppose, for example, that for the 10 percent of the population that knows it has health problems, health insurance is worth $300 and costs $270 to provide, and for the 90 percent of the population without preexisting conditions, health insurance is worth $100 and costs $90 to provide. Assume that individuals know whether they have problems or not, but employers cannot tell healthy from unhealthy individuals. Now consider what happens if employers do not offer health insurance. Any employer offering health insurance and a salary reduction of less than $100 would attract both classes of workers and would lose money, since the average cost of insurance would be $.9 x 90 + .1 x 270 = $108. Firms could offer insurance and reduce wages by between $270 and $300. This would attract only unhealthy individuals. Even leaving aside the consideration that for productivity reasons, firms might not prefer a personnel policy that was most likely to attract unhealthy workers, it is clear that the market solution will not provide universal insurance even though all individuals are willing to pay more than it costs to insure themselves.

The same argument holds in the case of other employee benefits. Workers know much better than their employers whether they are likely to go on parental leave or become disabled. They probably also know something about whether they are likely to become enmeshed in employment disputes. This suggests that there are efficiency arguments for limiting employers' ability to fire workers at will.

These two considerations suggest that it may be optimal for the government to intervene in the provision of goods that some employers provide their workers. [The question remains, however, whether goods such as health insurance should be provided directly by the government or whether the government should require employers to provide them.]

[A]t least some presumption should exist in favor of mandated benefits [over public provision]. Mandated benefits preserve employers' ability to tailor arrangements to their workers and to offer more than minimum packages. This avoids what might be called the "government provision trap".... Suppose that the government provides universal free health care of modest quality. This will be more attractive to many than paying the costs of high-quality care themselves, even though if they had to pay for all their care they would have selected high- rather than low-quality care.

Another argument in favor of mandated benefits [is that they] do not give rise to deadweight losses as large as those that arise from government tax collections. Suppose that the government required that all employers provide a certain benefit, say a leave policy, that cost employers $.10 per employee hour to provide. What would happen? Consider first employers whose employees previously valued the benefit at more than $.10 per hour and so had a leave package greater than $.10 per hour. They would not be affected at all by the government mandate, since they were previously in compliance with the law. For employees who valued the benefit at less than $.10 an hour, they would then receive the plan, at the cost of $.10.

What would happen to the wages of those receiving the benefit?.... Two special cases are instructive. First, suppose that the mandated benefit is worthless to employees. In this very special case, the change in employment and wages corresponds exactly to what would be expected from a $.10 tax on employers. Since the mandated benefit is worthless to employees, it is just like a tax from the point of view of both employers and employees. Second, consider the case where employees valuation of the policy is arbitrarily close to $.10. In this case, the mandated benefit does not affect the level of employment, the employer's total employee costs, or the employee's utility.

The general point should be clear from this example. In terms of their allocational effects on employment, mandated benefits represent a tax at a rate equal to the *difference* between the employer's cost of providing the benefit and the employee's valuation of it, *not* at a rate equal to the cost to the employer of providing the benefit.

With this in mind, contrast the effects of mandating benefits with the effects of taxing all employers and using the proceeds to finance a public parental leave program. In the latter case, employers would abandon their plans, and the government would end up paying for all parental leave. This would mean far more tax distortions than in the mandated benefits case for two reasons. First, employers and employees who were unaffected by the mandated benefit program would be taxed for the parental leave program. This creates a larger deadweight loss. Second, for those employers and employees who are affected, the tax levied is equal to the full cost of parental leave, not the difference between the employers' cost and the workers' benefit....

This analysis suggests at least two possible advantages of mandated benefits over public provision of benefits. First, mandated benefits are likely to afford workers more choice. Second, they are likely to involve fewer distortions of economic activity. Why then should not all social objectives be sought through mandated benefits?...

The most obvious problem with mandated benefits is that they only help those with jobs. Beyond the 25 million employed Americans without health insurance, another 13 million nonemployed Americans do not have health insurance. Mandated benefit programs obviously do not reach these people. There is certainly a case for public provision in situations where there is no employer who can be required to provide benefits.

A more fundamental problem comes when there are wage rigidities. Suppose, for example, that there is a binding minimum wage. In this case, wages cannot fall to offset employers' cost of providing a mandated benefit, so it is likely to create unemployment. This is a common objection to proposals for mandated health insurance, given that a large fraction of employees who are without health insurance are paid low wages. It is not clear whether this should be regarded as a problem with mandated benefits or minimum wages. Note that a payroll tax on employers directed at financing health insurance benefits publicly would have exactly the same employment displacement effects as a mandated health insurance program.

A different type of wage rigidity involves a requirement that firms pay different workers the same wage even though the cost of providing benefits differs. For example, the cost of health insurance is greater for older than for younger workers and the expected cost of parental leave is greater for women than men. If wages could freely adjust, these differences in expected benefit costs would be offset by differences in wages. If such differences are precluded, however, there will be efficiency consequences as employers seek to hire workers with lower benefit costs. It is thus possible that mandated benefit programs can work against the interest of those who most require the benefit being offered. Publicly provided benefits do not drive a wedge between the marginal costs of hiring different workers and so do not give rise to a distortion of this kind.

Another objection to mandated benefits is that they reduce the scope for government redistribution. Consider the example of old-age benefits. Many of the arguments I have discussed could be used to support a proposal to privatize Social Security. The principal problem with this proposal is that it would make the redistribution of lifetime income that is inherent in the operation of the current Social Security system impossible. Assuming perfectly flexible markets, wages for each type of worker would fall by the amount of benefits they could expect to receive from a mandated pension; there would be no transfer from [rich to poor]. If the government sought to prevent redistribution by preventing wage adjustments, unemployment among those most in need would result. The non-redistributive character of mandated benefit programs is a direct consequence of the fact that, as with benefit taxes, workers pay directly for the benefits they receive.

A different sort of objection to mandated benefits as a tool of social policy follows along the lines of the traditional conservative position that "the only good tax is a bad tax." If policymakers fail to recognize the costs of mandated benefits because they do not appear in the government budget, then mandated benefit programs could lead to excessive spending on social programs. There is no sense in which benefits become "free" just because the government mandates that employers offer them to workers. As with value-added taxes, it can plausibly be argued that mandated benefits fuel the growth of government because their costs are relatively invisible and their distortionary effects are relatively minor.

NOTES

1. *Who Are the Uninsured?* People without health insurance can be found in virtually every segment of American society. While people with low incomes are more likely to lack health insurance, many of the uninsured earn adequate incomes. In 1988, 54% of uninsured workers earned under $20,000, but 15% earned more than $40,000. Similarly, while the unemployed are more likely to be uninsured (50% of the unemployed lack insurance compared to 11% for full-time workers), the overwhelming majority of uninsured persons are employed (only 3% of all uninsured persons were unemployed, 76% had jobs, and the remainder were not in the labor force.) GAO, HEALTH INSURANCE COVERAGE: A PROFILE OF THE UNINSURED IN SELECTED STATES 33, 35, 37 (1991). *See also* GAO, HISPANIC ACCESS TO HEALTH CARE: SIGNIFICANT GAPS EXIST (1992) (one-third of Hispanics did not have health insurance in 1989, compared to 19% of African-Americans and 14% of Whites).

2. *The Employer's Interest.* Most economists believe that employers do not pay directly for increases in health insurance costs. Instead, those costs are passed on to workers in lower wages, often in the form of lower *increases* in

wages than employees would otherwise receive. Mark V. Pauly, *Taxation, Health Insurance and Market Failure in the Medical Economy*, 24 J. ECON. LITERATURE 629 (1986). In this view, employers have two primary interests in health care costs. First, employers are interested in avoiding unexpected shocks that cannot be smoothly passed on to workers. The *McGann* case can be viewed as an example of an employer avoiding a shock by passing it on to workers (although the transfer was not exactly smooth). This interest also explains heightened employer concern in years when health care inflation is especially high; employers are especially concerned then because when increases in costs are large and sudden, it is difficult to pass them on to employees in the form of lower wages. Second, employers are interested in formulating a wage/health insurance package that will attract and retain a desirable workforce. An employer that offers a lower wage and better health insurance than its competitors might find that it attracts a workforce that tends to be unhealthy. An employer that offers a high wage and no health insurance benefits is sacrificing tax benefits that, in effect, subsidize its compensation package.

   3. *Health Insurance and International Competitiveness.* Employers are often heard to complain that increases in the cost of health insurance will make them less able to compete internationally. In 1988, for example, Chrysler spent $700 per vehicle on employee health care, twice as much as German automakers and three times as much as the Japanese. Similarly, Canada has a nationalized health care system that is funded predominantly by general tax revenues (so the burdens on employers are less direct) and that controls costs better (so overall health care expenditures are considerably lower than in the United States).

   The claim that health care costs in the United States have adverse effects on international competitiveness, however, is very difficult to resolve. Those making the claim generally assume that increases in the costs of health care will increase the overall cost of labor for employers. But employers are able to shift some portion of the increase in costs to employees. If employers were able to shift all of the increase in health care costs to employees (for example, by lowering wages), total labor costs and American competitiveness would remain constant. Thus, the competitiveness claim requires difficult empirical assessments of the increase in health care costs both in the United States and elsewhere, and of the ultimate incidence of those costs in each country. *See* CBO, ECONOMIC IMPLICATIONS OF RISING HEALTH CARE COSTS (1992) (international competitiveness not hurt because employers have been able to shift higher health care costs to workers in the form of lower wages and less generous nonmedical benefits).

Part VIII

Prevention and Compensation of Workplace Injuries and Diseases

The forty-six men who were killed last year [1906] in the South Chicago plant of the United States Steel Corporation went to their deaths by a large number of different and divergent routes. Twelve of them were killed in the neighborhood of blast furnaces.... Three of them were electrocuted. Three of them were killed by falls from high places.... Four of them were burned to death by hot metal .... And ten of them were killed by railroad cars or by railroad locomotives.... The operating men who manage the Illinois Steel Company are human beings. They do not wish to commit either murder or suicide. But Steel is War. And it is also Dividends.... The figures that indicate production and profits are the only figures handled and scrutinized by the members of the board of directors....

> —William Hard, *Making Steel and Killing Men*, EVERYBODY'S MAGAZINE, Nov. 1907, *reprinted in* THE MUCKRAKERS 342, 347-48, 354 (Arthur & Lila Weinberg eds., 1961).

Government regulations often have significant impact on the income and wealth of workers. To the extent that firms cannot pass on regulatory compliance cost increases to consumers, firms will absorb these costs by cutting wages, and by reducing employment.... If government regulations force firms out of business or into overseas production, employment of American workers will be reduced, making workers less healthy by reducing their incomes. OSHA should estimate whether the possible effect of compliance costs on workers' health will outweigh the health improvements that may result from decreased exposure to the regulated substances.

> —James B. MacRae, Jr., of the Office of Management and Budget, in a March 1992 letter to the Labor Department suspending the proposed OSHA Air Contaminants Standard.

The issue of workplace safety and health is important and difficult. The stakes are high in terms of the human suffering and of the economic costs to workers, employers, and society.

What Has Happened to Workplace Safety and Health?

The peak in the number of fatalities resulting from workplace accidents was reached in 1907, the year Hard's article was published, when more than 7,000 workers were killed in just two industries: railroading and bituminous mines.[*] Fortunately, the fatality rate resulting from accidents significantly declined during the 20th century. Unfortunately, the workplace injury rate, unlike the fatality rate, has not continued to decline continuously throughout the 20th century. A substantial decline did occur between 1926 and 1932, but this was followed by an "overall plateau" from 1932 to 1946. The injury frequency rate then

---

[*]This section is based on John F. Burton, Jr. & James R. Chelius, *Workplace Safety and Health Regulations: Rationale and Results*, *in* GOVERNMENT REGULATION OF THE EMPLOYMENT RELATIONSHIP 253-93 (Bruce E. Kaufman ed., 1997). Copyright © 1997 by Industrial Relations Research Association. Reprinted with permission.

927

dropped significantly from 1948 to 1958, when the rate began to increase in a process that lasted until 1970. Since 1972, when the Bureau of Labor Statistics (BLS) introduced new measures of workplace safety, the data have provided a mixed picture.

While there are several reasons why the accuracy of the data on the frequency and severity of workplace injuries can be challenged, the data on workplace diseases and death are even more problematical. The BLS reported about 495,000 workplace illnesses in 1995, but an alternative estimate for 1992 reported 1.3 million cases of occupational diseases and almost 60,000 fatalities resulting from occupational diseases.

The essence of this review is that workplace fatalities from accidents have declined throughout the 20th century, but trends for workplace injuries show no such continuing improvement. The evidence on trends in occupational diseases is inconclusive, which complicates an overall assessment. At best there is no apparent improvement in workplace safety and health in the last twenty-five years.

The Costs of Workplace Injuries and Diseases

The national costs of the workers' compensation program, which provides medical care, cash benefits, and rehabilitation services to workers disabled by work-related injuries or diseases, have increased substantially since 1960, although the costs have moderated in recent years. Social Security Administration data indicate that the employers' costs of workers' compensation increased from 0.93% of payroll in 1960 to 2.17% of payroll in 1993, and then declined to 1.83% of payroll in 1995, when the total costs for employers were $57.1 billion.

While workers' compensation costs may have dropped in the 1990s following several decades of rapid increases in costs, it is important to recognize that there are other significant costs associated with workplace injures and diseases in addition to the expenses of the workers' compensation program. J. Paul Leigh estimates that the indirect costs — including lost wages not replaced by workers' compensation benefits and the expenses that employers incur for retraining replacement workers — were $106 billion in 1992. *Occupational Injury and Illness in the United States*, 157 Archives Internal Medicine 1557 (1997). These indirect costs plus direct costs (such as workers' compensation benefits) resulted in the total costs for workplace injuries and diseases of $171 billion in that year, which were far more than the combined costs for AIDS ($30 billion) and Alzheimer's disease ($67 billion). This emphasizes the importance of the topics examined in this Part.

The Goals of Health and Safety Programs

The basic goals of government health and safety programs are clear, at least if presented only in broad outline. The goals are, first, the *prevention* of workplace injuries and illnesses and, second, the *compensation* of workers when they do become injured or ill, including the provision of cash benefits, medical care, and rehabilitation services. The goals become less clear, however, as one begins to flesh out these goals: At what price, for example, should the prevention goal be pursued? What if eliminating a certain class of workplace injuries is so expensive it will mean the loss of significant numbers of jobs? Are slightly more dangerous jobs better than no jobs at all? Is government in a better position to make this kind of trade-off than workers and employers?

This Part considers four principal approaches that seek to achieve the basic goals:

(1) *The Labor Market.* — Workers will require a risk premium to induce them to accept a job that is likely to result in a workplace injury. The risk premium represents *ex ante* compensation for any injury that occurs. The employer has an incentive to improve workplace safety in order to reduce the risk premium. Thus, the labor market serves both the prevention and compensation goals.

(2) *Tort Suits.* — A worker who is injured on the job can bring a tort suit against the employer or other party responsible for the injury. The recovery from the suit provides *ex post* compensation for the injury. The employer has an incentive to improve safety in the workplace in order to avoid liability in a tort suit. Thus, tort suits also serve both the prevention and compensation goals.

(3) *Workers' Compensation.* — A worker who is injured on the job receives cash benefits, rehabilitation services, and medical care, which represent *ex post* compensation. The program is financed by premiums paid by employers that are experience rated — that is, an employer's premiums decrease if the program compensates fewer work injuries. Thus, workers' compensation also serves both the compensation and prevention goals.

(4) *Safety and Health Laws.* — The employer is required to provide a safe and healthy workplace. The immediate purpose of the program is prevention, although to the extent that workplace injuries and diseases are prevented, fewer workers will require compensation.

Three criteria are useful for comparing the principal approaches for addressing workplace safety and health concerns. First, is the approach *adequate*? That is, does it provide sufficient resources and incentives to achieve the compensation and prevention goals? Second, is the approach *equitable*? Are various classes of workers (such as unionized and non-unionized workers) and employers (such as large and small employers) treated fairly under the approach? And third, does the approach provide *delivery system efficiency*? (The delivery system is comprised of employers, insurance carriers, state and federal agencies, attorneys, doctors, and others who provide the benefits and services in the approach.) Is the approach administratively efficient, in the sense that it achieves the desirable levels of adequacy and equity with the least use of delivery system resources?

The four approaches to prevention and compensation do not have a clear chronological order. Indeed, all but the workers' compensation program were used in some form in the nineteenth century, and all four approaches have been used throughout most of the twentieth century. The order in which the approaches are treated in this Part differentiates between the "prestatutory approaches" — namely the labor market and tort suits (discussed in Chapter 20) — and the statutory approaches exemplified by workers' compensation, with most state statutes enacted between 1910 and 1920 (discussed in Chapter 21), and by safety and health acts, notably the Occupational Safety and Health Act (OSHA), enacted in 1970 (discussed in Chapter 22). (Some states had enacted safety statutes in the nineteenth century, but the major safety and health law dates from the enactment of OSHA.) This Part also examines the inter-relationships between the four approaches at several places, most notably in Chapter 23.

A. THE LABOR MARKET

RONALD G. EHRENBERG, WORKERS' COMPENSATION, WAGES, AND THE RISK OF INJURY, in NEW PERSPECTIVES IN WORKERS' COMPENSATION 71, 74-81 (John F. Burton, Jr. ed., 1988)[*]

Consider a simplified world in which the labor market is competitive, workers have perfect information about the risks of injury associated with each job, and there are no barriers to mobility between jobs. Suppose also that firms differ in their production technology; that each technology has certain inherent risks of injury associated with it, which can be reduced if firms expend resources to do so; and that the marginal cost (to the employer) of reducing risks varies across firms.

Assume also, initially, that workers value positively their expected earnings per period (earnings times the probability of not being injured) and value negatively the probability of being injured. Workers will move to firms whose wage rates-risk of injury combination maximizes their well-being and, if all workers have identical preferences, firms with higher risks of injury would have to pay higher wages to attract workers. The mobility of workers would thus lead to *fully compensating* wage differentials, or wage differentials that compensate workers for the disutility they would suffer from risk of injury.

In such a world, firms would offer the wage rates-risk of injury combination so that their marginal cost for injury reduction would equal their marginal benefits from injury reduction. The former includes the costs of resources devoted to preventing accidents, while the latter includes the lower bill for wages associated with the lower accident rate, less downtime in production, and reduced hiring and training costs of replacements for injured workers. If the marginal cost of preventing accidents varied across firms, different firms would offer different "wage-injury rate packages."...

Compensating Wage Differentials

The first issue is whether markets "work" in the sense that wage differentials arise to compensate workers for exposure to risk of injury. Numerous studies have ... attempted to ascertain if wage rates are positively associated with various measures of injury risk (fatal accident rates, nonfatal accident rates, work-days

---

lost as a result of accident rates, and so on), after other personal characteristics that should influence wages (e.g., education, experience) are controlled for.

These studies uniformly tend to find that there is a positive association between fatal accident rates and wages. The relationship between nonfatal accident rates and wages is less well established, however; it appears in some studies but not in others. Most studies indicate that the magnitude of compensating wage differentials is larger in the union sector than in the nonunion sector, an expected result given that accident rates tend to be higher in the union sector and that unions may serve the role of winning wage differentials at the bargaining table to compensate their members for unfavorable job characteristics when "the market" fails to produce such differentials....

Unfortunately, this voluminous literature provides very little that is of use for public policy. Presumably one wants to know if (1) the market is providing appropriate incentives for employers to take actions to reduce injury rates and (2) the market is *fully* compensating workers for risk of injury. As discussed below, no answer to either of these questions is provided by these studies.

With respect to the first question, the issue is really whether the positive association between wages and risk-of-injury measures reflects a compensating wage differential for risk of injury. Jobs may offer a variety of undesirable working conditions in addition to risk of injury; these may include having to work in a noisy environment, having to do repetitive tasks, being required to do heavy lifting, and lacking the opportunity to make independent judgments. Many of these job characteristics are probably highly correlated with risk of injury on the job, and workers may demand wage premiums to accept them. As a result, when one omits these other job characteristics from the analysis, any effect they have on wages is captured by the risk-of-injury variable. Thus one may well overstate the true magnitude of the compensating wage differentials for risk of injury. When a few investigators have included other working conditions along with risk of injury in wage equations, the risk-of-injury variables tended not to be significantly associated with wages. Whether this is due to the high collinearity of the working conditions variables (which makes estimates imprecise) or to the nonexistence of a true wage-risk of injury differential cannot be determined. In either case, the evidence on the existence of compensating wage differentials *for* risk of injury is not as well established as the various studies would have us believe.

Suppose we ignore this problem and assume that wage differentials for risk of injury do exist. How could one hope to decide that their magnitudes are sufficiently large to permit one to conclude that they *fully* compensate workers for the disutility associated with risk of injury? Only if they are, as is implicitly assumed in a discussion of the subject in chapter 6 of the 1987 *Economic Report of the*

President,[*] is the case for government intervention to improve occupational safety weakened....

Now, if one truly believes that all labor markets are competitive, it is a tautology that whatever wage differentials are generated by these markets will be "fully compensating" ones. Once one allows for market imperfections, however, the question becomes an empirical one. The mere existence of *some* wage differential does *not* imply that it is a fully compensating one.

Estimates of the compensating wage differentials associated with the risk of fatal injury at the workplace suggest that individuals are paid a premium of 1 to 4 percent of their wages to compensate them for existing risks of fatal injury; this leads (given the magnitude of fatal injury rates) to imputed values of lives in the range of $200,000 to $3,500,000. Researchers have no way of evaluating (nor have they even tended to consider) whether differentials in this range truly fully compensate workers for risk of fatal injury.

As a result, the potential usefulness for public policy in occupational safety of estimates of compensating wage differentials for injury risk is limited. On the one hand, if these estimates truly reflect differentials paid for risk of injury, they may provide only lower-bound estimates of the value of life. On the other hand, if they also reflect a premium paid for other unmeasured unfavorable job characteristics that are correlated with job risk, they may lead one to overstate the true value of life.

NOTES

1. *Further Evidence on Compensating Differentials.* There is a burgeoning literature on compensating wage differentials for the risks of workplace death and injury that supplements the results in the 1988 Ehrenberg analysis. A 1996 survey by Ehrenberg and Smith reports that studies have generally found that industries having the average risk of job fatalities (about one per 10,000 workers per year) pay wages that are 0.5% to 2% higher than the wages for comparable workers in industries with half that level of risk. This suggests that total elimination of the risk of fatalities would reduce wages by about 4% for the average worker. The total amount of risk premiums implied by such studies is substantial, ranging as high as $200 billion for 1993. As indicated by Ehrenberg, the data on wage premiums received by workers to accept risk can be used to calculated the implicit value that workers place on their lives. A 1994 survey by Viscusi of 24 labor market studies found that a majority of estimates for the implicit value of life are in the $3 million to $7 million range in 1990 dollars. *See generally* John F. Burton, Jr. & James R. Chelius, *Workplace Safety and Health Regulations: Rationale and Results*, in GOVERNMENT REGULATION OF THE EMPLOYMENT RELATIONSHIP 253-93 (Bruce E. Kaufman ed., 1997).

---

[*] Portions of Chapter 6 of the 1987 *Economic Report of the President* are included in Chapter 23 of this volume.

2. *Insufficient Wage Premiums for Dangerous Work?* For a number of reasons, workers may not ask for a wage premium that is high enough to offset their risk of injury. Consider the arguments of Professor Rose-Ackerman:

> [T]he market will only work efficiently if potential new employees can observe the riskiness of jobs. One way such information might be provided is through a learning process. The first round of employees are uninformed, but after they are injured, other members of the labor force observe their injuries and illnesses and demand that the company pay a wage premium or reduce workplace hazards.
>
> There are many reasons why this learning process will work poorly in the real world. First, many hazards take a long time to produce injuries. Second, even if they happen quickly, participants in a large labor market will not observe many of the injured. Third, the level of hazard depends on workers as well as workplaces. Some workers are more susceptible to hazards because of their genetic characteristics or their life style — for example, whether they smoke. Therefore, it may be difficult for job applicants correctly to infer their own risk by observing the harm suffered by others. Fourth, workplace conditions change with technology — so the past may be a poor guide to the future. For all these reasons, regulations that require employers to inform employees of hazards are easy to justify....
>
> But the mere provision of information may not be sufficient for two different reasons. The first turns on the limited information-processing capacities of people, especially regarding probabilistic information. Rather than engage in a massive educational campaign, it may be more efficient to regulate workplace health and safety directly ....
>
> A second reason why an information strategy may be inadequate concerns ... "local public goods." If dust collectors are installed, they will benefit all employees on a shop floor, [however, individual workers may understate how much they value the benefit in an attempt to minimize the extent to which their wages are reduced to pay for it.] If employers do not know the value workers place on safety, they may be unwilling to experiment with costly changes that may not pay off in lower wage increases or improved productivity....
>
> There is a final argument for regulating workplace health and safety. Given the widespread existence of health insurance, welfare and publicly subsidized health care for the poor and old, individuals do not bear all of the costs of their illnesses and injuries. Furthermore, individuals may not properly weigh the pain and suffering of their relatives and friends. [Hence,] individuals may fail to take into account all the social costs of their risky employment decisions.

Susan Rose-Ackerman, *Progressive Law and Economics — And the New Administrative Law*, 98 YALE L.J. 341, 355-57 (1988).[*]

3. ***Appropriate or Too High Wage Premiums for Dangerous Work?*** Reason and even evidence suggest that workers may ask for an appropriate wage premium or even a premium that more than offsets the risk of injury:

> The available evidence suggests that workers utilize diverse forms of information in a reasonable fashion to form their risk judgments. Although there are not available data on workers' perceptions of fatality risks, overall assessments of nonfatal risk levels follow expected patterns. In particular, workers' risk perceptions are strongly correlated with BLS [the U.S. Bureau of Labor Statistics] nonfatal injury risk measures and are influenced in the expected manner by opportunities for learning on the job. These influences include experiencing an injury oneself, hearing of injuries to other workers, seeing hazard warning signs, and observing whether the physical conditions at the workplace are pleasant.
>
> Comparable data are not available to assess the extent of the correspondence between subjective risk perceptions and actual fatality risk levels. It is, however, noteworthy that fatality risks are several orders of magnitude smaller than nonfatal risks. To the extent that any systematic bias arises in risk perceptions, it is that individuals generally display a tendency to overestimate small probabilities and underestimate large probabilities.

MICHAEL J. MOORE & W. KIP VISCUSI, COMPENSATION MECHANISMS FOR JOB RISKS 74-75 (1990).

4. ***An Evaluation of the Labor Market.*** How well does the labor market achieve the goals of prevention and compensation? The adequacy criterion would require that wage premiums for dangerous work be fully compensating, so that workers on average receive adequate compensation and employers accordingly receive the proper economic incentives to improve safety and health conditions at the workplace.

As the contrasting view of Rose-Ackerman versus Moore and Viscusi suggest, and as the selection from Ehrenberg attests, no clear answer exists as to whether the market is fully compensating workers for risk of injury. A particularly sharp attack on the compensating wage differential evidence was recently made by Dorman, who argues that most studies have been improperly specified and that, after controlling for industry level factors, the evidence for compensating wage differentials for most workers disappears. PETER DORMAN, MARKETS AND MORTALITY: ECONOMICS, DANGEROUS WORK, AND THE VALUE OF HUMAN LIFE (1996). And even those studies that do provide evidence of compensating differentials rely on a critical assumption:

---

[*] Reprinted by permission of The Yale Law Journal Company and Fred B. Rothman & Company from *The Yale Law Journal*, Vol. 98, pp. 341-68.

Furthermore, all of these results are premised on an assumption of individual rationality. If individuals do not fully understand the risk and respond to risks in a rational manner, then the risk tradeoff that people are actually making may not be those that researchers believe they are making based on objective measures of the risk.

W. Kip Viscusi, *The Value of Risks to Life and Health*, 31 J. ECON. LITERATURE 1912, 1938 (1993).

Since it is impossible to decide whether the wage differentials fully compensate workers for the risks of workplace injuries and diseases, a clear judgment on the adequacy criterion is impossible.

There is little doubt, however, that the labor market approach to prevention and compensation has serious equity problems. The evidence that union workers receive higher risk premiums than nonunion workers in jobs with comparable risks indicates an equity problem prior to the occurrence of any injuries that will, for example, distort the financial incentives for employers to improve workplace safety. Moreover, since injuries are to some extent due to chance, those workers who are injured are likely to experience much greater losses than the amount of the risk premiums they received before their injuries, while uninjured workers in the same facility will receive the risk premiums but experience no losses.

The deficiencies of the labor market as evaluated by the equity criterion are offset to some degree by the virtue of the approach in meeting the delivery system efficiency criterion. Measured by this standard — the minimal use of delivery system resources to achieve adequacy and equity — the labor market excels. Whether the superior record on the efficiency criterion justifies reliance on the labor market in light of the deficiencies on the equity criterion and the uncertainties on the adequacy criterion cannot be resolved "scientifically." Most observers, however, would probably be unwilling to rely solely on the market, which is one reason why we will examine the other approaches to prevention and compensation, such as reliance on tort suits.

B. TORT SUITS

FARWELL v. BOSTON & WORCESTER RAIL ROAD CORP.

Supreme Judicial Court of Massachusetts
45 Mass. (4 Met.) 49 (1842)

SHAW, C.J. This is an action of new impression in our courts, and involves a principle of great importance. It presents a case, where two persons are in the service and employment of one company, whose business it is to construct and maintain a rail road, and to employ their trains of cars to carry persons and merchandize for hire. They are appointed and employed by the same company to perform separate duties and services, all tending to the accomplishment of one and the same purpose — that of the safe and rapid transmission of the trains; and they are paid for their respective services according to the nature of their respective duties, and the labor and skill required for their proper performance. The question is, whether, for damages sustained by one of the persons so employed, by means of the carelessness and negligence of another, the party injured has a remedy against the common employer. It is an argument against such an action, though certainly not a decisive one, that no such action has before been maintained.

It is laid down by Blackstone, that if a servant, by his negligence, does any damage to a stranger, the master shall be answerable for his neglect. But the damage must be done while he is actually employed in the master's service; otherwise, the servant shall answer for his own misbehavior. This rule is obviously founded on the great principle of social duty, that every man, in the management of his own affairs, whether by himself or by his agents or servants, shall so conduct them as not to injure another; and if he does not, and another thereby sustains damage, he shall answer for it. If done by a servant, in the course of his employment, and acting within the scope of his authority, it is considered, in contemplation of law, so far the act of the master, that the latter shall be answerable *civiliter*. But this presupposes that the parties stand to each other in the relation of strangers, between whom there is no privity; and the action, in such case, is an action sounding in tort. The form is trespass on the case, for the consequential damage. The maxim *respondeat superior* is adopted in that case, from general considerations of policy and security.

But this does not apply to the case of a servant bringing his action against his own employer to recover damages for an injury arising in the course of that employment, where all such risks and perils as the employer and the servant respectively intend to assume and bear may be regulated by the express or implied contract between them, and which, in contemplation of law, must be presumed to be thus regulated.

The same view seems to have been taken by the learned counsel for the plaintiff in the argument; and it was conceded, that the claim could not be placed on the principle indicated by the maxim *respondeat superior,* which binds the master to indemnify a stranger for the damage caused by the careless, negligent or unskillful act of his servant in the conduct of his affairs. The claim, therefore, is placed, and must be maintained, if maintained at all, on the ground of contract. As there is no express contract between the parties, applicable to this point, it is placed on the footing of an implied contract of indemnity, arising out of the relation of master and servant. It would be an implied promise, arising from the duty of the master to be responsible to each person employed by him, in the conduct of every branch of business, where two or more persons are employed, to pay for all damage occasioned by the negligence of every other person employed in the same service. If such a duty were established by law — like that of a common carrier, to stand to all losses of goods not caused by the act of God or of a public enemy — or that of an innkeeper, to be responsible, in like manner, for the baggage of his guest; it would be a rule of frequent and familiar occurrence, and its existence and application, with all its qualifications and restrictions, would be settled by judicial precedents. But we are of opinion that no such rule has been established, and the authorities, as far as they go, are opposed to the principle.

The general rule, resulting from considerations as well of justice as of policy, is, that he who engages in the employment of another for the performance of specified duties and services, for compensation, takes upon himself the natural and ordinary risks and perils incident to the performance of such services, and in legal presumption, the compensation is adjusted accordingly. And we are not aware of any principle which should except the perils arising from the carelessness and negligence of those who are in the same employment. These are perils which the servant is as likely to know, and against which he can effectually guard, as the master. They are perils incident to the service, and which can be as distinctly foreseen and provided for in the rate of compensation as any others. To say that the master shall be responsible because the damage is caused by his agents, is assuming the very point which remains to be proved. They are his agents to some extent, and for some purposes; but whether he is responsible, in a particular case, for their negligence, is not decided by the single fact that they are, for some purposes, his agents. It seems to be now well settled, what ever might have been thought formerly, that underwriters cannot excuse themselves from payment of a loss by one of the perils insured against, on the ground that the loss was caused by the negligence or unskillfulness of the officers or crew of the vessel, in the performance of their various duties as navigators, although employed and paid by the owners, and, in the navigation of the vessel, their agents. I am aware that the maritime law has its own rules and analogies, and that we cannot always safely rely upon them in applying them to other branches of law. But the rule in question seems to be a good authority for the point, that persons are not to be responsible, in all cases, for the negligence of those employed by them.

If we look from considerations of justice to those of policy, they will strongly lead to the same conclusion. In considering the rights and obligations arising out of particular relations, it is competent for courts of justice to regard considerations of policy and general convenience, and to draw from them such rules as will, in their practical application, best promote the safety and security of all parties concerned. This is, in truth, the basis on which implied promises are raised, being duties legally inferred from a consideration of what is best adapted to promote the benefit of all persons concerned, under given circumstances. To take the well known and familiar cases already cited; a common carrier, without regard to actual fault or neglect in himself or his servants, is made liable for all losses of goods confided to him for carriage except those caused by the act of God or of public enemy, because he can best guard them against all minor dangers, and because, in the case of actual loss, it would be extremely difficult for the owner to adduce proof of embezzlement, or other actual fault or neglect on the part of the carrier, although it may have been the real cause of the loss. The risk is therefore thrown upon the carrier, and he receives, in the form of payment for the carriage, a premium for the risk which he thus assumes....

We are of opinion that these considerations apply strongly to the case in question. Where several persons are employed in the conduct of one common enterprise or undertaking, and the safety of each depends much on the care and skill with which each other shall perform his appropriate duty, each is an observer of the conduct of the others, can give notice of any misconduct, incapacity or neglect of duty, and leave the service, if the common employer will not take such precautions, and employ such agents as the safety of the whole party may require. By these means, the safety of each will be much more effectually secured, than could be done by a resort to the common employer for indemnity in case of loss by the negligence of each other. Regarding it in this light, it is the ordinary case of one sustaining an injury in the course of his own employment, in which he must bear the loss himself, or seek his remedy, if he have any, against the actual wrong-doer.

In applying these principles to the present case, it appears that the plaintiff was employed by the defendants as an engineer, at the rate of wages usually paid in that employment, being a higher rate than the plaintiff had before received as a machinist. It was a voluntary undertaking on his part, with a full knowledge of the risk incident to the employment; and the loss was sustained by means of an ordinary casualty, caused by the negligence of another servant of the company. Under these circumstances, the loss must be deemed to be the result of a pure accident, like those to which all men, in all employments, and at all times, are more or less exposed; and like similar losses from accidental causes, it must rest where it first fell, unless the plaintiff has a remedy against the person actually in default; of which we give no opinion.

It was strongly pressed in the argument, that although this might be so, where two or more servants are employed in the same department of duty, where each can exert some influence over the conduct of the other, and thus to some extent provide for his own security; yet that it could not apply where two or more are employed in different departments of duty, at a distance from each other, and where one can in no degree control or influence the conduct of another. But we think this is founded upon a supposed distinction, on which it would be extremely difficult to establish a practical rule. When the object to be accomplished is one and the same, when the employers are the same, and the several persons employed derive their authority and their compensation from the same source, it would be extremely difficult to distinguish, what constitutes one department and what a distinct department of duty. It would vary with the circumstances of every case. If it were made to depend upon the nearness or distance of the persons from each other, the question would immediately arise, how near or how distant must they be, to be in the same or different departments. In a blacksmith's shop, persons working in the same building, at different fires, may be quite independent of each other, though only a few feet distant. In a ropewalk, several may be at work on the same piece of cordage, at the same time, at many hundred feet distant from each other, and beyond the reach of sight and voice, and yet acting together....

Plaintiff nonsuit.

NOTES

1. *Economics and Irrelevance.* The court says the "legal presumption" is that the pay of workers is adjusted to compensate them for the risk that they will be injured by the negligence of a co-worker. If wages do adjust this way, then changing the legal rule is irrelevant as to whether employers receive adequate economic incentives to prevent workplace injuries and is also irrelevant as to whether on average workers receive adequate compensation. Either way, the employer pays and workers are compensated. With the fellow servant rule, workers are paid through an increase in their wages that compensates them for the risk of injury. Alternatively, if the employer is liable, the worker receives lower wages (because she no longer receives compensation for the risk of injury from the negligence of fellow servants), but is compensated after the injury occurs by the tort suit recovery.

2. *Winners and Losers: The Tort System as Insurance.* Assuming that the "legal presumption" describes reality, workers as a group are neither helped nor hurt by the fellow servant rule: workers receive compensation for injuries caused by fellow servants either *ex ante* if the fellow servant rule applies or *ex post* if it does not. Thus workers can in principle receive adequate protection regardless of the operation of the fellow servant rule. But *individual* workers can be either winners or losers, so an equity problem occurs. With the fellow servant rule limiting recovery, workers who accept the wage premium for absorbing the risk of injury, but who are not injured, are winners; workers who are injured are losers. One way of viewing abrogation of the fellow servant rule, then, is as employer-provided insurance designed to improve equity. Workers who are not injured are not winners because they did not receive a wage premium for accepting the risk of injury; workers who are injured are not losers because they are fully compensated for their injuries *ex post.*

3. *The Unholy Trinity.* The fellow servant rule was only one of three common law doctrines that severely limited the ability of workers at the turn of the century to recover from their employers for workplace injuries. The other two were contributory negligence and assumption of the risk.

The doctrine of contributory negligence barred recovery if the injured worker's negligence contributed at all to her injuries. Although a general defense in tort cases at the time, the doctrine was applied with special vigor in cases brought by injured workers. If the worker's negligence was 1% responsible for her injuries and the employer's negligence was 99% responsible, the worker could not recover.

The assumption of the risk doctrine barred recovery for the ordinary risks of employment; the extraordinary risks of employment, if the worker knew of them or might reasonably have been expected to know of them; and the risks arising from the carelessness, ignorance, or incompetency of fellow servants.

4. *Workers' Chances for Recovery.* A critical assessment of the reliance on tort suits to deal with workplace injuries was provided in C. ARTHUR WILLIAMS, JR. & PETER S. BARTH, COMPENDIUM ON WORKMEN'S COMPENSATION 11 (1973):

> Before 1910, in almost every State the laws determining employers' responsibility for industrial injuries had been handed down from the pre-industrial period in England and the United States. Under these laws an injured worker's only recourse was through the courts and his chances of recovery were slight. It has been estimated that not more than 13 percent of injured employees ever recovered damages under the common law, even though 70 percent of the injuries were estimated to have been related to working conditions or employer's negligence. This inability to recover damages was due to the changes "wrought by the factory system and modern industry which had strained, beyond their capacity for adoption, common law doctrines developed to meet the needs of a simple economy."

5. *An Evaluation of Tort Suits.* The failure of most workers to recover damages for their workplace injuries meant that reliance on tort suits provided inadequate financial incentives to employers to prevent injuries as well as inadequate compensation for workers. There were, moreover, serious equity problems: some workers — those who were successful in their suits — may have done well, but other workers experienced significant uncompensated losses. Finally, the tort suits typically required long delays and required workers to pay legal fees from their awards, thus raising serious questions about the delivery system efficiency of the tort suit approach to prevention and compensation. These criticisms were major reasons why the workers' compensation programs began to be adopted by the states around 1910. Whether the modern tort system would do a better job of compensation and prevention is examined in Chapter 23.

Chapter 21

A. THE ORIGINS OF WORKERS' COMPENSATION

C. ARTHUR WILLIAMS, JR. & PETER S. BARTH, COMPENDIUM ON WORKMEN'S COMPENSATION 13-18 (1973)

Employers' Liability Statutes

[Dissatisfaction with the labor market and tort suits as solutions to the problem of workplace safety and health resulted, first, in the enactment of employers' liability statutes, and only later in enactment of workers' compensation laws.]

The employer liability acts did not attempt to create a new system of liability in the industrial relationship. They were based on the theory that the employee must bear the economic loss of an industrial injury unless he could show that some other person was directly responsible, through a negligent act or omission, for the occurrence of the accident. The employer was liable only for his own negligence, or at most for the liability of someone for whom he was directly responsible under the doctrine of *respondeat superior*. These statutes were merely intended to restore the worker to a position no worse than that of a stranger injured by the negligence of an employer or his employees.

Effects on Employer Defenses

Many of these employer liability statutes were extremely narrow in scope, confining their modifications to a specific industry or a particular defense. For example, the Georgia Act of 1855, the first such statute enacted, abolished the fellow servant rule for railroad companies only. While later enactments were often broader than the Georgia statute, none attempted to abrogate all three of the employer defenses for every employer-employee relationship. By 1907, 26 States had enacted employer liability acts, with most of these abolishing the fellow-servant rule while a few limited the assumption of risk and contributory negligence doctrines as well.

It was natural that the defense most vigorously attacked was the fellow-servant rule, since this doctrine not only was the cause of tremendous inequities but also represented a marked departure from the common law principle of vicarious liability. Most liability statutes limited the scope of the fellow-servant doctrine, but did not totally eliminate it. Many State legislatures abrogated the defense as to railroads only; several modified it; and only a few abolished the fellow-servant defense altogether.

Another approach taken by the legislatures was to remove or lessen the unjust effects that stemmed from the doctrine of contributory negligence. One approach adopted by several States was to replace the common law defense of contributory negligence with the doctrine of comparative negligence. Under this

943

principle, an employee who, through his own negligence, contributed proximately to his injury was not barred from recovery but rather his negligence merely operated to mitigate damages. Some statutes modified this doctrine by shifting the burden of proof from the plaintiff to the defendant where the plaintiff had the burden of proving his own freedom from negligence. Finally, several acts abolished the defense whenever the employee's accident was related to the employer's violation of a safety statute.

The third principle modification embodied in the liability acts limited the assumption of risk doctrine. Several States abolished this defense whenever the risk which produced the accident was caused by the employer's fault. A number of States made it inapplicable to extraordinary risks or known defects in plant or machinery, especially in the case of railroads. Others abrogated this defense as to violations of safety statutes....

Deficiencies of Employers' Liability Statutes

Employers' liability statutes did not provide an adequate solution for the problems arising from industrial accidents. They were, in fact, a tremendous source of worry, dissatisfaction, and friction to the employers and workers. As accidents frequently arise from the methods of carrying on a business, the responsibility for the resulting injuries must be assigned to conditions rather than persons. In contrast, under these statutes, liability was based on personal fault. Thus the economic loss for accidents of this nature had to be borne by the injured worker. These uncompensated accidents often gave rise to dependency and destitution, with the worker and his family forced to seek relief through various charitable organizations. This resulting status of enforced pauperization had a dehumanizing effect upon the injured worker.

Another source of criticism of this system stemmed from the fact that liability could be established only by a suit at law. The application of the law to any given case is not a matter of certainty and the amount of a possible recovery is undetermined.... The employee, when he did recover damages, received compensation only after a long delay and even then was forced to sacrifice a large portion of the award to pay attorney's fees. The employer, on the other hand, had to pay out large sums of money for defense of these claims and for satisfaction of verdicts. In addition, friction between employee and employer often arose out of these claims for damages, whether or not they reached the stage of law suits.

The system of employer liability under these statutes was defective in that it failed to accomplish its fundamental purpose: A solution of the problems created by work-related accidents. The operation of the employer's liability system resulted in injustice to all classes. With the continuous increase in economic development, the injustice was aggravated. As a result, alongside this development there grew a new social philosophy which demanded recognition of changed conditions and sought some adequate and just compensation for workmen who suffered economic losses from work-related injuries....

Workmen's Compensation in the United States

In the United States, efforts to implement a system of compensation for industrial injuries lagged far behind the countries of Europe. As work-related injuries and diseases and their sequellae grew less and less tolerable towards the end of the 19th century, the situation became ripe for a radical change. The first evidence of interest in workmen's compensation was seen in 1893 when legislators seized upon John Graham Brooks' account of the German system as a clue to the direction of efforts at reform. This interest was further stimulated by the passage of the British Compensation Act of 1897.

Early Labor and Management Positions

In 1898 the Social Reform Club of New York drafted a bill proposing automatic compensation for some types of industrial accidents. This bill was opposed by various labor organizations who did not accept the concept of compensation at this time. They were fearful that State development of guildlike provisions for pensions and other welfare benefits would reduce the workers' loyalty to the unions. They supported legislation modifying the employers' common law defenses which they believed would produce court awards much higher than automatic compensation. Agitation along these lines resulted in the Reform Club's compensation bill "dying on the drawing board" and ultimately led to the passage of employer liability statutes.

In contrast to this opposition by labor leaders, many private corporations, particularly the railroads, had come to favor such plans. They instituted private compensation and welfare programs which varied in scope and effectiveness, as well as in methods. Some were no more than arrangements for medical care. Others provided compensation for disability and death. "The greatest criticism of these plans were that they were in all cases inadequate, making provision only for immediate needs, and that they were too often much more advantageous to the corporation than to the workman." Despite these shortcomings, these employer relief funds were significant in that they indicated a broadened attitude on the part of industry as to the practical and humanitarian gains of accident prevention and compensation.

The National Association of Manufacturers in 1910 openly endorsed the idea of workmen's compensation legislation. They realized that employer relief funds were too costly for small manufacturers and could not provide an adequate solution to the problem of industrial injuries....

By 1910 labor had shifted its position because of the failure of liability statutes to provide a remedy, and began to work actively for compensation legislation. The National Civic Federation, which claimed to represent business, labor, and the public, managed to unify the various labor organizations and gain the attention of the State legislatures. With labor and industry lobbying for effective compensation legislation, the movement toward reform was in full swing.

The First Laws

In 1902, Maryland passed an act providing for a cooperative accident insurance fund representing the first legislation embodying in any degree the compensation principle. The scope of the act was restricted. Benefits, which were quite meager, were provided only for fatal accidents. Within three years the courts declared the act unconstitutional....

By 1908, there was still no workmen's compensation act in the United States. President Theodore Roosevelt, realizing the injustice, urged the passage of an act for Federal employees in a message to Congress in January. He pointed out that the burden of an accident fell upon the helpless man, his wife, and children. The President declared that this was "an outrage." Later in 1908 Congress passed a compensation act covering certain Federal employees. Though utterly inadequate, it was the first real compensation act passed in the United States.

During the next few years agitation continued for State laws. A law passed in Montana in 1909, applying to miners and laborers in coal mines, was declared unconstitutional. Nevertheless, many States appointed commissions to investigate the feasibility of compensation acts and to propose specific legislation. The greater number of compensation acts were the result of these commissions' reports, all of which favored some form of compensation legislation, combined with recommendations from various private organizations. Widespread agreement on the need for compensation legislation unfortunately did not end all conflict over reform. Interest groups clashed over specific bills and over questions of coverage, waiting periods, and State versus commercial insurance.

In 1910 New York became the first State to adopt a workmen's compensation act of general application which was compulsory for certain especially hazardous jobs and optional for others. "Although most corporate leaders and politicians of prominence, such as Theodore Roosevelt and President Taft, had publicly endorsed workmen's compensation, there was a residue of conservative opposition to such 'radical' social legislation." This conservative view was expressed by the courts who felt that these acts were plainly revolutionary by common law standards. Thus, in 1911 in *Ives v. South Buffalo Railway Company*[, 94 N.E. 431 (N.Y. 1911),] the Court of Appeals of New York held the New York act unconstitutional on the grounds of deprivation of property without due process of law. This decision was met with an explosion of criticism from all sides. Theodore Roosevelt was so angry that he openly advocated the passage of laws which would permit the recall of judicial decisions. While even the supporters of compensation legislation considered this measure too extreme, fear of its passage prompted many conservatives to support compensation legislation by more traditional means.

Following the *Ives* decision many State courts adopted a more liberal attitude toward compensation. Unfortunately, this decision had residual effects on the system. The "fear of unconstitutionality impelled the legislatures to pass over the ideal type of coverage, which would be both comprehensive and compulsory, in

favor of more awkward and fragmentary plans ... [to] ensure [their] constitutional validity." Elective or optional statutes became the rule, and several
States limited their coverage to hazardous employment. By the time the U.S.
Supreme Court held in 1917 that compulsory compensation laws were constitutional, the pattern of elective statutes had been set....

The 1911 Wisconsin workmen's compensation act was the first law to become
and remain effective. The laws of four other States (Nevada, New Jersey, California, and Washington) also became effective that year. Although 24 jurisdictions had enacted such legislation by 1925, workmen's compensation was not
provided in every State until Mississippi enacted its law in 1948.

NEW YORK CENTRAL RAILROAD CO. v. WHITE

United States Supreme Court
243 U.S. 188 (1917)

MR. JUSTICE PITNEY delivered the opinion of the court.

A proceeding was commenced by defendant in error before the Workmen's
Compensation Commission of the State of New York, established by the Work-
men's Compensation Law of that State, to recover compensation from the New
York Central & Hudson River Railroad Company for the death of her husband,
Jacob White, who lost his life September 2, 1914, through an accidental injury
arising out of and in the course of his employment under that company. The
Commission awarded compensation in accordance with the terms of the law; its
award was affirmed, without opinion, by the Appellate Division of the Supreme
Court for the Third Judicial Department, whose order was affirmed by the Court
of Appeals, without opinion. Federal questions having been saved, the present
writ of error was sued out by the New York Central Railroad Company ....

The errors specified are based upon these contentions: (1) That the liability, if
any, of the railroad company for the death of Jacob White is defined and limited
exclusively by the provisions of the Federal Employers' Liability Act of April
22, 1908, and (2) that to award compensation to defendant in error under the
provisions of the Workmen's Compensation Law would deprive plaintiff in error
of its property without due process of law, and deny to it the equal protection of
the laws, in contravention of the Fourteenth Amendment.

The first point assumes that the deceased was employed in interstate commerce at the time he received the fatal injuries.... Decedent's work bore no direct
relation to interstate transportation, and had to do solely with construction work,
which is clearly distinguishable .... The first point, therefore, is without basis in
fact.

We turn to the constitutional question....

In a previous year, the legislature enacted a compulsory compensation law
applicable to a limited number of specially hazardous employments, and
requiring the employer to pay compensation without regard to fault. Laws 1910,

Chap. 674. This was held by the Court of Appeals in *Ives v. South Buffalo Ry. Co.*, 201 N.Y. 271, to be invalid because in conflict with the due process of law provisions of the state constitution and of the Fourteenth Amendment. Thereafter, and in the year 1913, a constitutional amendment was adopted, effective January 1, 1914, declaring:

> Nothing contained in this constitution shall be construed to limit the power of the legislature to enact laws for the protection of the lives, health, or safety of employees ....

In December, 1913, the legislature enacted the law now under consideration, and in 1914 reenacted it to take effect as to payment of compensation on July 1 in that year. The act was sustained by the Court of Appeals as not inconsistent with the Fourteenth Amendment in *Matter of Jensen v. Southern Pacific Co.*, 215 N.Y. 514; and that decision was followed in the case at bar.

The scheme of the act is so wide a departure from common-law standards respecting the responsibility of employer to employee that doubts naturally have been raised respecting its constitutional validity. The adverse considerations urged or suggested in this case and in kindred cases submitted at the same time are: (a) that the employer's property is taken without due process of law, because he is subjected to a liability for compensation without regard to any neglect or default on his part or on the part of any other person for whom he is responsible, and in spite of the fact that the injury may be solely attributable to the fault of the employee; (b) that the employee's rights are interfered with, in that he is prevented from having compensation for injuries arising from the employer's fault commensurate with the damages actually sustained, and is limited to the measure of compensation prescribed by the act; and (c) that both employer and employee are deprived of their liberty to acquire property by being prevented from making such agreement as they choose respecting the terms of the employment....

In considering the constitutional question, it is necessary to view the matter from the standpoint of the employee as well as from that of the employer. For, while plaintiff in error is an employer, and cannot succeed without showing that its rights as such are infringed yet, as pointed out by the Court of Appeals in the *Jensen Case,* 215 N.Y. 526, the exemption from further liability is an essential part of the scheme, so that the statute if invalid as against the employee is invalid as against the employer.

The close relation of the rules governing responsibility as between employer and employee to the fundamental rights of liberty and property is of course recognized. But those rules, as guides of conduct, are not beyond alteration by legislation in the public interest. No person has a vested interest in any rule of law entitling him to insist that it shall remain unchanged for his benefit. The common law bases the employer's liability for injuries to the employee upon the ground of negligence; but negligence is merely the disregard of some duty imposed by law; and the nature and extent of the duty may be modified by legislation, with corresponding change in the test of negligence. Indeed, liability may be imposed for the consequences of a failure to comply with a statutory duty, irrespective of negligence in the ordinary sense; safety appliance acts being a familiar instance....

But it is not necessary to extend the discussion. This court repeatedly has upheld the authority of the States to establish by legislation departures from the fellow-servant rule and other common-law rules affecting the employer's liability for personal injuries to the employee. A corresponding power on the part of Congress, when legislating within its appropriate sphere, was sustained in *Second Employers' Liability Cases,* 223 U.S. 1.

It is true that in the case of the statutes thus sustained there were reasons rendering the particular departures appropriate. Nor is it necessary, for the purposes of the present case, to say that a State might, without violence to the constitutional guaranty of "due process of law," suddenly set aside all common-law rules respecting liability as between employer and employee, without providing a reasonably just substitute.... The statute under consideration sets aside one body of rules only to establish another system in its place. If the employee is no longer able to recover as much as before in case of being injured through the employer's negligence, he is entitled to moderate compensation in all cases of injury, and has a certain and speedy remedy without the difficulty and expense of establishing negligence or proving the amount of the damages. Instead of assuming the entire consequences of all ordinary risks of the occupation, he assumes the consequences, in excess of the scheduled compensation, of risks ordinary and extraordinary. On the other hand, if the employer is left without defense respecting the question of fault, he at the same time is assured that the recovery is limited, and that it goes directly to the relief of the designated beneficiary. And just as the employee's assumption of ordinary risks at common law presumably was taken into account in fixing the rate of wages, so the fixed responsibility of the employer, and the modified assumption of risk by the employee under the new system, presumably will be reflected in the wage scale. The act evidently is intended as a just settlement of a difficult problem, affecting one of the most important of social relations, and it is to be judged in its entirety. We have said enough to demonstrate that, in such an adjustment, the particular rules of the common law affecting the subject-matter are not placed by the Fourteenth Amendment beyond the reach of the law making power of the State; and thus we are brought to the question whether the method of compensation that is established as a substitute transcends the limits of permissible state action.

We will consider, first, the scheme of compensation, deferring for the present the question of the manner in which the employer is required to secure payment.

Briefly, the statute imposes liability upon the employer to make compensation for disability or death of the employee resulting from accidental personal injury arising out of and in the course of the employment, without regard to fault as a cause except where the injury or death is occasioned by the employee's willful intention to produce it, or where the injury results solely from his intoxication while on duty; it graduates the compensation for disability according to a pre-scribed scale based upon the loss of earning power, having regard to the previous wage and the character and duration of the disability; and measures the death benefits according to the dependency of the surviving wife, husband, or infant children. Perhaps we should add that it has no retrospective effect, and applies only to cases arising some months after its passage.

Of course, we cannot ignore the question whether the new arrangement is arbitrary and unreasonable, from the standpoint of natural justice. Respecting this, it is important to be observed that the act applies only to disabling or fatal personal injuries received in the course of hazardous employment in gainful occupation. Reduced to its elements, the situation to be dealt with is this: Employer and employee, by mutual consent, engage in a common operation intended to be advantageous to both; the employee is to contribute his personal services, and for these is to receive wages, and ordinarily nothing more; the employer is to furnish plant, facilities, organization, capital, credit, is to control and manage the operation, paying the wages and other expenses, disposing of the product at such prices as he can obtain, taking all the profits, if any there be, and of necessity bearing the entire losses. In the nature of things, there is more or less of a probability that the employee may lose his life through some accidental injury arising out of the employment, leaving his widow or children deprived of their natural support; or that he may sustain an injury not mortal but resulting in his total or partial disablement, temporary or permanent, with corresponding impairment of earning capacity. The physical suffering must be borne by the employee alone; the laws of nature prevent this from being evaded or shifted to another, and the statute makes no attempt to afford an equivalent in compen-sation. But, besides, there is the loss of earning power; a loss of that which stands to the employee as his capital in trade. This is a loss arising out of the business, and, however it may be charged up, is an expense of the operation, as truly as the cost of repairing broken machinery or any other expense that ordi-narily is paid by the employer. Who is to bear the charge? It is plain that, on grounds of natural justice, it is not unreasonable for the State, while relieving the employer from responsibility for damages measured by common-law standards and payable in cases where he or those for whose conduct he is answerable are found to be at fault, to require him to contribute a reasonable amount, and according to a reasonable and definite scale, by way of compensation for the loss of earning power incurred in the common enterprise, irrespective of the question of negligence, instead of leaving the entire loss to rest where it may chance to fall — that is, upon the injured employee or his dependents. Nor can it be deemed arbitrary and unreasonable, from the standpoint of the employee's inter-est, to supplant a system under which he assumed the entire risk of injury in ordinary cases, and in others had a right to recover an amount more or less speculative upon proving facts of negligence that often were difficult to prove, and substitute a system under which in all ordinary cases of accidental injury he is sure of a definite and easily ascertained compensation, not being obliged to assume the entire loss in any case but in all cases assuming any loss beyond the prescribed scale.

Much emphasis is laid upon the criticism that the act creates liability without fault. This is sufficiently answered by what has been said, but we may add that liability without fault is not a novelty in the law. The common-law liability of the carrier, of the inn-keeper, of him who employed fire or other dangerous agency or harbored a mischievous animal, was not dependent altogether upon questions of fault or negligence. Statutes imposing liability without fault have been sustained....

Viewing the entire matter, it cannot be pronounced arbitrary and unreasonable for the State to impose upon the employer the absolute duty of making a moderate and definite compensation in money to every disabled employee, or in case of his death to those who were entitled to look to him for support, in lieu of the common-law liability confined to cases of negligence.

This, of course, is not to say that any scale of compensation, however insignificant on the one hand or onerous on the other, would be supportable. In this case, no criticism is made on the ground that the compensation prescribed by the statute in question is unreasonable in amount, either in general or in the particular case. Any question of that kind may be met when it arises.

But, it is said, the statute strikes at the fundamentals of constitutional freedom of contract; and we are referred to two recent declarations by this court. The first is this: "Included in the right of personal liberty and the right of private property — partaking of the nature of each — is the right to make contracts for the acquisition of property. Chief among such contracts is that of personal employment, by which labor and other services are exchanged for money or other forms of property. If this right be struck down or arbitrarily interfered with, there is a substantial impairment of liberty in the long-established constitutional sense." *Coppage v. Kansas*, 236 U.S. 1, 14. And this is the other: "It requires no argument to show that the right to work for a living in the common occupations of the community is of the very essence of the personal freedom and opportunity that it was the purpose of the [Fourteenth] Amendment to secure." *Truax v. Raich*, 239 U.S. 33, 41.

It is not our purpose to qualify or weaken either of these declarations in the least. And we recognize that the legislation under review does measurably limit the freedom of employer and employee to agree respecting the terms of employment, and that it cannot be supported except on the ground that it is a reasonable exercise of the police power of the State. In our opinion it is fairly supportable upon that ground. And for this reason: The subject matter in respect of which freedom of contract is restricted is the matter of compensation for human life or limb lost or disability incurred in the course of hazardous employment, and the public has a direct interest in this as affecting the common welfare....

Judgment affirmed.

NOTES

1. *Constitutional Limits.* The Fourteenth Amendment to the U.S. Constitution was the basis for the challenge to the New York law. Another significant constitutional limitation on federal involvement in workers' compensation statutes was the Supreme Court's interpretation of the commerce clause of the U.S. Constitution, which provides, in part, that "The Congress shall have Power ... To Regulate Commerce with foreign Nations and among the several States ...." U.S. Const. art. I, § 8, cl. 3. The interpretation of this clause by the Supreme Court prior to the 1930s meant that the authority of Congress to deal with this issue was quite limited, and hence that workers' compensation statutes dealing with most private-sector employees had to be enacted at the state level.

2. *The Workers' Compensation Principle.* The workers' compensation principle has two elements. Workers benefit from a no-fault system, which enables them to recover in many situations in which tort suits would be unsuccessful. Employers benefit from limited liability, which means that the limited benefits provided in the workers' compensation statute are the only liability of the employer to its employees. The trade-off that is the essence of the workers' compensation principle has been restated by Professor Epstein:

> [T]he basic structure of the bargain was well understood with passage of the Act. The broad coverage formula eliminated the need to determine negligence on both sides and assumption of the risk — all inquiries with a high degree of uncertainty. In exchange for the broad coverage formula, the workman received a level of compensation that, by design left him *worse off* than if the injury itself had never taken place. The low levels of the benefits doubtless proved nettlesome to workers *after* injuries. But to concentrate on that point is to miss the central role. First, low damages help keep down the overall costs of the plan, which will induce employers to continue to hire labor. Second, low benefits help prevent fraud against the plan, as there is less to gain by pretending that an injury, or its consequences, is work-related. Third, the low awards create additional incentives upon the worker for self-protection and therefore act as an implicit substitute for assumption of risk and contributory negligence.

Richard A. Epstein, *The Historical Origins and Economic Structure of Workers' Compensation Law,* 16 GA. L. REV. 775, 800 (1982).

3. *Who Pays for Workers' Compensation?* The national costs of the workers' compensation program were $57.1 billion in 1995. But who pays for the program? The dominant view among lawyers is found in the first paragraph of the leading legal treatise, ARTHUR LARSON, LARSON'S WORKER'S COMPENSATION § 1.00 (Desk ed. 1997):

> Worker's compensation is a mechanism for providing cash-wage benefits and medical care to victims of work-connected injuries, and for placing the

cost of these injuries ultimately on the consumer, through the medium of insurance, whose premiums are passed on in the cost of the product.

An alternative view — suggesting that employers bear at least a portion of the costs of the workers' compensation program — is found in Justice Pitney's opinion in *New York Central Railroad v. White,* 243 U.S. at 203-04:

> Who is to bear the charge? It is plain that, on grounds of natural justice, it is not unreasonable for the State, while relieving the employer from responsibility for damages measured by common-law standards and payable in cases where he or those for whose conduct he is answerable are found to be at fault, to require him to contribute a reasonable amount, and according to a reasonable and definite scale, by way of compensation for the loss of earning power incurred in the common enterprise, irrespective of the question of negligence, instead of leaving the entire loss to rest where it may chance to fall — that is, upon the injured employee or his dependents.

There is yet another view about who pays for workers' compensation. This position, largely espoused by economists, is that workers pay for much of the workers' compensation program. The mechanism is that workers are paid lower wages than they would have received in the absence of workers' compensation. The essence of the modern economists' position about who pays for workers' compensation was anticipated by Justice Pitney in his 1917 opinion, 243 U.S. at 201-02:

> And just as the employee's assumption of ordinary risks at common law presumably was taken into account in fixing the rate of wages, so the fixed responsibility of the employer, and the modified assumption of risk by the employee under the new system, presumably will be reflected in the wage scale.

4. *Early Statutes.* The New York workers' compensation statute described in *New York Central Railroad v. White* was typical of the original workers' compensation laws enacted in most states. A summary of the features of these early statutes is provided in C. ARTHUR WILLIAMS, JR. & PETER S. BARTH, COMPENDIUM ON WORKMEN'S COMPENSATION 18 (1973):

> Coverage of the early laws was limited: even when elective, most acts applied only to specified hazardous industries. None covered all classes of employees. Agricultural workers, domestic help, and casual workers were most commonly excluded. Only a few acts applied to public employment. In general, compensation laws limited indemnity benefits to maximum total amounts, even for permanent disability or death. Cash benefits were usually stated as a percent of wages at the time of injury, 50 percent being the most common, although a few acts provided for about two-thirds of wages, subject to statutory maximum compensation ranging from $10 weekly in several

states up to $15. Several states made no provision at all for medical benefits. Where provided they were limited in duration or amount or both.

None of the early State compensation acts expressly covered occupational diseases. Statutes which provided compensation for "injury" were frequently interpreted to include disability from disease, but those acts which limited compensability to "injury by accident" excluded occupational disease. All except Oregon's act required uncompensated waiting periods of one to nine weeks, with several providing retroactive payments after a prescribed period.

5. *The National Commission.* The initial workers' compensation statutes, whatever their limits, nonetheless represented the first social insurance program in the United States and thus meant that for the first two decades of the program (until the mid-1930s) the government was doing more for injured workers than for unemployed or retired workers. With the enactment of the unemployment insurance and Social Security programs in the 1930s and the expansion of those programs in subsequent decades, the "lustre" of workers' compensation faded. By the 1960s, the proportion of the workforce covered by workers' compensation was less than the coverage of Social Security and unemployment insurance. Moreover, workers' compensation cash benefit increases lagged behind increases in wages in the period between 1940 and the 1960s.

One result of these developments was increasing criticism of the workers' compensation program during the 1960s that in turn led to the creation of the National Commission on State Workmen's Compensation Laws by the Occupational Safety and Health Act of 1970. Despite the membership of the Commission (most were Republicans appointed by President Nixon), *The Report of the National Commission on State Workmen's Compensation Laws* was critical of state workers' compensation laws:

> The inescapable conclusion is that State workmen's compensation laws in general are inadequate and inequitable. While several States have good programs, and while medical care and some other aspects of workmen's compensation are commendable in most States, the strong points are too often matched by weak.

Id. at 119.

The National Commission identified five objectives for a modern workers' compensation program: (1) broad coverage of employees and work-related injuries and diseases; (2) substantial protection against interruption of income; (3) sufficient medical care and rehabilitation services; (4) promotion of safety; and (5) an effective delivery system. The National Commission made eighty-four specific recommendations for state workers' compensation programs, several of which will be discussed in this chapter. The Commission also identified nineteen recommendations as essential, and called for a significant improvement in state laws, compelled by federal workers' compensation standards if necessary to achieve these nineteen essential recommendations. Federal standards have not been enacted, but many states have improved their laws in response to the recommendations of the National Commission.

B. AN OVERVIEW OF CURRENT WORKERS' COMPENSATION PROGRAMS

1. COVERAGE OF EMPLOYEES AND EMPLOYERS

Not all employees and employers are covered by workers' compensation. Recent estimates indicate that nationally about 97% of workers are covered. Some states cover virtually all employees, while only about 80% of the workers are covered in Texas. The gaps in coverage occur because some states exempt: (1) employers with a limited number of employees (e.g. three or less); (2) certain industries, such as state and local government, and agriculture; and (3) certain occupations, such as household workers. In addition, three states (including Texas) have workers' compensation laws that are elective for employers.

In addition, the laws are designed to cover employees, which means that workers who are independent contractors normally are not covered. Moreover, certain employees — those who are casual workers or workers not engaged in the normal trade or business of the employer — may not be protected by the act even when their employers are within the scope of the act.

2. COVERAGE OF INJURIES AND DISEASES

Even workers who are covered by workers' compensation statutes must meet certain legal tests in order to receive benefits. There is a four-step test found in most state workers' compensation laws: (1) there must be a *personal injury*, which in some jurisdictions is interpreted to exclude mental illness; (2) that results from an *accident*, which is interpreted in some states to exclude injuries that develop over a long period of time, as opposed to those injuries resulting from a traumatic incident; (3) that must *arise out of employment*, which means that the source of the injury must be related to the job; and (4) that must occur during the *course of employment*, which normally requires that the injury occur on the employer's premises and during working hours. Most work-related injuries can meet these four tests, although there are thousands of cases testing the exact meaning of each of these four steps.

The coverage of diseases is a problem in workers' compensation. Many diseases could not meet the accident test because they developed over a prolonged period. In addition the statutes used to contain limited lists of diseases that were compensable. Fortunately, the restricted lists of diseases have now been abandoned in all jurisdictions. Now, typically, there is a list of specified occupational diseases followed by a general category permitting the compensation of other occupational diseases.

Nonetheless, there are restrictions in language pertaining to work-related diseases still found in many laws, such as statutes of limitations that require the claim to be filed within a limited period after the last exposure to the substance causing the disease, even if the disease did not manifest itself for a prolonged period. Also, some state courts have interpreted the general category of occupational diseases to only cover those diseases that are peculiar to or characteristic of the occupation of the employee seeking coverage.

3. MEDICAL CARE AND REHABILITATION SERVICES

Most state workers' compensation laws require the employer to provide full medical benefits without cost to the worker. This portion of the workers' compensation program has become increasingly expensive in the last decade, with medical benefits now accounting for close to half of all benefit payments, up from one-third in the early 1980s. Unlike most health care plans, there are no deductibles or co-insurance provisions that require employees to share the expense of medical care.

Fee schedules have been issued by many state workers' compensation agencies that limit medical charges, which have made some medical care providers reluctant or unwilling to provide services to injured workers. Other providers appear to react to fee schedules by increasing the quantity of health care services provided. There is disagreement about whether the fee schedules are effective in reducing expenditures on medical care.

Another approach to reducing workers' compensation health care expenditures used in a number of states is to allow the insurance carrier or employer (rather than the employee) to choose the treating physician. Again, there is disagreement about the effect of such limits on employee choice on the quality and cost of health care. In recent years, there has also been a rapid increase in the use of managed health care in the workers' compensation programs in a number of states, including such techniques as HMOs, PPOs, and utilization review. There is limited evidence about the effect of these cost containment efforts on medical costs in the workers' compensation system.

Medical rehabilitation, such as physical therapy, is likely to be provided by the workers' compensation laws. However, many states do not provide vocational rehabilitation services that may be necessary to equip the injured worker to handle a new job.

4. CASH BENEFITS

Cash benefits vary substantially among the states, with wide variations in maximum weekly benefits and in some instances limitations on the duration of benefits. Each state also provides a variety of types of cash benefits. A general characteristic of the cash benefits is that they are not subject to state or federal income taxes.

a. Temporary Total Disability Benefits

These benefits are paid to someone who is completely unable to work but whose injury is of a temporary nature. The weekly benefit in most jurisdictions is two-thirds of the worker's preinjury wage, subject to maximum and minimum amounts as prescribed by state law. There is also a waiting period during which the worker receives no benefits. However, if the worker is still disabled beyond a specified date, known as the retroactive date, then the benefits for the waiting period are paid on a retroactive basis.

b. Temporary Partial Disability Benefits

These benefits are paid to someone who is still recovering from a workplace injury or disease and who is able to return to work but has limitations on the amount or intensity of work that can be provided during the healing period. The weekly benefit in most jurisdiction is two-thirds of the difference between the worker's preinjury wage and the worker's current earnings, subject to a maximum amount as prescribed by state law.

c. Permanent Partial Disability (PPD) Benefits

PPD benefits are the most complicated, controversial, and expensive type of workers' compensation benefit. They are paid to a worker who has a permanent consequence of his or her work-related injury or disease that is not totally disabling. An example would be someone who has lost a hand in an accident.

There are two general approaches to permanent partial disability benefits. *Scheduled PPD benefits* are paid for those injuries that are included in a list found in the workers' compensation statute. In New York, for example, 100% loss of an arm entitles the worker to 312 weeks of benefits. The schedules are also applied to partial loss of the arm, so that a 50% loss of an arm in New York is worth 156 weeks of benefit. The schedules in most jurisdictions provide benefits whether the injury results in amputation or a loss of use of the body part. Normally the schedule is limited to the body extremities such as arms, legs, hand and feet, plus eyes and ears. (These schedules are sometimes referred to as "Meat Charts." In Australia, the schedules are known as "The Table of Maims.")

Nonscheduled PPD benefits are paid for those permanent injuries that are not on the schedule, such as back cases. The basis for these benefits depends on the jurisdiction. In states like New Jersey that use the "impairment approach," the back injury is rated in terms of the seriousness of the medical consequences. (In New Jersey, 25% of loss of the whole person in a medical sense translates into 25% of 600 weeks or 150 weeks of benefits). In states like Wisconsin that use the "loss of earning capacity approach," the back injury is rated considering the medical consequences as well as factors, such as age, education, and job experience, that affect the worker's earning capacity. (In Wisconsin, 25% of loss of earning capacity translates into 25% of 1000 weeks or 250 weeks of benefits).

These benefit durations for scheduled PPD benefits and for nonscheduled permanent partial benefits in those jurisdictions relying on the impairment approach or on the loss of earning capacity approach are fixed in the sense that the worker receives that duration of benefits whether or not she has actual wage loss for that period. During the period these types of the permanent partial benefits are being paid, the weekly benefit is normally calculated as $66^2/_3\%$ of preinjury wages, subject to maximum and minimum weekly benefit amounts.

The nonscheduled permanent partial disability benefits in New York rely on a fundamentally different approach, usually referred to as the "wage-loss approach." The worker only receives benefits if, in addition to having a injury with permanent consequences, the worker also has actual wage loss due to the work-injury. The weekly nonscheduled permanent partial disability benefit in New York is $66^2/_3\%$ of the difference between the worker's earnings prior to the injury minus the worker's earnings after the healing period is over, subject to a maximum weekly amount. In New York, these nonscheduled permanent partial disability benefits can continue for as long as the worker has earnings losses due to the work-related injury, which can be for the rest of the worker's life.

d. Permanent Total Disability Benefits

Permanent total disability benefits are paid to someone who is completely unable to work for an indefinite period. Permanent total status is assigned if the worker has specified types of injuries, such as the loss of two arms, or more generally if the facts in the case warrant an evaluation as a permanent total disability. This is a relatively uncommon type of case in workers' compensation. The weekly benefit for a permanent total disability is normally two-thirds of the preinjury wage, subject to maximum and minimum amounts as prescribed by state law. In most states, the permanent total disability benefits are paid for the duration of total disability or for life. In a number of states, however, there are arbitrary limits on total dollar amounts or duration of these benefits.

e. Death Benefits

Death benefits are paid to the survivor of a worker who was killed on the job. In many jurisdictions the weekly benefit depends on the number of survivors. For example, a widow or widower might receive a benefit that is 50% of the deceased worker's wage, while a widow or widower with a child might receive a weekly benefit that is $66^2/_3\%$ of the deceased worker's wage. These benefits are subject to minimum and maximum weekly amounts. Most states provide the benefits for the duration of the survivor's lifetime if the survivor is a widow or widower and for children's benefits at least until age twenty-one, but there are a number of states that have limits on the dollar amounts or on the durations of survivors' benefits.

5. FINANCING OF BENEFITS

Workers' compensation benefits are prescribed by state laws, but these laws assign the responsibility for the provision of the benefits to the employer. The employer in turn provides the benefits by one of three mechanisms: (i) by purchasing insurance from a private insurance carrier; (ii) by purchasing insurance from a state workers' compensation fund; or (iii) by qualifying as a self-insurer and paying its own employees directly. Some states, such as New York, have all three options available. (This is known as the three-way system.) Other states, such as Ohio, restrict the choices to the state fund (known as an exclusive or monopolistic state fund) or self-insurance. Still other states, such as Nebraska, New Jersey, and Wisconsin, restrict the choices to private insurance carriers or self-insurance. Nationally, about 50% of all benefits are paid by private insurance carriers, with self-insurance and state funds each accounting for about 25%.

The workers' compensation insurance premiums are experience rated. There are several steps in the experience rating process. Every employer who purchases insurance is assigned to a particular insurance classification (e.g. a bakery is assigned to class 2003); then the initial insurance rate can be determined by looking in an insurance manual that specifies the "manual rate" for each insurance classification. These manual rates are in terms of so many dollars per hundred dollars of payroll. (For example, a manual rate of $2.00 means that an employer who has a worker paid $300 a week must pay a $6.00 per week insurance premium for that worker.) The manual rates vary substantially within each state, reflecting the previous experience with benefit payments for all the employers in that classification. Manual rates in a particular state might range from $40 per $100 of payroll for logging to $.75 per $100 of payroll for clerical workers.

Those employers who are of medium or large size are eligible for firm-level experience rating. This means that they will pay more or less than the premiums suggested by the manual rates, depending on their own experience relative to other firms in the same insurance classification. For example, a bakery with a particularly adverse record of benefit payments might end up paying $6 per $100 of payroll even though the manual rate is $2 per $100 of payroll.

Employers that self-insure — that is, pay benefits to their own employees without use of an insurance carrier — represent an ultimate form of experience rating. (This needs to be qualified to some degree because self-insuring employers generally purchase excess risk policies that protect them against unusually adverse experience.)

6. ADMINISTRATION OF WORKERS' COMPENSATION

There are wide variations among the states in how the workers' compensation programs are administered. There are several dimensions of the differences among states.

a. The Initial Responsibility for Payment

Most states use what is known as the direct payment system, in which employers are obligated to begin payment as soon as the worker is injured and the employer accepts liability. Other states use the agreement system, where the employers have no obligation to begin payments until an agreement is reached with the employee concerning the amount due. The agreement system is likely to involve delays in many cases where the worker is unable to make a decision rapidly.

b. The Functions of the Administrative Agency

Most states have a workers' compensation agency that is responsible for administering the program. One function of the agency is adjudication of disputes between workers and employers or insurance carriers. In most agencies, the initial level of decision is made by an administrative law judge (ALJ) or an official with similar duties, such as a hearing examiner. The decisions of the ALJ normally can be appealed to an appeals board (or commission) within the workers' compensation agency. Then, appeals from the workers' compensation board typically enter the state court system at the appellate court level.

The state workers' compensation agencies vary considerably in their administrative styles. At one extreme are agencies, such as those in Illinois, that are passive. They essentially do nothing but wait for problems to arise and then perform the adjudication function. The other extreme is Wisconsin, where the agency can be characterized as active because it performs three functions in addition to adjudication. The Wisconsin agency engages in extensive record keeping, in monitoring of the performance of carriers and employers, and in providing evaluations (e.g., of the extent of permanent disability) that help the parties reach decisions without resorting to litigation.

c. Closing of Cases

In many states, cases are closed by private agreements of the parties. These are generally known as compromise and release agreements, because a compromise is reached on the amount of benefits paid and the employer is released from any further obligations. Normally the benefits are paid in a lump sum. These compromise and release agreements are often criticized, because they mean that workers who subsequently have additional need for medical care or income benefits cannot obtain them from the employer.

d. Extent of Litigation

States vary widely in the extent of litigation (defined here as the use of an attorney by the worker to help receive benefits). The worker's attorney's fee is almost always deducted from the cash benefit. Wisconsin is an extreme example of a state where lawyers are involved in only a small minority of cases. At the other extreme, states such as California and Illinois have lawyers involved in the great majority of cases, especially those that involve anything other than a relatively short period of temporary total benefits.

C. THE EXCLUSIVITY OF WORKERS' COMPENSATION

Exclusivity is one of the founding principles of workers' compensation. In exchange for a no-fault system (which benefited workers), workers' compensation became the exclusive remedy against the employer for a worker injured on the job (which benefited employers). As Professor Larson explains:

> The exclusiveness of the compensation remedy is a universal feature of American compensation law. It lies at the heart of the well-known quid pro quo, under which the employer enjoys tort immunity in exchange for accepting absolute liability for all work-connected injuries.... In recent years, however, selective attacks have been made on exclusiveness .... There have been six main lines of attack on exclusiveness: (1) nonphysical torts; (2) the dual-capacity doctrine; (3) the insurer as suable third party for negligent safety inspection or medical treatment; (4) suits against co-employees, including physicians and corporate officers; (5) attempts to stretch the concept of "intentional" injury to include willful and wanton negligence; and (6) recovery-over by third parties against the employer for contribution or implied indemnity....
>
> The five principal nonphysical torts that have figured in reported cases are false imprisonment, defamation, deceit, intentional infliction of emotional distress, and retaliation.

Arthur Larson, *Tensions of the Next Decade, in* NEW PERSPECTIVES IN WORKERS' COMPENSATION 21, 23-24 (John F. Burton, Jr. ed., 1988). The following cases examine the limits of the exclusivity principle.

1. TORT SUITS AND OTHER LEGAL ACTIONS AGAINST THE EMPLOYER

MILLISON v. E.I. du PONT DE NEMOURS & CO.

Supreme Court of New Jersey

501 A.2d 505 (1985)

CLIFFORD, J.

The New Jersey Workers' Compensation Act, *N.J.S.A.* 34:15-1 to -128 (Compensation Act), contains an exclusive-remedy provision in *N.J.S.A.* 34:15-8. The issue in these consolidated cases is whether that provision precludes employees who have suffered occupational diseases from maintaining a separate tort action against their employer and against company physicians. The employees charge the employer and physicians with intentionally exposing the employees to asbestos in the workplace, deliberately concealing from employees the risks of exposure to asbestos, and fraudulently concealing specific medical information obtained during employee physical examinations that reveal diseases already contracted by workmen. We hold that although the employees are limited to workers' compensation benefits for any initial occupational-disease disabilities related to the hazards of their employment experience, the Compensation Act does not bar plaintiffs' cause of action for aggravation of those illnesses resulting from defendants' fraudulent concealment of already-discovered disabilities....

II

....

The thrust of plaintiffs' allegations is that there was something akin to a conspiratorial agreement between du Pont and its medical staff that resulted in harm to plaintiffs. They assert generally that defendants, with knowledge of the adverse health consequences of asbestos use and exposure, and as part of a concerted plan for profit, deliberately exposed the plaintiffs to a dangerous work environment. Their claims focus on two separate situations, however.

The first count of the complaint avers that defendants knew or should have known of the dangers associated with asbestos exposure, that they therefore had a duty to inform plaintiffs and to protect them from those dangers, but that they nonetheless acted intentionally to conceal from plaintiffs all information regarding the health hazards of asbestos. In count two of their complaint, plaintiffs allege that du Pont and the company physicians fraudulently concealed from plaintiffs the fact that company medical examinations had revealed that certain plaintiffs-employees had contracted asbestos-related diseases. They assert that each year the du Pont doctors would give employees complete physical examinations, including chest x-rays, pulmonary function tests, electrocardiograms, urine analyses, and blood tests. Plaintiffs contend that the results of these physical exams indicated that plaintiffs-employees had contracted serious pulmonary and respiratory abnormalities associated with exposure to asbestos. They further maintain that rather than provide medical treatment for these ailing employees, defendants fraudulently concealed plaintiffs' asbestos-related diseases and sent them back into the workplace, where their initial infirmities were aggravated by additional exposure to asbestos. Plaintiffs claim that the time from defendants' first knowledge of the employee's condition to the time when the employee was told of the danger was as long as eight years.

III

It is undisputed that plaintiffs' injuries, if proven, are compensable under the Compensation Act. The controversy presented, however, calls for a determination of whether the legislature intended that the Compensation Act should serve as a worker's sole and exclusive remedy under circumstances such as those alleged. The pertinent statute, *N.J.S.A.* 34:15-8, declares that when, by express or implied agreement, the parties have accepted the provisions of the Compensation Act and the employee qualifies for benefits under the conditions of the Act, the employee shall ordinarily be barred from the pursuit of other remedies.[2] As the statute expressly indicates, however, an exception to the exclusivity provision is available when plaintiffs can prove an "intentional wrong."...

Plaintiffs argue that their charges that defendants knowingly and deliberately exposed employees to a hazardous work environment and fraudulently concealed existing occupational diseases are sufficient to fall within the Act's limited "intentional wrong" exception and to take their injuries outside the intended scope of the Compensation Act. However, as noted by the Appellate Division in granting defendants' motions to dismiss, in order to satisfy the Compensation Act's definition of "intentional wrong," claimants have heretofore been required to show a deliberate intention to injure.... This requirement of proving actual intent to injure in order to avoid the exclusivity of a workers' compensation act is the subject of comment by Professor Larson in his multivolume treatise on Workers' Compensation Law:

> Even if the alleged conduct goes beyond aggravated negligence, and includes such elements as knowingly permitting a hazardous work condition to exist, knowingly ordering claimant to perform an extremely dangerous job, willfully failing to furnish a safe place to work, or even willfully and unlawfully violating a safety statute, this still falls short of the kind of actual intention to injure that robs the injury of accidental character....
>
> If these decisions seem rather strict, one must remind oneself that what is being tested here is not the degree of gravity or depravity of the employer's conduct, but rather the narrow issue of intentional versus accidental quality of the precise event producing injury. The intentional removal of a safety device or toleration of a dangerous condition may or may not set the stage for an accidental injury later. But in any normal use of the words, it cannot be said, if such an injury does happen, that this was deliberate infliction of harm comparable to an intentional left jab to the chin.

[2A A. Larson, *The Law of Workmen's Compensation*, § 68.13 at 13-22 to 13-27 (1983) (footnotes omitted).]

The approach explicated by Professor Larson emphasizes the narrow or limited character of the exception.... The approach of construing and applying the exception in the most limited fashion consistent with the purpose of the law is followed by the vast majority of jurisdictions that have considered whether allegedly egregious employer conduct warrants the recognition of a separate cause of action outside the compensation system....

---

[2] Absent an express written statement to the contrary, *N.J.S.A.* 34:15-9 creates a presumption that the parties to every employment contract have agreed to be governed by the provisions of the Compensation Act.

V

Mindful of the origins of the Compensation Act and its subsequent development, we turn to the precise legal issue posed by this appeal: what categories of employer conduct will be sufficiently flagrant so as to constitute an "intentional wrong," thereby entitling a plaintiff to avoid the "exclusivity" bar of *N.J.S.A.* 34:15-8? Plaintiffs contend that du Pont and the doctors, in exposing the employees to asbestos and concealing medical information, acted knowingly and deliberately, not accidentally or negligently, so that defendants' conduct must be considered an "intentional wrong" within the meaning of the statute. Defendants, relying on the bulk of the authority on this topic, conversely assert that only conduct amounting to actual intent to injure employees will be sufficient to qualify as an "intentional wrong" in the context of a workers' compensation statute, and that the plaintiffs' complaints fall short of alleging "deliberate infliction of harm comparable to an intentional left jab to the chin." 2A *A. Larson, supra,* § 68.13 at 13-27.

Although we are certain that the legislature could not have intended that the system of workers' compensation would insulate actors from liability outside the boundaries of the Act for all willful and flagrant misconduct short of deliberate assault and battery, we are equally sure that the statutory scheme contemplates that as many work-related disability claims as possible be processed exclusively within the Act. Moreover, if "intentional wrong" is interpreted too broadly, this single exception would swallow up the entire "exclusivity" provision of the Act, since virtually all employee accidents, injuries, and sicknesses are a result of the employer or a co-employee intentionally acting to do whatever it is that may or may not lead to eventual injury or disease. Thus in setting an appropriate standard by which to measure an "intentional wrong," we are careful to keep an eye fixed on the obvious: the system of workers' compensation confronts head-on the unpleasant, even harsh, reality — but a reality nevertheless — that industry knowingly exposes workers to the risks of injury and disease.

The essential question therefore becomes what level of risk-exposure is so egregious as to constitute an "intentional wrong." We are confident that the *quid pro quo* of workers' compensation — employer makes swift and certain payment without regard to his own fault in exchange for immunity from liability at law — can best be preserved by applying the "intent" analysis of Dean Prosser to determine what is an "intentional wrong" within the meaning of the Act. According to Prosser,

> the mere knowledge and appreciation of a risk — something short of substantial certainty — is not intent. The defendant who acts in the belief or consciousness that the act is causing an appreciable risk of harm to another may be negligent, and if the risk is great the conduct may be characterized as reckless or wanton, but it is not an intentional wrong....

In adopting a "substantial certainty" standard, we acknowledge that every undertaking, particularly certain business judgments, involve some risk, but that willful employer misconduct was not meant to go undeterred. The distinctions between negligence, recklessness, and intent are obviously matters of degree, albeit subtle ones, as the thoughtful dissent so powerfully points out. In light of the legislative inclusion of occupational diseases within the coverage of the Compensation Act, however, the dividing line between negligent or reckless conduct on the one hand and intentional wrong on the other must be drawn with caution, so that the statutory framework of the Act is not circumvented simply because a known risk later blossoms into reality. We must demand a virtual certainty....

There is another significant component to the level of risk exposure that will satisfy the "intentional wrong" exception. Courts must examine not only the conduct of the employer, but also the context in which that conduct takes place: may the resulting injury or disease, and the circumstances in which it is inflicted on the worker, fairly be viewed as a fact of life of industrial employment, or is it rather plainly beyond anything the legislature could have contemplated as entitling the employee to recover *only* under the Compensation Act?

Examining the allegations in these cases in light of the foregoing principles, we conclude that count one of plaintiffs' complaints seeking damages beyond those available through workers' compensation for their initial work-related occupational diseases must fall. Although defendants' conduct in knowingly exposing plaintiffs to asbestos clearly amounts to deliberately taking risks with employees' health, as we have observed heretofore the mere knowledge and appreciation of a risk — even the strong probability of a risk — will come up short of the "substantial certainty" needed to find an intentional wrong resulting in avoidance of the exclusive-remedy bar of the compensation statute. In the face of the legislature's awareness of occupational diseases as a fact of industrial employment, we are constrained to conclude that plaintiffs-employees' initial resulting occupational diseases must be considered the type of hazard of employment that the legislature anticipated would be compensable under the terms of the Compensation Act and not actionable in an additional civil suit.

We acknowledge a certain anomaly in the notion that employees who are severely ill as a result of their exposure to asbestos in their place of employment are forced to accept the limited benefits available to them through the Compensation Act. Despite the fact that the current system sometimes provides what seems to be, and at times doubtless is, a less-than-adequate remedy to those who have been disabled on the job, all policy arguments regarding any ineffectiveness in the current compensation system as a way to address the problems of industrial diseases and accidents are within the exclusive province of the legislature....

Plaintiffs have, however, pleaded a valid cause of action for aggravation of their initial occupational diseases under the second count of their complaints. Count two alleges that in order to prevent employees from leaving the workforce, defendants fraudulently concealed from plaintiffs the fact that they were suffering from asbestos-related diseases, thereby delaying their treatment and aggravating their existing illnesses. As noted earlier, du Pont's medical staff provides company employees with physical examinations as part of its package of medical services. Plaintiffs contend that although plaintiffs' physical examinations revealed changes in chest x-rays indicating asbestos-related injuries, du Pont's doctors did not inform plaintiffs of their sicknesses, but instead told them that their health was fine and sent them back to work under the same hazardous conditions that had caused the initial injuries.

These allegations go well beyond failing to warn of potentially-dangerous conditions or intentionally exposing workers to the risks of disease. There is a difference between, on the one hand, tolerating in the workplace conditions that will result in a certain number of injuries or illnesses, and, on the other, actively misleading the employees who have already fallen victim to those risks of the workplace. An employer's fraudulent concealment of diseases already developed is not one of the risks an employee should have to assume. Such intentionally-deceitful action goes beyond the bargain struck by the Compensation Act. But for defendants' corporate strategy of concealing diseases discovered in company physical examinations, plaintiffs would have minimized the dangers to their health. Instead, plaintiffs were deceived — or so they charge — by corporate doctors who held themselves out as acting in plaintiffs' best interests. The legislature, in passing the Compensation Act, could not have intended to insulate such conduct from tort liability. We therefore conclude that plaintiffs' allegations that defendants fraudulently concealed knowledge of already-contracted diseases are sufficient to state a cause of action for aggravation of plaintiffs' illnesses, as distinct from any claim for the existence of the initial disease, which is cognizable only under the Compensation Act....

Those corporate medical departments that do their best to provide legitimate medical services to their workers, yet commit a negligent error along the way, have no reason to fear increased liability as a result of our holding. On the other hand, those corporations that would use their medical departments as a tool to prevent employees from learning of known injuries that are substantially certain to be aggravated by lack of disclosure must be deterred from embarking on such a course of conduct....

VIII

As to so much of plaintiffs' complaints as seek damages for deliberate exposure to asbestos and to the risks associated with that exposure, we hold that those claims are compensable exclusively under the Compensation Act. They were dismissed by the trial court and the judgment of dismissal was affirmed by the Appellate Division. So much of the Appellate Division's judgment as embraces dismissal of the first count of the complaint is affirmed.

Plaintiffs have pleaded a valid cause of action in their second count as against du Pont and its physicians, based on an intentional wrong.

HANDLER, J., concurring in part and dissenting....

The Court today recognizes that in order for an injured worker suffering from an occupation-related disease to bring a common-law action against his employer based upon "intentional wrong," thereby escaping the exclusivity provision of the Workers' Compensation Act under *N.J.S.A.* 34:15-8, the worker must prove that the employer's actions were "substantially certain" to cause the resultant disease. The Court also interprets the "intentional wrong" exception to the exclusive remedy of the Compensation Act as encompassing intentional wrongs committed by employers as well as a worker's co-employees.

I agree with these propositions of law. However, I think that the Court errs in applying its standard to the facts of this case. While the Court professes to endorse the "substantially certain" standard in construing the "intentional wrong" exception, its rejection of plaintiffs' common-law cause of action in the context of this case in effect requires that an employee demonstrate a much higher degree of knowledge on the part of the employer than "substantial certainty." The effect of the Court's decision is to impose a level of knowledge of resultant harm that is virtually akin to a showing of subjective intent or actual purpose to inflict injury. I take issue with the Court's application because, as I view the record, plaintiffs have presented a cause of action that genuinely and fairly raises the issue of whether or not defendants in this case possessed and concealed information indicating that exposure to asbestos was "substantially certain" to cause the occupational diseases that have debilitated the plaintiffs. I would thus reverse the lower court's disposition of plaintiffs' "initial intentional concealment and exposure" claims and permit that cause of action to proceed to a plenary trial.

The Court also upholds plaintiffs' claims against du Pont and its physicians for fraudulent failure to disclose the plaintiffs' contraction of asbestos engendered diseases and consequent aggravation of those diseases. I concur in the majority's disposition of this claim....

NOTES

1. *Deceit and Fraud as a Basis for Tort Recovery*. Deceit and fraud are emerging as important categories of exceptions to the exclusive remedy provision. These forms of tort serve as the principal vehicle for suits against employers when workers suffer from diseases caused by substances, such as asbestos, cotton dust, and uranium, for which the dangers to workers are not immediately obvious. According to Professor Larson, the key to whether these suits are successful is whether there is a single injury or a dual injury:

> In the single-injury cases, the employer deceives the employee as to the hazards of the job, such as chemicals, fibers, and dusts, and the employee is injured as a result. This kind of action is almost universally held barred, because the deceit merges into the compensable injury itself. *Johnson v.*

Kerr-McGee Oil Industries, Inc.,[5] for example, follows the present dual-injury analysis in holding that an action for tort would not lie for failure to warn the employee of the hazards to which he would be exposed in mining uranium.

Dual injury occurs when the employer deceives an employee after the employee has already incurred a work-connected injury, with the result that the employee suffers a second, additional or aggravated harm. An early case establishing the principle was *Ramey v. General Petroleum Corp.*[6] The employee charged that the employer and carrier had conspired to conceal the existence of the employee's cause of action against a third party with which the employer had a hold-harmless agreement. The statute ran, and the cause of action was destroyed. An action in deceit was held to lie.

The leading case applying the two-injury technique to asbestos-related cases is *Johns-Manville Products Co. v. Contra Costa Superior Court (Rudkin).*[7] Here the court held that, although an action would not lie against the employer for the consequences of the original failure to warn of asbestos hazards, an action would lie for deceiving employees as to their condition after the impact of asbestos exposure was known and thus depriving them of the opportunity to take appropriate steps to avoid further injury and to treat the illness promptly. This doctrine received important support in 1985 when the Supreme Court of New Jersey, on similar facts, reached a similar conclusion.[8] This dual-injury analysis is not, however, universally accepted. *Rivers v. New York Jets,*[9] for example, dismisses a suit against the employer for failing to inform the plaintiff football player of the true nature of his injuries.

Arthur Larson, *Tensions of the Next Decade, in* NEW PERSPECTIVES IN WORKERS' COMPENSATION 21, 24-25 (John F. Burton, Jr. ed., 1988).

While Larson indicates that the key to recovery in these fraud or deceit cases is whether there is a single injury or a dual injury, a more useful distinction may be whether the fraud or deceit precedes the injury to the worker (in which case the worker cannot recover in a tort suit) or whether the injury precedes the fraud or deceit (in which case a tort suit is possible).

2. *Fraud by Employer in Defending Claim.* Suppose a worker files a workers' compensation claim and the employer challenges the claim by filing false documents. Because of the employer's fraud, the Workers' Compensation Board initially denies the claim, requiring the worker to hire a lawyer to uncover the fraud and appeal the Board's ruling. Eventually the employee receives his workers'

---

[5] 631 P.2d 548 (Ariz. Ct. App. 1981).

[6] 343 P.2d 787 (Cal. Ct. App. 1950).

[7] 612 P.2d 948 (Cal. Ct. App. 1980).

[8] *Millison v. E.I. du Pont de Nemours & Co.,* 501 A.2d 505 (N.J. 1985).

[9] 460 F. Supp. 1233 (E.D. Mo. 1978), applying New York law.

compensation award. Should the employee be allowed to bring a fraudulent mis-representation action and, if so, what are the appropriate damages? The danger of such an action is that employers will be chilled from vigorously defending against compensation claims. *See Persinger v. Peabody Coal Co.*, 474 S.E.2d 887 (W. Va. 1996) (allowing action for full compensatory damages, including annoyance and inconvenience, plus punitive damages and attorney's fees).

3. *"Substantially Certain" or "Certain"?* The ability of injured workers to use the intentional injury exception successfully depends in part on the language in the particular state's workers' compensation statute. Michigan provides a good example of how that language can change over time. The Michigan Supreme Court in *Beauchamp v. Dow Chemical Co.*, 398 N.W.2d 882 (Mich. 1986), held that an intentional tort provided an exception to the exclusive remedy doctrine, and that "intention" included any injury in which the employer intended an act and believed that the injurious consequence was "substantially certain" to occur.

The Michigan legislature reacted in 1987 by amending the workers' compensation statute to provide that an intentional injury occurs only when "the employer had actual knowledge that an injury was certain to occur and willfully disregarded that knowledge." MICH. COMP. LAWS § 418.131(1). The Michigan Supreme Court interpreted this language in *Travis v. Dreis & Krump Manufacturing Co.*, 551 N.W.2d 132 (Mich. 1996). Travis had been assigned to work on an unfamiliar machine which her supervisor knew (but did not tell her) had a history of unpredictable malfunctions. The tool room supervisor had told the supervisor that the machine needed to be shut down and fixed or rebuilt, or that someone would be hurt. After this conversation, some repairs were made on the machine and the supervisor believed it was functioning properly. However, the machine malfunctioned and Travis suffered amputation of two fingers and multiple crushing injuries to both hands. The trial court granted summary disposition of the case because it could not find that the facts constituted an intentional injury, and the Michigan Supreme Court agreed because the 1987 legislation requires an "extremely high standard" of showing that an injury was "certain" to occur. *Id.* at 143.

Consider an alternative set of facts. An employee's job includes pouring wet scrap metal objects into a furnace containing molten aluminum. The employee warned the employer about the dangerous circumstances under which he was required to work and the lack of protective devices. He suffers minor burns from this task and is sent home. He is then called back the same day to perform the same job function, and is severely burned this time. Would this constitute an intentional injury under the 1987 Michigan legislation? *Golec v. Metal Exch. Corp.*, 551 N.W.2d 132 (Mich. 1996) (yes, because of actual knowledge of specific injury which had already been proven "certain" to occur).

4. *Sexual Harassment as a Basis for Tort Recovery.* In *Ford v. Revlon, Inc.*, 734 P.2d 580 (Ariz. 1987), an employee sued her employer for intentional infliction of emotional distress when her supervisor repeatedly sexually harassed her verbally and physically. The Arizona Supreme Court rejected the employer's exclusivity defense, reasoning that intentional acts causing mental injury were not "accidents" within the meaning of the Arizona Workers' Compensation law. Justice Feldman concurred with the result but not the reasoning of the majority:

> While the form of the action — intentional infliction of emotional distress — is not always outside workers' compensation, the essence of the tort in the case before us involves a violation of rights protected by law and policy. *See* [Title VII;] *Meritor Savings Bank, FSB v. Vinson,* 477 U.S. 57 (1986). By law, exposure to sexual harassment is not an inherent or necessary risk of employment, even though it may be or may have been endemic. The cost of such conduct ought not to be included in the cost of the product and passed to the consumer. If my employer invades my right to privacy by tapping my telephone, it is my employer who should pay the piper for such a wrong, not his compensation carrier.
>
> ... Thus, I believe [the employee] is entitled to maintain a tort action against her employer despite the exclusivity bar for the simple reason that her injury ought not to be compensable under the workers' compensation system and is one of those torts that ought to be compensable only at the expense of the wrongdoer and only upon a showing of the requisite degree of culpability.

734 P.2d at 591.

Several recent cases have barred tort claims for intentional infliction of emotional distress because of the exclusive remedy provision of workers' compensation statutes. In *Konstantopoulos v. Westvaco Corp.,* 112 F.3d 710 (3rd Cir. 1997), *cert. denied,* 118 S. Ct. 1079 (1998), the Court of Appeals affirmed dismissal of a claim for intentional infliction of emotional distress as well as a claim for sexual assault and battery based in part on a certification from the Supreme Court of Delaware that "an employee's claim against her employer for personal injuries sustained during the course of employment, even if the offending conduct was of a sexual nature, is limited to the compensation provided by the [Workers' Compensation] Act." The offensive conduct included sexually suggestive behavior directed towards Konstantopoulos and a request to her from a fellow employee with "his pants' flap open" to "look at this." In a similar fashion, the Court in *Reed v. Avian Farms, Inc.,* 941 F. Supp. 10 (D. Me. 1996), dismissed the count alleging intentional infliction of emotional distress because of the exclusive remedy provision of the Maine workers' compensation act. Reed had been subjected to unwelcome and lewd sexual comments from a fellow employee, including a threat of rape.

An interesting extension of the use of the exclusive remedy provision as a bar to a suit for negligent infliction of emotional distress was presented in *Weiss v. City of Milwaukee,* 559 N.W.2d 588 (Wis. 1997). Despite assurances to the contrary, the city provided Weiss's new address and home phone number to her abusive former husband. He then regularly called her at work to inform her that he knew her new address and that he would kill her and their two children. The court affirmed a dismissal of Weiss's claim against the city, reasoning "that when an attack occurs during the course of employment and arises from personal animus imported from a private relationship, the incident arises out of the claimant's employment if employment conditions have contributed to or facilitated the attack." *Id.* at 595. The court found that since Weiss had been required to provide her address to the city as a condition of employment, the information was accidentally released by the city to the former husband, and the disclosure enabled him to threaten Weiss, the injury arose out her employment.

5. *Other Remedies for Sexual Harassment.* While a worker may not be able to recover in a tort suit against the employer because of the workers' compensation exclusivity principle, recovery may be possible under Title VII or under a state fair employment statute. One reason exclusivity was so important in sexual harassment cases was that until the enactment of the Civil Rights Act of 1991, Title VII did not permit compensatory damages for sexual harassment. Workers thus attempted tort suits instead of bringing Title VII suits in order to receive adequate relief. For a recent examination of the relationships among workers' compensation and other remedies for sexual harassment, *see Sexual Harassment, Antidiscrimination Laws, and Workers' Compensation*, 1 LARSON'S WORKERS' COMP. NEWS 15 (1996).

6. *Goosing as a Basis for Tort Recovery?* Hazelwood, a journeyman pressman working in the pressroom of the Richmond Newspapers, on several occasions was grabbed in the buttocks or the genital area by his immediate supervisor. The pressman sued the newspaper for compensatory and punitive damages, accusing the supervisor of assault and battery and the employer of negligence in hiring and retaining an unfit person in the workplace. The newspaper submitted evidence that "goosing" was prevalent in its pressroom, that the practice had continued for more than forty years, and that goosing existed in the pressrooms of other newspapers. The employer then argued that since goosing was so common, the activity was an actual risk of the employment and therefore any recovery for the consequences was limited to workers' compensation benefits. The Virginia Supreme Court found instead that goosing in the pressroom "was of a personal nature and not directed against the recipients as employees or in furtherance of the employer's business." *Richmond Newspapers, Inc. v. Hazelwood*, 457 S.E.2d 56 (Va. 1995). As a consequence, the exclusive remedy provision of workers' compensation could not be invoked, and the court upheld a jury verdict awarding Hazelwood $40,000 in compensatory damages and $100,000 in punitive damages.

2. NO REMEDY AGAINST THE EMPLOYER?

LIVITSANOS v. SUPERIOR COURT

Supreme Court of California

828 P.2d 1195 (1992)

ARABIAN, J.

We granted review to consider whether the exclusive remedy provisions of the Workers' Compensation Act apply to bar an employee's claims for intentional and negligent infliction of emotional distress, where no physical injury or disability is alleged. We hold that claims for intentional or negligent infliction of emotional distress are preempted by the exclusivity provisions of the workers' compensation law, notwithstanding the absence of any compensable physical disability. We further conclude that, for unrelated reasons, the case must be remanded to the Court of Appeal for further proceedings consistent with the views set herein.

Facts

....

Plaintiff Apostol Livitsanos began his employment at Continental Culture Specialists, Inc. (Continental), a yogurt manufacturing company owned by Vasa Cubaleski (Cubaleski), in 1976 in the shipping department. Two years later, plaintiff was promoted to supervisor of the department and in 1980 he was made manager, with attendant salary increases....

In 1984, Continental's regular distributor went out of business, leaving Continental without a distributor. Plaintiff and another Continental employee, Andy Stylianou, formed a company, known as ABA, exclusively to distribute Continental's products. Plaintiff and Stylianou operated the distributorship with full knowledge and approval of defendants Continental and Cubaleski.

Throughout plaintiff's term of employment, defendant Cubaleski praised plaintiff's performance, telling him that he had "saved the company," and that he would "someday own Continental."

In late 1988 or early 1989, for no apparent reason, Cubaleski began a campaign of harassment against plaintiff. This campaign took several forms. Cubaleski falsely accused plaintiff, along with Continental's office manager, of writing fraudulent checks to an outside contractor as part of a scheme to siphon funds away from Continental. Cubaleski communicated this charge to other Continental employees, as well as to an employee of an outside accounting firm. In addition, Cubaleski told Continental employees and others that $800,000 was "missing" from Continental, implying that plaintiff had stolen the money. Cubaleski threatened to have plaintiff "put in jail" because of the "missing" money.

....

In August 1989, Cubaleski insisted that plaintiff and Stylianou sell their distributorship company, ABA, to another distributor that Continental wished to employ. At the time, one of the clients of ABA was indebted to the company because Continental had asked ABA to extend $100,000 credit to this customer. Cubaleski promised that, if plaintiff sold ABA, Continental would assume responsibility for the $100,000 credit. After plaintiff agreed to sell ABA, Cubaleski demanded that plaintiff sign a promissory note for the $100,000 credit and agree to personal liability or he would "be in trouble." Plaintiff signed the note. Approximately two weeks later, plaintiff was terminated.

Plaintiff was discharged with no warning, no explanation and no severance pay. After the termination, Cubaleski told other Continental employees that plaintiff's company had been improperly buying fruit toppings to resell, using Continental's money. The accusations were false. After the termination, Cubaleski also told other Continental employees that plaintiff had stolen $800,000 from Continental and that plaintiff was blackmailing Cubaleski.

Plaintiff filed suit against Continental and Cubaleski for breach of contract, defamation, intentional infliction of emotional distress, negligent infliction of emotional distress, and money lent. He alleged that defendants engaged in a campaign of harassment resulting in the wrongful termination of his employment. Defendants demurred to the causes of action for defamation and negligent and intentional infliction of emotional distress. The trial court sustained Continental's demurrers without leave to amend, apparently on the ground that the employer's conduct was "a normal part of the employment relationship" and therefore barred by the Workers' Compensation Act (*Cole v. Fair Oaks Fire Protection Dist.* (1987) 43 Cal. 3d 148, 160 (hereafter *Cole*)). Cubaleski's demurrers were also sustained, but leave to amend was granted as to limited issues. The Court of Appeal, citing *Cole,* summarily denied plaintiff's petition for writ of mandate.

Discussion

1. *Intentional Infliction of Emotional Distress*

Plaintiff contends that because he did not allege any physical injury or disability resulting from defendants' conduct, his cause of action for intentional infliction of emotional distress is outside the scope of the workers' compensation law, and thus not governed by *Cole*. He relies principally on *Renteria v. County of Orange* (1978) 82 Cal. App. 3d 833, 838 (hereafter *Renteria*), which held that a cause of action for intentional infliction of emotional distress is outside the scope of the workers' compensation scheme where the injury is purely "emotional," and no "physical" disability is alleged.

We have not heretofore been called upon to reconcile the principles of *Cole* and *Renteria*. In *Cole*, the employer engaged in a campaign of harassment which caused the plaintiff severe physical injury and disability. We held that the injuries were compensable under workers' compensation notwithstanding the egregious nature of the employer's misconduct, because such actions "are a normal part of the employment relationship." There was no allegation, however, that the plaintiff had suffered a "purely emotional" injury.... Here, plaintiff has not alleged any physical injury or disability resulting from the employer's conduct.[4] Thus ... we are called upon to construe the principles we adduced in *Cole* in the context of a case of purely emotional injury.

We begin with a review of *Renteria*. The plaintiff filed a civil action against his employer and fellow employees alleging numerous acts of harassment designed to discriminate against him because of his Mexican-American ancestry. The defendants successfully demurred on the ground the action was barred by the exclusive remedy provisions of the workers' compensation law. The Court of Appeal reversed, holding that the cause of action for intentional infliction of emotional distress was not barred.

The court first rejected the defendants' claim that emotional distress damages are generally recoverable in a workers' compensation proceeding. Although physical injury (e.g., a heart condition) caused by mental and emotional stress, or disabling mental illness caused by job pressures are compensable, the court held that "mental suffering, *as such*," without accompanying physical injury or disability, was not a compensable injury. (*Renteria, supra,* 82 Cal. App. 3d 833, 839; italics in original.) The court noted that the fact that an injury was non-compensable did not, "by itself, abrogate the exclusive remedy provisions of the Workers' Compensation Act." It determined, however, that the plaintiff's action was "not an isolated instance of a physical injury which is noncompensable, but an entire class of civil wrongs outside the contemplation of the workers' compensation system."

It reached this conclusion, evidently, in large part because the alleged wrong involved intentional injury. As the court stated: "While it is possible to believe that the Legislature intended that employees lose their right to compensation for certain forms of negligently or accidentally inflicted physical injuries in exchange for a system of workers' compensation featuring liability without fault, compulsory insurance, and prompt medical care, it is much more difficult to believe that the Legislature intended the employee to surrender all right to any form of compensation for mental suffering caused by extreme and outrageous misconduct by an employer." The *Renteria* court therefore concluded that the cause of action for intentional infliction of emotional distress constituted an implied exception to workers' compensation exclusivity under conditions where the "'essence of the tort, in law, [was] non-physical ....'"

....

[T]he proposition that intentional or egregious employer conduct is necessarily outside the scope of the worker's compensation scheme is erroneous. This was the precise problem which we addressed in *Cole,* where we noted that many intentional acts by an employer could be expected to cause emotional distress

---

[4] We reject defendants' suggestion that allegations plaintiff suffered "nervousness" necessarily constitute physical injury. Terms such as nervousness, anxiety, worry, humiliation, embarrassment, apprehension, and others, refer to subjective emotional states.

and yet do not lie outside the proper scope of workers' compensation. Even intentional "misconduct" may constitute a "normal part of the employment relationship."...

Furthermore, as we observed in *Cole,* the *Renteria* court's distinction between "physical" and "emotional" injury presents a glaring anomaly: If the employer's misconduct causes "purely emotional" distress, then the employee may maintain a civil action with full tort remedies; if the employer's conduct is so outrageous as to cause actual physical disability, however, the employee is limited to the recovery of workers' compensation. Thus, the more reprehensible the employer's conduct, the more likely that such conduct would be shielded by the workers' compensation exclusivity rule. It would then be in the employer's best interest to make conditions so intolerable for an employee and to cause such a level of emotional distress that the employee could not work as a result. Thus, the employer could avoid civil liability for the most egregious misconduct.

Clearly, the law should not, and need not, countenance such paradoxical results. The "physical" versus "emotional" dichotomy is logically insupportable. More importantly, it is contrary to the text and purposes of the workers' compensation law.

The touchstone of the workers' compensation system is industrial injury which results in *occupational disability* or death. Labor Code section 3208 defines "injury" as "*any* injury or disease arising out of the employment ...." (Italics added.) Labor Code section 3208.1 describes "specific" injuries "occurring as the result of one incident or exposure *which causes disability or need for medical treatment*" and "cumulative" injury as "occurring as repetitive mentally or physically traumatic activities extending over a period of time, the combined effect of *which causes any disability or need for medical treatment.*" (Italics added.) Thus, as the court in *Coca-Cola Bottling Co. v. Superior Court* (1991) 233 Cal. App. 3d 1273, observed, "a compensable injury is one which causes disability or need for medical treatments." (*Id.* at p. 1284.)

Moreover, the workers' compensation system is designed to compensate only for such disability or need for treatment as is occupationally related. "Temporary disability" benefits are a substitute for lost wages during a period of temporary incapacity from working; "permanent disability" payments are provided for permanent bodily impairment, to indemnify for impaired future earning capacity or decreased ability to compete in an open labor market. The basic purpose of the Workers' Compensation Act is to compensate for the disabled worker's diminished ability to compete in the open labor market, not to compensate every work-related injury.

Thus, compensable injuries may be physical, emotional or both, so long as they are disabling....

Compensation for psychiatric injury is not new.... An employee who suffers a disabling emotional injury caused by the employment is entitled, upon appropriate proof, to workers' compensation benefits, including any necessary disability compensation or medical or hospital benefits.

Thus, the *Renteria* court plainly erred in suggesting that emotional injury which results in an industrial disability is not compensable under the Workers' Compensation Act. So long as the basic conditions of compensation are otherwise satisfied, and the employer's conduct neither contravenes fundamental public policy (*Tameny v. Atlantic Richfield Co., supra,* 27 Cal. 3d 167) nor exceeds the risks inherent in the employment relationship (*Cole, supra,* 43 Cal. 3d 148), an employee's emotional distress injuries are subsumed under the exclusive remedy provisions of workers' compensation.

The conclusion that emotional injury lies within the scope of the workers' compensation law does not complete the analysis, however. For injury must also result in an industrial *disability* compensable under workers' compensation. It is theoretically possible to incur a work-related injury that results in no compensable industrial disability. Indeed, this was one of the concerns originally addressed in *Renteria.* And *Renteria* itself contains the answer: "The existence of a noncompensable injury does not, by itself, abrogate the exclusive remedy provisions of the Workers' Compensation Act."

This proposition was more fully explained by the court in *Williams v. State Compensation Ins. Fund* (1975) 50 Cal. App. 3d 116, where an employee who allegedly suffered a loss of sexual function as the result of an industrial injury asserted that his civil claim should go forward because such losses were not compensable under workers' compensation. The court rejected the argument, explaining as follows: "Plaintiff is correct in arguing that the statutory emphasis on *occupational* disability as a rating factor denigrates the compensability of nonoccupational handicaps. Decisions in other states hold that the workers' compensation law provides the exclusive remedy for industrial injury even though the resulting disability — for example, sexual impotence — is noncompensable. The theory underlying the out-of-state decisions is that the workers' compensation plan imposes reciprocal concessions upon employer and employee alike, withdrawing from each certain rights and defenses available at common law; the employer assumes liability without fault, receiving relief from some elements of damage available at common law; the employee gains relatively unconditional protection for impairment of his earning capacity, surrendering his common law right to elements of damage unrelated to earning capacity; the work-connected injury engenders a single remedy against the employer, exclusively cognizable by the compensation agency and not divisible into separate elements of damage available from separate tribunals; *a failure of the compensation law to include some elements of damage recoverable at common law is a legislative and not a judicial problem. (Id.* at 122, italics added.)[6]

---

[6] It should be noted that the portion of *Williams v. State Compensation Ins. Fund,* discussed in *Renteria,* apparently dealt with the question of rating factors with respect to an award of *permanent*

In sum, where the employee suffers annoyance or upset on account of the employer's conduct but is not disabled, does not require medical care, and the employer's conduct neither contravenes fundamental public policy nor exceeds the inherent risks of the employment, the injury will simply not have resulted in any occupational impairment compensable under the workers' compensation law or remediable by way of a civil action. To be sure, the theoretical class of cases which fit these criteria, in which there will be *no* remedy, would appear to be rather limited. Nevertheless, the possibility of a lack of a remedy in a few cases does not abrogate workers' compensation exclusivity. Not every aggravation in normal employment life is compensable.[7]

The question remains whether, in light of the foregoing principles, the demurrers to plaintiff's causes of action for intentional and negligent infliction of emotional distress were properly sustained. As discussed above, there is no merit to plaintiff's assertion that purely emotional injuries lie outside the scope of the workers' compensation system. The mere failure to allege physical disability will not entitle the injured employee to a civil action. To this extent, the demurrers were properly sustained.

Plaintiff's contention that defendants' misconduct exceeded the normal risks of the employment relationship is another matter. Plaintiff has alleged that defendants engaged in a campaign of outrageous and harassing conduct, which included falsely claiming that plaintiff embezzled money from Continental and tried to sabotage the company's product; compelling plaintiff to sell his independent distribution company, ABA, and demanding possession of its books and records; and forcing plaintiff to sign a $100,000 promissory note for a debt owed to ABA under threat of retaliation if he refused. The circumstances of the discharge were further complicated by the fact that plaintiff apparently occupied a dual status in his relationship with defendants: as employee, and as independent distributor of Continental's product.

---

disability benefits. An employee who suffered injury to the groin and thigh area from a machine used at work might well require medical treatment for the injuries and temporary disability benefits while off work. The employee would of course be entitled to such benefits, whether or not there was ultimately any residual ratable "permanent" disability. In addition, as the *Williams* court noted, Labor Code section 4660 provides that disfigurement, as well as occupational handicap, is a basis for an award of permanent disability. The court stated that "Whether disfigurement in the statutory sense requires visible mutilation or, on the contrary, comprehends a functional impairment without external manifestations, is an open question in California." (50 Cal. App. 3d at 123, fn. 3.) In *Williams,* the plaintiff did not urge that the injury to his genital organs constituted a disfigurement within the meaning of Labor Code section 4660, apparently because such a claim would have defeated his contention that his injury was not covered by workers' compensation and supported an independent action. The court accordingly did not address the disfigurement question.

[7] *Renteria* does not fall in this category. In that case, racial discrimination appears to have been the motivating force behind the employer's misconduct. Thus, the plaintiffs could have filed a civil suit based on a violation of fundamental public policy under principles set forth in *Tameny v. Atlantic Richfield Co., supra,* 27 Cal. 3d 167.

In summarily denying plaintiff's petition for writ of mandate, the Court of Appeal cited *Cole.* In so doing, however, it is unclear whether the court was concerned with the *Renteria* issue or the nature of defendants' alleged misconduct. *Cole,* of course, addressed both issues. Its central holding that workers' compensation provides the exclusive remedy for torts that comprise "a normal part of the employment relationship" has been discussed. However, as also noted, while *Cole* did not resolve the *Renteria* issue it acknowledged the "anomaly" which that decision had engendered.

Whatever the Court of Appeal's intentions in issuing a summary denial, it plainly failed to render a decision on the merits. In light of the serious allegations set forth in plaintiff's complaint, however, we conclude that the issue is an important one which should be addressed in a written opinion by the Court of Appeal. Accordingly, we shall remand the matter to the Court of Appeal with directions to consider whether, in this regard, the demurrers to the causes of action for negligent and intentional infliction of emotional distress were properly sustained.

2. Defamation

In addition to his claims of intentional and negligent infliction of emotional distress, plaintiff asserted a cause of action for defamation based on defendants' allegedly false statements accusing plaintiff of embezzlement and other misconduct against the company. Plaintiff claimed that the statements were slanderous per se, that he was "shocked and humiliated" by their publication, and that he suffered general damages to his reputation of $1 million.

The trial court ruled that the defamation claim was barred by the exclusive remedy provisions of the Workers' Compensation Act; the Court of Appeal denied plaintiff's petition for writ of mandate, citing *Cole.*

We have not heretofore ruled on the question whether defamation claims arising out of the course and scope of employment are barred by the exclusive remedy provisions of the Workers' Compensation Act.[9] We need not do so here. For even assuming, without deciding, that certain defamatory remarks in the employment context may be subject to workers' compensation, as we noted in the previous section the seriousness of the allegations in plaintiff's complaint and the hybrid nature of the relationship between plaintiff and defendants raise the further issue whether defendants' conduct was outside the scope and normal risks of employment. Therefore, on remand the Court of Appeal is directed to address these issues.

---

[9] A number of courts have apparently determined that the gravamen of an action for libel or slander is damage to "reputation," a "proprietary" as distinct from a physical or mental injury, and therefore have concluded that defamation does not lie within the purview of the workers' compensation law.... Other states have apparently concluded otherwise. Although the issue is an interesting and unsettled one, as explained above it is not one which necessarily requires resolution here.

Disposition

Plaintiff's contention that *Renteria* compels reversal of the order of the superior court sustaining the demurrer to his causes of action for negligent and intentional infliction of emotional distress is without merit. Nevertheless, the judgment of the Court of Appeal summarily denying plaintiff's petition for writ of mandate for relief from that order is reversed, and the case is remanded to the Court of Appeal to consider on the merits the remaining issues identified herein.

NOTES

1. *No Remedy Anywhere?* Normally, an employee injured at work will receive workers' compensation benefits and, because of the exclusive remedy principle, will be barred from a tort suit against the employer. But the California Supreme Court emphasizes that the test of exclusivity is not whether the particular employee will actually receive a workers' compensation award for a particular consequence of the injury. The court discusses a permanent physical consequence (sexual impotence) resulting from a work injury that does not affect the ability to work. Similar injuries are those to internal organs with permanent consequences that do not affect earning capacity. Presumably a work incident that resulted in permanent mental consequences, such as the worker's aversion to crowds, may result in no workers' compensation benefits (since the worker's earning capacity is not affected in the job she holds) and yet she may be barred by the exclusivity principle from a tort remedy.

2. *Are There Constitutional Limits to Constricted Coverage?* Earlier in this Part, we read the seminal case upholding the constitutionality of workers' compensation statutes, *New York Central Railroad Co. v. White*, 243 U.S. 188 (1917). One part of the Court's rationale was as follows:

> Viewing the entire matter, it cannot be pronounced arbitrary and unreasonable for the State to impose upon the employer the absolute duty of making a moderate and definite compensation in money to every disabled employee, or in case of his death to those who were entitled to look to him for support, in lieu of the common-law liability to cases of negligence.
>
> This, of course is not to say that any scale of compensation, however, insignificant on the one hand or onerous on the other, would be supportable. In this case, no criticism is made on the ground that the compensation prescribed by the statute in question is unreasonable in amount, either in general or in the particular case. Any question of that kind may be met when it arises.

Id. at 205-06.

Does this "ancient" pronouncement of a constitutional principle have any continuing validity? How would you reconcile this principle with the holding in *Livitsanos*? Suppose Kleinhesselink, who is a safety coordinator, experiences mental and physical conditions resulting from mental stress at the workplace because his safety recommendations were ignored, resulting in deaths and injuries. Suppose the case arose in a state that (1) made workers' compensation the exclusive remedy for work-related injuries and diseases, and (2) excluded the type of conditions Kleinhesselink experienced from coverage because their cause was mental rather than physical. Suppose that the employee files a tort suit alleging two counts of negligence against the employer. Can the employer have the counts dismissed because of the exclusive remedy provision? *Kleinhesselink v. Chevron*, 920 P.2d 108 (Mont. 1996) (no, because the trade-off of no-fault recovery for employees in return for protection from large damage awards for employers means that "it is axiomatic that there must be some possibility of recovery by the employee for the compromise to hold").

3. TO WHOM DOES THE EXCLUSIVE REMEDY PROVISION APPLY?

The exclusive remedy principle means that the only recovery of the injured worker against his or her employer is workers' compensation benefits, unless the worker can take advantage of one of the exceptions to exclusivity discussed in the previous subsections. The injured worker may, however, be able to bring a tort suit against a third party who was at least partially responsible for the injury. Since that third party did not participate in the exchange that established workers' compensation, which provided a no-fault program for employees in exchange for limited liability for the employer, the third party cannot claim immunity from a tort suit by invoking the exclusive remedy principle.

The claim against a third party can arise in a wide variety of circumstances. The third party, for example, may be the manufacturer of machinery that was defective in design and sold to the employer of the injured worker. In recent years, a number of third party suits have involved workers who contracted cancer or other diseases as a result of working with asbestos. Many of these workers have successfully sued manufacturers of asbestos, such as Johns-Manville, who did not provide adequate warnings about the danger of working with asbestos.

In general, the third party is liable for the entire amount of the damages experienced by the worker, including loss of wages, medical expenses, pain and suffering, and, where appropriate, punitive damages. In most states, the third party cannot require the employer to pay a portion of the damages, even when the employer is partially responsible for the damages to the employee. There might be, for example, joint negligence of the third party, who improperly designed a machine, and the employer, who removed a safety guard from the machine in order to speed production. Despite the joint negligence, in most jurisdictions the third party is liable for the entire amount of damages. The courts have reasoned that the exclusivity principle of workers' compensation would be jeopardized if the third party were allowed to require the employer to pay for part of the damages.

The employer is not only usually excused from responsibility for any portion of the damages when a third party is successfully sued by the employee, in most jurisdictions the employer can recover an amount from the award to reimburse the employer for any workers' compensation benefits that have been provided to the employee. Thus, if the employee sues the machine tool manufacturer whose negligence was partially responsible for the injury and recovers $100,000, the employer who has expended $40,000 on workers' compensation benefits can recoup those expenditures from the damage award in a subrogation action. The purpose of this recoupment is to prevent the worker from double recovery, since presumably the damages in the tort suit include payment for medical care and lost wages that were compensated for by the workers' compensation program.

The general principles involving the relationships among workers, third parties, and employers are not followed in every jurisdiction. A few jurisdictions, for example, require the injured worker to elect either workers' compensation or a tort suit. States vary about whether only the employee can bring the suit against the third party, or whether the employer also has this right, or whether both the employee and employer have the right.

In most jurisdictions, the comparative negligence of the employee but not the employer is used to establish the maximum liability of the third party in a suit brought by the employee. Thus, if the total damages were $500,000 and the third party was 50% responsible, while the employer and employee were each 25% responsible, then the employee could recover $375,000 in damages from the third party. In most jurisdictions, the employer would still be able to recover any workers' compensation benefits paid from this award in a subrogation action.

NOTES

1. *Federal Right to Subrogation.* Congress tried to balance the third party liability in tort suits with the employer's responsibility for workers' compensation benefits in the Product Liability Reform Act of 1996. Vetoed by President Clinton, Section 111 would have created a federal right of subrogation in favor of an employer or its insurer. The section would also have authorized a direct reduction of the employee's product liability recovery when the manufacturer proved by clear and convincing evidence that the injury was caused by the fault of either the employer or a fellow employee. *See* Thomas A. Eaton, *Revisiting the Intersection of Workers' Compensation and Product Liability: An Assessment of a Proposed Federal Solution to an Old Problem,* 64 TENN. L. REV. 881 (1997).

2. *Insurer as Third Party.* A few states allow employees to sue the employer's insurance carrier for negligent inspection of the workplace or negligent medical care. *See Nelson v. Union Wire Rope Corp.,* 199 N.E.2d 769 (Ill. 1964) (carrier can be sued for negligence in its voluntary inspection of employer's elevator cable). The large majority of jurisdictions, however, immunize insurance companies from such suits under the exclusive remedy principle. A recent case dismissing a tort suit against an insurer's negligent safety inspection because of the exclusive remedy principle is *Fleischmann v. Wausau Business Insurance Co.*, 671 N.E.2d 473 (Ind. Ct. App. 1996).

3. ***Emotional Distress Caused by Insurance Carriers.*** Employees sometimes sue insurance carriers for emotional distress caused by overly vigorous investigation of claims.

> A case whose melodramatic facts helped to popularize this cause of action was *Unruh v. Truck Insurance Exchange*, 498 P.2d 1063 (Cal. 1972). The carrier, suspecting employees of malingering, sent a team of two investigators to get evidence for its suspicions. One got the female plaintiff emotionally involved with him. The other clandestinely photographed their activities, including her negotiating barrel bridges and the like at Disneyland in a fashion inconsistent with continued back disability. The shock of this revelation in the hearing room caused the plaintiff to suffer a violent emotional collapse, leading to protracted hospitalization. A cause of action was held to lie against the carrier, free of the exclusiveness bar.
>
> In that picturesque situations like this are not very common, this category would perhaps deserve little attention were it confined to comparable acts of treachery by insurance carriers. But when the underlying principle is extended to deliberate delay or terminations of payments by carriers, the potential importance of the principle becomes painfully clear. The first major case to make this extension was *Stafford v. Westchester Fire Insurance Co.*, 526 P.2d 37 (Alaska 1974), involving an aggravated set of facts showing deliberate delay and harassment by the carrier. An action was held to lie. A rash of similar attempts followed. In several extreme cases, *Stafford* was followed. But the significant fact for these purposes is that in most subsequent cases the courts rejected the cause of action, seeing the danger of this development as an open-ended invitation to sue in tort for any delay in payment, merely by calling it intentional infliction of emotional distress, or "outrage," or some such term.

Arthur Larson, *Tensions of the Next Decade, in* NEW PERSPECTIVES IN WORKERS' COMPENSATION 21, 25-26 (John F. Burton, Jr. ed., 1988).

An example of the courts' resistance to broach the exclusive remedy provision because of alleged intentionally inflicted emotional distress is *Winterberg v. Transportation Insurance Co.*, 72 F.3d 318 (3rd Cir. 1995) (applying Pennsylvania law). The court affirmed dismissal of the tort suit because of the exclusive remedy doctrine even if the insurance carrier behaved egregiously in handling the workers' compensation claim. The carrier allegedly improperly terminated medical services and cash benefits, and sent her to a physician for a medical examination in which she was emotionally and physically abused. Winterberg asserted that she fell during the exam after the doctor roughly grabbed her foot, and that he refused to assist her even though she further injured herself because of the fall.

4. *Fellow Employee as Third Party.* In most, but not all, states, employees as well as the employer are immune from suits for workplace injuries they inflict on fellow employees. The protection for the fellow employee is provided by statutory language, such as that found in the New Jersey workers' compensation statute that provides immunity for "an act or omission occurring while such person was in the same employ as the person injured...." N.J. REV. STAT. § 34:15-8. Suppose Cadorette, a supervisor at Acme, improperly removes the safety tape from a computerized saw sometime in 1988 before he leaves the firm in November 1988. Suppose Estrada is hired in March 1989 and is injured in May 1989 because of Cadorette's removal of the safety tape. Can Estrada bring a tort suit against former employee Cadorette? *Estrada v. Hendricksaw Corp.*, 695 A.2d 323 (N.J. Super. Ct. App. Div. 1997) (no because the fellow-employee immunity applies to former as well as current employees).

5. *The Employer as a Third Party: The Dual Capacity Doctrine.* Some employees have attempted to sue their employers by characterizing them as something else — a supplier of goods or medical services. Occasionally, courts accept the dual characterization and allow the tort claim. For example, in *Mercer v. Uniroyal, Inc.*, 361 N.E.2d 492 (Ohio Ct. App. 1976), a truck driver employed by Uniroyal was injured when a Uniroyal tire blew out. The Ohio Appellate Court allowed his product liability suit against Uniroyal.

Today, dual capacity suits are rarely successful. In *McCormick v. Caterpillar Tractor Co.*, 423 N.E.2d 876 (Ill. 1981), for example, an employee sued the employer for malpractice by the company doctor. The Illinois Supreme Court held the claim barred by the exclusive remedy provision of workers compensation, reasoning that state law required the employer to provide medical services to the employee. The Illinois Court of Appeals did allow one count of a tort suit to proceed by relying on the dual capacity doctrine in *Goins v. Mercy Center for Health Care Services*, 667 N.E.2d 652 (Ill. Ct. App. 1996). Scott Goins, a hospital security officer, became infected with the HIV virus in the process of restraining a patient with AIDS. Goins alleged that Mercy Center violated the AIDS Confidentiality Act by disclosing his condition to other employees. The court allowed the cause of action, reasoning that at the time of the alleged violations of the Confidentiality Act, "Mercy Center's role had changed from that of an employer providing statutorily-required medical treatment to that of a medical provider which owed Scott the same duty that it owed to all other patients similarly situated, namely confidentiality regarding his AIDS test. Accordingly ... we find that Scott's claims for violations of the Confidentiality Act were not barred by the Workers' Compensation Act's exclusive remedy provisions." *Id.* at 657.

6. *For Whom is the Remedy Exclusive I? Family Members.* The exclusive remedy doctrine generally protects employers from suits by the worker's spouse, parents, or children for harm resulting from workplace incidents. However, the results depend in part on the language of the jurisdiction's exclusive remedy provision. In general, there are three types of clauses: (1) the narrowest limitation on suits by other family members, exemplified by the Massachusetts statute, which only says that the employee waives "his" common law rights by coming under workers' compensation; (2) the significant limitation by general language, illustrated by the California law, which says that the employee's remedy shall be "exclusive;" and (3) the significant limitation by detailed specification, typified by the New York workers' compensation act, which states that the excluded suits include those by "such employee, his personal representatives, spouse, parents, dependents, or next of kin, or anyone otherwise entitled to recover damages, at common law or otherwise on account of such injury or death." ARTHUR LARSON, LARSON'S WORKERS' COMPENSATION § 66.10 (Desk ed. 1997).

The California language was interpreted in two decisions. In *Bell v. Macy's*, 261 Cal. Rptr. 447 (Cal. Ct. App. 1989), the Court barred a suit by the mother (who was the employee), father, and baby who was born with significant brain damage and subsequently died. The mother had suffered severe abdominal pain at work. Her condition was misdiagnosed by the company nurse, and the ambulance did not arrive until some fifty minutes after Bell first began to feel sick. By the time she reached the hospital with a ruptured uterus, the baby had experienced significant injury that the evidence suggested would not have occurred had Bell received prompt attention. The trial court dismissed the claim, and the court of appeals affirmed, holding that workers' compensation provided the exclusive remedy. Among the arguments made by the court was that if the employer were held liable for damages to the fetus, one adverse consequence may be that "female employees ... could easily find themselves the victims of financially driven gender discrimination by liability-conscious employers." *Id.* at 455. The concern for discrimination against women did not deter the California Supreme Court from rejecting the outcome and rationale of the *Bell* decision in *Snyder v. Michael's Stores, Inc.*, 945 P.2d 781 (Cal. 1997). Naomi Snyder was exposed to carbon monoxide at work, including one incident in which twenty-one customers and employees became so ill they were conveyed to hospitals. Mikayla Snyder, who at the time of the exposure was in utero, was deprived of adequate oxygen as a result of the carbon monoxide exposure and experienced permanent damage to her brain and other parts of her body. The court endorsed the principle that workers' compensation proceedings are the exclusive remedy for third party actions deemed collateral to or derivative of the employee's injury, such as civil action by the employee's spouse for loss of the employee's services or consortium. However, the injury to Mikayla was not derivative from Naomi's injury, but was direct, and thus the exclusive remedy provision was inapplicable.

7. *For Whom is the Remedy Exclusive II? Independent Contractors.* General issues relating to the distinction between employee and independent contractor were considered in Chapter 2. The issue of whether an individual is an independent contractor or an employee is important in workers' compensation because only an employee is entitled to the protection of the program. A classic workers' compensation case that illustrates the application of the tests used to decide whether a worker is an employee or independent contractor is *Marcum v. State Accident Insurance Fund*, 565 P.2d 399 (Or. Ct. App. 1977).

Generally in cases of this type, the individual is attempting to demonstrate that he or she is an employee in order to receive benefits. Thus in *Hoste v. Shanty Creek Management, Inc.*, 561 N.W.2d 106 (Mich. Ct. App. 1997), the plaintiff was successful because he was able to convince the court that he was an employee. Hoste was a member of the National Ski Patrol who was asked by the ski school director to forerun the course to assure it was safe, which demonstrably it was not because he fell and fractured his vertebra causing paralysis from which he is unlikely to recover. Hoste did not receive any wages, but did receive a ski pass and discounts on food and beverages. The court said that compensation did not have to be in the form of wages in order for the employee to receive benefits, and that Hoste was an employee because he rendered services to Shanty Creek.

The interesting twist in workers' compensation is that sometimes the injured individual is attempting to convince the court that he is *not* an employee, so the exclusive remedy provision barring tort suits can be avoided. Consider the plight of Keith Hallal, who, as a full-time student pursuing a degree in sports management, received an internship with the Orlando Magic basketball team. He injured his ear when his head struck an antenna protruding from the wall of the supply room. Hallal claimed he was a volunteer because he did not receive monetary remuneration for his services. In Florida, a "volunteer" is specifically excluded from the definition of "employee" in the workers' compensation statute, and so Hallal appeared well down the road to a tort suit recovery. However, interns with the Magic are required to attend all home games for which they are paid $25 per game. The court, in *Hallal v. RDV Sports, Inc.*, 682 So. 2d 1235, 1237 (Fla. Dist. Ct. App. 1996), trenchantly disposed of the suit. "Such payment constitutes monetary remuneration. Therefore, Mr. Hallal was not a 'volunteer.' On this basis, final summary judgment was properly entered in favor of the Magic."

8. *For Whom is the Remedy Exclusive III? Employees Not Covered by a Workers' Compensation Statute.* Some employees are not covered by a workers' compensation statute and therefore, in general, their employers are not protected by the exclusive remedy provisions. Most workers' compensation statutes exclude certain industries (e.g., state and local government), or occupations (household workers), or small employers (e.g., those with three or fewer employees), or make the laws elective for employers (most notably in Texas). In addition, employees may not be covered if they are casual workers or do not work in the regular business of the employer.

Larson catalogs several approaches found in state workers' compensation statutes in dealing with casual employment and employment outside of the business of the employer:

(i) Four states exclude all casual employment;

(ii) Twenty-seven states (plus the District of Columbia) exclude employments that are both casual and not in the course of the employer's trade, business, or profession;

(iii) Eight states exclude all employments not in the course of the employer's trade, business, or profession;

(iv) Several states apparently cover all employees (not otherwise excluded) regardless of whether they are casual or not working in the course of the employer's trade, business, or profession.

ARTHUR LARSON, WORKMEN'S COMPENSATION FOR OCCUPATIONAL INJURIES AND DEATH § 50.10 (Desk ed. 1992).

D. WHICH INJURIES ARE COMPENSABLE?

Even a worker who has established that his employment is covered by the state workers' compensation statute will not receive workers' compensation benefits for every injury that affects the worker. The worker must establish that the injury was work-related. With only minor variations, almost all workers' compensation statutes provide the following definition of "work-related":

"Injury" and "personal injury" means only accidental injuries arising out of and in the course of employment ....

This language has been interpreted to encompass four legal tests, all of which must be met in order for the worker's injury to be considered compensable:

(i) an injury
(ii) resulting from an accident that
(iii) arose out of employment (the "AOE test") and
(iv) in the course of employment (the "COE test").

In this section, we consider these tests.

Several states have enacted laws during the 1990s that have made the legal tests for compensability more difficult to meet. An example of such language is Section 440.09(1) of the Florida workers' compensation law, which is included in the Statutory Supplement. The impact of the more restrictive legal tests will be examined in Section F, "Injuries and Diseases for Which Compensability is Problematic," since those conditions are the primary target of the recent legislation.

1. TEST ONE: "DURING THE COURSE OF EMPLOYMENT"

a. Activity: Mixed Social and Business Activities

EZZY v. WORKERS' COMPENSATION APPEALS BOARD

California Court of Appeals
194 Cal. Rptr. 90 (1983)

SMITH, ASSOCIATE JUDGE:

Petitioner, Marilyn Ezzy, sought and was granted a writ of review after the Workers' Compensation Appeals Board [hereafter WCAB] denied Ezzy's petition for reconsideration and affirmed the decision of the workers' compensation judge who found that petitioner's injury did not arise out of and in the course of her employment.

The sole issue before us is whether the injury to petitioner's finger, which occurred during a company-sponsored softball game, arises out of and in the course of her employment, and is therefore compensable.

Marilyn Ezzy (hereafter "Ezzy") at all relevant times was employed by the law firm of Gassett, Perry & Frank (hereafter "GPF") as a law clerk. On or about August 15, 1980, Ezzy participated in an employer-sponsored softball game, during which she injured the little finger on her right hand as she attempted to catch a fly ball.

The record of the WCAB hearing discloses that GPF participated in a softball league composed primarily of civil defense law firms. The rules of the league required that the teams be composed of both men and women, and required forfeiture if less than four women were present on each team.

John Burton (hereafter "Burton") is a partner in GPF, and was the team coach. Burton stated that he did not have to recruit players; a sign up was conducted of all those who wanted to play. Burton testified that it was not a requirement that everyone will play. Some of the older and less athletically inclined members of the firm did not play. Some, but not all, of the secretaries participated. Everyone in the GPF firm, player and non-player alike, was provided at the firm's expense a special teeshirt emblazoned with his or her GPF billing number. Burton testified that GPF paid for the balls, bats and post-game refreshments. A postseason awards banquet was provided by GPF to which all employees were invited. Burton stated that no one was ever reprimanded or fired for not playing.

Burton further testified that his secretary sent around memos reminding office personnel of games or practice. Burton stated that Administrative Director's Rule 9883, regarding off-duty recreational activities, was neither posted nor read to employees. Burton testified that "the better players were more encouraged to be present than some of the ones that were not so good. That would also depend on how many men we had and how many women we had." Burton stated that his team had never forfeited a game, and that he always had the correct number of female players there. He further testified that he did have one or two problems making sure one of their key women would be present at the games. Burton admitted that, although no business was derived from the games, they were very good for office spirit.

Ezzy testified that she did not volunteer but was "drafted" to join the team. On the first day after she returned from vacation, Burton approached Ezzy, handed her a teeshirt, a schedule of games and practices, and said, "At the next one we'll see you there." Ezzy understood there was a coed requirement, and when there appeared to be a shortage of women, the female members were urged to get out and play. Ezzy felt there was a spirit of camaraderie that the firm was trying to create, and that the strong urgings to play and the concern over having an adequate number of females led her to believe that she should play softball. Ezzy stated that the firm paid for post-game pizza and other refreshments. Ezzy testified that on one occasion home movies of a softball game were shown in the conference room of GPF offices during working hours, and that she and others were called in to watch. At the awards banquet, Burton received a whip as a gag-gift because he was such a "hard driver."

In his "Opinion On Decision," the workers' compensation judge stated that participation in the softball game, while encouraged, was not a requirement or a reasonable expectancy of petitioner's job. Petitioner contends that the workers' compensation judge erred in concluding that petitioner's injury did not occur in the course of employment. We agree.

Discussion

I

At the outset, we note that the application of Labor Code section 3600, subdivision (a)(8) to the instant factual setting presents a close case. We find nothing in the case law to guide us; no appellate court has yet construed section 3600, subdivision (a)(8).

Before examining the evidence as reflected by the record, we must consider the applicable statute, section 3600, subdivision (a)(8), which reads, in pertinent part, as follows:

> (a) Liability for the compensation provided by this division ... shall, without regard to negligence, exist against an employer for any injury sustained by his or her employees arising out of and in the course of the employment and for the death of any employee if the injury proximately causes death, in those cases where the following conditions of compensation concur: ...
>
> (8) Where the injury does not arise out of voluntary participation in any off-duty recreational, social, or athletic activity not constituting part of the employee's work-related duties, *except where these activities are a reasonable expectancy of, or are expressly or impliedly required by, the employment.* The administrative director shall promulgate reasonable rules and regulations requiring employers to post and keep posted in a conspicuous place or places a notice advising employees of the provisions of this subdivision. Failure of the employer to post such a notice shall not constitute an expression of intent to waive the provisions of this subdivision. (Emphasis added.)

The clear language of section 3600, subdivision (a)(8) first states the rule — recovery may be had for injuries arising out of and in the course of employment if those injuries do *not* arise out of voluntary participation in athletic activities. Stated conversely, no recovery may be had where the injury arises from voluntary participation in athletic activities. The section then states exceptions to the rule of non-compensability. Where athletic activities are either a "reasonable expectancy of, or are expressly or impliedly required by, the employment" injuries arising therefrom *are compensable.*

The key legal question to be decided here is whether Ezzy's participation was a reasonable expectancy of her employment at GPF.

Respondent erroneously assumes that the question of "reasonable expectancy" is one of fact. While factual findings form the foundation upon which a court bases its determination that a "reasonable expectancy" exists, the question requires a conclusion derived from those facts which is itself *legal* in nature. Furthermore, the question of "reasonable expectancy" is but a subset of the ultimate issue — whether the applicant's injury arose out of and in the course of her employment.

With respect to the ultimate issue, the scope of our review is clear: "Where ... there is no real dispute as to the facts, the question of whether an injury was suffered in the course of employment is one of law and a purported finding of fact on that question is not binding on an appellate court."

Other areas of the law have attempted to give a specific meaning to this phrase. In connection with insurance law, the "doctrine of reasonable expectations" has been applied so that ambiguities in an insurance policy are to be resolved in accordance with *the reasonable expectations of the insured.* With respect to Fourth Amendment law, a person's "reasonable expectation of privacy" is one which is *subjectively* held by the person searched, and which society recognizes as *objectively* reasonable. In the context of labor law, for purposes of establishing whether a person is an employee when determining whether a majority of employees have agreed to union representation, the determination is based upon *the employee's reasonable expectation* of future or continued employment.

In each of the situations mentioned above, the law looks to the expectations of the person who is being protected and measures his subjective understanding against a neutral and unbiased standard. It is our view that the test of "reasonable expectancy of employment" in the context of the case at bar consists of two elements: (1) whether the employee subjectively believes his or her participation in an activity is expected by the employer, and (2) whether that belief is objectively reasonable.

The effect of this test is to recognize *only* expectations which are objectively reasonable. Stated another way, the employer is protected from liability for injuries where an employee's belief that he or she is expected to participate in an activity is unreasonable. The burden rests upon an employer to insure that no subtle or indirect pressure or coercion is applied to induce involuntary participation by an employee. We do not find this burden to be an onerous one, for the employer's means of protecting himself are peculiarly within his own control.

We turn next to legislative intent. Prior to the enactment of section 3600, subdivision (a)(8), section 3600 made no specific reference to athletic or recreational activities.

Section 3600, subdivision (h), now section 3600, subdivision (a)(8), originated as Assembly Bill No. 2555 (1977-1978). The bill analysis prepared by the Assembly Committee on Finance, Insurance, and Commerce when that committee heard Assembly Bill No. 2555 stated "[t]he thrust of [the proposed legislation] appears to overrule ... *Goodman v. Fireman's Fund American Insurance Co.* (1974) 74 OAK 49472, [which] found that a water skiing injury to an airline stewardess during a four-day layover in Tahiti was an employment-related injury" and therefore compensable. According to the bill analysis, the legislation was also intended to overrule *Lizama v. Workmen's Comp. Appeals Bd.* (1974) 40 Cal. App. 3d 363, which held compensable an injury to a janitor, who, after receiving permission from his employer, used a company power saw after work hours. The committee report emphasized that the activities were held compensable because they were reasonably foreseeable or expectable in the work setting.

Section 3600, subdivision (a)(8) was therefore intended to draw a brighter line delimiting compensability by replacing the general foreseeability test with one of "reasonable expectancy" of employment.

At the time Assembly Bill No. 2555 was under consideration, two cases adjudicated by the WCAB in 1976 and 1977 were presumptively known to the Legislature, yet there is no hint in the committee analysis that the Legislature was displeased with those results.

In *Pacific Tel. & Tel. Co. v. Workers' Comp. Appeals Bd. (Brady)* (1976) 41 Cal. Comp. Cases 771, Ms. Brady, an employee of the phone company, was injured while playing softball on a team made up wholly of Pacific Telephone Company employees. The team played other phone company teams comprising the league. The games were played off the employer's premises after working hours. Ms. Brady was not a regular team member, but participated on this occasion because the team would otherwise have had to forfeit for lack of sufficient players. Ms. Brady felt job pressure to play when asked to do so by team members who included Ms. Brady's supervisor. The management of the telephone company permitted league formation meetings to be conducted on the premises, and promulgated safety rules. The company photocopy machine was used in the dissemination of league and team information. Also, raffles to benefit the league were conducted on company premises during working hours. The WCAB judge relied upon (1) substantial employment involvement in creation and operation of the league, (2) benefit to the employer of improved employee morale, and (3) the job-related pressure upon Ms. Brady which led to her participation. The Court of Appeal denied a petition for writ of review.

In *California Highway Patrol v. Workers' Comp. Appeals Bd.* (Loveless) (1977) 42 Cal. Comp. Cases 264, the WCAB found that a highway patrol officer's injury was compensable. Officer Loveless played on a softball team representing the Monterey area office of the CHP which participated in the Central Coast Counties Police League. Notices of games were posted in the locker room, play was encouraged by state and local CHP management. The WCAB judge concluded the softball activity was part and parcel of Loveless' job. The Court of Appeal denied CHP's petition for a writ of review.

Both the *Pacific Tel. & Tel.* and *California Highway Patrol* cases, in finding athletic injuries compensable, go beyond the broad "foreseeability" test of *Goodman* and *Lizama*. Rather these cases rely upon the more specific factors of employer involvement, benefit to employer, and job-related pressure to participate to find an activity within the course of employment....

We conclude that it was the Legislature's intent to eliminate from the workers' compensation scheme *only* those injuries which were remotely work-connected. The use of such terms as "reasonable expectancy" and "impliedly required" in section 3600, subdivision (a)(8) is evidence that the Legislature recognized the potential use by employers of indirect means to encourage participation in an activity, and that such indirect encouragement changes the voluntary character of such participation. The Legislature intended that injuries occurring under such circumstances should be considered work-connected, and must fall within the coverage of the workers' compensation scheme.

II

In the case at bar we conclude that facts evident from the record establish that petitioner's injury resulted from participation in an activity which was a "reasonable expectancy" of her employment, and therefore occurred in the course of her employment.

Petitioner was a part-time law clerk in her second year of law school, a position which is low in the legal profession's hierarchy. As such, petitioner was more than usually vulnerable to pressure or suggestion that she join the law firm's softball team. Thus, when she was urged to play by one of the firm's partners, who was also the team coach, it was reasonable for petitioner to feel that she was expected to participate.

There was relatively more pressure on female employees to participate because of the league's requirement that four women be present on the field at all times.

A substantial benefit to the firm was generated by participation in the softball team by virtue of improved office cooperation, spirit, morale and camaraderie.

The law firm paid for all equipment, for teeshirts for team members and other employees of the firm, as well as for post-game refreshments. The firm sponsored an awards banquet to which team members and other employees were invited.

It is also undisputed that the law-firm employer had neither posted nor read to its employees the contents of Administrative Director's Rule 9883, which reads as follows:

> *Notice to Employee Concerning Off-Duty Recreational Social, or Athletic Activity.* Every employer shall post and keep posted in a conspicuous place or places, the following notice:

> Your employer or its insurance carrier may not be liable for the payment of
> workers' compensation benefits for any injury which arises out of an
> employee's voluntary participation in any off-duty recreational, social, or
> athletic activity which is not a part of the employee's work-related duties.

Section 3600, subdivision (a)(8) states that "[f]ailure of the employer to post
such a notice shall not constitute an expression of intent to waive the provisions
of this subdivision." Nonetheless, in the case at bar, employer's failure to post
the required notice was contrary to a statutory directive which was intended to
inform an employee of the jeopardy of non-coverage by workers' compensation
insurance when voluntarily involved in athletic events. While not a waiver of the
subdivision's provisions, an employer's failure to post the required notice makes
any action by the employer which tends to encourage participation in athletic
events appear more coercive in effect.

The facts present a close case. We are, however, mindful of Labor Code section 3202 which mandates: "The provisions of Division 4 and Division 5 of this
code shall be liberally construed by the courts with the purpose of extending
their benefits for the protection of persons injured in the course of their employment."

In the case at bar, the record shows that petitioner subjectively believed that
her employer expected her to participate in the company sponsored baseball
activities. Petitioner so stated under oath. We have determined that her subjective belief was objectively reasonable, and, therefore, conclude that petitioner's
injury arose out of and in the course of her employment.

The decision of the Workers' Compensation Appeals Board is annulled and
the cause is remanded to that board for proceedings consistent with the views
expressed herein.

MILLER, J., concurs.

ROUSE, ASSOCIATE JUSTICE, concurring:
I concur, but not without comment.

Admittedly, the question of whether this particular activity was a reasonable
expectancy of petitioner's employment is a legal issue which this court may
properly redetermine, based upon facts set forth in the record. Nevertheless, I am
reluctant to "second guess" the workers' compensation judge (a specialist in that
field) whose adjudication has been reviewed and endorsed by the Workers'
Compensation Board, in what, in my perception, is a close case. Since substantial evidence supports that judge's conclusion I would hold that his determination of the matter must prevail were it not for those cases cited wherein awards
of compensation were made in situations which are, in my judgment, factually
indistinguishable from petitioner's case.

One of the functions of an appellate court in announcing its decision is to
ensure uniformity and consistency in the rules applied by various inferior

tribunals. I believe that is what the decision in this case seeks to accomplish, and it is for this limited reason that I concur in the opinion.

NOTE

Drawing the Boundary on Another Type of Recreational Activity. Jocquelyn Shunk was a real estate salesperson who was responsible for finding prospective lot purchasers and persuading them to fly to the real estate development in Naples, Florida. She had a dinner with Luther Tanly, a prospective lot purchaser, which ended about 12:30 a.m.. Then, according to her amended version of the story, she accompanied him to his apartment so she would know where to awaken him the next morning in order to make certain he got on the plane to Naples. Mrs. Shunk testified that she became nauseated because of shrimp she ate at dinner and used Tanly's bathroom to relieve her nausea. She alleged that he then made improper advances towards her and that, in an attempt to elude him, she fell from the window of the apartment, injuring herself at about 2:30 a.m. Mrs. Shunk's original version of her injury, made at the hospital, was that she had been accosted in a telephone booth by a male with a gun who took her to his apartment from which she jumped. Another version of what happened, which Tanly told the police after they took him into custody on suspicion of attempted homicide, was that he and Mrs. Shunk had been drinking at a list of bars. However, he was not charged and was released the same day. Howard Keller, who was Mrs. Shunk's supervisor, testified that it was definitely part of her job to get Mr. Tanly on the plane the morning following the dinner, and that "almost anything Mrs. Shunk or any of the other lady solicitors did in securing prospective customers was part of their jobs, for which they were paid. He stated they had no regular working hours but worked all the time getting people to go on the plane trips, and then seeing that they woke up and got on the planes."

Was the injury to Mrs. Shunk in the course of her employment, entitling her to workers' compensation benefits. Yes, according to the Judge of Industrial Claims, based on the candor and demeanor of the witnesses. No, according to the Industrial Commission on appeal, because "the facts clearly show that the claimant had deviated from her employment prior to the accident." Yes, according to the Supreme Court of Florida, in *Shunk v. Gulf American Land Corp.*, 224 So.2d 269, 271-72 (Fla. 1969):

> It is quite true that the particular circumstances related above present a suspicious inference that claimant was not acting in the course of her employment at the time of her injury.... However, a suspicious inference in these particular circumstances is not necessarily conclusive.... [I]t seems fairly well established that promotion of real estate sales to prospective customers of the kind here considered involves techniques and methods in a special class that have been found to be necessary in persuading prospective customers to agree to make the related plane trips.

In a debatable situation, such as this one, we conclude we should rest our judgment with the trier of the facts and lay aside our skepticism and natural inclination to be cynically suspicious.

How would you change the facts to strengthen the arguments for: (1) Gulf American? (2) Jocquelyn Shunk?

b. Activity: Horseplay

PROWS v. INDUSTRIAL COMMISSION

Supreme Court of Utah
610 P.2d 1362 (1980)

WILKINS, JUSTICE:

This is an appeal from an Order of the Industrial Commission (hereafter "Commission") denying the application for Workmen's Compensation benefits by Michael Prows (hereinafter "Petitioner").

The facts of this case are essentially undisputed. Petitioner was employed as a truck driver by Respondent Bergin Brunswig Company (hereafter "Bergin"). His duties included loading medical supplies onto his delivery truck and making deliveries to doctors, hospitals, and clinics.

The boxes containing the medical supplies measured approximately eleven and one-half by twenty-four inches, and each box was secured by elastic bands (also described as "rubber bands"). Each rubber band was approximately twelve inches long by three-eighths inch wide.

Testimony before the administrative law judge established that the rubber bands were used by some of Bergin's employees for "rubber bands fights." Petitioner and one of his co-employees testified that the "fights" were an almost daily occurrence. One of Bergin's supervisors testified that he observed such "fights" perhaps two or three times a month, and that when he observed one he discouraged its continuation.

On March 3, 1978, Petitioner was engaged in his usual assigned duties and was loading supplies on his delivery truck. As he was unloading boxes of supplies from a hand truck and onto his delivery truck, he was hit by one or two rubber bands which were flipped at him by two co-employees standing nearby. Petitioner thereupon flipped a rubber band back at his "attackers." One of the co-employees then ripped an approximately eighteen inch long piece of wood off a nearby pallet and came toward Petitioner brandishing the wood like a sword. Petitioner took the wood from his co-employee, placed a rubber band between the handles of his hand truck and attempted to shoot the wood into the air in a slingshot fashion. The piece of wood, instead of sailing into the air, struck Petitioner in the right eye, severely injuring him.

In denying compensation the administrative law judge found, *inter alia,* that there had been numerous incidents of "horseplay" indulged in by Bergin's employees, including flipping rubber bands, and that this type of activity had been discouraged and was not condoned by Bergin; that the horseplay represented a "complete abandonment of the employee's duties"; and that the petitioner had "failed to prove that his accident arose out of or was in the scope of his employment."[1] In denying Petitioner's Motion for Review, the Commission adopted the administrative law judge's Findings of Fact, Conclusions of Law, and Order.

Section 35-1-45 of Utah's Workmen's Compensation Act provides in pertinent part:

> Every employee ... who is injured by accident arising out of or in the course of his employment, wheresoever such injury occurred, provided the same was not purposely self-inflicted, shall be entitled to receive, and shall be paid such compensation for loss sustained on account of such injury ... as herein provided.[3]

In discussing construction of the act and the underlying purposes of the act this Court in *Chandler v. Industrial Commission,* [184 P. 1020, 1021-22 (Utah 1919)] stated:

> We are also reminded that our statute [now § 68-3-2] requires that the statutes of this state are to be "liberally construed with a view to effect the objects of the statutes and to promote justice."...

This Court, along with the courts of other jurisdictions, has recognized that concepts of negligence, contributory negligence, fault, and similar tort concepts have no place within the remedial framework of the compensation act. In *Twin Peaks Canning Co. v. Industrial Commission,* [196 P. 853 (Utah 1921)] this Court stated:

> Our statute only excluded those injuries which are "purposely self-inflicted." As we read the statute, therefore, it is not enough that the employé merely disregards some rule, regulation, or order of the master, since such conduct may constitute nothing more than ordinary negligence on the part of the employé, and mere negligence does not destroy the right to compensation.

---

[1] The concept of "Scope of Employment" is one foreign to the law of workmen's compensation, belonging rather in the law of master and servant. Therefore, petitioner can in no way be considered to have the burden of proving that the accident "was in the scope of his employment."

[3] It must be kept clearly in mind that the statute requires that the injury arise in the course of employment, not that the injured worker be in the course of his employment. A definition of the term "course of employment" is found in 1 Larson, *The Law of Workmen's Compensation* (1979), § 14: "when it takes place within the period of the employment at a place where the employee reasonably may be, and while he is fulfilling his duties or engaged in doing something incidental thereto."

... With these basic principles in mind, we turn now to an analysis of whether and under what circumstances injuries sustained as a result of "horseplay" on the part of an employee may not be compensated under the act.

In his treatise, *The Law of Workmen's Compensation* (1979), Professor Arthur Larson (hereafter "Larson") lists four "actual or suggested treatments of the problem" of participants in horseplay:

> 1. The "aggressor defense" which results in the denial of compensation in any case where the injured employee instigated or participated in the horseplay. It is reasoned that by instigating the horseplay the employee has voluntarily stepped aside from his employment.
>
> 2. The New York Rule which permits even an instigator of or participant in horseplay to recover if the horseplay was a regular incident of the employment as distinguished from an isolated act.
>
> 3. The view that an instigator or participant should be treated the same as a non-participant since it is the conditions of the employment that induce the horseplay.
>
> 4. The rule proposed by Larson that an instigator or participant should recover if, by ordinary "course of employment" standards, his indulgence in horseplay does not amount to a *substantial deviation* from the employment.

As the basis for the fourth approach above, Larson proposes a four-part test to analyze any particular act of horseplay to determine whether the horseplay constitutes such a substantial deviation as to justify denying compensation to a participant therein. Whether initiation of or participation in horseplay is a deviation from course of employment depends on (1) the extent and seriousness of the deviation, (2) the completeness of the deviation (i.e., whether it was commingled with the performance of duty or involved an abandonment of duty), (3) the extent to which the practice of horseplay had become an accepted part of the employment, and (4) the extent to which the nature of the employment may be expected to include some such horseplay.

This Court has heretofore had only one occasion to examine the issue of horseplay in the workmen's compensation setting. In *Twin Peaks Canning Company v. Industrial Commission, supra,* an award of compensation to the dependents of a worker who was killed as a result of horseplay in which "the deceased was the instigator and the principal, if not the sole actor" was affirmed by this Court. The analysis in *Twin Peaks* turned on whether the deceased employee could be said to have been killed while "in the course of" his employment in light of his activities in using an elevator located on the premises of his employer, the use of which elevator by the deceased was allegedly forbidden by the employer. Although the words "deviation from employment" are nowhere found in the *Twin Peaks* opinion, it is clear that the Court was wrestling with the question of when a deviation from the assigned duties of an employee was sufficient to take that employee out of the course of his employment. In our view, the analysis in *Twin Peaks* though lacking the formal structure of the test proposed by Larson, is founded on the same general principles.[15] We therefore adopt Larson's four-part test to determine whether a particular act of horseplay constitutes such a deviation that it can be said that the resulting injury did not arise in the course of the employment and hence is not compensable.

(1) *Extent and seriousness of the deviation.*

In *Twin Peaks* the Court observed:

> A careful reading of the decided cases will, however, disclose that the mere fact that the injured employe, at the time of the accident, was not in the discharge of his usual duties or was not directly engaged in anything connected with those duties, does not necessarily prevent him from recovering compensation in case of accidental injury. In that connection it must be remembered that, while a human being may do no more than what a machine might do, yet he can not be classed as a machine merely.

Recognizing that "a little nonsense now and then is relished by the best of [workers]," it is clear that the better reasoned decisions make allowances for the fact that workers cannot be expected to attend strictly to their assigned duties every minute they are on the job. That is not to say that substantial excursions from job assignments need be tolerated or if injury occurs during such excursions, compensation need be paid. In the case at bar, Petitioner was engaged in the performance of his assigned duties when he was playfully "attacked" by co-workers flipping rubber bands. Petitioner then momentarily set aside his duties and took up the challenge. In an exchange lasting a matter of minutes, Petitioner was injured. As Larson points out:

> The substantial character of a horseplay deviation should not be judged by the seriousness of its consequences in the light of hindsight, but by the extent of the work-departure in itself. This is not always easy to do, especially when a trifling incident escalates or explodes into a major tragedy.

We think the converse of this principle is likewise true; the fact that a major tragedy has occurred should not dictate an award of compensation when that tragedy resulted from a deviation so extensive and serious that the employment can be said to have been abandoned. However, it is our opinion that the deviation involved in the case at bar was short in duration and when disassociated from the serious consequences which resulted, relatively trivial.

---

[15] Mr. Justice Hall in his dissenting opinion distinguishes *Twin Peaks* from the case at bar and emphasizes that the Court there considered the case borderline. The dissent focuses particularly on the fact that *Twin Peaks* involved a 14-year old boy while Petitioner here was almost 22 years old at the time he was injured. A close reading of *Twin Peaks* reveals that the dicta concerning the worker's age were part of an analysis of the effect of the violation of a rule of the employer and whether the worker's death could be considered to have been "purposely self-inflicted."

(2) *Completeness of the deviation.*

Petitioner was, at the time he was "attacked" by his co-employees, engaged in the discharge of his duties. Had he not been injured, he would presumably have completed loading the truck and carried on with his deliveries. The horseplay he engaged in was clearly "commingled with the performance of duty" and hence did not constitute an "abandonment of duty." Larson points out:

> ... [T]he particular act of horseplay is entitled to be judged according to the same standards of [extent] and duration of deviation that are accepted in other [fields,] such as resting, seeking personal comfort, or indulging in incidental personal errands. If an employee momentarily walks over to a co-employee to engage in a friendly word or two, this would nowadays be called an insubstantial deviation. If he accompanies this friendly word with a playful jab in the ribs, surely it cannot be said that an entirely new set of principles has come into play. The incident remains a simple human diversion subject to the same tests of extent of departure from the employment as if the playful gesture had been omitted.
>
> At the other extreme, there are cases in which the prankster undertakes a practical joke which necessitates the complete abandonment of the employment and the concentration of all his energies for a substantial part of his working time on the horseplay enterprise. When this abandonment is sufficiently complete and extensive, it can only be treated the same as abandonment of the employment for any other personal purpose, such as an extended personal errand or an intentional four-hour nap.

(3) *Extent to which horseplay has become a part of the employment.*

The evidence adduced at the hearing before the administrative law judge was conflicting on the frequency of "rubber band fights," but clearly such "fights" had become a part of the employment, whether the "fights" occurred "daily" or "two or three times a month." As Larson points out:

> The controlling issue is whether the custom had *in fact* become a part of the employment; the employer's knowledge of it can make it neither more nor less a part of the employment — at most it is evidence of incorporation of the practice into the employment. (Italics in original.)

We do not consider the fact that apparently no employee of Bergin had ever attempted before to flip a piece of wood with a rubber band as indicating that such a practice could not be considered a part of the employment. The elements of the practice, which must be conceded to have been part of the employment, were not significantly enlarged or so modified so as to no longer constitute a part of the employment.

(4) *Extent to which nature of employment may be expected to include some such horseplay.*

This element of Larson's approach focuses on the foreseeability of horseplay in any given employment environment and on the particular act of horseplay involved. Considerations which may enter into the analysis of this point include whether the work involves lulls in employment activity or is essentially continuous, and the existence of instrumentalities which are part of the work environment and which are readily usable in horseplay situations. This list is not intended to be exhaustive but rather illustrative of the possibilities. In the present case all of the elements which joined to result in Petitioner's injury — the hand truck, the rubber bands, and the piece of wood — were part and parcel of the work environment. It therefore is not difficult to foresee that horseplay of the type engaged in by Petitioner was to be expected.

By adopting the approach suggested by Larson, this Court does not intend the adoption of a test which by mechanical application will in cases involving horseplay dictate a "correct result." Indeed this approach is not susceptible of mechanical application but rather is intended as a method of analysis to assist the Industrial Commission in consideration of future cases coming before it involving horseplay. It is this Court's view that when the underlying policy of the compensation act is effectuated in the light of the analysis suggested herein, a rational result can be expected.

While we remain committed to the proposition that this Court will examine the evidence in a compensation case only to ascertain whether there is any substantial evidence in support of the findings of the Commission and whether the Commission has acted without or in excess of its jurisdiction, under the facts of this case we believe as a matter of law that there was not a substantial deviation such that it can be said that the resulting injury did not arise in the course of the employment and hence is not compensable. The record herein reveals no substantial evidence supporting the finding of the Commission that by engaging in horseplay, Petitioner "completely abandoned" his duties and hence was not injured in the course of his employment. Therefore the Order of the Commission is reversed. Costs to Petitioner and against Bergin.

MAUGHAN and STEWART, JJ., concur.

HALL, JUSTICE, dissenting:
I respectfully dissent.

In reversing the order of the Commission, the majority opinion rules *"as a matter of law* that there was not a substantial deviation" from petitioner's course of employment (emphasis added). My primary concern with such a ruling is that a decision as to whether one is injured by accident arising out of or in the course of his employment is not a law matter, but a factual one. Once the Commission has found the facts, this Court has traditionally refrained from disturbing such findings whenever there is substantial evidence to support them.

The majority relies upon the case of *Twin Peaks Canning Company v. Industrial Commission* as being consistent with its holding. On the contrary, in *Twin Peaks* the Court affirmed the findings of the Commission and acknowledged the standard of review referred to *supra*. Furthermore, the facts in *Twin Peaks* are readily distinguishable in several particulars. For example, in *Twin Peaks,* the fatal injury occurred during a lull in the work, at a time when there was no work to perform; in the instant case, petitioner was actively engaged in his work when he abandoned it for the purpose of "horseplay." Also, at the time of the accident in *Twin Peaks* the injured party was a minor (14 years of age) whereas in the instant case, petitioner was 22 years of age. The Court specifically acknowledged that *Twin Peaks* was a borderline case (which further suggests the importance of the *factual* determination) and that "if the deceased had been a man of mature years and experience, we might have reached a different conclusion."

The approach suggested by Professor Larson may well assist in determining whether the accident arises out of or in the course of one's employment. However, even if this four-step analysis is applied, it is the fact-finder (not this Court) which must evaluate and weigh each element individually and collectively. This includes the element the majority treats as a law matter, that of substantial deviation from petitioner's course of employment.

. . . .

CROCKETT, CHIEF JUSTICE, concurs in the dissent of HALL, J.:

c. Time and Place: Going and Coming Rule

SANTA ROSA JUNIOR COLLEGE v. WORKERS' COMPENSATION APPEALS BOARD

Supreme Court of California
708 P.2d 673 (1985)

KAUS, JUSTICE:

The Workers' Compensation Act (Lab. Code, § 3201 et seq.) establishes the liability of an employer "for any injury sustained by his or her employees arising out of and in the course of the employment." Almost 70 years ago, we adopted the "going and coming rule" as an aid in determining whether an injury occurred in the course of the employment. Generally prohibiting compensation for injuries suffered by an employee while commuting to and from work, the going and coming rule has been criticized by courts and commentators alike as being arbitrary and harsh. It has generated a multitude of exceptions which threaten, at times, to defeat the rule entirely. This appeal confronts us with the question of whether one such exception should be dramatically expanded to create, in effect, a "white-collar" nullification of the rule.

Santa Rosa Junior College (college) challenges a decision of the Workers' Compensation Appeals Board (board) awarding death benefits to JoAnne Smyth, widow of a community college instructor who was killed in an automobile accident on his way home from the campus. At issue is the applicability of the going and coming rule to school teachers who regularly take work home. If, in such cases, the home may be fairly regarded as a "second jobsite," the rule does not apply and injuries sustained en route are compensable. If the fact that the employee regularly takes work home does not establish the home as a second jobsite, compensation is barred.

We conclude that — unless the employer requires the employee to labor at home as a condition of the employment — the fact that an employee regularly works there does not transform the home into a second jobsite for purposes of the going and coming rule.

Facts

Joseph Smyth was a mathematics instructor and head of the mathematics department at the college. About 6 p.m. on March 16, 1982, he was killed in an accident while driving his personal automobile home from work. His home was located in Ukiah, about 60 miles from the Santa Rosa campus. The family had moved to Ukiah six years earlier for their own convenience ....

It is undisputed that at the time of the accident Smyth had with him some student papers he intended to grade that evening. Indeed, Smyth regularly worked at home in the evenings. For several years before the accident, he stayed overnight in Santa Rosa once every two or three weeks and worked at home on some week nights. In 1981-1982, he assumed additional responsibilities as department head. In that school year, he worked late on campus once or twice per week, stayed overnight in Santa Rosa once or twice per week, and brought home one or two hours of work "about every night." At home, he worked in a section of the living room reserved for that purpose, where he kept duplicate copies of necessary books. The work usually consisted of grading papers or exams; occasionally, he would also prepare lesson plans or future class schedules at home. Mrs. Smyth testified that her husband worked at home rather than on campus because on campus, he was subject to interruption by students or other business, and, in addition, he wished to spend time with his family.

Smyth's habit of working at home in the evenings was not unusual for members of the college's faculty; working at home appears to have been the rule, not the exception. Patrick Boyle, one of Smyth's colleagues and a former department head, testified that he and many other instructors regularly took work home. In his opinion, the work could not be completed during normal working hours because teachers were subject to interruption in their offices by students (both during the day and at night) and no suitable alternatives for uninterrupted work existed on campus.

Richard Giles, another of Smyth's colleagues, echoed these concerns about the persistent interruptions on campus, testifying that he also took work home four or five nights per week....

Edmund Buckley, associate dean of instruction at the college, testified that the administration neither encouraged nor discouraged working at home. Noting that "it's common for many, many instructors to take work home," he stated that during his own four-year tenure as a departmental head he had been able to avoid interruptions in his office "to some degree — not to a great degree." Buckley had occasionally worked in the library grading papers, a solution he considered "satisfactory" because he found "study carrels that nobody else knew about." He had never received any complaints from instructors to the effect that their working facilities on campus were inadequate.

William Wilbur, dean of business services, agreed that there was no rule against taking work home and that working at home is "common to all disciplines." He also stated that neither Smyth nor any other staff member received financial or other consideration to account for the distance and time of their commutes. He knew of no benefit to the employer by reason of the work being done at home rather than on campus.

An office was provided for each instructor at the college. Undisputed evidence shows that Smyth could have eliminated or reduced student interruptions by posting office hours. Moreover, the record shows — not surprisingly — that Smyth was also subject to interruption while working at home.

The workers' compensation judge concluded that Smyth's death did not occur in the course of employment. He found that Smyth had adequate facilities and sufficient time to complete his work on campus and that it was Smyth's choice to work at home.

Acting on a petition for reconsideration, a three-member board panel, by a two-to-one vote, held that the death arose out of and occurred during the course of employment. The board concluded that because of the nature of the work and the frequent interruptions from students and phone calls, Smyth was "essentially required to maintain a second worksite in his home." It reasoned that in this case "[the] work at home was more a matter of business necessity than of personal convenience." Accordingly, the board awarded death benefits to Mrs. Smyth.

The college seeks review of the board's decision.

Discussion

As the employer, the college is liable for the death benefits provided under the act only if Smyth's accident arose "out of and in the course of the employment" and if certain "conditions of compensation" were present. (Lab. Code, § 3600.) We note at the outset that where, as here, there is no real dispute as to the facts, "the question of whether an injury was suffered in the course of employment is one of law and a purported finding of fact on that question is not binding on an appellate court."

We originally adopted the going and coming rule as one means of determining when an accident should be treated as an "accident arising out of and in the course of the employment." In *Ocean Accident etc. Co. v. Industrial Acc. Com.* (1916) 159 P. 1041, the issue was whether a fatal accident suffered by a seaman as he attempted to reboard his ship after going ashore for personal reasons arose out of and occurred within the scope of his employment. Observing that the language of the act was identical to that of the English Workmen's Compensation Act (enacted in 1897), we looked to English case law for guidance. We concluded that "there are excluded from the benefits of the act all those accidental injuries which occur while the employee is going to or returning from his work ...."

Of course, we recognized that in the broadest sense an injury occurring on the way to one's place of employment is an injury "growing out of and incident to his employment," since "a necessary part of the employment is that the employee shall go to and return from his place of labor." However, the right to an award is founded not "upon the fact that the injury grows out of and is incidental to his employment," but, rather, "upon the fact that the *service* he is rendering at the time of the injury grows out of and is incidental to the employment." (Emphasis original.) Therefore, we reasoned, "an employee going to and from his place of employment is not rendering any service, and begins to render such service only when [arriving at the place of employment]."

The going and coming rule resulted from the type of judicial line-drawing frequently required when construing and applying vague or open-ended statutory provisions. With its genesis in the practical need of drawing a "line" delineating an employee's "scope of employment," the rule was necessarily arbitrary, later explanations of its underlying rationale notwithstanding. California courts — manifesting much unease both in applying as well as in refusing to apply the rule — have recognized this essential arbitrariness and its potential harshness.

Indeed, it has become customary for courts to introduce each new discussion of the rule with a litany of reservations and qualifications: the rule is a "slippery concept" which is "riddled with exceptions"; "[much] criticized and subject to numerous exceptions, the rule is difficult to apply uniformly"; it has had a "tortuous history"; neither the rule nor its exceptions are susceptible to "automatic application"; each case "must be adjudged by the facts which are peculiarly its own"; "application of the rule has been especially difficult in 'borderline cases' ...." Finally, most attempts to exorcise or anesthetize the rule depart from or culminate in an invocation of Labor Code section 3202, which provides that the act "shall be liberally construed by the courts with the purpose of extending [its] benefits for the protection of persons injured in the course of their employment." Having shown that years of case law have properly eviscerated the going and coming rule, courts then go on to explain why the particular facts of the case fall into one of the many established exceptions to the rule.

The trouble is that the facts in this case do not fit convincingly into any of the established limitations or exceptions. (*See* fn. 11.) Because Smyth's accident occurred miles away from the Santa Rosa campus, exceptions to the "premises line" doctrine[11] cannot reasonably be invoked to render the going and coming rule inapplicable. Smyth received no special or additional compensation for his commute; therefore, the "wage payment or travel expense" exception cannot apply.[12] The college did not require Smyth to furnish his own vehicle on the job. If it had, the "required transportation" exception would have curtailed application of the going and coming rule.

Smyth's employment at the college in no way created a "special risk." Under that exception, an injury is compensable if, before entry upon the premises, an employee suffers injury from a special risk causally related to employment. (*Gen. Ins. Co. v. Workmen's Comp. App. Bd. (Chairez)* (1976) 16 Cal. 3d 595, 600 ....) "The facts that an accident happens upon a public road and that the danger is one to which the general public is likewise exposed, however, do not preclude the existence of a causal relationship between the accident and the employment if the danger is one to which the employee, by reason of and in connection with his employment, is subjected peculiarly or to an abnormal degree." (*Freire v. Matson Nav. Co.* (1941) 19 Cal. 2d 8, 12 ....) In *Chairez,* we devised a two-prong test to determine applicability of the special risk exception: the exception will apply (1) if "but for" the employment the employee would not have been at the location where the injury occurred and (2) if "the risk is distinctive in nature or quantitatively greater than risks common to the public." While the circumstances of Smyth's accident certainly meet the first requirement (i.e., the accident would not have occurred "but for" the employment), his employment at the college did not subject him to a risk which was distinct or quantitatively greater than that common to the public generally.

We also find no merit in the suggestion that Smyth's accident occurred while he was on "special mission" or "errand" which was reasonably undertaken at the

---

[11] For purposes of applying the going and coming rule, the employment relationship begins when the employee enters the employer's premises. We have reaffirmed the "premises line" rule, stating that it "has the advantage of enabling courts to ascertain the point at which employment begins — objectively and fairly." However, injuries sustained in close proximity to the employer's premises may, in fact arise out of the employment, especially when the accident occurs in the parking lot used by employees or on public property immediately adjacent to the workplace. Recognizing this, we have defined the course of employment to include a "reasonable margin of time and space necessary to be used in passing to and from the place where the work is to be done." Where the employment itself creates a danger to employees entering or leaving the premises, we have posited a "field of risk" or "zone of danger," the extent of which varies from case to case, depending on the degree to which the employer's conduct contributes directly as a proximate cause of the employee's injuries. This line of cases stems from one of the earliest attempts to circumvent or soften *Ocean Accident. (See Judson Mfg. Co. v. Ind. Acc. Com.* (1919) 181 Cal. 300, 302 ... ["It would be a harsh and indefensible rule that would withhold compensation from an employee engaged in traversing a dangerous pathway in his employer's building on his way to his own particular place of work therein, on the ground that he had not yet entered upon the real work of his employment"].)

[12] The fact that an employer compensates an employee for the commuting time implies an agreement that the employment relationship shall continue during the period of going and coming.

request or invitation of his employer.[13] In relation to his routine duties, there was nothing "extraordinary" about his commute on March 16, 1982. The accident occurred, quite simply, during his regular commute between the college and his home in Ukiah. Smyth's practice of taking work home with him in the evenings cannot convert a routine commute into a "special mission."

Finally, we have recognized a "home as a second jobsite" exception to the going and coming rule. It is this exception — or an extension of it — which the board used in concluding that the rule does not preclude compensation in this case. Generally, "[work] done at home may exempt an injury occurring during a regular commute from the going and coming rule if circumstances of the employment — and not mere dictates of convenience to the employee — make the home a second jobsite. If the home becomes a second business situs, the familiar rule applies that injury sustained while traveling between jobsites is compensable." (*Wilson v. Workmen's Comp. App. Bd.* (1976) 16 Cal. 3d 181, 184 ....) We noted that the commute does not constitute a business trip if the employees work at home for their own convenience "serving the employee's own convenience in selecting an off-premise place to work is a personal and not a business purpose."

The facts underlying Smyth's claim to a "home as a second jobsite" exception closely resemble those advanced by the applicant in *Wilson*. Like Smyth, Wilson was a teacher. She was injured in an automobile accident while driving to her school. Instructors at her school commonly graded papers and planned lessons outside class periods or at home in the evening, as the class schedule did not set aside a specific period for these activities. Although teachers could complete class preparation at school, they usually chose to work at home for their own convenience. At the time of the accident, Wilson's car contained miscellaneous supplies for use in her art class, materials graded at home the previous evening, and her teaching manual and other books.

In *Wilson*, we affirmed the board's determination that the applicant's home did not constitute a second jobsite warranting exemption from the going and coming rule. Her explicit job requirements demanded only that she report to the school premises, and "[her] employer's implicit requirement to work beyond classroom hours did not require labor at home."

---

[13] "An injury suffered by an employee during his regular commute is compensable if he was also performing a special mission for his employer." (*Chairez, supra,* 16 Cal. 3d at p. 601.) The employee's conduct is "special" if it is "extraordinary in relation to routine duties, not outside the scope of employment." The closely related "dual purpose" rule also appears inapplicable. In *Lockheed Aircraft Corp. v. Ind. Acc. Com.* (1946) 28 Cal. 2d 756 ..., we held that "where the employee is combining his own business with that of his employer, or attending to both at substantially the same time, no nice inquiry will be made as to which business he was actually engaged in at the time of injury, unless it clearly appears that neither directly or indirectly could he have been serving his employer." The dual purpose situation usually arises when the employees combine their personal business with a "special errand" or "mission."

Applicant in the present case contends that the board properly concluded that it was an implied term or condition of Smyth's employment contract that he take work home in the evenings — that it was "more a matter of business necessity than of personal convenience." On this basis, the board distinguished *Wilson,* wherein there was no claim that school facilities were not sufficient to allow completion of the required work.

It is not entirely clear whether the board's determination that Smyth was "implicitly required" to use his home as a second jobsite represents a conclusion of law or a finding of fact. Much of the language used by the board suggests that it was a legal conclusion which the board drew from the uncontradicted evidence in the record: *"The picture that emerges from the testimony* of the various witnesses is that the decedent was essentially required to maintain a second worksite in his home"; "... *we conclude that the decedent was implicitly author-ized* to perform part of his duties at home ..."; "clearly this was an accepted practice. *It appears* moreover, *that this was in effect an implied term or condi-tion* of the employment contract"; "his home was *in effect a second worksite* due to the fact that he was *implicitly required* to work at home". (Italics added.)

These passages suggest that the board concluded that where an employee works long hours and is subject to interruption at the workplace and where fellow employees commonly take work home with the knowledge and implicit permission of the employer, general principles of workers' compensation law establish that the employee is, as a matter of law, "implicitly required" to use his home as a second jobsite. There is no authority, however, to support such a proposition. *Wilson* makes quite clear that a home does not become a second jobsite simply because one's employment requires long working hours and the employer knows that the employee frequently brings work home. As we observed in *Wilson,* "[the] contemporary professional frequently takes work home. There, the draftsman designs on a napkin, the businessman plans at break-fast, the lawyer labors in the evening. But this hearthside activity — while commendable — does not create a white collar exception to the going and coming rule." Thus, to the extent that the board's "implicit requirement" determination amounts to a legal conclusion, it cannot be reconciled with *Wilson.*

Furthermore, we find little to commend the white-collar exception which we refused to establish in *Wilson.* It would, *a fortiori,* extend workers' compensation benefits to workers injured in the homes themselves, as well as en route to and from their regular work places. Ironically, a white collar exception would probably not diminish the controversy surrounding the going and coming rule; it would merely shift it to a new and equally arbitrary "line" defining the "course of employment."[16] Would the fact that an employee regularly took work-related

---

[16] The going and coming rule and its many exceptions are all "arbitrary" — judicial responses to the practical necessity of establishing guidelines for use in determining whether a worker's injury arose out of and in the course of employment. Like all arbitrary rules, they are, in borderline cases, widely perceived as unfair.... As one commentator observed, "[it] is a familiar problem in law, when a sharp, objective, and perhaps somewhat arbitrary line has been drawn ... to encounter

materials home suffice to create a second jobsite, or would the employee have to show that he *actually* worked at home? How would we treat employees who work at home on some evenings but not on others, depending on their personal inclinations? And, of course, new problems of the "frolics and detours" variety would plague the new exception.

On the other hand, insofar as the board's determination that the employee was "implicitly required" to maintain his home as a second jobsite was intended as a finding of fact, it is simply not supported by substantial evidence in the record. Although the evidence shows that most faculty members took work home and that the employer was well aware of this practice, there is nothing in the record which indicates that faculty members were *required* — implicitly or otherwise — to work at home rather than on campus. Rather, the evidence reveals that professors worked at home by choice, not because of the dictates of their employer. On this record, there is no room for a factual finding that working at home was a condition of Smyth's employment.

Therefore, applying established "going and coming rule" principles and precedents, we conclude that the board erred in awarding compensation. We could, of course, abrogate the rule or expand any of its exceptions, for they have evolved simply as "the product of judicial gloss on the statutory conditions of compensability." However, they have become an important part of our workers' compensation law. Although the Legislature has enacted significant changes in the Workers' Compensation Act during the last 70 years, it has not disturbed the going and coming rule or its judicially created exceptions. Unless the judiciary can devise rules which are fairer, less arbitrary, less problematic in application, and more clearly consistent with the public policies underlying the act, it should leave to the Legislature the major task of restructuring the rules governing employer liability.

Smyth's accident occurred during a routine commute from college to home. We conclude that the facts of this case are essentially indistinguishable from those of *Wilson v. Workmen's Comp. App. Bd.* and that our holding in *Wilson* should govern here.

The decision of the board is annulled.

---

demands that the line be blurred a little to take care of the closest cases. For example, one writer says that there is no reason in principle why states should not protect employees 'for a reasonable distance' before reaching or after leaving the employer's premises. This, however, only raises a new problem because it provides no standard by which the reasonableness of the distance can be judged. It substitutes the widely varying subjective interpretation of 'reasonable distance' by different administrators and judges for the physical fact of a boundary line. At the same time, it does not solve the original problem, because each time the premises are extended a 'reasonable distance,' there will inevitably arise new cases only slightly beyond that point — and the cry of unfairness of drawing distinctions based on only a few feet of distance will once more be heard." (1 Larson, Workmen's Compensation Law, § 15.12(a).) While the going and coming rule (and its exceptions) can hardly be considered to be as "sharp" and "objective" as the premises-line doctrine which Larson was defending, we believe that his reasoning is applicable to the issues in this case.

REYNOSO, JUSTICE, dissenting:

I respectfully dissent. Courts have fashioned the "going and coming" rule to aid in determining whether an injury occurred "in the course of the employment." In applying this rule, courts have held "non-compensable the injury that occurs during a local commute en route to a fixed place of business at fixed hours in the absence of special or extraordinary circumstances." By narrowly focusing on the rule and its numerous exceptions, however, the majority in this case has lost sight of the primary statutory test. Since Smyth's accident clearly occurred in the course of his employment, it should be compensable.

....

Smyth's accident during his Ukiah commute should be compensable because it was a dual purpose trip, serving both his personal purpose of making a trip home and the business purpose of reaching a second jobsite. In such a situation, the court should look for three principal indicia to establish a compensable injury: "the quantity and regularity of work performed at home; the continuing presence of work equipment at home; and special circumstances of the particular employment that make it necessary and not merely personally convenient to work at home." (1 Larson, The Law of Workmen's Compensation (1985) § 18.32 at p. 4-309.)

Here, testimony demonstrated that Smyth brought home one or two hours of work almost every night. In addition, part of the Smyths' living room was reserved as his work place, in which he kept duplicate copies of his books. Finally, it was more than a matter of personal convenience to work at home. To be an effective teacher, Smyth needed to be accessible to students while in his office. Frequent interruptions by students, however, made it impossible for him to complete his preparatory work on campus. Furthermore, Smyth served as head of the mathematics department. In this capacity, he assumed the responsibility of supervising and evaluating the night instructors as well as the burden of administrative work, which included receiving all telephone calls for the department. This evidence supports the board's finding that Smyth's home was a second jobsite.

....

NOTES

1. *Traveling to a Convention.* In *Ehrgott v. Jones,* 506 A.2d 40 (N.J. Super. Ct. App. Div. 1986), the plaintiff, Ehrgott, brought a tort suit against the estate of a fellow employee, Jones, as a result of an accident that occurred while Jones was driving them to the Newark Airport. Jones and another passenger in the car were killed and Ehrgott was seriously and permanently disabled. Both Ehrgott and Jones were employees of Hoechst-Roussel Pharmaceuticals, and were on the way to an annual meeting of the American Chemical Society in Las Vegas. Ehrgott and Jones would have been covered by workers' compensation while attending the meeting. The issue in the case was whether the trip to the airport fell within the definition of the "going and coming" rule (in which case workers' compensation coverage was not legally required) or whether this trip fell within the "special-mission provision" of the New Jersey statute (in which case Ehrgott was covered by workers' compensation and Jones was protected from a tort suit because the exclusive remedy provision in the New Jersey workers' compensation statute extends to fellow employees). The special-mission provision provides that the employee is deemed to be in the course of employment when he is both required by the employer to be away from his place of employment and is then actually engaged in the direct performance of duties assigned or directed by the employer. The court held that Ehrgott's trip fell within the special-mission provision and therefore the proper remedy was workers' compensation and not a tort suit. Note the irony of the case: Ehrgott was arguing that he did *not* have workers' compensation coverage in order to be able to bring a tort suit against the estate of a fellow employee.

2. *Arkansas Travelers.* The Arkansas workers' compensation law was amended in 1993 to eliminate the requirement that the act should be applied liberally and that all doubts should be resolved in favor of the worker. The amendment also requires evidence to be weighed impartially, without giving the benefit of the doubt to either party, and requires the courts to construe the provisions of the Act strictly. The Act also added a new definition: "Compensable injury" does not include an injury that was inflicted upon the employee at a time when employment services were not being performed. ARK. CODE ANN. § 11-9-102.

The Court of Appeals interpreted the amended workers' compensation law in *Hightower v. Newark Public School System*, 943 S.W.2d 608 (Ark. Ct. App. 1997). A teacher at a day-care center was ordered to report to work despite the encasement of the employer's parking lot in a sheet of ice. She slipped and fell, hurt her back, and missed two weeks of work. The court indicated that under the law prior to 1993, her injury would have been compensable because there was an exception to the going and coming rule for injuries that occurred on the employer's premises. However, the court said that the 1993 definition of compensable injury seemed clearly aimed at eliminating the premises exception to the going-and-coming rule. Under a strict construction of the law, "merely walking to and from one's car, even on the employer's premises, does not qualify as performing 'employment services.'"

Cheri Pettey was also injured in Arkansas after the 1993 amendments. She was a nursing assistant who traveled to patients' homes to provide nursing service. She was compensated according to the time spent at each patient's home. She did not receive compensation for travel expenses or for travel time, and used her own vehicle to travel to the patients' homes. Pettey had reported to the employer's office to pick up supplies and was on the way to her first patient of the day when she lost control of her auto and was injured. Is the injury compensable? *Olsten Kimberly Quality Care v. Pettey*, 944 S.W.2d 524 (Ark. 1997) (yes). The court recognized that an employee generally does not meet the course of employment test when traveling to and from the workplace. However, there are traditional exceptions to the "going and coming" rule, such as situations when the travel is an integral part of the job because the employee must travel from job site to job site. The court was not persuaded that the fact the employee was not paid for the travel time meant the trip was not in the course of employment (really, the triple negative was in the court's opinion!), in part because the employee was required to furnish her own conveyance and in part because the facts "clearly demonstrate that travel was a necessary part of her employment." *Id.* at 572.

2. TEST TWO: "ARISING OUT OF EMPLOYMENT"

The second test that a worker must meet in order to receive workers' compensation benefits is that there be an injury "arising out of employment." This test is used to distinguish among three types of risk that are associated with any workplace: (1) occupational risks, such as machinery breaking, that are universally compensable because they are associated with the employment; (2) personal risks, which are universally noncompensable since they are personal to the claimant, such as a heart seizure resulting from a drug overdose; and (3) "neutral" risks, where the cause of the injury is neither distinctly occupational nor distinctly personal in character or where the cause is unknown. Neutral risks may or may not be compensable depending on the legal doctrine used in a particular state and on the specific facts of the case.

Figure 21-1

Three Categories of Risk

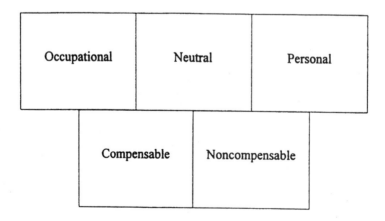

The first step in deciding whether a particular case meets the arising out of employment (AOE) test is to decide the category of risk involved in the case. Most cases will involve either occupational or personal risks, and therefore whether the case meets the AOE test is easily resolved. If the case is one of the unusual variety that involves a neutral risk, the legal inquiry become more complicated and two more steps are necessary.

The second step is to determine the type of neutral risk. This may affect the resolution of the case because some states use different legal tests for different types of neutral risks. (As will be discussed later in this section, more states used to differentiate among types of neutral risks than currently do, but the distinctions are still relevant in many jurisdictions.) Among the types of neutral risks are (1) an "Act of God" or (depending on your philosophical view) an "Act of Nature," such as a worker injured by lightning, a wild animal bite, an earthquake, a windstorm, a sunstroke, or a similar calamity of nature; (2) assault by a stranger; (3) "street risks," which are harms such as dog bites, police bullets, or other maladies associated with being on a public street; and (4) unexplained death.

The legal doctrine used in a jurisdiction to deal with a particular type of neutral risk (or used to decide all neutral risks in the state) is the third step that is crucial to the outcome of the case. Professor Larson has identified five lines of interpretation of the "arising out of employment" test. In increasing liberality these are:

(1) *The Proximate Cause Doctrine.* This rule, now obsolete, required that the harm be foreseeable as a hazard of this kind of employment and that an unbroken chain of causation connect the hazard and the injury without any intervening cause. This test would make all neutral risks (and even some occupational risks) noncompensable.

(2) *The Peculiar Risk Doctrine.* The rule used by most states in the past, but now largely abandoned, which requires that the hazard be peculiar to (and increased by) the employment.

(3) *The Increased Risk Doctrine.* The rule still used in many if not most states, which requires that the job increase the quantity of the risk, even if the risk is not peculiar to the occupation. A flag pole sitter struck by lightning would satisfy this test (although not the two previous tests).

(4) *The Actual Risk Doctrine.* The position of a substantial number of states, which allows compensation even if the risk that caused the injury was common to the public, as long as it was an actual risk of this employment. An alternative term for this test (and one that helps clarify the meaning) is the normal risk doctrine: the risk may be no greater than the risks faced by the public, but is compensable if it is a normal risk of this job. A worker in a 24-hour convenience store in a dangerous neighborhood may not face greater risk of assault by a stranger than anyone else in the area (which means that the increased risk doctrine would not be satisfied), but such an assault is an actual (or normal) risk of being a clerk in such a store, and thus would meet the actual risk doctrine.

(5) *The Positional Risk Doctrine.* The position of a growing minority of states, which allows compensation for all injuries that would not have

occurred but for the fact that the conditions of the employment placed claimant in the position where he or she was injured. A worker in a 24-hour convenience store who is in the back room sorting bottles and who is killed by a freak lightning bolt that ricochets through the store could meet this doctrine but not the other four tests.

See ARTHUR LARSON, LARSON'S WORKER'S COMPENSATION §§ 6.00-6.60 (Desk ed., 1997).

These tests are explicated in the succeeding cases, which were selected in part to illustrate the historical evolution of the legal approaches to deciding which neutral risks are compensable.

DONAHUE v. MARYLAND CASUALTY CO.

Supreme Judicial Court of Massachusetts
116 N.E. 226 (1917)

CROSBY, J.:

The evidence presented to the committee of arbitration was in substance as follows: The claimant, who was employed by the insured in the sale of church goods, on February 21, 1916, left his employer's place of business in Boston, and proceeded by train to Lowell and thence by electric cars to the village of Collinsville in Lowell. Upon leaving the electric cars, he went to the house of a clergyman, which was distant about ten minutes' walk from the car line, and after completing his business there left and started to walk back. He had proceeded about thirty-five or forty feet when he slipped on the ice and fell, sustaining a broken ankle. When injured he was walking in the middle of the street, the sidewalk being impassable on account of ice. He was employed principally as a traveling salesman, but worked in the store during the Christmas and Easter seasons. More than half of the time he was outside his employer's store visiting different places throughout New England for the purpose of selling church goods. He traveled by steam railroads, electric cars, and on foot — using cars when available. When he left the house of the clergyman he intended to take a car to Lexington to sell some goods there. The committee found that the employee received an injury in the course of and arising out of his employment.

At the hearing before the Industrial Accident Board in addition to the evidence before the committee above recited, the employee testified:

> I was going to get a car to Lexington when I fell. The street was a mass of ice. I never saw anything like it before or since.

The finding that the injury was received in the course of the employment was warranted. The question remains whether there was any evidence that the injury arose out of the employment. An injury arises out of the employment when there is a causal connection between the conditions under which the work is to be performed and the resulting injury. An injury cannot be found to have arisen out of the employment unless the employment was a contributing, proximate cause.

If the risk of injury to the employee was one to which he would have been equally exposed apart from his employment, then the injury does not arise out of it. As was said by this court in *McNicols' Case*[, 102 N.E. 697 (Mass. 1913)]:

> The causative danger must be peculiar to the work and not common to the neighborhood. It must be incidental to the character of the business and not independent of the relation of master and servant.

The undisputed evidence shows that while the employee was walking along the street in the course of his employment on his way to the electric car line, he slipped upon the ice and received the injury for which he seeks compensation. Manifestly the injury so received did not result in any proper sense from a risk incidental to the employment. It seems plain that the danger of the employee's slipping upon the ice in a public street was not peculiar to his work, but was a hazard common to persons engaged in any employment who had occasion to travel along the streets. The risk of slipping upon the icy pavement was common to the public who had occasion to pass over it on foot. It was a danger due to climatic conditions to which persons in that locality, however employed or if not employed at all, were equally exposed.

As the hazard of slipping on the ice in the street was not a causative danger peculiar to the claimant's employment, the injury received could not properly be found to have arisen out of the employment.

The decree of the superior court must be reversed, and a decree entered in favor of the insurer.

So ordered.

KATZ v. A. KADANS & CO.

New York Court of Appeals
134 N.E. 330 (1922)

POUND, J.

This is a workmen's compensation case. Louis Katz, the claimant, was a dairyman's chauffeur. On May 7, 1920, when he was driving his employer's car west on Canal street after delivering some cheese, an insane man stabbed him. A lot of people were running after the insane man and he stabbed any one near him. The question is whether claimant's injuries arose out of his employment.

If the work itself involves exposure to perils of the street, strange, unanticipated, and infrequent though they may be, the employee passes along the streets when on his master's occasions under the protection of the statute. This is the rule unequivocally laid down by the House of Lords in England:

> "When a workman is sent into the street on his master's business, ... his employment necessarily involves exposure to the risks of the streets and injury from such a cause [necessarily] arises out of his employment."

Dennis v. White, [1917] L.R. App. Cas. 479.

So we have to concern ourselves only with the question whether claimant's accident arose out of a street risk.

Cases may arise where one is hurt in the street, but where the risk is of a general nature, not peculiar to the street. Lightning strikes fortuitously in the street; bombs dropped by enemy aircraft do not expose to special danger persons in a street as distinguished from those in houses. The danger must result from the place to make it a street risk, but that is enough if the workman is in the place by reason of his employment, and in the discharge of his duty to his employer. The street becomes a dangerous place when street brawlers, highwaymen, escaping criminals, or violent madmen are afoot therein as they sometimes are. The danger of being struck by them by accident is a street risk because it is incident to passing through or being on the street when dangerous characters are abroad.

Particularly on the crowded streets of a great city, not only do vehicles collide, pavements become out of repair, and crowds jostle, but mad or biting dogs may run wild, gunmen may discharge their weapons, police officers may shoot at fugitives fleeing from justice, or other things may happen from which accidental injuries result to people on the streets which are peculiar to the use of the streets and do not commonly happen indoors.

The risk of being stabbed by an insane man running amuck seems in a peculiar sense a risk incidental to the streets to which claimant was exposed by his employment. *Matter of Heidemann v. Am. Dist. Tel. Co.,* 130 N.E. 302 [(N.Y. 1921)], does not hold that where the street risk is one shared equally by all who pass or repass, whether in or out of employment, it should be shown that the employment involves some special exposure; that the night watchman is exposed by his employment to the risk of being shot by accident as he nears a sudden brawl which it is his duty to investigate, while the night clerk whose business brings him on the street, but whose duty is not to seek danger, is not so exposed. We decided the case before us and no other, dwelling naturally upon those features of the situation which emphasized the connection between the risk and the employment. But the fact that the risk is one to which every one on the street is exposed does not itself defeat compensation. Members of the public may face the same risk every day. The question is whether the employment exposed the workman to the risks by sending him on to the street, common though such risks were to all on the street.

The order should be affirmed, with costs.

HOGAN, CARDOZO, and CRANE, JJ., concur.
HISCOCK, C. J., and MCLAUGHLIN and ANDREWS, JJ., dissent.

NOTES

1. *Evolution of the Street Risk Doctrine.* The *Donahue* and *Katz* cases present in a capsule view the evolution of the street risk doctrine. In *Donahue,* decided in 1917, street risks were treated like all other forms of neutral risks (and the peculiar risk test was used). In *Katz,* decided in New York in 1922 and still the approach used in some jurisdictions today (although not New York), the court differentiated street risks from other types of neutral risks and then used a more liberal doctrine for street risks than was being used contemporaneously for other neutral risks. The pattern in such states is to use the increased risk doctrine for most neutral risks, but a more liberal doctrine (typically the actual risk test) for street risks.

2. *The Street Risk Sequence.* In those states which use a different doctrine for street risks than for other types of neutral risks, the logical sequence in applying the AOE test is first to decide which of the three categories of risk is involved; then (assuming the risk is a neutral risk), decide which type of neutral risk is involved; and then decide which legal doctrine is applicable.

Assume that your client, Stu Stevens, a delivery person, is mauled by a bear while delivering a famous casebook to a customer. What additional evidence would allow Stu to meet the AOE test? What additional evidence would preclude Stu from meeting the AOE test?

HANSON v. REICHELT

Supreme Court of Iowa

452 N.W.2d 164 (1990)

LAVORATO, JUSTICE.

This appeal arises out of the death of a farm employee who suffered a heat-stroke while working. The Iowa industrial commissioner denied benefits, finding that the employee's injury did not arise out of his employment. In making this finding, the commissioner applied the general public-increased risk rule, a rule this court first approved in a workers' compensation case involving heatstroke more than fifty years ago.

....

We now adopt the actual risk rule in workers' compensation cases involving injuries from exposure to the elements. We think here, however, that the agency should be allowed to decide the liability issue in light of the rule we adopt today. So we affirm in part and vacate in part the decision of the court of appeals. We reverse the judgment of the district court and remand for further proceedings consistent with this opinion.

On June 24, 1983, D. Van Maanen agreed to buy some hay from Sherman Reichelt. Reichelt had already baled some of the hay. The remainder of the hay sold to Van Maanen had to be baled, and all of the hay had to be stacked on a hayrack and transported from Riechelt's field.

Reichelt hired Dennis L. Hanson to help with the baling. When the baling operation began, the weather was very hot; the recorded temperature that day reached a high of 95 degrees.

At about 2:30 p.m. on June 24, Van Maanen's wife, Van Maanen, Reichelt, and Hanson began working in the field. Hanson's job was twofold: he stacked bales and drove empty and full hayracks to and from the field. Each bale weighed about sixty pounds. Hanson did this for about an hour and a half. But at no time did he work more than twenty-five minutes without a break.

At some point Hanson quit and sat down in the field. About thirty minutes later, Reichelt drove up in his pickup and found Hanson passed out.

Reichelt called for medical assistance; an ambulance arrived about 5:00 p.m. and took Hanson to a hospital in Newton. The doctors there determined that Hanson had suffered a heatstroke. Later Hanson was transferred to Iowa Methodist Medical Center in Des Moines where he underwent extensive treatment and finally died on July 18, 1983.

Hanson's father and mother were appointed administrators of their son's estate. As such the parents filed a petition with the Iowa Industrial Commission in June 1984. They sought medical and death benefits from Reichelt and Reichelt's insurance carrier.

A deputy industrial commissioner in an arbitration decision found that Hanson's death did not arise out of his employment and denied benefits. The administrators appealed to the commissioner who affirmed.

The administrators then filed in the district court a petition for judicial review of the commissioner's decision. The district court affirmed.

The administrators appealed from the district court's decision, and we transferred the case to the court of appeals. The court of appeals found that Hanson's death did arise out of his employment. So it reversed the judgment of the district court.

. . . .

Reichelt and his carrier sought further review of the court of appeals decision, which we granted. The narrow issue we must decide is whether the agency properly applied the law when it found that Hanson's death did not arise out of his employment.

I

When we review a district court decision on the validity of agency action, we ask only whether the district court has correctly applied the law. The district court is itself acting in an appellate capacity to correct errors of law made by the agency. In our review of the district court's action in such capacity, we merely apply the standards of Iowa Code section 17A.19(8) to the agency action to determine whether our conclusions are the same as those of the district court. If our conclusions are the same, we must affirm. Likewise, if our conclusions differ, we must reverse.

II

In these proceedings the administrators had the burden to prove by a preponderance of the evidence that Hanson had suffered an injury that arose out of and in the course of his employment....

Both sides agree that Hanson's injury — the heatstroke — arose during the course of his employment. So, as we said, our sole issue is whether Hanson's injury arose out of his employment.

III

In the past this court addressed the issue whether a heatstroke is compensable in workers' compensation cases. *See, e.g., Wax v. Des Moines Asphalt Paving Corp.,* 263 N.W. 333 (Iowa 1935); *West v. Phillips,* 288 N.W. 625 (Iowa 1939). In *Wax* an employee suffered a heatstroke while digging a trench in 100+ degree temperatures. The industrial commissioner allowed benefits, and the district court affirmed. Viewing the same facts, we held as a matter of law that the heatstroke did not arise out of the employment. In other words, there was no causal connection between the employment and the injury.

In reaching this conclusion, we adopted and applied the general public-increased risk rule which provides that

> [i]f the employment brings with it no greater exposure to injurious results from natural causes, and neither contributes to produce these nor to aggravate their effect, as from lightning, severe heat or cold, than those to which persons generally in that locality, whether so employed or not, are equally exposed there is no causal connection between the employment and the injury. But where the employment brings a greater exposure and injury results, the injury does arise out of the employment.

Simply put, the rule permits recovery "only in cases where the [employee] is exposed to conditions of temperature unusual or more intense than those experienced by [employees] of the community in general."

Relying on the same rule, we reached an opposite result in *West v. Phillips.* There a bakery employee became ill while working the night shift. The employee died the next day. His doctor testified that the employee showed substantially all the symptoms of heat exhaustion. The doctor performed an autopsy. He found that the employee had severe heart trouble and that the heat exhaustion had hastened the employee's death.

In *West* experts testified that heat infiltration from the tar roof, an inefficient fan inside, and artificial heat from the oven combined to make it 10 to 12 degrees hotter inside. During the day, the temperatures outside had reached 108.

We thought that the testimony of the experts was sufficient to sustain a finding "that there was excessive heat in the bakeshop caused by artificial heat." Such a finding, of course, met the recovery requirement of the general public-increased risk rule: the employee must be exposed to conditions of temperature unusual or more intense than those experienced by employees of the community in general. In addition, we thought the doctor's testimony was sufficient to establish the necessary causal connection between the employee's death and the heat exhaustion.

The facts here are on all fours with the facts in *Wax*. So it is not surprising that the deputy reached the same conclusion as we did in *Wax*: no causal connection between the death and the injury.

One noted authority criticizes the general public-increased risk rule because of the way courts define the general public:

> The heart of the difficulty is almost entirely in defining the general public with which the comparison is made. It is here that many of the negative cases have gone wide of the mark. Clearly, since the object of the comparison between the exposure of this employee and the exposure of the public is to isolate and identify the distinctive characteristics of this employment, the comparison should be made with a broad cross section of the public having no characteristics specially selected because they resemble those of the employment. Because most of these cases arise during extreme hot, cold, rainy, or stormy weather, the most direct way to approach a working rule is to ask: What does the average man, free of the obligation of any particular employment, do when it is twenty below, or a hundred in the shade, or raining, sleeting or snowing violently? There may be various answers as to what he does, but there is one clear answer as to what he does not do. He does not stay outdoors all day.

1 Larson, *Workmen's Compensation Law,* § 8.42 (1984).

Larson gives an example of the proper application of the general public-increased risk rule from a Texas sunstroke case in which the court succinctly and clearly summed up the rule:

> In the case before us the very work which the decedent was doing for his employer exposed him to a greater hazard from heatstroke than the general public was exposed to for the simple reason that the general public were not pushing wheelbarrow loads of sand in the hot sun on that day.

Several jurisdictions have discarded the general public-increased risk rule in cases involving effects of exposure to the elements. In its place, these courts have adopted the actual risk rule.

In *Hughes* [*v. St. Patrick's Cathedral,* 156 N.E. 665 (N.Y. 1927)], the employee suffered heat prostration while working outdoors. In holding for the employee, the court summed up the actual risk rule in two sentences:

> Heat prostration is an accidental injury arising out of and during the course of the employment, if the nature of the employment exposes the workman to risk of such injury. Although the risk may be common to all who are

exposed to the suns [*sic*] rays on a hot day, the question is whether the employment exposes the employee to the risk.

Reaching the same result on similar reasoning in an accidental freezing case, the Wisconsin Supreme Court said:

> The injury in the instant case clearly grew out of and was incidental to the employment. It makes no difference that the exposure was common to all out of door employments in that locality in that kind of weather. The injury grew out of that employment and was incidental to it. It was a hazard of the industry.

Eagle River Bldg. & Supply Co., 225 N.W. at 691.

We think the actual risk rule is the better rule and more in line with how we construe our Workers' Compensation Act. We construe the Act liberally in favor of the employee; we resolve all doubts in favor of the employee.

Moreover, the actual risk rule makes no comparison between risks found by the employee and those found by the general public. So the rule is not subject to the same criticisms that have been voiced against the general public-increased risk rule.

We adopt the actual risk rule in cases involving injuries from exposure to the elements. If the nature of the employment exposes the employee to the risk of such an injury, the employee suffers an accidental injury arising out of and during the course of the employment. And it makes no difference that the risk was common to the general public on the day of the injury.

IV

Because the district court's judgment is based on a rule of law we now renounce, we must reverse. But we think the agency should be allowed to decide the liability issue in light of the actual risk rule. So we affirm that part of the court of appeals decision which reversed the judgment of the district court. We vacate that part of the court of appeals decision which held that Hanson's injury arose out of his employment. We reverse the judgment of the district court and remand for further proceedings consistent with this opinion.

NOTE

Evolution of the AOE Test in Iowa. James Miedema was a laborer at the Dial Corporation. He clocked in for his shift and then went to the restroom while getting ready to work. After turning to flush the toilet, he experienced severe pain in his lower back, was taken to the emergency room at the local hospital, and was out of work for a month. The injury occurred in the course of employment, but did it meet the arising out of the employment test? The Iowa Supreme Court, in *Miedema v. Dial Corp.*, 551 N.W.2d 309 (Iowa 1996), indicated that it had adopted the actual risk rule in *Hanson v. Reichelt* and that its analysis applies here. Would you consider experiencing a severe back strain as a result of flushing a toilet an actual risk of being a laborer? Or, to use the alternative formulation of the actual risk doctrine, would you consider the back strain a normal risk of being a laborer? Editors' response (for what it is worth): No, thereby suggesting that the decision of the court finding that Miedema did not meet the arising out of employment test is consistent with the actual risk rule. Next, consider this language from the decision: "Miedema fails to establish that use of Dial's restroom exposed him to any increased risk of injury." *Id.* at 311. Does the Iowa Supreme Court understand the distinction between the increased risk doctrine and the actual risk doctrine?

NIPPERT v. SHINN FARM CONSTRUCTION CO.

Supreme Court of Nebraska
388 N.W.2d 820 (1986)

PER CURIAM.

Dennis W. Nippert appeals the dismissal of a suit filed against his employer, Shinn Farm Construction Company, in the Nebraska Workers' Compensation Court. Nippert seeks compensation for total temporary disability and permanent partial disability suffered as a result of injuries sustained in a tornado on October 18, 1979.

A single judge of the compensation court found, under the "act of nature" doctrine, that the accident which caused Nippert's injury did not "arise out of" his employment as required for recovery under the Workers' Compensation Act.... On rehearing, a three-judge panel affirmed the order of dismissal. We reverse.

Nippert was employed by Shinn Farm Construction Company on October 18, 1979. On this date he and other workers were erecting a hog shed on a farm near Wamego, Kansas. The workers were inside the nearly completed building, preparing to leave the jobsite for the day, when a tornado approached the area at approximately 6 p.m. The weather service had issued tornado warnings, but the construction workers had received no such information. The wind force inside the building was so strong that the workers were unable to move, a phenomenon apparently resulting from the fact that the doors on the southeast and northeast corners of the building had not yet been installed.

At some point the walls of the 40- by 60-foot building collapsed, and the roof fell to the ground intact. Miraculously, no one was injured when the building fell. The wind then subsided for a few moments, but about a minute later the tornado picked Nippert up and hurled him to the ground some 30 feet away. Nippert's leg was fractured, and he later developed back problems.

The storm system that hit the jobsite injured 11 people and caused extensive property damage throughout northeast Kansas. On the farm where the company was erecting the hog shed, Roger Shinn observed extensive damage to two silos, the destruction of a large machine shed and barn, and damaged machinery and equipment, including a truck which was thrown into a feedlot. The storm had also destroyed or damaged buildings on two adjacent farms. The tornado's path was 2 to 12 miles wide, and it traveled approximately 58 miles.

Nippert was treated for his injuries, but he was unable to return to work until November 1980. Shinn Construction Company voluntarily paid Nippert's medical expenses as well as temporary total disability benefits and permanent partial disability benefits based on a 20-percent permanent disability of his left leg. It was not until Nippert filed a petition seeking additional benefits that the company raised a question of liability.

Based upon the increased risk doctrine, the Nebraska Workers' Compensation Court rejected Nippert's claim for benefits. We recently reviewed this doctrine in *McGinn v. Douglas County Social Services Admin.,* 317 N.W.2d 764 (Neb. 1982). In a 4-to-3 opinion, the majority held that an employee is entitled to benefits under the provisions of the Nebraska Workers' Compensation Act only when an accident arises both out of and in the course of employment: "The term 'arising out of' describes the accident and its origin, cause, and character, i.e., whether it resulted from the risks arising from within the scope or sphere of the employee's job." An injury caused by the elements arises out of employment only if the employee is exposed to a different hazard than others generally in the area where the injury occurred.

Nippert's theory on appeal is twofold. First, he asks this court to overrule the increased risk test and adopt the positional risk test. Second, if the court continues to apply the increased risk test, Nippert asks for reversal on the grounds that the dismissal was against the great weight of evidence that he was exposed to an increased risk of injury in his work environment and, therefore, that his injuries arose out of his employment.

We agree with Nippert's first theory, and to the extent that *McGinn* and earlier cases are inconsistent with it, they are overruled. In *McGinn* we were asked to adopt the positional risk test, the rationale being that an accident arises out of employment when an employee is where he is required to be at the time the act of nature occurs and causes the employee's injury. We rejected the argument and affirmed the increased risk doctrine as the law in this state. The increased risk doctrine requires an employee to demonstrate that his employment duties expose him to a greater risk or hazard than that to which the general public in the area is exposed.

After careful consideration we have concluded that the better rule is the positional risk test espoused by the dissent in *McGinn.* Under this theory an employee's injuries are compensable as long as his employment duties put him in a position that he might not otherwise be in which exposes him to a risk, even though the risk is not greater than that of the general public. In 1 A. Larson, The Law of Workmen's Compensation § 8.12 at 3-23 (1985), the positional risk test is stated as follows: "[W]hen one in the course of his employment is reasonably required to be at a particular place at a particular time and there meets with an accident, although one which any other person then and there present would have met with irrespective of his employment, that accident is one 'arising out of' the employment of the person so injured."

The record shows that Nippert's employment required him to be in the area where the tornado struck. The record also reflects that the storm caused Nippert's injuries. The judgment of the Workers' Compensation Court is reversed.

WHITE, J., participating on briefs.

CAPORALE, JUSTICE, dissenting.

I dissent and lament the wound inflicted by the majority upon a venerable but endangered friend: The Rule of Law.

Reasonable minds schooled in the law are certainly entitled to differ as to whether the "increased risk" or the "positional risk" rule is the better reasoned one. Thus, were this a case of first impression, a majority of this court would have both the right as well as the duty to choose one rule over the other. But this is not a case of first impression. Nor is it a case dealing with a nonstatutory principle of common law.

The Legislature enacted the compensation act 73 years ago. Thirteen years later, this court interpreted the "arising out of and in the course of" language of the act for the first time. *Gale v. Krug Park Amusement Co.,* 208 N.W. 739, 741 (Neb. 1926), determined that to be compensable an injury caused by the elements must result from a hazard "greater than that to which the public generally is subjected." During the intervening 60 years, the Legislature has seen fit to let that consistently applied judicial interpretation of its enactment stand. The most recent application was in *McGinn v. Douglas County Social Services Admin....*

The controlling rule of law is that where a judicial interpretation of a statute has not evoked a legislative amendment, it is to be presumed that the Legislature has acquiesced in the court's determination of the legislative intent....

It seems to me we are not free to ignore the legislative acquiescence rule at our whim. Such a selective application of any rule is arbitrary and capricious and robs the law of the predictability it needs....

The only significant thing which has changed since this court's first interpretation of the "arising out of and in the course of" language of the compensation act is the composition of this court. I respectfully submit that if the law depends upon nothing more than the predilections of those who happen to sit on this tribunal at any given time, there is no law.

The only mistake the compensation court made was to apply the law as this court had declared it to be. I would affirm.

BOSLAUGH and HASTINGS, JJ., join in this dissent.

NOTES

1. *The AOE Savant.* Rumors are circulating that you have mastered the substance of the "arising out of employment" test. Demonstrate your knowledge by developing a set of facts that would meet the general public-increased risk rule that was previously used in Iowa but that was rejected in *Hanson*. Now develop a set of facts that would meet the actual risk test as enunciated in *Hanson* but that would not meet the increased risk test. And finally, provide a set of facts that would meet the positional risk test as explained by the Nebraska court in *Nippert* but that would not meet the actual risk test from *Hanson*.

2. *Is the AOE Test a Relic?* A growing number of states have adopted the positional risk test. Does this mean that every injury meeting the other three legal tests (course of employment, injury, and accident) is compensable? In *Livingston v. Henry & Hall,* 59 So. 2d 892 (La. Ct. App. 1952), a worker was assaulted at work by an irate husband, who was not a fellow employee, because of a love affair. The court held that the AOE test was met using the positional risk doctrine. What is wrong with this line of reasoning?

3. *A Final Testament to the Vitality of the AOE Test.* Bruce Money was employed by Coin Depot Corporation as an armored truck security guard. He was required to carry a gun, with which he allegedly had a propensity to play Russian Roulette. On his last day at work, he "pulled out his gun, put a bullet in the cylinder, spun the cylinder, placed the gun against his chin, and pulled the trigger." On his second try, the gun fired and killed him instantly. The judge of compensation held the death was work-related, and compared the circumstances to "horseplay" cases in which the deviation from the normal course of employment can be considered minor. The appeals court in New Jersey reversed the decision in *Money v. Coin Depot Corp.,* 672 A.2d 751 (N.J. Super. Ct. App. Div. 1997). The court relied on the distinction among three categories of risk which may result in an accident arising out of employment: risks "distinctly associated" with the employment; "neutral" risks; and "personal" risks. In New Jersey, the first two types of risks are compensable, but personal risks are not. The court felt that a game of Russian Roulette represented a major deviation from the normal course of employment and thus constituted a personal risk. Under what circumstances would an accidental discharge of a gun by a guard or police officer be compensable?

3. TRADEOFFS BETWEEN TESTS ONE AND TWO

TECHNICAL TAPE CORP. v. INDUSTRIAL COMMISSION

Supreme Court of Illinois
317 N.E.2d 515 (1974)

WARD, JUSTICE:

This is a direct appeal ... by the employer-respondent, Technical Tape Corporation, from a judgment of the circuit court of Jackson County, which affirmed an award of the Industrial Commission in favor of the employee-claimant, Terry Crain, for temporary disability, partial incapacity and permanent disfigurement under the Workmen's Compensation Act.

On January 31, 1969, Terry Crain, who was working on the three-to-eleven p.m. shift at the Technical Tape Corporation, was told to clean the residue from a glue churn. The churn was five feet long, five feet wide, and three feet deep. It had a capacity of approximately 200 gallons and was completely enclosed except for a small opening on the top. The ingredients of the glue included toluene, which is a solvent, resins, and rubber.

When the claimant came out of the churn at 10:45 p.m., after working in it for over a half hour, he testified he felt a burning sensation in his feet and legs. He also felt nauseated. The record shows that after leaving the plant at the completion of his shift the claimant drove his car erratically for about five miles and then ran a stop sign and collided with another car. He suffered a disfigurement of his left ear, a fractured skull, and a partial loss of the use of his right foot.

The only witnesses at the hearing before the arbitrator were the claimant and his father, George Crain, who also was employed at the Technical Tape Corporation. The father testified he saw Terry as he was coming out of the churn after cleaning it. He noticed that there were "two big red streaks on both sides of Terry's neck." He said that he admonished Terry for doing that work because it was his experience that employees who worked in such churns would "get so drunk [they could] hardly get out of them." He testified that at that time Terry told him that he was dizzy and felt ill.

Because he was concerned about his son's condition, George Crain attempted to see Terry again before he left for home. However, upon reaching the parking lot he heard the motor of Terry's auto roar "as loud as it would go" and saw him speed out of the parking lot. He got into his car and began to follow Terry. He said Terry drove through a four-way stop intersection without stopping and minutes later narrowly missed hitting a railroad-crossing gate that was being lowered. Terry's car would have struck the gate if the crossing guard had not quickly raised it. The gate was re-lowered and the father had to wait for a crossing train to pass. When it did he continued his pursuit of Terry. He drove about five miles and came upon the scene of the collision.

Terry Crain testified that he hardly remembered climbing from the churn. He testified that the last thing he recalled the night of the accident was "clocking out of the plant" shortly after 11 p.m. He said he did not recall anything until he awakened in a hospital two weeks later. The employer did not offer any evidence at the hearing before the arbitrator. The arbitrator found in favor of the claimant and entered an award for 20 3/7 weeks of temporary total compensation, 6 weeks of compensation for the permanent disfigurement of the left ear, 60 weeks of compensation for a fracture of the skull and 85 1/4 weeks of compensation representing 55% permanent loss of the use of the right foot.

Upon the filing of a petition for review by the employer with the Industrial Commission, the deposition of Dr. Host von Paleske, who specializes in orthopedic surgery, was admitted into evidence in behalf of the claimant. Dr. Von Paleske stated that when he examined the claimant shortly before midnight on the night of the accident it was obvious that the claimant had been exposed to a large amount of toluene, because the odor of toluene came not only from his nostrils and mouth but from his skin and hair as well. He said that exposure to toluene for a long period of time could cause dizziness and "almost a drunken-type feeling." Dr. Von Paleske said that toluene produced an effect similar to that caused by alcohol. The respondent did not offer evidence before the Commission....

An injury must "arise out of" and "in the course of" employment to be compensable under the Workmen's Compensation Act.

"While the phrase 'in the course of employment' relates to the time, place and circumstances of the injury, the phrase 'arising out of the employment' refers to the requisite causal connection between the injury and the employment." In order for an injury to "arise out of" employment it must have had its origin in some risk connected with, or incidental to, the employment, so that there is a causal connection between the employment and the injury.

Professor Larson, in The Law of Workmen's Compensation, has observations which have relevance to this case. He comments:

> "...[I]n Workmen's Compensation the controlling event is something done *to*, not *by*, the employee, and since the real question is whether this something was an industrial accident, the *origin* of the accident is crucial, and the moment of manifestation should be immaterial....
>
> ...[The Act] does not say that the injury must 'occur' or 'be manifested' or 'be consumated' [*sic*] in the course of employment. It merely says that it must 'arise... in the course of employment.' 'Arising' connotes origin, not completion or manifestation. If a strain occurs during employment hours which produces no symptoms, and claimant suffers a heart attack as a result sometime after working hours, the injury is compensable." 1 A. Larson, The Law of Workmen's Compensation, sec. 29.22.

Dr. Von Paleske testified here that if a person were exposed to toluene for any length of time, it would be absorbed into the blood stream, the lungs and eventually into the fatty tissues, which could "cause a feeling of dizziness, almost a drunken-type feeling." He further testified that it was obvious that the claimant had been exposed to and had absorbed a high concentration of toluene. There was uncontradicted evidence that when the claimant had finished cleaning the churn he was dizzy and sick to his stomach. He behaved erratically and then drove his car bizarrely and recklessly before he was involved in the collision.

The evidence showed that the claimant's intoxication was a result of his cleaning the churn and that the injuries sustained in the collision had their origin in the intoxication. It cannot be reasonably said that the Commission's finding that the claimant's injuries arose out of and in the course of his employment was contrary to the manifest weight of the evidence....

Judgment affirmed.

NOTES

1. *Asleep at the Wheel: Variant I.* Snowbarger was required to work 86 out of a 100 hour period during an emergency created by an ice storm. He performed such tasks as cutting up trees and digging holes by hand. While driving home after leaving work at 1:00 a.m., he fell asleep. His car went over the center line of the highway and crashed head-on into another vehicle, and he died as a result of the accident. The scene of the crash was 22 miles from his place of employment. The Supreme Court of Missouri, in *Snowbarger v. Tri-County Electric Cooperative*, 793 S.W.2d 348 (Mo. 1990), awarded benefits to his dependents. The court held there was an exception to the statutory language narrowly defining the course of employment because the deceased "encountered an abnormal exposure to an employment related peril" as a result of the unusually long overtime hours he had worked.

2. *Asleep at the Wheel: Variant II.* Theurer worked his normal shift from 3:30 to 8:00 p.m. Then, in order to make some extra money, he voluntarily worked from midnight until 8:21 a.m. While driving home after leaving work, he fell asleep. His car went over the center line of the highway and crashed head-on into another vehicle, and he died as a result of the accident. The plaintiff, who was Theurer's mother, filed a wrongful death action alleging that the defendant negligently caused Theurer's death. The defendant argued that Theurer's injury and resulting death were compensable under the workers' compensation law, and therefore the negligence suit was barred by the exclusive remedy provision. The defendant argued that an injury does not have to satisfy both traditional requirements of "arising out of" and "in the course of" in order to be compensable. Instead, the defendant argued, the AOE and COE requirements are merged into a single concept of "work-connection" and, if a sufficient nexus exists between the accident and the employment, any resulting injury is "work-connected," and therefore is compensable. The Supreme Court of Oregon rejected the argument in *Krushwitz v. McDonald's Restaurants of Oregon, Inc.*, 919 P.2d 465 (Or. 1996). The court stated that, even though it had adopted the work-connected test, nonetheless both the AOE and COE elements of the compensability test must be satisfied to some degree. In this case, the factors supporting the AOE requirement were strong, but the court found that the COE requirement was not satisfied at all because Theurer had completed his work and was returning home at the time of his death, bringing his commute squarely within the going and coming rule. Since the COE test was not met, his mother was not entitled to workers' compensation benefits, and therefore the exclusivity provisions of the workers' compensation law did not bar her wrongful death action.

3. *Is Fungibility a Virtue?* One interpretation of *Technical Tape*, *Snowbarger*, and *Krushwitz* is that a "strong" case for the AOE test will offset a "weak" case for the COE test. Presumably the converse could also be true: a compelling COE case could offset a questionable AOE case. Such flexibility will allow some workers to receive workers' compensation benefits when their disabilities are evidently caused by the workplace, but the facts do not satisfy the normal requirements for one of the tests for compensability. But such flexibility may lead to greater uncertainty and more litigation if — instead of two independent tests with reasonably well defined legal doctrines — there are now two tests that relate to each other in an unpredictable way.

4. TEST THREE: "ACCIDENT"

MATTHEWS v. R.T. ALLEN & SONS

Supreme Judicial Court of Maine
266 A.2d 240 (1970)

WEATHERBEE, JUSTICE.

The Petitioner, a 43 year old woods-worker, testified that on November 13, 1967 he was employed loading pulpwood onto trucks by hand. He had worked at this since 7:00 A.M. and the lifting evidently involved bending and straightening the back. The sticks were four feet long and from four inches to two feet in diameter. At about 10:30 or 11:00 A.M. he felt pain in his back but he continued to work. During his noon lunch period while he ate his lunch in the truck, the pain became worse. He worked one to one and a half hours after lunch at which time the pain was so great that he reported to his employer that he was unable to continue and went home. During the next four days the back pain continued to increase in severity and he could not go to work. On November 18 he was admitted to the Maine Coast Memorial Hospital in Ellsworth and on December 10 he was transferred to the Maine Medical Center in Portland where a herniated disc was removed. He returned to work the first of May, 1968.

On cross-examination he testified that the pain began that morning gradually and was not associated with any "specific lifting, slipping or tripping." He admitted he had told an insurance company investigator that the pain came on while he was sitting in the truck at noon but he testified that he had noticed the pain while working that morning. "... [B]ut when I first noticed it why it didn't bother me to lift or anything. It was after when I started to straighten up to pull myself back." At noon it had become worse. He agreed that he told the doctors that the pain came on gradually and "got worse and worse and worse" as he worked. He also said that on previous occasions while doing woods work he had had low back pains but they were never disabling.

The doctors' reports and hospital discharge summaries add only that the Petitioner had been admitted to the Ellsworth hospital suffering such severe pain that he "could hardly move." During the next four days the pain increased in severity and also radiated down into his left leg and foot. After two weeks of conservative treatment his condition had only worsened. A myelogram showed a defect in the L4-5 interspace on the left and surgery disclosed an acutely herniated disc in that area, which was removed.

The doctors' reports expressed no opinion as to the precipitating cause of the injury, whether it may have developed prior to November 13, 1967 or, if so, whether the exertion of November 13 may have aggravated the condition except for one significant comment to be discussed later.

The Commissioner found:

> The evidence, we find, is insufficient to support a finding that Mr. Matthews sustained a personal injury by accident arising out of and in the course of his employment. We cannot conclude from the testimony that the disc condition which disabled him on November 13, 1967, resulted from any single episode, or traumatic incident. The medical history given by Mr. Matthews and his testimony on cross examination, indicate that the symptoms of the underlying disc condition became disabling on November 13, 1967, but that the herniated disc had developed prior to that time — probably gradually. It is our decision that the petition must be dismissed.

Our own findings lead us to an opposite conclusion.

The Petitioner has the burden of proving that he suffered a personal injury by accident arising out of and in the course of his employment.

The Workmen's Compensation Law represents a relatively recent concept of responsibility without negligence. While the early cases usually concerned accidental injuries where an external force was applied to an external portion of the body, our own Court decided early in the development of our law that the term injury by accident includes incidents where internal parts of the physical structure break down under external force, including the stress of labor. While this may more dramatically occur as a result of a slip, a fall or a single unusual strained effort, we have found other such internal breakdowns to have resulted from the usual work which the workman was performing in his usual, normal way. In short, we have construed the term "accident" to include not only injuries which are the results of accidents but also injuries which are themselves accidents. In *Brown's Case,* 123 A. 421 (Me. 1924) a fatal heart dilation resulted from the exertion of shovelling snow. In *Patrick v. J.B. Ham Co.,* 111 A. 912

(Me. 1921) the Petitioner's husband suffered a cerebral hemorrhage while performing his regular duties of lifting sacks of grain. In *Taylor's Case,* 142 A. 730 (Me. 1928) the Petitioner's husband had been lifting heavy objects in the course of his usual work and a particularly vigorous straining caused a pulmonary embolism.

This position is in agreement with that taken by the great majority of American jurisdictions and follows the rule recognized in England which in many respects furnished the model for our own Act. In England the Courts soon came to hold that an unexpected, unforeseen or unintended result from usual or customary exertion constitutes an injury by accident even though there is no unexpected or fortuitous cause.

In some of the earlier decisions holding that the breaking down of internal parts might be accidents under the statute, the death or incapacity occurred suddenly as the internal part dramatically gave way. This furnished another similarity to the usual concept of accident occurring when an external force is applied violently to an external part and assisted this Court in arriving at its conclusion that the Legislature intended both situations to be considered industrial accidents. "If a laborer performing his usual task, in his wonted way, by reason of strain, breaks his wrist, nobody would question the accidental nature of the injury. If instead of the wrist it is an artery that breaks, the occurrence is just as clearly an accident." Certainly the sudden quality of a mishap often makes it more clearly distinguishable from the mere malfunctioning of an organ which develops through natural progression, unrelated to the employment.

This thinking led our Court in early decisions to describe an accidental injury as being "unusual, undesigned, unexpected, sudden" (*Brown's Case, supra,* where the employee "suddenly became dizzy, faint and short of breath" while shovelling snow). As recently as in *Bernier v. Cola-Cola Bottling Plants, Inc.,* 250 A.2d 820 (Me. 1969) in pointing out that the Petitioner need not prove that his back strain resulted from "any unusual slip, fall, etc., in other words, external injury" we quoted *Brown's Case* to hold that "an internal injury that is itself sudden, unusual, and unexpected is none the less accidental because its external cause is a part of the victim's ordinary work."

This is not to say, however, that the internal accident must have demonstrated itself by a sudden, dramatic effect upon the victim.

In *Taylor's Case* the victim continued work until noontime when for the first time he complained of pain in his chest. He continued to work, although with difficulty, that afternoon but his condition worsened and he died some ten days later. It will be noted that this Court then stated the rule to be that

> ... [I]f the strain were not accidental, it is the unusual, undesigned, unexpected *or* sudden results of the strain, not necessarily the strain itself, which make the accidental injury necessary under the law. (Emphasis added.)

We concur in the statement found in 58 Am. Jur., Workmen's Compensation § 196:

While the concept of accident is ordinarily understood as embodying a certain degree of element of suddenness in the occurrence of the event, and is frequently so defined, it is not always required that the occurrence be instantaneous.

In our present case there is a dearth of medical opinion that might assist us regarding the probable onset of the Petitioner's disabling condition. We are not told how soon pain and disability would be expected to follow the herniation of an intervertebral disc. However, as valuable as medical opinion is, it is not always essential, and sound and rational conclusions in Workmen's Compensation matters may often be drawn from facts proven and inferences to be logically drawn therefrom although lacking the support of expert opinion....

We find no significant dispute in the testimony. It reveals a 43 year old woodsworker who had had low back pains in the past, usually associated with his work, but never to the extent of being disabling. On this occasion the pain began while he was loading sticks of pulpwood, some very heavy. He continued to work several hours while the pain got "worse and worse and worse." After he stopped working the pain continued to increase in severity and to extend in area until relieved by surgery. Surgery disclosed that an extruding mass from the ruptured disc was pressing against the nerve and obviously bowing it outward and upward....

We are called upon to decide whether Petitioner's disability, hospitalization and surgery were casually connected with his activities while loading pulpwood that November 13. Whether Petitioner's disc ruptured abruptly the morning of November 13 or whether the defective condition developed gradually during his previous episodes of low back pain is not controlling here. The scanty facts presented to us lead us to the conclusion that in either case the heavy labor of November 13 constituted the critical episode which completely incapacitated the man with increasing and unrelieved crippling pain until surgery removed the ruptured part.

While we do not know the moment when the actual herniation occurred its causal connection with the labor of November 13 seems apparent. In other words the personal injury appears either to have been caused by the exertions of November 13 or aggravated by them. We have repeatedly held that if stress of labor aggravates or accelerates the development of a preexisting infirmity causing an internal breakdown of that part of the structure a personal injury by accident occurs. The point is dramatized by the language of the Court in *Lachance's Case,* 118 A. 370, 372 (Me. 1922):

> If Lachance, but for the hurt, would not have died at the time at which, and in the way in which, he did die, then, within the meaning of the Workmen's Act, the unfortunate occurrence, though it merely hastened a deep-seated disorder to destiny, must be held to have resulted in an injury causing death.

Although neither the Ellsworth orthopedic surgeon who originally treated Petitioner nor the Portland neuro-surgeon who performed the surgery was called to testify, the orthopedic surgeon (who also assisted in the operation) commented tersely in his written report:

> Unfortunately, after the pain had developed he continued to work until the job was completed.

We infer from this that it was his opinion that Petitioner's exertion in loading the trucks at least contributed to his disability and to his need for surgery.

We find that Petitioner sustained a personal injury by accident arising out of and in the course of his employment on November 13, 1967.

Appeal sustained....

NOTES

1. *Accident Test Expanded.* Two subtests are normally read into the accident requirement: (1) there must be, in the language of a significant English case, *Fenton v. Thorley & Co.,* [1903] App. Cas. 443, "an unlooked for mishap or an untoward event which is not expected or designed"; and (2) the injury must be traceable, within reasonable limits, to a definite time, place, and cause.

These two tests can be further broken down as follows:

> I. Unexpectedness
>
>> A. Of Cause
>> B. Of Result
>
> II. Definite Time
>
>> A. Of Cause
>> B. Of Result.

To illustrate the meaning of these tests, if a court requires the unexpectedness to apply to the cause of the injury, then a worker who is injured because a machine falls on him can receive compensation, while compensation will be denied to a worker who is performing her normal duties of carrying heavy wheat sacks and suffers a heart attack, even though medical evidence confirms the attack was caused by heavy lifting. However, if the court says that the unexpected aspect of the accident requirement can be met by the nature of the result, then the heart attack caused by the normal but strenuous lifting would be compensable. Evaluate the decisions of the Industrial Accident Commissioner and the Supreme Judicial Court of Maine in *Matthews* using the distinctions drawn in this paragraph.

A similar two-way distinction applies to the requirement of a definite time or event. The cause may be gradual and the result precisely distinguishable, such as dust poisoning that causes a sudden collapse of a lung. Or the etiology may be easily specified, such as a fall into the river, while the pathology may intermittently progress to pneumonia. Again, the compensability of the lung collapse or the pneumonia depends on whether the court is looking for a definite time that can be assigned to the cause, the result, or both.

If both aspects of both the unexpectedness and the definite time requirements are met, such as might occur in an explosion, then the case for compensability is the clearest. The opposite extreme is the typical occupational disease, where all the elements are lacking. The problems posed by occupational diseases are examined in more detail in a later section.

2. *A Jaundiced View of the Accident Test.* THE REPORT OF THE NATIONAL COMMISSION ON STATE WORKMEN'S COMPENSATION LAWS 49 (1972) provided this analysis of the accident test:

> An "accident" has frequently been defined as a sudden unexpected event, determinate as to time and place. The "accident" requirement has been a bar to compensability, especially in the past, because of failure in a particular case to meet one or more requirements in this definition. Compensation, for example, has been denied when nothing unexpected or unusual occurred. If a man strained his back while doing regular work in the usual fashion, it was to be expected.
>
> This narrow interpretation of "accident" has to a large extent been discarded. Where it persists, it is undesirable as it serves to bar compensation for injuries that are clearly work-related.
>
> There should be no legal impediments to full coverage of all injuries which are work related.
>
> *We recommend that the "accident" requirement be dropped as a test for compensability.*

5. TEST FOUR: "PERSONAL INJURY"

The injury test can be conceptualized as the two-by-two matrix shown in Figure 21-2:

Figure 21-2

The Injury Test Matrix

CAUSE

	Physical	Mental
Physical	Physical-Physical	Mental-Physical
Mental	Physical-Mental	Mental-Mental

CONSEQUENCE

The injury test will be met when both the cause and the effect of the personal harm are physical: the "physical-physical" case. (The ballerina loses her toe because the theater scaffolding collapses.) Likewise, the injury test will be satisfied in almost all jurisdictions when the cause is physical and the result is both physical and mental: the "physical-mental" case. (The ballerina injures her toe when the scaffolding collapses and suffers a mental breakdown when she realizes that her career is over.) Similarly, most states hold the injury test to be satisfied when the mental cause leads to a physical consequence: the "mental-physical" case. (The ballerina is humiliated by the dance company director and slashes off her toes in a rage.) The most problematic cases are those that involve both a mental cause and a mental consequence: the "mental-mental" case. (The ballerina is humiliated by the dance company director and thinks about slashing off her toes, but instead suffers a mental collapse.) Some states deal with such cases as injuries and some as diseases: we return to these mental-mental cases in a later section after we introduce the complications of compensating work-related diseases.

E. WHICH DISEASES ARE COMPENSABLE?

TISCO INTERMOUNTAIN v. INDUSTRIAL COMMISSION

Supreme Court of Utah
744 P.2d 1340 (1987)

HALL, CHIEF JUSTICE:

Plaintiffs challenge the award of death benefits made to defendant Jean B. Werner under the provisions of the Utah Occupational Disease Disability Law.

Defendant Jean B. Werner is the widow of George Jakob Werner. Mr. Werner had been employed since 1947 as an insulation mechanic. Most insulation was asbestos-based until 1971, when the federal government banned the use of asbestos in insulation. Thus, Mr. Werner was continuously exposed to asbestos from 1947 until at least 1971. In 1977, Mr. Werner formed his own insulation company, Tisco Intermountain ("Tisco").

In December 1981, Mr. Werner noticed that his stomach was distended, his navel was red, and he was very tired. In February or March 1982, he sought medical treatment. In June 1982, he underwent surgery on his stomach, at which time a malignant tumor was found. Thereafter, he underwent chemotherapy, but died in January 1983 from complications attendant to peritoneal mesothelioma.

Mrs. Werner made a claim for death benefits under the Occupational Disease Disability Law, alleging that Mr. Werner developed cancer and died as a result of exposure to asbestos during the course of his employment with Tisco. The administrative law judge found that Mr. Werner was injuriously exposed to asbestos during the course of his employment with Tisco and that Mrs. Werner was therefore entitled to death benefits.

Plaintiffs filed a motion for review of the administrative law judge's order. The motion was denied by the Industrial Commission, and a final order was entered.

Plaintiffs' first point on appeal is that the Commission abused its discretion in awarding death benefits under the Occupational Disease Disability Law because there was no substantial credible evidence of exposure to asbestos during the deceased employee's period of employment with the employer against whom the award was made. It was undisputed that Mr. Werner was exposed to asbestos from 1947 until 1971. However, any claim against Mr. Werner's employers during that period was barred by the statute of limitations set forth in Utah Code Ann. § 35-2-13(b)(4) (1974). Furthermore, Utah Code Ann. § 35-2-14 (1974) states: "The only employer liable shall be the employer in whose employment the employee was last injuriously exposed to the hazards of such disease...."

The record, viewed in its entirety, does not contain sufficient evidence to support the conclusion that Mr. Werner was "last injuriously exposed" to asbestos while at Tisco. Only three witnesses were called, Mrs. Werner, Joseph Collins, and Darrell Kinder. Each witness recounted the many years Mr. Werner was employed as a mechanic by various insulation contractors and the frequent exposure he had to asbestos products prior to 1968 or 1969, when he accepted an office position with Mountain States Insulation. None of the witnesses related any specific exposure that Mr. Werner had to asbestos products from 1971 until his death. Rather, they spoke only in very general terms.

When asked if she had any knowledge of the insulation products used by Tisco, Mrs. Werner responded: "Not an awfully lot. I know that it was the kind they had — it was not the kind that they had used prior or previously because it had been outlawed, more or less, and so you had to go into new forms...." In response to the next question, whether the insulation material used by Tisco had an asbestos base, Mrs. Werner unequivocally stated that it did not.

Collins testified that transite pipe composed of one-half cement and one-half asbestos was utilized in the industry as a substitute for asbestos-based insulation used prior to 1971. When asked whether Mr. Werner ever engaged in an operation that included the cutting of transite pipe or sheets, his response was: "I personally never seen him, but knowing it was part of the trade and we all did it at one time or another, I'd have to say yes." When asked if he knew whether Mr. Werner used transite material in his business at Tisco, Collins responded that he did not.

Kinder's testimony reiterated the exposure Mr. Werner had to asbestos on various jobs through 1970. However, he expressed no knowledge of any such exposure at Tisco. He simply stated that he was aware that Tisco was engaged in the insulation business....

The medical issues were submitted to a medical panel, which concluded that the delay between first exposure to asbestos and the development of malignant mesothelioma can range from fifteen to twenty years. Any latency period less than fifteen years would cast doubt on the relationship of the disease to a particular occupational or environmental exposure. If fifteen years is accepted as the minimal latency period prior to development of malignant mesothelioma, Mr. Werner's exposures prior to 1968 were the main cause for his terminal condition. In theory, a cessation of exposure in 1968 may have decreased the risk for his development of the malignant mesothelioma....

The administrative law judge acknowledged in his findings that in the absence of evidence that Mr. Werner was injuriously exposed to asbestos at Tisco, Mrs. Werner's claim would fail since section 35-2-13 of the Occupational Disease Disability Law requires in subsection (b)(4) that in the absence of exceptions not relevant here, death from an occupational disease must result within three years from the last date on which the employee actually worked for the employer against whom benefits are claimed. Application of section 35-2-14 in this case would require that a claim be made against Mountain States Insulation, which claim would be barred since Mr. Werner last worked there in 1976.

Faced with such harsh circumstances, the administrative law judge strained to fashion a remedy. The following passage is extracted from his findings:

> Recognizing this insufficiency of remedy with respect to asbestos cases, and resolving the doubt in favor of the applicant and in favor of coverage, I find that George Jakob Werner was injuriously exposed to the hazards of asbestos while employed by the defendant Tisco Intermountain, Inc.

Policy considerations in workers' compensation cases dictate that statutes should be liberally construed in favor of an award. However, policy considerations have no application in the absence of any evidence to support an award, nor can they be used to controvert the clear meaning of the statutory requirements upon which an award must be based.

In the instant case, it clearly appears that the award of benefits is unsupported by substantial credible evidence, and that is the standard this court must apply. In awarding benefits, the administrative law judge also ignored competent medical evidence that negatives a finding of medical causation....

The award of benefits is vacated and set aside. No costs awarded.

STEWART, ASSOCIATE C.J., and DURHAM and ZIMMERMAN, JJ., concur.

HOWE, J., dissents.

NOTES

1. *The Continuing Vitality of the Statute of Limitations.* During his employment with Gulf Oil, Kenneth Cable was periodically exposed to the carcinogens coumene and benzene, most recently in July 1981. He was no longer employed by Gulf Oil after March 1983. In July 1988, he was diagnosed with bladder cancer and was advised that the cause was his exposure to coumene and benzene. The manifestation of the cancer occurred less than 300 weeks after he ended his

employment with Gulf, but more than 300 weeks after his last exposure to the carcinogens. The Pennsylvania workers' compensation act provides, in part, that "whenever occupational disease is the basis for compensation, for disability or death under this act, it shall apply only to disability or death resulting from such disease and occurring within three hundred weeks after the last date of employment in an occupation or industry to [*sic*] which he was exposed to hazards of such disease ..." 77 PA. CONS. STAT. § 411(2). The Supreme Court of Pennsylvania held the cancer was not compensable because the relevant employment for the statute of limitations is the employment in which the employee was exposed to the coumene and benzene, not the subsequent employment with the employer in which he was not exposed to the carcinogens. *Cable v. Workmen's Comp. Appeal Bd.*, 664 A.2d 1349 (Pa. 1995).

2. *A Humane Alternative.* The *Cable* and *Tisco Intermountain* cases provide examples of how a long latency period for a work-related disease can interact with a restrictive statute of limitations to defeat a claim for workers' compensation benefits. Workers in Utah and Pennsylvania who are exposed to toxic substances should be advised to die quickly. A more humane alternative would be for these states to adopt statutes of limitations that run from the date of impairment or disability rather than from the date of last exposure, as recommended by the National Commission on State Workmen's Compensation Laws:

> We recommend that the time limit for initiating a claim be three years after the date the claimant knows or, by exercise of reasonable diligence should have known, of the existence of the impairment and its possible relationship to his employment, or within three years after the employee first experiences a loss of wages which the employee knows or, by exercise of reasonable diligence should have known, was because of the work-related impairment.

NATIONAL COMMISSION ON STATE WORKMEN'S COMPENSATION LAWS, THE REPORT OF THE NATIONAL COMMISSION ON STATE WORKMEN'S COMPENSATION LAWS 107-08 (1972).

PETER S. BARTH with H. ALLAN HUNT, WORKERS' COMPENSATION AND WORK-RELATED ILLNESSES AND DISEASES 95-104 (1980)[*]

Even though considerable variation in the interpretation and application of "occupational disease" exists, several elements of the law are rather consistent across all states. Where there is a disabling injury involving an accident that arises out of and in the course of covered employment, if a disabling illness or disease develops due to the injury, it is compensable. An example is an infection that develops in a wound that occurred in a work-related injury.

Second, if an accident (a sudden, unforeseen event occurring at a definite place and time) injures a worker, and the injury involves a disease, it is compen-

---

sable. An eye disease from a welder's flash burn, a laboratory assistant's dermatosis from being splashed with a caustic substance, sudden hypoxia in an underwater occupation due to a mechanical failure all would be straightforward cases.

A third common element across states is to deny claims based on disability due to ordinary diseases of life and compensate, where other conditions permit, diseases that are peculiar or particular to some line of work....

The Role of Scheduled Diseases

The explicit legislative move to cover occupational disease in England took the form of a precise listing of diseases to be covered. The manner in which coverage was broadened attests to the reluctance to include many such disablements....

In the United States, schedules of diseases developed for similar reasons. By providing that diseases could be compensated, the states have broadened the overall coverage of workers' compensation, but by limiting claims only to those diseases enumerated on the schedule, they have served to preclude wholesale expansion of the system. Because such schedules have no obvious analog in the handling of accident-injury claims, however, confusion exists about the role that such schedules play.

Many states at one time depended heavily on schedules to determine compensability for disease, but very few do so today.... Thus where a schedule coexists with a provision that diseases are "broadly covered," the schedule actually can enlarge the number of successful claims by easing the burden of proof for a claimant....

There are several advantages in having a schedule of covered diseases. They eliminate some of the uncertainty about whether a disease is to be considered occupational or an ordinary disease of life. By limiting uncertainty they tend to reduce litigation and allow a larger number of worthy claims to be filed and compensated. They can provide a clear legislative direction to the courts and workers' compensation boards regarding the extent of coverage of diseases....

The primary problem of schedules, where not supplemented by broad disease coverage, is their restrictiveness. This means of limiting coverage often appears harsh, inflexible, and contrary to the nature of the compensation system. Limiting compensable diseases to a few dozen specified ailments seems an anachronism when viewed in terms of the myriad diseases medical science has conclusively shown are caused by occupation exposures....

Where schedules of diseases exist, it would seem desirable that the list be expanded: first, as medical science (and the law) discovers new links between work and the disease and, second, as the work environment is modified through the use of new processes or substances, or as new kinds of industry locate in a state. Unless a schedule becomes totally vestigial, one should expect to see it expanded frequently.

Infectious Disease Cases and the By-Accident Provision

The occupational diseases referred to in most statutes do not include most infectious diseases. Workers' compensation laws have been written and interpreted to exclude coverage of ordinary diseases of life, which include most infectious illnesses....

Virtually all the states eventually moved in the direction of explicitly covering occupational disease by schedules and/or specific provisions for such coverage. Yet the fear of excessively broadening coverage caused the states to limit the kinds of diseases that were considered occupational. State laws still force many infectious disease cases to be evaluated as injuries caused by accident. Consequently a most haphazard approach currently characterizes the handing of infectious disease and other disease claims based on the accidental nature of the injury. Messina has characterized the entire situation as a "Serbonian bog."...

The inconsistency of the compensation system in handling claims is obvious when comparing two decisions made less than one month apart by the same judicial body in the same state. In *Herdick v. New York Zoological Society*[, 356 N.Y.S.2d 706 (N.Y. App. Div. 1974)], the [court] awarded compensation to an animal keeper who had contracted tuberculosis. The claimant alleged that the disease was the result of contact with infected animals and the court allowed that such exposure is a natural incident of a particular occupation and attaches to that occupation a greater hazard than that attending employment in general. The same court then overturned a decision awarding compensation for disability due to tuberculosis to Middleton, a correction officer in a state facility. [*Middleton v. Coxsackie Correctional Facility*, 357 N.Y.S.2d 732 (N.Y. App. Div. 1974).] The court held that because the disease was not a natural and unavoidable result of the occupation, the claimant must establish that the inception of the disease is assignable to a determinate or single act, identified in space and time, and assignable to something extraordinary or catastrophic. Unlike *Herdick,* tuberculosis was not an occupational disease in this case and the claimant's burden was therefore to prove that this was an injury caused by accident. Since the mere exposure of the officer to a tubercular inmate was neither catastrophic nor extraordinary, the claim was denied.

The *Middleton* decision on its own may seem harsh, but coming immediately on the heels of *Herdick,* it also appears capricious. If one works with animals behind bars, tuberculosis is an occupational disease, but if one works with humans behind bars, it is not. The court of appeals later overturned *Middleton,* but it did not do so on the grounds that this was an occupational disease.

F. INJURIES AND DISEASES FOR WHICH COMPENSABILITY IS PROBLEMATIC

Workplace stress and back disorders are two conditions examined in this section for which the determination of compensability is most vexing. Other similar conditions not examined here include cumulative trauma (including carpel tunnel syndrome), respiratory diseases, heart disease, and many types of cancers.

There are several common characteristics of these maladies. First, workers' compensation law sometimes treats these conditions as injuries, sometimes as diseases, and sometimes as both. Second, the troublesome cases typically involve injuries or diseases resulting from an interaction of congenital, degenerative, work-related, and/or personal lifestyle factors. Third, the symptoms may include subjective complaints ("my back hurts") in addition to (or instead of) "objective" medical evidence (the MRI reveals a physical abnormality in the back). Fourth, there often are competing medical theories (and almost always competing medical testimony in serious cases) about the cause of the worker's disorder. Fifth, the legal rules used to decide whether a condition is work-related often are inconsistent with prevailing medical opinions about causation.

A sixth common characteristic of these conditions pertains to disabilities that result from the interaction of old (or underlying) medical problems and a new work-related accident or exposure. The traditional legal doctrine pertaining to disability resulting from a workplace accident or exposure interacting with a pre-existing medical problem that has not previously limited the worker's performance at work is that the employer is responsible for the entire resulting disability. (The doctrine is often summarized as: "the employer takes the worker as it finds her.") A few states have begun to limit the employer's liability for such injuries by requiring an apportionment of the causative factors between work-related and other factors, and only requiring the employer to provide benefits for the work-related portion of the disability.[*]

A seventh characteristic is that many states have amended their workers' compensation laws in the 1990s to make it more difficult for workers with these conditions to satisfy the legal requirements for compensability. Several of the cases and notes illustrate this constrictive tendency.

---

[*] Arguably another exception to the doctrine that "the employer takes the worker as it finds him" involves the use of second injury funds. For example, a workers' compensation law may provide that if the worker who had a previous impairment (such as the loss of an arm) experiences a new work-related injury (such as the loss of the other arm) which results in permanent total disability, then the employer is only responsible for the benefits for the loss of an arm and the second injury fund is responsible for the balance of the payments for permanent total disability. In this instance, while the employer is relieved of some financial liability for the extent of the disability resulting from the interaction of the previous and the new (or "second") injury, the worker receives workers' compensation benefits for the full extent of his or her disability.

1. WORKPLACE STRESS

CHICAGO BOARD OF EDUCATION v. INDUSTRIAL COMMISSION

Appellate Court of Illinois

523 N.E.2d 912, *appeal denied*, 530 N.E.2d 241 (Ill. 1988)

JUSTICE MCCULLOUGH delivered the opinion of the court:

Claimant, an elementary school teacher, filed two applications for adjustment of claim under the Workers' Compensation Act for separate incidents occurring on January 5, 1976, and January 5, 1978. During the course of the compensation proceedings claimant was allowed to amend his applications to seek compensation under the Occupational Diseases Act. The arbitrator awarded claimant $251.09 for $210^6/_7$ weeks of disability under section 19(b) of the Occupational Diseases Act. Claimant was also awarded medical benefits and respondent was ordered to provide rehabilitation services. On review, the Industrial Commission (Commission) affirmed the arbitrator, but vacated the rehabilitation award and remanded to the arbitrator for proceedings on the issue of permanent disability. On certiorari, the circuit court confirmed the Commission order. Respondent filed a timely notice of appeal. On appeal, the issue is whether claimant established he was exposed to or suffered from a compensable occupational disease.

Claimant, a 56-year-old school teacher, was employed by respondent from June 1967 to June 1978 and was assigned exclusively to the Hefferen Elementary School where he taught a variety of subjects. In September 1978, instead of returning to his teaching duties after the summer recess, claimant sought treatment at the Portage-Cragin Mental Health Center where he was counseled on a weekly basis by Deborah Gessner, a psychiatric social worker. Claimant took a 25-month leave of absence from the Chicago Board of Education (Board) and except for tutoring a blind student and selling hot dogs for a short time was not gainfully employed during that period. He applied for reinstatement to his teaching position in January 1981 but was rejected because he failed a psychiatric evaluation conducted by respondent's psychiatrist.

At the hearing before the arbitrator, Deborah Gessner testified she counseled claimant for a "great psychological debilitation" which she stated was caused by the gradual deterioration of claimant's work environment, chaos in the classroom, lack of support from the administration, physical assault by students, inability to comply with school regulations, unmanageable students, inability to control the classroom, and physical isolation in a mobile classroom detached from the main school facility. Gessner testified claimant's condition was a reactive depression characterized by feelings of hopelessness, failure and inadequacy emanating from claimant's work environment.

On cross-examination, Gessner discounted claimant's childhood experiences and the fact he had been hospitalized for psychiatric care while in the Army in 1944 as factors in claimant's present condition of ill-being. Gessner also believed claimant had a stable marital and family relationship with his wife and children which was not a source of claimant's depression.

Claimant testified before the arbitrator he graduated from high school in 1940 and worked until he was drafted into the Army in 1943. He was discharged from his noncombat position 18 months later after hospitalization for a psychiatric disorder. He subsequently attended several universities and worked principally as an insurance salesman, first for New York Life Insurance Company from 1953 to 1960, and from 1960 to 1967 as a self-employed insurance broker. He worked for respondent as a substitute teacher during the 1960's and became a full-time substitute in 1967.

Petitioner testified extensively concerning incidents of stress, assaults, and injuries he received in the course of his teaching duties. On March 4, 1974, while unloading teaching materials from his car, which he was forced to remove from a mobile classroom each evening because of vandalism, claimant was struck on his right shoulder by a piece of concrete.

On March 18, 1974, while performing the same task, he was robbed at knife point by three men. While cooperating with police in the investigation of this crime, he received an anonymous phone call directing him to drop the investigation.

On April 3, 1974, a female student engaged in a fight with another student, kicked and scratched him when he attempted to intervene.

On May 9, 1974, he was kicked and bitten by a student who was engaged in a fistfight.

On the last day of school in 1973 claimant was chased from the school yard by 12 to 15 students and was struck in the back with a rock.

In the fall of 1973, claimant slightly injured his leg when he stumbled out of the doorway of the mobile classroom when the steps leading to the unit had been moved away from the building.

On January 5, 1976, while in the main school building, after school hours, claimant saw a boy lying on the floor and went to his aid. Claimant testified the child was faking injury and pushed claimant causing him to fall and injure his back.

On January 5, 1978, a violent fight broke out between two boys in the classroom. While intervening, one child grabbed claimant's arm and struck it on a table. His right elbow was injured requiring medical attention, including a brace and sling. Claimant is still treated for the injury to his elbow and his back which he reinjured on October 25, 1977, while moving books at the direction of the principal.

Claimant also testified to a variety of working conditions which exacerbated his problems. In 1976 the school board made a change in the duties of teachers requiring more paperwork. Claimant maintained he spent two to four hours each night keeping up with the additional reports he was required to prepare. He had continuous difficulty keeping discipline in the classroom because of the nature of the students being taught and although unruly children were sent to the principal's office, they were often returned to the classroom without being disciplined or counseled. Claimant maintained this was a violation of the union contract.

Claimant was also a member of the teacher professional and problem committee, a group of faculty members who submitted problems to the principal. Claimant testified the principal did not resolve faculty complaints about increased paperwork and discipline.

Claimant also maintained the principal was abusive to him, citing a September 1976 incident when the principal yelled at him and cursed him for being late and leaving his class unattended for several minutes while the class went to recess. This incident occurred on the playground in full view of the entire school and claimant stated he felt humiliated.

In May 1978, claimant testified a female student was brought to his classroom and placed there for the remainder of the school year. The student had just broken the leg of another teacher by striking her with a chair. Although claimant objected to the inclusion of the student in his class, he was told there was nothing he could do about it. The child was violent and refused to do any work for the remainder of the school year.

Claimant testified he could not return to teaching in the fall of 1978 because he could not face the assignment citing, in particular, the incident in which his arm was injured which affected his ability to do his job because he was right-handed. He also found stressful the 1978 incident in which the female student was assigned to his class.

On cross-examination, claimant stated he grew up in a poor family and was raised by his mother after his father disappeared. He admitted being discharged from the Army because of psychiatric problems manifesting themselves in outbursts of crying and tremors. He acknowledged he was disappointed when he was denied a master's degree after failing the oral examination. He also stated he quit his job selling life insurance because he did not make enough money and did not like the pressure of selling because he had difficulty meeting new people and persuading them to buy insurance.

He nevertheless started his own insurance company in 1960, with his wife helping with clerical work. He stated there was a difference in the pressure of selling insurance when he worked for himself. He closed that business, however, because the business climate in the mid-1960's required that he be more aggressive and he did not believe insuring people's property furthered the goal he had set for himself of helping people.

Claimant also stated the increased work load at school caused him to stay late every evening. He denied ever conducting insurance-related business during these late night sessions although he admitted his insurance business consumed approximately 20% of his time for several years after he stopped actively soliciting new accounts. He also denied being constantly late for class although he occasionally got up late or bad weather prevented him from being at school on time.

Claimant admitted he did not have many friends and separated from his family in April 1979 because he was continually fighting with his wife and children. He denied any physical altercations occurred, however. He stated he moved out of the house to find a calmer atmosphere at the suggestion of one of his psychologists. He became upset when his teenage daughter brought friends to the house and caused a commotion. He was also disturbed by his adult son who lived at home and made noise playing the stereo. He denied telling a psychiatrist he and his wife engaged in physical fights. He also admitted that from 1970 through 1977 he received excellent ratings on his teacher evaluations, the second highest rating a teacher could achieve.

Ronald Gehrig, a vocational rehabilitation counselor, testified he interviewed claimant, had gone over his history, had spoken to claimant's social worker, and researched the job structure of the Board of Education. In Gehrig's opinion, claimant was a candidate for vocational rehabilitation and could become a teacher's aid as long as claimant did not have to assume primary responsibility for a classroom. In the absence of a teaching job, Gehrig thought claimant could perform retail sales as long as the tempo was low-key. Gehrig did not believe claimant could succeed at selling insurance because it was a high-pressure job.

Keith Van Wieren, a guidance counselor at the school where claimant taught, testified for respondent. Van Wieren had known claimant since 1966 and had no particular prior problems with him. It was Van Wieren's opinion the principal at the school was an individual who did not "make waves" keeping problems in-house. Van Wieren thought the principal was not arbitrary or disrespectful to teachers and did not play favorites among the faculty.

Van Wieren stated the Hefferen school was no different than any other inner-city school. It was not chaotic and Van Wieren was not in fear of his life. The student body by and large was manageable although individuals could become very disruptive. To Van Wieren's knowledge, no teachers other than claimant ever stayed after school to work on school business. Van Wieren stated claimant went "by the book" on discipline and had tried, without success, to establish a more rigorous disciplinary code. Van Wieren stated all teachers were frustrated when children were referred to the principal for discipline only to be returned to the classroom. In this respect, Van Wieren did not believe the union contract adequately spelled out the procedure for disciplining students.

Van Wieren maintained claimant once told him the paperwork for his school-related duties was overwhelming. Van Wieren once saw claimant working after hours on materials which did not appear to be school related. Van Wieren also had to substitute for claimant when he arrived late or missed work entirely.

Frances Sullivan, a first grade teacher, testified she did not remember the principal being disrespectful to any teacher, although she agreed the principal did not back up the faculty as much as they would have liked. She attributed this to the fact the principal did not interpret the union contract in the same way as the teachers. One such area of dispute was student discipline and Sullivan was concerned the policy was too lax. Sullivan never stayed late at school because of the fear for her safety. She believed it was unwise to either come to school early or stay late. Sullivan concluded claimant had a history of precise and copious record keeping and concern with discipline which was, in Sullivan's words, "fantastic."

The deposition of Myrtle Mason, a board-certified psychiatrist with the respondent, was admitted into evidence. Mason examined claimant in February of 1981 and denied his application for reinstatement on the basis two of claimant's psychiatrists disagreed about his ability to return to teaching duties given his mental condition. Mason felt claimant was less than candid about his progress and rehabilitation and was too eager to return to the classroom. There was also some indication and admission by claimant of prior physical alter-·cations with his wife. During the course of the deposition, Mason was confronted with the fact that one of the reports upon which she relied in reaching her diagnosis was one year old at the time she examined claimant. She had thought both reports were issued contemporaneous to her examination. Claimant's treating physician, two weeks before Mason's examination, had found claimant was fit to return to full-time duties. This mistake on the part of Mason might have changed her mind about claimant's condition had she realized it at the time.

As we have indicated, the arbitrator and Commission awarded benefits under the Occupational Diseases Act.

On appeal, the issue is whether claimant established he was exposed to the hazards of or sustained an injury from an occupational disease. Section 1(d) of the Occupational Diseases Act states in pertinent part:

> "In this Act the term 'Occupational Disease' means a disease arising out of and in the course of the employment or which has become aggravated and rendered disabling as a result of the exposure of the employment. Such aggravation shall arise out of a risk peculiar to or increased by the employment and not common to the general public. A disease shall be deemed to arise out of the employment if there is apparent to the rational mind, upon consideration of all the circumstances, a causal connection between the conditions under which the work is performed and the occupational disease. The disease need not to have been foreseen or expected but after its contraction it must appear to have had its origin or aggravation in a risk connected with the employment and to have flowed from that source as a rational consequence."

On appeal, respondent argues claimant has not established he suffers from an occupational disease within the meaning of the act and, alternatively, the Commission's decision to award compensation is against the manifest weight of the evidence. Relying upon *Pathfinder Co. v. Industrial Comm'n* (1976), 343 N.E.2d 913, and *Peoria County Belwood Nursing Home v. Industrial Comm'n* (1987), 505 N.E.2d 1026, claimant maintains compensation is available under the Occupational Diseases Act for mental disorders suffered in the absence of physical trauma or injury which develop gradually over a period of time without the necessity of finding that the injury occurred as a result of specific incidents traceable to a definite time, place, and cause.

The first issue we must resolve is whether on-the-job mental stress which results in emotional illness in the absence of physical trauma and sudden disablement traceable to a definite time, place, or cause is compensable under the Occupational Diseases Act. The language employed in the opening paragraph of section 1(d) of our Occupational Diseases Act speaks of diseases a worker is exposed to on the job causing disability as a result of that exposure. On-the-job stress, of itself, is not a disease. Events and conditions capable of producing stress exist in every employment environment. Stress occasioned in reaction to employment demands may, in turn, cause mental disorders. Whether mental illness qualifies as an occupational disease depends upon whether the employee can establish the risk to which he was exposed arose out of and in the course of his employment and has a clear causal relationship to the disability suffered. Under our diseases act the disease must flow from that risk as a rational consequence.

The causal connection between claimant's mental disability and the gradual mental stimuli which allegedly produced the disease is not readily apparent. Whereas the rational mind can perceive a clear connection between exposure to asbestos and the subsequent contraction of asbestosis, for instance, there is a much more tenuous link in a situation where a person suffers a gradually developing mental disability which, in retrospect, is attributed to factors such as worry, anxiety, tension, pressure, and overwork without proof of a specific time, place, and event producing the disability.

To recognize that our occupational disease law would allow compensation for any mental diseases and disorders caused by on-the-job stressful events or conditions would, in the words of one court, open a floodgate for workers who succumb to the everyday pressures of life. We reject claimant's argument the supreme court opinion in *Pathfinder* supports such a result. There, the supreme court, mindful of the potential for abuse in cases of alleged psychological injury through fabrication, allowed recovery on the basis the nonphysical traumatic events triggering the mental disability were uncommonly gruesome and the disability immediate and sudden. *Pathfinder* does not authorize compensation under the Workers' Compensation Act for anxiety, emotional stress or depression which develop over time in the normal course of an employment relationship.

Also *Peoria Belwood* does not support claimant's argument. There, an accidental injury claim under the Workers' Compensation Act for carpal tunnel syndrome was found compensable in the absence of a showing of complete disfunction due to a precisely identifiable event. As the supreme court stated, in such a case the employee must still meet the same standard of proof as other claimants alleging an accidental injury. There must be a showing that the injury is work related and not the result of a normal degenerative aging process. The precise holding in *Peoria Belwood* was that the date of an accidental injury in a repetitive-trauma compensation case is the date on which the injury "manifests itself" which means the date on which both the fact of injury and the causal relationship of the injury to the claimant's employment would have become plainly apparent to a reasonable person. In *Peoria Belwood* claimant sought treatment for her condition the day after she began experiencing physical symptoms consistent with carpal tunnel syndrome. In our view, *Peoria Belwood* only obviates the need for proof of a specific time, place, or event which triggers the disability if it is immediately apparent from the onset of symptoms that the disability is work related despite the fact there is no single event prior to the appearance of symptoms which is sufficient, of itself, to cause the disability. We therefore reject the contention that mental disorders are compensable as occupational diseases when the disorder allegedly was caused by general, work-related emotional pressures common to the employment relationship.

The issue then is under what circumstances our occupational disease statute provides compensation for mental disorders emanating from on-the-job stressful conditions. Section 1(d) of our Act requires that the disease must appear to have had its origin in a "risk connected with the employment and to have flowed from that source as a rational consequence." Many courts have considered this issue with varying results. (*See generally* 1B A. Larson, Workmen's Compensation Law § 42.23(b).) We conclude, upon examination of the several lines of precedent that if nontraumatically induced mental disorders due to a gradual deterioration of mental processes are compensable under our Occupational Diseases Act, a causal connection between the employment and the disability must be established by showing that the employment exposed the employee to an identifiable condition of the employment that is not common and necessary to all or to a great many occupations. Stated differently, mental disorders not resulting from trauma must arise from a situation of greater dimensions than the day to day emotional strain and tension which all employees must experience. As the Supreme Judicial Court of Maine reasoned in *Townsend v. Maine Bureau of Public Safety* (Me. 1979), 404 A.2d 1014: "[A] higher threshold level than simply the usual and ordinary pressures that exist in any working situation would erect an appropriate buffer between the employer and a host of malingering claims." Making this a requirement in an occupational disease claim is consistent with the ruling in *Pathfinder,* a compensation case which predicated recovery upon substantial evidence of a sudden, severe emotional shock precipitated by an uncommonly frightening event well beyond that to which the employee would otherwise be exposed in the normal employment environment.

It follows that if the conditions producing disability must be extraordinary, they must also, from an objective standpoint, exist in reality. The employee must establish that the stressful conditions actually exist on the job. It is not sufficient that the employee believe, although mistakenly, the conditions exist. Under our statute there must be an actual risk connected with the employment which produces the injury. An honest perception which does not factually exist is insufficient to demonstrate a causal connection between the occupation and the disease. We also agree with the Oregon Supreme Court in *McGarrah* [*v. State Accident Insurance Fund Corp.* (1983), 675 P.2d 159,] that the worker must prove that employment conditions, when compared with nonemployment conditions, were the "major contributory cause" of the mental disorder. Such a requirement comports with the statutory provision of the Occupational Diseases Act that the disability must flow from a risk as a rational consequence.

Applying this test to the facts of this case, we conclude claimant has not established he suffers an occupational disease within the meaning of the act. The conditions allegedly producing the injury are no greater than those any teacher might face in an educational setting. Unruly students, an unresponsive administration, and the burdens of paperwork and record keeping are not unusual. Although claimant expressed fear for his safety, we find it significant that none of the events he described occurring over an extended period of years produced any demonstrable symptoms of mental disturbance coextensive with the events allegedly precipitating the fear. In fact, claimant's breakdown did not occur while in the course of employment with the Board. Rather, the first evidence of mental disability surfaced at the conclusion of summer vacation prior to the start of a new school year.

We also discount the testimony of the psychiatric social worker that claimant's problem emanated solely from his work environment. Her opinion was rendered without benefit of all the facts and was based, in part, on faulty information. The social worker, for instance, minimized claimant's relationship with his family, believing it was harmonious, when in fact, claimant was having severe marital difficulties. The social worker also based her opinion, in part, on claimant's perception that the principal was demeaning to claimant when there is no objective evidence, other than claimant's perception, to support this claim and testimony was presented directly refuting it by other faculty members. Under these circumstances, we do not believe claimant established that the events giving rise to the disability were out of the ordinary in relation to the normal workplace environment or that some objectively existed in reality or that they were the predominating cause of his illness. Accordingly, we do not believe claimant has proved his depressive disorder arose out of and in the course of his employment or was the consequence of an accidental injury.

For the foregoing reasons, the judgment of the circuit court and the decision of the Industrial Commission are reversed.

BARRY, P.J., and MCNAMARA, WOODWARD and CALVO, JJ., concur.

NOTES

1. *State Approaches to Stress Claims.* Stress claims are a subcategory of the mental cause and mental consequence (or mental stimulus-mental injury) cases, which are shown in Figure 21-2 and which are generally referred to as "mental-

mental" cases. Larson's treatise identifies four approaches that states use to analyze stress claims. The seven states in Group One find mental injury produced by mental stimulus compensable even if the stress is gradual and not unusual by comparison with that of ordinary life or employment. The twelve states in Group Two hold "mental-mental" cases compensable even if the stimulus is gradual, but only if the stress is unusual. The six states in Group Three find "mental-mental" cases compensable, but only if the stimulus is sudden. The nine states in Group Four never compensate "mental-mental" cases; there must be some physical component in the injury. Sixteen states have yet to decide the compensability of mental-mental cases. LARSON'S WORKERS' COMPENSATION § 42.25 (Desk ed. 1997).

2. *The Recent Trend to Limit Compensability.* A number of jurisdictions have enacted legislation in the 1990s limiting the number of stress claims that qualify for workers' compensation benefits. Lex Larson, 2 Larson's Workers' Comp. News 120 (1996).

Montana appears to have undertaken the most extreme reform since it now denies coverage for a mental injury even accompanied by a disabling physical injury (the physical-mental category identified in Figure 21-2), which is probably compensable in all other jurisdictions. Thus in *Yarborough v. Montana Municipal Insurance Authority*, 938 P.2d 679 (Mont. 1997), a firefighter was denied compensation for his post-traumatic stress disorder after he was struck by an exploding ball of fire in a burning home that caused first and second degree burns on his hands and face.

Most states have confined themselves to tightening the standards for mental-mental injuries. These claims have been totally eliminated by statutory amendments in states such as Kentucky, Florida, Oklahoma, Wyoming, and West Virginia, several of which previously compensated stress claims under some circumstances. Other states have not totally eliminated stress claims, but have enacted a variety of limitations that Larson places in five categories: (1) requiring a set amount or type of stress, such as the Arkansas requirement that the claimant be the victim of a crime of violence, Ark. Code Ann. § 11-9-113; (2) raising the standard of causation, such as the Colorado requirement that the stress be "proximately caused solely by hazards to which the worker would not have been equally exposed outside the employment," Colo. Rev. Stat. Ann. § 8-41-302; (3) increasing the burden of proof, such as the Maine requirement that the stress claims must be shown by clear and convincing evidence, Me. Rev. Stat. Ann. tit. 39A, pt. 1, ch. 5 § 201(3); (4) imposing specific diagnostic guidelines; and (5) limiting benefits, such as the twenty-six weeks limit in Arkansas. Ark. Code Ann. § 11-9-113(b)(1). A number of states, such as Arkansas, California, and Oregon have incorporated more than one of these restrictions.

3. *Stress from Personnel Decisions.* Many workers' compensation stress claims arise from personnel decisions, such as layoffs or transfers. Most jurisdictions are unwilling to compensate for such mental injuries, for fear of an avalanche of claims.

A typical case is *Lapare v. Industrial Commission,* 742 P.2d 819 (Ariz. Ct. App. 1987). Lapare was a Trailways bus driver for over twenty years. In 1984, the drivers were informed that the company was in financial difficulty and wanted to reduce their pay. Rumors spread concerning pay cuts, layoffs, and the insolvency of the pension plan. During a stopover, Lapare attended an impromptu union meeting, where several drivers concluded they were about to lose their jobs. When Lapare resumed driving after the meeting, he became disoriented and considered crashing the bus. After reaching the next stop, he had to be replaced by another driver. Lapare later consulted two psychiatrists, who agreed that he had suffered a mental breakdown from the anxiety of job loss. The court upheld the denial of benefits, declining "to hold that notice of a possible job loss or reduction in pay is sufficiently unexpected, unusual or extraordinary in modern society to justify compensation benefits for a worker's resulting emotional injury."

Arizona is listed in Larson's Group Two category of states, which find mental-mental cases compensable only if caused by an unusual stimulus. In Arizona, impending loss of your job after twenty years with the same employer apparently is not considered unusual.

An outlying decision that allowed compensation for being laid off or transferred is *Kelly's Case,* 477 N.E.2d 582 (Mass. 1985). Kelly had worked twenty-two years for her firm when she was told she would be laid off due to company cutbacks in the department. Kelly became upset, departed from work early, and remained upset over the weekend. Upon returning to work on Monday, she was informed that she could transfer to the cable department. Kelly was not satisfied with that proposal, and the same day became depressed, developed chest pains, and was transported to a hospital where she was placed on medication. She did not return to work for six weeks. Nine days after beginning work in the cable department, she experienced chest pains and was again taken to the hospital. She subsequently lost weight, had problems sleeping, and underwent psychiatric treatment for depression.

The Massachusetts Supreme Judicial Court held that Kelly could receive compensation, because her disability arose out of and in the course of employment. The court then rejected the argument that Kelly's emotional disability need result from an "unusual and objectively stressful or traumatic event" in order to be entitled to workers' compensation. Regardless of the particular vulnerabilities to injury a worker may have, the employer takes that individual "as is."

The court concluded that stress from layoffs should be viewed as a cost of doing business:

> We recognize that layoffs and job transfers are frequent events, and that emotional injuries are more prone to fabrication and less susceptible to sub-stantiation than are physical injuries. Nevertheless, it is within the Legis-

lature's prerogative to determine, as a matter of public policy, whether one of the costs of doing business in this Commonwealth shall be the compensation of those few employees who do suffer emotional disability as a result of being laid off or transferred, and it is also the Legislature's prerogative to say whether determination of the existence of such a disability is appropriately left to the expertise of the Industrial Accident Board.

Id. at 585.

The Massachusetts legislature responded by enacting legislation in 1985 that precluded workers' compensation benefits for personnel actions:

No mental or emotional disability arising principally out of a bona fide, personnel action including a transfer, promotion, demotion, or termination except such action which is the intentional infliction of emotional harm shall be deemed to be a personal injury within the meaning of this chapter.

MASS. GEN. LAWS ch. 152, § 29.

4. *Compensable Stress From a Single Incident.* Mental stress is most likely to be compensable when caused by a single workplace incident other than notice of firing or layoff. For example, in *Jones v. City of New Orleans,* 514 So. 2d 611 (La. Ct. App. 1987), a home health care nurse went to a housing project to see a patient. Upon arriving there she was told to call her supervisor, who told her that an anonymous phone call had threatened her safety. The nurse was then escorted from the housing project by the police. This incident greatly disturbed her, and she awoke that night in hysterics. She became frightened and paranoid, and did not return to work the next day. When notifying his wife's employer, Jones' husband learned that a man on a roof of the housing project had been using binoculars to watch his wife. Jones became frightened and withdrawn, and was not able to leave her house unless accompanied. She experienced recurrent nightmares about armed men, and had flashbacks about another nurse who had been killed in the housing project. Her family physician referred her to a psychiatrist, and she was diagnosed as suffering from Post Traumatic Stress Disorder resulting from the housing project incident.

Louisiana was a Group Four state that never found mental-mental cases compensable. Nevertheless, the court upheld an award of benefits, reasoning that the nurse had been subjected to an "unforeseen event" and noting "the scientific fact that mental disorders constitute an injury to the physical capabilities of a worker." *Id.* at 613.

2. BACK DISORDERS

JOHN F. BURTON, JR., COMPENSATION FOR BACK DISORDERS, Workers' Compensation Monitor, April 1988, at 11-12*

The Legal Approach to Back Disorders

1. *The Work-Related Test.* Backs are almost always treated as injuries rather than diseases. Consequently, the four legal tests [(1) there is a personal injury (2) resulting from an accident (3) that arises out of employment and (4) that occurs in the course of employment] normally are used to decide whether the back injuries are work-related. The most difficult legal test for claims involving back disorders is the accident requirement. The accident test involves two elements. First, the injury must be unexpected or unusual, an element that can be divided into unexpectedness in cause and in result. Second, the injury must be traceable, within reasonable limits, to a definite time, place, and occasion, which again can be divided into definiteness in cause and result.

According to Larson (§ 37.20) "If both parts of both elements are satisfied, one has the clearest example of a typical industrial accident, in the colloquial sense: collisions, explosions, slips, falls and the like, leading to obvious traumatic injuries." As far as back disorders are concerned, those involving fractures and dislocations will almost always satisfy these elements of the "typical industrial accident" and will not be examined here.

"At the other extreme, if all elements are missing, one sees the typical occupational disease. The cause is characteristic harmful conditions of the particular industry. The result is a kind of disability which is not unexpected if work under these conditions continues for a long time. And the development is usually gradual and imperceptible over an extended period." As noted, few back disorders are treated as diseases in workers' compensation and therefore this extreme case also is outside of my scope of inquiry. The main concerns of the inquiry thus are strains, sprains, and diseases of the back that are treated as if they were injuries.

As the accident test has been applied to back cases, normally the *result* is considered unexpected. For most courts, this will satisfy the unexpectedness element. However, some courts require the *cause* to be unexpected, which commonly is equated with the employee engaging in some unusual exertion at work prior to the onset of the back problem.

The other element of the accident test often involved in cases with back disorders concerns whether there is a definite effect or result. A definite result is equated with breakage, that is, "an obvious sudden mechanical or structural change in the body," as opposed to "generalized conditions," that is, "conditions not displaying overt breakage."

Definite result. The legal approach distinguishes slipped discs from other types of back disorders. According to Larson (§ 38.20), the reason is that "a so-called 'slipped intervertebral disc' is a herniation or rupture, and thus mechanically comparable to an inguinal hernia...." Because the result is definite, "a heavy preponderance of jurisdictions afford compensation for this type of injury without exacting proof of unusual exertion or mishap as a cause."

Generalized results. The other category of back disorders involves those with "generalized conditions." Larson (§ 38.33) includes in this category all back conditions except those with sufficient breakage content, notably disc herniations. Examples are back strain, back sprain, aggravation of a congenital back condition, and such diagnoses as "hurt her back."

For generalized conditions, essentially all states provide compensation if there is evidence of unusual exertion. Where the indefinite result is coupled with usual exertion, a majority of states also will consider the accident test met, but a substantial minority will not.

2. *An evaluation of the work-related tests.* In this subsection, the present legal doctrines used to decide whether back disorders are work-related are evaluated in light of the medical knowledge on backs.

There appear to be little problem with reconciling the medical knowledge concerning fractures and dislocations with the legal approach to these back disorders. There is normally an external traumatic event that causes the back problem, and the application of the four legal tests, including the accident requirement, is no more difficult than in most workers' compensation cases. However, fractures and dislocations represent only a small proportion of the back disorders handled by workers' compensation, and so there is little consolation to be derived from this congruence of the medical and legal approaches.

The current distinction in the law between herniated discs and other back disorders is medically unwarranted. It represents in part an outmoded view of causation in which external trauma was assumed to be the cause of discal herniation. The distinction also reflects an inaccurate view that the consequences of discal herniation can be distinguished from the consequences of other back disorders because there is breakage rather than generalized conditions. Probably the most serious problem, however, with the legal approach is the implicit assumption that herniated discs can be differentiated from other sources of back disorder. The medical approach recognizes that many back cases simply cannot be diagnosed because of factors such as the multiplicity of diseases that can produce particular symptoms and the finding that many persons with X-ray evidence of a particular back disease are asymptomatic.

The current legal approach of distinguishing between unusual and usual exertion as a precipitant of the back disorder is also inappropriate in light of current medical knowledge. Aside from cases involving obvious trauma, there is little proof that pattern of use causes lower back disease. As indicated by Kelsey, usage may be a factor in precipitating an underlying back disease. However, even this finding is of little value in deciding which back disorders are sufficiently work-connected to warrant compensation. The evidence indicates, for example, that some diseases are induced by sedentary work such as prolonged sitting. Moreover, ordinary physical activity can place tremendous stress on the back and trigger underlying degenerative conditions.

The conclusions that result from this review of the legal rules used to decide which back disorders are work-related cannot be too comforting to those who support workers' compensation. The current legal tests that distinguish specific and generalized results, and the roles assigned to discrete precipitants and evidence of prior disease, seem to have little scientific validity.

G. CASH AND MEDICAL BENEFITS

The workers' compensation program in each jurisdiction provides several types of cash benefits, depending on the extent and duration of the worker's disability, or whether the worker is killed. This section begins with an introduction to cash benefits, and then, in turn, examines temporary disability, permanent partial disability, permanent total disability, and death benefits. The section also reviews the medical and rehabilitation benefits provided by workers' compensation programs.

1. INTRODUCTION TO CASH BENEFITS

Three distinct time periods are pertinent in determining the amount and type of cash benefits that will be paid to a worker with a compensable injury or disease, as shown in Figure 21-3.

Figure 21-3

Three Time Periods in a Workers' Compensation Case Where the Injury has Permanent Consequences

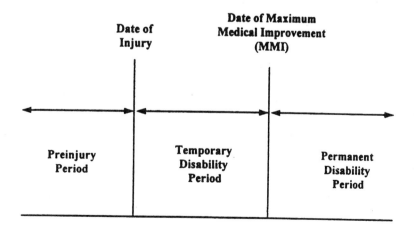

The employee's average wage in the *preinjury period* is used in calculating the cash benefits paid by the workers' compensation program. The consequences of a work-related injury or disease can be categorized as temporary or permanent, a distinction that has an important bearing on the types of cash benefits that are provided.

The *temporary disability period* refers to the time from the occurrence of the injury until the date of maximum medical improvement (MMI). During this period, which is often referred to as the healing period, the worker will receive temporary total disability or temporary partial disability benefits.

Most workers completely recover by the end of the healing period, and so only qualify for temporary disability benefits. A substantial minority of workers have permanent consequences of their injury or disease that persist after the date of MMI. For such a worker, there is a period following MMI that is referred to as the *permanent disability period*. During this period, the worker will receive permanent partial disability (PPD) or permanent total disability benefits.

The distinction between the temporary disability period and the permanent disability period can be significant for workers with permanent consequences of the injury or disease. A number of states, for example, have lower maximum weekly benefits for PPD benefits than for temporary total disability benefits. Also, as will be examined later in this section, once a worker qualifies for PPD benefits, the benefits may terminate even if the worker continues to experience loss of earnings due to the work-related injury or disease.

Many states do not use the term "maximum medical improvement." Most states, however, either use similar terms that denote the existence of MMI (such as the injury is "permanent and stationary") or have practices that indicate that the healing period is over (e.g., the date when the case is considered ready to schedule for a hearing to determine the amount of PPD benefits).

2. TEMPORARY DISABILITY BENEFITS

a. Temporary Total Disability Benefits

These benefits are paid to an injured worker who is completely unable to work during the period between the date of injury and the date of maximum medical improvement. There is a waiting period before the temporary total disability benefits begin. However, if the worker is still disabled beyond a specified date, known as the retroactive date, then the benefits for the waiting period are paid on a retroactive basis. In insurance terminology, the waiting period is a form of deductible during which time the worker bears the loss of wages resulting from the injury.

The National Commission on State Workmen's Compensation Laws recommended that "the waiting period for benefits be no more than three days and that a period of no more than 14 days be required to qualify for retroactive benefits for days lost." As of January 1, 1997, thirteen states met this recommendation, including California, Minnesota, and Wisconsin. There were twenty-three states with seven-day waiting periods, including New York, with a retroactive date of fourteen days, Texas, with a retroactive date of four weeks, and Louisiana and Nebraska, with a retroactive date of six weeks.

In most states, after the waiting period for benefits is satisfied, the weekly benefit is two-thirds of the preinjury wage, subject to maximum and minimum amounts as prescribed by state law. The worker will receive two-thirds of his or her preinjury wage or the state maximum weekly benefit, whichever is less. Or, for a low-wage worker, the worker will receive two-thirds of his or her preinjury wage, or the state minimum benefit, whichever is more. In insurance terminology, the one-third share of lost wages borne by the worker is a form of coinsurance.

The National Commission on State Workmen's Compensation Laws recommended that after July 1, 1975, the maximum weekly benefit for temporary total disability benefits should be at least 100% of the state's average weekly wage. As of January 1, 1997, 32 states plus the District of Columbia met or exceeded this recommendation. Important exceptions were California, where the maximum weekly benefit of $490 was only 86% of the state's average weekly wage; New Jersey, where the maximum weekly amount of $496 was only 78% of the state's average weekly wage; and New York, where the weekly maximum of $400 was only 62% of the state's average weekly wage.

Workers' compensation benefits are not subject to income tax. Because of the progressive federal income tax plus the income tax imposed by many states, the temporary total disability benefits, if calculated as two-thirds of gross wages, can represent a higher proportion of take-home pay. In some instances, the workers' compensation benefits can represent more than 100% of lost take-home pay. In recognition of the work disincentives that such high replacement rates may cause for some workers, the National Commission on State Workmen's Compensation Laws recommended that temporary total disability benefits should be 80% of the worker's spendable weekly earnings. Spendable earnings were defined as gross wages minus the deductions for the federal income tax and the federal Social Security tax (FICA). As of January 1997, seven jurisdictions (Alaska, Connecticut, the District of Columbia, Iowa, Maine, Michigan, and Rhode Island) used the spendable earnings approach to calculating temporary total disability benefits, although several of these states do not comply with the recommendation of the National Commission since they also subtracted state income taxes in calculating spendable earnings (e.g., Michigan) or the replacement rate was less than 80% of spendable earnings (e.g., Connecticut).

b. Temporary Partial Disability Benefits

CARR v. VIRGINIA ELECTRIC & POWER CO.

Court of Appeals of Virginia
487 S.E.2d 878 (1997)

FITZPATRICK, J.:

Dennis L. Carr (claimant) appeals a decision of the Workers' Compensation Commission denying him an award of temporary partial disability benefits. He contends that the commission erred in failing to award him benefits for the time periods during which he performed light duty work but received no opportunities for overtime. For the reasons that follow, we reverse the decision of the commission.

I. BACKGROUND

Claimant was employed with Virginia Power (employer) as a lineman for approximately twenty-three years. During his employment as a lineman, claimant's duties included "climb[ing] poles," "work[ing] out of a bucket truck," trouble shooting, building lines, and "restor[ing] service customers when they're out of lights." Claimant typically worked more than forty hours per week and regularly received overtime compensation. Additionally, claimant received bonus or incentive pay when he "filled other shifts" or worked "outside of his department of geographic area." On July 5, 1995, claimant, who is left-handed, suffered a compensable injury resulting in the amputation of his left ring finger.

Subsequently, claimant was paid wages in lieu of compensation for periods of total incapacitation from July 6, 1995 through August 5, 1995, and from September 26, 1995 through October 15, 1995. Claimant performed light duty work from August 6, 1995 through September 25, 1995, and from October 16, 1995 and continuing. Claimant testified that he returned only to light duty work "because my doctor says I can't do line work anymore." A letter from one of claimant's doctors states that claimant's injury "precludes him from performing all of his regular duties as an electrician." Claimant's light duty work included the following responsibilities: "some inspection work on [the] equipment, visual, just visual inspections, and ... reading some meters from time to time." During the light duty work, claimant worked "eight hours a day, 40-hour week." He received, during his light duty work, approximately $114.16 less per week than he received at his pre-injury work. However, during his light duty work, he was neither offered overtime work, nor paid additional wages; nor did he receive any "shift differential."

At the hearing on April 12, 1996 before the deputy commissioner, claimant admitted that he sometimes declined or was unavailable to work overtime, that he had been disciplined for having low acceptance rates for overtime, and that he did not know exactly how much overtime he would have been offered. Finally, claimant testified that he knew that overtime had been offered to other linemen during the time period in question, and stated that he would have accepted such an opportunity if it had been offered.

David H. Driggs (Driggs), the construction superintendent, testified that there was no way to predict how much overtime would be available to any given employee from year to year, and that, in the past, claimant failed to maintain the amount of overtime required by the company. However, Driggs also testified that, during the past ten years, overtime had always been offered to linemen.

Following the hearing, the deputy commissioner denied claimant's request for temporary partial disability benefits for the wage loss allegedly resulting from his lack of overtime work, and found that "the reduction in earnings stems from purely economic factors unrelated to the accident. Therefore, the claimant has failed to prove a causal nexus between the accident and his loss of earnings."

On November 4, 1996, the full commission reviewed the record and found that "the claimant was not medically restricted from working overtime and had not proven that his wage loss was due to medical restrictions from the industrial accident." The commission made no finding or classification as to the job title of claimant's light duty position relative to his pre-injury title of lineman. Accordingly, the commission affirmed the decision of the deputy commissioner that denied claimant temporary partial benefits for wages lost due to a lack of overtime work or shift differential.

II. WAGE LOSS

Claimant contends that because he was offered light duty work without the opportunity to work overtime, shift differential, or out-of-business-area pay, he suffered a wage loss below his pre-injury wage. Additionally, claimant argues that his wage loss is properly attributable to his occupational injury, as medically imposed restrictions prevented him from performing his pre-injury job and receiving extra earnings, and it is therefore compensable under Code § 65.2-502.[2]

We recently addressed the issue of the impact of economic or business conditions on a partially disabled claimant's right to compensation. *See Consolidated Stores Corporation v. Graham*, 486 S.E.2d 576 (Va. App. 1997). In that case, some time after her injury, claimant was authorized to perform light duty work.

---

[2] Code § 65.2-502, Compensation for partial incapacity, provides as follows:

Except as otherwise provided in § 65.2-503 or § 65.2-510, when the incapacity for work resulting from the injury is partial, the employer shall pay, or cause to be paid, as hereinafter provided, to the injured employee during such incapacity a weekly compensation equal to $66^2/_3$ percent of the difference between his average weekly wages before the injury and the average weekly wages which he is able to earn thereafter, but not more than 100 percent of the average weekly wage of the Commonwealth as defined in § 65.2-500. In no case shall the period covered by such compensation be greater than 500 weeks. In case the partial incapacity begins after a period of total incapacity, the latter period shall be deducted from the maximum period herein allowed for partial incapacity.

CH. 21: WORKERS' COMPENSATION

She was offered and she accepted a position as a sales clerk in which she made the same hourly wage as her pre-injury position as a "stocker." However, "due to economic conditions, [employer] assigned [claimant] a reduced number of hours, resulting in an average weekly wage of less than $108." *Id.* at 577. Although the deputy commissioner found that "any diminution in hours worked was a product of the down turn in business," the full commission reversed and found that the claimant had not been "released to her pre-injury job and that she was not performing all her pre-injury duties" and that the "fact that the availability of light duty work is limited due to economic conditions does not diminish the claimant's right to compensation when the injury prevents her from performing her regular job." *Id.* at 577.

Finding that claimant was not released to her pre-injury employment and that her light duty responsibilities as a store clerk were not commensurate with her pre-injury position of a stocker, we held that "the employer's financial condition and the availability of alternative work do not affect *the claimant's right to compensation due to an impaired capacity to perform his pre-injury duties.*" *Id.* at 578 (emphasis added). In reaching this decision, we relied on Code § 65.2-502:

> During a period of partial incapacity, a claimant performing work remains entitled to compensation benefits, determined in part by calculating the difference between the claimant's average weekly wage before and after the injury. Thus, by providing suitable alternative employment to a claimant, an employer may avoid paying compensation benefits.

Id. Accordingly, we held that because claimant was neither released to return to her pre-injury duties, nor restored to her pre-injury capacity by the employer's offered alternative light duty work, the employer remained liable to fulfill its duty to compensate claimant.

The circumstances in *Consolidated* are remarkably similar to those of the instant case. Here, employer offered claimant light duty work similar in pay to his pre-injury employment as a lineman. As in *Consolidated*, however, claimant suffered a wage loss at the light duty position that he would not have incurred at his pre-injury placement. "The threshold test for compensability is whether the employee is 'able fully to perform the duties of his pre[-]injury employment.'" ... Under the holding in *Consolidated*, the employer is relieved of its duty to compensate the claimant only if it offers the claimant employment in his or her "pre-injury capacity" and the claimant has been released to perform the work. In both *Consolidated* and this case, the employer failed to make this offer. Claimant, who made at least some overtime in his previous position, now makes none. The evidence demonstrated that other linemen continue to receive overtime and that claimant's range of duties in his light duty work is not equivalent to his pre-injury duties as a lineman. Thus, claimant has not been released to his pre-injury capacity as a lineman. Accordingly, employer's inability to predict the available overtime to the linemen during the period in question does not diminish claimant's right to compensation, as his work-related injury prevents him from performing lineman duties, and employer remains liable for the wage loss suffered by claimant....

For the foregoing reasons, the decision of the commission is reversed and the case remanded for the commission to enter an order consistent with this opinion.

Reversed and remanded.

3. PERMANENT PARTIAL DISABILITY BENEFITS

a. Introduction

Permanent partial disability benefits are paid to those workers who have injuries that are serious enough to have permanent consequences but that are not serious enough to be totally disabling.

What Are the Permanent Consequences?

For those workers with relatively serious injuries, several permanent consequences are possible. There may be a persistence of pain and suffering and a continuing need for medical care and rehabilitation. Of particular interest are the other permanent consequences shown in Figure 21-4 because they are the focus of most of the debate concerning the design of permanent disability benefits in a workers' compensation program.

Figure 21-4

Permanent Consequences of an Injury or Disease

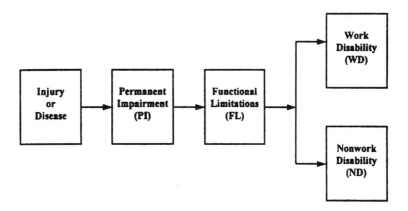

A permanent impairment (PI) is any anatomic or functional abnormality or loss that remains after maximum medical improvement has been achieved. Examples of permanent impairments are an amputated limb or an enervated muscle. The impairment probably causes the worker to experience functional limitations (FL). Physical performance may be limited in such activities as walking, climbing, reaching, and hearing, and, in addition, the worker's emotional and mental performance may be limited. Functional limitations, in turn, are likely to result in disability, of which two types should be recognized. Work disability (WD) refers to the loss of earning capacity or loss of actual earnings that results from the functional limitations, while nonwork disability (ND) includes the loss of the capacities for other aspects of life, including recreation and the performance of household tasks.

Work disability, as indicated, can be conceptualized as either the loss of earning capacity or the actual loss of earnings. In a strict sense, these two aspects of work disability must accompany one another. An actual loss of earnings only occurs if there is loss of earning capacity. Nevertheless, the distinction is important because (as discussed later in this subsection) some types of workers' compensation benefits are based solely on a determination of a *presumed* loss of earning capacity.

What Should Be the Operational Basis for Benefits?

States use several different operational approaches for permanent disability benefits depending on which of the permanent consequences shown in Figure 21-4 is used as a proxy for work disability. In most jurisdictions, the choice of an operational approach first depends on whether the worker's injury is a scheduled or nonscheduled injury.

Scheduled v. Nonscheduled Injuries

The workers' compensation statutes in most states contain a schedule that lists the number of weeks or the dollar amounts of compensation benefits to be paid for the physical loss or (in most jurisdictions) the loss of use of specified parts of the body. A scheduled injury is any injury that is specifically enumerated in the workers' compensation statute. In addition to listing the upper and lower extremities (the arm, leg, hand, foot, fingers, and toes), states commonly schedule benefits for the enucleation of an eye and for hearing and vision loss.

Injuries to the trunk, internal organs, nervous system, and other body systems usually are not included in the list of injuries found in the statutes; these are nonscheduled injuries. In some states, they are referred to as "unscheduled" injuries.

In the next subsection, we examine the handling of scheduled injuries. The following three subsections then examine three categories of states that differ in their handling of nonscheduled injuries.

b. Scheduled Permanent Partial Disability Benefits

The worker who suffers the physical loss of a part of the body included in the schedule is evaluated in terms of the seriousness of the impairment. In New Jersey — which equates the loss of an arm with 330 weeks of benefits — a worker who loses half of an arm by amputation will be entitled to 165 weeks of benefits.

An injury that leads to the loss of use of a body part found in the schedule is evaluated in terms of the extent of functional limitations that result. Thus in New Jersey — which equates the loss of a hand with 245 weeks of benefits — a worker with an injury that causes a 20% loss of the use of a hand will receive forty-nine weeks of benefits. Most states (including New Jersey) pay scheduled benefits if the worker experiences either a physical loss or a loss of use of the body part found in the schedule, but there are some states that confine scheduled benefits to amputations. Also, in most jurisdictions, the worker is not entitled to benefits after the scheduled duration expires even if the worker continues to experience actual wage loss because of the work-related injury. In some states, such as Michigan, there are exceptions to this generalization. *Van Dorpel v. Haven-Busch Co.*, 85 N.W.2d 97 (Mich. 1957).

c. Category I: Nonscheduled PPD Benefits Based on Impairment

Three categories of operational approaches for nonscheduled permanent partial disability benefits can be identified. The Category I approach is represented in Figure 21-5. New Jersey is in this category, although some aspects of the state's program make the designation less than perfect.

Figure 21-5

Permanent Partial Disability Benefits in Impairment States (Category I)

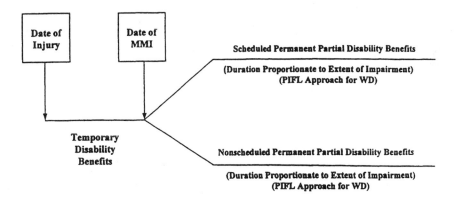

In the Category I approach, an injury with permanent consequences must first be classified as scheduled or nonscheduled. The New Jersey provisions for scheduled PPD benefits were discussed in the previous subsection. The Category I approach to nonscheduled permanent injuries evaluates them in terms of the resulting permanent impairments (PI) or functional limitations (FL). For example, a worker may experience structural damage to a vertebra and the spinal column, which are injuries not found on the schedule. The impairment itself may be evaluated (the disc is herniated) or the consequent functional limitation may be assessed (the worker is restricted in his ability to lift, stoop, or perform certain motions that he was able to make before the injury). This approach to nonscheduled injuries usually produces a percentage rating that relates the worker's condition to that of a whole person (or to a "totally disabled" person). Thus, in New Jersey the statute equates a whole person to 600 weeks, and a worker with an impairment rating of 25% would receive 150 weeks of permanent partial disability benefits.

d. Category II: Nonscheduled PPD Benefits Based on Loss of Earning Capacity

The second general approach to nonscheduled permanent partial disability benefits is illustrated in Figure 21-6. Category II is exemplified by Wisconsin, although again the assignment overlooks some characteristics of the state's law.

Figure 21-6

Permanent Partial Disability Benefits in Loss of Earning Capacity States (Category II)

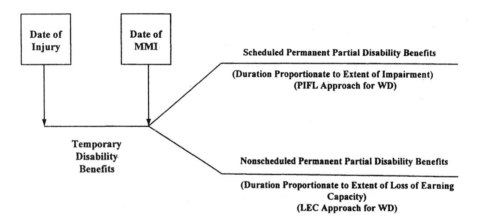

As in the first approach, an injury with permanent consequences must first be classified as scheduled or nonscheduled in the Category II approach. The distinction in Wisconsin is similar to that in New Jersey, with arms, legs, hands, etc., in the statutory schedule, while backs and internal organs are nonscheduled injuries. The scheduled durations in the two jurisdictions differ, however. An arm, for example, is worth 500 weeks in Wisconsin compared to 330 weeks in New Jersey. Nonetheless, scheduled injuries in Categories I and II are handled fundamentally the same way.

The distinctive attribute of the Category II approach to permanent partial disability benefits concerns the treatment of nonscheduled benefits. In states using this approach, an assessment is made of the worker's loss of earning capacity resulting from the work-related injury or disease. This evaluation takes into account the seriousness of the worker's permanent impairments and functional limitations plus such factors as the worker's age, education, and prior work experience. This approach to nonscheduled injuries usually produces a rating indicating the percentage loss in earning capacity due to the injury. The statute equates full earning capacity to a specified duration, which in Wisconsin is 1000 weeks. Thus, a Wisconsin worker with a 25% loss of earning capacity would receive 250 weeks of permanent partial disability benefits.

SJOBERG'S CASE

Appeals Court of Massachusetts
462 N.E.2d 353 (1984), *aff'd*, 476 N.E.2d 196 (Mass. 1985)

DREBEN, JUSTICE.

The insurer appeals from a judgment in favor of the employee affirming a decision of the Industrial Accident Board (board) which awarded the employee forty dollars a week partial compensation .... At issue is whether an employee whose earning capacity is impaired by industrial injuries is precluded, as matter of law, from obtaining benefits because, by working more than fifty hours a week, his average post-injury earnings exceed his average pre-injury weekly wage. We hold that he is not so precluded.

On October 22, 1977, and again on June 12, 1978, the employee suffered severe back pain while performing work as a pressman and molder. The board, affirming and adopting the findings of the single member, found that as a result of his injuries, the employee could not perform any work which made heavy physical demands on his back and that, prior to these injuries, he had had no such limitation. The board also found that the various jobs held by the employee since leaving his employer each paid a significantly lower hourly wage than his former job. It was only by working more than fifty hours a week, including overtime, that the employee could match, and even slightly exceed, his former earnings. While considering the weekly wages before and after the injury "as important pieces of evidence" the single member, and the reviewing board, viewed the post-injury earnings of the employee as "not conclusive on the issue of loss of earning capacity" and awarded him forty dollars a week for such loss.

We think the board's decision comports with the statute and its purpose. The award under G.L. c. 152, § 35, is for impairment of earning capacity, and is measured with certain upper limits not now relevant, as follows: "While the incapacity for work resulting from the injury is partial, the insurer shall pay the injured employee a weekly compensation equal to the entire difference between his average weekly wage before the injury and the average weekly wage he is able to earn thereafter ...."

The dollar amount actually received is not conclusive in determining the average weekly wage. In some cases this is true even for pre-injury wages. Thus, in *Shaw's Case,* 141 N.E. 858 (Mass. 1923), the court, albeit without discussion, excluded overtime in computing the employee's average weekly wage before the injury. The cases concerning post-injury earnings emphasize that compensation "is to be measured by the amount the employee was capable of earning and not necessarily by what he actually earned." The employee is to be paid "for the loss of earnings caused by the injury" and not for a loss of earnings caused by other factors. Thus, if an employee's earnings are reduced because he works less than a normal work week, he is entitled to partial compensation only if the diminution is due to his injuries and not because of a lack of demand for his labor.

Similarly, if an employee's income is higher because of factors other than his earning capacity, the income due to these factors is not to be taken into account. In *Shaw's Case,* it was held that even though an employee's wages were elevated to the same level as before by reason of a gratuity from his employer, the employee could still recover for his impaired earning capacity. Although he received full wages, he was not able to earn them, and the gratuity was irrelevant....

Where, as here, the board found an impairment of earning capacity and a reduced per hour wage, we see no reason to deny compensation because the diminution of earning capacity is concealed by the longer hours worked.... The statute bids comparison of pre- and post-injury weekly wages. A fair comparison is possible only if like factors are considered. "[O]nly by the elimination of all variables except the injury itself" can "a reasonably accurate estimate ... be made of the impairment of earning capacity attributable to the injury." *Arizona Pub. Serv. Co. v. Industrial Comm'n.,* 492 P.2d 1212 (Ariz. 1972).

Inflation of post-injury earnings by reason of longer working hours interjects, in our opinion, an extraneous factor. *See* 2A Larson, Workmen's Compensation § 57.33 (1982).[4] ... Accordingly, we hold the award for impaired earning capacity under G.L. c. 152, § 35, was not "tainted by error of law."

METROPOLITAN STEVEDORE CO. v. RAMBO

Supreme Court of the United States
117 S. Ct. 1953 (1997)

JUSTICE SOUTER delivered the opinion of the Court.

This case under the Longshore and Harbor Workers' Compensation Act is before us a second time, now raising the question whether the Act bars nominal

---

[4] Larson states (footnotes omitted), "Most obviously of all, although the wage comparison is usually on a weekly or monthly basis, it would not be fair to offset loss due to physical impairment by earnings attributable solely to claimant's having worked more hours per week. Overtime worked after the injury should be omitted from consideration if overtime was not included in the calculation of the preinjury wage basis. Similarly, if claimant's hourly wage has fallen, he is entitled to a partial award even if the reduction has been offset by his working longer hours."

compensation to a worker who is presently able to earn at least as much as before he was injured. We hold nominal compensation proper when there is a significant possibility that the worker's wage-earning capacity will fall below the level of his pre-injury wages sometime in the future.

I

Respondent John Rambo injured his back and leg in 1980 while doing longshore work for petitioner Metropolitan Stevedore Company. Rambo claimed against Metropolitan for compensation under the Longshore and Harbor Workers' Compensation Act (LHWCA or Act), 33 U.S.C. § 901 et seq., and the parties stipulated that Rambo had sustained a $22\frac{1}{2}\%$ permanent partial disability, which would normally reflect a $120.24 decline in his pre-injury $534.38 weekly wage. This, in turn, was reduced to an award of $80.16 per week under § 8(c)(21) of the Act, 33 U.S.C. § 908(c)(21), providing for compensation at the rate of $66\frac{2}{3}\%$ of the difference between an employee's pre-injury wages and post-injury wage-earning capacity. An Administrative Law Judge (ALJ) entered an order incorporating this stipulated award. *Metropolitan Stevedore Co. v. Rambo (Rambo I)*, 515 U.S. 291, 293 (1995).

Rambo was later trained as a longshore crane operator and got full-time work with his new skills, with occasional stints as a heavy-truck operator to earn extra pay. His resulting annual earnings between 1985 and 1990 were about three times what he had made before his injury. As a consequence, Metropolitan moved in 1989 to modify Rambo's earlier disability award, and a hearing was held before an ALJ. While there was no evidence that Rambo's physical condition had improved, the ALJ ordered the disability payments discontinued based on the tripling of Rambo's pre-injury earnings:

> "After taking into consideration the increase in wages due to the rate of inflation and any increase in salary for the particular job, it is evident that [Rambo] no longer has a wage-earning capacity loss. Although [Rambo] testified that he might lose his job at some future time, the evidence shows that [Rambo] would not be at any greater risk of losing his job than anyone else. Moreover, no evidence has been offered to show that [Rambo's] age, education, and vocational training are such that he would be at greater risk of losing his present job or in seeking new employment in the event that he should be required to do so. Likewise, the evidence does not show that [Rambo's] employer is a beneficent one. On the contrary, the evidence shows that [Rambo] is not only able to work full time as a crane operator, but that he is able to work as a heavy lift truck operator when the time is available within which to do so."

The Benefits Review Board affirmed the modification order, but the Court of Appeals for the Ninth Circuit reversed on the ground that § 22 authorizes modification of an award only for changed physical conditions, *Rambo v. Director,*

OWCP, 28 F.3d 86 (1994). We in turn reversed in *Rambo I*, holding that "the fundamental purpose of the Act is to compensate employees (or their beneficiaries) for wage-earning capacity lost because of injury; where that wage-earning capacity has been reduced, restored, or improved, the basis for compensation changes and the statutory scheme allows for modification." *Rambo I*, 515 U.S. at 298. Since the essence of wage-earning capacity is economic, not physical, that capacity may be affected "even without any change in the employee's physical condition," *id.*, at 301.

On remand, the Court of Appeals again reversed the order discontinuing compensation payments. It recognized that when a worker suffers a significant physical impairment without experiencing a present loss of earnings, there may be serious tension between the statutory mandate to account for future effects of disability in determining a claimant's wage-earning capacity (and thus entitlement to compensation), and the statutory prohibition against issuing any new order to pay benefits more than one year after compensation ends or an order is entered denying an award. The Court of Appeals reconciled the two provisions by reading the statute to authorize a present nominal award subject to later modification if conditions should change. *Rambo v. Director, OWCP*, 81 F.3d 840, 844 (CA9 1996). The court reversed the order ending Rambo's benefits as unsupported by substantial evidence, due to "overemphasi[sis on] Rambo's current status and failure to consider the effect of Rambo's permanent partial disability on his future earnings," *ibid.*, and it remanded for entry of a nominal award reflecting Rambo's permanent partial disability, *id.*, at 845. We granted certiorari. While we agree that nominal compensation may be awarded under certain circumstances despite the worker's present ability to earn more than his pre-injury wage, we vacate the judgment of the Court of Appeals directing entry of such an award and remand for factfinding by the ALJ.

II

The LHWCA authorizes compensation not for physical injury as such, but for economic harm to the injured worker from decreased ability to earn wages. The Act speaks of this economic harm as "disability," defined as the "incapacity because of injury to earn the wages which the employee was receiving at the time of injury in the same or any other employment," 33 U.S.C. § 902(10). Such incapacity is conclusively presumed for certain enumerated or "scheduled" injuries, which are compensated at $66^2/_3$% of the worker's pre-injury wages over specified periods of time. For other, so-called "unscheduled" injuries resulting in less than total disability, the Act sets compensation at "$66^2/_3$ per centum of the difference between the average weekly [pre-injury] wages of the employee and the employee's wage-earning capacity thereafter." 33 U.S.C. § 908(c)(21) (permanent partial disability). *See also* 33 U.S.C. § 908(e) (temporary partial disability). For figuring this difference, § 8(h) explains that the claimant's post-injury "wage-earning capacity" is to be determined "by his actual earnings if such actual earnings fairly and reasonably represent his wage-earning capacity: Provided, however, That if the employee has no actual earnings or his actual earnings do not fairly and reasonably represent his wage-earning capacity, the deputy commissioner may, in the interest of justice, fix such wage-earning capacity as shall be reasonable, having due regard to the nature of his injury, the degree of physical impairment, his usual employment, and any other factors or circumstances in the case which may affect his capacity to earn wages in his disabled condition, including the effect of disability as it may naturally extend into the future." ...

We may summarize these provisions and their implications this way. Disability is a measure of earning capacity lost as a result of work-related injury. By distinguishing between the diminished capacity and the injury itself, and by defining capacity in relation both to the injured worker's old job and to other employment, the statute makes it clear that disability is the product of injury and opportunities in the job market. Capacity, and thus disability, is not necessarily reflected in actual wages earned after injury, and when it is not, the fact-finder under the Act must make a determination of disability that is "reasonable" and "in the interest of justice," and one that takes account of the disability's future effects, § 8(h).

In some cases a disparity between the worker's actual post-injury wages and his job-market capacity will be obvious, along with the reasons for it. If a disabled worker with some present capacity chooses not to work at all, or to work at less than his capacity, a windfall is avoided by determining present disability and awarding a benefit accordingly. *See, e.g., Penrod Drilling Co. v. Johnson*, 905 F.2d 84, 87-88 (CA5 1990). At the other extreme, a worker with some present disability may nonetheless be fortunate enough to receive not merely the market wages appropriate for his diminished capacity, but full pre-injury wages (say, because an employer is generous, for whatever reason). *See, e.g., Travelers Ins. Co. v. McLellan*, 288 F.2d 250, 251 (CA2 1961); *see also Edwards v. Director, OWCP*, 999 F.2d 1374, 1375-1376 (CA9 1993) (holding that wages from short-lived employment do not represent actual earning capacity on open market). Once again, the present disability may still be calculated and a corresponding award made.

A problem in applying the provisions applicable when there is a disparity between current wages and wage-earning capacity arises in a case like this one, however. The worker now receives appropriate market wages as high or higher than those before his injury, thus experiencing no decline in present capacity. And yet (we assume for now) there is some particular likelihood that in the future the combination of injury and market conditions may leave him with a lower capacity. The question is whether such a person is presently disabled within the meaning of the statute, and if so, what provision should be made for the potential effects of disability in the future.

There are two reasons to treat such a person as presently disabled under the statute. The first follows from the provision of law that on its face bars an injured worker from waiting for adverse economic effects to occur in the future before bringing his disability claim, which generally must be filed within a year of injury. 33 U.S.C. § 913(a); *Pillsbury v. United Engineering Co.*, 342 U.S. 197 (1952). He is also barred from seeking a new, modified award after one year from the date of any denial or termination of benefits. 33 U.S.C. § 922. Because an injured worker who has a basis to anticipate wage loss in the future resulting from a combination of his injury and job-market opportunities must nonetheless claim promptly, it is likely that Congress intended "disability" to include the injury-related potential for future wage-loss. And because a losing claimant loses for all time after one year from the denial or termination of benefits, it is equally likely that Congress intended such a claimant to obtain some award of benefits in anticipation of the future potential loss.

This conclusion is confirmed by the provision of § 8(h) that in cases of disparity between actual wages and earning capacity, the natural effects of disability that will occur in the future must be given "due regard" as one of the "factors or circumstances in the case which may affect [a claimant's] capacity to earn wages in his disabled condition." Although this mandate is phrased in general terms, its practical effect is limited to the class of cases at issue here, where the worker is presently able to earn at least as much as before his injury. In all other cases, when injury depresses the claimant's wage-earning capacity under the conditions prevailing at the time of an award, so that the present effects of his disability are unquestionably compensable immediately, the Act already makes provision for the future effects of disability by means of § 22, which liberally permits modification of awards in response to changed conditions that occur within one year of the last payment of compensation (or a denial or termination of benefits). 33 U.S.C. § 922. *Rambo I* held that this provision allows modification whenever a changed combination of training and economic (let alone physical) circumstances reduces, restores, or improves wage-earning capacity. 515 U.S. at 296-297. Since ongoing awards may be modified if future possibilities become present realities, there is no need to account for such possibilities in calculating a worker's immediately compensable disability; the Act plainly takes a wait-and-see approach to future contingencies here. The first award in this case was a standard illustration of the proper practice of basing capacity determinations and compensation awards on present reality. If Rambo's initial award had already been discounted to reflect the odds of his obtaining less strenuous but higher-paying work in the future, *Rambo I* could hardly have held that the Act permitted reduction of that initial award again when Rambo actually received training as a crane operator and found work using his new skills. The first award simply reflected the degree of diminished capacity operative at the time it was made, and it was proper to revise it when conditions changed.

Thus, if § 8(h)'s admonition to consider future effects when calculating capacity has any practical application, it must be because it may apply in a case such as this one, in which there is no present wage loss and would thus be no present award if compensation were to be based solely on present employment conditions. If the future were ignored and compensation altogether denied whenever present earning capacity had not (yet) declined, § 22 would bar modification in response to future changes in condition after one year. To implement the mandate of § 8(h) in this class of cases, then, "disability" must be read broadly enough to cover loss of capacity not just as a product of the worker's injury and present market conditions, but as a potential product of injury and market opportunities in the future. There must, in other words, be a cognizable category of disability that is potentially substantial, but presently nominal in character.

There being, then, a need to account for potential future effects in a present determination of wage-earning capacity (and thus disability) when capacity does not immediately decline, the question is which of two basic methods to choose to do this. The first would be to make a one-time calculation of a periodic benefit following the approach of the common law of torts, which bases lump-sum awards for loss of future earnings on an estimate of "the difference ... between the value of the plaintiff's services as they will be in view of the harm and as they would have been had there been no harm." Restatement (Second) of Torts § 924, Comment d, p. 525 (1977). This predictive approach ordinarily requires consideration of every possible variable that could have an impact on ability to earn, including "environmental factors such as the condition of the labor market, the chance of advancement or of being laid off, and the like." 4 F. Harper, F. James, & O. Gray, Law of Torts § 25.8, pp. 550-551 (2d ed. 1986) (footnote omitted). Prediction of future employment may well be the most troublesome step in this wide-ranging enquiry. As the tripling of Rambo's own earnings shows, a claimant's future ability to earn wages will vary as greatly as opportunity varies, and any estimate of wage-earning potential turns in part on the probabilities over time that suitable jobs within certain ranges of pay will actually be open. In these calculations, there is room for error. *Cf. id.*, § 25.8, at 553 (to determine lost wage-earning capacity, juries must often "use their judgment (in effect, ... speculate)"). That juries in tort cases must routinely engage in such difficult predictions (compounded further by discounting for present value) is the price paid by the common-law approach for the finality of a one-time lump-sum judgment.

The second possible way to account for future developments would be to do in this situation just what the Act already does through the modification provision in the run of cases: to wait and see, that is, to base calculation of diminished wage-earning capacity, and thus compensation, on current realities and to permit modifications reflecting the actual effects of an employee's disability as manifested over time. This way, finality is exchanged for accuracy, both in compensating a worker for the actual economic effects of his injury, and in charging the employer and his insurer for that amount alone.

Metropolitan denies that the second, wait-and-see alternative is even open, arguing that § 8(h) gives the factfinder only two choices: either deny compensation altogether because a claimant's actual wages have not diminished, or, if the ALJ concludes that the worker's current income does not fairly represent his present wage-earning capacity, calculate the extent of the worker's disability (and his consequent entitlement to compensation) in toto based on all relevant factors, including the future effects of the disability. What we have already said, however, shows the unsoundness of Metropolitan's two options.

The practical effect of denying any compensation to a disabled claimant on the ground that he is presently able to earn as much as (or more than) before his injury would run afoul of the Act's mandate to account for the future effects of disability in fashioning an award, since those effects would not be reflected in the current award and the one-year statute of limitations for modification after denial of compensation would foreclose responding to such effects on a wait-and-see basis as they might arise. On the other hand, trying to honor that mandate by basing a present award on a comprehensive prediction of an inherently uncertain future would, as we have seen, almost always result in present over- or undercompensation. And it would be passing strange to credit Congress with the intent to guarantee fairness to employers and employees by a wait-and-see approach in most cases where future effects are imperfectly foreseeable, but to find no such intent in one class of cases, those in which wage-earning ability does not immediately decline.[7]

There is moreover an even more fundamental objection to Metropolitan's proposed options. They implicitly reject the very conclusion required to make sense of the combined provisions limiting claims and mandating consideration of future effects: that a disability whose substantial effects are only potential is nonetheless a present disability, albeit a presently nominal one. It is, indeed, this realization that points toward a way to employ the wait-and-see approach to provide for the future effects of disability when capacity does not immediately decline. It is simply "reasonable" and "in the interest of justice" (to use the lan-

---

[7] The legislative history to the 1938 amendments to the Act, which added § 8(h), indicates that Congress understood that the reference to future effects in the new subsection would interact with § 22 by allowing compensation for permanent partial disability for employees whose job opportunities are narrowed by injury but whose wages have not declined:

"[Section 8(h)] provides for consideration of the effects of an injury ... upon the employee's future ability to earn.... Often an employee returns to work earning for the time being the same wages as he earned prior to injury, although still in a disabled condition and with his opportunity to secure gainful employment definitely limited.... It is clear that in such a case the employee's ability to compete in the labor market has been definitely affected; and, though at present the employee is paid his former full-time earnings, he suffers permanent partial disability which should be compensable under the ... Act ....

"In a case such as that ..., an unscrupulous employer might with profit to himself continue the original wages ... until the ... right of review of the case (sec. 22) had run, ... thus defeating the beneficent provisions of the ... Act." H. R. Rep. No. 1945, 75th Cong., 3d Sess., No. 5-6 (1938); S. Rep. 1988, 75th Cong., 3d Sess. (1938).

guage of § 8(h)) to reflect merely nominal current disability with a correspondingly nominal award. Ordering nominal compensation holds open the possibility of a modified award if a future conjunction of injury, training, and employment opportunity should later depress the worker's ability to earn wages below the pre-injury level, turning the potential disability into an actual one. It allows full scope to the mandate to consider the future effects of disability, it promotes accuracy, it preserves administrative simplicity by obviating cumbersome enquiries relating to the entire range of possible future states of affairs, and it avoids imputing to Congress the unlikely intent to join a wait-and-see rule for most cases with a predict-the-future method when the disability results in no current decline in what the worker can earn.

Our view, as it turns out, coincides on this point with the position taken by the Director of the Office of Workers' Compensation Programs (OWCP), who is charged with the administration of the Act, and who also construes the Act as permitting nominal compensation as a mechanism for taking future effects of disability into account when present wage-earning ability remains undiminished....The Secretary of Labor has delegated the bulk of her statutory authority to administer and enforce the Act, including rule-making power, to the Director, ... and the Director's reasonable interpretation of the Act brings at least some added persuasive force to our conclusion,....

There is, of course, the question of how high the potential for disability need be to be recognized as nominal, but that is an issue not addressed by the parties, and it would be imprudent of us to address it now with any pretense of settling it for all time. Here it is enough to recall that in those cases where an injury immediately depresses ability to earn wages under present conditions, the payment of actual compensation holds open the option of modification under § 22 even for future changes in condition whose probability of occurrence may well be remote at the time of the original award. Consistent application of the Act's wait-and-see approach thus suggests that nominal compensation permitting future modification should not be limited to instances where a decline in capacity can be shown to a high degree of statistical likelihood. Those courts to have dealt with the matter explicitly have required a showing that there is a significant possibility that a worker's wage-earning capacity will at some future point fall below his pre-injury wages, ... and, in the absence of rulemaking by the agency specifying how substantial the possibility of future decline in capacity must be to justify a nominal award, we adopt this standard.

We therefore hold that a worker is entitled to nominal compensation when his work-related injury has not diminished his present wage-earning capacity under current circumstances, but there is a significant potential that the injury will cause diminished capacity under future conditions.

III

The application of this legal standard to the case before us depends in part on how the burden of persuasion is allocated. Section 7(c) of the APA, 5 U.S.C. § 556(d), which applies to adjudications under the Act, ... places the burden of persuasion on the proponent of an order...; when the evidence is evenly balanced, the proponent loses.... On the initial claim for nominal compensation under the Act, then, the employee has the burden of showing by a preponderance of the evidence that he has been injured and that the odds are significant that his wage-earning capacity will fall below his pre-injury wages at some point in the future. But when an employer seeks modification of previously awarded compensation, the employer is the proponent of the order with the burden of establishing a change in conditions justifying modification. In a case like this, where the prior award was based on a finding of economic harm resulting from an actual decline in wage-earning capacity at the time the award was entered, the employer satisfies this burden by showing that as a result of a change in capacity the employee's wages have risen to a level at or above his pre-injury earnings. Once the employer makes this showing, § 8(h) gives rise to the presumption that the employee's wage-earning capacity is equal to his current, higher wage and, in the face of this presumption, the burden shifts back to the claimant to show that the likelihood of a future decline in capacity is sufficient for an award of nominal compensation. We emphasize that the probability of a future decline is a matter of proof; it is not to be assumed pro forma as an administrative convenience in the run of cases.

In this case, the first award of compensation was based on the parties' stipulation that Rambo suffered $22^{1}/_{2}\%$ permanent partial disability as a result of his injury, whereby Rambo established that the injury impaired his ability to undertake at least some types of previously available gainful labor and thus prevented him from earning as much as he had before his accident. Metropolitan sought termination of the award based solely on evidence, which the ALJ found persuasive, that Rambo is now able to earn market wages as a crane operator significantly greater than his pre-injury earnings. There is therefore substantial evidence in the record supporting the ALJ's decision to terminate actual (as opposed to nominal) benefits, since under present conditions Rambo's capacity to earn wages is no longer depressed. But the ALJ failed to consider whether there is a significant possibility that Rambo's wage-earning capacity will decline again in the future. Because there is no evidence in the record of the modification proceedings showing that Rambo's physical condition has improved to the point of full recovery, the parties' earlier stipulation of permanent partial disability at least raises the possibility that Rambo's ability to earn will decline in the event he loses his current employment as a crane operator. The ALJ's order altogether terminating benefits must therefore be vacated for failure to consider whether a future decline in Rambo's earning capacity is sufficiently likely to justify nominal compensation. Since the ALJ is the factfinder under the Act, see

§ 21(b)(3), (c), 33 U.S.C. §§ 921(b)(3), (c), however, the Court of Appeals should have remanded to the agency for further findings of fact, *see, e.g., Randall v. Comfort Control, Inc.*, 725 F.2d at 799-800 (remanding for consideration of nominal award), instead of directing entry of a nominal award based on its own appraisal of the evidence. We therefore vacate the Ninth Circuit's judgment insofar as it directs entry of an award of nominal compensation and remand for further proceedings consistent with this opinion.

It is so ordered.

JUSTICE O'CONNOR, with whom JUSTICE SCALIA and JUSTICE THOMAS join, dissenting.

The Court holds today that an administrative law judge can award nominal worker's compensation benefits to an injured longshoreman whose wage-earning capacity has not dropped, and probably will never drop, below his pre-injury capacity. Because I believe that § 8(h) of the Longshore and Harbor Workers' Compensation Act (LHWCA or Act), 33 U.S.C. § 908(h), requires that a worker be compensated if and only if a preponderance of the evidence demonstrates that he has a reduced wage-earning capacity — that is, a present or future loss of earning power — I respectfully dissent.

As an initial matter, I note my agreement with some of the starting points for the Court's analysis. It is common ground that "disability" under the LHWCA is an economic, rather than a medical, concept.... Likewise, I agree that a worker's eligibility for compensation (i.e., his disability) under the LHWCA turns on his wage-earning capacity, which depends on his ability to earn wages now and in the future. That is, I agree that an injured worker who is currently receiving high wages, but who is likely to be paid less in the future due to his injury, is disabled under the LHWCA and is therefore eligible for compensation today....

I part company with the Court first because, in my view, § 8(h) of the LHWCA, 33 U.S.C. § 908(h), requires an administrative law judge (ALJ) to make an up-front finding that "fixes" the worker's wage-earning capacity (and hence his eligibility for compensation) by taking into account both the worker's present and future ability to earn wages. Second, a finding of future economic harm must be supported by a preponderance of the evidence pursuant to the Administrative Procedure Act (APA), 5 U.S.C. § 551 et seq., in order to affect a claimant's wage-earning capacity. Finally, because I read the ALJ's decision as expressly finding that respondent Rambo will probably suffer no future loss of earning power, and because that finding is supported by substantial evidence, I would reverse the decision of the Court of Appeals and direct the entry of judgment for petitioner Metropolitan Stevedore Co.....

NOTE

The Prospective Benefit Approach. Both the scheduled and nonscheduled benefits in the Category I and II approaches rely on the *ex ante* or prospective benefit approach. There are distinctive features of the *ex ante* approach. First, although the presumed rationale for the permanent disability benefits is the actual loss of wages resulting from the work-related injury or disease, all of these benefits rely on proxies for that actual wage loss. As suggested by the chain of causation shown in Figure 21-4, such a use of proxies is not logically flawed since presumably the actual wage loss will result from the other permanent consequences.

The second feature of the *ex ante* approach is that the decision about the amount of the benefits is made after the medical condition has stabilized but before most or all of the actual wage loss occurs for which benefits are intended. That is, the amount of the permanent disability benefits is determined near the beginning of the period of permanent disability and once the determination is made, the amount is seldom adjusted. Thus the permanent disability benefits are paid for expected wage loss during the period of permanent disability on a prospective (or *ex ante*) basis.

The Supreme Court decision in *Rambo* provides a qualification to this characterization of the nature of the *ex ante* approach, since the decision provides an example of how adjustments in the extent of loss of earning capacity can be made over time in response to factors such as the worker's experience in the labor market. The decision indicates that the line between the Category II and Category III approaches to PPD benefits is somewhat blurry rather than perfectly bright.

e. Category III: Nonscheduled PPD Benefits Based on Actual Wage Loss

The third approach to permanent partial disability benefits is represented in Figure 21-7. New York probably is the only state for which the figure is applicable. However, the distinctive feature of the New York approach for non-scheduled permanent partial disability benefits — the use of the wage-loss approach — is found in a somewhat different guise in several other jurisdictions, including Pennsylvania, Michigan, and several of the Canadian provinces.

Figure 21-7

Permanent Partial Disability Benefits in Actual Wage-Loss States
(Category III)

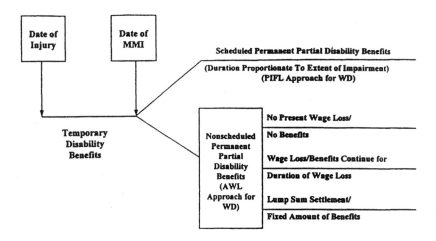

In New York, the first step in determining the applicable benefits for an injury with permanent consequences is to determine whether the injury is scheduled or nonscheduled. The distinction is similar to that used in New Jersey and Wisconsin, with arms, legs, and other bodily extremities scheduled and internal organs and the back nonscheduled. The scheduled durations are, to be sure, different among the states, with the New York arm worth only 312 weeks.

The major differences among the states pertain to the nonscheduled permanent partial disability benefits. The Category III states rely on the wage-loss approach, which requires the worker to demonstrate that he or she has experienced an actual loss of earnings because of the work-related injury or disease. In contrast, the Category I and II approaches will pay nonscheduled benefits even if there is no actual loss of earnings so long as the worker can demonstrate that the work injury caused a diminution in one of the proxies for actual wage-loss. (In the Category I approach, the proxy is an impairment or functional limitation; in the Category II approach, the proxy for actual wage loss is loss of earning capacity.)

KACHINSKI v. WORKMEN'S COMPENSATION APPEAL BOARD (VEPCO CONSTRUCTION CO.)

Supreme Court of Pennsylvania
532 A.2d 374 (1987)

MCDERMOTT, JUSTICE.

Joseph Kachinski was a mechanic employed by Vepco Construction Company. On January 19, 1981, while working on employer's premises, Mr. Kachinski was injured when a paint can exploded. The explosion caused Mr. Kachinski to fall off the machine he was working on, thereby injuring his back. The explosion also caused extensive facial burns.

Mr. Kachinski was awarded workmen's compensation benefits due to the burns he received, but no award was made related to his back injury. On April 9, 1981, Mr. Kachinski filed a petition to review the notice of compensation, alleging that his back was injured in the same accident, and that he was entitled to coverage for that injury as well. The employer denied that Mr. Kachinski had injured his back. Furthermore, on September 24, 1981, employer filed a petition to modify the compensation payments, alleging that as of June 30, 1981 claimant had sufficiently recovered from his original work-related injury as to be capable of returning to gainful employment which was then presently available in the market place.

The two petitions were considered together, and after a hearing the referee concluded that Mr. Kachinski's burns had healed, and that Mr. Kachinski did in fact injure his back in the accident, but that his back injury had improved to a point where he could no longer be considered totally disabled. The latter conclusion was based on the referee's determination that the employer had introduced sufficient evidence to establish the existence of "available work" which claimant was capable of performing. Accordingly, the referee reduced Mr. Kachinski's benefits from those appropriate for total disability to a level appropriate for a partial disability. This decision was affirmed by the Board.

On appeal, the Commonwealth Court reversed the order of the Board, effectively reinstating Mr. Kachinski's benefits. Upon petition we granted allowance of appeal.

The narrow issue presented to us is whether the evidence in this case was sufficient to sustain the employer's burden to show available work prior to effecting a reduction in benefits. However, this issue bespeaks a larger issue, which is whether an employer can sustain his burden of showing available work by demonstrating the existence of jobs in the marketplace, as opposed to demonstrating jobs which have actually been made available to the claimant.

In the case of *Barrett v. Otis Elevator Co.,* 246 A.2d 668 (1968), this Court held that once a claimant has discharged his burden of proving that because of his work-related injury he is unable to do the type of work he was engaged in when injured, the employer has the burden of proving that other work is available to the claimant which he is capable of obtaining. The *Barrett* rule was an extension of the Court's decision in *Petrone v. Moffat Coal Co.,* 233 A.2d 891 (1967), in which the issue concerned the determination of total disability in a situation where the claimant possessed residual capabilities despite his work-related injury.

In *Petrone,* the claimant was seeking total disability benefits due to his long-term exposure to coal dust. The Board and the Superior Court agreed that he was unfit to continue as a coal miner, but ruled that his residual capabilities made him able to do light work, and that such work was presumptively "available." This Court, however, ruled that a presumption that light work was available had no place in the law of workmen's compensation, and that the employer was required to demonstrate the availability of such work. Unfortunately the Court did not explain what evidence was required to show availability, but alluded to the proof method utilized under the Social Security disability program. Although the *Petrone* Court did not expressly adopt the federal approach the reference thereto seems to have fostered the development of an analogous method of analyzing availability of work issues under the Pennsylvania Workmen's Compensation Act. Because this analysis flows from an incorrect premise it has led to some confusion, and inconsistent decisions.

Social Security is a "comprehensive contributory insurance plan," the purpose of which "is to protect workers and their dependents from the risk of loss of income due to the insureds' old age, death or disability." The plan represents a "form of social insurance ... whereby persons gainfully employed, and those who employ them, are taxed in order to permit the payment of benefits."... "The right to social security benefits is in a sense 'earned,' for the entire scheme rests on the legislative judgment that those who in their productive years were functioning members of the economy may justly call upon that economy ... for protection from the rigors of poverty." Hence, the amount of disability benefits paid can be tied to the amount of contributions an employer makes.

On the other hand, the workmen's compensation program is *not* a contributory insurance plan. Rather it is a means for the obtainment of compensation for injuries which has been substituted for common law tort actions between employees and employers.

Unlike Social Security, where the cause of a claimant's disability can be unrelated to any work activity, a workmen's compensation claimant may only collect for those injuries arising out of his employment. Similarly, a claimant's benefits are tied to his wage at the time of the injury, as opposed to contributions to a fund. Finally, entitlement to workmen's compensation is not earned *per se*; rather, it is caused by an injury in the workplace.

In order to be eligible for disability benefits under the Social Security Act one must be unable "to engage *in any* substantial, gainful activity." However, a workmen's compensation claimant, while he must prove that he was injured during the course of his employment, need only demonstrate that his injury causes him lost earning power. This distinct economic injury burden reflects the compromise which the Workmen's Compensation Act fashioned between employees and employers: employees receiving immediate set benefits as opposed to the potentially greater benefits which could result from a successful tort action; and employers being protected from exorbitant unexpected costs which could result from employee lawsuits.

Therefore, whereas the theory behind Social Security is to tax presently employed workers for the inevitable day when they become either too old or too disabled to support themselves, the theory behind workmen's compensation is to include within the cost of production the unpredictable expenses of occasional injuries caused during the production process. It is because of the nature of workmen's compensation as *compensation* for an injury done that the claimant stands on a distinct level as compared with a social security recipient....

The federal courts have consistently interpreted the Social Security Act to require a showing of potential availability of jobs. Thus, if work exists in the economy which the claimant is realistically capable of performing, the claimant cannot be considered disabled. This conclusion is derived from the governing statutory language which defines disability as the inability "to engage in any substantial activity." Thus, to rebut a claim of disability it is enough to show that there exists in the economy "substantial gainful activity" which claimant is capable of obtaining. Such a showing is distinct from demonstrating that there are job openings in the economy; and a person cannot be considered disabled if his residual capabilities enable him to obtain a job which happens to be filled.

For example, let us assume a secretary was so injured as to ruin her typing ability, and she was unable to continue in a secretarial position. Let us further assume that this woman's residual skills made her capable of working as a receptionist. Regardless of whether any receptionist jobs were available, she would not receive Social Security benefits, since: (a) receptionist jobs do exist in the economy; (b) such jobs do constitute substantial gainful employment; and (c) the claimant's residual skills enable her to fill such a job.

In workmen's compensation cases we have refused to define "available" in terms of potential, at least from the time of *Petrone*. This different approach flows from our definition of disability, i.e., the "loss, total or partial, of earning power [resulting] from the injury," *Woodward v. Pittsburgh Engineering and Construction Co.*, 143 A. 21, 22-23 (1928), by which we determine the degree of a worker's disability by reference to how the injury affected his earning power.

Thus, if our fictional secretary's injury occurred in a work-related accident, and no receptionist jobs were vacant, she would be considered totally disabled because she could no longer work. The mere fact that receptionist jobs exist in the economy would not affect her entitlement to benefits. Only the existence of job vacancies which were available to the claimant would affect her entitlement....

A recipient of workmen's compensation is by definition a person who has been injured during the operation of the employer's business. Although the employer is not personally responsible for an employee's injury, the employer, as the owner of the production process, nonetheless bears a responsibility to those who are injured while operating it. That responsibility, though not without its limits, requires at a minimum some effort on the part of the employer to make the injured employee whole. To impose on the injured party the duty to find alternative work under pain of foregoing the compensation to which he has become entitled is to condition one's receipt of compensation on something other than the injury itself: a concept far removed from the salutary purpose of workmen's compensation to provide relief due to injuries caused in the workplace. Thus as Mr. Justice Musmanno wrote in *Petrone*:

[T]he law does not require that the claimant must visit every building and house in his community to inquire if he is needed as an elevator operator or engineer on a power lawn mower. If light work is available, it is easier for the defendant to prove its existence than for the claimant to prove its non-existence.

Therefore, we adopt the Commonwealth Court's interpretation of "available" as requiring a showing of actual availability....

It is obvious that in this sensitive area of evaluating when an injured employee can return to work there is a need for some concrete guidelines which consider both the employees' interest in receiving the compensation due him, and the employer's interest in not being held responsible in excess of the injury caused. Therefore we today state the following procedure as governing the return to work of injured employees:

1. The employer who seeks to modify a claimant's benefits on the basis that he has recovered some or all of his ability must first produce medical evidence of a change in condition.

2. The employer must then produce evidence of a referral (or referrals) to a then open job (or jobs), which fits in the occupational category for which the claimant has been given medical clearance, *e.g.*, light work, sedentary work, etc.

3. The claimant must then demonstrate that he has in good faith followed through on the job referral(s).

4. If the referral fails to result in a job then claimant's benefits should continue.

Obviously, the viability of this system depends on the good faith of the participants. The referrals by the employer must be tailored to the claimant's abilities, and be made in a good faith attempt to return the injured employee to productive employment, rather than a mere attempt to avoid paying compensation. By the same token, employees must make a good faith effort to return to the work force when they are able, and their benefits can be modified for failure to follow up on referrals or for willfully sabotaging referrals. If an employee refuses a valid job offer his benefits can also be modified if it is found he had no basis upon which to do so. Of course medical evidence which rebuts the employer's evidence of a change in condition, or indicates the unacceptability of the offered employment, can be a basis for a determination that claimant had a valid reason for refusing a job offer.

Though we seem to have almost moved to a point where the employer must produce a job offer, that is not quite true since the refusal of the employee to pursue a valid job referral can provide a reason for altering benefits. Nonetheless, to require an injured employee to receive no less than a job referral is consonant with the purposes of the Workmen's Compensation Act and this Court's prior comments on the issue. One injured at work, stranded into partial disability, deserves more than a generic list describing where he might find some suitable work.

Turning to the facts of this case, the employer presented evidence of eleven positions which were purportedly available to the claimant. Of these, three jobs were listed as being available in 1981 which was almost two years prior to the employer's medical evidence that claimant was fit to return to work. Therefore these jobs are excluded. Of the remaining eight, two were never called to claimant's attention, and these are also excluded; and two were not found by the referee to be suitable, a determination that has not been challenged on appeal. Of the remaining four jobs there was evidence that when these jobs became available general inquiries were sent to claimant's counsel. To these inquiries there was no response, and apparently the information about possible work was never conveyed to the claimant. Hence, there was no evidence that claimant himself was ever apprised of available work generally, and it is undisputed that he was never advised of the specific jobs here in issue. However, after the employer's vocational expert testified at the hearing claimant's counsel sought a continuance to investigate the job openings. Employer's counsel objected as to the jobs about which inquiries had been sent, but offered no objection to a recess for the claimant to pursue the two job openings, of which he had not been given prior notice. Somewhat inexplicably the referee refused the continuance as to all job referrals. Although we understand the referee's ruling as to the first group of job openings, it seems to have been an abuse of discretion to refuse a continuance as to the second group: an action which may have resulted in Mr. Kachinski returning to the work force and obviating the need for this continuing litigation.

Nevertheless, we think it was inexcusable for claimant's counsel in this case to fail to follow up on the employer's initial inquiries, and especially to fail to advise his client about the employer's overtures. Such actions can be grounds for modifying a claimant's benefits, in which case the claimant may have a malpractice action against his attorney. However, under the facts of this case, and given the unclear status of the law at the time regarding claimant's duty, it would be onerous to punish this claimant for the dereliction of his attorney where no actual job referral was made. It would be especially harsh since when claimant was presented with the actual information regarding the job he offered to pursue them and was refused permission by the referee.

Therefore, we will affirm the order of the Commonwealth Court on the basis that the employer's efforts which were primarily directed at showing available jobs in the workplace, were not adequate to show that actual jobs had been made available to the claimant.

HUTCHINSON, J., notes his dissent.
[The concurring opinion of Justice Larsen is omitted.]

NOTES

1. ***Reform or Counter-Reformation in the Keystone State?*** The Pennsylvania workers' compensation law was amended in 1996. One change was that "[u]nder current law, the employer can reduce the amount of an injured worker's benefits by offering or finding someone else to offer the worker light-duty or other suitable work. Under the reform legislation ..., an injured worker's benefits may be reduced if the employer can establish that light-duty work is available within commuting distance." *Reform Bill Passes Legislature, Is Expected to Reduce Premiums*, 7 Workers' Comp. Rep. (BNA) 319 (1996). The supporters of the legislation claimed that enactment would curb the "skyrocketing cost of wage loss benefits." *Id.*

2. ***Traits of the Wage-Loss Approach.*** Several of the traits of a "pure" wage-loss approach are worth emphasizing. One trait is that, unless the worker has actual earnings after the date of MMI that are less than the worker's preinjury earnings, no benefits are paid even if the work injury has resulted in an impairment, functional limitation, or loss of earning capacity. This is a crucial difference between the true wage-loss approach (Category III) and the loss of earning capacity approach (Category II); a worker who experiences a loss of earning capacity but no actual loss of earnings is precluded from benefits in the wage-loss approach but is not precluded in the loss of earning capacity approach. The "no present wage loss/no benefits" outcome shown in Figure 21-7 is not a mere hypothetical result: in a recent year, almost 10% of all nonscheduled cases in New York were closed with no permanent disability benefits because the workers were experiencing no actual loss of earnings at the date of the hearing, even though they had other permanent consequences of their injuries.

Another characteristic of the wage-loss approach is that the total duration of the permanent disability benefits is *not* determined shortly after the date of MMI, as in Categories I and II. Instead, the duration of benefits depends on the length of time the worker experiences actual losses of earnings due to the work injury. In New York, this duration can range from zero weeks (for those cases closed with no present wage loss) to the balance of the worker's life. If at the time the case is initially classified as a nonscheduled permanent partial disability in New York, the worker experiences a wage loss, benefits commence under the option entitled "wage loss — benefits continue for duration of wage loss." The length of time these benefits will continue is unknown because the duration of subsequent wage loss is unknown. Furthermore, the worker's eligibility for nonscheduled benefits can change through time. For example, a worker whose case is initially closed with no benefits because of no present wage loss can reopen the case for up to eighteen years after the date of injury or eight years after the last benefit payment. Permanent partial benefits can commence after the reopening if the work injury is then causing lost earnings. This approach can be described as a retrospective or *ex post* approach to permanent disability benefits because the amount and duration of permanent disability benefits are not known until the period of permanent disability is over (or the period for reopening has expired).

There is a third outcome for a nonscheduled permanent partial disability case shown in Figure 21-7, namely the lump sum settlement. The lump sum settlement in New York is essentially a compromise and release (C & R) agreement, in which the parties reach a compromise concerning the amount of benefits to be paid, the worker receives a lump-sum payment, and the employer is released from any further liability for the particular injury. The use of a C & R agreement or a lump-sum settlement basically transforms a case from one relying on a Category III approach (where the amount of permanent disability benefits in a case is unknown until the end of the period of permanent disability or the period for reopening has expired) into a Category II approach (where the amount of permanent disability benefits is determined near the beginning of the period of permanent disability based on an assessment of the extent of loss of earning capacity).

f. The Hybrid Approach to Permanent Partial Disability Benefits

Some states determine the amount and duration of permanent partial disability benefits by a hybrid approach that begins with a period of PPD benefits based on the seriousness of the worker's impairment, and then provides additional benefits based on the wage loss approach for cases with unusually serious economic consequences. The hybrid approach is represented in Figure 21-8, which illustrates the approach used in Florida since 1994.

Figure 21-8

**Permanent Partial Disability Benefits in Florida Since 1994:
The Hybrid Approach**

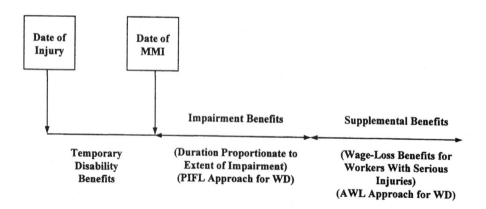

The hybrid approach in Florida pays two types of PPD benefits after the date of MMI. Three weeks of impairment benefits are paid for each 1% permanent impairment rating. The weekly benefits are 50% of the worker's average temporary total disability benefit. Those workers who have a permanent impairment rating of at least 20% have an opportunity to qualify for wage-loss benefits after the impairment benefits have expired (i.e., at least sixty weeks after the initial eligibility date for impairment benefits). The wage-loss benefits are paid to workers who experience at least a 20% drop in wages between the preinjury period and the period of permanent disability; 80% of the wage loss in excess of the 20% threshold is compensated.

The hybrid approach (although not specifically the Florida variant of hybrid PPD benefits) received significant support in a Policy Statement on Permanent Partial Disability that was prepared by the Blue Ribbon Panel on Workers' Compensation of the National Conference of State Legislatures:[*]

> It is widely agreed that states ... usually face problems with a category of cases know as permanent partial disabilities....
>
> The evidence regarding the problematic nature of permanent partial disability claims is clear. Compared with temporary total disability claims, permanent partial disability claims require about six times the medical expense, but 17 times the average indemnity expense....
>
> Perhaps it is because of the difficulties that many states have had with their permanent partial disability programs, that so much interstate variation exists. Few, if any, areas of workers' compensation exhibit so much variation in approach, allowing these to serve as experiments in operating these benefit programs....
>
> Broadly speaking, particular benefit approaches can be fitted into three categories:
>
> Impairment. Providing compensation based upon physical or mental loss of use of bodily function....
>
> Wage loss. The compensation benefit is based on the actual loss of earnings experienced as the result of the permanent impairment, with the amount of the compensation calculated and paid as the loss is actually experienced.
>
> Loss of wage earning capacity. This approach takes into consideration the impact that factors such as age, education and work experience, when combined with a permanent impairment, have on the worker's ability to compete in the labor market. In some states, it is viewed as a predictor of

---

[*] The "Policy Statement on Permanent Partial Disability" by the Blue Ribbon Panel on Workers' Compensation of the National Conference of State Legislatures is reprinted at 5 WORKERS' COMPENSATION MONITOR, July/Aug. 1992, at 7-11.

the earnings loss that is expected to occur as the result of the permanent injury.

We believe that there is widespread acceptance of the proposition that the most important justification for compensation in such cases is actual loss of income....

Because the impairment based approach determines benefit amounts through the evaluation of loss of physical (and possibly mental) function, on its face this approach may appear to have little value in a system that seeks to replace lost income. However, it may actually accomplish this. The dollar value accorded to a degree of impairment can be considered as the compensation level deemed appropriate to compensate for the *average* income loss sustained by a person with such impairment. Historical evidence indicates that the development of scheduled impairment benefits was based upon this concept. In addition, impairment is as good a predictor of who will suffer income loss as the combination of factors which are used in the loss of earning capacity approach.

Each of the basic compensation approaches has significant flaws:

... Impairment benefits do not respond directly to the economic impact of the injury. The pianist and the attorney both receive the same benefits for the loss of a finger.

Each approach also has certain advantages:

... Impairment can (though it need not) be estimated with relative ease, and with small disparities among evaluators, especially if the evaluators use the same standard.

Having described in very basic form each of the three approaches, it must be observed that variations on each theme exist....

[I]t would seem desirable, in most cases, to limit benefits to be paid for impairment, with the door left ajar for those rare instances where an egregious injustice has occurred. In those instances, the worker would be paid, initially, an impairment-based benefit, and when those benefits expired, a supplemental income award based on their actual wage loss.

4. PERMANENT TOTAL DISABILITY BENEFITS

Permanent total disability benefits are paid to an injured worker who is completely unable to work after the date of maximum medical improvement. Most workers' compensation statutes provide that a worker will be classified as permanently and totally disabled if specified losses occur, which can be considered a form of "scheduled" permanent total disability benefits. Thus, the New Jersey workers' compensation statute provides that "The loss of both hands, or both arms, or both feet, or both legs, or both eyes, or any two thereof as the result of any one accident, shall constitute total and permanent disability ...." N.J. REV. STAT. § 34:15-12(20). A worker can also be classified as permanently and totally disabled based on the facts in the case: this might be done by using the "odd-lot" doctrine, which will be examined in the *Guyton* case below.

In most states, the weekly benefit is two-thirds of the preinjury wage, subject to maximum and minimum weekly benefits as prescribed by state law. The National Commission on State Workmen's Compensation Laws recommended that after July 1, 1975, the maximum weekly benefit for permanent total disability should be at least 100% of the state's average weekly wage. As of January 1, 1997, thirty states plus the District of Columbia met or exceeded this standard. Most states have the same maximum for permanent total disability as for temporary total disability, and so the relatively low temporary total maximums cited earlier for California, New Jersey, and New York also apply to permanent total disability cases. Two states (Utah and Wyoming) have maximums for temporary total disability that are at least 100% of the state's average weekly wage, but have lower maximum weekly benefits for permanent total disability that do not meet the National Commission's recommendation. What rationale can you provide for a lower maximum for permanent total disability than for temporary total disability benefits?

The National Commission also recommended that "total disability benefits be paid for the duration of the worker's disability, or for life, without any limitations as to dollar amount or time." As of January 1, 1997, forty-two states plus the District of Columbia met this recommendation. Noncomplying states (as of January 1997) included Indiana (which limited permanent total disability benefits to $214,000)and Mississippi (which limited permanent total disability benefits to 450 weeks or $121,801). What rationale can you provide for these limits on the duration or dollar amount of permanent total disability benefits?

GUYTON v. IRVING JENSEN CO.

Supreme Court of Iowa
373 N.W.2d 101 (1985)

MCCORMICK, JUSTICE.

In this case of first impression we adopt the "odd-lot doctrine" in workers' compensation cases....

Petitioner Frank Guyton, Jr.... hurt his back on May 5, 1978, while working for respondent Irving Jensen Company in Sioux City, when he was struck in the left hip by a cement truck. Workers' compensation benefits were paid during three months in 1978. In the review-reopening proceeding, he sought benefits for permanent disability, and the dispute concerns the extent of his compensable disability.

The industrial commissioner ... determined Guyton's disability to be twenty percent. In accordance with these findings, the commissioner awarded Guyton benefits based on a twenty percent industrial disability.

Thus the commissioner equated Guyton's ability to obtain employment with his ability to perform physical activity in "junking." In this context, Guyton's industrial disability was determined to be approximately the same as his fifteen to twenty percent functional disability. The availability of suitable employment was not discussed.

The commissioner did not in his analysis address any of the other factors to be considered in determining industrial disability. Industrial disability means reduced earning capacity. Bodily impairment is merely one factor in gauging industrial disability. Other factors include the worker's age, intelligence, education, qualifications, experience, and the effect of the injury on the worker's ability to obtain suitable work. When the combination of factors precludes the worker from obtaining regular employment to earn a living, the worker with only a partial functional disability has a total industrial disability.

Abundant evidence concerning the other factors was adduced in this case. Guyton is a black man approximately 40 years old who does not know his age. He grew up in Mississippi where he had about one month of formal education. He cannot read or write or make change. The evidence included results of psychological tests administered for social security disability purposes. The tests showed Guyton to be mildly retarded. Considering his retardation with his lack of education and illiteracy, the examiner concluded Guyton "will be limited in competitive employment to jobs of an unskilled, repetitive nature requiring no literacy."

Guyton's employment history before his injury included work as a farm hand in Mississippi, fertilizer bagger in Waterloo, laborer in a Waterloo bottling plant for six years, city garbage man, and janitor at the Waterloo sewage plant. He was working as a laborer on highway construction when he was injured.

The uncontroverted medical evidence was that Guyton received a lower back sprain in the truck mishap, resulting in some percentage of permanent physical impairment due to recurrent pain. Substantial evidence supports the commissioner's finding that this impairment is fifteen to twenty percent of the body. Guyton's physician testified that he would have good days and bad days but could not do any job on a regular basis that involved bending, prolonged sitting, or even lifting as little as ten or fifteen pounds. He believed Guyton could not perform the work in the kind of jobs he previously had.

Testimony was received from a vocational counselor. Based on the medical and psychological data and her study of the job market, she said that before his injury Guyton could expect to obtain elemental employment in the bottom ten percent of the job market. After his injury she did not believe he could even obtain jobs of that type. She said Guyton might find work in a sheltered workshop that would pay approximately $1430 a year. In a normal economic climate, she believed most employers would eliminate him as a job applicant. If he were hired, she thought he would be put in a "last hired, first fired" category. His physical and mental limitations would combine to screen him out of job opportunities. She concluded that Guyton had "little, if any, possibility of job placement in substantial gainful activity." As a result, she said she considered him to be 100 percent vocationally disabled.

The record contains substantial evidence of Guyton's efforts since his injury to find employment. He applied for work with the assistance of a friend at numerous places in the Waterloo area and up to 150 miles away. He had not found employment in this period of more than four years. He subsisted by earning small amounts through his junking activities and through social security disability compensation. There was no evidence that jobs were available to persons with his combination of impairments....

In determining the correct rule of law to be applied to this record we must address Guyton's contention that Iowa recognizes the "odd-lot doctrine." He argued this contention before the commissioner and in district court. The commissioner believed that doctrine is implicit in the industrial disability standard enunciated in our cases, and we agree. We now formally adopt the doctrine.

Under that doctrine a worker becomes an odd-lot employee when an injury makes the worker incapable of obtaining employment in any well-known branch of the labor market. An odd-lot worker is thus totally disabled if the only services the worker can perform are "so limited in quality, dependability, or quantity that a reasonably stable market for them does not exist...." *Lee v. Minneapolis Street Railway Co,* 41 N.W.2d 433, 436 (Minn. 1950). A person who has no reasonable prospect of steady employment has no material earning capacity. This concept ... is recognized in virtually every jurisdiction. *See* 2 A. Larson, *The Law of [Workers'] Compensation,* § 57.51 at 10-164.24 (1983). The evidence in the present case would permit the finder of fact to find Guyton is an odd-lot employee.

In most jurisdictions, the odd-lot doctrine involves an allocation of the burden of production of evidence that has not been addressed in our prior cases. Professor Larson states the general rule as follows:

> A suggested general-purpose principle on burden of proof in this class of cases would run as follows: If the evidence of degree of obvious physical impairment, coupled with other facts such as claimant's mental capacity, education, training, or age, places claimant prima facie in the odd-lot category, the burden should be on the employer to show that some kind of suitable work is regularly and continuously available to the claimant. Certainly in such a case it should not be enough to show that claimant is physically capable of performing light work, and then round out the case for non-compensability by adding a presumption that light work is available. It is a well-known fact of modern economic life that the demand for unskilled and semi-skilled labor has been rapidly declining with the advent of the age of mechanization and automation, and that the great bulk of the persistent hard-core unemployment of the United States is in these categories.

2 A. Larson, *supra,* at 10-164.95 to 10-164.113. Our cases make it clear that the burden of persuasion on the issue of industrial disability always remains with the worker. The cases, however, have distinguished between burden of persuasion and burden of production in other workers' compensation situations. Before today we were not required to decide whether a presumption exists that suitable work is available to an odd-lot employee or whether evidence must be adduced on that subject.

We adopt the burden of proof allocation enunciated in Professor Larson's statement of the general rule. We emphasize that this rule merely allocates the burden of production of evidence. It is triggered only when the worker makes a prima facie case for inclusion in the odd-lot category....

We therefore hold that when a worker makes a prima facie case of total disability by producing substantial evidence that the worker is not employable in the competitive labor market, the burden to produce evidence of suitable employment shifts to the employer. If the employer fails to produce such evidence and the trier of fact finds the worker does fall in the odd-lot category, the worker is entitled to a finding of total disability.

The court of appeals, without using the burden-shifting aspect of the odd-lot employee doctrine, nevertheless found Guyton carried his burden to prove total disability as a matter of law. We do not agree. Even under the odd-lot doctrine that we adopt today the trier of fact is free to determine the weight and credibility of the evidence in determining whether the worker's burden of persuasion has been carried. Only in an exceptional case would evidence be sufficiently strong to compel a finding of total disability as a matter of law. The evidence in the present case is not that strong. As demonstrated in the analysis of the commissioner, a dispute existed in the evidence concerning the effect of Guyton's injury on his ability to hold and keep a job. Although Guyton clearly made a prima facie case that he is totally disabled, the evidence was not strong enough to compel that holding as a matter of law. The evidence would permit a finding that his inability to obtain employment was attributable to unsatisfactory work history unrelated to his injury.

Upon remand, in view of the burden-shifting aspect of the odd-lot doctrine we adopt today, the commissioner shall give the parties an opportunity to offer such additional evidence as they wish on the issue of availability of suitable employment for Guyton. The commissioner shall make new findings of fact and conclusions of law in accordance with today's holding.

Decision of court of appeals vacated; judgment of district court reversed and remanded.

All Justices concur except WOLLE, J., who takes no part.

5. DEATH BENEFITS

Death benefits are paid to the survivor or survivors of a worker killed on the job. In some jurisdictions, the weekly benefit depends on the number of survivors. For example, a widow or widower might receive a benefit that is 50% of the deceased worker's wage, while a widow or widower with a child might receive a weekly benefit that is $66^2/_3$% of the deceased worker's wage. The National Commission on State Workmen's Compensation Laws recommended that in all death cases, the weekly benefit should be at least two-thirds of the worker's weekly wage before death. As of January 1, 1997, thirty-two states met this recommendation. States not complying with this recommendation included Arizona (where a surviving spouse without dependents only receives 35% of the worker's wage before death) and New Jersey (where a surviving spouse only receives 50% of the worker's wage before death).

The death benefits are subject to minimum and maximum weekly amounts. The National Commission recommended that after July 1, 1975, the maximum weekly benefit for death benefits should be at least 100% of the state's average weekly wage (SAWW). As of January 1, 1997, twenty-seven states plus the District of Columbia met this standard. States not meeting the recommendation included Arizona (where the maximum weekly benefit was $145.40, which was 32% of the SAWW) and Idaho (where the maximum weekly benefit was $259.80, which was 63% of the SAWW). Several states had maximums for temporary total and permanent total disability that met the National Commission's recommendations (that the maximums be at least 100% of the state's average weekly wage) but had lower maximum weekly amounts for death benefits that did not meet the National Commission's standard for death benefits. For example, Kentucky provided maximum weekly benefits of $447.03 for temporary and permanent total disability benefits, but a maximum of only $223.52, which was 52% of the SAWW, for death benefits.

The National Commission also recommended that death benefits be paid to a widow or widower for life or until remarriage and to a dependent child until at least age eighteen (or at least until age twenty-five if enrolled as a full-time student). As of January 1, 1997, thirty-two states plus the District of Columbia met this recommendation as it applied to widows or widowers, but only fourteen states met the standard as it applied to full-time students. Examples of noncomplying states are Indiana and Idaho, where death benefits are limited to 500 weeks.

6. MEDICAL AND REHABILITATION BENEFITS

Most state workers' compensation laws require the employer to provide medical benefits without cost to the workers. Unlike many health care plans (and unlike workers' compensation cash benefits), there are no deductibles or co-insurance provisions that require employees to share the expenses of medical benefits. Fee schedules have been issued by many state workers' compensation agencies that limit medical charges, which have made some medical care providers reluctant or unwilling to provide services to injured workers. During the 1990s, managed care has been introduced into the workers' compensation health care delivery systems in many states.

Medical rehabilitation, such as physical therapy, is provided in most states by the workers' compensation program. However, many states do not provide vocational rehabilitation services that may be necessary to equip the injured worker to return to the former job or, where necessary, to handle a new job.

While in general medical care and medical rehabilitation are provided to injured workers in all states, there are limits to what the workers' compensation programs will cover.

PETRILLA v. WORKMEN'S COMPENSATION APPEAL BOARD (PEOPLE'S NATURAL GAS)

Commonwealth Court of Pennsylvania
692 A.2d 623 (1997)

OPINION BY JUDGE DOYLE

Robert J. Petrilla (Claimant) appeals from an order of the Workmen's Compensation Appeal Board (Board) which affirmed the referee's decision denying his petition for review. The issues raised on appeal are: (1) whether under Section 306(f) of the Workers' Compensation Act (Act), Claimant is entitled to reimbursement for home nursing care provided by his wife; and (2) whether a van equipped with special devices designed to enable Claimant to travel in his wheelchair constitutes "orthopedic appliances" under Section 306(f) of the Act. Claimant, while employed by People's Natural Gas Company (Employer), sustained a work-related injury on January 23, 1979 and began receiving total disability benefits pursuant to a notice of compensation payable. Due to the work injury, Claimant became a paraplegic, and he is currently confined to a wheelchair.

On December 11, 1991, Claimant filed a petition for review, alleging that Employer refused to provide medically necessary transportation and pay for reasonably incurred medical expenses for home nursing care provided by his wife. In its answer, Employer alleged that it had offered to retrofit Claimant's vehicle with hand controls or other modifications to enable him to drive, that it had no obligation to provide the vehicle itself, and that it had no obligation to pay for the services provided by Claimant's wife, who was not a duly licensed practitioner of the healing arts.

To support the petition, Claimant and his wife testified at the hearing. Claimant also presented the deposition testimony of his treating physician, Gilbert Brenes, M.D. The following facts found by the referee are undisputed. Claimant needs home nursing care for regular catheterization, daily bowel training and assistance in getting in and out of bed, getting dressed and his daily exercises. In addition, Claimant must be turned in his bed every two hours to avoid skin problems. Claimant's wife received training for home nursing care at the Harmarville Center where Claimant was treated. She provided home care for Claimant until she left him in April 1990. Employer thereafter provided nursing care until Claimant was discharged from the Harmarville Center on August 16, 1990 upon his wife's return. Claimant's wife again left Claimant in August 1991, and Employer has since provided nursing care for Claimant. Claimant requested reimbursement for the services provided by his wife in the amount of $100 per day.

The Harmarville Center prescribed a specially equipped van for Claimant because he could no longer transport himself in a standard size car with modified controls due to his medical conditions. Claimant requested $37,940 for such a van.

The referee denied Claimant's petition, concluding that the services provided by Claimant's wife did not fall within "services rendered by duly licensed practitioners of the healing arts" under Section 306(f)(1) of the Act, and further, that the requested van similarly did not fall within "orthopedic appliances" under Section 306(f)(4). On appeal, the Board affirmed the referee's decision.

Claimant first contends that the home nursing care provided by his wife is recoverable under Section 306(f)(1) of the Act in effect when Claimant filed the petition. Section 306(f)(1) provided that "[t]he employer shall provide payment for reasonable surgical and medical services, services rendered by duly licensed practitioners of the healing arts, medicines, and supplies, as and when needed ...." Services provided to a claimant by someone who is not a licensed practitioner of the healing arts, to be recoverable under Section 306(f)(1), must be provided under the supervision of a practitioner, or at a minimum, by a referral from the practitioner....

In this matter, it is undisputed that Claimant's wife provided the care without any supervision of Dr. Brenes or any other licensed practitioner. Moreover, the mere fact that Claimant's wife received training for the home nursing care of her husband at the Harmarville Center does not make her services compensable under Section 306(f)(1).

In *Linko v. Workmen's Compensation Appeal Board (Roadway Express, Inc.),* 621 A.2d 1188 (Pa. Cmwlth. 1993), after the claimant sustained the work injury, his wife left her job as a nurse's aide to care for the claimant. The claimant later sought reimbursement for the services provided by his wife during his convalescence. This Court held that the claimant was not entitled to reimbursement, noting, *inter alia*, that the claimant did not actually pay for the services rendered by his wife, and that her care for her husband was not different from that which husband or wife would perform for an injured spouse.

As in *Linko*, Claimant did not hire his wife for the home nursing care, nor did he pay for her services. Rather, she voluntarily provided the care to her injured husband. As the Supreme Court observed, "[t]he plaintiff cannot recover for the nursing and attendance of the members of his own household, unless they are hired servants" because such care by family members "involves the performance of the ordinary offices of affection, which is their duty ...." *Goodhart v. Penn-*

sylvania Railroad Co., 35 A. 191, 192 (Pa. 1896). Hence, the referee and the Board properly concluded that Claimant is not entitled to reimbursement for the services provided by his wife under Section 306(f) of the Act.

Claimant next contends that Employer must provide a specially equipped van to enable him to travel in his wheelchair. Section 306(f)(4) provides that the employer must pay for "medicines and supplies, hospital treatment, services and supplies *and orthopedic appliances*, and prostheses." 77 P.S. § 531(4) (emphasis added). Employer is willing to provide the necessary modifications to a van, but refuses to provide a van itself. Employer contends that the van requested by Claimant does not fall within "orthopedic appliances" under Section 306(f)(4).

In *Rieger v. Workmen's Compensation Appeal Board (Barnes & Tucker Co.)*, 521 A.2d 84 (Pa. Commw. Ct. 1987), this Court held that a wheelchair is an "orthopedic appliance," and that devices which will aid the claimant in the use of his wheelchair, such as the bars placed in a bathroom, ramps leading to and from his home, as well as retrofitting of claimant's automobile with hand controls, also fall within the definition of "orthopedic appliances" under Section 306(f)(4). The Court reasoned:

> [A] wheelchair was in fact a necessity for the claimant, and if a wheelchair is necessary, then it logically follows that minor modifications needed to facilitate the use of the appliance must also be considered a necessity....
>
> [T]he intent of the Act is not that a claimant be forced either to rely upon the charity of his family and friends or to rely upon hired assistance in order to perform those daily tasks, duties and business that he was previously able to perform, when a simple, inexpensive remedy is available at hand. If the claimant's injuries make it impossible to leave his home, the remedial nature of the Act would be frustrated by a failure to provide a one-time expenditure.

521 A.2d at 87.

In the matter *sub judice*, the referee accepted Dr. Brenes' testimony and found that due to his conditions of bilateral carpal tunnel syndrome and rotator cuff syndrome in his right shoulder, which are related to the 1979 work injury, Claimant was no longer able to transport himself in a standard size automobile with modified controls, and that he therefore needed a van with various modifications. Dr. Brenes stated in his July 21, 1992 medical report:

> I have, therefore, prepared a prescription for the type of vehicle that will be necessary to allow Mr. Petrilla to transport himself from place to place. I believe that such a vehicle is a medical necessity as it will enable him to obtain treatment without assistance and possibly alleviate the existing home care needs.

Employer has acknowledged and agreed that it is responsible for the necessary modifications to a motor vehicle, including a van, which would be necessary because of Claimant's handicaps. However, Employer argues that it should not have to pay for the cost of the van itself. The WCJ agreed and reached the conclusion that the issue was one of pure law and statutory interpretation and that a van was not an "orthopedic appliance" within the meaning of Section 306(f)(4) of the Act. The Board affirmed and the issue now presented on appeal is a further extension of this Court's holding in *Rieger*; one which has not been squarely addressed in this Commonwealth, but has recently been addressed in our sister state of Maryland.

In *R & T Construction Co. v. Judge*, 594 A.2d 99 (Md. 1991), a quadriplegic injured worker filed a workers' compensation claim for a specially equipped van and, *inter alia*, the cost of enlarging and remodeling his home to accommodate his "sip and puff" controlled wheelchair. In an extensive and wide-ranging opinion which considered the case law and similar compensation statutes in a number of other states, including this Court's decisions in *Rieger* and *Bomboy*, the Maryland Court of Appeals held that a specially equipped van is not compensable "medical equipment or apparatus" under Article 101, § 37(a) of the Maryland Code (1957, 1985 Repl. Vol.), which is Maryland's equivalent of our Workers' Compensation Act provision. The *R & T* Court went further and, quoting A. Larson, 2 *The Law of Workmen's Compensation* § 61.13(a), at 10-863 (1989), summarized the case law on the issue by stating that "as to specially-equipped automobiles for paraplegics, the cases have uniformly denied reimbursement, on the ground that an automobile is simply not a medical apparatus or device." 594 A.2d at 108 (footnote omitted).

While not controlling the resolution of the issue in this Commonwealth, of course, the statutory language in Maryland's statue is strikingly similar to ours and compels the same logical analysis. First, "medical apparatus or prosthetic appliance" (Md.) and an "orthopedic appliance" (Pa.) have, for our purposes, almost identical definitions and are thus very similar in scope. Obviously, neither the phrase "*medical* apparatus or prosthetic *appliance*" nor the term "orthopedic *appliance*," in this context, refers to a motor vehicle for general transportation use. The general use of a vehicle must, of course, be distinguished from the retrofitting of that vehicle, without which the vehicle could not be operated by the claimant. It is the modifications and additional "appliances," not the vehicle itself, which are necessary to accommodate the claimant's work-related injury. Thus, the special retrofitting is an "orthopedic appliance," *Rieger*, while a van itself is not.

Second, by analogy, while the special remodeling of an injured worker's home to make it wheelchair accessible might be analogous to the cost of retrofitting a motor vehicle so that the vehicle is accessible to a paraplegic, the cost of the van itself might also be analogized to the cost of purchasing the home itself, which is noncompensable; to argue that these latter costs should be compensable is simply untenable.

Finally, considering only the cost of the van in this case, i.e., $37,940, which would have a limited life expectancy, we would have to further conclude that the expenditure would be prohibitive under *Bomboy*, where the Court found that a cost of $30,000 to $35,000 for additional modifications in the home to accommodate the claimant's wheelchair were unreasonable after the employer had already spent $5,000 to convert the claimant's basement into living quarters. The *Bomboy* Court opined:

> Moreover, in *Rieger*, the employer modified the claimant's home at a cost of $433.02. In this case, the employer had already provided approximately $5,000.00 in modifications, and the claimant now seeks additional modifications, at a cost of approximately $30,000.00 to $35,000.00
>
> Because additional home modifications would result in a substantial cost burden on the employer, and because the claimant proposed no alternatives, we conclude that *Rieger* does not support the claimant's request for an attached garage and a wheelchair lift.

572 A.2d at 250. The cost of providing a $37,940 vehicle would be equally as burdensome.

Accordingly, we affirm the determination of the Board.

Dissenting Opinion by SENIOR JUDGE MIRARCHI [omitted].

NOTES

1. *Limits on Van Modifications.* The holding in *Petrilla* that the employer is only responsible for the cost of modifying a van for a disabled worker, but not for the cost of the van itself is in agreement with decisions in most jurisdictions. *See, e.g., Strickland v. Bowater, Inc.*, 472 S.E.2d 635 (S.C. Ct. App. 1996). Strickland sustained an accident to his head and neck. He was not initially disabled, but underwent surgery to remove a herniated disc. As a result of complications during the surgery, he was rendered a quadriplegic and was awarded permanent total disability benefits. Bowater agreed to pay for the cost of modifying a van for Strickland's use and for the difference in cost between an average mid-sized automobile and an unmodified van. The court decided that Bowater was not required to pay the full cost of the unmodified van.

2. *Limits on Spousal Reimbursement.* The other holding in *Petrilla*, that the employer was not entitled to reimbursement for home nursing care provided by his wife, is not as consistently followed in other jurisdictions. The differences in statutes and facts among cases are important. In *Close v. Superior Excavating Co.*, 693 A.2d 729 (Vt. 1997), the Supreme Court of Vermont affirmed an order of the Commissioner of the Vermont Department of Labor and Industry requiring the employer to pay the worker $207,312 for nursing services provided by his spouse. Close suffered a severe head injury and was subject to seizures, severe disorientation, and memory loss. As a result, he required supervision twenty-four hours a day, as well as assistance in dressing, eating, and taking his

medication. Close's wife was assigned a number of tasks by his physician, which she provided between March 1989, when he was discharged from the hospital, and March 1995, when he was admitted to an assisted-living facility. The court indicated that this was the first case that required an interpretation of the Vermont workers' compensation statute requiring an employer to "furnish reasonable surgical, medical and nursing services." The court reviewed a number of decisions in other states, and found that they reflected a flexible approach, considering such factors as the nature of the services provided, the need for continuous care, the medical condition of the injured worker, and whether a reasonable value can be assigned to the services provided. Using these factors for guidance, the court concluded that the facts in this case justified the payment to the spouse.

3. *Should the Injured Worker be Required to Accept Medical Care and Rehabilitation Services?* In *Turner v. Neeb Kearney & Co.*, 139 So. 2d 3 (La. Ct. App. 1962), the worker recovered to the extent possible through medical treatment. His further recovery would have required exercise or use of the injured shoulder, which he refused to do. The court refused his claim for temporary total disability benefits because "to allow him three or four hundred weeks compensation will destroy all incentive to rehabilitate his arm by exercise." For a discussion of the various incentives for rehabilitation faced by employers and workers, *see* LARSON'S WORKERS' COMPENSATION, § 61.20 (Desk ed. 1997). Are there circumstances when a worker's failure to undergo medical treatment or accept rehabilitation services is warranted, such as a refusal due to a religious dictate?

SHAWNEE MANAGEMENT CORP. v. HAMILTON

Court of Appeals of Virginia
480 S.E.2d 773, *aff'd en banc,* 492 S.E.2d 456 (Va. 1997)

Opinion by CHIEF JUDGE NORMAN K. MOON

Shawnee Management Corporation appeals the decision of the commission awarding Rhonda C. Hamilton benefits. The dispositive question is whether Shawnee must continue paying disability benefits to Hamilton who did not stop smoking cigarettes and/or lose weight as required by her treating physician in order to undergo surgery. We find that because Hamilton's failure to quit smoking renders her unable to receive medical treatment for her compensable injury, her refusal to stop smoking constitutes refusal of medical treatment, and therefore precludes her right to compensation until she complies.

On October 25, 1991, Hamilton, a resident of Winchester Virginia, slipped on a wet floor at her place of employment and injured her back. By agreement, an award was entered for temporary total disability benefits beginning November 2, 1991.

On January 25, 1993, Hamilton underwent back surgery to correct her injuries. About early April she moved from Winchester, Virginia, to Manassas, Virginia, but continued to travel back and forth to Winchester for treatment by Dr. Zoller. On July 20, 1993 Dr. Zoller released her to return to light work with several restrictions. In August, 1993, Shawnee sent a job description to Dr. Zoller, describing a cashier position at a Winchester Hardees. Shawnee intended to offer Hamilton the position pending Dr. Zoller's approval of the job. Dr. Zoller noted in Hamilton's medical records that:

> I got a job description from Shawnee Corporation and I read it to [Hamilton] and I said that there was no way I could legitimately say no to this offer. They are bending over backwards to accommodate her and it certainly seems like it would be doable by anybody other than possibly a quadriplegic.

Hamilton testified that in late August Shawnee offered her the cashier position. She testified that she declined to take the position because her back still hurt and the hour and one-half commute each direction was excessive given that she would only work two or three hours each day. She testified, "I told [Dr. Zoller], you know, since I was so far away that I was going to try to babysit my daughter's kids. I didn't really look at as [sic] refusing, I just — it would have been too far to have drove [sic]." Hamilton also testified that she had looked for work within her capabilities. She testified: "I've applied for jobs. But, ... they don't really want someone that they have to limit. So, I didn't — I wasn't accepted." She also testified that during the two year period in which she could have returned to work, she did not register with the Virginia Employment Commission and applied for work with only three stores.

On September 14, 1993, Shawnee filed an application to suspend Hamilton's benefits on the basis that she had refused selective employment within her residual capacity. Hamilton's benefits were suspended as of September 13, 1993, not on the basis of Shawnee's application, but because Hamilton had failed to keep the commission informed of her mailing address. In December, 1993, Hamilton moved back to Winchester, Virginia.

In August, 1994, Dr. Zoller referred Hamilton to Dr. John P. Kostuik at Johns Hopkins for a second opinion. Dr. Kostuik determined that additional surgery was needed. Both doctors agreed that the procedure should not be undertaken until Hamilton stopped smoking and lost some weight. On or about August 25, 1994, Dr. Zoller wrote to Shawnee's insurance carrier and reiterated that Hamilton could return to work and that she was once again living in Winchester. Dr. Zoller noted that the restrictions for work remained "totally unchanged" from July, 1993.

Hamilton testified that she had previously quit smoking in order to undergo the original back surgery in January, 1993. She stated that she refrained from smoking for sixteen to eighteen months, but explained that "my son got in trouble and my sister kept on, here take a drag and calm your nerves, calm your nerves. So I started up again." Hamilton testified that she smoked two packs of cigarettes a day at the time. Drs. Zoller and Kostuik instructed her to stop in order to undergo the additional surgery. Since that time, Hamilton testified, she has reduced her smoking to five or so cigarettes a day. She has also gained approximately sixty pounds.

On January 3, 1995, Dr. Zoller wrote to Shawnee's insurer explaining that he had changed his mind regarding Hamilton's ability to return to work, stating that "it probably would have been more worthwhile to keep her on with off-work from that time [July 20, 1993] until the present time.... I feel that [Hamilton] should be considered off work the entire period of time, never having been allowed to go back to work." Dr. Zoller noted on February 22, 1995 that Hamilton had not stopped smoking and that they could not proceed with surgery until she stopped.

On January 31, 1995, Hamilton filed a change in condition application seeking temporary total disability benefits beginning September 14, 1993. The deputy commissioner considered Hamilton's application and Shawnee's application still pending from September 14, 1993. The deputy commissioner found Hamilton's failure to stop smoking warranted continued suspension of her benefits until such time as she stopped in order to undergo the corrective surgery. The deputy commissioner specifically declined to reach the other defenses raised by Shawnee or Shawnee's application, although evidence was presented by the parties on these issues.

On Hamilton's appeal, the full commission reversed the deputy commissioner's ruling and summarily disposed of every defense raised by Shawnee and Shawnee's application.

Smoking as Refusal of Medical Care

Workers' compensation benefits may be suspended where a claimant refuses medical treatment. *Davis v. Brown & Williamson Tobacco Co.*, 348 S.E.2d 420, 422 (Va. App. 1986).

Here, Hamilton's continued smoking completely prohibits her from receiving treatment. Hamilton was informed unequivocally that before she could have surgery she must "quit [smoking] altogether." Her doctor explained to her that the surgery she required could not be performed while she continued to smoke and to suffer the effects of routine cigarette use. Until she quits smoking, she will remain totally disabled because of her injury and consequently unable to work. Hamilton's continued smoking constitutes a complete and total bar to her treatment and therefore bars her ability to reenter the work force.

Hamilton is faced with the choice of having to quit smoking entirely or to continue her current condition without treatment. No evidence in the record proved that Hamilton is so addicted to tobacco that she cannot stop smoking. To the contrary, Hamilton testified that she had, on her doctor's order, previously stopped smoking for a period of sixteen to eighteen months. Further, Hamilton

testified that she had reduced her smoking from two packs a day to five cigarettes a day. This record does not support a finding that Hamilton should be
entitled to continue drawing benefits while she chooses to forgo the medical
treatment determined by her doctor. Hamilton's decision to keep smoking,
knowing it prevents her from having surgery, is no more or less than a decision
not to undergo the medical treatment proscribed by her treating physician. Therefore, her benefits should be suspended.

Holding that Hamilton's claim for compensation was properly denied, we need
not reach the additional issue raised by Shawnee concerning whether Hamilton
may refuse selective employment because she has moved away from her original
job location.

Reversed.

Dissent by ELDER, J. [omitted]

H. THE DELIVERY SYSTEM

SANDERS v. BROYHILL FURNITURE INDUSTRIES

Court of Appeals of North Carolina
478 S.E.2d 223 (1996)

LEWIS, JUDGE.

On 16 November 1992, plaintiff filed a request for hearing with the Industrial
Commission seeking compensation for injuries allegedly arising from a work-
related accident occurring on 17 December 1991. After hearing, Deputy Commissioner Dillard found plaintiff not credible and denied his claim. The full
Commission, with Commissioner Sellers dissenting, reversed the Deputy Commissioner and awarded plaintiff temporary total benefits. Defendant-employer
appeals.

At the hearing before the Deputy Commissioner on 23 February 1994, plaintiff
testified that he had worked for defendant Broyhill Furniture Industries
("Broyhill") for about thirty-two years. He testified that in December 1991, he
hurt his back while pulling a truck loaded with stock. He explained that one of
the standards which holds the stock on the truck broke, causing him to fall.
Plaintiff testified that he worked the rest of the day and recalled telling Dwight
Davis, his job supervisor, that he had hurt his back. Mr. Sanders testified that he
could barely walk when he got home that evening, but returned to work the next
day and worked a full day. However, Mr. Sanders testified that he was helped a
great deal by his co-worker, Morris Parsons. Mr. Sanders worked the rest of that
week until Christmas vacation. He worked only two days after Christmas and
was not able to return to work thereafter.

Mr. Parsons, plaintiff's co-worker, testified that he helped Mr. Sanders on the
job during December 1991 but Mr. Sanders never told him that he needed the
help because he had injured his back at work. Dwight Davis, plaintiff's super-

visor at Broyhill, testified that plaintiff never reported to him that he had suffered an injury at work. He further testified that after plaintiff was out of work for several weeks, he tried to contact him to find out how he was doing. Mr. Davis stated that he was told plaintiff was out of work because he was sick.

Reba Cobb, an insurance clerk for Broyhill, testified that Mr. Sanders did not report an injury to her in December 1991. She further testified that she received an out-of-work slip from plaintiff's doctor dated 1 January 1992 explaining that plaintiff was not able to work because of hip pain. Therefore, she testified that it was her understanding that the reason Mr. Sanders was out of work in January 1992 was due to arthritis in his hip. She testified that although she was in close contact with plaintiff and his wife, neither of them told her about an accident at work. The first time she was notified that plaintiff alleged to have suffered a work-related accident was in September 1992.

Plaintiff's medical records, which were stipulated into evidence, contain contradictory accounts of how plaintiff received his injury.

Defendant-employer first argues on appeal that the Industrial Commission erred in finding and concluding that plaintiff suffered a compensable injury by accident on 17 December 1991. Defendant-employer contends that it was error for the Commission to rely solely on plaintiff's testimony, which is not credible. Broyhill maintains that the full Commission should have upheld the finding of the Deputy Commissioner that plaintiff was not credible because only the Deputy Commissioner could observe personally the witnesses.

N.C. Gen. Stat. section 97-85 empowers the full Commission, after application, to review an award of a deputy commissioner and "if good ground be shown therefor, [to] reconsider the evidence, receive further evidence, rehear the parties or their representatives, and, if proper, amend the award." N.C. Gen. Stat. § 97-85 (1991). These powers are "plenary powers to be exercised in the sound discretion of the Commission" and should not be reviewed on appeal absent a manifest abuse of discretion. *Lynch v. Construction Company*, 254 S.E.2d 236, 238 (N.C. App.), *disc. review denied*, 259 S.E.2d 914 (N.C. 1979).

Ordinarily, the full Commission is the sole judge of the credibility of witnesses.... However, in cases where the full Commission does not conduct a hearing and reviews a cold record, this Court has recognized the general rule that "the hearing officer is the best judge of the credibility of witnesses because he is a firsthand observer of witnesses whose testimony he must weigh and accept or reject." *Pollard v. Krispy Waffle*, 304 S.E.2d 762, 764 (N.C. App. 1983).

In *Pollard*, this Court held that the full Commission "has the power to review determinations made by deputy commissioners on the credibility of witnesses" under G.S. 97-85. *Id.* We leave this holding undisturbed. However, we believe that when the Commission reviews a deputy commissioner's credibility determination on a cold record and reverses it without considering that the hearing officer may have been in a better position to make such an observation, it has committed a manifest abuse of its discretion. Accordingly, we hold that prior to reversing the deputy commissioner's credibility findings on review of a cold record, the full Commission must, as it did in *Pollard*, demonstrate in its opinion that it considered the applicability of the general rule which encourages deference to the hearing officer who is the best judge of credibility.

... While the Commission is entitled to overrule the deputy commissioner's ruling on credibility, its determination cannot be made lightly when the deputy commissioner is the only person who has observed the witnesses. Credibility can be decisive in deciding a party's success or failure. Our holding today recognizes this fact and reinforces the widely-held belief that credibility is best judged by those who are present when the record is made.

In civil and criminal trials, trial judges are considered to be the best judge of credibility since they are present to observe the witnesses.... In *Sessoms*, we offered the following explanation for this deference:

> We can only read the record and, of course, the written word must stand on its own. But the trial judge is present for the full sensual effect of the spoken word, with the nuances of meaning revealed in pitch, mimicry and gestures, appearances and postures, shrillness and stridency, calmness and composure, all of which add to or detract from the force of spoken words.

Sessoms, 458 S.E.2d at 203. This reasoning is equally true in the context of Industrial Commission hearings.

In her dissent, Commissioner Sellers voiced concern over the full Commission's treatment of the credibility issue, expressing her opinion that "Commissioners sitting as the Full Commission should exercise great restraint when tempted to replace the evaluation of a deputy, who was actually present to observe the witnesses who testified under oath, with the opinion of a Commissioner, who has reviewed only a cold record and the brief arguments of the party or their counsel." We agree.

We stress that our holding is limited strictly to situations where the full Commission reviews the evidence on a cold record. Clearly, if the witnesses appear before the full Commission, it may make credibility findings without regard to any findings of credibility made by the deputy commissioner. Neither do we lessen the Commission's discretion in determining whether to uphold the deputy commissioner's credibility findings. The Commission is free to reach an opposite conclusion. What we require today is documentation that sufficient consideration was paid to the fact that credibility may be best judged by a first-hand observer of the witness when that observation was the only one. In doing so, we encourage the full Commission to include findings showing why the deputy commissioner's credibility determination should be rejected.

In the present case, the Deputy Commissioner made the following finding: "Plaintiff's testimony regarding the alleged accident is not credible. Plaintiff did not sustain an injury by accident within the course of his employment." The majority of the full Commission, without mention of plaintiff's credibility or its reasons for reversing the deputy commissioner's finding, relied solely on plaintiff's testimony to find that he had suffered an injury by accident within the scope of his employment. For the reasons stated above, we hold that this is a manifest abuse of the Commission's discretion.

We therefore reverse the Industrial Commission's award and remand this case to the Industrial Commission for consideration of the Deputy Commissioner's findings of credibility.

Reversed and remanded.

NOTES

1. *The Scope of Review.* On appeals within a workers' compensation agency (e.g., from an ALJ to a workers' compensation board), the scope of review normally includes both legal and factual determinations made by the ALJ. On appeals from the workers' compensation agency to the courts, the scope of review normally is confined to legal issues, while factual determinations made by the board (or the ALJ) are not subject to review. But what happens if the factual determination is arguably or patently wrong? Consider the following guidance from *Lawrence v. Industrial Commission,* 62 N.E.2d 686, 688 (Ill. 1945):

> [I]f there is any evidence showing or tending to show [an employer-employee] relationship, then the question is one of fact and it is the exclusive duty and province of the commission to weigh the evidence and to draw any and all reasonable inferences therefrom, and its conclusion in such case is final and not subject to review; but where the evidence affecting such question is undisputed and is reasonably susceptible of but a single inference, the question what relation is thereby shown to exist is one of law. If the undisputed facts permit an inference either way, that is, if one reasonable mind may draw one inference and another reasonable mind a different inference from such facts, then the commission alone is empowered to draw the inference and its decision as to the weight of the evidence will not be disturbed on review. While in compensation cases the courts review all questions of law and fact presented by the record, yet it is only where the decision of the Industrial Commission is without substantial foundation in the evidence or its finding is manifestly against the weight of the evidence that such finding is set aside.

Consider three possible holdings by a workers' compensation commission on the issue of whether an injured person is an employee or an independent contractor (a distinction that will determine whether the injured party is eligible for workers' compensation benefits): (1) the commission holds the person is an employee and the undisputed evidence makes patently clear the person is an employee; (2) the commission holds the person is an employee and the undisputed evidence makes patently clear the person is an independent contractor; and

(3) the commission holds the person is an employee and the conflicting evidence indicates that the person probably is an independent contractor. The guidance from the *Lawrence* decision suggests that only in the second situation could the holding of the commission properly be reversed by the court to which the decision has been appealed. Notice, however, that the factual determination of the North Carolina Industrial Commission was challenged by the Court of Appeals in the *Sanders* case, which suggests that courts will sometimes ignore the guidance offered by the *Lawrence* court.

2. *The Courts' Sub Silentio Subversion of the Law-Fact Rubber Stamps.* Is the law-fact distinction strong enough to constrain judicial decision-making? Consider:

> [T]he traditional high court strategy is to hide behind procedure: to first choose, for reasons not stated, whether to give limited or full review to an appellate coverage issue, and then afterwards to attach to that issue, artificially and without regard to plain English meanings, the label of either fact or law. These law-fact rubber stamps sport too many chameleon-like qualities to adequately serve as explanations for the appellate choice of roles; law and fact are instead stand-ins for meaningful appellate accountings. The good news in all this is that law-fact elasticity facilitates the ongoing fine tuning of the legal process by which courts seek, sub silentio, just and efficient means to distribute the power of decision.

John Kenneth Vinson, *Disentangling Law and Fact: Echoes of Proximate Cause in the Workers' Compensation Coverage Formula*, 47 ALA. L. REV. 723-725 (1996).

3. *Justice Delayed is Justice Denied?* One rationale for the substitution of workers' compensation for negligence suits was the long delays associated with the use of the court system. Consider then the plight of Bob Manning. Manning was paralyzed from the neck down and has been granted several awards, the largest being $1.2 million. However, the awards have been tied up in litigation. He has received benefits through the years, but a continuing dispute exists concerning the liability of the carrier to pay for the care that Manning receives from his wife, who is a registered nurse. By May, 1997, all of his benefits had been stopped for a month. In November 1996, a New York appellate panel had ruled that Manning was due the money for his wife's services, but the carrier refused to make the payments because it is appealing the case to the New York Court of Appeals. The lawyer for the carrier was quoted as stating there were "several avenues of new appeals, which he said would take years to resolve, and stated that until those appeals were over, Utilities Mutual 'really is not obligated to make any payments at all.'" Of special interest for this note, though, is that Manning's injury occurred in 1962. David Cay Johnston, *Paralyzed Since Fall in 1962, Man Is Still Seeking Benefits*, N.Y. TIMES, May 5, 1997, at A1.

One interesting aspect of the Manning case is that the case had not been resolved by use of a compromise and release agreement. Such an agreement usually involves three elements: a compromise between the worker's claim and the employer's previous offer concerning the amount of benefits to be paid; the payment of the compromised amount in a lump sum; and the release of the employer from further liability. Compromise and release agreements are commonly used in most states to resolve complicated and/or expensive cases. A likely reason that a compromise and release agreement was not used in *Manning* is that in New York such agreements are limited to nonscheduled PPD cases and are not available for permanent total disability cases such as this. The compromise and release agreements are known as lump-sum settlements in New York.

4. *Bypass of Procedures in Unionized Firms.* An interesting innovation in the administration of workers' compensation has recently emerged in several states, partially due to the frustration of some employers and workers with the delays and expenses associated with processing claims through state workers' compensation agencies. Five states (California, Florida, Kentucky, Maine, and Massachusetts) have enacted laws allowing firms with unions to negotiate their own medical delivery systems and dispute resolution procedures. A favorable review of the initial experience under the Massachusetts law is provided in John H. Lewis, *Improving Workers' Compensation Through Collective Bargaining*, in 1995 Workers' Compensation Year Book I-131 to I-136 (John F. Burton, Jr. & Timothy P. Schmidle eds., 1994).

TERRY THOMASON & JOHN F. BURTON, JR., ECONOMIC EFFECTS OF WORKERS' COMPENSATION IN THE UNITED STATES: PRIVATE INSURANCE AND THE ADMINISTRATION OF COMPENSATION CLAIMS, 11 Journal of Labor Economics, Part 2, S1-S37 (January 1993) [The digest appeared in Workers' Compensation Monitor, Nov.-Dec. 1993, at 21-22.][*]

Digest. The article examines two aspects of the administrative process related to the payment of nonscheduled PPD benefits in New York. One is insurer claims adjustment activity, such as suspension or modification of benefits. The other is the use of compromise and release (C&R) agreements, which involve three elements: a compromise between the worker and the employer (or carrier) about the amount of benefits to be paid; the payment of the compromised amount in a lump sum; and the release of the employer from further liability. Technically, New York does not allow C&R agreements since the lump sum settlements do not involve a release, but the authors (together with Dane Partridge) had previously demonstrated that in practice the New York lump sums are equivalent to C&R agreements. There are distinctive attributes of the New York C&R agreements, however: they are only used for nonscheduled PPD

---

benefits, and they are only available after liability has been established and three months have elapsed since medical treatment was required.

Thomason and Burton provide a literature review on (1) the theory of work injuries, including the empirical studies of the effects of higher benefits on claims frequency and duration and on employer safety activity; and (2) the causes and consequences of C&R agreements, including their use by carriers. The authors also develop a theory concerning the settlement of New York non-scheduled PPD benefits and the determinants of insurer claims adjustment activity. The theory was then tested on a sample of 977 New York compensation claims using regression analysis.

The statistical results support some of the authors' hypotheses. For example, workers with higher preinjury wages and with longer periods of temporary total disability benefits receive higher lump sum awards or, for those cases resolved by Administrative Law Judges, higher adjudicated awards. Also, as predicted, the insurer claims adjustment activity increases the probability of a C&R settlement. However, while insurer adjustment activity tended to reduce the size of lump sum settlements and the size of the adjudicated awards, these relationships were not statistically significant.

Another of the authors' findings is too sensitive to paraphrase:

> As predicted, retention of legal counsel increases the probability of settlement and decreases settlement size, indicating that claimant attorneys are acting contrary to their clients' interests. Specifically, attorneys appear to undervalue the claim, inducing claimants to accept smaller settlements. However, if the claim does go to a hearing, attorneys appear to be successful in obtaining larger judgments for their claimants, although this result is not statistically significant.

Other results are that lump sum settlements are less likely for self-insuring employers and the state insurance fund than for private insurance carriers, and that private carriers offer significantly smaller lump sums than self-insured employers or the state fund. The authors also found, however, that the state fund pursued a more aggressive claims adjustment strategy than private carriers or self-insured employers, which is a result that the authors found "particularly difficult to explain."

The authors used their regression results on the determinants of the size of lump sum settlements and of the amount of weekly benefits for those cases with adjudicated awards to estimate the effect of settlements on the amount of benefits paid to workers. Thus, for a worker who received a lump sum settlement, Thomason and Burton estimated the amount the worker would have received if the worker had decided instead to obtain an adjudicated award, given the worker's personal characteristics, preinjury wage, seriousness of injury, and other explanatory variables. This adjudicated award would have resulted in a weekly award paid over an extended duration of time. The authors found that the discount rate needed to make the present value of the periodic payments equivalent to the amount of the lump sum award ranged from 24 to 25 percent. The authors conclude their article with this translucent paragraph:

Whether discount rates of 24%-25% are excessive is a vexing question. The New York Workers' Compensation Board relies on actuarial tables that translate future income payments into a lump sum amount using a 6% discount rate, and obviously our results indicate that much higher discount rates are used in practice. Interest rates of 20%-30% are, however, commonly paid by low- and middle-income people in transactions outside the workers' compensation context. Judgment as to whether the discount rates estimated for our sample of workers' compensation recipients are excessive thus depends on whether the standard for a just rate is taken from the workers' compensation program or from the market place. As economists, we understand the allure of the market. As students of social insurance, we recognize that workers' compensation reflects society's judgment that sole reliance on the market to deal with work-related injuries is unacceptable. Is the market the lady or the tiger?

NOTE

Attorneys in Workers' Compensation Programs. The results of this study must be used with caution since they are derived from only one state. Nonetheless, New York has certain features — such as a relatively stringent set of criteria before a lump sum agreement will be approved — which may mean that the deleterious effects of C&R agreements are even worse in many other jurisdictions, where agreements are approved by workers' compensation agencies with much less scrutiny than in New York.

One compelling implication of this study — at least for New York — is that workers' compensation policy makers need to carefully evaluate the method used to compensate claimants' attorneys. Casual inspections of workers' compensation data reveals that cash benefits tend to be higher in cases in which attorneys are involved, and there is a natural tendency to assume that attorneys are therefore responsible for the higher benefits. However, this assumption overlooks the likelihood that more serious injuries both result in higher benefits and attract lawyers, which means that the lawyers may not be a source of higher benefits. The article asked several questions: what is the contribution of lawyers to the likelihood of lump sum settlements, to the size of the lump sum awards, and to the size of the awards if the case is adjudicated — after controlling for the severity of the injury and other relevant factors? The findings that attorneys increase the probability of lump sum settlements, reduce the amounts of those settlements, and have no statistically significant effect on the size of litigated awards are disturbing. Unfortunately, these findings are not surprising, given the method used to determine claimants' attorneys' fees in New York (and in most jurisdictions), namely a contingency fee system with the amount of the fee tied to the size of the lump sum settlement.

Suppose we were to use a system for compensating attorneys that tied the amount of the fee to the degree of success in reemploying the worker after the work injury. Or suppose we were to pay attorneys who negotiate lump sum settlements (or, more generally, C&R agreements) as if the benefits were being paid on continuing basis. These fee systems would likely lead to drastic changes in the behavior of attorneys and to the operation of the workers' compensation programs. These methods of compensating attorneys need not result in lower overall fees for attorneys, but should make the incentives for attorneys more consonant with the basic objectives of the workers' compensation program, such as long-term income protection for seriously injured workers, and reemployment of injured workers who are capable of being rehabilitated.

I. ASSESSMENT OF WORKERS' COMPENSATION

MONROE BERKOWITZ & JOHN F. BURTON, JR., PERMANENT DISABILITY BENEFITS IN WORKERS' COMPENSATION 379-82 (1987)*

Efficient Permanent Disability Benefits

The question of efficiency concerns the administrative costs of providing benefits incurred by the participants in the workers' compensation delivery system, including employers, insurance carriers, workers, attorneys, and governmental agencies. The term *efficiency* is used to describe two concepts.... One meaning of efficiency, termed *myopic efficiency,* is that administrative costs are at the lowest possible level without regard to the quality of benefits provided. Although this disregard for quality is usually not made explicit, it appears that what some people mean by maximum efficiency is the cheapest delivery system. The other meaning of efficiency, termed *panoramic efficiency,* is that a particular quality of benefits is provided at the least possible administrative costs. Thus, if two delivery systems provide benefits of equal adequacy and equity, the delivery system that does so with lower administrative costs has greater panoramic efficiency.

We do not believe it is meaningful to say that one delivery system has lower administrative costs than another delivery system unless the differences in the quality of the benefits are specified. Only with the latter information can judgments be made about the relevant concept, namely the panoramic efficiency of the delivery systems....

Evaluation using the efficiency criterion is especially difficult. For one thing, data on the expenses of administering the program that are borne by employers and others in the private sector, the amount of attorneys' fees, and the lags in payments of permanent disability benefits after a workers' condition is permanent and stationary, as well as a variety of other types of data relevant to the assessment of the efficiency of the delivery system, are scarce. Another reason the efficiency criterion is hard to apply is that the quality of benefits and the administrative costs must be simultaneously considered in order to evaluate the panoramic efficiency of a state's workers' compensation program. It would be foolish, for example, to prefer one jurisdiction merely because its administrative costs are lower than the costs in a second jurisdiction. The first jurisdiction's administrative costs may result from lower-quality benefits, and thus represent no greater panoramic efficiency....

Application of the Efficiency Test. An important aspect of the efficiency test concerns the types of delivery system used to provide workers' compensation benefits. One model (typified by Wisconsin) relies on an active state agency that makes many decisions itself, closely supervises the operation of employers and private carriers, and limits the role for attorneys. A considerably different model (typified by the federally operated Longshore and Harbor Workers' Compensation Act) relies on the private parties, particularly attorneys, to make most of the decisions about benefit payments. The agency is essentially passive, although it will resolve disputes brought to it by the private parties. An intermediate model (typified by Florida prior to the 1979 reforms and by California) involves a state agency that conducts a minimal review of the decisions made by the private parties and that resolves disputes in a relatively high proportion of the cases, but that nonetheless relies on extensive attorney involvement to make the delivery system operate.

How attorneys are used is an important feature differentiating these three delivery system models. As recounted by many commentators on the history of workers' compensation, the original notion was that the elimination of the fault concept and the prescription of benefits by statute would enable employees to protect their interest without external assistance. From that standpoint, the substantial reliance on lawyers in California and Florida before 1979 suggests at the minimum a lack of myopic efficiency. And yet, the involvement of attorneys can also be viewed as a *prima facie* indictment of the idea that workers' compensation laws can be self-administering; attorneys may be in the system because they help achieve the criteria of adequate and equitable benefits. In other words, their involvement may represent a lack of myopic efficiency but not a lack of panoramic efficiency. Whether, in fact, attorneys help achieve the equity and adequacy of benefits is not clear *a priori*. On one hand, they receive fees that generally are subtracted from the workers' awards, which, in a nominal sense, reduces the adequacy of the benefits. On the other hand, attorneys increase the awards in some cases in which they are involved and probably have an indirect impact on the amount of benefits in other cases in which they are not involved (similar to the "threat" effect that unions have on wages in nonunionized firms). Thus on *a priori* grounds, the impact of attorneys on the adequacy of benefits is unclear. Likewise, the impact of attorneys on the equity of benefits is unclear. They may take cases in which benefits would otherwise be inappropriately low, or alternatively their involvement may be on a basis unrelated to the relative undercompensation of the case, such as the worker's membership in a union.

The data from Wisconsin, Florida, and California shed some light on the question of whether the use of attorneys improves panoramic efficiency. In terms of the ability to deliver benefits without litigation, Wisconsin clearly surpassed California and Florida before 1979.... More than 5 out of 6 permanent partial disability cases in Wisconsin were resolved without a contest ([a "contest" includes] use of compromise and release agreements). By contrast more than 2 out of 3 Florida permanent disability cases were controverted, and only 1 in 10 California permanent disability cases was resolved by use of informal ratings rather than reliance on a more litigious approach, such as use of a compromise and release agreement or a formal hearing before an Administrative Law Judge. A related finding is that legal fees amounted to only about 3 percent of benefits for the workers in our Wisconsin sample, compared to about 12 percent in Florida and about 6 percent in California.

Wisconsin thus appeared to be superior to California and Florida in the handling of permanent partial disability benefits without excessive litigation, thus providing some evidence that it had greater myopic efficiency. Moreover, the Wisconsin benefits for the workers in our samples were more adequate and more equitable than the Florida and California benefits, suggesting that the Wisconsin delivery system also provided greater panoramic efficiency than the delivery systems in the other two states. We believe this conclusion is valid even when consideration is taken of the administrative expenditures in both the public and private sectors, including the expenses of operating the state workers' compensation agencies and state courts as well as the cost of attorneys' fees for claimants, employers, and carriers. The Wisconsin agency has a particularly impressive record in terms of budget and staff compared to the other jurisdictions in our study ....

The Florida and California delivery systems are representative of the systems in most of the jurisdictions in our 10-state study. There appears to be a general concern for myopic efficiency in workers' compensation, which manifests itself in inadequate resources for state agencies and undue reliance on litigation. The consequence of this narrow concern appears to be a loss of panoramic efficiency.

JOHN F. BURTON, JR. & JAMES R. CHELIUS, WORKPLACE SAFETY AND HEALTH REGULATIONS: RATIONALE AND RESULTS, in GOVERNMENT REGULATION OF THE EMPLOYMENT RELATIONSHIP 253, 264-67 (Bruce E. Kaufman ed., 1997)[*]

Workers' compensation and experience rating. The workers' compensation program in each state relies on two levels of experience rating to promote safety. Industry-level experience rating establishes an insurance rate for each industry that is largely based on prior benefit payments by the industry. Firm-level experience rating determines the workers' compensation premium for each firm above a minimum size by comparing its prior benefit payments to those of other firms in the industry....

The essence of the "pure" neoclassical economics approach is that the introduction of workers' compensation (1) will lead to reduced incentives for workers to avoid injuries, assuming that they did not purchase private disability insurance plans prior to the introduction of workers' compensation, and (2) will lead to reduced incentives for employers to prevent accidents, if assumptions such as perfect experience rating are dropped.

In contrast, the OIE ["old" institutional economics] approach argues that the introduction of workers' compensation with experience rating should improve safety because the limitations of knowledge and mobility and the unequal bargaining power for employees mean that the risk premiums generated in the labor market are inadequate to provide employers the safety incentives postulated by the pure neoclassical economics approach. Commons ..., a leading figure in the OIE approach ... asserted that experience rating provides employers economic incentives to get the "safety spirit" that would otherwise be lacking. [JOHN R. COMMONS, INSTITUTIONAL ECONOMICS: ITS PLACE IN POLITICAL ECONOMY 804-5 (1934).] The modified neoclassical economics approach would also accept the idea that experience rating should help improve safety by providing stronger incentives to employers to avoid accidents.... Where the OIE theorists would probably disassociate themselves from the modified neoclassical economics theorists would be the latter contingent's emphasis on the moral hazard problem aspect of workers' compensation, which could result in more injuries.

A number of recent studies of the workers' compensation program provide evidence that should help us evaluate the virtues of the pure neoclassical economics, the modified neoclassical economics, and the OIE approaches. However, the evidence is inconclusive. One survey of the literature by Boden concluded that: "research on the safety impacts has not provided a clear answer to whether workers' compensation improves workplace safety." [Leslie I. Boden, *Creating Economic Incentives: Lessons from Workers' Compensation Systems, in* PROCEEDINGS OF THE FORTY-SEVENTH ANNUAL MEETING 282, 285 (Industrial Relations Research Association, 1995).] In contrast, a recent survey by Butler found that, with the exception of the study by Chelius and Smith, most recent studies provide statistically significant evidence that experience rating "has had at least some role in improving workplace safety for large firms." [Richard J. Butler, *Safety Incentives in Workers' Compensation, in* 1995 WORKERS' COMPENSATION YEAR BOOK I-82, I-87 (John F. Burton, Jr. & Timothy P. Schmidle eds., 1994); James R. Chelius & Robert S. Smith, *Experience-Rating and Injury Prevention, in* SAFETY AND THE WORKFORCE 128 (John D. Worrall ed., 1983).] Based on our knowledge of the literature, we believe the Butler conclusion is more reasonable, although additional research is clearly warranted in order to support this finding. Some estimates of the magnitude of the safety effect are substantial: Durbin and Butler suggest that a 10% increase in workers' compensation costs may reduce fatality rates by 4.1% to 15.4%. [David Durbin & Richard Butler, *Prevention of Disability from Work Related Sources, in* DISABILITY IN THE WORKPLACE: PREVENTION, COMPENSATION, AND CURE (Terry Thomason et al. eds., forthcoming).] This evidence on experience rating is consistent with the positive impact on safety postulated by the OIE approach and the modified neo-classical economists, and inconsistent with the pure neoclassical view that the use of experience rating should be irrelevant or may even lead to reduced incentives for employers to improve workplace safety.

There is also evidence that the presence of workers' compensation benefits leads to changes in worker behavior. Thomason and Burton summarize a number of studies that found the reported frequency and severity of workers' compensation claims increase in response to higher benefits, which suggests that a moral hazard problem exists. [Terry Thomason & John F. Burton, Jr., *Economic Effects of Workers' Compensation in the United States: Private Insurance and the Administration of Compensation Claims, in* J. LAB. ECON., January 1993, at S1, S8.] Caution is needed in interpreting these studies, however, since the increased frequency or severity reported in the claims can result from a "true injury effect" (workers take more risks as a result of higher benefits and as a result actually experience more injuries) or from the "reporting effect" (workers report claims that would not have been reported as a result of the higher benefits, and/or extend their period of reported disability because of the higher benefits). Most studies of the relationship between workers' compensation benefits and the frequency and severity of claims have not distinguished between the true injury and reporting effects. Durbin and Butler conclude that the latter effect dominates, which implies that the concerns of modified neoclassical economists that the use of workers' compensation benefits to provide ex post compensation for injured workers will lead to more injuries may be exaggerated.

NOTE

Evaluation of Workers' Compensation. Evaluation of the workers' compensation program by use of the criteria of adequacy, equity, and delivery system efficiency is complicated by the decentralized nature of the program. Each state has its own statute and set of practices and so generalizations are difficult. With that caveat in place, what brief assessment is possible?

The compensation goal for workers' compensation requires that two-thirds of income lost because of work-related injuries or diseases be replaced by workers' compensation benefits in order to meet the adequacy standard established by the National Commission on State Workmen's Compensation Laws. At the time the National Commission submitted its report in 1972, only one state met the commission's essential recommendation that the maximum weekly benefit for temporary total disability in each state be at least 100% of that state's average weekly wage. (Since the typical workers' compensation statute provides that the worker gets the *lesser* of two-thirds of the worker's pre-injury wage or the maximum weekly benefit prescribed by the state statute, a low maximum can limit a worker's recovery.) Indeed, at the time the National Commission submitted its report, a majority of states had weekly benefit amounts so low that the most workers in those states could receive was below the national poverty level for a non-farm family of four persons ($79.56 a week). As of January 1997, thirty-two states plus the District of Columbia had maximum weekly benefits that were at least 100% of the jurisdiction's average weekly wage. Thus — with some notable exceptions — most states now probably provide benefits that are generally adequate.*

Workers' compensation has serious equity problems in meeting the compensation goal. While benefits may be generally adequate nationally, significant interstate differences in liberality of benefits mean that workers with similar earnings losses are treated differently depending on where they receive benefits. Consider this westward journey as of January 1997: the maximum weekly benefit for a worker who was permanently and totally disabled was $428 in Indiana, $781 in Illinois, and $873 in Iowa.

The equity problem in workers' compensation involves much more than interstate differences in statutory levels of benefits. There are also significant intrastate differences in how workers are treated. This is particularly true for those workers who receive permanent partial disability benefits. As discussed in MONROE BERKOWITZ & JOHN F. BURTON, JR., PERMANENT DISABILITY BENEFITS IN WORKERS' COMPENSATION 373-78 (1987), the approaches used to provide permanent partial disability benefits do a poor job of matching benefits to actual losses of earnings. Some workers receive more benefits than they experience in lost wages, while other workers have only a small proportion of lost wages replaced by workers' compensation benefits.

The delivery system efficiency criterion as applied to the compensation goal of workers' compensation is also widely violated, as indicated in the Berkowitz and Burton analysis. The costs of the legal system in California — including attorneys' fees, payments to doctors to prepare reports for litigation purposes and to testify, and the state's expenditures for administrative law judges and support personnel for workers' compensation cases — exceeded $1 billion per year in the early 1990s, before declining rapidly in recent years. The irony is that California workers' compensation benefits are relatively inadequate, especially for serious injuries.**

---

* A necessary qualification is that the benefits a workers' compensation statute appears to provide may differ significantly from the benefits that workers actually receive.

** The maximum weekly benefit for a permanently and totally disabled worker was $490 in California as of January 1997.

The prevention goal may be better served by workers' compensation, according to the evidence presented by Burton and Chelius in the preceding article. The workers' compensation approach to prevention may be efficient, since the incentives to safety are produced by the experience rating plans that are relatively easy to administer. However, the approach may not provide adequate incentives for safety because many firms do not qualify for firm-level experience rating. Moreover, an equity problem exists with the workers' compensation approach to promoting safety: it is generally small firms that are not eligible for experience rating and thus receive muted economic incentives to improve safety and health conditions in the workplace.

Chapter 22

THE OCCUPATIONAL SAFETY AND HEALTH ACT

Statutes regulating workplace safety were (along with laws dealing with child labor) the earliest types of protective labor legislation enacted by the states, with many of the statutes dating to the nineteenth century. Workplace safety legislation did not receive significant attention through the first half of the twentieth century, however. This lack of attention was in part due to the generally improving safety statistics for several decades after the introduction of the workers' compensation programs in most states between 1910 and 1920. In addition, with the onset of the depression in the 1930s, other aspects of the labor market received primary attention. Thus the 1930s and the immediate postwar period of the 1940s had significant legislation enacted dealing with areas such as labor-management relations, wages and work hours, unemployment, and retirement income.

Attention shifted to workplace safety and health in the 1960s in part because other areas of the workplace had been dealt with by federal legislation. An even more important explanation for the new focus on safety was the reversal of the downward trend in the injury rate in the manufacturing sector during the 1960s. Although it was not entirely clear what caused the deterioration in workplace safety, a virtual consensus was reached at the federal level that some action was necessary to reverse the trend and that states were unable or unwilling to enact the strict regulations necessary to improve workplace safety and health.

Numerous bills were introduced in Congress in the late 1960s. Leading figures were Senator Harrison Williams, a Democrat from New Jersey, and Congressman William Steiger, a Republican from Wisconsin. The ultimate result was the Occupational Safety and Health Act of 1970 (OSHAct, or the Act), which represented a compromise among the proposals of Williams and Steiger and of ideas from others in Congress and the Nixon administration. The OSHAct was passed with large majorities in both the House and Senate and signed with a strong endorsement by President Nixon on December 29, 1970. The Act became effective 120 days later and soon became one of the most controversial pieces of federal legislation dealing with the workplace. Yet, despite almost three decades of criticism from virtually every interest group concerned about workplace safety and health, the Act has not been significantly amended — in part because the criticisms from parties such as organized labor about lack of vigor in enforcement have been countered by charges from participants such as employer groups about excessive stringency of regulation.

A. AN OVERVIEW OF THE ACT

1. COVERAGE

The OSHAct covers virtually all private sector workers. *See* OSHAct § 4. The primary exceptions are workers covered by other federal safety legislation, such as railroad workers. Federal employees are not covered. State and local government employees are likewise not covered; however, if a state has an approved plan (as described below), state and local employees must be covered. In addition, since fiscal year 1977, Congress has limited or eliminated some aspects of normal enforcement activities for certain employers. Examples are small employers (those with ten or fewer employees) with good safety records, who are exempt from regular inspections, and small farms, which are entirely exempt from the Act.

2. OSHA'S ADMINISTRATIVE STRUCTURE

The OSHAct created three major federal agencies to implement federal policy in occupational safety and health.

First, it created within the Department of Labor the Occupational Safety and Health Administration (OSHA). OSHA is headed by an Assistant Secretary for Occupational Safety and Health and is responsible for promulgating standards, inspecting workplaces for compliance, and prosecuting violations.

Second, it created the National Institute for Occupation Safety and Health (NIOSH) as part of the Department of Health and Human Services (known in 1970 as the Department of Health, Education and Welfare). *See* OSHAct § 22. NIOSH conducts research and makes proposals for new health and safety standards.

Third, it established a new independent agency, the Occupational Safety and Health Review Commission (OSHRC or the Commission). *See* OSHAct § 12. The Commission has three members who are appointed by the President (subject to Senate confirmation). The Commission also contains administrative law judges responsible for the initial level of dispute adjudication between OSHA and a party (usually an employer) charged with a violation of the Act.

In addition, the Act established the National Advisory Committee on Occupation Safety and Health (NACOSH) as a permanent committee of twelve members that represents management, labor, safety and health professionals, and the public. *See* OSHAct § 7(a). The NACOSH advises the Secretaries of Labor and of Health and Human Services on matters relating to the Act. Finally, there are Advisory Committees that assist the Secretary of Labor in evaluating specific proposed health or safety standards.

This separation of functions among agencies differs from the usual agency model. Congress hoped to assure employers that the separation of functions would prevent any one agency from wielding too much power.

3. PROMULGATIONS OF STANDARDS

Congress, in enacting the OSHAct, did not directly prohibit or require specific actions by employers. Instead, section 5(a)(1) subjects the employer to a general duty to "furnish to each of his employees employment and a place of employment which are free from recognized hazards that are causing or are likely to cause death or serious physical harm ...." In addition, section 5(a)(2) requires each employer to "comply with occupational safety and health standards promulgated under this Act."*

The OSHAct approach to standards stands in contrast to some other legislation dealing with the workplace. For example, the National Labor Relations Act (NLRA) contains standards for employer and union behavior in the text of the law, such as the detailed specification in section 8(d) of what the "duty to bargain" entails. The OSHAct text has no equivalent detailed standard, only the vague general duty clause and the requirement to comply with OSHA-promulgated standards. The Act requires that the Secretary of Labor (acting through OSHA) promulgate standards under the administrative procedures specified in the Act, and the Secretary has issued several thousand such occupational safety and health standards. Again, in contrast, under the NLRA, the National Labor Relations Board has issued almost no substantive standards using its rule-making procedure during the sixty years the NLRA has been in effect.

OSHA standards consist of three types: interim standards, emergency temporary standards, and permanent standards. Later sections of this chapter examine each type of standard in detail.

a. Interim Standards

Section 6(a) of the OSHAct authorized the Secretary of Labor to issue interim standards during the first two years of the Act without adhering to the formal rule-making procedure required for new permanent standards. Sometimes referred to as start-up standards, the interim standards were to be derived from either "established Federal standards," which were those already issued by the Federal government under other laws, or from "national consensus standards," which were those already issued by a nationally recognized standards-producing organization. Once promulgated, interim standards remain in effect until revoked or revised using the procedure for new permanent standards.

---

* Section 5(b) requires that each employee shall comply with OSHA standards and all rules, regulations, and orders issued pursuant to the Act. As discussed later in the chapter, court decisions have made this provision unenforceable.

b. Permanent Standards

Permanent standards (including revisions or revocations of interim standards) are covered by section 6(b) of the OSHAct. The procedure for promulgating a permanent standard is elaborate, consisting of several steps:

(i) A standard can be proposed by the Secretary or by any interested party. NIOSH, for example, may conduct research that leads to a proposed standard that is forwarded to the Secretary, who will review and may publish the proposed standard.

(ii) (Optional) An Advisory Committee can assess the proposed standard and provide recommendations to the Secretary.

(iii) The Secretary announces the proposed standard in the Federal Register.

(iv) Any interested party may submit written data or comments on the proposed standard.

(v) Any interested party can file written objections to the proposed rule and request a public hearing, which must be held by the Secretary.

(vi) The Office of Management and Budget, another Executive agency, will review the proposed standard. This step, while not enumerated in the Act, has nonetheless occurred for a number of proposed standards.

(vii) The Secretary shall either issue the proposed standard or a modified standard, or shall make a determination that a standard should not be issued.

(viii) If a standard is promulgated, any person who may be adversely affected may obtain a pre-enforcement review of the standard by filing a petition challenging its validity with the court of appeals for the circuit in which the person resides or has a principal place of business.

(ix) The court of appeals is to uphold the determinations of the Secretary that resulted in the standard "if supported by substantial evidence in the record considered as a whole."

(x) The Supreme Court, at its discretion, may review the decision of the circuit court.

The Small Business Regulatory Enforcement Fairness Act of 1996 (discussed below) has added even more hurdles to the promulgation process for permanent standards. The elaborate procedure plus the difficulties the Secretary has faced in meeting the substantive requirements has resulted in a listless pace of promulgating standards. After twenty-five years, OSHA has issued fewer than 100 health and safety standards after rulemaking. Moreover, most of the health standards and some of the safety standards have been challenged in court, and two of the challenges — those involving the benzene standard and the cotton dust standard — have reached the Supreme Court.

c. Emergency Temporary Standards

Section 6(c) of the OSHAct authorizes the Secretary to issue an emergency temporary standard (ETS) after a much simpler procedure than required under section 6(b) for permanent standards. For an ETS, OSHA need not conduct hearings or use advisory committees. The ETS is effective immediately upon publication in the Federal Register. It can remain in effect for six months (unless replaced earlier by a permanent standard).

To promulgate an ETS, the Secretary must determine "(A) that employees are exposed to grave danger from exposure to substances or agents determined to be toxic or physically harmful or from new hazards, and (B) that such emergency standard is necessary to protect employees from such danger."

4. VARIANCES

Variances to standards can be requested by an employer by filing an application with the Secretary of Labor. There are two types of variances.

Temporary variances are governed by section 6(b)(6)(A). They are granted for a maximum of two years. The employer must satisfy several requirements: (1) the employer cannot meet the standard by its effective date because of a shortage of technical or professional personnel or because construction cannot be completed on time; (2) employees are being protected in the interim; and (3) the standard will be complied with as soon as possible.

Permanent variances are covered by section 6(d). A permanent variance can be granted if the Secretary determines that the employer has provided alternative means to provide a workplace that is as safe and healthful as it would be if the employer had complied with the standard.

5. ENFORCEMENT

The OSHAct gives the Secretary of Labor broad powers to inspect workplaces. *See* OSHAct § 8(a). OSHA has developed a regular inspection program, and will also inspect a particular employer on the basis of an employee complaint. The inspection process is governed by a series of rules, such as the prohibition on advance notice to an employer of an impending inspection. We examine in this chapter other aspects of the inspection process, such as the warrant requirement and the right of an employee to participate in the inspection.

If an OSHA compliance officer finds a violation of the Act, the employer can be cited and sent a notice of a proposed penalty. The penalty can consist of (1) an order to comply with the Act within a specified abatement period, and/or (2) an order to pay a fine.

The fines for employers vary depending on the severity of the offense. For a nonserious violation, the fine is from $0 to $7,000; for a serious violation, the fine is from $1 to $7,000; for a repeat violation, the fine is from $0 to $70,000; for a willful violation, the fine is from $5,000 to $70,000; and for a failure to abate, the fine is from $0 to $7,000 per day. The only criminal penalty under the Act is for a willful violation that results in death, which can result in a fine of up to $70,000 plus a jail sentence of up to six months.

6. PROCEDURE IN CONTESTED CASES

The employer may file a notice of contest within fifteen days of receipt of the notice of the proposed penalty. *See* OSHAct § 10(b). The case will then be referred to the Occupational Safety and Health Review Commission, an agency independent of the Department of Labor. *See* OSHAct § 10(c). The case will be assigned to an Administrative Law Judge at the Commission. A representative of the Secretary of Labor will prosecute the case. Most contested cases are settled without a hearing. If the case does result in a hearing, the ALJ will issue a decision.

The decisions of the ALJ may be appealed to the Commission. There is no right to a review by the Commission, but the ALJ decisions may be reviewed on the basis of a petition for a discretionary review filed by any aggrieved party or a Commission member may direct a review of the ALJ's decision. The Commission has ultimate responsibility for making findings of fact, but will normally defer to the ALJ's findings of fact. If the employer contests the citation, the abatement requirement is tolled until the Commission issues a final order.

The decision of the Commission may in turn be appealed to a United States court of appeals. *See* OSHAct § 11. Any person adversely affected or aggrieved by a final order of the Commission may file a petition for review in the circuit in which the alleged violation occurred, where the employer has its principal office, or in the Court of Appeals for the District of Columbia Circuit. The Secretary may seek review only in the first two of these choices. The filing of a petition with the court of appeals does not automatically operate as a stay on the Commission's order, but the employer can request such a postponement from the court. After the court of appeals issues its decision, the losing party can seek discretionary review from the Supreme Court by filing a petition for a writ of certiorari.

7. IMMINENT DANGER

An imminent danger is defined by section 13(a) as a danger "which could reasonably be expected to cause death or serious physical harm immediately or before the imminence of such danger can be eliminated through the enforcement procedures otherwise provided by this Act." When there is an imminent danger and the employer will not eliminate the danger immediately or remove the employees from the location of the imminent risk, then the OSHAct provides for a special procedure. The Secretary of Labor can seek a temporary restraining order from a U.S. district court on an ex parte basis (i.e., the employer need not be involved) for a period of up to five days. The district court can then provide injunctive relief pending the outcome of the normal enforcement activity described above.

8. STATE PLANS

The OSHAct preempts most state safety and health activities, subject to certain exceptions examined in later sections. Even in those areas where federal preemption operates, however, states can run their own safety and health program if:

> (i) a state agency is designated to run the program;
> (ii) the state agency has sufficient funds and legal authority to conduct the program; and
> (iii) the state health and safety standards are at least as effective as the Federal standards. *See* OSHAct § 18(c).

9. OTHER PROVISIONS OF THE OSHACT

The OSHAct has numerous other provisions. Directly related to workplace safety are the recordkeeping requirements imposed on employers. There are some exceptions to this requirement, including (since 1983) the virtual elimination of recordkeeping responsibilities for employers in the retail trade, finance, insurance, real estate, and services sectors. Other sections of the Act are less relevant for workplace safety and health, such as the provision in section 31 dealing with emergency locator beacons for fixed-wing, powered aircraft.

10. THE SMALL BUSINESS REGULATORY ENFORCEMENT FAIRNESS ACT

In 1996, Congress enacted the Small Business Regulatory Enforcement Fairness Act (SBREFA), Pub. L. No. 104-121, 110 Stat. 857, which will have a major impact on the promulgation of standards under the OSHAct and on the Act's enforcement.

Subtitle A requires OSHA to develop "small entity compliance guides" for essentially all standards. The Act allows the Small Business Administration (SBA) to establish the definition of a small entity (i.e., a small business), and based on prior SBA practice, firms of 100 or fewer employees are likely to fall within the definition. 110 Stat. at 858-59.

Subtitle B requires the SBA to establish an Ombudsman who will act as an advocate for small business in their dealings with OSHA and other regulatory agencies. The Ombudsman will develop ratings for OSHA regional and area offices based on the comments of representatives of small businesses that have been inspected. OSHA is also required to establish a program to provide reductions in, and even waivers of, penalties for small businesses. 110 Stat. at 860-62.

Subtitle C requires OSHA to reimburse small businesses for fees and expenses incurred during agency enforcement actions when a court finds that OSHA actions are unreasonable. This would require OSHA to reimburse the employers' litigation expenses in some instances when the proposed fines have been reduced during the litigation process, even though the employers are found to have violated the law. 110 Stat. at 862-64.

Subtitle D expands the provisions of the Regulatory Flexibility Act (RFA), 5 U.S.C. §§ 601-12, which had been enacted in 1980. The RFA required agencies, such as OSHA, to prepare a regulatory flexibility analysis ("reg-flex") to accompany any notice of a rule that affects small businesses. The reg-flex analysis is required *inter alia* to describe the impact of the rule on small businesses, the objectives and legal basis for the rule, and significant alternatives to the rule that could accomplish the stated objectives while minimizing significant economic impacts on small businesses. The 1980 statute only provided for judicial review of the reg-flex analysis under restricted circumstances. Subtitle D of the SBREFA significantly expands the opportunities for judicial review of rules affecting small businesses, including the agency's responsibility to undertake a periodic review of promulgated rules to see if they should be continued. 110 Stat. 864-68.

Subtitle E requires OSHA, as soon as it issues a new standard, to send a report containing the rule, as well as any supporting analysis, to the House, Senate, and the General Accounting Office (GAO). Within fifteen days, the GAO must report to Congress whether OSHA has properly followed all procedures in developing the rule. Congress then has sixty session days to review the rule. A joint resolution of disapproval can be passed by Congress and a rejected rule cannot take effect or be reissued in substantially the same form except by an Act of Congress or a determination by the President that the rule is in the public interest. 110 Stat. 868-74.

B. SUBSTANTIVE CRITERIA FOR EVALUATION OF OSHA STANDARDS

A recurring issue under the OSHAct is the goals or criteria OSHA should use when creating standards. The most prominent substantive criteria that have been used or proposed are technological feasibility, economic feasibility, benefits to workers' health or safety, and cost-benefit analysis.

These substantive criteria are usually considered in the context of permanent standards issued under section 6(b), but they also apply to some degree to the interim standards under section 6(a), the emergency temporary standards under section 6(c), and the application of the section 5(a) general duty clause. After we review the criteria in this section, we will examine their use for permanent standards and the general duty clause.

1. TECHNOLOGICAL AND ECONOMIC FEASIBILITY

AFL-CIO v. BRENNAN

United States Court of Appeals, Third Circuit
530 F.2d 109 (1975)

GIBBONS, CIRCUIT JUDGE:

The American Federation of Labor and Congress of Industrial Organizations and the Industrial Union Department, AFL-CIO (Petitioners), by a petition filed pursuant to § 6(f) of the Occupational Safety and Health Act (OSHA), challenge the action of the Secretary of Labor (the Secretary) in promulgating on December 3, 1974 a revision of the safety standards applicable to mechanical power presses.... At issue is the Secretary's decision to eliminate the "no hands in dies" standard for mechanical power presses, adopted in 1971....

We conclude that each of the Secretary's reasons for his departure from the no hands in dies standard, whatever its legal merit may be, is supported by substantial evidence in the record as a whole. Thus we now address petitioner's legal challenges.

B. *Relevancy of the Secretary's Reasons*

Petitioner contends that the Secretary's reliance on technological and economic infeasibility, even though his findings to that effect are supported by substantial evidence, was impermissible in standard setting proceedings under OSHA.

(1) *Technological Infeasibility*

Acknowledging that for many applications the no hands in dies standard is technologically infeasible, and that the result of its universal application will be the elimination of some businesses and some jobs, petitioner urges that this is exactly the result that Congress sought to accomplish. Neither this court nor, so far as our research discloses any other court, has construed OSHA in so Procrustean a fashion. Undoubtedly the most certain way to eliminate industrial hazards is to eliminate industry. But the congressional statement of findings and declaration of purpose and policy in § 2 of the Act shows that the upgrading of working conditions, not the complete elimination of hazardous occupations, was the dominant intention. In an enforcement context we have noted that while Congress in enacting OSHA intended to reduce the number of workplace injuries, it did not intend to impose strict liability on employers for unavoidable occupational hazards. *Brennan v. OSHRC*, 502 F.2d 946, 951 (3d Cir. 1974). We do not question that there are industrial activities involving hazards so great and of such little social utility that the Secretary would be justified in concluding that their total prohibition is proper if there is no technologically feasible method of eliminating the operational hazard. But while Congress gave the Secretary license to make such a determination in specific instances, it did not direct him to do so in every instance where total elimination of risk is beyond the reach of present technology. Section 6(b)(5) of the Act, dealing with standards for toxic materials, explicitly confines the Secretary's rule-making authority within technologically feasible boundaries. If the Secretary may consider technological feasibility with respect to the elimination of hazards from toxic materials, then a fortiori he must be permitted to do so with respect to other hazards under the more general language of § 6(a).

Although we hold that the Secretary may, consistent with the statute, consider the technological feasibility of a proposed occupational health and safety standard promulgated pursuant to § 6(a), we agree with the Second Circuit in *Society of Plastics Industry, Inc. v. OSHA,* [509 F.2d 1301, 1308 (2d Cir.), *cert. denied,* 421 U.S. 992 (1975)], that, at least to a limited extent, OSHA is to be viewed as a technology-forcing piece of legislation. Thus the Secretary would not be justified in dismissing an alternative to a proposed health and safety standard as infeasible when the necessary technology looms on today's horizon. Nevertheless, we are satisfied that the Secretary in this case has placed this factor in its proper perspective. The Secretary found, and we believe there is substantial evidence to support such a finding, that compliance with no hands in dies is not technologically feasible in the "near future." This finding necessarily implies consideration both of existing technological capabilities and imminent advances in the art. We do not believe that the Act imposes any heavier obligation.

(2) *Economic Infeasibility*

This court has not yet considered whether OSHA permits the Secretary, in adopting standards, to take into account the likely economic impact of those standards. The text of the statute does not address the point specifically, and the legislative history is at best cloudy. In *Industrial Union Department, AFL-CIO v. Hodgson,* [499 F.2d 467 (D.C. Cir. 1974)], Judge McGowan addresses the issue:

> There can be no question that OSHA represents a decision to require safeguards for the health of employees even if such measures substantially increase production costs. This it not, however, the same thing as saying that Congress intended to require immediate implementation of all protective measures technologically achievable without regard for their economic impact. To the contrary, it would comport with common usage to say that a standard that is prohibitively expensive is not 'feasible.' Senator Javits, author of the amendment that added the phrase in question to the Act, explained it in these terms:
>
> > As a result of this amendment the Secretary, in setting standards, is expressly required to consider feasibility of proposed standards. This is an improvement over the Daniels bill, which might be interpreted to require absolute health and safety in all cases, regardless of feasibility, and the Administration bill, which contains no criteria for standards at all.

The thrust of these remarks would seem to be that practical considerations can temper protective requirements. Congress does not appear to have intended to protect employees by putting their employers out of business — either by requiring protective devices unavailable under existing technology or by making financial viability generally impossible.

This qualification is not intended to provide a route by which recalcitrant employers or industries may avoid the reforms contemplated by the Act. Standards may be economically feasible even though, from the standpoint of employers, they are financially burdensome and affect profit margins adversely. Nor does the concept of economic feasibility necessarily guarantee the continued existence of individual employers. It would appear to be consistent with the purposes of the Act to envisage the economic demise of an employer who has lagged behind the rest of the industry in protecting the health and safety of employees and is consequently financially unable to comply with new standards as quickly as other employers. As the effect becomes more widespread within an industry, the problem of economic feasibility becomes more pressing. For example, if the standard requires changes that only a few leading firms could quickly achieve, delay might be necessary to avoid increasing the concentration of that industry. Similarly, if the competitive structure or posture of the industry would be otherwise adversely affected — perhaps rendered unable to compete with imports or with substitute products — the Secretary could properly consider that factor. These tentative examples are offered not to illustrate concrete instances of economic unfeasibility but rather to suggest the complex elements that may be relevant to such a determination.

Judge McGowan has, we believe, arrived at a proper construction of the statute. Congress did contemplate that the Secretary's rulemaking would put out of business some businesses so marginally efficient or productive as to be unable to follow standards otherwise universally feasible. But we will not impute to congressional silence a direction to the Secretary to disregard the possibility of massive economic dislocation caused by an unreasonable standard. An economically impossible standard would in all likelihood prove unenforceable, inducing employers faced with going out of business to evade rather than comply with the regulation. The Act does vest the Secretary with authority to enforce his regulations, but the burden of enforcing a regulation uniformly ignored by a majority of industry members would prove overwhelming. We therefore conclude that the Secretary may in the weighing process consider the economic consequences of his quasi-legislative standard-setting. We reject the petitioner's contrary contention....

III. *Conclusion*

We conclude that the Secretary's statement of reasons does not adequately disclose why the rule he adopted will better effectuate the purposes of OSHA than would the national consensus standard which it supplants. The cause will be remanded to the Occupational Safety and Health Administration of the Department of Labor for the preparation of a more complete statement of reasons in accordance with this opinion.

NOTE

Regulatory Winners and Losers. In the *Hodgson* case, Judge McGowan argued that OSHA standards may be appropriate even if they drive some employers out of business. He speculated that one concern with such an OSHA standard would be the increased concentration in the industry, which might lead to monopoly pricing. This leads to the more general question: do OSHA standards harm all firms in an industry, or might some firms actually benefit by being relatively lightly hit with the costs of compliance?

Professors Bartel and Thomas have explained the competing influences this way:

> A common error in popular expressions of political economy is the presumption that all firms oppose environmental and safety regulations because these edicts raise business costs. The flaw in this presumption arises from an exclusive focus on what we will call the "direct effects" of regulation — the isolated, partial equilibrium effects of regulation on single firms or individuals. Examples of the direct effects of environmental and safety regulations include increased safety of products and workplaces, decreased emissions of pollutants, and increased manufacturing costs. While direct effects dominate popular perceptions of regulation, the often pronounced heterogeneity among firms gives rise to additional, general equilibrium effects that we will call "indirect effects" — the competitive advantages that arise from the asymmetrical distributions of regulatory effect among different groups of firms and workers. For example, if the cost burden of certain regulations falls heavily on one group of firms and lightly on a second group, then an indirect effect of these regulations is to provide cost advantage to the second group of firms. It is extremely important to recognize that, for many firms and workers, the indirect effects of regulation can outweigh (in terms of economic importance) the direct effects. If the competitive advantage gained through indirect effects is sufficiently large, it can more than offset any direct costs, producing a net benefit for the regulated firm and its workers.... [T]he Occupational Safety and Health Administration (OSHA) cotton dust standard [is] among the many regulations where indirect effects have been shown to predominate.[2]

---

[2] ... On OSHA, see Michael Maloney & Robert McCormick, *A Positive Theory of Environmental Quality Regulation,* 25 J.L. & ECON. 99 (1982); and John Hughes, Wesley Magat, & William Ricks, *The Economic Consequences of the OSHA Cotton Dust Standard,* 29 J.L. & ECON. 29 (1986).

Ann P. Bartel & Lacy Glenn Thomas, *Predation Through Regulation: The Wage and Profit Effects of the Occupational Safety and Health Administration and the Environmental Protection Agency*, 30 J.L. & ECON. 239, 239-40 (1987).

Bartel and Thomas divide indirect effects of OSHA regulation into two types: First is the compliance asymmetry whereby some firms suffer a greater cost burden per unit of output. Generally, firms experience large economies of scale in complying with OSHA regulations, so that the compliance burden falls hardest on smaller firms. Second are enforcement asymmetries. Bartel and Thomas found that the OSHAct was enforced more intensely (per worker) against small, nonunion, and Sun Belt firms.

2. BENEFITS TO WORKERS' HEALTH OR SAFETY

The Secretary must demonstrate through scientific evidence the benefits to workers' health or safety from a proposed standard under section 6 or an enforcement action under the section 5(a) general duty clause. If a proposed standard deals with a substance that is alleged to be carcinogenic (i.e., cancer causing), then the evidence must demonstrate the medical risks associated with current exposure levels and the benefits to health that will result from reduced exposure to the substance.

The scientific evidence can be produced in an epidemiological study, which examines the effect of exposure to the substance on humans, or in animal experiments, which are used to project the likely effect of exposure on humans. Each approach has advantages and disadvantages.

Epidemiological studies have the obvious advantage of relying on direct evidence of the effect on humans of exposure to the substance. There are several disadvantages, however. Historical exposure levels are likely to be high relative to current exposure levels or, more likely, to the levels proposed in a new standard, and so direct evidence on the health benefits of the proposal are unavailable. In addition, many workers have been exposed to a variety of potential carcinogens, and separating the effects of the substance being considered for regulation from the effects of other substances is difficult. The problem is compounded because the data are likely to be incomplete on exposure levels that workers were subjected to in an earlier period, perhaps decades ago — especially if the substance was not a suspected carcinogen at that time.

Another disadvantage of epidemiological studies is that creating a large enough sample of workers to derive statistically reliable results may be difficult, especially if the substance did not have widespread use or if the workers were in an industry with high labor turnover. Overcoming these factors in combination also means that epidemiological studies are likely to be expensive. Finally, but of great significance, most scientists are reluctant to deliberately expose different groups of workers to different levels of exposure to a suspected carcinogen in order to produce compelling evidence about the benefits of reduced exposure that could result from a proposed health standard.

Animal studies allow scientists to overcome some of the difficulties of studies of humans. Animals such as rats or mice are relatively inexpensive and so relatively large numbers can be used to ferret out the differential effects of various exposure levels. Moreover, scientists can restrict exposure to other known carcinogens so the contribution to cancer of the substance of particular interest can be isolated.

One typical characteristic of animal studies does cause a problem, namely the practice of exposing animals to relatively high levels of the suspected substance in order to increase the likelihood that some of the animals in the sample will develop cancer. The projection of the results to lower exposure levels is controversial. An even more serious extrapolation is from animals to humans: mice, rats, and rabbits may be more (or less) susceptible to cancer from a particular substance than humans. Primates, such as monkeys or baboons, may be better sources of data that can be extrapolated to humans, but these animals are more expensive than rodents and thus sample sizes are likely to be smaller. Finally, all animal studies inevitably involve sacrifices of life, and animal rights advocates may object to the studies, even when human lives may thereby be saved.

"Quantitative risk assessment" and "risk analysis" are the terms commonly used in the occupational safety and health area to describe the procedure to establish the benefits to workers of a proposed OSHA standard. Broadly defined, quantitative risk assessment is a method to estimate the likelihood that a particular amount of exposure to a substance will cause cancer.

Quantitative risk assessment (QRA) usually involves two extrapolations: (1) from animals to humans (because most data are from animal studies), and (2) from high doses (exposure levels) to low doses (because most studies involved high levels of exposure). The controversies involving the second extrapolation are represented in Figure 22-1, which involves a hypothetical substance, an industrial soap sold under the tradename of "Grimeoff." The horizontal axis represents the dose levels (in annual washings per worker (wpw)), with greater exposure levels to the suspected carcinogen shown as further to the right on the graph. The vertical axis represents the excess mortality rates (in excess deaths per year per 100,000 workers), with higher death rates shown as further up on the graph.

Figure 22-1

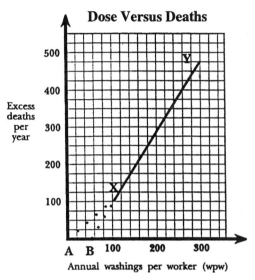

Dose Versus Deaths

Excess deaths per year (vertical axis): 100, 200, 300, 400, 500

Annual washings per worker (wpw) (horizontal axis): A B 100 200 300

The solid line XY is a dose-response curve, which shows the relationship between exposure levels to Grimeoff and excess deaths derived from actual data (which may involve animals or possibly humans). The line XY shows that there is a positive relationship between dose levels of 100 wpw to 300 wpw. But what about the relationship between exposure to Grimeoff of less than 100 wpw? This may be relevant if there is a proposal to adopt an OSHA standard that would reduce the exposure level to 10 wpw. Can such a low exposure level be justified on the basis of quantitative risk assessment?

The answer depends on one's choice of two scientifically competing views. One view is that once a substance has been established as carcinogenic, there is no safe level of exposure to that substance. This view appears to be appropriate for some carcinogens, such as asbestos, for which even a minuscule level of exposure poses some risk of cancer. In terms of Figure 22-1, this view is represented by line AX, which represents a projection of the dose-response curve from the lowest value on line XY (that is, the lowest value for which actual data exist concerning the relationship between exposure to Grimeoff and cancer) through the origin.

A competing view is that even for a substance that is known to be carcinogenic in substantial amounts, there may be a lower threshold below which exposure does not pose a risk of cancer. Most readers will hope this is the accurate description of sunlight, which is known to produce excess skin cancer in those who have had incidents of sunburn. In terms of Figure 22-1, this view is represented by line BX, which represents a straight-line extrapolation from the lowest value on line XY through the horizontal axis at a value of 50 wpw. This extrapolation suggests that there is no risk of cancer associated with 50 or fewer washings per year using Grimeoff.

Alternatively stated, QRA would suggest that a proposed health standard of 10 wpw has a beneficial effect on workers' health if Grimeoff has no safe level of exposure, while the proposed standard is unnecessarily stringent if Grimeoff has a safe threshold of exposure of 50 wpw.

3. COST-BENEFIT ANALYSIS

Another possible criterion for evaluating a proposed health or safety standard is cost-benefit analysis. A standard would be considered desirable or valid if the benefits of the standard equal or exceed its cost. At a certain level of abstraction, it would be hard to argue with the proposition that benefits should equal or exceed costs. As the approach is used by economists, however, there are skeptics.

One controversial aspect is that a monetary value must be assigned to the possible advantages and disadvantages of a proposed activity. In theory, the proper way to measure the benefits of a proposed government program is to determine the maximum amount that beneficiaries are willing to pay for the program. But determining the value that citizens receive from a government program is not easy. Suppose, for example, the government surveys possible beneficiaries of a flood control project. If the government might possibly use the survey results to allocate the costs of the project, then those surveyed have an incentive to understate the true value they place on the project. They know that if the project is completed, they cannot readily be excluded from the benefits of the project even if they have not paid the full value to them. This is referred to as the "free rider" problem.

The free rider problem is one reason why the value of some health or safety standards is difficult to determine. If, for example, a pollution control is installed in a plant that reduces emissions, a particular worker who actually prefers the lower risks of respiratory disease may claim the lower emissions are of no value to her if she thinks the costs of the pollution control may be reflected in a lower wage. Another problem of determining the monetary benefits of a proposed health or safety standard is that most workers are likely to have a hard time answering a question such as: "How much would you be willing to pay for a safety guard on your machine that will reduce the probability of your being killed this year by one chance in ten thousand?"

The economist's solution to the problems of obtaining information from workers about the value they place on safety and health is to rely on information from the labor market. After taking into account all other factors that should affect wages (such as skill levels, education, experience, job stability, working conditions), the economist compares the wages of jobs that differ in their rate of workplace injuries or fatalities. If higher risk jobs pay higher wages, *ceteris paribus,* then the risk premium provides an indirect measure of the value that workers place on their own lives and by inference the amount they are willing to pay for health and safety standards that reduce the chance of losing one's life by a certain probability. Thus, if a wage premium of $300 is typically paid for each increase in the yearly death rate of 1 in 10,000, then a proposed health standard that would reduce the probabilities of death by 2 in 10,000 annually would be worth $600 per year per worker.

Several reasons for skepticism about compensating wage differentials and their use in public policy were provided in the Ehrenberg selection in Chapter 20. Here, we assume that, despite the problems with measuring compensating wage differentials, we can use the measures of risk premium to assign a value to life and in turn to place a monetary value on proposed OSHA health or safety standards. (An alternative source of the value of human life might be the monetary damages found by juries in wrongful death suits.) The value to each worker of reducing the probability of death by 1 in 10,000 times the expected reduction in the probability of death resulting from the OSHA standard times the number of workers who would be affected provides a total dollar figure for the expected annual benefits of the standard. Figure 22-2 plots the total benefits from OSHA standards of different levels of effectiveness. The vertical axis measures total annual benefits (or costs) in dollars, while the horizontal axis measures the size of the OSHA program (with increasingly stringent standards further to the right). The marginal benefits (or costs) are measured by the slope of the total benefits (or total costs) lines.

Figure 22-2

Costs and Benefits of an OSHA Program

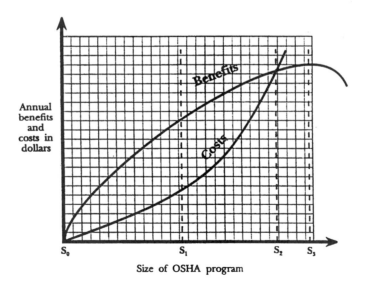

Size of OSHA program

Cost-benefit analysis also requires that costs of the government programs be measured. The costs represent a measure of all the resources used to provide the program, which in the case of an OSHA standard would include matters such as wages of personnel involved in administering or supervising the standard, capital expenditures for safety equipment or for pollution control devices, and costs of training workers. The annual costs of the various size government programs are also plotted in Figure 22-2.

The final step in cost-benefit analysis is to determine the appropriate size of the program (which in the context of OSHA can be understood as the stringency of the standard). Three solutions can be contrasted: (1) the economist's solution, (2) the nontransferable resources solution, and (3) the maximum-safety-at-all-costs solution.

The economist's solution would choose the size of the OSHA program for which the marginal benefit of the program is equal to the marginal cost. In terms of the graph, this occurs where the slopes of the total benefit and cost curves are equal (which is also where the vertical distance between the two programs is greatest). In Figure 22-2, the optimal size of the program is S_1.

The reason why S_1 is the optimal size and not a larger program (such as S_2, where the benefit and cost curves intersect) goes to the essence of the rationale for cost-benefit analysis. Economists argue that the costs are opportunity costs — that is, the resources used for this particular program have alternative uses in the economy. For example, if OSHA did not promulgate a particular standard, the resources thus released could be used elsewhere in the economy to improve highway safety, or support medical research or law school scholarships, or implement an OSHA standard for some other substance. The increase in the OSHA program shown in Figure 22-2 between S_0 and S_1 is pulling resources from elsewhere in the economy at a cost that is less than the benefit of this program: i.e., the marginal benefit of increasing the program exceeds the marginal cost until the program reaches size S_1. Beyond that point, the additional benefits on a larger program are less than the costs of the expanded program: the alternative uses of the resources have greater value than their use in expanding this OSHA program beyond S_1.

The ultimate purpose of cost-benefit analysis is thus to achieve the best possible use of resources in the economy by not using resources on a particular program that have a higher value elsewhere in the economy. An OSHA standard should not be more stringent than the standard represented by program size S_1 because society would be better off using the resources needed for a larger OSHA program in some alternative use. Conversely, an OSHA standard should not be less stringent than the standard represented by S_1 because the additional resources needed to expand this OSHA program to S_1 have lower value in some alternative use.

The nontransferable resources solution rejects the assumption used by economists that resources used for a particular OSHA standard have an opportunity cost. The rejection could be based on a view that society often has unused resources in the form of unemployed workers or idle plant and equipment (or perhaps uninvested savings) that could be used to expand the OSHA program without reducing the size of any other program. An alternative justification for rejecting the opportunity costs approach is a perception that the amount of resources devoted to uses other than OSHA is determined by political factors, and that expanding (or contracting) OSHA will not affect the sizes of these other programs. In this nontransferable resources solution approach, the size of the OSHA program should be expanded until the total costs of the program equal the total benefits, which occurs at size S_2 in Figure 22-2. Between S_1 and S_2, increasing the size of the OSHA program makes the workplace safer. So long as the total costs of OSHA do not exceed the total benefits of the program, supporters of this approach would advocate expanding the program.

The maximum-safety-at-all-costs solution would increase the size of the OSHA program until additional resources devoted to expanding the program would lead to a reduction in safety. This would represent size S_3 in graph 22-2, where the total benefits curve peaks. The downturn in benefits of an expanded OSHA program beyond S_3 might occur if, for example, regulations became so complex that employers began a campaign of massive evasion of the program rather than even trying to comply. Between S_2 and S_3 the excess of the total costs of the OSHA program over the total benefits continues to grow. One possible justification for expanding the program beyond S_2 is that the procedure used to derive the benefits of the OSHA program shown in the graph assumes that the value of life is finite. If, to the contrary, the value of human life is assumed to be infinite, then there is ample justification for expanding the size of the OSHA program so long as one additional life is saved.

Despite the compelling logic (!) that justifies the use of the economist's solution to cost-benefit analysis, the approach is controversial, especially in the context of occupational safety and health. Some persons object to the notion that a monetary value can be placed on life, which is a necessary assumption of this approach. In addition, many object to the validity and usefulness of the research results concerning compensating wage differentials. A number of technical problems associated with cost-benefit analysis makes the approach complicated in practice.[*] Last, but not least, is the issue of the legal status of cost-benefit analysis under the OSHAct. Does OSHA permit, require, or prohibit cost-benefit analysis? We examine that issue in Section D.

---

[*] One example is the treatment of multi-year projects. If, for example, the costs of a new health standard will largely occur in the first five years (while capital equipment is installed and new processes installed) while the benefits may accrue more evenly over twenty years, then deciding the appropriate size of the project is contingent on the size of the discount rate used to determine the present value of the benefits and the costs. With costs concentrated in early years and benefits distributed evenly over the life of the project, the higher the discount rate used to calculate present values, the lower is the ratio of benefits to costs.

C. INTERIM STANDARDS AND EMERGENCY TEMPORARY STANDARDS

1. INTERIM STANDARDS

As noted in Section A of this chapter, section 6(a) of the OSHAct authorized the Secretary of Labor to issue interim standards during the first two years of the Act without adhering to the formal rule-making procedure required for new permanent standards. These start-up standards were to be derived from either "established Federal standards" or from "national consensus standards," which were those already issued by a nationally recognized standards-producing organization. Once promulgated, interim standards remain in effect until revoked or revised using the procedure for new permanent standards.

The Act became effective in April, 1971. In May 1971, the Secretary of Labor promulgated all 4,400 established federal standards, twenty-three months before the deadline for the promulgation of interim standards. Although it is doubtful the Secretary could have carefully scrutinized that many standards even if he had taken the full two years, the immediate adoption of all the potential interim standards caused great controversy.

One source of the controversy was the overwhelming complexity of the rules that employers were suddenly subject to. The interim standards required over 300 pages in the Federal Register, not including some standards that were incorporated by reference. Some of the interim standards were criticized as too vague, while others were attacked as unnecessarily specific and even meddlesome. The mandate for split toilet seats and the prohibition on ice water for drinking became part of the litany of the caustic attacks on the interim standards.

> 29 C.F.R. § 1910.141 (1971). Sanitation.
> (b) Water supply — (1) Potable water
>   (iii) In all instances where water is cooled by ice, the construction of the container shall be such that the ice does not come in direct contact with the water.
> (c) Toilet facilities — (2) Construction and installation of toilet facilities.
>   (ii) Every water closet shall have a hinged openfront seat made of substantial material having a nonabsorbent finish.[*]

In response to the widespread criticism of the interim standards, OSHA deleted approximately 600 safety standards in 1978 on the grounds that the standards were either obsolete, directed to comfort rather than safety, directed to the public rather than to employees, enforced by other agencies, contingent on manufacturer approval, too detailed, or covered by other standards.

---

[*] The ice water standard was rescinded in 1973. The open-front toilet-seat standard was revised in 1973 to apply only to seats installed or replaced after June 4, 1973. The standard was rescinded in 1978.

Another problem was that many of the consensus standards from which the interim standards were derived contained advisory rather than mandatory language. For example, the American National Standards Institute (ANSI) scaffolding standard suggested that "[g]uardrails and toeboards *should* be installed on all open sides and ends of platforms more than 10 feet above the ground or floor." In promulgating the interim scaffolding standard, the Secretary of Labor altered the ANSI standard to read: "Guardrails and toeboards *shall* be installed on all open sides and ends of platforms more than 10 feet above the ground or floor" (emphasis added). In *Usery v. Kennecott Copper Corp.,* 577 F.2d 1113, 1117-18 (10th Cir. 1977), the court struck down the standard because of the alteration:

> We hold that the Secretary did not comply with the statute by reason of his failure to adopt the ANSI standard verbatim or by failure to follow the appropriate due process procedure. The promulgation of the standard with the use of *shall* rather than *should* did not constitute the adoption of a national consensus standard. It is, therefore, unenforceable. In order for the Secretary to have rendered the standard enforceable with the change in language, he was obliged to observe the rulemaking procedures contained in the Act [for a permanent standard].

The problems resulting from unenforceable interim standards were compounded by a decision of the Commission in *A. Prokosch & Sons Sheet Metal,* 8 O.S.H. Cas. (BNA) 2077 (1980). Most courts have held that the general duty clause (which will be examined in Section E) cannot be used as a basis for a citation against an employer when there is a specific standard applicable to the hazard.* In *Prokosch,* the Commission held that use of the general duty clause was blocked even if the standard itself was unenforceable because the Secretary had converted a "should" in the consensus standard into a "shall" in the interim standard. In response to this decision, in 1984 OSHA formally removed 153 provisions of the general industry standards that had adapted advisory standards from ANSI. Rather than promulgate permanent standards in their place, OSHA decided to rely on other general industry standards with mandatory language, or upon the general duty clause, to enforce the Act in these areas.

Despite these deletions, the remaining interim standards adopted in 1971 constitute the bulk of the OSHA standards that are currently in effect.

2. EMERGENCY TEMPORARY STANDARDS

In enacting the OSHAct, Congress contemplated that OSHA might have to react to a grave danger with a quickly promulgated standard. Thus, in section

---

* The D.C. Circuit Court of Appeals has permitted a citation against an employer based on the general duty clause even when a specific standard applied to the hazard. The decision, *UAW v. General Dynamics Land Systems Division,* 815 F.2d 1570 (D.C. Cir. 1987) is discussed in Section E.

6(c) it authorized the Secretary to issue an emergency temporary standard (ETS) after a much simpler procedure than required under section 6(b) for permanent standards. For an ETS, OSHA need not conduct hearings or use advisory committees. The ETS is effective immediately upon publication in the Federal Register. It can remain in effect for six months (unless replaced earlier by a permanent standard).

OSHA has issued only nine emergency temporary standards in the history of the Act. Of these, only three were not challenged in court and went into effect. One ETS — for acrylonitrile, a chemical used in textile production — was challenged but went into effect when the Sixth Circuit denied a stay. The other five ETSs were vacated or stayed by the courts.

The 1983 asbestos ETS. The experience with the 1983 ETS for asbestos indicates the extreme difficulty that OSHA has experienced with the courts, and in particular with the Fifth Circuit, in issuing emergency temporary standards. OSHA issued the original asbestos standard in 1971 as an interim standard under section 6(a). It provided for a permissible exposure limit (PEL) of 12 fibers per cubic centimeter (12 f/cc). OSHA issued a new permanent standard in 1972 that provided for a PEL of 2.0 f/cc after four years. In 1975, OSHA proposed an even more stringent permanent standard for asbestos with a PEL of 0.5 f/cc, but that standard was never promulgated.

In 1983, OSHA revisited the asbestos health issue and issued an emergency temporary standard, which also lowered the PEL for asbestos to 0.5 f/cc. OSHA wrote a preamble to the proposed ETS indicating that the standard was based on information that postdated the 1975 proposal and therefore was a "new regulatory initiative."

The 1983 ETS for asbestos was invalidated by the Fifth Circuit in *Asbestos Information Ass'n/N.A. v. OSHA,* 727 F.2d 415 (5th Cir. 1984). The court noted that OSHA had relied on quantitative risk assessments (QRAs) to conclude that a grave danger existed if exposure to asbestos continued at the PEL of 2.0 f/cc. OSHA concluded that eighty lives could be saved by lowering the PEL to 0.5 f/cc for six months. The conclusion was based on eleven epidemiological studies that had been used for QRAs for lung cancer. Four of these studies were also used to compute risk assessments for mesothelioma, another type of cancer. The epidemiological studies were based on data for approximately 53,000 workers, and the QRAs derived from these studies were favorably reviewed by several experts selected by OSHA.

The Fifth Circuit indicated that the ETS provision is "an extraordinary power to be used only in 'limited situations' in which a grave danger exists, and then, to be 'delicately exercised.' The Agency cannot use its ETS powers as a stop-gap measure." The court nonetheless agreed with OSHA that new awareness of the danger of asbestos derived from QRAs could justify the Secretary's action to issue an ETS. Moreover, the court indicated that formal cost-benefit analysis was not required before OSHA could promulgate an ETS, although "an ETS must, on balance, produce a benefit the costs of which are not unreasonable." The court agreed that OSHA had demonstrated that the cost of compliance with the asbestos ETS was not unreasonable "if the ETS in fact alleviates a grave danger." In addition, the Fifth Circuit stated that "[t]he Secretary determined that eighty lives at risk is a grave danger. We are not prepared to say it is not."

Nevertheless, while QRA is an acceptable means to determine the benefits of a proposed ETS, and while eighty lives at risk constitutes a grave risk, the court was not persuaded that OSHA had demonstrated that the asbestos ETS would save eighty lives. The court concluded that the standard under which it would review the consequences of the asbestos PEL "is whether the Agency's action is supported by substantial evidence in the record considered as a whole." The court stated that:

> OSHA has made the *number* of deaths avoided — at least 80 — the basis for its rulemaking. Yet it is apparent from an examination of the record that the actual number of lives saved is uncertain, and is likely to be substantially less than 80. Both the gravity of the risk as defined by OSHA and the necessity of an ETS to protect against it are therefore questionable.

Id. at 425.

The Fifth Circuit specifically questioned the use of QRA to project the savings in life from a six-month period. While the court indicated that

> risk assessment analysis is an extremely useful tool, especially when used to project lifetime consequences of exposure, the results of its application to a small slice of time are speculative because the underlying data-base projects only long-term risks. Epidemiologists generally study only the consequences of long-term exposure to asbestos. Indeed, OSHA concedes some unreliability and uncertainty to be inherent in risk assessment generally. Applying the risk assessment process to a period of six months, one-ninetieth of OSHA's estimated working lifetime, only magnifies those inherent uncertainties.

Id. at 425-426.

The court also found uncertainty concerning the beneficial effect of the ETS from the fact that OSHA was not fully enforcing the current asbestos standard. The court stated that because of "the added saving obtainable by application of the current regulations, we must assume that OSHA's claimed benefit should be discounted by some additional, uncertain amount." Because of these various uncertainties concerning the benefits that would result from the proposed ETS, the court held that "an ETS that lacks support in the record for the basis OSHA has articulated must be declared invalid."

Criticism of the Fifth Circuit. The data on the consequences of exposure to asbestos are better than the data for most other substances, and the consequences of such exposure are particularly lethal. If OSHA cannot convince a court of the need for an ETS for asbestos, it will be hard to get any ETS approved. As one scholar commented:

> The court's opinion is subject to a variety of criticisms. Simply stated, the court is requiring OSHA to do the impossible. If the ETS were not accompanied by a quantitative risk assessment of the expected benefits, undoubtedly the court would have held the ETS to be invalid. OSHA, however, performed a detailed risk assessment based on epidemiological evidence and calculated the number of lives expected to be saved. Differences of opinion over mathematical models should not obscure the fact that under any model a substantial number of lives would be saved by the ETS. It is *never* possible to predict precisely the effects of exposure on thousands of workers — nor is such evidence required.

MARK ROTHSTEIN, OCCUPATIONAL SAFETY AND HEALTH ACT § 80 (3d ed. 1990).

Requiem for emergency temporary standards. As a practical matter, the ETS provision in the OSHAct is probably moribund. The challenge of convincing the courts that employees are exposed to a grave danger and that the emergency temporary standard is necessary to protect the employees from the danger is formidable. Moreover, the ETS expires no later than six months after publication, and given the long delays in issuing permanent standards (discussed in the next section), the ETS would probably lapse long before a new permanent standard could take effect.

Efforts by unions and other groups to persuade the Secretary of Labor to issue ETSs have been unsuccessful in the 1990s. Thus, in 1992, the Secretary denied a petition to issue an ETS on ergonomic hazards in an effort to deal with the rapid increase in cumulative trauma disorders. She justified her denial in part on the traditional view that only conditions posing life-threatening, incurable, or fatal injury or illnesses would constitute a grave danger warranting an ETS. Cumulative trauma disorders, in contrast, only produce conditions such as carpal tunnel syndrome, which can lead to permanent damage to the wrist and hand, but is not life threatening.

D. PROMULGATING PERMANENT STANDARDS

The development and promulgation of new standards was to be at the heart of the OSHAct. After more than a quarter century, however, OSHA has promulgated only about fifty permanent health and safety standards. In large part, this glacial pace is due to the elaborate procedure for creating permanent standards, outlined in Section A of this chapter.

1. SCOPE OF JUDICIAL REVIEW

One reason for the slow pace of the promulgation of new standards under section 6(b) is the amount of effort that OSHA has devoted to defending the standards in court. After the Secretary has promulgated the standard, any person who may be adversely affected may obtain pre-enforcement review of the standard by filing a petition challenging the validity of the standard.

Section 6(f) of the OSHAct instructs the reviewing court to uphold the Secretary's determinations "if supported by substantial evidence in the record considered as a whole." The congressional command to use "substantial evidence" review is unusual for agency proceedings like OSHA's. Normally, courts review for substantial evidence when agencies have made determinations of fact in the course of formal, trial-like proceedings.* It is unclear how courts should review for substantial evidence when the agency decision is based on a policy preference. The more common standard for courts in reviewing informal rulemaking — a standard contemplated by the Administrative Procedure Act section 706(2) — is to uphold the agency decision unless it is "arbitrary and capricious."

The landmark OSHA case concerning the standard of review is *Industrial Union Department v. Hodgson*, 499 F.2d 467 (D.C. Cir. 1974). In reviewing an OSHA standard for asbestos, the court noted that the administrative record differed from one "customarily conceived of as appropriate for substantial evidence review,"** and emphasized that the Secretary's determinations "are on the frontiers of scientific knowledge, and consequently ... depend to a greater extent upon policy judgments and less upon purely factual analysis." The court declared that it would use the substantial evidence standard to review the facts underlying the Secretary's determinations. But when reviewing policy judgments, it would "approach our reviewing task with a flexibility informed and shaped by sensitivity to the diverse origins of the determinations that enter into a legislative judgment."

At the opposite extreme, the Fifth Circuit has been unwilling to disavow the substantial evidence formulation. In *National Grain & Feed Ass'n v. OSHA*, 858

---

* Usually agencies use formal proceedings (complete with on-the-record oral hearings and right to cross-examine witnesses) when adjudicating whether an individual has complied with existing rules. An example is an OSHRC proceeding to determine whether an employer has violated its duties under the Act. OSHAct § 11(a) is typical in instructing courts, in reviewing Commission orders, to treat Commission findings of fact as conclusive "if supported by substantial evidence on the record considered as a whole."

** As the court in *Hodgson* noted, section 6(b)(3) of the OSHAct requires the Secretary upon request to hold a public hearing about the proposed standard. In part to provide a record to which a reviewing court could meaningfully apply the substantial evidence test, the Secretary by regulation has given this hearing some of the attributes of the adjudicatory or formal rulemaking model. In particular, the Secretary called for a hearing examiner to preside and allowed an opportunity for cross-examination "on crucial issues."

F.2d 1019 (5th Cir. 1988), *on reconsideration,* 866 F.2d 717 (5th Cir. 1989), *cert. denied,* 490 U.S. 1065 (1989), the court declared that it would apply the substantial evidence test to OSHA's legislative policy decisions as well as to its factual findings.

The real question, of course, is whether the choice of a review standard makes any difference. In 1970, when Congress required "substantial evidence" review of OSHA standards, Congress may have been signaling courts to engage in a more intense review than was traditionally done under the arbitrary and capricious standard. However, during the 1970s (after Congress enacted the OSHAct), the federal courts of appeals began to put more teeth into the arbitrary and capricious standard, requiring a "hard look" into the results of informal agency rulemaking. With the "hard look" gloss, there has come to be less difference in intensity between the arbitrary and capricious standard of review and review using the substantial evidence test.

The Supreme Court has sent conflicting signals about "hard look." For example, in *Motor Vehicle Manufacturers Ass'n v. State Farm Mututal Automobile Insurance Co.,* 463 U.S. 29 (1983), the Court employed much of the terminology of "hard look" in holding that a Department of Transportation decision to rescind its seat-belt safety standard was arbitrary and capricious. That same term, however, the Supreme Court applied a deferential arbitrary and capricious standard in upholding an agency determination that the environmental uncertainties in storing nuclear waste should not affect the decision to license a particular nuclear power plant. *Baltimore Gas & Electric Co. v. NRDC,* 462 U.S. 87 (1983). The Court, citing its 1980 case reviewing OSHA's benzene standard, warned that when an agency "is making predictions, within its area of special expertise, at the frontiers of science..., a reviewing court must generally be at its most deferential." If the deferential style of arbitrary and capricious review again becomes more common, Congress's 1970 decision to require "substantial evidence" review of OSHA standards could again have the effect of subjecting OSHA to more stringent judicial review than that typically accorded agency rulemaking.

Color Pigments Manufacturers Ass'n v. OSHA, 16 F.3d 1157 (11th Cir. 1994), examined the standard of review for OSHA standards. The court endorsed an interpretation of the substantial evidence standard that does not require OSHA to prove there is but one possible conclusion:

> The existence of a viable alternative does not preclude the acceptance of an agency determination as supported by substantial evidence. All that needs to be shown is that OSHA's determination is supported by evidence presented to or produced by it and does not rest on faulty assumptions or factual foundations.
>
> Nevertheless, while the standard is not so stringent as a preponderance of the evidence test, it does require us "to take a 'harder look' at OSHA's action than we would if we were reviewing the action under the more defer-

ential arbitrary and capricious standard applicable to agencies governed by the Administrative Procedure Act.'"

Id. at 1160.

2. SUBSTANTIVE CRITERIA FOR STANDARDS

The Act does not clearly enunciate the substantive criteria to be used by OSHA in setting standards. Section 6(b)(5) provides in part that:

> The Secretary, in promulgating standards dealing with toxic material or harmful physical agents under this subsection, shall set the standard which most adequately assures, to the extent feasible, on the basis of the best available evidence, that no employee will suffer material impairment of health or functional capacity .... In addition to the attainment of the highest degree of health and safety protection for the employee, other considerations shall be the latest available scientific data in the field, the feasibility of the standards, and experience gained under this and other health and safety laws. Whenever practicable, the standard promulgated shall be expressed in terms of objective criteria and of the performance desired.

If that language does not guarantee full employment for lawyers in litigating phrases such as "to the extent feasible" and "the feasibility of the standards," consider the further guidance provided in section 3(8), the definitions section for the Act:

> The term "occupational safety and health standard" means a standard which requires conditions, or the adoption or use of one or more practices, means, methods, operations or processes, reasonably necessary or appropriate to provide safe or healthful employment and places of employment.

The key legal issue here is the meaning of feasibility. As discussed above, feasibility might mean:

(1) technological feasibility;
(2) economic feasibility;
(3) benefits to workers' health or safety; and
(4) cost-benefit analysis.

Is OSHA forbidden, permitted, or required to use any of these criteria? The greatest controversy surrounds the meaning of benefits to workers' health or safety, and the permissibility of cost-benefit analysis.

Industrial Union Dep't v. American Petroleum Inst. (The Benzene Case), 448 U.S. 607 (1980). The Supreme Court's first attempt at these issues arose in its review of OSHA's benzene standard, a substance known (at least at high dosages) to cause leukemia. Promulgated in 1978, that standard revised an interim standard, reducing the maximum permissible exposure level (PEL) for benzene from 10 parts per million (ppm) averaged over 8 hours to 1 ppm averaged over 8 hours. The new standard also reduced the short-term exposure level to a maximum of 5 ppm over any 5 minutes. OSHA had no animal data on benzene and the epidemiological data primarily involved human exposures at concentrations well above the previous standard's level of 10 ppm. In the absence of data concerning the excess risk of leukemia at exposure levels below 10 ppm, OSHA assumed a positive dose-response relationship between exposure to benzene and excess mortality and also assumed that there was no safe level of benzene. In essence, OSHA argued that the only limits on the degree of stringency of the standard were technological and economic feasibility.

Upon review under section 6(f), the Court of Appeals for the Fifth Circuit vacated the benzene standard[*] on two grounds: (1) OSHA had failed to provide evidence concerning the expected benefits that would result from reducing the PEL, and (2) OSHA had failed to compare the benefits and costs of the proposed standard.

The Supreme Court affirmed the judgment of the Court of Appeals, but without a majority opinion. Justice Stevens wrote the plurality opinion, joined by Justices Burger and Stewart. In that opinion, Justice Stevens finessed the cost-benefit issue by finding that section 3(8) imposes a threshold burden upon OSHA to show that the new benzene standard would benefit the health of workers by alleviating a significant risk, a burden that OSHA did not carry.

> Our resolution of the issues in these cases turns, to a large extent, on the meaning of the relationship between § 3(8), which defines a health and safety standard as a standard that is "reasonably necessary and appropriate to provide safe or healthful employment," and § 6(b)(5), which directs the Secretary in promulgating a health and safety standard for toxic materials to "set the standard which most adequately assures, to the extent feasible, on the basis of the best available evidence, that no employee will suffer material impairment of health or functional capacity...."
>
> By empowering the Secretary to promulgate standards that are "reasonably necessary or appropriate to provide safe or healthful employment and places of employment," the Act implies that, before promulgating any standard, the Secretary must make a finding that the workplaces in question are not safe. But "safe" is not the equivalent of "risk-free." There are many activities that we engage in every day — such as driving a car or even breathing city air — that entail some risk of accident or material health

---

[*] In 1977, OSHA had issued an Emergency Temporary Standard for benzene. The Fifth Circuit issued a temporary restraining order preventing the emergency standard from taking effect.

impairment; nevertheless, few people would consider these activities "unsafe." Similarly, a workplace can hardly be considered "unsafe" unless it threatens the workers with a significant risk of harm.

Therefore, before he can promulgate *any* permanent health or safety standard, the Secretary is required to make a threshold finding that a place of employment is unsafe — in the sense that significant risks are present and can be eliminated or lessened by a change in practices. This requirement applies to permanent standards promulgated pursuant to § 6(b)(5), as well as to other types of permanent standards. For there is no reason why § 3(8)'s definition of a standard should not be deemed incorporated by reference into § 6(b)(5). The standards promulgated pursuant to § 6(b)(5) are just one species of the genus of standards governed by the basic requirement. That section repeatedly uses the term "standard" without suggesting any exception from, or qualification of, the general definition; on the contrary, it directs the Secretary to select *"the* standard" — that is to say, one of various possible alternatives that satisfy the basic definition in § 3(8) — that is most protective. Moreover, requiring the Secretary to make a threshold finding of significant risk is consistent with the scope of the regulatory power granted to him by § 6(b)(5), which empowers the Secretary to promulgate standards, not for chemicals and physical agents generally, but for *"toxic* materials" and *"harmful* physical agents."

In applying this threshold test to the benzene standard, Justice Stevens first rejected OSHA's carcinogen policy. OSHA's carcinogen policy, never formally promulgated as a standard, states that whenever a carcinogen is involved, in the absence of definitive proof of a safe level OSHA will assume that any level above zero presents some increased risk of cancer. In rejecting the carcinogen policy, Justice Stevens pointed out that "there are literally thousands of substances used in the workplace that have been identified as carcinogens or suspect carcinogens, [and] the Government's theory would give OSHA power to impose enormous costs that might produce little, if any, discernible benefit."

Justice Stevens also rejected OSHA's contention that even if its carcinogen policy was found to be invalid, the benzene standard was still valid under OSHA's mandate to regulate hazardous materials. While OSHA's written explanation of the standard filled 184 pages of the printed appendix, Stevens found it "noteworthy" that at no point in its explanation did OSHA quote or cite section 3(8) of the Act, and OSHA never made a finding that the new standard was reasonably necessary or appropriate to provide safe or healthful employment.

Justice Powell, concurring in part, was the only Justice expressly reaching the cost-benefit question. Justice Powell agreed with the plurality that OSHA had not met the threshold requirement of section 3(8). But even if OSHA had properly met this burden, Justice Powell argued, the statute also requires OSHA to determine that "the economic effects of its standard bear a reasonable relationship to the expected benefits." Justice Powell found this type of cost-benefit

analysis necessary since "an occupational standard is neither 'reasonably necessary' nor 'feasible' ... if it calls for expenditures wholly disproportionate to the
expected health and safety benefits."

Justice Rehnquist provided the fifth vote to strike down the benzene standard,
but he refused to join Justice Stevens's analysis. Instead, he would have struck
down OSHA's authority to promulgate standards under section 6(b)(5) as an
unconstitutional delegation of Congress's authority to legislate, a position he
repeated the following year in the *Cotton Dust* case.

Justice Marshall, on behalf of four Justices, dissented in the case. He would
have upheld the benzene standard as being properly based on "feasibility
analysis."

NOTES

1. *Significant Risk Test.* Justice Stevens's threshold test, in essence, demands
that the proposed OSHA standard must benefit workers' health. This test, usually
referred to as the significant risk test, requires that OSHA (1) show that the
current exposure level for a substance (such as benzene) represents a significant
risk to workers, and (2) demonstrate by substantial evidence that the new standard would eliminate or reduce the risk. This evidence cannot rely on extrapolations of the type represented by line AX in Figure 22-1, which, as you will
recall, ultimately rested on an assumption that there is no safe exposure level to a
carcinogen.

OSHA soon adapted to the requirements imposed by the *Benzene* decision.
Within months after the *Benzene* decision, the Court of Appeals for the District
of Columbia, in *United Steelworkers v. Marshall,* 647 F.2d 1189 (D.C. Cir.
1980), *cert. denied,* 453 U.S. 913 (1981), upheld OSHA's 50-microgram
standard for lead exposures and indicated that OSHA clearly met the significant
risk test by providing substantial evidence that the previous exposure level to
lead posed a significant risk to workers and that the proposed standard would
reduce this risk.

2. *What Constitutes a Significant Risk?* The plurality opinion by Justice
Stevens in the *Benzene* case contains this passage:

> It is the Agency's responsibility to determine, in the first instance, what it
> considers to be a "significant" risk. Some risks are plainly acceptable and
> others are plainly unacceptable. If, for example, the odds are one in a billion
> that a person will die from cancer by taking a drink of chlorinated water, the
> risk clearly could not be considered significant. On the other hand, if the
> odds are one in a thousand that regular inhalation of gasoline vapors that are
> 2% benzene will be fatal, a reasonable person might well consider the risk
> significant and take appropriate steps to decrease or eliminate it. Although
> the Agency has no duty to calculate the exact probability of harm, it does
> have an obligation to find that a significant risk is present before it can
> characterize a place of employment as "unsafe."

448 U.S. at 607. The courts and OSHA have used this language as a starting point for defining the meaning of significant risk. The Supreme Court's formulation is ambiguous concerning the period during which the exposure is to be measured. The chlorinated water example ("taking a drink") sounds as if the risk is to be determined for a single exposure to the carcinogen, while the gasoline vapors example ("regular inhalation") indicates that the risk is to be measured over an extended time period. The Court's formulation is also unclear about the time period during which the cancer is supposed to occur. Does the "one in a thousand" refer to the odds of developing cancer in a short period, such as a month or a year, or to the odds of developing cancer over a longer period, such as a lifetime?

The court in *United Auto Workers v. Pendergrass,* 878 F.2d 389 (D.C. Cir. 1989), helped answer these questions. The case involved new standards for formaldehyde, which reduced the permissible exposure limit ("PEL") to one part per million ("ppm") as an 8-hour time-weighted average and the short-term exposure limit ("STEL") to 2 ppm. The court remanded the case to OSHA for reconsideration of its calculation of the risk of cancer from formaldehyde at 1 ppm. OSHA had failed to explain its finding that the 1 ppm level of exposure resulted in an insignificant risk. The opinion indicated that a significant risk exists if (1) there is a one in a thousand chance that a worker will develop cancer during the worker's lifetime, and (2) that risk results from exposure during a working career to formaldehyde at the PEL of 1 ppm. The issue of what constitutes a significant risk is examined further in the next case.

AMERICAN TEXTILE MANUFACTURERS INSTITUTE
v. DONOVAN

United States Supreme Court
452 U.S. 490 (1981)

JUSTICE BRENNAN delivered the opinion of the Court.

... In 1978, the Secretary, acting through the Occupational Safety and Health Administration (OSHA), promulgated a standard limiting occupational exposure to cotton dust, an airborne particle byproduct of the preparation and manufacture of cotton products, exposure to which induces a "constellation of respiratory effects" known as "byssinosis."...

Petitioners in these consolidated cases, representing the interests of the cotton industry, challenged the validity of the "Cotton Dust Standard" in the Court of Appeals for the District of Columbia Circuit pursuant to § 6(f) of the Act. They contend in this Court, as they did below, that the Act requires OSHA to demonstrate that its Standard reflects a reasonable relationship between the costs and benefits associated with the Standard. Respondents, the Secretary of Labor and two labor organizations, counter that Congress balanced the costs and benefits in the Act itself, and that the Act should therefore be construed not to require

OSHA to do so. They interpret the Act as mandating that OSHA enact the most protective standard possible to eliminate a significant risk of material health impairment, subject to the constraints of economic and technological feasibility. The Court of Appeals held that the Act did not require OSHA to compare costs and benefits. *AFL-CIO v. Marshall,* 617 F.2d 636 (1979). We granted certiorari to resolve this important question, which was presented but not decided in last Term's *Industrial Union Dept. v. American Petroleum Institute,* 448 U.S. 607 (1980), and to decide other issues related to the Cotton Dust Standard.

I

Byssinosis, known in its more severe manifestations as "brown lung" disease, is a serious and potentially disabling respiratory disease primarily caused by the inhalation of cotton dust.... In its most serious form, byssinosis is a chronic and irreversible obstructive pulmonary disease, clinically similar to chronic bronchitis or emphysema, and can be severely disabling. At worst, as is true of other respiratory diseases including bronchitis, emphysema, and asthma, byssinosis can create an additional strain on cardiovascular functions and can contribute to death from heart failure....

Estimates indicate that at least 35,000 employed and retired cotton mill workers, or 1 in 12 such workers, suffer from the most disabling form of byssinosis. The Senate Report accompanying the Act cited estimates that 100,000 active and retired workers suffer from some grade of the disease. One study found that over 25% of a sample of active cotton-preparation and yarn-manufacturing workers suffer at least some form of the disease at a dust exposure level common prior to adoption of the current Standard. Other studies confirm these general findings on the prevalence of byssinosis....

The Cotton Dust Standard promulgated by OSHA establishes mandatory PEL's [Permissible Exposure Limit] over an 8-hour period of 200 μ g/m^3 [micrograms per cubic meter of air] for yarn manufacturing, 750 μ g/m^3 for slashing and weaving operations, and 500 μ g/m^3 for all other processes in the cotton industry. These levels represent a relaxation of the proposed PEL of 200 μ g/m^3 for all segments of the cotton industry.

OSHA chose an implementation strategy for the Standard that depended primarily on a mix of engineering controls, such as installation of ventilation systems, and work practice controls, such as special floor-sweeping procedures. Full compliance with the PEL's is required within four years, except to the extent that employers can establish that the engineering and work practice controls are infeasible. During this compliance period, and at certain other times, the Standard requires employers to provide respirators to employees. Other requirements include monitoring of cotton dust exposure, medical surveillance of all employees, annual medical examinations, employee education and training programs, and the posting of warning signs. A specific provision also under challenge in the instant case requires employers to transfer employees unable to wear respirators to another position, if available, having a dust level at or below the Standard's PEL's, with "no loss of earnings or other employment rights or benefits as a result of the transfer."

On the basis of the evidence in the record as a whole, the Secretary determined that exposure to cotton dust represents a "significant health hazard to employees," and that "the prevalence of byssinosis should be significantly reduced" by the adoption of the Standard's PEL's. In assessing the health risks from cotton dust and the risk reduction obtained from lowered exposure, OSHA relied particularly on data showing a strong linear relationship between the prevalence of byssinosis and the concentration of lint-free respirable cotton dust. Even at the 200 μ g/m^3 PEL, OSHA found that the prevalence of at least Grade 2 byssinosis would be 13% of all employees in the yarn manufacturing sector.

In promulgating the Cotton Dust Standard, OSHA interpreted the Act to require adoption of the most stringent standard to protect against material health impairment, bounded only by technological and economic feasibility. OSHA therefore rejected the industry's alternative proposal for a PEL of 500 μ g/m^3 in yarn manufacturing, a proposal which would produce a 25% prevalence of at least Grade 2 byssinosis. The agency expressly found the Standard to be both technologically and economically feasible based on the evidence in the record as a whole. Although recognizing that permitted levels of exposure to cotton dust would still cause some byssinosis, OSHA nevertheless rejected the union proposal for a 100 μ g/m^3 PEL because it was not within the "technological capabilities of the industry." Similarly, OSHA set PEL's for some segments of the cotton industry at 500 μ g/m^3 in part because of limitations of technological feasibility. Finally, the Secretary found that "engineering dust controls in weaving may not be feasible even with massive expenditures by the industry," and for that and other reasons adopted a less stringent PEL of 750 μ g/m^3 for weaving and slashing.

The Court of Appeals upheld the Standard in all major respects. The court rejected the industry's claim that OSHA failed to consider its proposed alternative or give sufficient reasons for failing to adopt it. The court also held that the Standard was "reasonably necessary and appropriate" within the meaning of § 3(8) of the Act, because of the risk of material health impairment caused by exposure to cotton dust. Rejecting the industry position that OSHA must demonstrate that the benefits of the Standard are proportionate to its costs, the court instead agreed with OSHA's interpretation that the Standard must protect employees against material health impairment subject only to the limits of technological and economic feasibility. The court held that "Congress itself struck the balance between costs and benefits in the mandate to the agency" under § 6(b)(5) of the Act, and that OSHA is powerless to circumvent that judgment by adopting less than the most protective feasible standard. Finally, the court held that the agency's determination of technological and economic feasibility was supported by substantial evidence in the record as a whole.

We affirm in part, and vacate in part.[25]

II

The principal question presented in these cases is whether the Occupational Safety and Health Act requires the Secretary, in promulgating a standard pursuant to § 6(b)(5) of the Act, to determine that the costs of the standard bear a reasonable relationship to its benefits. Relying on §§ 6(b)(5) and 3(8) of the Act, petitioners urge not only that OSHA must show that a standard addresses a significant risk of material health impairment, see *Industrial Union Dept. v. American Petroleum Institute*, 448 U.S., at 639 (plurality opinion), but also that OSHA must demonstrate that the reduction in risk of material health impairment is significant in light of the costs of attaining that reduction.[26] Respondents on

---

[25] The postargument motions of the several parties for leave to file supplemental memoranda are granted. We decline to adopt the suggestion of the Secretary of Labor that we should "vacate the judgment of the court of appeals and remand the case so that the record may be returned to the Secretary for further consideration and development." We also decline to adopt the suggestion of petitioners that we should "hold these cases in abeyance and ... remand the record to the court of appeals with an instruction that the record be remanded to the agency for further proceedings."

At oral argument, and in a letter addressed to the Court after oral argument, petitioners contended that the Secretary's recent amendment of OSHA's so-called "Cancer Policy" in light of this Court's decision in *Industrial Union Dept. v. American Petroleum Institute*, 448 U.S. 607 (1980), was relevant to the issues in the present cases. We disagree.

OSHA amended its Cancer Policy to "carry out the Court's interpretation of the Occupational Safety and Health Act of 1970 that consideration must be given to the significance of the risk in the issuance of a carcinogen standard and that OSHA must consider all relevant evidence in making these determinations." 46 Fed. Reg. 4889, col. 3 (1981). Previously, although lacking such evidence as dose-response data, the Secretary presumed that no safe exposure level existed for carcinogenic substances. Following this Court's decision, OSHA deleted those provisions of the Cancer Policy which required the "automatic setting of the lowest feasible level" without regard to determinations of risk significance. 46 Fed. Reg. 4890, col. 1 (1981).

In distinct contrast with its Cancer Policy, OSHA expressly found that "exposure to cotton dust presents a significant health hazard to employees," 43 Fed. Reg. 27350, col. 1 (1978), and that "cotton dust produced significant health effects at low levels of exposure," *id.*, at 27358, col. 2. In addition, the agency noted that "grade ½ byssinosis and associated pulmonary function decrements are significant health effects in themselves and should be prevented in so far as possible." *Id.*, at 27354, col. 2. In making its assessment of significant risk, OSHA relied on dose-response curve data (the Merchant Study) showing that 25% of employees suffered at least Grade ½ byssinosis at a 500 μ g/m^3 PEL, and that 12.7% of all employees would suffer byssinosis at the 200 μ g/m^3 PEL standard. *Id.*, at 27358, cols. 2 and 3. Examining the Merchant Study in light of other studies in the record, the agency found that "the Merchant study provides a reliable assessment of health risk to cotton textile workers from cotton dust." *Id.*, at 27357, col. 3. OSHA concluded that the "prevalence of byssinosis should be significantly reduced" by the 200 μ g/m^3 PEL. *Id.*, at 27359, col. 3; *see id.*, at 27359, col. 1 ("200 μ g/m^3 represents a significant reduction in the number of affected workers"). It is difficult to imagine what else the agency could do to comply with this Court's decision in *Industrial Union Dept. v. American Petroleum Institute*.

[26] Petitioners ATMI et al. express their position in several ways. They maintain that OSHA "is required to show that a reasonable relationship exists between the risk reduction benefits and the costs of its standards." Petitioners also suggest that OSHA must show that "the standard is expected

the other hand contend that the Act requires OSHA to promulgate standards that eliminate or reduce such risks "to the extent such protection is technologically and economically feasible."[27] To resolve this debate, we must turn to the language, structure, and legislative history of the Act.

A

The starting point of our analysis is the language of the statute itself. Section 6(b)(5) of the Act (emphasis added), provides:

> The Secretary, in promulgating standards dealing with toxic materials or harmful physical agents under this subsection, shall set the standard which most adequately assures, *to the extent feasible,* on the basis of the best available evidence, that no employee will suffer material impairment of health or functional capacity even if such employee has regular exposure to the hazard dealt with by such standard for the period of his working life.

---

to achieve a *significant reduction in* [the significant risk of material health impairment]" based on "an assessment of the costs of achieving it." Allowing that "[this] does not mean that OSHA must engage in a rigidly formal cost-benefit calculation that places a dollar value on employee lives or health," petitioners describe the required exercise as follows:

> First, OSHA must make a responsible determination of the costs and risk reduction benefits of its standard. Pursuant to the requirement of Section 6(f) of the Act, this determination must be factually supported by substantial evidence in the record. The subsequent determination whether the reduction in health risk is "significant" (based upon the factual assessment of costs and benefits) is a judgment to be made by the agency in the first instance.

Respondent Secretary disputes petitioners' description of the exercise, claiming that any meaningful balancing must involve "placing a [dollar] value on human life and freedom from suffering," and that there is no other way but through formal cost-benefit analysis to accomplish petitioners' desired balancing. Cost-benefit analysis contemplates "systematic enumeration of all benefits and all costs, tangible and intangible, whether readily quantifiable or difficult to measure, that will accrue to all members of society if a particular project is adopted." E. Stokey & R. Zeckhauser, A Primer for Policy Analysis 134 (1978); *see* Commission on Natural Resources, National Research Council, Decision Making for Regulating Chemicals in the Environment 38 (1975). *See generally* E. Mishan, Cost-Benefit Analysis (1976); Prest & Turvey, *Cost-Benefit Analysis,* 300 Economic Journal 683 (1965). Whether petitioners' or respondent's characterization is correct, we will sometimes refer to petitioners' proposed exercise as "cost-benefit analysis."

[27] As described by the union respondents, the test for determining whether a standard promulgated to regulate a "toxic material or harmful physical agent" satisfies the Act has three parts:

> First, whether the "place of employment is unsafe — in the sense that significant risks are present and can be eliminated or lessened by a change in practices." Second, whether of the possible available correctives the Secretary has selected "*the* standard ... that is most protective." Third, whether that standard is "feasible."

We will sometimes refer to this test as "feasibility analysis."

Although their interpretations differ, all parties agree that the phrase "to the extent feasible" contains the critical language in § 6(b)(5) for purposes of these cases.

The plain meaning of the word "feasible" supports respondents' interpretation of the statute. According to Webster's Third New International Dictionary of the English Language 831 (1976), "feasible" means "capable of being done, executed, or effected." *Accord,* the Oxford English Dictionary 116 (1933) ("Capable of being done, accomplished or carried out"); Funk & Wagnalls New "Standard" Dictionary of the English Language 903 (1957) ("That may be done, performed or effected"). Thus, § 6(b)(5) directs the Secretary to issue the standard that "most adequately assures ... that no employee will suffer material impairment of health," limited only by the extent to which this is "capable of being done." In effect then, as the Court of Appeals held, Congress itself defined the basic relationship between costs and benefits, by placing the "benefit" of worker health above all other considerations save those making attainment of this "benefit" unachievable. Any standard based on a balancing of costs and benefits by the Secretary that strikes a different balance than that struck by Congress would be inconsistent with the command set forth in § 6(b)(5). Thus, cost-benefit analysis by OSHA is not required by the statute because feasibility analysis is.[29] *See Industrial Union Dept. v. American Petroleum Institute,* 448 U.S., at 718-719 (MARSHALL, J., dissenting).

When Congress has intended that an agency engage in cost-benefit analysis, it has clearly indicated such intent on the face of the statute. [The Court then discusses several other statutes, including the Flood Control Act of 1936 and the Outer Continental Shelf Lands Act Amendments of 1978.] These and other statutes demonstrate that Congress uses specific language when intending that an agency engage in cost-benefit analysis. Certainly in light of its ordinary meaning, the word "feasible" cannot be construed to articulate such congressional intent. We therefore reject the argument that Congress required cost-benefit analysis in § 6(b)(5).

---

[29] In these cases we are faced with the issue whether the Act requires OSHA to balance costs and benefits in promulgating a *single* toxic material and harmful physical agent standard under § 6(b)(5). Petitioners argue that without cost-benefit balancing, the issuance of a single standard might result in a "serious [misallocation] of the finite resources that are available for the protection of worker safety and health," given the other health hazards in the workplace. This argument is more properly addressed to other provisions of the Act which may authorize OSHA to explore costs and benefits for deciding between issuance of several standards regulating different varieties of health and safety hazards, e.g., § 6(g) of the Act, 29 U.S.C. § 655(g); or for promulgating other types of standards not issued under § 6(b)(5). We express no view on these questions.

B

Even though the plain language of § 6(b)(5) supports this construction, we must still decide whether § 3(8), the general definition of an occupational safety and health standard, either alone or in tandem with § 6(b)(5), incorporates a cost-benefit requirement for standards dealing with toxic materials or harmful physical agents. Section 3(8) of the Act (emphasis added) provides:

> The term "occupational safety and health standard" means a standard which requires conditions, or the adoption or use of one or more practices, means, methods, operations, or processes, *reasonably necessary or appropriate* to provide safe or healthful employment and places of employment.

Taken alone, the phrase "reasonably necessary or appropriate" might be construed to contemplate some balancing of the costs and benefits of a standard. Petitioners urge that, so construed, § 3(8) engrafts a cost-benefit analysis requirement on the issuance of § 6(b)(5) standards, even if § 6(b)(5) itself does not authorize such analysis. We need not decide whether § 3(8), standing alone, would contemplate some form of cost-benefit analysis. For even if it does, Congress specifically chose in § 6(b)(5) to impose separate and additional requirements for issuance of a subcategory of occupational safety and health standards dealing with toxic materials and harmful physical agents: it required that those standards be issued to prevent material impairment of health *to the extent feasible.* Congress could reasonably have concluded that *health* standards should be subject to different criteria than *safety* standards because of the special problems presented in regulating them.

Agreement with petitioners' argument that § 3(8) imposes an additional and overriding requirement of cost-benefit analysis on the issuance of § 6(b)(5) standards would eviscerate the "to the extent feasible" requirement. Standards would inevitably be set at the level indicated by cost-benefit analysis, and not at the level specified by § 6(b)(5). For example, if cost-benefit analysis indicated a protective standard of 1,000 μ g/m^3 PEL, while feasibility analysis indicated a 500 μ g/m^3 PEL, the agency would be forced by the cost-benefit requirement to choose the less stringent point. We cannot believe that Congress intended the general terms of § 3(8) to countermand the specific feasibility requirement of § 6(b)(5). Adoption of petitioners' interpretation would effectively write § 6(b)(5) out of the Act. We decline to render Congress' decision to include a feasibility requirement nugatory, thereby offending the well-settled rule that all parts of a statute, if possible, are to be given effect. Congress did not contemplate any further balancing by the agency for toxic material and harmful physical agents standards, and we should not "'impute to Congress a purpose to paralyze with one hand what it sought to promote with the other.'"[32]

---

[32] This is not to say that § 3(8) might not require the balancing of costs and benefits for standards promulgated under provisions other than § 6(b)(5) of the Act. As a plurality of this Court

C

The legislative history of the Act, while concededly not crystal clear, provides general support for respondents' interpretation of the Act. The congressional Reports and debates certainly confirm that Congress meant "feasible" and nothing else in using that term. Congress was concerned that the Act might be thought to require achievement of absolute safety, an impossible standard, and therefore insisted that health and safety goals be capable of economic and technological accomplishment. Perhaps most telling is the absence of any indication whatsoever that Congress intended OSHA to conduct its own cost-benefit analysis before promulgating a toxic material or harmful physical agent standard. The legislative history demonstrates conclusively that Congress was fully aware that the Act would impose real and substantial costs of compliance on industry, and believed that such costs were part of the cost of doing business. We thus turn to the relevant portions of the legislative history.

[The Court then analyzes wording changes in various drafts of the statute.]

Not only does the legislative history confirm that Congress meant "feasible" rather than "cost-benefit" when it used the former term, but it also shows that Congress understood that the Act would create substantial costs for employers, yet intended to impose such costs when necessary to create a safe and healthful working environment. Congress viewed the costs of health and safety as a cost of doing business. Senator Yarborough, a cosponsor of the Williams bill, stated: "We know the costs would be put into consumer goods but that is the price we should pay for the 80 million workers in America." He asked:

> One may well ask too expensive for whom? Is it too expensive for the company who for lack of proper safety equipment loses the services of its skilled employees? Is it too expensive for the employee who loses his hand or leg or eyesight? Is it too expensive for the widow trying to raise her children on meager allowance under workmen's compensation and social security? And what about the man — a good hardworking man — tied to a wheel chair or hospital bed for the rest of his life? That is what we are dealing with when we talk about industrial safety....

---

noted in *Industrial Union Dept.,* if § 3(8) had no substantive content, "there would be no statutory criteria at all to guide the Secretary in promulgating either national consensus standards or permanent standards other than those dealing with toxic materials and harmful physical agents." Furthermore, the mere fact that a § 6(b)(5) standard is "feasible" does not mean that § 3(8)'s "reasonably necessary or appropriate" language might not impose additional restraints on OSHA. For example, all § 6(b)(5) standards must be addressed to "significant risks" of material health impairment. In addition, if the use of one respirator would achieve the same reduction in health risk as the use of five, the use of five respirators was "technologically and economically feasible," and OSHA thus insisted on the use of five, then the "reasonably necessary or appropriate" limitation might come into play as an additional restriction on OSHA to choose the one-respirator standard. In this case we need not decide all the applications that § 3(8) might have, either alone or together with § 6(b)(5).

We are talking about people's lives, not the indifference of some cost accountants.

Senator Eagleton commented that "[the] costs that will be incurred by employers in meeting the standards of health and safety to be established under this bill are, in my view, *reasonable and necessary costs of doing business.*" (emphasis added).

Other Members of Congress voiced similar views. Nowhere is there any indication that Congress contemplated a different balancing by OSHA of the benefits of worker health and safety against the costs of achieving them. Indeed Congress thought that the *financial costs* of health and safety problems in the workplace were as large as or larger than the *financial costs* of eliminating these problems. In its statement of findings and declaration of purpose encompassed in the Act itself, Congress announced that "personal injuries and illnesses arising out of work situations impose a substantial burden upon, and are a hindrance to, interstate commerce in terms of lost production, wage loss, medical expenses, and disability compensation payments." The Senate was well aware of the magnitude of these costs:

> "[The] economic impact of industrial deaths and disability is staggering. Over $1.5 billion is wasted in lost wages, and the annual loss to the Gross National Product is estimated to be over $8 billion. Vast resources that could be available for productive use are siphoned off to pay workmen's compensation benefits and medical expenses." S. Rep. No. 91-1282, p. 2 (1970), Leg. Hist. 142.

Senator Eagleton summarized: "Whether we, as individuals, are motivated by simple humanity or by simple economics, we can no longer permit profits to be dependent upon an unsafe or unhealthy worksite."

III

Section 6(f) of the Act provides that "[the] determinations of the Secretary shall be conclusive if supported by substantial evidence in the record considered as a whole." Petitioners contend that the Secretary's determination that the Cotton Dust Standard is "economically feasible" is not supported by substantial evidence in the record considered as a whole. In particular, they claim (1) that OSHA underestimated the financial costs necessary to meet the Standard's requirements; and (2) that OSHA incorrectly found that the Standard would not threaten the economic viability of the cotton industry.

In statutes with provisions virtually identical to § 6(f) of the Act, we have defined substantial evidence as "such relevant evidence as a reasonable mind might accept as adequate to support a conclusion." *Universal Camera Corp. v. NLRB,* 340 U.S. 474, 477 (1951). The reviewing court must take into account contradictory evidence in the record, but "the possibility of drawing two inconsistent conclusions from the evidence does not prevent an administrative agency's finding from being supported by substantial evidence," *Consolo v. FMC,* 383 U.S. 607, 620 (1966). Since the Act places responsibility for determining substantial evidence questions in the courts of appeals, we apply the familiar rule that "[this] Court will intervene only in what ought to be the rare instance when the [substantial evidence] standard appears to have been misapprehended or grossly misapplied" by the court below. Therefore, our inquiry is not to determine whether we, in the first instance, would find OSHA's findings supported by substantial evidence. Instead we turn to OSHA's findings and the record upon which they were based to decide whether the Court of Appeals "misapprehended or grossly misapplied" the substantial evidence test.

... On the basis of the whole record, we cannot conclude that the Court of Appeals "misapprehended or grossly misapplied" the substantial evidence test.

IV

The final Cotton Dust Standard places heavy reliance on the use of respirators to protect employees from exposure to cotton dust, particularly during the 4-year interim period necessary to install and implement feasible engineering controls. One part of the respirator provision requires the employer to give employees unable to wear a respirator the opportunity to transfer to another position, if available, where the dust level meets the Standard's PEL. When such a transfer occurs, the employer must guarantee that the employee suffers no loss of earnings or other employment rights or benefits. Petitioners do not object to the transfer provision, but challenge OSHA's authority under the Act to require employers to guarantee employees' wage and employment benefits following the transfer. The Court of Appeals held that OSHA has such authority. We hold that, whether or not OSHA has this underlying authority, the agency has failed to make the necessary determination or statement of reasons that its wage guarantee requirement is related to the achievement of a safe and healthful work environment.

... OSHA never explained the wage guarantee provision as an approach designed to contribute to increased health protection. Instead the agency stated that the "goal of this provision is to minimize any adverse economic impact on the employee by virtue of the inability to wear a respirator." Perhaps in recognition of this fact, respondents in their briefs argue:

> Experience under the Act has shown that employees are reluctant to disclose symptoms of disease and tend to minimize work-related health problems for fear of being discharged or transferred to a lower paying job.... It may reasonably be expected, therefore, that many employees incapable of using respirators would continue to breathe unhealthful air rather than request a transfer, thus destroying the utility of the respirator program.

Whether these arguments have merit, and they very well may, the *post hoc* rationalizations of the agency or the parties to this litigation cannot serve as a sufficient predicate for agency action. For Congress gave OSHA the responsibility to protect worker health and safety, and to explain its reasons for its actions. Because the Act in no way authorizes OSHA to repair general unfairness to employees that is unrelated to achievement of health and safety goals, we conclude that OSHA acted beyond statutory authority when it issued the wage guarantee regulation.

V

When Congress passed the Occupational Safety and Health Act in 1970, it chose to place pre-eminent value on assuring employees a safe and healthful working environment, limited only by the feasibility of achieving such an environment. We must measure the validity of the Secretary's actions against the requirements of that Act. For "[the] judicial function does not extend to substantive revision of regulatory policy. That function lies elsewhere — in Congressional and Executive oversight or amendatory legislation." *Industrial Union Dept. v. American Petroleum Institute,* 448 U.S., at 663 (BURGER, C. J., concurring).[75]

Accordingly, the judgment of the Court of Appeals is affirmed in all respects except to the extent of its approval of the Secretary's application of the wage guarantee provision of the Cotton Dust Standard at 29 CFR § 1910.1043 (f)(2)(v) (1980). To that extent, the judgment of the Court of Appeals is vacated and the case remanded with directions to remand to the Secretary for further proceedings consistent with this opinion.

It is so ordered.

JUSTICE POWELL took no part in the decision of these cases.

JUSTICE STEWART, dissenting.

... Everybody agrees that under [§ 6(b)(5)] the Cotton Dust Standard must at least be *economically* feasible, and everybody would also agree, I suppose, that in order to determine whether or not something is economically feasible, one must have a fairly clear idea of how much it is going to cost. Because I believe that OSHA failed to justify its estimate of the cost of the Cotton Dust Standard on the basis of substantial evidence, I would reverse the judgment before us without reaching the question whether the Act requires that a standard, beyond

---

[75] Even had JUSTICE REHNQUIST correctly characterized the Court's opinion — and there were three possible constructions of the phrase "to the extent feasible" — this would hardly have been grounds for invalidating § 6(b)(5) under the delegation doctrine. After all, this would not be the first time that more than one interpretation of a statute had been argued. *See, e.g., Pennhurst State School v. Halderman,* 451 U.S. 1 (1981); *Watt v. Alaska,* 451 U.S. 259 (1981).

being economically feasible, must meet the demands of a cost-benefit examination.

The simple truth about OSHA's assessment of the cost of the Cotton Dust Standard is that the agency never relied on any study or report purporting to predict the cost to industry of the Standard finally adopted by the agency. OSHA did have before it one cost analysis, that of the Research Triangle Institute, which attempted to predict the cost of the final Standard. However, as recognized by the Court, the agency flatly rejected that prediction as a gross overestimate. The only other estimate OSHA had, the Hocutt-Thomas estimate prepared by industry researchers, was not designed to predict the cost of the final OSHA Standard. Rather, it assumed a far less stringent and inevitably far less costly standard for all phases of cotton production except roving. The agency examined the Hocutt-Thomas study, and concluded that it too was an overestimate of the costs of the less stringent standard it was addressing. I am willing to defer to OSHA's determination that the Hocutt-Thomas study was such an overestimate, conceding that such subtle financial and technical matters lie within the discretion and skill of the agency. But in a remarkable non sequitur, the agency decided that because the Hocutt-Thomas study was an overestimate of the cost of a less stringent standard, it could be treated as a reliable estimate for the more costly final Standard actually promulgated, never rationally explaining how it came to this happy conclusion. This is not substantial evidence. It is unsupported speculation.

Of course, as the Court notes, this Court will re-examine a court of appeals' review of a question of substantial evidence "only in what ought to be the rare instance when the standard appears to have been misapprehended or grossly misapplied." But I think this is one of those rare instances where an agency has categorically misconceived the nature of the evidence necessary to support a regulation, and where the Court of Appeals has failed to correct the agency's error....

Unlike the Court, I think it clear to the point of being obvious that, as a matter of law, OSHA's prediction of the cost of the Cotton Dust Standard lacks a basis in substantial evidence, since the agency did not rely on even a single estimate of the cost of the actual Standard it promulgated. Accordingly, I respectfully dissent.

JUSTICE REHNQUIST, with whom THE CHIEF JUSTICE joins, dissenting.

A year ago I stated my belief that Congress in enacting § 6(b)(5) of the Occupational Safety and Health Act of 1970 unconstitutionally delegated to the Executive Branch the authority to make the "hard policy choices" properly the task of the legislature. *Industrial Union Dept. v. American Petroleum Institute,* 448 U.S. 607, 671 (1980) (concurring in judgment). Because I continue to believe that the Act exceeds Congress' power to delegate legislative authority to nonelected officials, see *J. W. Hampton & Co. v. United States,* 276 U.S. 394 (1928), and *Panama Refining Co. v. Ryan,* 293 U.S. 388 (1935), I dissent.

I will repeat only a little of what I said last Term....

As the Court correctly observes, the phrase "to the extent feasible" contains the critical language for the purpose of these cases. We are presented with a remarkable range of interpretations of that language. Petitioners contend that the statute *requires* the Secretary to demonstrate that the benefits of its "Cotton Dust Standard," in terms of reducing health risks, bear a reasonable relationship to its costs. Respondents, including the Secretary of Labor at least until his post-argument motion, counter that Congress itself balanced costs and benefits when it enacted the statute, and that the statute *prohibits* the Secretary from engaging in a cost-benefit type balancing. Their view is that the Act merely requires the Secretary to promulgate standards that eliminate or reduce such risks "to the extent ... technologically or economically feasible." As I read the Court's opinion, it takes a different position. It concludes that, at least as to the "Cotton Dust Standard," the Act does not require the Secretary to engage in a cost-benefit analysis, which suggests of course that the Act *permits* the Secretary to undertake such an analysis if he so chooses....

[In enacting § 6(b)(5)] Congress had at least three choices. It could have required the Secretary to engage in a cost-benefit analysis prior to the setting of exposure levels, it could have prohibited cost-benefit analysis, or it could have permitted the use of such an analysis. Rather than make that choice and resolve that difficult policy issue, however, Congress passed. Congress simply said that the Secretary should set standards "to the extent feasible." Last year, JUSTICE POWELL reflected that "one might wish that Congress had spoken with greater clarity." *American Petroleum Institute,* 448 U.S., at 668 (POWELL, J., concurring in part and in judgment). I am convinced that the reason that Congress did not speak with greater "clarity" was because it could not. The words "to the extent feasible" were used to mask a fundamental policy disagreement in Congress. I have no doubt that if Congress had been required to choose whether to mandate, permit, or prohibit the Secretary from engaging in a cost-benefit analysis, there would have been no bill for the President to sign.

The Court seems to argue that Congress *did* make a policy choice when it enacted the "feasibility" language. Its view is that Congress required the Secretary to engage in something called "feasibility analysis." But those words mean nothing at all. They are a "legislative mirage, appearing to some Members [of Congress] but not to others, and assuming any form desired by the beholder." Even the Court does not settle on a meaning. It first suggests that the language requires the Secretary to do what is "capable of being done." But, if that is all the language means, it is merely precatory and "no more than an admonition to the Secretary to do his duty ...." Leg. Hist. 367 (remarks of Sen. Dominick). The Court then seems to adopt the Secretary's view that feasibility means "technological and economic feasibility." But there is nothing in the words of § 6(b)(5), or their legislative history, to suggest why they should be so limited. One wonders why the "requirement" of § 6(b)(5) could not include considerations of administrative or even political feasibility. As even the Court recognizes, when Congress has wanted to limit the concept of feasibility to technological and economic feasibility, it has said so. Thus the words "to the extent feasible" provide no meaningful guidance to those who will administer the law.

In believing that § 6(b)(5) amounts to an unconstitutional delegation of legislative authority to the Executive Branch, I do not mean to suggest that Congress, in enacting a statute, must resolve all ambiguities or must "fill in all of the blanks." Even the neophyte student of government realizes that legislation is the art of compromise, and that an important, controversial bill is seldom enacted by Congress in the form in which it is first introduced. It is not unusual for the various factions supporting or opposing a proposal to accept some departure from the language they would prefer and to adopt substitute language agreeable to all. But that sort of compromise is a far cry from this case, where Congress simply abdicated its responsibility for the making of a fundamental and most difficult policy choice — whether and to what extent "the statistical possibility of future deaths should ... be disregarded in light of the economic costs of preventing those deaths." That is a "quintessential legislative" choice and must be made by the elected representatives of the people, not by nonelected officials in the Executive Branch. As stated last Term:

> In drafting § 6(b)(5), Congress was faced with a clear, if difficult, choice between balancing statistical lives and industrial resources or authorizing the Secretary to elevate human life above all concerns save massive dislocation in an affected industry. That Congress recognized the difficulty of this choice is clear .... That Congress chose, intentionally or unintentionally, to pass this difficult choice on to the Secretary is evident from the spectral quality of the standard it selected.

In sum, the Court is quite correct in asserting that the phrase "to the extent feasible" is the critical language for the purposes of these cases. But that language is critical, not because it establishes a general standard by which those charged with administering the statute may be guided, but because it has precisely the opposite effect: in failing to agree on whether the Secretary should be either mandated, permitted, or prohibited from undertaking a cost-benefit analysis, Congress simply left the crucial policy choices in the hands of the Secretary of Labor.[1] As I stated at greater length last Term, I believe that in so doing Congress unconstitutionally delegated its legislative responsibility to the Executive Branch.

---

[1] Contrary to the suggestion of the Court, I do *not* argue that the existence of several plausible interpretations of the statute is a ground for invoking the delegation doctrine: I invoke the delegation doctrine because Congress failed to *choose* among those plausible interpretations.

NOTES

1. *Legality of Cost-Benefit Analysis.* Does the majority opinion in *Cotton Dust* prohibit OSHA from using cost-benefit analysis? Justice Rehnquist, citing the last sentence of part II.A. of the Court's opinion, reads the court as permitting cost-benefit analysis.

In reading the Supreme Court tea leaves, it may help to consider the unusual briefing procedure in the case. The government submitted its briefs defending the cotton dust standard under the Carter Administration. Oral argument was held on January 21, 1981, the first day of the Reagan administration. President Reagan later issued an executive order requiring the use of cost-benefit analysis for any government regulation. OSHA then asked the Supreme Court to refrain from further consideration of the *Cotton Dust* case until the cost-benefit analysis was completed. The AFL-CIO and the Amalgamated Clothing and Textile Workers Unions, the union respondents in the case, opposed the OSHA request for a delay. The Supreme Court's response rejecting a delay appears in note 25, where the court declares it "difficult to imagine" what else the agency could do. Does this indicate that the Supreme Court rejected the claim that OSHA could engage in cost-benefit analysis if it so chose?

2. *Cost-Effectiveness Principle.* As a result of the Supreme Court decision in the *Cotton Dust* case, OSHA announced that it would now rely on the principle of cost effectiveness to assess proposed OSHA standards. This principle requires OSHA to determine the level of protection from exposure to a particular substance by using criteria other than cost-benefit analysis. Once this level of desired protection has been reached, then OSHA is able to select the least expensive means of compliance that will achieve that level of protection. Thus, if OSHA decided that a PEL of 500 provides the desirable level of protection from substance X, and this PEL can be achieved either by redesigning the ventilation system or by encapsulating the oven that produces the emissions, then OSHA can choose the least expensive means to reach the PEL.

3. *Cost-Benefit Analysis in Other OSHA Areas.* Footnote 29 of the *Cotton Dust* opinion contemplates a greater role for cost-benefit analysis in areas other than section 6(b)(5) standards for toxic materials and harmful physical agents. In *National Grain & Feed Ass'n v. OSHA,* 866 F.2d 717 (5th Cir.), *cert. denied,* 490 U.S. 1065 (1989), the Fifth Circuit held that the Court would defer to the Secretary's position that the grain dust, which was covered by the grain handling standard, is not a "harmful physical agent" within the meaning of section 6(b)(5). The court therefore imposed a requirement that the grain handling standard must be "reasonably necessary or appropriate" to protect worker safety, using the language in section 3(8) of the Act. The court said that this requirement is intermediate between feasibility and a strict cost-benefit analysis. The intermediate requirement meant that costs must be "reasonably related" to benefits.

A similar result was reached by the D.C. Circuit in *UAW v. OSHA*, 938 F.2d 1310 (D.C. Cir. 1991). This case involved the OSHA standard requiring employers to lockout or tagout machines that are being serviced so they cannot inadvertently be turned on. The court held that this standard was not covered by section 6(b)(5), since the lockout/tagout standard dealt with an immediately noticeable physical harm rather than "toxic materials or harmful physical agents." The court rejected the argument made by industry that the "reasonably necessary or appropriate" language of section 3(8) required the use of cost-benefit analysis, but nonetheless held that cost-benefit analysis is permissible. The court also rejected the OSHA position that under section 3(8) the agency was free to impose any restriction it chooses so long as it is feasible. The case was remanded to OSHA with a request for the agency to reveal the reasoning behind its choice of an appropriate rule to evaluate standards governed by section 3(8).

The remanded case returned to the D.C. Circuit in *UAW v. OSHA*, 37 F.3d 665 (D.C. Cir. 1994). OSHA on remand had indicated six principles that constrained its discretion in choosing a safety standard: (1) the standard will substantially reduce a significant risk of harm; (2) and (3) compliance will be economically and technologically feasible; (4) the standard employs the most cost-effective protection measures; (5) OSHA would publish its reasons for adopting any standard differing from an existing national consensus standard; and (6) OSHA would support its choice of a standard with evidence. The court expressed its skepticism about whether these six principles sufficiently limited OSHA's discretion in establishing standards to avoid violation of the nondelegation doctrine, which would make the OSHA promulgation of standards unconstitutional. However, the court found that OSHA's response had gone beyond these six principles. For example, OSHA had indicated that its interpretation of the law requires it to enact a safety standard once it has identified a significant safety risk; OSHA is not permitted under these circumstances to do nothing at all. In addition, while OSHA had rejected "formal cost-benefit analysis," and the court found no logical relationship between the six principles offered by OSHA, nonetheless in this instance OSHA had found "that the relationship between the benefits secured by the lockout/tagout standard and the costs it imposes is reasonable." While the court stated that "the current case does not require us to decide whether the statute requires a reasonable relationship between a rule's costs and its benefits," the assurance by OSHA that the relationship between the benefits and costs for this standard was reasonable apparently was an important factor that persuaded the court to dismiss the petition for review of the OSHA lockout/tagout standard.

4. *A Rose by Any Other Name, or the Saga of "Risk-Risk" Analysis.* An interesting effort to introduce cost-benefit analysis into OSHA decisions occurred in 1992. The Office of Management and Budget (OMB) directed the

Labor Department to conduct a "risk-risk" analysis to determine whether a proposed OSHA standard dealing with air contaminants in construction, maritime, agriculture, and general industries would result in more deaths than lives saved. The OMB approach argues that the costs of more stringent regulations are largely absorbed by consumers through higher prices and by workers through lower wages. The consequence, according to this approach, is that workers and consumers will have lower incomes and will be forced to purchase less health care, to eat poorer diets, and to invest in fewer safety devices, such as home fire alarms. The OMB cited research results suggesting that each $7.25 million in regulatory costs leads to worker and consumer adjustments in healthful lifestyles that result in one additional fatality. Thus, the OMB argues, unless the additional $7.25 million in regulatory cost associated with a new OSHA standard saves at least one life, the net impact of the new standard would be an increase in fatalities.

The reaction to the OMB proposal was predictable. Skepticism if not downright hostility swelled about economists and cost-benefit analysis in general, and risk-risk analysis in particular. Moreover, Congressional critics and others were quick to point out that the Supreme Court had held that cost-benefit analysis, regardless of its nom de plume, was prohibited in determining the stringency of section 6(b)(5) OSHA standards. *GAO Criticizes Budget Office Theory on 'Risk-Risk' Analysis for OSHA Rule*, 10 BNA'S EMPLOYEE RELATIONS WEEKLY 769 (1992).

5. *The Continued Irrelevance of Cost-Benefit Analysis.* The use of cost-benefit analysis for evaluating OSHA health standards was one of the issues considered in *American Dental Ass'n v. Martin*, 984 F.2d 823 (7th Cir.), *cert. denied*, 510 U.S. 859 (1993). The majority opinion was written by Judge Posner and endorsed by Judge Easterbrook. They expressed reservations about the arguments that had been made by OSHA to justify the rule on occupational exposure to bloodborne pathogens. Nonetheless, they stated the standard for reviewing an OSHA health standard:

> In deciding to impose this extensive array of restrictions on the practice of medicine, nursing, and dentistry, OSHA did not (indeed it is not authorized to) compare the benefits with the costs and impose the restrictions on finding that the former exceeded the latter. Instead it asked whether the restrictions would materially reduce a significant workplace risk to human health without imperiling the existence of, or threatening massive dislocation to, the health care industry. For this is the applicable legal standard.

Id. at 825.

Persuaded by this argument? Consider then the response by Judge Coffey who expressed this view:

> I disagree with my two colleagues, who are both properly recognized and respected as experts in the field of economics as well as law, but who have

overlooked the lack of marginal benefit in the final rule. The majority maintains that OSHA "is not authorized to ... compare the benefits with the costs and impose the restrictions [the Bloodborne Pathogens Standard] on finding that the former exceeded the latter." ... As I have previously mentioned ... the Supreme Court has recommend that OSHA pursuant to § 3(8) of the Act, consider drafting the less costly of two equally effective proposals ... Furthermore, had OSHA considered and analyzed the marginal costs and benefits of its regulations as applied to the dental, home health care and personnel services professions, they would have foregone promulgation of the rule, because less costly, less intrusive regulations are available and have effectively reduced the risk of exposure to bloodborne pathogens.

Id. at 838 (concurring in part and dissenting in part).

3. GENERIC RULEMAKING

Almost all of the OSHA standards currently in effect are the interim standards that were issued in 1971, shortly after the OSHAct was effective. The new permanent standards issued under section 6(b) of the Act have been sparse: only about fifty have been issued in almost three decades. The slow pace is at least partially explained by the considerable resources that OSHA had to devote to building a factual record supporting each standard so it would withstand the careful scrutiny of the courts.

Whatever the justification, the glacial pace of issuing new standards has led to criticisms of OSHA. One response has been the emergence of generic rulemaking. Most permanent OSHA standards deal with a single substance (such as cotton dust) that is used in a limited set of industries (such as cotton mills and yarn manufacturers). Generic rulemaking, in contrast, regulates a process that is common to many industries or regulates a broad range of substances.

There have been four efforts at generic rulemaking. According to Mintz, "A successful generic regulatory effort was OSHA's 1983 regulation on access to employee exposure and medical records, which requires that employers provide access to employees and to OSHA to existing employer-maintained exposure and medical records relevant to employees exposed to a broad range of toxic substances and harmful physical agents." BENJAMIN W. MINTZ, OSHA: HISTORY, LAW, AND POLICY 86 (1984). Another apparent success was the hazard communications standard, which is discussed in Section H of this chapter.

A less successful effort at generic rulemaking was the 1980 Carcinogens Policy (Cancer Policy), which provided procedures for the identification, classification, and regulation of potential carcinogens, and two "model standards" for emergency temporary and permanent standards for carcinogens. In addition to the beating by Justice Stevens in the *Benzene* case, the Carcinogens Policy suffered direct challenges in several courts and was never implemented in a rulemaking proceeding. *See* MINTZ, *supra,* at 86-88.

The latest effort at generic rulemaking by OSHA was the 1989 Air Contaminant Standard, which set permissible exposure limits for 428 toxic substances. OSHA described the standard as "its most significant workplace exposure action ever." 35 O.S.H. Rep. (BNA) 1475-76 (Jan. 18, 1989). Despite this accolade, the Air Contaminants Standard was challenged in 28 suits, a number which was eventually reduced by settlements to 11 cases. The Eleventh Circuit was picked by random selection to hear the consolidated cases.

AFL-CIO v. OSHA

United States Court of Appeals, Eleventh Circuit
965 F.2d 962 (1992)

Before FAY and COX, CIRCUIT JUDGES, and JOHNSON, SENIOR CIRCUIT JUDGE.

FAY, CIRCUIT JUDGE:

In 1989, the Occupational Safety and Health Administration ("OSHA"), a division of the Department of Labor, issued its Air Contaminants Standard, a set of permissible exposure limits for 428 toxic substances. Air Contaminants Standard, 54 Fed. Reg. 2332 (1989) (codified at 29 C.F.R. § 1910.1000). In these consolidated appeals, petitioners representing various affected industries and the American Federation of Labor and Congress of Industrial Organizations ("AFL-CIO" or "the union") challenge both the procedure used by OSHA to generate this multi-substance standard and OSHA's findings on numerous specific substances included in the new standard. For the reasons that follow, we vacate the Air Contaminants Standard and remand to the agency.

I. *Background*

... Section 6(a) of the Act provided that in its first two years, OSHA should promulgate "start-up" standards, on an expedited basis and without public hearing or comment, based on "national consensus" or "established Federal standard[s]" that improve employee safety or health. *Id.* § 655(a). Pursuant to that authority, OSHA in 1971 promulgated approximately 425 permissible exposure limits ("PELs") for air contaminants, 29 C.F.R. § 1910.1000 (1971), derived principally from federal standards applicable to government contractors under the Walsh-Healey Act, 41 U.S.C. § 35.

The Act then provides two mechanisms to update these standards. Most new standards or revised existing standards must be promulgated under the requirements of section 6(b) of the OSH Act. 29 U.S.C. § 655(b). This section sets forth both procedural requirements and substantive criteria which the standards must meet. In promulgating these standards, OSHA must follow a procedure that is even more stringent than that in the federal Administrative Procedure Act, 5 U.S.C. § 553. OSHA must provide notice of proposed rulemaking, give interested parties an opportunity to comment, and hold a public hearing if requested. As of 1988, OSHA had issued only twenty-four substance-specific and three "generic" health standards under section 6(b).[7]

OSHA may also issue Emergency Temporary Standards under section 6(c) of the OSH Act, 29 U.S.C. § 655(c), when it determines "that employees are exposed to grave danger from exposure" to toxic substances. However, once OSHA has published an emergency standard, proceedings must commence for issuance of a regular standard under section 6(b).

On June 7, 1988, OSHA published a Notice of Proposed Rulemaking for its Air Contaminants Standard. In this single rulemaking, OSHA proposed to issue new or revised PELs for over 400 substances. OSHA limited the scope of this rulemaking to those substances for which the ACGIH [American Conference of Governmental Industrial Hygienists] recommended limits that were either new or more protective than the existing PELs. There was an initial comment period of forty-seven days, followed by a thirteen-day public hearing. Interested parties then had until October 7, 1988 to submit post-hearing evidence and until October 31, 1988 to submit post-hearing briefs.

OSHA then issued its revised Air Contaminants Standard for 428 toxic substances on January 19, 1989. This standard, which differs from the proposal in several respects, lowered the PELs for 212 substances, set new PELs for 164 previously unregulated substances, and left unchanged PELs for 52 substances for which lower limits had originally been proposed. The standard established an approximately four-year period for employers to come into compliance with the new standard using engineering and work practice controls. Until that time, employers may use respirators or any other reasonable methods to comply with the standards.

Various industry groups, the AFL-CIO, and specific individual companies filed challenges to the final standard in numerous United States Courts of Appeals. Pursuant to 28 U.S.C. § 2112(a), all petitions for review of the Air Contaminants Standard were transferred to this court, where they have been consolidated for disposition....

III. *Discussion*

In challenging the procedure by which OSHA promulgated the Air Contaminants Standard, a group of industry petitioners complain that OSHA's use of generic findings, the lumping together of so many substances in one rulemaking, and the short time provided for comment by interested parties, combine to create a record inadequate to support this massive new set of PELs. The union also challenges the rulemaking procedure utilized by OSHA for the Air Contaminants Standard. Not surprisingly, however, the union claims that this procedure

---

[7] The three "generic" rulemakings were: Cancer Policy, 29 C.F.R. Part 1990; Access to Employee Exposure and Medical Records Regulation, 29 C.F.R. § 1910.20; Hazard Communication Standard, 29 C.F.R. § 1910.1200.

resulted in standards that are systematically underprotective of employee health....

A. *"Generic" Rulemaking*

Unlike most of the OSHA standards previously reviewed by the courts, the Air Contaminants Standard regulates not a single toxic substance, but 428 different substances. The agency explained its decision to issue such an omnibus standard in its Notice of Proposed Rulemaking:

> OSHA has issued only 24 substance-specific health regulations since its creation. It has not been able to review the many thousands of currently unregulated chemicals in the workplace nor to keep up with reviewing the several thousand new chemicals introduced since its creation. It has not been able to fully review the literature to determine if lower limits are needed for many of the approximately 400 substances it now regulates.

> Using past approaches and practices, OSHA could continue to regulate a small number of the high priority substances and those of greatest public interest. However, it would take decades to review currently used chemicals and OSHA would never be able to keep up with the many chemicals which will be newly introduced in the future.

53 Fed. Reg. at 20963. For this reason, "OSHA determined that it was necessary to modify this approach through the use of *generic* rulemaking, which would simultaneously cover many substances." 54 Fed. Reg. at 2333 (emphasis added).

"Generic" means something "common to or characteristic of a whole group or class; typifying or subsuming; not specific or individual." *Webster's Third New International Dictionary* 945 (1966). Previous "generic" rulemakings by OSHA have all dealt with requirements that, once promulgated, could be applied to numerous different situations. For example, OSHA's Hazard Communication Standard, 29 C.F.R. § 1910.1200, mandates that employers inform employees of potentially hazardous materials. The regulation includes a basic list of substances which employers must treat as hazardous, but requires that the employers themselves also evaluate substances produced in their workplaces to determine if they are potentially hazardous based on available scientific evidence. Similarly, OSHA has issued standards regulating employee access to medical and toxic substance exposure records, 29 C.F.R. § 1910.20, and setting forth uniform criteria for application in future regulation of exposure to carcinogens, 29 C.F.R. Part 1990.

By contrast, the new Air Contaminants Standard is an amalgamation of 428 unrelated substance exposure limits. There is little common to this group of diverse substances except the fact that OSHA considers them toxic and in need of regulation. In fact, this rulemaking is the antithesis of a "generic" rulemaking; it is a set of 428 specific and individual substance exposure limits. Therefore,

OSHA's characterization of this as a "generic" rulemaking is somewhat misleading.

Nonetheless, we find nothing in the OSH Act that would prevent OSHA from addressing multiple substances in a single rulemaking. Moreover, because the statute leaves this point open and because OSHA's interpretation of the statute is reasonable, it is appropriate for us to defer to OSHA's interpretation. However, we believe the PEL for each substance must be able to stand independently, i.e., that each PEL must be supported by substantial evidence in the record considered as a whole and accompanied by adequate explanation. OSHA may not, by using such multi-substance rulemaking, ignore the requirements of the OSH Act. Both the industry petitioners and the union argue that such disregard was what in essence occurred. Regretfully, we agree.

B. *Significant Risk of Material Health Impairment*

Section 3(8) of the OSH Act defines "occupational health and safety standard" as "a standard which requires conditions, or the adoption or use of one or more practices, means, methods, operations, or processes, *reasonably necessary or appropriate* to provide safe or healthful employment and places of employment." 29 U.S.C. § 652(8) (emphasis added). The Supreme Court has interpreted this provision to require that, before the promulgation of any permanent health standard, OSHA make a threshold finding that a significant risk of material health impairment exists at the current levels of exposure to the toxic substance in question, "and that a new, lower standard is therefore 'reasonably necessary or appropriate to provide safe or healthful employment and places of employment.'" *Benzene*, 448 U.S. at 615. OSHA is not entitled to regulate *any* risk, only those which present a "significant" risk of "material" health impairment. OSHA must therefore determine: (1) what health impairments are "material," and (2) what constitutes a "significant" risk of such impairment....[15]

Once OSHA finds that a significant risk of material health impairment exists at current exposure levels for a given toxic substance, any standard promulgated to address that risk must comply with the requirements of section 6(b)(5) of the OSH Act, 29 U.S.C. § 655(b)(5). That section provides that the agency

> in promulgating standards dealing with toxic materials or harmful physical agents under this subsection, shall set the standard which *most adequately assures, to the extent feasible, on the basis of the best available evidence, that no employee will suffer material impairment of health or functional*

---

[15] The Court in *Benzene* gave an example, stating that "if the odds are one in a thousand that regular inhalation of gasoline vapors that are 2% benzene will be fatal, a reasonable person might well consider the risk significant and take appropriate steps to decrease or eliminate it." *Benzene*, 448 U.S. at 655. OSHA has apparently incorporated that example "as a policy norm, at least in the sense of believing that it *must* regulate if it finds a risk at the 1/1000 level." *International Union v. Pendergrass*, 878 F.2d 389, 392 (D.C. Cir. 1989).

capacity even if such employee has regular exposure to the hazard dealt with by such standard for the period of his working life....

Id. (emphasis added). In other words, section 6(b)(5) mandates that the standard adopted "prevent material impairment of health to the extent feasible." *ATMI,* 452 U.S. at 512 (emphasis omitted).

1. *Material Impairment*

In this rulemaking, OSHA grouped the 428 substances into eighteen categories by the primary health effects of those substances, for example, neuropathic effects, sensory irritation, and cancer. Industry petitioners charge that for several categories of substances OSHA failed to adequately justify its determination that the health effects caused by exposure to these substances are "material impairments." We disagree.

Petitioners cite the category of "sensory irritation" as a particularly egregious example. At the beginning of the discussion for each category, the agency summarized the types of health effects within that category, and discussed why those effects constituted "material impairments." The "Description of Health Effects" for the "sensory irritation" category includes the following discussion:

> The symptoms of sensory irritation include stinging, itching, and burning of the eyes, tearing (or lacrimation), a burning sensation in the nasal passages, rhinitis (nasal inflammation), cough, sputum production, chest pain, wheezing, and dyspnea (breathing difficulty)....
>
> These effects may cause severe discomfort and can be seriously disabling, as is the case with dyspnea or wheezing. The tearing and eye irritation associated with exposure to sensory irritants are often severe and can be as disabling as the weeping caused by exposure to tear gas. In addition to these primary effects, workers distracted by material irritant effects are more likely than nonexposed workers to have accidents and thus to endanger both themselves and others. (These adverse health effects also clearly have substantial productivity impacts.).
>
> ....
>
> During the rulemaking, the question arose as to the level of irritation that constitutes a significant risk of material impairment.... Some commentators are of the opinion that transient irritant effects should not be considered material impairment of health....
>
> Most commentators, however, recommended that these signs and symptoms be regarded as material health impairments....
>
> ....
>
> [A]ccording to NIOSH [National Institute of Occupational Safety and Health], sensory irritants interfere with job performance and safety, cause inflammation, may increase the victim's susceptibility to other irritants and infectious agents, lead to permanent injury or dysfunction, or permit greater

absorption of hazardous substances.... OSHA concludes that exposure limits are needed for those substances for which PELs are being established in this rulemaking to protect against sensory irritant effects that result in objective signs of irritation, such as coughing, wheezing, conjunctivitis, and tearing. Such levels of mucous membrane irritation may require medical treatment, adversely affect the well-being of employees, and place the affected individuals at risk from increased absorption of the substance and decreased resistance to infection. Exposing workers repeatedly to irritants at levels that cause subjective irritant effects may cause workers to become inured to the irritant warning properties of these substances and thus increase the risk of overexposure.

54 Fed. Reg. at 2444-45 (citations omitted). In addition, in the more general discussion of OSHA's approach to this rulemaking, OSHA also recognized that

irritation also covers a spectrum of effects, some serious and some trivial. Hence, complaints of minor irritation would not in and of itself constitute material impairment.

In addition, OSHA would weigh irritation with physical manifestations more heavily than irritation with purely subjective responses. This does not mean that purely subjective responses would not constitute material impairment. That judgment would depend on the magnitude of the irritation.

Id. at 2362. We interpret this explanation as indicating that OSHA finds that although minor irritation may not be a material impairment, there is a level at which such irritation becomes so severe that employee health and job performance are seriously threatened, even though those effects may be transitory. We find this explanation adequate. OSHA is not required to state with scientific certainty or precision the exact point at which each type of sensory or physical irritation becomes a material impairment. Moreover, section 6(b)(5) of the Act charges OSHA with addressing all forms of "material impairment of health *or functional capacity,*" and not exclusively "death or serious physical harm" or "grave danger" from exposure to toxic substances. Overall, we find that OSHA's determinations of what constitute "material impairments" are adequately explained and supported in the record.

2. *Significant Risk*

However, the agency's determination of the extent of the risk posed by individual substances is more problematic.... OSHA has a responsibility to quantify or explain, at least to some reasonable degree, the risk posed by *each* toxic substance regulated. Otherwise, OSHA has not demonstrated, and this court cannot evaluate, how serious the risk is for any particular substance, or whether *any* workers will in fact benefit from the new standard for any particular substance. If each of these 428 toxic substances had been addressed in separate rulemakings, OSHA would clearly have been required to estimate in some fashion the risk of harm for each substance. OSHA is not entitled to take short-cuts with statutory requirements simply because it chose to combine multiple substances in a single rulemaking.

However, OSHA's discussions of individual substances generally contain no quantification or explanation of the risk from that individual substance. The discussions of individual substances contain summaries of various studies of that substance and the health effects found at various levels of exposure to that substance. However, OSHA made no attempt to estimate the risk of contracting those health effects. Instead, OSHA merely provided a conclusory statement that the new PEL will reduce the "significant" risk of material health effects shown to be caused by that substance, *see, e.g.*, 54 Fed. Reg. at 2508 (bismuth telluride), without any explanation of how the agency determined that the risk was significant. However, OSHA did make a generic finding that the Air Contaminants Standard as a whole would prevent 55,000 occupational illnesses and 683 deaths annually.

Moreover, a determination that the new standard is "reasonably necessary or appropriate," 29 U.S.C. § 652(8), and that it is the standard that "most adequately assures ... that no employee will suffer material impairment of health or functional capacity," *id.* § 655(b)(5), necessarily requires some assessment of the level at which significant risk of harm is eliminated or substantially reduced. Yet, with rare exceptions, the individual substance discussions in the Air Contaminants Standard are virtually devoid of reasons for setting those individual standards. In most cases, OSHA cited a few studies and then established a PEL without explaining why the studies mandated the particular PEL chosen. For example, the PEL for bismuth telluride appears to be based on a single study that showed almost no effects of any kind in animals at several times that concentration. Similarly, the PEL for ferrovanadium dust was based on pulmonary changes at exposure levels many hundreds of times higher than OSHA's new standard. For some substances, OSHA merely repeated a boilerplate finding that the new limit would protect workers from significant risk of some material health impairment. For example, OSHA did not cite any studies whatsoever for its aluminum welding fume standard, or its vegetable oil mist standard.

"While our deference to the agency is at a peak for its choices among scientific predictions, we must still look for *some* articulation of reasons for those choices." *Pendergrass,* 878 F.2d at 392 (emphasis added).

> Explicit explanation for the basis of the agency's decision not only facilitates proper judicial review but also provides the opportunity for effective peer review, legislative oversight, and public education. This requirement is in the best interest of everyone, including the decision-makers themselves. If the decision-making process is open and candid, it will inspire more confidence in those who are affected. Further, by opening the process to public scrutiny and criticism, we reduce the risk that important information will be overlooked or ignored.

AFL-CIO v. Marshall, 617 F.2d at 651-52. Mere conclusory statements, such as those made throughout the Air Contaminants Standard, are simply inadequate to support a finding of significant risk of material health impairment.

On the other hand, OSHA established PELs for carbon tetrachloride and vinyl bromide, both carcinogens, at levels where OSHA itself acknowledged that the risk of material health impairment remained significant. For carbon tetrachloride, OSHA stated that at the new level, "residual risk continues to be significant ... 3.7 excess deaths per 1,000 workers exposed over their working lifetimes." For vinyl bromide, OSHA stated that the new PEL "will not eliminate this significant risk, because ... residual risk [at the new level] is 40 excess deaths per 1,000 exposed workers ... [and thus] is clearly significant." The only explanation given by OSHA in the final rule for setting its standard where a significant risk of material health impairment remains was that the time and resource constraints of attempting to promulgate an air contaminants standard of this magnitude prevented detailed analysis of these substances. OSHA did not claim in the final rule that the PELs for these two substances were necessary because of feasibility concern.

The agency's response to this criticism is unpersuasive. OSHA first contends that quantitative risk analysis using mathematical models like the ones developed for carcinogens was impossible for this rulemaking because no such models exist for noncarcinogens.

> Dose-response models have often been used in the quantitative assessment of the risks associated with exposures to carcinogenic substances. However, less scientific effort has been devoted to models to be used with non-carcinogenic substances. Mathematically precise methods to establish the true no-effect level or to define the dose-response curves have not been developed for most of the more than 400 substances involved in this rulemaking.
>
> Most of the scientific work that has been done was designed to identify lowest observed effect or no-effect levels for a variety of acute effects.... It is possible to use these data, combined with professional judgment and OSHA's expertise and experience, to determine that significant risk exists at current levels of exposure and that a reduction in these levels will substantially reduce this risk of material impairment of health.

54 Fed. Reg. at 2399-2400. Yet, in several previous rulemakings, OSHA apparently succeeded in determining how many workers were exposed to a particular substance or how much risk would be alleviated by a new standard, even though those particular substances were *not* carcinogens. *See United Steelworkers*, 647 F.2d at 1245-51 (lead poisoning); *AFL-CIO v. Marshall*, 617 F.2d at 646 (byssinosis caused by cotton dust); *see also Building & Constr.*, 838 F.2d at 1263 (asbestosis and cancer). It is therefore unclear whether the lack of a method to quantitatively assess the risk for noncarcinogens is a cause or a result of the agency's approach. In this rulemaking, OSHA concluded that current exposure to 428 substances posed a "significant" risk of material health impairment, and that

its new standards were required for most of these substances to eliminate or substantially reduce that risk. It is not unreasonable to require that the agency explain how it arrived at that determination, and, indeed, this is precisely what Congress required.

The agency further claims that no quantification was required because OSHA's final standards "'fall[ ] within a zone of reasonableness.'" However, without *any* quantification or any explanation, this court cannot determine what that "zone of reasonableness" is or if these standards fall within it.

OSHA also responds by noting that it incorporated "uncertainty" or "safety" factors into many PELs. However, OSHA did not use a uniform safety factor, but instead claims to have made a case-by-case assessment of the appropriate safety factor. "Studies are often of small size and, since there is a large variation in human susceptibility, a study because of its small size may not demonstrate an effect that actually exists.... For this reason, it is not uncommon to set a limit below that level which the study may have indicated showed no effect." *Id.* at 2365. OSHA claims that use of such uncertainty factors "has been the standard approach for recommending exposure limits for non-carcinogens by scientists and health experts in the field for many years." *Id.* In this rulemaking, the difference between the level shown by the evidence and the final PEL is sometimes substantial. We assume, because it is not expressly stated, that for each of those substances OSHA applied a safety factor to arrive at the final standard. Nevertheless, the method by which the "appropriate" safety factor was determined for each of those substances is not explained in the final rule.

We find OSHA's use of safety factors in this rulemaking problematic. First, OSHA's use of safety factors in this rulemaking is very similar to the approach criticized by the Supreme Court in *Benzene.* Second, even assuming that the use of safety factors is permissible under the Act and *Benzene,* application of such factors without explaining the method by which they were determined, as was done in this case, is clearly not permitted.

From OSHA's description, safety factors are used to lower the standard below levels at which the available evidence shows no significant risk of material health impairment because of the *possibility* that the evidence is incorrect or incomplete; i.e., OSHA essentially makes an assumption that the existing evidence does not adequately show the extent of the risk. That may be a correct assumption, but beyond a general statement that the use of safety factors is common in the scientific community, OSHA did not indicate how the existing evidence for individual substances was inadequate to show the extent of the risk from those substances. Such a rationale is very reminiscent of the "benefits are likely to be appreciable" rationale rejected in *Benzene* as insufficient to satisfy the agency's obligations under the OSHAct. In *Benzene,* the Supreme Court noted that "[t]he evidence in the administrative record of adverse effects of benzene exposure at 10 ppm [the former PEL] is sketchy at best...." Comparing

OSHA's rationale for using safety factors in this rulemaking with the Court's discussion of their use in the *Benzene* case, we find little appreciable difference.

The Supreme Court in *Benzene* did recognize that absolute scientific certainty may be impossible when regulating on the edge of scientific knowledge, and that "so long as they are supported by a body of reputable scientific thought, the Agency is free to use conservative assumptions in interpreting the data ..., risking error on the side of overprotection rather than underprotection." [448 U.S.] at 656. However, the Court also discussed the use of monitoring and medical testing as a "backstop," permitting the agency to "keep a constant check on the validity of the assumptions made in developing the permissible exposure limit, giving it a sound evidentiary basis for decreasing the limit if it was initially set too high." *Id.* at 658.

The lesson of *Benzene* is clearly that OSHA may use assumptions, but only to the extent that those assumptions have some basis in reputable scientific evidence. If the agency is concerned that the standard should be more stringent than even a conservative interpretation of the existing evidence supports, monitoring and medical testing may be done to accumulate the additional evidence needed to support that more protective limit. *Benzene* does not provide support for setting standards below the level substantiated by the evidence. Nor may OSHA base a finding of significant risk at lower levels of exposure on unsupported assumptions using evidence of health impairments at significantly higher levels of exposure. Overall, OSHA's use of safety factors in this rule-making was not adequately explained by this rulemaking record.

More generally, OSHA defends its failure to make more specific findings for each individual substance, as well as its decision to set the standards for several substances at levels where significant risks of material health impairment remain, by citing its authority to set priorities, 29 U.S.C. § 655(g), and the discretion permitted the agency in making policy decisions. There were warning signs of this position in the Notice of Proposed Rulemaking, where OSHA expressed its view that "to review and regulate many substances in a reasonable period requires some narrowing of the issues, focus of analysis, and reducing the length of the discussions in the preamble." 53 Fed. Reg. at 20963.... Moreover, the agency stated that

> [i]n response to both the court challenges and the need to face difficult issues, OSHA has engaged in detailed and extensive analyses. These have resulted in lengthier preamble discussions and in-depth analyses for all issues....
>
> Now that OSHA has reviewed these issues in depth several times, has experience "gained under this ... law" (sec. 6(b)(5)) on these issues, and has had its analysis upheld in the Courts, somewhat less detailed chemical-by-chemical analyses should be appropriate. The accumulated judicial guidance and agency experience reduces the need for as extensive a discussion of some of the issues.

Id. at 20964. This implies that OSHA need no longer perform detailed analysis and explanation when promulgating PELs because the agency's analysis for other substances has been upheld in prior rulemakings. Besides displaying more than a touch of hubris, this passage reveals a fundamental misperception of the OSH Act and the caselaw [*sic*] interpreting that act.

While OSHA has probably established that most or all of the substances involved do pose a significant risk at some level, it has failed to establish that existing exposure levels in the workplace present a significant risk of material health impairment or that the new standards eliminate or substantially lessen the risk.

C. *Feasibility*

The Supreme Court has defined "feasibility" as "'capable of being done, executed, or effected,'" *ATMI,* 452 U.S. at 508-09 (quoting *Webster's Third New International Dictionary* 831 (1976)), both technologically and economically. Again, the burden is on OSHA to show by substantial evidence that the standard is feasible, although OSHA need not prove feasibility with scientific certainty. Despite OSHA's repeated claims that it made feasibility determinations on an industry-by-industry basis, it is clear that the agency again proceeded "generically."

1. *Technological Feasibility*

To show that a standard is technologically feasible, OSHA must demonstrate "that modern technology has at least conceived some industrial strategies or devices which are likely to be capable of meeting the PEL and which the industries are generally capable of adopting." *United Steelworkers,* 647 F.2d at 1266. Further, "the undisputed principle that feasibility is to be tested industry-by-industry demands that OSHA examine the technological feasibility of each industry individually." *Id.* at 1301. Courts have remanded OSHA determinations where the agency has not sufficiently analyzed the abilities of different industries to meet proposed standards.

In this rulemaking, OSHA first identified the primary air contaminant control methods: Engineering controls are methods such as ventilation, isolation, and substitution. Complementing the engineering controls are work practices and administrative reforms (e.g., housekeeping, material handling or transfer procedures, leak detection programs, training, and personal hygiene). Finally, personal protective equipment such as respirators and gloves may become necessary when these other controls are not fully effective.

OSHA then organized its discussion of technological feasibility by industry sector using the Standard Industrial Classification (SIC) groupings. The SIC codes classify by type of activity for purposes of promoting uniformity and comparability in the presentation of data. As the codes go from two and three digits to four digits, the groupings become progressively more specific. For example,

SIC Code 28 represents "Chemicals and Allied Products," SIC Code 281 represents "Industrial Inorganic Chemicals," and SIC Code 2812 includes only "Alkalies and Chlorine." OSHA primarily relied on the more general two-digit codes in its feasibility analysis. For most of the SIC codes discussed, OSHA provided only a general description of how generic engineering controls might be used in a given sector. Then, relying on this generic analysis, OSHA concluded

> that existing engineering controls are available to reduce exposure levels to the new levels.
>
> In reviewing the comments and hearing testimony on the technological feasibility of achieving the PELs and other limits, OSHA has found that for the overwhelming majority of situations where air contaminants are encountered by workers, compliance can be achieved by applying known engineering control methods and work practice improvements.

54 Fed. Reg. at 2289. However, OSHA made no attempt to show the ability of technology to meet specific exposure standards in specific industries. Except for an occasional specific conclusion as to whether a particular process control could meet a particular PEL, OSHA merely presented general conclusions as to the availability of these controls in a particular industry.

OSHA correctly notes that all it need demonstrate is "a general *presumption* of feasibility for *an industry*." *United Steelworkers,* 647 F.2d at 1266 (second emphasis added); *see also ASARCO,* 746 F.2d at 496. However, as this quote indicates, "a general presumption of feasibility" refers to a specific industry-by-industry determination that a "typical firm will be able to develop and install engineering and work practice controls that can meet the PEL in most of its operations." *United Steelworkers,* 647 F.2d at 1272. OSHA can prove this "by pointing to technology that is either already in use or has been conceived and is reasonably capable of experimental refinement and distribution within the standard's deadlines." *Id.* Only when OSHA has provided such proof for a given industry does there arise "a presumption that industry can meet the PEL without relying on respirators, a presumption which firms will have to overcome to obtain relief in any secondary inquiry into feasibility."

... Thus, it is clear that the concept of "a general presumption of feasibility" does not grant OSHA a license to make overbroad generalities as to feasibility or to group large categories of industries together without some explanation of why findings for the group adequately represent the different industries in that group. We find that OSHA has not established the technological feasibility of the 428 PELs in its revised Air Contaminants Standard.

2. *Economic Feasibility*

Nor has OSHA adequately demonstrated that the standard is economically feasible.... The determination of economic feasibility is governed by the same principles as technological feasibility. It must be supported by substantial evidence and OSHA must demonstrate its applicability to the affected industries.

In this rulemaking, although OSHA ostensibly recognized its responsibility "to demonstrate economic feasibility for *an industry*," 54 Fed. Reg. at 2367 (emphasis added), the agency nevertheless determined feasibility for each industry "*sector*" (i.e., two-digit SIC code), without explaining why such a broad grouping was appropriate. OSHA's economic feasibility determinations therefore suffer from the same faults as its technological feasibility findings. Indeed, it would seem particularly important not to aggregate disparate industries when making a showing of economic feasibility. OSHA admits that its economic feasibility conclusions only "have a high degree of validity on a sector basis," as opposed to a subsector or more industry-specific basis. *See also id.* at 2374 ("OSHA concludes that this approach is accurate on an industry sector by industry sector basis for individual processes."). OSHA then stated that "[t]he costs are sufficiently low per sector to demonstrate feasibility not only for each sector but also for each subsector."

However, reliance on such tools as average estimates of cost can be extremely misleading in assessing the impact of particular standards on individual industries. Analyzing the economic impact for an entire sector could conceal particular industries laboring under special disabilities and likely to fail as a result of enforcement. Moreover, for some substances, OSHA failed even to analyze all the affected industry sectors. *See, e.g., id.* at 2686-89 (perchloroethylene). We find that OSHA has not met its burden of establishing that its 428 new PELs are either economically or technologically feasible.

D. *The Perc Example*

OSHA's analysis of perchloroethylene (perc) is a prime example of the problems with OSHA's approach to this rulemaking. Perc is a widely used solvent in the drycleaning and industrial degreasing industries. Petitioners, the International Fabricare Institute ("IFI") and the Halogenated Solvents Industry Alliance, argue that OSHA's determination that perc presents a significant cancer risk is not supported by substantial evidence. On the other hand, the union argues that the final PEL adopted by OSHA, 25 ppm, though lower than the 50 ppm limit originally proposed, still leaves workers exposed to a significant cancer risk. Indeed, as OSHA recognized, the quantitative risk assessment on which the agency relied showed that even at an exposure level of 10 ppm, an excess risk of 6.4 deaths per 1000 workers would remain, which by OSHA's own admission is considered significant. OSHA, however, cited feasibility concerns for its decision not to lower the PEL even further. If supported by substantial evidence in the record, this would satisfy the requirements of the OSH Act.

Although OSHA stated that it "does not believe that information in the record at the present time demonstrates that it is feasible to reduce exposures to lower levels," OSHA's feasibility analysis for perc is grossly inadequate. For technological feasibility, OSHA limited its discussion to showing that its new PEL of 25 ppm was achievable. OSHA stated that 25 ppm can be achieved with newer equipment and engineering and work practice controls. OSHA also stated that "a significant percentage of operations, including smaller operations, have installed" the newer equipment, and that the industry as a whole "is gradually replacing older equipment with newer equipment." However, there is no explanation or evidence cited in the final rule to support the proposition that an even lower PEL is not technologically feasible.

On the other hand, OSHA's economic feasibility determination for perc cannot support either the new PEL of 25 ppm or the agency's decision not to set an even lower PEL. OSHA used the two-digit SIC code, SIC 72 — Personal Services, to define the industries affected by the perc standard. This creates two problems. First, drycleaning is the only industry in SIC 72 affected by the perc standard. SIC 72 covers numerous other industries, including funeral services, shoe repairs, barber and beauty shops, and photography studios. Nevertheless, OSHA took the costs of compliance with the new perc standard, which would be borne only by the drycleaning industry subsector (SIC code 7216), and compared those costs to the profits and sales of the entire personal services sector (SIC 72). As a result, OSHA must have significantly understated the costs of compliance for the drycleaning industry. Indeed, petitioners claim that the actual economic impact on this industry would be more than ten times OSHA's estimate.

Moreover, while the drycleaning industry received at least some feasibility analysis for perc, the other major user of that chemical, industrial degreasing operations, received none. This industry is not in SIC 72, which was the only industry sector reviewed for technological or economic feasibility for the new perc standard. Therefore, OSHA clearly has not fulfilled its duty to examine the feasibility of its perc standard for each affected industry.

Accordingly, while OSHA has determined that significant risk remains for exposure to perc at a level of 25 ppm, it is not clear from the record that 25 ppm is the lowest feasible level. The union claims that it would be feasible to set the standard lower than 25 ppm, perhaps as low as 10 ppm. Industry, on the other hand, claims that even 25 ppm is not feasible. From the record and final rule as presented, it is impossible for this court to determine which claim is correct.

E. *Other Union Issues*

Union petitioners raise several other issues that deserve comment.

1. *Use of ACGIH Recommendations*

[The court rejected the union's claim that OSHA should not have relied on the American Conference of Governmental Industrial Hygienists' recommendations to limit the substances to be included in the generic rulemaking.]

2. *Exclusion of Monitoring and Medical Surveillance*

[The court also rejected a union challenge to OSHA's decision to defer issuing standards for monitoring and medical surveillance of the new PELs until a later rulemaking.]

3. *Four-year Compliance Period*

The union also challenges OSHA's decision to allow four years, until December 31, 1992, for the implementation of engineering and work practice controls to bring industry into compliance with the new standards, while in the interim permitting compliance through the use of respirators. As a transitional provision, OSHA specified that employers must continue to achieve the 1971 PELs by adhering to the hierarchy of controls in 29 C.F.R. § 1910.1000(e), as they have been required to do since 1971. In adopting this four-year time period, OSHA stated that the agency's "experience is that for substances of normal difficulty, one to two years is sufficient," 54 Fed. Reg. at 2916, but that a four-year period "takes into account that some employers will have to control several substances and also considers those few substances where compliance may take greater efforts for some employers," *id.* That conclusory analysis falls short of justifying an across-the-board four-year period of delay, but is fully consistent with OSHA's treatment of this standard as a "generic" standard, without adequate consideration of individual substances or the effect of the new standards on individual industries.

This "generic" four-year compliance period is simply not adequately supported in the record. Unlike other standards where OSHA has exercised its "technology-forcing" authority and required that industries develop the technology to achieve the new standards, in this standard, "OSHA's feasibility analysis was based on what industry is already achieving or what could be achieved with standard 'off-the-shelf' technology, [and] there are few if any cases where OSHA is attempting to force technology." 54 Fed. Reg. at 2366. If the technology exists and is in many cases already being used, it is difficult to understand why four years is required for the implementation of this standard for all industries. If OSHA's concern was primarily economic feasibility, that too needed to be addressed for each industry or for each appropriate industrial grouping.

To the extent that there may be any unusual situations in which a feasibility problem exists, the OSH Act and the standard itself provide appropriate means of dealing with such problems without resorting to the extreme expedient of an across-the-board four-year compliance period. First, section 6(b)(6) allows an employer to obtain a temporary variance if that employer "is unable to comply with a standard by its effective date because of unavailability of professional or technical personnel or of materials and equipment needed to come into compliance with the standard or because necessary construction or alteration of facilities cannot be completed by the effective date." Furthermore, if the rulemaking record establishes that specific industries will need an extended period of time to comply with PELs for certain substances, OSHA could so provide, just as it allows respirator use after December 1992 for four substances in specified operations. 54 Fed. Reg. at 2335, 2916 (carbon monoxide, carbon disulfide, styrene, and sulfur dioxide). We find insufficient explanation in the record to support this across-the-board four-year delay in implementation of this rule.

IV. *Conclusion*

It is clear that the analytical approach used by OSHA in promulgating its revised Air Contaminants Standard is so flawed that it cannot stand. OSHA not only mislabeled this a "generic" rulemaking, but it inappropriately treated it as such. The result of this approach is a set of 428 inadequately supported standards. OSHA has lumped together substances and affected industries and provided such inadequate explanation that it is virtually impossible for a reviewing court to determine if sufficient evidence supports the agency's conclusions. The individual substances discussed in this opinion are merely examples of what is endemic in the Air Contaminants Standard as a whole.

OSHA does have the authority to set priorities for establishing standards under the OSH Act. *See* 29 U.S.C. § 655(g). That priority-setting authority permits OSHA to combine rulemaking for multiple substances in one rulemaking, to limit the scope of this rulemaking in a rational manner, and to defer issuance of regulations for monitoring and medical surveillance until a later rulemaking. It does not, however, give OSHA blanket authority to pick and choose what statutory requirements it will follow. The OSH Act mandates that OSHA promulgate the standards that "most adequately" assure that workers will not be exposed to significant risks of material health impairment "to the extent feasible" for the affected industries. Further, section 6(e) and caselaw [*sic*] require OSHA to adequately explain its determinations. Section 6(b) of the Act does not provide an exception to these requirements for administrative convenience. The only exceptions to the strict statutory criteria are the start-up provisions of section 6(a), the applicability of which has long since passed, and the emergency provisions of section 6(c), neither of which are implicated in this case.

Therefore, although we find that the record adequately explains and supports OSHA's determination that the health effects of exposure to these 428 substances are material impairments, we hold that OSHA has not sufficiently explained or supported its threshold determination that exposure to these substances at previous levels posed a significant risk of these material health impairments or that the new standard eliminates or reduces that risk to the extent feasible. OSHA's overall approach to this rulemaking is so flawed that we must vacate the whole revised Air Contaminants Standard.

We have no doubt that the agency acted with the best of intentions. It may well be, as OSHA claims, that this was the only practical way of accomplishing a much needed revision of the existing standards and of making major strides towards improving worker health and safety. Given OSHA's history of slow progress in issuing standards, we can easily believe OSHA's claim that going through detailed analysis for each of the 428 different substances regulated was not possible given the time constraints set by the agency for this rulemaking. Unfortunately, OSHA's approach to this rulemaking is not consistent with the requirements of the OSH Act. Before OSHA uses such an approach, it must get authorization from Congress by way of amendment to the OSH Act. Legislative decisions on the federal level are to be made in the chambers of Congress. It is not for this court to undertake the substantial rewriting of the Act necessary to uphold OSHA's approach to this rulemaking.

Therefore, for the reasons stated above, we vacate the revised Air Contaminants Standard, and remand to the agency.

NOTE

New Permanent Standards. The *AFL-CIO v. OSHA* opinion seems to doom efforts to expedite the process of promulgating generic standards that apply to a multiplicity of toxic substances. The alternative route is to issue a series of standards, each dealing with a particular toxic substance, harmful physical agent, or some other threat to workers' safety or health.

An example of a permanent standard dealing with a particular risk is the process safety management (PSM) standard that requires companies to adopt detailed management plans to prevent catastrophic chemical explosions, which was issued in February 1992. 29 C.F.R. § 1910.119. The rule primarily affects petrochemical and chemical companies, natural gas manufacturers, and other industries that transport or mix chemicals. The OSHA standard requires industries to analyze potential hazards in each step of chemical processes and take any necessary action to avoid chemical releases or explosions.

The most significant developments in recent years concerning permanent standards have involved the efforts by Congress to limit OSHA's ability to promulgate and enforce the standards. As described in Section A of this chapter, Subtitle E of the Small Business Regulatory Enforcement Fairness Act of 1996 has created a new opportunity for Congress to review and reject new permanent standards after they are promulgated by OSHA. In addition, Congress has used its authority to delay the promulgation of an ergonomics standard that would require employers to reduce the incidence of cumulative or repetitive trauma disorders from lifting, assembly, and other stresses to muscles, nerves, and tendons. Repetitive strain injuries are the fastest growing category of occupational illnesses, with an annual cost of $20 billion a year, according to one estimate. Employers have vigorously resisted the notion that OSHA should issue an ergonomics standard, and apparently will succeed in having Congress add a provision to the 1998 fiscal year appropriation for the Department of Labor that will prohibit OSHA from issuing an ergonomics standard for one year. Earlier Congressional riders had prohibited OSHA from even working on a possible ergonomics standard for much of 1995 and 1996.

The 1998 appropriations for the Department of Labor apparently will also contain a rider limiting OSHA's authority to enforce the methylene chloride standard during the 1998 fiscal year. The standard, issued in January 1997, reduced the permissible exposure level for methylene chloride from 500 parts per million (ppm) to 25 ppm measured over an eight-hour period. The budget language would largely prevent OSHA from enforcing the standard for most employers with 150 or fewer employees.

E. THE GENERAL DUTY CLAUSE

NATIONAL REALTY & CONSTRUCTION CO. v. OSHRC

United States Court of Appeals, D.C. Circuit

489 F.2d 1257 (1973)

Before WRIGHT and ROBB, CIRCUIT JUDGES, and MATTHEWS, SENIOR DISTRICT JUDGE.

WRIGHT, CIRCUIT JUDGE.

We review here an order of the Occupational Safety and Health Review Commission which found National Realty and Construction Company, Inc. to have committed a "serious violation" of the "general duty clause" of the Occupational Safety and Health Act of 1970, for which a civil fine of $300 was imposed. Unable to locate substantial evidence in the record to support the Commission's finding of a violation, we reverse.

I. *The Proceedings and the Evidence*

....

An employer's duties under the Act flow from two sources. First, by 29 U.S.C. § 654(a)(2) [§ 5(a)(2)], he must conform to the detailed health and safety standards promulgated by the Secretary of Labor under 29 U.S.C. § 655 [§ 6]. Second, where no promulgated standards apply, he is subject to the general duty to

> furnish to each of his employees employment and a place of employment which are free from recognized hazards that are causing or are likely to cause death or serious physical harm to his employees.

[§ 5(a)(1),] 29 U.S.C. § 654(a)(1). Breach of the general duty opens an employer to fines of up to $1,000 per violation, some fine in this range being mandatory if the violation is "serious," 29 U.S.C. § 666(b) and (c). Employer duties are enforced through citations and proposed penalties issued by the Secretary of Labor, contested matters being adjudicated by the Commission, an independent body of safety experts.

On September 24, 1971 the Secretary cited National Realty for serious breach of its general duty

> in that an employee was permitted to stand as a passenger on the running board of an Allis Chalmers 645 Front end loader while the loader was in motion.

After National Realty filed timely notice of contest, the Secretary entered a formal complaint charging that National Realty had

> permitted the existence of a condition which constituted a recognized hazard that was likely to cause death or serious physical harm to its employees. Said condition, which resulted in the death of foreman O. C. Smith, arose when Smith stood as a passenger on the running board of a piece of construction equipment which was in motion.

At an administrative hearing, held before an examiner appointed by the Commission, William Simms, the Labor Department inspector who cited National Realty, testified in person, and counsel read into the record a summary of stipulated testimony by several employees of National Realty. The evidence is quickly restated.

On September 16, 1971, at a motel construction site operated by National Realty in Arlington, Virginia, O. C. Smith, a foreman with the company, rode the running board of a front-end loader driven by one of his subordinates, Clyde Williams. The loader suffered a stalled engine while going down an earthen ramp into an excavation and began to swerve off the ramp. Smith jumped from the loader, but was killed when it toppled off the ramp and fell on him. John Irwin, Smith's supervisor, testified that he had not seen the accident, that Smith's safety record had been very good, that the company had a "policy" against equipment riding, and that he — Irwin — had stopped the "4 or 5" employees he had seen taking rides in the past two years. The loader's driver testified that he did not order Smith off the vehicle because Smith was his foreman; he further testified that loader riding was extremely rare at National Realty. Another company employee testified that it was contrary to company policy to ride on heavy equipment. A company supervisor said he had reprimanded violators of this policy and would fire second offenders should the occasion arise. Simms, the inspector, testified from personal experience that the Army Corps of Engineers has a policy against equipment riding. He stated he was unaware of other instances of equipment riding at National Realty and that the company had "abated" its violation. Asked to define abatement, Simms said it would consist of orally instructing equipment drivers not to allow riding.

The hearing examiner dismissed the citation, finding that National Realty had not "permitted" O. C. Smith to ride the loader, as charged in the citation and complaint.... Upon reviewing the hearing record, the Commission reversed its examiner by a 2-1 vote, each commissioner writing separately. Ruling for the Secretary, Commissioners Burch and Van Namee found inadequate implementation of National Realty's safety "policy." Rejecting the hearing examiner's factual findings in part, Commissioner Burch stated that it was "incredible" that an oral safety policy could have reduced equipment riding to a rare occurrence. Commissioner Van Namee reasoned that the Smith incident and the "4 or 5" occurrences shown on the record "put respondent on notice that more was required of it to obtain effective implementation of its safety policy." The majority commissioners briefly suggested several improvements which National Realty might have effected in its safety policy: placing the policy in writing, posting no-riding signs, threatening riders with automatic discharge, and providing alternative means of transport at the construction site. In dissent, Commissioner Moran concluded that the Secretary had not proved his charge that National Realty had "permitted" either equipment riding in general or the particular incident which caused Smith's death.

II. *The Issues*

....

Thus, despite the awkwardness of his charges and pleadings, the Secretary could properly have produced evidence at the hearing on the question whether National Realty's safety policy failed, in design or implementation, to meet the standards of the general duty clause. Under the clause, the Secretary must prove (1) that the employer failed to render its workplace "free" of a hazard which was (2) "recognized" and (3) "causing or likely to cause death or serious physical harm." The hazard here was the dangerous activity of riding heavy equipment. The record clearly contains substantial evidence to support the Commission's finding that this hazard was "recognized"[32] and "likely to cause death or serious physical harm."[33] The question then is whether National Realty rendered its construction site "free" of the hazard. In this case of first impression, the meaning of that statutory term must be settled before the sufficiency of the evidence can be assessed.

---

[32] An activity may be a "recognized hazard" even if the defendant employer is ignorant of the activity's existence or its potential for harm. The term received a concise definition in a floor speech by Representative Daniels when he proposed an amendment which became the present version of the general duty clause:

> A recognized hazard is a condition that is known to be hazardous, and is known not necessarily by each and every individual employer but is known taking into account the standard of knowledge in the industry. In other words, whether or not a hazard is "recognized" is a matter for objective determination; it does not depend on whether the particular employer is aware of it.

116 Cong. Rec. (Part 28) 38377 (1970). The standard would be the common knowledge of safety experts who are familiar with the circumstances of the industry or activity in question. The evidence below showed that both National Realty and the Army Corps of Engineers took equipment riding seriously enough to prohibit it as a matter of policy. Absent contrary indications, this is at least substantial evidence that equipment riding is a "recognized hazard."

[33] Presumably, any given instance of equipment riding carries a less than 50% probability of serious mishap, but no such mathematical test would be proper in construing this element of the general duty clause. *See* Morey, *The General Duty Clause of the Occupational Safety and Health Act of 1970*, 86 Harv. L. Rev. 988, 997-998 (1973). If evidence is presented that a practice could eventuate in serious physical harm upon other than a freakish or utterly implausible concurrence of circumstances, the Commission's expert determination of likelihood should be accorded considerable deference by the courts. For equipment riding, the potential for injury is indicated on the record by Smith's death and, of course, by common sense.

Construing the term in the present context presents a dilemma. On the one hand, the adjective is unqualified and absolute: A workplace cannot be just "reasonably free" of a hazard, or merely as free as the average workplace in the industry. On the other hand, Congress quite clearly did not intend the general duty clause to impose strict liability: The duty was to be an achievable one. Congress' language is consonant with its intent only where the "recognized" hazard in question *can be* totally eliminated from a workplace. A hazard consisting of conduct by employees, such as equipment riding, cannot, however, be totally eliminated. A demented, suicidal, or willfully reckless employee may on occasion circumvent the best conceived and most vigorously enforced safety regime. This seeming dilemma is, however, soluble within the literal structure of the general duty clause. Congress intended to require elimination only of preventable hazards. It follows, we think, that Congress did not intend unpreventable hazards to be considered "recognized" under the clause. Though a generic form of hazardous conduct, such as equipment riding, may be "recognized," unpreventable instances of it are not, and thus the possibility of their occurrence at a workplace is not inconsistent with the workplace being "free" of recognized hazards.

Though resistant to precise definition, the criterion of preventability draws content from the informed judgment of safety experts. Hazardous conduct is not preventable if it is so idiosyncratic and implausible in motive or means that conscientious experts, familiar with the industry, would not take it into account in prescribing a safety program. Nor is misconduct preventable if its elimination would require methods of hiring, training, monitoring, or sanctioning workers which are either so untested or so expensive that safety experts would substantially concur in thinking the methods infeasible. All preventable forms and instances of hazardous conduct must, however, be entirely excluded from the workplace. To establish a violation of the general duty clause, hazardous conduct need not actually have occurred, for a safety program's feasibly curable inadequacies may sometimes be demonstrated before employees have acted dangerously. At the same time, however, actual occurrence of hazardous conduct is not, by itself, sufficient evidence of a violation, even when the conduct has led to injury. The record must additionally indicate that demonstrably feasible measures would have materially reduced the likelihood that such misconduct would have occurred.

C. *Deficiencies in This Record*

The hearing record shows several incidents of equipment riding, including the Smith episode where a foreman broke a safety policy he was charged with enforcing. It seems quite unlikely that these were unpreventable instances of hazardous conduct. But the hearing record is barren of evidence describing, and demonstrating the feasibility and likely utility of, the particular measures which National Realty should have taken to improve its safety policy. Having the burden of proof, the Secretary must be charged with these evidentiary deficiencies.

The Commission sought to cure these deficiencies *sua sponte* by speculating about what National Realty could have done to upgrade its safety program. These suggestions, while not unattractive, came too late in the proceedings. An employer is unfairly deprived of an opportunity to cross-examine or to present rebuttal evidence and testimony when it learns the exact nature of its alleged violation only after the hearing. As noted above, the Secretary has considerable scope before and during a hearing to alter his pleadings and legal theories. But the Commission cannot make these alterations itself in the face of an empty record.[40] To merit judicial deference, the Commission's expertise must operate upon, not seek to replace, record evidence.

Only by requiring the Secretary, at the hearing, to formulate and defend *his own* theory of what a cited defendant should have done can the Commission and the courts assure even-handed enforcement of the general duty clause.[41] Because employers have a general duty to do virtually everything possible to prevent and repress hazardous conduct by employees, violations exist almost everywhere, and the Secretary has an awesomely broad discretion in selecting defendants and in proposing penalties. To assure that citations issue only upon careful deliberation, the Secretary must be constrained to specify the particular steps a

---

[40] It is patently unfair for an agency to decide a case on a legal theory or set of facts which was not presented at the hearing. The Commission suggested that National Realty should have posted "no-riding" signs or reduced its safety policy to writing, but the Secretary introduced no testimony indicating the value of such precautions relative to "orally" disseminated safety policies. The Commission [made several other suggestions, without the Secretary introducing evidence on point]. In short, the Commissioners attempted to serve as expert witnesses for the Secretary. This is not their role. The Secretary should have called his own expert or experts at the hearing.

[41] Such precautions will not, of course, make the broad commands of the general duty clause any more precise and clear to *prospective* violators of the clause. But any statute or rule of law imposing general obligations raises certain problems of fair notice. [T]he Commission can ameliorate the fair notice problem by attending carefully to the statutory definition of a "serious violation": ... 29 U.S.C. § 666(j). Where the hazard involved is a form of hazardous conduct by employees, an employer's safety program is in "serious" violation of the general duty clause only if (1) the misconduct involves a substantial risk of harm and is substantially probable under the employer's regime of safety precautions, or (2) the employer, with the exercise of reasonable diligence, could have known that its safety program failed the standards of the clause by failing to preclude the occurrence of preventable misconduct. If either condition applies, it is hardly unfair for the Commission to assume that the defendant-employer had at least constructive notice that the law required more than was being done. Only if a violation is serious is a penalty necessarily imposed. *Compare* 29 U.S.C. § 666(b) *with* 29 U.S.C. § 666(c). While the Commission has the clear authority to impose a penalty even if the violation is not serious, a zero penalty, coupled with an abatement order, would obviously be the proper response where the Commission determined that the defendant-employer had no notice, i.e., no duty to know, that its safety regime was defective.

Given our disposition of this case, there is no occasion to decide if National Realty's violation, properly proved, would be "serious."

cited employer should have taken to avoid citation, and to demonstrate the feasibility and likely utility of those measures.

Because the Secretary did not shoulder his burden of proof, the record lacks substantial evidence of a violation, and the Commission's decision and order are, therefore,

Reversed.

NOTES

1. *The Four Elements of a General Duty Violation.* The *National Realty* decision articulated three elements that OSHA must prove to establish a general duty violation. Subsequent decisions by the Review Commission and the courts have established four elements of general duty violation, in effect bifurcating the first element discussed in *National Realty*. OSHA's 1983 Field Operations Manual enumerated the four elements of a section 5(a)(1) violation:

(1) The employer failed to keep the workplace free of a hazard to which employees of that employer were exposed;

(2) The hazard was recognized;

(3) The hazard was causing or was likely to cause death or serious physical harm; and

(4) There was a feasible and useful method to correct the hazard.

2. *Element One: The Hazard Must Affect the Cited Employer's Employees.* This element is usually not a major issue unless there is a complex situation, such as a multi-employer worksite.

3. *Element Two: The Hazard Must Be Recognized.* What is the meaning of a recognizable hazard? Suppose, for example, that the workers and the employer who manufacture Grimeoff, an industrial soap, do not realize that the odorless fumes that spew from the soap vat are carcinogenic, although this fact is known to epidemiologists. Is the hazard recognizable? In note 32 of the *National Realty* decision, Judge Wright stated that "an activity may be a 'recognized hazard' even if the defendant employer is ignorant of the activity's existence or its potential for harm." Contrast this view with that of Representative Steiger, one of the primary authors of the OSHAct. In explaining the Act on the House floor, he defined the term "recognized hazards" as hazards "that can readily be detected on the basis of the basic human senses. Hazards which require technical or testing devices to detect them are not intended to be within the scope of the general duty requirement." 116 Cong. Rec. H42,206 (Daily ed. Dec. 17, 1970).

Despite this warning that recognized hazards must be detectable by the human senses, OSHA has consistently treated section 5(a)(1) as also covering hazards whose detection requires monitoring devices. This policy was upheld in *American Smelting & Refining Co. v. OSHRC*, 501 F.2d 504 (8th Cir. 1974). *See generally* BENJAMIN W. MINTZ, OSHA: HISTORY, LAW, AND POLICY 446 (1984). So much for legislative intent!

As a policy matter, do we want to hold employers responsible under the general duty clause for hazards that are not immediately obvious? Should not employer responsibility for these types of nonobvious hazards only result from the violation of a permanent standard issued under section 6(b), the promulgation of which will put the employer on notice of possible liability?

4. *Element Three: Likelihood of Death or Serious Harm.* The courts and the Commission have tried several approaches to defining a likelihood of death or serious injury, which can perhaps be better understood by distinguishing among three statistical measures. *Pe* is the probability of a harmful event occurring (e.g., an injury) per unit of exposure (e.g., per use of a machine or per year). *Pdsh* is the probability of death or serious harm occurring, assuming that a harmful event has occurred. *Pzap* is the product of *Pe* and *Pdsh* and represents the probability of death or serious harm occurring per unit of exposure.

The legal issue is: what values of *Pe, Pdsh,* or *Pzap* constitute a sufficient "likelihood of death or serious injury" that a violation of section 5(a)(1) has occurred? A warning: the courts have not explicitly adopted the concepts (and surely have not adopted the terminology) in this note, and may be skeptical of the approach. Review, if you will, the language in note 33 of the *National Realty* decision.

Note 33 provides an admonition against a mathematical test, but nonetheless offers some guidance about the level of *Pzap* necessary for a violation. That "a given instance of equipment riding carries a less than 50% probability of serious mishap" does not preclude a finding of a violation so long as serious physical harm (*Pzap*) is not "freakish or utterly implausible." Does this mean that *Pzap* could be as low as .001? How about .0001?

While the court in *National Realty* framed the statistical test in terms of the necessary level of *Pzap,* the Commission thereafter began to examine the components *Pe* and *Pdsh.* In *Secretary of Labor v. R. L. Sanders Roofing Co.,* 7 O.S.H. Cas. (BNA) 1566 (1979), *rev'd on other grounds,* 620 F.2d 97 (5th Cir. 1980), the Commission held that *Pdsh* was the critical variable: "The proper question is not whether an accident is likely to occur but whether, if an accident does occur, the result is likely to be death or serious physical harm." In effect, *Pe* could be low (as low as .0001?) so long as *Pdsh* was greater than .5 (if an accident occurs, the likely result is death or serious harm). Some courts have termed this the "possibility" test, because a general duty violation is made out by showing a mere possibility of a serious accident. Then in *Secretary of Labor v. Bomac Drilling,* 9 O.S.H. Cas. (BNA) 1681 (1981), the Commission held that the "incident" creating the hazard must be "reasonably foreseeable." Presumably this meant that *Pe* must be more than just possible, but less than probable (*Pe* must be more than .001 but less than .5?). The requirement for *Pdsh* was not changed (i.e., death or serious harm must be the likely result of an incident). The Secretary of Labor adopted this "reasonable foreseeability" test for enforcement activities.

In *Pratt & Whitney Aircraft v. Secretary of Labor,* 649 F.2d 96 (2d Cir. 1981), the Second Circuit rejected both the "possibility" test and the "reasonable foreseeability" test as being too easy for the Secretary of Labor to prove. Instead, the court endorsed a "significant risk of harm" test that was adapted from the test used in the *Benzene* case for promulgation of a new standard under section 6(b). Although the court was not clear about the meaning of a "significant risk of harm" in the context of a general duty violation, one interpretation is that the required level for *Pzap* was .001 or greater.

The Commission again dealt with the meaning of the likelihood of death or serious physical harm in *Secretary of Labor v. Kastalon, Inc.,* 12 O.S.H. Cas. (BNA) 1928 (1986), and embraced the "significant risk" test. The commission threw out a citation of *Kastalon* and held that "in order to establish a significant risk in a Section 5(a)(1) case involving a carcinogen, the Secretary must show the probability that employees will contract cancer under the conditions present in the workplace. This is consistent with the Supreme Court decision in the *Benzene* Case." As discussed in note 2 after the *Benzene* case [*Industrial Union Dep't v Am. Petr. Inst.,* 448 U.S. 607 (1980)], the significant risk test requires at least a one in a thousand chance of developing cancer from exposure to a carcinogen during a working career. Thus, in terms of the statistical measures used in this note, the Commission in *Kastalon* appeared to be requiring a *Pzap* of at least 0.001 in order to find a violation of the general duty clause.

This interpretation must be tempered by the Commission's explanation of the *Kastalon* decision in *Secretary of Labor v. Waldon Healthcare Center,* 16 O.S.H. Cas. (BNA) 1052 (1993). Waldon was issued a citation alleging a violation of the general duty clause because nurses and nursing assistants were exposed to Hepatitis B virus ("HBV") through possible direct contact with blood or other bodily fluids. The Commission concluded that "the evidence establishes that the risk of contacting blood during the various nursing home procedures is rather low ..." [Using our terminology, this could be interpreted as meaning that *Pe* was low.] The Commission also concluded that the "evidence amply demonstrates that a person who contracts the HBV virus is likely to suffer death or serious physical harm." [Using our terminology, this is equivalent to saying that *Pdsh* is high.]

The Commission then explained the legal test that is applicable to decide whether there is a likelihood of death or serious harm, as required by the general duty clause. The Commission stated that "[t]he essence of the *Kastalon* holding is that when citing a violation of the general duty clause, the Secretary must establish that the cited condition actually poses a hazard to employees.... Therefore, when the Secretary proceeds under the general duty clause, he must meet the same minimal criterion regarding the nature of the alleged hazards he does when promulgating a section 5(a)(2) standard." The Commission stated that those minimal criterion are provided in the *Benzene* case, and provided this guidance as to the meaning:

> Contrary to ARA's [the respondent's] argument, to be consistent with the Supreme Court decision in the '*Benzene* Case,' there is no requirement that there be a 'significant' risk of the hazard coming to fruition, only that if the hazardous event occurs, it would create a 'significant risk' to employees.

This passage from *Waldon* appears to endorse the "possibility" test for determining whether element three of the general duty clause has been satisfied. And the required probability of *Pe* appears to be quite low, perhaps no more than one chance in ten thousand (.0001). This interpretation of *Waldon* is strengthened by the Commission's citation of *R.L. Sanders Roofing Co.* as authority, since this was the decision that established the "possibility" test. One problem with this interpretation is that the Commission treats the holding in *Waldon* as if it were consistent with the *Benzene* case. However, while the Commission in *Waldon* interpreted the *Benzene* case as imposing "no requirement that there be a 'significant risk' of the hazard coming to fruition," the general interpretation of the significant risk test imposed by the *Benzene* case is that there must be at least a one in a thousand chance that the worker will develop cancer or some other serious harm during the worker's lifetime. *Pzap* cannot be at least one in a thousand unless *Pe* is at least one in a thousand since the value of *Pdsh* must be one or less. Thus the Commission now appears to be requiring a lower *Pe* for a general duty clause violation than the *Pe* that the federal courts require to meet the significant risk test for permanent standards.

Congratulations! You have been hired as a consultant to OSHA to blend the best of statistics and law. What values of *Pe*, *Pdsh*, and *Pzap* would you require for a violation of the general duty clause?

5. *Element Four: A Feasible Method to Correct the Hazard.* What responsibilities does an employer have to deal with recognized hazards at the worksite? For example, suppose that an employer operates in an area subject to earthquakes. Is an earthquake a hazard for which the employer is responsible under section 5(a)(1)? The *National Realty* decision suggests that "hazard" means "preventable hazard," which presumably would absolve an employer from liability for an injury resulting from an earthquake because there is no feasible method to correct the hazard.

But what about hazardous conduct by an employee? *National Realty* indicates that hazardous conduct "is not preventable if it so idiosyncratic and implausible in motive or means that conscientious experts, familiar with the industry, would not take it into account in prescribing a safety program." Did the conduct of the supervisor who was injured in the case meet this test? As a policy matter, should OSHA make employers responsible only for hazards that are preventable? If National Realty had been made responsible for the supervisor's injury, perhaps under a standard of absolute liability, the costs of the hazardous conduct would have been reflected in the price of the firm's product, which in turn would have resulted in less consumption of the product. Should the OSHAct be interpreted to encourage reduced consumption and production of products that involve hazards to workers, even when, from the standpoint of the employer, the hazard is not preventable? An absolute liability standard would also force employers to implement the latest technology and training methods in order to avoid injuries and fatalities.

Further examination of the fourth element of a section 5(a)(1) violation raises an equity issue. Suppose, for example, that the manufacturer of Grimeoff is in an industry that routinely allows impurities in the soap that are causing the health problem. Nonetheless, the engineers for the manufacturer of Grimeoff have identified a relatively expensive process that will remove the impurities. Is Grimeoff required to use this process when the industry practice is to leave the impurities in the soap? The *National Realty* decision represents the majority view, namely that an employer's obligations are not limited by industry practice. But is it appropriate to put an employer at a competitive disadvantage by imposing a higher standard of performance on the firm through the general duty clause? As will be discussed in the next section dealing with enforcement, other firms in the industry may not be inspected for years or even decades, and so the competitive disadvantage of the firm cited for a general duty violation that imposes standards on the firm higher than those used elsewhere in the industry is likely to persist for an extended period.

REICH v. ARCADIAN CORP.

United States Court of Appeals, Fifth Circuit
110 F.3d 1192 (1997)

STEWART, CIRCUIT JUDGE:

Today we interpret the meaning of the General Duty Clause of the Occupational Safety and Health Act of 1970 (OSH Act) (29 U.S.C. §§ 651-678). This case presents the question of whether the Secretary of Labor (Secretary) was correct when he decided to fine Arcadian Corporation (Arcadian) on a per-employee basis for violating the Clause. The Occupational Safety and Health Review Commission (Commission) reversed the Secretary's decision, holding that the unit of prosecution under the Clause is the *condition* that poses a hazard to employees, and not the affected employee(s). The Secretary filed this petition for review. We deny the petition and hold that the General Duty Clause unambiguously provides that the violative condition, not the employee, is the unit of prosecution.

Background

Arcadian Corporation (Arcadian) manufactures fertilizer at a plant in Lake Charles, Louisiana. A terrible accident occurred on July 28, 1992. That day, a urea reactor at the plant exploded, scattering the reactor and its contents over a 600-acre area. The reactor's 19,000 pound steel head was blown 500 feet, and ammonia and carbon dioxide, heated to 370 degrees F, were released into the atmosphere. According to the Secretary, Arcadian had detected leaks in the liner of the reactor's pressure vessel prior to the explosion and failed to take steps to eliminate the hazard, such as shutting down the reactor, implementing a program to monitor the vessel's leak detection system, and assuring that critical welds were performed according to industry standards and design specifications. Eighty-seven Arcadian employees were exposed to the danger of being struck by flying debris, suffering heat and chemical burns, and asphyxiation by toxic gases.

Procedural History

In January 1993, the Occupational Health and Safety Administration (OSHA) cited Arcadian for violations of the OSH Act. The Secretary of Labor argued that Arcadian willfully violated the OSH Act's General Duty Clause, which requires employers to provide a place of employment free from hazards that cause or are likely to cause death or serious physical harm to employees. 29 U.S.C. § 654(a)(1). Citation 2, Item 1 alleged that Arcadian had failed to provide Mary Poullard Smith with safe employment because the catastrophic explosion in the pressure vessel constituted a violation of the General Duty Clause. OSHA alleged that the violation was willful and proposed a penalty of $50,000 and several other corrective measures.[1] Items 2 through 87 of Citation 2 were identical to Item 1 except for the identity of the employee exposed to the hazard. When all was said and done, Arcadian was assessed a penalty of $4,350,000.

Pursuant to the OSH Act, Arcadian contested the citations before an administrative law judge (ALJ) on the ground that the unit of prosecution for violating the General Duty Clause is the violative condition, not the employee or employees exposed to that condition. After some discovery, Arcadian moved for partial summary judgment and requested that Items 2 through 87 be vacated and their allegations consolidated with Item 1. The Secretary of Labor filed a cross-motion for summary judgment. At the time the motions were filed, the record consisted essentially of the citations and a deposition transcript of Raymond Donnelly, Director of OSHA's Office of General Industry Compliance Assistance. Donnelly provided uncontradicted evidence that the number 87 was a "multiplier" which represented the number of employees exposed to a single hazardous condition. He admitted that Arcadian was only required to correct the condition once, not 87 times.

The ALJ sided with Arcadian, holding that Arcadian's failure to properly inspect and maintain the reactor was a single course of conduct that could support only one violation of the General Duty Clause. The Occupational Safety and Health Review Commission (Commission) affirmed the ALJ. In a 2-1 decision, the majority concluded that the General Duty Clause unambiguously

---

[1] 29 U.S.C. § 666(a) provides that "any employer who willfully or repeatedly violates the requirements of section 5 of this Act [i.e., the General Duty Clause] ... may be assessed a civil penalty of not more than $70,000 for each violation, but not less than $5,000 for each willful violation." In 1990, Congress increased the fine from $10,000 to $70,000 and added the $5,000 minimum penalty for willful violations.

provided that employers should be fined on a per-violation, rather than a per-employee, basis. Four reasons justified the Commission's conclusion. First, the majority argued that issuing identical abatement orders for each employee exposed to the same hazard would increase administrative and legal costs and would be inconsistent with congressional intent. Second, according to the majority, the General Duty Clause referred to employees as a group, rather than as individuals; the phrase "each of his employees" in § 654(a) merely refers to all employees as opposed to some. Third, the majority viewed the Secretary's interpretation of the General Duty Clause as a departure from previous practices, which had allowed separate citations for each individual hazard but not for each exposed employee. This approach was unreasonable, concluded the Commission, because the Secretary had not explained the reason for his departure from earlier practice. Finally, the Commission concluded that it did not owe deference to the Secretary's interpretation of the General Duty Clause because the Commission viewed itself as the final adjudicator of the OSH Act and because the statutory authority to assess penalties rested squarely with the Commission.

The Chairman of the Commission dissented. He argued that the Commission had upheld violation-by-violation citations in other cases, including per-employee citations, under various OSH Act standards. In his opinion, the permissibility of such citations depends on the language of the cited provision. He concluded that the Secretary's interpretation was compatible with the Act and did not conflict with the plain language of the General Duty Clause. The Chairman also stated that although the Secretary's interpretations of the OSH Act are not generally entitled to deference from the Commission, deference was due here because "whether and how to cite under [the General Duty Clause] relates directly to the Secretary's prosecutorial discretion and goes to the heart of his enforcement authority."

The Commission ultimately remanded the case to the ALJ to provide the Secretary an opportunity to amend the citations. The Secretary, however, declined to do so. The ALJ thereafter reentered an order vacating Items 2-87 and severing them from the rest of the case. The order became the final order of the Commission, and the Secretary filed this petition for review.

Discussion

I. *Standard of Review*

We begin with the now-familiar two-step process for reviewing an administrative agency's interpretation of a statute. Our guide is the Supreme Court's decision in *Chevron, U.S.A., Inc. v. Natural Resources Defense Council, Inc.*, 467 U.S. 837 (1984), in which the Court held that we must first apply traditional principles of statutory construction to determine congressional intent. "If the intent of Congress is clear," wrote the Court, "that is the end of the matter; for the court, as well as the agency, must give effect to the unambiguously expressed intent of Congress." *Id.* at 843. Second, assuming the plain language of the statute is ambiguous (i.e., susceptible of two reasonable interpretations) or silent on the matter at issue, "the question for the court is whether the agency's answer is based on a permissible construction of the statute." *Id.*

II. *Is the General Duty Clause Ambiguous?*

A. *Principles of Statutory Construction*

Step one of *Chevron* requires us to apply "traditional principles of statutory construction" to determine whether Congress expressed a clear intent with regard to the meaning of the General Duty Clause. "In a statutory construction case, the beginning point must be the language of the statute, and when a statute speaks with clarity to an issue[,] judicial inquiry into the statute's meaning, in all but the most extraordinary circumstances, is finished." *Estate of Cowart v. Nicklos Drilling Co.*, 505 U.S. 469, 475 (1992). When we evaluate the terms of a statute, the Supreme Court has cautioned us to abide by a "fundamental principle of statutory construction (and, indeed, of language itself) that the meaning of a word cannot be determined in isolation, but must be drawn from the context in which it is used." *Deal v. United States*, 508 U.S. 129, 132 (1993). As such, a term is not ambiguous, even though the term may be susceptible to different interpretations, when "all but one of the meanings is ordinarily eliminated by context." *Deal*, 508 U.S. at 131-32. At the same time, "a statute must, if possible, be construed in such fashion that every word has some operative effect." *United States v. Nordic Village, Inc.*, 503 U.S. 30, 36 (1992); *United States v. Rodriguez-Rios*, 14 F.3d 1040, 1044 (5th Cir. 1994) (en banc). Finally, "[i]n ascertaining whether the agency's interpretation is a permissible construction of the language, a court must look to the structure and language of the statute as a whole." *National R.R. Passenger Corp. v. Boston and Maine Corp.*, 503 U.S. 407, 417 (1992).

B. *The General Duty Clause*

Section 654(a) of the OSH Act, known as the General Duty Clause, states simply:

(a) Each employer —
(1) shall furnish to *each of his employees* employment and a place of employment which are free from *recognized hazards* that are causing or likely to cause death or serious physical harm to his employees;
(2) shall comply with *occupational safety and health standards* promulgated under this Act.

29 U.S.C. § 654(a)(1), (2) (emphasis added). Before addressing the arguments of the parties, we find it helpful to place the Clause in proper context. It is well-settled that the Secretary has essentially two weapons in its arsenal of enforcement. First, the Secretary may issue a citation for violations of specific standards promulgated (through rulemaking) by the Secretary. Alternatively, where the Secretary has not promulgated standards, he may rely on the General Duty Clause as a "catchall provision." *Pratt & Whitney Aircraft, Div. of United Tech-*

nologies Corp. v. Secretary of Labor, 649 F.2d 96, 98 (2d Cir. 1981). Courts have held that enforcement through the application of standards is preferred because standards provide employers notice of what is required under the OSH Act....

In this case, it is undisputed that the Secretary did not promulgate standards which would have governed the accident at the Arcadian plant, and so the case was brought under the General Duty Clause. We must decide how far the Secretary may go in enforcing the Clause, for it is clear that a per-employee unit of prosecution carries far heavier penalties than a per-violative-condition unit of prosecution. After carefully considering the arguments of the parties, we proceed no further than step one of the *Chevron* analysis and conclude that the Clause is not ambiguous because it provides that a violative condition, not an employee, is the proper unit of prosecution for a General Duty Clause violation. Three justifications support our conclusion.

1. *The Plain Meaning of the General Duty Clause*

First, a plain reading of the Clause reveals that its focus is on an employer's duty to prevent hazardous conditions from developing in the employment itself or the physical workplace. Indeed, the central thrust of § 654(a)(1) concerns "recognized hazards" that cause or may cause "death or serious physical harm to ... employees." Subsection (a)(2) — the enforcement provision of the Clause — is consistent with this interpretation. It suggests that employers must "comply with occupational safety and health standards promulgated" by the Secretary. Section 652(8) defines an "occupational safety and health standard" as "a standard which requires *conditions*, or the adoption or use of one or more *practices, means, methods, operations*, or *processes*, reasonably necessary or appropriate to provide safe or healthful *employment* and *places of employment*." (Emphasis added). Thus, taken together, subsections (a)(1) and (a)(2) of the General Duty Clause are exclusively focused on an employer's duty to prevent hazardous conditions from developing, either in employment or the place of employment.

Our conclusion is reinforced by examining the elements the Secretary must prove in a General Duty Clause prosecution. Seizing on the plain terms of the Clause, courts (including our own) have held that the Secretary must prove three elements: "(1) that the employer failed to render its workplace 'free' of a hazard which was (2) 'recognized' and (3) 'causing or likely to cause death or serious physical harm.'" *National Realty & Constr. Co. v. OSHRC*, 489 F.2d 1257, 1265 (D.C. Cir. 1973). Plainly, the Secretary need not prove that a *particular* employee in fact was exposed to a hazardous condition. Consistent with the OSH Act generally, the mere fact that a recognized hazardous condition exists and is "likely to cause" death or serious physical harm constitutes a sufficient showing that an employer has breached the General Duty Clause.... If it were otherwise — if proof that a particular employee was exposed to a hazard is not required under standards promulgated by the Secretary, but is required for General Duty Clause violations — we would produce the anomalous result that the "catchall" provision of the OSH Act (the General Duty Clause) provides *less* protection for employees (because actual employee exposure must be shown) than the more narrow regulatory framework constructed by the Secretary.

The Secretary argues that if Congress intended to create a single duty running to employees in the aggregate, then Congress "could have omitted the words 'each of' in the general duty clause, for those words serve no purpose unless they mean that the employer's duty runs to each individual employee rather than to employees as a group." We simply cannot accept this construction of the Clause. First, we have not read "each of" out of the General Duty Clause. In the context of the Clause as a whole, with its principal (if not exclusive) focus on hazardous conditions, "each of" simply means that an employer's duty extends to all employees, regardless of their individual susceptibilities (i.e., age or pregnancy). Second, if we were to accept the Secretary's view that an employee is the proper unit of prosecution for a General Duty Clause violation, we would be compelled to conclude that, despite Arcadian's alleged egregious violation of the Clause, if a particular employee had not *in fact* been exposed to the hazardous condition at the Arcadian plant, Arcadian would not have violated the General Duty Clause. Such a result is flatly inconsistent with the OSH Act's central purpose of protecting workers from hazardous conditions in employment and the workplace, regardless of whether a particular employee has in fact been injured or exposed to a hazard....

The Secretary also argues that if the General Duty Clause does not run to each employee, we would be undermining the deterrence function of the OSH Act generally and the General Duty Clause in particular. "The congressional intent that civil penalties serve as a meaningful deterrent will not be fulfilled," argues the Secretary, "if a single $70,000 penalty is the most that can be assessed against a large employer who willfully exposes numerous employees to a known hazard in violation of the general duty clause." Because we have concluded that an employer's duty under the Clause is to avoid hazardous conditions, the Secretary's argument is best addressed to Congress rather than this court.... In 1990, Congress increased the civil penalty for General Duty Clause violations from $10,000 per violation to $70,000, and added a $5,000 minimum penalty for willful violations. It is simply not our place in the constitutional scheme to ignore the plain meaning of the Clause and offer our own free-wheeling policy judgment about the proper monetary deterrence for a General Duty Clause violation.

2. *The General Duty Clause in Context*

Second, our construction of the General Duty Clause is consistent with other provisions of the OSH Act. Section 666(a) provides that an employer "may be assessed a civil penalty of not more than $70,000 *for each violation*." (Emphasis added). Because violations of the Clause are considered "serious," we look to § 666(k), which (like § 652(8)) speaks of "condition[s]," "practices," "means," "methods," "operations," and "processes." Here again, Congress focused on the presence of hazardous conditions as a "violation" for purposes of assessing the maximum $70,000 penalty. Therefore, it must logically follow that a violation of the General Duty Clause must carry per-violative-condition penalties, and not per-employee penalties.

By contrast, the Secretary's position that the employee is the unit of prosecution for General Duty Clause enforcement actions runs counter to § 652(8) of the OSH Act. Section 652(8) permits the Secretary to promulgate standards governing "conditions" and "practices" of employment and within the workplace. See *International Union, UAW v. Occupational Safety & Health Admin.*, 938 F.2d 1310, 1316 (D.C.Cir.1991). As such, the Secretary cannot set a unit of prosecution because, in most cases, a unit of prosecution has nothing to do with employment or workplace practices or conditions. An employee could be a unit of violation, however, only if the regulated condition or practice is unique to the employee (i.e., failure to train or remove a worker).... It would therefore be anomalous for us to hold that per-employee penalties, generally unavailable for violations of OSHA standards, are *always* available for violations of the General Duty Clause — especially in light of the fact that courts have consistently held that standards are the preferred enforcement mechanism and that the General Duty Clause serves as an enforcement tool of last resort.

3. *The General Duty Clause and Penalty Assessment*

Finally, our interpretation of the Clause properly recognizes the respective roles played by the Secretary and the Commission in penalty assessment. It is well-settled that the Commission has the exclusive authority to assess penalties once a penalty proposed by the Secretary is contested.[8] It is also well-established that in assessing a penalty, the Commission is guided by the four criteria provided in § 666(j). In particular, the Commission must "giv[e] due consideration to the appropriateness of the penalty with respect to [1] the size of the business of the employer being charged, [2] the gravity of the violation, [3] the good faith of the employer, and [4] the history of previous violations." 29 U.S.C. § 666(j). When appropriate, the Commission includes the number of employees exposed to a hazardous condition in its analysis of prong two of the § 666(j) inquiry.... Our holding that the General Duty Clause contemplates per-violative-condition as opposed to per-employee units of prosecution goes hand-in-hand with the Commission's authority to adjust (up or down) penalties depending upon the number of employees injured or exposed to a hazardous condition. By contrast, if we were to agree with the Secretary's construction of the General Duty Clause and hold that OSH Act penalties for violations of the

---

[8] 29 U.S.C. § 666(j) ("The Commission shall have authority to assess *all* civil penalties provided in this section ...." (emphasis added)); § 659(a) (stating that the Secretary's penalty is merely a "propos[al]"); § 659(c) ("If an employer notifies the Secretary that he intends to contest a citation ... [t]he Commission shall thereafter issue an order ... affirming, modifying, or vacating the Secretary's citation or *proposed penalty* ...." (emphasis added)); ...

Clause should be fixed on a per-employee basis, we would be usurping the Commission's statutorily ordained power to assess "all" penalties. 29 U.S.C. § 666(j). This we decline to do.

Conclusion

Finding that the General Duty Clause of the OSH Act unambiguously provides that a hazardous condition is the proper unit of prosecution, we DENY the Secretary's petition for review and AFFIRM the decision of the Commission.

NOTES

1. *Per-employee Violations of the General Duty Clause for Ergonomics Conditions?* As discussed in the previous section, the Secretary of Labor has been stymied in the effort to issue a permanent standard for ergonomic conditions. Can the Secretary then use the general duty clause to cite an employer because of ergonomic problems? The Commission, in *Secretary of Labor v. Pepperidge Farm, Inc.*, 17 O.S.H. Cas. (BNA) 1993 (1997), held that the Secretary may utilize section 5(a)(1) to address lifting and repetitive motion hazards. The lifting items included employees handling 100 pound bags of sugar and roll stocks weighing up to 165 pounds. The repetitive motion items involved employees performing in quick succession such tasks as dropping paper cups from a stack with one hand and filling them with baked cookies with the other hand. The members of the Commission agreed on the amount of the total penalty for the lifting violations ($20,000), but disagreed on whether this amount resulted from twenty-one violations based on twenty-one employees (the view of Chairman Weisberg) or from four violations based on the number of different lifting tasks that were cited (the view of Commissioners Guttman and Montoya). This decision is likely to be appealed because of the importance of the holdings on the ergonomics and per-employee violation issues (as well as other issues not noted here), which will undoubtedly add to its distinction in terms of thoroughness of consideration. The decision by the Administrative Law Judge was 244 pages, and the unofficial version of the Commission decision exceeded 250 pages.

2. *Inadequate Research as a Violation of the General Duty Clause.* The Sixth Circuit, in *Wiley Organics, Inc. v. Occupational Safety & Health Review Commission*, 124 F.3d 201 (6th Cir. 1997) (unpublished table decision) (opinion reported at 17 O.S.H. Cas. (BNA) 2125), held that inadequate research can serve as a basis for a violation of Section 5(a)(1). Wiley changed its manufacturing process by substituting a formaldehyde mixture, Formalin, for sodium metabisulfite before Formalin was fully tested. Subsequently a chemical reactor vessel exploded and killed one employee.

3. *Ignoring Advice as a Violation of the General Duty Clause.* An employee was seriously injured when a steel stud broke and a nine-pound fragment flew 121 feet through the air and struck him in the back of his head. Flying studs had nearly injured workers in two previous incidents. A tradesman with a good safety record had been assigned to perform the task that resulted in the studs breaking, and he had repeatedly requested management to implement safety precautions, but his suggestions were ignored. The Seventh Circuit affirmed the Commission's finding that this employer behavior constituted a willful violation of the general duty clause in *Caterpillar Inc. v. Occupational Safety & Health Review Commission,* 122 F.3d 437 (7th Cir. 1997).

4. *The Relationship Between Section 5(a)(1) and Section 6 Standards.*
Suppose a permanent standard has been issued under section 6(b) that limits the use of Grimeoff to ten washes per week. NIOSH then develops evidence that any exposure greater than five washes per week causes an excess mortality rate. OSHA decides against an emergency temporary standard under section 6(c) because of the courts' pillorying of that approach. OSHA also despairs of the delays that will occur if a revised permanent standard is promulgated under section (6)(b). Can OSHA use the general duty clause to impose a more stringent exposure rule for Grimeoff than is provided in the permanent standard?

The general rule is that a citation under section 5(a)(1) is only proper if no specific standard applies. In *United Auto Workers v. General Dynamics Land Systems Division,* 815 F.2d 1570 (D.C. Cir.), *cert. denied,* 484 U.S. 976 (1987), the court reviewed an order of the Commission that had vacated a citation for violation of the general duty clause for exposing workers to freon vapors in confined spaces. The Commission vacated the general duty citation because there was a specific standard limiting the amount of exposure to freon. There was evidence indicating that the employer was aware that workers were experiencing serious medical problems from freon at exposure levels below the level required by the standard. The court remanded the case to the Commission and directed it to address the merits of the section 5(a)(1) citation with these instruction:

> Therefore if (as is alleged in this case) an employer knows a particular safety standard is inadequate to protect his workers against the specific hazard it is intended to address, or that the conditions in his place of employment are such that the safety standard will not adequately deal with the hazards to which his employees are exposed, he has a duty under section 5(a)(1) to take whatever measures may be required by the Act, over and above those mandated by the safety standard, to safeguard his workers. In sum, if an employer knows a specific standard will not protect his workers against a particular hazard, his duty under section 5(a)(1) will not be discharged no matter how faithfully he observes that standard. Scienter is the key.

Id. at 1577.

F. ENFORCEMENT

OSHA enforces the Act through inspections conducted by a compliance officer. OSHA is not allowed to hold on-site "consultations" with employers; section 9(a) and OSHA regulations require that OSHA issue citations for all violations detected.[*] After the inspection, OSHA proposes a penalty for each alleged violation. The employer can contest the proposed penalty, in which case the case will be heard by the Occupational Safety and Health Review Commission. Commission decisions can be appealed to the Federal courts.

Inspection Activity

The inspection task of OSHA is daunting. OSHA has jurisdiction over some five million workplaces, and in recent years there have been only about 3,000 federal and state safety inspectors. The number of inspections has varied considerably during the past twenty-five years.

The OSHAct became effective in 1971, and inspection activity increased rapidly during the Nixon-Ford Administrations, peaking at 91,516 inspections in fiscal year 1976. During the four years of the Carter Administration (fiscal years 1977 to 1980), the total number of inspections dropped dramatically and averaged about 60,000 per year. During the Reagan Administration, the annual number of inspections increased to about 70,000 in the mid-1980s, and then averaged about 60,000 per year in the last two years of the Administration (fiscal years 1987 and 1988). During the Bush Administration (fiscal years 1989 to 1992), the annual number of inspections averaged about 45,000.

The number of inspections has declined considerably during the Clinton Administration, from about 40,000 per year in fiscal years 1993 and 1994 to a record low of 24,024 in fiscal year 1996. This decline was in part due to budgetary constraints imposed by Congress and, as the fiscal situation for OSHA has improved somewhat in fiscal year 1997, the number of inspections has increased.

The relatively low level of inspections has sparked criticism. An AFL-CIO study found that, on average, OSHA inspects workplaces only once every 84 years. Surprise inspections of high-hazard workplaces occur on average only once every 25 years. Colleen M. O'Neill, *OSHA Inspection Once-in-Lifetime Experience, Study Shows,* AFL-CIO NEWS, May 11, 1992, at 1. Moreover, some states with their own safety and health plans have even lower inspection rates. According to the AFL-CIO, North Carolina would need 119 years to get to each jobsite at its current inspection rate.

---

[*] States with approved OSHA plans can provide on-site consulting. The Secretary of Labor has also issued regulations allowing states without approved state plans to use independent consultants to provide on-site consultation with employers. One requirement of such consultations is that if an imminent danger is discovered, the employer must abate the hazard immediately.

Penalties

As a result of an inspection, the employer can be cited and sent a notice of a proposed penalty. The penalty can consist of an order to comply with the OSHAct within a specified abatement period or an order to pay a fine. The fines vary depending on the severity of the offense. As a result of changes included in the Omnibus Budget Reconciliation Act of 1990, a nonserious violation can be fined from $0 to $7,000; a serious violation can be fined from $1 to $7,000; a repeated violation from $0 to $70,000; a willful violation from $5,000 to $70,000; and a failure to abate, from $0 to $7,000 per day. (Prior to March 1991, the fines were considerably lower. For example, the maximums for willful and repeat violations were previously only $10,000.)

OSHA has exercised its discretion concerning penalties several times in recent years. Since 1994, all willful violations are assessed either as serious (with penalties ranging from $25,000 to $70,000) or as other-than serious (with a minimum penalty of $5,000). Since 1995, this policy has been adjusted for the benefit of small employers. Employers with fewer than fifty employees are no longer subject to the $25,000 minimum for willful violations. In addition, there are now reductions in the penalties for serious violations for small employers, such as a 30% reduction for employers with twenty-five or fewer employees.

The only criminal penalty under the Act is for a willful violation that results in death, which can result in a fine of up to $70,000 plus a jail sentence of up to six months.

The total number and composition of alleged violations of the Act have changed significantly in the last decade. In fiscal year 1986, 69% of the approximately 129,000 alleged violations were nonserious, 27% were serious, and only 1% were willful. In fiscal year 1996, 39% of the 55,000 alleged violations were nonserious, 59% were serious, and 2% were willful.

As these changes in the composition of charges would suggest, the magnitude of penalties proposed by OSHA has also increased. From a total of $4.3 million in fiscal year 1982, the figures have grown to $11.4 million in fiscal year 1986, to $116.1 million in fiscal year 1992 (the last year of the Bush Administration), and to $119.9 million in fiscal year 1994. The figure subsequently declined to $66.8 million in fiscal year 1996. The 1996 figure includes such megafines as $3.8 million for DeCoster Egg Farms and $1.0 million for Richter's Bakery. The rapid increases in the amounts of proposed penalties has led to criticisms from some employers.

It should be noted, however, that the full amount of the proposed penalty is often not paid by the employer. Once an employer receives an OSHA citation with a proposed penalty, the employer can either (1) accept the citation, abate the hazard, and pay the penalty, or (2) have an informal conference with OSHA officials and negotiate an informal settlement, or (3) formally contest the citation before the Commission. DeCoster Egg Farms, for example, negotiated a settlement that reduced its fine from $3.8 million to $2.0 million. In a comprehensive study by the Government Accounting Office (GAO) of almost 170,000 citations issued in fiscal year 1989, 67% of the employers accepted the citation and paid the proposed penalty; 27% of the employers negotiated an informal settlement with OSHA and had the proposed penalties reduced by an average of 45%; and 6% of the employers formally contested their citations and had their proposed penalties reduced by an average of 57% by the Commission. U.S. GENERAL ACCOUNTING OFFICE, OCCUPATIONAL SAFETY AND HEALTH: PENALTIES FOR VIOLATIONS ARE WELL BELOW MAXIMUM ALLOWABLE PENALTIES (1992).

While settlements often reduce the amount of the proposed penalties, there are circumstances under which the employer's liability can be increased. For example, interest on penalties assessed by the Commission begins to accrue at the time of assessment, rather than at the time a court issues a ruling enforcing the penalty assessment. *Reich v. Sea Sprite Boat Co.*, 50 F.3d 413 (7th Cir. 1995). In addition, employer resistance that is too vigorous can lead to contempt sanctions. In *Sea Sprite*, the original penalty was $135,000, while the sanction for contempt of court for failure to obey an order to abate the violation and pay the penalty was $1,452,000.

OSHA as the Bad Cop

Despite *Reich v. Arcadian Corp.*, OSHA has continued to rely on an "egregious" case policy, in which the agency multiplies the penalties for willful or repeat violations, either by the number of employees exposed to the hazards or by the number of times the hazardous condition exists. The policy was used for more than twenty-five cases annually in fiscal years 1987 and 1988, but the annual number of cases has consistently been below 25 since then, dropping to only six cases in fiscal year 1996.

Despite the low number of "egregious" cases in recent years, the policy has been controversial and has been strongly criticized by the business community. A good example of Commission approval of the use of the "egregious" case policy is *Caterpillar, Inc.*, 15 O.S.H. Cas. (BNA) 2153 (1993), in which separate penalties were upheld for 167 violations of the OSHA reporting requirements for injuries and illnesses, even though the Commission did not find the failures to report were willful. *Secretary of Labor v. Pepperidge Farm, Inc.*, 17 O.S.H. Cas. (BNA) 1993 (1997), in which the Review Commission upheld the use of the general duty clause to cite an employer for per-employee violations, was discussed in the previous section. However, the decision in *Reich v. Arcadian Corp.*, 110 F.3d 1192 (5th Cir. 1997), in which the Circuit Court held that OSHA cannot use the general duty clause as a basis for per-employee violations, raises serious obstacles to continued use of the "egregious" case policy. OSHA decided not to appeal the decision because the use of the general duty clause to support per-employee violations is extremely rare. Apparently, OSHA plans to continue to use the "egregious" case policy in other circumstances, such as repeated or willful violations of permanent standards. As evidence of OSHA's continued reliance on the policy, OSHA reported thirteen "egregious" cases through the end of the third quarter of fiscal year 1997, up from six for the entire fiscal year 1996.

Since 1986, OSHA has also been identifying "significant" cases in which penalties of $100,000 or more are proposed. The number of significant cases averaged about twenty-five per year between fiscal years 1986 and 1991, and then the incidence sharply increased, reaching 69, 125, and 165 cases in the three most recent fiscal years (1994-96). The number of "significant" cases in the first three quarters of fiscal year 1997 also was up considerably from the corresponding period in the previous fiscal year (152 compared to 104), suggesting that the recent emphasis on serious violators is continuing.

OSHA as the Good Cop

While OSHA has been increasing its enforcement activity for "egregious" cases and for "significant" cases, it has also been attempting to promote a less contentious relationship with the business community. President Clinton announced his plans for reinventing OSHA in 1995 by eliminating duplicative and unnecessary regulations and by instituting penalty reductions for small businesses.

The proposal for reduced penalties for small employers was implemented in 1995, although there are still complaints from the small business community about OSHA enforcement. Another example of a new approach to OSHA enforcement is the cooperative compliance programs (CCPs) that were operating in nine states as of mid-1997, with plans to expand coverage to all twenty-nine states with federal (as opposed to state) responsibility for OSHA enforcement by fiscal year 1998. The CCPs are statewide programs that attempt to reduce injury and illness rates by encouraging employers with relatively bad health and safety records to work with the agency and implement safety and health programs. The CCP approach was instituted in 1993 with the "Maine 200" partnership with 200 large employers in Maine that offered them the choice between increased OSHA enforcement or a partnership with OSHA that relied on employer self-inspection and employee involvement, including the use of safety committees. In 1995, OSHA reported that the pilot program was a success, with employers finding and fixing hazards at a rate that was fourteen times the success that OSHA had previously achieved. The approach has rapidly been extended to other jurisdictions, with some variations to account for different types of industries and sizes of businesses.

NOTE ON OPTIMAL FINES

The recent megafine strategy of OSHA is in marked contrast to the notoriously low fines in the early days of OSHA. The question arises, what is the optimal level of fines?

Presumably, profit-maximizing employers will try harder to comply with OSHA regulations as the size of the penalty and the probability of being penalized increase. OSHA, then, has two basic policy instruments for inducing employers to comply with its standards: (1) it can increase the probability of catching violators by increasing the number of inspectors and inspections; and (2) it can increase the size of the fines.

Suppose for a moment that OSHA could detect and penalize every violation of its standards. In such a case, what would the appropriate penalty be? One possibility would be to set the fine equal to the damages suffered by workers should they be injured by the dangerous condition (analogous to the damages a tort suit would award to a victim). One problem is that this high fine is being assessed for every violation, whether or not the violation causes actual injury. For example, suppose a machine violating OSHA standards will cut off a worker's hand an average of once a year. Should the daily OSHA fine be the full damages for a lost hand, say $100,000? This would require the employer, over the course of the year, to pay 365 times the actual damages caused by the dangerous condition. Still, if the goal is to eliminate all OSHA violations, such a penalty scheme may be appropriate (but an even higher fine might work even better).

Is elimination of all OSHA violations the appropriate goal? Such a high penalty structure will cause employers to spend large sums not to violate OSHA. In the hand example, the employer may spend up to $36,500,000 to be sure of not violating OSHA (or more realistically, the employer might eliminate that job and machine). The cost of compliance may outweigh the benefits: the high penalty structure over-deters employers. If OSHA were to penalize every workplace violation, then rather modest fines might be appropriate. To continue with the example, a daily fine of $100,000/365, or $274, might be appropriate. This would induce employers to spend up to $100,000 a year to keep the machine in compliance, which is exactly the benefits of a safe machine.

Given OSHA's low operating budget, contemplating anything close to perfect detection is ridiculous. The government would have to spend vast sums to detect even a considerable fraction of all OSHA violations. OSHA does have various strategies to increase the "effective" rate of detection, such as targeting inspections for those industries most likely to have violations, or where the violations will have the worst consequences. Nevertheless, in order to keep the cost of detection low, OSHA must increase the level of fines to ensure adequate compliance with its standards.

To continue with our hand example, OSHA could keep the same deterrence by reducing (random) inspections to once a year and increasing the fine to $100,000. Better yet, OSHA could save even more by inspecting once a decade and imposing a million dollar fine. OSHA will minimize inspection costs by setting the fine as high as possible (an employer's entire assets?) and reducing the probability of detection proportionately, so that the expected yearly fine for a non-compliant machine remains at $100,000.

Should OSHA have any limit on its megafine policy? One problem occurs if employers are risk averse. Risk-averse persons suffer real damage simply from the threat of such a large fine, and will spend real money to avoid the risk. In our situation, this will lead to employers again spending more than $100,000 to ensure they are not hit with a megafine. A second problem, analytically similar to risk aversion, comes from legal error. Suppose OSHA occasionally fines employers who in fact are in compliance with the safety standard. This imposes a cost on employers that is magnified as the amount of the fine increases. A third problem is that megafines — whatever their merits for deterrence — provoke political opposition among employers, which may lead to amendments in the Act or changes in administrative zeal that reduce the overall effectiveness of OSHA. In summary, a trade-off exists between minimizing inspection costs (which calls for megafines) and minimizing risk bearing, legal error, and political costs (which calls for more modest fines).

OSHA conducts two types of inspections: First are the programmed inspections of targeted high-hazard industries and workplaces. Second are unprogrammed inspections triggered by accident reports, employee complaints, referrals, or other publicity. The inspection is governed by a series of rules, such as the prohibition on advance notice to an employer of an impending inspection. The purpose of this requirement is to maximize the effectiveness of OSHA inspections, since most employers are unlikely to be inspected more than once a decade. But what happens if the employer who is surprised by a visit from the OSHA inspector refuses to allow entry to the plant? The next case explores this issue.

MARSHALL v. BARLOW'S, INC.

United States Supreme Court
436 U.S. 307 (1978)

MR. JUSTICE WHITE delivered the opinion of the Court.

Section 8(a) of the Occupational Safety and Health Act of 1970 (OSHA or Act) empowers agents of the Secretary of Labor (Secretary) to search the work area of any employment facility within the Act's jurisdiction. The purpose of the search is to inspect for safety hazards and violations of OSHA regulations. No search warrant or other process is expressly required under the Act.

On the morning of September 11, 1975, an OSHA inspector entered the customer service area of Barlow's, Inc., an electrical and plumbing installation business located in Pocatello, Idaho. The president and general manager, Ferrol G. "Bill" Barlow, was on hand; and the OSHA inspector, after showing his credentials, informed Mr. Barlow that he wished to conduct a search of the working areas of the business. Mr. Barlow inquired whether any complaint had been received about his company. The inspector answered no, but that Barlow's, Inc., had simply turned up in the agency's selection process. The inspector again asked to enter the nonpublic area of the business; Mr. Barlow's response was to inquire whether the inspector had a search warrant. The inspector had none. Thereupon, Mr. Barlow refused the inspector admission to the employee area of his business. He said he was relying on his rights as guaranteed by the Fourth Amendment of the United States Constitution.

Three months later, the Secretary petitioned the United States District Court for the District of Idaho to issue an order compelling Mr. Barlow to admit the inspector. The requested order was issued on December 30, 1975, and was presented to Mr. Barlow on January 5, 1976. Mr. Barlow again refused admission, and he sought his own injunctive relief against the warrantless searches assertedly permitted by OSHA. A three-judge court was convened. On December 30, 1976, it ruled in Mr. Barlow's favor. Concluding that *Camara v. Municipal Court,* 387 U.S. 523, 528-529 (1967), and *See v. Seattle,* 387 U.S. 541, 543 (1967), controlled this case, the court held that the Fourth Amendment required a warrant for the type of search involved here and that the statutory authorization for warrantless inspections was unconstitutional. An injunction against searches or inspections pursuant to § 8(a) was entered. The Secretary appealed, challenging the judgment, and we noted probable jurisdiction.

I

The Secretary urges that warrantless inspections to enforce OSHA are reasonable within the meaning of the Fourth Amendment. Among other things, he relies on § 8(a) of the Act, which authorizes inspection of business premises without a warrant and which the Secretary urges represents a congressional construction of the Fourth Amendment that the courts should not reject. Regrettably, we are unable to agree.

The Warrant Clause of the Fourth Amendment protects commercial buildings as well as private homes. To hold otherwise would belie the origin of that Amendment, and the American colonial experience. An important forerunner of the first 10 Amendments to the United States Constitution, the Virginia Bill of Rights, specifically opposed "general warrants, whereby an officer or messenger may be commanded to search suspected places without evidence of a fact committed." The general warrant was a recurring point of contention in the Colonies immediately preceding the Revolution. The particular offensiveness it engendered was acutely felt by the merchants and businessmen whose premises and products were inspected for compliance with the several parliamentary revenue measures that most irritated the colonists.... Against this background, it is untenable that the ban on warrantless searches was not intended to shield places of business as well as of residence.

This Court has already held that warrantless searches are generally unreasonable, and that this rule applies to commercial premises as well as homes. In *Camara v. Municipal Court, supra,* at 528-529, we held:

> [Except] in certain carefully defined classes of cases, a search of private property without proper consent is "unreasonable" unless it has been authorized by a valid search warrant.

On the same day, we also ruled:

> As we explained in *Camara,* a search of private houses is presumptively unreasonable if conducted without a warrant. The businessman, like the occupant of a residence, has a constitutional right to go about his business free from unreasonable official entries upon his private commercial property. The businessman, too, has that right placed in jeopardy if the decision to enter and inspect for violation of regulatory laws can be made and enforced by the inspector in the field without official authority evidenced by a warrant.

See v. Seattle, supra, at 543.

These same cases also held that the Fourth Amendment prohibition against unreasonable searches protects against warrantless intrusions during civil as well as criminal investigations. The reason is found in the "basic purpose of this Amendment ... [which] is to safeguard the privacy and security of individuals against arbitrary invasions by governmental officials." *Camara, supra,* at 528. If the government intrudes on a person's property, the privacy interest suffers whether the government's motivation is to investigate violations of criminal laws or breaches of other statutory or regulatory standards. It therefore appears that unless some recognized exception to the warrant requirement applies, *See v. Seattle* would require a warrant to conduct the inspection sought in this case.

The Secretary urges that an exception from the search warrant requirement has been recognized for "pervasively regulated [businesses]," *United States v. Biswell,* 406 U.S. 311, 316 (1972), and for "closely regulated" industries "long subject to close supervision and inspection." *Colonnade Catering Corp. v. United States,* 397 U.S. 72, 74, 77 (1970). These cases are indeed exceptions, but they represent responses to relatively unique circumstances. Certain industries have such a history of government oversight that no reasonable expectation of privacy, see *Katz v. United States,* 389 U.S. 347, 351-352 (1967), could exist for a proprietor over the stock of such an enterprise. Liquor (*Colonnade*) and firearms (*Biswell*) are industries of this type; when an entrepreneur embarks upon such a business, he has voluntarily chosen to subject himself to a full arsenal of governmental regulation.

Industries such as these fall within the "certain carefully defined classes of cases," referenced in *Camara,* 387 U.S., at 528. The element that distinguishes these enterprises from ordinary businesses is a long tradition of close government supervision, of which any person who chooses to enter such a business must already be aware. "A central difference between those cases [*Colonnade* and *Biswell*] and this one is that businessmen engaged in such federally licensed and regulated enterprises accept the burdens as well as the benefits of their trade, whereas the petitioner here was not engaged in any regulated or licensed business. The businessman in a regulated industry in effect consents to the restrictions placed upon him." *Almeida-Sanchez v. United States,* 413 U.S. 266, 271 (1973).

The clear import of our cases is that the closely regulated industry of the type involved in *Colonnade* and *Biswell* is the exception. The Secretary would make it the rule. Invoking the Walsh-Healey Act of 1936, 41 U.S.C. § 35 et seq., the Secretary attempts to support a conclusion that all businesses involved in interstate commerce have long been subjected to close supervision of employee safety and health conditions. But the degree of federal involvement in employee working circumstances has never been of the order of specificity and pervasiveness that OSHA mandates. It is quite unconvincing to argue that the imposition of minimum wages and maximum hours on employers who contracted with the Government under the Walsh-Healey Act prepared the entirety of American interstate commerce for regulation of working conditions to the minutest detail. Nor can any but the most fictional sense of voluntary consent to later searches be found in the single fact that one conducts a business affecting interstate commerce; under current practice and law, few businesses can be conducted without having some effect on interstate commerce.

The Secretary also attempts to derive support for a *Colonnade-Biswell*-type exception by drawing analogies from the field of labor law. In *Republic Aviation Corp. v. NLRB,* 324 U.S. 793 (1945), this Court upheld the rights of employees to solicit for a union during nonworking time where efficiency was not compromised. By opening up his property to employees, the employer had yielded so much of his private property rights as to allow those employees to exercise § 7 rights under the National Labor Relations Act. But this Court also held that the private property rights of an owner prevailed over the intrusion of nonemployee organizers, even in nonworking areas of the plant and during nonworking hours. *NLRB v. Babcock & Wilcox Co.,* 351 U.S. 105 (1956).

The critical fact in this case is that entry over Mr. Barlow's objection is being sought by a Government agent. Employees are not being prohibited from reporting OSHA violations. What they observe in their daily functions is undoubtedly beyond the employer's reasonable expectation of privacy. The Government inspector, however, is not an employee. Without a warrant he stands in no better position than a member of the public. What is observable by the public is observable, without a warrant, by the Government inspector as well. The owner of a business has not, by the necessary utilization of employees in his operation, thrown open the areas where employees alone are permitted to the warrantless scrutiny of Government agents. That an employee is free to report, and the Government is free to use, any evidence of noncompliance with OSHA that the employee observes furnishes no justification for federal agents to enter a place of business from which the public is restricted and to conduct their own warrantless search.

II

The Secretary nevertheless stoutly argues that the enforcement scheme of the Act requires warrantless searches, and that the restrictions on search discretion contained in the Act and its regulations already protect as much privacy as a warrant would. The Secretary thereby asserts the actual reasonableness of OSHA searches, whatever the general rule against warrantless searches might be. Because "reasonableness is still the ultimate standard," *Camara v. Municipal Court,* 387 U.S., at 539, the Secretary suggests that the Court decide whether a warrant is needed by arriving at a sensible balance between the administrative necessities of OSHA inspections and the incremental protection of privacy of business owners a warrant would afford. He suggests that only a decision exempting OSHA inspections from the Warrant Clause would give "full recognition to the competing public and private interests here at stake." *Ibid.*

The Secretary submits that warrantless inspections are essential to the proper enforcement of OSHA because they afford the opportunity to inspect without prior notice and hence to preserve the advantages of surprise. While the dangerous conditions outlawed by the Act include structural defects that cannot be quickly hidden or remedied, the Act also regulates a myriad of safety details that may be amenable to speedy alteration or disguise. The risk is that during the interval between an inspector's initial request to search a plant and his procuring a warrant following the owner's refusal of permission, violations of this latter type could be corrected and thus escape the inspector's notice. To the suggestion that warrants may be issued *ex parte* and executed without delay and without prior notice, thereby preserving the element of surprise, the Secretary expresses concern for the administrative strain that would be experienced by the inspection system, and by the courts, should *ex parte* warrants issued in advance become standard practice.

We are unconvinced, however, that requiring warrants to inspect will impose serious burdens on the inspection system or the courts, will prevent inspections necessary to enforce the statute, or will make them less effective. In the first place, the great majority of businessmen can be expected in normal course to consent to inspection without warrant; the Secretary has not brought to this Court's attention any widespread pattern of refusal.[11] In those cases where an owner does insist on a warrant, the Secretary argues that inspection efficiency will be impeded by the advance notice and delay. The Act's penalty provisions

---

[11] We recognize that today's holding itself might have an impact on whether owners choose to resist requested searches; we can only await the development of evidence not present on this record to determine how serious an impediment to effective enforcement this might be.

for giving advance notice of a search, 29 U.S.C. § 666 (f), and the Secretary's own regulations, 29 CFR § 1903.6 (1977), indicate that surprise searches are indeed contemplated. However, the Secretary has also promulgated a regulation providing that upon refusal to permit an inspector to enter the property or to complete his inspection, the inspector shall attempt to ascertain the reasons for the refusal and report to his superior, who shall "promptly take appropriate action, including compulsory process, if necessary." 29 CFR § 1903.4 (1977). The regulation represents a choice to proceed by process where entry is refused; and on the basis of evidence available from present practice, the Act's effectiveness has not been crippled by providing those owners who wish to refuse an initial requested entry with a time lapse while the inspector obtains the necessary process. Indeed, the kind of process sought in this case and apparently anticipated by the regulation provides notice to the business operator. If this safeguard endangers the efficient administration of OSHA, the Secretary should never have adopted it, particularly when the Act does not require it. Nor is it immediately apparent why the advantages of surprise would be lost if, after being refused entry, procedures were available for the Secretary to seek an *ex parte* warrant and to reappear at the premises without further notice to the establishment being inspected.

Whether the Secretary proceeds to secure a warrant or other process, with or without prior notice, his entitlement to inspect will not depend on his demonstrating probable cause to believe that conditions in violation of OSHA exist on the premises. Probable cause in the criminal law sense is not required. For purposes of an administrative search such as this, probable cause justifying the issuance of a warrant may be based not only on specific evidence of an existing violation but also on a showing that "reasonable legislative or administrative standards for conducting an ... inspection are satisfied with respect to a particular [establishment]." *Camara v. Municipal Court,* 387 U.S., at 538. A warrant showing that a specific business has been chosen for an OSHA search on the basis of a general administrative plan for the enforcement of the Act derived from neutral sources such as, for example, dispersion of employees in various types of industries across a given area, and the desired frequency of searches in any of the lesser divisions of the area, would protect an employer's Fourth Amendment rights. We doubt that the consumption of enforcement energies in the obtaining of such warrants will exceed manageable proportions....

Nor do we agree that the incremental protections afforded the employer's privacy by a warrant are so marginal that they fail to justify the administrative burdens that may be entailed. The authority to make warrantless searches devolves almost unbridled discretion upon executive and administrative officers, particularly those in the field, as to when to search and whom to search. A warrant, by contrast, would provide assurances from a neutral officer that the inspection is reasonable under the Constitution, is authorized by statute, and is pursuant to an administrative plan containing specific neutral criteria. Also, a warrant would then and there advise the owner of the scope and objects of the search, beyond which limits the inspector is not expected to proceed. These are important functions for a warrant to perform, functions which underlie the Court's prior decisions that the Warrant Clause applies to inspections for compliance with regulatory statutes.[22] *Camara v. Municipal Court,* 387 U.S. 523 (1967); *See v. Seattle,* 387 U.S. 541 (1967). We conclude that the concerns expressed by the Secretary do not suffice to justify warrantless inspections under OSHA or vitiate the general constitutional requirement that for a search to be reasonable a warrant must be obtained.

III

We hold that Barlow's was entitled to a declaratory judgment that the Act is unconstitutional insofar as it purports to authorize inspections without warrant or its equivalent and to an injunction enjoining the Act's enforcement to that extent. The judgment of the District Court is therefore affirmed.

So ordered.

MR. JUSTICE BRENNAN took no part in the consideration or decision of this case.

---

[22] Delineating the scope of a search with some care is particularly important where documents are involved. Section 8(c) of the Act provides that an employer must "make, keep and preserve, and make available to the Secretary [of Labor] or to the Secretary of Health, Education and Welfare" such records regarding his activities relating to OSHA as the Secretary of Labor may prescribe by regulation as necessary or appropriate for enforcement of the statute or for developing information regarding the causes and prevention of occupational accidents and illnesses. Regulations requiring employers to maintain records of and to make periodic reports on "work-related deaths, injuries and illnesses" are also contemplated, as are rules requiring accurate records of employee exposures to potential toxic materials and harmful physical agents.

In describing the scope of the warrantless inspection authorized by the statute, § 8(a) does not expressly include any records among those items or things that may be examined, and § 8(c) merely provides that the employer is to "make available" his pertinent records and to make periodic reports.

The Secretary's regulation, 29 CFR § 1903.3 (1977), however, expressly includes among the inspector's powers the authority "to review records required by the Act and regulations published in this chapter, and other records which are directly related to the purpose of the inspection." Further, § 1903.7 requires inspectors to indicate generally "the records specified in § 1903.3 which they wish to review" but "such designations of records shall not preclude access to additional records specified in § 1903.3." It is the Secretary's position, which we reject, that an inspection of documents of this scope may be effected without a warrant.

The order that issued in this case included among the objects and things to be inspected "all other things therein (including but not limited to records, files, papers, processes, controls and facilities) bearing upon whether Barlow's, Inc. is furnishing to its employees employment and a place of employment that are free from recognized hazards that are causing or are likely to cause death or serious physical harm to its employees, and whether Barlow's, Inc. is complying with ..." the OSHA regulations.

MR. JUSTICE STEVENS, with whom MR. JUSTICE BLACKMUN and MR. JUSTICE REHNQUIST join, dissenting.

Congress enacted the Occupational Safety and Health Act to safeguard employees against hazards in the work areas of businesses subject to the Act. To ensure compliance, Congress authorized the Secretary of Labor to conduct routine, nonconsensual inspections. Today the Court holds that the Fourth Amendment prohibits such inspections without a warrant. The Court also holds that the constitutionally required warrant may be issued without any showing of probable cause. I disagree with both of these holdings.

The Fourth Amendment contains two separate Clauses, each flatly prohibiting a category of governmental conduct. The first Clause states that the right to be free from unreasonable searches "shall not be violated"; the second unequivocally prohibits the issuance of warrants except "upon probable cause." In this case the ultimate question is whether the category of warrantless searches authorized by the statute is "unreasonable" within the meaning of the first Clause....

I

... The routine OSHA inspections are, by definition, not based on cause to believe there is a violation on the premises to be inspected. Hence, if the inspections were measured against the requirements of the Warrant Clause, they would be automatically and unequivocally unreasonable.

Because of the acknowledged importance and reasonableness of routine inspections in the enforcement of federal regulatory statutes such as OSHA, the Court recognizes that requiring full compliance with the Warrant Clause would invalidate all such inspection programs. Yet, rather than simply analyzing such programs under the "Reasonableness" Clause of the Fourth Amendment, the Court holds the OSHA program invalid under the Warrant Clause and then avoids a blanket prohibition on all routine, regulatory inspections by relying on the notion that the "probable cause" requirement in the Warrant Clause may be relaxed whenever the Court believes that the governmental need to conduct a category of "searches" outweighs the intrusion on interests protected by the Fourth Amendment.

The Court's approach disregards the plain language of the Warrant Clause and is unfaithful to the balance struck by the Framers of the Fourth Amendment — "the one procedural safeguard in the Constitution that grew directly out of the events which immediately preceded the revolutionary struggle with England."...

Since the general warrant, not the warrantless search, was the immediate evil at which the Fourth Amendment was directed, it is not surprising that the Framers placed precise limits on its issuance. The requirement that a warrant only issue on a showing of particularized probable cause was the means adopted to circumscribe the warrant power. While the subsequent course of Fourth Amendment jurisprudence in this Court emphasizes the dangers posed by warrantless searches conducted without probable cause, it is the general reasonableness standard in the first Clause, not the Warrant Clause, that the Framers adopted to limit this category of searches. It is, of course, true that the existence of a valid warrant normally satisfies the reasonableness requirement under the Fourth Amendment. But we should not dilute the requirements of the Warrant Clause in an effort to force every kind of governmental intrusion which satisfies the Fourth Amendment definition of a "search" into a judicially developed, warrant-preference scheme....

II

Even if a warrant issued without probable cause were faithful to the Warrant Clause, I could not accept the Court's holding that the Government's inspection program is constitutionally unreasonable because it fails to require such a warrant procedure. In determining whether a warrant is a necessary safeguard in a given class of cases, "the Court has weighed the public interest against the Fourth Amendment interest of the individual ...." *United States v. Martinez-Fuerte,* 428 U.S., at 555. Several considerations persuade me that this balance should be struck in favor of the routine inspections authorized by Congress.

Congress has determined that regulation and supervision of safety in the workplace furthers an important public interest and that the power to conduct warrantless searches is necessary to accomplish the safety goals of the legislation. In assessing the public interest side of the Fourth Amendment balance, however, the Court today substitutes its judgment for that of Congress on the question of what inspection authority is needed to effectuate the purposes of the Act. The Court states that if surprise is truly an important ingredient of an effective, representative inspection program, it can be retained by obtaining *ex parte* warrants in advance. The Court assures the Secretary that this will not unduly burden enforcement resources because most employers will consent to inspection.

The Court's analysis does not persuade me that Congress' determination that the warrantless-inspection power as a necessary adjunct of the exercise of the regulatory power is unreasonable. It was surely not unreasonable to conclude that the rate at which employers deny entry to inspectors would increase if covered businesses, which may have safety violations on their premises, have a right to deny warrantless entry to a compliance inspector. The Court is correct that this problem could be avoided by requiring inspectors to obtain a warrant prior to every inspection visit. But the adoption of such a practice undercuts the Court's explanation of why a warrant requirement would not create undue enforcement problems. For, even if it were true that many employers would not exercise their right to demand a warrant, it would provide little solace to those charged with administration of OSHA; faced with an increase in the rate of refusals and the added costs generated by futile trips to inspection sites where entry is denied, officials may be compelled to adopt a general practice of obtaining warrants in advance. While the Court's prediction of the effect a warrant requirement would have on the behavior of covered employers may turn out to be accurate, its judgment is essentially empirical. On such an issue, I would defer to Congress' judgment regarding the importance of a warrantless-search power to the OSHA enforcement scheme.

NOTES

1. *Semi-surprised Employers.* OSHA regulations were amended in 1980 to allow OSHA to obtain an *ex parte* warrant to enter the premises of a recalcitrant employer and to permit OSHA to seek such a warrant prior to attempting to enter the premises. After the 1980 Presidential elections, the policy was changed to provide that, except under special circumstances, OSHA would not attempt to obtain a warrant until after the employer objected to an OSHA inspection. How surprised would an employer be by an OSHA inspection under this policy?

2. *Probable Cause for a Warrant.* The Fourth Amendment of the U.S. Constitution provides that "no warrants shall issue but upon probable cause." The majority opinion in *Barlow's* indicated that "probable cause in the criminal law sense is not required. For purposes of an administrative search such as this, probable cause justifying the issuance of a warrant may be based not only on specific evidence of an existing violation but also on a showing that 'reasonable legislative or administrative standards for conducting an ... inspection are satisfied with respect to a particular [establishment].'" 436 U.S. at 320.

The "probable cause" requirement is not a serious obstacle for OSHA when an employer is selected on the basis of a programmed inspection targeted at a high-hazard industry. OSHA has experienced more difficulty in satisfying the probable cause requirement for those unprogrammed inspections that result from events such as accident reports and employee complaints. In *Donovan v. Federal Clearing Die Casting Co.*, 655 F.2d 793 (7th Cir. 1981), the court held that two newspaper articles describing an industrial accident, in which one of Federal's employees allegedly had his hands severed while operating a hydraulic punch press, did not satisfy the probable cause requirement for specific evidence of a violation of the Act. A subsequent case from the same circuit, *In re Establishment Inspection of Microcosm*, 951 F.2d 121 (7th Cir. 1991), *cert. denied* 506 U.S. 815 (1992), provides an extreme contrast. OSHA received an anonymous complaint about the use of solvents at Microcosm in a letter purportedly written by a friend of an employee. OSHA obtained an inspection warrant based on the complaint, which the company refused to honor. The court found the warrant to be valid and found the company in contempt for refusing to honor the warrant. The Seventh Circuit also upheld the validity of a search warrant in a more recent case, *In re Establishment Inspection of Kelly-Springfield Tire Co.*, 13 F.3d 1160 (7th Cir. 1994), when OSHA based the warrant on three interviews with a complaining employee after receiving a two-sentence written complaint about working conditions in the plant.

An interesting case arose after Joseph Dear, then OSHA Administrator, looked out of his hotel room and observed workers performing their job eighty feet above the ground without fall protection. Dear notified OSHA, and a compliance officer went to the roof of the hotel (with permission) and videotaped the workers. The officer then went to the work site and interviewed the employees and their foreman. The Commission held that the compliance officer did not violate the Fourth Amendment or the OSHAct when he videotaped employees from an off-site location before presenting his credentials to the employer, and the Fourth Circuit affirmed on that issue. *Secretary of Labor v. L.R. Willson & Sons, Inc.*, 17 O.S.H. Cas. (BNA) 2059 (1997), *aff'd in part and rev'd in part*, 134 F.3d 1235 (4th Cir. 1998).

3. *The Scope of the Inspection.* What portion of the employer's premises can OSHA inspect when entry is obtained? If the employer has been chosen on the basis of a programmed inspection, the OSHA compliance officer has access to the entire premises. If the employer was selected for an unprogrammed inspection, the Commission and circuit courts have taken several positions. In *Burkhart Randall Division of Textron, Inc. v. Marshall*, 625 F.2d 1313 (7th Cir. 1980), the Seventh Circuit allowed a general inspection of the whole plant in response to an employee complaint about a specific violation. The same circuit later adopted a more restrictive view in *Donovan v. Fall River Foundry Co.*, 712 F.2d 1103 (7th Cir. 1983), in which the court said that, when a complaint was received about an area separate from the rest of the building, a warrant to inspect the entire premises was not appropriate unless OSHA presented some evidence to show that hazardous conditions existed elsewhere in the plant. At one time, the Review Commission had adopted an even more restrictive position. In *Secretary of Labor v. Sarasota Concrete Co.*, 9 O.S.H. Cas. (BNA)1608 (1981), *aff'd*, 693 F.2d 1061 (11th Cir. 1982), the Commission held that when probable cause for the warrant is based on a specific violation, OSHA must limit its inspection to an examination of the alleged violative condition. That decision must be read in light of a subsequent decision from the same court, *Reich v. Montana Sulphur & Chemical Co.*, 32 F.3d 440 (11th Cir. 1994), *cert. denied*, 514 U.S. 1015 (1995). An individual complained that the company did not x-ray welds or certify its welders. The court approved a subpoena for information relating to a range of procedures for welding as well as more general information, such as minutes of safety and health meetings. The court indicated that OSHA was not confined to inquiries limited to violations of specific standards applicable to welding, but could rely on the general duty clause as a basis for its subpoena. The court also said that OSHA could expand its inquiry into welding activities beyond the specific allegations made by the informant.

The Sixth Circuit scrutinized a full-scope inspection that was triggered by an employee complaint of a specific problem in *Trinity Industries, Inc. v. OSHRC*, 16 F.3d 1455 (6th Cir. 1994). OSHA had established a plan that calls for a full-scope inspection if: (1) an employee complaint sets forth reasonable grounds to believe a violation or danger exists; (2) the establishment is in an industry with a high injury rate; (3) a complete inspection of the facility has not been conducted in the last two years; and (4) the facility has an injury rate at or above the national average. The court held that a full-scope inspection was not permitted. The search must be limited in scope to the employee complaint that triggered the inspection, plus a review of the employer's injury and illness rewards. If the limited search and the injury and illness rewards lead OSHA to suspect that a further inspection is necessary, then a second warrant authorizing a full-scope inspection must be obtained.

4. *Challenging the OSHA Standard in Enforcement Actions.* As examined in Section D of this chapter, employers often seek pre-enforcement judicial review of an OSHA standard under section 6(f). In addition, an employer cited for violating a standard can challenge its validity before the Commission under section 10(c), and on judicial review of the Commission's decision under section 11(a). The courts of appeal have split on whether an employer can challenge procedural defects in the underlying OSHA standard. *Compare National Indus. Constr., Inc. v. OSHRC,* 583 F.2d 1048 (8th Cir. 1978) (procedural attacks on newly-promulgated standards must be raised in section 6(f) review or are deemed waived) *with Marshall v. Union Oil Co.,* 616 F.2d 1113 (1980) (procedural validity of OSHA regulation can be challenged in section 10(c) proceeding). More important is the possibility of challenging the substance of the OSHA standard in an enforcement action, particularly on the issue of whether compliance with the standard is feasible. Here, some courts have placed a greater burden on the Secretary in enforcing a standard against a particular employer than in defending the whole standard in a section 6(f) review. For example, in *Boise Cascade Corp. v. Secretary of Labor,* 694 F.2d 584 (9th Cir. 1982), the court noted that in promulgating a standard, the Secretary can satisfy the technological feasibility requirement by adopting a technology that is merely "looming on today's horizon." In an enforcement proceeding, however, the Secretary must show that "specific, technically feasible controls exist to abate the violation."

G. EMPLOYEE RIGHTS AND RESPONSIBILITIES

ATLANTIC & GULF STEVEDORES, INC. v. OSHA

United States Court of Appeals, Third Circuit
534 F.2d 541 (1976)

GIBBONS, CIRCUIT JUDGE.

The petitioners are stevedoring companies operating in the Port of Philadelphia. They employ longshoremen. The Secretary of Labor, pursuant to statutory authority, has adopted safety and health regulations for longshoring. Among those regulations is the so called "longshoring hardhat" standard:

> Employees shall be protected by protective hats meeting the specifications contained in the American National Standard Safety Requirements for Industrial Head Protection, Z89.1 (1969).

29 C.F.R. § 1918.105(a) (1975).

On April 10-11, 1973 an OSHA compliance officer inspected the Camden, New Jersey docks and discovered that nearly all of petitioners' longshoremen were working without hardhats. The Secretary cited petitioners for violation of § 5(a)(2) of OSHA, and proposed that civil penalties aggregating $455 be levied against the petitioners. Each citation also ordered immediate abatement of violations. Petitioners filed notices of contest, which resulted in a hearing before the Commission's Administrative Law Judge.

At the hearing the OSHA compliance officer testified that on the dates of his inspections, only a very small proportion of the longshoremen were wearing hardhats, that none of the petitioners had previously been cited for a violation of the hardhat standard, and that no injuries were involved. He also testified that between 1971, when the standard was adopted, and April 1973 there had been a moratorium in the Secretary's enforcement of it, because the longshoremen's unions opposed it and the rank-and-file preferred not to wear hardhats....

Witnesses for the petitioners testified that stevedores in the Port of Philadelphia had, beginning in 1971, undertaken strenuous but unsuccessful efforts to obtain compliance with the standard by their longshoring employees; had furnished the required hardhats; had encouraged use of the headgear at regular safety meetings; had posted hardhat signs on their working premises; had used payroll envelope stuffers advocating hardhat wearing; and had placed hardhat safety messages on the hiring tapes. All this was to little avail, and each employer witness testified to a firm belief that wildcat strikes or walkouts would attend attempts to enforce the standard by firing employees who refused to comply. There is undisputed testimony that in another port a strike over that issue did occur.[4] There is, however, no testimony that these petitioners ever denied work to a longshoreman for his refusal to wear a hardhat.

The petitioners urged that the Secretary's citations and proposed penalties should be vacated because in view of the longshoremen's intransigent opposition to and their union's lukewarm support for the standard, compliance *by them* with the hardhat standard was not achievable. The Administrative Law Judge found the three employers in violation of 29 C.F.R. § 1918.105(a), but vacated the Secretary's proposed penalties....

[On review, t]he Commission voted 2-1 to affirm the Administrative Law Judge's decision finding violations and vacating proposed penalties, but each

---

[4] This strike occurred in the Port of New York in 1970, prior to the enactment of OSHA. The record also disclosed that stevedoring companies have successfully enforced the mandatory use regulation in the Port of Norfolk, but that longshoremen in the Port of San Francisco have resisted the use of hardhats.

Commissioner filed a separate opinion. Commissioner Cleary announced the decision of the Commission. He rejected as "largely speculative" the petitioners' contention that they had done all they could do without causing labor strife. In addition, he concluded that, at least when non-compliance by employees was neither unpredictable nor idiosyncratic, final responsibility for compliance with the Act's requirements rested with the employers.

Commissioner Van Namee, concurring, did not agree that the evidence of potential labor unrest was speculative. Nor did he agree that employers could under the Act be held strictly liable in all instances of technical non-compliance. Yet he concluded that in this instance the employers would, because of the terms of their collective bargaining agreements, have a remedy under § 301 of the Labor Management Relations Act, 29 U.S.C. § 185, against a wildcat strike. Commissioner Van Namee surmised that the availability of such a remedy made the fear of a strike, or at least an effective one, "nothing more than an illusion."[6] He recognized, however, that the applicability of a particular safety and health standard should not turn on whether the parties to the collective bargaining agreement agreed upon a grievance-arbitration procedure that was broad enough to permit a *Boys Markets* injunction. Such an approach would admit of selective enforcement of OSHA safety standards. To meet this objection Commissioner Van Namee said that irrespective of the existence of a *Boys Markets* remedy, the Commission itself had the statutory authority to issue cease and desist orders running against employees. These orders could be enforced by injunction in the Courts of Appeals pursuant to §§ 11(a) and (b) of the Act.

Chairman Moran dissented. Like Commissioner Van Namee, he rejected Commissioner Cleary's assessment of the evidence concerning the likelihood of walkouts over attempts to enforce the hardhat requirement. He concluded that the employers had taken all steps required of them under the Act. He also expressed doubt as to the availability of § 301 injunctive relief.

In summary, although the Commission order affirmed the citations, there is no opinion which can be said to represent a concensus. Two Commissioners, Moran and Van Namee, agree that the record contains substantial evidence tending to show that a work stoppage will occur if the petitioners take additional steps to enforce the hardhat requirement. Commissioner Van Namee concludes, however,

---

[6] That a *Boys Markets, Inc. v. Retail Clerks, Local 770,* 398 U.S. 235 (1970) remedy is available does not, of course, by itself conclusively answer petitioners' objection that employee recalcitrance makes compliance with the longshoring hardhat safety standard impossible. The stevedores could obtain a § 301 injunction only if they agreed to submit the hardhat dispute to arbitration. There can be no assurance, for example, that an arbitrator would decide that an employee who defied an express directive of his employer and ignored validly promulgated federal regulations could be discharged or otherwise disciplined for such conduct. We assume, however, that arbitration would most often sustain the employer prerogative in this regard. Where the collective bargaining agreement empowers the employer to seek § 301 relief, therefore, that remedy is likely to prove adequate. In those instances where it is demonstrably inadequate, the employers may nevertheless seek relief from liability by petitioning for a variance from the standard, 29 U.S.C. § 655(d), or for an extension of time in which to abate a cited violation 29 U.S.C. § 659(c). See Part IIIB, *infra.*

that the availability of relief before the Commission against spontaneous employee obduracy renders this body of evidence irrelevant. Chairman Moran evidently does not share Commissioner Van Namee's expansive view of the Commission's powers, although he did not in this case address the issue. Commissioner Cleary flatly rejects any interpretation of OSHA that would permit the Commission to issue cease and desist orders against employees. Nevertheless, he regards the threat of work stoppages posed in this instance as largely speculative. In any event, Commissioner Cleary suggests that where, as here, employee non-compliance is neither unpredictable nor idiosyncratic, the employer has an absolute statutory duty to enforce the terms of the Act.

II

Section 11(a) of the Act directs the reviewing court to accept "[t]he findings of the Commission with respect to questions of fact, if supported by substantial evidence on the record considered as a whole ...." *Brennan v. OSHRC (Interstate Glass Co.)*, 487 F.2d 438 (8th Cir. 1973). Because there is no opinion in which a majority of the Commission joined, there is no Commission finding of fact with respect to the likelihood that enforcement of the hardhat standard would provoke a work stoppage. But two Commissioners appear to have credited the testimony of the petitioners' witnesses that such a work stoppage was likely if not inevitable. We believe that such a finding would be supported by substantial evidence on the record as a whole.[7] Indeed, Commissioner Cleary's rejection of the evidence as "largely speculative," if it represented a finding of the Commission, probably would have to be dismissed as unsupported by substantial record evidence. Thus we assume, for purposes of this petition for review, that the longshoremen in the Port of Philadelphia are intransigent on the hardhat issue and are likely to strike if more vigorous enforcement efforts are undertaken.

This assumption serves to focus the specific and relatively narrow issue presented by this petition, viz., whether when employee non-compliance with an occupational safety or health standard is both predictable and virtually uniform, the employer must nevertheless enforce compliance even at the risk of concerted employee work stoppages. Because any answer to this inquiry is an adjudicatory conclusion, the scope of our review is less narrowly jacketed than with factual

---

[7] In addition to the evidence of the employers' futile attempts at friendly persuasion, and of the longshoremen's resistance in the Port of Philadelphia and elsewhere, the evidence showed that while initial compliance in 1971 with the regulation was good (about 80%), the rate of compliance quickly deteriorated. Apparently many workers tried the hats, found them uncomfortable or cumbersome, and discontinued their use.

The evidence also showed that although the stevedores had never actually denied employment to a longshoreman who refused to wear a hardhat, a 1971 threat of such action triggered an angry demonstration of longshoring foremen. Statistics showing that head injuries comprised only a small fraction (perhaps 1%) of total longshoring injuries fueled employee sentiment that hardhats did not protect against a significant occupational hazard and hence were unnecessary.

determinations. The law of this circuit is that we may set aside such conclusions if we find them to be arbitrary, capricious, an abuse of discretion or otherwise not in accordance with law. *Brennan v. OSHRC (Hanovia Lamp Div.),* 502 F.2d 946, 951 (3d Cir. 1974).

A

In urging us to vacate the citations, petitioners place principal reliance on our decision in the *Hanovia Lamp* case. There we followed the holding of the District of Columbia Circuit in *National Realty & Construction Co. v. OSHRC,* 489 F.2d 1257 (1973), rejecting a construction of the Act which would effectively make employers strictly liable for violations arising from employee misconduct. In *Hanovia Lamp* we held that an employer could be held answerable for a violation resulting from such misconduct only when "demonstrably feasible measures" existed for materially reducing its incidence. 502 F.2d at 952. In reply the Secretary correctly points out that both *National Realty Construction* and *Hanovia Lamp* involved citations for violation of the Act's general duty clause, while this case involves a citation for violation of a specific safety standard. It seems to be the Secretary's position that employers are to be held to a higher standard of care under specific regulations than under the general duty clause. We decline to bifurcate the statute in such a manner, and attach no significance to the proffered distinction.... [T]he employer's task of guarding against the aberrational action of specific employees who violate specific safety standards is essentially no less difficult than under the general duty clause. Thus the *Hanovia Lamp* standard governing employer responsibility applies, in our view, to 29 C.F.R. § 1918.105(a) to the same extent as to the general duty clause.

But while *Hanovia Lamp* [and] *National Realty Construction* ... supply us with the standard of liability to be applied to the facts of this case, they offer precious little insight into the question whether the petitioner stevedoring companies have breached their statutory duty of care. Those cases involved the unpredictable and unforeseeable actions of individual employees. This case involves the predictable, nearly universal actions of all the longshoremen. There is a demonstrably feasible measure which can be taken to prevent such concerted disobedience: the employer can refuse employment to those who insist on violating the standard. The discussions of strict liability in the cases referred to have no application to the instant situation, except to the extent that they are authority for the proposition that we will not construe OSHA to impose completely unreasonable burdens on employers within the Act's coverage.

We find guidance on this difficult question in our recent decision in *AFL-CIO v. Brennan,* 530 F.2d 109 (3d Cir. 1975). In that case we reviewed action of the Secretary adopting a "no hands in dies" standard for the mechanical power press industry. We recognized that the economic feasibility of an occupational safety and health standard was relevant to our assessment of its statutory validity. We pointed out that an economically impossible standard would in all likelihood prove unenforceable, and that the burden of policing a regulation uniformly ignored by a majority of industry members would prove to be overwhelming. Thus we held that in promulgating regulations the Secretary could take into account the economic impact of a proposed standard....

III

In this case the petitioners contend that the longshoring hardhat safety standard, insofar as it is applied to them, is invalid because attempts at enforcement would provoke a wildcat strike by their employees. The standard is, in their view, economically infeasible. They produced evidence tending to support this position in the proceeding before the Administrative Law Judge. We believe that petitioners have carried their burden of proof on the issue. The remaining question is the legal sufficiency of the defense. We turn, then, to the several grounds relied upon by the Commission in rejecting petitioners' challenge to the hardhat safety standard.

A

If Commissioner Van Namee is correct that the Commission has the power to issue cease and desist orders against employees as well as employers, then the economic infeasibility argument against the standard disappears from this case. Unlike the no hands in dies standard which we reviewed in *AFL-CIO v. Brennan, supra,* the infeasibility claim in this case is bottomed not on the cost of forcing the technological change, but on the cost of a work stoppage caused by employee discontent with a simple, inexpensive and facially reasonable safety standard. If the Commission, and in turn this court, can issue coercive process against employees directly, the threat is eliminated and the defense overcome. It is far from clear, however, that the Commission enjoys the power for which Commissioner Van Namee argues.

Commissioner Van Namee finds the source of such coercive authority in a combination of § 2(b)(2) of the Act, § 5(b), and § 10(c). The latter provision authorizes the Commission to issue orders "affirming, modifying, or vacating the Secretary's citation ... or directing other appropriate relief ...." Section 2(b)(2), in the section of the Act setting forth congressional findings and a declaration of policy, provides:

> (b) The Congress declares it to be its purpose and policy ... to assure so far as possible every working man and woman in the Nation safe and healthful working conditions and to preserve our human resources —
>
> ....
>
> (2) by providing that employers and employees have separate but dependent responsibilities and rights with respect to achieving safe and healthful working conditions ....

Section 5(b) provides that

> [e]ach employee shall comply with occupational safety and health standards and all rules, regulations, and orders issued pursuant to this chapter which are applicable to his own actions and conduct.

According to Commissioner Van Namee the employees' separate responsibilities under § 5(b) would be "meaningless and a nullity" if the Commission and this court, in an enforcement proceeding, were powerless to sanction employee disregard of safety standards and commission orders....

With considerable misgivings, we conclude that Congress did not intend to confer on the Secretary or the Commission the power to sanction employees. Sections 2(b)(2) and 5(b) cannot be read apart from the detailed scheme of enforcement set out in §§ 9, 10 and 17 of the Act. It seems clear that this enforcement scheme is directed only against employers. Sections 9(a) and 10(a) provide for the issuance of citations and notifications of proposed penalties only to employers. Section 10(a) refers only to an employer's opportunity to contest a citation and notification of proposed penalty. Only after an employer has filed a notice of contest does the Commission obtain general jurisdiction. Employees and their representatives may then elect to intervene under § 10(c). The only independent right granted employees by § 10(c) is to contest before the Commission the reasonableness of any time period fixed by the Secretary in a citation for the abatement of a violation. Section 17 provides for the assessment of civil monetary penalties only against employers. That the Act's use of the term "employer" is truly generic is made plain in § 3, the definitional section, where "employer" and "employee" are separately defined. We find no room for loose construction of the term of art.

We are likewise unable to find support in § 5(b) for the proposition that the Act's sanctions can be directed at employees. Although this provision's injunction to employees is essentially devoid of content if not enforceable, we reluctantly conclude that this result precisely coincides with the congressional intent.... The Senate Report on the employee duty section ... says:

> The committee recognizes that accomplishment of the purposes of this bill cannot be totally achieved without the fullest cooperation of affected employees. In this connection, Section 5(b) expressly places upon each employee the obligation to comply with standards and other applicable requirements under the act....
>
> The committee does not intend the employee-duty provided in section 5(b) to diminish in any way the employer's compliance responsibilities or his responsibility to assure compliance by his own employees. Final responsibility for compliance with the requirements of this act remains with the employer.

We simply cannot accept the argument that a remedy for violations of § 5(b) can be implied from its terms. All the evidence points in the other direction.[18]

Nor do we believe that the language in § 10(c) authorizing the Commission to issue orders "directing other appropriate relief" can be stretched to the point that it includes relief against employees. Rather, the generality of that language must be deemed limited by its context — relief in connection with the Secretary's citation. The Secretary appears not to have authority to issue a citation against an employee, and the Commission's powers cannot be any broader. "Other appropriate relief" refers to other appropriate relief against an employer.

This court's power under § 11(a) of the Act is framed in somewhat broader terms:

> Upon [the filing of a petition for review], the court shall have jurisdiction of the proceeding and of the question determined therein, and shall have power to grant such temporary relief or restraining order as it deems just and proper, and to make and enter upon the pleadings, testimony, and proceedings set forth in such record a decree affirming, modifying, or setting aside in whole or in part, the order of the Commission and enforcing the same to the extent that such order is affirmed or modified.

Clearly we can, in deciding whether and to what extent we will enforce a Commission order affirming a Secretary's citation, take into account the fact that employee intransigence in spite of employer best efforts would make enforcement inequitable. In such a case we could deny or limit enforcement. But § 11(a) does not grant to this court any independent authority to sanction employees.

B

We hold, then, that Commissioner Van Namee's reason for rejecting the petitioners' economic infeasibility defense cannot withstand analysis. We must face squarely the issue whether the Secretary can announce, and insist on employer

---

[18] Our conclusion is fortified by reference to the following post-enactment colloquy between Representative Steiger, a co-sponsor of OSHA, and Representative Hungate:

> MR. HUNGATE: Now, employer-employee. We have had a line of testimony about, tell this guy to wear a hardhat, or there are six guys on the job and five of them do and the other guy tosses it out, it is a hot day. And they come through and the employer gets fined and the employee does not. What can we do about that?

> MR. STEIGER: Well, Mr. Chairman when this bill was being considered, that was a question on which we spent a considerable amount of time. I would have to say the business community, at the time the bill was under consideration, took a very hard line that they did not want the Federal government to be in the business of disciplining their employees .... But on balance, Mr. Chairman, I would not want to see us amend the law to impose Federal government discipline on employees. I think that is something left between management and labor....

Hearings before the Subcomm. on Environmental Problems Affecting Small Business of the Select Comm. on Small Business, 92d Cong., 2d Sess. 490-91 (1972).

compliance with a standard which employees are likely to resist to the point of concerted work stoppages. To frame the issue in slightly different terms, can the Secretary insist that an employer in the collective bargaining process bargain to retain the right to discipline employees for violation of safety standards which are patently reasonable, and are economically feasible except for employee resistance?

We hold that the Secretary has such power. As Part IIIA of this opinion has indicated, the entire thrust of the Act is to place primary responsibility for safety in the work place upon the employer. That, certainly, is a decision within the legislative competence of Congress. In some cases, undoubtedly, such a policy will result in work stoppages. But as we observed in *AFL-CIO v. Brennan, supra,* the task of weighing the economic feasibility of a regulation is conferred upon the Secretary. He has concluded that stevedores must take all available legal steps to secure compliance by the longshoremen with the hardhat standard.

We can perceive several legal remedies which employers in petitioners' shoes might find availing. An employer can bargain in good faith with the representatives of its employees for the right to discharge or discipline any employee who disobeys an OSHA standard. Because occupational safety and health would seem to be subsumed within the subjects of mandatory collective bargaining — wages, hours and conditions of employment — the employer can, consistent with its duty to bargain in good faith, insist to the point of impasse upon the right to discharge or discipline disobedient employees. *See NLRB v. American National Insurance Co.,* 343 U.S. 395 (1952). Where the employer's prerogative in such matters is established, that right can be enforced under § 301. Should discipline or discharge nevertheless provoke a work stoppage, *Boys Markets* injunctive relief would be available if the parties have agreed upon a no-strike or grievance and arbitration provision. And even in those cases in which an injunction cannot be obtained, or where arbitration fails to vindicate the employer's action, the employer can still apply to the Secretary pursuant to § 6(d) of the Act, for a variance from a promulgated standard, on a showing that alternative methods for protecting employees would be equally effective. Moreover, under § 10(c) the Secretary has authority to extend the time within which a violation of a standard must be abated.

In this case petitioners have produced no evidence demonstrating that they have bargained for a unilateral privilege of discharge or discipline, that they have actually discharged or disciplined, or threatened to discharge or discipline, any employee who defied the hardhat standard, or that they have petitioned the Secretary for a variance or an extension of the time within which compliance is to be achieved. We conclude that as a matter of law petitioners have failed to establish the infeasibility of the challenged regulation.

The order of the Commission enforcing the Secretary's citations will be affirmed. The petition for review will be denied.

WHIRLPOOL CORP. v. MARSHALL

United States Supreme Court

445 U.S. 1 (1980)

MR. JUSTICE STEWART delivered the opinion of the Court.

The Occupational Safety and Health Act of 1970 (Act) prohibits an employer from discharging or discriminating against any employee who exercises "any right afforded by" the Act.[2] The Secretary of Labor (Secretary) has promulgated a regulation providing that, among the rights that the Act so protects, is the right of an employee to choose not to perform his assigned task because of a reasonable ap, hension of death or serious injury coupled with a reasonable belief that no less drastic alternative is available.[3] The question presented in the case before us is whether this regulation is consistent with the Act.

---

[2] Section 11(c)(1), 29 U.S.C. § 660(c)(1).

[3] The regulation, 29 CFR § 1977.12 (1979), provides in full:

(a) In addition to protecting employees who file complaints, institute proceedings, or testify in proceedings under or related to the Act, section 11(c) also protects employees from discrimination occurring because of the exercise "of any right afforded by this Act." Certain rights are explicitly provided in the Act; for example, there is a right to participate as a party in enforcement proceedings (sec. 10). Certain other rights exist by necessary implication. For example, employees may request information from the Occupational Safety and Health Administration; such requests would constitute the exercise of a right afforded by the Act. Likewise, employees interviewed by agents of the Secretary in the course of inspections or investigations could not subsequently be discriminated against because of their cooperation.

(b)(1) On the other hand, review of the Act and examination of the legislative history discloses that, as a general matter, there is no right afforded by the Act which would entitle employees to walk off the job because of potential unsafe conditions at the workplace. Hazardous conditions which may be violative of the Act will ordinarily be corrected by the employer, once brought to his attention. If corrections are not accomplished, or if there is dispute about the existence of a hazard, the employee will normally have opportunity to request inspection of the workplace pursuant to section 8(f) of the Act, or to seek the assistance of other public agencies which have responsibility in the field of safety and health. Under such circumstances, therefore, an employer would not ordinarily be in violation of section 11(c) by taking action to discipline an employee for refusing to perform normal job activities because of alleged safety or health hazards.

(2) However, occasions might arise when an employee is confronted with a choice between not performing assigned tasks or subjecting himself to serious injury or death arising from a hazardous condition at the workplace. If the employee, with no reasonable alternative, refuses in good faith to expose himself to the dangerous condition, he would be protected against subsequent discrimination. The condition causing the employee's apprehension of death or injury must be of such a nature that a reasonable person, under the circumstances then confronting the employee, would conclude that there is a real danger of death or serious injury and that there is insufficient time due to the urgency of the situation, to eliminate the danger through resort to regular statutory enforcement channels. In addition, in such circumstances, the employee, where possible, must also have sought from his employer, and been unable to obtain, a correction of the dangerous condition.

I

The petitioner company maintains a manufacturing plant in Marion, Ohio, for the production of household appliances. Overhead conveyors transport appliance components throughout the plant. To protect employees from objects that occasionally fall from these conveyors, the petitioner has installed a horizontal wire-mesh guard screen approximately 20 feet above the plant floor. This mesh screen is welded to angle-iron frames suspended from the building's structural steel skeleton.

Maintenance employees of the petitioner spend several hours each week removing objects from the screen, replacing paper spread on the screen to catch grease drippings from the material on the conveyors, and performing occasional maintenance work on the conveyors themselves. To perform these duties, maintenance employees usually are able to stand on the iron frames, but sometimes find it necessary to step onto the steel mesh screen itself.

In 1973, the company began to install heavier wire in the screen because its safety had been drawn into question. Several employees had fallen partly through the old screen, and on one occasion an employee had fallen completely through to the plant floor below but had survived. A number of maintenance employees had reacted to these incidents by bringing the unsafe screen conditions to the attention of their foremen. The petitioner company's contemporaneous safety instructions admonished employees to step only on the angle-iron frames.

On June 28, 1974, a maintenance employee fell to his death through the guard screen in an area where the newer, stronger mesh had not yet been installed.[4] Following this incident, the petitioner effectuated some repairs and issued an order strictly forbidding maintenance employees from stepping on either the screens or the angle-iron supporting structure. An alternative but somewhat more cumbersome and less satisfactory method was developed for removing objects from the screen. This procedure required employees to stand on power-raised mobile platforms and use hooks to recover the material.

On July 7, 1974, two of the petitioner's maintenance employees, Virgil Deemer and Thomas Cornwell, met with the plant maintenance superintendent to voice their concern about the safety of the screen. The superintendent disagreed with their view, but permitted the two men to inspect the screen with their foreman and to point out dangerous areas needing repair. Unsatisfied with the petitioner's response to the results of this inspection, Deemer and Cornwell met on

---

[4] As a result of this fatality, the Secretary conducted an investigation that led to the issuance of a citation charging the company with maintaining an unsafe walking and working surface in violation of 29 U.S.C. § 654(a)(1). The citation required immediate abatement of the hazard and proposed a $600 penalty. Nearly five years following the accident, the Occupational Safety and Health Review Commission affirmed the citation, but decided to permit the petitioner six months in which to correct the unsafe condition. A petition to review that decision is pending in the United States Court of Appeals for the District of Columbia Circuit.

July 9 with the plant safety director. At that meeting, they requested the name, address, and telephone number of a representative of the local office of the Occupational Safety and Health Administration (OSHA). Although the safety director told the men that they "had better stop and think about what [they] were doing," he furnished the men with the information they requested. Later that same day, Deemer contacted an official of the regional OSHA office and discussed the guard screen.

The next day, Deemer and Cornwell reported for the night shift at 10:45 p.m. Their foreman, after himself walking on some of the angle-iron frames, directed the two men to perform their usual maintenance duties on a section of the old screen.[6] Claiming that the screen was unsafe, they refused to carry out this directive. The foreman then sent them to the personnel office, where they were ordered to punch out without working or being paid for the remaining six hours of the shift.[7] The two men subsequently received written reprimands, which were placed in their employment files.

A little over a month later, the Secretary filed suit in the United States District Court for the Northern District of Ohio, alleging that the petitioner's actions against Deemer and Cornwell constituted discrimination in violation of § 11(c)(1) of the Act. [The District Court held that the employees met the requirements of the regulation, but denied relief holding that the regulation was inconsistent with the Act. The Court of Appeals for the Sixth Circuit reversed, holding that the regulation was valid and that the actions of Deemer and Cornwell were justified under it.]

II

The Act itself creates an express mechanism for protecting workers from employment conditions believed to pose an emergent threat of death or serious injury. Upon receipt of an employee inspection request stating reasonable grounds to believe that an imminent danger is present in a workplace, OSHA must conduct an inspection. 29 U.S.C. § 657(f)(1). In the event this inspection reveals workplace conditions or practices that "could reasonably be expected to cause death or serious physical harm immediately or before the imminence of such danger can be eliminated through the enforcement procedures otherwise provided by" the Act, 29 U.S.C. § 662(a), the OSHA inspector must inform the affected employees and the employer of the danger and notify them that he is recommending to the Secretary that injunctive relief be sought. § 662(c). At this juncture, the Secretary can petition a federal court to restrain the conditions or practices giving rise to the imminent danger. By means of a temporary restraining order or preliminary injunction, the court may then require the

---

[6] This order appears to have been in direct violation of the outstanding company directive that maintenance work was to be accomplished without stepping on the screen apparatus.

[7] Both employees apparently returned to work the following day without further incident.

employer to avoid, correct, or remove the danger or to prohibit employees from working in the area. § 662(a).

To ensure that this process functions effectively, the Act expressly accords to every employee several rights, the exercise of which may not subject him to discharge or discrimination. An employee is given the right to inform OSHA of an imminently dangerous workplace condition or practice and request that OSHA inspect that condition or practice. 29 U.S.C. § 657(f)(1). He is given a limited right to assist the OSHA inspector in inspecting the workplace, §§ 657(a)(2), (e), and (f)(2), and the right to aid a court in determining whether or not a risk of imminent danger in fact exists. See § 660(c)(1). Finally, an affected employee is given the right to bring an action to compel the Secretary to seek injunctive relief if he believes the Secretary has wrongfully declined to do so. § 662(d).

In the light of this detailed statutory scheme, the Secretary is obviously correct when he acknowledges in his regulation that, "as a general matter, there is no right afforded by the Act which would entitle employees to walk off the job because of potential unsafe conditions at the workplace." By providing for prompt notice to the employer of an inspector's intention to seek an injunction against an imminently dangerous condition, the legislation obviously contemplates that the employer will normally respond by voluntarily and speedily eliminating the danger. And in the few instances where this does not occur, the legislative provisions authorizing prompt judicial action are designed to give employees full protection in most situations from the risk of injury or death resulting from an imminently dangerous condition at the worksite.

As this case illustrates, however, circumstances may sometimes exist in which the employee justifiably believes that the express statutory arrangement does not sufficiently protect him from death or serious injury. Such circumstances will probably not often occur, but such a situation may arise when (1) the employee is ordered by his employer to work under conditions that the employee reasonably believes pose an imminent risk of death or serious bodily injury, and (2) the employee has reason to believe that there is not sufficient time or opportunity either to seek effective redress from his employer or to apprise OSHA of the danger.

Nothing in the Act suggests that those few employees who have to face this dilemma must rely exclusively on the remedies expressly set forth in the Act at the risk of their own safety. But nothing in the Act explicitly provides otherwise. Against this background of legislative silence, the Secretary has exercised his rulemaking power under 29 U.S.C. § 657(g)(2) and has determined that, when an employee in good faith finds himself in such a predicament, he may refuse to expose himself to the dangerous condition, without being subjected to "subsequent discrimination" by the employer.

The question before us is whether this interpretative regulation constitutes a permissible gloss on the Act by the Secretary, in light of the Act's language, structure, and legislative history. Our inquiry is informed by an awareness that the regulation is entitled to deference unless it can be said not to be a reasoned and supportable interpretation of the Act.

A

The regulation clearly conforms to the fundamental objective of the Act — to prevent occupational deaths and serious injuries. The Act, in its preamble, declares that its purpose and policy is "to assure so far as possible every working man and woman in the Nation safe and healthful working conditions and to *preserve* our human resources ...." 29 U.S.C. § 651(b). (Emphasis added.)

To accomplish this basic purpose, the legislation's remedial orientation is prophylactic in nature. The Act does not wait for an employee to die or become injured. It authorizes the promulgation of health and safety standards and the issuance of citations in the hope that these will act to prevent deaths or injuries from ever occurring. It would seem anomalous to construe an Act so directed and constructed as prohibiting an employee, with no other reasonable alternative, the freedom to withdraw from a workplace environment that he reasonably believes is highly dangerous.

Moreover, the Secretary's regulation can be viewed as an appropriate aid to the full effectuation of the Act's "general duty" clause. That clause provides that "[e]ach employer ... shall furnish to each of his employees employment and a place of employment which are free from recognized hazards that are causing or are likely to cause death or serious physical harm to his employees." 29 U.S.C. § 654(a)(1). As the legislative history of this provision reflects, it was intended itself to deter the occurrence of occupational deaths and serious injuries by placing on employers a mandatory obligation independent of the specific health and safety standards to be promulgated by the Secretary. Since OSHA inspectors cannot be present around the clock in every workplace, the Secretary's regulation ensures that employees will in all circumstances enjoy the rights afforded them by the "general duty" clause.

The regulation thus on its face appears to further the overriding purpose of the Act, and rationally to complement its remedial scheme. In the absence of some contrary indication in the legislative history, the Secretary's regulation must, therefore, be upheld, particularly when it is remembered that safety legislation is to be liberally construed to effectuate the congressional purpose.

B

In urging reversal of the judgment before us, the petitioner relies primarily on two aspects of the Act's legislative history.

1

Representative Daniels of New Jersey sponsored one of several House bills that led ultimately to the passage of the Act. As reported to the House by the Committee on Education and Labor, the Daniels bill contained a section that was soon dubbed the "strike with pay" provision. This section provided that employees could request an examination by the Department of Health, Education, and Welfare (HEW) of the toxicity of any materials in their workplace. If that examination revealed a workplace substance that had "potentially toxic or harmful effects in such concentration as used or found," the employer was given 60 days to correct the potentially dangerous condition. Following the expiration of that period, the employer could not require that an employee be exposed to toxic concentrations of the substance unless the employee was informed of the hazards and symptoms associated with the substance, the employee was instructed in the proper precautions for dealing with the substance, and the employee was furnished with personal protective equipment. If these conditions were not met, an employee could "absent himself from such risk of harm for the period necessary to avoid such danger without loss of regular compensation for such period."

This provision encountered stiff opposition in the House. Representative Steiger of Wisconsin introduced a substitute bill containing no "strike with pay" provision. In response, Representative Daniels offered a floor amendment that, among other things, deleted his bill's "strike with pay" provision. He suggested that employees instead be afforded the right to request an immediate OSHA inspection of the premises, a right which the Steiger bill did not provide. The House ultimately adopted the Steiger bill.

The bill that was reported to and, with a few amendments, passed by the Senate never contained a "strike with pay" provision. It did, however, give employees the means by which they could request immediate Labor Department inspections....

The petitioner reads into this legislative history a congressional intent incompatible with an administrative interpretation of the Act such as is embodied in the regulation at issue in this case. The petitioner argues that Congress' overriding concern in rejecting the "strike with pay" provision was to avoid giving employees a unilateral authority to walk off the job which they might abuse in order to intimidate or harass their employer. Congress deliberately chose instead, the petitioner maintains, to grant employees the power to request immediate administrative inspections of the workplace which could in appropriate cases lead to coercive judicial remedies. As the petitioner views the regulation, therefore, it gives to workers precisely what Congress determined to withhold from them.

We read the legislative history differently. Congress rejected a provision that did not concern itself at all with conditions posing real and immediate threats of death or severe injury. The remedy which the rejected provision furnished employees could have been invoked only after 60 days had passed following HEW's inspection and notification that improperly high levels of toxic substances were present in the workplace. Had that inspection revealed employment conditions posing a threat of imminent and grave harm, the Secretary of Labor would presumably have requested, long before expiration of the 60-day period, a court injunction pursuant to other provisions of the Daniels bill. Consequently, in rejecting the Daniels bill's "strike with pay" provision, Congress was not rejecting a legislative provision dealing with the highly perilous and fast-moving situations covered by the regulation now before us.

It is also important to emphasize that what primarily troubled Congress about the Daniels bill's "strike with pay" provision was its requirement that employees be paid their regular salary after having properly invoked their right to refuse to work under the section.[29] It is instructive that virtually every time the issue of an employee's right to absent himself from hazardous work was discussed in the legislative debates, it was in the context of the employee's right to continue to receive his usual compensation.

When it rejected the "strike with pay" concept, therefore, Congress very clearly meant to reject a law unconditionally imposing upon employers an obligation to continue to pay their employees their regular paychecks when they absented themselves from work for reasons of safety. But the regulation at issue here does not require employers to pay workers who refuse to perform their assigned tasks in the face of imminent danger. It simply provides that in such cases the employer may not "discriminate" against the employees involved. An employer "discriminates" against an employee only when he treats that employee less favorably than he treats others similarly situated.[31]

2

The second aspect of the Act's legislative history upon which the petitioner relies is the rejection by Congress of provisions contained in both the Daniels and the Williams bills that would have given Labor Department officials, in imminent-danger situations, the power temporarily to shut down all or part of an

---

[29] Congress' concern necessarily was with the provision's compensation requirement. The law then, as it does today, already afforded workers a right, under certain circumstances, to walk off their jobs when faced with hazardous conditions. Under Section 7 of the National Labor Relations Act, 29 U.S.C. § 157, employees have a protected right to strike over safety issues. *See NLRB v. Washington Aluminum Co.,* 370 U.S. 9. Similarly, Section 502 of the Labor Management Relations Act, 29 U.S.C. § 143, provides that "the quitting of labor by an employee or employees in good faith because of abnormally dangerous conditions for work at the place of employment of such employee or employees [shall not] be deemed a strike." The effect of this section is to create an exception to a no-strike obligation in a collective-bargaining agreement. *Gateway Coal Co. v. Mine Workers,* 414 U.S. 368. The existence of these statutory rights also makes clear that the Secretary's regulation does not conflict with the general pattern of federal labor legislation in the area of occupational safety and health.

[31] Deemer and Cornwell were clearly subjected to "discrimination" when the petitioner placed reprimands in their respective employment files. Whether the two employees were also discriminated against when they were denied pay for the approximately six hours they did not work on July 10, 1974, is a question not now before us. The District Court dismissed the complaint without indicating what relief it thought would have been appropriate had it upheld the Secretary's regulation. The Court of Appeals expressed no view concerning the limits of the relief to which the Secretary might ultimately be entitled. On remand, the District Court will reach this issue.

employer's plant. These provisions aroused considerable opposition in both Houses of Congress. The hostility engendered in the House of Representatives led Representative Daniels to delete his version of the provision in proposing amendments to his original bill. The Steiger bill that ultimately passed the House gave the Labor Department no such authority. The Wil ns bill, as approved by the Senate, did contain an administrative shutdown provision, but the Conference Committee rejected this aspect of the Senate bill.

The petitioner infers from these events a congressional will hostile to the regulation in question here. The regulation, the petitioner argues, provides employees with the very authority to shut down an employer's plant that was expressly denied a more expert and objective United States Department of Labor

As we read the pertinent legislative history, however, the petitioner misconceives the thrust of Congress' concern. Those in Congress who prevented passage of the administrative shutdown provisions in the Daniels and Williams bills were opposed to the unilateral authority those provisions gave to federal officials, without any judicial safeguards, drastically to impair the operation of an employer's business. Congressional opponents also feared that the provisions might jeopardize the Government's otherwise neutral role in labor-management relations.

Neither of these congressional concerns is implicated by the regulation before us. The regulation accords no authority to Government officials. It simply permits private employees of a private employer to avoid workplace conditions that they believe pose grave dangers to their own safety. The employees have no power under the regulation to order their employer to correct the hazardous condition or to clear the dangerous workplace of others. Moreover, any employee who acts in reliance on the regulation runs the risk of discharge or reprimand in the event a court subsequently finds that he acted unreasonably or in bad faith. The regulation, therefore, does not remotely resemble the legislation that Congress rejected.

C

For these reasons we conclude that 29 CFR § 1977.12(b)(2) (1979) was promulgated by the Secretary in the valid exercise of his authority under the Act. Accordingly, the judgment of the Court of Appeals is affirmed.

It is so ordered.

H. FEDERAL VERSUS STATE AUTHORITY FOR WORKPLACE SAFETY AND HEALTH

1. STATE AUTHORITY CEDED UNDER OSHA

The OSHAct preempts state safety and health activities, although, as later subsections indicate, there are controversies about the limits of federal preemption of certain areas of state responsibility, such as criminal laws, that have an indirect effect on workplace safety and health. Even in those areas where federal preemption clearly operates, however, namely the promulgation and enforcement of occupational health and safety standards, states can run their own safety and health programs if certain conditions are met. Section 18(c) of the Act provides that the Secretary of Labor may approve a state plan for the development and enforcement of occupational safety and health standards if, in the judgment of the Secretary, the state plan meets a number of conditions, including:

　　(i) a state agency is designated to run the program;
　　(ii) the state agency has sufficient funds and legal authority to conduct the program; and
　　(iii) the state health and safety standards are at least as effective as the federal standards.

Approved state plans must cover state and local government employees as well as the private sector workers subject to the Act. The Secretary of Labor has the authority to decide whether to accept a state's plan, to monitor the state's performance, and to revoke a state's authority to operate its own plan.

As of 1997, there were twenty-three approved state plans (including "state" plans in the Virgin Islands and Puerto Rico). In addition, New York and Connecticut had approved plans for state employees only. Federal funds reimburse states for up to 50% of the operating costs of approved state plans. If a state does not have an approved state plan, then OSHA is responsible for enforcing all health and safety standards in the state at no cost to the state's taxpayers. This was one reason why California revoked its state plan in 1977 — only to reverse its decisions thereafter on the basis of a state referendum.

The status of the state plans received considerable attention in the aftermath of the September 1991 fire at the Imperial Food Products' poultry processing plant in Hamlet, North Carolina. That disaster killed twenty-five workers who were trapped behind exit doors that were locked in violation of a safety standard. North Carolina, one of the twenty-three jurisdictions that runs its own safety and health program, had never inspected the Imperial Food Products' plant. OSHA terminated North Carolina's state plan operational status in October 1991 and assumed concurrent enforcement authority with the state for all safety and health matters. In April 1992, OSHA announced it was taking preliminary steps to withdraw approval of North Carolina's state plan. Then in July 1992, OSHA relented and indicated that enough improvements had been made in North Carolina to warrant the state's continued operation of the plan.

The North Carolina disaster prompted OSHA to evaluate the other twenty-two state plans. In January 1992, OSHA announced that all of the state plans had structural deficiencies. The structural features that OSHA considers essential to an effective state plan include: the ability to adopt comparable state standards within six months after the federal OSHA promulgates new standards; meeting federal benchmarks for the number of state compliance officers; and enactment of seven-fold increases in state penalties to parallel the increases contained in the 1990 amendments to the federal OSHAct. OSHA indicated that states must demonstrate substantial improvements in their plans within six months. OSHA indicated that failure of a state to take corrective action could lead to withdrawal of the plan's operational status. Since North Carolina was identified as the state with the most deficiencies in its state safety and health plan, and since OSHA subsequently decided not to revoke that state's authority to run its plan, OSHA's ultimate decision not to revoke the state plan in any of the other jurisdictions was not surprising.

OSHA's oversight of the state-operated safety and health programs was sharply criticized in 1994 by the United States General Accounting Office (GAO) in a report to Congress entitled Occupational Safety and Health: Changes Needed in the Combined Federal-State Approach. According to the GAO, the most fundamental weakness in OSHA's oversight of state programs is that the focus was on program activities (such as numbers of inspections conducted and penalties levied) rather than on outcomes or results (such as numbers of workplace injuries and diseases). Moreover, OSHA treated all 115 measures of program activities as equally important, according to the GAO critique.

2. OTHER SOURCES OF STATE AUTHORITY

The OSHAct preempts state health and safety plans that directly compete with OSHA standards unless, as discussed in the previous subsection, the Secretary of Labor has approved a state plan that meets certain conditions spelled out in section 18 of the Act. But what about state laws with "dual impacts," one of which involves regulation of workplace safety and health? Two examples of such state laws are "right-to-know" acts and occupational licensing acts, which protect both workers and the general public.

"Right-to-know" laws were enacted in about thirty states during the 1980s to provide information about hazardous substances in the workplace. An example is the New Jersey Worker and Community Right to Know Act, N.J. STAT. ANN. § 34:5A14, which required employers to disclose information about toxic chemicals to public safety officers, workers, and environmental control officials. One rationale for such disclosure to nonworkers is that police or firefighters who are summoned to a plant need to know what chemicals are present in order to decide if fumes are life-threatening and to know what firefighting techniques are appropriate.

OSHA promulgated the Hazard Communication Standard (HCS) for the manufacturing sector in 1983, and then extended the HCS to nonmanufacturing employers in 1987. 29 C.F.R. 1910.1200 (1986). The standard requires, *inter alia,* that employers prepare lists of hazardous chemicals, that all hazardous chemicals leaving a chemical manufacturing plant be labeled, that material safety data sheets (MSDS) be provided to each customer of the chemical firm, that employers who use these chemicals make the MSDSs available to employees, and that employees using the hazardous chemicals be trained about how to safely use the chemicals.

The Hazard Communication Standard is one of the most significant requirements that the OSHAct has placed on employers. For example, the two OSHA standards most frequency cited in OSHA violations during fiscal year 1996 were the HCSs for general industry and for construction. Nonetheless, one of the reasons why OSHA issued the HCS was to preempt state right-to-know laws and thus reduce burdens for employers.

A series of decisions by the Third Circuit drew distinctions between those portions of the right-to-know laws that were preempted by OSHA and those portions of the state laws that could remain operative. In *New Jersey State Chamber of Commerce v. Hughey (Hughey I),* 774 F.2d 587 (3d Cir. 1985), for example, the court held that the provision requiring manufacturing employers to complete workplace surveys was preempted, but that the provisions requiring reports of environmental hazards to agencies concerned with public health were not preempted. The Pennsylvania Right to Know law was challenged in *Manufacturers Ass'n of Tri-County v. Knepper,* 801 F.2d 130 (3d Cir. 1986), *cert. denied,* 484 U.S. 815 (1987). In this decision, the Third Circuit again distinguished between certain provisions that were preempted (such as education and training requirements for employees in manufacturing) and other provisions that were not (such as a hazard survey that was more inclusive than the HCS list of hazardous chemicals).

OSHA amended the Hazard Communication Standard in 1987. In addition to expanding coverage to nonmanufacturing employers, the preemption language was strengthened: thus state provisions concerning MSDSs, labeling of chemicals, and training programs "for the primary purpose" of assuring worker safety and health were explicitly preempted. The Third Circuit considered this language in *New Jersey Chamber of Commerce v. Hughey (Hughey II),* 868 F.2d 621 (3d Cir.), *cert. denied,* 492 U.S. 920 (1989), and decided that the container-labeling provision of the New Jersey right-to-know law would not be preempted because the state law would not serve as an obstacle to the accomplishment of the federal standard.

The "successful" efforts of the Third Circuit to distinguish between those portions of a state's right-to-know law that are preempted by OSHA and those portions that are not serve as a backdrop to the next case. *Gade v. National Solid Wastes Management Ass'n* deals with Illinois' efforts simultaneously to regulate workplace safety and health and to license certain occupations. The Court of Appeals for the Seventh Circuit held that the OSHAct preempted the state licensing laws. The plurality opinion by Justice O'Connor indicates that the Supreme Court granted certiorari in order to resolve the conflict between the Seventh Circuit opinion holding the Illinois law preempted and "decisions in which other Courts of Appeals have found the OSH Act to have a much narrower pre-emptive effect on 'dual impact' state regulations." Among the cases cited by Justice O'Connor in this category were the *Knepper* and *Hughey I* decisions discussed above. After you read the *Gade* decision, you can reassess the characterization of the Third Circuit's efforts as "successful."

GADE v. NATIONAL SOLID WASTES MANAGEMENT ASSOCIATION

United States Supreme Court
505 U.S. 88 (1992)

JUSTICE O'CONNOR announced the judgment of the Court and delivered an opinion, Parts I, III, and IV of which represent the views of the Court, and Part II of which is joined by THE CHIEF JUSTICE, JUSTICE WHITE, and JUSTICE SCALIA.

In 1988, the Illinois General Assembly enacted the Hazardous Waste Crane and Hoisting Equipment Operators Licensing Act and the Hazardous Waste Laborers Licensing Act (together, licensing acts). The stated purpose of the acts is both "to promote job safety" and "to protect life, limb and property." In this case, we consider whether these "dual impact" statutes, which protect both workers and the general public, are pre-empted by the federal Occupational Safety and Health Act of 1970 (OSH Act), and the standards promulgated thereunder by the Occupational Safety and Health Administration (OSHA).

I

The OSH Act authorizes the Secretary of Labor to promulgate federal occupational safety and health standards. In the Superfund Amendments and Reauthorization Act of 1986 (SARA), Congress directed the Secretary of Labor to "promulgate standards for the health and safety protection of employees engaged in hazardous waste operations" pursuant to her authority under the OSH Act. In relevant part, SARA requires the Secretary to establish standards for the initial and routine training of workers who handle hazardous wastes.

In response to this congressional directive, OSHA, to which the Secretary has delegated certain of her statutory responsibilities, promulgated regulations on "Hazardous Waste Operations and Emergency Response," including detailed regulations on worker training requirements. The OSHA regulations require, among other things, that workers engaged in an activity that may expose them to hazardous wastes receive a minimum of 40 hours of instruction off the site, and a minimum of three days actual field experience under the supervision of a trained supervisor. Workers who are on the site only occasionally or who are working in areas that have been determined to be under the permissible exposure limits must complete at least 24 hours of off-site instruction and one day of actual field experience. On-site managers and supervisors directly responsible for hazardous waste operations must receive the same initial training as general employees, plus at least eight additional hours of specialized training on various health and safety programs. Employees and supervisors are required to receive eight hours of refresher training annually. Those who have satisfied the training and field experience requirement receive a written certification; uncertified workers are prohibited from engaging in hazardous waste operations.

In 1988, while OSHA's interim hazardous waste regulations were in effect, the State of Illinois enacted the licensing acts at issue here. The laws are designated as acts "in relation to environmental protection," and their stated aim is to protect both employees and the general public by licensing hazardous waste equipment operators and laborers working at certain facilities. Both acts require a license applicant to provide a certified record of at least 40 hours of training under an approved program conducted within Illinois, to pass a written examination, and to complete an annual refresher course of at least eight hours of instruction. In addition, applicants for a hazardous waste crane operator's license must submit "a certified record showing operation of equipment used in hazardous waste handling for a minimum of 4,000 hours." Employees who work without the proper license, and employers who knowingly permit an unlicensed employee to work, are subject to escalating fines for each offense....

Shortly before the state licensing acts were due to go into effect, the [National Solid Waste Management Association (the Association)] brought a declaratory judgment action in United States District Court against [The Director] of the Illinois Environmental Protection Agency (IEPA). The Association sought to enjoin IEPA from enforcing the Illinois licensing acts, claiming that the acts were pre-empted by the OSH Act and OSHA regulations and that they violated the Commerce Clause of the United States Constitution. The District Court held [that the Illinois acts were not preempted. The Seventh Circuit reversed in part, and remanded for further consideration.]...

We granted certiorari to resolve a conflict between the decision below and decisions in which other Courts of Appeals have found the OSH Act to have a much narrower pre-emptive effect on "dual impact" state regulations. *See Associated Industries of Massachusetts v. Snow,* 898 F.2d 274, 279 (CA1 1990); *Environmental Encapsulating Corp. v. New York City,* 855 F.2d 48, 57 (CA2 1988); *Manufacturers Assn. of Tri-County v. Knepper,* 801 F.2d 130, 138 (CA3 1986), *cert. denied,* 484 U.S. 815 (1987); *New Jersey State Chamber of Commerce v. Hughey,* 774 F.2d 587, 593 (CA3 1985).

II

Before addressing the scope of the OSH Act's pre-emption of dual impact state regulations, we consider petitioner's threshold argument ... that the Act does not pre-empt nonconflicting state regulations at all....

In the OSH Act, Congress endeavored "to assure so far as possible every working man and woman in the Nation safe and healthful working conditions." 29 U.S.C. § 651(b). To that end, Congress authorized the Secretary of Labor to set mandatory occupational safety and health standards applicable to all businesses affecting interstate commerce, and thereby brought the Federal Government into a field that traditionally had been occupied by the States. Federal regulation of the workplace was not intended to be all-encompassing, however. First, Congress expressly saved two areas from federal pre-emption. Section 4(b)(4) of the OSH Act states that the Act does not "supersede or in any manner affect any workmen's compensation law or ... enlarge or diminish or affect in any other manner the common law or statutory rights, duties, or liabilities of employers and employees under any law with respect to injuries, diseases, or death of employees arising out of, or in the course of, employment." Section 18(a) provides that the Act does not "prevent any State agency or court from asserting jurisdiction under State law over any occupational safety or health issue with respect to which no [federal] standard is in effect."

Congress not only reserved certain areas to state regulation, but it also, in § 18(b) of the Act, gave the States the option of pre-empting federal regulation entirely. That section provides:

> Submission of State plan for development and enforcement of State standards to preempt applicable Federal standards.
>
> Any State which, at any time, desires to assume responsibility for development and enforcement therein of occupational safety and health standards relating to any occupational safety or health issue with respect to which a Federal standard has been promulgated [by the Secretary under the OSH Act] shall submit a State plan for the development of such standards and their enforcement.

About half the States have received the Secretary's approval for their own state plans as described in this provision. Illinois is not among them.

In the decision below, the Court of Appeals held that § 18(b) "unquestionably" pre-empts any state law or regulation that establishes an occupational health and safety standard on an issue for which OSHA has already promulgated a standard, unless the State has obtained the Secretary's approval for its own plan. Every other federal and state court confronted with an OSH Act pre-emption challenge has reached the same conclusion, and so do we.

Pre-emption may be either expressed or implied, and "is compelled whether Congress' command is explicitly stated in the statute's language or implicitly contained in its structure and purpose." Absent explicit pre-emptive language, we have recognized at least two types of implied pre-emption: field pre-emption, where the scheme of federal regulation is "'so pervasive as to make reasonable the inference that Congress left no room for the States to supplement it,'" and conflict pre-emption, where "compliance with both federal and state regulations is a physical impossibility," *Florida Lime & Avocado Growers, Inc. v. Paul,* 373 U.S. 132, 142-143 (1963), or where state law "stands as an obstacle to the accomplishment and execution of the full purposes and objectives of Congress." *Hines v. Davidowitz,* 312 U.S. 52, 67 (1941).

Our ultimate task in any pre-emption case is to determine whether state regulation is consistent with the structure and purpose of the statute as a whole. Looking to "the provisions of the whole law, and to its object and policy," *Pilot Life Ins. Co. v. Dedeaux,* 481 U.S. 41, 51 (1987), we hold that nonapproved state regulation of occupational safety and health issues for which a federal standard is in effect is impliedly pre-empted as in conflict with the full purposes and objectives of the OSH Act. The design of the statute persuades us that Congress intended to subject employers and employees to only one set of regulations, be it federal or state, and that the only way a State may regulate an OSHA-regulated occupational safety and health issue is pursuant to an approved state plan that displaces the federal standards. The principal indication that Congress intended to pre-empt state law is § 18(b)'s statement that a State "shall" submit a plan if it wishes to "assume responsibility" for "development and enforcement ... of occupational safety and health standards relating to any occupational safety or health issue with respect to which a Federal standard has been promulgated." The unavoidable implication of this provision is that a State may not enforce its own occupational safety and health standards without obtaining the Secretary's approval, and petitioner concedes that § 18(b) would require an approved plan if Illinois wanted to "assume responsibility" for the regulation of occupational safety and health within the State. Petitioner contends, however, that an approved plan is necessary only if the State wishes completely to replace the federal regulations, not merely to supplement them. She argues that the correct interpretation of § 18(b) is that ... a State may either "oust" the federal standard by submitting a state plan to the Secretary for approval or "add to" the federal standard without seeking the Secretary's approval.

Petitioner's interpretation of § 18(b) might be plausible were we to interpret that provision in isolation, but it simply is not tenable in light of the OSH Act's surrounding provisions.... The OSH Act as a whole evidences Congress' intent to avoid subjecting workers and employers to duplicative regulation; a State may develop an occupational safety and health program tailored to its own needs, but only if it is willing completely to displace the applicable federal regulations.

Cutting against petitioner's interpretation of § 18(b) is the language of § 18(a), which saves from pre-emption any state law regulating an occupational safety and health issue with respect to which no federal standard is in effect. Although this is a saving clause, not a pre-emption clause, the natural implication of this provision is that state laws regulating the same issue as federal laws are not saved, even if they merely supplement the federal standard. Moreover, if petitioner's reading of § 18(b) were correct, and if a State were free to enact nonconflicting safety and health regulations, then § 18(a) would be superfluous: there is no possibility of conflict where there is no federal regulation.... [W]e conclude that § 18(a)'s preservation of state authority in the absence of a federal standard presupposes a background pre-emption of all state occupational safety and health standards whenever a federal standard governing the same issue is in effect.

Our understanding of the implications of § 18(b) is likewise bolstered by § 18(c) of the Act, which sets forth the conditions that must be satisfied before the Secretary can approve a plan submitted by a State under subsection (b). State standards that affect interstate commerce will be approved only if they "are required by compelling local conditions" and "do not unduly burden interstate commerce." If a State could supplement federal regulations without undergoing the § 18(b) approval process, then the protections that § 18(c) offers to interstate commerce would easily be undercut. It would make little sense to impose such a condition on state programs intended to supplant federal regulation and not those that merely supplement it: the burden on interstate commerce remains the same.

Section 18(f) also confirms our view that States are not permitted to assume an enforcement role without the Secretary's approval, unless no federal standard is in effect. That provision gives the Secretary the authority to withdraw her approval of a state plan. Once approval is withdrawn, the plan "ceases to be in effect" and the State is permitted to assert jurisdiction under its occupational health and safety law only for those cases "commenced before the withdrawal of the plan." Under petitioner's reading of § 18(b), § 18(f) should permit the continued exercise of state jurisdiction over purely "supplemental" and nonconflicting standards. Instead, § 18(f) assumes that the State loses the power to enforce all of its occupational safety and health standards once approval is withdrawn.

The same assumption of exclusive federal jurisdiction in the absence of an approved state plan is apparent in the transitional provisions contained in § 18(h) of the Act. Section 18(h) authorized the Secretary of Labor, during the first two years after passage of the Act, to enter into an agreement with a State by which the State would be permitted to continue to enforce its own occupational health and safety standards for two years or until final action was taken by the Secretary pursuant to § 18(b), whichever was earlier. Significantly, § 18(h) does not say that such an agreement is only necessary when the State wishes fully to supplant federal standards....

Looking at the provisions of § 18 as a whole, we conclude that the OSH Act precludes any state regulation of an occupational safety or health issue with respect to which a federal standard has been established, unless a state plan has been submitted and approved pursuant to § 18(b). Our review of the Act persuades us that Congress sought to promote occupational safety and health while at the same time avoiding duplicative, and possibly counterproductive, regulation. It thus established a system of uniform federal occupational health and safety standards, but gave States the option of pre-empting federal regulations by developing their own occupational safety and health programs. In addition, Congress offered the States substantial federal grant monies to assist them in developing their own programs. *See* OSH Act § 23, 29 U.S.C. §§ 672(a), (b), and (f) (for three years following enactment, the Secretary may award up to 90% of the costs to a State of developing a state occupational safety and health plan); 29 U.S.C. § 672(g) (States that develop approved plans may receive funding for up to 50% of the costs of operating their occupational health and safety programs). To allow a State selectively to "supplement" certain federal regulations with ostensibly nonconflicting standards would be inconsistent with this federal scheme of establishing uniform federal standards, on the one hand, and encouraging States to assume full responsibility for development and enforcement of their own OSH programs, on the other.

We cannot accept petitioner's argument that the OSH Act does not pre-empt nonconflicting state laws because those laws, like the Act, are designed to promote worker safety. In determining whether state law "stands as an obstacle" to the full implementation of a federal law, *Hines v. Davidowitz,* 312 U. S., at 67, "it is not enough to say that the ultimate goal of both federal and state law" is the same. *International Paper Co. v. Ouellette,* 479 U.S. 481, 494 (1987). "A state law also is pre-empted if it interferes with the methods by which the federal statute was designed to reach that goal." *Ibid.; see also Michigan Canners & Freezers Assn., Inc. v. Agricultural Marketing and Bargaining Bd.,* 467 U.S. 461, 477 (1984) (state statute establishing association to represent agricultural producers pre-empted even though it and the federal Agricultural Fair Practices Act "share the goal of augmenting the producer's bargaining power"); *Wisconsin Dept. of Industry v. Gould Inc.,* 475 U.S. 282, 286-287 (1986) (state statute preventing three-time violators of the National Labor Relations Act from doing business with the State is pre-empted even though state law was designed to reinforce requirements of federal Act). The OSH Act does not foreclose a State from enacting its own laws to advance the goal of worker safety, but it does restrict the ways in which it can do so. If a State wishes to regulate an issue of worker safety for which a federal standard is in effect, its only option is to obtain the prior approval of the Secretary of Labor, as described in § 18 of the Act.[2]

---

[2] JUSTICE KENNEDY, while agreeing on the pre-emptive scope of the OSH Act, finds that its pre-emption is express rather than implied. The Court's previous observation that our pre-emption categories are not "rigidly distinct," *English v. General Electric Co.,* 496 U.S. 72, 79 n.5 (1990), is proved true by this case. We, too, are persuaded that the text of the Act provides the strongest indication that Congress intended the promulgation of a federal safety and health standard to pre-empt all nonapproved state regulation of the same issue, but we cannot say that it rises to the level of express pre-emption. In the end, even JUSTICE KENNEDY finds express pre-emption by relying on the negative "inference" of § 18(b), which governs when state law will pre-empt federal law. We cannot agree that the negative implications of the text, although ultimately dispositive to our own analysis, expressly address the issue of federal pre-emption of state law. We therefore prefer to

III

Petitioner next argues that, even if Congress intended to pre-empt all non-approved state occupational safety and health regulations whenever a federal standard is in effect, the OSH Act's pre-emptive effect should not be extended to state laws that address public safety as well as occupational safety concerns. As we explained in Part II, we understand § 18(b) to mean that the OSH Act pre-empts all state "occupational safety and health standards relating to any occupational safety or health issue with respect to which a Federal standard has been promulgated." We now consider whether a dual impact law can be an "occupational safety and health standard" subject to pre-emption under the Act.

The OSH Act defines an "occupational safety and health standard" as "a standard which requires conditions, or the adoption or use of one or more practices, means, methods, operations, or processes, reasonably necessary or appropriate to provide safe or healthful employment and places of employment." 29 U.S.C. § 652(8). Any state law requirement designed to promote health and safety in the workplace falls neatly within the Act's definition of an "occupational safety and health standard." Clearly, under this definition, a state law that expressly declares a legislative purpose of regulating occupational health and safety would, in the absence of an approved state plan, be pre-empted by an OSHA standard regulating the same subject matter. But petitioner asserts that if the state legislature articulates a purpose other than (or in addition to) workplace health and safety, then the OSH Act loses its pre-emptive force. We disagree.

Although "part of the pre-empted field is defined by reference to the purpose of the state law in question, ... another part of the field is defined by the state law's actual effect." *English v. General Electric Co.,* 496 U.S. 72, 84 (1990). In assessing the impact of a state law on the federal scheme, we have refused to rely solely on the legislature's professed purpose and have looked as well to the effects of the law. As we explained over two decades ago:

> We can no longer adhere to the aberrational doctrine ... that state law may frustrate the operation of federal law as long as the state legislature in passing its law had some purpose in mind other than one of frustration. Apart from the fact that it is at odds with the approach taken in nearly all our Supremacy Clause cases, such a doctrine would enable state legislatures to nullify nearly all unwanted federal legislation by simply publishing a

---

place this case in the category of implied pre-emption. Although we have chosen to use the term "conflict" pre-emption, we could as easily have stated that the promulgation of a federal safety and health standard "pre-empts the field" for any nonapproved state law regulating the same safety and health issue. Frequently, the pre-emptive "label" we choose will carry with it substantive implications for the scope of pre-emption. In this case, however, it does not. Our disagreement with JUSTICE KENNEDY as to whether the OSH Act's pre-emptive effect is labelled "express" or "implied" is less important than our agreement that the implications of the text of the statute evince a congressional intent to pre-empt nonapproved state regulations when a federal standard is in effect.

legislative committee report articulating some state interest or policy — other than frustration of the federal objective — that would be tangentially furthered by the proposed state law.... Any state legislation which frustrates the full effectiveness of federal law is rendered invalid by the Supremacy Clause.

Perez v. Campbell, 402 U.S., at 651-652.

Our precedents leave no doubt that a dual impact state regulation cannot avoid OSH Act pre-emption simply because the regulation serves several objectives rather than one. As the Court of Appeals observed, "it would defeat the purpose of section 18 if a state could enact measures stricter than OSHA's and largely accomplished through regulation of worker health and safety simply by asserting a non-occupational purpose for the legislation." Whatever the purpose or purposes of the state law, pre-emption analysis cannot ignore the effect of the challenged state action on the pre-empted field. The key question is thus at what point the state regulation sufficiently interferes with federal regulation that it should be deemed pre-empted under the Act.

In *English v. General Electric Co., supra,* we held that a state tort claim brought by an employee of a nuclear-fuels production facility against her employer was not pre-empted by a federal whistle-blower provision because the state law did not have a "direct and substantial effect" on the federal scheme. In the decision below, the Court of Appeals relied on *English* to hold that, in the absence of the approval of the Secretary, the OSH Act pre-empts all state law that "constitutes, in a direct, clear and substantial way, regulation of worker health and safety." We agree that this is the appropriate standard for determining OSH Act pre-emption. On the other hand, state laws of general applicability (such as laws regarding traffic safety or fire safety) that do not conflict with OSHA standards and that regulate the conduct of workers and non-workers alike would generally not be pre-empted. Although some laws of general applicability may have a "direct and substantial" effect on worker safety, they cannot fairly be characterized as "occupational" standards, because they regulate workers simply as members of the general public. In this case, we agree with the court below that a law directed at workplace safety is not saved from pre-emption simply because the State can demonstrate some additional effect outside of the workplace.

In sum, a state law requirement that directly, substantially, and specifically regulates occupational safety and health is an occupational safety and health standard within the meaning of the Act. That such a law may also have a non-occupational impact does not render it any less of an occupational standard for purposes of pre-emption analysis. If the State wishes to enact a dual impact law that regulates an occupational safety or health issue for which a federal standard is in effect, § 18 of the Act requires that the State submit a plan for the approval of the Secretary.

IV

We recognize that "the States have a compelling interest in the practice of professions within their boundaries, and that as part of their power to protect the public health, safety, and other valid interests they have broad power to establish standards for licensing practitioners and regulating the practice of professions." *Goldfarb v. Virginia State Bar,* 421 U.S. 773, 792 (1975). But under the Supremacy Clause, from which our pre-emption doctrine is derived, "any state law, however clearly within a State's acknowledged power, which interferes with or is contrary to federal law, must yield." *Felder v. Casey,* 487 U.S., at 138. We therefore reject petitioner's argument that the State's interest in licensing various occupations can save from OSH Act pre-emption those provisions that directly and substantially affect workplace safety.

We also reject petitioner's argument that the Illinois acts do not regulate occupational safety and health at all, but are instead a "pre-condition" to employment. By that reasoning, the OSHA regulations themselves would not be considered occupational standards. SARA, however, makes clear that the training of employees engaged in hazardous waste operations is an occupational safety and health issue, and that certification requirements before an employee may engage in such work are occupational safety and health standards. Because neither of the OSH Act's saving provisions are implicated, and because Illinois does not have an approved state plan under § 18(b), the state licensing acts are pre-empted by the OSH Act to the extent they establish occupational safety and health standards for training those who work with hazardous wastes. Like the Court of Appeals, we do not specifically consider which of the licensing acts' provisions will stand or fall under the pre-emption analysis set forth above.

The judgment of the Court of Appeals is hereby

Affirmed.

JUSTICE KENNEDY, concurring in part and concurring in the judgment.

Though I concur in the Court's judgment and with the ultimate conclusion that the state law is pre-empted, I would find express pre-emption from the terms of the federal statute. I cannot agree that we should denominate this case as one of implied pre-emption. The contrary view of the plurality is based on an undue expansion of our implied pre-emption jurisprudence which, in my view, is neither wise nor necessary....

Our decisions establish that a high threshold must be met if a state law is to be pre-empted for conflicting with the purposes of a federal Act.... In my view, this type of pre-emption should be limited to state laws which impose prohibitions or obligations which are in direct contradiction to Congress' primary objectives, as conveyed with clarity in the federal legislation.

I do not believe that supplementary state regulation of an occupational safety and health issue can be said to create the sort of actual conflict required by our decisions. The purpose of state supplementary regulation, like the federal standards promulgated by the Occupational Safety and Health Administration (OSHA) is to protect worker safety and health. Any potential tension between a scheme of federal regulation of the workplace and a concurrent, supplementary state scheme would not, in my view, rise to the level of "actual conflict" described in our pre-emption cases. Absent the express provisions of § 18 of the Occupational Safety and Health Act of 1970 (OSH Act), I would not say that state supplementary regulation conflicts with the purposes of the OSH Act, or that it "interferes with the methods by which the federal statute was designed to reach [its] goal."

Nonetheless, I agree with the Court that "the OSH Act pre-empts all state 'occupational safety and health standards relating to any occupational safety or health issue with respect to which a Federal standard has been promulgated.'" I believe, however, that this result is mandated by the express terms of § 18(b) of the OSH Act. It follows from this that the pre-emptive scope of the Act is also limited to the language of the statute. When the existence of pre-emption is evident from the statutory text, our inquiry must begin and end with the statutory framework itself....

The statute is clear: When a State desires to assume responsibility for an occupational safety and health issue already addressed by the Federal Government, it must submit a state plan. The most reasonable inference from this language is that when a State does not submit and secure approval of a state plan, it may not enforce occupational safety and health standards in that area. Any doubt that this is what Congress intended disappears when subsection (b) is considered in conjunction with subsections (a), (c), and (f). I will not reiterate the plurality's persuasive discussion on this point. Unartful though the language of § 18(b) may be, the structure and language of § 18 leave little doubt that in the OSH statute Congress intended to pre-empt supplementary state regulation of an occupational safety and health issue with respect to which a federal standard exists.

In this regard I disagree with the dissent, and find unconvincing its conclusion that Congress intended to allow concurrent state and federal jurisdiction over occupational safety and health issues....

As a final matter, I agree that the Illinois Acts are not saved because they operate through a licensing mechanism rather than through direct regulation of the workplace. I therefore join all but Part II of the Court's opinion, and concur in the judgment of the Court.

JUSTICE SOUTER, with whom JUSTICE BLACKMUN, JUSTICE STEVENS, and JUSTICE THOMAS join, dissenting....

At first blush, respondent's strongest argument might seem to rest on § 18(a) of the Act, the full text of which is this:

(a) Assertion of State standards in absence of applicable Federal standards

Nothing in this chapter shall prevent any State agency or court from asserting jurisdiction under State law over any occupational safety or health issue with respect to which no standard is in effect under section 655 of this title.

That is to say, where there is no federal standard in effect, there is no pre-emption. The plurality reasons that there must be pre-emption, however, when there is a federal standard in effect, else § 18(a) would be rendered superfluous because "there is no possibility of conflict where there is no federal regulation."

The plurality errs doubly. First, its premise is incorrect. In the sense in which the plurality uses the term, there is the possibility of "conflict" even absent federal regulation since the mere enactment of a federal law like the Act may amount to an occupation of an entire field, preventing state regulation. Second, the necessary implication of § 18(a) is not that every federal regulation pre-empts all state law on the issue in question, but only that some federal regulations may pre-empt some state law. The plurality ignores the possibility that the provision simply rules out field pre-emption and is otherwise entirely compatible with the possibility that pre-emption will occur only when actual conflict between a federal regulation and a state rule renders compliance with both impossible. Indeed, if Congress had meant to say that any state rule should be pre-empted if it deals with an issue as to which there is a federal regulation in effect, the text of subsection (a) would have been a very inept way of trying to make the point. It was not, however, an inept way to make the different point that Congress intended no field pre-emption of the sphere of health and safety subject to regulation, but not necessarily regulated, under the Act. Unlike the case where field pre-emption occurs, the provision tells us, absence of a federal standard leaves a State free to do as it will on the issue. Beyond this, subsection (a) does not necessarily mean anything, and the provision is perfectly consistent with the conclusion that as long as compliance with both a federal standard and a state regulation is not physically impossible, each standard shall be enforceable. If, indeed, the presumption against pre-emption means anything, § 18(a) must be read in just this way.

Respondent also relies on § 18(b).... Respondent argues that the necessary implication of this provision is clear: the only way that a state rule on a particular occupational safety and health issue may be enforced once a federal standard on the issue is also in place is by incorporating the state rule in a plan approved by the Secretary.

As both the plurality and JUSTICE KENNEDY acknowledge, however, that is not the necessary implication of § 18(b). The subsection simply does not say that unless a plan is approved, state law on an issue is pre-empted by the promulgation of a federal standard. In fact it tugs the other way, and in actually providing a mechanism for a State to "assume responsibility" for an issue with respect to which a federal standard has been promulgated (that is, to pre-empt federal law), § 18(b) is far from pre-emptive of anything adopted by the States. Its heading, enacted as part of the statute and properly considered under our canons of construction for whatever light it may shed, speaks expressly of the "development and enforcement of State standards to preempt applicable Federal standards." The provision does not in any way provide that absent such state pre-emption of federal rules, the State may not even supplement the federal standards with consistent regulations of its own. Once again, nothing in the provision's language speaks one way or the other to the question whether promulgation of a federal standard pre-empts state regulation, or whether, in the absence of a plan, consistent federal and state regulations may coexist. The provision thus makes perfect sense on the assumption that a dual regulatory scheme is permissible but subject to state pre-emption if the State wishes to shoulder enough of the federal mandate to gain approval of a plan.

Nor does the provision setting out conditions for the Secretary's approval of a plan indicate that a state regulation on an issue federally addressed is never enforceable unless incorporated in a plan so approved. Subsection (c)(2) requires the Secretary to approve a plan when in her judgment, among other things, it will not "unduly burden interstate commerce." 29 U.S.C. § 667(c)(2). Respondent argues, and the plurality concludes, that if state regulations were not pre-empted, this provision would somehow suggest that States acting independently could enforce regulations that did burden interstate commerce unduly. But this simply does not follow. The subsection puts a limit on the Secretary's authority to approve a plan that burdens interstate commerce, thus capping the discretion that might otherwise have been read into the congressional delegation of authority to the Secretary to approve state plans. From this restriction applying only to the Secretary's federal authority it is clearly a non sequitur to conclude that pre-emption must have been intended to avoid the equally objectionable undue burden that independent state regulation might otherwise impose. Quite the contrary; the dormant Commerce Clause can take care of that, without any need to assume pre-emption.

The final provision that arguably suggests pre-emption merely by promulgation of a federal standard is § 18(h), 29 U.S.C. § 667(h):

(h) Temporary enforcement of State standards

The Secretary may enter into an agreement with a State under which the State will be permitted to continue to enforce one or more occupational health and safety standards in effect in such State until final action is taken by the Secretary with respect to a plan submitted by a State under subsection (b) of this section, or two years from December 29, 1970, whichever is earlier.

This provision of course expired in 1972, but its language may suggest something about the way Congress understood the rest of § 18. Since, all are agreed, a State would not have had reason to file a plan unless a federal standard was in place, § 18(h) necessarily refers to a situation in which there is a federal standard. Respondent argues that the provision for agreements authorizing continued enforcement of a state standard following adoption of a federal standard on the issue it addresses implies that, absent such agreement, a State would have been barred from enforcing any standard of its own.

Once again, however, that is not the necessary implication of the text. A purely permissive provision for enforcement of state regulations does not imply that all state regulations are otherwise unenforceable. All it necessarily means is that the Secretary could agree to permit the State for a limited time to enforce whatever State regulations would otherwise have been pre-empted, as would have been true when they actually so conflicted with the federal standard that an employer could not comply with them and still comply with federal law as well. Thus, in the case of a State wishing to submit a plan, the provision as I read it would have allowed for the possibility of just one transition, from the pre-Act state law to the post-Act state plan. Read as the Court reads it, however, employers and employees in such a State would have been subjected first to state law on a given issue; then, after promulgation of a federal standard, to that standard; and then, after approval of the plan, to a new state regime. One enforced readjustment would have been better than two, and the statute is better read accordingly.

In sum, our rule is that the traditional police powers of the State survive unless Congress has made a purpose to pre-empt them clear. The Act does not, in so many words, pre-empt all state regulation of issues on which federal standards have been promulgated, and respondent's contention at oral argument that reading subsections (a), (b), and (h) could leave no other "logical" conclusion but one of pre-emption is wrong. Each provision can be read consistently with the others without any implication of pre-emptive intent. They are in fact just as consistent with a purpose and objective to permit overlapping state and federal regulation as with one to guarantee that employers and employees would be subjected to only one regulatory regime. Restriction to one such regime by precluding supplemental state regulation might or might not be desirable. But in the absence of any clear expression of congressional intent to pre-empt, I can only conclude that, as long as compliance with federally promulgated standards does not render obedience to Illinois' regulations impossible, the enforcement of the state law is not prohibited by the Supremacy Clause. I respectfully dissent.

3. CRIMINAL PROSECUTIONS OF EMPLOYERS

PEOPLE v. CHICAGO MAGNET WIRE CORP.

Supreme Court of Illinois
534 N.E.2d 962, *cert. denied*, 493 U.S. 809 (1989)

JUSTICE WARD delivered the opinion of the court:

The issue we consider on this appeal is whether the Occupational Safety and Health Act of 1970 (OSHA) preempts the State from prosecuting the defendants, in the absence of approval from OSHA officials, for conduct which is regulated by OSHA occupational health and safety standards.

Indictments returned in the circuit court of Cook County charged the defendants, Chicago Magnet Wire Corporation, and five of its officers and agents, with aggravated battery and reckless conduct. The individual defendants were also charged with conspiracy to commit aggravated battery. In substance, the indictments alleged that the defendants knowingly and recklessly caused the injury of 42 employees by failing to provide for them necessary safety precautions in the workplace to avoid harmful exposure to "poisonous and stupefying substances" used by the company in its manufacturing processes. On the defendants' motion, the trial court dismissed the charges, holding that OSHA has preempted the State from prosecuting the defendants for the conduct alleged in the indictments. The appellate court affirmed and we granted the State's petition for leave to appeal ....

Defendant Chicago Magnet Wire Corporation is an Illinois corporation whose principal business is the coating of wire with various substances and chemical compounds. [The individual defendants] are officers or managerial agents of the corporation.

The indictments charged that the defendants unreasonably exposed 42 employees to "poisonous and stupefying substances" in the workplace and prevented the employees from protecting themselves by "failing to provide necessary safety instructions and necessary safety equipment and sundry health monitoring systems." The indictments also alleged that the defendants improperly stored the substances, provided inadequate ventilation and maintained dangerously overheated working conditions....

The circuit court dismissed the indictments, holding that OSHA preempts the States from prosecuting employers for conduct which is governed by Federal occupational health and safety standards, unless the State has received approval from OSHA officials to administer its own occupational safety and health plan. The court stated that because the conduct of the defendants set out in the indictments was governed by OSHA occupational health and safety standards, and the State had not received approval from OSHA officials to administer its own plan, it could not prosecute the defendants for such conduct.

The extent to which State law is preempted by Federal legislation under the supremacy clause of the Constitution of the United States is essentially a question of congressional intendment. Thus, if Congress, when acting within constitutional limits, explicitly mandates the preemption of State law within a stated situation, we need not proceed beyond the statutory language to determine that State law is preempted. Even absent an express command by Congress to preempt State law in a particular area, preemptive intent may be inferred where "the scheme of federal regulation is sufficiently comprehensive to make reasonable the inference that Congress 'left no room' for supplementary state regulation," or where the regulated field is one in which "the federal interest is so dominant that the federal system will be assumed to preclude enforcement of state laws on the same subject." Congressional intent to preempt State law may also be inferred where "'the object sought to be obtained by the federal law and the character of obligations imposed by it may reveal the same purpose.'"

The declared purpose of OSHA is "to assure so far as possible every working man and woman in the Nation safe and healthful working conditions and to preserve our human resources." (29 U.S.C. § 651(b).) To this end, Congress gave the Secretary of Labor the authority "to set mandatory occupational safety and health standards" for the workplace and to secure compliance with those standards by imposing civil and criminal sanctions for their violation. An "occupational health and safety standard" is defined as "a standard which requires conditions, or the adoption or use of one or more practices, means, methods, operations, or processes, reasonably necessary or appropriate to provide safe or healthful employment and places of employment." (29 U.S.C. § 652(8).) OSHA also imposes a duty on employers, separate and independent from specific standards set by the Secretary, to provide a workplace "free from recognized hazards that are causing or are likely to cause death or serious physical harm to his employees." 29 U.S.C. § 654(a).

Congress also authorized the Secretary to conduct investigations and on-site inspections of workplaces and to institute enforcement proceedings for violations of OSHA standards. For violations of specific OSHA standards or section 5(a), OSHA authorizes the imposition of civil fines ranging from $1,000 to $10,000. Criminal fines of $10,000 may be imposed for giving unauthorized advanced notification of an OSHA inspection or knowingly making false statements on any OSHA filing. OSHA also provides for prison terms of up to six months for wilful violations of OSHA standards that result in an employee's death.

The defendants read section 18(a) of OSHA to mean that under it Congress explicitly provided that the States are preempted from asserting jurisdiction over any occupational health and safety issue that is governed by OSHA occupational health and safety standards unless the State obtains approval from OSHA officials to administer its own occupational health and safety plan under section 18(b). Section 18 provides:

> (a) Nothing in this chapter shall prevent any State agency or court from asserting jurisdiction under State law over any occupational safety or health issue with respect to which no standard is in effect under section 655 of this title.
>
> (b) Any State which, at any time, desires to assume responsibility for development and enforcement therein of occupational safety and health standards relating to any occupational safety or health issue with respect to which a Federal standard has been promulgated under section 655 of this title shall submit a State plan for the development of such standards and their enforcement.

The defendants state that the conduct alleged in the indictments is governed by OSHA occupational health and safety standards. Specifically, they claim that OSHA standards define permissible exposure limits for the toxic substances which allegedly injured their employees and that OSHA also regulates the conduct that the prosecution says rendered the company's workplace unsafe. The defendants contend that therefore the trial court correctly held that, because the State had not received approval from OSHA officials pursuant to section 18(b) to prosecute the conduct set out in the indictments, the charges must be dismissed. We disagree.

Contrary to this argument, we cannot say that the language of section 18 of OSHA can reasonably be construed as explicitly preempting the enforcement of the criminal law of the States as to conduct governed by OSHA occupational health and safety standards. The language of section 18 refers only to a State's development and enforcement of "occupational health and safety standards." Nowhere in section 18 is there a statement or suggestion that the enforcement of State criminal law as to federally regulated workplace matters is preempted unless approval is obtained from OSHA officials.

The defendants argue, however, that because the charges set out in the indictments are based on conduct related to an alleged failure to maintain a safe work environment for their employees, in practical effect, the State is attempting to enforce occupational health and safety standards. They contend that the primary purpose of punishing conduct under criminal law is to deter conduct that society deems harmful and to secure conformity with acceptable norms of behavior. In that way, the criminal law establishes standards of care in society. When applied to conduct in the workplace, the defendants argue, criminal law serves the same purpose as OSHA, i.e., to compel adherence to a particular standard of safety that will minimize the risk of injury....

We cannot accept the defendants' contention that it must be concluded that Congress intended to preempt the enforcement of State criminal laws in regard to conduct of employers in the workplace because the State criminal laws implicitly enforce occupational health and safety standards.

Although the imposition of sanctions under State penal law may effect a regulation of behavior as OSHA safety standards do, regulation through deterrence, however, is not the sole purpose of criminal law. For example, it also serves to punish as a matter of retributive justice. Too, whereas OSHA standards apply only to specific hazards in the workplace, criminal law reaches to regulate conduct in society in general. In contrast, occupational health and safety standards are promulgated under OSHA primarily as a means of regulating conduct to prevent injuries in the workplace.

It is to be observed also that for the most part OSHA imposes strict liability for violation of its standards, and that the criminal charges here allege that the defendants knowingly or recklessly injured several of their employees by unreasonably exposing them to toxic substances in the workplace. In order to be convicted of the charges, the State must establish that the defendants not only committed acts causing injury but that they also had the charged mental state, i.e., that they recognized the risk of injury and nevertheless wilfully failed to take precautions to prevent injury. Thus, the criminal charges here do not set any new or other standards for workplace safety but rather seek to impose an additional sanction for an employer's conduct that, if proved, would certainly violate the duty set out in section 5(a) of OSHA.

There is nothing in the structure of OSHA or its legislative history which indicates that Congress intended to preempt the enforcement of State criminal law prohibiting conduct of employers that is also governed by OSHA safety standards. We would observe that the Supreme Court declared in *Jones v. Rath Packing Co.* (1977), 430 U.S. 519, 525, that "[w]here ... the field which Congress is said to have pre-empted has been traditionally occupied by the States, ... 'we start with the assumption that the historic police powers of the States were not to be superseded by the Federal Act unless that was the clear and manifest purpose of Congress.'"

Certainly, the power to prosecute criminal conduct has traditionally been regarded as properly within the scope of State superintendence. The regulation of health and safety has also been considered as "primarily, and historically" a matter of local concern. It cannot be said that it was the "clear and manifest" purpose of Congress to preempt the application of State criminal laws for culpable conduct of employers simply because the same conduct is also governed by OSHA occupational health and safety standards.

Although the provisions of OSHA are comprehensive, that Congress, in section 18, invited the States to administer their own occupational health and safety plans demonstrates that it did not intend to preclude supplementary State regulation. Indeed, section 2 of OSHA provides that the States are "to assume the fullest responsibility for the administration and enforcement of their occupational safety and health laws." It seems clear that the Federal interest in occupational health and safety was not to be exclusive.

Too, considering that until the recently increased interest in environmental safety charges were rarely brought under State law for conduct relating to an employer's failure to maintain a safe workplace, it would be unreasonable to say that Congress considered the preemption of State criminal law when enacting OSHA. Indeed, OSHA provides principally civil sanctions and only a few minor criminal sanctions for violations of its standards. Even for wilful violations of OSHA standards which result in an employee's death an employer can be sentenced only to a maximum of six months' imprisonment. There is no penalty provided for conduct which causes serious injury to workers. It seems clear that providing for appropriate criminal sanctions in cases of egregious conduct causing serious or fatal injuries to employees was not considered. Under these circumstances, it is totally unreasonable to conclude that Congress intended that OSHA's penalties would be the only sanctions available for wrongful conduct which threatens or results in serious physical injury or death to workers.

We judge that the purpose underlying section 18 was to ensure that OSHA would create a nationwide floor of effective safety and health standards and provide for the enforcement of those standards. It was not fear that the States would apply more stringent standards or penalties than OSHA that concerned Congress but that the States would apply lesser ones which would not provide the necessary level of safety.... While additional sanctions imposed through State criminal law enforcement for conduct also governed by OSHA safety standards may incidentally serve as a regulation for workplace safety, there is nothing in OSHA or its legislative history to indicate that Congress intended to preempt the enforcement of State criminal law simply because of its incidental regulatory effect.

A question with resemblance to the one here was before the Supreme Court in *Silkwood v. Kerr-McGee Corp.* (1984), 464 U.S. 238. There, the Court addressed the issue of whether State courts are preempted under the Atomic Energy Act from assessing punitive damages against defendants that cause injuries by excessive radiation.... [T]he Court had held [previously] that under the Atomic Energy Act the States are precluded from regulating the safety aspects of nuclear energy. The defendant argued that a "State-sanctioned award of punitive damages ... punishes and deters conduct relating to radiation hazards" and therefore should be preempted by the Atomic Energy Act. The Court upheld the award notwithstanding the fact that it would have an incidental regulatory effect ....

We note, too, that Congress expressly stated that OSHA was not intended to preempt two bases of liability that, like criminal law, operate to regulate workplace conduct and implicitly set safety standards — State workers' compensation and tort law. Section 4(b)(4) of OSHA provides:

> Nothing in this chapter shall be construed to supersede or in any manner affect any workmen's compensation law or to enlarge or diminish or affect in any other manner the common law or statutory rights, duties, or liabilities of employers and employees under any law with respect to injuries, diseases, or death of employees arising out of, or in the course of, employment.

There is little if any difference in the regulatory effect of punitive damages in tort and criminal penalties under the criminal law. We see no reason, therefore, why what the Court declared in *Silkwood* should not be applied to the preemptive effect of OSHA. Also, if Congress, in OSHA, explicitly declared it was willing to accept the incidental regulation imposed by compensatory damages awards under State tort law, it cannot plausibly be argued that it also intended to preempt State criminal law because of its incidental regulatory effect on workplace safety.

It is a contention of the defendants that it is irrelevant that the State is invoking criminal law jurisdiction as long as the conduct charged in an indictment or information is conduct subject to regulation by OSHA. The defendants argue that the test of preemption is whether the conduct for which the State seeks to prosecute is in any way regulated by Federal legislation. The defendants assert that because the conduct charged in the indictments is conduct regulated under OSHA, a State prosecution for that conduct is preempted by OSHA. The contention is not convincing.

Simply because the conduct sought to be regulated in a sense under State criminal law is identical to that conduct made subject to Federal regulation does not result in State law being preempted. When there is no intent shown on the part of Congress to preempt the operation of State law, the "inquiry is whether 'there exists an irreconcilable conflict between the federal and state regulatory schemes.'" A conflict arises where "compliance with both federal and state regulations is a physical impossibility," or when State law "stands as an obstacle to the accomplishment and execution of the full purposes and objectives of Congress."

The defendants argue that the prosecutions here would conflict with the purposes of OSHA. They say that Congress intended that under OSHA the Federal government was to have exclusive authority to set occupational health and safety standards. The standards were to be set only after extensive research to assure that the standards would minimize injuries in the workplace but at the same time not be so stringent that compliance would not be economically feasible. The defendants correctly point out that although the States are given the opportunity to enforce their own occupational health and safety standards, the plan submitted must contain assurances that the State will develop and enforce standards "at least as effective" as OSHA's. Even after a State plan is approved, the Occupational Safety and Health Administration retains jurisdiction to enforce its own standards until it determines, based on three years of experience, that the State's administration of the plan is "at least as effective" as OSHA's.

The defendants maintain that Federal supervision over State efforts to enforce their own workplace health and safety programs would be thwarted if a State, without prior approval from OSHA officials, could enforce its criminal laws for workplace conduct of employers which is also subject to OSHA standards. They say that the States would thus be permitted to impose standards so burdensome as to exceed the bounds of feasibility or so vague as not to provide clear guidance to employers.

We believe the concern of the defendants is unfounded. We cannot see that State prosecutions of employers for conduct which is regulated by OSHA standards would conflict with the administration of OSHA or be at odds with its goals or purposes. On the contrary, prosecutions of employers who violate State criminal law by failing to maintain safe working conditions for their employees will surely further OSHA's stated goal of "assur[ing] so far as possible every working man and woman in the Nation safe and healthful working conditions." State criminal law can provide valuable and forceful supplement to insure that workers are more adequately protected and that particularly egregious conduct receives appropriate punishment.

The defendants' statements that the State will now have the ability to enforce more stringent standards than OSHA's does not persuade. As stated, the charges here are based on the defendants' alleged willful failure to remove workplace hazards which create a substantial probability that they will cause injuries to their employees. Thus, employers are not left without guidance as to what standard of care they must meet. Too, in practical terms, if a defendant were in compliance with OSHA standards it is unlikely that the State would bring prosecutive action. Enforcement of State criminal law in the workplace will not "stand as an obstacle to the accomplishment and execution of the full purposes and objectives of Congress."

To adopt the defendants' interpretation of OSHA would, in effect, convert the statute, which was enacted to create a safe work environment for the nation's workers, into a grant of immunity for employers responsible for serious injuries or deaths of employees. We are sure that that would be a consequence unforeseen by Congress.

The question here has been considered by a few courts. The appellate court of Wisconsin in *State ex rel. Cornellier v. Black* (Wis. App. 1988), 425 N.W.2d 21, held that the State's authority to enforce its criminal laws in the workplace has not been preempted by OSHA.... (A divided court held to the contrary in *People v. Hegedus* (Mich. App. 1988), 425 N.W.2d 729, *leave to appeal granted in part* (Mich. App. 1988), 429 N.W.2d 593; *Sabine Consolidated, Inc. v. State* (Tex. App. 1988), 756 S.W.2d 865, citing the opinion of our appellate court in this case (510 N.E.2d 1173), also held *contra.*)

We would note that on September 27, 1988, the congressional committee on government operations approved and adopted a report on the question of whether State criminal prosecutions for workplace safety violations are preempted by OSHA. The committee concluded that inadequate use has been made of the criminal penalty provisions of the Act and recommended to Congress that "OSHA should take the position that the States have clear authority under the Federal OSH Act, as it is written, to prosecute employers for acts against their employees which constitute crimes under State law." Report of House Comm. on Government Operations, Getting Away with Murder in the Workplace: OSHA's Nonuse of Criminal Penalties for Safety Violations, H.R. Rep. No. 1051, 100th Cong., 2d Sess. 9 (1988)....

For the reasons given, the judgments of the appellate court and circuit court are reversed and the cause is remanded to the circuit court of Cook County for further proceedings.

NOTES

1. *Criminal Prosecution Under the Occupational Safety and Health Act.* The OSHAct primarily relies on a civil enforcement scheme to assure safe and healthful working conditions. The OSHAct does contain some provisions establishing criminal penalties, however. The most significant is Section 17(e), which provides for criminal liability in the event of a willful violation of a standard, rule, order, or regulation that causes the death of an employee. Section 17(e) originally imposed a fine of not more than $10,000 or imprisonment for not more than six months for a first offense; these maximums were doubled for subsequent violations. As a result of the passage of the Comprehensive Crime Control Act in 1984, the maximum fine was raised to $250,000 for an individual and $500,000 for an organization.

The scope of the criminal provisions is limited. Coverage only extends to employer violations that result in a worker's death and that are willful. A willful violation requires deliberate action taken with knowledge of the OSHA standard or with plain indifference to its requirements. Thus an employer who repeatedly violates a standard without meeting the willful test or who commits a violation that only results in a serious permanent injury is not subject to criminal prosecution.

The OSHAct criminal provisions are infrequently invoked. A 1988 report of the U.S. House Committee on Government Operations was quite critical of enforcement activity to that date, as evidenced by the document's title: *Getting Away With Murder in the Workplace: OSHA's Nonuse of Criminal Penalties for Safety Violations.* The report indicated that OSHA had, since its creation in 1970, referred only forty-two cases to the U.S. Department of Justice for possible criminal actions. Of these cases, the Justice Department only prosecuted fourteen, which resulted in ten convictions but no jail sentences. *Id.* at 4.

The *Getting Away With Murder* report was transmitted from the House Committee on Government Operations to the Criminal Division of the U.S. Department of Justice. The Justice Department's response was provided by Assistant Attorney General Thomas M. Boyd, in a letter dated December 9, 1988:

> [The Justice Department] shares the committee's concern about the adequacy of the penalties provided by statute for criminal violations of OSHA safety standards.... [The Department] would be happy to see an increase in the period of imprisonment authorized for a criminal violation of OSHA safety standards. We would also be inclined to give serious consideration to proposals to expand the application of criminal sanctions to include violations which lead to serious injuries, in addition to those which lead to the death of an employee.

Boyd also explained why only a limited number of the cases referred to the Justice Department by OSHA had been prosecuted, and offered an implicit forecast about the number of future prosecutions:

> As a general matter, the deterrent value of prosecution is often a strong factor in favor of prosecution.... [A] countervailing factor is whether a sentence sufficient to the seriousness of the offense and to the necessary investment of prosecutorial resources could be obtained in the event of a conviction. In this regard, we think it likely that the increased fines available [under the Comprehensive Crime Control Act] will increase the prosecutive appeal of OSHA cases.

There was an increase in criminal prosecution referrals by OSHA to the Department of Justice in the early 1990s to around fifteen cases per year. However, no more than six cases per year were prosecuted in those years, and the annual number of referrals has declined to less than ten per year since 1992.

A decision by the Seventh Circuit, *United States v. Doig*, 950 F.2d 411 (7th Cir. 1991), limited the scope of prosecutions under Section 17(e) to a corporate officer or director acting as a corporation's agent. As a result, the defendant, who was the manager of a tunnel project where an explosion killed three workers, could not be prosecuted under the OSHAct.

    2. *Criminal Prosecutions Under State OSHA Plans.* The Secretary of Labor has approved twenty-three state plans that provide for criminal penalties for violations of state health and safety programs. Some of these state plans contain criminal provisions significantly more comprehensive than those included in Section 17(e) of the OSHAct. Minnesota has a particularly broad provision that permits fines and/or imprisonment of up to six months for *any* willful or repeated violations of the state plan — not just, as in the OSHAct, those that are willful and result in an employee's death. Additional jurisdictions that have state plans providing criminal penalties for violations beyond those encompassed by Section 17(e) of the OSHAct include Alaska, California, Indiana, and Washington.

Some states have been relatively aggressive in enforcing their criminal provisions for violations of safety and health programs, at least relative to the federal government's record in enforcing the OSHAct. California was singled out for praise in the House committee's *Getting Away With Murder* report for having "prosecuted over 250 cases [since 1973] involving workplace related deaths, injuries, and illnesses, and [because] in the past eight years there have been 112 successful prosecutions."

    3. *Criminal Prosecutions Under General Criminal Laws of the States.* The most interesting recent developments concerning the use of criminal penalties against employers responsible for workplace safety and health violations pertain to efforts by state and local officials to use their jurisdictions' general criminal laws. The holding of the Illinois Supreme Court in *People v. Chicago Magnet Wire Corp.*, 534 N.E.2d 962 (Ill. 1989) is probably still valid despite the holding in *Gade v. National Solid Wastes Management Ass'n*, 505 U.S. 88 (1992), because the *Chicago Magnet Wire* prosecutions were based on general criminal laws. In contrast, state criminal penalties explicitly related to violations of occupational safety and health requirements are of doubtful validity. Thus, in the aftermath of the *Gade* decision, the Supreme Judicial Court of Massachusetts held in *Commonwealth v. College Pro Painters (U.S.) Ltd.*, 640 N.E.2d 777 (Mass. 1994) that state regulations, which provided for criminal sanctions for failing to comply with scaffold safety standards for painters, were preempted by OSHA construction industry standards.

4. *The Role of Criminal Prosecutions in Workplace Safety.* Criminal prosecutions, it is clear, will never be a common method of encouraging workplace safety. At most, after almost four decades, only two or three individuals have spent time in jail for violating the OSHAct. Thus, criminal prosecutions are unlikely to have any significant direct effect in encouraging workplace safety. Moreover, substantial resources are needed to prosecute criminal cases, resources that could be used more effectively in promulgating standards, inspecting workplaces, or enforcing civil penalties. What then is the appropriate role of criminal prosecutions?

On deterrence, the argument would have to be that criminal prosecutions tend to focus attention on workplace safety, and especially the attention of high-level executives who may not worry much about relatively modest civil fines paid out of corporate coffers, but may well worry about personal criminal consequences. The deterrence argument cannot be limited to the fate of the few who are actually prosecuted, but must also consider the extent to which the prosecutions raise public consciousness about workplace safety issues and about the extent of corporate responsibility for them, especially among corporate executives themselves. *See generally* V.S. Khanna, *Corporate Criminal Liability: What Purpose Does It Serve?*, 109 HARV. L. REV. 1477 (1996).

The criminal law also serves an important expressive function which must be considered in this context. Even if criminal prosecutions have no deterrent effect whatsoever, it may be that criminal prosecutions are justified as a societal statement of its strong disapproval of the types of conduct that result in prosecution. JOEL FEINBERG, DOING & DESERVING: ESSAYS IN THE THEORY OF RESPONSIBILITY 95-118 (1970).

4. TORT SUITS

TEAL v. E.I. DuPONT DE NEMOURS & CO.

United States Court of Appeals, Sixth Circuit
728 F.2d 799 (1984)

CELEBREZZE, SENIOR CIRCUIT JUDGE.

Richard and Tina Teal (plaintiffs-appellants) brought this diversity action against E.I. DuPont de Nemours and Company (defendant-appellee) to recover for injuries sustained as a consequence of an accident that occurred at DuPont's plant in Old Hickory, Tennessee. At the conclusion of a five day jury trial, a verdict was returned in favor of DuPont. On appeal, appellants raise two issues which merit discussion. First, appellants claim that the trial court erred by instructing the jury that a landowner owes no duty to invitees to furnish protection against hazards on the landowner's premises. Second, appellants assert that the trial court erred by refusing to instruct the jury on the issue of negligence *per se*. Although the instruction concerning a landowner's duty to invitees is ambiguous, we conclude that such ambiguity is harmless. We hold, however, that the court's refusal to instruct the jury on the issue of negligence *per se* was improper and prejudicial. Accordingly, this case is affirmed in part, reversed in part and remanded for a trial solely on the issue of negligence *per se*.

The Daniel Construction Company (Daniel Construction) entered into a contract with DuPont to dismantle and remove hydraulic bailers from DuPont's plant. The bailers occupied three floor levels within the plant and were used to compress synthetic Dacron fiber. Hydraulic "rams" provided the force necessary to compress the fiber. The rams were located below the ground floor in a "bailer pit," access to which was provided by a straight and permanently affixed ladder. On March 14, 1979, Richard Teal, an employee of Daniel Construction, fell approximately seventeen feet from the ladder to the floor of the bailer pit. Richard Teal brought this action against DuPont alleging that his fall and injuries were the direct and proximate result of DuPont's negligence....

Appellants' second argument concerns their negligence *per se* claim. During the course of the trial, appellants introduced evidence which indicated that DuPont's ladder failed to conform to federal regulations promulgated pursuant to the Occupational Safety and Health Act of 1970. Specifically, OSHA regulations require a clearance of not less than seven inches "from the centerline of the rungs, cleats or steps to the nearest permanent object in back of the ladder." The uncontroverted testimony of Robert B. Taylor, a director of the Division of Occupational Safety and Health for the Tennessee Department of Labor, indicated that the ladder failed to conform with the seven inch clearance requirement. Because DuPont had breached a regulatory obligation, appellants requested the trial court to instruct the jury on the issue of negligence *per se*. The trial court refused; instead, it informed the jury that the OSHA regulation "may be considered ... as some evidence ... of the (appropriate) standard of care." Appellants claim that the district court's refusal to charge on the issue of negligence *per se* is reversible error.

....

Pursuant to Tennessee case law, a breach of a duty imposed by statute or regulation is negligence *per se* if the party injured is a member of the class of persons the statute or regulation was intended to protect. In this case, the parties agree that Richard Teal was, at the time of the accident, an employee of Daniel Construction, an independent contractor, and that Teal fell from a permanently affixed ladder in DuPont's plant. Further, the parties agree that the OSHA regulation established a duty owed by DuPont and that DuPont breached its duty to conform with the specifications of the regulation.[4] Accordingly, the primary dispute is whether an employee of an independent contractor is a member of the class of persons that the OSHA regulation was intended to protect.

DuPont argues that the stated purposes for the Occupational Safety and Health Act of 1970 reveal that Congress did not intend to impose a duty upon employers to protect the safety of an independent contractor's employees who work in the employer's plant. In support of this proposition, DuPont relies upon the plain language of the Act which provides that "each employer shall furnish to each of his employees employment and a place of employment which are free from recognized hazards that are causing or are likely to cause death or serious physical harm to *his* employees." 29 U.S.C. Sec. 654(a)(1) (emphasis added). Although DuPont's legal position is not without support, we believe that an employer's duty to comply with OSHA regulations is broader than DuPont suggests.

Congress' primary purpose for enacting the Occupational Safety and Health Act is "to assure so far as possible every working man and woman in the Nation safe and healthful working conditions." 29 U.S.C. Sec. 651(b). To further this primary goal, Congress imposed statutory duties on employers and employees. Under the Act, an employer's duty is two-fold:

> Each employer —
> (1) Shall furnish to each of his employees employment and a place of employment which are free from recognized hazards that are causing or are likely to cause death or serious physical harm to his employees;
> (2) Shall comply with Occupational Safety and Health standards promulgated under this chapter.

29 U.S.C. Sec. 654(a). The first duty is a "general duty" imposed on an employer to protect its employees from hazards that are likely to cause death or serious bodily injury. The second duty is a "specific duty" imposed on employers to

---

[4] DuPont concedes that it breached the regulatory obligation. DuPont argues, however, that its breach is *"de minimis"* and, thus, that the variance from the clearance specifications established by 29 C.F.R. Sec. 1910.27(c)(4) is not negligence *per se*. In contrast, appellants claim that even a slight variation from standards established by regulation is negligence per se. Furthermore, appellants argue that the trial court erred by permitting any testimony which characterized DuPont's breach of duty as *"de minimis."* We agree with appellants' assertion that even a *de minimis* breach of a statutory or regulatory duty is negligence *per se*. We disagree, however, with appellants' claim that the court permitted improperly testimony concerning the *de minimis* nature of DuPont's breach of duty. If the plaintiff proves that the defendant breached a statutory or regulatory obligation, and that the statutory or regulatory duty was enacted for the plaintiff's benefit, then the defendant is considered negligent as a matter of law. A determination that the defendant is negligent *per se*, however, does not require necessarily an award of damages. Negligence *per se* only establishes a defendant's duty and breach thereof. The question whether the breach of the duty is a proximate cause of a plaintiff's injury and the question concerning the extent, if any, of injury are jury questions that survive a determination that the defendant is negligent *per se*. In our view, testimony that a defendant's breach of duty is *de minimis* concerns the issue of proximate cause, and thus, is admissible.

comply with the OSHA regulations. These separate duty clauses have been subject to varying interpretations.

The difficulty which courts have experienced in attempting to define a particular employer's responsibilities under the Act is due primarily to the varying nature of the separate duty provisions. The general duty clause was intended by Congress to cover unanticipated hazards; Congress recognized that it could not anticipate all of the potential hazards that might affect adversely the safety of workers. Accordingly, it enacted the general duty clause to cover serious hazards that were not otherwise covered by specific regulations. Pursuant to Sec. 654(a)(1), every employer owes a duty of reasonable care to protect his employees from recognized hazards that are likely to cause death or serious bodily injury. The protection from exposure to serious hazards is the primary purpose of the general duty clause, and every employer owes this duty regardless of whether it controls the workplace, whether it is responsible for the hazard, or whether it has the best opportunity to abate the hazard. In contrast, Sec. 654(a)(2) is the specific duty provision. The class of employers who owe a duty to comply with the OSHA regulations is defined with reference to control of the workplace and opportunity to comply with the OSHA regulations. Accordingly, an employers' responsibilities under the Act depend upon which duty provision the employer is accused of breaching. Similarly, the class of persons for whom each of these duty provisions was enacted must be determined with reference to the particular duty in dispute.

In this case, DuPont is accused of breaching the specific duty imposed on employers by Sec. 654(a)(2). Accordingly, DuPont's reliance on the plain language of the general duty clause is misplaced. The very narrow question on appeal does not concern the scope of an employer's general duty to protect employees from exposure to recognized hazards, but rather, the scope of an employer's duty to comply with the specific OSHA regulations. If the special duty provision is logically construed as imposing an obligation on the part of employers to protect all of the employees who work at a particular job site, then the employees of an independent contractor who work on the premises of another employer must be considered members of the class that Sec. 654(a)(2) was intended to protect. In other words, one cannot define the scope of an employer's obligation under Sec. 654(a)(2) as including the protection of another's employees and, at the same time, claim that these "other" employees are unintended beneficiaries.

We believe that Congress enacted Sec. 654(a)(2) for the special benefit of all employees, including the employees of an independent contractor, who perform work at another employer's workplace. The specific duty clause represents the *primary* means for furthering Congress' purpose of assuring "so far as possible every working man and woman in the Nation safe and healthful working conditions." 29 U.S.C. Sec. 651(b). The broad remedial nature of the Occupational Health and Safety Act of 1970 is the Act's primary characteristic. Consistent with the broad remedial nature of the Act, we interpret the scope of intended beneficiaries of the special duty provision in a broad fashion. In our view, once an employer is deemed responsible for complying with OSHA regulations, it is obligated to protect every employee who works at its workplace. Thus, Richard Teal, an employee of an independent contractor, must be considered a member of the class of persons that the special duty provision was intended to protect.

As we have indicated, Tennessee case law establishes that the breach of a duty imposed by regulation is negligence *per se* if the plaintiff is a member of the class of persons which the regulation was intended to protect. DuPont concedes that it owed a duty to comply with the OSHA regulation in question and that it breached this duty. Because Richard Teal is a member of the class of persons that the OSHA regulation was intended to protect, the appellants were entitled to a jury instruction on their negligence *per se* claim. Accordingly, we hold that the district court erred by refusing to give the requested instruction on the issue of negligence *per se*.

NOTES

1. *A Per Se Violation?* Recall that most current OSHA standards are the interim standards that were issued by the Secretary of Labor in 1971. These interim standards were derived from either the "established Federal standards" then in existence or the "national consensus standards" that had already been issued by a nationally recognized standards-producing organization, such as the American National Standards Institute (ANSI). Also recall that the ANSI standards had been voluntary standards and that after their adoption as OSHA standards, many were criticized and some were revoked. Does this history influence your attitude about whether even a de minimis violation of an OSHA standard should be considered negligence *per se*? Perhaps the distinction drawn in note 4 of *Teal* among questions of breach of duty, proximate cause, and the extent of injury, if any, can assuage any concerns you might have about the origins of the OSHA standards and their use in tort suits. A finding of negligence *per se* is of little consequence if the injured worker cannot establish proximate cause or any injury.

2. *Tort Suits for OSHA Negligence.* An injured worker successfully sued the federal government under the Federal Tort Claims Act in *Irving v. United States*, 942 F. Supp. 1483 (D.N.H. 1996). During two inspections, compliance officers for OSHA failed to inspect a die-out machine. The worker was subsequently injured when her hair became caught in the unguarded rotating drive shaft on the machine. The court stated that OSHA breached its duty to perform the inspection in a non-negligent manner, and the worker recovered a damage award of $1 million.

I. ASSESSMENT OF THE OCCUPATIONAL SAFETY AND HEALTH ACT

JOHN F. BURTON, JR. & JAMES R. CHELIUS, WORKPLACE SAFETY AND HEALTH REGULATIONS: RATIONALE AND RESULTS, in GOVERNMENT REGULATION OF THE EMPLOYMENT RELATIONSHIP 253, 276-80 (Bruce E. Kaufman ed., 1997)[*]

The evidence suggests that the OSHAct has done little to improve workplace safety. The workplace fatality rate declined by 57% between 1970 (the year the OSHAct was enacted) and 1993. However, Kniesner and Leeth point out that the drop in the frequency of workplace fatalities from 1947 to 1970 (the thirteen years prior to OSHA) was 70% larger than the drop in the thirteen years after OSHA, and assert that "OSHA might actually have slowed the downward trend in fatal injuries." Kniesner and Leeth also found "no downward trend in either the total frequency of workplace injuries or the frequency of injuries resulting in at least one lost workday." ... [Thomas J. Kniesner & John D. Leeth, *Abolishing OSHA*, REGULATION, Vol. 18, No. 4, 1995, at 46, 49.]

Several possible reasons have been offered for the apparent failure of the OSHAct to improve workplace safety. Kniesner and Leeth note that the self-employed account for about 9% of the workforce but about 20% of all workplace fatalities; these workers are not covered by the OSHAct. In addition, [the Bureau of Labor Statistics] found that 40% of recent workplace fatalities were from transportation accidents and about 20% from assaults and other violent acts, and Kniesner and Leeth argue these leading causes of work-place deaths "are unlikely to be reduced much by OSHA inspections." [*Id.*]

OSHA's ineffectiveness in part may be due to the lack of inspection activity, since the average establishment is only inspected once every 84 years. According to Kniesner and Leeth, "the federal government has six times more fish and game inspectors than workplace health and safety inspectors." [*Id.* at 48.] But the evidence also suggests that transferring resources from walleye inspection to wall-to-wall plant inspections may be imprudent. Kniesner and Leeth reviewed the empirical studies of OSHA inspections and concluded "that OSHA has reduced injuries by no more than 4.6%. OSHA's impact, however, may be considerably smaller than 4 to 5%, considering that the majority of studies have found neither an abatement nor a deterrence effect from OSHA inspections." [*Id.* at 50.] Smith provided a more exhaustive review of the studies of OSHA inspections, and reached a similar conclusion: the studies "suggest that inspections reduce injuries by 2 to 15%" although the estimates often are not statistically significant (and thus cannot be confidently distinguished from zero effect). [Robert S. Smith, *Have OSHA and Workers' Compensation Made the*

---

[*] Copyright © 1997 by Industrial Relations Research Association. Reprinted with permission.

Workplace Safer?, in RESEARCH FRONTIERS IN INDUSTRIAL RELATIONS AND HUMAN RESOURCES 557, 566-71 (David Lewin et al. eds., 1992).]

Several recent studies have provided a more favorable assessment of the OSHA inspection process. Weil examined the custom woodworking industry and found that OSHA inspections resulted in improved compliance with a set of OSHA standards particularly relevant for that industry. However, Weil was unable to determine if the improved compliance with OSHA standards resulted in lower injury rates. [David Weil, *If OSHA Is So Bad, Why Is Compliance So Good?*, 27 RAND J. ECON. 618 (1996).] Even more promising results were provided by Gray and Scholz, who examined firms that had been inspected more than once for exceeding OSHA exposure limits for dangerous substances and found that the effect of an inspection leading to a penalty was to reduce the firm's injury rate by 20% over the following three years. [WAYNE B. GRAY & JOHN T. SCHOLZ, DO OSHA INSPECTIONS REDUCE INJURIES? A PANEL ANALYSIS (National Bureau of Economics Research, Working Paper No. 3774, 1991).] However, even Dorman, who supports an aggressive public policy to reduce workplace injuries, provided a qualified interpretation of such evidence: "these new results portray an OSHA with unfulfilled potential for improving working conditions ... however, even the most optimistic reading indicates that ... more vigorous enforcement alone cannot close the gap between US safety conditions and those in other OECD countries." [PETER DORMAN, MARKETS AND MORTALITY: ECONOMICS, DANGEROUS WORK, AND THE VALUE OF HUMAN LIFE 196 (1996).]

Supporters of the government mandate theory, as represented by McGarity and Shapiro, are more optimistic about the potential impact of OSHA inspections:

> Analysts who have attempted to isolate OSHA's impact using econometric models have produced inconsistent results. To the abolitionists these equivocal results suggest that OSHA is ineffective. However, a more plausible interpretation is that they demonstrate OSHA's unrealized potential.

[Thomas O. McGarity & Sidney A. Shapiro, *OSHA's Critics and Regulatory Reform*, 31 WAKE FOREST L. REV., 587, 596 (1996).]

OSHA inspections might be more effective if the size of the monetary penalties were increased or if criminal sanctions were utilized more frequently. But some critics of OSHA are skeptical this would help; Kniesner and Leeth argue that "the economic incentives to improve safety by reducing compensating wage differentials and workers' compensation expenses far surpass the safety-enhancing incentives from the relatively small fines currently imposed by OSHA." [Kniesner & Leeth, *supra,* at 55.] Even if OSHA fines were doubled, the amounts would be far surpassed by these other sources of economic incentives.

While the inspection and fines approach to improving safety relied on by OSHA is thus of questionable effectiveness based on the evidence concerning trends in workplace fatalities and injuries, and the studies of the impact of inspections, some critics of OSHA have identified other problems. Kniesner and Leeth argue that the annual compliance costs with OSHA health and safety standards are $11 billion (considering the effect on productivity and the cost of OSHA-mandated capital equipment), while the upper range of the benefits of OSHA in terms of reducing injuries is $3.6 billion a year. [Kniesner & Leeth, *supra,* at 50-51.] This unimpressive cost-benefit ratio is in part a result of the excessive stringency of some of the various safety and health standards that have been promulgated by OSHA. Viscusi examined OSHA standards using an implicit value of life of $5 million as the standard for efficient regulation. [W. Kip Viscusi, *Economic Foundations of the Current Regulatory Reform Efforts*, J. ECON. PERSP., Summer 1996, at 119, 124-25.] Four of the five OSHA safety regulations adopted as final rules had costs per life saved of less than $5 million; only the 1987 grain dust standard with $5.3 million per life saved failed the efficiency test proposed by Viscusi. In contrast, only one of the five OSHA health regulations adopted as final rules had costs per life saved of less than $5 million, namely the 1983 Hazard Communication Standard that cost $1.8 million per life saved. The four health standards that failed the efficiency tests had costs that ranged from $17.1 million per life saved (the 1987 benzene standard) to $72,000 million per life saved (the 1987 formaldehyde standard).

The Viscusi analysis has been challenged by Stone, who specifically focuses on the formaldehyde standard. Viscusi confined his analysis of the benefits of the standard to the number of lives saved without considering the other beneficial effects of OSHA standards, such as reductions in the number of injuries and illnesses. Stone indicates that the OSHA regulations typically prevent roughly 5 to 25 injuries for every life saved. However the formaldehyde standard has an extraordinarily high ratio of reduced illnesses to reduced fatalities. According to OSHA's estimates, the standard prevents approximately 17,000 illnesses per year and 0.6 deaths per year, for a ratio of 30,000 avoided illnesses for every life saved. Stone, using an implicit value of a typical avoided illness or injury of $20,000 to $50,000 (which he attributes to Viscusi) calculates that the illness-reduction benefits of the OSHA formaldehyde standard are between $340 million and $850 million annually, with a midpoint of about $600 million. Since OSHA estimates that the annualized cost of the standard is only $64 million, Stone argues that the cost-benefit test of efficiency is clearly met. [Robert F. Stone, *Correspondence on Benefit-Cost Analysis*, J. ECON. PERSP., Spring 1997, at 187-88.]

To be sure, cost-benefit analysis of health standards issued under the OSHAct is not legal, and so those standards that fail the cost-benefit test (considering both lives saved plus injuries and illnesses avoided) do not violate the letter and presumably the purpose of the law. But to the extent that the rationale offered by the government mandate theorists for regulation of health is that workers lack enough information to make correct decisions and therefore the government is in a better position to make decisions about how to improve workplace health, the evidence on the variability and magnitude of the cost/benefit ratios for OSHA health standards is disquieting. Rather than OSHA standards reflecting interventions in the market place that overcome deficiencies of the market, the explanation of why the stringency of regulation varies so much among industries would appear at best to be a result of technology-based decisions that could well aggravate the alleged misallocation of resources resulting from operation of the market, and at worst could reflect relative political power of the workers and employers in various industries.

NOTE

Evaluation of OSHA. The goal of the OSHAct is the prevention of workplace injuries and diseases. The failure of the OSHAct to reduce the frequencies of workplace injuries or the number of lost workdays per 100 workers in the last twenty-five years indicate that the OSHA program has not met the adequacy criterion. The studies discussed in the excerpt from the Burton and Chelius chapter suggest that simply hiring more OSHA inspectors will probably not do much to reduce the injury rate. What may help is the relatively new policy of megafines, which have now raised the consequences for flagrant violations of the Act into the million-dollar range. However, one continuing problem that OSHA faces is the inability to promulgate new standards at a reasonable pace. This problem has been aggravated in recent year by Congressional mandates directing OSHA not to adopt or enforce certain standards, most notably an ergonomics standard.

Equity is also a serious problem for OSHA. Most of the current OSHA standards are the "interim standards" that were derived from preexisting federal standards or voluntary organization guidelines. Some industries were affected more than others by this hodgepodge of regulations, and twenty-five years of promulgation of new standards has not reduced the disparity among industries in the effect of the standards. The new standards promulgated in this period have had varying success in the courts, and again, failure of the generic rulemaking approach has left the permissible exposure levels for some substances vastly out of date, while other substances have more appropriate standards based on our current knowledge of health risks. Economists have used one of their favorite analytical tools — cost-benefit analysis — to point out that the compliance costs per life saved vary considerably among different OSHA standards.

The delivery system efficiency of the OSHA approach to prevention is also a problem. The evidence from most studies of OSHA suggests that the payoff from additional inspections is not very high. Moreover, a cynic might argue that the main beneficiary of the effort to promulgate new standards has been lawyers, who are marshaled to defend or, more likely, attack the proposals. Perhaps greater efficiency will result from the efforts to use the general duty clause to deal with ergonomic problems. Perhaps the megafine policy will improve efficiency. Perhaps there are other approaches to preventing workplace injuries and diseases that are more efficient (as well as more adequate and equitable). The quest for better approaches is the subject of the next chapter.

Chapter 23

RETHINKING THE APPROACHES TO THE PREVENTION AND COMPENSATION OF WORKPLACE INJURIES AND DISEASES

The subject of Part VIII is the prevention and compensation of work-related injuries and diseases. The Introduction to Part VIII introduced four approaches to reach these goals: the labor market, tort suits, workers' compensation, and safety and health laws. These approaches can be evaluated using the criteria of adequacy, equity, and delivery system efficiency.

This final chapter returns to this theme and asks for an assessment of the current approaches, as well as consideration of how the approaches can be improved. To supplement the material in previous chapters, four selections primarily concerned with the prevention of workplace injuries and diseases are provided. First, an excerpt from the 1987 *Economic Report of the President* provides a paean to the labor market as a source of prevention. Then two selections provide contrasting views on the role of tort suits in reducing accidents. Finally, one brave commentator provides grades for the record of the four approaches in promoting workplace safety.

ECONOMIC REPORT OF THE PRESIDENT 181-201 (1987)

Protection Against Risk

Every individual can reduce risk by exercising personal care. If responsible adults voluntarily undertake risky activities, such as hang gliding, their choices must be respected in a society that values individual liberty and autonomy. This general principle of respecting personal choice is compatible, however, with governmental action to reduce risk in particular circumstances, especially when the actions of some increase the risks to others.

The institutional means for increasing safety and reducing risk are provided through three social arrangements — markets, the legal system, and government regulation. Markets create incentives for safe behavior and allow individual choice in decisions involving risk.... The market also promotes safety in the workplace. All other things equal, employers must pay higher wages for riskier jobs, which creates an incentive to reduce occupational hazards.

Private insurance enables individuals and firms to protect themselves against the costs of various risks. Consumers purchase insurance against losses from death, illness and accidents, and some kinds of natural disasters.... By spreading the costs of risk, insurance can also undermine incentives for safe behavior; but where premiums are closely linked to the likelihood of events insured against, safety incentives are substantially preserved.

Markets cannot entirely protect an individual from being harmed by the actions of others. The legal system, specifically tort law, provides victims the opportunity to be compensated. By transferring to those who cause harm the costs they impose on others, tort law creates incentives for individuals to behave responsibly.

Government Management of Risk

Government provides the legal and judicial framework for the market and tort systems, offers insurance against some risks, imposes regulatory standards, and operates programs to control risk directly....

Several circumstances may provide a rationale for government regulation. First, consumers may lack the information or the ability to assess particular risks accurately. Second, individuals or firms fail in some cases to take account of the costs of harm they impose on others. The tort system may not be able to force a person who causes harm to bear these costs if the person's wealth is insufficient to compensate the victim, the cost of using the tort system is too high, or the person who caused the harm cannot be identified. Third, if markets and the tort system cannot adequately control externalities such as those leading to environmental pollution, government regulation may be warranted....

The Tort System

In addition to self-inflicted injury, harm can result from the actions of others. Tort law, the civil law governing harms other than breach of contract, serves to compensate persons injured by the negligent or wrongful conduct of others, and also to deter such conduct.

Two general rules of liability guide accident law — negligence and strict liability. Negligence is determined by reasonableness of conduct. If the injurer acted unreasonably, that is, failed to exercise due care, then ordinarily the injurer would be required to compensate the victim. Strict liability, on the other hand, focuses on whether a product that caused an injury was defective in such a way as to make it unreasonably dangerous for its intended use. Both standards seek to impose a duty of care; strict liability, however, allows demonstration of the breach of that duty by examination of the product itself.

The product user's degree of care also can affect the risk of accidents. In certain instances, the user can more easily eliminate or reduce the risk of injury than can the manufacturer. The rule of contributory negligence limits the scope of liability so that an injurer is not liable for harm that could have been avoided had the victim not been negligent. Many States have adopted the rule of comparative fault, under which an injurer is liable only for that share of the harm corresponding to the injurer's share of responsibility. Determining the reasonableness of a party's conduct depends in part on the costs of avoiding the accident. When both parties can affect the probability or seriousness of an accidental injury, the rule of negligence (or the rule of strict liability accompanied by the defense of contributory negligence or comparative fault) leads both the potential injurer and potential victim to behave reasonably to avoid accidents....

Occupational Safety

Risks of death from work accidents, along with other types of safety hazards, have declined sharply. Injury rates, which are less reliably measured than death rates, have also declined, but less rapidly. As people demanded better working conditions and safety on the job, they also sought increased government regulation of workplace safety. Among the many laws and regulations that address job safety, the major ones are State workers' compensation acts and the Federal Occupational Safety and Health Act. Both workers' compensation and the OSHA statute were expected to reduce work injuries, but many of their possible effects on costs were overlooked.

Labor Market Safety Incentives

... The labor market provides strong incentives for employers to improve safety. In order to make a hazardous job attractive to workers, a firm must offer higher wages than it would have to pay otherwise. Wage premiums are a critical device for controlling job hazards because they provide employers with incentives to reduce hazards in order to reduce wage costs....

In efficient labor markets, wage premiums result in appropriate matching of workers and jobs based on risk and other factors.... Imperfect information may militate against fully efficient labor market outcomes, thus providing a rationale for regulation or other government intervention. However, studies have found evidence that job safety information, although not perfect, is generally adequate. Workers have reasonably accurate perceptions of risks, and if they acquire new information suggesting risks greater than they originally had expected, their likelihood of quitting increases.

Workers' knowledge of health risks is probably less accurate than their knowledge of safety risks.... Government also has limited knowledge of occupational health hazards, but it can improve the information available to both employees and employers by supporting research on job safety and disseminating the results. Government, however, has no clear advantage over workers, labor unions, and employers in using this information to determine appropriate levels of workplace safety or the best way to reduce hazards.

Pecuniary costs of job injuries are commonly shifted to the general public by income transfers such as social security disability payments, welfare, and food stamps. This reduces firms' incentives to take safety measures, by enabling them to pay lower wage premiums. Even where information is not perfect or pecuniary externalities exist, however, wage premiums serve a useful function in providing safety incentives and in matching workers with jobs.

Workers' Compensation

... Except for the largest firms, which are allowed to self-insure, employers must buy insurance from a private carrier or a State insurance fund to cover their workers' compensation liabilities.... Premiums are experience-rated — that is, linked to past loss experience — only for larger firms....

Although the impetus for adoption of workers' compensation was to replace employers' tort liability with a no-fault system, safety incentives were an additional consideration. Workers' compensation was expected to induce employers to provide greater workplace safety because each firm would assume the costs of its workers' injuries more predictably than under tort liability. The costs of industrial injuries thus would be included among other business costs, and employers would be motivated to reduce them by increasing job safety. This expectation of improved safety, however, overlooked factors that would undermine safety: reduced wage premiums in response to lower but more certain recovery of damages, and reduced incentives for employers to increase safety when workers' compensation premiums are not closely related to the injuries suffered by employees.

A growing body of research has found that workers' compensation benefits have unfavorable effects on safety. Higher benefits appear to increase both the frequency of work injuries and the number of compensation claims filed. One explanation for the positive connection is the claim effect. Even if actual injuries remain constant, workers are more likely to file claims when benefits are higher, thereby producing more reported injuries.

Lack of experience rating of workers' compensation premiums reduces an employer's incentive to invest in safety measures. A firm that is not forced to bear the full costs of compensating its workers for their injuries has a diminished incentive to make expenditures that promote safety.... Employers' safety incentives could be strengthened by requiring them to make a deductible payment and copayment on each claim....

Workers' compensation has improved the reliability of compensation to injured workers. By replacing lost wages, it also has enabled injured workers to recuperate more fully before returning to work. There is evidence, however, analogous to findings on the effects of unemployment insurance, that higher levels of workers' compensation benefits create work disincentives. Recipients whose benefits are relatively high compared with their previous wages have longer durations of work disability. Work disincentive effects can be important: because benefits are not taxable, the after-tax rate of wage replacement for some workers exceeds 100 percent of their prior wages.

Although one goal of workers' compensation was to reduce the high transactions costs of litigation, many workers' compensation claims are still contested. Workers, moreover, are making liability claims with increasing frequency against suppliers of inputs, commonly in situations where adverse effects on health, such as those related to cancer, may be delayed. Such suits are not barred under the no-fault workers' compensation system.

Regulation of Job Safety

The Occupational Safety and Health Act's sweeping mandate is to ensure that "so far as possible every working man and woman in the Nation [has] safe and healthful working conditions." OSHA has issued several thousand workplace standards, the large majority of which were adopted soon after OSHA's formation and formalized existing industry practices. Some of the most obviously ineffective of these have since been revoked. Most of OSHA's rules deal with safety rather than health hazards. Employers continue to complain that OSHA's regulations are costly, but no comprehensive estimates of compliance costs have been made.

Compared with the magnitude of safety incentives provided in the market, OSHA's fines and enforcement activities are small. One estimate of wage premiums generated by job risks is approximately $90 billion per year, which compares with about $9 million in OSHA fines. By comparison, workers' compensation benefits are about $20 billion annually.

A number of studies have found that OSHA's activities have not been effective in promoting workplace safety.... Over recent decades, the job fatality rate has declined fairly steadily by more than 2 percent per year. OSHA has not made an identifiable difference in this rate of decline. One recent study, however, has found that OSHA's activities have resulted in a small reduction in work injuries. It is more difficult to assess OSHA's effects on health, because of the time lag between a worker's exposure to a toxic chemical or environmental hazard and the manifestation of disease. This Administration has taken steps to enhance the effectiveness and reduce the burdens of OSHA's inspections. Inspections are now less confrontational and are targeted toward high-risk firms and serious workplace hazards.

OSHA's effects on health and safety may be small because of the type of regulations it has promulgated. Many require specific changes in the physical work environment rather than encouraging safe behavior. For example, OSHA has not required the use of automobile safety belts, although motor vehicle fatalities account for about one-third of total work deaths .... Even in manufacturing, motor vehicle deaths are close to 20 percent of work deaths....

Although precise causation of work injuries is difficult to establish, studies show that individual behavior is a major factor in many work accidents. Studies of occupational fatalities have found that 9 to 40 percent are alcohol-related.

Executive Order No. 12291 broadly required the use of cost-benefit criteria for agency rulemaking, to the extent permitted by law. The Supreme Court has interpreted OSHA's legislative mandate as prohibiting the balancing of costs and benefits in formulating health regulations. OSHA has adopted a restricted cost-effectiveness approach in accordance with this decision, allowing lowest cost methods of compliance in achieving a given technical standard. Studies of past OSHA rules show that costs typically exceed expected benefits. The recent OSHA hazard communication standard, requiring that workers be informed of workplace hazards, is an important exception.

A major criticism of OSHA is that many of its regulations have unnecessarily increased costs by preventing employers from using flexible means to meet health and safety goals. In contrast, OSHA's hazard communication rule requires that workers be informed about chemical hazards, but leaves employers leeway in implementation.

Many of OSHA's standards increase costs and reduce productivity and competitiveness. Where OSHA's rules increase capital requirements, they also reduce employment opportunities, by encouraging the substitution of capital for labor. Where OSHA's rules specify characteristics of workplace design, they impose fixed costs that tend to favor larger firms over smaller ones.

The evidence on whether workers' compensation and OSHA have improved safety is mixed at best. Most studies indicate that these programs have failed to reduce job injuries in the aggregate. Although workers' compensation achieved some of its goals, it also may have undermined safety incentives. Both workers' compensation and OSHA have generated costs and indirect effects that have tended to reduce productivity....

NOTES

1. *Economists' Logic, or Run That by Me Again, Please.* The *Economic Report of the President* recognizes the distinction between two possible consequences of statutory increases in workers' compensation benefits: a "true injury effect," in which the actual level of workplace risk may rise, and a "reporting effect," in which injured workers are more likely to report their injuries and press for higher payments. Which of these two possible explanations for a positive relationship between higher benefits and higher reported injuries should be of primary concern to policymakers? Which of these possible explanations is represented in the first sentence of the following passage from the *Economic Report*? Which is represented in the second sentence? The third? The fourth? What difference is there between the implications of the first and fourth sentence for the consequences of higher workers' compensation benefits in achieving the goal of promoting workplace safety? Of some interest is that the explanation in the first sentence appears to dominate the balance of the selection from the *Economic Report*:

> A growing body of research has found that workers' compensation benefits have unfavorable effects on safety. Higher benefits appear to increase both the frequency of work injuries and the number of compensation claims filed. One explanation for the positive connection is the claim effect. Even if actual injuries remain constant, workers are more likely to file claims when benefits are higher, thereby producing more reported injuries.

2. *Overwhelmed by the Market?* The *Economic Report of the President* indicates that, "Compared with the magnitude of safety incentives provided in the market, OSHA's fines and enforcement activities are small." How small? The ratio of wage premiums to OSHA fines in the data provided by the *Report* is 10,000 to 1 — $90 billion in wage premiums to $9 million in OSHA fines. With ratios like those, who could deny the efficacy of the market?

JAMES A. LOWE, THIRD PARTY LIABILITY, IN SAFE WORK: PREVENTING INJURY AND DISEASE IN THE WORKPLACE 32-33 (1991)[*]

The workers' compensation system represents nothing more than a failure in the ability of society to prevent worker injury. Our job is not to compensate people for injuries, but to prevent them in the first place. We haven't done very well.

The first premise, therefore, is that compensation is the only available method of social engineering. The second premise is that expense to somebody is an incentive to prevent injury and death. That is where the Association of Trial Lawyers of America, and my practice in particular, come in. We use the tort system, not to aggrandize anyone, but to prevent injury and death that is preventable. We believe that expense is a mighty incentive to safety engineering.

We have spent most of the day talking about OSHA, yet there is no OSHA for manufacturers. There is, at best, self-regulation through industry standards.

The American National Standards Institute says that the ultimate responsibility for worker safety rests with the employers. But workers themselves, for the most part, have no idea what is in the chemicals they work with, and certainly they have no idea how a press or a shear machine could be designed to prevent the possibility of injury.

Just as we can design automobiles that respect the fact that people can fall asleep at the wheel, we can design equipment that recognizes that momentary inadvertence and lack of attention can occur after twelve hours of running the same piece of equipment. We can prevent people from injuring themselves in foreseeable circumstances.

Workers' compensation never was a reflection of social consciousness. It was, in fact, a reaction to the effectiveness of the tort system. It scared employers, even at the time when defenses abounded. There was the complete defense of assumption of the risk, the defense of contributory negligence. If the employee was responsible for his own injury in whole or in part, he could be denied compensation. It was a much tougher system, yet the costs to the employer still were not predictable.

Workers' compensation does provide a kind of no-fault system, but the level of compensation is far below what is adequate. Even though the costs go up, they don't go up in terms of the net for the employee. They go up in terms of medical expenses, which are uncontrollable, and other kinds of expenses. But the employee does not necessarily take home an amount that increases with inflation.

One of our problems is trying to regulate safety in the workplace through the tort system. In the absence of tort system, who would do anything to prevent injury and disease from occurring? Can we permit a manufacturer to produce and supply an unguarded press, hoping that the employer will guard it because OSHA requires this? Or can we make it so expensive for the manufacturer that it doesn't pay to manufacture defective and unreasonably dangerous equipment?

We have found that industry makes what are called value analyses. We have discovered memoranda in which manufacturers made an analysis of the actual cost to make a safer product versus the cost of litigation to defend the acknowledged defective products, and found that it was cheaper to defend the lawsuits and pay the victim than to make a safer product.

It is the function of our ability to sue the manufacturer that permits us to keep that from being a viable alternative and to make the workplace safer in the first instance, before you get to the compensation system.

JOHN F. BURTON, JR. & JAMES R. CHELIUS, WORKPLACE SAFETY AND HEALTH REGULATIONS: RATIONALE AND RESULTS, in GOVERNMENT REGULATION OF THE EMPLOYMENT RELATIONSHIP 253, 272-74 (Bruce E. Kaufman ed., 1997)[*]

Theoretical stimulus of tort law to safety. When negligence is the legal standard used for tort suits, an injured employee may sue his employer for damages when the employer is at fault. If the employer has not taken proper measures to prevent accidents and thus is at fault, the employer will be liable for all of the consequences of the injury. The standard for the proper prevention measure was developed by Judge Learned Land and restated by Posner as:

> the judge (or jury) should attempt to measure three things in ascertaining negligence: the magnitude of the loss if an accident occurs; the probability of the accident's occurring; and the burden [cost] of taking precautions to prevent it. If the product of the first two terms, the expected benefit, exceeds the burden of precautions, the failure to take those precautions is negligence.

[Richard A. Posner, *A Theory of Negligence*, 1 J. LEGAL STUD. 29, 32 (1972).]

Posner argued that proper application of this standard will result in economically efficient incentives to avoid accidents. As Chelius notes, the added costs of determining liability in a court may appear to be inconsistent with achieving an efficient use of resources, since legal fees are usually a significant percentage of the total award. [JAMES R. CHELIUS, WORKPLACE SAFETY AND HEALTH 34-35 (1977).] The benefits of legal proceedings, however, *may* outweigh their costs if the incentives created by such a system are more accurate than those present under alternative systems.

Evidence on the tort law stimulus to safety. The generally accepted view is that tort suits were largely ineffective as remedy for workplace injuries in late 1880s and early 1900s. Not only were workplace injuries and fatalities increasing, but employees were generally unsuccessful in suits, in large part because of legal defenses available to employers, such as the contributory negligence defense that eliminated any recovery if the worker was negligent, even if the employer was negligent to a greater degree. The leading legal treatise on workers' compensation concludes that "the precompensation loss-adjustment system for industrial accidents was a complete failure ...." [ARTHUR LARSON & LEX K. LARSON, LARSON'S WORKERS' COMPENSATION: DESK EDITION § 4.50 (1997).] However, Berkowitz and Berkowitz indicate that workers were beginning to enjoy considerable success with tort suits at the beginning of the workers' compensation era. [Edward D. Berkowitz & Monroe Berkowitz, *Challenges to Workers' Compensation: An Historical Analysis, in* WORKERS' COMPENSATION BENEFITS: ADEQUACY, EQUITY, AND EFFICIENCY 158, 160 (John D. Worrall & David Appell eds., 1985).] Perhaps the tort system if left in place for workplace injuries would have evolved and produced a major stimulus to workplace safety.

There are two type of empirical evidence that indicate skepticism is nonetheless warranted about the stimulus to workplace safety from tort suits. First, as previously discussed, Chelius found that the replacement of the negligence remedy with workers' compensation led to a reduction in workplace fatalities. [CHELIUS, *supra.*] Second, in other areas of tort law, there is a major controversy among legal scholars about whether the theoretical incentives for safety resulting from tort suits actually work. One school of thought is exemplified by Landes and Posner, who state that "although there has been little systematic study of the deterrent effect of tort law, what empirical evidence there is indicates that tort law ... deters, even where, notably in the area of automobile accidents, liability insurance is widespread ... and personal safety might be expected to be of greater concern than the potential financial consequences of an accident." [WILLIAM M. LANDES & RICHARD A. POSNER, THE ECONOMIC STRUCTURE OF TORT LAW 10 (1987).]

An opposing view on the deterrent effects of tort law is provided by Priest, who finds almost no relationship between liability payouts and the accident rate for general aviation, and states that: "This relationship between liability payouts and accidents appears typical of other areas of modern tort law as well, such as medical malpractice and products liability." [George L. Priest, *The Modern Expansion of Tort Liability: Its Sources, Its Effects, and Its Reform*, J. ECON. PERSP., Summer 1991, at 31, 44.]

A survey of the deterrent effects of tort laws by Schwartz distinguished between a strong form of deterrence (as postulated by Landes and Posner) and a moderate form of deterrence, in which "tort law provides a significant amount of deterrence, yet considerably less than the economists' formulae tend to predict." [Gary T. Schwartz, *Reality in the Economic Analysis of Tort Law: Does Tort Law Really Deter?*, 42 UCLA L. REV. 377, 378-79 (1994).] Schwartz surveys a variety of areas where tort law is used, including motorist liability, medical malpractice, and product liability, and concludes that sector by sector the evidence undermines the strong form of deterrence but provides adequate support for the deterrence argument in its moderate form. As to workers' injuries, Schwartz ... concludes "it is unclear whether a tort system or workers' compensation provides better incentives for workplace safety; in an odd way ... [the studies are consistent] with the general idea that a properly designed set of liability rules can produce beneficial results."

Based on both the ambiguous historical experience of the impact of workers' compensation on workplace safety, and the current controversy over the deterrence effect in other areas of tort law, the law and economics theory concerning tort law does not provide much assistance in designing an optimal policy for workplace safety and health. We will be even more assertive in our assessment of the virtues of tort law as a strategy for improving workplace safety and health: we are sufficiently persuaded of the favorable effects of workers' compensation experience on safety, and sufficiently skeptical of the deterrent effects of tort suits, that we would resist the use of tort suits to deal with work injuries unless much more compelling evidence of the deterrent effect if produced.

JOHN F. BURTON, JR., EVALUATING WORKERS' COMPENSATION SYSTEMS, IN SAFE WORK: PREVENTING INJURY AND DISEASE IN THE WORKPLACE 28-32 (1991)[*]

The U.S. experience with workplace injuries and disease can be divided into three historical periods. From about the Civil War until World War I, there was a rapid deterioration of workplace safety and health associated with industrialization. Death rates went up dramatically. It was recognized around the turn of the century that we had a serious problem.

From about World War I until 1960, in general, the frequency and severity rates for workplace injuries improved. And then we began a period of deterioration, an apparent decline in safety, which has accelerated in recent years. The injury frequency rates went up during the 1960s. This was one of the factors cited in the enactment of OSHA.

The data collected by the Labor Department since 1972 show an apparent decline in workplace safety. For example, the number of lost workdays per 100 workers per year in 1972 was a little under 48. By 1980 that number was 65. By 1989 it was almost 79. We have thus had an apparent 50 percent increase in the number of lost workdays.

It is important to use these data with considerable caution. But they are probably still the best indicator we have of what's going on. They probably exaggerate the extent of the deterioration, but they certainly suggest that we've had a problem for the last twenty or thirty years that is getting worse.

How do we go about improving workplace safety and health?

One alternative is to rely upon economic incentives generated in the marketplace. This is the theory economists use: workers would recognize that certain jobs are associated with higher risks; there would be a wage premium paid for those jobs; and employers would have an incentive to improve workplace health and safety because they could reduce wages as a result. If you have an unhealthy workplace, you've got to pay more.

That theory of compensating wage differentials was certainly not working in the years after the Civil War and until the early part of this century.

For many workers today — low-skilled workers, non-unionized workers — I think we could say that the compensating wage differential model still doesn't work very well. I would give it a D-minus or F as an approach to dealing with occupational safety and health for these workers.

On the other hand, for some workers — skilled workers and in particular unionized workers — there is evidence that higher wages are paid in response to higher risk. The magnitude of the compensating wage differentials runs into billions of dollars. Their annual magnitude is at least a thousand times larger than the total OSHA fines. Probably the major factor of improving safety and health over the course of the twentieth century has been the economic incentives to employers to improve the workplace in order to save money. So for more skilled workers, and for unionized workers in particular, I'd give a grade of B to market forces.

I want to make clear that, in my view, reliance on market forces is not a sufficient approach to dealing with workplace safety and health. The question is: What else do we need?

A second general approach is the use of legislation — safety and health rules and regulations. Here we have a history that goes back to the mid-nineteenth century. Our earliest labor-standards legislation was state safety laws. Safety laws have been used for over a century, culminating in the enactment of OSHA in 1970.

The empirical evidence about the effect of the OSHA Act on safety is not very encouraging. In general, the evidence suggests that OSHA has had little or no effect on improving safety. One would have to say that the scorecard for OSHA to date is a D-minus. OSHA probably does better on health, but we ought not to delude ourselves into thinking that OSHA has made much of a contribution to improving safety.

The third general approach to promoting workplace safety is tort suits against employers for workplace safety and health violations. This was the approach originally used. Before about 1915, we allowed workers to sue their employers in tort and try to recover damages. The pre-1915 version of tort was generally recognized as a failure in compensating workers, although there are some conflicting views on that. It appears to have been ineffective as a force for safety. There were other drawbacks associated with the reliance on tort suits: delays, expense, arbitrary outcomes, low recovery rates by employees. Looking at the historical record, I would have to give the use of tort suits as a way of improving safety a grade of F.

Tort law has evolved in the last seventy-five years. Thus it's not quite fair to grade on the basis of our historical experience. We ought to say that some modified forms of tort law might have a better effect on safety. However, some of the other problems, such as delays and arbitrary outcomes, would still be present. My view is that even a modified version of tort suits as a way of dealing with safety would be a D-minus.

Workers' compensation emerged in most states around 1915 to 1920 because of dissatisfaction with tort suits, among other things. It was supposed to promote safety, by and large, by the financing mechanism. Employers' costs depend upon the amount of benefits paid to workers. There is, in theory, a strong incentive for employers to improve safety in the workplace in order to reduce their workers' compensation insurance premiums.

Studies suggest that the introduction of workers' compensation did in fact improve safety considerably. However, studies done in the last ten years, primarily by economists, have been mixed. Some have found support for the notion that workers' compensation promotes safety. Others have found no such evidence. One should be a little skeptical about the effect to date of workers' compensation on safety.

There are some things now going on in workers' compensation that relate to safety incentives.

One is that over the last fifteen or twenty years there has been, in most states, a substantial improvement in cash benefits. More than any other social insurance program, workers' compensation benefits have increased substantially in most states. This has translated into much higher costs for employers. In 1970 the national average of payroll spent on workers' compensation was about 1.10 percent. In the latest data, from 1988, it is 2.15 percent of payroll. In many states it is higher, and many firms pay considerably more.

In a sense, whatever the pros and cons of these higher costs for employers, it is a plus for safety. Workers' compensation is a lot more expensive than it used to be, and therefore employers have a lot more incentive to improve the workplace and save money. It is no longer cheap to kill and maim workers.

Some recent trends, however, undermine the ability of workers' compensation to promote safety. One is the emergence of conditions and diseases such as carpal tunnel syndrome and stress. Such conditions are particularly difficult to identify in the workplace. As a result, it is harder to draw the line between work-related and non-work-related sources of disability. To the extent that distinction breaks down, it reduces the experience-rating feedback mechanism that gets employers to improve workplace conditions in order to reduce costs.

Another recent development undermining the ability of workers' compensation to provide safety incentives is the increasing importance of medical costs within workers' compensation. It has gone from about a third of all benefits a decade ago to about 40 percent now. The emergence of escalating medical costs has led to proposals in some jurisdictions (and in at least one jurisdiction, Florida, to legislative enactment) that would break down the distinction between work-related and non-work-related sources of the need for medical care. We may be moving in the direction of twenty-four-hour medical care for workers.

There are some real advantages to that. In general, I would support the movement. But one downside is that to the extent you have a program cutting across all sources of need for medical care, you reduce the feedback mechanism for incentives to employers to improve workplace health.

Workers' compensation as a promotion device for workplace safety and health thus gets a grade of C-minus to D-plus.

I've given a lot of low grades. I think we don't know very well what to do to improve workplace safety and health. We're going to have to try our best to improve a variety of approaches. OSHA needs to be restructured. Workers' compensation needs some improvement. Eula Bingham [former Assistant Secretary of Labor for Occupational Safety and Health] mentioned the use of criminal penalties, which is another possible avenue to promote safety. The one thing I'd be most skeptical about as a way to promote safety and health would be increased reliance on tort suits.

NOTES

1. *The Labor Market.* How well is the labor market doing in achieving the goals of preventing workplace injuries and compensating those workers who are injured? (Use of the criteria of adequacy, equity, and delivery system efficiency will enhance your answer.) What, if anything, could be done to improve the operation of the labor market in achieving these goals? Would you place primary (or even sole) reliance on the labor market as the approach to achieve these goals?

2. *Tort Suits.* How well did the tort law of the early twentieth century do in achieving the goals of prevention and compensation? How well would modern tort law do in achieving the goals? (Again, the criteria troika of adequacy, equity, and delivery system efficiency should be utilized in order to place your answer in proper context and show your erudition.)

What, if anything, could be done to improve the role of tort suits in promoting safety and improving compensation? Would you expand the circumstances under which workers injured on the job could sue their own employers? Would you, for example, make it possible for employees to bring a tort suit against the employer when there was gross negligence? What would that do to the exclusive remedy provision? What would the expanded ability to sue the employer do to the prospects of legislators increasing workers' compensation benefits?

Would you expand the ability of an injured employee to bring a tort suit against a third party for injuries that occur at the workplace? Or would it make sense to establish a no-fault program for harm to workers caused by third parties? Should the benefits in such a plan be limited, as in the workers' compensation program?

Would you place primary (or even sole) reliance on a redesigned tort system to achieve the goals of injury prevention and compensation of injured workers?

3. *Workers' Compensation.* How well is the workers' compensation program doing in preventing workplace injuries and compensating injured workers? What would you do to improve the performance of the workers' compensation program? How would you deal with the argument that efforts to improve the adequacy of workers' compensation benefits undermines efforts to reduce workplace injuries?

How do you resolve the tradeoff between equity (in the sense of matching benefits to losses experienced by individual workers) and efficiency (and, in particular, delivery system efficiency, which seeks to reduce the costs of the delivery system)? Is there merit to the claim that, in comparison to tort suits, which hold out the promise of individual equity in conjunction with high transaction costs, workers' compensation provides benefits with a rough form of social justice together with much lower transactions costs than tort suits, and that workers' compensation thus represents a better use of society's resources?

What other changes would you recommend for the workers' compensation program? Would you place primary (or even sole) reliance on a revamped workers' compensation program to achieve the goals of injury prevention and compensation of injured workers?

4. *Safety and Health Laws.* How well is the Occupational Safety and Health Act doing in achieving the goal of reducing workplace injuries and diseases? How would you change the OSHA program to improve its record? Would you change the process and criteria used to promulgate new OSHA standards?

Would you expand (or contract) the role of the states in achieving workplace safety? Would you place greater emphasis on criminal prosecutions of employers responsible for workplace injuries and diseases? If so, would you expand the criminal activities at the federal or state level, or both? Would you mandate safety committees including workers and employers in every facility covered by OSHA? What would be the roles of the committees?

What other changes would you recommend for the OSHA program? Would you place primary (or even sole) reliance on an expanded OSHA program to achieve the goal of workplace safety?

5. *General Equilibrium Analysis.* What is the proper mix of approaches to achieve the goals of prevention of workplace injuries and compensation for those workers who are injured? Should we, for example, solely rely on OSHA to achieve safe and healthy workplaces, and have workers' compensation solely concentrate on providing cash benefits and medical care to injured workers? Or should OSHA be declared a failed experiment and terminated, in order for the marketplace, workers' compensation, and (perhaps) an expanded array of tort suits to serve the goals of prevention and compensation? Unfortunately, the authors of this casebook are unable to provide unassailable answers to these questions — even in the instructor's manual!

Table of Cases

References are to page numbers. Principal cases and the pages
where they appear are in italics.

INDEX

A

AGE DISCRIMINATION.
Disparate treatment model.

AIDS.

AMERICAN RULE.
Employment at will.

ARBITRATION.
Fair labor standards act (FLSA).

ATTORNEYS AT LAW.
In-house counsel.

AT WILL EMPLOYMENT.
See EMPLOYMENT AT WILL.

B

BACK DISORDERS.
Workers' compensation.

BFOQ DEFENSE.
Age discrimination.

BLACKSTONE'S RULE.
Employment at will.

C

CHILD LABOR.

CONTRACT LAW.
See EMPLOYMENT CONTRACTS.

1007